The New International Commentary
on the
New Testament

General Editors

NED B. STONEHOUSE
(1946-1962)

F. F. BRUCE
(1962-1990)

GORDON D. FEE
(1990-   )

The Epistle to the

ROMANS

DOUGLAS J. MOO

WILLIAM B. EERDMANS PUBLISHING COMPANY
GRAND RAPIDS, MICHIGAN / CAMBRIDGE, U.K.

© 1996 Wm. B. Eerdmans Publishing Co.
255 Jefferson Ave. S.E., Grand Rapids, Michigan 49503 /
P.O. Box 163, Cambridge CB3 9PU U.K.

Printed in the United States of America

01 00 99 98   7 6 5 4 3 2

Library of Congress Cataloging-in-Publication Data

Moo, Douglas J.
The Epistle to the Romans / Douglas J. Moo
p.   cm.
— (The new international commentary on the New Testament)
Includes bibliographical references and indexes.
ISBN 0-8028-2317-3 (alk. paper)
1. Bible. N.T. Romans — Commentaries. I. Title. II. Series.
BS2665.3.M55   1966
227′.107 — dc20   96-26077
                                                          CIP

CONTENTS

EDITOR'S PREFACE

With this volume a new day has dawned for this series of commentaries. Not only is it the first volume (not counting my own *Philippians*) to appear under the third editorship of the series, but it is also the first among several of the new and/or replacement volumes that represent a younger generation of evangelical scholars, thus signaling in part the "coming of age" of evangelical scholarship at the end of the present millennium.

Dr. Moo, for many years a teacher at the Trinity Evangelical Divinity School (Deerfield, Illinois) and editor of the *Trinity Journal,* brings to this commentary the rigors of a first-rate exegete who is equally concerned for the theological and practical implications of the text of Romans. In his "Author's Preface," he details the happy circumstances by which his (now completed) commentary became a part of the present series.

But if this volume in some ways inaugurates a new day for the series, it also has some strong ties to the past. This series began in a context of evangelical theology that was also decidedly within the Reformed tradition. It is therefore fitting that the replacement commentary on Romans in particular, originally written by John Murray (professor of systematic theology at Westminster Theological Seminary), should be written by someone whose theological sympathies lie in this direction. Although it will be clear to the perceptive reader that Dr. Moo has struck an independent course at many significant places (most notably with his interpretation of 7:7-25), he has nonetheless here articulated a (more traditional) view of Romans that is not notably popular among Romans specialists these days. In so doing, he has put everyone in his debt with his careful and clear articulation of this view, and with his equally knowledgeable and gracious interaction with those who take different views. And his careful work on the details of the text, which made it such a joy to edit, also makes it a "must" commentary for those who want to get at the meaning of this crucial Pauline letter.

GORDON D. FEE

AUTHOR'S PREFACE

The "traditions-history" of this commentary is convoluted. In 1983 I was asked by Moody Press to contribute a commentary on Romans to their new Wycliffe Exegetical Commentary series. I began work and produced the first volume of that commentary in 1991 *(Romans 1–8)*. Shortly after the appearance of that volume, however, Moody Press decided the cancel the series. I therefore began searching desperately for a publisher who would be willing to republish *Romans 1–8* along with the second volume of the commentary, on which I was already at work. In the providence of God, the William B. Eerdmans Publishing Company was at that very time seeking an author to write a revised commentary on Romans for their New International Commentary on the New Testament series. I gladly accepted their offer to put my commentary in their series.

    The very different natures of the two commentary series required rather extensive revisions of my first volume. This I found to be both a curse and a blessing. The curse was having to transfer much detailed argumentation of my Wycliffe volume into footnotes in the New International Commentary series — requiring extensive rewriting of both text and notes. But the blessing was that this rewriting enabled me to sharpen my arguments and improve my style at a number of places. Readers of my Wycliffe *Romans 1–8* should know, however, that I made few substantive changes — a nuance here, a caveat there, and, of course, interaction with scholarly literature that had appeared since *Romans 1–8*.

    I wrote in the preface to my Wycliffe volume that I did not (in 1990) regret my decision to write a commentary on the much-worked-over letter of Paul to the Romans. I still do not. For what makes study of Romans so challenging is just what makes it so rewarding — being forced to think about so many issues basic to Christian theology and practice. At the same time I am more convinced than ever of the need for interaction with the "new perspective on Paul" that I feature in this commentary. I pray that what I have written will be of service to the church and that readers of this commentary will grow in that "practical divinity" which counts before God: "the doctrine of living to God," as the Puritan divine William Ames put it.

Many people contributed to this commentary. Several research assistants at Trinity Evangelical Divinity School helped compile bibliography and proofread various part of the MS: Joe Anderson, Harrison Skeele, David Johnson, Jay Smith, and George Goldman. Many students, too numerous to mention, sharpened my thinking about the text through their papers and class interaction. I am grateful to the Board and Administration of Trinity for their generous sabbatical program. The editors of the Wycliffe volume, Moisés Silva and Ken Barker, helped me think through several issues and polish my grammar; their contributions may still be discerned in this revised commentary. And I want especially to thank Milton Essenburg at Eerdmans and Gordon Fee, series editor, for taking my commentary on and interacting fully with my work.

Most of all, I thank my family, who have supported me and prayed for my work: my wife Jenny, and my children Jonathan, David, Lukas, Rebecca, and Christy. My youngest daughter (twelve years old), Christy, brought home to me just how long they have given this support when she commented as I finished the MS that my Romans was as old as she was.

Douglas J. Moo

ABBREVIATIONS

AAR	American Academy of Religion
AB	Anchor Bible
'Abot R. Nat.	*'Abot de Rabbi Nathan*
'Abod. Zar.	*'Aboda Zara*
A.D.	*anno Domini* (in the year of our Lord)
Add. Esth.	Additions to Esther
Adv. Haer.	*Adversus Haereses* (Irenaeus)
Ag. Ap.	*Against Apion* (Josephus)
Against Jul.	*Against Julian* (Augustine)
ALBO	Analecta lovaniensia biblica et orientalia
AnBib	Analecta Biblica
Ann.	*Annales* (Tacitus)
ANRW	*Aufstieg und Niedergang der römischen Welt*
Ant.	*Antiquities* (Josephus)
Ant. Rom.	*Antiquities of Rome* (Dionysius of Halicarnassus)
Apoc. Abr.	*Apocalypse of Abraham*
2 Apoc. Bar.	Syriac *Apocalypse of Baruch*
Apoc. Mos.	*Apocalypse of Moses*
Apol.	*Apology* (Justin)
Apost. Const.	*Apostolic Constitutions*
As. Mos.	*Assumption of Moses*
ATANT	Abhandlungen zur Theologie des Alten und Neuen Testaments
AusBR	*Australian Biblical Review*
AUSS	*Andrews University Seminary Studies*
BAGD	W. Bauer, W. F. Arndt, F. W. Gingrich, and F. W. Danker, *Greek-English Lexicon of the NT and Other Early Christian Literature*
Bar.	Baruch
Barn.	*Barnabas*

BBB	Bonner biblische Beiträge
BBET	Beiträge zur biblischen Exegese und Theologie
B.C.	before Christ
BDB	F. Brown, S. R. Driver, and C. A. Briggs, *Hebrew and English Lexicon of the OT*
BDF	F. Blass, A. Debrunner, and R. W. Funk, *A Greek Grammar of the NT*
BDR	F. Blass, A. Debrunner, and F. Rehkopf, *Grammatik des neutestamentlichen Griechisch*
BECNT	Baker Exegetical Commentary on the NT
BET	Bibliotheca ecclesiastica. Torino
BETL	Bibliotheca ephemeridum theologicarum lovaniensium
BEvT	Beiträge zur evangelischen Theologie
BFCT	Beiträge zur Förderung christlicher Theologie
Bib.	*Biblica*
Bib. Ant.	*Biblical Antiquities* (Pseudo-Philo)
BJRL	*Bulletin of the John Rylands Library of Manchester*
B. Meṣ.	*Baba Meṣiʿa*
BSac	*Bibliotheca Sacra*
BT	*Bible Translator*
BTB	*Biblical Theology Bulletin*
BWANT	Beitrage zur Wissenschaft vom Alten und Neuen Testament
BZ	*Biblische Zeitschrift*
BZHT	Beihefte zur historischen Theologie
BZNW	Beihefte zur Zeitschrift für die neutestamentliche Wissenschaft
c.	*circa* (around)
CBNT	Coniectanea biblica. NT
CBQ	*Catholic Biblical Quarterly*
CD	*Church Dogmatics*
CD	Cairo Damascus (Document)
cent.	century
cf.	confer (compare)
chaps.	chapters
1 Clem.	*1 Clement*
col.	column
CRINT	Compendia rerum iudaicarum ad Novum Testamentum
Cyr.	*Cyropaedia* (Xenophon)
Did.	*Didache*
diss.	dissertation
Diss.	*Dissertationes* (Epictetus)
DSS	Dead Sea Scrolls

Ebib	Etudes bibliques
Ecclus.	Ecclesiasticus
ed.	editor, edition
EDNT	H. Balz and G. Schneider (eds.), *Exegetical Dictionary of the NT*
e.g.	*exempli gratia* (for example)
EKKNT	Evangelisch-katholischer Kommentar zum Neuen Testament
Ep. Arist.	*Epistle of Aristeas*
Eph.	*Ephesians* (Ignatius)
Eq. Mag.	*De Equitum Magistro* (Xenophon)
1 Esdr.	1 Esdras
esp.	especially
ET	English translation
ETL	*Ephemerides theologicae lovanienses*
ETR	*Etudes théologiques et religieuses*
EvQ	*Evangelical Quarterly*
EvT	*Evangelische Theologie*
Exod. Rab.	*Exodus Rabbah*
ExpTim	*Expository Times*
FBBS	Facet Books, Biblical Series
FRLANT	Forschungen zur Religion und Literatur des Alten und Neuen Testaments
FzB	Forschungen zur Bibel
GEL	J. Louw and E. Nida (eds.), *Greek-English Lexicon*
Gen. Rab.	*Genesis Rabbah*
Germ.	German
Gk.	Greek
Haer.	*Haereses* (Epiphanius)
HBT	*Horizons in Biblical Theology*
H.E.	*Historia Ecclesiastica* (Eusebius)
Heb.	Hebrew
Herm. *Sim.*	Hermas, *Similitudes*
Herm. *Vis.*	Hermas, *Visions*
Hist.	*Historia* (Polybius)
HKNT	Handkommentar zum Neuen Testament
HNT	Handbuch zum Neuen Testament
HNTC	Harper's NT Commentaries
HTKNT	Herders theologischer Kommentar zum Neuen Testament
HTR	*Harvard Theological Review*
HUCA	*Hebrew Union College Annual*
HUTh	Hermeneutische Untersuchungen zur Theologie

IB	*Interpreter's Bible*
ICC	International Critical Commentary
IDBSup	G. A. Buttrick (ed.), *Interpreter's Dictionary of the Bible, Supplementary Volume*
i.e.	*id est* (that is)
Int	*Interpretation*
ITQ	*Irish Theological Quarterly*
JAAR	*Journal of the American Academy of Religion*
JAC	Jahrbuch für Antike und Christentum
JB	Jerusalem Bible
JBL	*Journal of Biblical Literature*
JETS	*Journal of the Evangelical Theological Society*
Jos. and As.	*Joseph and Asenath*
JPS	Jewish Publication Society
JR	*Journal of Religion*
JSNT	*Journal for the Study of the NT*
JSNTSup	*Journal for the Study of the NT,* Supplementary Volume
JSOT	*Journal for the Study of the OT*
JTS	*Journal of Theological Studies*
Jub.	*Jubilees*
Jud.	Judith
KD	*Kerygma und Dogma*
1, 2, 3, and 4 Kgdms.	1, 2, 3, and 4 Kingdoms
KJV	King James Version
J.W.	*Jewish War* (Josephus)
Lat.	Latin
LD	Lectio divina
lit.	literally
LSJ	Liddell-Scott-Jones, *Greek-English Lexicon*
LUÅ	Lunds universiteits årsskrift
LW	*Lutheran World*
LXX	The Septuagint
1, 2, 3, and 4 Macc.	1, 2, 3, and 4 Maccabees
Mek.	*Mekilta*
MeyerK	H. A. W. Meyer, *Kritisch-exegetischer Kommentar über das Neue Testament*
Midr. Qoh.	*Midrash Qohelet*
mg.	margin
MM	J. H. Moulton and G. Milligan, *The Vocabulary of the Greek Testament*

MNTC	Moffatt NT Commentary
MS(S)	manuscript(s)
MT	Massoretic Text
MTZ	*Munchener theologische Zeitschrift*
NA	Nestle-Aland, *Novum Testamentum Graece,* 27th ed.
NAB	New American Bible
NASB	New American Standard Bible
n.d.	no date
NEB	New English Bible
Neot	*Neotestamentica*
New Docs.	*New Documents Illustrating Early Christianity*
NICNT	New International Commentary on the NT
NICOT	New International Commentary on the OT
NIDNTT	*New International Dictionary of NT Theology*
NIGTC	New International Greek Testament Commentary
NIV	New International Version
NJB	New Jerusalem Bible
NKZ	*Neue kirchliche Zeitschrift*
n(n).	note(s)
NovT	*Novum Testamentum*
NovTSup	*Novum Testamentum,* Supplements
NPNF	*Nicene and Post-Nicene Fathers*
NRSV	New Revised Standard Version
NRT	*La nouvelle revue théologique*
n.s.	new series
NT	New Testament
NTA	*New Testament Abstracts*
NTAbh	Neutestamentliche Abhandlungen
NTD	Das Neue Testament Deutsch
NTS	*New Testament Studies*
NTTS	New Testament Tools and Studies
Odes Sol.	*Odes of Solomon*
OL	Old Latin
OT	Old Testament
par(s).	parallels
Par. Jer.	*Paralipomena Jeremiou*
Pesaḥ.	*Pesahim*
Pesiq. R.	*Pesiqta Rabbati*
PG	J. Migne, *Patrologia Graeca*
PL	J. Migne, *Patrologia Latina*
Plant.	*De Plantis* (Aristotle)
Pol.	*Politica* (Aristotle)

P.Oxy.	*Oxyrhynchus Papyri*
Prel. Stud.	*Preliminary Studies* (Philo)
Pr. Man.	Prayer of Manasseh
Ps.-Clem. Hom.	*Pseudo-Clementine Homilies*
Pss. Sol.	*Psalms of Solomon*
Qidd.	*Qiddushin*
1QH	*Hôdāyôt* (Thanksgiving Hymns) from Qumran Cave 1
1QM	*Milḥāmāḥ* (War Scroll) from Qumran Cave 1
1QpHab	Pesher on Habakkuk (Habakkuk Commentary) from Qumran Cave 1
1QpNah	Pesher on Nahum (Nahum Commentary) from Qumran Cave 1
1QS	*Serek hayyaḥad* (Rule of the Community) from Qumran Cave 1
4QFlor	*Florilegium* from Qumran Cave 4
4QMMT	*Miqsat Maʿaseh Torah* from Qumran Cave 4
11QMelch	*Melchizedek* text from Qumran Cave 11
RB	*Revue biblique*
REB	Revised English Bible
Res.	*De Resurrectione Carnis*
RestQ	*Restoration Quarterly*
rev. ed.	revised edition
RevExp	*Review and Expositor*
RevistB	*Revista biblica*
RevQ	*Revue de Qumran*
RevThom	*Revue thomiste*
Rh.	*Rhetorica* (Aristotle)
RHPR	*Revue d'histoire des religions*
RNT	Regensburger Neues Testament
rpt.	reprint
RSPT	*Revue des sciences philosophiques et theologiques*
RSR	*Recherches de science religieuse*
RSV	Revised Standard Version
RTP	*Revue de théologie et de philosophie*
Sanh.	*Sanhedrin*
SANT	Studien zum Alten und Neuen Testament
SB	Sources bibliques
SBLDS	Society of Biblical Literature Dissertation Series
SBS	Stuttgarter Bibelstudien
SBT	Studies in Biblical Theology
SD	Studies and Documents
SE	*Studia Evangelica*

SEÅ	*Svensk exegetisk årsbok*
S-H	W. Sanday and A. C. Headlam, *A Critical and Exegetical Commentary on the Epistle to the Romans*
Shabb.	*Shabbat*
Sib. Or.	*Sibylline Oracles*
Sifre Deut.	*Sifre Deuteronomy*
Sipre Lev.	*Sipre Leviticus*
Sipre Num.	*Sipre Numbers*
Sir.	Sirach
SJLA	Studies in Judaism in Late Antiquity
SJT	*Scottish Journal of Theology*
Smyrn.	*To the Smyrneans* (Ignatius)
SNT	Studien zum Neuen Testament
SNTSMS	Society for NT Studies Monograph Series
SPB	Studia postbiblica
SPCIC	*Studiorum Paulinorum Congressus Internationalis Catholicus*
ST	*Studia Theologica*
StrB	H. Strack and P. Billerbeck, *Kommentar zum Neuen Testament*
SUNT	Studien zur Umwelt des Neuen Testaments
Tanch. B.	*Tanchuma Buber*
TBei	*Theologische Beiträge*
TBl	*Theologische Blätter*
TBü	Theologische Bücherei
TDNT	*Theological Dictionary of the NT*
TDOT	*Theological Dictionary of the OT*
TEV	Today's English Version
T. 12 Patriarchs	*Testaments of the Twelve Patriarchs* (listed individually)
T. Job	*Testament of Job*
T. Mos.	*Testament of Moses*
Tg. Ket.	*Targum of the Writings*
Tg. Neof.	*Targum Neofiti*
THKNT	Theologischer Handkommentar zum Neuen Testament
TLZ	*Theologische Literaturzeitung*
TNTC	Tyndale NT Commentary
TOTC	Tyndale OT Commentary
TP	*Theologie und Philosophie*
Tob.	Tobit
trans.	translated by
TrinJ	*Trinity Journal*
TToday	*Theology Today*

TynBul	*Tyndale Bulletin*
TZ	*Theologische Zeitschrift*
UBS	United Bible Societies *Greek New Testament,* 4th ed.
UNT	Unterschungen zum Neuen Testament
USQR	*Union Seminary Quarterly Review*
v.l.	varia lectio (variant reading)
vol.	volume
v(v.)	verse(s)
WBC	Word Biblical Commentary
WEC	Wycliffe Exegetical Commentary
WH	Westcott and Hort, *Greek New Testament*
Wis.	Wisdom of Solomon
WMANT	Wissenschaftliche Monographien zum Alten und Neuen Testament
WTJ	*Westminster Theological Journal*
WUNT	Wissenschaftliche Untersuchungen zum Neuen Testament
WW	*Word and World*
Yad.	*Yadayim*
Yebam.	*Yebamot*
Z-G	M. Zerwick and M. Grosvenor, *A Grammatical Analysis of the Greek NT*
ZNW	*Zeitschrift für die neutestamentliche Wissenschaft*
ZTK	*Zeitschrift für Theologie und Kirche*

BIBLIOGRAPHY

I. A NOTE ON THE USE OF PRIMARY SOURCES

Unless otherwise noted, I have used *Novum Testamentum Graece* (ed. Kurt Aland, Johannes Karavidopoulos, Carlo M. Martini, and Bruce M. Metzger; 27th ed., 1993) for the text of Romans and other NT literature, *Biblia Hebraica Stuttgartensia* (ed. K. Elliger and W. Rudolf, 1977) for the Hebrew OT, *Septuaginta* (ed. A. Rahlfs, 1971) for the Septuagint, *Die Texte aus Qumran* (ed. E. Lohse, 1964) for the Dead Sea Scrolls, the Loeb Classical Library editions for the works of Josephus and Philo, *The Oxford Annotated Apocrypha* (RSV trans., 1957) for English translations of the Apocrypha, and *The Old Testament Pseudepigrapha* (ed. J. Charlesworth; 2 vols., 1983, 1985) for English translations of the Pseudepigrapha.

I have cited texts from the OT according to the versification of the English translations, even when the MT or LXX verse number differs.

II. A NOTE ON THE USE OF SECONDARY SOURCES

The interpreter of Romans is faced with the danger that the text of what Paul himself wrote will become obscured by the reams and reams of material that other people have written about the text. Thomas Hobbes is reputed to have said, "If I read as many books as most men do, I would be as dull-witted as they are." Certainly it is easy for the interpreter of Scripture to substitute broad reading in books about the text for deep reading in the text itself. In no book of the Bible is this more of a temptation than in Romans, and I hope I have not succumbed to it.

In any case, I have tried to keep the focus on the text while, at the same time, interacting with as much of the secondary literature as possible.

Even here, however, I have been quite selective, citing scholars who are representative of a particular view or who have argued a view particularly well. With respect to this point, the reader should note the difference between a simple reference to a work and a reference preceded by "see especially." The former indicates nothing more than that the work in question is representative of those who argue the particular position mentioned, but the latter means that the work in question provides a particularly good argument for the point in question.

I have cited commentaries by the last name of the commentator only; the reader may assume, unless noted, that the reference is to the commentator's notes on the relevant verse. I have cited several other frequently used volumes in the same way; these are listed under "Other Significant Works" below.

III. COMMENTARIES

The following list of commentaries is far from exhaustive: Romans, by virtue of its theological importance, has attracted uncountable numbers of commentators (Cranfield [1.30-44] has a particularly good survey of commentaries up to 1973). These range from technical, scholarly tomes, replete with Latin and Greek and extensive interaction with other scholars, to homilies designed to apply, rather than analyze, the message of the letter.

The reader will find few references to the second type because such books, by their very nature, say little new about the meaning of the text. A noted exception, however — if indeed they belong in this category at all — are the edited sermons of D. M. Lloyd-Jones. His very relevant homiletical applications grow out of insightful, theologically informed exegesis, and the reader can see from the notes how much his exegesis has informed my own thinking about the text.

On the other hand, I have consulted as many of those works on Romans that might be accurately termed "commentary" as I could lay my hands on. Realizing early on in my work that it was both impractical and unnecessary to cite all these works consistently — for there is much repetition of argument and conclusion — I selected twelve commentators for particularly careful study. Three factors informed my selection: exegetical excellence, theological sophistication, and representative significance. These commentaries may be called — to borrow a phrase from textual criticism — the "constant witnesses" in my commentary, and they are preceded in the list that follows with and asterisk (*). I regard these scholars as my exegetical "sparring partners," and I refer the reader to them consistently.

Achtemeier, Paul J. *Romans.* Interpretation: A Bible Commentary for Teaching and Preaching. Atlanta: John Knox, 1985.

Alford, Henry. *The Greek Testament.* 4 vols. 1845-60. Reprint. Chicago: Moody, 1958.

Althaus, Paul. *Der Brief an der Römer übersetzt und erklärt.* NTD. Göttingen: Vandenhoeck & Ruprecht, 1978.

Ambrosiaster, in *PL* 17.45-184.

Augustine. *Augustine on Romans: Propositions from the Epistle to the Romans and Unfinished Commentary on the Epistle to the Romans.* Chico, CA: Scholars, 1982.

Barclay, William. *The Letter to the Romans.* The Daily Study Bible. Edinburgh: St. Andrew, 1957.

*Barrett, C. K. *A Commentary on the Epistle to the Romans.* HNTC. San Francisco: Harper & Row, 1957.

Barth, Karl. *The Epistle to the Romans.* London: Oxford University, 1933.

———. *A Shorter Commentary on Romans.* Richmond: John Knox, 1959. (Cited as *Shorter.*)

Baulès, R. *L'Evangile puissance de Dieu.* LD 53. Paris: Cerf, 1968.

Bengel, J. A. *Gnomon of the New Testament.* 5 vols. 1742. Reprint. Edinburgh: T & T Clark, 1860.

Best, Ernest. *The Letter of Paul to the Romans.* Cambridge Bible Commentary. Cambridge: Cambridge University, 1967.

Black, Matthew. *Romans.* NCB. London: Oliphants, 1973.

Boylon, Patrick. *St. Paul's Epistle to the Romans.* Dublin: M. H. Gill, 1934.

Bruce, F. F. *The Letter of Paul to the Romans.* TNTC. Grand Rapids: Eerdmans, 1985.

Brunner, Emil. *The Letter to the Romans: A Commentary.* Philadelphia: Westminster, 1959.

*Calvin, John. *Commentaries on the Epistle of Paul the Apostle to the Romans.* 1540. Reprint. Grand Rapids: Eerdmans, 1947.

Chrysostom, John. *Homilies on Romans.* PG 60.391-682; *NPNF* 11.335-564.

*Cranfield, C. E. B. *A Critical and Exegetical Commentary on the Epistle to the Romans.* ICC, n.s. 2 vols. Edinburgh: T & T Clark, 1975, 1979.

Denney, James. "St. Paul's Epistle to the Romans." In *The Expositor's Greek New Testament,* vol. 2. 1904. Reprint. Grand Rapids: Eerdmans, 1970.

Dodd, C. H. *The Epistle of Paul to the Romans.* MNTC. New York: Harper and Bros., 1932.

*Dunn, James D. G. *Romans 1-8, Romans 9-16.* Word Biblical Commentary. Waco, TX: Word, 1988.

*Fitzmyer, Joseph. *Romans: A New Translation with Introduction and Commentary.* AB. New York: Doubleday, 1993.

————. "The Letter to the Romans." In *The Jerome Biblical Commentary.* Ed. Raymond E. Brown, Joseph A. Fitzmyer, and Roland E. Murphy. Englewood Cliffs, NJ: Prentice-Hall, 1968.

Garvie, Alfred E. *Romans.* The Century Bible. London: Caxton, n.d.

Gaugler, E. *Der Römerbrief.* Prophezei. 2 vols. Zurich: Zwingli, 1945, 1952.

Gifford, E. H. *The Epistle of St. Paul to the Romans.* London: John Murray, 1886.

*Godet, Frederic Louis. *Commentary on Romans.* 1879. Reprint. Grand Rapids: Kregel, 1977.

Gore, Charles. *St. Paul's Epistle to the Romans. A Practical Exposition.* 2 vols. London: John Murray, 1899.

Haldane, Robert. *Exposition of the Epistle to the Romans.* 1839. Reprint. London: Banner of Truth, 1958.

Harrison, Everett F. "Romans." In *The Expositor's Bible Commentary,* vol. 10. Grand Rapids: Zondervan, 1976.

Harrisville, Roy A. *Romans.* Augsburg Commentary on the New Testament. Minneapolis: Augsburg, 1980.

Hendriksen, William. *Exposition of Paul's Epistle to the Romans.* 2 vols. Grand Rapids: Baker, 1980.

Hodge, Charles. *Commentary on the Epistle to the Romans.* 1886. Reprint. Grand Rapids: Eerdmans, 1950.

Huby, J. *Saint Paul: Epître aux Romains.* Ed. Stanilas Lyonnet. Paris: Beauchesne, 1957.

Johnson, Alan F. *Romans: The Freedom Letter.* Everyman's Bible Commentary. Rev. ed. 2 vols. Chicago: Moody, 1984, 1985.

*Käsemann, Ernst. *Commentary on Romans.* Grand Rapids: Eerdmans, 1980 (ET of *An die Römer* [Tübingen: Mohr, 1980]).

Kirk, K. E. *The Epistle to the Romans.* Clarendon Bible. Oxford: Clarendon, 1937.

Knox, John. "The Epistle to the Romans." *IB,* vol. 9. New York: Abingdon, 1954.

*Kuss, Otto. *Der Römerbrief.* 3 vols. Regensburg: Pustet, 1963-78.

Lagrange, M.-J. *Saint Paul: Epître aux Romains.* Ebib. Paris: Gabalda, 1950.

Lapide, Cornelius à. *Commentaria in Epistolarum ad Romanos Commentarii. Sacram Scriptorum,* vol. 9. 1614. Reprint. Paris, 1859.

Leenhardt, Franz J. *The Epistle to the Romans.* 1957. ET, London: Lutterworth, 1961.

Lenski, R. C. H. *The Interpretation of St. Paul's Epistle to the Romans.* Minneapolis: Augsburg, 1936.

Liddon, H. P. *Explanatory Analysis of St. Paul's Epistle to the Romans.* London: Longmans, Green, 1893.

Lietzmann, Hans. *An die Römer.* HNT. Tübingen: Mohr, 1933.

Lightfoot, J. B. *Notes on Epistles of St. Paul.* 1895. Reprint. Grand Rapids: Baker, 1980.

Lipsius, R. A. *Briefe an die Galater, Römer, Philipper.* HKNT. Freiburg: Mohr, 1892.

Lloyd-Jones, D. M. *Romans.* 7 vols., variously titled, on chaps. 1 and 3:20–8:39. Grand Rapids: Zondervan, 1970-88.

Luther, Martin. *Lectures on Romans: Glosses and Scholia.* Luther's Works 25. St. Louis: Concordia, 1972.

Meyer, H. A. W. *The Epistle to the Romans.* MeyerK. 2 vols. 1872. Reprint. Edinburgh: T & T Clark, 1881, 1884.

(*)Michel, Otto. *Der Brief an die Römer.* MeyerK. Göttingen: Vandenhoeck & Ruprecht, 1978.

Morris, Leon. *The Epistle to the Romans.* Pillar New Testament Commentary. Grand Rapids: Eerdmans, 1988.

Moule, H. C. G. *The Epistle to the Romans.* The Cambridge Bible for Schools and Colleges. Cambridge: Cambridge University, 1887.

√ (*)Murray, John. *The Epistle to the Romans.* NICNT. 2 vols. Grand Rapids: Eerdmans, 1959, 1965.

Nygren, Anders. *Commentary on Romans.* 1944. Reprint. Philadelphia: Fortress, 1949.

O'Neill, J. C. *Paul's Letter to the Romans.* Pelican New Testament Commentaries. Baltimore: Penguin, 1975.

Pesch, R. *Römerbrief.* Die neue Echter Bibel. Wurzburg: Echter, 1983.

Ridderbos, Herman N. *Aan de Romeinen.* Commentaar op het Nieuwe Testament. Kampen: Kok, 1959.

Robinson, John A. T. *Wrestling with Romans.* Philadelphia: Westminster, 1979.

√ (*)Sanday, William, and Arthur C. Headlam. *A Critical and Exegetical Commentary on the Epistle to the Romans.* ICC. Edinburgh: T & T Clark, 1902.

Schelkle, Karl Hermann. *Paulus, Lehrer der Väter. Die altkirchliche Auslegung von Römer 1–11.* Düsseldorf: Patmos, 1956.

Schlatter, Adolf. *Gottes Gerechtigkeit.* Stuttgart: Calwer, 1959.

Schlier, H. *Der Römerbrief Kommentar.* HTKNT. Freiburg: Herder, 1977.

Schmidt, Hans Wilhelm. *Der Brief des Paulus an die Römer.* THKNT. Berlin: Evangelische, 1963.

Schmithals, W. *Der Römerbrief. Ein Kommentar.* Gütersloh: Mohn, 1988.

Shedd, William G. T. *A Critical and Doctrinal Commentary upon the Epistle of St. Paul to the Romans.* New York: Scribner's, 1879.

Sickenberger, Joseph. *Die beiden Briefe des heiligen Paulus an die Korinther und sein Brief an die Römer.* Die Heiligen Schriften des Neuen Testaments. Bonn: Peter Hanstein, 1923.

Smart, James. *Doorway to a New Age: A Study of Paul's Letter to the Romans.* Philadelphia: Westminster, 1972.

Stuart, Moses. *A Commentary on the Epistle to the Romans.* Ed. and rev. by R. D. C. Robbins. Andover, MA: Warren F. Draper, 1862.

Stuhlmacher, P. *Paul's Letter to the Romans. A Commentary.* Louisville: Westminster/John Knox, 1994.

Theodoret, in *PG* 82.43-226.

Thomas, W. H. Griffith. *St. Paul's Epistle to the Romans.* 1946. Reprint. Grand Rapids: Eerdmans, 1962.

Tholuck, F. A. G. *Exposition of St. Paul's Epistle to the Romans.* Philadelphia: Sorin and Ball, 1844.

Viard, A. *Saint Paul: Epître aux Romains.* SB. Paris: Gabalda, 1975.

Wesley, John. *Explanatory Notes upon the New Testament.* 1754. Reprint. London: Epworth, 1950.

Westcott, Frederick Brooke. *St. Paul and Justification, being an Exposition of the Teaching in the Epistles to Rome and Galatia.* London: Macmillan, 1913.

*Wilckens, Ulrich. *Der Brief an die Römer.* EKKNT. 3 vols. Neukirchen/Vluyn: Neukirchener and Zürich: Benziger, 1978-81.

Zahn, Theodor. *Der Brief des Paulus an die Römer.* Leipzig: A. Deichertsche, 1910.

Zeller, Dieter. *Der Brief an die Römer.* RNT. Regensburg: Pustet, 1985.

IV. OTHER SIGNIFICANT WORKS

Beker, J. C. *Paul the Apostle: The Triumph of God in Life and Thought.* Philadelphia: Fortress, 1980.

Bultmann, Rudolf. *Theology of the New Testament.* 2 vols. New York: Scribner's, 1951, 1955.

Burton, E. de W. *Syntax of the Moods and Tenses in New Testament Greek.* 3d ed. Edinburgh: T & T Clark, 1898.

Byrne, Brendan. *'Sons of God' — 'Seed of Abraham.' A Study of the Idea of Sonship of God of All Christians in Paul against the Jewish Background.* AnBib 83. Rome: Pontifical Biblical Institute, 1979.

Cambier, J. *L'Evangile de Dieu selon L'épître aux Romains. Exégèse et théologie biblique. Vol. I: L'Evangile de la justice et de la grace.* Brussels/Louvain: Desclée de Brouwer, 1967.

Dahl, Nils Alstrup. *Studies in Paul: Theology for the Early Christian Mission.* Minneapolis: Augsburg, 1977.

Davies, W. D. *Paul and Rabbinic Judaism.* London: SPCK, 1948.

Deidun, T. J. *New Covenant Morality in Paul.* AnBib 89. Rome: Pontifical Biblical Institute, 1981.

Donfried, Karl P., ed. *The Romans Debate.* 2d ed. Peabody, MA: Hendrickson, 1991.

Gamble, Harry, Jr. *The Textual History of the Letter to the Romans: A Study in Textual and Literary Criticism.* SD 42. Grand Rapids: Eerdmans, 1977.

Gundry, R. H. *Sōma in Biblical Theology with Emphasis on Pauline Anthropology.* SNTSMS 29. Cambridge: Cambridge University, 1976. Reprint. Grand Rapids: Zondervan, 1987.

Hagner, Donald A., and Harris, Murray J., eds. *Pauline Studies: Essays Presented to Professor F. F. Bruce on His 70th Birthday.* Grand Rapids: Eerdmans, 1980.

Hays, Richard B. *Echoes of Scripture in the Letters of Paul.* New Haven: Yale University, 1989.

Hübner, Hans. *Law in Paul's Thought.* Edinburgh: T & T Clark, 1984.

Koch, D.-A. *Die Schrift als Zeuge des Evangeliums: Untersuchungen zur Verwendung und zum Verständnis der Schrift bei Paulus.* BZHT 69. Tübingen: Mohr, 1986.

Kühl, E. *Der Brief des Paulus an die Römer.* Leipzig: Quelle & Meyer, 1913.

Longenecker, Richard N. *Paul, Apostle of Liberty.* 1964. Reprint. Grand Rapids: Baker, 1976.

Lorenzi, Lorenzo de, ed. *Battesimo e Giustizia in Rom 6 e 8.* Monographic Series of "Benedictina," Biblical-ecumenical Section, 2. Rome: St. Paul's Abbey, 1974.

————, ed. *Die Israelfrage nach Röm 9–11.* Monographic Series of "Benedictina," Biblical-ecumenical Section, 3. Rome: St. Paul's Abbey, 1977.

————, ed. *Dimensions de la vie chrétienne (Rm 12–13).* Monographic Series of "Benedictina," Biblical-ecumenical Section, 4. Rome: St. Paul's Abbey, 1979.

————, ed. *The Law of the Spirit in Rom 7 and 8.* Monographic Series of "Benedictina," Biblical-ecumenical Section, 1. Rome: St. Paul's Abbey, 1976.

Luz, U. *Das Geschichtsverständnis bei Paulus.* BEvT 49. Munich: Kaiser, 1968.

Metzger, Bruce M. *A Textual Commentary on the Greek New Testament.* New York: United Bible Societies, 1971.

Minear, Paul S. *The Obedience of Faith: The Purposes of Paul in the Epistle to the Romans.* London: SCM, 1971.

Moulton, James Hope. *Prolegomena.* Vol. 1 of *A Grammar of New Testament Greek.* Edinburgh: T & T Clark, 1908.

Munck, Johannes. *Paul and the Salvation of Mankind.* 1954. London: SCM, 1959.

Ortkemper, F.-J. *Leben aus dem Glauben: Christliche Grundhaltungen nach Römer 12–13.* NTAbh n.s. 14. Münster: Aschendorff, 1980.

Piper, John. *The Justification of God: An Exegetical and Theological Study of Romans 9:1-23.* Grand Rapids: Baker, 1983.

Räisänen, Heikki. *Paul and the Law.* WUNT 29. Tübingen: Mohr, 1983.

Robertson, A. T. *A Grammar of the Greek New Testament in the Light of Historical Research.* New York: George H. Doran, 1915.

Schoeps, H.-J. *Paul. The Theology of the Apostle in the Light of Jewish Religious History.* 1959. Philadelphia: Westminster, 1961.

Turner, Nigel. *Syntax.* Vol. 3 of *A Grammar of New Testament Greek,* by J. H. Moulton. Edinburgh: T & T Clark, 1963.

Watson, Francis. *Paul, Judaism and the Gentiles: A Sociological Approach.* SNTSMS 56. Cambridge: Cambridge University, 1986.

Westerholm, Stephen. *Israel's Law and the Church's Faith: Paul and His Recent Interpreters.* Grand Rapids: Eerdmans, 1988.

Zerwick, Maximilian. *Biblical Greek.* Rome: Pontifical Biblical Institute, 1963.

—————, and Grosvenor, Mary. *A Grammatical Analysis of the Greek New Testament.* Rome: Biblical Institute Press, 1981.

Zuntz, G. *The Text of the Epistles: A Disquisition upon the Corpus Paulinum.* The Schweich Lectures, 1946. London: British Academy, 1953.

INTRODUCTION

"The quintessence and perfection of saving doctrine."[1] This description of Romans by Thomas Draxe, a seventeenth-century English Puritan, has been echoed by theologians, commentators, and laypeople throughout the centuries. When we think of Romans, we think of doctrine. Moreover, this response is both understandable and appropriate. As we will see, Paul's letter to the Romans is thoroughly doctrinal: the "purest Gospel," as Luther put it.[2] But, like every book in the NT, Romans is rooted in history. It is not a systematic theology but a letter, written in specific circumstances and with specific purposes. The message of Romans is, indeed, timeless; but to understand its message aright, we must appreciate the specific context out of which Romans was written. In the pages that follow, I want to fill out this context as a basis for my interpretation and application of the letter.

I. GENERAL CIRCUMSTANCES

A. PAUL

Romans claims to be written by Paul (1:1), and there has been no serious challenge to this claim. In keeping with regular ancient custom, Paul used an amanuensis, or scribe, to write the letter, identified in 16:22 as Tertius. Ancient authors gave to their amanuenses varying degrees of responsibility in the composition of their works — from word-for-word recording of what they

---

1. Quoted in W. Haller, *The Rise of Puritanism* (Philadelphia: University of Pennsylvania, 1972), p. 87.
2. Luther, "Preface to the Epistle to the Romans" (1522).

dictated to quite sweeping responsibility for putting ideas into words. Paul's method in Romans is certainly far toward the "dictation" end of this spectrum. For the style of Romans is very close to that of Galatians and 1 Corinthians — and we have no evidence that Tertius was involved in the composition of either of these letters (indeed, see Gal. 6:11).

If the authorship of Romans is not in doubt, neither is the general situation in which it was written. Paul tells us in 15:22-29 that three localities figure in his immediate plans: Jerusalem, Rome, and Spain. Jerusalem is his immediate destination. Paul has completed his collection of money from his largely Gentile churches and is now on his way to Jerusalem to deliver the money to the Jewish saints there. This collection was an important project for Paul, as may be gauged from the fact that he talks about it in every letter written on the third missionary journey (cf. also 1 Cor. 16:1-4; 2 Cor. 8–9). Its importance goes beyond meeting the material needs of the poor Christians in Judea; Paul views it as a practical way to cement the fractured relationship between the Gentile churches of the mission field and the Jewish churches in the "home" country. In chap. 15 Paul demonstrates his concern about how this collection will be received by the "saints" in Jerusalem. Will they accept the gift and so acknowledge the links that bind Jewish and Gentile believers together in one people of God? Or will they reject it, out of suspicion of Paul and the "law-free" churches he has planted?

Rome is the second stage in Paul's itinerary (15:24, 28). But, while sincere in his desire to visit the Christians in Rome, Paul views Rome as little more than a stopping-off point in his projected journey to Spain. This is not to minimize the importance of the Christian community in Rome but reflects Paul's understanding of his call: "to preach the gospel in regions where Christ has not yet been named" (15:20). This task of initial church-planting is one that Paul has completed in the eastern Mediterranean: "from Jerusalem and as far around as Illyricum [modern-day Albania and the former Yugoslavia] I have 'fulfilled' the gospel of Christ" (15:19). As a result of the first three missionary journeys, churches have been planted in major metropolitan centers throughout southern and western Asia Minor (Tarsus, Pisidian Antioch, Lystra, Iconium, Derbe, and Ephesus), Macedonia (Philippi and Thessalonica), and Greece (Corinth). These churches can now take responsibility for evangelism in their own areas, while Paul sets his sights on virgin gospel territory in the far western end of the Mediterranean.

When we compare these indications with Luke's narrative in Acts, it is clear that Romans must have been written toward the end of the third missionary journey, when Paul, accompanied by representatives from the churches he had founded, prepared to return to Jerusalem (Acts 20:3-6). Since Luke tells us that Paul spent three months in Greece before beginning his homeward journey, we can also surmise that while staying here, with the next stage of his missionary career about to unfold, Paul wrote his letter to the Romans. It was probably in Corinth that Paul stayed while in Greece (see 2 Cor. 13:1, 10); and that Romans was written from here is suggested by the fact that Paul commends to the Romans a woman, Phoebe, from Cenchrea, a seaport adjacent to Corinth (16:1-2). Moreover, the Gaius with whom Paul is apparently staying (16:23) is probably the same Gaius whom Paul baptized at Corinth (1 Cor. 1:14). (And is the city-treasurer Erastus who sends greetings to the Romans [16:23] the same Erastus who is identified in an inscription as an *aedile* [city commissioner] at Corinth?[3]) The date at which Romans was written will depend, accordingly, on the dating of Paul's three-month stay in Greece; and this dating, in turn, is dependent on the hazardous process of constructing an absolute chronology of the life of Paul. The best alternative is probably A.D. 57,[4] though leeway of a year or two either way must be allowed.[5]

What emerges as especially significant from this sketch of Paul's own situation is that he writes his letter to the Romans at an important transition point in his missionary career. For almost twenty-five years, Paul has planted churches in the eastern Mediterranean. Now he prepares to bring to Jerusalem a practical fruit of that work, one that he hopes will heal the most serious social-theological rift in the early church — the relationship between Jew and Gentile in the people of God. Beyond Jerusalem, Spain, with its "fields ripe for the harvesting," beckons. On the way is Rome.

B. THE CHRISTIAN COMMUNITY IN ROME

In reconstructing Paul's situation when he wrote Romans, we can build on his own statements in Romans, as well as on the evidence from his other letters and from the book of Acts. We have no such direct evidence to use in

---

3. See the notes on 16:23.

4. Cf. esp. F. F. Bruce, *Paul: Apostle of the Heart Set Free* (Grand Rapids: Eerdmans, 1977), p. 475, for the general chronology.

5. E.g., G. Ogg dates Paul's stay in Corinth to A.D. 58-59 (*The Odyssey of Paul* [Old Tappan, NJ: Revell, 1968], p. 139). If the evidence of Acts is dismissed in constructing a Pauline chronology, a much wider time frame is possible: G. Luedemann dates Romans in A.D. 51/52 or 54/55 (*Paul: Apostle to the Gentiles, Studies in Chronology* [Philadelphia: Fortress, 1984], p. 263); C. Buck and G. Taylor in A.D. 47 (*Saint Paul: A Study of the Development of His Thought* [New York: Scribner's, 1969], pp. 170-71); J. R. Richards before 1 Corinthians in A.D. 52-54 ("Romans and 1 Corinthians: Their Chronological Relationship and Comparative Dates," *NTS* 13 [1966-67], 14-30); A. Suhl in A.D. 55, but from Thessalonica rather than Corinth (*Paulus and seine Briefe, Ein Beitrag zur paulinischen Chronologie* [SNT 11; Gütersloh: Mohn, 1957], pp. 264-82).

reconstructing the situation of the Christian community in Rome at the time of Paul's letter. Its origin is obscure and its composition and nature in Paul's day unclear.

The tradition that the church in Rome was founded by Peter (or Peter and Paul together) cannot be right.[6] It is in this very letter that Paul enunciates the principle that he will "not build on another person's foundation" (15:20). This makes it impossible to think that he would have written this letter, or planned the kind of visit he describes in 1:8-15, to a church that was founded by Peter. Nor is it likely that Peter could have been at Rome early enough to have founded the church there. Since the traditions we possess associate no other apostle with the church at Rome, the assessment of the fourth-century church father Ambrosiaster is probably correct: the Romans "have embraced the faith of Christ, albeit according to the Jewish rite, without seeing any sign of mighty works or any of the apostles."[7] The most likely scenario is that Roman Jews, who were converted on the day of Pentecost in Jerusalem (see Acts 2:10), brought their faith in Jesus as the Messiah back with them to their home synagogues. In this way the Christian movement in Rome was initiated.

Ambrosiaster is probably also right, then, when he identifies the synagogue as the starting point for Christianity in Rome. Enough Jews had emigrated to Rome by the end of the first century B.C. to make up a significant portion of the population.[8] They were not bound together in any single organizational structure. Their many synagogues apparently were independent of one another.[9] An important event in the history of the Jews in Rome is mentioned by the Roman historian Suetonius. In his *Life of Claudius,* he says that Claudius "expelled the Jews from Rome because they were constantly rioting at the instigation of Chrestus" (25.2). Most scholars agree that "Chrestus" is a corruption of the Greek *Christos* and that the reference is probably to disputes within the Jewish community over the claims of Jesus to be the

---

6. The *Catalogus Liberianus* (A.D. 354) names Peter as the founder and first bishop of the Roman church, but earlier tradition associates both Peter and Paul with the founding of the church (cf. Irenaeus, *Adv. Haer.* 3.1.2; 3.3.1). Because this earlier version is obviously incorrect, the later version is even more suspect (see O. Cullmann, *Peter: Disciple, Apostle, Martyr* [Philadelphia: Westminster, 1962], pp. 72-157).

7. *PL* 17, col. 46.

8. Philo (*Embassy to Gaius* 23.155) claims that the nucleus of the Jewish community in Rome was made up of enslaved prisoners of war. This is disputed, however, by H. J. Leon (*The Jews of Ancient Rome* [Philadelphia: Jewish Publication Society, 1960], pp. 4-5; cf. pp. 5-9); also see W. Wiefel, "The Jewish Community in Ancient Rome and the Origins of Roman Christianity," in Donfried, 86-92; S-H, xviii-xxv.

9. Leon, *Jews,* pp. 135-70; Romano Penna, "Les Juifs à Rome au temps de l'apôtre Paul," *NTS* 28 (1982), 327-28; Wiefel, "Jewish Community," pp. 89-92.

Christos, the Messiah. There is less agreement over whether the fifth-century writer Orosius is right in dating this incident in A.D. 49. But the date is probably correct[10] and receives incidental confirmation from Acts 18:2, where Luke says that Aquila and Priscilla had recently come to Corinth from Italy "because Claudius had commanded all the Jews to leave Rome." As with similar expulsions of specific groups from Rome, this one did not stay in force for long. Jews, like Aquila and Priscilla (cf. Rom. 16:3), were able to return to Rome within a short period of time, certainly soon after Claudius's death in A.D. 54.

Nevertheless, since the Roman authorities would not have distinguished between Jews and Jewish Christians, this expulsion, however temporary, must have had a significant impact on the development of the church at Rome. Specifically, the Gentile element in the churches, undoubtedly present before the expulsion, would have come into greater prominence as a result of the absence for a time of all (or virtually all) the Jewish Christians.[11] Theologically this would also have meant an acceleration in the movement of the Christian community away from its Jewish origins. The decentralized nature of the Jewish community from which the Christian community sprang would also make it likely that the Christians in Rome were grouped into several house churches. Confirmation that this was the case comes from Rom. 16, where Paul seems to greet several different house churches.[12] It is also possible, though more speculative, that these different house churches were divided theologically.[13]

II. INTEGRITY, LITERARY HISTORY, AND TEXT

Is the letter to the Romans as it is now printed in our Bibles identical to the letter that Paul sent to the Christians in Rome? Many scholars answer no. Of these a few base their conclusions on internal literary considerations alone. Two scholars, for instance, conclude that internal inconsistencies within Romans can be explained only if our present letter is composed of two or more

10. See esp. E. M. Smallwood, *The Jews under Roman Rule* (SJLA 20; Leiden: Brill, 1976), pp. 210-16; also F. F. Bruce, "The Romans Debate — Continued," *BJRL* 64 (1982), 338-39. On the other hand, Leon (*Jews,* pp. 23-27) thinks there was an expulsion of rioters only in A.D. 41 (cf. also Penna, "Les Juifs," p. 331).

11. Cf. especially Wiefel, "Jewish Community," pp. 92-101.

12. See esp. P. Lampe, *Die stadtrömischen Christen in den ersten beiden Jahrhunderten: Untersuchungen zur Socialgeschichte* (2d ed.; WUNT 2.18; Tübingen: Mohr, 1989), pp. 301-2.

13. E.g., Drane, "Why Did Paul Write Romans?" in Hagner and Harris, 215-18.

separate letters.[14] Others have identified interpolations in the text: single verses, or more, that have been added to the letter after the time of Paul.[15] But none of these theories can be accepted. They have no textual basis, and Romans has none of those somewhat awkward transitions that have led scholars to question the integrity of other Pauline letters.

But a more serious question is raised by the textual evidence. This evidence has led a significant number of scholars to think that the 16-chapter form of the letter we have in our Bibles was not the form of the letter that Paul sent to the Roman Christians. We can begin by listing the several forms of the text as it appears in the MSS tradition:

1. 1:1–14:23, 15:1–16:23, 16:25-27: P[61]?, ℵ, B, C, D, 1739, etc.
2. 1:1–14:23, 16:25-27, 15:1–16:23, 16:25-27: A, P, 5, 33, 104
3. 1:1–14:23, 16:25-27, 15:1–16:24: Ψ, the "majority" text, sy[h]
4. 1:1–14:23, 15:1–16:24: F, G [archetype of D?], 629
5. 1:1–14:23, 16:24-27: vg[1648,1792,2089]
6. 1:1–15:33, 16:25-27, 16:1-23: P[46]

Ostensibly, the major problem is whether the doxology (16:25-27) should be included, and if so, where — at the end of chap. 14, chap. 15, or chap. 16? If this were the extent of the problem, we would be faced with a relatively minor textual question. But the different placements of the doxology combine with other textual and literary issues to raise serious questions about the origin and literary history of this letter as a whole. As can be seen above, for instance, several MSS of the Latin Vulgate omit 15:1–16:23 entirely, an omission for which evidence is also found in another Vulgate codex[16] and in the absence of reference to chaps. 15 and 16 in

---

14. W. Schmithals posits a "Romans A" made up of 1:1–4:25; 5:12–11:36; and 15:8-13 and a "Romans B" made up of 12:1-21; 13:8-10; 14:1–15:4a, 7, 5-6; 15:14-23; 16:21-23; and 15:33, with 16:1-20 a letter to Ephesus and the rest of the text made up of various minor interpolations and fragments (*Der Römerbrief als historisches Problem* [SNT 9; Gütersloh: Gerd Mohn, 1975], summary on pp. 180-211; cf. also his commentary, pp. 25-29). For a critique see Hübner, 65-69. J. Kinoshita identifies the "original letter" as composed of chaps. 1; 2:6-16; 3:21-26; 5:1-11; 8; 12; 13; 15:14-33, with chap. 16 a letter commending Phoebe and the remainder a "manual of instruction" on Jewish problems ("Romans — Two Writings Combined — A New Interpretation of the Body of Romans," *NovT* 7 [1964], 258-77).

15. In addition to those treated in the commentary, I should mention O'Neill's constant recourse to theories of interpolation to explain large parts of the letter. See N. M. Watson, "Simplifying the Righteousness of God: A Critique of J. C. O'Neill's *Romans*," *SJT* 30 (1977), 464-69, for a pertinent critique.

16. Codex Amiatinus has all 16 chapters, but the section summaries corresponding to 15:1–16:24, taken from an earlier Latin version, are not included.

Tertullian,[17] Irenaeus, and Cyprian. All this raises the possibility that the 16-chapter form of the letter we now have in our Bibles is secondary to an original 14- or 15-chapter form. When we add to this the fact that a few MSS (G and the Old Latin g) omit the only references to Rome that occur in the letter (1:7, 15), we can understand why various theories of a shortened and more "universal" form of the letter have arisen.

Lake, for instance, argues that Paul's original letter was made up of chaps. 1–14 and that he added chap. 15 when he sent it to Rome.[18] But a more popular theory is that the original letter, addressed to Rome, consisted of 1:1–15:33. In both reconstructions, however, chap. 16 is considered to be no part of Paul's letter to the Romans. This conclusion, which is quite widespread, is based on both textual and literary considerations. The placement of the doxology after chap. 15 in P[46] can be accounted for, it is argued, only if the letter had at one time ended there.

But more important is the internal evidence of chap. 16 itself. The warning about people causing dissensions in 16:17-20 seems out of place with chaps. 1–15. Particularly striking are the extensive greetings in vv. 3-15. In addition to Phoebe, Paul greets twenty-five individuals, two families, one "church," and an unspecified number of "fellow believers" and "saints" — all these in a community that he had never visited. Surely chap. 16, it is argued, must be addressed to a church that Paul knows well — Ephesus being the best candidate because Paul singles out for a greeting "the first convert in Asia" (16:5; Ephesus was in the Roman province of Asia) and because we last meet Aquila and Priscilla there (Acts 18:19). According to one variation of this interpretation, chap. 16 was a separate letter of commendation for Phoebe.[19] According to another view, associated particularly with T. W. Manson, the chapter was added when Paul sent a copy of his original letter to Rome (chaps. 1–15) to Ephesus.[20]

---

17. Tertullian refers to 14:10 as being in the last part of the epistle (*Contra Marcion* 5.14).

18. K. Lake, *The Earlier Epistles of St. Paul* (London: Rivingtons, 1919), pp. 350-66.

19. E.g., E. J. Goodspeed, "Phoebe's Letter of Introduction," *HTR* 44 (1951), 55-57; Schmithals, *Römerbrief,* pp. 125-51 (see also his commentary, 544-53); J. Moffatt, *An Introduction to the Literature of the New Testament* (Edinburgh: T & T Clark, 1912), pp. 135-39; A. Jülicher, *An Introduction to the New Testament* (London: Smith and Elder, 1904), pp. 109-12; S. Davidson, *An Introduction to the Study of the New Testament* (London: Longmans, Green, 1868), pp. 137-40; Fitzmyer, in *Jerome Biblical Commentary,* pp. 292-93 (he has changed his mind in his later Anchor Bible commentary); Käsemann, 415, 419-20. Gifford (pp. 27-30) thinks that 16:3-20 was a letter written to Rome after Paul's imprisonment there. J. I. H. McDonald ("Was Romans XVI a Separate Letter?" *NTS* 16 [1969-70], 369-72) has shown that such a compact and greetings-oriented letter is possible.

20. Manson, "To the Romans — and Others"; cf. Zuntz, 276-77; W. Manson, "Notes on the Argument of Romans (Chapters 1–8)," in *New Testament Essays: Studies in Honour of T. W. Manson* (ed. A. J. B. Higgins; Manchester: Manchester University,

These theories, however, are almost certainly wrong.[21] Although there is definite evidence of a 14-chapter form of Romans in the early church,[22] the intimate connection between chaps. 14 and 15 makes it impossible to think that Paul's original letter was without chap. 15.[23] How, then, did the 14-chapter form of the letter originate? Lightfoot thought that Paul himself may have abbreviated his letter to the Romans, omitting the references to Rome in 1:7 and 1:15 at the same time, in order to universalize the epistle.[24] But it is unlikely that, had this been Paul's purpose, he would have cut off his epistle in the middle of his argument.[25] The same objection applies to Gamble's theory that the text of Romans was shortened after Paul's time in order to make the letter more universally applicable.[26] The earliest explanation for the shortened form is given by Origen, who claims that Marcion cut off *(dissecuit)* the last two chapters. Since this explanation offers the best rationale for breaking off the letter at 15:1 (for there is much from 15:1 onward that would have offended Marcion's anti-Jewish sentiments), I tentatively adopt it as the most likely explanation for the 14-chapter form of the letter.[27]

What, then, of the alleged 15-chapter form? Textually, this theory is on shaky ground from the outset, for there is no single MS of Romans that contains only 15 chapters. Its only textual evidence is the placement of the doxology in P[46] after chap. 15; but P[46] does not omit chap. 16. Furthermore, the internal arguments for omitting the chapter are not strong. The last-minute warning about false teachers in vv. 17-20 has some parallel with Paul's procedure in other letters; and the special circumstances of Romans explain why it occurs only here.[28] The number of people greeted poses a greater problem. But the expulsion of the Jews and Jewish Christians from Rome would have given Paul opportunity to meet a number of these people (like

---

1952), pp. 152-53; A. H. McNeile, *An Introduction to the Study of the New Testament,* rev. ed. with C. S. C. Williams (Oxford: Clarendon, 1953), pp. 154-58; R. P. Martin, *New Testament Foundations: A Guide for Christian Students* (2 vols.; Grand Rapids: Eerdmans, 1978), 2:194-96; F. Refoulé, "A Contre-Courant Romains 16,3-16," *RHPR* 70 (1990), 409-20.

21. Almost all recent treatments of Romans accept the 16-chapter form of the letter as original. See, for a recent treatment, Lampe, *Stadtrömischen Christen,* pp. 124-35.

22. E.g., Gamble, 16-21.

23. E.g., S-H, xci; Gamble, 84.

24. "The Structure and Destination of the Epistle to the Romans," *Biblical Essays* (London: Macmillan, 1893), pp. 287-320, 352-74; cf. Denney, 576-82.

25. Cf. Hort's comments, included in *Biblical Essays,* ed. Lightfoot, pp. 321-51.

26. Gamble, 115-24.

27. E.g., W. G. Kümmel, *Introduction to the New Testament* (London: SCM, 1975), p. 316; D. Guthrie, *New Testament Introduction* (Downers Grove, IL: InterVarsity, 1981), p. 413; S-H, lxvi; Barrett, 143 (?); Morris, 21-24 (?); Fitzmyer, 55-65.

28. For details, see the notes on 16:17-20.

Priscilla and Aquila) during the time of their exile in the east. It has even been argued that Paul would be more likely to greet individuals by name in an unfamiliar church where he knew only those whom he greeted than to risk offending the majority by greeting only selected members in a church he knew well.[29] At any rate, the problem posed by the number of greetings is not great enough to overcome the external evidence in favor of including chap. 16 in Paul's original letter to the Romans.

We conclude that the letter Paul wrote to Rome contained all sixteen chapters found in modern texts and translations.[30]

III. AUDIENCE

As we have seen, Christianity in Rome began among Jews (see "General Circumstances"). And, although the expulsion under Claudius eliminated the Jewish element in the church for a time, we can be certain that by the date of Romans at least some Jewish Christians (like Priscilla and Aquila) would have returned. We have no direct knowledge of the origins of Gentile Christianity in Rome; but, if the pattern of the Pauline mission was followed, we can surmise that "God fearers," Gentiles who were interested in Judaism and attended synagogue without becoming Jews,[31] were the first to be attracted to the new faith. Certainly by the date of Romans Gentiles made up a significant portion of the church in Rome (cf. 11:13-32 and 15:7-12). We may, then, be fairly certain that when Paul wrote Romans the Christian community in Rome was made up of both Jewish and Gentile Christians. This does not necessarily mean, however, that Paul had both groups in mind as he wrote his letter. It is to the evidence of the letter that we must turn to determine the audience.

Unfortunately, the letter appears to send out mixed signals on this issue. On the one hand, there is evidence to suggest that Paul had Jewish Christians in mind as he wrote: (1) he greets the Jewish-Christians Priscilla and Aquila and his "kinfolk" *(syngeneis)* Andronicus, Junia, and Herodion in chap. 16 (vv. 3, 7, 11); (2) he directly addresses "the Jew" in chap. 2 (cf. v. 17); (3) he

---

29. Lightfoot, "Structure and Destination," p. 298. Cf. Gamble, 48-49. On this issue, see also B. N. Kaye, " 'To the Romans and Others' Revisited," *NovT* 18 (1976), 37-77; Donfried, "A Short Note on Romans 16," in Donfried, 44-52; Lietzmann, 123.

30. For the question of the doxology, see the notes on 16:25-27.

31. A few scholars have cast doubt on the significance of this group in the first century, but without good reason; see T. M. Finn, "The God-fearers Reconsidered," *CBQ* 47 (1985), 75-84; A. Segal, *Paul the Convert: The Apostolate and Apostasy of Saul the Pharisee* (New Haven: Yale University, 1990), p. 94.

associates his readers closely with the Mosaic law (6:14: "you are no longer under the law"; 7:1: "I am speaking to those who know the law"; 7:4: "you have died to the law"); (4) he calls Abraham *"our* forefather according to the flesh" (4:1); and (5) he spends much of the letter on issues of special interest to the Jewish people: their sin and presumption of divine favor (2:1–3:8), the failure of their law (3:19-20, 27-31; 4:12-15; 5:13-14, 20; 6:14; 7; 8:2-4; 9:30–10:8), the significance of Abraham their "forefather" (chap. 4), and their place in the unfolding plan of God (chaps. 9–11).

Indications of a Gentile-Christian audience are also, however, evident: (1) in his address for the letter as a whole, Paul includes the Roman Christians among the Gentiles to whom he has been called to minister (1:5-6; cf. also 1:13 and 15:14-21); (2) Paul claims that his argument about the place of Jews in God's plan (11:11-24) is directed "to you Gentiles" (v. 13; and note the second person plurals throughout vv. 14-24); (3) Paul's plea to "receive one another" in 15:7 appears to be directed especially to Gentile Christians (cf. vv. 8-9).

We appear to be faced with a paradox. As Kümmel puts it, "Romans manifests a double character: it is essentially a debate between the Pauline gospel and Judaism, so that the conclusion seems obvious that the readers were Jewish Christians. Yet the letter contains statements which indicate specifically that the community was Gentile-Christian."[32] Several options are open to us.

First, we may dismiss or downplay the evidence of a Gentile-Christian readership and conclude that the letter is addressed solely, or at least mainly, to Jewish Christians.[33] But this will not do. Rom. 11:13 may suggest that Gentiles are only one part of the church, but 1:5-6 cannot be evaded (by, for instance, translating "among whom [Gentiles] you [Roman Christians] are located" — see the exegesis). This verse, standing in the introduction to the

---

32. Kümmel, *Introduction,* p. 309.

33. Cf. esp. F. C. Baur, "Über Zweck und Veranlassung des Römerbriefes und die damit Zusammenhängenden Verhältnisse der römischen Gemeinde," in *Historisch-Kritische Untersuchungen zum Neuen Testament* (2 vols.; Stuttgart: Friedrich Frommann, 1963), 1.147-266 (originally published in 1836 in *Tübinger Zeitschrift für Theologie*); idem, *Paul the Apostle of Jesus Christ: His Life and Work, His Epistles and His Doctrine* (2d ed.; 2 vols.; London: Williams and Norgate, 1876), 1.331-65; T. B. Zahn, *An Introduction to the New Testament* (3 vols.; Edinburgh: T & T Clark, 1909), 1.421-34; M. Kettunen, *Der Abfassungszwecke des Römerbriefes* (Annales Academiae Scientarum Fennicae; Dissertationes Humanarum Litterarum 18; Helsinki: Suomalainen Tiedeakatemin, 1979), pp. 73-81; W. Bindemann, *Die Hoffnung der Schöpfung. Römer 8,18-27 und die Frage einer Theologie der Befreiung von Mensch und Natur* (Neukirchener Studien 14; Neukirchen/Vluyn: Neukirchener, 1983), pp. 55-66; A. J. Guerra, "Romans: Paul's Purpose and Audience, with Special Attention to Romans 9–11," *RB* 97 (1990), 220-24; Watson, 103-7.

letter, suggests strongly that Paul regarded his addressees as Gentile Christians.

A much better case can be made, then, for the view that Paul's readers were Gentile Christians.[34] Not only does 1:5-6 appear to be decisive, but the evidence for a Jewish-Christian readership is not particularly strong. The greetings in chap. 16 show that there were Jewish Christians in the Roman community, but they do not require that the letter be addressed to them. The second singular address in Rom. 2 is a literary device and reveals nothing about the actual readers of the letter (see the introduction to 2:1–3:8). When Paul calls Abraham "our" forefather (4:1), he may be including with himself other Jews or Jewish Christians rather than his readers. That Paul associates his readers with the law is clear; but, as we argue (see the notes on 6:14 and 7:4), Paul thinks that Gentiles are "under the law" in some sense. And, even in 14:1–15:13, where reference to Jewish Christians can probably not be excluded, Paul's argument is directed mainly to the "strong in faith."

Finally, while some of the letter is, indeed, a debate, or dialogue, with Judaism (e.g., 1:18–4:25), it is not necessary that Jews or Jewish Christians be the intended audience for the debate. Paul's purpose may be to rehearse the basic issues separating Jews and Christians and to show what his gospel has to say about them, with the purpose of helping Gentile Christians understand the roots of their faith and their own situation vis-à-vis both Jews and Jewish Christians.[35] This purpose certainly becomes evident in chaps. 9–11, where Paul sketches the place of Israel in salvation history to stifle the arrogance of the Gentiles. Galatians, too, demonstrates clearly enough that teaching about the failure of the law and the inadequacy of circumcision was necessary for Gentile Christians to hear.[36] Moreover, the Gentiles themselves would have had a more personal interest in these matters than we have sometimes realized. For, as we have suggested, Christianity in Rome began in the synagogue, and the first Gentiles converted were almost certainly "God-fearing" synagogue attenders. This Jewish matrix for Christianity in Rome meant that even Gentile Christians would have "known the law" (7:1)

34. Cf. esp. Munck, 200-209; Schmithals, *Römerbrief,* pp. 9-89; Jülicher, *Introduction,* pp. 112-15. Dunn (p. xiv), while saying that "Paul is clearly writing to Gentiles," appears to allow for Jewish Christians among Paul's audience (cf. his statement later in the same paragraph that one of the matters Paul was writing about was "how gentile and Jewish Christians should perceive their relationship to each other").

35. D. Fraikin, "The Rhetorical Function of the Jews in Romans," in *Paul and the Gospels* (Vol. 1 of *Anti-Judaism in Early Christianity,* ed. P. Richardson; Studies in Christianity and Judaism 2; Waterloo, Ont.: Canadian Corporation for Studies in Religion, 1986), pp. 91-105.

36. E.g., Denney, 562-66; Munck, 204-7.

and that many of them would likely have been curious about how the gospel related to their previous understanding of circumcision and the law.[37]

Although this interpretation of the data is generally satisfactory, it must be questioned whether we can eliminate Jewish Christians entirely from Paul's audience. Paul claims in 1:7 that he is addressing "*all* those beloved of God in Rome," and it is clear that there were Jewish Christians in Rome. Moreover, Paul's exhortation to the "strong" and the "weak" makes best sense if both groups — roughly equivalent to Gentile and Jewish Christians respectively — were in his audience. And, while Paul's "dialogue with Judaism" in 1:18–4:25 and his sketch of the inadequacy of the law in chap. 7 can be accounted for on the basis of a solely Gentile audience, we must wonder whether these texts are not more adequately explained if there were at least some Jewish Christians in Paul's audience. These considerations make it likely that the audience to which Paul writes was composed of both Jewish and Gentile Christians.

Granted such a mixed audience, it is possible to suppose that Paul directs different parts of his letter to different groups within the Roman church. The most elaborate and best-defended version of this viewpoint is that of Paul Minear. He distinguishes five separate groups in the community, attributing each section of the letter to one or another of these groups.[38] While providing a salutary reminder that the community in Rome should not be simplistically divided into two groups according to ethnic origin, Minear's thesis goes beyond the evidence. The existence of several of his groups is unclear, and the progressive flow of Paul's argument in the letter renders a constant shifting in audience unlikely. This means that, with certain exceptions (e.g., 11:13-24), we must assume that Paul has the whole community, a mixed group of Jewish and Gentile Christians, in mind as he writes.

Along with the majority of commentators, then, we think that Paul addresses a mixed group of Jewish and Gentile Christians in Romans. Some

---

37. Cf. Schmithals, *Römerbrief,* pp. 69-82; N. T. Wright, "The Messiah and the People of God: A Study of Pauline Theology with particular reference to the Argument of the Epistle to the Romans" (Ph.D. diss., Oxford University, 1980), pp. 232-35; Dunn, xlvii-xlviii. Brown and Meier go too far, however, when they argue that Paul's letter presupposes that the Christianity in Rome "was a Christianity appreciative of Judaism and loyal to its customs" (R. E. Brown and J. P. Meier, *Antioch and Rome: New Testament Cradles of Catholic Christianity* [New York: Paulist, 1983], p. 110). Rom. 11 and 14–15 demonstrate that at least many Roman Christians had abandoned Jewish customs and were, indeed, negative toward Jews and/or Jewish Christians.

38. See his *Obedience of Faith.* Minear's groups are: (1) a mainly Jewish-Christian group that was condemning the "strong in faith" (cf. chap. 14); (2) a mainly Gentile-Christian group that scorned the "weak in faith" (the first group); (3) "doubters" who shared some of the same concerns as the "weak in faith"; (4) the "weak in faith" who did not, however, condemn the "strong"; (5) the "strong in faith" who did not despise the "weak in faith" (pp. 8-15).

decline to estimate the relative proportion of the two groups,[39] but the considerations advanced above show that Gentile Christians were in the majority, perhaps an overwhelming majority.[40] There is, however, one major problem with this reconstruction: Why, if there were Jewish Christians in the community, and especially if they were being slighted by the Gentile-Christian majority (cf. 11:13-24), would Paul have addressed the community as a *Gentile* one (1:5-6)?[41] The answer is probably that the community as a whole had by this date taken on the complexion of Gentile Christianity.[42] Indeed, it is perhaps just this shift from the earlier Jewish matrix of Roman Christianity to a more purely "Gentile" framework (a process accelerated by the enforced exile of Jewish Christians under Claudius) that has given rise to a sense of inferiority on the part of the Jewish segment. Moreover, the purpose of Paul in 1:5-6 (and 1:13) is not so much to identify the national complexion of the community as to locate it within the scope of his commission to the Gentiles. These texts, then, do not stand in the way of the conclusion that the audience Paul addresses in Romans is made up of a Gentile-Christian majority and a Jewish-Christian minority.

IV. NATURE AND GENRE

Romans is, of course, an epistle, but what kind? Many types of letters were written in the ancient world, ranging from brief, intimate, and informal notes to friends and family members to carefully crafted treatises designed for a large audience. Where within this range we should situate the Pauline letters has been much debated, but they clearly fall somewhere between these extremes.[43] Even the Pauline letters addressed to individuals — 1 and 2 Timothy, Titus, and Philemon (though cf. v. 2) — have broadly pastoral purposes. And the most general of his letters — Ephesians and Romans — are not only addressed to specific communities (at least in their present form) but also include material, like greetings to individuals, that would be of limited interest.

39. E.g., Cranfield, 1.17-21.

40. This is the view of a majority of scholars. See, for a representative statement, Kümmel, *Introduction,* pp. 309-11.

41. Gifford, in fact, urges this consideration as a reason for thinking that ἔθνη in 1:5 and 1:13 must mean "nations," so that the word would embrace the whole community.

42. See J. Becker, *Paul: Apostle to the Gentiles* (Louisville: Westminster/John Knox, 1993), pp. 336-37.

43. For a recent survey, see S. K. Stowers, *Letter Writing in Greco-Roman Antiquity,* Library of Early Christianity (Philadelphia: Westminster, 1986), p. 25. He also gives a good survey of the history and present status of the question.

Nevertheless, while Romans displays clear evidence of its "occasional" nature in its epistolary opening (1:1-15 [-17]) and closing (15:14–16:27), the really striking feature of the letter is the general and sustained argument of 1:16–11:36. Unlike, for instance, 1 Corinthians, where Paul's agenda is set by questions and issues raised by his readers, these chapters in Romans develop according to the inner logic of Paul's own teaching. Even the questions and objections that periodically interrupt the argument arise naturally from the flow of Paul's presentation.[44] Not once in these chapters does Paul allude to a circumstance peculiar to the community at Rome, and even the direct addresses of his audience are so general as to be applicable to almost any church: "fellow believers" (7:4; 8:12; 10:1; 11:25), "those who know the law" (7:1), "you Gentiles" (11:13). Nor does the situation change much in 12:1–15:13. None of the issues addressed is clearly local or particular in scope. Some even argue that the section about the "strong" and the "weak" (14:1–15:13) has no specific local situation in view.[45]

These features show that the main body of Romans is what we may call a "treatise," or "tractate." It addresses key theological issues against the backdrop of middle first-century Christianity rather than within the context of specific local problems. Nevertheless, Romans is no timeless treatise. We must not forget that Romans as a whole is a *letter,* written on a specific occasion, to a specific community. As we have seen, these specifics have not played a large role in Paul's presentation, but they have undoubtedly determined the agenda of theological and practical issues with which Paul deals. In this regard, we must note that Romans is far from being a comprehensive summary of Paul's theology. Many issues near and dear to him are absent, or only allusively mentioned: the church as the "body of Christ," the parousia, and Christology (in the "formal" sense). Moreover, the issues that Paul does treat are oriented to a specific, though broad, theological topic: the relationship between Jew and Gentile, law and gospel (see, further, the section on "Theme" below).

Romans, then, is a tractate letter and has at its heart a general theological argument, or series of arguments.[46] More specific genre identification is perilous. R. Bultmann compared Romans to the "diatribe," an argumentative

44. Cf. esp. Bornkamm, "The Letter to the Romans as Paul's Last Will and Testament," in Donfried, 25. Becker (p. 364) notes the general agreement in order of topics between Rom. 3:21–8:17 and Galatians as evidence that the agenda in Romans is set by Paul's own understanding of the gospel.

45. See R. J. Karris, "Romans 14:1–15:13 and the Occasion of Romans," in Donfried, 65-84; Drane, "Why Did Paul Write Romans?" in Hagner and Harris, 220.

46. R. N. Longenecker, "On the Form, Function, and Authority of the New Testament Letters," in *Scripture and Truth* (ed. D. A. Carson and J. Woodbridge; Grand Rapids: Zondervan, 1983), p. 104; cf. also Lightfoot, *Biblical Essays,* p. 315.

genre particularly popular with Cynic-Stoic philosophers (the best example is probably the *Discourses* of Epictetus, 1st-2d cent. A.D.).[47] Features of the diatribe include "fictional" conversations and debates, rhetorical questions, and the use of *mē genoito* ("may it never be!")[48] to reject a line of argument. Bultmann thought that the diatribe had a polemical purpose and read Romans accordingly. But S. Stowers argues that instruction and clarification rather than polemics were the purposes of the diatribe.[49] Recent research also suggests that "diatribe" was not so much a genre as a style.[50] In any case, while parts of Romans use this diatribe style (e.g., 2:1–3:8), the letter as a whole cannot be classified as a diatribe.

Scholars have suggested many other genre classifications for Romans: "memorandum,"[51] "epideictic" letter,[52] ambassadorial letter,[53] "protreptic letter,"[54] and "letter essay,"[55] to name only a few. None quite fits. Certainly Romans has similarities to these genres and to a large number of other ancient Hellenistic and Jewish genres and styles. But these resemblances mean nothing more than that Paul has effectively utilized various literary conventions of his culture to get his message across. Romans cannot finally be put into any single genre; as Dunn says, "the distinctiveness of the letter far outweighs the significance of its conformity with current literary or rhetorical custom."[56]

---

47. A. J. Malherbe has demonstrated the similarities between the use of μὴ γένοιτο in Paul and in Epictetus ("MH GENOITO in the Diatribe and Paul," *HTR* 73 [1980], 231-40).

48. *Der Stil der paulinischen Predigt und die kynisch-stoische Diatribe* (FRLANT 13; Göttingen: Vandenhoeck & Ruprecht, 1910).

49. S. K. Stowers, *The Diatribe and Paul's Letter to the Romans* (SBLDS 57; Chico, CA: Scholars Press, 1981); T. Schmeller, however, questions Stowers's conclusions on this point (*Paulus und die "Diatribe": Eine vergleichende Stilinterpretation* [NTAbh n.s. 19; Münster: Aschendorff, 1987], p. 436).

50. Stowers, *Diatribe;* Schmeller, *Diatribe;* K. P. Donfried, "False Presuppositions in the Study of Romans," in Donfried, 102-24.

51. K. Haacker, "Exegetische Probleme des Römerbrief," *NovT* 20 (1978), 2-3.

52. W. Wuellner, "Paul's Rhetoric of Argumentation," in Donfried, 128-46.

53. R. Jewett, "Romans as an Ambassadorial Letter," *Int* 36 (1982), 5-20; cf. also idem, "Following the Argument of Romans," in Donfried, 266-74.

54. See esp. D. Aune, "Romans as a *Logos Protreptikos* in the Context of Ancient Religions and Philosophical Propaganda," in *Paulus und das antike Judentum* (ed. M. Hengel and U. Heckel; Tübingen: Mohr, 1991), pp. 91-121; also Stowers, *Letter Writing,* pp. 113-14; Stuhlmacher, 13-14. The *Logos Protreptikos* is a speech of exhortation designed to win converts and attract people to a certain way of life (see Aune, p. 91).

55. M. L. Stirewalt, Jr., "The Form and Function of the Greek Letter-Essay," in Donfried, 147-71; Fitzmyer, 68-69.

56. Dunn, lix; idem, "Paul's Epistle to the Romans: An Analysis of Structure and Argument," *ANRW* 2.5.25, p. 2845.

V. PURPOSE

The interesting mixture of the general and the occasional outlined in the last section gives rise to one of the most debated questions about Romans: Why has Paul written *this* letter to *this* particular church?[57] This question can, of course, be bypassed by those who view Romans as a timeless theological treatise, a "compendium of Christian doctrine" (Melanchthon). But, however general and systematic its presentation may be, Romans is a letter, and the question of why Paul has written it cannot be evaded.

The question of the purpose of Romans has been given so many different answers because Paul says almost nothing on the subject. In the introduction (1:1-15), Paul talks about his plans to visit Rome and preach the gospel there, but he says nothing about the purpose of the letter. The conclusion of the letter elaborates these plans to come to Rome. Having "completed" his mission in the eastern Mediterranean, Paul is going next to Jerusalem to deliver the collection, and from there he plans to visit Rome on his way to Spain. But about the purpose of the letter he says only that he "has written on some points by way of reminder" (15:15). This statement is so general and stereotyped that little can be gleaned from it.

Paul's purpose in writing, then, can be determined only by fitting the contents of the letter with its occasion. We have sketched the general occasion for the letter earlier in the introduction and, briefly, in the last paragraph. But it is the specific occasion, in the sense of Paul's motivation for writing, that will give us the clue to the purpose of the letter. Opinions on this matter may be divided into two basic types: (1) those that stress Paul's own situation and circumstances as the occasion for Romans; and (2) those that focus on problems within the Roman community as the occasion for the letter. Few scholars completely ignore either of these occasions; but their reconstructions differ in the degree of importance accorded to each one.

A. FOCUSING ON PAUL'S CIRCUMSTANCES

Alternatives that focus on circumstances within Paul's own situation as his motivation for writing to the Romans may be conveniently, if somewhat simplistically, categorized by reference to the *location* that is Paul's focus.

---

57. On this whole question, see particularly the essays gathered together in Donfried and the especially complete survey of views in Morris, 8-17.

1. Spain

Most scholars, whatever weight they give to other circumstances, think that one of Paul's purposes in writing to the Romans was to prepare for his mission to Spain. A church-planting enterprise so far from Paul's home base in Antioch would create all kinds of logistical problems. It would be natural for Paul to try to enlist the help of the vital and centrally located Roman community for this mission. In fact, Paul alludes to his hopes for such support in 15:24, using the verb *propempō,* which connotes "help on the way with material support." We may, then, view Romans as Paul's "letter of introduction" to a church that he hopes to add to his list of "sponsors." This would explain the general theological focus of the letter, for Paul would want to assure the Romans that they would be sponsoring a missionary whose orthodoxy was without question.[58]

Preparation for the mission to Spain was certainly one of Paul's purposes in writing, probably even a major purpose. But it cannot stand alone as an explanation for the epistle. For one thing, had this been Paul's sole concern, we would have expected him to mention the visit to Spain more prominently — in the introduction, not just in the conclusion of the letter. For another, it is difficult on this interpretation to account for Paul's focus on questions of Jew and Gentile within salvation history.

2. Corinth/Galatia

One way of accounting for this emphasis on Jewish issues is to regard Romans as Paul's summary of the position he had hammered out in the course of his struggle with Judaizers in Galatia and Corinth. Paul's three-month stay in Greece came after the resolution of intense battles for the gospel in these churches; before he enters a new stage of missionary work, with fresh challenges and problems, Paul may well have decided to put in writing his settled views on these issues. Supporting this way of viewing the matter is the neutral and balanced stance that Paul in Romans takes on issues such as the law and circumcision — a balance that suggests no particular viewpoint was forcing Paul into a polemical position on these matters.[59]

---

58. Some of those who emphasize preparation for the Spanish mission as the most important purpose of the letter are D. Zeller, *Juden und Heiden in der Mission des Paulus: Studien zür Römerbrief* (Stuttgart: Katholisches, 1976), pp. 75-77; T. Borman, "Die dreifache Würde des Völkerapostels," *ST* 29 (1975), 63-69; Morris, 17. J. Blank calls Romans "the theological calling-card of Paul" ("die theologische Visitenkarte des Paulus"; "Gesetz and Geist," in Lorenzi, *Law of the Spirit,* 77).

59. Bornkamm, "Last Will and Testament," p. 25; Munck, 199; Kümmel, *Introduction,* pp. 312-13 (with, however, some modifications); Manson, "To the Romans — and Others," p. 4; Kaye, " 'To the Romans and Others' Revisited," pp. 41-50.

Again, there is probably much to this suggestion. But it leaves too much unexplained. Most important, why send this "last will and testament" (as Bornkamm calls it) to Rome?[60]

3. Jerusalem

The same objection applies to the suggestion that Romans contains the "speech" that Paul is preparing to deliver in Jerusalem when he arrives with the collection. As we have seen, Paul viewed this collection as a practical means to cement the fractured and sometimes bitter relationships between Jews and Gentiles in the early church. And, since Paul expressly requests the Romans to pray for the success of this mission (15:30-33), what is more natural than that he would outline his own theological position on the issue to the church?[61] Paul's impending visit to Jerusalem clearly loomed large in his mind as he wrote Romans. But there is no evidence that it was his overriding concern. Moreover, both this suggestion and the last fail to come to grips with Paul's stress on his desire to visit the community in Rome — an emphasis in both the introduction and conclusion to the letter. Surely this suggests that the letter had something specific to do with this planned visit.

B. FOCUSING ON PROBLEMS IN ROME

F. C. Baur inaugurated a new approach to Romans by insisting, against the prevalent tendency to consider Romans as a timeless theological manifesto, that this letter, like all the other letters of Paul, must be directed to specific issues in the church addressed.[62] To be sure, Paul had never visited the church in Rome. But there is sufficient evidence that he was acquainted with the situation there (see 1:8; 7:1; 11:13; 14–15; Prisca and Aquila would have been good sources of information).[63] Baur's general approach has enjoyed a resurgence in the last three decades. However, though Baur thought Romans had

---

60. See Zeller, *Juden und Heiden,* p. 42. B. Weiss suggested that it was the significance of Rome as the "capital of the world" that led Paul to send this "manifesto" there (*A Manual of Introduction to the New Testament* [2 vols.; New York: Funk & Wagnalls, n.d.], 1.300-307). But Paul gives no indication that he accorded Rome this kind of significance.

61. See esp. J. Jervell, "The Letter to Jerusalem," in Donfried, 53-64. Cf. also Dahl, 77.

62. Baur, "Zweck und Veranlassung des Römerbriefes," pp. 153-60.

63. Cf. K. H. Rengstorf, "Paulus und die älteste römische Christenheit," *SE* 2 (ed. F. L. Cross; Berlin: Akademie, 1964), pp. 447-64; contra, e.g., Bornkamm, "Last Will and Testament," p. 19.

a polemical purpose, contesting the claims of Jewish Christians, modern scholars have focused on other concerns as primary.

G. Klein thinks that Paul wrote with the purpose of providing the necessary apostolic foundation for the creation of a "church" in Rome. Significant, according to Klein, is the absence of the word "church" *(ekklēsia)* from the address of the letter (1:7). The Christians in Rome lacked the apostolic "imprimatur" that was necessary to constitute a church. In Romans, Paul provides this apostolic stamp of approval by rehearsing the "fundamental kerygma" that would turn a Christian community into a Christian church.[64] Klein's thesis does not stand up to scrutiny. Paul's failure to address the Romans as a church proves nothing; Philippians, Colossians, and Ephesians share the same omission.[65] More fundamentally, however, Klein's supposition that a church could not exist without a *personal* "apostolic foundation" is baseless.

Most of those who think that Paul writes with the needs of the Roman church uppermost in his mind seize on the implications of 14:1–15:13 as the key to the purpose of the letter. This passage reveals a split in the Roman community between Jewish and Gentile Christians. Here it is, many scholars think, that we find the central concern of the letter. The treatise in chaps. 1–11 supplies the theological basis for Paul's appeal for unity in chaps. 14–15, while chaps. 12–13 provide its general parenetic basis. According to F. Watson, Paul writes specifically to convert the Jewish Christians in the community to his view of a "law-free" gospel so that they will separate completely from Judaism and join the Gentile Christians in forming one Pauline congregation.[66] It is more popular, though, to view Romans as addressed to both Jewish and Gentile Christians, with the emphasis, if anything, on the latter group. This fits better with both the focus on Gentiles in the letter (1:5-6, 13; 11:13 — see above) and the probably increasingly dominant position of Gentiles in the church. Paul would then be writing to correct the Gentiles' indifference, even arrogance, toward the Jewish minority at the same time that he tries to show the Jews that they must not insist on the law as a normative factor in the church.[67]

---

64. "Paul's Purpose in Writing the Epistle to the Romans," in Donfried, 29-43.

65. Cf. Kettunen, *Abfassungsweck,* pp. 30-35.

66. Watson, 97-98; see also Boman, "Dreifache Würde," p. 69.

67. W. Marxsen, *Introduction to the New Testament* (Philadelphia: Fortress, 1968), pp. 92-104; W. S. Campbell, "Why Did Paul Write Romans?" *ExpTim* 85 (1974), 264-69; H.-W. Bartsch, "The Historical Situation of Romans. With Notes by W. Gray," *Encounter, Creative Theological Scholarship* 33 (1972), 329-38; Donfried, "A Short Note on Romans 16," in Donfried, 46-48; D. Patte, *Paul's Faith and the Power of the Gospel: A Structural Introduction to the Pauline Letters* (Philadelphia: Fortress, 1983), pp. 244-50; J. Marcus, "The Circumcision and the Uncircumcision in Rome," *NTS* 35 (1989), 67-81.

We think that Paul does, indeed, write with an eye on specific problems in the community at Rome. What he says in 14:1–15:13 is too specific to allow us to consider it as general "paraenesis," with no direct application to the Roman community.[68] And his direct address of Gentiles in 11:13-24 shows that Paul intends the theology he is developing to have direct practical relevance to his audience. But we also think that the divisions in the Roman church mirrored the tensions of the church at large in Paul's day. It would be going too far to say that the specific problem in Rome gave Paul a good excuse to write about this widespread tension. But it is the case that Romans is far less tied to issues bound up with a particular church than is any other Pauline letter (with the possible exception of Ephesians). We have noted that the major part of the body of Romans, chaps. 1–11, develops by its own internal logic: Paul's focus is on the gospel and its meaning rather than on the Romans and their needs.[69] The complete omission of any direct reference to the Romans until 11:13 makes it very difficult to think that the problems of the Roman church were foremost in Paul's mind. Then, too, there is much in this treatise that does not relate to the situation implied in chaps. 14 and 15. Nor is it fair to argue that Romans must be directed to the needs of the congregation in the same way that Paul's other letters are. For one thing, Romans stands apart, by definition, as being the only letter Paul wrote to a church for which he did not have established "pastoral" responsibility.[70] For another, we have too few letters of Paul to make black-and-white judgments about the kind of letter he could or could not have written.

The purpose of Paul in Romans, then, cannot be confined to any one of these suggestions; Romans has several purposes.[71] But the various purposes share a common denominator: Paul's missionary situation.[72] The past battles in Galatia and Corinth; the coming crisis in Jerusalem; the desire to secure a missionary base for his work in Spain; the need to unify the Romans around "his" gospel to support his work in Spain — all these forced Paul to write a letter in which he carefully rehearsed his understanding of the gospel, espe-

---

68. Cf. Donfried, "False Presuppositions," in Donfried, 107-10; contra Karris, "Romans 14:1–15:13," in Donfried, 65-84.

69. See, e.g., Aune, "Romans as a *Logos Protreptikos*," p. 112; Hays, 35.

70. E.g., E. P. Sanders, *Paul and Palestinian Judaism: A Comparison of Patterns of Religion* (Philadelphia: Fortress, 1977), p. 488; Drane, "Why Did Paul Write Romans?" p. 212.

71. See esp. A. J. M. Wedderburn, *The Reasons for Romans* (Edinburgh: T & T Clark, 1991); note also Fitzmyer, 80.

72. See, for a similar suggestion, L. A. Jervis, *The Purpose of Romans: A Comparative Letter Structure Investigation* (JSNTSup 55; Sheffield: JSOT, 1991), esp. pp. 158-63 (summary).

cially as it related to the salvation-historical questions of Jew and Gentile and the continuity of the plan of salvation.[73]

There may have been another reason for Paul to give such prominence to these particular issues. Paul's battle against Judaizers (cf. Galatians; 2 Corinthians) had gained for him a reputation as being "anti-law" and perhaps even "anti-Jewish." Rumors of Paul's stance on these matters had probably reached Rome, as 3:8 might suggest (Paul mentions people who are "blasphemously" charging him with saying, "Let us do evil that good may come"). As Paul introduces his gospel to the Roman community, he is aware that he must defuse these rumors and perhaps even win over some who were already hostile toward him.[74] But, unlike the situations he faced in Galatia and elsewhere, at Rome these doubts about Paul and his gospel did not, apparently, come from only one side.[75] As 14:1–15:13 suggests, he was contending both with Jewish Christians who were still tied to the law and with Gentile Christians who scorned everything Jewish — and very likely with a number of intermediate positions. Hence Paul fights on two fronts: criticizing Judaism for its overemphasis on the law and its presumption of "most favored nation" status, while affirming Israel as the "root" of the church and emphasizing its continuing place within the plan of God.

One more thing about the occasion and purpose of Romans should be mentioned. The legitimate desire to pin down as precisely as possible the historical background and purpose of the letter should not obscure the degree to which Romans deals with theological issues raised by the nature

---

73. See for this general approach Sanders, *Paul and Palestinian Judaism,* p. 488; Cranfield, 2.814; Fitzmyer, 68-83; Drane, "Why Did Paul Write Romans?" pp. 212-23; H. Moxnes, *Theology in Conflict: Studies in Paul's Understanding of God in Romans* (NovTSup 53; Leiden: Brill, 1980), p. 34; U. Wilckens, "Über Abfassungszweck und Aufbau des Römerbriefes," in *Rechtfertigung als Freiheit: Paulusstudien* (Neukirchen-Vluyn: Neukirchener, 1974), pp. 110-43; A. Wikenhauser and J. Schmid, *Einleitung in das Neue Testament* (6th ed.; Freiburg/Basel/Vienna: Herder, 1973), pp. 456-58; A. J. M. Wedderburn, "The Purpose and Occasion of Romans Again," *ExpTim* 90 (1979), 137-41; Beker, 71-74; Dunn, 1.lv-lviii; S. K. Williams, "The 'Righteousness of God' in Romans," *JBL* 99 (1980), 245-46.

74. Jülicher, *Introduction,* pp. 115-18; F. F. Bruce, "Romans Debate — Continued," in Donfried, 182-83; P. Stuhlmacher, "The Apostle Paul's View of Righteousness," in *Reconciliation, Law and Righteousness: Essays in Biblical Theology* (Philadelphia: Fortress, 1986), pp. 76-77; idem, his commentary, 3-10; Käsemann, 19-20 (though in more "existential" terms). We should probably not go so far, however, as to posit the existence of Judaizers in Rome, as, e.g., Stuhlmacher does (cf. also Fitzmyer, 34; M. Seifrid, *Justification by Faith: The Origin and Development of a Central Pauline Theme* [NovTSup 68; Leiden: Brill, 1992], pp. 192, 209).

75. E.g., H. J. van der Minde, *Schrift und Tradition bei Paulus: Ihre Bedeutung und Funktion im Römerbrief* (Paderborner Theologische Studien 3; Munich: Schöningh, 1976), pp. 190-94.

of God's revelation itself. Perhaps the earliest comment on the purpose of Romans comes in the Muratorian Canon (A.D. 200?): "to the Romans he [Paul] wrote at greater length [than in Corinthians or Galatians], concerning the plan of the Scriptures, showing at the same time that their foundation is Christ."

We moderns must beware the tendency to overhistoricize: to focus so much on specific local and personal situations that we miss the larger theological and philosophical concerns of the biblical authors.[76] That Paul was dealing in Romans with immediate concerns in the early church we do not doubt. But, especially in Romans, these issues are ultimately those of the church — and the world — of all ages: the continuity of God's plan of salvation, the sin and need of human beings, God's provision for our sin problem in Christ, the means to a life of holiness, and security in the face of suffering and death.[77] Augustine, Luther, Calvin, and Wesley, whatever their failings as exegetes, saw this; and perhaps they understood more clearly than many of their latter-day critics.[78] We need to recognize that Romans is God's word to *us* and read it seeking to discover the message that God has for us in it. As Luther said, "[Romans] is worthy not only that every Christian should know it word for word, by heart, but occupy himself with it every day, as the daily bread of the soul. It can never be read or pondered too much, and the more it is dealt with the more precious it becomes, and the better it tastes."[79]

VI. THEME

At the risk of oversimplification, we can chart the history of the discussion of the theme of Romans as a movement from a focus on the beginning of the epistle to its end. The Reformers and their followers, following the lead of Luther, almost universally gave pride of place to chaps. 1–5, with their

76. For all the problems with "canonical criticism," B. Childs has a point when he warns about the danger of allowing specific historical contexts to blot out the larger theological dimensions of Romans (*The New Testament as Canon: An Introduction* [Philadelphia: Fortress, 1985], p. 51).

77. Cf. Denney (570): "Is it not manifest that when we give [the 'conditions' under which Paul wrote] all the historical definiteness of which they are capable, there is something in them which rises above the casualness of time and place, something which might easily give the epistle not an accidental or occasional character, but the character of an exposition of principles?"

78. For similar remarks, although in a different context, see Westerholm, 222.

79. Luther, "Preface to the Epistle to the Romans" (1522).

theme, justification by faith, as the center of the letter.[80] At the beginning of this century, however, Schweitzer and others argued that justification by faith was no more than a "battle doctrine" *(Kampflehre),* a theological concept that Paul used simply to oppose Judaizers. The real center of Paul's thinking is to be found in chaps. 5–8, in his doctrine of union with Christ and the work of God's Spirit.[81] Others objected to the traditional focus on justification by faith because they thought that it illegitimately read back into Paul's day a modern and Western preoccupation with the individual and his conscience. "How can a sinful person be made right with God?" was Luther's problem, but it was not Paul's. Rather, the question Paul sought to answer was: "How can Gentiles be incorporated with Jews into God's people without jeopardizing the continuity of salvation history?" For these scholars, Rom. 9–11, far from being a detour from the real theme of the letter,[82] was the heart of the letter.[83] Finally, as we have seen, the last thirty years have witnessed an emphasis on Romans as an occasional letter, directed to the needs of the Roman church. For many of those who advocate this approach to the letter, Paul's exhortation to unity in 14:1–15:13 expresses the major purpose of the letter (see above on Purpose).

Forms of each of these positions are argued in the current literature on Romans. H. Hübner and others have vigorously reasserted, against its critics, the centrality of justification in Romans and in Paul generally.[84] In the approach associated especially with E. Käsemann, justification language is subsumed under the category of "the righteousness of God," interpreted broadly to mean God's intervention to reclaim his creation for himself and to bring salvation to his people.[85] Indeed, he claims that this interpretation is the theme

---

80. It may be questioned, however, whether all those usually cited for this view are claiming that justification is the theme of the letter or whether they are singling it out as a crucial teaching within the letter. Note, e.g., that Calvin makes justification the main topic of the first five chapters only (xxix, 66).

81. See, e.g. (though with differences in detail), H. Lüdemann, *Die Anthropologie des Apostels Paulus und ihre Stellung innerhalb seiner Heilslehre* (Kiel: Universitäts-Buchhandlung, 1872); P. Wernle, *Der Christ und die Sünde bei Paulus* (Freiburg: Mohr, 1904); W. Wrede, *Paul* (London: Philip Green, 1907), pp. 123-25; A. Schweitzer, *The Mysticism of Paul the Apostle* (London: A & C Black, 1931), pp. 205-26.

82. As many scholars who put the center of Romans in chaps. 1–4 or 5–8 thought; see, e.g., S-H, who claim that chaps. 9–11 belong to "the circumference of Paul's thought" (xlv).

83. See particularly K. Stendahl, "The Apostle Paul and the Introspective Conscience of the West," *HTR* 56 (1963), 199-215.

84. H. Hübner, "Pauli Theologiae Proprium," *NTS* 26 (1980), 445-73; Seifrid, *Justification;* Nygren, 10-17.

85. E.g., E. Käsemann, "The Righteousness of God in Paul," in *New Testament Questions of Today* (Philadelphia: Fortress, 1969), p. 168; Beker's view is somewhat similar (p. 92).

of Romans. E. P. Sanders has reemphasized the importance of the "participationist" categories of Rom. 5–8.[86] Perhaps the most popular recent viewpoint is that Romans is about the role of Jews in salvation history.[87] Many other focal points for the letter have also been advocated: "God,"[88] "hope,"[89] and "salvation,"[90] to name only a few.

Before commenting on these proposals, two cautions are in order. First, we must be careful not to impose on Romans a single theme when Paul may never have thought in those terms. It is true that the tractate nature of the letter encourages the supposition that Paul may have had a single overarching theme in view. But such a supposition is not necessary, particularly when we recognize that the tractate style recedes into the background after chap. 11. In other words, a theme that fits 1:16–11:36 may not fit the letter as a whole. Romans may, then, have several themes without having any single, unifying topic. Second, we must define what we mean when we talk about *the* "theme," or "center," of the letter. Do we mean the doctrine that serves to ground and unify the various topics of the letter, the theological framework of Paul's thinking, or the most important, or critical, topic in the letter — or something else? Some of the debate on this issue is no more than shadow-boxing, because scholars are confusing categories and are not arguing about the same thing.

To avoid confusion, we will define "theme" as the overarching topic that is able to stand as the heading of Romans as a whole. Before further exploring the issue of theme per se, we need to comment on some of the related issues that we raised above.

---

86. Sanders, *Paul and Palestinian Judaism*, pp. 434-42.

87. E. P. Sanders, *Paul, the Law and the Jewish People* (Philadelphia: Fortress, 1983), p. 30; cf. Jervell, "Letter to Jerusalem," pp. 59-60; H. Boers, "The Problem of Jews and Gentiles in the Macro-Structure of Romans," *Neot* 15 (1981), 1-11; idem, *The Justification of the Gentiles: Paul's Letters to the Galatians and Romans* (Peabody, MA: Hendrickson, 1994), pp. 80-142; R. B. Hays, " 'Have We Found Abraham to be Our Forefather according to the Flesh?' A Reconsideration of Rom 4:1," *NovT* 27 (1985), 84-85; R. D. Kaylor, *Paul's Covenant Community. Jew and Gentile in Romans* (Atlanta: John Knox, 1988), pp. 18-19, passim; Dunn, 1.lxii-lxiii ("the integrating motif").

88. L. Morris, "The Theme of Romans," in *Apostolic History and the Gospel: Biblical and Historical Essays presented to F. F. Bruce on his 60th Birthday* (ed. W. W. Gasque and R. P. Martin; Grand Rapids: Eerdmans, 1970), pp. 250-62; cf. Wright, "Messiah and the People of God," p. 53; A. Feuillet, "La vie nouvelle du chrétien et les trois Personnes divines d'après Rom. I–VIII," *RevThom* 83 (1983), 7.

89. J. P. Heil, *Romans: Paul's Letter of Hope* (AnBib 112; Rome: Pontifical Biblical Institute, 1987).

90. Cambier, 34.

A. THE THEOLOGICAL STARTING POINT

Christology is the theological ground and starting point of the letter. Paul's understanding of Christ is the only topic broad enough to unify his various emphases. And, though no paragraph is devoted to Christology per se in the doctrinal portion of the letter, we must not neglect the importance of Rom. 1:3-4, where Paul describes the content of his gospel in terms of Christology.[91] Other passages make God's act in Christ the center of God's eschatological revelation (3:21-26; 5:12-21), and all the topics in the letter are grounded in Christ (note the constant refrain in chaps. 5–8: "through Jesus Christ our Lord"). God's act in Christ is the starting point of all Paul's thinking and is so basic to the early church that he could assume that the Roman Christians shared this conviction with him. In this sense, while Christology is nowhere in Romans the expressed *topic,* it is everywhere the underlying point of departure.

B. THE CONCEPTUAL FRAMEWORK

Second, the theological framework within which Paul expresses his key ideas in Romans can be called salvation history. The phrase "salvation history," or "redemptive history" (Germ. *Heilsgeschichte*), is used to designate several different and sometimes contradictory concepts. We are using the phrase in a rather untechnical fashion to denote a conceptual framework that Paul uses to describe what has taken place in Christ. In focusing on Paul, we do not intend to confine the conception exclusively to him; on the contrary, it is basic to the NT and perhaps the OT as well.[92]

---

91. See Wright, "Messiah and People of God," p. 51.

92. Some of the more important studies are O. Cullmann, *Christ and Time* (Philadelphia: Westminster, 1950) and *Salvation in History* (London: SCM, 1967); G. E. Ladd, *A Theology of the New Testament* (Grand Rapids: Eerdmans, 1974), cf. pp. 369-75; L. Goppelt, *Theology of the New Testament* (2 vols.; Grand Rapids: Eerdmans, 1975, 1976), cf. 1.280-81; and esp. H. Ridderbos, *Paul: An Outline of His Theology* (Grand Rapids: Eerdmans, 1974), cf. pp. 44-90. Nygren employs the two-age scheme extensively in his commentary, as does E. Käsemann, although with modifications introduced by his more existential approach. (See the interchange between Käsemann and Stendahl over the nature and importance of "salvation history" in Paul — Stendahl, "Introspective Conscience"; Käsemann, "Justification and Salvation History in the Epistle to the Romans," in *Perspectives on Paul* [Philadelphia: Fortress, 1971], pp. 60-78; Stendahl, "Introspective Conscience," also in *Paul among Jews and Gentiles* [Philadelphia: Fortress, 1976].) A useful introduction to some of these perspectives at a more popular level is L. Smedes's *Union with Christ: A Biblical View of the New Life in Jesus Christ* (Grand Rapids: Eerdmans, 1983).

Justification for the salvation-historical approach begins with due appreciation for the fact that God has accomplished redemption as part of a historical process. God's work in Christ is the center of history, the point from which both past and future must be understood. The cross and resurrection of Christ are both the fulfillment of the OT and the basis and anticipation of final glory. With Christ as the climax of history, then, history can be divided into two "eras," or "aeons," each with its own founder — Adam and Christ, respectively — and each with its own ruling powers — sin, the law, flesh, and death on the one hand; righteousness, grace, the Spirit, and life on the other. All people start out in the "old era" by virtue of participation in the act by which it was founded — the sin of Adam (cf. Rom. 5:12, 18-19). But one can be transferred into the "new era" by becoming joined to Christ, the founder of that era, thereby participating in the acts through which that era came into being — Christ's death, burial, and resurrection (cf. 6:1-6). This *corporate* element in Paul's thinking is vital to understanding his argument at a number of points in Romans.

The division of history into two ages was popular in Jewish apocalyptic, and Paul probably drew his conception from that background. But his understanding of God's work in Christ introduces a key qualification in the scheme. Although Jewish apocalyptic conceived of the transition from old age to new as taking place in the field of actual history, Paul's conception is necessarily more nuanced. For, contrary to Jewish expectation, the Messiah has accomplished the work of redemption, the Spirit has been poured out, yet evil has not been eradicated, the general resurrection is still future, and the final state of God's kingdom has not been established. In other words, the new era has begun — has been inaugurated — but it has not yet replaced the old era. Both ages exist simultaneously; and this means that "history," in the sense of temporal sequence, is not ultimately determinative in Paul's salvation-historical scheme.[93] Thus, the "change of aeons," while occurring historically at the cross (cf. 3:21), becomes real for the individual only at the point of faith. The "change of aeons" that took place in Christ is experienced only "in Christ." Therefore, the person who lives *after* Christ's death and resurrection and who has not appropriated the benefits of those events by faith lives in the old era yet: enslaved to sin, in the flesh, doomed to eternal death. On the other hand, Abraham, for example, though living many centuries *before* Christ, must, in light of Rom. 4,

---

93. See esp. K. Stalder, *Das Werk des Geistes in des Heiligung bei Paulus* (Zürich: EVZ, 1962), pp. 240-48; V. P. Furnish, *Theology and Ethics in Paul* (Nashville: Abingdon, 1968), pp. 134-35; J. M. G. Barclay, *Obeying the Truth: Paul's Ethics in Galatians* (Edinburgh: T & T Clark, 1988), pp. 99, 104-5; Beker, 135-81. As M. Silva points out, "Paul is not concerned about purely chronological differences but about the difference in *character* between the two ages: the age of the flesh (= self-confidence and sin) and the age of the Spirit (= promise and salvation)" (*Philippians* [WEC; Chicago: Moody, 1988], p. 186 n. 28).

be considered to belong, in some sense at least, to the new era. This circumstance introduces a confusing factor, making it difficult to come up with an overall system that is capable of integrating all of Paul's applications of salvation history. At this point, however, it is important to recall that, while rooted in the nature of God's redemptive work, the salvation-historical scheme we have delineated is largely a useful conceptual tool for Paul, a tool that he uses to make different points in different places.[94] But it serves Paul well in Romans, where it perfectly serves his purpose to make clear the finality and uniqueness of the gospel as well as its connections with the revelation of God in the OT.[95]

C. THE THEME

The trend in recent scholarship to make the relationship of Jews and Gentiles within the new covenant people of God central to Romans is understandable and, to a considerable extent, justified. For Romans is permeated with concern for the Jews, their law, and their relationship to the revelation of the righteousness of God and to the increasingly Gentile-oriented church. The word "law," usually referring to the Mosaic law, occurs more times in Romans (74) than in all the other letters of Paul combined (47); Paul devotes an entire chapter to it (7), and it recurs in relationship to almost every topic Paul treats (cf., e.g., 2:12-16; 4:13-15; 5:13-14, 20; 6:14, 15; 8:2-4; 9:31–10:5; 13:8-10).[96] Because the law is central to the Mosaic covenant, Paul's discussion of law becomes a discussion of the Mosaic covenant and its relationship to the New Covenant initiated in Christ. Rom. 9–11 is no excursus then, but brings to a climax a theme that has been present in the letter since its opening verses: "the gospel of God which he promised beforehand through his prophets in the holy scriptures" (1:1b-2). For the issue of the Jew is, finally, the issue of continuity in God's salvation plan and, consequently, of God's faithfulness to his promises (cf. 3:1-8; 9:6). In Romans, Paul teaches both the newness of God's intervention in Christ — which means a "no" to the law and the Mosaic covenant as permanent features of salvation history — and the connections between the new act and the OT — which means a "yes" to the Abrahamic promise and to the future of Israel. Paul, then, both denies to the Jew

---

94. Cf. L. Goppelt, "Paulus und Heilsgeschichte: Schlussfolgerungen aus Röm. IV und I Kor. X.1-13," *NTS* 13 (1966-67), 31-42.

95. See esp. T. Hoppe, *Die Idee der Heilsgeschichte bei Paulus mit besonderer Berücksichtigung des Römerbriefes* (BFCT 2.30; Gütersloh: Bertelsmann, 1926), pp. 26-27, 81, etc.

96. Bornkamm says that Paul's explanation of his claims that Christ is the "end of the law" (10:4) and that "faith establishes the law" (3:31) is the theme of the letter ("Wandlungen im alt- und neutestamentlichen Gesetzsverständnis," in *Geschichte und Glaube*, part 2: *Gesammelte Aufsätze* [Munich: Kaiser, 1971], 4.106).

an "advantage" (3:9) and affirms that Israel has certain inalienable rights (3:1-2; 11:11-32); affirms the universality of God's righteousness — "to *all* who believe" — and its particular relevance to the Jew — "to the Jew first"; and claims that the righteousness of God has been revealed "apart from the law" (3:21) and that the gospel first provides for the true fulfillment of the law (3:31; 8:4). These are not contradictions but the two sides of the relationship of continuity and discontinuity between the testaments that Paul sets forth in Romans. We can understand, then, why many scholars call Romans a "dialogue with Judaism."[97]

But to make the relationship between the two peoples — Jews and Gentiles — the theme of Romans, with the transformation of the individual a subordinate, supporting concept, is to reverse their relationship in the letter, to confuse background with foreground. The scholars who have put "people" questions at the center of Romans have overreacted to the neglect of these matters among some earlier interpreters. The bulk of Romans focuses on how God has acted in Christ to bring the *individual* sinner into a new relationship with himself (chaps. 1–4), to provide for that *individual's* eternal life in glory (chaps. 5–8), and to transform that *individual's* life on earth now (12:1–15:13). Since it is essential to Paul's message that God acts, in a way that he has not previously, to include on an equal basis both Jew and Gentile in this transforming operation, Paul must pay constant attention to the implications of this new equality of treatment. He must explain how his message of individual transformation relates to God's focus on Israel in the OT. This explanation thus becomes a constant motif in the letter and occupies an important section of the letter (chaps. 9–11) in its own right. But it remains the background, as Paul presents in the foreground the way in which God has acted to transform rebellious sinners into obedient saints.

Is, then, justification by faith the theme of the letter? Certainly a good case can be made for it. But I do not finally think that it can stand as the overarching theme. This is not because I would thereby be foisting an anachronism on Paul. The individual and his relationship to God are important in Romans; and there is not as much difference between the thought world of Paul and that of Luther or ourselves as Stendahl and others think.[98] On the other hand, there is too much in Romans that cannot, without distortion, be subsumed under the heading of justification: the assurance

---

97. E.g., J. Jeremias, "Zur Gedankenführung in den paulinischen Briefen," in *Abba: Studien zur Neutestamentlichen Theologie und Zeitgeschichte* (Göttingen: Vandenhoeck & Ruprecht, 1966), pp. 269-71 (with reference to chaps. 1–11); Beker, 86; Wilckens, 1.34.

98. See particularly J. M. Espy, "Paul's 'Robust Conscience' Re-examined," *NTS* 31 (1985), 161-88.

and hope of the believer (chaps. 5 and 8); freedom from sin and the law (chaps. 6 and 7); God's purpose for Israel (chaps. 9–11); and the life of obedience (chaps. 12–15). To be sure, we can relate all of these to justification, as its fruits, or implications, or requirements; and Paul makes this connection himself at several points (cf. 5:1, 9; 8:33; cf. 9:30–10:8). But he does not do so often enough to make us think that justification, or "the righteousness of God," is his constant reference point. In fact, as we have implied above, it is only in 1:18–4:25 that justification is highlighted in Romans.

But while it is not the theme of Romans, justification by faith is nevertheless of critical importance in the letter. For, as we will argue below, the theme of the letter is the gospel. And the message of the gospel is that God brings guilty sinners into relationship with himself and destines them to eternal life when they believe in his son, Jesus the Messiah. Moreover, this message is nothing more than what we call justification by faith. And justification by faith is central to Romans and to Paul's theology also because it expresses, in the sphere of anthropology, a crucial element in Paul's understanding of God's work in Christ: its entirely gracious character. Justification by faith is the necessary implicate of the grace of God (e.g., 4:5, 16). Not only, then, does justification by faith guard against the Jewish attempt to make works of the law basic for salvation in Paul's day; it expresses the resolute resistance of Paul, and the NT authors, to the constant human tendency to make what people do decisive for salvation. It is in this sense, then, that we uphold justification as a doctrine of critical importance in Romans.[99]

What, then, is the theme of the letter? The gospel.[100] The word "gospel" and the cognate verb "evangelize" are particularly prominent in the introduction (cf. 1:1, 2, 9, 15) and conclusion (15:16, 19) of Romans — its epistolary "frame." And this is the word that has pride of place in Paul's statement of the theme of the letter: 1:16-17. "For I am not ashamed of the gospel. . . ." True, Paul goes on to speak of the interplay of salvation,

---

99. E.g., Westerholm, 167-69.

100. Note Wilckens, e.g., 1.91: "Above all else, the whole letter has the purpose of bringing about an agreement about the gospel in the only form in which Paul can and must preach it" ("Der ganze Brief dient zunächst dem Ziel, Einverständnis über das Evangelium zu erzielen, wie Paulus es nicht anders verkündigen kann und darf"). See also Blank, "Gesetz und Geist," p. 82; P. Stuhlmacher, "The Theme of Romans," in Donfried, 333-45; idem, "The Purpose of Romans," in Donfried, 231-42; idem, commentary, 10-12 (although he quickly defines "gospel" in terms of "the righteousness of God"); J. A. D. Weima, "Preaching the Gospel in Rome: A Study of the Epistolary Framework of Romans," in *Gospel in Paul: Studies on Corinthians, Galatians and Romans for Richard N. Longenecker* (ed. L. A. Jervis and P. Richardson; Sheffield: JSOT, 1994), pp. 337-38.

the interplay of Jew and Gentile, and justification by faith; and each has been advanced as the theme of the letter. But they are all elaborations of the main topic of these verses, the gospel.[101] And we require a theme as broad as "the gospel" to encompass the diverse topics in Romans. Moreover, as we have seen, Romans grows out of Paul's own missionary situation; and the gospel Paul preaches would naturally be the focus of attention in any letter that arises from such a situation. Romans is Paul's summary of the gospel that he preaches. But because he writes this summary in a context charged with uncertainty and controversy over the gospel's relationship to the OT — especially the torah — and its embrace of both Jew and Gentile, he nuances his summary with constant reference to these issues.

VII. TEXT AND TRANSLATION

The textual basis for the commentary is the United Bible Societies' *The Greek New Testament,* fourth edition (which prints the same text as the Nestle-Aland *Novum Testamentum Graece,* twenty-seventh edition). Readers may find discussion of every variant cited in UBS[4] in the footnotes to the translations; I have also discussed a number of significant variants that do not appear in UBS[4].

The Greek MSS witnesses to the text of Romans are:

Papyri

P[46], "Chester Beatty II." This very early (c. A.D. 200) papyrus codex exhibits what Aland and Aland call a "free" text,[102] one that does not clearly line up consistently with any of the "families" that developed at a later period.[103] It unfortunately includes only parts of Romans: 5:17–6:14; 8:15–15:9; 15:11–16:27.

The other papryi witnesses to the text of Romans (P[10, 26, 27, 31, 40, 61, 94]) include only small parts of the letter.

---

101. See further the additional note on 1:16-17.

102. K. and B. Aland, *The Text of the New Testament: An Introduction to the Critical Editions and to the Theory and Practice of Modern Textual Criticism* (2d ed.; Grand Rapids: Eerdmans, 1989), cf. p. 99.

103. My own rather unscientific survey confirms this. I collated the number of times each major MS of the text of Romans agreed with every other major MS. The numbers for P[46] are: ℵ — 48; A — 64; B — 61; C — 34; D — 91; F — 96; G — 99; L — 9; P — 20; Ψ — 39; 33 — 5; 1739 — 38; Majority Text — 37.

Uncials

א (01), "Sinaiticus." This is one of the great fourth-century uncials, containing the entire NT (as well as most of the OT and Apocrypha). It is a primary witness to the Alexandrian text.

A (02), "Alexandrinus." This fifth-century MS contains most of the NT, including all of Romans, and is a slightly less valuable witness to the Alexandrian text (Aland and Aland's category II).

B (03), "Vaticanus." With Sinaiticus, Vaticanus is the most important witness to the Alexandrian textual tradition. It contains most of the NT, including all of Romans.

C (04), "Ephraemi Rescriptus." A fifth-century palimpsest, it contains most of Romans and is a secondary witness to the Alexandrian text.

D (06), "Claromontanus." To be distinguished from the "D" uncial of the Gospels and Acts (Bezae), this sixth-century uncial is one of the most important witnesses to the western text in Romans. It lacks only a few verses of Rom. 1.

F (010), "Augiensis." A ninth-century witness to the western text, it contains all of Romans except chaps. 1–2 and parts of chap. 3.

G (012), "Boernerianus." This ninth-century MS, containing all of Romans except parts of chaps. 1 and 2, has a text very close to that of "F." They might well be "sister" MSS, copied from the same (now lost) MS.

P (025), "Porphyrianus." Containing most of Romans, this ninth-century codex displays a text that does not line up consistently with any of the major textual families (Aland and Aland's category III).

Ψ (044), "Athous Lavrensis." This eighth- or ninth-century uncial, like P, is not a consistent witness to any text family. It includes all of Romans.

Several other uncials contain all or most of Romans: K (018), L (020), 049, 056, 0142, and 0151. But they are late (ninth century or later) and are part of what textual critics call the "majority text."

Minuscules

Twenty-nine minuscules contain all or part of the text of Romans. The three most important are 33 (ninth century), 81 (eleventh century), and 1739 (tenth century), all of which are important secondary witnesses to the Alexandrian text.[104]

104. For description, dates, and evaluation of these MSS, we have relied primarily on Aland and Aland, *Text,* pp. 96-163; cf. also M. Holmes, "Textual Criticism," in *Dictionary of Paul and His Letters* (ed. G. F. Hawthorne and R. P. Martin; Downers Grove: InterVarsity, 1993), p. 928; Fitzmyer, 44-47.

All the important witnesses identified above will be cited (where extant and relevant) as we deal with variants in the text of Romans. Following the practice of NA[27] and UBS[4], I will cite the majority of late MSS that belong to the Byzantine text by reference to the "majority text" (= "Byz" in UBS[4]).

The translation printed at the heading of each section is my own. It is very literal, my purpose being to give the non-Greek-speaking reader as much sense as possible of the structure and ambiguity of the underlying Greek.

VIII. STRUCTURE

Because the main body of Romans is a "theological tractate," outlines of the structure of the letter tend to resemble the headings in systematic theologies. Beker has objected to this procedure, arguing that the pursuit of a "systematic thought structure" imposes an "architectonic rigor" on what is, after all, an occasional letter.[105] To the extent that scholars subsume everything in the letter under a single theological doctrine (e.g., justification by faith), or attach the labels of later dogmatic structures to the letter (e.g., dividing Rom. 1–8 into the topics of justification and sanctification, or making predestination the topic of chaps. 9–11), or ignore the occasional and practical elements in the letter (especially chaps. 12–16), this objection is warranted. But this should not deter us from searching for logical movement in the letter, especially in chaps. 1–11, where, as we have seen, the course of Paul's argument owes more to the "inner logic" of the gospel than to occasional matters. In these chapters, I am convinced, Paul is arguing — and arguing theologically. We should not impose our own theological categories on Paul, but neither should we ignore those that he may be using.

My own outline reflects what I think is the theme of the letter: the gospel. There is general agreement over the major sections of the letter, with one significant exception: the place of chap. 5. Many interpreters, especially in the Reformed Protestant tradition, made this chapter the conclusion to Paul's argument about justification by faith in chaps. 1–4. But gaining in popularity has been the decision to take chap. 5 with chaps. 6–8, a part of Paul's "two-age" presentation of Christian existence and hope. As I argue in the introduction to chaps. 5–8, I am are convinced that the latter alternative is correct.

105. Beker, 64-69.

IX. ANALYSIS OF ROMANS

The Epistle to the ROMANS

Text, Exposition, and Notes

I. THE LETTER OPENING (1:1-17)

The main body of Romans is a treatise on Paul's gospel, bracketed by an epistolary opening (1:1-17) and conclusion (15:14–16:27). These opening and concluding statements have many similarities, not the least of which is the emphasis on the *gospel*. (Eight of the 11 occurrences in Romans of *euangelion* ["gospel"] and *euangelizomai* ["to evangelize"] are in these passages.) Paul's special relationship to this gospel, a relationship that encompasses the Roman Christians, both opens and closes the strictly "epistolary" introductory material in this section (vv. 1-5, 13-15).[1]

A. PRESCRIPT (1:1-7)

> 1*Paul, a slave of Christ Jesus,*[2] *called to be an apostle, set apart for the gospel of God,* 2*which was promised beforehand through his prophets in the holy Scriptures,* 3*concerning his son, who came from the seed of David according to the flesh,* 4*who was designated Son of God in power according to the Spirit of holiness on the basis of the resurrection of the dead, Jesus Christ our Lord,* 5*through whom we received grace and apostleship for the obedience of faith among all the Gentiles for the sake of his name,* 6*among whom you also are called*

1. Cf. Wuellner, "Paul's Rhetoric of Argumentation," p. 133.
2. The order Χριστοῦ Ἰησοῦ is attested in only three Greek MSS, P[10], the primary Alexandrian uncial B, and the secondary Alexandrian 81. All the other MSS have the order Ἰησοῦ Χριστοῦ. But, while its external testimony is slim, the reading adopted here has strong internal support: this is the order of terms that Paul almost always uses in these kinds of context (see n. 9 below).

of Jesus Christ, 7to all of you in Rome,[3] beloved by God, called to be saints. Grace to you, and peace from God our Father and the Lord Jesus Christ.

The letters of Paul must have been greeted with considerable perplexity by their first-century recipients. To the extent that this perplexity was due to the theological complexity of the letters, contemporary readers can share the reaction of their first-century counterparts. But the very form of the letters would have been further grounds for puzzlement to the early Christians. Paul's letters are far longer than most first-century letters — so long that they make exact literary classification difficult. And Romans, with 7,114 words, is the longest of Paul's letters. Fittingly, Romans also has the longest prescript. The typical Greek letter began simply with a one-sentence identification of the sender and recipients, and a greeting: A to B, "greetings" (*chairein;* Acts 15:23; 23:26; Jas. 1:1). Paul expands this form considerably in all his letters but nowhere more than in Romans.[4] The superscription, or identification of the sender, is particularly long, occupying the first six verses.

Paul introduces himself by stating his divine call (v. 1), the message that he has been called to proclaim (vv. 2-4), and the specific task with which he is occupied (vv. 5-6). Finally comes the address in v. 7a, followed by the usual Pauline salutation in v. 7b. The length and theological orientation of this prescript are due mainly to the fact that Paul was introducing himself to a church that he had neither founded nor visited. He wanted to establish his credentials as an apostle with a worldwide commission to proclaim the good news of Jesus Christ. Whether this elaborate prescript had a polemical motive (as, e.g., Murray thinks) is not clear.

1 Paul[5] introduces himself to the Roman church with three parallel designations that, respectively, identify his master, his office, and his purpose. All three lack articles, a style typical of the introductions of letters.[6] "Slave

---

3. The omission of ἐν Ῥώμῃ in G, 1739^{mg}, and a few other MSS here and in 1:15 is almost certainly a later attempt to "universalize" Romans by ridding it of its specific destination. See the Introduction, pp. 5-9.

4. Michel and Käsemann, following E. Lohmeyer ("Probleme paulinischer Theologie. 1 Briefliche Grussüberschriften," *ZNW* 26 [1927], 158-73), suggest that the lengthier form of prescript employed by Paul may be derived from a Jewish-oriental model of letter writing (cf. 2 Macc. 1:1-6). This is, however, contested by O. Roller (*Das Formular des paulinischen Briefe. Ein Beitrag zur Lehre vom antiken Briefe* [BWANT 4.6; Stuttgart: Kohlhammer, 1933], pp. 213-38) and Cranfield.

5. The name Παῦλος is likely to have been Paul's Latin *cognomen* (Cranfield; Bruce, *Paul,* p. 38) rather than a special Christian name or a name taken from his first famous convert, Sergius Paulus (cf. Acts 13:9), as Lagrange suggests.

6. BDF 252.

of Christ Jesus" is patterned on the familiar OT phrase "slave," or "servant," of Yahweh.[7] The phrase connotes total devotion, suggesting that the servant is completely at the disposal of his or her Lord. That great honor attaches to the service of so exalted a master is of course true, and many commentators stress this side of the title in Paul's application of it to himself.[8] But the connotations of humility, devotion, and obedience are never absent from the OT phrase and are surely primary here also. Indicative of Paul's high Christology is the fact that he replaces the "Lord" of the OT phrase with "Christ Jesus."[9] The sequence "Christ Jesus" draws particular attention to the *Messiah* Jesus and may also suggest the corporate and universal significance of this Messiahship.

Only in the prescripts of Titus and Philippians (where Timothy is also mentioned) does Paul call himself a "slave." But the second designation in Rom. 1:1, "apostle," is used in every Pauline prescript except those in Philippians, 1 and 2 Thessalonians, and Philemon. Paul occasionally uses "apostle" in a general way to mean simply "messenger" (Phil. 2:25; 2 Cor. 8:23), and more often to refer to accredited missionaries (e.g., Rom. 16:7). But here the title carries a stronger sense, marking Paul as one among that unique group appointed by Christ himself to have the salvation-historical role as the "foundation" of the church (Eph. 2:20).[10] For the risen Christ appeared to him

---

7. This phrase, or parallels (e.g., "your servant"), is occasionally applied to Israel generally (Neh. 1:6; Isa. 43:10) and sometimes to the prophets (2 Kings 9:7; 17:23), but it more often depicts a particularly significant and outstanding "servant": Moses (e.g., Josh. 14:7; 2 Kings 18:12), Joshua (Josh. 24:29), Elijah (2 Kings 10:10), Nehemiah (Neh. 1:6), and, especially frequently, David.

8. E.g., Käsemann.

9. The order of the titles may be significant. Unlike the rest of the NT authors, who prefer Ἰησοῦ Χριστοῦ to Χριστοῦ Ἰησοῦ (47 times to 7), Paul prefers the order Χριστοῦ Ἰησοῦ (80 times to 25). This significant difference in word order suggests that — contrary to the opinion of some — Paul uses Χριστός as a title with important theological meaning: "the Messiah, Jesus." But there may be further significance to the order. Paul tends to use "Christ Jesus" — rather than "Jesus Christ" — in two contexts: in descriptions of his apostolic services (as here) and after the prepositions εἰς ("into") or ἐν ("in"), to denote his characteristic motif of incorporation into Christ. See esp. Wright, "Messiah and People of God," pp. 19-31; also Schlier. W. Kramer (*Christ, Lord, Son of God* [SBT 50; London: SCM, 1966], pp. 203-6) suggests that Paul may have put Χριστός first to indicate the grammatical case of the phrase, but more is needed to explain the variety of Paul's order. M. Hengel, on the other hand, doubts whether the order of the titles has any significance ("Erwägungen zum Sprachgebrauch von Χριστός bei Paulus und in der 'vorpaulinischen' Überlieferung," in *Paul and Paulinism: Essays in Honour of C. K. Barrett* [ed. M. Hooker and S. G. Wilson; London: SPCK, 1982], p. 137).

10. Since ἀπόστολος is not used in a technical sense in the LXX or in secular Greek, many interpreters have suggested as the background for the NT titular use of the word the Jewish-rabbinic use of שָׁלִיחַ ("one sent") to describe an authorized representative

(1 Cor. 15:8) and chose him for his special mission to the Gentiles (Rom. 11:13; cf. 1 Tim. 2:7; 2 Tim. 1:11). This divine initiative in Paul's apostleship is made evident here by the verbal adjective "called."[11] What Paul intends by this is spelled out in the polemically oriented opening of Galatians: "Paul, an apostle — sent not from men nor by man, but by Jesus Christ and God the Father, who raised him from the dead . . ." (NIV). As is Paul's custom, then, he specifies at the very beginning of his letter that he writes not as a private individual, nor even as a gifted teacher, but as a "called apostle" whose words bear the authority of God himself. Any reading of this great theological treatise that ignores this claim to authority will fail to come to grips with the ultimate purpose of its writing.

Paul's final description of himself in v. 1, "set apart for the gospel of God," may allude to his being set aside for his great apostolic task even from "the womb of his mother" (cf. Gal. 1:15).[12] But the word order here makes it more likely that the "set apart" clause is simply a further definition of "called."[13] The verb is used in the LXX of God's "separating" and calling of Israel from among other nations (Lev. 20:26) and in Acts 13:2 of the "setting apart" of Barnabas and Saul for missionary service. Similarly, Paul, as a "called apostle," has been set aside by God for a special purpose in God's plan for history. Paul here specifies this purpose with the words "for[14] the gospel of God." "Gospel" here might denote the activity of preaching the gospel (cf. TEV: "called by God to preach the Good News"),[15] or it might

---

or messenger (e.g., K. H. Rengstorf, *TDNT* I, 414-20; see examples in Str-B, 3.2-4). But the late date of the sources in which the term is used, combined with the general lack of missionary emphasis in the rabbis, makes this suggestion questionable (cf. D. Müller, *NIDNTT* I, 134; cf., however, R. W. Herron, Jr., "The Origin of the New Testament Apostolate," *WTJ* 45 [1983], 101-31). On Paul's use of ἀπόστολος, see further the note on 16:7.

11. Gk. κλητός; cf. also 1 Cor. 1:1.

12. See, e.g., Bruce, Cranfield. In the Galatians passage, Paul uses κλητός to refer to his calling on the Damascus Road and ἀφορίζω for his being "set apart" for this task even from his mother's womb (Paul here alludes to Jeremiah's famous description of his call; cf. Jer. 1:5).

13. The "effectual dedication that occurred in the actual call to apostleship" (Murray; cf. also Meyer). Some commentators (Zahn; Barrett; Nygren; Black; Fitzmyer) think the word ἀφορίζω may contain a play on the supposed root of "Pharisee," פָּרַשׁ: while thinking himself "separated" as a Pharisee, Paul now realizes that it is only in Christ that he has become *truly* "separated." But Cranfield is right to dismiss such an interpretation as improbable. Even less probable is the implicit law/gospel contrast Nygren sees in these words.

14. Gk. εἰς, with a telic sense.

15. Godet; Wilckens.

simply refer to the message of the gospel itself.[16] What makes a decision difficult is that the dynamic sense fits well with v. 1 but badly with vv. 2-3, while the more static connotation suffers from just the reverse problem. Cranfield suggests that the word contains both connotations here. This is certainly on the right track, but perhaps we can refine this suggestion further. Paul uses "gospel" so generally in some contexts (cf. Rom. 1:9; Phil. 1:27; Eph. 3:6; 6:19) that it becomes functionally equivalent to "Christ" or God's intervention in Christ. In other words, Paul can sometimes expand the scope of "gospel" to include the very events of which the message speaks. God's sending his Son for the salvation of the world is itself "good news."[17] Since the context makes it difficult to choose either the active or the static sense alone, there is good reason to adopt this broad meaning of the word here. In saying that he has been "set apart for the gospel of God," then, Paul is claiming that his life is totally dedicated to God's act of salvation in Christ — a dedication that involves both his own belief in, and obedience to, that message as well as his apostolic proclamation of it. With this meaning, "of God" probably can be paraphrased "sent by God."[18] This genitive addition should not be overlooked. As L. Morris has reminded us, Romans is ultimately a book about *God:* how *he* acted to bring salvation, how *his* justice is preserved, how *his* purposes are worked out in history, how *he* can be served by his people.[19]

2 In a relative clause dependent on "gospel" *(euangelion),* Paul further defines the gospel as something promised in the OT. In a manner typical of Paul's emphasis throughout Romans, he draws a line of continuity

---

16. Zahn; Murray. εὐαγγέλιον is a typically Pauline word — 60 of the 76 NT occurrences are his. Since the LXX never uses the word with theological significance, some have argued that the NT usage must be derived from the use of the term in the imperial cult (e.g., U. Becker, *NIDNTT* II, 109). However, although the term may have had such allusions for Paul and his readers, its derivation from such a source is unlikely. Rather, the use of the term in the NT should be traced to the verb בָּשַׂר ("bring good news"), used in the OT to describe the eschatological victory of Yahweh (Joel 2:32; Nah. 1:15; Isa. 40:9; 42:7; 60:6; 61:1 [cf. Luke 4:18]) (see esp. P. Stuhlmacher, *Das paulinische Evangelium. I: Vorgeschichte* [FRLANT 95; Göttingen: Vandenhoeck & Ruprecht, 1968], pp. 152-53, 177-79, 204-6; also R. P. Martin, *ISBE* II, 530). The noun in the NT denotes the "good news" of the saving intervention of God in Christ, referring usually to the message about Christ (1 Cor. 15:1; Gal. 1:11; 2:2) and, by extension, to the act of preaching that message (1 Cor. 9:14 [second occurrence]; 2 Cor. 2:12; 8:18; Phil. 1:5[?]; 4:3[?]).

17. G. Friedrich says, "The Gospel does not merely bear witness to salvation history; it is itself salvation history" (*TDNT* II, 731).

18. E.g., the genitive would be subjective. See Turner, 211; BDF 163; H. Schlier, "Εὐαγγέλιον in Römerbrief," in *Wort Gottes in der Zeit (für K. H. Schelkle)* (ed. H. Feld and J. Nolte; Düsseldorf: Patmos, 1973), p. 128. Close to this sense is the "source" genitive suggested by Murray and Cranfield. S-H argue for a "general" genitive, which would include "all aspects . . . in which the Gospel is in any way related to God."

19. Morris, "The Theme of Romans," pp. 249-63.

between the new work of God in his Son, the content of the gospel (vv. 3-4), and the OT. By adding the redundant "ahead of time" to the verb "promise,"[20] Paul emphasizes the temporal sequence of promise and fulfillment. He therefore touches on what will become two key themes in Romans: the promise (cf. Rom. 4), and the grounding of God's salvific revelation in his previous purposes and work.[21] The "prophets" through whom God promised the gospel include men like Moses (cf. Acts 3:21-22) and David (cf. Acts 2:30), in addition to those we would ordinarily classify as "prophets" per se. In Paul's perspective, as Luther puts it, "Scripture is completely prophetical." The phrase "holy Scriptures"[22] occurs only here in Paul.[23] It is doubtful whether Paul has any particular OT passages in mind here; his purpose is general and principial, to allay possible suspicion about "his" gospel as new and innovative by asserting its organic relationship to the OT.

3 Whether the prepositional phrase that introduces v. 3, "concerning his Son," depends on "promise ahead of time" in v. 2[24] or on "gospel" in v. 1,[25] the meaning is much the same: the focus of the gospel is a person, God's Son. "Son of God" is a title not used often by Paul, but as M. Hengel notes, it is used in key places and assumes thereby an importance disproportionate to its frequency.[26] As we would expect, the title focuses on Jesus' uniquely intimate relationship to God.[27] "His Son" is further defined in vv.

---

20. In the Greek we have the rare compound verb προεπαγγέλλομαι (its only other NT occurrence is in 2 Cor. 9:5), where the prefixed preposition πρό accentuates the temporal priority connoted already by the simple verb.

21. Greek words beginning with πρό are especially prominent in the book.

22. Gk. γραφαῖς ἁγίαις. The phrase may correspond to the rabbis' כִּתְבֵי הַקֹּדֶשׁ (Str-B, 3.14). The anarthrous phrase is not, of course, indefinite (one "holy Scriptures" as opposed to others) but continues the style employed in v. 1 (Cranfield). Others take the anarthrous construction to have a qualitative force (S-H; Murray). The tendency to omit articles after prepositions (cf. BDF 255) could also play a role.

23. Paul uses the plural γραφαί ("Scriptures") four other times (Rom. 15:4; 16:26 [v.l.]; 1 Cor. 15:3, 4).

24. E.g., Godet.

25. E.g., Zahn.

26. M. Hengel, *The Son of God: The Origin of Christology and the History of Jewish-Hellenistic Religion* (Philadelphia: Fortress, 1976), pp. 59-66.

27. Paul calls Jesus υἱός 17 times, his focus being particularly on Jesus' relationship to the Father and to those who belong to him. The former is evident from the use of the title to highlight God's sending of his Son (Rom. 8:3; Gal. 4:4, 6) and his handing him over to death on our behalf (Rom. 5:10; 8:32; Gal. 2:20). Contrary to Dunn (*Christology in the Making: A New Testament Inquiry into the Origin of the Doctrine of the Incarnation* [Philadelphia: Westminster, 1980], pp. 38-45), several of these texts presume the preexistence of the Son. Paul also uses the title to express the fellowship between Christ and those who are God's "sons" in him (Rom. 1:9; 8:29; 1 Cor. 1:9; Eph. 4:13; Col. 1:13). The background for the title can be traced to the OT, where "Son" is used of the King

3b-4 with two parallel participial clauses. Their close parallelism is evident when they are set side by side:

"who has come"   "who was appointed"
"from the seed of David"   "Son of God in power"
"according to the flesh"   "according to the Spirit of holiness"
                      "from the resurrection of the dead"[28]

This parallelism, coupled with the presence of several words and phrases unique or unusual in Paul,[29] raises the possibility that Paul is here quoting from, or adapting, an earlier tradition. Such use of traditional material is unobjectionable in itself, paralleled in other Pauline texts, and entirely appropriate as a means to establish some common ground with the unfamiliar Roman church.[30] Nevertheless, we should be cautious about drawing exegetical conclusions from this necessarily uncertain hypothesis. The meaning of these verses, then, is to be determined against the background of Paul and his letters, not against a necessarily hypothetical traditions-history.[31]

---

and often with messianic significance (Ps. 2:7; 2 Sam. 7:14; though the rabbis did not use "Son" as a messianic title [Str-B, 3.15-20], 4QFlor attests continuing messianic interest in these OT "Son" passages; cf. also 4Q246 2:1). Ultimately, however, Jesus' own understanding of and teaching about his unique relationship to the Father decisively conditioned its meaning. In this context, the title bears not so much an official significance (as if "Son" were simply equivalent to "Messiah") as an ontological significance. On this, see further Hengel, *Son of God;* O. Cullmann, *The Christology of the New Testament* (Philadelphia: Westminster, 1963), pp. 270-305; I. H. Marshall, *The Origins of New Testament Christology* (Downers Grove, IL: InterVarsity, 1976), pp. 111-29; Ridderbos, *Paul,* pp. 68-78.

    28. Gk.: τοῦ γενομένου
            τοῦ ὁρισθέντος

            ἐκ σπέρματος Δαυίδ
            υἱοῦ θεοῦ ἐν δυνάμει

            κατὰ σάρκα
            κατὰ πνεῦμα ἁγιωσύνης

            ἐξ ἀναστάσεως νεκρῶν.
    29. πνεῦμα ἁγιωσύνης, σπέρματος Δαυίδ.
    30. Most recent interpreters argue for, or assume, the existence of a pre-Pauline tradition (see, e.g., Fitzmyer).
    31. That Paul in vv. 3-4 is quoting an early Christian tradition, or hymn, or creed is widely held, but considerable uncertainty attaches to the original form and meaning of the tradition. Most are convinced that the creed originated in the early Jewish church and that it had a distinctly "adoptionist" tone. Paul would then have added περὶ υἱοῦ αὐτοῦ and ἐν δυνάμει in order to remove this element of adoptionism. Much of the debate has focused on the two

The first participial clause (v. 3b) focuses on the Son of God coming into human existence. This clause assumes the preexistence of the Son.[32] How specifically Paul may allude to the incarnation depends on the meaning to be given the word *genomenon*, "has come." Although it is not the usual word for "give birth,"[33] it can sometimes take this meaning, and some argue for it here.[34] But this probably reads too much into the verb. Perhaps Paul uses the more general term to suggest that more than a simple "birth" was entailed in the "becoming" of the Son; a change in existence also took place. This appearance of the Son on the human scene is qualified as being "from the seed of David," a clear allusion to the messianic stature of the Son.[35] Finally,

---

κατά phrases, which some take to be Pauline additions (e.g., K. Wengst, *Christologische Formeln und Lieder des Urchristentums* [SNT 7; Gütersloh: Mohn, 1972], pp. 112-14), while an increasingly large majority attribute them to the original creed (see esp. E. Schweizer, "Röm. 1,3f, und der Gegensatz von Fleisch und Geist vor und bei Paulus," in *Neotestamentica* [Zürich/Stuttgart: Zwingli, 1963]; note also P.-E. Langevin, "Une Confession prépaulinienne de la 'Seigneurie' du Christ. Exégèse de Romains 1, 3-4," in *Le Christ hier, aujourd'hui, et demain* [ed. R. Laflamme and M. Gervais; Quebec: Université Laval, 1976], pp. 284-91; P. Stuhlmacher, "Theologische Probleme des Römerbriefpräskripts," *EvT* 27 [1967], 382; I. Dugandzic, *Das 'Ja' Gottes in Christus. Eine Studie zur Bedeutung des Alten Testaments für das Christusverständnis des Paulus* [FzB 26; Würzburg: Echter, 1977], pp. 137-42; van der Minde, *Schrift und Tradition,* pp. 40-43). Still others posit a three-stage development, with the κατά phrases being added in a second, but still pre-Pauline, stage (R. Jewett, *Paul's Anthropological Terms: A Study of Their Use in Conflict Settings* [AGJU 10; Leiden: Brill, 1971], pp. 136-38; note also his later "The Redaction and Use of an Early Christian Confession in Romans 1:3-4," in *The Living Text: Essays in Honor of Ernest W. Saunders* [ed. D. E. Groh and R. Jewett; Lanham, MD: University Press of America, 1985], pp. 99-122).

However, some questions must be raised about this process of reconstruction. The current trend in scholarship is to find many pieces of tradition in the NT, but the criteria by which they can be identified are not accurate enough to allow for much confidence in the process. In this case, while the evidence that Paul is using traditional language is strong, it is not clear that he is quoting a set creed or hymn (see V. S. Poythress, "Is Romans 1:3-4 a Pauline Confession after All?" *ExpTim* 87 [1975-76], 180-83; J. M. Scott, *Adoption as Sons of God: An Exegetical Investigation into the Background of* ΥΙΟΘΕΣΙΑ *in the Pauline Corpus* [WUNT 2.48; Tübingen: Mohr, 1992], pp. 227-36). Methodologically, it is necessary at least to maintain that whatever Paul quotes, he himself affirms (see Wright, "Messiah and People of God," pp. 51-55).

32. Contra Dunn.

33. γεννάω is the usual Greek word for "give birth to"; it is found here in a poorly attested variant.

34. Cf., e.g., BAGD; Godet. Note the somewhat parallel use of the word in Gal. 4:4: "God sent forth his Son, born [γενόμενον] of a woman, born [γενόμενον] under the law."

35. The promise to David that his seed would have an eternal reign (2 Sam. 7:12-16) became the prime focus of messianic expectation in the OT (cf. Isa. 11:1, 10; Jer. 23:5-6; 30:9; 33:14-18; Ezek. 34:23-24; 37:24-25) and in Judaism (cf. esp. *Pss. Sol.* 17:21; 4QFlor; and cf. John 7:42; Matt. 9:27, passim). According to consistent NT testimony, this promise finds its fulfillment in Jesus (Matt. 1:1-16; Luke 1:27, 32, 69; 2 Tim. 2:8; Rev. 5:5; 22:16).

this "coming" of the Son is qualified as being "according to the flesh." "Flesh" *(sarx)* is a key Pauline theological term. It refers essentially to human existence, with emphasis on the transitory, weak, frail nature of that existence.[36] "According to the flesh," used 21 times in Paul, denotes being or living according to the "merely human." Neutral in itself, the phrase nevertheless suggests that only one perspective is being considered and that other aspects must be taken into account to get the whole picture.[37] The phrase here, then, while obviously far toward the neutral end of the spectrum, also suggests that we have not arrived at a full understanding of Jesus if we look at him only from the standpoint of "the flesh." Verse 4 goes on to fill out this picture of Jesus by looking at him from another perspective.

4 Although the claim that v. 4 sets forth "the whole message of the epistle in a nutshell" (Nygren) may be exaggerated, the verse is theologically important. But its meaning is debated and can be determined only after answering three basic exegetical questions. First, what is the meaning of the word we have translated "designated"? Some think it should be translated "declared": the resurrection declared that Jesus was "Son of God."[38] But the verb does not appear to have this meaning in first-century Greek.[39] In its seven other NT occurrences, the verb means "determine, appoint, fix,"[40] and we

---

36. Paul never uses σάρξ in its simplest meaning: the soft tissues of the human body. As in secular Greek, however, Paul can use the word to refer to the human body as a whole (e.g., 1 Cor. 5:5[?]; 6:16; 2 Cor. 7:1; 12:7; Gal. 4:13; Eph. 5:31) but more often of the person generally (e.g., Rom. 3:20; Gal. 1:16 — this usage arises from equivalence with the Heb. בָּשָׂר). Paul's more theologically significant uses of the term occupy a spectrum of meaning from a rather neutral use, designating human nature or existence as such (e.g., Rom. 4:1; 8:3; 9:8; 1 Cor. 1:29; 15:50), to a much more negative (or ethical) meaning: human life, or the material world considered as independent of, and even in opposition to, the spiritual realm (e.g., Rom. 7:5; 8:8; 13:14; Gal. 5:13-18 — see esp. J. D. G. Dunn, "Jesus — Flesh and Spirit: An Exposition of Romans I.3-4," *JTS* 24 [1973], esp. 44-51). T. Laato helpfully contrasts these two main emphases: the human person in distinction from God; the human person in contrast to God (T. Laato, *Paulus und das Judentum: Anthropologische Erwägungen* [Åbo: Åbo Academy, 1991], p. 95). See, further, for Paul's teaching about the flesh, A. Sand, *Der Begriff 'Sarx' in den paulinischen Hauptbriefen* (Biblische Untersuchungen 2; Regensburg: Pustet, 1967); E. Brandenburger, *Fleisch und Geist. Paulus und die dualistische Weisheit* (WMANT 29; Neukirchen/Vluyn: Neukirchener, 1968); W. D. Stacey, *The Pauline View of Man in Relation to Its Judaic and Hellenistic Background* (London: Macmillan, 1956), pp. 154-80; E. Schweizer, *TDNT* VII, 99-124.

37. See esp. Dunn, "Jesus — Flesh and Spirit," esp. pp. 44-51; idem, his *Romans*. Dunn may, however, err in giving the phrase *too* negative a nuance here (Fitzmyer).

38. E.g., BAGD; Chrysostom; S-H. The verb ὁρίζω means, basically, to "mark out" or "fix" a boundary (cf. LXX Num. 34:6; Ezek. 47:20).

39. Lagrange.

40. Luke 22:22; Acts 2:23; 10:42; 11:29; 17:26, 31; Heb. 4:7.

must assume that the word has this meaning here also: the Son (the subject of the participle; cf. v. 3a) has been "appointed" Son of God by God the Father[41] by virtue of his resurrection.

This notion appears at first sight to be theologically troublesome (is the eternal sonship of Christ being denied?), but several considerations remove any difficulty. The idea that the resurrection caused Jesus to be, in some sense, appointed Son has parallels elsewhere in the NT. See, particularly, Paul's proclamation to the synagogue worshipers in Pisidian Antioch: "this ['what God promised to the fathers'] he has fulfilled to us their children by raising Jesus; as also it is written in the second psalm, 'Thou art my Son, today I have begotten Thee'" (Acts 13:33). Rom. 1:4 probably alludes to this Psalm verse (2:7), which speaks of the coronation of the Davidic messianic King (cf. also Heb. 1:5).[42] In speaking this way, Paul and the other NT authors do not mean to suggest that Jesus becomes the Son only at the time of his resurrection. In this passage, we must remember that the Son is the subject of the entire statement in vv. 3-4: It is the *Son* who is "appointed" Son. The tautologous nature of this statement reveals that being appointed Son has to do not with a change in essence — as if a person or human messiah becomes Son of God for the first time — but with a change in status or function.

At this point we must consider the second key exegetical issue in this verse: the function of the phrase "in power."[43] The phrase could modify either "declared" — "declared with power to be the Son of God" (NIV)[44] — or "Son of God" — "declared Son-of-God-in-power."[45] But the need to demarcate the second occurrence of "Son of God" from the first — "his Son" in v. 3 — strongly favors the latter connection.[46] What Paul is claiming, then, is that the preexistent Son, who entered into human experience as the promised Messiah, was appointed on the basis of (or, perhaps, at the time

---

41. The passive ὁρισθέντος has God as its implied agent (Fitzmyer).

42. Cf. esp. M.-E. Boismard, "Constitué Fils de Dieu (Rom. I.4)," *RevistB* 60 (1953), 5-17. Note also Langevin, "Confession," pp. 302-3; P. Beasley-Murray, "Romans 1:3f: An Early Confession of Faith in the Lordship of Jesus," *TynBul* 31 (1980), 151-52; P. E. Hughes, *The True Image: The Origin and Destiny of Man in Christ* (Grand Rapids: Eerdmans, 1989), p. 384; Calvin. There is probably also an allusion to 2 Sam. 7:14, a messianic text that predicts that a "seed" of David would be adopted as Son of God (see Scott, *Adoption,* pp. 241-42).

43. Gk. ἐν δυνάμει.

44. See also NASB; TEV; S-H; Godet; Meyer; Hodge. Chrysostom thinks the phrase refers to the miracles that accompanied Jesus' earthly ministry.

45. So most recent commentators.

46. See especially the extensive discussion in Langevin, "Confession," pp. 298-305. Mark 9:1 may feature a parallel construction (and concept): Jesus proclaims, "There are some standing here who will not taste death until they see the kingdom of God come in power" (τὴν βασιλείαν τοῦ θεοῦ ἐληλυθυῖαν ἐν δυνάμει; cf. Michel).

of[47]) the resurrection to a new and more powerful position in relation to the world. By virtue of his obedience to the will of the Father (cf. Phil. 2:6-11) and because of the eschatological revelation of God's saving power in the gospel (1:1, 16), the Son attains a new, exalted status as "Lord" (cf. v. 4b). Son of God from eternity, he becomes Son of God "in power," "able [*dynatai*] for all time to save those who draw near to God through him" (Heb. 7:25, RSV). The transition from v. 3 to v. 4, then, is not a transition from a human messiah to a divine Son of God (adoptionism) but from the Son as Messiah to the Son as both Messiah *and* powerful, reigning Lord.

This brings us to the third and most difficult question: What is the meaning of "according to the Spirit of holiness"? This phrase is the antithetical parallel to "according the flesh" in v. 3. We may then explore this question by assessing the meaning of the contrast. Although a bewildering variety of views are found,[48] they fall into three basic categories.

The first understands "flesh/spirit" to suggest a contrast between Jesus' human and divine natures. It is because of Jesus' human descent that he is "seed of David"; and because of "the divine nature, or Godhead, that dwelt in Jesus Christ" he is the Son of God.[49] While having a respectable pedigree, this interpretation suffers from fatal objections. Not only must it take *horizō* to mean "demonstrate" or "manifest," which we have seen to be unlikely, but it also gives to "spirit" a connotation unexampled elsewhere in Paul.

The second interpretation avoids the latter problem by understanding "spirit of holiness" as the obedient, consecrated spirit that Jesus manifested throughout his earthly life. The contrast in vv. 3-4 is that between the outward and physical, by virtue of which Jesus is qualified as "seed of David," and the inward, spiritual perfection, which qualifies Jesus to be the Son of God in power.[50] While suffering from fewer difficulties than the first, this interpretation is open to the objection that it does not give to the "flesh/spirit" antithesis the meaning it most often has in Paul.

The contrast of "flesh" and "Spirit" is part of Paul's larger salva-

---

47. ἐξ is probably causal (see below), but it could have a temporal reference (Lietzmann; Käsemann; Cranfield); some suggest both (Beasley-Murray, "Romans 1:3f," p. 153; Kuss).

48. A useful classification is found in B. Schneider, "Κατὰ Πνεῦμα Ἁγιωσύνης (Romans 1,4)," *Bib* 48 (1967), 369-70.

49. Hodge; Haldane; Shedd; Gifford.

50. S-H; Meyer; Lagrange; O. Pfleiderer, *Paulinism: A Contribution to the History of Primitive Christian Theology* (2 vols.; London: Williams & Norgate, 1891), 1:126-27; S. L. Johnson, "The Jesus That Paul Preached," *BSac* 128 (1971), 128, 134; Schweizer, "Röm. 1,3f," pp. 187-89, and esp. Dunn, "Jesus — Flesh and Spirit," pp. 49-57. Langevin ("Confession," pp. 310-15) argues that ἁγιωσύνης should be given a dynamic sense: it is Christ's Spirit that sanctifies people.

tion-historical framework, in which two "aeons" or eras are set over against one another: the old era, dominated by sin, death, and the flesh, and the new era, characterized by righteousness, life, and the eschatological gift of the Holy Spirit.[51] The third interpretation of the contrast takes its starting point from this framework and is thereby to be preferred.[52] In Jesus' earthly life (his life in "the realm of the flesh"), he was the Davidic seed, the Messiah. But while true and valuable, this does not tell the whole story. For Christians, Jesus is also, in "the realm of the Spirit," the powerful, life-giving Son of God. In Christ the "new era" of redemptive history has begun, and in this new stage of God's plan Jesus reigns as Son of God, powerfully active to bring salvation to all who believe (cf. 1:16).[53] The major objection to this interpretation is that "spirit of holiness" is never used of the Holy Spirit in the NT; indeed, the phrase is found only here in biblical Greek.[54] However, the Semitic-flavored expression may reflect traditional language.[55] As is usual in Paul, the inauguration of this new age is attributed to Christ's resurrection.[56]

With "Jesus Christ our Lord," Paul returns to the beginning of v. 3: "his Son," the inner content of the gospel, is now finally and climactically identified. This identification builds on the christological formula of vv. 3b-4, since Jesus' lordship is linked to his investiture in power after and because of his resurrection (Phil. 2:6-11; Acts 2:31-36). For Paul, "Lord," expressing both Jesus' cosmic majesty and his status as master of the believer, is the single best title to express the true significance of Jesus. Verses 3-4 leave the

---

51. For this approach, see esp. Ridderbos, *Paul*, pp. 64-68; and G. Vos, "The Eschatological Aspect of the Pauline Conception of the Spirit," in *Redemptive History and Biblical Interpretation* (rpt.; Phillipsburg, NJ: Presbyterian and Reformed, 1980), pp. 103-5.

52. See esp. Nygren and Vos, "Eschatological Aspect," pp. 103-5; in addition Murray; Schneider, "Κατὰ Πνεῦμα Ἁγιωσύνης," p. 386; Käsemann; Barrett; Bruce.

53. This approach is able to maintain what seems to be the intentional parallelism between κατὰ σάρκα and κατὰ πνεῦμα ἁγιωσύνης and gives κατά its natural meaning, "according to." Similarly, ἐκ/ἐξ will denote in both verses the origin of the respective stages of the Son's existence.

54. ἁγιωσύνη is found only five times in the LXX and two other times in the NT (2 Cor. 7:1; 1 Thess. 3:13), both with reference to the sanctification of believers.

55. The Greek is a literal translation of Heb. רוּחַ קֹדֶשׁ; cf. Ps. 51:11; Isa. 63:10, 11; 1QS 4:21; 8:16; 9:3; 1QH 7:6, 7; 9:32; cf. *T. Levi* 18:7. The genitive may be objective: "the Spirit who gives/supplies holiness" (G. D. Fee, *God's Empowering Presence: The Holy Spirit in the Letters of Paul* [Peabody, MA: Hendrickson, 1994], p. 483).

56. ἐξ ἀναστάσεως νεκρῶν, lit. "out of resurrection of dead persons." While the plural νεκρῶν has been taken to indicate the eschatological idea of the general resurrection that Jesus' resurrection initiates (e.g., S. H. Hooke, "The Translation of Romans 1.4," *NTS* 9 [1962-63], 370-71; Nygren), the plural form is, in fact, usual when describing Jesus' resurrection (cf., e.g., Rom. 4:24). The genitive is partitive: "resurrection from among dead persons."

reader, then, with an impressive accumulation of christological titles: Son of God, Seed of David, Messiah, and Lord. Here, Paul makes clear, is the heart of the gospel that he will be setting forth in great detail for the Romans. Since Christology does not, apparently, figure in the issues with which Paul and the Romans are concerned, Paul provides no detailed attention to Christology per se in the rest of the letter. But these verses remind us that the gospel cannot be understood without reference to the person of Christ, whose resurrection ushers in the new age of redemption.

5 Paul's description of himself, interrupted by the theologically loaded excursus about the gospel to which he has been dedicated (vv. 2-4), continues in this verse with an indication of the purpose of his apostolic call. "Jesus Christ our Lord" (v. 4b) is the mediator[57] of this apostleship. Paul may use the plural "we received"[58] because he includes other Christians as recipients of grace[59] or because he includes his fellow apostles.[60] But it is better, since the description of mission in the rest of the verse is so typical of Paul's conception of his own call, to view the plural as editorial.[61] What Paul has received is "grace and apostleship."[62] Paul may have in view two separate things,[63] but it is more likely that the second term explains the first: Paul has received the special gift of being an apostle.[64]

Paul then draws attention to three aspects of his apostleship in prepositional phrases.[65] First, Paul's purpose in his apostolic ministry is to bring about[66] "obedience[67] of faith." Scholars debate the exact relationship of these two words. Many think that Paul intends to present faith as the basis for, or motivating force of, obedience: "obedience that springs from

---

57. διά, "through."

58. Gk. ἐλάβομεν.

59. E.g., Barrett.

60. E.g., S-H.

61. So most commentators. Paul often uses a plural form to speak of himself alone.

62. "Grace" (χάρις) is, of course, common in Paul; but ἀποστολή ("office of apostle") occurs only here and in 1 Cor. 9:2; Gal. 2:8 (see also Acts 1:25).

63. See, e.g., S-H; Murray; Barrett.

64. See Z-G; Michel; Käsemann; Cranfield. For Paul's use of χάρις in this sense, see esp. Rom. 12:3; 15:15; cf. 1 Cor. 3:10; 15:10.

65. Michel views the three prepositional phrases in this verse as parallel to the three qualifications of υἱὸς θεοῦ in v. 4 and finds in this an example of Paul's rhetorical artistry. It is questionable, however, whether the parallelism is intentional.

66. The εἰς denotes purpose.

67. Half of Paul's uses of ὑπακούω and ὑπακοή are found in Romans. The terms are used of Christ's willing commitment to his destiny (5:19), of the commitment to God generally that should characterize believers (1:5; 16:19), of the initial act of submission to the gospel (10:16), and, with particularly high density, of the call for Christians to live out the victory over sin won for them by Christ (6:12, 16 [3 times], 17).

faith."[68] This rendering places the emphasis on postconversion commitment: the obedience of the Christian that is to follow and be the fruit of faith. The other major option[69] is to take "faith" as a definition of "obedience": "the obedience which is faith."[70] In support of this last interpretation can be mentioned the numerous places where obedience and faith occur in parallel statements,[71] as well as those instances where Paul speaks of "obeying" the gospel.[72] However, this view, by evaporating "obedience" into faith, gives insufficient emphasis to this part of Paul's ministry. But by effectively putting faith into a subordinate position, the first option illegitimately downplays the priority of evangelism in Paul's apostleship. Paul saw his task as calling men and women to submission to the lordship of Christ (cf. vv. 4b and 7b), a submission that began with conversion but which was to continue in a deepening, lifelong commitment. This obedience to Christ as Lord is always closely related to faith, both as an initial, decisive step of faith and as a continuing "faith" relationship with Christ.[73] In light of this, we understand the words "obedience" and "faith" to be mutually interpreting: obedience always involves faith, and faith always involves obedience. They should not be equated, compartmentalized, or made into separate stages of Christian experience. Paul called men and women to a faith that was always inseparable from obedience — for the Savior in whom we believe is nothing less than our Lord — and to an obedience that could

68. That is, πίστεως would be a source or subjective genitive. See, e.g., Lagrange; Bruce; Black; Hendriksen; G. N. Davies, *Faith and Obedience in Romans: A Study in Romans 1–4* (JSNTSup 39; Sheffield: JSOT, 1990), pp. 25-30. D. Garlington argues that the phrase picks up concepts found widely in the OT and Judaism and that it denotes fidelity to the covenant. No longer, Paul suggests, is covenant fidelity tied to the law; it is now "transferred" to the realm of Christian faith and available for all (D. B. Garlington, *"The Obedience of Faith": A Pauline Phrase in Historical Context* [WUNT 2.38; Tübingen: Mohr, 1991], esp. pp. 242-48, 254; cf. also idem, *Faith, Obedience, and Perseverance: Aspects of Paul's Letter to the Romans* [WUNT 79; Tübingen: Mohr, 1994], 10-31).

69. A few scholars have suggested that πίστεως might denote a body of doctrine that one is to obey (objective genitive; cf. Kuss) or that is to be preached (G. Friedrich, "Muss ὑπακοὴ πίστεως Röm 1.5 mit 'Glaubensgehorsam' übersetz werden?" *ZNW* 72 [1981], 118-23). Neither option is lexically probable.

70. E.g., an epexegetic genitive. See Käsemann: "Obedience of faith means acceptance of the message of salvation"; cf. also, e.g., Calvin; Zahn; Nygren; Cranfield.

71. Rom. 1:8 and 16:19; 10:16a and 10:16b; 11:23; and 11:30, 31.

72. Rom. 10:16; 2 Thess. 1:8; 3:14.

73. See esp. Leenhardt and Dunn; note also the discussions in W. Mundle, *Der Glaubensbegriff der Paulus. Eine Untersuchung zur Dogmengeschichte des ältesten Christentums* (rpt.; Darmstadt: Wissenschaftliche, 1977), pp. 29-34; W. Wiefel, "Glaubensgehorsam? Erwägungen zu Röm. 1,5," in *Wort und Gemeinde. Festschrift für Erdman Schott zur 65. Geburtstag* (Berlin: Akademie, n.d.), pp. 137-44; R. Dabelstein, *Die Beurteilung der 'Heiden' bei Paulus* (BBET 14; Frankfurt: Peter Lang, 1981), pp. 109-11.

never be divorced from faith — for we can obey Jesus as Lord only when we have given ourselves to him in faith. Viewed in this light, the phrase captures the full dimension of Paul's apostolic task, a task that was not confined to initial evangelization but that included also the building up and firm establishment of churches.

The second prepositional phrase specifies the arena of Paul's apostolic labors: "among[74] all the Gentiles [*ethnesin*]." The word *ethnē* could mean "nations" in a strictly geographical sense,[75] but this would run contrary to the semantic focus of the term in Paul when it is used of the sphere of his apostolic work.[76] Paul's call was not so much to minister in many different nations as it was to minister to Gentiles in distinction from Jews.

The third modifier of "grace and apostleship" is "for the sake of his name." The phrase expresses the ultimate focus of Paul's ministry: the *name* of Jesus his Lord.[77] As generally in Scripture, "name" connotes the person in his or her true character and significance. Ultimately, Paul ministers not for personal gain or even the benefit of his converts, but for the glory and benefit of Jesus Christ his Lord.

6 This verse, inasmuch as it characterizes the readers before Paul actually addresses them in v. 7, is somewhat parenthetical. It is connected grammatically to "Gentiles" in v. 5 by the relative pronoun "whom" and is most naturally punctuated, as Godet shows, with a comma after "you": "among whom also are you, [you] who are called of Jesus Christ" (cf. NRSV, as opposed to NASB and NIV). We may also follow Godet in identifying the purpose of this remark: to show the Roman Christians that they belong within the sphere of Paul's apostolic commission. Paul is sent to "*all* the Gentiles"; and the Romans are "among" the Gentiles. They are thereby subject to his authority, as mediated in the letter that follows and in his personal presence

---

74. As often, ἐν followed by a plural object means "among."

75. Zahn; Hodge; Gifford.

76. See Rom. 15:16, 18 [in light of 15:9-12, 25-29]; Gal. 1:16; 2:1-11; Eph. 3:1, 6, 8; 1 Thess. 2:16; 1 Tim. 2:7; 2 Tim. 4:17; see esp. Godet. Paul's only uses of the singular ἔθνος come in a single OT quotation (Rom. 10:19 [= Deut. 32:21]). While the plural ἔθνη can mean "nations," including the Jews (1 Tim. 3:16; probably Rom. 4:17, 18), the vast majority of occurrences clearly designate "Gentiles" as opposed to Jews (Rom. 2:14, 24; 3:29 [twice]; 9:24, 30; 11:11, 12, 13 [twice], 25; 15:9 [twice], 10, 11, 12 [twice], 16 [twice], 18, 27; 16:4, 26 [v. 1.]; 1 Cor. 1:23; Gal. 1:16; 2:2, 8, 9, 12, 14, 15; 3:8 [twice], 14; Eph. 2:11; 3:1, 6, 8; 1 Thess. 2:16). Even some references that are unclear because of the OT context (particularly Rom. 15:11 and Gal. 3:8) are best taken as narrowly focusing on Gentiles (cf. K. L. Schmidt, *TDNT* II, 369-70). By extension from the typical Jewish perspective, Paul can also use ἔθνη to refer to those outside the Christian community (1 Cor. 5:1; 12:2; 2 Cor. 11:26; Eph. 4:17; Col. 1:27; 1 Thess. 4:5; 2 Tim. 4:17). This dominance of the meaning "Gentile as opposed to Jew" suggests that we should take ἔθνη in the sense "non-Jews" unless context demands otherwise.

77. The antecedent of αὐτοῦ must be Ἰησοῦ Χριστοῦ τοῦ κυρίου ἡμῶν in v. 4b.

when he visits them. Greater difficulty attaches to the exact meaning of the phrase "among the Gentiles." Cranfield argues that Paul is simply identifying the Romans as living in the midst of Gentiles.[78] On this view, the verse would imply nothing about the Roman Christians' national origin. This interpretation has the advantage of leaving open the vexing question of the makeup of the Roman church (see the Introduction), but it must be rejected.[79] We take it, then, that Paul designates the Roman Christians to whom he is writing as (at least mainly) Gentile.[80] This interpretation also agrees with the most natural reading of v. 13 (see below).

More important than the Roman Christians' ethnic origin is their spiritual destination. They have been "called to belong to Jesus Christ."[81] As Paul has been "called" to be an apostle (v. 1), so the Roman Christians have been "called" to be people who name Jesus as Christ and Lord. "Call" and its cognates are used by Paul to express an "effectual" calling. What is meant is not an "invitation" but the powerful and irresistible reaching out of God in grace to bring people into his kingdom.[82]

7 With v. 7 Paul finally returns to the standard letter opening begun in v. 1 and identifies those to whom the letter is being written: "to all in Rome." Not much should be made of Paul's failure to address himself to the "church" in Rome, since Paul does not consistently use the word in his letter openings.[83] But its absence may reflect the fact that the Roman Christians met in several house churches.

In designating the Roman Christians as "beloved by God" and "called to be saints," Paul implies that they are God's chosen people; for both phrases echo OT designations of Israel.[84] In so transferring language used of Israel

---

78. He bases his conclusion on Paul's use of the preposition ἐν rather than ἐκ. See also Schlatter; Schlier; Käsemann; Wilckens; Watson, 103; W. Bindemann, *Die Hoffnung der Schöpfung: Römer 8,18-27 und die Frage einer Theologie der Befreiung von Mensch und Natur* (Neukirchener Studien 14; Neukirchen/Vluyn: Neukirchener, 1983), pp. 55-66; Kettunen, *Abfassungszweck,* pp. 40-43.

79. The argument from the use of ἐν rather than ἐκ is weak since Paul is not stressing the origin of the Roman Christians but the category to which they belong. Further, the καί ("also") is difficult on Cranfield's view, implying as it does that the Roman Christians are *part of* — not just "in the midst of" — the Gentiles of v. 5.

80. See, e.g., S-H; Barrett.

81. Taking the genitive Ἰησοῦ Χριστοῦ with predicate force: cf. Z-G, 457; Murray; Feuillet, "La vie nouvelle," pp. 8-9.

82. See W. W. Klein, "Paul's Use of *Kalein:* A Proposal," *JETS* 27 (1984), 53-64.

83. Contra Klein, who thinks that Paul writes the letter to provide the necessary apostolic foundation for a "church" in Rome ("Paul's Purpose in Writing the Epistle to the Romans," p. 41). For further discussion of this proposal, see the Introduction.

84. Schlier; Deidun, 4-8. κλητοῖς ἁγίοις resembles the OT מִקְרָא קֹדֶשׁ = LXX κλητὴ ἁγία (O. Procksch, *TDNT* I, 107).

in the OT to Christians, Paul initiates an important theme of the first eight chapters of the letter. In addition, these two descriptions remind the readers that who they are depends on *God's* love and call. Paul uses "saints" at least 38 times to designate Christians (four other times in salutations), the focus being not on behavior but on status: Christians are those who *have been* sanctified "in the name of the Lord Jesus Christ and in the Spirit of our God" (1 Cor. 6:11).

As we noted in commenting on v. 4, the importance of Christology in this opening paragraph should not be missed. Paul shares with his Roman audience the conviction that Jesus is the heart of the gospel. He is the promised Messiah of Israel ("seed of David"), the Son of God, the Lord. Confessing the gospel in our own day requires that we subscribe to Paul's exalted view of Jesus; it is failure to do so that spawns many heresies. But Paul's attention, as we have also seen, is especially on the activity of this Jesus: his coming to earth as the Messiah; his exaltation through resurrection to Lord of all; his dispensing power as the Son of God. It is what Jesus has done, not just who he is, that makes the gospel the "good news" that it is. But make no mistake: what Jesus has done cannot be severed from who he is. Ours is an age not too much interested in theology; but correct theology — in this case, the person of Jesus — is vital to salvation and to Christian living.

B. THANKSGIVING AND OCCASION:
PAUL AND THE ROMANS (1:8-15)

> 8*First, I am thanking my God through Jesus Christ for all of you, because your faith is being proclaimed in all the world.* 9*For God is my witness, whom I serve in my spirit in the gospel of his Son, that without ceasing I remember you,* 10*always in my prayers praying if somehow, now at last, in the will of God, I might succeed in coming to you.* 11*For I long to see you, so that I might share with you some spiritual gift to strengthen you.* 12*That is, to be mutually encouraged among you through the faith that is in one another, both yours and mine.*
>
> 13*Now I do not wish[1] you to be ignorant, brothers and sisters, for I have often wanted to come to you (but I have been hindered until now) so that I might have a harvest also among you, even as I have had among the rest of the Gentiles.* 14*To both Greeks and barbarians,*

---

1. One Greek MS (the original hand of the western uncial D) and a few MSS of the OL read οὐκ οἴομαι, "I do not expect," in place of οὐ θέλω, "I do not wish."

to both the wise and the unlearned, I am a debtor. 15*And so my desire is to preach the gospel also to you in Rome.*[2]

Greek letters often had an expression of thanks or petition to the gods in the "proem," the second main part of the letter. Paul adapts this form for his own purposes, generally including a thanksgiving and, often, a prayer for his readers at an early point in his letters.[3] After thanking God for the widespread knowledge of the Romans' faith (v. 8), Paul mentions his frequent prayer that he might visit them (vv. 9-10). The reason for this desire is given in vv. 11-13: that Paul and the Romans might strengthen and comfort one another in their faith. Finally, as both an explanation of his wish to visit Rome and a transition to the statement of the letter's theme, Paul expresses his strong sense of obligation to preach the gospel to all sorts of people (vv. 14-15).[4]

What is remarkable about this section is a certain awkwardness on Paul's part in stating his reasons for wanting to come to Rome. After mentioning his wish to strengthen the Romans' faith (v. 11), Paul almost corrects himself, acknowledging that he anticipates a *mutual* benefit (v. 12). This note should not be seen as mere rhetorical flourish — as if Paul did not really believe that the Romans could contribute anything to his own Christian walk. Nevertheless, it is unparalleled in Paul's other letters. Such hesitation to assert his authority (cf. also 15:14-17) may reflect his desire to tread warily in light of doubts among the Roman Christians about his message and ministry.[5] But it is mainly attributable to his caution about "building on another's foundation" (15:20).[6]

---

2. The phrase τοῖς ἐν Ῥώμῃ is omitted in one Greek MS (G), in one MS of the OL, and by Origen (according to the Latin trans.). The omission is secondary; cf. the similar variant in v. 7 and the Introduction.

3. Cf. esp. P. T. O'Brien, *Introductory Thanksgivings in the Letters of Paul* (NovT-Sup 49; Leiden: Brill, 1977); and the older study by P. Schubert, *The Form and Function of the Pauline Thanksgivings* (BZNW 20; Berlin: Akademie, 1939).

4. Some scholars put a major break between vv. 13 and 14, with the "disclosure statement" (οὐ θέλω δὲ ὑμᾶς ἀγνοεῖν, "I do not wish you to be ignorant") introducing the next section (see J. L. White, *The Body of the Greek Letter* [SBLDS 2; Missoula, MT: Scholars Press, 1972], pp. 52-53; Schmithals). But O'Brien is surely correct to argue that the close thematic relationship of vv. 11-12 and 13 demands that they be kept together (*Introductory Thanksgivings,* pp. 201-2). Moreover, attempts to fit Pauline epistolary procedures neatly into the categories of Greek style are often, as Dunn notes, "overrefined."

5. See, e.g., Michel; Wilckens; Stuhlmacher. These scholars think that the Roman Christians were suspicious of Paul because of his stance on the law and other related issues. This could well have been the case; but the evidence for this supposition is not strong (see, e.g., Fitzmyer).

6. See also 2 Cor. 10:15-16; and cf. Barrett; Murray; Cranfield; E. Trocmé, "L'Épître aux Romains et la Methode missionaire de L'Apôtre Paul," *NTS* 7 (1970-71),

8   The opening word, "first," implies a series, but Paul never comes
to a "second" or "next." It is hard to know whether Paul simply forgets to
maintain the sequence he begins or whether the phrase functions here simply
to highlight what Paul considers of primary importance (cf. NEB, "Let me
begin . . .").[7] In either case, Paul draws special attention to his thanksgiving,
a feature typical of Paul's letters. He offers his thanks to "my God," a note
of personal piety that may reflect the language of the Psalms.[8] Only in Romans,
however, does Paul offer his thanks "through Jesus Christ." Although this
might mean that Christ, as High Priest, is the mediator of his thanks before
God,[9] it is better taken as an indication that Christ is the one who has created
the access to God for such thanks to be offered.[10]

Corresponding to his apostolic commission (1:5, 14-15) and the
universality of the gospel (1:16*b*), Paul includes all the Christians in Rome
in his thanksgiving. Paul's reason[11] for giving thanks is that "your faith is
being proclaimed in the whole world." Nothing is implied in this about
their faith being particularly strong; the very fact of their faith is sufficient
reason for giving thanks to God, the author of faith.[12] A measure of hyperbole is undoubtedly present in the phrase "in all the world"; but it must
be remembered that Paul is thinking of fellow Christians[13] and thus of
places where the gospel had already been preached. That people in the
Roman capital had bowed the knee to the Lord Jesus is something that
would be widely known, and perhaps highlighted, by the early missionaries.[14]

9-10   "For"[15] introduces further remarks about Paul's prayers for the
Romans. Paul often follows his thanksgivings with assertions about the con-

---

148. Other scholars, however, think that there may be more going on here than this.
G. Klein, e.g., finds in v. 15 the key to Paul's purpose in both his writing to the Romans
and in his projected visit to the city: Paul must preach the gospel to the Romans to provide
the church with apostolic foundations ("Paul's Purpose"). Käsemann finds evidence here
of a kind of existential "Angst" on Paul's part with regard to his person and ministry:
"The most important theological epistle in Christian history is undoubtedly also the record
of an existence struggling for recognition and of an apostolicity called into question."

7. Parallel occurrences of πρῶτον μέν are found in Rom. 3:2 and 1 Cor. 11:18,
and in all three cases the exact force of the phrase is unclear. See the discussions in BDF
447(4); Robertson, 1152; Fitzmyer.

8. See also Phil. 1:3; Phlm. 4; and cf. O'Brien, *Introductory Thanksgivings,* pp. 203-4.

9. E.g., S-H; Fitzmyer.

10. E.g., Käsemann.

11. The ὅτι is causal.

12. See also Eph. 1:16; Col. 1:3; 1 Thess. 1:2; 2 Thess. 1:3; Phlm. 4.

13. This must be the implied subject of καταγγέλλεται, "is being proclaimed."

14. O'Brien, *Introductory Thanksgivings,* pp. 207-8.

15. Gk. γάρ.

stancy of his prayer and concern for his readers[16] as well as petitions for their spiritual growth.[17] Here Paul's unceasing prayer for the Romans (v. 9b) has a more personal focus: his own desire to minister personally to them (v. 10). Since the "witness formula" that introduces the verse is used by Paul when he is particularly concerned to attest to the truth of what he is saying,[18] it would seem that Paul is eager that the Romans know of his heartfelt concern for them and desire to see them. Perhaps there were some in the church who felt slighted that the "Apostle to the Gentiles" had not yet deigned to visit the capital of the Gentile world.

Before stating what it is that he calls God to witness, Paul digresses in a relative clause that affirms the sincerity of his service of God. The word Paul uses for "serve" focuses attention on his service in its vertical aspect as an offering of worship to God.[19] Paul qualifies his worshipful service of God as being "in my spirit" and "in the gospel of his Son." The former phrase is particularly unclear. A few take *pneuma* as a reference to the Holy Spirit,[20] but Paul's use of *pneuma* qualified by a first or second person pronoun is against it. Others suggest that the phrase may denote prayer, the inward or "spiritual" aspect of Paul's ministry,[21] but this, too, is unlikely. What fits Pauline usage and makes sense in the context is an emphasis on the engagement of Paul's "deepest" person in the ministry to which he has been called.[22] As this inward part of Paul's person is the instrument of his service, the gospel of God's Son is the sphere of that ministry. "Gospel" has an active sense here: Paul's service consists particularly in preaching the good news about God's Son (cf. 15:16-21 for many of these same emphases).[23]

16. 1 Cor. 1:4; Eph. 1:16; Phil. 1:4; Col. 1:3b; 1 Thess. 1:2; 2 Thess. 1:3; Phlm. 4.

17. Eph. 1:16b-19; Phil. 1:9-11; Col. 1:9-11; Phlm. 6.

18. Cf. 2 Cor. 1:23; Phil. 1:8; 1 Thess. 2:5, 10.

19. The Greek verb is λατρεύω, which is used in the LXX, e.g., in the second commandment of the Decalogue, which prohibits God's people from "serving" other gods (Exod. 20:5; Deut. 5:9), and in the statements about Israel's desire to leave Egypt and "serve" God in the wilderness (Exod. 7:16; 8:1, passim). Paul's other uses of the verb (Rom. 1:25; Phil. 3:3; 2 Tim. 1:3), as well as his use of the cognate noun λατρεία in Rom 9:4; 12:1, have the same connotation.

20. Schlatter. Jewett (*Paul's Anthropological Terms,* pp. 197-98) suggests a reference to what he calls the "apportioned spirit": the Spirit of God apportioned to Paul. Fee (*God's Empowering Presence,* pp. 485-86) sees a reference to both the human spirit and the Holy Spirit.

21. Str-B (3.26) mention that "serving in the heart" is used in the rabbis with reference to prayer; cf. Zahn; Cranfield.

22. Fitzmyer: that aspect of Paul that is especially open to the influence of God's Spirit. Some view πνεῦμα as the organ of Paul's service (Godet; S-H), others as highlighting the sincerity and wholeheartedness of that service (Michel; Käsemann). I am combining these emphases in my interpretation.

23. The genitive τοῦ υἱοῦ (αὐτοῦ) is objective.

The end of v. 9 — "that[24] without ceasing I remember you"[25] — resumes the main thought from the beginning of the verse — "God is my witness." In a context like this, the word "unceasingly,"[26] as well as "always" in v. 10a, does not refer to "unceasing petition, or the like, but to prayer offered at frequent and regular intervals."[27] Paul's reticence to claim any authority over the Romans is again evident in his unusual failure to spell out any specific petitions for the Christians there. Rather, in v. 10 Paul shares with the Romans a petition he often brings before God, which, though related to the Romans, has more to do with his own plans: he regularly[28] prays that he might "somehow, now at last,"[29] "succeed"[30] in coming to them.

11 With "for," Paul introduces several verses (11-15) in which he explains why he wants to come to Rome. Paul really advances only one reason, which he delineates in three roughly parallel purpose statements: "to share some spiritual gift" (v. 11); "to have a harvest" (v. 13); "to preach the gospel" (v. 15). "Spiritual gift" is a literal translation of the Greek[31] and may refer to that kind of spiritual gift which Paul elsewhere denotes simply with "gift" (*charisma;* cf., e.g., Rom. 12:6; 1 Cor. 12, passim).[32] But Paul never elsewhere uses the combination "spiritual" and "gift" with this meaning, and the indefinite focus here — "some"[33] — makes it difficult to think that Paul has in mind his special ministerial gift(s).[34] Others think that Paul refers to "spiritual blessings" that he hopes will result from his ministry in Rome.[35] But we

24. Gk. ὡς here is equivalent to ὅτι (cf. BAGD, IV.4).

25. The construction using the middle of ποιέω with μνείαν followed by the genitive is classical, being found only here in the NT. See Z-G, 458.

26. Gk. ἀδιαλείπτως. Paul's three other uses of the adverb are all also applied to prayer: 1 Thess. 1:2; 2:13; 5:17.

27. O'Brien, *Introductory Thanksgivings,* p. 214.

28. Since πάντοτε would create a tautology with ἀδιαλείπτως if the phrase πάντοτε ἐπὶ τῶν προσευχῶν μου ("always in my prayers") were taken with what precedes (NIV), it is better to take it with the petitionary clause that follows (NASB).

29. Paul's use of hypothetical language at this point (combining εἰ ["if"], πως ["somehow"], and ἤδη ποτέ ["now at last"]) shows that he is uncertain about the fulfillment of the request and impatient about the delay.

30. The verb is εὐδόω. It literally means "lead along a good road," a meaning that would be most appropriate here (cf. NIV: "the way may be opened"). But Paul's other use of the word is metaphorical (1 Cor. 16:2; cf. 3 John 2), and since it is followed by the infinitive ἐλθεῖν, it must mean simply "succeed" here (Denney).

31. χάρισμα πνευματικόν.

32. See also 1 Tim. 4:14; 2 Tim. 1:6; cf., e.g., S-H; Barrett. Some go so far as to suggest that Paul is trying to accredit himself as a "Spirit person" (Germ. *Pneumatiker*) before some like-minded Roman Christians (Michel).

33. Gk. τι.

34. One would have expected a μου ("my") if this were the meaning.

35. Cranfield; Fitzmyer; cf. χαρίσματα in 11:29 and πνευμάτιχος in 15:27.

should think rather of an insight or ability, given Paul by the Spirit, that Paul hopes to "share" with the Romans. What gift Paul may want to share with the Romans cannot be specified until he sees what their needs may be. Whatever it is, its purpose will be to "strengthen"[36] their faith.

12 "But that is,"[37] used only here in the NT, implies that what follows in some sense "corrects" what has just been said.[38] What is being corrected is probably the last phrase of v. 11, "in order to strengthen you."[39] It is not that Paul wants to withdraw this statement but that he wants to expand it by recognizing the *mutual* gain that will accrue from his visit. The verb Paul uses[40] could refer to mutual exhortation, but probably here refers to mutual "comfort" or "encouragement."[41] This mutual encouragement[42] will be accomplished through faith — "both yours and mine." This rather cumbersome expression suggests both commonality — Paul and the Romans share the same faith — and distinction — the faith they share brings with it different perspectives and gifts, which, when shared, bring mutual edification. Paul's wish that his visit would bring spiritual encouragement to him as well as to the Roman Christians is no mere literary convention or "pious fraud" (as Erasmus called it) but is sincerely meant (and he returns to it in the letter closing: see 15:32). But the fact that he mentions it here — in contrast to his habit elsewhere — signals Paul's diplomacy. For he is dealing with a church that, while certainly within the scope of his authority (cf. 1:5-6; 15:15), is built on another person's foundation (cf. 15:20). If Paul is to gain a sympathetic ear for "his" gospel from the Roman Christians and enlist their support for his Spanish mission (15:24), he must exercise tact in asserting his authority.

13 Conveying a degree of solemnity by the use of a disclosure formula, "I do not wish you to be ignorant, brothers and sisters,"[43] Paul reaffirms his concern for the Roman Christians and his desire to minister with them. Not only has he longed to see them (v. 11a) and prayed that he might be able to make the trip (v. 10), but he has often made specific plans to that

---

36. Gk. στηριχθῆναι — cf. 1 Thess. 3:2, 13; 2 Thess. 2:17; 3:3.

37. Gk. τοῦτο δέ ἐστιν.

38. τουτ' ἐστιν has a more purely explanatory force (cf. Lightfoot).

39. E.g., Godet.

40. συμπαρακαλέω. Note that the simple verb παρακαλέω occurs with στηρίζω (cf. v. 11b) in 1 Thess. 3:2 and 2 Thess. 2:17.

41. This translation is suggested by the fact that "faith" is the means (διά) by which the action of the verb will be carried out.

42. The ἐν ὑμῖν is probably local ("among you") rather than instrumental ("by you").

43. Gk. οὐ θέλω δὲ ὑμᾶς ἀγνοεῖν, ἀδελφοί. Paul uses this, or a similar formula, in Rom. 11:25; 1 Cor. 10:1; 12:1; 2 Cor. 1:8; and 1 Thess. 4:13.

end.[44] In a parenthetical clause,[45] Paul mentions that these plans have been hindered — probably by the demands on Paul of his ministry in the eastern Mediterranean ("from Jerusalem all the way around to Illyricum," 15:19).[46] With the last clause of v. 13, Paul expresses the purpose of coming to the Romans — to "have a harvest" among the Romans. "Harvest" refers to the product of his apostolic labors (cf. Phil. 1:22), including here probably both an increase in the number of Christians through evangelization "among" the Romans and a strengthening of the faith of the Roman Christians themselves (cf. v. 11b).[47] By adding the phrase "as among the rest of the Gentiles," Paul makes clear again that he views the Roman Christians as belonging to a "Gentile" church.[48] Paul's forthright reaffirmation of his intention to bring spiritual benefit to the Roman Christians demonstrates that the mutuality of v. 12, while genuine, takes nothing from Paul's view of the importance of his apostolic labors in Rome.

14 The lack of a connecting particle between vv. 13 and 14 lends a certain emphasis to what follows, but the logical connection between the verses is clear. Paul's plan to have a harvest among the Roman Christians has its source not in a desire for personal aggrandizement but in his sense of missionary "obligation." Paul is deeply conscious of his calling, of his being "set apart for the gospel" (1:1), and it is this *divine* obligation to use his gift (Eph. 3:8) that motivates Paul — "Woe to me if I do not preach the gospel!" (1 Cor. 9:16b). The two pairs of peoples mentioned in this verse — "Greeks and barbarians," "wise and foolish" — have been variously understood. Each pair may include all of humanity, one being essentially synonymous with the other or each classifying humanity according to different criteria. However, while Paul frequently uses "Greeks" to designate Greeks-as-opposed-to-Jews (1:16; 2:9, 10; 3:9; 10:12 in Romans), his pairing the word here with "barbarians" suggests a different meaning. "Barbarian" is an onomatopoeic word (a word that sounds like what it means), mocking the way "uncouth" foreign languages would sound

---

44. προεθέμην (aorist middle of προτίθημι), "I proposed," "I intended," conveys a strong sense of intention; cf. Rom. 3:25; Eph. 1:9.

45. This clause is introduced with a καί; an unusual but by no means unexampled use of that conjunction (cf. BAGD, I.2.i; BDF 465[1]).

46. Cf. Luther's gloss: "I have been burdened with a large number of places where preaching had to be done."

47. Paul uses καρπός 11 times. Twice Paul uses the word in its literal sense as part of an analogy (1 Cor. 9:7; 2 Tim. 2:6). When he uses the word metaphorically, Paul usually does so to denote the behavior of the believer (cf. Rom. 6:21, 22; Gal. 5:22; Eph. 5:9; Phil. 1:11), sometimes as the result of his own ministry (Phil. 1:22; 4:17). Based on its use in 15:28, M. A. Kruger suggests that it refers here to the collection for the "poor" in Jerusalem ("Tina Karpon, 'Some Fruit,' in Rom. 1:13," *WTJ* 49 [1987], 168-70).

48. As in vv. 5 and 6, ἔθνη must refer to "Gentiles," not "nations" (see the notes there and, e.g., in Dunn).

to Greek ears. Accordingly, it is widely used in Greek literature of all non-Greek-speaking peoples and, by derivation, often connotes the supposedly inferior culture of such peoples. Paul applies the word in its general linguistic sense to the incomprehension attendant on exercising the gift of tongues without an interpretation (1 Cor. 14:11) and uses it in a list embracing all humanity (Col. 3:11). Greeks would, of course, include Jews among the "barbarians," but it is more than probable that Paul followed the general practice of Philo and Josephus in excluding them from such an "inferior" grouping.[49]

Probably, then, Paul intends in the first pair to designate all of *Gentile* humanity, divided according to linguistic/cultural criteria.[50] Many of the Romans would undoubtedly place themselves in the first class. But, recognizing the appeal of Christianity to the lower classes and the influx of foreigners into Rome, there would also be some who would count themselves "barbarians" (and perhaps Paul thinks also of those people in Spain to whom he hopes to preach the gospel[51]). Whether the terms in the second pair are simply explanatory equivalents to the first pair,[52] embrace the same people as the first pair but from a different perspective,[53] or designate a wider group beyond but including the first pair[54] is difficult to decide. But the reference to "Gentiles" in v. 13b makes it probable that Paul has in mind only Gentiles in v. 14. Perhaps Paul's use of "wise" in 1 Cor. 1 (19, 20, 26, 27) to designate those who prided themselves on their knowledge of God and the world, and his reference in Rom. 1:22 to people who thought they were "wise" by virtue of their own thoughts, suggests that the contrast is between those who claimed some intellectual attainment and those who did not.

15 Paul now relates what he has said generally in v. 14 to the specific situation of his desire to come to Rome: "and so[55] my desire[56] is to preach the gospel also to you in Rome." That Paul includes the Roman Christians among those to whom he wants to preach the gospel is, at first sight, strange. Some commentators therefore think that Paul is talking here about what he had planned

---

49. H. Windisch, *TDNT* I, 546-53 (552).

50. See, e.g., Fitzmyer.

51. Windisch, *TDNT* I, 552; Leenhardt; O'Brien, *Introductory Thanksgivings*, p. 223 n. 119.

52. E.g., Kuss; Schlier.

53. E.g., S-H; Cranfield.

54. Huby; Fitzmyer.

55. Gk. οὕτως, which here introduces an inference from what precedes (BAGD 1.b).

56. τὸ . . . πρόθυμον ("the desire") is probably an example of Paul's penchant for using neuter adjectives as substantives (cf. τὸ γνωστόν [1:19] and τὰ ἀόρατα [1:20]). κατ' ἐμέ (lit. "according to me") is a well-known Hellenistic Greek equivalent for the genitive (here μου, "my"; cf. BDF 224; Lietzmann). The whole phrase is the subject of the sentence (BAGD; Cranfield).

to do in the past when he had hoped to come to Rome.[57] But v. 15 is tied to v. 14, which uses a present tense.[58] Others think that he is indicating his desire to preach the gospel in Spain, on behalf of the Roman Christians.[59] But this requires us to import too much from the end of the letter. Another possibility is that "you" refers generally to Romans and that Paul is speaking of his desire to evangelize in Rome.[60] But it is more natural to take "you" to refer to the Roman Christians; in this case, "preach the gospel" will refer to the ongoing work of teaching and discipleship that builds on initial evangelization.[61] As P. Bowers has pointed out, "the gospel" in Paul includes "not simply an initial preaching mission but the full sequence of activities resulting in settled churches."[62]

C. THE THEME OF THE LETTER (1:16-17)

> 16*For I am not ashamed of the gospel,*[1] *for it is the power of God for salvation to everyone who believes, to the Jew first and then to the Greek.* 17*For in it the righteousness of God is being revealed, from faith for faith, even as it is written, "The one who is righteous by faith will live."*[a]

> a. Hab. 2:4

These theologically dense verses are made up of four subordinate clauses, each supporting or illuminating the one before it. Paul's pride in the gospel (v. 16a) is the reason why he is so eager to preach the gospel in Rome (v. 15). This pride, in turn, stems from the fact that the gospel contains, or mediates, God's saving power for everyone who believes (v. 16b). Why the gospel brings salvation is explained in v. 17a: it manifests God's righteousness, a righteous-

---

57. Stuhlmacher.

58. See Schmithals.

59. E.g., Kruger, " 'Some Fruit,' " p. 171. On this view, ὑμῖν is a dative of advantage and the implied object of the verb εὐαγγελίσασθαι is the people in Spain (cf. 15:28).

60. E.g., Godet.

61. Dunn; cf. Munck, 298; Seifrid, *Justification by Faith,* p. 189; S. Pedersen, "Theologische Überlegungen zur Isogogik des Römerbriefes," *ZNW* 76 (1985), 47-67. The latter two rely especially on the parallel to this text in 15:20-21.

62. P. Bowers, "Fulfilling the Gospel: The Scope of the Pauline Mission," *JETS* 30 (1987), 198; cf. also G. Friedrich, *TDNT* II, 719-20; Cranfield; Mundle, *Der Glaubensbegriff,* pp. 45-54. See esp. 1 Thess. 2:2-4, 8-12. It must be said, however, that this interpretation, while attractive, has against it Paul's normal use of εὐαγγελίζομαι, which he rarely uses for anything except initial evangelistic preaching.

1. The KJV addition "of Christ" reflects a secondary reading found in the corrector of D, Ψ, and the majority text.

ness based on faith. Verse 17b, finally, provides scriptural confirmation for this connection between righteousness and faith.

This chain of subordinate clauses is tied both to what comes before it and to what comes after it (note the "for" in both v. 16 and v. 18); from the standpoint of syntax alone, this means that the main statement of the sequence is Paul's assertion of desire to preach the gospel in Rome (v. 15). Some interpreters accordingly question the common opinion that vv. 16-17 state the theme of the letter.[2] Isolating these verses as the theme of the letter, it is argued, betrays a preoccupation with theology at the expense of the argumentative and syntactical flow of the text.

But the syntax does not tell the whole story. Grammatically subordinate clauses frequently stand out in importance by virtue of their content — especially in Greek, with its love of subordinate clauses (hypotaxis).[3] In the present case, the language of v. 16a implies a shift in focus. Up to this point, Paul has been telling the Romans about his call to ministry and how that ministry relates to the Romans. Since the gospel is the very essence of his ministry (vv. 1, 9) and is also the message that Paul wants to bring to Rome (v. 15), it has naturally figured prominently in these verses. Now, however, using v. 16a to make the transition, Paul turns his attention away from his own ministry and focuses it on the gospel as such. After this, nothing more is said of Paul's mission plans or the Romans (except for brief interjections — 7:1, 4; 8:12; 10:1; 11:13, 25; 12:1) until the "strong and the weak" section in 14:1–15:13 and the final summing up of Paul's plans and prospects in 15:14-33. In other words, the epistolary material of 1:1-15 and 15:14ff. "frames" what appears to be a theological treatise.

Therefore, while vv. 16-17 are technically part of the proem of the letter,[4] they serve as the transition into the body by stating Paul's theme. Most scholars would agree with this conclusion;[5] but they would not agree

2. See esp. Achtemeier.

3. Hence Achtemeier's assertion that "Grammatically, 1:17 cannot function" as the central theme of Romans is wrong (cf. Dunn).

4. See Wilckens; Käsemann.

5. See, e.g., the recent complete discussion, with reference to possible literary parallels, in J.-N. Aletti, *Comment Dieu est-il juste? Clefs pour interpréter l'épître aux Romains* (Parole de Dieu; Rome: Editions du Seuil, 1991), pp. 1-24, 38-40. A few interpreters, however, think that these verses introduce only the first major section of the letter. Calvin calls justification by faith, introduced in 1:17, the "main hinge" of the first part of the epistle. J. Dupont sees 1:16 (salvation) as relating to chap. 5, and 1:17 (justification by faith) linked with 3:21–4:25 ("Le problème de la structure littéraire de l'Epître aux Romains," *RB* 62 [1955], 372, 382). J. I. McDonald links "power of God to salvation" with 1:18-32 by antithesis, "to the Jew first and then to the Greek" with 2:1–3:20, "righteousness of God revealed" with 3:21-31, and "the just will live by faith" with chap. 4 (*Kerygma and Didache: The Articulation and Structure of the Earliest Christian Message* [SNTSMS 37; Cambridge: Cambridge University, 1979], pp. 55-57).

about just where within vv. 16-17 this theme is to be found. Protestant exegetes have traditionally focused on either "the righteousness of God is being revealed" or "the one who is righteous by faith will live," understanding them as assertions of the theological theme of "justification by faith."[6] E. Käsemann and his many followers also see in "the righteousness of God" the theme of the letter, but they give the phrase a much broader meaning than it has in traditional Protestantism (see the excursus below). A few interpreters place the concept of "salvation" in v. 16b at the center.[7] Still others are impressed by the way in which the phrase "to the Jew first and then to the Greek" (v. 16b) encapsulates two of the letter's key themes: the incorporation of Gentiles within the people of God and the continuing significance of Israel.[8] It is also possible to view the individual elements of vv. 16-17 as each summing up different parts of the letter.[9] However, as we argued in the Introduction, the breadth of the letter's contents requires a correspondingly broad theme. And standing out by virtue of its importance in vv. 1-15 as well as by its leading position in the structure of vv. 16-17 is the term "gospel" (for further exploration of the theme of the letter, see the Introduction).

16 As we have noted, v. 16a explains (cf. the "for") why Paul is eager to preach the gospel in Rome (v. 15). But it also picks up the various descriptions of Paul's commitment to the ministry of the gospel in vv. 1-15 (cf. vv. 1, 5, 9, 14). The negative form of Paul's assertion, "I am not ashamed of the gospel," may be a literary convention (litotes), justifying our rendering it as a straightforward positive statement (cf. TEV: "I have complete confidence").[10] However, "the foolishness of the word of the cross" (1 Cor. 1:18) would make some degree of embarrassment about the gospel natural — par-

6. Cf., e.g., Hodge; Godet; Murray; Bruce; S-H (including both human justification and divine "righteousness"); Barrett; Michel.

7. Dahl, *Studies,* p. 82; cf. also Lagrange; J. Cambier, *L'Evangile de Dieu selon L'Épître aux Romains. Exégèse et théologie biblique. Vol. 1: L'Évangile de la justice et de la grace* (Brussels/Louvain: Desclée de Brouwer, 1967), p. 34; Hoppe, *Die Idee der Heilsgeschichte,* pp. 26-27. These scholars then sometimes argue that the dual revelations of righteousness (v. 17) and wrath (v. 18) are subthemes.

8. Sanders, *Paul, the Law and the Jewish People,* p. 30; Schmithals, *Römerbrief,* pp. 12-13; cf. Beker, 72.

9. E.g., "salvation for *all*" = chaps. 9–11; "justified by faith" = chaps. 1–4; "live" = chaps. 5–8; cf. Wesley, p. 514; P. Rolland, *Epître aux Romains: Texte grec structure* (Rome: Pontifical Biblical Institute, 1980), p. 3.

10. Michel; Bruce; Wilckens. This interpretation is particularly attractive to those who see a close connection between this statement and Jesus' affirmation in Mark 8:38/Luke 9:26 (cf. C. K. Barrett, "I am not Ashamed of the Gospel," in *Foi et salut selon S. Paul* [AnBib 42; Rome: Pontifical Biblical Institute, 1970], pp. 19-41; Dunn).

ticularly in the capital of the Gentile world.[11] It may also be that accusations to the effect that Paul's gospel was antinomian or anti-Jewish lie behind this denial (cf. 3:8; 9:1-5).[12]

The second clause in v. 16 explains ("for") why Paul is not ashamed of the gospel. For this gospel, whose content is Jesus Christ, "appointed Son-of-God-in-power" (v. 4), mediates "the power of God leading to salvation." The term "power," as one might expect, is used widely in Greek philosophy and religion,[13] but its NT background is undoubtedly to be sought in the OT teaching about a personal God who uniquely possesses power and who manifests that power in delivering (Exod. 9:16; Ps. 77:14-15) and judging (Jer. 16:21) his people.[14]

"Salvation" and its cognates are widely used in both the Greek world and the LXX to depict deliverance from a broad range of evils.[15] The NT as a whole uses "salvation" and its cognates with much of the same broad range of

11. E.g., Murray. Moreover, evidence for the use of ἐπαισχύνομαι ("confess") in confessions is slight (Mark 8:38 and 2 Tim. 1:8 are usually cited). G. Herold (*Zorn und Gerechtigkeit Gottes bei Paulus: Eine Untersuchung zu Röm 1,16-18* [Europäische Hochschulschriften 23.14; Bern: Peter Lang, 1973], pp. 28-138) points out that litotes is rare in Paul. He argues for a forensic meaning of "shame" against the background of OT and Jewish laments. But the texts he cites have little in common with Rom. 1:16-17.

12. K. Grayston, " 'Not ashamed of the Gospel,' Romans 1,16a and the Structure of the Epistle," *SE* 1, Part 1 (1964), 569-73.

13. The Greek is δύναμις. Cranfield quotes *P.Oxy.* 11.1381.215-18: δύναμις . . . θεοῦ εἰς σωτηρίαν. On the OT use of δύναμις, see Cambier, *L'Evangile,* pp. 28-33.

14. David, praying for deliverance, addresses the Lord as "the power of my salvation" (Ps. 140:7; LXX δύναμις τῆς σωτηρίας μου). Paul frequently ascribes δύναμις to the word of the gospel (1 Cor. 2:4-5; 4:19, 20; 1 Thess. 1:5) and derivatively to his ministry (2 Cor. 4:7; 6:7; 12:9; Eph. 3:7). Particularly close to our passage is 1 Cor. 1:18, where "the word of the cross" is said to be δύναμις θεοῦ . . . τοῖς σῳζομένοις ("power of God . . . to those who are being saved"). Since Paul in this Corinthians text is countering false conceptions of power held by the Corinthians, a few scholars suggest that the ascription of power to the gospel in Rom. 1:16 may have a similar polemical thrust, countering the rabbinic ascription of salvific power to the law (W. Grundmann, *TDNT* II, 309; Nygren; cf. *Mek.* 15:13, 26). Cranfield objects to this interpretation, noting that the context reveals no polemical purpose. But the idea is certainly Pauline (cf. 8:3 — "what the law could not do [ἀδύνατον]") and should not be ruled out entirely.

15. In the OT, as we might expect, salvation is usually attributed to God, who delivers his people from their enemies (cf. Exod. 14:13; 15:2; Judg. 15:18; 1 Sam. 11:9). The peculiar OT interplay between the historical/temporary and the spiritual/eternal, and the frequent use of the former to represent the latter, makes it difficult to determine the degree of spiritual significance in the use of this word group. Some texts, however, clearly use σωτηρία ("salvation") to depict God's eschatological deliverance (cf. Isa. 12:2; 25:9; 46:13; 49:6; 52:7, 10). Of these, Isa. 52:7 is particularly significant: in addition to σωτηρία, it also uses εὐαγγελίζομαι ("preach good news"); note that Paul quotes it later in the letter (10:15). See the survey in W. Foerster and G. Fohrer, *TDNT* VII, 965-1024.

meaning as the OT, whereas Paul uses the words only of spiritual deliverance. Moreover, his focus is eschatological: "salvation" is usually the deliverance from eschatological judgment that is finalized only at the last day.[16] Characteristic, however, of Paul's (and the NT's) outlook is the conviction that these eschatological blessings are, to some extent, enjoyed by anyone the moment he or she trusts Jesus Christ as Savior and Lord. It is because of this "already" focus in Paul's salvation-historical perspective that he can speak of Christians as "saved" in this life.[17] "Salvation" often has a negative meaning — deliverance *from* something — but positive nuances are present at times also, so that the term can denote generally God's provision for a person's spiritual need. Particularly, in light of Rom. 3:23 and the use of "save" in 8:24 (cf. vv. 18-23), "salvation" here must include the restoration of the sinner to a share of the "glory of God."

The last part of v. 16 introduces themes that recur as key motifs throughout Romans. First, God's salvific power is available "to everyone who believes." "Believe"[18] and "faith"[19] are key words in Romans; they are particularly prominent in 3:21–4:25.[20] The lack of an explicit object after "believe" is also characteristic of Romans. This does not mean that Paul depreciates the centrality of Christ as the object of faith, but that the language of faith has become so tied to what God has done in Christ that further specification is not needed. To "believe" is to put full trust in the God who "justifies the ungodly" (4:5) by means of the cross and resurrection of Christ. Though intellectual assent cannot be excluded from faith, the Pauline emphasis is on surrender to God as an act of the will (cf., e.g., 4:18; 10:9). Pauline (and NT) faith is not (primarily) agreement with a set of doctrines but trust in a person. Though not explicit here, another focus of Romans is the insistence that faith is in no sense a "work."[21] Therefore, although we must never go to the extreme of making the person a totally passive instrument through whom "believing" occurs — for Paul makes clear that people are responsible to believe — we must also insist that believing is not something we *do* (in the sense of "works") but is always a response, an accepting of the gift God holds out to us in his grace (see especially 4:1-8). As Calvin puts it, faith is "a kind of vessel" with which we "come empty and with the mouth of our soul open to seek God's grace."[22]

---

16. Cf. Rom. 13:11; 1 Thess. 5:9; cf. also the use of σῴζω ("save") in Rom. 5:9-10 and the contrast between "those being saved" and "those who are perishing" in 1 Cor. 1:18; 2 Cor. 2:15; 2 Thess. 2:10.

17. 2 Cor. 6:2: "now is the day of salvation"; cf. Rom. 8:24; Eph. 2:5, 8.

18. Gk. πιστεύω.

19. Gk. πίστις.

20. Of the 21 occurrences of πιστεύω in Romans, 7 are in this section; for πίστις the figures are 18 out of 37.

21. See esp. 3:20, 27-28; 4:1-8; 9:31–10:8.

22. *Institutes* 3.11.7; cf. also Nygren on this point.

"Believing," then, while a genuinely human activity, possesses no "merit" or worth for which God is somehow bound to reward us; for salvation is, from first to last, *God's* work.[23]

But this same phrase introduces another recurring motif of Romans: the availability of God's "power for salvation" for "*all* who believe." This phrase occurs four other times in Romans (3:22; 4:11; 10:4, 11), in each case with particular reference to the breaking down of barriers between Jew and Gentile. Paul's ministry to Gentiles derives from his understanding of the gospel itself as eschatological revelation that fulfills the OT promises about the universal reign of Yahweh.[24] This required the elimination of those barriers between Jew and Gentile laboriously erected by the oral (and written — cf. Eph. 2:15) law. Nowhere does this principle receive more emphasis than in Romans, as Paul seeks to validate his gospel before a skeptical audience.

Yet it is typical also of Romans that Paul does not rest content with a reminder of the universalism of the gospel but immediately introduces a note of particularism: "to the Jew first and then to the Greek." It is only a slight exaggeration to say that the key to understanding Romans lies in successfully untangling the two connected strands of universalism — "to *all* who believe" — and particularism — "to the Jew *first*." The attempted resolution of this apparent paradox must await our comments on Rom. 9–11, but we must say something here about this particular phrase. In opposition to "Jew," "Greek" must indicate, broadly, any non-Jew.[25] What is the nature of the Jew's priority ("first") over the Gentile? Some scholars, indeed, have sought to remove any sense of priority from the phrase,[26] but without success. Paul clearly accords some kind of priority to the Jew. Some suggest that no more is involved than

23. Contrast the traditional Roman Catholic "Semi-Pelagianism" that attributes "intrinsic moral value" to faith (cf. F. Prat, *The Theology of Saint Paul* [2 vols.; Westminster, MD: Newman, 1952], 2:238-40). See the excellent discussion of this point in Hughes, *The True Image,* pp. 185-214.

24. See esp. (with an exaggerated emphasis on Paul's personal role) Munck, *Paul and the Salvation of Mankind.*

25. Paul probably uses Ἕλλην ("Greek") because he has no singular of ἔθνη ("Gentiles") as part of his own word stock (Schlier). In v. 14, Ἕλλην is contrasted with "barbarian," indicating that the word denotes a certain *kind* of Gentile. While, then, v. 14 describes the universality of the gospel from the point of view of the contemporary secular division of humankind, v. 16 makes the same point from the perspective of salvation history.

26. Marcion, to no one's surprise, removed πρῶτον ("first") from the text; Zahn suggested that πρῶτον modified the whole phrase (Zahn; see on this Zeller, *Juden und Heiden in der Mission des Paulus,* pp. 142-43); and Lietzmann dismissed the word as "a factually valueless concession to the 'chosen people of God' " ("Eine faktisch wertlose Konzession an das 'auserwählte Volk Gottes' ").

the historical circumstance of the apostolic preaching, which, according to Acts, began with the Jews and moved to the Gentiles.[27] But Paul must intend more than simple historical fact in light of the theological context here. If we ask what precedence Paul accords Israel elsewhere in Romans, we find that his emphasis is on the special applicability of the promise of God to that people whom he chose (3:2; 9–11). However much the church may seem to be dominated by Gentiles, Paul insists that the promises of God realized in the gospel are "first of all" for the Jew. To Israel the promises were first given, and to the Jews they still particularly apply. Without in any way subtracting from the equal access that all people now have to the gospel, then, Paul insists that the gospel, "promised beforehand . . . in the holy Scriptures" (1:2), has a special relevance to the Jew.

17 Verse 17 shows why (see again the "for") the gospel is God's saving power to everyone who believes (v. 16b): "in it [the gospel], the righteousness of God is being revealed." The verb translated "is being revealed"[28] is an important biblical term. Meaning originally "uncover," this verb and its cognate noun, "revelation," are typically used by Paul to refer to the eschatological disclosure of various aspects and elements of God's redemptive plan. Sometimes this disclosure is an "uncovering" to the intellect of various truths relating to God's purposes.[29] But in other places, picking up the language and concepts of Jewish apocalyptic, Paul uses the word to denote the "uncovering" of God's redemptive plan as it unfolds on the plane of human history.[30] If the former, "cognitive," meaning is adopted here, then Paul is speaking about the way in which the gospel makes known to us, or informs us, of "the righteousness of God." If we accept the more "historical" meaning of "reveal," however, Paul's point will be that the gospel in some way actually makes manifest, or brings into existence, "the righteousness of God." This latter, "historical" meaning is to be preferred in 1:17. This is the most frequent meaning of the verb in Paul, and it matches both the most likely meaning of "reveal" in 1:18 ("the wrath of God is being revealed [e.g., is being inflicted] from heaven") and the related statement in 3:21: "the righteousness of God has been made manifest." One key difference between 3:21 and 1:17, however, is the tense of the verb. The perfect tense in 3:21 focuses

---

27. Barrett; Hendriksen.

28. Gk. ἀποκαλύπτεται.

29. Cf. 1 Cor. 2:10; 14:30; Eph. 3:5 (parallel with γνωρίζω, "make known"); Phil. 3:15.

30. Cf. Rom. 2:5; 8:18, 19; 1 Cor. 1:7; Gal. 1:16; 3:23; 2 Thess. 1:7; 2:3, 6, 8. See, for discussion, e.g., Ridderbos, *Paul,* p. 47; A. Oepke, *TDNT* III, 583; D. Lührmann, *Das Offenbarungsverständnis bei Paulus und in paulinischen Gemeinden* (WMANT 16; Neukirchen/Vluyn: Neukirchener, 1965), cf. pp. 154-62 (Lührmann, however, overemphasizes the anthropological dimension of Paul's revelation language).

attention on the cross as the time of God's decisive intervention to establish his righteousness. In 1:17, on the other hand, the present tense suggests that Paul is thinking of an ongoing process, or series of actions, connected with the preaching of the gospel. Wherever the gospel is being proclaimed, the "righteousness of God" in its eschatological fullness is being disclosed.[31]

But what is this "righteousness of God" *(dikaiosynē theou)?*[32] Occurring only eight times in Romans (1:17; 3:5, 21, 22, 25, 26; 10:3 [twice]), the phrase bears an importance out of proportion to its frequency, and for three reasons. First, with the exception of 2 Cor. 5:21, Paul uses the phrase "righteousness of God" only in Romans, so that the phrase might give us a clue to the distinctive message of the letter. Second, the phrase is prominent in precisely those texts that are often considered to state the central theme of the letter: 1:16-17 and 3:21-26. And, third, the meaning of "the righteousness of God" has played a significant role in the interpretation of Paul and of the gospel generally — from Augustine to Luther to E. Käsemann. There are three main options for the meaning of the phrase.

(1) The expression might refer to *an attribute of God.*[33] Under this general heading are to be included two distinct possibilities. According to the first, "righteousness" is God's justice, or rectitude *(iustitia distributiva,* "distributive justice"). This interpretation was widespread in the early church, where it owed its popularity somewhat to the meaning of the Greek term *dikaiosynē* and its Latin equivalent.[34] Contemporary scholars, while often giving this meaning to the phrase in 3:5 and 3:25-26, rarely do so in 1:17; for the context requires a positive meaning for the phrase. The second possibility takes its point of departure from the alleged OT meaning of "God's righteousness": God's faithfulness, especially to his covenant with Israel. This interpretation also has an ancient pedigree,[35] but it is particularly popular in recent studies. While again the occurrences in 3:5 and 3:25-26 are most often interpreted in this way, a few scholars think that 1:17 could be understood in the same way: for example, the gospel reveals "the faithfulness of God [to his promises of salvation]."[36]

---

31. See, e.g., Dunn.

32. Despite the lack of articles, the phrase is clearly definite; Paul may omit articles here and throughout v. 17 as part of a "definition style" (BDF 252).

33. With this meaning, θεοῦ is probably a possessive genitive: "God's own righteousness."

34. See A. E. McGrath, *Iustitia Dei: A History of the Christian Doctrine of Justification* (2 vols.; Cambridge: Cambridge University, 1986, 1987), 1.52.

35. See McGrath, *Iustitia Dei,* 1:52, who cites Ambrosiaster.

36. Williams, "Righteousness of God," pp. 241-90; P. T. O'Brien, "Justification in Paul and Some Crucial Issues of the Last Two Decades," in *Right with God: Justification in the Bible and the World* (ed. D. A. Carson; Grand Rapids: Baker, 1992), pp. 70-78.

(2) "Righteousness of God" in 1:17 might refer to a *status given by God*.[37] Luther's personal spiritual struggle ended with his realization that God's righteousness meant not "the righteousness by which he is righteous in himself but the righteousness by which we are made righteous by God." Not the strict "distributive justice" *(iustitia distributiva)* by which God impartially rules and governs the world, but a righteousness that is not one's own *(iustitia aliena),* a new standing imparted to the sinner who believes — this was what made Paul's message "good news" to Luther. In contrast to both Augustine and most medieval theologians, Luther viewed this righteousness as purely forensic — a matter of judicial standing, or status, and not of internal renewal or moral transformation.[38] This understanding of "righteousness of God" stands at the heart of Luther's theology and has been a hallmark of Protestant interpretation.[39] On this view, Paul is asserting that the gospel reveals "the righteous status that is from God."

(3) "Righteousness of God" might denote *an activity of God*.[40] The English word "righteousness" naturally designates an abstract quality, but the use of the equivalent Greek term *(dikaiosynē)* in the LXX has a much broader range of meaning — including the dynamic sense of "establishing right." Especially significant are the many places in the Psalms and Isaiah where God's "righteousness" refers to his salvific intervention on behalf of his people (see section A.2 in the Excursus). If Paul is using this "biblical" meaning of the word, then his point here would be that the gospel manifests "the saving action of God."[41]

37. This interpretation usually takes θεοῦ as a genitive of source — "righteousness from God" — but a few have followed Luther and taken it as an objective genitive — "righteousness that is valid before God" (cf. A. Oepke, "ΔΙΚΑΙΟΣΥΝΗ ΘΕΟΥ bei Paulus in neuer Beleuchtung," *TLZ* 78 [1953], 263 [idem, *TDNT* III, 583]; O'Neill).

38. McGrath argues that it was this "deliberate and systematic distinction . . . between justification and regeneration" that distinguished Protestant from medieval Roman Catholic theology *(Iustitia Dei,* 1.183-86).

39. As we have seen, however, the occurrences in 3:5 and 3:25-26 are usually exempted and understood to refer to God's justice. A sample of recent expositors who argue that "righteousness of God" in 1:17 is a status given to human beings by God includes more "traditional" Protestants — Nygren; Ridderbos; Cranfield; G. E. Ladd, "Righteousness in Romans," *Southwest Journal of Theology* 19 (1976), 6-17; Seifrid, *Justification,* pp. 214-15 — as well as R. Bultmann ("Διχαιοσύνη Θεοῦ," *JBL* 83 [1964], 12-16) and many of his followers, such as H. Conzelmann *(An Outline of the Theology of the New Testament* [London: SCM, 1969], pp. 214-20); G. Klein ("Righteousness in the NT," in *IDBSup* [New York: Abingdon, 1976], pp. 750-52); and Zeller *(Juden und Heiden,* pp. 161-80).

40. On this view, θεοῦ is a subjective genitive: "the righteousness that is being shown by God."

41. Cambier, *L'Evangile de Dieu,* pp. 39-40; J. H. Roberts, "Righteousness in Romans with Special Reference to Romans 3:19-31," *Neot* 15 (1981), 18; Dodd; Michel; Barrett; Dunn.

These options are neither exhaustive nor mutually exclusive, and two or more of them are often combined in the interpretation of 1:17. In fact, every possible combination of the three basic interpretations is found in the literature: God's action in making people right and the status of people so made right;[42] God's attribute of "being in the right" and his making sinners right before him;[43] both his being in the right and his gift of righteousness;[44] and, combining all three, God's being in the right, his action of making people right before him, *and* the resultant status of those made right.[45] A particularly attractive and popular combination is that found in the interpretation of Käsemann. He argues that "God's righteousness" is "God's salvation-creating power,"[46] a concept that incorporates the ideas of status given by God and activity exercised by God — with the emphasis on the latter — and the addition of nuances such as God's reclaiming of creation for his lordship (see B.4 in the Excursus for details).

Three factors influence the decision we reach on this issue: the OT background; the use of "righteousness" words generally in Romans[47]; and the immediate context. The difficulty is that they do not all point in the same direction. Whereas the OT provides warrant for each of the main alternatives,

42. H. S. Songer, "New Standing Before God. Romans 3:21–5:21," *Review and Expositor* 73 (1976), 416; G. N. Davies, "Faith and Obedience in Romans" (Ph.D. diss. University of Sheffield, 1987), p. 18.

43. D. Hill, *Greek Words and Hebrew Meanings: Studies in the Semantics of Soteriological Terms* (SNTSMS 5; Cambridge: Cambridge University, 1967), p. 160; S-H; Bruce.

44. L. Morris, *The Apostolic Preaching of the Cross* (Grand Rapids: Eerdmans, 1955), p. 252; C. A. A. Scott, *Christianity according to St. Paul* (Cambridge: Cambridge University, 1939), p. 63.

45. J. H. Ropes, " 'Righteousness' and 'The Righteousness of God' in the Old Testament and in St. Paul," *JBL* 22 (1903), 225-26; Wedderburn, *Reasons,* pp. 108-23.

46. Germ. "Heilsetzende Macht." For Käsemann's view, see esp. "Gerechtigkeit Gottes," pp. 367-78 (ET "Righteousness of God," pp. 168-82); *Romans,* 23-30; the appendix to "Justification and Salvation History" (in *Perspectives on Paul* [Philadelphia: Fortress, 1971], pp. 76-78). A few of the more important works that defend this general approach — though with differences in specifics — are P. Stuhlmacher, *Gerechtigkeit Gottes bei Paulus* (FRLANT 87; Göttingen: Vandenhoeck & Ruprecht, 1966) (see, however, the important qualifications he introduces in his essay "Paul's View of Righteousness," pp. 91-92); C. Müller, *Gottes Gerechtigkeit und Gottes Volk. Eine Untersuchung zu Römer 9–11* (FRLANT 86; Göttingen: Vandenhoeck & Ruprecht, 1964), esp. pp. 65-72 and 109-14; K. Kertelge, *'Rechtfertigung' bei Paulus. Studien zur Struktur und zum Bedeutungsgehalt der paulinischen Rechtfertigungslehre* (NTA n.s. 3; Münster: Aschendorff, 1967); J. A. Ziesler, *The Meaning of Righteousness in Paul: A Linguistic and Theological Investigation* (SNTSMS 20; Cambridge: Cambridge University, 1972), pp. 170-71, 187-88; A. Hultgren, *Paul's Gospel and Mission: The Outlook from His Letter to the Romans* (Philadelphia: Fortress, 1985), p. 31; Beker, 263-64.

47. These include, in addition to the noun δικαιοσύνη, the adjective δίκαιος ("righteous") and the verb δικαιόω ("justify").

there is no doubt that the third — God's saving activity — receives strongest support. When "righteousness" is attributed to God, it has this meaning more than any other; and it is God's "righteousness" in this sense — a saving, vindicating intervention of God — that the prophets say will characterize the eschatological deliverance of God's people (cf. Mic. 7:9; Isa. 46:13; 50:5-8; and see section A.2 in the Excursus for detailed substantiation). Granted the OT roots of Paul's conception of "righteousness" (cf. 3:21), we would expect this notion of saving activity to be included when he announces the revelation of "the righteousness of God."

Paul uses "righteousness" words in Romans in several different ways (see, again, the survey in section A.2 in the Excursus). But one thing emerges as characteristic: the connection between righteousness and faith. It is no exaggeration to call this a leitmotif of the letter. The references to "righteousness of God" evidence a definite pattern at this point: those in 3:5 and 3:25-26 are not tied directly to faith, and — as our exposition will show — they refer to God's attribute of "faithfulness to his person and promises." On the other hand, Paul links "righteousness of God" closely with the response of faith in 1:17, in 3:21-22, and (cf. 10:6) in 10:3. This ties the idea of "righteousness" in the phrase "righteousness of God" to Paul's use of the word generally in Romans, where it is typically linked to faith.[48] And "righteousness" is used most often in Romans to denote the "gift of righteousness" (5:17) — a righteous status that God bestows on the one who believes (chap. 4, passim; note also the parallel between "righteousness of God" and "righteousness based on faith" in 10:3-6, and the reference to "righteousness *from*[49] God" in Phil. 3:9). Paul's use of "righteousness" language in Romans, then, strongly suggests that "righteousness of God" in 1:17; 3:21, 22; and 10:3 includes reference to the status of righteousness "given" to the believer by God.

If these first two factors point in two different directions, the consideration of the context only confuses matters further by giving some support to *each* possibility. On the one hand, Paul's use of "reveal" — particularly if it has the dynamic meaning we have suggested — makes better sense if "righteousness of God" denotes a divine activity than if it refers to a divine gift. Furthermore, the "revelation of God's wrath" in v. 18 appears to parallel v. 17, and "wrath" in v. 18 is clearly a divine activity. On the other hand, the "gift" character of "righteousness" receives support from the prepositional addition "on the basis of faith" and from the quotation of Hab. 2:4 at the end of the verse, where the cognate word "righteous" designates human status. And this

---

48. This is an important methodological point, for Käsemann and many of his followers insist that δικαιοσύνη θεοῦ be treated as a technical phrase with a meaning all its own.

49. Gk. ἐκ.

stress on faith as the means by which the righteousness of God is received binds this verse closely to those many others in Romans in which righteousness is clearly a status given to the one who believes (see above). The contexts in which the related occurrences of "righteousness of God" are found evidence the same ambiguity: God's righteousness is "manifested" (3:21), and people are to "submit" to it (10:3) — suggesting activity; and yet it is also "based on" faith — suggesting gift or status.

Most interpreters make a decision at this point, choosing either activity or status and offering more or less convincing explanations of the data that appear to conflict with the view they have chosen. But must we make this choice? Do we have to choose between theology (*God* acting) and anthropology (the *human being* who receives) — as some have stated the dilemma? Could we not take "righteousness of God" here to include *both* God's activity of "making right" — saving, vindicating — *and* the status of those who are so made right, in a relational sense that bridges the divine and the human? The LXX usage, out of which Paul's use of the phrase grows, makes it likely that "the righteousness of God" is first of all the saving intervention of God in history, predicted by the prophets, manifested on the cross, and constantly made effective in the preaching of the gospel. But God's righteousness never operates in a vacuum, and the OT occurrences often allude also to the situation or status of those who experience God's saving intervention (see section A.2 in the Excursus). Partly because he needs to distance his interpretation of God's righteousness from the prevalent Jewish view, in which works and the law play so prominent a role (cf. 3:21; 10:3), Paul insists that God's righteousness can be experienced only through faith: "For Paul the righteousness of God is essentially a righteousness that comes by faith."[50] His theology also leads him to develop the idea of righteousness as an enduring, judicial status far beyond anything found in the OT. This emphasis shifts the focus of the phrase a bit with respect to its OT usage, although, as we have said, the dual aspect of God's righteousness as both divine activity and human status does have its antecedents in the OT.

For Paul, as in the OT, "righteousness of God" is a relational concept. Bringing together the aspects of activity and status, we can define it as *the act by which God brings people into right relationship with himself.*[51] With Luther, we stress that what is meant is a status *before* God and not internal moral transformation — God's activity of "making right" is a purely forensic activity, an acquitting, and not an "infusing" of righteousness or a "making

50. Stuhlmacher, "Paul's View of Righteousness," p. 80.
51. See especially also Stuhlmacher, who argues that "righteousness of God" in Paul includes "both poles of the event of justification. . . . The gracious activity of God himself and the end result of the divine work in the form of the righteousness granted to the sinner" ("Theme," p. 339).

right" in a moral sense (see the Excursus). To be sure, the person who experiences God's righteousness does, necessarily, give evidence of that in the moral realm, as Paul makes clear in Rom. 6. But, while "sanctification" and "justification" are inseparable, they are distinct; and Paul is badly misread if they are confused or combined. To use the imagery of the law court, from which righteousness language is derived, we can picture God's righteousness as the act or decision by which the judge declares innocent a defendant: an activity of the judge, but an activity that is a declaration of status — an act that results in, and indeed includes within it, a gift. In this sense, the noun "righteousness" in this phrase can be understood to be the substantival equivalent of the verb "justify."[52]

This more comprehensive interpretation of "righteousness of God" in 1:17 has several advantages. First, it is built on the most frequent meaning of the phrase in the OT, so that Paul's readers in Rome would have an immediate starting point for their understanding of Paul's language. Second, it does justice to the nuances of both divine activity and human receptivity that occur in the text. Third, it enables us to relate the phrase to Paul's broader use of "righteousness," where he frequently highlights the end result of the process of justification in the believer's status of righteousness.

Verse 16 has already indicated that God's salvation comes only to those (though to all) who believe. The same point is underscored in the present verse with the phrase "from faith to faith" and the quotation from Hab. 2:4. Just what the prepositional phrase modifies is not clear. Coming immediately after, the phrase could modify the verb "is being revealed."[53] But the Habakkuk quotation that follows — where "on the basis of faith" probably modifies "the one who is righteous" — and Paul's persistent linking of righteousness words with faith throughout Rom. 1–4 point toward a connection with "righteousness of God." Both concerns can be met if we construe the double prepositional phrase as an almost independent phrase that resumes Paul's discussion of righteousness.[54]

---

52. A factor that makes this situation difficult for the English reader is the use of two different roots, "just" and right," for words from one root, δικ-, in Greek. Thus, to make clear the relationship in English, one could translate δικαιόω as "declare righteous" and δικαιοσύνη θεοῦ as "the 'righteousing' of God" or translate δικαιόω as "justifying" and δικαιοσύνη θεοῦ as "the justifying activity of God." However, the former is horrendous English, while the latter is cumbersome. A rather close linguistic parallel can be found in the words ἁγιόω ("sanctify") and ἁγιωσύνη ("sanctification"; often, the process of becoming sanctified).

53. See, e.g., Seifrid, *Justification*, p. 218.

54. Nygren; Cranfield. Similar is the suggestion that the double prepositional phrase modifies the entire clause (Käsemann; Schlier). Oepke ("ΔΙΚΑΙΟΣΥΝΗ ΘΕΟΥ bei Paulus," p. 263) and Leenhardt take ἐκ πίστεως with δικαιοσύνη and εἰς πίστιν with ἀποκαλύπτεται, but word order is decisively against this.

Thus, the NIV: "For in the gospel a righteousness from God is revealed, a righteousness that is by faith . . ." (v. 17).

Paul's addition of "for faith"[55] to "on the basis of faith" has been the subject of endless discussion. Many of the Fathers explained the double reference as meaning that God's righteousness was "from the faith in the law to the faith in the gospel."[56] Augustine gave several explanations, among them that Paul wished to include both the faith of the preacher and the faith of the hearer.[57] Calvin and others see a reference to the growth of faith in the individual, enabling the Christian to appreciate and enjoy more and more the righteousness of God.[58] Barth argues that the first "faith" refers to God's faithfulness, and the second the faith of the individual person.[59] Some commentators compare Rom. 3:22, concluding that Paul wants to stress both that righteousness is received by faith and is for all who believe,[60] or (on another reading of Rom. 3:22) that Paul attributes our righteousness both to Christ's faithfulness ("on the basis of faith") and to our own believing.[61] Others find a thrust against Judaism: righteousness is both received by faith and has faith, not works, as its goal.[62] Probably, however, in light of the only clear NT parallel to the construction,[63] the combination is rhetorical and is intended to emphasize that faith and "nothing but faith" can put us into right relationship with God.[64]

The quotation from Hab. 2:4 confirms (cf. "even as") the truth that righteousness is to be attained only on the basis of faith. There are textual differences between Paul's wording and the original text of Habakkuk,[65] but

55. Gk. εἰς πίστιν.

56. E.g., Augustine, *The Spirit and the Letter* 11.18 (*NPNF* 5.90); cf. also Schelkle.

57. Augustine, *The Spirit and the Letter* 11.18.

58. See also Tholuck; Gifford; S-H; Huby; Kuss; Schmithals; Fitzmyer.

59. See also Dunn; Davies, *Faith and Obedience,* pp. 42-43. An interpretation gaining ground recently is the idea that this first "faith" refers to the faithfulness of Christ (see M. D. Hooker, "ΠΙΣΤΙΣ ΧΡΙΣΤΟΥ," *NTS* 35 (1989), 321-42; D. A. Campbell, "Romans 1:17 — A *Crux Interpretum* for the Πίστις Χριστοῦ Debate," *JBL* 113 [1994], 265-85).

60. E.g., Murray; Leenhardt.

61. For documentation and further discussion of the πίστις Χριστοῦ issue, see the notes on 3:22.

62. Zahn; Schlatter; Michel.

63. See 2 Cor. 2:16, οἷς μὲν ὀσμὴ ἐκ θανάτου εἰς θάνατον, οἷς δὲ ὀσμὴ ἐκ ζωῆς εἰς ζωήν; "to those an odor of 'death leading to death,' to others an odor of 'life leading to life.' "

64. See, e.g., Barrett; Cranfield.

65. The textual history of Hab. 2:4 is complex. The relevant data are as follows (see esp. J. Fitzmyer, "Habakkuk 2:3-4 and the New Testament," in *To Advance the Gospel: New Testament Studies* [New York: Crossroad, 1981], pp. 236-45):

the main problem is that Paul appears to give the words a different meaning. Hab. 2:4 is God's response to the prophet's complaint about God's inaction and injustice. It instructs the person who is already righteous how to face the difficulties of life and, especially, the apparent contradictions between God's promises and what takes place in history. In Paul, the quotation functions to characterize how it is that one can attain right standing with God and so live eternally. Another key difference is found if we take "on the basis of faith"

MT: וְצַדִּיק בֶּאֱמוּנָתוֹ יִחְיֶה, "but the righteous one by his faith will live"
1QpHab 7:17 = MT
LXX: ὁ δὲ δίκαιος ἐκ πίστεώς μου ζήσεται, "But the righteous one on the basis of my faith will live"
LXX, MSS A and C: ὁ δὲ δίκαιός μου ἐκ πίστεως ζήσεται, "but my righteous one on the basis of faith will live"
8HevXIIgr (a Greek scroll of the minor prophets, generally exhibiting a proto-Theodotionic text), col. 12: [δίκ]αιος ἐν πίστει αὐτοῦ ζήσετ[αι], "a righteous one in his faith will live"
Aquila: δίκαιος ἐν πίστει αὐτοῦ ζήσεται, "a righteous one in his faith will live"
Symmachus: δίκιαος τῇ ἑαυτοῦ πίστει ζήσεται, "a righteous one by his own faith will live"
Heb. 10:38: ὁ δὲ δίκαιός μου ἐκ πίστεως ζήσεται, "but my righteous one on the basis of faith will live" (a number of MSS omit μου, whereas others place it after πίστεως)
Gal. 3:11 and Rom. 1:17: ὁ δὲ δίκαιος ἐκ πίστεως ζήσεται (Gal. omits δέ), "but the righteous one on the basis of faith will live"

The most interesting variation is in the choice and placement of the personal pronoun. The LXX differs from the MT in reading a first person pronoun, thereby apparently attributing πίστις to God as his "faithfulness." Hebrews reads the pronoun but (if P[46], ℵ, A, etc. are followed) places it after δίκαιος, thus approximating the meaning of the MT. Paul is unique in omitting any personal pronoun. His quotation is closest to the text of the MT, and since the third person pronominal suffix refers to the "righteous one," Paul's text does not differ in any important respect from the MT. Since he usually follows the LXX in his quotations (see the most recent study, C. D. Stanley, *Paul and the Language of Scripture: Citation Technique in the Pauline Epistles and Contemporary Literature* [SNTSMS 69; Cambridge: Cambridge University, 1992], cf. pp. 253-64), this may be a deliberate omission to facilitate his application of the verse. See, e.g., E. E. Ellis, "Midrash Pesher in Pauline Hermeneutics," in *Prophecy and Hermeneutic* [the article appeared originally in *NTS* 2 (1955-56)], pp. 174-77; B. Lindars, *New Testament Apologetic: The Doctrinal Significance of the Old Testament Quotations* (London: SCM, 1961), p. 231; D.-A. Koch, "Der Text von Hab 2.4b in des Septuaginta und im Neuen Testament," *ZNW* 76 (1985), 68-85. There is no evidence that Paul has been drawn to Hab. 2:4 through a Jewish eschatological scheme based on Hab. 2:3 (as is argued by A. Strobel, *Untersuchungen zum eschatologischen Verzögerungproblem auf Grund der spätjüdisch-urchristlichen Geschichte von Habakuk 2,2ff* [NovTSup 2; Leiden: Brill, 1961], pp. 173-202).

with "the righteous one" rather than with "will live." Indeed, a large number of scholars deny that we should do this. They argue that Paul, like Habakkuk, connects "by faith" with "live" (KJV: "The just shall live by faith"; also NASB; NIV).[66] But a better case can be made for connecting "the one who is righteous" with "on the basis of faith" (RSV: "He who through faith is righteous will live"; also TEV; NEB).[67] Of greatest significance is the way Paul in Rom. 1–8 consistently links faith with righteousness (cf. the summary in 5:1) and shows how "life" is the product of that righteousness (cf. 5:18 and 8:10). These connections favor the translation "the one who is righteous by faith will live."[68]

In both the meaning of the terms and their connections, then, Paul's quotation differs from the meaning of the original. But the differences should not be magnified. The point in Habakkuk is that faith[69] is the key to one's relationship to God. The meaning of faith in the NT is deepened through its intimate relationship to Christ as the object of faith,[70] but the OT concept, in verses like Gen. 15:6 and Hab. 2:4 especially, shares with NT "faith" the

66. This, its advocates argue, is the most natural way to interpret the word order. If Paul had meant to connect δίκαιος and ἐκ πίστεως he would have written ὁ δὲ ἐκ πίστεως δίκαιος and removed all ambiguity. Further, they claim, ζήσεται by itself is rather a weak anticlimax. See esp. Lightfoot; Godet; S-H; Murray; Michel; and on Gal. 3:11, H. C. C. Cavallin, " 'The Righteous Shall Live by Faith.' A Decisive Argument for the Traditional Interpretation," *ST* 32 (1978), 33-43. An unlikely alternative is to understand ὁ δίκαιος as Jesus (Campbell, "Romans 1:17," pp. 281-84).

67. See esp. A. Feuillet, "La citation d'Habaccuc II.4 et les huit premiers chapitres de l'Epître aux Romains," *NTS* 6 (1959-60), 52-80; Cranfield; Nygren; Käsemann; Wilckens. R. M. Moody ("The Habakkuk Quotation in Romans 1:17," *ExpTim* 92 [1981], 205-8) and Dunn take ἐκ πίστεως with *both* δίκαιος and ζήσεται.

68. "Life" in this sense being virtually equivalent to salvation (see Scott, *Christianity according to Saint Paul*, pp. 135-41). Both sides appeal to Gal. 3:11 (Paul's only other quotation of Hab. 2:4), but, since Paul's purpose there is to deny that justification comes "by the law," it is likely that "on the basis of faith," as a contrast to "by the law," modifies "the one who is righteous." This argument would be even stronger if, as Nygren and Cranfield claim, the quotation functions as the "heading" for Rom. 1–8. Specifically, they argue that "righteous by faith" summarizes the argument of chaps. 1–4 and "shall live" that of chaps. 5–8 (see also Byrne, 90). However, while the first point especially has merit, Paul fails to show clearly enough that the theme of "life" can stand as the heading for chaps. 5–8.

69. Heb. אֱמוּנָה. This word is only infrequently used to depict human response to God (1 Sam. 26:23; 2 Chron. 19:9; 31:12; Ps. 37:3) and generally means to be "faithful." The cognate verb (particularly in the hiphil), however, is used more often to depict a person's acceptance of God's words and promises and trust in and reliance upon him (Gen. 15:6; Exod. 14:31; Num. 20:12; 2 Chron. 20:20; Ps. 116:10; etc.).

70. For further discussion of this characteristic relationship between the testaments, see my "The Problem of Sensus Plenior," in *Hermeneutics, Canon and Authority* (ed. D. A. Carson and J. Woodbridge; Grand Rapids: Zondervan, 1986), pp. 179-211.

quality of absolute reliance on God and his Word rather than on human abilities, activities, or assurances.[71] Rom. 4 will bring out more fully how Christians are to exhibit this "faith of Abraham."

EXCURSUS: "RIGHTEOUSNESS" LANGUAGE IN PAUL

No set of words is more important for a correct understanding of Paul's message to the Romans than those that share the root *dik-*, especially *dikaioō* ("justify"), *dikaiosynē* ("righteousness"), and, to a lesser extent, *dikaios* ("righteous"). Although individual occurrences must be treated in context in the commentary proper, a discussion of the general background and meaning of the word group as a whole is necessary as a foundation.

A. THE OT AND JEWISH BACKGROUND

1. Words from the Dik- Root Generally

a. Dikaioō ("Justify")

Dikaioō and its cognates were used in secular Greek,[1] but the widespread and theologically significant use of the terminology in the LXX, along with Paul's frequent appeal to the OT in discussing the words (e.g., Rom. 3:22; 4:1-25), shows that the OT/Jewish background is decisive. In the LXX *dikaioō* normally translates two Hebrew words, *ṣedeq* and *ṣᵉdāqâ*, which are generally interchangeable.[2] Likewise, *dikaioō* usually translates *ṣādaq*, whereas *dikaios* renders *ṣaddîq*.[3] By the same token, words from the Hebrew root *sdq* are translated by Greek words from the *dik-* root in the large majority of cases. This considerable linguistic overlap suggests that the meaning of *dik-* words for Greek-speaking Jews like Paul was decisively influenced by the meaning of *ṣdq* words. The long-standing debate over whether the basic meaning of

---

71. C. F. Keil, *The Minor Prophets,* vol. 10 of *Commentary on the Old Testament* by C. F. Keil and F. Delitzsch (rpt., 2 vols. in one; Grand Rapids: Eerdmans, 1973), 2.73; Ridderbos, *Paul,* p. 172. O. P. Robertson (" 'The Justified (by faith) shall live by his steadfast Trust': Habakkuk 2:4," *Presbyterion* 9 [1983], 52-71) argues that "faith" should be construed with both "righteous" and "live."

1. See the survey in G. Schrenk, *TDNT* II, 178-225.

2. N. H. Snaith, *The Distinctive Ideas of the Old Testament* (Philadelphia: Westminster, 1946), p. 90. A distinction is maintained, however, by F. Crüsemann, "Jahwes Gerechtigkeit *(ṣedāqā/ṣädäq)* im Alten Testament," *EvT* 36 (1976), 427-50.

3. Ziesler (*Righteousness,* pp. 22-67) gives a full survey of the OT data.

the root *ṣdq* is "conformity to a norm"[4] or "mutual fulfillment of claims arising from a particular relationship"[5] may be bypassed if we agree with Ziesler that the "norm" in question is the demands that stem from God's relationship with his people in the covenant.[6]

Dikaioō occurs 44 times in the LXX, and in all but six occurrences where there is a Hebrew original it translates a form of *ṣādaq*. In the qal this verb means "to be righteous," in the piel "to be demonstrated as righteous," and in the hiphil "to declare righteous."[7] The nine times *dikaioō* translates the hiphil of *ṣādaq* are particularly significant for Paul's usage. The verb is used almost always with a judicial or forensic flavor. Sometimes the "judge" who "pronounces righteous," or acquits, is human (Deut. 25:1; Isa. 5:23), and at other times divine (Exod. 23:7; 1 Kings 8:32; 2 Chron. 6:23; Ps. 82:3; Isa. 50:8). Even when the term is not used with explicit reference to the law court, the forensic connotations remain (cf. Gen. 38:26; 44:16; Jer. 3:11; Ezek. 16:51-52). The high degree of translation correspondence between *dikaiosynē* and *ṣedeq/ṣᵉdāqâ* means that these can be considered together.

b. Dikaiosynē ("Righteousness")

Dikaiosynē, which occurs more than 300 times in the LXX, is applied both to God and to human beings. Leaving the former for consideration below in conjunction with *dikaiosynē theou* ("righteousness of God"), we note that the forensic flavor is much less obvious in the case of the human being's *dikaiosynē* in the LXX. The word becomes a general way of describing what is "well pleasing" to God and takes on definitely ethical connotations.[8] Nevertheless, the notion of right relationship is not completely lost. As most scholars emphasize, *dikaiosynē* language has its context in the covenant and designates most often that form of life which is the Israelite's appropriate response to the covenant.[9]

---

4. This view is associated especially with E. Kautzsch, *Die Derivate des Stammes* צדק *im alttestamentlichen Sprachgebrauch* (Tübingen, 1881). Modern scholarship has tended to move away from this derivation — though cf. Snaith, *Distinctive Ideas,* pp. 90-97; Hill, *Greek Words,* p. 83; and L. J. Kuyper, "Righteousness and Salvation," *SJT* 3 (1977), 233-34 (however, the latter two understand the "norm" involved to be the terms of the covenant). For a concise survey, see Piper, *Justification,* pp. 82-83.

5. The work of H. Cremer, *Die paulinische Rechtfertigungslehre im Zusammenhange ihrer geschichtlichen Voraussetzungen* (2d ed.; Gütersloh: Bertelsmann, 1900), is above all credited with this proposal. It has been followed by a large number of modern OT scholars.

6. Ziesler, *Righteousness,* pp. 36-39.

7. See Ziesler, *Righteousness,* pp. 18-22.

8. Cf. Isa. 5:7: [Israel] ἐποίησεν ἀνομίαν καὶ οὐ δικαιοσύνη ("Israel has done what is against the law and not righteousness").

9. Ziesler, *Righteousness,* pp. 24-27; Morris speaks more broadly of conformity to God's standard (*Apostolic Preaching,* p. 234).

In intertestamental Judaism, *dikaiosynē* usually has this more "ethical" flavor, a usage reflected in Matthew's Gospel especially.[10] *Dikaios,* the most common *dik-* word in the LXX (almost 400 occurrences), is used of the person who is characterized by *dikaiosynē*. It is the standard way by which the godly, or pious, person is denoted (cf., e.g., Prov. 10–13).

2. *"The Righteousness of God" (dikaiosynē theou)*

The complexity of the issues surrounding this phrase makes it necessary to consider it on its own. The actual phrase *dikaiosynē theou* never occurs in the LXX; *dikaiosynē kyriou* ("righteousness of the Lord") occurs twice (1 Sam. 12:7; Mic. 6:5). But 48 times, mainly in the Psalms and Isaiah, we find *dikaiosynē* modified by a personal pronoun whose antecedent is "God" or "the Lord."[11] In all but six of these occurrences, *dikaiosynē* translates *ṣedeq* (12 times) or *ṣᵉdāqâ* (32 times).[12] In addition to these specific references to "God's righteousness" are more than 50 places where *dikaiosynē* is ascribed to God or where God is said to do or speak *dikaiosynē,* or the like. The high degree of translation equivalence between the *dik-* and *ṣdq* roots means that a study of the one is virtually a study of the other also. Since our concern is to explain the Greek phrase in Romans, we will take the LXX occurrences as our basic material.

God's *dikaiosynē* in secular Greek usually designates an attribute of God, although most of the biblical occurrences possess a more active or relational meaning. For instance, in Ps. 51:14 David prays, "Deliver me from those who seek my blood, O God, the God of my salvation; my tongue will rejoice in your righteousness [*tēn dikaiosynēn sou*]" (LXX 50:16). Similarly, God promises through the prophet Isaiah: "I bring near my righteousness [*tēn dikaiosynēn mou*], and my salvation will not delay" (Isa. 46:13). As the parallel with "salvation" shows, "God's righteousness" in these verses is his saving intervention on behalf of his people. Probably 16 other occurrences of the phrase have this same general sense.[13]

What is sometimes overlooked at this point is that this saving activity can also be considered from the standpoint of the human being who receives

---

10. Cf. B. Pryzybylski, *Righteousness in Matthew and His World of Thought* (SNTSMS 41; Cambridge: Cambridge University, 1980), p. 105 passim.

11. Of these, two are textually uncertain. In 1 Sam. 12:7, some MSS read the plural δικαιοσύνας, and the phrase is omitted entirely in some MSS in Ps. 71:21.

12. The exceptions are Exod. 15:13 and Isa. 63:7 (where the Hebrew is חֶסֶד), Isa. 38:19 and Dan. 9:13ᴸˣˣ (where the Hebrew is אֱמֶת), and Bar. 4:13 and Ps. 71:21 (where there is no corresponding Hebrew word).

13. Pss. 22:31; 35:28; 40:10; 69:27; 71:15, 16, 19, 24; 88:12; 98:2; 119:123; Mic. 6:5; 7:9; Isa. 51:5, 6, 8.

"God's righteousness." In these contexts, God's righteousness clearly includes the aspect of gift or status enjoyed by the recipient. The clearest instance is Ps. 35:27-28: "Let those who desire *my* righteousness shout and be glad. . . . And my tongue will declare *your* righteousness." Cf. also 51:14, where the psalmist speaks of the "God of *my* salvation" and of "*your* [God's] righteousness," and the references to the psalmist's righteousness in 4:1 and 37:6, and to Israel's righteousness in Isa. 62:2. The important occurrences of the phrase in Isa. 46:13 and 50:5-8 may also include reference to the continuing enjoyment of God's righteousness, since this righteousness meets the need brought by Israel's being "far from righteousness" (Isa. 46:12) and is said to be eternal (50:8).

Recognizing that these texts constitute the largest single category among those that we are considering, and that both Micah and Isaiah predict the arrival of this righteousness at the time of God's eschatological deliverance (Mic. 7:9; Isa. 46:13; 54:5-8), we are justified in thinking that this meaning of the phrase must have considerable influence on Paul's *dikaiosynē theou*.

A second meaning is closely related to this first, and, indeed, is not always easy to distinguish from it. In a number of texts, God's *dikaiosynē* is not his saving activity but the basis, or the motivation, for that saving activity. Psalm 31:1 is characteristic: "in your righteousness [*en tē dikaiosynē sou*] deliver me and lead me out." At least 14 other occurrences probably fit here.[14] In these passages, God's "righteousness" is his faithfulness, his commitment to fulfill the promises he has made to his people. Since it is generally thought that OT righteousness language has to do with meeting commitments imposed by the covenant relationship, this dimension of God's righteousness is often said to be his covenant faithfulness.[15] In a number of verses where righteousness is attributed to God (e.g., Ps. 88:12; 145:7), it is difficult to know whether God's commitment to help his people or the help itself is meant.[16] In some cases, at least, we may surmise that elements of both are present.

Thus far, it would appear that God's *dikaiosynē* is exclusively beneficial in its operation; and, indeed, scholars such as von Rad conclude just that.[17]

---

14. Exod. 15:13; Ps. 35:24; 36:6, 10; 71:2; 89:16; 103:17; 111:3; 119:40; 143:1, 11; 145:7; Isa. 38:19; 63:7. In these texts, δικαιοσύνη translates Heb. חֶסֶד ("loving-kindness") twice (Exod. 15:13; Isa. 63:7), אֱמֶת ("truth") once (Isa. 38:19), and is paralleled by words such as ἀλήθεια ("truth"; Ps. 36:6; 88:12; 98:2; 143:1; Isa. 38:19), ἔλεος ("mercy"; Ps. 31:1; 36:6, 10; 88:12; 98:2; 103:17; 143:11), and χρηστότης ("goodness"; Ps. 145:7). Note, e.g., Ps. 36:5-6a: "Lord, your mercy [ἔλεος] is in heaven, and your truth [ἀλήθεια] unto the clouds; your righteousness [δικαιοσύνη] is as the mountains of God."

15. Cf. Hill, *Greek Words,* p. 156.

16. Cf. esp. Cremer, *Die paulinische Rechtfertigungslehre;* note also G. von Rad, *Old Testament Theology* (2 vols.; New York: Harper & Row, 1962), 1:370-77.

17. von Rad, *Old Testament Theology,* 1:370-77.

But a number of texts show how shortsighted such a conclusion would be. First, several of the passages that highlight the salvific benefits of God's righteousness also refer to the judgment that it brings on the wicked. In Ps. 50, for instance, God summons the heavens and the earth as witnesses as he sits in judgment over his people (v. 4). Verse 6 then reads: "And the heavens declare his righteousness, for God himself is judge." There follows in the rest of the psalm an indictment of Israel, with a call for repentance. Here God's *dikaiosynē* is virtually his justice, in a neutral sense — his commitment to deliver those who have met the standards of the covenant and reject those who have not (similar to this are Ps. 7:17; 9:4, 8; 97:2; Isa. 59:17). It is God's righteousness in this sense that is given to the king, so that he will be able to "vindicate the afflicted, save the children of the needy, and crush the oppressor" (Ps. 72:1). God's *dikaiosynē* bears this meaning also in the expression that occurs five times in Ps. 119 — *ta krimata tou dikaiosynēs sou,* "the judgments of your righteousness" (vv. 7, 62, 106, 160, 164) — and in those places where God is said to judge "in righteousness."[18] God's covenant commitment, these passages suggest, is a commitment to do what is "right" with reference to that covenant. When Israel's enemies are in view, or when Israel breaks the terms of the covenant, God's righteousness naturally takes on a negative, judgmental aspect (cf. Isa. 5:16; 10:22).

This more neutral meaning of *dikaiosynē* colors even those texts where God's righteousness is salvific. In many of those passages, the saving righteousness of God is pictured as God's vindicating his people — his granting to them a deliverance to which they can lay claim, either because of their own "righteousness" (Ps. 7:8; 9:8; 18:20, 24; 35:24; 37:6) or because of God's promises. The righteousness of God, then, while having the same positive connotation as salvation in these instances, stresses that the deliverance in view has the character of vindication, an establishing of what is "right." The phrase is used positively so often because God's promises to his people in the covenant mean that the pious Israelite can expect God's "doing what is right" to bring deliverance from his or her enemies.

That such a conception creates tensions even with the OT is clear. In Ps. 143:1, for instance, the psalmist pleads for deliverance on the basis of God's righteousness, while acknowledging that no one can claim God's help on the basis of one's own righteousness (v. 2). Similarly, in Dan. 9, God is acknowledged to be righteous in the disasters he has brought on his unfaithful people (vv. 7, 14), while at the same time the prophet can appeal to God's righteousness as the motivation for turning his wrath away from his people (v. 16). Here God's establishing of what is right does not take place within

18. Cf. Pss. 67:4; 94:15; and 89:14 and 97:2, where δικαιοσύνη appears to be parallel to εὐθύτης, "uprightness."

the terms of the covenant as such but with reference to something more basic. Piper argues that it is God's determination to act for the glory of his name that is this more basic element (see Dan. 9:17-19).[19] Piper is certainly on the right track but perhaps narrows the conception more than is justified. More broadly, in view of the clearly forensic focus of righteousness language in the OT,[20] the "more basic element" is God's always acting in accordance with the norm of his own person and promises.[21]

A frequent objection to any such view of God's righteousness as an "attribute" is that it "intrudes conceptions quite foreign to the Hebrew mind, and for which there is no basis in the naïvely realistic thinking of the Israelite."[22] But such objections, while understandable as a reaction against the tendency of some scholars (particularly in the past) to read European medieval legal norms into the OT, surely have gone too far. What the "Hebrew mind" could or could not conceive can be known only from the pages of the OT. Nor are we seeking to revive the notion that God's righteousness in the OT is a conformity to an ideal ethical norm, as if God were being forced to conform to something outside himself. Nor are we arguing that righteousness is attributed to God as a result of ontological speculation. It is, as we may put it, an experienced attribute, stating the conviction of the Israelites that God can always be depended upon to act in accordance with what is right, as defined by God's person and promises.[23]

To summarize, then, we find that God's *dikaiosynē* in the OT can denote God's character as that of a God who will always do what is right, God's activity of establishing right, and even, as a product of this activity, the state of those who have been, or hope to be, put right.[24] While the expectation that God would act to put his people in the right is usually founded on the covenant commitment,

---

19. Piper, *Justification,* p. 100.

20. Cf. Morris, *Apostolic Preaching,* pp. 226-33; G. Quell, *TDNT* II, 177.

21. The same is true with God's "mercy" (חֶסֶד). This term is often viewed in terms of God's "obligation" to do such and such within the terms of the covenant (e.g., N. Glueck, *Hesed in the Bible* [Cincinnati: Hebrew Union College, 1967]). But the dimension of God's unrestricted, unconstrained "free mercy" must also be seen (F. Andersen, "Yahweh the Kind and Sensitive God," in *God Who is Rich in Mercy. Essays presented to Dr. D. B. Knox* [ed. P. T. O'Brien and D. G. Peterson; Homebush West, Australia: Anzea, 1986], pp. 41-88).

22. W. Eichrodt, *Theology of the Old Testament* (2 vols.; Philadelphia: Westminster, 1967), 1.240.

23. Evidence of the "cosmic" significance of the phrase, posited, e.g., by Käsemann and his followers, is not forthcoming (cf. Fitzmyer, 106-7).

24. Cf. Ropes's similar summary: "God's vindication of man can be described either as the righteousness of man or the righteousness of God. It belongs to man as a state into which he is, or hopes to be put; it belongs to God as an attribute, and as the act in which that attribute is exercised" ("Righteousness," pp. 218-19).

some texts, such as Ps. 143, Dan. 9, and probably Isa. 46 and 50, anticipate an irruption of God's righteousness that cannot be tied to the covenant as such.

Further evidence pertaining to Paul's use of *dikaiosynē theou* is found in intertestamental Jewish texts. Particularly significant, because singled out by the "Käsemann school" as the clearest evidence for the pre-Christian technical, apocalyptic use of the phrase, is chap. 11 in the Dead Sea Scroll "The Manual of Discipline" (1QS).[25] "God's/his righteousness" occurs five times in the chapter.[26] Moreover, in what some claim to be a striking anticipation of Paul's theology, this righteousness of God is in four of these verses said to be the basis for human justification.[27] This last point, however, is questionable. The translation "justification" for the Hebrew *mišpāṭ* is problematic, and the stress on the law throughout the scrolls creates a wholly different atmosphere from that of Paul's teaching.[28] Nor does the use of the phrase "God's righteousness" signal an advance on the OT teaching. It probably means "mercy" or "saving faithfulness" in 1QS 11 and is used with other meanings elsewhere in the scrolls, showing that the phrase has not taken on a fixed meaning.[29] The situation is the same in other possibly pre-Christian texts where the phrase occurs (1QM 4:6; *T. Dan* 6:10[30]; *1 Enoch* 71:14; 99:10; 101:3). In *1 Enoch,* for instance, "God's righteousness" refers to his faithfulness (71:14) and is parallel to the simple "righteousness" (cf. 71:16), his moral strictures (99:10), and his merciful works (101:3). In all this, there is little that substantiates a key supposition of the "Käsemann" approach: that "righteousness of God" is a fixed, apocalyptic *terminus technicus.*[31] Nor does

25. Cf. Stuhlmacher, *Gottes Gerechtigkeit,* pp. 165-66.

26. צדקת אל in v. 12; the third person singular pronominal suffix form in vv. 3, 5, 14, and 15; cf. צדקת אמתו ("the righteousness of his truth") in v. 14.

27. Cf. S. Schulz, "Zur Rechtfertigung aus Gnaden in Qumran und bei Paulus," *ZTK* 56 (1959), 106-7; Dahl, *Studies in Paul,* pp. 97-100.

28. Sanders, *Paul and Palestinian Judaism,* pp. 308-12; Fitzmyer, "Justification by Faith," p. 201; cf. also O. Betz, "Rechtfertigung in Qumran," in *Rechtfertigung. Festschrift für Ernst Käsemann zum 70. Geburtstag* (ed. J. Friedrich, W. Pöhlmann, and P. Stuhlmacher; Tübingen: Mohr/Göttingen: Vandenhoeck & Ruprecht, 1976), p. 36.

29. Sanders, *Paul and Palestinian Judaism,* pp. 308-9, Pryzybylski, *Righteousness in Matthew,* pp. 13-38.

30. M. L. Soards ("Käsemann's 'Righteousness' Reexamined," *CBQ* 49 [1987], 264-67) disputes Käsemann's appeal to *T. Dan* 6:10 in support of his interpretation.

31. Cf. E. Lohse, "Die Gerechtigkeit Gottes in der paulinischen Theologie," in *Battesimo e Giustizia in Rom 6 e 8* (ed. L. de Lorenzi; Monographic Series of "Benedictina," Biblical-ecumenical Section, 2; Rome: St. Paul's Abbey, 1974), pp. 14-15, 21-24; E. Güttgemanns, " 'Gottesgerechtigkeit' und strukturale Semantik. Linguistische Analyse zu δικαιοσύνη θεοῦ," in *Studia Linguistica neotestamentica* (BEvT 60; Munich: Kaiser, 1973), pp. 63-82; Wright, "Messiah and People of God," p. 64; Sanders, *Paul and Palestinian Judaism,* p. 494. Stuhlmacher now admits that he gave too much emphasis to this point in his monograph (see "Paul's View of Righteousness," p. 91).

the NT give any basis for interpreting *dikaiosynē theou* as a *terminus technicus*. It occurs only twice outside Paul's letters, and then with a meaning different from Paul's (Matt. 6:33; Jas. 1:20).

B. "JUSTIFY," "RIGHTEOUSNESS," AND "RIGHTEOUS" IN PAUL

1. "Justify" (Dikaioō)

In Paul, it is always God who justifies and the human being who is justified (except in the probably traditional 1 Tim. 3:16). Particularly characteristic of Paul's usage is his insistence that justification takes place by faith[32] and not by "works" (Rom. 4:2), or "works of the law" (Rom. 3:20, 28; Gal. 2:16). That Paul preserves the thoroughly forensic flavor of the word is clear from his addition of the phrase "before God" to the verb (Rom. 2:13; 3:20) and from the contrast between *dikaioō* and *katakrinō* ("condemn") in Rom. 8:33. It is now generally agreed, then, that *dikaioō* in Paul means not "make righteous" but "declare righteous," or "acquit," on the analogy of the verdict pronounced by a judge.[33] To justify signifies, according to forensic usage, to acquit a guilty one and declare him or her righteous.[34]

Roman Catholic scholars who agree that *dikaioō* means "declare righteous" nevertheless often insist that this declaration, being God's powerful word, must be effectual, and include thereby moral transformation.[35] It is indeed the case that God's declaration is effectual, but there is nothing about the act that suggests this effect must extend beyond its forensic sphere. So also the criticism that a strictly forensic meaning of *dikaioō* makes the action

32. ἐκ πίστεως: Rom. 3:30; 5:1; Gal. 2:16; 3:8, 24; πίστει: Rom. 3:28; ἐκ πίστεως, διὰ τῆς πίστεως: Rom. 3:30.

33. So most Protestant exegetes. See particularly Morris, *Apostolic Preaching*, pp. 224-74; J. Morison, *A Critical Exposition of the Third Chapter of Paul's Epistle to the Romans* (London: Hamilton, Adams, 1866), pp. 163-98; and, interacting with recent discussion, R. Y.-K. Fung, "The Forensic Character of Justification," *Themelios* 3 (1977), 16-21.

34. Melanchthon, *Apology for the Augsburg Confession*, 4.184.

35. E.g., the Council of Trent says of justification: ". . . not the remission of sins merely, but also the sanctification and renewal of the inward man" (chap. 7). Cf. Fitzmyer, "Justification by Faith," p. 208; F. Amiot, *The Key Concepts of St. Paul* (New York: Herder and Herder, 1962), pp. 122-23; L. Cerfaux, *The Christian in the Theology of St. Paul* (London: Geoffrey Chapman, 1967), pp. 392, 424-27; Prat, *Theology*, 2.247, 249; and even, for all his agreement with Barth, H. Küng, *Justification: The Doctrine of Karl Barth and a Catholic Reflection* (Philadelphia: Westminster, 1964), pp. 208, 213.

a "legal fiction" is wide of the mark: legal it is, but it is no more fiction than is the release from imprisonment experienced by the pardoned criminal.

Despite his debt to the OT and Judaism in his use of *dikaioō*, Paul differs from the normal OT/Jewish usage in three important respects. First, the verdict pronounced by a judge, according to the OT, was required to be in accordance with the facts (cf. especially Exod. 23:7; 1 Kings 8:32). It is a keystone of Paul's doctrine, however, that "God justifies the ungodly" (Rom. 4:5). His realization of the seriousness of sin and concern to maintain the absolute grace of God manifested in Christ led him to see that God's justifying verdict could never be forthcoming if the human being were regarded in himself. It is not that God acts "unjustly," against the facts; but his justifying takes into account a larger set of facts, including the atoning character of Jesus' death and the righteousness he thereby acquired.[36]

Second, the Jewish view was that the verdict of "justification" would be pronounced only at the judgment.[37] Indeed, Sanders disputes this, noting the frequency with which Jewish writings speak of people as "righteous" in this life.[38] But what is meant by "righteous" in these writings is something different from what Paul means. Moreover, Sanders's own argument, which stresses the importance of obedience to the law as a condition for remaining in the covenant, shows implicitly that the final verdict according to Jewish theology cannot be pronounced until the judgment. Paul, however, transfers the final verdict into the present.[39] (For a discussion of the difficulties caused in this regard by Rom. 2:13, see the discussion there.) The moment a sinner places his or her faith in Christ, he or she is justified — the final verdict is read back into his or her present experience in a characteristic example of NT "inaugurated eschatology."

Third, the justification offered the sinner in the gospel goes beyond "acquittal," by putting the sinner into a relationship with God in which *all* sins — future as well as past — are accounted for.

2. *"Righteousness" (Dikaiosynē)*

Ziesler contends that *dikaioō* in Paul is always forensic, but that *dikaiosynē* usually has both ethical and forensic dimensions. But Ziesler has been justly criticized for too often finding two meanings in *dikaiosynē* that are not clearly

---

36. C. S. Lewis beautifully captures the idea in his distinction between the witch's insistence on absolute justice and the "deeper magic" (*The Lion, the Witch and the Wardrobe* [New York: Macmillan, 1950], pp. 153-63).

37. See, e.g., Isa. 43:9; 45:25; 50:8; Bultmann, *Theology,* 1:274-75. In the NT, Matt. 12:37 and, probably, Jas. 2:20-26 bear witness to this usage (cf. D. Moo, *The Letter of James* [TNTC; Grand Rapids: Eerdmans, 1985], pp. 108-11).

38. Sanders, *Paul and Palestinian Judaism,* p. 494.

39. On this, see esp. Ladd, *Theology,* pp. 441-43.

supported from the context.[40] Some of Paul's uses of *dikaiosynē* are difficult to categorize (particularly those in Rom. 6), but most fall clearly into one category or the other.[41]

3. *"Righteous" (Dikaios) and Other Terms*

In comparison with the frequency of the word in the LXX, Paul's 17 uses of *dikaios* seem paltry. As in the LXX, Paul can use the word to mean "what is right" (Eph. 6:1; Phil. 1:7; 4:8; Col. 4:1), but he rarely uses it as is customary in the LXX, to denote the person who is "right" with God. When Paul does so use it, forensic connotations are again to the fore (cf. Rom. 1:17; 2:13; 3:10; 5:19; Gal. 3:11). One is "right" not because of behavior that is pleasing to God but because of faith in Jesus Christ. God is called "just" several times (2 Thess. 1:5, 6; 2 Tim. 4:8), as is the law (Rom. 7:12). Paul uses several other words with a *dik-* root in Romans, and these are also generally forensic in nature: *dikaiōma* ("just decree"; cf. 1:32; 2:26; 5:16, 18; 8:4); *dikaiōsis* ("justifying"; cf. 4:25; 5:18); *dikaiokrisia* ("righteous judgment"; cf. 2:5); *endikos* ("just"; cf. 3:8). The antonyms *adikia* ("unrighteousness") and *adikos* ("unrighteous") are generally used of humans, with moral force (although cf. 3:5; 9:14).

4. *A Note on E. Käsemann's Interpretation of "The Righteousness of God"*

We allude to E. Käsemann's influential interpretation of *dikaiosynē theou* in the exposition above; here we want to describe it in more detail. Käsemann argues that "righteousness of God" is a technical phrase in Jewish apocalyptic, where it denotes God's saving power and activity as it is exercised in commitment to the covenant. Paul picks up the phrase from this apocalyptic context but modifies its meaning by expanding the sphere of God's saving activity from the covenant people to all of creation. God in Jesus acts to reclaim his sovereignty over the world. Particularly important to Käsemann, who is reacting to what he perceives to be an excessive concern with anthropology in Bultmann, is that God's righteousness always remains God's. Even when Paul portrays this righteousness as a gift, it is a gift that is never separate from the giver. We are taken up

40. Cf. N. M. Watson, Review article of J. A. Ziesler's *The Meaning of Righteousness in Paul, NTS* 20 (1973-74), 220; Reumann, *Righteousness,* pp. 56, 57, 58-59.

41. Almost certainly purely forensic are those occurrences in Rom. 4 that are connected with Gen. 15:6, and those in Rom. 9:30–10:13. Romans 5:17, significantly, speaks of δικαιοσύνη as a "gift"; and note δικαιοσύνη ἐκ θεοῦ in Phil. 3:9. The meaning of δικαιοσύνη in Rom. 14:17 is probably also forensic, while those in Rom. 6:13, 16, 18, 19, and 20 are probably ethical.

into righteousness as a sphere of power and are called to its service (Rom. 6). Käsemann's interpretation, therefore, includes the ideas of status given by God and activity exercised by God, with the emphasis on the latter and the addition of nuances such as power and the reclaiming of creation that shift the focus of these ideas. It is a powerful and coherent interpretation and is the lifeblood of his impassioned interpretation of Romans and of Paul.

Since there are some similarities between our own interpretation and that of Käsemann, the differences should be noted: (1) our explanation is not dependent on the background of a fixed apocalyptic term but on the broad OT usage; (2) faithfulness or activity directed to the creation as a whole is not included — in fact, Paul's righteousness language appears to be concentrated solely on the relationship of God to people;[42] (3) the idea of "power" is not clearly present; (4) it is not so clear that the occurrences of "righteousness" in texts such as Rom. 6 have to be merged with this conception — they may reflect a relatively independent conception, based on the OT, Jewish, and NT (see Matthew) use of *dikaiosynē* to designate what is ethically right; (5) the phrase "righteousness of God" cannot be made the center, or starting point, of Paul's theology.

C. JUSTIFICATION BY FAITH IN ROMANS AND IN PAUL'S THEOLOGY

For Luther, and many Protestant interpreters who have followed him, "justification by faith" is the center of Romans, of Paul's theology, and indeed of the Bible. This view of the matter has, however, been subjected to severe criticism, most notably by W. Wrede and A. Schweitzer at the beginning of this century, and by K. Stendahl, E. P. Sanders, and others more recently. Wrede considered "justification by faith" to be a doctrine with only polemical import, devised to counter the claims of Judaism,[43] whereas Schweitzer, noting the relative absence of justification language in Rom. 5–8, labeled justification by faith a "subsidiary crater" in Paul's thinking, much less important than his "Christ-mysticism."[44] Stendahl is representative of many contemporary exegetes who insist that questions of "people" — Jew and Gentile; who belongs to the people of God — rather than questions of an individual's being right with God dominate Romans and Paul's thinking.[45] Sanders, wanting to integrate Paul's justification language into his central concerns more than Schweitzer did, nevertheless agrees

42. Cf. Lohse, "Gerechtigkeit Gottes," pp. 24-25; Fitzmyer, "Justification by Faith," pp. 199-210, 210-11.

43. Wrede, *Paul,* pp. 122-37.

44. Schweitzer, *Mysticism,* pp. 205-26 (esp. 219-26).

45. Stendahl, *Paul among Jews and Greeks,* pp. 26-27.

with Schweitzer that "participationist," not forensic, justification categories are central to Paul.[46] These views have, naturally, sparked considerable response from those who want to defend the traditional position that justification by faith is central to Paul's thought, especially in Romans.[47]

A decision on this question depends greatly on what is meant by "center." If by this one means the organizing focus of Paul's thinking, then Christology should probably be put at the center. If one means, however, the basic theological framework within which Paul expresses his theology, then salvation history should be made central. But there is something to be said for the centrality of justification by faith in another sense. Though it is true, as opponents of the traditional view tirelessly point out, that "justification by faith" occurs mainly in passages where Paul is countering Jewish tendencies and that the doctrine has, for that reason, a distinctly polemical thrust, it is also true that the doctrine guards Paul's theology at an absolutely vital point. Justification by faith is the anthropological reflex of Paul's basic conviction that what God has done in Christ for sinful human beings is entirely a matter of grace (see especially 3:24; 4:1-8, 16). If, then, justification by faith is not the center of Romans or of Paul's thought in the logical sense, in another sense it expresses a central, driving force in Paul's thought (see, further, the Introduction, under "Theme"). In this respect, the Reformers were not far wrong in giving to justification by faith the attention they did.

II. THE HEART OF THE GOSPEL: JUSTIFICATION BY FAITH (1:18–4:25)

In his statement of the theme of the letter (vv. 16-17), Paul moves quickly from the gospel to the salvation mediated by the gospel to the "righteousness of God" revealed in the gospel. It is now this righteousness, God acting to bring people into a right relationship with himself, that occupies Paul's attention in the first major section of the body of Romans, 1:18–4:25.[1] "Righ-

---

46. Sanders, *Paul and Palestinian Judaism,* pp. 434-42.

47. See esp. Seifrid, *Justification;* also O'Brien, "Justification," pp. 78-85; Hübner, "Pauli Theologiae Proprium," pp. 445-73; Reumann, *Righteousness,* p. 185 passim. Reumann gives a good survey of the main options (cf. pp. 181-85); cf. also R. Y.-K. Fung, "The Status of Justification by Faith in Paul's Thought: A Brief Survey of a Modern Debate," *Themelios* 6/3 (1981), 4-11.

1. Ellis's theory that 1:17 is the "proem text" of a midrashic structure in 1:17–4:25 (E. E. Ellis, "Exegetical Patterns in 1 Corinthians and Romans," *Prophecy and Hermeneutic,* pp. 217-18) correctly identifies the theme but finds connections in the material that are not as clear as one would wish.

teousness" *(dikaiosynē)* and its cognates "justify" *(dikaioō)* and "righteous" *(dikaios)* occur 24 times in these verses, being particularly prominent (6 occurrences) in the passage that is the heart of this section, 3:21-26. But even more prominent is another word group: "faith" *(pistis)* and its (in Greek) cognate verb, "believe" *(pisteuō),* occur 27 times, and usually in close conjunction with "righteousness" or "justify." Word frequency does not, of course, tell the whole story, but in this case the statistics are indeed indicative of the theme of these chapters: God's righteousness as the righteousness of faith.

OT prophets and psalmists predicted that God's righteousness, his intervention in history to establish Israel's "right," would be revealed in the last days. And Jews in Paul's day continued to look for this act of God on their behalf. Paul announces the coming of this righteousness in the gospel of Christ. But he also emphasizes two aspects of this righteousness that were not widely accepted in his day. First, being an entirely gracious act on God's part, God's righteousness could be experienced only by faith. Second, *anyone* — Jew or Gentile — could, and *needed* to, experience it on exactly the same terms. These points, which for Paul are intertwined (for, as he argues, in 3:28-30, if God is to be God of all people, his righteousness must be offered to all on the same basis), are what he wants to get across to the Romans in this part of his letter. The argument takes the form of a "dialogue with Judaism."[2] Not only does Paul address "the Jew" directly (2:17-29; cf. 2:1-5), but the issues of the law and circumcision dominate much of the discussion. The language of "righteousness" itself is OT-Jewish. Even Paul's indictment of humanity (1:18–3:20) focuses on the Jew (2:1–3:20). As we argue in the Introduction, the fact that Paul dialogues with Judaism here does not mean that the dialogue is itself directed to Jews, or even to Jewish Christians. Paul wants the Christian community in Rome to listen in to this dialogue so that they may understand his gospel. The points he argues in this section are those points for which Paul had to contend throughout his missionary career. It is therefore no wonder that "the Apostle to the Gentiles," when setting forth his gospel to Christians with whom he had had no contact, would emphasize just these points.

A. THE UNIVERSAL REIGN OF SIN (1:18–3:20)

Our claim that righteousness, or justification, by faith is the focus of 1:18–4:25 might seem odd in light of the statistics that emerge from 1:18–3:20: "righteousness" words occur only six times and references to faith or believ-

2. See esp. Beker, 78-83.

ing only twice — and then without reference to human faith. It is, in fact, only beginning with 3:21 that "righteousness by faith" becomes central; in 1:18–3:20, sin, wrath, and judgment occupy center stage. Paul implicitly acknowledges that 1:18–3:20 is an interruption in his exposition of the righteousness of God by reprising 1:17 in 3:21: "But now the righteousness of God has been manifested. . . ." Why this interruption? What is the purpose of this step-by-step indictment of humanity? Some think that the "revelation of God's wrath" is a product of the preaching of the gospel, so that 1:18–3:20 is as much "gospel" as is 3:21–4:25 (see below, on v. 18). But, although Paul clearly considers warning about judgment to come to be related to his preaching of the gospel (2:16),[3] his generally positive use of "gospel" language forbids us from considering God's wrath and judgment to be *part of* the gospel.

We must consider 1:18–3:20 as a preparation for, rather than as part of, Paul's exposition of the gospel of God's righteousness. But it is a necessary preparation if what Paul wants to emphasize about this righteousness is to be accepted by the Romans. For only if sin is seen to be the dominating, ruling force that Paul presents it to be in this section (cf. 3:9) will it become clear why God's righteousness can be experienced only by humbly receiving it as a gift — in a word, by faith. "Only those who are prepared to acknowledge that they are unworthy can put faith in the Giver of grace."[4] And only if Jews as much as Gentiles are understood to be subject to this imprisoning effect of sin will it become clear that all people need to experience this righteousness of God.

This dual focus of 1:18–3:20 is succinctly stated in 3:9: "all people, both Jews and Gentiles, are under the power of sin." So absolute is sin's power over people that only God's power, available in the gospel, can rescue them. And so universal is sin's power that it has gained sway even over God's chosen people, the Jews. As we argue below (see the introduction to 1:18-32), Paul's indictment of humanity in 1:18–3:8 proceeds as if it were moving inward through a series of concentric circles: from the whole of humanity (1:18), to humanity apart from special revelation — mainly, then, Gentiles (1:19-32), to the "righteous" person — but mainly the Jew (2:1-16), to the Jew explicitly (2:17–3:8).[5]

---

3. P. Stuhlmacher argues that 1:18–3:20 has the purpose of convincing opponents of Paul that he *does* preach judgment ("Paul's Understanding of the Law in the Letter to the Romans," *SEÅ* 50 [1985], 96).

4. J. Moffatt, *Grace in the New Testament* (London: Hodder, 1931), p. 132.

5. R. Dabelstein (*Die Beurteilung der 'Heiden' bei Paulus* [BBET 14; Frankfurt: Peter Lang, 1981], pp. 64-73) and Davies (*Faith and Obedience in Romans,* pp. 44-46) argue that Paul works against a Jewish background in which the crucial distinction was not between Jews and Gentiles but between the "righteous" and the "unrighteous." But the distinction that Paul explicitly states throughout these chapters is the former.

This section, then, may practically be divided into two main parts: 1:18-32, which targets Gentiles mainly; and 2:1–3:8, which is preoccupied with the Jews. It is obvious that Paul has carefully formulated an argument in each of the first two sections that will meet the needs of the different people addressed. To counter Paul's indictment of them, the Gentiles might well claim to have had no chance to make things right with God; thus Paul insists that all people have some knowledge of God and of his will for them. Moreover, Jews might well claim exemption from judgment by virtue of their covenant privileges; so Paul shows that these privileges, though real, do not help them in the judgment because they have broken that covenant through disobedience.[6]

While, then, 1:18–3:20 brings charges against all humanity, the structure and relative weight of Paul's indictment reveal that the Jew is his main "target."[7] After all, few people would have to be convinced that Gentiles were in need of God's righteousness. Except for "God-fearers," few Gentiles would have ever had any pretense of a relationship to the God of the Bible. But the case was different with the Jews. Were they not God's people? Had not God already

---

6. Our understanding of the theme of 1:18–3:20 is traditional; but several alternative interpretations have been advanced in recent years. J. Bassler, e.g., initiated a trend that singled out divine impartiality as the central theme of Rom. 1–2, and perhaps of 1:16–3:20 as a whole (*Divine Impartiality: Paul and a Theological Axiom* [SBLDS 59; Chico, CA: Scholars Press, 1982], cf. esp. pp. 122-37, 154-65; idem, "Divine Impartiality in Paul's Letter to the Romans," *NovT* 26 [1984], 43-58; anticipating some of her findings was M. Pohlenz, "Paulus und die Stoa," *ZNW* 42 [1949], 73-74). According to Bassler, 2:11, "for there is no partiality with God," is the hinge verse in 1:16–2:29; and the theme of impartiality is sounded repeatedly in the emphasis on both Jew and Gentile in the section. And since this theme continues to be prominent throughout the letter, divine impartiality, its theological basis, is also to be seen as prominent throughout.

Bassler and others who argue a similar view are correct to emphasize that divine impartiality undergirds at least two of the key arguments in the section: the equality of Jew and Greek and the impartial standard of works as the basis for judgment. However, divine impartiality is not the central theme of the section, but a principle used by Paul to place Jews on the same footing as Gentiles and so to establish the broader conclusion that Jews, like Gentiles, are in need of the righteousness of God and can attain it only through faith. Specifically, Bassler's division of the section at 2:11 is based on some verbal similarities that are interesting but insufficient to establish her point. And although the transition from 1:18-32 to 2:1 is a problem for the traditional structure, her own scheme does not take seriously enough the shift in tone signaled by the second person singular (cf. also 2:17). Rom. 1:17 and 3:21 are so clearly parallel that the material between them should be grouped as one large unit. The climax of the argument of that unit, to which all the material is driving, is that "all are under sin" (3:9) and "no one will be justified by works of the law" (3:20). Universal human guilt, not divine impartiality, is the theme of 1:18–3:20.

7. As Aletti notes in his discussion of the structure of 1:18–3:20, the indictment of Gentiles in 1:19-32 is an "assumed point" that is really prefatory to the real argument (cf. *Comment Dieu est-il juste?* pp. 55-72).

promised them his righteousness through the terms of the Old Covenant? Can it be said that Jews stand in the same hopeless condition as do godless Gentiles? So might the questions run, questions that Paul had to confront often in the course of his missionary work. And so Paul must argue that Jews are as much subject to sin's power as are Gentiles and that the old system of the law, in itself, is quite insufficient to provide for release from sin's power (cf. 3:20). As Beker puts it, "What is argued is the equal status of Jew and Gentile under sin; what is presupposed is the self-evident character of the Gentile under sin."[8]

But why this preoccupation with unbelieving Jews in a letter that is written to Christians, and mainly Gentile Christians at that? Although Paul is undoubtedly rehearsing themes from his missionary preaching,[9] it is not unconverted Jews but the Roman Christians who are the real audience of what he says in this letter.[10] To a considerable extent, of course, Paul's focus is due to his desire to set before the Romans, in preparation for his visit and request for support, the gospel he preaches — and the need for God's righteousness on the part of both Jews and Gentiles is an important component of that gospel. Add to this Paul's concern about his upcoming visit to Jerusalem (cf. 15:30-33), and it is no wonder he says as much about the situation of Jews as he does.

But there were factors within the Roman church that made the discussion quite relevant to the Christians there. We must assume that Paul already had his eye on the tensions between the Gentile-Christian majority and the Jewish-Christian minority that he attacks in 14:1–15:13. In this regard, we should not overlook the fact that Paul balances his attack on the Jewish presumption of superiority with affirmations of the Jews' salvation-historical prerogatives (3:1-2), the legitimate demand of the law (3:31), and the OT roots of the gospel (3:21, 31; 4:1-25). Paul is also aware that perverted information about his teaching on these matters was circulating in the community at Rome (cf. 3:8). If the Christians in Rome were to be united in support of Paul's ministry, they would have to be convinced of the logical coherence of Paul's gospel on this central, early Christian issue. Throughout Romans, then, Paul preaches the equality of Jew and Gentile in both sin and righteousness, at the same time as he insists that Israel retains inalienable salvation-historical privileges. In the present section, Paul's overriding concern is to show that, like Gentiles, Jews are locked up under sin and can receive the righteousness available in the gospel only by faith in Jesus.[11]

8. Beker, 80.

9. This point is emphasized by E. Weber, *Die Beziehungen von Röm 1–3 zur Missionspraxis des Paulus* (BFCT 9/2; Gütersloh: Bertelsmann, 1905).

10. Cf. Stowers, *Diatribe,* pp. 179-84.

11. See esp. Beker, 77-80; Sanders, *Paul and Palestinian Judaism,* pp. 489-91; E. Synofzik, *Die Gerichts- und Vergeltungsaussagen bei Paulus: Eine traditionsgeschichtliche Untersuchung* (Göttinger Theologische Arbeiten 8; Göttingen: Vandenhoeck

1. All Persons Are Accountable to God for Sin (1:18-32)

18For the wrath of God is being revealed from heaven against all ungodliness and unrighteousness of human beings, who suppress the truth in unrighteousness, 19for what can be known about God is manifest among them — for God has made it manifest to them. 20For since the creation of the world his invisible attributes — his eternal power and his deity — have been seen, being understood through the things he has made, so that they are without excuse.

21Because, having known God, they did not glorify him as God or give thanks but became foolish in their reasonings, and their hearts, lacking understanding, were darkened. 22Supposing themselves to be wise, they became fools, 23and exchanged the glory of the immortal God for the likeness of the image of mortal man, and birds, and animals, and reptiles. 24Therefore, God handed them over in the passions of their hearts to uncleanness, to the dishonoring of their bodies among themselves. 25They exchanged the truth of God for a lie, worshiping and serving the creature rather than the Creator, who is blessed forever. Amen. 26Because of this, God handed them over to dishonorable passions, for women exchanged the natural use of their bodies for that use which is against nature. 27Likewise, men, leaving natural use of the woman, burned in their desire for one another, men with men doing that which is shameful and receiving in themselves the just penalty that was necessary for their error. 28And even as they did not see fit to retain God in knowledge, God handed them over to a worthless mind, so that they do what is not right, 29being filled with all manner of unrighteousness, evil, greed, wickedness;[12] full of envy, murder, strife, deceit, malice; gossips, 30maligners, haters of God, proud, ar-

---

& Ruprecht, 1977), pp. 887-90; Watson, passim; W. Popkes, "Zum Aufbau und Charakter von Römer 1.18-32," *NTS* 28 (1982), 494. Minear, 46-56, in keeping with his theory of the audience of Romans, thinks all of 1:18–4:25 is directed to the Jewish Christian "weak in faith" group who are judging the Gentile Christians.

12. The order of πονηρία ("evil"), πλεονεξία ("greed"), and κακία ("wickedness") varies in the MS tradition. Some witnesses put κακία first (the secondary Alexandrian uncial C, and the minuscules 33, 81, and 1506); others reverse πλεονεξία and κακία (the primary Alexandrian uncial ℵ and the secondary Alexandrian uncial A). One uncial (K) omits πονηρία. Several MSS add πορνεία ("fornication"), either in place of πονηρία (conjectured for the western uncial D; cf. also the western uncial G) or as a fourth item in the list (the uncial Ψ and the majority text; note, e.g., the KJV translation here). The variation in order of terms is natural, given the difficulties of reproducing such a list. The presence of πορνεία in some MSS is probably due to assimilation to similar lists.

rogant, overbearing, devisers of evil, disobedient to parents, 31*without understanding, without faithfulness, without affection,*[13] *without mercy.*

32*These people, knowing the righteous decree of God, that those who do such things are worthy of death, not only do these things themselves, but commend those who do them.*

This passage divides into three main parts. In the first (vv. 18-20), Paul announces the "revelation" of God's wrath and explains why that wrath is justified: people commit ungodly and unrighteous acts, "suppressing" the truth (v. 18). Paul can accuse people of *suppressing* the truth because God has given people a knowledge of himself (vv. 19-20a); therefore, when they sin, they are "without excuse" (v. 20b). The second section, vv. 21-31, describes in more detail the ways in which people have suppressed the truth of God and draws out some of their consequences. Paul uses three generally parallel "retribution" sequences to make his point:[14]

> Vv. 21-24: People *"exchange"*[15] the truth of God for idols — God *"hands them over"*[16]
> Vv. 25-26a: People *"exchange"* the truth of God for a lie — God *"hands them over"*
> Vv. 26b-31: People *"exchange"* natural sexual practices for the unnatural — God *"hands them over"*

Verse 32 makes up the third section. Though related to vv. 28-31, it stands somewhat independently as a concluding indictment and transition to 2:1ff.

Whose experience does Paul describe in these verses? Traditionally, it has been assumed almost without argument that Paul is depicting the situation of Gentiles. However, the tendency of recent scholarship is to reject, or at least qualify, this conclusion. It is pointed out that the objects of God's wrath are called "people," not "Gentiles"; indeed, the word "Gentiles" *(ethnē)* never occurs in the passage. Moreover, their turn to idolatry is described in language reminiscent of OT descriptions of the Fall, suggesting that all humanity is in view, and of the golden calf incident, suggesting that Jews must be

13. A sizable number of MSS add after ἀστόργους the word ἀσπόνδους ("irreconcilable") (the Byzantine second corrector of the uncial ℵ, the secondary Alexandrian uncial C, uncial Ψ, minuscules 81 and 104, and the majority text [hence see again KJV]), but the addition is almost certainly due to assimilation to 2 Tim. 3:3.

14. See esp. E. Klostermann, "Die adäquate Vergeltung in Röm 1.22-31," *ZNW* 32 (1933), 1-6; J. Jeremias, "Zu Röm 1.22-32," *ZNW* 45 (1954), 119-21.

15. The Greek verb in v. 23 is ἀλλάσσω; the compound μεταλλάσσω is used in vv. 25 and 27.

16. The Greek verb in each place (vv. 24, 26, and 28) is παραδίδωμι.

included in Paul's purview. Finally, the transition from 1:32 to 2:1 would make better sense if the people indicted in 2:1-4 were already included in 1:18-32; but those depicted in 2:1-4 cannot be confined to Gentiles.[17]

Despite the force of some of these points, two considerations, in particular, favor a reference mainly to Gentiles. First, the passage is reminiscent of Jewish apologetic arguments in which Gentile idolatry was derided and the moral sins of the Gentile world were traced to that idolatry.[18] Second, the knowledge of God rejected by those depicted in 1:18-32 comes solely through "natural revelation" — the evidences of God in creation and, perhaps, the conscience. The situation with Jews is, of course, wholly different, for Paul holds them responsible for the special revelation they have been given in the law (cf. 2:12-13, 17-29).

This last point, especially, makes it improbable that Paul is thinking specifically of Jews in 1:19-32. It may not be, however, that Jews are entirely excluded either. The argument of 1:18–2:29 is best viewed as a series of concentric circles, proceeding from the general to the particular. Verse 18, the outermost circle, begins with a universal indictment: *all* people stand condemned under the wrath of God. It is the "heading" of 1:18–3:20 as a whole.[19] Romans 1:19-32, likewise, includes in its scope all people, but it looks at them from the standpoint of their responsibility to God apart from special revelation. This qualification, even though not removing Jews in principle from the focus, means that Paul is not speaking directly about them. He is still speaking *to* them, however, since he uses this section to set up the indictment of the Jews that follows. The focus in 2:1-11 becomes more specific as Paul indicts the "moral person," but implicitly, as we will see, the Jew. Romans 2:17-29 finally targets Jews explicitly, accusing them on the basis of the clearest revelation of God available: the law of Moses.

17. See esp. J. Jervell, *Imago Dei: Gen 1,26f. im Spätjudentum, in der Gnosis und in den paulinischen Briefen* (FRLANT 58; Göttingen: Vandenhoeck & Ruprecht, 1960), pp. 316-19; Bassler, *Divine Impartiality,* p. 122; Zahn; Cranfield. A. Willer thinks 1:18-32 must be directed to humanity generally because the text alludes to the Decalogue (*Der Römerbrief — eine dekalogische Komposition* [Stuttgart: Calwer, 1981], p. 63), but the allusions he finds are not very obvious.

18. See esp. Wis. Sol. 12–15. The author of this first-century-B.C. Jewish tract details the idolatry and sinfulness of the Gentiles and shows that God's judgment of them is entirely just (chaps. 12–14). He then claims exemption from that judgment for the Jewish people on the grounds of God's special relationship with them (chap. 15). The argument of chaps. 12–14 is similar both in general and in many details (for which see S-H, 51-52) to Rom. 1:18-32, while that of chap. 15 may lie behind Paul's polemic in 2:1-11 (see the notes on those verses). Paul may well have Wisdom of Solomon directly in view as he writes Rom. 1–2, although it is also possible that he depends more broadly on a common Jewish tradition that finds expression in Wisdom (as Davies [pp. 27-30] points out, the same basic tradition is found in the rabbis).

19. Cf. Dabelstein, *Beurteilung der 'Heiden,'* pp. 76-77 (who views 1:18 as the heading of 1:19–3:20); Wilckens; Dunn; Schmithals.

Can we isolate more specifically the experience(s) depicted in 1:19-32? The sequence of tenses is relevant to this question. In vv. 18-19a and 32, Paul uses the present tense, suggesting that the revealing of God's wrath, the suppression of the knowledge of God available in creation, and the recognition that certain sins deserve God's judgment are constant aspects of human experience. Throughout vv. 19b-31, however (except in v. 20, which asserts a universal truth), Paul uses a tense (the aorist) normally rendered in English with a past tense: people *turned* from God; he *handed* them over. This may suggest that vv. 19b-31 have in view a specific event: either the original fall of humanity into sin (Gen. 3), or a kind of mythical "Ur-fall" of the Gentiles.[20] This view has certain undeniable strengths but cannot finally be accepted. The tense Paul uses in vv. 19-31 need not indicate a single past experience;[21] and, more important, this view fails to explain the heart of this passage: the characterization of all those upon whom the wrath of God falls as those who possessed the truth of God but turned from it.

Paul says more than that all people experienced the consequences of an original turning away from God, or even that all people shared such an original turning away. He insists that those who turned were also those who knew better, and who are consequently deserving of God's wrath. This, coupled with the obviously universal thrust of vv. 18 and 32, makes clear that this foolish and culpable rejection of the knowledge of God is repeated in every generation, by every individual. *Every person* is "without excuse" because every person — whether a first-century pagan or a twentieth-century materialist — has been given a knowledge of God and has spurned that knowledge in favor of idolatry, in all its varied manifestations. All therefore stand under the awful reality of the wrath of God, and all are in desperate need of the justifying power of the gospel of Christ. We will never come to grips with the importance of the gospel, or be motivated as we should be to proclaim it, until this sad truth has been fully integrated into our worldview.[22]

---

20. See, e.g., Althaus.

21. Scholars have long recognized that the Greek aorist tense does not, in itself, indicate "one-time" action; it can depict action of all kinds, including continuous and repeated action. Some grammarians would go even further and claim that the aorist (even in the indicative mood) has, in itself, no indication of time of action either. See esp. S. E. Porter, *Verbal Aspect in the Greek of the New Testament, with Reference to Tense and Mood* (Studies in Biblical Greek 1; Frankfurt: Peter Lang, 1989). He claims that the aorists in vv. 19-28 are "timeless" (p. 236). Without buying into Porter's whole particular "aspect" scheme, his warnings about too quickly finding particular temporal significance in the aorist tense has some point.

22. For the missionary implications of this section, see A. F. Walls, "The First Chapter of the Epistle to the Romans and the Modern Missionary Movement," in *Apostolic History and the Gospel,* pp. 346-57.

18 In light of the stark contrast between the "revelation of the righteousness of God" (v. 17) and "the revelation of the wrath of God," we would expect v. 18 to begin with a strong adversative — "but" or "however."[23] Instead, v. 18 is linked to the preceding verses with the word "for,"[24] which normally introduces a reason or explanation for a previous statement. It may be that the word here has lost its normal causal meaning and that we should simply ignore it (note that it is untranslated in NIV, TEV, and NJB).[25] Some scholars, however, think that the close biblical connection between righteousness and wrath allows Paul to claim the reality of God's righteousness *because* the wrath of God is present.[26] But Paul is not using the word "righteousness" in v. 17 in a way that would make this connection likely. It is best, then, to retain the usual force of "for," but to view it as introducing the answer to a question implicit in what Paul has just said: Why has God manifested his righteousness and why can it be appropriated only through faith?[27] Viewed in this light, this conjunction introduces the entire argument of 1:18–3:20 — which, indeed, is encapsulated in v. 18.

Since the time of certain Greek philosophers, the idea that God would inflict wrath on people has been rejected as incompatible with an enlightened understanding of the deity.[28] The second-century Christian heretic Marcion omitted "of God" in v. 18,[29] and many others since would like to omit the verse altogether. In our day, C. H. Dodd is representative of those who have rejected or drastically modified the traditional conception of God's wrath. Criticizing the conception of a God who personally exercises wrath as "archaic," he argues that Paul's "wrath of God" is no more than "an inevitable process of cause and effect in a moral universe."[30] But such a conception of God has more in common with the Greek philosophical abstraction of God than the biblical presentation of a personal, active God.

In the Bible wrath is an aspect of God's person, as is clear from the many OT texts that make the "kindling" of God's wrath the basis for his judgment. God's wrath is necessary to the biblical conception of God: "As

---

23. Dodd, in fact, translates "but"; cf. also Fitzmyer.

24. Gk. γάρ.

25. See, e.g., Lietzmann.

26. Barrett; Herold, *Zorn und Gerechtigkeit,* pp. 226, 270-74.

27. See also Dabelstein, *Die Beurteilung der 'Heiden,'* pp. 74-75, who argues that the γάρ relates to the announcement of salvation in v. 16.

28. Cf. H. Kleinknecht, *TDNT* V, 386-87.

29. Cf. Schelkle.

30. Cf. also A. T. Hanson, *The Wrath of the Lamb* (London: SPCK, 1957), pp. 84-85; G. H. C. MacGregor, "The Concept of the Wrath of God in the New Testament," *NTS* 7 (1960-61), 101-9.

long as God is God, He cannot behold with indifference that His creation is destroyed and His holy will trodden underfoot. Therefore He meets sin with His mighty and annihilating reaction."[31] The OT regularly pictures God as responding to sin with wrath;[32] but, particularly in the prophets, the wrath of God is associated with the Day of the Lord as a cosmic, climactic outbreak of judgment. Although Paul works with this same conception of God's wrath, he stresses the working and effects of God's wrath. Paul speaks of wrath as a present reality under which people outside Christ stand,[33] and often, following the OT prophets, predicts the outpouring of God's wrath on the future day of judgment.[34] If the main verb in v. 18 is a "futuristic present," Paul could here also be predicting this climactic outbreak of wrath at the end of history, as in 2:5.[35] But the verb is most likely depicting a present-time situation.[36]

If, then, Paul presents God's wrath as a present reality, how are we to understand that that wrath is now being manifested? And what is the relationship between the two "revelations" — of the righteousness of God in v. 17 and of the wrath of God in v. 18?[37] Taking the last question first, a determinative issue is whether the verb "reveal" means "reveal [a truth] to the mind" or "manifest [an action] in history." One provocative interpretation that takes the verb in the first sense is associated with Karl Barth. He argues that the revelation of both God's righteousness and wrath takes place in the preaching of the gospel. For the gospel proclaims the cross, and Jesus' death on the cross

---

31. Nygren.

32. E.g., when Moses tries to avoid the task God has given him (Exod. 4:14); when Pharaoh and the Egyptians refuse to obey his command to let his people go (Exod. 15:7); when Israel turns to idolatry at Sinai (Exod. 32:10-12). Often God's wrath strikes in the course of historical events: in a fire that destroys rebellious Israelites (Num. 11:1); in the Babylonian conquest of Jerusalem (Jer. 21:3-7).

33. Rom. 3:5; 4:15; 9:22; Eph. 2:3.

34. Rom. 2:5, 8; 5:9; Col. 3:6; 1 Thess. 1:10. Only in the difficult 1 Thess. 2:16 does Paul speak of a present infliction of the wrath of God.

35. This would be in keeping with his usual perspective on God's wrath and finds support from the allegedly "apocalyptic" language of the verse ("reveal"; "from heaven"). Adding to the attractiveness of this interpretation is the way in which 1:18 and 2:5 would then frame the material between with descriptions of the future infliction of God's wrath. See, e.g., Chrysostom(?) and other Fathers; S-H; and, most fully, H.-J. Eckstein, " 'Den Gottes Zorn wird vom Himmel her offenbar werden.' Exegetische Erwägungen zu Röm 1:18," *ZNW* 78 (1987), 74-89.

36. It is difficult to give the same form of the same verb, ἀποκαλύπτεται, a present reference in one verse (17) and a future reference in the next. See esp. Dunn.

37. On this issue, see particularly the penetrating analysis of G. Bornkamm, "The Revelation of God's Wrath (Romans 1-3)," in *Early Christian Experience* (London: SCM, 1969), pp. 47-50, 62-64.

reveals both the possibility for a new righteousness *and* the seriousness of God's wrath against human sin.[38] Although this view does justice to the parallelism between vv. 17 and 18, it suffers from some fatal objections.[39] Barth's interpretation also requires that "reveal" have a cognitive sense: "make known, disclose." But as we have seen, this same verb in v. 17 has a "historical" sense: "come into historical reality" (from the "hiddenness" of God's purpose). It is probable that this is the meaning of the verb in v. 18 also, especially since the object of this "revealing" is not people but the sins of people, or people as sinners: God's wrath is revealed "upon all godlessness and unrighteousness of human beings."[40]

If, then, "reveal" indicates the actual inflicting of God's wrath, when, and how, does it take place? Although God will inflict his wrath on sin finally and irrevocably at the end of time (2:5), there is an anticipatory working of God's wrath in the events of history. Particularly, as vv. 24-28 suggest, the wrath of God is now visible in his "handing over" of human beings to their chosen way of sin and all its consequences. As Schiller's famous aphorism puts it, "The history of the world is the judgment of the world." It is this judgment of the world that the present infliction of God's wrath is intended to reveal. For the present experience of God's wrath is merely a foretaste of what will come on the day of judgment. Furthermore, what both the warning of "wrath to come" and the present experience of wrath demonstrate is the sentence of condemnation under which all people outside Christ stand. It is this reality that Paul wants to get across to this readers here.

What, then, of the parallel between vv. 17 and 18? Some would go so far as to make this exercise of wrath a part of the righteousness of God.[41] But only if righteousness is taken broadly as an attribute of God is this possible, and we have seen good reason to reject this interpretation. On the other hand, the parallel with v. 17 may suggest that this condemning activity is particularly bound up with the eschatological breaking in of the new age

---

38. Barth, *Shorter;* cf. also Gaugler; Cranfield; Wilckens; D. Guthrie, *New Testament Theology* (Downers Grove, IL: InterVarsity, 1981), p. 102.

39. E.g., Paul does not generally include in the gospel the negative concepts of judgment or wrath. If he were to do so here, particularly in light of v. 16, a clear contextual indicator to that effect would be expected — e.g., the phrase ἐν αὐτῷ καί, "in it also."

40. See, e.g., M. Lachmann, *Vom Geheimnis der Schöpfung: Die Geschichte der Exegese von Römer I,18-23, II,14-16 und Acta XIV,15-17, XVII,22-29 vom 2. Jahrhundert bis zum Beginn der Orthodoxie* (Stuttgart: Evangelisches, 1952), pp. 177-80. If Paul had wanted to say that God's wrath over sin is revealed *to believers* (as S. H. Travis [*Christ and the Judgment of God* {Foundations for Faith; Basingstoke: Marshall Pickering, 1986}, p. 36] thinks), we would have expected a dative modifier of ἀποκαλύπτεται indicating this. The presence of the ἐπί phrase by itself strongly implies that it contains the object of the revelation.

41. Black; Wright, "Messiah and People of God," pp. 67-69.

in Christ.[42] Though it is clear that God has inflicted his wrath in the past,[43] the inauguration of "the last days" means that the final, climactic wrath of God is already making itself felt.[44] The wrath of God falls more deservedly than ever before on people now that God's righteousness in Christ is being publicly proclaimed.

Paul's mention of the fact that God's wrath is being revealed "from heaven" adds weight to what Paul is saying: it "significantly implies the majesty of an angry God, and His all-seeing eye, and the wide extent of His wrath: whatever is under heaven, and yet not under the Gospel, is under this wrath."[45] Paul specifies two objects of God's wrath: "ungodliness" and "unrighteousness." Some distinguish the two words, arguing that the former refers to sins of a religious nature and the latter to sins of a moral nature.[46] Paul would then be following a sequence similar to that of the Decalogue, which focuses on a person's duty to God in the first four commandments and on one's duty to others in the second six.[47] Moreover, it is claimed that 1:19-32 picks up this same sequence, as Paul concentrates first on people's rejection of God (vv. 19-27) and then on the disruption of human relations that flows from this rejection.[48] The point would be, as S. L. Johnson puts it, "immorality in life proceeds from apostasy in doctrine."[49] Although this interpretation is attractive and theologically sound, it does not have sufficient basis in the meaning of the words Paul uses.[50]

Paul further characterizes the people who are guilty of "ungodliness"

42. Michel; Kuss; Käsemann; Nygren; G. Stählin, *TDNT* V, 431-32.

43. R. V. G. Tasker, *The Biblical Doctrine of the Wrath of God* (London: Tyndale, 1951), pp. 10-11.

44. Ridderbos, *Paul,* p. 110.

45. Bengel. "From heaven" (ἀπ' οὐρανοῦ) could qualify θεοῦ ("God from heaven") (Stuart; Cranfield) but is more likely to modify ἀποκαλύπτεται ("is being revealed from heaven"; see 2 Thess. 1:7: ἐν τῇ ἀποκαλύψει τοῦ κυρίου ᾿Ιησοῦ ἀπ' οὐρανοῦ, "in the revelation of the Lord Jesus from heaven"). Whether "from heaven" has the further purpose of distinguishing the source of God's wrath from the source of God's righteousness — cf. vv. 16-17, "in the gospel" (e.g., Meyer) — is not clear (cf. Wilckens).

46. E.g., Godet; Griffith Thomas.

47. Schlatter; Michel.

48. E.g., Harrison.

49. S. L. Johnson, "Paul and the Knowledge of God," *BSac* 129 (1972), 66.

50. The words are etymologically distinct, ἀσέβεια denoting "ir-religion" and ἀδικία "in-justice," but there is evidence both in the LXX (see Ps. 73:6; Prov. 11:5; Hos. 10:13; Mic. 7:18; Ezek. 18:30, in all of which the two words occur together) and in Paul that this distinction is not usually maintained. Certainly ἀδικία in Paul cannot be confined to sins against others; it often refers to sin in its widest aspect (see Rom. 2:8; 6:13; 1 Cor. 13:6; 2 Thess. 2:10, 12; 2 Tim. 2:19). If a distinction between the words is to be pressed (and it is not clear that it should be), we are on firmer ground with Cranfield's suggestion that ἀσέβεια characterizes sin as "an attack on the majesty of God," whereas ἀδικία labels it also as "a violation of God's just order" (cf. also Nygren; Wilckens; Fitzmyer).

and "unrighteousness" as those who "suppress the truth of God in unrighteousness."[51] "Truth" in the NT is not simply something to which one must give
mental assent; it is something to be done, to be obeyed. When people act sinfully,
rebelling against God's just rule, they fail to embrace the truth and so suppress
it.[52] In this case, as Meyer says, they "do not let it develop itself into power and
influence on their religious knowledge and moral condition."

19 Verses 19-20 have two purposes. On the one hand, Paul justifies
his assertion that people "suppress" the truth (v. 18b).[53] On the other hand,
he wants to show that people who sin and are correspondingly subject to
God's wrath are responsible for their situation. They are "without excuse"
(v. 20b). He accomplishes both purposes by asserting that people have been
given a knowledge of God: "for[54] what can be known[55] about God is manifest
among[56] them." For Jews, as Paul will acknowledge later (2:18, 20), this

---

51. ἐν ἀδικίᾳ ("in unrighteousness") may be adverbial ("they suppress the truth
unrighteously") (Godet) but is more likely to be instrumental: "through unrighteousnes
[e.g., unrighteous acts] they suppress the truth" (e.g., Murray).

52. The verb κατέχω here probably means "suppress." While the verb can mean
"possess" or "retain" (1 Cor. 7:30; 11:2; 15:2; 2 Cor. 6:10; 1 Thess. 5:21), and Lightfoot, e.g.,
argues for this meaning here, the qualification ἐν ἀδικίᾳ favors the meaning "suppress" or
"hinder" (BAGD; cf. 2 Thess. 2:6, 7; Phlm. 13). Cranfield gives the verb a conative force —
"attempt to suppress" — in order to preserve the concept of the "inherent futility of sin." But
although it might be true that all sin is *ultimately* futile, in that it can never dethrone God or
deflect him from his purposes, the truth does not in fact accomplish what God intends for it
when it is not obeyed and lived by. In that sense, people *do* "hinder" the truth, and this is the
point that Paul is demonstrating in the following verses.

53. Murray; Johnson, "Paul and the Knowledge of God," pp. 67-68.

54. διότι does not have as strong a causal force as it often possesses, being
equivalent here to ὅτι, "for" (BDF 456 [1]).

55. In its 13 other NT occurrences, γνωστός (the lexical form of Paul's neuter abstract
τὸ γνωστόν) means "what *is* known" (Luke 2:44; 23:49; John 18:15, 16; Acts 1:19; 2:14; 4:10,
16; 9:42; 13:38; 15:18; 19:17; 28:22, 28); this is its normal meaning in the LXX and secular
Greek as well. Because Paul explicitly attributes to people actual knowledge of God in this
passage (vv. 20, 28, and 32), a strong case can be made for this translation (Meyer; H. Rosin,
"To gnoston tou theou," *TZ* 17 [1961], 162). But to translate "what is known of God is manifest,
or visible, among them" creates a tautology. Since γνωστός can mean "what can be known"
(Gen. 2:9; Sir. 21:7[?]; cf. also LSJ), and we have no other Pauline usages to go by, the needs
of the context legitimately take precedence here over the general NT usage.

56. Gk. ἐν. The word could refer to a "manifesting" of knowledge of God "in"
each individual, a revelation to the conscience (Calvin; S-H). Or ἐν could connote the
indirect object: "to" (Fitzmyer). But it probably has the meaning it often has with a plural
object, "among": God makes himself known "among" people, through his works of
creation and providence (Michel; Barrett; Cranfield). This is because of the word φανερός
("manifest"), which usually means "making visible," "bringing to light" (Rom. 2:28;
1 Cor. 3:13; 11:19; 14:25; Gal. 5:19; Phil. 1:13; 1 Tim. 4:15; cf. R. Bultmann/D. Lührmann, *TDNT* IX, 2-3) and because of the references to God's creation in v. 20.

knowledge of God comes above all through the law of Moses. Here, however, he is interested in the knowledge of God available to all people through the nature of the world itself. Therefore, what Paul says in the following verses, though not limited to Gentiles (since Jews, too, have knowledge of God through nature), has particular relevance to them.

The last clause of v. 19 explains "is manifest": what can be known of God has been made visible *because* God has "made it known."[57] Only by an act of revelation from above — God "making it known" — can people understand God as he is.

20 The "for"[58] introducing this verse shows that Paul continues the close chain of reasoning about the knowledge of God that he began in v. 19. He has asserted that what can be known of God is visible among people generally and that this is so only because God has acted to disclose himself. Now he explains how it is that God has made this disclosure. Two different connections among the main elements in the verse are possible: (1) "his invisible attributes . . . have been seen through the things he has made, being understood";[59] (2) "his invisible attributes . . . have been seen, being understood through the things he has made."[60] Probably the latter makes better sense because, on the former rendering, the word "being understood" is somewhat redundant.[61] The subject of this complex clause, "his invisible attributes,"[62] is further defined in the appositional addition, "his eternal power and his deity."[63] What is denoted is that God is powerful and that he possesses those properties normally associated with deity. These properties of God that

57. The Greek verb here is φανερόω. Fitzmyer claims that the choice of this verb, in place of ἀποκαλύπτω (used in vv. 17 and 18), signals a move away from divine "revelation." But this is not clear; for Paul often uses φανερόω with fully as much emphasis on divine revelation as ἀποκαλύπτω (see esp. Rom. 3:21; Eph. 5:13, 14; Col. 1:26; 3:4 (twice); 1 Tim. 3:16; 2 Tim. 1:10; Tit. 1:3 (Paul also uses the verb in Rom. 16:26 [v.l.]; 1 Cor. 4:5; 2 Cor. 2:14; 3:3; 4:10, 11; 5:10, 11 [twice]; 7:12; 11:6; Col. 4:4). See *GEL* 28.36 and 38.

58. Gk. γάρ.

59. See NEB. On this reading, τοῖς ποιήμασιν ("the things that have been made") is an instrumental modifier of the main verb, καθορᾶται ("seen"), with the participle νοούμενα ("being understood") modifying the main verb.

60. See NIV. On this interpretation, τοῖς ποιήμασιν goes with νοούμενα, the whole modifying καθορᾶται.

61. E.g., A. Fridrichsen, "Zur Auslegung von Röm 1,19f," *ZNW* 17 (1916), 161.

62. Gk. τὰ ἀόρατα αὐτοῦ, lit. "his invisible things." Paul refers to the attributes of God, who in keeping with OT and Jewish teaching is regarded as invisible to human beings (cf. Col. 1:15; 1 Tim. 1:17; Heb. 11:27). Cf. Str-B 3:31-32.

63. Gk. ἥ τε ἀΐδιος αὐτοῦ δύναμις καὶ θειότης. The language reflects Paul's dependence in this text on Hellenistic Jewish traditions. The key terms are rare in the NT (θειότης only here in the NT; ἀΐδιος only here and in Jude 6).

cannot be "seen" *(aorata)* are "seen" *(kathoratai)* — an example of the literary device called oxymoron, in which a rhetorical effect is achieved by asserting something that is apparently contradictory. God in his essence is hidden from human sight, yet much of him and much about him can be seen through the things he has made. Paul is thinking primarily of the world as the product of God's creation (see, e.g., Ps. 8), though the acts of God in history may also be included.[64]

But just what does Paul mean when he claims that human beings "see" and "understand" from creation and history that a powerful God exists? Some think that Paul is asserting only that people have around them the evidence of God's existence and basic qualities; whether people actually perceive it or become personally conscious of it is not clear. But Paul's wording suggests more than this. He asserts that people actually come to "understand" something about God's existence and nature.[65] How universal is this perception? The flow of Paul's argument makes any limitation impossible. Those who perceive the attributes of God in creation must be the same as those who suppress the truth in unrighteousness and are therefore liable to the wrath of God. Paul makes clear that this includes all people (see 3:9, 19-20).

The last clause of v. 20, "so that they are without excuse," states a key element in our interpretation of vv. 19-20.[66] For Paul here makes clear

---

64. Schlatter; Schlier; Michel. Reference to historical events would be excluded if ἀπὸ (κτίσεως αὐτοῦ) indicates source (e.g., the creation itself is the source of our knowledge of God; cf. Gifford). But Pauline usage would suggest that ἀπό has a temporal meaning: God's invisible attributes have been seen *since* the creation of the world (Fitzmyer).

65. καθοράω, "see," occurs only here in the NT and 4 times in the LXX (Num. 24:2; Job 10:4; 39:26; 3 Macc. 3:11) but is found more frequently in secular Greek. The evidence of the LXX is mixed, but in secular Greek the word more often denotes physical seeing than mental perception. The verb νοέω, on the other hand, connotes an inner recognition, often without any reference to physical sight. None of the other 13 NT occurrences includes physical seeing (see Matt. 15:17; 16:9, 11; 24:15; Mark 7:18; 8:17; 13:14; John 12:40; Eph. 3:4, 20; 1 Tim. 1:7; 2 Tim. 2:7; Heb. 11:3); and note the contrast in John 12:40 between "seeing" (ὁράω) with the eye and "understanding" (νοέω) in the heart.

66. The Greek is εἰς τὸ εἶναι αὐτοὺς ἀναπολογήτους (ἀναπολόγητος occurs only here and in Rom. 2:1 in biblical Greek). It is difficult to decide whether the infinitival construction is consecutive — "with the result that" (cf. Burton, 411) — or final — "with the purpose that." Turner, e.g., argues for the latter (p. 43), claiming that εἰς τό + infinitive in Paul means "hardly anything but purpose" (cf. p. 143). But Turner's claim is overstated. Of 49 occurrences of the construction in Paul, we estimate that 22 are probably final (Rom. 1:11; 3:26; 4:16; 7:4; 8:29; 11:11; 15:8; 1 Cor. 9:18; 10:6; 11:33; 2 Cor. 1:4; 8:6; Eph. 1:12, 18; 1 Thess. 3:2 [twice], 5, 13; 2 Thess. 1:5; 2:6, 11; 3:9), nine are probably consecutive (Rom. 4:18; 6:12; 7:5; 1 Cor. 8:10; 2 Cor. 7:3 [twice]; Gal. 3:17; 1 Thess. 2:16; 2 Thess. 2:10), seven could be either final or consecutive (Rom. 1:20; 4:11 [twice]; 12:2;

Result not purpose

that "natural revelation," in and of itself, leads to a negative result. That Paul teaches the reality of a revelation of God in nature to all people, this text makes clear. But it is equally obvious that this revelation is universally rejected, as people turn from knowledge of God to gods of their own making (cf. vv. 22ff.). Why this is so, Paul will explain elsewhere (cf. Rom. 5:12-21). But it is vital if we are to understand Paul's gospel and his urgency in preaching it to realize that natural revelation leads not to salvation but to the demonstration that God's condemnation is just: people are "without excuse." That verdict stands over the people we meet every day just as much as over the people Paul rubbed shoulders with in the first century, and our urgency in communicating the gospel should be as great as Paul's.

21 This verse provides the missing link in the argument of v. 20. The refusal of people to acknowledge and worship God (v. 21) explains why the revelation of God in nature (v. 20a) leads to their being "without excuse" (v. 20b).[67] Paul accentuates the accountability of people by claiming that their failure to "glorify" and "give thanks to" God took place "even though they knew God."[68] Paul's claim that people through natural revelation "know" God is unexpected. Such language is normally confined to the intimate, personal relationship to God and Christ that is possible only for the believer.[69] In light of the use to which this knowledge is put, this is plainly not the case here. "Knowing God" must therefore be given a strictly limited sense compatible with Paul's argument in this passage. But how limited? Cranfield suggests a greatly weakened sense: "in their awareness of the created world it is of him that all along, though unwittingly, they have been — objectively — aware." But the elimination of any subjective perception from the meaning of the verb has no basis in Paul's usage.[70] People do have some knowledge of God. But this knowledge, Paul also makes clear, is limited, involving the

---

15:13; 2 Cor. 4:4; Phil. 1:10), whereas 11 have other functions (Rom. 12:3; 15:16; 1 Cor. 11:22 [twice]; Phil. 1:23 [twice]; 1 Thess. 2:12; 3:10 [twice]; 4:9; 2 Thess. 2:2). (See the survey in I. T. Beckwith, "The Articular Infinitive with εἰς," *JBL* 15 [1896], 155-67.) Pauline usage therefore favors the final sense but is not conclusive. Perhaps the difference is not overly significant. If God's revelation of himself in nature results in all being without excuse when they turn from that knowledge, it is a small step to suggest that at least one of the purposes of God in providing that revelation was to render all people responsible for their condemnation.

67. As in v. 19, διότι has a weak causal force.

68. γνόντες τὸν θεόν ("knowing God") is concessive. The verb is in the aorist because "knowing God" precedes the refusal to revere God that is stated in the main clause.

69. In Paul, see Gal. 4:9; Phil. 3:8, 10; 2 Cor. 5:16. Note also 1 Cor. 1:21: "in the wisdom of God the world did not know God through that wisdom."

70. D. L. Turner, "Cornelius van Til and Romans 1:18-21. A Study in the Epistemology of Presuppositional Apologetics," *Grace Theological Journal* 2 (1981), 55-58.

narrow range of understanding of God available in nature: they "knew of God" (Phillips: "They knew all the time that there is a God").[71] The outward manifestation of God in his created works was met with a real, though severely limited, knowledge of him among those who observed those works.

This limited knowledge of God falls far short of what is necessary to establish a relationship with him. Knowledge must lead to reverence and gratitude. This it has failed to do. Instead of acknowledging God "as God," by glorifying him and thanking him, human beings perverted their knowledge and sank into idolatry. That idolatry, explicitly discussed in v. 23, might already be in Paul's mind in this verse is suggested by his claim that people "became futile."[72] It is in the "reasonings"[73] of people that this futility has taken place, showing that, whatever their initial knowledge of God might be, their natural capacity to reason accurately about God is quickly and permanently harmed. Parallel to, and descriptive of, this futility in thinking is the darkening of the "un-understanding heart."[74] In the NT, "heart" is broad in its meaning, denoting "the thinking, feeling, willing ego of man, with particular regard to his responsibility to God."[75] We can understand, then, how Paul can describe the heart as being "without understanding" and recognize also how comprehensive is this description of fallen humanity. At the very center of every person, where the knowledge of God, if it is to have any positive effects, must be embraced, there has settled a darkness — a darkness that only the light of the gospel can penetrate.

22 This verse initiates three parallel descriptions of people's rejection of God and the corresponding punitive response of God (vv. 22-24, 25-27, 28-31; see the introduction to the section).[76] The degeneration in

---

71. See esp. Fitzmyer.

72. The verb Paul uses here, ματαιόω, refers to idolatry in three of its seven LXX occurrences (2 Sam. 17:15; Jer. 2:5; 51:17 [= LXX 28:17]), and the cognate τὰ μάταια is used several times to denote idols. Nevertheless, caution is necessary because Paul does not use these and other cognate words with any clear reference to idolatry. The translation reflects the judgment that the aorist tense is ingressive.

73. Gk. διαλογισμοῖς. The word refers to "thoughts," "reasoning" in Matt. 15:19; Mark 7:21; Luke 2:35; 5:22; 6:8; 9:47; Rom. 14:1; Jas. 2:4; to "doubt," "dispute" in Luke 24:38; 9:46; Phil. 2:14; 1 Tim. 2:8. See BAGD. See esp. 1 Cor. 3:20, quoting Ps. 94:11: "The Lord knows the reasonings of the wise, that they are futile."

74. Gk. ἡ ἀσύνετος αὐτῶν καρδία.

75. See the use of לֵב in the OT. Cf. T. Sort, NIDNTT II, 182.

76. Although the correspondences are not as close, Paul may also be hinting at a parallel between the sin of people and the response of God. The failure of people to give God "honor" (δόξα) (v. 23) leads to a "dis-honoring" (ἀτιμάζεσθαι) of their bodies; people's "exchange" of the true God for idols (v. 25) leads to an "exchange" of proper sexual roles for improper ones (v. 26); and the failure of human beings to "approve" (ἐδοκίμασαν) God (v. 28a) leads to an "unapproved" (ἀδόκιμον) mind (v. 28b). See M. D. Hooker, "A Further Note on Romans I," NTS 13 (1966-67), 182.

people's understanding of God, asserted in v. 21, is characterized further in v. 22 by a contrast between illusion and reality. In refusing to pay homage to God when his works are recognized, people claim to be acquiring wisdom.[77] In reality, however, it is the opposite: they are "becoming foolish."[78] From v. 23, it is clear that this foolishness involves not only refusing to worship the true God but also embracing false gods.[79] This contrast, in which what people think is wisdom God considers foolishness, and vice versa, is elaborated in 1 Cor. 1–4. In that this "becoming foolish" involves the various idolatrous religions that people invent for themselves (v. 23), Paul's estimation of non-Christian religions also becomes clear in this verse. Far from being a preparatory stage in the human quest for God, these religions represent a descent from the truth and are "evidence of man's deepest corruption."[80]

23 Continuing the sentence begun in v. 22, this verse graphically portrays the folly of idolatry that lies at the heart of all religions that are not based on a reverent response to the revelation of the one true God. Paul pictures the fall into idolatry as an "exchange" of the glory of God for the images of human beings and beasts. "Glory" signifies the splendor and majesty that belong intrinsically to the one true God.[81] Given the opportunity to bask in the glory of the immortal[82] God, people have rather chosen, in their folly, to worship the images of mortal human beings and beasts. Paul's description of the fall into idolatry is reminiscent of several OT texts, particularly Ps. 106:20, "and they exchanged their glory for the likeness of a bull that eats grass"; cf. also Jer. 2:11, "has a nation exchanged its gods? . . . yet my people have

---

77. The nominative σοφοί after the infinitive is allowed because of the predicative function of εἶναι (BDF 405[2]).

78. Gk. ἐμωράνθησαν, another ingressive aorist.

79. Murray suggests an instrumental relationship between the participle φάσκοντες ("claiming") and the main verb ἐμωράνθησαν: "*by* pretending to be wise they made themselves fools." Note *Ep. Arist.* 137: "Those who have invented these fabrications and myths are usually ranked to be the wisest of the Greeks" (137).

80. Nygren.

81. The Greek is δόξα. In secular Greek, the word means "opinion," "judgment," "estimation" (cf. LSJ). But the LXX translators used it for the Heb. כָּבוֹד, and it is through this correspondence that its typical NT sense develops. From its basic meaning "be weighty," כָּבוֹד came to denote the "honor" or "importance" or "prestige" of people (e.g., Ps. 49:16; Isa. 16:14; cf. Matt. 4:8) and, when applied to God, his "weighty" and magnificent presence — as revealed in nature (Ps. 97:1-6), the tabernacle (Exod. 40:34), and the climax of history, to all peoples (Isa. 40:5; 66:18) (see G. von Rad, *TDNT* II, 238-42). John claims that this eschatological manifestation of God's glory has taken place in the person of the Word-become-flesh (John 1:14).

82. Paul only once elsewhere calls God "immortal" (ἀφθάρτος; cf. 1 Tim. 1:17); he does so here in order to accentuate the contrast with "mortal" (φθαρτός) human beings.

exchanged its glory."[83] Paul wishes his readers to see how foolish it is to substitute for direct contact with God's awesome presence the indirect, shadowy relationship found in idolatry.

Paul's description of the fall into idolatry in this verse draws from a variety of sources and traditions. There are allusions to the creation story in the threefold division of the animal kingdom. Ps. 106:20, which, as we have seen, Paul uses, comments on the "fall" of Israel into idolatry when she constructed the golden calf (Exod. 32). But Paul is not describing either the fall of Israel[84] or the fall of humankind in Adam.[85] Rather, in a somewhat

---

83. The LXX of Ps. 106:20 reads καὶ ἠλλάξαντο τὴν δόξαν αὐτῶν ἐν ὁμοιώματι μόσχου ἔσθοντος χόρτου; and Jer. 2:11, εἰ ἀλλάξανται ἔθνη θεοὺς αὐτοῦ; . . . ὁ δὲ λαὸς μου ἠλλάξαντο τὴν δόξαν αὐτοῦ. Like the LXX translator, Paul uses ἐν after ἀλλάσσω as equivalent to the Hebrew בְּ. Unlike the Psalm verse, however, Paul adds the genitive εἰκόνος ("image") to ὁμοιώματι ("likeness"). Why he does so is not clear, since the words are similar in meaning. Both are used frequently in the LXX to refer to idolary: εἰκών in most of its occurrences and ὁμοίωμα a little less than half the time (see Deut. 4:15-16, where they are used interchangeably). This significant semantic overlap means that εἰκόνος could be epexegetic (Z-G, 460; Zahn), it being added, perhaps, to stress the insubstantial and inferior nature of idolatry (Barrett; Käsemann; Dunn). Others suggest that ὁμοίωμα may mean "likeness," "copy" (a meaning the word has frequently in the LXX; see the comments on 5:14) and εἰκών the actual "form" or "prototype" that is copied (G. Kittel, *TDNT* II, 395; Cranfield; cf. Jervell, *Imago Dei,* pp. 320-21). But perhaps the former is preferable since Paul may be influenced by Wis. 13-14, where εἰκών is used to denote idols four times.

84. Contra, e.g., Zahn.

85. Those who think that Paul is describing the fall of the original human couple into sin in these verses note: (1) the threefold description of the "animal kingdom" (πετεινά, τετράποδα, ἑρπετά) is similar to LXX Gen. 1:20, 24; (2) the words εἰκών and ὁμοίωμα remind one of Gen. 1:26 (the creation of humankind in the "form" [LXX εἰκών] and "image" [ὁμοίωσις] of God (cf. N. Hyldahl, "A Reminiscence of the Old Testament at Romans i 23," *NTS* 2 [1955-56], 285-88); (3) the aorist tenses are naturally indicative of a past series of events. Thus, it is argued, Paul "is describing man's sin in relation to its true biblical setting — the Genesis narrative of the Creation and the Fall" (M. D. Hooker, "Adam in Romans I," *NTS* [1959-60], 300; cf. also Jervell, *Imago Dei,* pp. 316-29; D. J. W. Milne, "Genesis 3 in the Letter to the Romans," *Reformed Theological Review* 39 [1980], 10-12). On this view, Paul would be tracing the sinfulness of the world of his day to the corporate fall of humanity in the Garden and God's consequent punishment ("handing them over"). However, while theologically attractive, this interpretation does not survive close scrutiny. In Gen. 1–3, "idolatry" (the desire to "be like God") precedes the Fall; in Rom. 1, a "fall" (the refusal to honor God, v. 21) precedes idolatry. Then also, as we have seen, Rom. 1 focuses on human neglect of "natural revelation," whereas Rom. 5:13-14 shows that Paul linked Adam with Israel in being responsible for "special revelation." Moreover, it is significant that, although allusions to Gen. 1 are found in Rom. 1:18-32, there are no clear allusions to Gen. 3 — except, perhaps, with "death" in v. 32 (Dunn; cf. A. J. M. Wedderburn, "Adam in Paul's Letter to the Romans," in *Studia Biblica 1978, III: Papers on Paul and Other New Testament Authors* [ed. E. A. Livingstone; JSNTSup 3; Sheffield: JSOT, 1980], pp. 413, 419). Even εἰκὼν φθαρτοῦ ἀνθρώπου may depend on the

idealized, paradigmatic fashion, he describes the terrible proclivity of all people to corrupt the knowledge of God they possess by making gods of their own. This tragic process of human "god-making" continues apace in our own day, and Paul's words have as much relevance for people who have made money or sex or fame their gods as for those who carved idols out of wood and stone. Thus, as vv. 24-31 show, the whole dreadful panoply of sins that plague humanity has its roots in the soil of this idolatry.[86]

24 The "therefore"[87] at the beginning of this verse shows that God's "handing over" of human beings is his response to their culpable rejection of the knowledge of himself that he has made generally available (vv. 21-23). Paul's use of the verb "hand over" to describe this retribution has its roots in the OT, where it is regularly used in the stereotyped formula according to which God "hands over" Israel's enemies so that they may be defeated in battle.[88] And, in an ironic role reversal, the same formula is used when God hands his own people over to another nation as punishment for their sins.[89] Somewhat similarly, Paul here alleges that God has "handed over" people to "uncleanness."[90] What does Paul mean by this? Clearly he cannot be saying that God impelled people to sin. Not only would this contradict the biblical depiction of God (cf. Jas. 1:13), but the phrase that qualifies this "handing over to uncleanness," "in the passions of their hearts," shows that those who were handed over were already immersed in sin. Paul's purpose in this verse is to highlight the divine side of the cycle of sin; but it must be balanced with

---

description of idolatry in Jewish polemic (cf. Wis. 13:13d: ἀπείκασεν αὐτὸ εἰκόνι ἀνθρώπου) rather than on Gen. 1:26. That Paul may view the "fall" of individual human beings as analogous *in some ways* to the Fall of the first human pair is likely, but the text does not warrant the conclusion that he is specifically describing the latter. Cf. the similar conclusion of R. Scroggs, *The Last Adam: A Study in Pauline Anthropology* (Philadelphia: Fortress, 1966), pp. 75-79; Fitzmyer.

86. See esp. Achtemeier.

87. Gk. διό.

88. The Greek verb is παραδίδωμι. For examples of this formula, see, e.g., Exod. 23:31; Deut. 7:23. In the NT, παραδίδωμι is very common (119 occurrences) and is used (1) of the "handing over" or "entrusting" various things to people (e.g., 1 Cor. 13:3, "if I hand over my body to be burned"); (2) of the "handing over" of people into judicial custody (e.g., Judas "hands over" Jesus to the Jewish authorities; Matt. 26:15; John 19:11, etc.); (3) of the "handing over" or "committing" of Christian tradition (e.g., 1 Cor. 15:3). See BAGD.

89. E.g., Lev. 26:25; Josh. 7:7; Judg. 2:14; 6:1, 13, etc.; and note Job 2:6. Acts 7:42, where Stephen says that, because of Israel's idolatry, God "turned and gave them over [παρέδωκεν] to worship the host of heaven," picks up this use of the verb and provides the closest parallel to Paul's language.

90. Gk. ἀκαθαρσίαν. The only literal use in the NT is Matt. 23:27; the others, which are all in Paul, refer generally to immorality, and esp. sexual immorality (see Murray; Rom. 6:19; 2 Cor. 12:21; Gal. 5:19; Eph. 4:19; 5:3; Col. 3:5; 1 Thess. 2:3; 4:7).

the human side, presented in Eph. 4:19, where Paul says that Gentiles "gave themselves up"[91] to licentiousness, leading to all kinds of "uncleanness."[92] Dodd, in keeping with his interpretation of God's wrath, thinks the "handing over" is no more than the outworking of the natural processes of history. But so impersonal a procedure does justice neither to the biblical teaching about God's sovereign activity in history nor to Paul's active language. Chrysostom interprets this handing over in a passive sense: by withdrawing his influence over these disobedient idolaters, God permits them to continue in, and indeed to plunge more deeply into, the sin they had already chosen. As Godet puts it: "He [God] ceased to hold the boat as it was dragged by the current of the river."[93]

No doubt such a withdrawal of divine influence would produce this result. But the meaning of "hand over" demands that we give God a more active role as the initiator of the process.[94] God does not simply let the boat go — he gives it a push downstream. Like a judge who hands over a prisoner to the punishment his crime has earned, God hands over the sinner to the terrible cycle of ever-increasing sin.[95] Is this punishment reformatory in purpose? Chrysostom thought so; the depths of sin in which the idolater is plunged are designed to awaken the sinner to the awful seriousness of his or her situation.[96] In that God's handing over of his people in the OT was not the final word, and in light of the possible parallel to this action in the temporary confining of Israel under sin through the law (Gal. 3:21-25), this might be the case. But it must be added that both biblical and secular history afford us many examples in which such punishment has not led to spiritual reformation.

The sexual nuance present in the term "uncleanness" is elaborated in the last clause of the verse: "to the dishonoring of their bodies among themselves." The significance of this clause is not clear. Does it indicate the purpose for which God handed people over?[97] Its result?[98] Or does it simply give a

91. Gk. παρέδωκεν.
92. Gk. ἀκαθαρσία.
93. See also, e.g., Wesley; Haldane; Cranfield.
94. Calvin; Gifford; Meyer; S-H; Murray; S. L. Johnson, "'God Gave Them Up'": A Study in Divine Retribution," *BSac* 129 (1972), 131-32. Tholuck takes a mediating position: the "handing over" consists in God's not suspending the law of his moral government that he had already established.
95. Note Wis. 11:15-16: "In return for their [the Gentiles'] foolish and wicked thoughts, which led them astray to worship irrational serpents and worthless animals, you sent upon them a multitude of irrational creatures to punish them, that they might learn that one is punished by the very things by which he sins."
96. See also Cranfield.
97. E.g., Godet.
98. BDF 400(2); Cranfield.

fuller definition of the word "uncleanness"?[99] Certainty is impossible, but the last is probably the best option.[100]

25 The first clause of this verse might continue the sentence begun in v. 24 and have a causal meaning: "God handed them over [v. 24] . . . *because* they exchanged the truth of God for a lie."[101] But since v. 23 has already expressed the reason for this handing over, it is preferable to see v. 25 as initiating a new sentence.[102] Rather than looking backward, then, v. 25 looks ahead, providing, as does v. 23 in relation to v. 24, the basis for God's judicial "handing over" of sinners to the consequences of their choices. Moreover, the bases are very similar. If in v. 23 Paul accuses people of exchanging "the glory of the immortal God for the likeness of the image of mortal man, and birds, and animals, and reptiles," so here he claims that they have "exchanged[103] the truth of God for a lie." "The truth of God" is not "the truth God has made known and belongs to him,"[104] but the reality, the fact of God as he has revealed himself.[105] The Thessalonian Christians, Paul

99. E.g., Barrett; Murray.

100. The Greek construction is the genitive article τοῦ, followed by an infinitive (ἀτιμάζεσθαι). Paul's use of this construction does not point decisively to any one conclusion. Although it is often categorized as a purpose construction, Paul, at least, uses it only rarely with such meaning. Not including Rom. 1:24, Paul uses τοῦ with the infinitive 16 times. Many are debated, but we would classify only one as clearly final (1 Cor. 10:13); three are probably consecutive (Rom. 7:3; 11:10; Gal. 3:10), two could be either (Rom. 6:6; 1 Cor. 10:13), whereas ten have other functions, often epexegetic (Rom. 8:12; 11:8 [twice]; 15:22, 23; 1 Cor. 9:10; 16:4; 2 Cor. 8:11; Phil. 3:10, 21). See BDF 400 for a slightly different classification. With this view of the infinitive, it is most natural to take ἀτιμάζεσθαι as middle rather than passive (Godet; contra BAGD) and to translate ἐν αὐτοῖς "among them" (S-H; contra Käsemann, who suggests an instrumental meaning). The RSV captures well the resultant meaning: "God gave them up . . . to impurity, to the dishonoring of their bodies among themselves."

101. See RSV; JB; NEB; Michel; Murray. Verse 25 is not explicitly linked (e.g., by a conjunction or particle) to v. 24 (asyndeton). Paul generally uses the indefinite relative pronoun οἵτινες ("who") to introduce a subordinate clause.

102. See, e.g., NIV; Cranfield. Paul uses οἵτινες to connect a virtually independent clause or sentence with a previous discussion elsewhere (cf. Rom. 1:32; 2:15; Gal. 4:24; Phil. 3:7). As is typical in NT Greek, the pronoun lacks indefiniteness (Moule, *Idiom Book*, pp. 123-24) but may convey a qualitative nuance: "Such people."

103. Paul uses the compound verbal form μετάλλασσω here with no change of meaning from the simple verb ἀλλάσσω in v. 23.

104. Murray.

105. Cf. *As. Mos.* 5:3b-4: "they [the Jews] will pollute the house of their worship with the customs of the nations; and they will play the harlot after foreign gods. For they will not follow the truth of God . . ."; note also Philo's description of Moses' reaction to the idolatry of the Israelites: "[he] marvelled at the sudden apostasy of the multitude and [how] they had exchanged [ὑπηλλάξαντο] so great a lie [ψεῦδος] for so great a truth [ἀληθείας]" (*Life of Moses* 2.167); and cf. Käsemann; Cranfield.

writes, have reversed this exchange; they "turned to God from idols, to serve a living and true God" (1 Thess. 1:9).

In the second clause of v. 25, Paul concisely defines the "lie" of idolatry: "worshiping and serving the creature rather than[106] the Creator." The two verbs are mutually interpreting and together sum up all that is involved in the veneration of idols.[107] It is this putting some aspect of God's creation — whether it be an animal, a human, or a material object — in place of God that is the essence of idolatry. Perhaps it is to underline the folly of this exchange that Paul adds a blessing formula, "who is blessed forever. Amen."[108]

26 In many Jewish polemical works, the gross sexual immorality that the Jews found rampant among the Gentiles was traced directly to idolatry. Thus, to cite Wisdom of Solomon: "the idea of making idols was the beginning of fornication, and the invention of them was the corruption of life" (14:12). Paul follows this genre by making the same connection but differs from it by attributing the connection to the act of God. As in vv. 23-24, people's "exchange" of the true God for idols (v. 25) is the cause[109] of God's retributive "handing them over."[110] And that to which they are handed over, "dishonorable passions,"[111] here corresponds to the "uncleanness" of v. 24. Paul's use of the word "passions,"[112] combined with what he says in vv. 26b-27, makes clear that he refers to illicit sexual

---

106. Gk. παρά. Because this preposition followed by the accusative normally has a comparative meaning, Paul might be accusing the Gentile idolaters of worshiping the creatures represented by their idols "more than" the Creator (cf. KJV). But παρά, by a natural extension of its comparative force, sometimes means "instead of"; cf. BAGD, who cite Luke 18:14; Rom. 1:25; Rom. 12:3; 1 Cor. 3:11; 2 Cor. 8:3; Heb. 1:9; 11:11; and *Ep. Arist.* 139, where the author says that the Jews worship τὸν μόνον θεὸν παρ' ὅλην τὴν κτίσιν ("the only God instead of the whole creation"). This meaning fits better Paul's emphasis on the "exchange" that idolaters have made (hence the translation found in most modern English versions).

107. The second verb, λατρεύω ("serve"), is used by Paul elsewhere to denote true worship (Rom. 1:9; Phil. 3:3; 2 Tim. 1:3; in the LXX, the verb is applied to the worship of both Yahweh and idols). The first verb, ἐσεβάσθησαν (the first aorist passive form has an active meaning [BAGD]), is from σεβάζομαι ("worship"), a rare word (the form σέβομαι is more common in the NT period). Perhaps Paul uses it to add a "pagan" connotation to the first verb.

108. Paul uses such a blessing only two other times (Rom. 9:5; 2 Cor. 11:31), but it is common in the rabbinic literature (usually taking the form הַקָּדוֹשׁ בָּרוּךְ הוּא, "the Holy One, blessed be he" [Str-B, 3.64]).

109. διὰ τοῦτο, "because of this."

110. The verb is again παραδίδωμι; see the notes on v. 24.

111. Taking the genitive ἀτιμίας as qualitative.

112. Gk. πάθη, plural of πάθος. Paul uses this word elsewhere only in Col. 3:5 and 1 Thess. 4:5; both have a sexual nuance. See also BAGD.

passions. For the last clause of the verse illustrates these "dishonorable passions."[113] In yet another similarity to Jewish criticisms of the Gentile world, the sexual sin that Paul singles out is homosexuality: "women[114] exchanged the natural use of their bodies for that use which is against nature." The verb "exchange," which has been used twice to depict the fall into idolatry (vv. 23, 25), is now used to characterize this tragic reversal in sexual practice. The "natural use" has been replaced with one that is "against nature."[115]

The extent to which Paul characterizes this exchange as a violation of God's created order depends on the significance of the words "natural" and "nature" in this verse. Paul generally uses the word "nature" to describe the way things are by reason of their intrinsic state or birth, and in these cases there is no clear reference to divine intention.[116] Some scholars in recent years especially, noting this, have argued that Paul does not here brand homosexuality as a violation of God's will. He is only, they argue, following his own cultural prejudices by characterizing homosexual relations as being against what is "usually" the case.[117] But Paul's use of the word "nature" in this verse probably owes much to Jewish authors,

---

113. The τε introducing this clause is correlative with the τε in v. 27 ("both . . . and"). The connecting particle γάρ ("for") is not causal — as if Paul were giving a reason for God's handing them over — but explanatory — the clause that follows explains the πάθη ἀτιμίας.

114. Gk. αἱ θήλειαι αὐτῶν, lit. "their female ones." Paul's use of the antonyms θῆλυς/ἄρσην (v. 27) rather than, e.g., γύνη/ἀνήρ, stresses the element of sexual distinctiveness and throws into relief the perversity of homosexuality by implicitly juxtaposing its confusion of the sexes with the divine "male and female he created them." For the pair θῆλυς/ἄρσην is consistently associated with the creation narrative (cf. Gen. 1:27; Matt. 19:4; Mark 10:6; although the only other occurrence of the pair in Paul [Gal. 3:28] does not clearly allude to creation).

115. The contrasting Greek phrases are τὴν φυσικὴν χρῆσιν and τὴν παρὰ φύσιν. On this use of χρῆσις to denote sexual relationships, see BAGD.

116. See Rom. 2:14; 11:21, 24 (3 times); Gal. 2:15; 4:8; Eph. 2:3; 1 Cor. 11:14 (debated).

117. To cite a representative work, R. Scroggs, in *The New Testament and Homosexuality: Contextual Background for Contemporary Debate* (Philadelphia: Fortress, 1983), holds that Paul's criticism of homosexuality cannot be taken too seriously. He sketches the attitude of the Greeks to homosexuality, which was generally positive. Pederasty, in particular, was widely practiced, accepted, and even honored in some circles. On the other hand, homosexual prostitution was generally condemned (pp. 17-65). In light of this background, Scroggs suggests that, while Paul opposes homosexuality in Rom. 1, Paul gives no real rationale, implying that he is simply following his Hellenistic Jewish model and that Paul himself is not "particularly upset" by the practice of homosexuality (pp. 109-18). Scroggs also thinks that Paul condemns only homosexual prostitution in 1 Cor. 6:9 (pp. 101-9).

particularly Philo, who included sexual morality as part of "natural law" and therefore as a divine mandate applicable to all people.[118] Violations of this law, as in the case of Sodom, are therefore considered transgressions of God's will.[119] In keeping with the biblical and Jewish worldview, the heterosexual desires observed normally in nature are traced to God's creative intent. Sexual sins that are "against nature" are also, then, against God, and it is this close association that makes it probable that Paul's appeal to "nature" in this verse includes appeal to God's created order.[120] Confirmation can be found in the context. In labeling the turning from "the natural use" to "that [use] which is against nature" an "exchange," Paul associates homosexuality with the perversion of true knowledge of God already depicted in vv. 23 and 25. In addition, we must remember that the clause in question is a description of "sinful passions," a phrase plainly connoting activities that are contrary to God's will. When these factors are considered, it is clear that Paul depicts homosexual activity as a violation of God's created order, another indication of the departure from true knowledge and worship of God.[121]

27 This verse is connected to the last part of v. 26 with "likewise," as Paul shows that the same "sinful passions" that lead women to engage in unnatural homosexual acts are also operative among men, with similar ef-

---

118. See, e.g., Fitzmyer. Paul's dependence on Jewish patterns of teaching throughout Rom. 1:18-32 renders it certain that he is influenced more by the OT-Jewish tradition than by the secular Greek view of homosexuality. Both the OT and Judaism condemned homosexual practice as a violation of God's order and will (cf. the story of Sodom and Gomorrah [Gen. 19:1-28]; Lev. 18:22; 20:13; Deut. 23:17-18; Wis. 14:26; *T. Levi* 17:11; *Sib. Or.* 3.596-600; and Str-B, 3.68-74 on the rabbis). Scroggs's contention that Paul's use of Hellenistic Jewish language and teaching in Rom. 1 distances him from his condemnation of homosexuality must be rejected. Paul does not uncritically take over everything that happens to appear in the traditions he uses; he always uses them selectively. Paul's possible dependence on these teachings in Rom. 1 demonstrates nothing more than that he fully agreed with them, and he needed to add little rationale of his own because he could assume his audience would regard the point as self-evident. Scroggs's interpretation, and others like it, are vain attempts to avoid the obvious: Paul criticized homosexual activity as a particularly clear example of the extent to which people have fallen from a true knowledge of God.

119. See *T. Naph.* 3:4-5. Philo's denunciation of homosexuality includes some of the same key terms that Paul uses here: φύσις, χρῆσις, and πάθος (*Change of Names* 111-12; *Special Laws* 4.79, *Decalogue* 142, 150). Both Philo (*Special Laws* 3.39) and Josephus (*Ag. Ap.* 2.273) use παρὰ φύσιν to describe homosexuality. Cf. H. Köster, *TDNT* IX, 267-71.

120. Contra, e.g., Scroggs, *The New Testament and Homosexuality,* pp. 114-15.

121. Cranfield; Wilckens; J. B. Souček, "Zur Exegese von Röm. 2,14ff," in *Antwort: Karl Barth zum siebzigsten Geburtstag am 10. Mai 1956* (Zollikon/Zürich: Evangelischer Verlag, 1956), pp. 108-9.

fect.[122] Homosexuality among "males,"[123] like that among "females," is characterized as a departure from nature.[124] As in the previous verse, "nature" denotes the natural order, but as reflective of God's purposes. Paul uses strong language to characterize male homosexuality: "they burned[125] in their desire[126] for one another, men with men[127] doing[128] that which is shameful[129] and receiving in themselves the just penalty[130] that was necessary for their error." In calling the homosexual activity that brings about this penalty an "error," Paul does not diminish the seriousness of the offense, for this word often denotes sins of unbelievers in the NT.[131] In claiming that this penalty for homosexual practice is received "in themselves," Paul may suggest that the sexual perversion itself is the punishment.[132] On the other hand, this could be a vivid way of saying that those who engage in such activities will suffer eternal punishment; they will receive "in their own persons" God's penalty for violation of his will.[133] This punishment, Paul says, was "necessary," by

---

122. We cannot know why Paul has mentioned women first. It is unlikely that the sequence in Gen. 3 has had anything to do with it (contra Michel).

123. Gk. ἄρσενες. In addition to possible allusion to the creation narrative (see n. 114), Paul may have chosen to use the word "male" in this verse because the same word occurs in the LXX in condemnations of homosexuality (Lev. 18:22; 20:13).

124. Gk. τὴν φυσικὴν χρῆσιν τῆς θηλείας, "natural relations with women" (NIV).

125. Gk. ἐξεκαύθησαν, from ἐκκαίω, a verb used only here in the NT but which occurs outside the NT in a metaphorical sense with reference to the "kindling" of sin (cf. Sir. 16:6, and Paul's use of πυρόω in 1 Cor. 7:9).

126. Gk. ὀρέξει, another word that occurs only here in the Greek NT.

127. The phrase ἄρσενες ἐν ἄρσεσιν is better taken with the participial clause that follows (cf. NA[26]) than with the main clause that precedes (WH).

128. The verb here is κατεργάζομαι, which sometimes stresses the end result ("produce") more than the simple ἐργάζομαι. Here, however, no such difference can be maintained. (These verbs are discussed in more detail in our comments on 7:15.)

129. The Gk. τὴν ἀσχημοσύνην has an abstract sense. Used only one other time in the NT (Rev. 16:15), this word, in the way Paul uses it, finds its closest parallels in intertestamental Judaism (cf. Sir. 26:8; 30:13).

130. The Gk. ἀντιμισθία (lit. "a payment in place of") can be used in a positive sense ("reward"), a neutral sense (cf. 2 Cor. 6:13), or a negative sense — "penalty," as here.

131. Eph. 4:14; 1 Thess. 2:3; 2 Thess. 2:11; 2 Pet. 2:18; 3:17; 1 John 4:6; Jude 11; cf. also Matt. 27:64 and Jas. 5:20.

132. E.g., Chrysostom; Dunn.

133. In 1 Cor. 6:9-10, Paul warns that those who practice homosexuality (*not* just homosexual prostitution) "will not inherit the kingdom of God." Some Christians think that AIDS may be a manifestation of this just recompense of the Lord. But (1) AIDS strikes many more than homosexual offenders; (2) AIDS does not afflict all homosexual offenders; and Paul must be referring to a general penalty that is imposed on those who engage in homosexual relationships. The most we could say is that AIDS may be an additional manifestation of the wrath of God against rebellious and sinful humanity.

which he probably means that God could not allow his created order to be so violated without there being a just punishment.[134]

28 In vv. 22-24 and 25-27 Paul has shown how the sexual immorality that pervades humanity has its roots in the rejection of the true God in favor of gods of their own making. In the third and final portrayal of this sin-retribution sequence (vv. 28-32), he traces sins of inhumanity, of man's hatred of his fellow man in all its terrible manifestations, to this same root sin of idolatry.

In keeping with the relation between human sin and divine retribution in the previous two sections, the first clause in this verse might have a causal force: "*because* they did not see fit to retain God in knowledge, God handed them over" (see NIV; NRSV).[135] But the lack of clear evidence for a causal meaning of the word Paul uses here[136] leads us to prefer the normal correlative sense of the word: "Even as people did not retain knowledge of God, God handed them over to a worthless mind."[137] This correlative relationship underlines the close correspondence in this verse between sin and retribution, a relationship Paul enhances with a wordplay in Greek between "see fit" and "worthless."[138] "To have God in knowledge" means to acknowledge God, to retain and respond to the knowledge of himself that God has given in his creation. The Greek word for "knowledge" that Paul uses here sometimes connotes "practical" or "applied" (as opposed to theoretical) knowledge.[139] Perhaps, then, we could distinguish the "theoretical" knowledge of God that Gentiles were given (vv. 19, 21) from the practical, experiential knowledge of God that would have been involved in glorifying and thanking God.[140]

---

134. Cf. Godet.

135. BAGD; BDF 453(2); Käsemann.

136. καθώς. BAGD cite John 17:2; Rom. 1:28; 1 Cor. 1:6; 5:7; Eph. 1:4; 4:32; Phil. 1:7. But in none is a causal meaning obvious.

137. Cf. Wilckens.

138. The Greek words are, respectively, ἐδοκίμασαν and ἀδόκιμον. The verb δοκιμάζω usually means "approve, test," but takes on the meaning "see fit" when followed by an infinitive (BAGD; they cite as a parallel the construction ἐν ὀργῇ ἔχειν τινα, "to be angry with someone" [cf. Thucydides, 2.18.5, etc.])

139. Paul uses the compound form ἐπιγνώσις rather than the simple γνῶσις. Some scholars think that Paul generally distinguishes between γνῶσις/γινώσκω and ἐπιγινώσκω/ἐπιγνώσις, the latter denoting a "deeper," more advanced knowledge than the former (see, e.g., Trench, *Synonyms,* pp. 285-86; on this verse specifically, K. Sullivan, "Epignosis in the Epistles of St. Paul," *SPCIC* 2.405-16; H. Clavier, "Recherche exégétique et théologique sur la notion paulinienne d'Epignosis," *SE* 6 [ed. E. A. Livingstone; Berlin: Akademie, 1973], pp. 37-52); Kuss. But any such distinction simply does not hold in Paul. As J. A. Robinson has shown, the ἐπι- prefix indicates not intensity, but direction; and Paul thus uses ἐπιγνώσις customarily with an object of the "knowing" (*St. Paul's Epistle to the Ephesians* [2d ed.; London: James Clarke, n.d.], pp. 248-54). Here, of course, the object of the "knowing" is God.

140. See Cranfield.

117

For the third time Paul describes God's response to people's spurning of him with the words "God handed them over" (cf. also vv. 24, 26). Whereas in the previous instances it was to immoral acts that God consigned people, in this case it is to a "worthless mind."[141] People who have refused to acknowledge God end up with minds that are "disqualified" from being able to understand and acknowledge the will of God. The result, of course, is that they do things that are "not proper."[142] As in 1:21, Paul stresses that people who have turned from God are fundamentally unable to think and decide correctly about God and his will. This tragic incapacity is the explanation for the apparently inexplicable failure of people to comprehend, let alone practice, biblical ethical principles. Only the work of the Spirit in "renewing the mind [*nous*]" (Rom. 12:2) can overcome this deep-seated blindness and perversity.

29-31 Paul includes a long list of immoral activities in "things that are not proper" in vv. 29-31. Such a listing of sins is called a "vice list," a literary form widespread in secular moral writings as well as in the NT.[143] As is typical of such lists, this one exhibits no rigid logical arrangement, since rhetorical concerns play a role in the ordering of the list. Nor is it possible to give each term in the list a meaning distinct from every other term — some are virtually synonymous, and a considerable degree of overlap in meaning occurs. Nevertheless, we can note some structural as well as logical order. Structurally, the list falls into three parts:

> "filled with[144] all manner[145] of unrighteousness, evil, greed, wickedness;

---

141. The Greek for "mind" is νοῦς. This word refers to more than intellectual capacity; it is the organ of moral reasoning and willing (cf. Rom. 7:23, 25; 11:34; 12:2; 14:5; 1 Cor. 1:10; 2:16; 14:14, 15, 19; Eph. 4:17, 23; Phil. 4:7; Col. 2:18; 2 Thess. 2:2; 1 Tim. 6:5; 2 Tim. 3:8; Tit. 1:15). The word occurs outside of Paul in the NT only in Luke 24:45 and Rev. 13:18; 17:9. See J. Behm, *TDNT* IV, 958-59.

142. Gk. τὰ καθήκοντα. τὸ καθῆκον was a "technical term with the Stoics" (S-H), the plural of which Paul uses (as in 2 Macc. 6:4 and 3 Macc. 4:16) to denote actions that are morally wrong.

143. Cf. Matt. 15:19; Gal. 5:19-21; Col. 3:5, 8; 1 Tim. 1:9-10; 2 Tim. 3:2-4; 1 Pet. 2:1; 4:3. See the study of E. Kamlah, *Die Form der katalogischen Paränese im Neuen Testament* (WUNT 7; Tübingen: Mohr, 1964), some of whose results are, however, a bit speculative.

144. Gk. πεπληρωμένους. Paul uses the perfect tense to emphasize the notion of an existing state (see on this meaning of the perfect, Porter, *Verbal Aspect*, pp. 251-59). The masculine plural accusative form of this participle, as well as of μεστούς ("full of") and of the 12 final words in the series, shows that they are grammatically dependent on αὐτούς in v. 28, though in sense they explicate τὰ καθήκοντα.

145. Gk. πάσῃ. It almost surely governs the following four nouns; for its qualitative significance ("all manner of"), see BAGD, 1.a.β.

"full of envy, murder, strife, deceit, malice;
"gossips, maligners, haters of God, proud, arrogant, overbearing, devisers of evil, disobedient to parents, without understanding, without faithfulness, withoutaffection, without mercy."

A general logical sequence matches this structure. The first four nouns are rather general in their focus, the second five revolve around envy and its consequences, while the last twelve begin with two words depicting slander, move on to four that focus on arrogance, and conclude with six less closely related. Throughout the list, Paul focuses on social ills, leaving out sins relating to sexual conduct and, for the most part, sins against God directly. The purpose of this recital, which is the longest of its kind in the NT, is to show the general scope of social evils produced by the "unqualified mind" to which God has handed sinners over. The harm done by people to other people is thus added to idolatry and sexual perversion to complete Paul's sketch of the world outside Christ.

On "unrighteousness,"[146] see 1:18.

"Evil" cannot easily be delimited to anything specific.[147]

"Greed" is more specific than the other three words in this first group but is perhaps included because greed is basic to so many other sins.[148]

The first two words of the second part of the list are probably put together because of the assonance they create — phthonou ("envy")/phonou ("murder") — but the two have a logical relation as well. "Envy" was the subject of many moral treatises both in the secular Greek world and in Hellenistic Judaism,[149] and to it were frequently ascribed acts of violence such as "murder."[150]

Perhaps the other three sins in this section, "strife," "deceit," and "malice,"[151] are also to be subsumed under envy,[152] although the logical relationship is not so clear for the last two.

146. Gk. ἀδικία.
147. Trench argued that the word (πονηρία) conveys a more active nuance than κακία — an evil that corrupts others (Synonyms, pp. 315-17). But the distinction does not hold up under scrutiny.
148. See esp. Col. 3:5, "greed [πλεονεξία], which is idolatry"; cf. also 2 Cor. 9:5; Eph. 4:19; 5:3; 1 Thess. 2:5.
149. See particularly T. Simeon 3–4; T. Gad 3–5.
150. See the connection in Jas. 4:1-3.
151. A few scholars have suggested that κακοηθεία, used only here in the NT, may have the narrow meaning "putting the worst construction on everything" (Trench, Synonyms, pp. 38-40; S-H; they refer to Aristotle, Rh. 1389b.20; 1416b.10b). But this meaning is not so widespread as to create the presumption that this is what Paul intends. In its LXX occurrences (Add. Esth. 16:6; 3 Macc. 3:22; 7:3; 4 Macc. 1:4; 3:4 [twice]), κακοηθεία means "malice" generally.
152. Cranfield.

The final part of the vice list begins with two terms that denote slander. The first[153] is the more specific, suggesting the "whispering" of the person who spreads "confidential" rumors about others.

The word translated "maligners" could more clumsily be paraphrased "one who speaks against."[154] The next word is the most difficult in the list to define. It is composed of words that mean "hate" and "God," but it is not clear whether God is the hater or the one hated. In classical Greek it is invariably passive, "hated by the gods," and some give it this meaning here.[155] But it is more likely that the word has an active sense, "haters of God."[156]

The sin of human self-exaltation before both God and other people is conveyed in the next three words, "proud," "arrogant," and "overbearing." Trench distinguishes them, arguing that the first focuses on activities, the second on thoughts, and the third on words.[157] Without making these distinctions absolute, they capture accurately enough the nuances of the words.[158]

Rhetoric rather than logic dictates the sequence of the next two vices, each denoted by a phrase rather than by a single word: "devisers of evil"[159] and "disobedient to parents." Because "disobedient to parents" occurs in 2 Tim. 3:2 along with "overbearing" and "proud," we may conclude that its presence here continues the theme of arrogance found earlier in v. 30.

The last four items are listed together to create assonance.[160] "Without understanding" describes those who, because of their rejection of God (cf.

153. ψιθυριστάς.

154. κατάλαλος. It appears nowhere else in the Bible, but its meaning can be gauged from the use of καταλαλέω in the LXX (cf. Ps. 44:16; Prov. 20:13) and the NT (Jas. 4:11; 1 Pet. 2:12; 3:16) and καταλαλία in the NT (2 Cor. 12:20; 1 Pet. 2:1).

155. Lightfoot; Meyer; Barrett. Barrett, indeed, suggests that it should be taken adjectivally, modifying καταλάλους. That the word functions as an adjective, however, is unlikely in light of the series of nouns and adjectives used as nouns in the context.

156. BAGD; Black. This meaning is attested in post-Christian literature (Ps.-Clem. Hom. 1.12; cf. the noun θεοστυγία in 1 Clem. 35:5) and fits better the emphasis throughout vv. 29-31 on the sinful attitudes and activities of people.

157. Trench, Synonyms, pp. 98-105.

158. ὑβριστής suggests a violent, proud person, such as Paul was in his former life (1 Tim. 1:13). ὑπερήφανος connotes the attitude that is the antithesis of humility (cf. Luke 1:51; 2 Tim. 3:2; Jas. 4:6; 1 Pet. 5:5). ἀλαζόνης appears only once elsewhere in the NT (2 Tim. 3:2), but the cognate noun, ἀλοζονεία, is associated with boastful speech in Jas. 4:16 (cf. also 1 John 2:16).

159. Gk. ἐφευρετὰς κακῶν. ἐφευρετής is a rare word, found only here in the LXX and NT. Cranfield suggests that we consider "devisers of evil things" to be those who find "ever more hateful methods of hurting and destroying their fellow men."

160. Each begins with the prefix α- (alpha privative); we have tried to duplicate the effect by using the preposition "without" to translate this prefix.

1:21, 28), can no longer comprehend the will of God. They are like the "fool" of Proverbs who ignores wisdom and pursues activities harmful both to herself and to others. "Without faithfulness" means literally one who refuses to abide by covenants and treaties.[161] "Without affection" may have reference particularly to the lack of affection for family members.[162] The failure of people to exhibit even the affection natural to family relationships shows how deep is the corruption of morals.

32 As in v. 25, Paul reverts to the subject of the earlier verses — human beings generally — by using a pronoun that focuses attention on their character.[163] Even though those in view are the people Paul has been describing throughout vv. 19-31,[164] this verse is linked particularly closely with vv. 28-31, since "such things" has its antecedent in the vices listed in vv. 29-31. The function of this concluding verse is to bring out even more fully the willful rebellion against God that pervades humanity. Toward this end, Paul notes that those who engage in the activities he has listed know that what they are doing is wrong. They act "knowing[165] the righteous decree of God, that those who do such things are worthy of death." "Righteous decree" translates a word that Paul uses several other times in Romans, the closest parallel being 8:4, where Paul speaks of the "righteous decree of the law" that believers fulfill by the Spirit.[166] The lack of reference here to "the law" is significant: Paul speaks of what all people, whether blessed with special revelation or not, can know of God's just judgment. "Death" denotes here a divinely imposed punishment and reminds us, as does the earlier part of this passage, of Gen. 3.[167] As Michel rightly emphasizes, the present tenses in this verse show that Paul is speaking not only of what has been true in the past or of what will be true in the future. People generally, Paul claims, have some degree of aware-

---

161. See the only LXX occurrences, in Jer. 3:7-11, where Judah is accused of following Israel in ignoring the demands of the covenant.

162. The root word, στοργέω, often refers to the love of relatives for one another (LSJ).

163. Gk. οἵτινες.

164. Paul's use of οἵτινες does not permit a change of subject; contra, e.g., Kamlah (*Katalogischen Paränese,* pp. 18-19) and F. Flückiger ("Zur Unterscheidung von Heiden und Juden in Röm. 1,18–2,3," *TZ* 10 [1954], 154-58), who think Paul begins talking about Jews in v. 32.

165. The participle ἐπιγνόντες has a concessive force ("although they know"); ἐπιγινώσκω has no different meaning than the simple γινώσκω (see the note on 1:28; compare Rom. 2:18; 1 Cor. 8:3; and Gal. 4:9; cf. R. Bultmann, *TDNT* I, 703-4).

166. The Greek word is δικαίωμα. In addition to 8:4, Paul uses the plural in 2:26 to denote those things commanded in the Mosaic law and the singular in 5:16, 18 of a "righteous act" performed by Christ.

167. Dunn.

168. See also Murray.

ness that the moral outrages they commit are wrong and hence deserve to be punished by God.[168]

The last part of the verse poses a certain difficulty. For by characterizing people as those "who not only do these things themselves, but commend those who do[169] them," Paul appears to suggest that "commending" evil is worse than doing it. Some have attempted to avoid the difficulty by rearranging the text or translating it differently, but these solutions are not convincing.[170] After all, is the traditional interpretation so large a problem? Granted that commending evil is not, in the ultimate sense, worse than doing it, it is also true that in a certain respect the person who commits a sin under the influence of strong temptation is less reprehensible than the one who dispassionately agrees with and encourages a sin for which he or she feels no strong attraction him- or herself. As Murray says, "we are not only bent on damning ourselves but we congratulate others in the doing of those things that we know have their issue in damnation."[171] Although it does not feature the same ascensive emphasis, *T. Asher* 6:2 is both verbally and conceptually close to Paul's statement: "The two-faced are doubly punished because they both practice evil and approve of others who practice it; they imitate the spirits of error and join in the struggle against mankind."

In Paul's concern to demonstrate the responsibility of all human beings for their sin and fallen state, he says some important things about what theologians call the doctrine of "natural revelation" — the knowledge of God that he has made available in the very creation and working of the world. Yet theologians disagree quite dramatically on the extent and significance of this revelation in nature. Roman Catholic theologians have traditionally been very open to the possibility of persons coming to know God through the evidence of nature and the conscience.[172] Against any such notion, Barth has reacted vigorously. For him all knowledge of God must come through Christ; Rom. 1:19-21 speaks not of Gentiles knowing God through nature, but of Gentiles who, confronted with the gospel, have revealed the objective condition that has been theirs all

---

169. The Greek verb here is πράσσω; in the immediately previous clause Paul uses ποιέω. Some posit a slight difference in meaning between them (e.g., S-H), but it is unlikely that any distinction exists (on these verbs, see further our comments on 7:15).

170. As the NA apparatus reveals, some ancient scribes rearranged key parts of the verse. Barrett argues that the οὐ μόνον . . . ἀλλὰ καί ("not only . . . but also") construction may contrast those of whom he has been speaking in vv. 28-31 with those whom he will address in 2:1ff. But to change the subject in the middle of the series of verbs in v. 32 is even more difficult than the alternative.

171. Cf. also, e.g., Chrysostom; Calvin.

172. See the documents of Vatican I (1870), Session III; and the historical survey in B. A. Demarest, *General Revelation: Historical Views and Contemporary Issues* (Grand Rapids: Zondervan, 1982), pp. 25-42.

along.[173] Others, noting that Paul elsewhere accuses the Gentiles of his day of being ignorant of God (cf. 1 Thess. 4:5; 2 Thess. 2:8; Gal. 4:8), suggest that the knowledge of God possessed by Gentiles was a stage in the past, before a collective fall into idolatry.[174] Support for this view is found in the aorist tenses of vv. 19b-28. Still others insist that the knowledge of God that Paul speaks of in these verses is a matter only of "objective" reality, but not of "subjective" awareness.[175]

What can we conclude from the text? First, against Barth, Rom. 1:19-21 teaches that true knowledge of God is available in nature and that people apart from God's revelation in Christ come to know this truth about God. Moreover, the emphasis on the "mind" in v. 19 strongly implies that the inner reason contributes to this knowledge *(sensus divinitatis)*. Second, the aorist tenses of vv. 19b-28 do not allow us to conclude that only a past generation is in view. For the argument of these verses supports the contention of v. 18b that people in Paul's day are suppressing the truth. For this argument to work, the people who have some kind of access to knowledge of God must be the same ones who suppress that knowledge. Thus, while the possibility that Paul describes a collective fall of humankind into idolatry in vv. 19-21 cannot be completely discounted, it does not, by itself, explain adequately the way the passage functions in Rom. 1. It can be concluded, then, that the text teaches that all people have, by reason of God's revelation in creation, access to some degree of knowledge about God (v. 19) and that, to however limited an extent, they subjectively perceive this knowledge (v. 20). "(M)an becomes guilty because something essential does reach him."[176]

But this knowledge is both limited and impure; it is confined to those basic attributes of God that may be discerned in nature (v. 20) and is so mixed with false perceptions that it is almost immediately perverted. Further, it is vitally important, if the passion of Paul's gospel is to be correctly appreciated and the argument of this section correctly understood, to see that the knowledge of God that people possess outside special revelation is woefully inadequate, of itself, to save. Paul makes clear that, rather than being a help to people in their search for God, the evidence of nature and conscience (cf. 2:14-16) serves only to render them "without excuse" before the wrathful God. That this is the result of natural revelation follows from the sinfulness of human beings, who without grace are unable to respond appropriately to whatever knowledge of God they

173. Barth, *CD* II/1, pp. 107-41; *Shorter,* pp. 26-28; cf. also Cranfield.

174. A. Feuillet, "La connaissance naturelle de Dieu par les hommes, d'après Rom 1,18-23," *Lumière et Vie* 14 (1954), 63-80; D. M. Coffey, "Natural Knowledge of God: Reflections on Romans 1,18–2," *TS* 31 (1970), 680-82.

175. P. Helm, *The Divine Revelation* (Westchester, IL: Crossway, 1982), p. 15; Cranfield.

176. H. Berkhof, *Christian Faith: An Introduction to the Study of the Faith* (Grand Rapids: Eerdmans, 1979), pp. 48-49; cf. also Turner, "Romans 1:18-21."

may possess. Paul, then, teaches a natural revelation, but, at least in this passage, the purpose and effect of that revelation are wholly negative.[177]

Another question is how long this knowledge remains with a person. When a person refuses to respond properly to the knowledge of God, is that knowledge immediately effaced or does it remain in some form, whether perverted or not? This question is more difficult to answer on the basis of the discussion in Rom. 1. But v. 32 strongly implies that some knowledge of God remains even after a person has fallen into the degenerate state that Paul depicts in these verses. For the present tenses of that verse, along with the fact that Paul is trying to establish the seriousness of the sinning he has depicted, make it probable that "knowing the righteous ordinance of God" is contemporaneous with the panoply of sinning outlined in vv. 29-31.[178]

Calvin, whose treatment of this topic in the *Institutes* (1.3-5) can hardly be improved on, may be quoted briefly on these points:

> It is therefore in vain that so many burning lamps shine for us in the workmanship of the universe to show forth the glory of its Author. Although they bathe us wholly in their radiance, yet they can of themselves in no way lead us into the right path. Surely they strike some sparks, but before their fuller light shines forth these are smothered. . . . But although we lack the natural ability to mount up unto the pure and clear knowledge of God, all excuse is cut off because the fault of dullness is within us.[179]

Paul's teaching about natural revelation in these verses has some parallels with Greek Stoicism and Hellenistic Judaism. The Greek traditions have

177. Some scholars think that the negative result of natural revelation is Rom. 1 contradicts the more positive tone found in Paul's "Areopagus Speech" in Acts 17. But the differences pertain to the contrast in situations, and no ultimate contradition is present. See B. E. Shields, "The Areopagus Sermon and Romans 1:18ff: A Study in Creation Theology," *Restoration Quarterly* 20 (1977), 23-40.

178. Cf. Murray.

179. *Institutes* 1.5.14, 15. On Calvin's teaching on this matter, which has been the topic of some dispute, see esp. B. B. Warfield, *Calvin and Augustine* (rpt. ed.; Philadelphia: Presbyterian and Reformed, 1956), pp. 29-48; and W. Niesel, *The Theology of Calvin* (rpt. ed.; Grand Rapids: Baker, 1980), pp. 39-53. Other treatments of natural, or general, revelation that defend the general view argued for here are: Demarest, *General Revelation,* pp. 22-23, 227-47; E. Brunner, *Revelation and Reason* (Philadelphia: Westminster, 1946 [original German ed., 1941]), pp. 58-77; Helm, *Divine Revelation,* pp. 15-17; A.-M. Dubarle, *La manifestation naturelle de Dieu d'après l'Ecriture* (LD 91; Paris: Cerf, 1976), pp. 201-24; Turner, "Romans 1:18-21," pp. 45-58; H. P. Owen, "The Scope of Natural Revelation in Rom. I and Acts XVII," *NTS* 5 (1958-59), 138; W. C. Martin, "The Bible and Natural Law," *Restoration Quarterly* 17 (1974), 215; B. Reicke, "Natürliche Theologie nach Paulus," *SEÅ* 22 (1957), 154-67; Nygren, pp. 101-7. For a history of interpretation, see, in addition to Demarest, Wilckens (1:117-21) and Lachmann, *Von Geheimnis der Schöpfung,* pp. 44-88.

mainly a positive purpose, however, encouraging people to pursue the knowledge of God through their reason. This is far from Paul's exclusively negative use of the language.[180] As Bornkamm puts it, "the intention of the Apostle is not to infer God's being from the world, but to uncover the being of the world from God's revelation."[181] The Hellenistic Jewish teachings differ widely, but some, at least, are much closer to Paul. Wisdom 13–14, for instance, criticizes Gentiles for not recognizing "the craftsman while paying heed to his works" (13:1) and for falling into the foolish worship of "homemade" gods. The author can even say that those who failed to recognize God are "not to be excused" (13:8). Paul has undoubtedly been influenced by this tradition and shares with it the generally negative verdict about the knowledge of God among the Gentiles.[182] At one crucial point, however, Paul dissents from the Jewish view: he criticizes Jews as well as Gentiles for failing to respond appropriately to God's self-revelation.[183]

2. Jews Are Accountable to God for Sin (2:1–3:8)

In 1:18-32, Paul describes those people whom he accuses of perverting their knowledge of God (Gentiles, primarily) in the third person: "they" turned away from God; God handed "them" over. In chap. 2, however, it is the second person singular, "you," that Paul uses in making his accusation (2:1-5, 17-29). This does not mean that Paul is now accusing his readers of these things; were he to do that, the second person plural would have been needed. Rather, Paul utilizes here, and sporadically throughout the letter, a literary style called *diatribe*. Diatribe style, which is attested in several ancient authors as well as elsewhere in the NT (e.g., James), uses the literary device of an imaginary dialogue with a student or opponent. Elements of this style include frequent questions, posed by the author to his conversation partner or by the conversation partner, emphatic rejections of possible objections to a line of argument using *mē genoito* ("May it never be!"), and the direct address of one's conversation partner or opponent.[1]

---

180. Cf. Pohlenz, "Paulus und die Stoa," pp. 71-82; Bornkamm, "Revelation of God's Wrath," pp. 50-55.

181. Bornkamm, "Revelation of God's Wrath," p. 59.

182. Cf. H. Bietenhard, "Natürliche Gotteserkenntnis bei des Heiden?" *TZ* 12 (1956), 275-88, for a survey of Jewish teaching. His conclusions are, perhaps, too negative with respect to the Jewish view about the Gentiles' knowledge of God, but his overall thesis, that none of the Jewish literature propagates a "natural theology," is well established.

183. Lührmann, *Offenbarungsverständnis,* pp. 21-26.

1. The best ancient example of diatribe style is found in the Discourses of Epictetus (c. A.D. 1-2). The key studies of the diatribe and Romans are Bultmann, *Der Stil des paulinischen Predigt;* T. Schmeller, *Paulus und die Diatribe;* and Stowers, *Diatribe.* See also the section "Nature and Genre" in the Introduction.

Romans 3:1-8 is a particularly clear example of this dialogical style; and chap. 2, while not containing any true dialogue, is similar to those parts of the diatribe in which the "teacher" rebukes his or her conversation partner by exposing his or her presumption and inconsistency (cf. 2:1: "you are without excuse, O person"; 2:3: "Do you reckon this, O person"; 2:17: "If you call yourself a Jew," etc.). However, the dialogue that Paul records in this part of the letter, while imaginary, undoubtedly reflects accurately many actual debates and conversations with those to whom he was preaching the gospel. The "conversations" and indictments that we find in this section are not verbatim reports of actual dialogues, but they reflect real-life situations.[2]

Who, then, is the person that Paul addresses in this section? Although some application to self-righteous Gentiles cannot be entirely removed from what Paul says in 2:1-11, it is clear that Paul's main target is the Jew (see the introduction to 2:1-16). His indictment of the Jew proceeds in two stages (2:1-16; 2:17-29), with 3:1-8 being a parenthetical response to possible misconceptions of what Paul has said. Both parts of Paul's indictment accuse the Jews of committing sins (2:1-5; 2:17-24) and then show that those sins are not excused by God simply by virtue of the Jews' belonging to the people of Israel, e.g., by possessing the law (2:12-16) or by being circumcised (2:25-29). Just as people in general have turned away from the revelation that God has given in nature (1:20-32), so the Jews have turned away, through their disobedience, from the revelation that God has given them specially (2:17-24).

Contrary to popular Jewish belief, the sins of the Jews will not be treated by God significantly differently from those of the Gentiles. For God is impartial and judges every person "according to his works" (2:6-11). Like John the Baptist (Matt. 3:7-10) and Jesus (cf. Matt. 21:28-32) before him, Paul denies that belonging to the covenant people per se ensures acceptance with God. Neither possession of the law nor circumcision marks a person as truly belonging to God. Only repentance (2:4) and an inner, heartfelt commitment to God (2:28-29) — in a word, faith — ultimately count before the Lord. Like the bark of the dog in the Sherlock Holmes story "Silver Blaze," the word "faith," introduced in 1:17 as the way in which God's righteousness can be appropriated, is conspicuous in 2:1–3:8 by its absence. Yet, as Paul shows in chap. 4, it has always been faith — and only faith — that enables *anyone* to belong to the people of God and so escape his wrath. Scholars have introduced the phrase "covenantal nomism" to describe the Jews' conviction that their corporate election, combined with sincere intention to obey the law, sufficed for salvation. This belief Paul implicitly denies in chap. 2. He then goes on to claim that the OT itself teaches not "covenantal nomism" but "promissory pistism" — that a *saving* relationship with God comes, as it did for Abraham, through human

2. See, e.g., Dabelstein, *Beurteilung der 'Heiden,'* pp. 96-97; Barrett, p. 43.

126

response to God's grace expressed in his promise and not through the Mosaic covenant. (See, in more detail, the Excursus after 3:20.)

a. The Jews and the Judgment of God (2:1-16)

Paul develops his critique of the Jews in these verses in three paragraphs. The first, vv. 1-5, uses the second person singular to accuse the Jews of earning for themselves the same wrath that is already falling on Gentile sinners. This accusation is the main point of 2:1-16. God's judgment is "according to truth," and he must fairly assess the works of every person (v. 2). And this criterion of impartial "fairness" applies even to the Jew who is proud of being a member of God's people (vv. 3-5).

The second two paragraphs (vv. 6-11 and 12-16) interrupt the second person "accusation" style (it is resumed in v. 17) with explanation (in the third person plural) of the indictment in vv. 1-5. Both paragraphs serve to validate the inclusion of Jews along with Gentiles under sentence of God's wrath by showing that Jews stand on the same basic ground as Gentiles when it comes to God's judgment. For, in the first place, God's impartiality demands that he treat all people the same, judging every person according to what he has done (vv. 6-11). To this, the Jews may object that they possess, in the Mosaic law, a distinct advantage over the Gentiles. So, in the second place, Paul shows that possession of the Mosaic law will make no difference in this judgment (v. 12) — for (1) it is not the possession but the doing of the law that matters (v. 13); and (2) the Gentiles also have "law" in some sense (vv. 14-16).

Paul therefore "levels the playing field" between Jew and Gentile. Both stand condemned before God because of their transgressions of God's Word. It is because Jews *do* "the same things" as Gentiles that God will judge them (2:1-3); because they disobey the law in which they boast that they "dishonor God" (2:17-24); because they transgress the law that they lose any value in their circumcision (2:25; see also 3:10-18). Factual transgressions are the reason Jews stand condemned and need the righteousness of God available in the gospel; the lack of security in their "covenant status" is the reason, in turn, why these transgressions will "count" before God.

i. Critique of Jewish Presumption (2:1-5)

1*Therefore, you are without excuse, O person, each one of you who is judging. For in what you are condemning the other person, you are condemning yourself, for you who are judging are doing the very same things. 2Now we know that the judgment of God upon those who do such things is according to truth. 3Or do you reckon this, O person* *who is judging those doing such things and doing the same things, that you will escape the judgment of God? 4Or are you showing contempt for the riches of his goodness and forbearance and patience, being ignorant that the goodness of God is leading you to repentance? 5Because of your hard and unrepentant heart you are storing up for yourself wrath on the day of wrath and the revelation[3] of the righteous judgment of God.*

Paul begins by turning his attention to a person who is standing in judgment over the people whom he has described in chap. 1. Cheering Paul on in his indictment of Gentiles, this person, although he thinks himself superior to the "heathen" idolater of 1:18-32, is nevertheless just as much in danger of the wrath of God, for he is doing "the same things" as those whom he condemns (2:1-2). Who is this "superior" person? A few interpreters, noting that Paul calls this person a "judge" (v. 1), have thought that Paul might be addressing an actual civil judge.[4] But this misses the import of Paul's accusation and is too narrow an application. Much more popular is the identification of this person with any self-consciously "moral" person, whether Jew or Gentile.[5] But this identification is a bit too broad. Without necessarily excluding application to the moral person generally, we think it is clear that it is the Jew who is the real target of Paul's indictment in these verses.[6]

Paul's accusation in vv. 1-3 could apply to anyone, but v. 4 draws on language from Wis. 12–15 that makes best sense if the passage is directed against the Jew. This same conclusion emerges from the fact that vv. 6-11 and 12-16, in which Paul lays the basis for the charge he has made in vv. 1-5, have the purpose of relativizing the position of the Jew vis-à-vis the Gentile. But this makes sense only if vv. 1-5 have been directed primarily against the Jew.[7] Therefore, although Paul does not explicitly identify his target until 2:17, it is clear that already in 2:1-11 the Jew is his "hidden target." By beginning his indictment in such general terms — "O person, each one of you" (v. 1) — Paul enables his readers in Rome to share in the "discovery" process that he probably used when he

---

3. Several MSS (the Byzantine second corrector of ℵ, the second corrector of the western D, Ψ, and the majority text) add a καί between ἀποκαλύψεως and δικαιοκρισίας.

4. E.g., Pelagius; Chrysostom; Luther (as one of several interpretations).

5. Calvin; Barrett. Dabelstein (*Beurteilung der 'Heiden,'* pp. 86-94) thinks that Paul refers to both Jews and Gentile "God-fearers."

6. See esp. Bengel; Michel; Nygren; Murray; Cranfield; Dunn; Hoppe, *Heilsgeschichte,* pp. 39-45; P. W. Livermore, "The Setting and Argument of Romans 1:18–3:20: The Empirical Verification of the Power of Sin" (Ph.D. diss., Princeton Theological Seminary, 1978), p. 278, passim.

7. See B. C. Wintle, "The Law of Moses and the Law of Christ" (Ph.D. diss., University of Manchester, 1977), p. 40.

preached his gospel to mixed audiences. We can imagine many self-professed "moral" people adding their "Amen" to the kind of denunciation of "heathen" sins that we find in 1:18-32. Suddenly, however, Paul turns on these people and accuses them of doing "the very same things." Only as he moves on in his denunciation will it emerge that it is the Jew whom Paul has really in mind. Such a technique would have enabled Paul to gain the sympathy of the Jews in his audience and keep them interested in his message.

1 The "therefore"[8] that connects the opening of Rom. 2 with Rom. 1 creates a problem for our conclusion that 1:18-32 is directed mainly against Gentiles and 2:1-16 mainly against Jews. For if Paul has shifted targets in this manner, we would expect the transition to be made with something like "in the same manner also." But how can the sin and guilt of Gentiles establish the conclusion ("therefore") that Jews who judge them are also "without excuse"? Several scholars seize on this problem as another reason for thinking that 1:18-32 must depict humanity generally; for if all people have been condemned there, the sin of those from among them who judge can follow as a logical conclusion.[9] But Paul's assertion that those who judge others do "the very same things" shows that he is distinguishing between those he described at the end of chap. 1 and those he now condemns. Others, then, argue that the word Paul uses at the beginning of this chapter has no inferential force here,[10] or that it states the conclusion of an argument that follows in vv. 1b-2,[11] or even that v. 1 should be removed from the text as a later gloss.[12] But none of these suggestions can muster convincing lexical or textual support. There is more to be said for the possibility that the word connects 2:1ff. with 1:32.[13] But the change of subject between 1:32 and 2:1 renders this connection logically questionable.

The best solution is to understand the "therefore" to relate, not to the description of (mainly) Gentile sin in 1:21-32, but to the announcement of God's wrath and the reality of the knowledge of God in 1:18-19. For 1:18-19, which functions as a kind of heading for all of 1:18–3:20, includes reference to all humanity. On this reading, Paul would be saying in 2:1 that *because* God's wrath is revealed against *all* people, and *because all* people have been given knowledge of God, *therefore* even the person who judges is "without

---

8. Gk. διό.

9. Zahn; Cranfield; Bassler, *Divine Impartiality,* pp. 131-34.

10. Lietzmann; Althaus; Michel; Schlier.

11. Murray.

12. Bultmann, "Glossen," p. 281; Käsemann.

13. Specifically, the logic might be (1) that those who judge others prove themselves to be among those who know "the just decree of God" (v. 32a; cf. Barrett); or (2) that those who condemn others for sinning while sinning themselves are, *a fortiori,* to be condemned even more than those who only "commend" sin (Godet; cf. also Livermore ["Romans 1:18–3:20," p. 181], who connects 2:1 with the vice list in 1:29-31).

excuse" before God.[14] Although it might be objected that connecting 2:1 with 1:18-19 skips over too much intervening material, it can be said in response that 1:18-19 establishes what is Paul's main point in 1:18-32, so that the "therefore" in 2:1 resumes the main sequence of Paul's argument.

Paul's accusation that the person who judges another is "without excuse" gives further support for this conclusion. In 1:20, Paul directed this accusation against those who spurned the knowledge of God available in nature. Paul now brings the same accusation against those who reveal by their act of judging that they also have access to the knowledge of God. The person whom Paul so accuses, addressed with the second person singular in diatribe style, is "O person,[15] each one of you who is judging."[16] Paul invites anyone who might judge another to include himself or herself in the scope of his accusation. But he particularly wants Jews to realize that they cannot be excused from this category. It is *anyone* — including the Jew — who "condemns"[17] another that is "without excuse."

In the second part of the verse, Paul tells why[18] one who judges is without excuse before God: in the very act[19] of judging another, a person is "condemning" himself because he does the same things as the other. It is not clear what Paul means in accusing the judgmental person of doing "the very same things" as "the other." If "the other" is to be identified with the Gentile of 1:21-32, as seems clear, how can it be said that highly moral people like the Jews are doing "the very same things"? Barrett suggests that this takes place in the act of judging itself, for to judge another is to seize God's prerogative and thus to be guilty of idolatry (cf. 1:23, 25). But this interpretation does not adequately explain the plural "these things." Minear suggests that failing to glorify and thank God and making a false claim to wisdom, which he views as the key sins in 1:18-32, are intended by Paul.[20] Another possibility is that Paul thinks in terms of sins "according to their essential

14. For a similar view, cf. Dunn; Fitzmyer; and Hoppe, *Heilsgeschichte*, p. 45.

15. Watson, 109-10, suggests that Paul might use the word ἄνθρωπε ("person") to stress the creatureliness of the human being who presumes to stand in judgment over others. But this is unlikely, since ἄνθρωπος is very common in the diatribe style (cf. Jas. 2:20).

16. The combination of the direct address ὦ ἄνθρωπε ("O person") with the participial appositive πᾶς ὁ κρίνων ("everyone who judges") is awkward. Paul clearly wants to say something like "every person who judges" (πᾶς ἄνθρωπε ὁ κρίνων), but the adjective in front of ἄνθρωπε would have taken away from the force of the address.

17. The Greek verb is κρίνω. This word has a wide variety of nuances in the NT, but here it clearly means "condemn" and is indistinguishable in meaning from κατακρίνω later in the verse.

18. Cf. Gk. γάρ.

19. Gk. ἐν ᾧ. The ἐν could also have a causal force (cf. Fitzmyer).

20. Minear, 48-49.

moral categories," perhaps in dependence on Jesus' manner of interpreting the commandments (Matt. 5:21-48).[21] In this sense, the Jews' reverence for their traditions is not essentially different from the idolatry of the Gentiles, nor is the lust in the hearts of Jews any less culpable than the perverse sexual practices of the Gentiles. There is some truth to this observation; but the similarity of "you are doing the very same things" and "those who are doing these things" in 1:32 suggests that we should look to 1:29-31 rather than to 1:20-28 for the sins Paul has in mind here in 2:1.[22] Many of these sins — for example, pride, arrogance, gossiping, maligning others, and lack of affection — are as prevalent in the Jewish as in the Gentile world. In fact, Paul will accuse the Jews of some of these same sins in vv. 17-24.

2 Having accused the self-righteous person of doing the same things as the "wicked" Gentiles, Paul now affirms[23] as a general principle the fact and fairness of God's judgment of such practices: "Now[24] we know that the judgment[25] of God upon those who do such things is according to truth." In claiming that God's judgment is "according to truth," Paul is affirming that God's judgment against sin is fully in accord with the facts, that it is just.[26] This tenet was one on which both Paul and his dialogue partner could agree, it being a standard Jewish teaching.[27] Where the disagreement between Paul and the Jew comes is in Paul's application of the principle to the Jews on the same basis as to the Gentiles. In other words, the Jews would want to include as part of the "truth" on the basis of which God judges the special relationship that they enjoy with God. Paul does not deny this relationship (cf. 3:1-8), but claims that it does not shield the Jews from the consequences of their sins (cf. the generally parallel vv. 6, 11, 13, and 16).

3 Having established common ground with his discussion partner (cf. "we know" in v. 2), Paul now uses the doctrine of God's "truthfulness" in judging to criticize the person who proudly stands in judgment over others (v. 1). And since he is moving again to the attack, Paul shifts back to the second person

---

21. Cf. Meyer; Cranfield; Best.

22. See Dunn.

23. Barrett takes the verse as the statement of an objector; cf. the NRSV: "You say, 'We know. . . .' " But the flow of the argument and the use of οἴδαμεν ("we know") (cf. also 3:19; 7:14; 8:22, 28) show that Paul continues his own exposition.

24. Gk. δέ, which has here a continuative sense (cf. NASB, "and"; NIV, "now"; RSV leaves it untranslated).

25. Gk. κρίμα, which means, as it usually does in Paul, the judicial verdict of condemnation (3:8; 5:16; 13:2; 1 Cor. 11:29, 34; Gal. 5:10; 1 Tim. 3:6; 5:12 — Rom. 11:33 and 1 Cor. 6:7 are different).

26. The context makes it unlikely that Paul refers to "*the* truth," e.g., the gospel, or to God's reliability toward Israel (as Dunn thinks).

27. Cf., e.g., *2 Apoc. Bar.* 85:9; *m. 'Abot* 3:16; and Str-B, 3.76.

singular form of address: "Or do you[28] reckon this, O person who is judging those doing such things and doing the same things, that you will escape the judgment of God?" The sense of the verse shows that Paul is questioning this person's belief that he or she will be able to escape this judgment of God. Such a question is legitimately put to the Gentile moralist or philosopher who thinks he or she can please God by his or her good life, but it is particularly the Jew who would be likely to make such an assumption. This is just the attitude revealed in the intertestamental Jewish writing *The Psalms of Solomon,* where the author asserts that "those who do lawlessness will not escape the judgment of the Lord"[29] (15:8) but then goes on to exempt the "righteous" from that same judgment. What Paul is calling into question is precisely whether anyone can claim that exemption, at least as traditionally defined in terms of the Mosaic covenant.[30]

The logic of the first three verses of the chapter may then be set forth as follows:

> God's judgment falls on those who do "these things."
> Even the self-righteous judge does "these things."
> Therefore: even the self-righteous judge stands under God's judgment.

4 The "or"[31] at the beginning of this verse does not set forth an alternative to v. 3 but introduces a rhetorical question that brings to light the false assumptions of the person who is addressed in v. 3.[32] Paul wants to show the person who thinks she can sin and yet avoid judgment that she is, in fact, "showing contempt for"[33] God's mercy. Three terms, all dependent on "riches," describe this mercy of God. "Goodness"[34] is attributed to God by Paul in Rom. 11:11a and c (where its opposite is "severity") and in Eph. 2:7; Tit. 3:4. It is used several times in the LXX of the Psalms to designate God's goodness toward his people.[35] "Forbearance"[36] and "patience"[37] denote the

---

28. The use of the nominative personal pronoun σύ is emphatic and pointed here: "Do *you* think that. . . ?"

29. The Greek shows similarities to Paul's wording: οὐκ ἐκφεύξονται οἱ ποιοῦντες ἀνομίαν τὸ κρίμα κυρίου.

30. See also Dunn.

31. Gk. ἤ.

32. BAGD.

33. The Greek verb is καταφρονέω, used elsewhere in the NT in Matt. 6:24; 18:10; Luke 16:13; 1 Cor. 11:22; 1 Tim. 4:12; 6:2; Heb. 12:2; 2 Pet. 2:10.

34. Gk. χρηστότης.

35. Pss. 25:7; 31:19; 68:10; 119:48; 145:7; cf. also *Pss. Sol.* 5:18.

36. Gk. ἀνοχή, used only here and in 3:26 in the NT (and only in 1 Macc. 12:25 in the LXX).

37. Gk. μακροθυμία. Paul uses this term with reference to God only once else (Rom. 9:22), holding it up as a human virtue elsewhere (in 2 Cor. 6:6; Gal. 5:22; and Col. 3:12, he uses

expression of God's goodness in his patient withholding of the judgment that is rightfully due the sinner.[38]

As we have noted, several of the words Paul uses in v. 4a are found in OT and Jewish descriptions of God's goodness and mercy toward Israel. But the text that stands out as particularly significant, in the light of parallels between Wis. 11–15 and 1:18-32, is Wis. 15:1-2. After a long exposé of Gentile idolatry and sin (chaps. 11–14), the author says in these verses: "But thou, our God, art kind[39] and true, patient,[40] and ruling all things in mercy. For even if we sin we are thine, knowing thy power." That Paul has this text in mind is probable; but even if he does not, it is the attitude expressed in the passage, and by no means confined to Wisdom of Solomon, that Paul rebukes in these verses. Certainly the OT encourages God's people to regard God as merciful and forgiving (e.g., Ps. 145). But the assumption of God's special favor toward his people had already in the OT period become a source of false security for those within Israel who were not living faithfully within the covenant, as the preaching of the prophets abundantly indicates. The literature of intertestamental Judaism, while consistently stressing the need for Jews to repent of sin, also tended to highlight Israel's favored position to the extent that its security in God's judgment was virtually unassailable.[41] It is this assumption that Paul, in agreement with the prophets, calls into question. As the passage unfolds, however, we will find Paul going beyond the prophets in asserting that Jews are no better off than Gentiles in the judgment. This is a radical departure from all Jewish tradition and implies not only a critique of the prevailing understanding of God's covenant with Israel but also that a new era in salvation history had dawned.

The participial clause in the last part of the verse — "being ignorant that the goodness of God is leading[42] you to repentance" — shows that God's purpose in his kindness is not to excuse sin but to stimulate repentance. This notion, too, has parallels in Jewish teaching (cf. Wis. 11:23), and Paul criticizes his rhetorical partner for willfully ignoring this truth. Repentance plays a

---

it in this way along with χηρστότης). Trench suggests that Paul may intend a difference in meaning between ἀνοχή and μακροθυμία, the former conveying more of a provisional and temporary suspension of judgment than does the latter (*Synonyms,* p. 199). But it is unlikely that Paul intends any significant distinction between the terms (cf. F. S. Spencer, "Beyond Trench's Study of Synonyms," *ExpTim* 99 [1987-88], 140). It is typical of both Greek and Hebrew style to pile up such generally synonymous terms to make a point.

38. Käsemann notes *2 Apoc. Bar.* 59:6, where "the abundance of long-suffering [ἀνοχή]" is coordinate with "the suppression of wrath." Note also 1 Cor. 13:4, where Paul attributes both qualities to Christian love.

39. Gk. χρηστός.

40. Gk. μακρόθυμος.

41. See, e.g., *Pss. Sol.* 9–10.

42. The Greek verb ἄγει uses the present tense with a gnomic, or "omnitemporal," denotation and is conative: God is "seeking to lead you to repentance" (S-H).

surprisingly small part in Paul's teaching, considering its importance in contemporary Judaism. Probably this is because the coming of Christ had revealed to Paul that acceptance with God requires a stronger action than the word "repentance" often connoted at the time.

5 God's patience with sin must not be taken as a sign that he is weak[43] or that he will withhold his judgment forever. In this verse, Paul warns his complacent addressee that a time of judgment is indeed coming, and that instead of mercy, it is wrath that the person who presumes on God's kindness is accumulating in advance of that judgment. It serves, then, as a solemn confirmation of the answer implied by the rhetorical question in v. 3. Such a person will certainly not "escape the judgment of God." Specifically, Paul claims that "because of[44] your hard[45] and unrepentant heart you are storing up for yourself[46] wrath." The metaphorical application of "store up" was well established.[47] But since what is "stored up" is almost always something good, the verb possesses an ironical flavor here: the recalcitrant sinner is storing up for himself not blessing or life[48] but wrath.[49]

When will this situation become evident? Noting that Paul speaks in this context (1:18) of a present infliction of the wrath of God, some commentators think that the last phrase in the verse, "on the day of wrath and the revelation of the righteous judgment of God," modifies "storing up." In this case, Paul would be qualifying the current period of salvation history as the "day of wrath."[50] But "day of wrath" is quasi-technical biblical language for the time of final judgment.[51] This strongly suggests that Paul is looking here at the climactic outpouring of wrath at the end of history; and the Jew who

---

43. Note the similar concern in *2 Apoc. Bar.* 21:20: "Therefore command mercifully and confirm all that you have said that you would do so that your power will be recognized by those who believe that your long-suffering means weakness."

44. The Greek preposition κατά has a causal nuance here (BAGD).

45. The Greek word is σκληρότης, which occurs only here in the NT. But several of its cognates are used in the NT to designate spiritual obduracy and rebellion: σκληρύνω ("to be hard"; Acts 19:9; Rom. 9:19; Heb. 3:8, 13, 15; 4:7); σκληροκαρδία ("hardness of heart"; Matt. 19:8; Mark 10:5); σκληροτράχηλος ("stiff-necked"; Acts 7:51). All have their roots in the OT, and σκληροτής is used in Deut. 9:27 of the spiritual "stubbornness" of Israel. This background is further evidence that Paul is thinking particularly of the Jewish sinner (Michel).

46. The negative connotation of "store up" here (see below) means that σεαυτῷ is a dative of disadvantage ("against yourself").

47. Cf., e.g., Prov. 2:7 and Matt. 6:19.

48. Contrast *Pss. Sol.* 9:5: "The one who does what is right saves up [θησαυρίζω] life for himself with the Lord."

49. Cf. Jas. 5:3, where the verb may have a similar ironical twist with reference to judgment.

50. See, e.g., Barth.

51. E.g., Ps. 110:5; Zeph. 1:14-15; Rev. 6:17.

refuses to repent is even now accumulating the wrath that on that day will be revealed.[52] Also to be revealed on that day, claims Paul, is "the righteous judgment of God."[53] This word also continues a central theme of this section of Romans: the reality of God's judgment and the fact that this judgment will be absolutely just (cf. v. 2). Paul thus calls into question the Jewish tendency to confine God's "righteous judgment" to Gentile sinners.[54]

ii. The Impartiality of Judgment (2:6-11)

6*For he will render to each person according to that person's works.* 7*On the one hand, to those who by their persistence in a good work are seeking glory and honor and immortality [he will render] eternal life;* 8*but, on the other hand, for those who are characterized by selfishness and who disobey the truth while obeying unrighteousness, there will be wrath and fury.* 9*There will be tribulation and distress for every soul of a person who does evil, for the Jew first and then for the Greek;* 10*but there will be glory and honor and peace for everyone who does good, for the Jew first and then for the Greek.* 11*For there is no partiality with God.*

These verses form a self-contained thought unit, as their chiastic arrangement demonstrates:

A.	God will judge everyone equitably	v. 6
B.	Those who do good will attain eternal life	v. 7
C.	Those who do evil will suffer wrath	v. 8
C'.	Wrath for those who do evil	v. 9
B'.	Glory for those who do good	v. 10
A'.	God judges impartially	v. 11[1]

52. The phrase, then, should be taken with ἡμέρᾳ, with ἐν given its normal temporal sense: "you are storing up against yourself wrath, which will fall on the day of wrath." (Käsemann, who apparently takes ἐν . . . with θησαυρίζεις, suggests that it is used in place of εἰς with the meaning "for." But the grammars give little support to an interchange between these prepositions in this particular sense.)

53. Gk. δικαιοκρισίας τοῦ θεοῦ. That Paul is thinking of the final judgment is suggested also by the word δικαιοκρισία, since it has this reference in *T. Levi* 3:2; 15:2 (cf. v.l. in 2 Thess. 1:5). MM note that the word emphasizes the character of the judge.

54. Even in *T. Levi* 15:2, where Israel is included in the judgment, v. 4 asserts that Jews will receive mercy through Abraham, Isaac, and Jacob (Wilckens).

1. K. Grobel ("A Chiastic Retribution-formula in Romans 2," in *Zeit und Geschichte. Dankesgabe an Rudolf Bultmann zum 80. Geburtstag* [ed. E. Dinkler; Tübingen: Mohr, 1964], pp. 255-61) thinks that Paul has taken over a self-contained tradition.

Unlike some chiastically structured paragraphs, the main point of vv. 6-11 occurs not at the center but at the beginning and the end (vv. 6, 11): God will judge every person impartially, assessing each according to the same standard — works. The paragraph therefore elaborates "the righteous judgment of God" in v. 5b. The verses that are sandwiched between the main assertions in vv. 6 and 11 illustrate the two possible outcomes of this judgment. In applying "the Jew first, then the Greek" sequence of salvation (1:16) to judgment (vv. 9, 10), Paul brings into the light the Jew as the hidden target of his polemic. On the other hand, the style of direct address is dropped — to be resumed in 2:17 — in favor of a more dispassionate expositional style.

6 Paul signals that he is continuing the general discussion of vv. 1-5 by connecting this verse grammatically with v. 5.[2] Paul's assertion that God "will render" or "recompense" every person according to what that person has done[3] reflects common OT and Jewish teaching.[4] And this teaching, though set in a new context as a result of the revelation of God's grace in Christ, is not retracted (cf. Matt. 16:27; 2 Cor. 11:15; 2 Tim. 4:14).

7-8 Verses 7 and 8 outline the two possible outcomes of God's rendering to "each" according to works.[5] On the one hand, to "those who by their persistence in a good work are seeking[6] glory and honor and immortal-

---

2. The "he" in our translation represents, in fact, the relative pronoun "who" (ὅς); cf. NASB.

3. The Greek here is τὰ ἔργα, which Paul uses to describe general human conduct, whether good (assumed in most texts) or bad (cf. esp. Rom. 9:10-12; also 4:2, 6; 9:32; 11:6; Eph. 2:9; 2 Tim. 1:9 [all absolute]; Tit. 1:16; 3:5; with qualifier denoting that the "works" are positive: Eph. 2:10; 1 Tim. 2:10; 5:10, 25; 6:18; Tit. 2:7, 14; 3:8, 14; with a qualifier that the "works" are negative: Rom. 13:12; Gal. 5:19; Eph. 5:11; Col. 1:21). Paul makes "works" the criterion of judgment also in 2 Cor. 11:15 and 2 Tim. 4:14 (note also the use of the singular ἔργον in Rom. 2:7; 1 Cor. 3:13a, b, 14, 15). On the theological significance of the word in Paul, see, further, D. J. Moo, " 'Law,' 'Works of the Law,' and Legalism in Paul," *WTJ* 45 (1983), 73-100.

4. See esp. Ps. 62:12; Eccl. 1:14; Hos. 12:2; *m. 'Abot* 3:15. Paul's language is closest to Prov. 24:12 LXX, which he may be quoting: ὃς ἀποδίδωσιν ἑκάστῳ κατὰ τὰ ἔργα αὐτοῦ. But the commonality of the teaching makes it improbable that Paul has any particular text in mind (cf. R. Heiligenthal, *Werke als Zeugen: Untersuchungen zur Bedeutung der menschlichen Taten im Frühjudentum, Neuen Testament und Frühchristentum* [WUNT 2.9; Tübingen: Mohr, 1983], pp. 171-74).

5. The verses are joined by a μέν . . . δέ ("on the one hand . . . on the other hand") construction.

6. The dative substantive participles in vv. 7-8 — τοῖς . . . ζητοῦσιν ("those . . . who are seeking"), τοῖς . . . ἀπειθοῦσι ("those . . . who are disobeying"), and [τοῖς] πειθομένοις ("those who are obeying") are grammatically related to the dative ἑκάστῳ in v. 6.

ity"[7] he will "render"[8] eternal life.[9] Paul's suggestion that a person's "good work" might lead to eternal life seems strange in light of his teaching elsewhere; and we will deal with this question below in conjunction with v. 10. It might be noted, however, that Paul goes out of his way to stress that the work that God so rewards is a persistent lifestyle of godliness.[10] In contrast to these people are "those who are characterized by selfishness, and who disobey the truth while obeying[11] unrighteousness, there will be wrath and fury."[12] As the contrast in these verses makes clear, there are two, and only two, fates in store for "every person" at the time of God's "righteous judgment." Those who do not receive eternal life receive the punishment of God's wrath.[13] Paul describes these latter people from the standpoint of their basic

7. "Glory" (δόξα), "honor" (τιμή), and "immortality" (ἀφθαρσία) denote blessings the righteous can hope to receive in the eschatological future. The first two have OT antecedents (and cf. 1 Pet. 1:7), whereas "immortality" has its roots in Greek soil (cf. Wis. 2:23 and Paul's use of the term in 1 Cor. 15:42, 50, 53-54; Eph. 6:24; 2 Tim. 1:10).

8. Both the subject [God understood] and the verb in v. 6, ἀποδώσει, must be carried over into v. 7.

9. An alternate translation of the verse would run, "to those who are seeking eternal life, [he will render] glory, honor, and immortality." On this reading, δόξαν καὶ τιμὴν καὶ ἀφθαρσίαν are objects of the understood verb ἀποδώσει, while ζωὴν αἰώνιον is the object of ζητοῦσιν (see Zahn). In favor of this rendering is the fact that "glory and honor" describe what God gives to those who do good in the parallel v. 10. But the syntax, with δόξαν καὶ τιμὴν καὶ ἀφθαρσίαν enclosed by the article τοῖς and the participle ζητοῦσιν, strongly favors the reading that we adopt above (which is reflected also in the major English translations).

10. The Greek phrase in question is καθ' ὑπομονὴν ἔργου ἀγαθοῦ. The κατά may have a causal nuance here (cf. BAGD). ὑπομονή often indicates the "patient fortitude" necessary in the face of suffering (5:3-4; 8:25; cf. 15:4, 5; 2 Cor. 1:6; 6:4) but indicates here a more active "perseverance in" (cf. 15:4; 1 Thess. 1:3). ἔργου ἀγαθοῦ must, then, be an objective genitive. In light of the plural ἔργα in v. 6, the singular ἔργον here is somewhat unexpected. Probably it is to be seen as a collective, summing up the "good works" of a person's life as a single dominating goal — "doing good" (e.g., S-H; Murray).

11. Gk. πειθομένοις. The verb πείθω usually means "convince," "persuade," "depend on." Here, however, the contrast with ἀπειθέω shows that it means "disobey" (cf. BAGD).

12. The nominative case of the nouns ὀργὴ καὶ θυμός (contrast the accusative ζωὴν αἰώνιον in v. 7) shows that v. 8 is more loosely tied to v. 6 than is v. 7. The participles [τοῖς] ἀπειθοῦσι and πειθομένοις may be in apposition to ἑκάστῳ in v. 6, with ὀργὴ καὶ θυμός being a pendant ("hanging," or independent) nominative, or the participles could be the indirect object of an implied verb (ἔσται, "will be"), with ὀργὴ καὶ θυμός the subject of the sentence (e.g., "wrath and anger will be to those who . . .").

13. "Wrath and anger," as a contrast to "eternal life" in v. 7, denote the punishment to be inflicted on the unrighteous at the judgment. They remind us that the judgment is the reaction of a personal God to the violation of his just order. θυμός occurs with ὀργή frequently in the LXX (Ps. 77:9; Dan. 3:13; Mic. 5:15) and in the NT (Eph. 4:31; Col. 3:8; Rev. 19:15), where attempts to distinguish the two in meaning are pointless.

motivating principle — selfishness[14] — and from the standpoint of their allegiance: they give themselves in obedience to unrighteousness rather than to the truth. Paul here describes opposite sides of the same coin. These people are refusing to subject themselves to the truth as God has revealed it and prefer rather to give themselves over to "unrighteousness" (cf. 1:18). As often in Romans, Paul singles out obedience as indicative of one's true spiritual state (cf. 1:5; 2:25-27; 6:15-23).

9-10 Paul now reiterates these two contrasting outcomes of judgment, taking them in reverse order.[15] And within this larger chiasm (vv. 7-8/9-10), we have a smaller chiasm linking vv. 8-9:

> v. 8 "there will be for those . . .   wrath and fury"
> v. 9 "tribulation and distress   for those who . . ."

Paul generally uses "tribulation" of the trials and suffering experienced by Christians in this life,[16] but here it clearly designates the suffering of es-

---

14. The Greek is ἐξ ἐριθείας, where the ἐκ denotes the motive "out of" which people live or act (cf. Phil. 1:16, 17 for a similar use of ἐκ). The meaning of the term ἐριθεία is debated. Its only pre-NT occurrences are in Aristotle, where it designates the attitude of those who seek political office for private gain rather than the public good (*Pol.* 5:3). These occurrences suggest that ἐριθεία might mean "factiousness" or "contentiousness," a meaning that makes sense in every one of its NT occurrences (Gal. 5:20; 2 Cor. 12:20; Phil. 1:16; 2:3; Jas. 3:14, 16) (S-H; Murray [Murray further suggests that this factiousness relates to our relation to God]). The probability that this meaning is correct would be strengthened if it could be shown that ἐριθεία is derived from ἔρις ("strife"); but this is unlikely. The word probably derives from ἐριθεύομαι, and hence ἔριθμος ("hired worker"); cf. W. F. Howard, *Accidence and Word-Formation,* vol. 2 of *A Grammar of New Testament Greek,* by J. H. Moulton (Edinburgh: T & T Clark, 1919-29), p. 339; BAGD; F. Büchsel, *TDNT* II, 660. With this derivation in mind, Barrett suggests that in this verse the word might connote a desire to gain righteousness on the basis of one's own works. But the context does not enable us to give the word so specific a meaning. Since hired workers in antiquity were often scorned because they worked solely for their own benefit, many think that the word connotes "selfishness" (Büchsel, ibid.). This meaning works as well as "factiousness" in Aristotle and in the NT occurrences. And it can be argued that it is preferable in Gal. 5:20 and 2 Cor. 12:20, where the occurrence of both ἔρις and ἐριθεία would be somewhat repetitive if the latter meant "factiousness." However, considering the amount of repetition that occurs in vice lists, this point is not a strong one (Murray). Ultimately, it is the context of Rom. 2:8 that makes the meaning "selfishness" most likely in this verse. A contrast with the attitude of those described in v. 7 is probably intended, and though "factiousness" does not create such a contrast, "selfishness" does. Those who receive eternal life are those who seek "the things above" (cf. Col. 3:1); those who receive wrath are those who seek only their own immediate gain. Cf. especially Büchsel, ibid.

15. The asyndeton (lack of conjunction or particle to connect v. 9 with v. 8) contributes to the sense of repetition and new beginning.

16. Cf. 5:3; 8:35; 12:12 in Romans; the Greek word is θλῖψις.

chatological condemnation (cf. 2 Thess. 1:6). "Distress," though close in meaning to "tribulation," may focus on the (subjective) suffering caused by the (objective) tribulation.[17] As eternal life was the reward for those who persisted in "good work" (v. 7), so this distress of divine judgment will[18] come "upon every soul of a person who does[19] evil."[20] In using the phrase "every soul of a person," Paul apparently wants to emphasize again the utter impartiality of God's judgment. And, once again, this point is directed particularly to the Jew, as the last phrase of the verse — "for the Jew first and then for the Greek" — indicates. In an ironic twist, Paul uses the same phrase that maintained the priority of the Jew as the recipient of the good news of salvation (1:16) to assert the same priority in judgment. As the word of the promise has gone "first" to the Jew, so does punishment for failure to respond to that word go "first" to the Jew. In contrast to the Jews' tendency to regard their election as a guarantee that they would be "first" in salvation and "last" in judgment, Paul insists that their priority be applied equally to both.

Verse 10 repeats the substance of v. 7, with only minor changes. "Glory and honor," which in v. 7 denoted the goal pursued by the righteous, now denote the blessing of God's salvation. And Paul adds a further term to describe this blessing, "peace," the state of perfect well-being created by God's eschatological intervention and enjoyed by the righteous.[21] And, more simply than in v. 7, Paul describes those who inherit these blessings as "everyone who does[22] good." But he also continues the theme of v. 9 with his addition of the phrase "for the Jew first and then for the Greek."

We now must ask who it is that Paul has in mind in vv. 7 and 10, where he promises salvation to those who engage in persistent "doing good." The question is an important one because these promises would seem at first sight to conflict with Paul's insistence elsewhere that "no one will be justified by works of the law" (cf. 3:20). Answers to this question can be

---

17. Godet; Cranfield; Wilckens. The Greek term is στενοχωρία. It is used with θλῖψις in more than half its LXX occurrences and in three of its four NT occurrences (8:35; 2 Cor. 6:4; cf. also 2 Cor. 12:10). Some scholars therefore think the two are synonymous (e.g., G. Bertram, *TDNT* VII, 607).

18. As in v. 8, ἔσται must be supplied.

19. The articular construction (τοῦ κατεργαζομένου) modifying an anarthrous noun (ἀνθρώπου) is a feature of Hellenistic Greek (Zerwick, 192).

20. The singular τὸ κακόν ("the evil thing") may not be generic but collective, matching "good work" in v. 7.

21. Gk. εἰρήνη, derived from Heb. שָׁלוֹם; cf. Isa. 43:7; Jer. 29:11; and the notes on 5:1.

22. Gk. τῷ ἐργαζομένῳ. The simple form of the verb here probably means the same thing as the compound form κατεργάζομαι in v. 9 (cf. 2 Cor. 7:10, where they are also used together).

divided into three categories, according to the identification of those who are doing good.

(1) Quite popular in the patristic period was the identification of these people with *faithful Jews and "moral" Gentiles* before the coming of Christ.[23]

(2) The majority of commentators have argued that Paul refers to *any non-Christian*. But within this interpretation, five approaches, differing in vital respects, are to be distinguished.

    (a) Some think that Paul sets out as a possibility the salvation of some people through their works apart from faith in Christ and that this principle stands in irreconcilable tension with his teaching of justification by faith alone.[24]

    (b) Others argue, similarly, that God rewards with eternal life those who respond obediently to "the light they have received" and that as long as the works are regarded as produced with the aid of God's grace no contradiction with Paul's teaching elsewhere is created.[25]

    (c) Another variation holds that those who earnestly seek eternal peace are granted the faith that brings justification and that this faith — the missing "middle term" in Paul's argument — is what brings eternal life.[26]

    (d) A few have viewed the principle as purely hypothetical, a statement of the way things would be if Christ had not come and the law could be fulfilled.[27]

    (e) Finally, others argue that the promise of eternal life for those who do good is fully valid, but that the power of sin prevents anyone from doing that good to the degree necessary to merit salvation. Verses 7 and 10 set out the condition, apart from Christ, for

---

23. E.g., Chrysostom.

24. H. Braun, *Gerichtsgedanke und Rechtfertigungslehre bei Paulus* (UNT 19; Leipzig: J. C. Hinrichs's, 1930), pp. 90-99; Räisänen, *Paul and the Law,* p. 107 ("a formidable tension"); Sanders, *Paul, the Law and the Jewish People,* pp. 123-35. R. Pregeant ("Grace and Recompense: Reflections on a Pauline Paradox," *JAAR* 47 [1979], 73-96) uses a "process hermeneutic" drawn from the logic of Whitehead to explain the tension.

25. Augustine, *On Grace* 7.17; K. Snodgrass, "Justification by Grace — to the Doers: An Analysis of the Place of Romans 2 in the Theology of Paul," *NTS* 32 (1986), 72-93.

26. Godet.

27. Lietzmann.

salvation; Paul's subsequent argument shows that no one is able to fulfill those conditions.[28]

(3) Growing in popularity is the view that Paul is thinking in these verses specifically of *Christians.* They, and only they, are those who, through union with Christ, are able to produce works acceptable to God in the judgment.[29]

We think that the choice lies between the last two of these alternatives. That Paul is considering only people before the coming of Christ (view 1) or that he considers them completely apart from the coming of Christ (view 2d) is unlikely because the revelation of God's wrath of which Paul is speaking is addressed clearly to Jews and Greeks in Paul's own day. Furthermore, the principle that all people, even Christians, will, in some sense, be judged by works is clearly taught in the NT and cannot be dismissed as a "pre-Christian" viewpoint. To adopt a view that creates a contradiction in Paul's teaching (view 2a) is a last resort and one that is unnecessary in the present instance. If they are to harmonize Paul, those who claim that Paul teaches a salvation based on obedience to the light each person has received (view 2b) must argue that Paul does not exclude *all* works from having the power to justify, but only "works of the law," understood in some sort of restricted sense (cf. 3:20, 28), and that Paul does not regard everyone who has not been justified by faith as condemned. But these positions cannot be maintained. Paul's denial that "works of the law" can justify is meant to exclude all "works," *anything* that a person does, as a basis for salvation (see our comments on 3:20). And the verdicts of 3:19 ("the whole world is held accountable to God") and 3:23 ("*all* have sinned and fallen short of God's glory"), in relationship to 3:21-22, 24-26, show that only by receiving God's righteousness through faith can a person be saved. The suggestion that we should supply justifying faith as the middle term in the promise of vv. 7 and 10 (view 2c) overcomes this objection

28. Melanchthon; Hodge; Wilckens; Murray, 1.78-79(?); L. Mattern, *Das Verständnis des Gerichtes bei Paulus* (ATANT 47; Zürich: Zwingli, 1966), pp. 136-38; Longenecker, 116-22; G. B. Stevens, *The Pauline Theology: A Study of the Origin and Correlation of the Doctrinal Teachings of the Apostle Paul* (New York: Scribner's, 1892), pp. 179-82; G. Vos, "The Alleged Legalism in Paul's Doctrine of Justification," in *Redemptive History and Biblical Interpretation,* ed. R. B. Gaffin, Jr. (Phillipsburg, NJ: Presbyterian & Reformed, 1980 [rpt. from *Princeton Theological Review* 1 (1903)]), pp. 387-94; F. Thielman, *From Plight to Solution: A Jewish Framework to Understanding Paul's View of the Law in Galatians and Romans* (NovTSup 61; Leiden: Brill, 1989), pp. 92-96.

29. Althaus; Viard; Black; Cranfield; Travis, *Judgment of God,* pp. 58-64; Watson, 119-21; T. R. Schreiner, *The Law and Its Fulfillment: A Pauline Theology of Law* (Grand Rapids: Baker, 1993), pp. 179-204. Davies (*Faith and Obedience,* pp. 54-57) argues that the reference is to the righteous before the coming of Christ.

but implies more than the context allows. It suggests a relationship between human effort and God's grace that is at least questionably Pauline (cf. 4:1-8; 9:10-13).

Whether we regard these verses as describing Christians (view 3), or view them as setting forth the unrealizable condition for salvation apart from Christ (view 2e), consistency in Paul's teaching is maintained. For Paul teaches, in agreement with the OT and Judaism, that judgment will be based on works, for Christians as well as for non-Christians (cf. 2 Cor. 5:10 and the Excursus: The Law, Justification, and Judgment in Paul). Moreover, he upholds faithful obedience to God, or the law as a *theoretical* means of attaining justification (cf. 2:13; 7:10). But the context strongly suggests that Paul is not directly describing Christians in vv. 7 and 10. Paul's purpose in 2:6-11 is to establish the principle that God will judge every person on the same basis — by works, not by religious heritage or national identity. Paul's focus is on the standard of judgment.

It is a continual seeking after eternal rewards, accompanied by a persistent doing of what is good, that is the condition for a positive verdict at the judgment. Paul never denies the validity of this principle, but he goes on to show that no one meets the conditions necessary for this principle to become a reality. This is the conclusion to which Paul is driving throughout this part of Romans (cf. 3:9, 19-20). It is true, of course, that a person in Christ does meet these conditions as the fruit of faith comes to expression in his life; and, while the principle in its context has the function of condemning all apart from Christ, Paul will show subsequently in Romans that it is, in fact, Christians who fulfill these conditions.[30] This may be right, but there is reason to be hesitant; the works of the Christian that are valid in the judgment are the "fruit" of union with Christ and manifestations of God's grace. But the stress in v. 6 on man's works as *the* criterion in the determination of a person's salvation or condemnation makes it difficult to fit grace into the situation at all (see the final paragraph in this section).

We think, therefore, that vv. 7 and 10 set forth what is called in traditional theological (especially Lutheran) language "the law." Paul sets forth the biblical conditions for attaining eternal life apart from Christ. Understood this way, Paul is not speaking hypothetically. But once his doctrine of universal human powerlessness under sin has been developed (cf. 3:9 especially), it becomes clear that the promise can, in fact, never become operative because the condition for its fulfillment — consistent, earnest seeking after good — can never be realized.

11 With this verse, Paul returns to the main theme of the paragraph. The principle that God treats all people equally in the judgment has been

30. Cf., e.g., Dunn.

made positively, with respect to the criterion of judgment, in v. 6. Now Paul makes the same point negatively, by claiming that "there is no partiality[31] with God."

This paragraph raises the question about the relationship between justification and judgment — an intricate theological topic. On the one hand, it is vital that the finality and determinacy of justification not be mitigated[32] and that salvation, from first to last, be ascribed to God's grace.[33] Paul believed that justification, in this life, was perfectly sufficient for deliverance from wrath at the judgment (cf. 5:9-10; 8:28-39). On the other hand, we cannot ignore the serious warnings addressed *to Christians* about the importance that their works will have at the final judgment (cf. 1 Cor. 3:10-14; 2 Cor. 5:10; Jas. 2:14-26; cf. Matt. 12:37; 25:31-46). Some seek to reconcile these by attributing different purposes to the initial "judgment" of justification and the final judgment,[34] others by attributing the two strands of teaching to different audiences or different purposes;[35] but none of these is completely convincing. Without becoming involved in the intricacies of theological nuance (and they are important here), we would follow those who maintain that the justification by faith granted the believer in this life is the sufficient cause of those works that God takes into account at the time of the judgment. The initial declaration of the believer's acquittal before the bar of heaven at the time of one's justification is infallibly confirmed by the judgment according to works at the last assize.

---

31. Gk. προσωπολημψία. This word and its cognates are used only in Christian literature: this word also in Eph. 6:9; Col. 3:25; Jas. 2:1; προσωπολημτέω, "treat with partiality," in Jas. 2:9; προσωπολήμπτης, "one who shows partiality," in Acts 10:34 (it might be, however, that the occurrence of the term in *T. Job* 4:8, 11 is an exception). It is possible that the word was coined by Christians. It is derived from the LXX πρόσωπον λαμβάνειν, "receive the face," which was used to translate the Hebrew phrase for partiality. However, although the word may have been new, the concept was not. As we have noted, Paul is here asserting a principle about God that was widely taught in the OT and Judaism (note Sir. 35:12: "for the Lord is the judge, and there is 'no glory of the face' with him"; cf. also *T. Job* 4:8; 43:13; see the thorough survey of the OT and Jewish teaching in Bassler, *Divine Impartiality,* pp. 7-119).

32. This is the tendency in the formulation of K. P. Donfried, "Justification and Last Judgment in Paul," *ZNW* 67 (1976), 90-110; cf. the attempt to "soften" Donfried's distinction between justification and judgment by Byrne ("Living Out the Righteousness of God," pp. 577-79) and Wilckens's salutary caution (1.143).

33. Contra, e.g., Watson, 120, who argues that Paul's stress on the judgment of Christians' works shows that Paul did not teach that salvation was by grace alone.

34. Cf. Mohrlang, *Matthew and Paul,* pp. 58-60.

35. E.g., Joest, *Gesetz und Freiheit,* pp. 170-88; N. M. Watson, "Justified by Faith, Judged by Works — An Antinomy?" *NTS* 29 (1983), 209-21.

iii. Judgment and the Law (2:12-16)

12*For as many as sin without the law will also perish without the law. And as many as sin in the law will be judged through the law. 13For it is not the hearers of the law who are just before God, but it is the doers of the law who will be justified. 14For whenever the Gentiles who do not have the law do by nature the things of the law, they are a law to themselves, even though they do not have the law. 15They show that the work of the law is written on their hearts, their conscience bearing witness and their thoughts among themselves both accusing and excusing them; 16on that day when God, through Christ Jesus,[1] will judge the secret things of people, according to my gospel.*

Some interpreters think that this paragraph belongs with what follows, 2:17-29, rather than with what precedes, 2:1-11. They note that Paul first introduces in this paragraph the topic of the law and that this topic continues to be important in the subsequent verses. Furthermore, Paul's purpose in vv. 12-16 appears to be similar to his concern in 2:25-29: to deny that the Jews can find refuge from God's judgment simply by virtue of possessing covenant "markers" — whether it be the law or circumcision.[2] These points have some force, but the connections with 2:1-11 are also very close. For Paul is continuing in vv. 12-16 to treat the standard of God's judgment and to defend its impartial application to both Jew and Gentile. Verse 16, indeed, with its reference to the last judgment, forms an inclusio with the focus on judgment in vv. 1-5. While recognizing that the paragraph has connections in both directions, therefore, we prefer to attach it to 2:1-11.[3]

The "for"[4] that introduces this paragraph connects it specifically with the principle of God's impartial judgment stated in v. 11. In these verses Paul defends the equality of all people before God's judgment seat against the charge that the Jews' possession of the law gives to them a decisive

---

1. Instead of the order Χριστοῦ Ἰησοῦ (read in the two key Alexandrian MSS, ℵ [original hand] and B, as well as in the later Alexandrian minuscule 81), many MSS have the order Ἰησοῦ Χριστοῦ (the first corrector of ℵ, the secondary Alexandrian MSS A, 33, and 1739, the uncial Ψ, and the majority text), while the western uncial D has Ἰησοῦ Χριστοῦ τοῦ κυρίου ἡμῶν ("Jesus Christ our Lord"). This last reading is clearly a secondary expansion; and Pauline style favors the order Χριστοῦ Ἰησοῦ in this kind of context (see the note on 1:1).

2. Cf. Schmithals, 90. Many commentators (e.g., Käsemann, 61-62; Wilckens, 1.131-32; Dunn, 1.94-95; Schlier, 76; Fitzmyer, 305) treat vv. 12-16 as a separate paragraph, parallel to 2:1-11.

3. Godet, 121; Murray, 1.68-69; cf. Cranfield, 1.153.

4. Gk. γάρ.

advantage.[5] This is not the case, Paul argues, because (1) it is doing, not hearing or possessing, the law that matters (v. 13); and (2) even the Gentiles, who do not have God's law in written form, are not without "law" (vv. 14-15). The law, then, gives to the Jews no true advantage when it comes to salvation.

12 The division of the world into those who sin "without the law" and those who sin "in the law"[6] corresponds to the distinction between Jews and Gentiles (cf. vv. 10, 14). This means that the "law" in question is the law of Moses, the body of commandments given by God through Moses to the people of Israel at Mt. Sinai. Modern scholars often use the transliterated Hebrew word "torah" to denote this law, in an effort to make clear the distinctly Jewish, salvation-historical nature of the law that Paul is talking about. While we will maintain the more traditional term "law" it will be important to keep in mind that, for Paul the converted Jew, "law" refers, unless other qualifications are present, to this specific, historical, body of commandments that functioned, more than anything else, to give Israel its particular identity as a "people apart."[7] Therefore, Paul is not here accusing

---

5. As C. H. Giblin (*In Hope of God's Glory: Pauline Theological Perspectives* [New York: Herder and Herder, 1970], pp. 339-40) points out, the impartiality of God's judgment entails a universal norm by which works can be judged.

6. "Without the law" translates the Greek adverb ἀνόμως, while "in the law" translates ἐν νόμῳ.

7. Paul's use of νόμος is decisively influenced by the OT/Jewish use of תּוֹרָה, which is usually translated by νόμος in the LXX. Although some have suggested that this translation introduced a harder, more legalistic conception than is fair to the Hebrew word (e.g., S. Schechter, *Aspects of Rabbinic Theology* [New York: Schocken, 1961 {original edition, 1909}], pp. 117-19; C. H. Dodd, "The Law," in *The Bible and the Greeks* [London: Hodder & Stoughton, 1935], pp. 25-41), νόμος is a fair equivalent for תּוֹרָה in its usual OT meaning — the body of commands, with sanctions, given through Moses at Sinai (cf. esp. S. Westerholm, "*Torah, nomos,* and law: A Question of 'Meaning'," *SR* 15 [1986], 327-36). That Paul uses νόμος in this way is clear from his own writings. Particularly significant are Gal. 3, where Paul claims that the law "came four hundred thirty years after Abraham" (v. 17; cf. also Rom. 5:13-14, 20), and Rom. 2:12; 3:19; 1 Cor. 9:20-21, where the difference between having νόμος and not having it is the difference between Jew and Gentile. More than 90 percent of the occurrences of νόμος in Paul refer to the Mosaic law.

This is not to preclude, however, the possibility that Paul might use νόμος with other meanings or referents. Because the Mosaic law was, for the Jews, the heart of the OT, Paul can use νόμος to designate the Pentateuch, or the OT as a whole (cf. Rom. 3:19a; 1 Cor. 9:8, 9; 14:21, 34; Gal. 4:21b). In other passages, νόμος, by synecdoche, designates the Mosaic covenant, or the "law-administration" of the OT (Rom. 3:21a; 6:14-15; 7:4, 6[?]). In another extension from its reference to the Mosaic law, it can designate divine "law" generally (Rom. 2:14; 8:7[?]) or the "Christian" form of God's law (Gal. 6:2 and cf. ἔννομος Χριστοῦ in 1 Cor. 9:21). More debated is the question whether Paul ever uses νόμος without direct reference to "law" of some kind. Yet there is ample warrant in Hellenistic Greek for using the term to mean

the Gentiles of being "lawless" (that is, notorious criminals or outlaws)[8] but of being "law-less" — by definition, as Gentiles, they do not possess the law of Moses. They are "alienated from the commonwealth of Israel, strangers to the covenants of promise" (Eph. 2:12).[9] In contrast, then, Jews live "in the sphere of," within the boundaries defined by, the law.[10] From the Jewish point of view, of course, this difference in possession of God's law is absolutely basic. The Gentile, so most Jews maintained, could experience God's favor only by taking on "the yoke of the law." Outside Israel, the sphere of the law, there is no salvation. The Jews who live within the domain of law, on the other hand, often considered themselves virtually assured of salvation.

Paul relativizes this difference between Jew and Gentile by arguing, in two parallel sentences, that "as many as[11] sin[12] without the law will also perish[13] without the law" and "as many as sin in the law will be judged through the law." The parallelism between the sentences and the contrast with "justify" in v. 13 show that "will be judged" in the second sentence must denote the negative verdict of condemnation.[14] Verse 23 of chap. 3 — "all have sinned" — shows

---

"principle," "norm," or "force" (see the notes on 3:27), and several of Paul's uses fit best here (Rom. 3:27; 7:21, 23[?], 25[?]; 8:2). Even in these cases, however, this general use of νόμος usually involves a rhetorical play on words with the term as used of the Mosaic law. (See also M. Winger, *By What Law? The Meaning of* Νόμος *in the Letters of Paul* [Atlanta: Scholars Press, 1992], who uses linguistic criteria to analyze Paul's use of the word. Particularly important is his conclusion that Paul closely correlates "law" and "people.")

Scholars from the time of Origen have attempted to distinguish the meanings of νόμος on the basis of the presence or absence of the article (e.g., S-H in the present text; cf. also Gifford; Stevens, *The Pauline Theology,* pp. 160-62), but these attempts have been unsuccessful. Paul does not generally use articular νόμος to mean anything different from anarthrous νόμος (see E. Grafe, *Die paulinische Lehre vom Gesetz nach den vier Haupt-briefen* [Freiburg and Tübingen: Mohr, 1884], pp. 5-8; Longenecker, 118-19). On this whole issue, see particularly my " 'Law,' 'Works of the Law,' and Legalism."

8. This is what ἄνομος means in Luke 22:37; Acts 2:23; 2 Thess. 2:8; 1 Tim. 1:9; 2 Pet. 2:8.

9. Cf. Paul's use of ἄνομος in 1 Cor. 9:21.

10. The ἐν in the phrase is locative.

11. Gk. ὅσοι.

12. The verb in both sentences is ἥμαρτον, with the aorist tense connoting "in-definite past" action (English generally uses the perfect tense for this kind of action). See Burton, 54. Porter (*Verbal Aspect,* p. 237) prefers to think of them as "timeless aorists."

13. Gk. ἀπολοῦνται, a middle form of ἀπόλλυμι, "destroy." The Scriptures frequently use this verb to depict the results of a negative verdict in the eschatological judgment (e.g., Pss. 9:5; 37:20; 1 Cor. 1:18, 19; 8:11; 15:18; 2 Cor. 2:15; 4:3; 2 Thess. 2:10). The metaphorical nature of the term precludes any conclusion about the final state of those who are so judged (e.g., one cannot build a case for "annihilationism" from this term).

14. The verb in the second sentence is κρίνω; it is used in this sense also in 3:7; John 3:17; Acts 7:7; 2 Thess. 2:12; Heb. 10:30; 13:4; Jas. 5:9; 1 Pet. 4:6 (cf. BAGD). No distinction in meaning between ἀπόλλυμι and κρίνω is to be made in this verse (contra Godet).

that Paul would exempt no one from the verdict he here imposes. It is clear from these verses that Paul argues for universal human sinfulness, and a sinfulness of such a nature that condemnation must be the outcome.

13 Paul explains why[15] even those who possess the law will nevertheless be condemned when they sin. It is because the law can justify only when it is obeyed; reading it, hearing it taught and preached, studying it — none of these, nor all of them together, can justify. This is the first time in Romans that Paul uses the verb "justify." As scholars now generally agree, it connotes the judicial decision of God to regard a sinner as "just" or "right" or "innocent" before him.[16] God's abhorrence of any hearing of the law without doing it is a very customary Jewish teaching: for example, "Not the expounding [of the law] is the chief thing, but the doing [of it]."[17] The NT embraces the principle as well (cf. Matt. 7:24-27; 12:50; Jas. 1:22-25). Whereas the principle in these examples has a hortatory purpose — to encourage obedience to the law or to the Word of God — Paul uses the principle to remind Jews of the standard of God's judgment. Only those who are "*doers* of the law" will be declared right in the judgment.

The question arises here again (as in vv. 7 and 10): Who are those whom Paul views as vindicated in the judgment by their doing of the law? Again, many interpreters think that Paul refers implicitly to Christians in whom, Paul says later in Romans, "the just decree of the law is fulfilled" (8:4).[18] The "doing of the law" spoken of here would then have to designate a faith-oriented obedience to God.[19] But, as we argued in our comments on v. 10, it would be surprising for Paul to connect vindication in the judgment so closely to the doing of the law. "Doers of the law" are no more and no less than those who "do the works of the law"; and "works of the law," Paul claims, cannot justify (cf. 3:20, 28). To be sure, there is NT precedent for applying the term "justify" *(dikaioō)* to vindication at the final judgment;[20] and Paul might then be thinking here not of the entry into salvation but of the ultimate vindication at the last judgment. However, Paul does not generally use "justify" in this restricted sense;[21] and the context here suggests that he

---

15. Note the γάρ.

16. For further discussion of δικαιόω ("justify") and its cognates, see the Excursus after 1:17.

17. *m. 'Abot* 1.17. Many more examples can be found in Str-B, 3.84-88.

18. J.-M. Cambier, "Le jugement de tous les hommes par Dieu seul, selon la verité, dans Rom 2:1–3:20," *ZNW* 67 (1976), 197-98; Godet; Cranfield; Watson, 119-21.

19. Cf. Dunn.

20. Cf. Jas. 2:20-26; and my *James,* pp. 107-10.

21. See, e.g., O'Brien, "Justification in Paul," pp. 90-95. Of course, Paul affirms that Christians must stand before God on the day of judgment (e.g., 2 Cor. 5:10). But he uses terms other than "justify" to denote this event; and the works that are taken into account in that judgment are the product of justifying faith and not the basis for justification itself.

uses it in his customary manner to denote the decisive salvific event in its broadest sense. As in vv. 7 and 10, therefore, we think it more likely that Paul is here simply setting forth the standard by which God's justifying verdict will be rendered.[22] This verse confirms and explains the reason for the Jews' condemnation in v. 12b; and this suggests that its purpose is not to show how people can be justified but to set forth the standard that must be met if a person is to be justified. As he does throughout this chapter, Paul presses typical Jewish teaching into the service of his "preparation for the gospel." Jews believed that "doing" the law, or perhaps the intent to do the law, would lead, for the Jew already in covenant relationship with God, to final salvation. Paul affirms the principle that doing the law can lead to salvation; but he denies (1) that anyone can so "do" the law;[23] and (2) that Jews can depend on their covenant relationship to shield them from the consequences of this failure.

14 Verses 14-15 are a self-contained unit, linked to the preceding verses with a "for."[24] The nature of this connection depends on the identity of the "Gentiles" who are the subjects of these verses. From earliest times, three basic alternatives have been proposed:[25] (1) Gentiles who fulfill the law and are saved apart from explicit faith in Christ;[26] (2) Gentiles who do some part of the law but who are not saved;[27] (3) Gentile Christians who fulfill the

---

22. Cf. also Barrett; Murray; Wilckens.

23. As Calvin paraphrases, "If righteousness be sought from the law, the law must be fulfilled; for the righteousness of the law consists in the perfection of works."

24. Gk. γάρ.

25. See the surveys of the history of interpretation in Riedl, *Das Heil des Heiden,* pp. 7-172 (cf. also Riedl, "Die Auslegung von R 2,14-16 in Vergangenheit und Gegenwart," *SPCIC,* 1.271-81) and Lachmann, *Vom Geheimnis,* pp. 95-140.

26. Usually this salvation was seen as contingent on God's work of grace apart from special revelation, although Pelagius (cf. Schelkle) attributed this power to natural ability, stressing φύσει; cf., for the majority view, Chrysostom; Gore; Amiot, *Key Concepts,* p. 72; Riedl, *Das Heil des Heiden,* pp. 202-24; Snodgrass, "Justification by Grace," pp. 72-93; X. Jacques, "La conscience et le Christ: Lettre aux Romains 2,14-16.26-29," *Christus* 28 (1981), 414-21; Davies, *Faith and Obedience,* pp. 61-67.

27. Melanchthon; Calvin; Haldane; Hodge; Leenhardt; Kuss; Murray; Käsemann; Wilckens; Fitzmyer; Bassler, *Divine Impartiality,* pp. 141-45; F. Kuhr, "Römer 2[14f.] und die Verheissung bei Jeremias 31[31ff.]," *ZNW* 55 (1964), 243-61; G. Bornkamm, "Gesetz und Natur (Röm 2:14-16)," in *Studie zu Antike und Urchristentum. Gesammelte Aufsätze, Band II* (Munich: Kaiser, 1963), p. 110; T. Schreiner, "Did Paul Believe in Justification by Works? Another Look at Romans 2," *Bulletin for Biblical Research* 3 (1993), 131-58. Luther's view of these verses is not clear, but he seems to conclude in favor of this view (see the scholium on 2:14 and L. Grane, "Luther's Auslegung von Röm 2,12-15 in der Römerbriefvorlesung," *Neue Zeitschrift für systematische Theologie und Religionsphilosophie* 17 [1975], 22-32).

law by virtue of their relationship to Christ.[28] As in the related vv. 7, 10, and 13, we think the second alternative is best. Our reasons for this conclusion will emerge as we analyze the details of the verses.

Those who think that the Gentiles to whom Paul alludes are Christians generally connect vv. 14-15 with v. 13: Paul now explains that Gentiles, like Jews, can be "doers of the law" and hence justified.[29] If, as we think, the Gentiles are unbelievers, these verses are best taken as an explanation and qualification of the phrase "without the law" that Paul has used in v. 12a. Gentiles are, indeed, "without the law" when one is thinking from the typical Jewish perspective of the law as the law of Moses. But to say that non-Christian Gentiles are "without *the* law" is one thing; to say they are "without law" is another. For Gentiles certainly have some knowledge of God's moral demands — "law" in the generic sense. And when God condemns them, he does not do so without their having any understanding of his demands upon them.[30] On this view, Paul is speaking not of all Gentiles nor of only a very small number of Gentiles, but, generically, of Gentiles *qua* Gentiles. And some of these Gentiles, Paul alleges, "do by nature the things of the law."[31] Some commentators think that "by nature" modifies "Gentiles who do not have the law" and so think that Paul is distinguishing between Gentiles before and after Christ. Before Christ, Gentiles, "by reason of their birth," do not have the law; but after conversion, through the ministry of the Holy Spirit, they *do* have the law.[32] But taking "by nature" with the verb "do" makes better sense (as do all major English translations).[33] For

28. Augustine, *Spirit and Letter* 26.43-45 (*NPNF* 5.101-4); Viard; Cranfield; Barth, *Shorter;* P. Feine, *Das gesetzesfreie Evangelium des Paulus* (Leipzig: J. C. Hinrichs, 1899), pp. 113-29; F. Flückiger, "Die Werke des Gesetzes bei den Heiden (nach Röm 2,14ff.)," *TZ* 8 (1952), 17-42; W. Mundle, "Zur Auslegung von Röm 2,13ff," *TBl* 13 (1934), 249-56; Souček, "Röm. 2,14ff," pp. 99-113; Minear, 51; Watson, 117-21.

29. E.g., Riedl, *Das Heil des Heiden,* p. 199; Cranfield.

30. See Haldane; Hodge; Murray; Käsemann; R. Walker, "Die Heiden und das Gericht. Zur Auslegung von Röm 2,12-16," *EvT* 20 (1960), 304; Bornkamm, "Gesetz und Natur," p. 100.

31. The construction is indefinite. Paul is not asserting that all, or most, Gentiles do the law (contra Walker, "Die Heiden und das Gericht," p. 304); nor does he claim that only a few exceptional Gentiles do (contra Gifford; Zahn). The number who may do so is simply left open (cf. Käsemann; Laato, *Paulus und das Judentum,* pp. 100-104).

32. See esp. Cranfield; and P. J. Achtemeier, " 'Some Things in Them Hard to Understand.' Reflections on an Approach to Paul," *Int* 38 (1984), 255-59; Flückiger, "Die Werke des Gesetzes," p. 32. Augustine's interpretation, that "by nature" refers to the new nature of Christians (*Against Jul.* 4.3.25) has no basis in Pauline usage (cf. Kuhr, "Römer 2¹⁴," p. 255).

33. The debated term is φύσει. Its placement between τὰ μὴ νόμον ἔχοντα and τὰ τοῦ νόμου ποιῶσιν provides no help in determining which of the two phrases it should be taken with. Cranfield uses in support of taking the word with the former clause Paul's use of the word with reference to what a person is by birth (cf. 2:27; Gal. 2:15; Eph. 2:3). But this could argue equally well for the opposite interpretation.

Paul is almost certainly pressing into service a widespread Greek tradition to the effect that all human beings possess an "unwritten" or "natural" law — an innate moral sense of "right and wrong."[34] Paul is "baptizing" this popular Greek conception, one that had already been taken over by Hellenistic Jews for the purpose of rendering Gentiles responsible for basic moral standards.[35] What Paul is then asserting is that certain Gentiles "do the things of the law" through a natural, inborn capacity; cf. NJB: "through their own innate sense." On this view of the text, it is very unlikely that Paul has in view Gentile Christians, for they, of course, do the law not "by nature" but "by grace."[36] "The things of the law" is a general way of stating certain of those requirements of the Mosaic law that God has made universally available to human beings in their very constitution.[37] Paul's point is that Gentiles outside of Christ regularly obey their parents, refrain from murder and robbery, and so on.[38]

Paul goes on to claim that those who do these things reveal the exis-

---

34. See, e.g., Godet; Dunn; Cambier, "Le jugement," p. 200. Among the Greeks, the "natural law," or "unwritten law" (νόμος ἀγράφος), was set forth as the basis and norm of the legal and social order, thereby providing for the possibility of universal standards. The Stoics rooted this law in nature (φύσις). Hellenistic Jews, like Philo, used the concept to demonstrate the universal applicability of the Mosaic "moral" standards. Philo says, "All right reason is an infallible law engraved not by this mortal or that, and thus perishable, nor on lifeless parchment or slabs, and therefore soulless as they, but by immortal nature on the immortal mind, never to perish" (*Every Good Man* 46; see also *Special Laws* 1.36-54; *Abraham* 276; cf. H. Köster, *TDNT* IX. 267-69); natural law was adopted also in Palestinian Judaism, particularly as an explanation for how the patriarchs could obey the law (cf. *2 Apoc. Bar.* 57.2; cf. I. Heinemann, "Die Lehre vom ungeschriebenen Gesetz im jüdischen Schriftum," *HUCA* 4 [1927], 149-71). Verses 14-15 clearly draw on this tradition, with several linguistic similarities, but apply it, in contrast to Greek sources, in a purely negative way. See, on the whole matter, esp. Bornkamm, "Gesetz und Natur," pp. 101-17.

35. Paul does not, however, take over the philosophical baggage that accompanied the conception. He uses the language (e.g., φύσις) in an untechnical way (Nygren; Käsemann; Ridderbos, *Paul,* p. 106; H.-J. Eckstein, *Der Begriff Syneidesis bei Paulus. Eine neutestamentlich-exegetische Untersuchung zum 'Gewissensbegriff'* [WUNT 2.10; Tübingen: Mohr, 1983], pp. 150-51).

36. See Kuhr, "Römer 2¹⁴," pp. 255-57. If Paul had had Gentile Christians in view, we would also have expected him to speak of their "fulfilling" (cf. 8:4) rather than their "doing" the law.

37. Contra, e.g., Barrett, who thinks the reference is to "believing obedience," a concept better indicated with the singular τὸν τοῦ νόμου.

38. See Zahn; Murray; Kuss; Käsemann; Bassler, *Divine Impartiality,* pp. 145-46. Paul is therefore clearly thinking here mainly of what has traditionally been called the "moral" dimensions of the law (cf. Riedl, *Das Heil des Heiden,* p. 200). Paul may also owe his conception to the Jewish notion of the "Noahic commandments," according to which God gave to Noah for all human beings certain basic moral requirements (see, e.g., Segal, *Paul the Convert,* pp. 194-201).

tence of that law and are "a law to themselves."[39] By this, Paul does not mean that these people need nothing to guide them[40] but that they attest knowledge of divine moral standards. Here, we think, Paul clearly uses the term *nomos* in an extended sense, to denote the "demand of God" generally.[41] These Gentiles, while not possessing *the* law of Moses, nevertheless have access to knowledge of God's will for them. By applying to Gentiles a term reserved in this context for Jews ("law"), Paul pursues his policy of putting Jews and Gentiles on the same footing.[42] The Jew does not have in the law a decisive advantage when it comes to knowing and doing the will of God, Paul suggests; for Gentiles have some of the same benefits.

15 Paul continues to speak of those Gentiles who manifest in their behavior an innate awareness of God's moral demands. In contrast to the often positive use of the "unwritten law" tradition among the Greeks, Paul follows Jewish writers in using the concept negatively: knowledge of God's moral demands among the Gentiles simply demonstrates their guilt.[43] The standpoint of the last judgment in v. 16 is sometimes read into the present tense verb "show,"[44] so that it, too, refers to a demonstration before the bar of God.[45] But, although the implicit testimony of the works of Gentiles reaches its climax in the judgment, Paul's focus in this verse is still on the implications of these works in this life. "The work of the law" written on the heart of the Gentiles could refer to love, the basic intention of the law (cf. 13:8-10),[46] or to the "effect" that the law produces,[47] but it is probably no more than a "collective" variant of "the things of the law" in v. 14: the "work," the conduct, that the law demands.[48]

In saying that this work of the law has been "written on their hearts,"[49] Paul might be alluding to the "new covenant" prophecy of Jer. 31:31-34,

---

39. Gk. ἑαυτοῖς εἰσιν νόμος. The dative may be dative of advantage ("for themselves") or possessive (cf. NEB: "their own law").

40. Aristotle uses language that some have found parallel to Paul's conception here (e.g., *Ethics* 4.14; *Pol.* 3.13; cf. H. Kleinknecht, *TDNT* IV, 1032). But the parallel is not close, for Aristotle is referring to the superior person for whom laws are both inappropriate and unnecessary.

41. Although some interpreters think that νόμος refers to the Mosaic law throughout this paragraph (e.g., Walker, "Die Heiden und das Gericht," pp. 308-9; Ridderbos, *Paul,* p. 106; Räisänen, 25-26).

42. J. Fitzmyer, "Paul and the Law," in *To Advance the Gospel: New Testament Studies* (rpt.; New York: Crossroad, 1981), pp. 186-87.

43. Cf. Pohlenz, "Paulus und die Stoa," pp. 71-77.

44. Gk. ἐνδείκνυνται.

45. E.g., Wilckens.

46. E.g., Michel.

47. On this view, τοῦ νόμου is a subjective genitive; cf. Barrett.

48. Käsemann; Wilckens; Deidun, 165.

49. Gk. γραπτὸν ἐν ταῖς καρδίαις.

which promises that God will "write his law" on the hearts of his people. Advocates of the view that finds Gentile Christians in these verses naturally use this as support for their interpretation.[50] But Jeremiah speaks about the *law's* being written on the heart and the complete knowledge of God that will result from it. Paul, however, makes reference to the "*work* of the law" being written on the heart and makes clear that this process still leaves the issue of final judgment in doubt (vv. 15b-16).[51] As Luther puts it, "the knowledge of the work is written, that is, the law that is written in letters concerning the works that have to be done, but not the grace to fulfill this law."

Some of the results of the Gentiles' knowledge of God's demand are spelled out in the last part of the verse: "their conscience bearing witness and their thoughts both accusing and excusing them."[52] The word "conscience" comes from the Greek rather than from the biblical world.[53] The word had an important technical role in Stoic philosophy, but Paul's conception does not go beyond the more popular usage.[54] The conscience could be the source of moral norms (as in our popular use of the term), but it is usually viewed as a reflective mechanism by which people can measure their conformity to a norm.[55] If, then, the "law" is that norm, the conscience of individual Gentiles reveals within each

50. Cf., e.g., Viard; Cranfield.

51. Calvin; Michel; Murray; Wilckens; Kuhr, "Römer 2¹⁴," pp. 259-60.

52. The syntax of the end of v. 15 is complex. The first participle, συμμαρτυρούσης, is a genitive absolute, with τῆς συνειδήσεως as its subject. The second and third participles, κατηγορούντων ("accusing") and ἀπολογουμένων ("excusing"), are bound closely to one another with ἢ καί ("or even") and together form a second genitive absolute construction. But the relationship of these last two participles to the first one is not clear. They could be a loose addition to συμμαρτυρούσης, in which case τῶν λογισμῶν ("the thoughts") might go with συνειδήσεως as the subject of συμμαρτουρούσης: "their conscience and their thoughts, which accuse or perhaps excuse, bearing witness" (Eckstein, *Syneidesis,* pp. 164-66). B. Reicke takes τῶν λογισμῶν as the object of συνειδήσεως, which he translates "Gefühl," "consciousness" ("Syneidesis in Röm. 2,15," *TZ* 12 [1956], 157-61). But it is more straightforward to take τῶν λογισμῶν as the subject of the last two participles, resulting in two coordinate genitive absolute constructions: "their conscience bearing witness and their thoughts accusing or perhaps excusing" (Godet; Jewett, *Paul's Anthropological Terms,* pp. 442-43).

53. It occurs in the LXX only in Ecclus. 10:20; Sir. 42:18 [although there is a v.l.]; Wis. 17:11; cf. also *T. Reub.* 4:3.

54. Cf. esp. C. A. Pierce, *Conscience in the New Testament* (SBT 15; London: SCM, 1955), pp. 10-22; Eckstein, *Syneidesis,* pp. 50-66. Paul uses the word elsewhere in Rom. 9:1; 13:5; 1 Cor. 8:7, 10, 12; 10:25, 27, 28, 29 (twice); 2 Cor. 1:12; 4:2; 5:11; 1 Tim. 1:5, 19; 3:9; 4:2; 2 Tim. 1:3; Tit. 1:15.

55. Pierce, *Conscience,* argues that the "conscience" always has a retrospective and not a prospective function (cf. Eckstein, *Syneidesis,* pp. 170-79, 311-17). But his claim is too rigid; see, e.g., M. E. Thrall, "The Pauline Use of ΣΥΝΕΙΔΗΣΙΣ," *NTS* 14 (1967-68), 124. Her claim that "conscience" in this text has the same function among Gentiles that the law had among the Jews is not clear, however.

of them the extent to which that norm is being followed. Paul uses "bear witness"[56] of this process, and the meaning of "conscience" would imply that this "witness" is first of all to the individuals themselves. In the light of v. 16, however, there may be a secondary reference to a witness before the heavenly judgment seat. The clause "their thoughts among themselves[57] both accusing and excusing them" might add a second, independent idea to the witness of the conscience,[58] but it probably expands it: the witness of the conscience consists in the mixed verdict of one's thoughts.[59]

This debate among the thoughts goes on constantly, but its ultimate significance will be revealed in the last judgment, as v. 16 shows.[60] The excusing and accusing testimony of the thoughts within each person's conscience portends the verdict of the one who will bring every thought to light. Some have seized on the reference to "excusing" as evidence that this final verdict could bring salvation to some Gentiles apart from the gospel. But this misses the connection in which the idea stands. Bengel is on the mark: "The concessive particle, *even,* shows that the thoughts have far more to accuse, than defend, and the defense itself . . . does not extend to the whole, but only to a part of the conduct, and this very part in turn proves us to be debtors as to the whole. . . ."

16 Some scholars consider the relationship between v. 16 and the preceding context so awkward that they eliminate the verse as a later, post-Pauline addition.[61] Once this unwarranted and textually unsupported expedient

---

56. The Greek verb is συμμαρτυρέω. It is not clear whether the prepositional prefix should be pressed, so that Paul designates the conscience as witnessing "along with" either the law (e.g., Barrett) or one's thoughts (e.g., Wilckens). Cranfield, citing the parallel in Rom. 9:1, argues that the prefix does not have any "with" significance, and he is probably right (see also, e.g., Fitzmyer).

57. A further syntactical issue is the question of the referent of ἀλλήλων in the phrase μεταξὺ ἀλλήλων, "among themselves" (μεταξύ functions here as an improper preposition with the meaning "among" or "between"; cf. BAGD). If it is referring to αὐτῶν ("their"), the meaning is that people stand in judgment over one another (S-H; Meyer; Dubarle, *La manifestation naturelle de Dieu,* p. 229). But it is better to take it with λογισμῶν ("thoughts"), which immediately follows, the sense being that people's thoughts are engaged in a continual debate among themselves (Godet; Käsemann).

58. E.g., Dunn.

59. E.g., Cranfield. A few commentators have thought that, by citing the law, the conscience, and the thoughts, Paul might want to signal a fulfillment of the requirement of Deut. 19:15, "on the evidence of two or three witnesses a matter shall be confirmed" (Lietzmann; Wilckens; Watson, 116). But this is uncertain.

60. We can understand, then, why Paul uses words like ἀπολογέομαι and κατηγορέω, which connote the defense and prosecution that go on in the law court (for the former, cf. Luke 12:11; 21:14; Acts 19:33; 24:10; 25:8; 26:1, 2, 24; 2 Cor. 12:19; for the latter, *inter alia,* Matt. 27:12; Acts 22:30; Rev. 12:10).

61. R. Bultmann, "Glossen im Römerbrief," in *Exegetica* (Tübingen: Mohr, 1967), pp. 282-83; Bornkamm, "Gesetz und Natur," p. 117; Schmithals.

is eliminated, several alternatives remain, of which five deserve mention. (1) Verse 16 could depend directly on the verbs in v. 15 if the processes described there are considered to be future.[62] But we have seen good reason to attribute these activities to the circumstances of this life. (2) Verse 16 could depend directly on the verbs in v. 15 if v. 16 is taken noneschatologically as a reference to any "time" of judgment.[63] But Pauline usage shows that "the day when the secret thoughts are judged" must be the last assize. (3) A popular alternative has been to take v. 16 with v. 13: "doers of the law will be justified . . . on the day when. . . ."[64] But vv. 14-15 are too important to Paul's argument to be viewed as a parenthesis, and v. 16 is too far from v. 13 to think that a syntactical relationship exists. (4) Verse 16 could go loosely with the whole paragraph.[65] But this sounds too much like a counsel of despair and gives to the opening prepositional phrase an unlikely function. (5) The final possibility, and the one we think is correct, is to take v. 16 with the verbs of v. 15, in the sense that the continual self-criticism of the Gentiles (v. 15) also relates to, and finds its ultimate meaning in, the final judgment (v. 16).[66] As Käsemann points out, v. 16 is necessary to Paul's argument because his purpose, as we saw in v. 12, is to demonstrate the reality of the condemnation under which the Gentiles stand. As degree of conformity to the law is the criterion of judgment for Jews (vv. 12b-13), so the extent to which Gentiles have conformed to the "law" they possess will be the standard by which they are judged. Their conscience and thoughts reveal to them how well they have done, but in the judgment of God even the secret thoughts will be used as evidence.

That God's judgment will take into account not only outward actions but also the "hidden things"[67] is a natural inference from his knowledge of the secrets of people's hearts.[68] Jesus reminded his disciples that God's reward will be based on what is done "in secret."[69] In the present context, this shows particularly that the inner witness of the conscience and conflicting thoughts (v. 15) are known to God and destined to be revealed on the day of judgment.

62. Lietzmann; Wilckens.

63. Viard; Haacker, "Exegetische Probleme," pp. 7-9.

64. Cf. the NIV translation and, e.g., Godet; S-H; Riedl, *Das Heil des Heiden,* p. 205. Dodd and O'Neill suggest that vv. 14-15 may have been added by Paul to what was originally a Jewish sermon.

65. E.g., Murray; Kuss.

66. E.g., Bengel; Cranfield; Käsemann; Bassler, *Divine Impartiality,* p. 148; H. Saake, "Echtheitskritische Überlegungen zur Interpolationshypothese von Römer ii.16," *NTS* 19 (1972-73), 486-89.

67. Gk. τὰ κρυπτά.

68. Cf. 1 Sam. 16:7; Ps. 139:1-2; Jer. 17:10.

69. ἐν κρυπτῷ; Matt. 6:4, 6, 18.

The two prepositional phrases are not clear as to their connections and relationship. Some connect "according to my gospel" to "will judge" and take "through Christ Jesus" with "my gospel": "God will judge, according to my gospel, which is through Christ Jesus."[70] Others suggest a similar sequence, only with "according to my gospel" dependent particularly on the fact that God will judge the "secret things."[71] Finally, it is possible to take "through Christ Jesus" with "will judge," with "according to my gospel" dependent on the whole statement, and particularly on the reference to the christological element in the judgment: "It is through Christ Jesus that God will judge, as my gospel teaches."[72] This last alternative does most justice to the somewhat unexpected reference to the gospel. Paul teaches that it is before the "judgment seat of Christ" that we will have to stand (2 Cor. 5:10). When Paul refers to "my gospel," he does not mean a particular form of teaching peculiar to him, but the gospel, common to all Christians, which has been entrusted by God to Paul for his preservation and proclamation (cf. 1:1).[73]

Paul's assertion in v. 13 that "the doers of the law will be justified" raises two broad theological issues.

First, to what degree and in what sense does Paul regard the law as a means of justification? The view that God gave the law to Israel as a means of justification is now generally discredited, and rightly so. The OT presents the law as a means of regulating the covenant relationship that had already been established through God's grace. But, granted that the law was not given for the purpose of securing one's relationship before God, it may still be questioned whether it sets forth in theory a means of justification. We would argue that it does.[74] Verses such as Rom. 2:7, 10, 13, and 7:10 suggest that Paul agreed with the Jewish belief that justification could, in theory, be secured through works. Where Paul disagreed with Judaism was in his belief that the power of sin prevents any person, even the Jew who depends on his or her covenant status, from actually achieving justification in that manner.[75] While, therefore, one could be justified by doing the law in theory, in practice it is impossible (see also the additional note on 3:20). This issue is related in traditional Reformed theology to the debate over the existence and nature of

---

70. E.g., Murray.

71. E.g., Barrett.

72. E.g., Cranfield.

73. Cf. G. Friedrich, *TDNT* II, 733.

74. Cf. Westerholm, 145-46, and R. T. Beckwith, "The Unity and Diversity of God's Covenant," *TynBul* 38 (1987), 112-13, to cite only two recent studies. Beckwith speaks of a "hypothetical covenant of works."

75. Cf. Wilckens; Ridderbos, *Paul,* p. 134; Vos, "Legalism," p. 393.

the "covenant of works" and the place of the Mosaic law within that covenant.[76]

Second, how does our suggestion that Paul assumes the impossibility of fulfilling the law square with contemporary Jewish beliefs? Sanders claims that they cannot be reconciled. He argues that Jews in Paul's day considered it possible, indeed easy, to "do the law." Perfection was not considered necessary; the *intention* to obey was what was important, along with repentance and other means of atonement when failures occurred. How, then, could Paul assume that no one can do the law?

Sanders's own answer is to call into question whether Paul indeed teaches that it is impossible to do the law.[77] But, contrary to Sanders, Gal. 3:10-13, along with 5:3, seems to imply just this.[78] It must be said, however, that Paul never makes this clear in Romans. But what he does make clear is that everyone has failed to match up to the standard necessary to secure justification (compare 2:13 with 3:9, 19-20, and see the additional note on 3:20).[79] Another possible answer is to say that Paul views the law as impossible to do only after the coming of Christ. But Paul's whole purpose in this part of Romans is to justify the need of "the revelation of the righteousness of God" in Christ (1:17; 3:21). He can hardly establish the need for this revelation by citing the problems people face after it has arrived.

The best answer appears to be that Paul takes a more radical viewpoint of what "doing the law" involves. Because he denies any salvific value to the Mosaic law and the covenant of which it is a part, he recognizes that it is not enough — and never has been — to seek to do the law, however sincerely. For, from the first, it has been faith in the promise of God, and only faith, that justifies (cf. chap. 4). This being the case, only a *perfect* doing of the law would suffice to justify a person before God. True, an insistence on perfect obedience is a departure from the Jewish view. But this is just what Paul has implied by putting Jews and Gentiles on the same footing with respect to

---

76. For a variety of views, see H. Heppe, *Reformed Dogmatics Set Out and Illustrated from the Sources* (rpt.; Grand Rapids: Baker, 1978), pp. 281-319. On the modern debate, see particularly Wilckens, 1.142-46 and "Was heißt bei Paulus: 'Aus Werken des Gesetzes wird kein Mensch gerecht'?" in *Rechtfertigung als Freiheit: Paulusstudien* (Neukirchen/Vluyn: Neukirchener, 1974), pp. 77-109. Wilckens contests the idea that Paul viewed the attempt to fulfill the law in itself as wrong (for this view, see, e.g., G. Klein, "Sündenverständnis und theologica Crucis bei Paulus," in *Theologica Crucis — Signum Crucis (für Erich Dinkler zum 70 Geburtstag)* [ed. C. Andressen and G. Klein; Tübingen: Mohr, 1979], pp. 249-82).

77. Sanders, *Paul and Palestinian Judaism*, p. 499, passim.

78. Cf., e.g., T. R. Schreiner, "Paul and Perfect Obedience to the Law: An Evaluation of the View of E. P. Sanders," *WTJ* 47 (1985), 245-78.

79. It is not unreasonable to think that Paul views this standard as complete conformity to the law of God; cf. Espy, "Paul's 'Robust Conscience,'" pp. 178-79.

works and judgment in 2:1-16. What he says here plainly implies that the covenantal structure within which the Jews thought their sins could be taken care of was itself denied by Paul. The enormity of God's Son being crucified led Paul to take a far more pessimistic view of human sin than was typical of Judaism: sins that, for the Jews, simply needed to be atoned for within the covenant meant for Paul a breaking of the covenantal structure itself.

b. The Limitations of the Covenant (2:17-29)

In this section Paul resumes the diatribe style of 2:1-5, using direct address and a series of rhetorical questions in his polemic. The person he addresses, though easily enough recognized from what Paul has said in 2:1-16, is now for the first time explicitly identified as a Jew. A sharpening of the attack is thereby indicated. This section has similarities to the diatribe in substance as well as in style. For the author of the diatribe would often criticize his "opponent" for not "practicing what he preached." Just as, then, Epictetus contests the claims of some to be "true Stoics" because they do not live the philosophy they teach, so Paul questions whether one who does not obey the law has any right to claim the title "Jew."[1]

The function of these verses in the argument of chap. 2 is not clear. Murray thinks that this section resumes the indictment of those who sin "in the law" in vv. 12b-13 after the "digression" about the Gentiles and the law in vv. 14-16. Verses 17-29 would, then, demonstrate that Jews cannot claim to be "doers of the law" and that they cannot, therefore, be justified by doing the law. Wilckens, on the other hand, thinks that vv. 17-29 prove the point Paul made in 2:3, that Jews do "the same things" as the Gentiles. While admitting an element of truth in both these suggestions, we prefer to relate vv. 17-29 to the argument of vv. 1-16 more broadly. Paul's main point in 2:1-16 is that, because Jews will be assessed by God in the judgment on the same basis as Gentiles (works, doing "the law"), they cannot assume, any more than Gentiles, that they will escape God's wrath (2:4). Paul is, however, well aware that his argument ignores a crucial matter: the Jews' claim to possess a status by virtue of the covenant that puts them in a position entirely different from that of the Gentiles. In vv. 17-29, Paul takes up this matter.

Without dismissing the Jews' claim entirely (3:1-2), Paul insists that their privileges do not exempt them from God's judgment. In two paragraphs with roughly parallel arguments (vv. 17-24, 25-29), Paul takes up those two things that, more than any others, pointed to the Jews' special status: the law and circumcision. In both paragraphs, without dismissing them as worthless, Paul argues that neither knowledge of the law nor physical circumcision has

---

1. Cf. esp. *Diss.* 2.19-20; 3.7, 17; and Stowers, *Diatribe,* p. 112.

value unless the law is obeyed. Again, it is what is actually *done* that is critical in determining every person's destiny — for the Jew as well as for the Gentile (2:13).

To be sure, Paul does not prove, or even explicitly assert, in these paragraphs that all Jews are transgressors, or even that they are all serious enough transgressors to invalidate their hope for salvation through the covenant. Paul does assert this later (3:9), but his point in this section is not to demonstrate that Jews commit sins (no Jew would deny that) but that these sins, despite possession of the law and circumcision, make Jews just as liable to God's judgment as Gentiles.[2] In arguing in this manner, Paul is implicitly contesting the traditional Jewish understanding of the covenant. Whereas Jews tended to rely on their election and works of the law, Paul insists that it is faith — only and always — that is the basis for a righteous standing with God. Therefore, the "signs" of election — the law and circumcision — are of no value without this faith. Only if the law is "done," and, Paul implies, done perfectly, will the election on the basis of the Mosaic covenant be of value to the Jew (see also the Excursus after 3:20).

i. The Law (2:17-24)

> 17*Now if you call yourself a Jew, and take pride in the law, and boast in God,* 18*and know his will and approve those things that are best, being instructed by the law,* 19*and being convinced that you are a guide to the blind, a light for those who are in darkness,* 20*an instructor of the foolish, a teacher of the immature, having the embodiment of knowledge and truth in the law —* 21*therefore will you who teach another, not teach yourself? Do you who preach against stealing, steal?* 22*Do you who say not to commit adultery, commit adultery? Do you who detest idols, rob temples?* 23*You who are boasting in the law are, through your transgression of the law, dishonoring God.* 24*For "the name of God is being blasphemed among the nations because of you,"*[a] *even as it is written.*
>
> a. Isa. 52:5.

Paul begins the paragraph with an "if," introducing a protasis of a conditional sentence. But the matching apodosis — the "then" clause — is not immediately evident. Godet thinks that all of vv. 17-24 may form the protasis, with the apodosis left unexpressed: "What value then is the law?" But the "therefore" at the beginning of v. 21 suggests that a break occurs at that point. It is

---

2. Westerholm, 155-64.

still difficult to decide whether Paul simply abandons his conditional sentence at that point (anacolouthon),[3] or whether vv. 21-24 are the apodosis.[4] In either case, vv. 21-24 expose the failure of the Jew to live up to the privileges that Paul enumerates in vv. 17-20. There is some measure of irony in the way Paul presents these privileges as items in which the Jew boasts. But the irony is not directed against the claim to these privileges as such, for each of them is, according to the OT, a rightful possession of the Jew.[5] Rather, the irony emerges in the piling up of these distinctives and in the anticipation of the point that will be made in vv. 21-24. Paul here claims for the Jew nothing more than what the Jews of his day were claiming for themselves; every item on the list in vv. 17-20 is paralleled in Jewish literature of the time.

17   The three privileges in this verse are listed in ascending order: belonging to the chosen people, reliance on the law, and a special relationship with God.[6] Each is presented from the standpoint of the Jew, Paul's debating partner, who advances them as evidence of his special relationship with God. The name "Jew," which originally referred to a person from the region occupied by the descendants of Judah, was applied to Israelite people generally after the Exile, when the territory occupied by the Jews encompassed not much more than the original Judah. By Paul's day, "Jew" had become a common designation of anyone who belonged to the people of Israel. It suggests the special status enjoyed by the people of Israel, in distinction from all other peoples (cf. 1:16; 2:9, 11).[7] "To be named a Jew,"[8] then, refers to the religious status shared by anyone who belonged to the covenant people.

Paul phrases the second privilege enjoyed by the Jews in such a way as to suggest the root problem he addresses. Possession of the law was certainly a genuine blessing. But the problem came because the Jews "rely on[9] the law." Paul makes a point very similar to that of the prophet Micah, who, after rebuking the leaders of Israel for their sin, says, "Yet they lean on[10] the LORD saying, 'Is not the LORD in our midst? Calamity will not come

---

3. E.g., Cranfield.

4. E.g., S-H; Murray.

5. See Fitzmyer.

6. Cf. Michel.

7. Cf. W. Gutbrod, *TDNT* III, 359-65; and cf. the note on 9:4.

8. The Greek verb is ἐπονομάζω, "impose a name." The word occurs only here in the NT, but is used 36 times in the LXX, all, however, in the active. The passive form here may have an intransitive force ("bear the name") or a reflexive sense ("call yourself"; cf. BAGD). Although Ἰουδαῖος was used as an actual surname, this is not its meaning here (contra, e.g., Michel).

9. The Gk. verb is ἐπαναπαύω, which is usually deponent middle in the LXX, as it is here and in its one other NT occurrence (Luke 10:6).

10. The LXX uses the same verb, ἐπαναπαύω, that Paul uses.

upon us'" (3:11). So, in Paul's day, Jews thought their reliance on the law would exempt them from judgment.

The final privilege enumerated in v. 17 is that the Jew "boasts[11] in God." "Boasting" is not in itself wrong, as Jer. 9:23-24 (alluded to by Paul in 1 Cor. 1:31 and 2 Cor. 10:17) makes clear: "Thus says the LORD, 'Let not the wise man boast of his wisdom, and let not the mighty man boast of his might, let not the rich man boast of his riches, but let him who boasts boast of this, that he understands and knows me.'" Thus, the Jews' "boasting in God" is not wrong in itself — an instance of human pride and arrogance — but a legitimate pride and joy in the God who had given to Israel so many good things.[12]

18 Paul continues the conditional construction from v. 17, adding two more distinguishing marks of the Jew to his list: the Jew "knows his will"[13] and "approves those things that are best." What Paul attributed to all people in 1:19 — that knowledge of God was available through his revelation — he attributes to the Jew. The translation "approve those things that are best"[14] is one of three possible renderings,[15] the other two being (1) "distin-

---

11. This is the first occurrence in Romans of the verb χαυχάομαι, a peculiarly Pauline word (35 of the 37 NT usages are his) that is prominent in his criticism of the Jews. The root idea is "boast," make a claim for oneself, but the word takes on the sense "glory in" (cf. Rom. 5:2, 3, 11) and "trust in, rely on" (cf. Phil. 3:3). In classical Greek, χαυχάομαι almost always denotes an arrogant boasting, but the situation is somewhat different in the LXX. There also the word often has a negative connotation (cf. Ps. 52:1; 74:4), but a more neutral meaning is beginning to prevail, with the key issue being what it is in which one boasts.

12. Paul's enumeration of blessings thus resembles many in Jewish literature. Cf. *Pss. Sol.* 17:1: "LORD, you are our king forevermore, for in you, O God, does our soul take pride"; *2 Apoc. Bar.* 48:20-24:

> For these are the people whom you have elected,
> and this is the nation of which you found no equal.
> But I shall speak to you now,
> and I will say as my heart thinks.
> In you we have put our trust, because, behold, your Law is with us,
> and we know that we do not fall as long as we keep your statutes.
> We shall always be blessed; at least, we did not mingle with the nations.
> For we are all a people of the Name;
> we, who received one Law from the One.
> And that Law that is among us will help us,
> and that excellent wisdom which is in us will support us.

13. Gk. τὸ θέλημα, the article being possessive, with reference to θεῷ ("God") at the end of v. 17. The absolute use of "the will" to denote God's will was also a customary Jewish expression (1QS 8:6; 9:23; cf. 1 Cor. 16:12).

14. Adopted also by Murray.

15. The Greek is δοκιμάζεις τὰ διαφέροντα. The ambiguity arises from the fact that each of the two key Greek terms can be interpreted in two basic ways, with a variety

guish the things that differ [from God's will]" (cf. NEB: "know right from wrong");[16] (2) "distinguish the things that really matter."[17] The former is unlikely here,[18] but the second has much to be said for it.[19] In fact, however, the difference in meaning between this rendering and the one we have adopted is slight.

The final clause of the verse explains why the Jew "knows his will" and "approves those things that are best": he is "instructed[20] by the law."[21] The Jews' knowledge of God's will and their approval of the things that mattered the most came through their exposure to the instruction of the law in the synagogue and elsewhere.

19-20 In vv. 17-18 Paul has listed five blessings personally enjoyed by the Jews by virtue of their being God's covenant people. Now, with a change in construction, he enumerates four prerogatives that Jews enjoy in relation to other people because of these blessings.[22] Paul continues his direct address of a representative Jewish person: "being convinced[23] that you are a

---

of other nuances possible (the same ambiguity applies to the occurrence of the clause in Phil. 1:10). δοκιμάζω means "test, distinguish" (1 Cor. 11:28; 1 Thess. 5:21) or "approve [as the result of a test]" (Rom. 1:28; 1 Cor. 16:3), whereas διαφέρω, when used intransitively, can mean "differ" (1 Cor. 15:41) or "be worth more" (Matt. 6:26; 10:31; 12:12; Luke 12:7, 24).

16. Godet; Hodge. Both these scholars suggest that Paul might be referring to the casuistry of the rabbis, who sought to determine very precisely the will of God for the Jew. Michel suggests an allusion to the things that separate Jew and Gentile.

17. On this view, διαφέροντα has as its implied opposite *adiaphora;* cf., e.g., Käsemann; Cranfield; Dunn.

18. διαφέρω is more likely to mean "excel" than "differ" in a passage where no explicit comparison is made.

19. Some favor this translation because they think that Matt. 23:23, Christ's singling out of "the weightier matters of the law," is parallel; but the parallel is not at all certain.

20. The Greek verb is κατέχω, which means "teach," "instruct" (cf. Acts 21:21, 24), and is often used in the NT of religious instruction (Luke 1:4; Acts 18:25; Gal. 6:6a, b; 1 Cor. 14:19). In later usage, it became the technical word for the instruction of new converts (hence "catechism," "catechetical").

21. On this view, the adverbial participle κατηχούμενος ("instructed") modifies both γινώσκεις ("know") and δοκιμάζεις ("approve"); cf. Cranfield. The participle could also modify only the last verb.

22. The participle πέποιθας is loosely joined to vv. 17-18 with a τε (it is possible, though less likely, that it joins πέποιθας directly with κατηχούμενος ["instructed"]). It is followed by a complementary infinitive, εἶναι, to which Paul adds four parallel predicate nouns (in the accusative, agreeing with σεαυτόν, the subject of the infinitive) describing the Jewish prerogatives.

23. The perfect form of the participle πέποιθας has a present meaning, "being persuaded, or convinced" (BAGD).

guide to the blind, a light[24] for those who are in darkness, an instructor of the foolish,[25] a teacher[26] of the immature." It is their uniquely detailed knowledge of God's will, revealed in the law, that renders Jews responsible to teach others. Paul's description of this role uses language drawn particularly from Jewish propaganda directed to the Hellenistic world.[27]

The Jews' sense of mission toward the rest of the world is rooted in the OT. When, therefore, Paul asserts that the Jew was convinced he was a "guide to the blind" and a "light for those in darkness," we think of the duty of God's servant — to some degree at least identified with Israel — to be a "light to the nations" and "to open the eyes of the blind."[28] The Jews, however far short of their responsibility to enlighten the Gentile world they may have fallen, continued to boast in these mandates as a means of highlighting their importance and the value of their law in the eyes of a skeptical and sometimes hostile Gentile world.[29]

As he did in v. 18, Paul adds to his list of Jewish prerogatives a participial clause in which he traces the benefits enjoyed by the Jews to the law. Paul highlights the sufficiency of the law by claiming that it contains "the embodiment[30] of knowledge and truth." Paul has asserted that all people,

---

24. "Light" was connected with the law (Wis. 18:4), and conversion from paganism to Judaism was pictured as a moving from darkness to light (e.g., *Jos. and As.* 8.10).

25. Gk. παιδευτὴν ἀφρόνων. The παιδευ- word group generally describes the activity of chastisement in the NT, particularly the chastisement of children (cf. Acts 22:3; Eph. 6:4; Heb. 12:5-11). Although παιδευτής here means "train" rather than "chastise" (for which see παιδεύω in Tit. 2:12), the activity is yet directed to those who, in terms of their religious understanding, are "very young children" (cf. the word νηπίων in the next phrase). This word, then, defines what Paul means by the "foolish": not scornful rejecters of God's truth but the ignorant, untrained, and immature. Thus do Jews regard Gentiles; cf. *1 Enoch* 105:1: "In those days, he says, 'The LORD will be patient and cause the children of the earth to hear. Reveal it to them with your wisdom, for you are their guides.' "

26. Gk. διδάσκαλον. While the διδασκ- word group usually denotes a more positive and intellectual activity than the παιδευ- group, there is little difference in meaning between παιδευτής and διδάσκαλος here.

27. Str-B, 3.96-105; Michel. That it is this Diaspora milieu that provides the context for these ascriptions is suggested also by Paul's saying nothing about the cultus (Käsemann).

28. Isa. 42:6-7; cf. also 49:6. Jesus gave an ironical twist to these ascriptions when he accused the Pharisees of being "blind guides" [τυφλοὶ ὁδηγοί] (Matt. 15:14; cf. also Acts 26:18, where Paul claims that he has the commission to "open their [i.e., both the people of Israel's and the Gentiles'] eyes").

29. Cf. *Sib. Or.* 3:194-95: "the people of the great God will again be strong who will be guides in life for all mortals."

30. Gk. μόρφωσιν. This word is used only one other time in the NT, and there it means "outward form [not matching the inward reality]" (2 Tim. 3:5); here it designates the "result of an impression" (Käsemann), hence "embodiment" (BAGD).

including especially those without special revelation, have access to "knowledge" and "truth" (1:18-19, 25, 28, 32) and are hence "without excuse" when they turn from it. The Jew has this knowledge and truth embodied in far clearer and more detailed form in the law, a claim he acknowledges, and indeed boasts of. Even more than the Gentile, therefore, the Jewish person is "without excuse" before God (2:1).

21-22   The four sentences in these verses are best taken as rhetorical questions, in keeping with the diatribe style. They expose the Jew who has made the lofty claims of vv. 17-20 as inconsistent and hypocritical, as failing "to practice what he preaches." Such a charge was certainly not new. The OT (cf. Ps. 50:16-21), Judaism (cf. *'Abot R. Nat.* 29[8a]), and Jesus (e.g., Matt. 23:3) made similar accusations. Paul's stress on "doing" as what ultimately counts before God surfaces here again. All the privileges, distinctions, and gifts that the Jew may claim are meaningless if they are not responded to with a sincere and consistent obedience. And it is just this obedience that is lacking.

The first charge, that the Jew who teaches others should teach himself, is a heading and is broken down into three specific examples in the questions that follow. Paul cites three flagrant violations of the law as evidence of the Jew's failure to "teach himself." The prohibitions of stealing and adultery[31] are, of course, included in the Ten Commandments. The third sin is more difficult to identify. Paul's claim that the Jew "detests[32] idols" is clear enough, and captures an important element of Jewish religion in the first century. The threat to Jewish existence posed by the inroads of Hellenism and the dispersion of Jews throughout pagan society had led to increased emphasis on the need to avoid such pagan practices. Idolatry, in the technical sense, was generally unknown among Jews at this time. Indeed, what Paul accuses the Jew of doing is not specifically worshiping idols, but "robbing temples." What Paul means by this accusation is not clear.[33]

---

31. A few interpreters (e.g., Barrett) have suggested that "committing adultery" might have a metaphorical sense here — worshiping false gods. But it is more likely that the simple sexual meaning is intended.

32. Gk. βδελυσσόμενος, a substantival participle: "[you] who detest." The verb (used in the NT only elsewhere in Rev. 21:8) is often used in the LXX with reference to idols (cf. Deut. 7:26).

33. The verb is ἱεροσυλέω. It does not appear elsewhere in the NT, but the cognate ἱερόσυλος occurs in Acts 19:37, where the Ephesian town official defends Paul and his companions as not being "temple-robbers" or "blasphemers." Usage in the LXX is confined to 2 Maccabees, where it refers to the robbing of the Jerusalem Temple (4:39, 42), pagan temples (9:2), and perhaps more generally of temple robbing and associated acts of sacrilege (13:6). Both Philo and Josephus use the verb, and its cognates ἱεροσυλία and ἱερόσυλος, with reference to both literal and metaphorical robbery of pagan temples, as well as of the Jewish Temple.

(1) He might use the word in its natural, literal sense. While evidence that Jews engaged in the robbing of temples is scarce, there is some reason to think that the strictures against using the precious metals from idolatrous articles (cf. Deut. 7:26) were being relaxed and disobeyed.[34] Paul could, then, be citing the use of such articles stolen from pagan temples as an example of a practice that contradicted the Jews' avowed abhorrence of idolatry.[35]

(2) Paul might apply the word to the robbing of the Jerusalem Temple, which would be taking place when Jews failed to pay the "temple tax" that was required of all Jews for the support of the worship of the Lord.[36]

(3) Paul might apply the word to sacrilege in a general sense.[37] For Paul's accusation to make sense, this sacrilege would have to involve various acts (or attitudes) of impiety toward the God of Israel — as, for instance, elevating the law to such an extent that it infringed on the rights and honor of the Lord himself.[38] Each of these alternatives has its problems. Both the second and the third suffer from the difficulty that an act committed against the Jewish Temple or God is not a contradiction to the Jews' abhorrence of idols.[39] If we adopt the first alternative, on the other hand, Paul would be accusing his Jewish target of an offense that was, at best, rare. Nevertheless, this difficulty is not as great as the one faced by the second and third alternatives. Moreover, this interpretation places this third accusation on the same footing as the first two (see below).

Why has Paul chosen examples of such serious and relatively infrequent activities to accuse Jews generally of failing to live out the law they reverence? How could his accusations be convincing to those Jews, surely in the majority, who had never stolen, committed adultery, or robbed a temple? Some interpreters conclude that Paul must view each of these activities in the

---

34. Cf. Str-B, 3.113-15.

35. E.g., Chrysostom; Godet; S-H; Michel; Murray; Käsemann; Wilckens; Dunn; Watson, 114; G. Schrenk, *TDNT* III, 256.

36. Hodge (?). Failure to pay this "temple tax" was, apparently, widespread and frequently criticized (cf. *Pss. Sol.* 8:11-13; *T. Levi* 14:5).

37. For evidence that the word could have this meaning, see 2 Macc. 13:6; Acts 19:37.

38. See esp. D. B. Garlington, "ΙΕΡΟΣΥΛΕΙΝ and the Idolatry of Israel (Romans 2.22)," *NTS* 36 (1990), 142-51; cf. also Calvin; Barrett; Cranfield; Fitzmyer. Bengel sees a reference to the Jews' refusal to honor God by responding to the gospel (cf. also Barth, *Shorter*). Philo accuses murderers of "temple-robbing" (ἱεροσυλία) in the sense that the taking of a person's life robs God of what is most valuable to him (*Decalogue* 133; *Special Laws* 3.83).

39. Kuss.

light of the "deepening" of the law taught by Jesus (Matt. 5:21-48). "When theft, adultery, and sacrilege are strictly and radically understood, there is no man who is not guilty of all three."[40] But there is nothing in the context to make such an understanding of these activities likely, and much that is against it. Paul's purpose in Rom. 2 is to convince Jews of the inadequacy of their works, defined according to the standard of the law itself. For him to accuse them of breaches of the law in the radicalized sense in which Jesus taught it would be to leave this intent behind.

Another suggestion is made by Watson, who notes that the context especially stresses the teaching activity of Jews. He thinks that Paul may be criticizing leaders of the Jewish community in Rome who had been active in proselytizing, but whose immorality had led to their expulsion from the city.[41] Watson's interpretation grows out of his reconstruction of the social situation addressed by Paul in Romans, a reconstruction that reads more into the text than is justified. Nevertheless, there may be an element of truth in his suggestion, in the sense that Paul's intention seems to be to cite these breaches of the law as exemplary of the contrast between words and works, possession of the law and obedience of it, that is the *leitmotif* of Rom. 2.[42] It is not, then, that all Jews commit these sins, but that these sins are representative of the contradiction between claim and conduct that *does* pervade Judaism. Paul may, then, have chosen these particular sins in order to make a contrast with the commands of the Decalogue (if "robbing temples" can be construed as a violation of the first commandment)[43] or to follow the pattern of other "vice lists," in which items such as murder, adultery, and sacrilege often appeared,[44] or, perhaps most likely, to show the equivalence between the sins of Jews and of Gentiles (cf. 2:3).[45]

23 This verse, which is probably a statement (NA[27], NEB, JB) rather than another rhetorical question (KJV, NASB, RSV, NIV, TEV), brings home to Paul's Jewish addressee the accusation developed in vv. 17-22. Whereas v. 17 spoke of the Jew "relying on" the law, this verse heightens the sense by speaking of the Jew as "boasting"[46] in it. All such pride in the law —

---

40. Barrett; Luther; Cranfield; Ridderbos, *Paul,* pp. 136-37; L. Goppelt, "Der Missionar des Gesetzes: Zu Röm. 2, 21f.," in *Christologie und Ethik: Aufsätze zum Neuen Testament* (Göttingen: Vandenhoeck & Ruprecht, 1968), pp. 137-46.

41. Watson, 114.

42. See Achtemeier; Kuss; Dunn. Käsemann sees evidence of an apocalyptic perspective in which the activities of some become representative of the community.

43. Cf. Harrisville.

44. See Philo, *Confusion of Tongues* 163 (and note ἱεροσυλία in *Special Laws* 2.13; 4.87); cf. G. Schrenk, *TDNT* III, 256.

45. Livermore, "Romans 1:18–3:20," p. 213.

46. Gk. καυχᾶσαι; on this word, see the note on v. 17.

claims as to its antiquity and perfection, boasts about Israel as the people entrusted with the law — becomes insignificant and, indeed, damaging when the law is not obeyed.[47] It is not boasting in the law that brings honor to God but obedience to it.

24 Paul uses an OT quotation to confirm the conclusion he has drawn in v. 23. The quotation is probably from Isa. 52:5.[48] In Isaiah, the blaspheming of God's name occurs through the oppression of Israel, God's chosen people, by foreign powers. Paul ascribes the cause of the blasphemy to the disobedient lives of his people.[49] Perhaps Paul intends the reader to see the irony in having responsibility for dishonoring God's name transferred from the Gentiles to the people of Israel.

ii. Circumcision (2:25-29)

25*For circumcision is of profit if you practice the law. But if you are a transgressor of the law, your circumcision has become uncircumcision.* 26*If, then, the person who is uncircumcised guards the just decrees of the law, will not that person's uncircumcision be considered as circumcision?* 27*And the person who is uncircumcised by nature who completes the law will judge you who, though having the letter and circumcision, are a transgressor of the law.* 28*For it is not the Jew who is one outwardly who is the Jew, nor is it the outward circumcision, in the flesh, that is circumcision,* 29*but it is the Jew who is in secret who is the Jew, and who has the circumcision of the heart, in the Spirit, not in letter. That Jew has praise not from human beings, but from God.*

As vv. 12-24 have shown that the Jews' possession of the law will not shield them from judgment because it is the doing of the law, not simply the possession of the law, that matters, so vv. 25-29 argue that circumcision also is of no benefit unless the law is obeyed. Circumcision, like the law, was a sign of the Jew's privileged position as a member of the chosen people, participant

47. It is, Paul says, διὰ τῆς παραβάσεως τοῦ νόμου that the Jew "dishonors" God. Paul consistently uses the word παράβασις to connote the "transgression" of a revealed law or commandment (cf. Rom. 4:15; 5:14; Gal. 3:19; 1 Tim. 2:14).

48. The LXX of Isa. 52:5 reads δι' ὑμᾶς διὰ παντὸς τὸ ὄνομά μου βλασφημεῖται ἐν τοῖς ἔθνεσιν (the MT has no equivalent to δι' ὑμᾶς or ἐν τοῖς ἔθνεσιν).

49. This shift in application has caused some commentators to suggest that Paul might be quoting Ezek. 26:20, which is conceptually closer to Paul and which was used by the rabbis in a way similar to Paul (e.g., *Mek. Exod.* 15:2[44b]; cf. Calvin). However, the Isaiah text is linguistically much closer to Paul's words, and it is best to assume that Paul has chosen the words of Isaiah as a suitable means of expressing his point.

in the covenant that God established with Abraham (Gen. 17). Later Judaism claimed that "no person who is circumcised will go down to Gehenna,"[1] and the importance of the rite throughout the Second Temple period suggests that this view was prevalent in Paul's day also. But Paul goes even further. Not only does disobedience of the law endanger the circumcised Jew's salvation;[2] obedience of the law can bring salvation to the uncircumcised Gentile. Moreover, while Paul's central concern is again (as in vv. 7, 10, and 14-15) to set forth the impartial standard of judgment outside of Christ, he here for the first time in the chapter also hints that it is the Christian, circumcised in the heart by God's Spirit, who is the "true" Jew (v. 29).

25 The "for"[3] at the beginning of v. 25 relates this whole paragraph to an implied Jewish objection: How can we be treated the same as Gentiles (vv. 6-11), even to the point of being in danger of the wrath of God (cf. v. 5), when our circumcision marks us as belonging to God's chosen people, heirs of the Abrahamic promises? Paul responds: circumcision "is of profit"[4] only if the law is done; if, on the other hand,[5] the law is transgressed, one's circumcision "has become[6] uncircumcision." Paul is clearly contesting the value of circumcision per se. But his precise meaning is open to question. First, what specific "profit" of circumcision is Paul contesting? In light of the context, with its focus on judgment and wrath, Paul must have in mind the efficacy of circumcision in shielding the Jew from the wrath of God. This meaning is confirmed by 3:1-2, where the question "Does circumcision have

---

1. *Exod. Rab.* 19 (81c); cf. also *Tanch. B.* 60b, 8; *Gen. Rab.* 48 (30a). The struggle for Jewish existence at the time of the Maccabees led to increased insistence on circumcision as an indispensable mark of Jewishness, one that a person must be willing to die for. And while, in response to criticism and ridicule, Hellenistic Judaism tended toward a more spiritualized approach to Jewish institutions, physical circumcision was nevertheless insisted upon. Philo, for all his allegorizing, insists on the physical rite, although he mentions some Jews who did not (*Special Laws* 1.1-11, 304-6; *Abraham* 92). That some Jews may have exempted Gentile converts from the rite is possible (cf. the story of the conversion of Izates in Josephus [*Ant.* 20.17-48]), but the prevailing opinion was that only circumcised Gentiles could be considered true proselytes (cf. G. F. Moore, *Judaism in the First Centuries of the Christian Era* [rpt.; 2 vols.; New York: Schocken, 1971], 1.323-35).

2. As Seifrid (*Justification,* pp. 64-65) notes, the issue of circumcision goes beyond the question of ethnic or "people" status: "Circumcision was indeed a 'national boundary marker,' but Paul here assumes that it also was a claim to religious preeminence mediated by the Law, and consequently constituted an assurance of salvation."

3. Gk. γάρ.

4. Gk. ὠφελεῖ.

5. The δέ here is correlative with the μέν in the first sentence of the verse.

6. Gk. γέγονεν, its perfect tense connoting the "state" that exists in relation to one's circumcision when the condition is fulfilled. Str-B (3.119) and Michel trace this use of the word to the rabbinic phrase כְּ נַעֲשָׂה, but Käsemann is probably correct to contest the identification because of syntactical differences.

any profit?"[7] makes sense only if Paul has denied its value in some vital respect in vv. 25-29 — and denied it for all Jews. In light of 3:9 and 19, this value must have to do with the efficacy of circumcision to rescue the Jew from the tyranny of sin and the judgment of God.

This conclusion has important implications for a second question, the meaning of the phrase "if you practice the law." Two interpretations fit the context: (1) a heartfelt, faith-filled obedience to the stipulations of the covenant;[8] (2) a perfect conformity to the letter of the law.[9] If the former is adopted, then Paul would presumably regard this kind of "doing the law" as possible, and his point would be that it is only when accompanied by this sincere and faithful response to God's covenant stipulations that circumcision, the sign of the covenant, is of any value. With the second meaning, on the other hand, Paul would be setting forth the standard by which God judges, a standard of perfect conformity to God's demands that no one can meet. In this case, circumcision would be of no "profit" (in the sense of salvific profit) to anyone. A decision between these two options is very difficult. In favor of the former is the undeniable stress in the OT itself on the heart attitude necessary for a true doing of the law, a stress that Paul in vv. 28-29 appears to reflect. Certainly, first-century Judaism regarded the law as doable; and most Jews would, presumably, read Paul as calling, not for perfect obedience, but for heartfelt, sincere obedience. Moreover, "doing" the law is something that Paul in vv. 26 and 27 appears to set forth as a genuine possibility.

These are strong arguments; but I am still inclined to adopt the second interpretation. My main reason for doing so is the crucial distinction between faith on the one hand and "the law," "works," or "doing," on the other, that Paul maintains throughout Romans, as well as in his other letters. Whereas "doing the law" in Judaism could well include faith, "doing the law" in Paul is definitely and emphatically separated from faith (cf. 3:27-28 [and our comments there]; 4:2-5, 13-16; 10:5-8; and perhaps most clearly, Gal. 3:12). True, Paul thereby drives a wedge between two human responses — faith and obedience to the law — that were intertwined in Judaism. But he does this knowingly and on the basis of conviction, for Paul views any mixing, any synergism, of faith and works as damaging to the grace of God (cf. especially 4:1-5). In light of this concern, it is unlikely that Paul would include faith in "doing the law" here. And in light of the inference Paul draws from his argument in this section of the epistle — "no one is justified before God through works of the law" (3:20) — it is equally unlikely that he intends to accord salvific value to circumcision or doing the law. Paul's

7. Here again Paul uses a form of ὠφελέω.
8. E.g., Murray; Cranfield.
9. E.g., Calvin; Hodge; Bruce.

purpose in this section is not to indicate how circumcision is of value with respect to the covenant but to remove circumcision from the list of those things that the Jew might think would afford him an automatic pardon from the wrath of God.[10]

These decisions help us to determine the meaning of Paul's claim that transgressing the law turns one's circumcision into "uncircumcision." If the profit of circumcision consists in protection from divine wrath, this phrase must, as its contrary, signify exposure to that wrath.[11] To become uncircumcised means to become like a Gentile and to forfeit any defense that one's membership in the people of God might provide on the day of judgment. Michel is right to underscore the polemical tone of this assertion.[12] For in contrast to Jewish teachers, who held that only a radical decision to renounce the covenant invalidated one's circumcision,[13] Paul argues that simple transgressions of the law can have the same effect. Although Paul is more radical, his polemic resembles that of the prophets, who warned the people of Israel that their cavalier disregard of their covenant obligations rendered null and void the security from foreign domination and divine judgment that they hoped to find in covenant signs.[14]

26   If it is not circumcision but obedience to the law that determines whether one will be saved at the judgment, it follows as a consequence[15] that a Gentile, "the uncircumcised person,"[16] can, if he or she obeys the law, be saved. This uncircumcision, signifying that the Gentile is "alienated from the commonwealth of Israel, [a] stranger[s] to the covenants of promise, having no hope and without God in the world" (Eph. 2:12), "will be considered"[17] as circumcision if he "guards the just decrees of the law."

Who are these uncircumcised Gentiles who keep the law and are saved on the day of judgment? We have already dismissed the possibility that Paul would describe Gentiles apart from faith in Christ as saved through their

10. Cf. Calvin.

11. Hodge; Michel; Nygren.

12. Cf. Livermore, "Romans 1:18–3:20," p. 226.

13. Cf. Sanders, *Paul and Palestinian Judaism,* pp. 157-82.

14. Cf., e.g., Jer. 7; Amos 5:18-27; Hos. 6–9.

15. Hence Paul's use of οὖν, "therefore."

16. Paul uses the abstract word ἀκροβυστία to denote "one who is in the state of being uncircumcised" (BAGD).

17. Paul borrows the combination λογίζομαι εἰς from Gen. 15:6 to denote, rather technically, the "imputation" of faith in Rom. 4 (cf. vv. 3, 9, and 22). Here, however, the phrase lacks this technical sense, being equivalent to Heb. לְ חָשַׁב (cf. 1 Sam. 1:13; Isa. 29:17; 32:15; Hos. 8:12 [with בְּ]; cf. also Wis. 3:17; 9:6). Paul may use a future form of the verb here (λογισθήσεται) because the "considering" follows the doing of the law (a "logical" future), but he more likely does so because he is thinking of final judgment (cf. 2:5, 16; see Kuss; Riedl, *Das Heil des Heiden,* p. 209).

obedience to the light they have received (see the notes on 2:11).[18] However, if one finds a reference to Gentile Christians in earlier verses of the chapter where a similar positive assessment of Gentiles is made (2:7, 10, 14-15), it is natural to make the same identification here.[19] But even some who do not think these earlier verses refer to Gentile Christians are persuaded that they are in view here.[20] Partly, this is because of the apparent realism of v. 27 and the fact that v. 29 alludes, however ambiguously, to Christians. But it is also argued that the phrase "guards the just decrees of the law" is a stronger expression than, for instance, "do the things of the law" (v. 14) and signifies a full and complete fulfillment of the law such as is possible only for Christians. This is questionable. Although Paul says that Christians who are walking by the Spirit have fulfilled in them "the just decree of the law" (Rom. 8:4), both the singular noun and the passive verb differentiate that statement from what Paul says here.[21] Yet Paul does not depict the Christian as one who is under obligation to the specific stipulations of the Mosaic law. The Christian is no longer "under the [Mosaic] law" (6:14, 15; see our comments there),

---

18. Riedl, *Das Heil des Heiden,* pp. 209-10; Snodgrass, "Justification by Grace," p. 83.

19. E.g., Godet; Barth, *Shorter;* Cranfield; Barrett; Schreiner, "Did Paul Believe in Justification by Works?"

20. E.g., Luther; Zahn; Murray; Laato, *Paulus und das Judentum,* pp. 104-5.

21. The phrase Paul here uses is φυλάσσω τὰ δικαιώματα τοῦ νόμου. A similar phrase (φυλάσσω τὰ διακιώματα αὐτοῦ [with reference to the Lord]) occurs frequently in Deuteronomy to denote the doing of the law (4:40; 6:2; 17:19; 28:45; 30:10, 16); and it is often in strict parallelism with similar phrases that use the verb ποιέω ("do") (cf. Deut. 26:16-17). The phrase is best understood, then, as another of several essentially synonymous phrases that designate in Rom. 2 obedience to the Mosaic law. In fact, the phrases that Paul uses to denote obedience to the law are few and unsystematized. The most frequent is [τὰ] ἔργα [τοῦ] νόμου, "works of the law," which Paul uses in contexts where he is denying that justification can be based on obedience to the law (Gal. 2:16; 3:2, 5, 10; Rom. 3:20, 28 — and see the notes on 3:20). He also uses several verbs with the word νόμος or equivalent words or phrases as their object: ποιέω, "do" (Gal. 3:10, 12; 5:3; Rom. 2:14; 10:5; cf. also ποιηταί in Rom. 2:13); φυλάσσω, "keep," "guard" (Gal. 6:13; Rom. 2:26); πράσσω, "practice" (Rom. 2:25); ἐμμένω, "remain in" (Gal. 3:10 [quoting Deut. 27:26]); τελέω, "complete" (Rom. 2:27). Some scholars think that there are distinctions in the meaning of these phrases (many especially putting "works of the law" in a separate category; e.g., Snodgrass, "Justified by Grace," pp. 83-85), but this is not at all clear. Most of the phrases were already being used by Jews to denote obedience to the law; and most have close equivalents in the Hebrew of the later rabbinic literature. They are all different ways of expressing the general idea of obedience to the law of Moses. To be put in a separate category, however, are those phrases in Paul that employ the word πληρόω, "fulfill," or a cognate of that term (cf. Rom. 8:4; 13:8, 10; Gal. 5:14; cf. Gal. 6:2). Paul reserves this language for the eschatological "filling up" of the basic demand of the law that has been made possible with the coming of Christ.

but under "the law of Christ" (Gal. 6:2; cf. 1 Cor. 9:20). Finally, the context suggests that as transgression of the law disbars the Jew from salvation (v. 25), so obedience to the law grants the Gentile membership among the saved. But it is impossible that Paul would have described any Christian as having been granted this status as a result of obeying the law.

We therefore conclude that Paul is again here citing God's standard of judgment apart from the gospel as a means of erasing the distinction at this point between Jew and Gentile. Paul is not pointing the way to salvation but is showing Jews that their position, despite their covenant privileges, is essentially no different from that of the Gentiles: disobedience brings condemnation; obedience brings salvation. Paul's way of putting the matter in this context could, of course, suggest that there actually are people who meet this requirement for salvation; but his later argument quickly disabuses us of any such idea (cf. 3:9, 20).[22]

Nevertheless, we should not miss the revolutionary implications of what Paul suggests here. Circumcision was, after all, commanded in the law — yet Paul can say that people who are not circumcised can do the law. This assumption looks toward a new understanding of what the covenant is and what God requires of his people, an understanding that arises from the conviction that a new stage in salvation history has begun.[23] Without directly describing Christians here, then, Paul's logic anticipates his teaching that it is faith and the indwelling of the Spirit that meet God's demand and so bring people into relationship with God. We may paraphrase: "if it should be that there were an uncircumcised person who perfectly kept the law (which in this sense there is not, though in another sense, as we will see, there is), that person would be considered a full member of the people of God."

27 The belief that the righteous would sit in judgment over the unrighteous was widespread.[24] But the Jewish tradition naturally cast Jews in the role of the righteous and Gentiles in that of the unrighteous. Paul reverses this customary scheme and, continuing his argument from v. 26, asserts that "the uncircumcised person by nature[25] who completes the law will judge[26]

---

22. For this general approach, see, e.g., Calvin; Käsemann; Wilckens; Kuss; Fitzmyer; Schmithals; S. Westerholm, "Letter and Spirit: The Foundation of Pauline *Ethics*," *NTS* 30 (1984), 235. I am indebted to B. Fisk, in an unpublished paper, for stimulating my thinking about this text.

23. See, e.g., Barrett.

24. Cf., in Paul, 1 Cor. 6:2; and note, e.g., *1 Enoch* 91:12; 98:12; *Apoc. Abr.* 29:19-21; Wis. 3:8; additional examples in Str-B, 3.124.

25. The word order makes it clear that ἐκ φύσεως, "by nature," modifies ἡ . . . ἀκροβυστία rather than τελοῦσα (Murray; contra Burton, 427; Denney). This qualification implies a contrast between what a person is by birth, by "natural" origin, and what the Jew is by birth (cf., for a similar use of φύσις, Gal. 2:15).

26. The Greek verb κρίνω clearly has a negative, condemnatory, sense.

you [e.g., the Jew][27] who, though having the letter and circumcision, are a transgressor of the law." Whether Paul suggests that these righteous Gentiles will be appointed as judges by God[28] or that their obedience to the law itself will stand as accusatory evidence against the disobedient Jew[29] is difficult to say. But the latter might be more likely in view of the parallel with Jesus' rebuke of the Jews who rejected him: "The men of Nineveh will arise at the judgment with this generation and condemn it; for they repented at the preaching of Jonah, and behold, something greater than Jonah is here. The queen of the south will arise at the judgment with this generation and condemn it; for she came from the ends of the earth to hear the wisdom of Solomon, and behold, something greater than Solomon is here" (Matt. 12:41-42; cf. Luke 11:31-32).

The matter-of-fact nature of this assertion gives support to those who think that Paul is here depicting a real rather than a hypothetical situation. Moreover, Paul's description of this person as one who "*completes* the law" might point in the same direction.[30] But this phrase is simply another way of describing obedience to the commandments of the law;[31] and, for the reasons outlined above, I prefer to see the verse as a vivid reminder of the equality between Jew and Gentile with respect to judgment.

A debated point in this verse is the phrase that Paul uses to qualify "a transgressor of the law": "through letter and circumcision." Two related issues arise: the meanings of the word "letter" and of the preposition we here translate "through." The Greek word *gramma* means "that which is inscribed or written," and Paul is the only biblical author to use the term with reference to the law.[32] In each case, he contrasts *gramma* with *pneuma*, "spirit" (cf. v. 29 and Rom. 7:6; 2 Cor. 3:6-7). If the preposition Paul uses here *(dia)* has its normal instrumental meaning, then "letter" must have a negative connotation: it is "through the letter" that transgression of the law occurs.[33] "Letter" will then connote "an understanding of the law which

27. The second person singular σέ maintains the diatribe style of the paragraph (cf. the second person singular verbs in v. 25).

28. Cf. BAGD, κρίνω 4.B.β.

29. E.g., Murray; Cranfield.

30. Schlier, e.g., thinks that Paul makes the transition in this verse from a hypothetical situation (vv. 25-26) to the actual situation of the Christian (vv. 27-29).

31. Paul never elsewhere uses τελέω with reference to the doing of the law; nor is it so used in the LXX. But Josephus (*J.W.* 2.495) and other NT authors (Luke 2:39; Jas. 2:8) use the verb with this kind of reference.

32. The plural γράμματα does have this reference in Judaism; particularly common is the phrase τὰ ἱερὰ γράμματα (= Heb. כִּתְבֵי הַקֹּדֶשׁ), "the holy writings" (G. Schrenk, *TDNT* I, 765).

33. See Cranfield; Dunn.

stays at the level of the ritual act and outward deed,"[34] a superficial and therefore incomplete understanding of the law.[35] But the wider context points in a different direction. Paul is arguing in Rom. 2 that Jews cannot depend on their covenant status, symbolized by the law and circumcision, for salvation. And the reason they cannot, he argues, is that they have transgressed the law by disobeying its precepts. Of course, a wrong heart attitude is one aspect of this problem (cf. vv. 28-29). But nothing Paul has said in this chapter suggests that a faulty understanding of the law is part of the problem. Indeed, vv. 17-24, with their contrast between "knowing God's will, being instructed through the law," and "breaking the law," show that it is not at the level of understanding but at the level of *doing* that the problem lies. This is typical of Paul's teaching throughout Romans, where the solution to the problem of sin is not a new or deeper understanding of the law, but faith in Christ, leading to the indwelling of the Spirit and the breaking of sin's stranglehold over human beings.

The context therefore makes it more likely that "letter" will have a neutral meaning, referring simply to the law as that which had been written down in letters.[36] And confirming this conclusion is the likelihood that "letter" has this same neutral meaning in Paul's other uses of it with reference to the law.[37] "Letter" and circumcision mark off the Jew from the Gentile, and Paul's point is that disobedience of the law cancels out these undeniable advantages. The preposition here should then be translated not "through," but "with" or "even though."[38]

28-29 Verses 28-29 explain why ("for") circumcision does not guarantee salvation and why its lack does not bar one from salvation. Though God's verdict is based on "works," these works reveal "the secret things" (cf. 2:16), the inner reality of a person's heart relationship to God. And it is this heart attitude that ultimately matters — not a rite that affects only the flesh. Paul argues by means of a contrast, with two denials in v. 28 being matched by two assertions in v. 29:

A For it is not the Jew who is one outwardly who is the Jew,
B nor is it the outward circumcision, in the flesh, that is circumcision
A but the Jew who in secret who is the Jew,

34. Dunn.

35. See also Cranfield. See also Calvin, who takes γράμματος καὶ περιτομῆς as a hendiadys, "legalistic circumcision."

36. As Winger argues, γράμμα and νόμος refer to the same thing — the law of Moses — but view it in different ways (*By What Law?* p. 41).

37. See the notes on vv. 28-29.

38. That is, διά indicates "attendant circumstances" (cf. BDF 223[3]); see also NIV; NASB; TEV; NRSV.

B and circumcision of the heart, in the Spirit, not in letter, is circumcision[39]

The basic contrast in these verses is an "inner"/"outer" contrast; a contrast between what can be seen with the eye (physical circumcision, Jewish birth) and what only God ultimately sees (the changed heart; "true" Jewishness).[40] The contrast between outward circumcision (done "in the flesh") and the circumcision "done to the heart"[41] is well known in the OT and Judaism. From the earliest history of Israel, God called on the people to display the kind of inner transformation that could be called a "circumcision of the heart" (e.g., Deut. 10:16; cf. Jer. 4:4). Significantly, it was also recognized that only God could ultimately bring about this heart transformation (Deut. 30:6). There thus grew up in Judaism the expectation that God would one day circumcise the hearts of his people through the work of the Spirit.[42] Thus Paul's call for a "circumcision of the heart, in the Spirit," is not entirely original. But the unprecedented addition of the negative phrase "not in letter" raises the question whether or not he is using the concept with a deeper significance.

The "letter/spirit" contrast Paul uses here has played a prominent role in church history, where it was often applied to interpretation: the "letter" denoting the literal, surface meaning of a text and the "spirit" its deeper, allegorical sense. Paul, however, never uses the contrast with this application. As we have seen (see v. 27), Paul uses "letter" to refer to the law of Moses "as written." In the current context, because of its proximity to "heart" and apparent contrast with "manifest," some interpreters think that "spirit" might refer to the inner aspect of the human being.[43] But the immediate contrast here is with "letter"; and this suggests that "spirit," like "letter," refers to a God-given entity. Thus, as in the other Pauline "letter/spirit" passages (Rom. 7:6; 2 Cor. 3:6-7), "spirit" should be capitalized: it refers to God's Holy Spirit.

---

39. Paul writes these verses elliptically, with key syntactical elements needing to be supplied. The key words Ἰουδαῖος ("Jew") and περιτομή ("circumcision") must be repeated in each verse; and whether we regard the words Paul wrote or the ones we must supply as the grammatical subjects makes very little difference (see Godet, S-H, and Cranfield for different schemes).

40. Paul uses the Greek words φανερός ("manifest," "visible") and κρυτός ("hidden," "secret"). Note especially here Jesus' use of the word κρυπτός to highlight the importance of sincere piety (Matt. 6:4, 6, 18; cf. 1 Pet. 3:4).

41. The genitive καρδίας after περιτομή in v. 29 is probably objective.

42. See esp. *Jub.* 1:23; *Odes Sol.* 11:2.

43. E.g., Sanders, *Paul, the Law and the Jewish People*, p. 127. Barrett thinks that ἐν πνεύματι might mean "in a spiritual way," a reference to the inner nature of Christianity as opposed to Judaism (cf. also Griffith Thomas).

Paul's "letter"/"Spirit" contrast is a salvation-historical one, "letter" describing the past era in which God's law through Moses played a central role and "Spirit" summing up the new era in which God's Spirit is poured out in eschatological fullness and power.[44] It is only the circumcision "in the Spirit"[45] that ultimately counts.

For the first time, then, in Rom. 2, Paul alludes to Christians. But even here it is only an allusion, since Paul is not so much describing a group of people as specifying what it is that qualifies a person to be a "true Jew" and so to be saved. No outward rite can bring a person into relationship with God; with that many Jews would have agreed. But Paul goes beyond any first-century Jewish viewpoint in suggesting that physical circumcision is no longer required and in implicitly applying the term "Jew" to those who were not ethnically Jews. As Ridderbos puts it, we find here "a radicalizing of the concept Jew, and thereby of the definition of the essence of the people of God."[46] Paul in these verses reaches ahead to the argument that he will unfold in 3:21–4:25. It is "an advance sounding of the message of salvation," as Bornkamm puts it.[47]

The last clause in v. 29 picks up the outward/inward contrast of vv. 28-29a. The "true" Jew, like the sincere worshiper (cf. Matt. 6:2-18), is praised not by people but by God.[48] This praise, in keeping with the focus on judgment throughout Rom. 2, is probably that praise with which God will honor his own people on the last day.[49]

---

44. Note that Paul first uses the contrast when speaking of covenants (2 Cor. 3:6). On this view of the contrast, see, e.g., Ridderbos, *Paul,* pp. 215-19; Westerholm, "Letter and Spirit," pp. 229-48; E. Käsemann, "The Spirit and the Letter," in *Perspectives on Paul* (Philadelphia: Fortress, 1971), pp. 138-66; S. Lyonnet, " 'La circumcision du coeur, celle qui relève de l'Esprit et non de la lettre' (Rom. 2:29)," in *L'Evangile, hier et aujourd'hui: Mélanges offerts zu Franz-J. Leenhardt* (Geneva: Labor et Fides, 1968), pp. 89-92; G. Schrenk, *TDNT* I, 765-66; Godet; Cranfield; Wilckens; Murray; Schlier. Paul's consistent alignment of "Spirit" with the new era and the contrast here with "letter" make it unlikely that he is referring to those Jews throughout history who were genuinely committed to the Lord (contra Kuhr, "Römer 2¹⁴," p. 253; Snodgrass, "Justification by Grace," p. 81).

45. The ἐν in this phrase could be instrumental — the circumcision is accomplished "by" the Spirit — but this meaning does not fit well with the other object of the preposition: γράμματι. It is preferable, therefore, to think that it denotes sphere.

46. Ridderbos, *Paul,* p. 334.

47. "Einen Vorausklang der Heilsbotschaft" (Bornkamm, "Gesetz und Natur," p. 110).

48. The Greek word ἔπαινος may contain a play on the word Ἰουδαῖος, which in Hebrew (יְהוּדִי) is very close to the hiphil of the verb "praise" (יָדָה; cf. Gen. 29:35; 49:8) (Haldane; Gifford).

49. Cranfield.

Paul's argument against the Jews in Rom. 2 has come in for severe criticism. These critics charge that the argument of the chapter is basically "un-Christian," or at least "un-Pauline," in its assumptions. Few have gone as far as O'Neill, who dismisses large sections of the chapter as later glosses. But it is more widely believed that Paul's teaching in this chapter cannot be easily harmonized, or perhaps harmonized at all, with his teaching elsewhere.[50] Some have been so struck by these differences that they think Paul may have taken over almost intact a synagogue homily.[51] Why so radical a conclusion? Three areas of difficulty are singled out: the teaching that justification can come by works (2:6-11, 13, 26-27), that the law can be fulfilled (2:14-15, 26-27), and, related to both of these, that Gentiles also have ability and virtue. These points, it is suggested, are the product of Paul's excessive zeal to remove any distinction between Jews and Gentiles. To this end, the Gentiles are presented in as positive a light as possible. Paul's conviction that Christ was the only solution is what came first, and that conviction required that he accuse all people of being lost in sin.

This criticism can only be met by a demonstration, through careful exegesis, that the teachings of the chapter found to be incompatible with Paul's theology are not, in fact, there. I hope to have made at least a start on this demonstration above. But a general criticism might be noted here: such a view of Rom. 2 requires either that Paul was unaware that he was creating a contradiction with Rom. 1:18-32 and 3:9, 19-20[52] or that he was not ultimately interested in a logically coherent theology.[53] Both suppositions are problematic. The former makes Paul into an obtuse person indeed — so obtuse that it is hard to know how he could ever have written a letter like Romans, let alone convince anyone to embrace his teaching. The latter, while justly stressing the need to recognize the social and contingent factors behind Paul's teaching, errs in thinking that Paul could have accomplished these social objectives with a logically contradictory theology. Surely those groups whom he was seeking to persuade would have spotted the inconsistencies and used them as an excuse to ignore his teaching.

Finally, although the direction of Paul's original thinking was probably from "solution to plight," the argumentation of Rom. 1–3, as Sanders admits, moves "from plight to solution." Thus, it is overwhelmingly probable that Paul devoted more attention to the nature of this plight, and found more reason

---

50. See, particularly, Sanders, *Paul, the Law and the Jewish People,* pp. 123-32; Räisänen, 99-108.

51. Sanders, *Paul, the Law and the Jewish People,* p. 129; cf. Dodd; O'Neill; Schmithals.

52. Räisänen, 106.

53. This is a central thesis of Watson, which he applies to Rom. 2 (cf. pp. 112-14).

in human inability for the necessity of the solution, than Sanders has allowed.[54] In a legitimate reaction against the excessively anthropological focus of Bultmann, Sanders and others have gone too far in eliminating anthropology from its structural role in Paul's theology.

c. God's Faithfulness and the Judgment of Jews (3:1-8)

1*What, then, is the advantage of being a Jew, or what is the profit of circumcision? 2Much, in every way. First of all, they have been entrusted with the oracles of God. 3For what then? Though some of them were unfaithful, their unfaithfulness will not nullify the faithfulness of God, will it? 4By no means! Let God be true, though every person is a liar, just as it is written, "so that you may be justified in your words, and that you might triumph when you judge."*[a]

5*But if our unrighteousness commends the righteousness of God, what shall we say? God is not unjust to inflict his wrath, is he? I am speaking in a human fashion. 6By no means! For how, then, would God judge the world? 7And*[1] *if the truth of God abounded to his glory through my lie, why am I yet being judged as a sinner? 8And why not conclude — as some are slanderously reporting that we say — "Let us do evil things, in order that good things might come"? God's judgment of such people is just.*

a. Ps. 51:4

The unwary commentator approaches this paragraph thinking to find rather clear sailing after the exegetical whirlpools of chap. 2 and before the theological storms of 3:21. He or she quickly realizes (or at least this commentator

---

54. E.g., Westerholm, 151-64.

1. This translation assumes that δέ (found in the primary Alexandrian uncial ℵ, and the secondary Alexandrian MSS A and 81) is the original reading. True, the alternative reading, γάρ, can marshal the largest number of witnesses, including the primary Alexandrian uncial B, the secondary Alexandrian minuscules 33 and 1739, the western D and G, the uncial Ψ, and the majority text. The UBS committee regards γάρ as "a rather inept scribal substitution, perhaps of western origin," but their reason for this conclusion is revealing: the parallelism between vv. 5 and 7 requires that δέ be read (Metzger, 507). Beyond this matter, which is precisely what needs to be determined, internal considerations are not conclusive. On the one hand, it could be argued that the presence of εἰ δέ in the generally parallel v. 5 might have led a copyist to substitute δέ for an original γάρ. On the other hand, the frequency of the εἰ γάρ combination in Paul may have stimulated the reverse procedure. If, as we argue in the exegesis, v. 7 is parallel to v. 5, then some preference for δέ might be indicated. While still not impossible, it is much more difficult to adopt this explanation if γάρ is read (correctly stressed by Godet).

did) the justice of Godet's claim: the paragraph 3:1-8 is "one of the most difficult, perhaps, in the Epistle." The chief cause of the obscurity is the rapid-fire sequence of questions, cast in a dialogical style. Is Paul citing and rejecting false consequences as he follows the "inner logic" of his own argument?[2] or is he reproducing a debate with a definite opponent?[3] In either case, which points are the false statements Paul rejects and which the correct teaching that he is defending? The difficulty of the passage is revealed in the fact that even this question is hotly debated. Stowers has shown that this passage manifests many of the characteristics of the diatribe style and can be compared with the use of questions and false conclusions typical of that style.[4] But few solid exegetical results come from this identification, not least because the diatribe style itself is quite amorphous and variable; and as Stowers notes, Paul shows evidence of having adapted it rather considerably.[5]

The difficulties presented by this passage have led one commentator to brand Paul's argument as "obscure and feeble" (Dodd). Others, convinced that Paul does argue coherently, nevertheless disagree dramatically on the nature of that argument. Without exploring these differences in detail,[6] we might note two

---

2. D. R. Hall, "Romans 3:1-8 Reconsidered," *NTS* 29 (1983), 184. Käsemann sees vv. 1-4 as a diatribe style, without any real opponent, while he finds in vv. 5-8 a genuine controversy.

3. E.g., Wilckens.

4. Stowers, *Diatribe,* pp. 119-20; idem, "Paul's Dialogue with a Fellow Jew in Romans 3:1-9," *CBQ* 46 (1984), 710-14. Hall's view that the text is not a diatribe reflects a more narrow definition of the genre ("Romans 3:1-8," pp. 183-84).

5. *Diatribe,* p. 137.

6. We may here, however, note three recent reconstructions of the progress of the dialogue.

(1) Traditionally, vv. 1, 3, 5, and most of 7-8 are attributed to Paul's opponent, or dialogue partner, with vv. 2, 4, 6, and 8b giving Paul's responses. Piper (pp. 103-13), while following this general scheme, argues that we must take into account the difference between Paul's opponents' understanding of "righteousness of God" and Paul's own view. In v. 5, "righteousness of God" means saving righteousness, since this is the opponents' understanding, but the logic of vv. 2-4 demonstrates that Paul holds a broader view of this concept, incorporating the judicial punishment as well as the saving power of God. The parallel with "glory" in v. 7 suggests, furthermore, that this broader conception of righteousness involves God's commitment always to act for his own glory (a meaning of "righteousness of God" that Piper finds to be basic in the OT). While Piper is correct to argue that Paul holds a conception of God's righteousness that involves something intrinsic to God and that it includes God's punitive justice, the connection with glory is not so clear (nor is it in the OT). It is likely, furthermore, that this, Paul's, meaning, rather than the opponents', is to be attributed to "righteousness" in v. 5. This makes better sense of the connection between v. 4b and v. 5 and also of the question about God's unrighteousness in v. 5b. Moreover, Paul always uses τί ἐροῦμεν ("what shall we say?") to introduce an objection to his own teaching.

(2) Hall ("Romans 3:1-8"), who does not find any real dialogue partner here,

broadly different approaches to the text. The first, the more "traditional" model, posits a shift in subjects at v. 5 (or v. 4). In vv. 1-4 (or 1-3), Paul focuses on the Jewish people, affirming the continuing faithfulness of God to them despite their widespread unfaithfulness. The strength of this affirmation, however, leads to another, far broader, question about the ways of God with humankind generally: How is it "right" for God to judge people when their sin magnifies his goodness and glory? On this view, the antecedent of the pronouns in vv. 5-8 ("our," "us," "my") is "people" or "man"/"woman." The other approach, which, while not unknown in the history of exegesis, has become more popular recently, insists that Paul's focus remains on the Jews throughout the paragraph. Verses 5-8, on this view, do not take up a general objection to the fairness and consistency of God, but affirm the faithfulness of God to Israel or the "right" of God to judge even his own covenant people.

In my view, this second approach is nearer to the truth. Verses 1-4a reject the inference that the judgment under which disobedient Jews stand (2:17-29) means that the Jews have no advantage at all. Rather, Paul insists, they have a great advantage, in possessing the words of God (vv. 1-2). The widespread unfaithfulness of the Jews in no way annuls God's faithfulness to those words (vv. 3-4a). Then, with the quotation of Ps. 51:4b in v. 4b, Paul's argument takes a decisive turn. Here he shows that God's faithfulness, or

---

follows the traditional scheme up to v. 5b. Here, however, he suggests that the question "God is not unjust. . . ?" is Paul's answer to the question in v. 5a rather than an opponent's question that follows from v. 5a. He also diverges from the usual interpretation in viewing vv. 7-8 as Paul's responses rather than as further questions from an objector. In neither of these points can he be followed. The sequence of τί ἐροῦμεν ("what shall we say?") — question — μὴ γένοιτο ("by no means!") (vv. 5b-6a) makes it clear that the question must represent an objector's viewpoint — even if it is phrased by Paul (as the μή implies). And the parallel between v. 7a and what Paul has taught in vv. 2-5 makes it clear that this must be a summary of Paul's own view, in which case the question of v. 7b is an objection to Paul. If this is so, then v. 8, connected to v. 7 with καί ("and"), must also embody an objection against Paul.

(3) The proposal of Stowers (cf. "Dialogue, p. 715) is built on his understanding of the usual function and development of the diatribe. In keeping with his view of this style as more at home in the philosophical "school" than in popular rhetoric and debate, he finds in 3:1-9 a "conversation" between Paul and a "student." As in the typical diatribe, Paul, the "teacher," does not simply respond to questions, but asks questions himself to guide the discussion. Stowers, then, attributes the questions in vv. 3, 5, and 7-8 to Paul, with v. 2 as Paul's initial response to the interlocutor's question (v. 1) and v. 9b as Paul's answer to v. 9a. Verses 4 and 6, in addition to vv. 1 and 9a, are then attributed to the interlocutor. Since in Stowers's view the interlocutor is not so much an opponent as a student, the attributing of verses to the interlocutor that are usually regarded as Paul's does not make a great difference in the meaning. It would, however, be unusual for Paul to give to the interlocutor so much of the "dialogue," including what is perhaps the decisive step in the argument, the OT quotation in v. 4b.

"righteousness," is manifested even through the sin of his people, for God's words promise judgment for disobedience as well as blessing for obedience. Verse 5, then, is Paul's formulation of a Jewish objection to the effect that Jewish sin, since it manifests God's righteousness, should not be subject to the wrath of God. This inference Paul rejects, simply noting that it is incompatible with the biblical doctrine that God is a just judge (v. 6). The objector repeats his or her objection again, however (v. 7), and adds to it the claim that Paul's doctrine actually encourages sinning (v. 8a). Paul again curtly rejects this line of reasoning, announcing the justice of God's condemnation (v. 8b). Taken as a whole, then, the passage both affirms the continuing faithfulness of God to his covenant people and argues that this faithfulness in no way precludes God from judging the Jews. Provoking this discussion is the Jewish tendency to interpret God's covenant faithfulness solely in terms of his salvific promises. Paul meets that conception with a broader and deeper view of God's faithfulness — his faithfulness to remain true to his character and to *all* his words: the promises of cursing for disobedience as well as blessing for obedience.[7]

What begins, then, as an attempt to answer an objection to Paul's ironing out of distinctions between Jews and Gentiles (vv. 1-2) becomes a frustratingly brief discussion of the relationship between Israel's unbelief and God's righteousness and, ultimately, between human sin and God's purposes. Indeed, many of our difficulties in interpretation are caused by the fact that Paul is touching here very briefly and sometimes allusively on themes that he develops at greater length elsewhere in the letter — especially chaps. 9–11.[8] The paragraph as a whole, then, while something of an "excursus" in Paul's exposition, contributes in important ways to our understanding of Paul's view of God's righteousness in its relationship to Israel's unbelief. In thus allowing the Roman Christians to "listen in" on this dialogue, Paul warns his mainly Gentile audience that they should not interpret the leveling of distinctions between Jew and Gentile in terms of God's judgment and salvation as the canceling of all the privileges of Israel. As Rom. 11:11-24 makes clear, Paul knows that the Gentile Christians, in Rome and elsewhere, need to hear this caution.

1 Paul frequently uses the words "what, then,"[9] in Romans to raise questions about what he has taught and so further his argument. While it is

---

7. For this general approach, see esp. Wilckens; Livermore, "Romans 1:18–3:20," pp. 232-33; Piper, 111-13; Stowers, "Dialogue," p. 718; Hall, "Romans 3:1-8," pp. 183-97.

8. See esp. Dunn.

9. Gk. τί οὖν. Sometimes Paul uses the phrase absolutely (3:9; 6:15; 7:7; 11:7); other times he adds ἐροῦμεν (6:1; 9:14, 30); and still other times, as here, he uses it to introduce a substantive question (4:1; 8:31; 9:19 [v.l.])

possible that Paul "quotes" a real interlocutor, it is more likely that he himself poses these questions to his readers. In other words, Paul is not so much reproducing for his readers an argument between himself and another person as he is posing questions and objections to himself in order to make his views clear to the Romans. Remembering Paul's own rich Jewish heritage, we might even regard the dialogue as one between Paul the Jew and Paul the Christian.[10] In chap. 2, Paul, writing from the vantage point of the fulfillment of salvation history in Christ, has asserted that possession of the law and circumcision — in a word, being Jewish — makes no essential difference for the day of judgment. The question in v. 1 is therefore entirely natural: "What, then, is the advantage[11] of being a Jew, or what is the profit[12] of circumcision?"

2 Dodd maintains that the logical reply to the questions of v. 1 is "none," and that it is only because of Paul's Jewish prejudice that he insists on continuing prerogatives for the Jews. But Dodd's opinion illustrates his failure to understand the particular purpose of chap. 2. Paul's intention there was not to deny that the Jews have privileges that the Gentiles do not have, but to contest the notion that these privileges give to the Jew an advantage in the judgment. Therefore, while acknowledging that the Jews have unparalleled access to God's truth in their law (vv. 17-20), he insists that it is only the doing of the law, not the simple possession of the law, that will satisfy God. There is nothing at all inconsistent, then, with Paul's positive response in v. 2, "much,[13] in every way." "In every way," if taken literally, claims an advantage for the Jew "in every respect," but Paul's meaning is more likely to be that the Jews' advantage extends to a significant number of matters.[14] What specific matters Paul may have in mind, in addition to the one advantage actually listed in this verse, can be gathered from 9:4-5: "adoption, the glory, the covenants, the giving of the law, the worship, and the promises; . . . the patriarchs, and of their race according to the flesh, . . . Christ." That Paul

---

10. See Dunn, 1.91.

11. Gk. περισσόν, a neuter substantive derived from περισσός, which means "exceeding the usual number or size" (BAGD). "What then is the advantage" means, then, "in what way does the Jew 'surpass' the usual person"; "what advantage does the Jew have [over the Gentile]?"

12. Gk. ὠφέλεια. This word provides a linguistic connection between the argument in 3:1-8 and 2:25-29, ὠφελέω ("to profit") being used in 2:25. These clear links with 2:17-29, along with the apparent inclusion of all Jews in v. 2, make it unlikely that 3:1 turns to a new audience — e.g., those Jews who have been faithful to the covenant (contra C. H. Cosgrove, "What If Some Have Not Believed? The Occasion and Thrust of Romans 3:1-8," *ZNW* 78 [1987], 90-92).

13. The Gk. πολύ is neuter, answering to the neuter περισσόν in v. 1. In sense, of course, it responds to both questions in v. 1.

14. The phrase is κατὰ πάντα τρόπον; cf. its use in Num. 18:7; Ign. *Eph.* 2:2; *Trall.* 2:3; *Smyrn.* 10:1.

intended to list more than the one item he actually includes is suggested by the phrase "first of all."[15] Indeed, some think the word may mean simply "chiefly,"[16] or be used to single out that advantage which stands supreme among the other privileges,[17] but it is likely that Paul intended to give a longer list, only to be forestalled by his concern about the Jews' response to "the oracles" and its implications.[18]

Even if the syntax does not justify our translating "chiefly," it is clear that the first advantage Paul enumerates is the supreme privilege granted to the Jews: "they have been entrusted with[19] the oracles of God." Paul uses the third person ("they") because, as in 9:1-5, he is thinking not of all Jews, including Jewish-Christians like himself, but only of unbelieving Jews. The word "oracles" (e.g., "divine utterances")[20] is used in the LXX of Balaam's "oracle" (Num. 24:4, 16) and frequently of God's "words" to his people.[21] The general meaning of the word gives rise to a plethora of suggestions about its specific reference here: "unmistakably divine" utterances of the OT;[22] God's self-revelation in both the OT and NT;[23] the law, especially the Decalogue;[24] and the promises of the OT,[25] or the OT as a whole, with special reference, perhaps, to the promises.[26] Of these alternatives, the last suits best the general application of the word in the LXX and the NT. Paul sets forth

15. Gk. πρῶτον μέν.

16. E.g., Calvin; Schmithals.

17. Godet, J. Morison, *A Critical Exposition of the Third Chapter of Paul's Epistle to the Romans: A Monograph* (London: Hamilton, Adams, 1866), pp. 9-11.

18. E.g., S-H; Barrett; Cranfield; Wilckens; Fitzmyer; Stuhlmacher.

19. Gk. ἐπιστεύθησαν. When used in the passive with an accusative following, the verb πιστεύω means "entrusted with" (cf. 1 Cor. 9:17; Gal. 2:7; 1 Thess. 2:4; 1 Tim. 1:11).

20. Gk. λογία.

21. Sometimes it refers to a specific word (Ps. 105:19), but more often to the revelation of God generally (cf., e.g., Deut. 33:9 and the 24 occurrences in Ps. 119). It usually translates words from the roots אמר and דבר. In the NT, λογία refers to the law of Moses (Acts 7:38), to the "teachings" (presumably Christian) about God (Heb. 5:12), and to "God's oracles" generally (probably oral) (1 Pet. 4:11).

22. S-H.

23. Zahn; Barth, *Shorter;* Cranfield.

24. Schlatter.

25. Meyer; Denney; Lietzmann; Leenhardt; Michel; Käsemann; Piper, 105; S. L. Johnson, "Studies in Romans. Part VII: The Jews and the Oracles of God," *BSac* 130 (1973), 240-45; Williams, "Righteousness of God," pp. 266-67 (as the Abrahamic promise specifically).

26. Cf. esp. J. W. Doeve, "Some Notes with Reference to ΤΑ ΛΟΓΙΑ ΤΟΥ ΘΕΟΥ in Romans III²," in *Studia Paulina in honorem Johannis de Zwaan septuagenarii* (Haarlem: F. Bohr, 1953), pp. 111-23; also Hodge; Godet; Morison, *Exposition,* pp. 14-18; Barrett; Murray; Dunn; Hall, "Romans 3:1-8," p. 185; Fitzmyer.

as the greatest of Jewish distinctions the fact that God has spoken to them and entered, with these words, into a special relationship with them. Material, though not linguistic, parallels to Paul's assertion are found in Deut. 4:8 — "What other nation is so great as to have such righteous decrees and laws as this body of laws I am setting before you today?" — and Ps. 147:19-20 — "He has revealed his word to Jacob, his laws and decrees to Israel. He has done this for no other nation; they do not know his laws." That the promises of God are included in "the oracles" is, of course, obvious; and Paul has probably chosen to use this word, rather than, for example, "the Scriptures," because he wants to highlight those "sayings" of the OT in which God committed himself to certain actions with reference to his people.[27] This nuance is suggested also by the words "unbelief" and "unfaithfulness" (v. 3) to designate Israel's failure and the words "faithfulness" and "reliability" to denote God's commitment.

3   Being entrusted with the stewardship of God's revelation is a great distinction. But in light of the sad history of Israel's rebellion, a rebellion that has (largely) continued right up to the present time, it could be asked whether this distinction any longer has meaning. This is the question raised in v. 3, as Paul departs from his "script" to deal with implications of, and objections to, his assertion of Jewish "advantage."[28] The precise form of that question, however, hinges on how the verse is punctuated and whether any of it is to be attributed to an objector. One alternative is to follow most English translations and divide the verse into two substantive questions: "What if some were unfaithful? Will their faithlessness nullify the faithfulness of God?" (NRSV). On this reading, the first question could be that of an objector to Paul, with the second, rhetorical, question being his response. The objector: "But Paul, what of the fact that some Jews have not proven faithful?" Paul: "What of it — their unfaithfulness cannot cancel God's faithfulness, can it?" Another option is to attribute both questions to Paul: "What, you might ask, of the fact that some Jews have not proven faithful? This does not mean, does it, that God will be any less faithful on his part?"[29] It is also possible, however, to divide the verse into a short interjectory question — "For what then?"[30] — and a longer substantive question — "Though some of them were unfaithful, their unfaithfulness will not nullify the faithfulness of God, will it?" The substantive question may then be that

27. τὰ λογία here may, then, be shorthand for those privileges of Israel that Paul enumerates in 9:4-5a.

28. Cf. H. Räisänen, "Zum Verständnis von Röm 3, 1-8," in *The Torah and Christ* (Publications of the Finnish Exegetical Society 45; Helsinki: Kirjapaino Raamattutalu, 1986), p. 200.

29. Morison, *Exposition,* pp. 20-22.

30. Cf. Phil. 1:18.

of an objector[31] or be Paul's own.[32] Paul's preference for short, pointed, questions when he writes in the dialogical style favors this second punctuation, and it is probable that Paul himself formulates the question.[33]

Paul's use of "some"[34] to designate the unfaithful Jews must be motivated partially by a desire to lessen the offense, since Rom. 9–11 shows that he regarded most Jews as having failed to respond appropriately to God's word.[35] By using the words "be unfaithful" and "unfaithfulness" to denote the Jews' failure, Paul creates an ironic antithesis to "entrust" in v. 2: God's "entrusting" of "the oracles" to Israel has not met with a corresponding "trust" on their part.[36] But, more importantly, these words point up the contrast between Israel's "faith*less*ness" and God's "faith*ful*ness."[37] This faithfulness of God, a concept that Paul picks up from the OT, refers especially to God's commitment to carry out the terms of the covenant with Israel. In contrast, then, the Jews' "faithlessness" will denote particularly their failure to meet their covenant obligations.[38] "Faith" in God and the promises is, of course, a significant and indispensable ingredient of true faithfulness to the covenant, and in that sense "lack of belief" is not excluded by this translation. Particularly, especially in light of 11:17, we should include in this "unfaithfulness" to the word of God the Jews' failure to embrace Jesus as the Messiah promised by that word.[39] While, then, Paul's

---

31. E.g., Wilckens.

32. E.g., Godet.

33. Attribution to Paul himself is suggested by the μή, which shows that the question expects a negative answer and is therefore in continuity rather than in contrast with v. 2. In addition, we would have expected a (presumably) Jewish objector to have used the first person plural rather than the third person plural.

34. Gk. τινες.

35. Calvin. Note the similar use of τινες in 11:17: "But [what] if *some* of the branches were broken off?"

36. Matching the verb ἀπιστεύω in v. 2 are the words ἀπιστεύω ("refuse to believe," "lack faith") and ἀπιστία ("lack of belief or faith").

37. Gk. τὴν πίστιν. In keeping with the usual meaning of πίστις in the LXX (where it always translates forms of אמן), this phrase means "God's faithfulness" (the genitive θεοῦ is subjective). In the LXX, God's πίστις is especially associated with his commitment to bless his people, in accordance with the terms of the covenant (Ps. 33:4; Jer. 32:41; Lam. 3:23; Hos. 2:20; cf. also *Pss. Sol.* 8:28).

38. Especially those commentators who think that τὰ λογία refers to God's promises argue that we should translate the terms in question as "disbelieve" and "unbelief" (S-H; Godet; Gifford; Meyer; Murray; Cranfield; Morison, *Exposition,* p. 23). This option has solid lexical support, since both words are used most often with this meaning in the NT. On the other hand, the contrast with God's πίστιν (cf. also 2 Tim. 2:13), the broader meaning that probably must be given τὰ λογία, and the heavy emphasis on the Jews' failure to obey the law in chap. 2 suggest that Paul is referring to the unfaithfulness of Israel to her covenant obligations (BAGD; Käsemann).

39. Cf. Dunn.

reference cannot be confined to the failure of Jews to believe in Christ, this would certainly be a prominent component of his meaning.[40] But, as is also the case in some of the key OT passages, Paul affirms that the failure of "some" Jews to abide by the terms of the covenant does not "nullify"[41] God's continuing care for and commitment to his people.

4 The form of the question in v. 3 has already anticipated its answer; but Paul leaves no doubt. He uses a formula of emphatic rejection, variously translated "God forbid" (KJV), "Of course not!" (Phillips), and, most literally, "May it never be!" (NASB).[42] The contrast in v. 4a between God's being "true" and the human being a "liar" restates the contrast between Israel's unfaithfulness and God's faithfulness in v. 3. When the OT speaks of God being "true," it usually means not that he is honest but that he is reliable, or trustworthy; "true" to his word.[43] And, while the promise to which God is "true" is usually his promise of blessing for his people, God's truth is also displayed when he carries out his threat of judgment for disobedience. Note especially Neh. 9:32-33, where the Levites acknowledge that God has "done truth" in bringing judgment upon Israel.[44] It is possible, then, that Paul may already be suggesting what is made explicit in v. 4b: that God is "reliable," faithful in fulfilling his word, even when people suffer his judgment.

40. Those who emphasize, with varying degrees, the application of Paul's language to failure to believe in Christ include Godet; Murray; Mundle, *Glaubensbegriff des Paulus*, p. 10; Cosgrove, "Romans 3:1-8," p. 97; Räisänen, "Röm 3,1-8," pp. 189-90.

41. The Greek verb is καταργέω, a distinctively Pauline word. It occurs only rarely in pre-NT secular Greek, where it means "to leave or cause to be idle" (LSJ), and only four times in the LXX, all in 2 Esdras, where it means "destroy." In the NT, it occurs in Luke 13:7; Heb. 2:14; and 25 times in Paul. Paul uses the word to mean "destroy" (1 Cor. 6:13), "pass away," "become outmoded" (1 Cor. 13:8, 10, 11; 2 Cor. 3:7, 11, 13, 14), "release from" (Rom. 7:6; Gal. 5:4), and "nullify," "render powerless" (Rom. 6:6; 1 Cor. 15:24; Gal. 3:17). See, e.g., G. Delling, *TDNT* I, 452-54. This last meaning makes best sense in the present context: the unfaithfulness of Israel will not "nullify" the faithfulness of God.

42. The Greek is μὴ γένοιτο (an optative form), a negative oath. Paul uses the same formula frequently in Romans (cf. 3:6, 31; 6:2, 15; 7:7, 13; 9:14; 11:1, 11). He probably takes it from the diatribe style; Epictetus uses the phrase frequently in the same way as Paul. See esp. Malherbe, "*Mē genoito*," 231-40. A few scholars (e.g., Str-B, 3.133; Murray) think that Paul may derive the expression from Heb. חָלִילָה לִי (cf., e.g., Gen. 44:7, 17), but that word does not have the same independent function that is typical of Paul's use of the phrase μὴ γένοιτο (cf. Käsemann).

43. The Greek in the LXX is ἀλήθεια ("truth") or ἀληθής ("true"), translating Heb. אֱמֶת.

44. Cf. also Ps. 45:4; 54:5; 96:13; 119:75. Fitzmyer cites Amos 3:2: "You alone have I known of all the families of the earth; therefore I will chastise you for all your iniquities."

Paul continues to enhance the contrast between God and human beings by again (cf. "unfaithfulness" versus "faithfulness" in v. 3) choosing linguistic opposites to make his point: "Let God be true, though every person is a liar."[45] Just as "true" characterizes God as being one who is reliable, so "liar," by contrast, and with analogies in the LXX, designates human beings as "unreliable, perfidious, faithless."[46] The precise meaning of this assertion is not clear.[47] Cranfield thinks that it refers generally to the nature of human beings as opposed to God. Wilckens confines the reference to Jews, arguing that Paul is condemning them all as covenant breakers. Käsemann, finding in "every" evidence of a significant move from Israel to the world at large, and interpreting v. 4b as an apocalyptic trial scene, argues that v. 4a pictures God as the victor and the human being as the loser in this trial. However, a concessive translation ("though," as in most of the English versions) makes perhaps best sense. Not only is God faithful when "some" are unfaithful, but he remains true *even if* every person should prove unreliable.

Paul uses his customary introductory formula — "just as it is written"[48] — to introduce a quotation from Ps. 51:4 that substantiates his point about the reliability and consistency of God: "so that you may be justified in your words, and that you might triumph when you judge."[49] Psalm 51 is David's moving

---

45. Paul's use of the imperative γινέσθω in this verse creates some difficulty. If we give the verb its "normal" dynamic meaning, Paul would be calling on God to "become" true. But Paul clearly believes God to always have been "true." Therefore, some paraphrase "let God be *recognized* as true" (Morison, *Exposition,* p. 36; Hodge; Murray), or "let God become more and more true [as more and more of his promises are fulfilled]" (Godet), or, with allusion to v. 4b, "let God's victory have its final manifestation [at the end of history]" (Käsemann). But it is more likely that γίνομαι has lost its dynamic meaning and is used, as often in the NT, as equivalent to εἶναι ("to be"). The imperative will then be "a vigorous way of stating the true situation," in contrast to v. 3, and the clause may be paraphrased, as Cranfield suggests, "We confess rather that God is true." If this is the case, then the second clause (where the verb is assumed) will not express the wish that all people become liars (contra Nygren), but affirms that they are.

46. See Black.

47. Paul may allude to Ps. 116:11, "I said in my consternation, 'Everyone is a liar'" (LXX, πᾶς ἄνθρωπος ψευστής), but, if so, it does not help explain the function of the clause here.

48. A few commentators (e.g., O'Neill) take the formula with what precedes, on the supposition that v. 4a quotes Ps. 116:11 (see the note above).

49. Paul's wording matches the LXX (Ps. 50:6b) exactly, with the exception that Paul has the indicative νικήσεις ("you will triumph") rather than the subjunctive νικήσῃς (although a fairly well-attested variant has the subjunctive in Rom. 3:4 [cf. the NA[27] apparatus]). The LXX translation of Ps. 51:4b differs from the MT (51:5b) in four respects, only two of which affect the meaning. Neither change in the first line affects the sense: the use of the passive δικαιωθῇς for the Qal stative תִּצְדַּק, and the substantive λόγοις for the verbal form בְּדָבְרֶךָ. In the second line, however, the LXX speaks of God's

confession of his sin with Bathsheba, and v. 4b is a purpose clause in which David expresses the intention either of his confession (v. 3) or of his sin (v. 4a).[50] This purpose is that God might be "right"[51] in the sentence he has pronounced over David (cf. 2 Sam. 12:9-14) and "be clear" in his judgment of him. What makes Paul's quotation of this verse difficult is that the negative application of God's justice in the Psalm — God is right when he judges — is used to support what is apparently a positive revelation of God's faithfulness to his people (vv. 3-4a). It is possible, of course, that Paul uses the quotation very generally to support the notion that God is faithful. But if this were so, it is peculiar that he would include the troublesome "in order that" or the second line in his quotation. If we seek a closer connection between the quotation and the context, three main possibilities present themselves.

(1) Paul might ignore the original meaning of the Psalm verse and quote it with a positive meaning. On this view, the second line would be

---

"being victorious" (νικήσῃς), while the MT has God being "in the clear" (תִזְכֶּה), a change perhaps due to the influence of Aramaic and Syriac (cf. F. Delitzsch, *Psalms,* in *Commentary on the Old Testament,* by C. F. Keil and F. Delitzsch [3 vols. in one; Grand Rapids: Eerdmans, n.d.], 2.136; Morison, *Exposition,* pp. 40-41). While this does change the sense slightly, the difference is not great, since both forms assert the moral rightness of God in his judgments. Finally, the active בְשָׁפְטֶךָ is translated in the LXX with the ambiguous κρίνεσθαι. If this verb is a passive, the LXX introduces the idea of God's winning when he is put on trial. But it could well be middle, in which case no difference from the MT is present.

50. In fact, the clause introduced by לְמַעַן could be connected to its context in four different ways. (1) The word could have a final sense and go with the confession of David in v. 3. On this reading, David's confession of his sin has the purpose of showing forth the justice of God's judgment (C. A. Briggs and E. B. Briggs, *A Critical and Exegetical Commentary on the Book of Psalms* [ICC; 2 vols.; Edinburgh: T & T Clark, 1906, 1907], 2.6. Cf. Morison, *Exposition,* pp. 44-45; Cranfield). (2) The word could have a final sense but connect the clause with David's emphasis in v. 4a that his sin was against God. This has the purpose of vindicating the judgment that God pronounces on that sin (cf. Murray; Godet). (3) The word could have a final sense but refer to the purpose of God rather than of David. David's sin, then, not only leads to but is, in some deeper sense, allowed by God for the purpose of revealing his justice (A. F. Kirkpatrick, *The Book of the Psalms* [Grand Rapids: Baker, 1982 {original edition, 1902}], pp. 289-90). (4) Finally, we could take the word to indicate consequence rather than purpose: as a result of David's sin, God is shown to be just in judging (Calvin; Hall, "Romans 3:1-8," p. 187). While this last makes best sense of the verse, lexicographers and commentators do not provide much basis for translating לְמַעַן as a consecutive conjunction (cf. BDB). A decision among these alternatives is difficult, but it is clear that Paul, at any rate, following the LXX, gives the clause a purpose force (ὅπως).

51. Gk. δικαιωθῇς, Heb. תִצְדָּק. This meaning of צָדַק is typical of the word in the qal and reflects the forensic background of the root (cf. esp. Müller, *Gottes Gerechtigkeit,* pp. 65-67, who stresses the notion of a judicial process in which God wins the victory over the unrighteous world).

translated "and that you might triumph *when you are judged.*"[52] While this interpretation gives a satisfactory sense, it suffers from the necessity to give the words in Romans a very different meaning from what they have in the Psalm. While Paul can sometimes quote the OT without reproducing the exact meaning of the original, it is not wise to suggest such a solution unless it becomes necessary. Moreover, it is likely that we should translate the key verb "when you judge."[53]

(2) A second possibility, then, is to understand the quotation to be demonstrating "what sins do *not* do to God (abrogate his faithfulness) by showing what in fact they *do* do to God (justify his judgment)."[54] This view has the merit of maintaining the original meaning of Ps. 51:4b, but must take it as supporting, not v. 4a, with which it is directly connected, but v. 3.

(3) We are left, then, with the third alternative — that Paul quotes a verse expressing the faithfulness of God when he judges sin because the "truthfulness" of God in v. 4a itself includes this negative aspect of God's faithfulness to his word.[55] "The oracles of God" include warnings that God will judge sin as well as promises that he will bless his people. Because of this, the OT insists that God is equally faithful when he judges his people's sin and when he fulfills his promises.[56] We must assume, then, a transition of sorts between vv. 3 and 4. The faithfulness of God is expressed generally in v. 3 and would undoubtedly imply, to a Jewish objector as well as to the readers, a commitment on God's part to maintain Israel's special and blessed place in God's purpose. In v. 4, however, Paul shows that God's faithfulness must also be recognized when he judges his people's sins. As Paul has shown at length in chap. 2, the special place of the Jews in God's plan does not protect them from the judgment of God. In 3:1-4, Paul reaffirms their special status by appealing to the invariability of God with respect to his word. But he also reminds us that this word includes warnings of judgment as well as promises of blessing. It is "the Jew first," but in judgment (2:9) as well as blessing (1:16; 2:10).

---

52. E.g., taking κρίνεσθαι as passive rather than middle; cf. Schlier; Dunn; Käsemann. Käsemann's view is flavored by his conviction that Paul uses the language of the Psalm to state his apocalyptic conception of the final victory of God over the entire creation. For Käsemann, then, the text is a key support for his overall conception of the cosmic and apocalyptic dimensions of God's righteousness.

53. That is, κρίνεσθαι is middle, the verb having the sense "go to law" — cf. Matt. 5:40; 1 Cor. 6:6; so most commentators.

54. Piper, 111.

55. So, substantially, Haldane; Morison, *Exposition,* pp. 46-47; Hall, "Romans 3:1-8," pp. 186-88; Davies, *Faith and Obedience,* p. 80.

56. Cf. esp. Neh. 9:32-33; Lam. 1:18. This becomes a key motif in the first-century-B.C. *Psalms of Solomon,* where δικαιόω ("be just," "justify") is used, as in Ps. 51:4b, to state the "justness" of God in his judgment of his people (cf. 2:18; 3:5; 4:8; 8:7).

5 Verse 5, which is parallel in form to v. 3, is Paul's statement of a possible objection to his teaching in vv. 1-4: "But if our unrighteousness commends the righteousness of God, what shall we say?" Paul is himself responsible for the formulation of this objection, as is clear from (1) the transitional clause "what shall we say," which Paul always uses to introduce his own conclusion or question, (2) the form of the question,[57] and (3) the "apology" at the end of the verse for the "human" way of putting the problem. While the objection Paul formulates in this question may come in response to the argument in vv. 3-4a,[58] its basis is more likely to be found in v. 4b. This is suggested by the similarity between v. 5a and v. 4b in both vocabulary[59] and content: the issue in both is the causal relationship between human sin and God's righteousness. It is hard to know whether "our unrighteousness" has a general meaning — human sinfulness[60] — or a narrower focus — Jewish unfaithfulness.[61] On the one hand, Paul never elsewhere uses "unrighteousness"[62] to denote specifically Jewish unfaithfulness, and the first person plural "our," in light of "every person" in v. 4, could naturally denote Paul, his readers, and people in the most general sense. On the other hand, "unrighteousness" is parallel to "unfaithfulness" (v. 3) and "liar" (v. 4), both of which specify Jewish unfaithfulness to the covenant. What tips the scales slightly in favor of the latter view is the concern of Paul with the implications of Jewish disobedience throughout this passage.

Just as "our unrighteousness" parallels "unfaithfulness," so we would expect "God's righteousness" to parallel "the faithfulness of God" (v. 3). God's "righteousness" can denote his faithfulness, as LXX usage makes clear (see the excursus after 1:17 for details). But this is not to say that the phrase must denote God's *covenant* faithfulness specifically or that this faithfulness must be limited to God's "saving" faithfulness. In fact, the context points to a broader notion, since the cognate verb "be in the right" in v. 4b designates God's being in the right when he *judges*. Of course, this argument would not apply if Paul were quoting an objector here. But we have seen that, even if an objection lies below the surface, it is Paul who is responsible for the formulation of the verse. In light of v. 4b, then, "God's righteousness" cannot

---

57. Paul uses μή to show that he expects a negative response.

58. Cf., e.g., Calvin.

59. θεοῦ δικαιοσύνην ("righteousness of God") reflects δικαιωθῇς ("be just"), συνίστησιν (which means here "manifest" or "demonstrate" [cf. Rom. 5:8; Gal. 2:18]; see BAGD; W. Kasch, *TDNT* VII, 898) picks up ὅπως ("in order that").

60. E.g., Godet; Dunn.

61. Cf. esp. Käsemann; Wilckens; Hall, "Romans 3:1-8," pp. 188-89; Räisänen, "Röm 3:1-8," pp. 196-97.

62. Gk. ἀδικία. See Rom. 1:18 (twice), 29; 2:8; 6:13; 9:14; 1 Cor. 13:6; 2 Cor. 12:13; 2 Thess. 2:10, 12; 2 Tim. 2:19.

refer to God's saving righteousness,[63] nor to his "[distributive] justice" (his "fairness"),[64] nor to his fidelity and forensic victory over all creation.[65] Nor is he using the phrase in the same way as he did in 1:17, to describe the activity by which God justifies people.[66] Rather, "God's righteousness" here designates God's faithfulness to his own person and word, particularly, as v. 4b reveals, as this is revealed in his judgment of sin.[67] This broad application of the phrase has parallels in the OT, and God's being "true" in v. 4a, as we suggested, may already encompass this dimension of God's reliability.

If human sin has "manifested" something good — for even if God's righteousness is expressed in judgment, that righteousness is still good[68] — it might well be asked if God is not "unjust" when he punishes that sin. The reference is to the eschatological wrath that God will "inflict"[69] on the last day; and since "unrighteousness" in v. 5a refers to the sin of Jews, they are also the objects of this wrath. It is generally assumed that Paul uses "unjust"[70] with the meaning "unfair," "acting against principles of justice." But several expositors argue that the word continues the covenantal emphasis of the previous verses. They maintain that the question raised in this verse has behind it the Jewish conviction that God's "righteousness" guarantees salvation to

---

63. This view has the support of many recent interpreters; cf., e.g., Watson, 126; S. Lyonnet, *Les Etapes de l'histoire du salut selon L'Epître aux Romains* (Bibliothèque Oecumenique 8; Paris: Cerf, 1969), pp. 26, 46-53. Piper, 107-8, gives the phrase this meaning but attributes it to Paul's opponents; cf. also Wilckens. Williams interprets the phrase to mean God's commitment to the Abrahamic promises, in line with his understanding of τὰ λογία ("Righteousness of God," pp. 265-70).

64. For this interpretation, see, e.g., Godet; Hodge; Murray; Ridderbos, *Paul,* p. 74; G. Bornkamm, "Theologie als Teufelskunst, Römer 3:1-9," in *Geschichte und Glaube, Band II. Gesammelte Aufsätze* (Munich: Kaiser, 1971), p. 145.

65. This view is identified especially with Käsemann; cf. also Reumann, *Righteousness in the New Testament,* p. 73.

66. Contra Haldane.

67. Cf. esp. Hall, "Romans 3:1-8," pp. 186-88; Stuhlmacher, "Paul's View of Righteousness," pp. 78-79. D. Hill (*Greek Words with Hebrew Meanings: Studies in the Semantics of Soteriological Terms* [SNTSMS 5; Cambridge: University Press, 1967], p. 158), Morris (*Apostolic Preaching,* p. 252), and Cosgrove ("Romans 3:1-8," p. 95) hold similar views. Although Piper does not interpret the phrase in this verse in this way, his interpretation of Paul's concept of God's righteousness as it unfolds in the passage as a whole is very close to ours (cf. pp. 109-13 on 3:1-8).

68. Even when the focus is on the judgmental side of "God's righteousness," the term is, as Stuhlmacher puts it, "semantically positive" ("The Apostle Paul's View of Righteousness," p. 79). This cancels Piper's objection (p. 107) that the view defended above does not make logical sense.

69. For this meaning of ἐπιφέρω, see BAGD. They cite *Ep. Arist.* 253 and Josephus, *Ant.* 2.296.

70. Gk. ἄδικος.

Israel. Is not, then, God in violation of this covenant agreement — *a-dikos*, "acting against his commitment to Israel" — if he inflicts wrath on his covenant people?[71] This interpretation correctly sees a certain Jewish view of divine righteousness behind the passage and establishes continuity with vv. 3-4. But it cannot give a satisfactory explanation for the sequence of sentences in vv. 5-6a. If v. 5 is attributed to an objector, who assumes that God's righteousness is purely salvific,[72] it is hard to understand why v. 5a speaks of human sin "manifesting" God's righteousness. In addition, as we have seen, it is unlikely that v. 5 can be construed as the statement of an objector.

On the other hand, if v. 5 is attributed to Paul, with v. 5b the logical conclusion to be drawn from the assertion of God's punitive righteousness in v. 5a,[73] these difficulties are avoided, but others are encountered. Primary among these is the emphatic "By no means!" in v. 6a, which always rejects a false conclusion in Paul. This strong rejection makes little sense if Paul has already stated his conclusion in v. 5b. The only way to make sense of the sequence of thought, then, is to view the issue in v. 5 as the "justness" of God's condemning Jews for sins that manifest his righteousness. This "justness," in keeping with the theocentric focus of Scripture, is not God's conformity to some external norm, but his acting in accordance with his own character. Paul has already used *dik-* language in this broader sense in 2:5, where he affirmed that the judgment of God will be just, being based on the works of each person. Now the question is posed whether this principle can still hold when the sinful works of God's people manifest his own righteousness. But Paul's concern to distance himself from any suggestion that God might be unrighteous leads him immediately to add the parenthetical "I am speaking in a human fashion."[74]

6 With his characteristic "By no means," Paul makes emphatically explicit what was already implicit in the way he formulated the matter in v. 6: God certainly does not act "unjustly" if he inflicts wrath on his people.[75] And

---

71. Cf. esp. Wilckens; Piper, 108-9; Hall, "Romans 3:1-8," pp. 189-91; Watson, 126.

72. Wilckens; Piper, 108-9; Watson, 126.

73. Hall, "Romans 3:1-8," pp. 189-91.

74. Gk. κατὰ ἄνθρωπον λέγω. Paul uses the same phrase in 1 Cor. 9:8 and Gal. 3:15 and a similar one in Rom. 6:19. In Gal. 3:15 and Rom. 6:19, the point is that a human analogy is being used, while 1 Cor. 9:8 and the present verse are more negative, asserting the purely human perspective from which something is being viewed.

75. The assertion of God's absolute justice, even in the face of his judgment of his people, is familiar in the OT. Particularly noteworthy, because of the many linguistic parallels with 3:1-8 and because it is followed by a recitation of the disasters brought on Israel by their unfaithfulness, is Deut. 32:4: "The Rock! His work is perfect (LXX ἀληθινά), for all his ways are just (κρίσεις); a God of faithfulness (πιστός) and without injustice (οὐκ ἀδικία). Righteous (δίκαιος) and upright is he."

191

Paul explains his rejection with a counterquestion: "For how, then, would God judge the world?" The point of this question is to draw out the absurd and clearly impossible consequences of the supposition stated in v. 5. It is certainly not the case that God is unjust to inflict wrath, for if it were otherwise[76] (that is, if God were unjust), how could God judge the world? While Paul clearly appeals to a principle that he, his readers, and any objectors would agree to, the exact purpose of the citation in unclear. Most expositors think that Paul alludes to the OT doctrine that "the Judge of all the earth must deal justly" (Gen. 18:25). And while some commentators have suggested more pointed or more subtle interpretations,[77] it is probably simply this point that Paul wants to make. Since the justice of God as judge has been questioned, it is reasonable for Paul to allude to the common OT postulate that attributes absolute justice to God.[78]

7 Uncertainty about the logical progression of the passage arises again in v. 7. And since this verse is joined to v. 8 by "and,"[79] a decision about the function of v. 7 will determine also the function of v. 8. There are two main possibilities. First, these verses may repeat and elaborate the objection in v. 5: How is it fair for God to judge me if my sin brings him glory (v. 7); and does not this viewpoint of yours, Paul, actually encourage sin (v. 8a)? To these renewed objections, Paul replies simply with a pronouncement of judgment (v. 8b).[80] The second possibility is that these verses explain v. 6. The reason why God could not judge the world if it were unfair for him to punish sins that manifest his righteousness (v. 6) is that anyone ("I") could come before God with the same excuse (v. 7). Moreover, Paul reasons, does not such a view actually encourage sin (v. 8a)?[81] The issue, then, is whether these verses contain further objections to Paul's teaching, or Paul's reply to his objectors. Both interpretations are

76. Gk. ἐπεί; for this meaning of the word, see BDF 456(3).

77. E.g., that God must use his wrath if he is to judge the world (suggested, although not apparently adopted, by Barrett), or that God must include Jews in his judgment if he is to be judge of the *world* (Wilckens; Hall, "Romans 3:1-8," pp. 191-92), or that God could not judge the Gentiles (e.g., κόσμος) if he is not to judge the Jews (Bengel). Or, more subtly, is he suggesting that God could not judge anyone if he never judged those sins that manifest his righteousness, since all sins have that ultimate effect (Godet)? Each of these interpretations makes sense of the context, but each must also read into the context more than is plain. Paul's use of "world" rather than, e.g., "Gentiles" or "all people," suggests that he has in view God's judgment in the broadest sense.

78. In addition to Gen. 18:25, see Job 8:3; 32:10-12.

79. Gk. καί.

80. Most commentators adopt some form of this interpretation.

81. See Morison, *Exposition,* pp. 67-68, 73, 74-75; Godet; Alford; Gifford; Hodge; Hall, "Romans 3:1-8," pp. 192-94.

compatible with the viewpoints that Paul and his interlocutor have adopted in the paragraph.[82]

One of the major disadvantages of finding in these verses further objections to Paul's teaching is the apparent failure of Paul to make any reply to them. Would Paul have cited such serious accusations about his doctrine and been content simply to condemn their advocates? The second reading, to its undeniable advantage, avoids this problem. But it suffers from an even greater one: v. 7 does not naturally read as an explanation of v. 6. If this had been Paul's intention, we would have expected him to have made explicit a key link in the argument — that the sins of all people lead to God's glory — and to have phrased the question in these general terms (e.g., "who, then, could be judged as a sinner?"). Verse 7 reads much more naturally as a reiteration ("from the side of man" [S-H]) of the objection stated in v. 5. Both vv. 5-6 and vv. 7-8, then, take up the problem created by Paul in v. 4, the former verses relating to v. 4b and the latter to v. 4a, in a chiastic arrangement.[83]

I take it, then, that Paul in v. 7 is restating the basic objection heard already in v. 5: "if the truth of God abounded[84] to his glory through[85] my lie, why am I[86] yet[87] being judged as a sinner?" This being the case, his use of

82. If we were sure what conjunction Paul used to connect vv. 7-8 with v. 6, it would be easier to make a decision: reading δέ favors the former alternative; reading γάρ favors the latter. Unfortunately, the external evidence for these readings is so evenly divided that the best reading can be determined only after the argument of the passage is understood (see n. 1 above).

83. Cf. J. Jeremias, "Chiasmus in den Paulusbriefen," in *Abba: Studien zur Neutestamentlichen Theologie und Zeitgeschichte* (Göttingen: Vandenhoeck & Ruprecht, 1966), pp. 287-89.

84. Paul may use the aorist tense (ἐπερίσσευσεν) because the objector is regarding the matter from the perspective of the last judgment (Morison, *Exposition,* p. 71). More likely, however, the past history of Jewish infidelity is being viewed from the standpoint of the present demonstration of God's glory in the fulfillment of his promises: if that infidelity has been the instrument through which God's promises have come to fruition, why should God judge the Jew? On the other hand, ἐπερίσσευσεν may be an example of a non-past-referring aorist (cf. Porter, *Verbal Aspect,* p. 299).

85. The ἐν is instrumental.

86. Gk. κἀγώ. It is not clear why Paul uses this compound form. This word normally implies a contrast between ἐγώ ("I") and some other person or persons ("I also," "even I"). Particularly on the supposition that Paul is continuing his own argument in this verse, ἐγώ could designate Paul himself, with καί emphasizing that "even" he is not immune from judgment (Denney; Hall, "Romans 3:1-8," pp. 193-94). There is also some precedent for taking the καί in κἀγώ with the verb (cf. 1 Thess. 3:5), in which case the word would heighten the unfairness of God "also" in judging the one whose sin increased his glory (Meyer; Käsemann). In some verses, καί is virtually redundant (Eph. 1:15), so it may be that no significance in particular should be attached to it. If, however, a Jewish objector is represented as speaking in the verse, the implied comparison could be with

the first person singular is a rhetorical variant of the first person plural in v. 5. It is clear, however, from the formulation of the objection, that Paul is speaking more in the person of the objector himself than he was in v. 5. This objector is likely once again to be the Jew, who questions why God should treat him like other "sinners" when his unfaithfulness has been the occasion for God's faithfulness and led to an increase in his glory. The contrasting words "truth" and "lie" are picked up from v. 4a, and the covenantal flavor of the words there will be present here also. The new word in the verse, "glory," makes more specific the positive implications of "righteousness" in v. 5, and thereby sharpens the objection. As in vv. 4b and 5a, the central concern is again the relationship between Jewish unrighteousness and divine righteousness/glory.

8 If v. 7 is an objector's question, then v. 8 can be understood in one of two basic ways: either it adds a second objection, parallel to the one in v. 7,[88] or it responds to the objection of v. 7 with a rhetorical counterquestion.[89] In favor of taking the verse as an additional objection is the "and" that joins the verses and the fact that "let us do evil that good may come" is a natural reaction to Paul's stress on God's providential use of even human sin, as the parenthetical statement clearly shows. Construing the verse as Paul's reply to the objection of v. 7, on the other hand, supplies a response from Paul that would otherwise be missing, and provides a more natural explanation for the form of the question[90] and for the shift from the first person singular of v. 7 to the plural of v. 8. If Paul intended v. 8 as a reply to v. 7, however, it is almost inconceivable that he would have introduced it with "and" rather than "but"[91] or even "By no means!" This "and" suggests that the main clause of v. 8 is coordinate with v. 7 and thus continues the Jewish objector's criticism of Paul's doctrine.[92] If vv. 7-8 are then

---

Gentiles: why should *I,* the Jew whose sin has manifested God's glory, be judged like Gentiles? Some slight support for this view might be gathered from Paul's use of ἁμαρτωλός ("sinner"), which he uses in Gal. 2:15, 17 with direct reference to Gentiles (on the other hand, the word is used more generally in 5:8, 19; 7:13; 1 Tim. 1:9, 15). Cf. Hall, "Romans 3:1-8," pp. 193-94, whose view of the verse, however, differs from ours.

87. ἔτι expresses the logical inference to be drawn from the apodosis (BAGD).

88. Morison (*Exposition,* pp. 75-83) gives a particularly thorough defense of this interpretation.

89. See esp. Cranfield. On either reading, the double καθώς ("even as") clause must be taken as a parenthesis, with ποιήσωμεν ("let us do"), or perhaps ὅτι ("that"), resuming the main clause again.

90. Paul again uses a μή to imply a negative response.

91. Gk. either ἀλλά or δέ.

92. Paul may then have used μή because the verb ποιήσωμεν is subjunctive (cf. BDF 427[4]), or because, as in v. 5, Paul's paraphrase of the opponent already anticipates his answer. The switch from first person singular to plural reflects the difference between an example, where individualization is normal (v. 7), and a suggested course of action, in which all those considered in the category might take part.

connected in this manner, it is better to view v. 8 as a separate question than as a continuation of the sentence of v. 7.[93] The verse presents certain other syntactical problems, but they are best resolved in the way reflected in the NIV: "Why not say — as we are being slanderously reported and as some claim that we say — 'Let us do evil that good may result'?"[94]

   Paul wants to say two things: that he (and other apostles?) has been accused of teaching the very doctrine that the Jewish objector claims is the logical conclusion of his viewpoint, and that such accusations are "blasphemous."[95] Paul indicates that the objection to his teaching that he puts here in the mouth of a Jewish objector is one that he has heard before and one, more than likely, that the Roman Christians had also heard.[96] Why, then, does Paul not answer the objection? A very common suggestion is that Paul does so, but not until Rom. 6 — note the similarity between what is said here and 6:1: "should we continue in sin in order that grace might increase?" However, 6:1 is the question of a Christian in light of the abundance of God's grace; the objection here is posed by a Jew, questioning whether his or her actions really have any meaning in light of Paul's assertion that even sin leads to God's glory.[97] And Paul's response in Rom. 6 is not really appropriate to the issue raised here. We must suppose, then, that Paul intends the very absurdity of the objection to imply its dismissal. The viewpoint taken by the Jewish objector, that it would not be right for God to punish his people for their sins, is implied to be fallacious, and, indeed, blasphemous, by the absurd conclusion to which his objection leads.[98]

---

93. Käsemann; contra Godet; S-H; Barrett; H. Ljungvik, "Zum Römerbrief 3:7-8," *ZNW* 32 (1933), 207-10.

94. The problem is whether to carry over the τι from v. 7b and to supply the verb λέγομεν from the verb in the parenthesis — "And why should we not say 'Let us do evil that good may come'" (Cranfield) — to carry over the τι only — "Why might we not do evil that good may come?" (Morison, *Exposition,* p. 80) — or to leave the question without these additions — "And shall we not do evil that good may come?" (Piper, 257-58). This last suggestion may be the simplest. The syntax of the parenthetical clause is made awkward by the repetition of καθώς ("even as"), which occurs apparently because Paul wants to shift from the passive to the active voice in mid-sentence.

95. Paul uses the Greek verb βλασφημέω. He could refer specifically to the "slander" of Paul involved in such an accusation, or to the blasphemy, the impugning of the character of God, implicit in their accusation (Wilckens). Perhaps, however, there are elements of both in the word, as in 1 Tim. 6:1: "in order that the name of God and the teaching not be blasphemed."

96. Stuhlmacher is especially insistent that Paul's teaching here (and elsewhere in the letter) is occasioned by "Paul's Jewish-Christian opponents and their sympathizers," who have been active even in Rome (cf. p. 50).

97. Cf. Murray; Cosgrove, "Romans 3:1-8," pp. 99-100.

98. Hodge; Stowers, "Paul's Dialogue," p. 718.

Depending on what we identify as the antecedent of "whose,"[99] the final sentence of v. 8 may state the "justness" of God's condemnation[100] of the evil actions of people, such as are mentioned in vv. 7-8,[101] or of some particular people who have been mentioned in vv. 7-8 — those who have maligned Paul,[102] the person claiming exemption from God's judgment in v. 7,[103] or the people arguing "let us do good that evil may come" in v. 8.[104] Or, if we understand this curt sentence of judgment as the capstone to Paul's argument in 2:1–3:8, the antecedent could be the Jews generally.[105] The closest, and most natural, antecedent is the subject of the main clause in v. 8 — those who object that Paul's doctrine encourages the practice of sin. But, since these people are expressing essentially the same viewpoint as the "I" in v. 7, Paul's sentence of condemnation embraces the objectors in vv. 7-8 as a whole. Paul, then, both rejects the excuse put forward in v. 7 — God *is* "just" to judge the sinner whose "lie" brings God glory — and imposes the sentence appropriate for the "blasphemy" of those who have maligned Paul and, by implication, the God who has manifested his righteousness in Christ. This paragraph concludes on the note that sounds throughout Rom. 1:18–3:20 as a key theme: the "justness"[106] of God's judgment.

In sum: Paul begins by warning his readers not to draw the wrong conclusion from his invective against Jewish presumption of salvation through circumcision and the law (chap. 2). God is faithful to his promises to Israel; his "righteousness" is steady and dependable. But Paul quickly turns from defense of Israel to further attack, reminding the Roman Christians that God's faithfulness is ultimately not to Israel but to his own person and promises. God is therefore "righteous" when he punishes his people for their sin as well as when he rewards them for obedience. But this does not mean, Paul concludes, that we should excuse sin simply because it always magnifies God's righteousness. Such an attitude brings God's own name into disrepute.

The problem Paul attacks in these verses is not confined to the people of God of his day. All too often we Christians have presumed that God's grace to us exempts us from any concern about our sin. Particularly is this a danger among Christians who share with me the belief that God sovereignly maintains

---

99. Gk. ὦν.

100. This is the meaning of κρίμα here.

101. Achtemeier, "Some Things in Them Hard to Understand," pp. 261-62.

102. Cf. τινες; Godet; Michel; Barrett; Cranfield; Dunn.

103. That is, ἐγώ; cf. Gifford; S-H.

104. That is, the subject of the verb ποιήσωμεν, "let us do" (cf. Morison, *Exposition*, p. 88; Alford).

105. Watson, 127.

106. Gk. ἔνδικος.

the regenerate in their salvation till the end. Too easily do we forget that God's ultimate concern is for his own glory and not for our blessing; that his righteousness is beautifully displayed when he judges as well as when he saves. We want to "stand on the promises" — and this is entirely appropriate. But we must not forget that God promises (in the NT as well as in the OT) to rebuke and chastise his people for sin as well as to bless them out of the abundance of his grace.

3. The Guilt of All Humanity (3:9-20)

9*What then? Do we have an advantage? By no means!*[1] *For we have already accused all people, whether Jews or Greeks, of being under sin.* 10*Even as it is written,*

> *There is no one who is righteous,*
> 11*there is no one who understands,*
> *there is no one who seeks for God.*
> 12*All have turned aside and together gone wrong.*
> *There is no one who is doing good,*
> *there is not*[2] *even one person.*[a]
> 13*Their throat is an open grave,*
> *they speak deceptively with their tongues,*[b]

1. The text between the opening question Τί οὖν ("what then?") and the last part of the verse, beginning with προητιασάμεθα ("we have already accused") occurs in four basic forms:

1. προεχόμεθα; οὐ πάντως: — found in the Alexandrian family (cf. the primary witnesses ℵ and B, and the secondary witnesses 33, 81, and 1739), in modified form in one western witness (the second corrector of D), and in the majority text.
2. προεχώμεθα; οὐ πάντως: — read by the secondary Alexandrian uncial A.
3. προεχόμεθα; — read in the uncial P
4. προκατέχομεν περισσόν — read in two western uncials (D* and G) and one other uncial (Ψ)

Not only does the first have solid external support, but it seems clear that the other readings are attempts to avoid the difficulties of the first (cf. Lietzmann and the commentary). N. A. Dahl, however, opts for the third reading, translating "What, then, do we plead as a defense?" the "we" being Christians ("Romans 3:9: Text and Meaning," in *Paul and Paulinism,* pp. 184-204; cf. also Dunn).

2. Two witnesses to the Alexandrian text (the primary B and the secondary 1739) omit οὐκ ἔστιν ("there is not"). In favor of the originality of this omission is the fact that the inclusion of the words conforms the text to Ps. 14:3, from which Paul is quoting. But the support for the omission is quite slight, and the fact that οὐκ ἔστιν does *not* conform to the LXX is greatly in its favor.

and the poison of asps is under their lips.[c]
14*Their mouth is filled with curses and bitterness,*[d]
15*their feet are swift to shed blood,*
16*ruin and misery are in their paths,*
17*and they do not know the way of peace.*[e]
18*There is no fear of God in their eyes.*[f]

19*Now we know that whatever the law says, it speaks to those who
are in the law, in order that every mouth might be stopped and the
whole world be held accountable to God.* 20*For no human being will
be justified before him by works of the law, for through the law comes
knowledge of sin.*

    a. Ps. 14:1-3
    b. Ps. 5:9
    c. Ps. 140b*b*
    d. Ps. 10:7
    e. Isa. 59:7-8a
    f. Ps. 36:1b

While the brief questions that open v. 9 connect it with the dialogue of vv.
1-8,[3] it is also clear that Paul is moving toward a summary and application
of the teaching he has been developing since 1:18. He labels this long section
an "accusation." In it, he charges all people, Jews and Gentiles, with being
"under the power of sin" (v. 9b). A string of loosely related OT quotations
confirms the universality and describes the variety of the sin that so characterizes all humanity (vv. 10-18). Finally, in vv. 19-20, Paul draws out the
implications of this universal bondage to sin: all stand condemned before the
divine bar of judgment and are unable to escape that condemnation by anything
they do. Thus is the way prepared for the proclamation of God's righteousness
in Christ (vv. 21-26).

    9 The opening words of v. 9 present several related problems, in-
volving the original text, the punctuation, and the meaning. Assuming the text
printed in UBS[4] and NA[27], and accepted by the great majority of scholars, to
be correct,[4] it is most natural to divide the opening words of the verse into
two questions — "What then?" "Do we have an advantage?" — with a short
answer to the second — "By no means!" Following the diatribe style, Paul
uses the brief transitional "What then?"[5] to introduce a question stimulated
by something that has been said in the previous discussion. Precisely what in

---

    3. Accordingly, Stowers ("Dialogue," p. 720) and Fitzmyer keep v. 9a with the
paragraph 3:1-8.
    4. See the note on v. 9 above.
    5. Gk. τί οὖν.

his earlier teaching it is that stimulates the question depends on just what this question is. For both the meaning of the verb Paul uses[6] and the identity of the persons he has in mind with his first person plural form — "we Jews," "we Gentiles," "we Christians," "we apostles," Paul himself? — are uncertain. Four main possibilities must be considered.

(1) "Am I [Paul] making an excuse for the Jews?"[7] Since the second verb in this verse — "we have already accused" — has Paul as its subject, we might well think that the first verb does also. This solution makes good contextual sense also: in reply to the question whether Paul is trying to excuse the Jews, he responds, "No! For I have already accused both Jews and Greeks. . . ." But this rendering has an insuperable lexical problem: it must assume, against all evidence of usage, that the object of the "excusing" — the Jews — is different from its subject — Paul.

(2) "Are we Jews trying to excuse ourselves?"[8] If Paul is not the subject of the verb, then the next most likely option would seem to be that the Jews are. For, as we have seen, the Jews are probably the subject in most of the first person verbs in vv. 5-8. But to make the Jews the subject of the verb would require that we paraphrase the question to mean something like "Do we Jews have anything to protect us from God's wrath?"[9] And this reads more into the verb than is justified.

(3) "Are we Jews surpassed [by them]"; "Are we Jews at a disadvantage?" (see NRSVmg, REBmg).[10] Such a question might seem inappropriate to the context, since 3:1-8 has stressed the privileges, not the disadvantages, of the Jews.[11] But such an objection fails to reckon with the polemic against Jewish covenant security in vv. 4-8. In light of Paul's stress in those verses on the reality of God's judgment of his people (vv. 4, 5b, 8b), it would be quite natural for Paul's Jewish discussion partner to ask whether Jews were, then, at a disadvantage, and for Paul to reject that inference with a reminder that he had already condemned Gentiles as well as Jews. On the other hand,

---

6. Gk. προεχόμεθα, which could be either middle or passive. The verb προέχω occurs only here in biblical Greek (it is a v.l. in Job 27:6). Derived from its basic meaning "hold before," προέχω means, in the active, "have an advantage," "surpass, excel," and in the middle "hold before oneself," thus "put forward as an excuse" (LSJ).

7. This translation assumes that the verb is middle in meaning; cf. Morison, *Exposition,* p. 93; and BAGD, who mention this as one option.

8. This translation again assumes that the verb is middle in meaning; cf. Godet; Meyer; Murray; Stuhlmacher.

9. Moreover, when προέχομαι has this meaning, it is followed by an object that specifies the excuse (cf. A. Feuillet, "La situation privilégiée des Juifs d'après Rm 3,9. Comparison avec Rm 1,16 et 3,1-2," *NRT* 105 [1983], 34).

10. This translation takes προεχόμεθα as a passive; cf. S-H; Lightfoot; Black; Fitzmyer; Stowers, "Dialogue," pp. 719-20.

11. Cf., e.g., Cranfield.

nothing in the previous context has suggested that the Jews might be *worse off* (even if they are no better off) than the Gentiles.[12]

(4) "Do we Jews have an advantage?"[13] On this view, the question would be stimulated by the assertion of Jewish "advantage" in vv. 1-3, an assertion that Paul wants to qualify by warning again that, whatever historical privileges the Jews may have, these do not place Jews in a superior position in God's judgment. Since affirming distinguishing privileges for the Jewish people after the polemic of 2:17-29 is Paul's main intention in 3:1-8 (however far from that he may have strayed with qualifications and discussion), tying the question of v. 9 back to that point presents no difficulty. The main problem with this view is linguistic: no other example of this form of the verb with this meaning has been found,[14] and no early Christian interpreter apparently took the verb this way.[15] This makes a decision between the third and the fourth views very difficult. Fortunately, though the translations are at opposite poles, these alternatives do not materially alter the central point: Gentile and Jew are on equal terms when it comes to the judgment of God.

Whether Paul asks if the Jews are at a disadvantage or an advantage, his answer is a negative one.[16] At first sight, it might seem that this answer conflicts

---

12. Furthermore, the use of προέχω in the passive with this meaning is rare, and, were it so used, we might have expected it to be followed by ὑπό ("by") to express the agent.

13. This translation, taking προεχόμεθα as a middle form with active meaning, is adopted by most modern English versions (cf. TEV and REB explicitly) and commentators.

14. Although it is not uncommon in the NT to find verbs in the middle where actives would have been expected (cf. Turner, 106-7 [who mentions this verse as an example]; BDF 316).

15. Cf. Schelkle.

16. Gk. οὐ πάντως. The force of the negative is uncertain. The most natural meaning is a qualified negative: "not entirely" or "not altogether." This translation follows the rule that a negative preceding an adverb generally modifies that adverb (cf. BDF 433); and this is the probable meaning of οὐ πάντως in its only other NT occurrence (1 Cor. 5:10). This meaning is possible if προεχόμεθα means "do we [Jews] have an advantage?" Paul would then be responding, "Not in every respect, for while Jews do have the advantage of possessing the 'oracles of God' (v. 2), their advantage does not extend to protection from divine judgment" (cf. NAB; so Zahn; Michel; Huby; Cranfield; Feuillet, "La privilégiée des Juifs," pp. 33-46; S. L. Johnson, Jr., "Studies in Romans, Part IX. The Universality of Sin," *BSac* 131 [1974], 166). However, οὐ πάντως might be an example of hyperbaton — the reversal of the normal order of words — in which case it would be an emphatic negative: "altogether not," "certainly not" (so most modern English translations; and see Alford; BDF 433[3]; Robertson, 423; S-H; Barrett; Wilckens). (Morison *Exposition*, p. 107 and Godet suggest that the words be separated: "No, certainly.") This answer would seem to be required if προεχόμεθα has a passive significance, for Paul could not very well respond to the question "are we Jews at a disadvantage?" with a qualified negative. Even if the verb is given the active signification, the emphatic negative might be preferable, in the sense that Paul is rejecting any advantage for the Jews with respect to the point at issue.

with what Paul has said in vv. 1-2. But Paul is making complementary, not contradictory, points. The Jews have an unassailable salvation-historical advantage: God has spoken to them and he has given them promises that will not be retracted (vv. 1-2). But, as Paul has repeatedly emphasized in chap. 2, the Jews have no advantage at all when it comes to God's impartial judgment of every person "according to his or her works." And this is the issue that Paul is addressing in v. 9, as his explanation[17] of his negative response indicates: "we have already accused[18] all people, whether Jews or Greeks, of being under sin." Paul is referring to the comprehensive indictment of humanity in 1:18–2:29, as first the Greek or the Gentile (1:19b-32) and then the Jew (2:1-29) were brought before the divine bar and found wanting. We have, then, in this statement, Paul's own comment on his purpose in this section of his letter. All people who have not experienced the righteousness of God by faith are "under sin": that is, they are helpless captives to its power.[19] However arrived at, Paul's understanding that all people, Jews as well as Gentiles, were not just sinners but helpless pawns under sin's power, distinguished him sharply from his Jewish contemporaries.[20] Nothing that Paul has said suggests that there are exceptions to this rule, and nothing shows more clearly the desperate need for the message of the gospel. For the problem with people is not just that they commit sins; their problem is that they are enslaved to sin. What is needed, therefore, is a new power to break in and set people free from sin — a power found in, *and only in,* the gospel of Jesus Christ.

17. Note the γάρ, "for."

18. Gk. προητιασάμεθα, from προαιτιάομαι, used only here in the NT. It is worth noting that Paul characterizes his argument not as a proof of guilt but as an accusation of guilt (Johnson, "Universality of Sin," p. 167). Criticisms of 1:18–2:29, then, to the effect that Paul has not logically demonstrated the guilt of all people are wide of the mark.

19. It is commonplace to characterize Paul's teaching on sin as dominated by the concepts of bondage and power. And there is reason for this. Paul typically uses ἁμαρτία in the singular rather than in the plural and presses into service to describe the human condition images drawn from the world of slavery. The non-Christian is a "slave to sin" (Rom. 6:17); becoming a Christian means being "set free" from sin (6:18) and no longer having sin as one's "lord" (6:14a).

20. Cf., e.g., Sanders, *Paul and Palestinian Judaism,* pp. 546-47; Beker, 243; Livermore, "Romans 1:18–3:20," p. 324; and esp. T. Laato, *Paulus und das Judentum.* In G. Theissen's interesting classification of Paul's soteriological symbols, the ὑπό language is part of Paul's liberation symbolism ("Soteriologische Symbolik in den paulinischen Scriften," *KD* 20 [1974], 282-304). It is important to note, however, that the difference has to do more with the extent and seriousness than with the nature of sin. As 1:22–2:29 shows, Paul retains the traditional understanding of sin as transgression against God's will. It is not, then, that he has replaced one notion of sin with another (cf. R. H. Gundry, "Grace, Works, and Staying Saved in Paul," *Bib* 66 [1985], 28-30). Rather, he has chosen to conceptualize the depths of human sinfulness with the picture of sin as an enslaving master.

10a "Even as it is written"[21] is the formula Paul typically uses to introduce quotations of the OT. But nowhere else does Paul use a quotation so long or one drawn from so many different (at least six) OT passages. There are resemblances between this collection of thematically linked verses and what the rabbis called "pearl-stringing," and some have suggested that Paul is quoting an early Christian psalm or "florilegium."[22] This is not clear, however; and, in any case, Paul's purpose in citing these verses is clearly to substantiate the accusation of v. 9, and, in particular, his claim that sin is universal. Thus, the "all" of v. 9 is taken up in the repeated "there is no"[23] of the quotations; and the way is prepared, in turn, for the application of vv. 19-20: "*every* mouth," "*all* flesh." While the collection appears at first sight to be haphazard, there is evidence of attention to structure and sequence. The first line (v. 10) is the heading of what follows, with the last line (v. 18) coming back to the same theme in an inclusio.[24] Verses 11-12 develop the first line with a series of five generally synonymous repetitions of the theme "there is no one righteous," all introduced with "there is no," and with a reference to "all people"[25] breaking them up in the middle (v. 12a). The next four lines (vv. 13-14) describe sins of speech, each line referring to a different organ of speech. Verses 15-17, on the other hand, focus on sins of violence against others. The fact that many of these quotations denounce only the wicked or unrighteous within Israel — and hence do not seem to fit Paul's universalistic intention — has been taken as indication that Paul's intention is not to condemn *all* people.[26] But Paul's actual intention is probably more

---

21. Gk. καθὼς γέγραπται.

22. This thesis is developed in most detail by L. E. Keck, "The Function of Rom 3,10-18. Observations and Suggestions," in *God's Christ and His People. Studies in Honor of Nils Alstrup Dahl* (ed. J. Jervell and W. A. Meeks; Oslo: Universitetsforleget, 1977), pp. 141-57. He goes so far as to suggest that the catena may be "the theological starting-point for Paul's reflection" in 1:18–3:8 (p. 153). Cf. also van der Minde, *Schrift und Tradition*, pp. 54-58; Käsemann; Michel; Wilckens; Schmithals (who thinks Paul may have taken it from the synagogue). Koch, 180-84, and Stanley, *Paul and the Language of Scripture*, 88-89, think that Paul may have composed the passage before he inserted it here. Cf. also A. T. Hanson (*Studies in Paul's Technique and Theology* [Grand Rapids: Eerdmans, 1974], pp. 21-29), who suggests a number of ingenious (and improbable) connections between the OT contexts and Paul's purposes.

23. Gk. οὐκ ἔστιν.

24. Note the οὐκ ἔστιν, establishing something of a frame around the series.

25. Gk. πάντες.

26. See Davies, *Faith and Obedience*, pp. 82-96. Davies has a definite point, of course: surely Paul does not believe that there were absolutely no "righteous" people before Christ (cf. his references to Abraham and David in chap. 4). But Paul appears to be looking at all human beings as they appear before the Lord apart from his saving grace. Even Abraham and David, then, are, in themselves, "unrighteous."

subtle; by citing texts that denounce the unrighteous and applying them, implicitly, to all people, including all Jews, he underscores the argument of 2:1–3:8 that, in fact, not even faithful Jews can claim to be "righteous."[27]

10b-12   The quotations begin with a series of phrases taken from Ps. 14:1-3 (LXX 13:1-3) (Ps. 53:1-3 is almost identical). As is the case with most of the quotations in this series, Paul's wording agrees closely with the LXX.[28] But there is one important difference: where the Psalms text has "there is no one who does *good,*" Paul has "there is no one who is *righteous.*" Granted the importance of the language of "righteousness" in this part of Romans (cf. 3:4, 5, 8, 19, 20), the word is almost certainly Paul's own editorial change.[29] It will thus carry with it Paul's specifically forensic nuance (cf. 1:17). What he means is that there is not a single person who, apart from God's justifying grace, can stand as "right" before God. This meaning is not far from David's intention in the Psalm, as he unfolds the myriad dimensions of human folly.

13-14   In the rest of the quotations, the focus on the universality of sin is abandoned in favor of a description of representative sins. The inclusion of these verses, which are not directly related to Paul's purpose, is one of the main arguments for regarding the collection of quotations as pre-Pauline. Taken from three similar denunciations of the wicked in the Psalms, vv. 13-14 depict the sinfulness of human speech. The order of the quotations may intentionally reproduce the sequence of organs involved in producing speech: throat — tongue — lips — mouth.[30] The LXX of Ps. 5:9 (MT, LXX 5:10) provides the source for the first two lines of v. 13. Describing the throat[31] as an "open grave" highlights both the inner corruption and the deadly effects of the speech of the

---

27. See esp. Dunn.

28. The LXX (Ps. 13:1c-3b) runs: οὐκ ἔστιν ποιῶν χρηστότητα, οὐκ ἔστιν ἕως ἑνός. κύριος ἐκ τοῦ οὐρανοῦ διέκυψεν ἐπὶ τοὺς υἱοὺς τῶν ἀνθρώπων τοῦ ἰδεῖν εἰ ἔστιν συνίων ἢ ἐκζητῶν τὸν θεόν. πάντες ἐξέκλιναν, ἅμα ἠχρεώθησαν, οὐκ ἔστιν ποιῶν χρηστότητα, οὐκ ἔστιν ἕως ἑνός. The LXX is a fair translation of the MT. In addition to Paul's modification of v. 1c (for which see above), Paul eliminates the reference to the Lord's looking from heaven (v. 2a) and gives the coordinate substantival participles συνίων and ἐκζητῶν separate lines. But the substance of the OT verse is unchanged. In v. 12, on the other hand, Paul reproduces the LXX of Ps. 14:3 exactly (with the probable exception of the article before ποιῶν [the article is omitted in a few MSS, but the reading is probably an accommodation to the LXX]). The inclusion of Rom. 3:13-18 in several MSS of the LXX of Psalm 14 is a striking example of the influence of Christian scribes on the transmission of the LXX (see S-H for a thorough discussion).

29. It is less likely that "there is no one righteous, not even one" are Paul's own words (this would be unusual, coming after the introductory formula καθὼς γέγραπται) or that Paul refers to Eccl. 7:20 LXX — ἄνθρωπος οὐκ ἔστιν δίκαιος ἐν τῇ γῇ (e.g., Dunn).

30. Cf. Morison, *Exposition,* p. 129.

31. Gk. λάρυγξ, a NT hapax.

psalmist's enemies. "They speak deceptively[32] with their tongues" refers to the deceptive flatteries of those who intend evil. The last line of v. 13 reproduces the LXX of Ps. 140:3b (MT 140:4b; LXX 139:4b). The last quotation in this sequence, in v. 14, is adapted from Ps. 10:7 (LXX 9:28).[33]

15-17 The three lines in these verses are all taken from Isa. 59:7-8a, with the LXX again being the source for the quotations. Verse 15 is an abridgment of Isa. 59:7a.[34] That this, rather than Prov. 1:16 (which has in common with Isa. 59:7 the words that Paul quotes), is Paul's source, is probable because vv. 16-17 continue to use Isa. 59. Verses 16-17, in contrast, contain almost exact quotations of the LXX of Isa. 59:7b-8a.[35] While Ps. 14, quoted in vv. 10-12, describes human beings generally and the Psalm verses cited in vv. 13-14 characterize the enemies of the psalmists, Isa. 59:7-8a is directed against the unrighteous in Israel. Again, then, Paul implies that Israel as a whole must now be considered in this category of the "wicked."

18 The final quotation, from Ps. 36:1b (MT 36:2b; LXX 35:2b), reverts to the introductory "there is not"[36] of vv. 10-12, acting therefore as a kind of concluding frame for the series. The text exposes the root error that gives rise to the manifold sins of humanity: lack of "fear of God." Paul's wording is again very close to that of the LXX.[37]

19 Paul now draws out the implications of the series of quotations for the position of human beings before the divine judge.[38] "We know" introduces a circumstance that would be generally acknowledged by Paul and his readers.[39] In this case, the circumstance is the applicability of "whatever the law says"[40] to those who are "in the law." The first occurrence of "law"

---

32. Gk. ἐδολιοῦσαν, translating the Heb. יַחֲלִיקוּן.

33. Paul's quotation differs from the LXX (which accurately renders the MT) in word order, the elimination of δόλον ("deceit") as a third object of γέμει ("filled"), and the use of the plural ὧν ("whose") instead of the singular οὗ.

34. Why Paul uses ὀξεῖς ("swift") rather than the ταχινοί ("quick") of the LXX is impossible to determine.

35. The only difference is that Paul uses ἔγνωσαν in place of the LXX οἴδασιν (both mean "they know").

36. Gk. οὐκ ἔστιν.

37. The only change is Paul's use of the plural αὐτῶν ("their") in place of the generic singular αὐτοῦ ("his") of the LXX.

38. The δέ introducing the verse will have, then, a loose consecutive meaning; "now," "then" (cf. BAGD).

39. See 2:2; 7:14; 8:22, 28; 2 Cor. 5:1; 1 Tim. 1:8. The Greek is οἴδαμεν.

40. The shift from the verb λέγω — "whatever the law *says*" — to λαλέω — "it *speaks* to those in the law" — may not be significant since a distinction between these verbs cannot be maintained consistently in the NT. But Paul may intend a difference here, with λέγω emphasizing more the content of what is said and λαλέω the act of speaking itself (cf., e.g., Godet; Cranfield; Morison, *Exposition*, p. 138).

(*nomos*) refers to the series of quotations just concluded. Since these quotations are drawn from the Psalms and Isaiah, *nomos* does not designate, as it usually does in Paul, the law of Moses, the torah, but the OT canon (cf. also 1 Cor. 9:8, 9; 14:21, 34; Gal. 4:21b).[41] The second occurrence of *nomos* — "it speaks to those who are in the *law*" — may also refer to the OT as a whole,[42] or it may revert to the more usual narrower meaning, "Mosaic law."[43] The difference is not great since in either case "those in the law" are the Jews, who live within the sphere of[44] the revelation of God given in the Scripture/law. This interpretation is preferable to giving *nomos* the more broad signification of divine law in any form, and, in line with 2:14-15, expanding "those in the law" to include all people.[45] For, while the explicitly universal terms of the last part of the verse might suggest so broad a scope, this view has against it the close identification of *nomos* with the written Scripture in this context (cf. vv. 10-18). And it is clear that, whatever access to God's law Gentiles may have, it does not come in this "written," "inscripturated" form. Paul's purpose is to insist that the OT passages quoted in vv. 10-18, while not all originally directed to Israel as a whole, are, indeed, "speaking to" the Jews generally. They cannot be excluded from the scope of sin.

The purpose for which the words of Scripture address the Jews is "that every mouth might be stopped and the whole world be held accountable to God." The terminology of this clause reflects the imagery of the courtroom. "Shutting the mouth" connotes the situation of the defendant who has no more to say in response to the charges brought against him or her.[46] The Greek word translated "accountable"[47] occurs nowhere else in the Scriptures, but it is used in extra-biblical Greek to mean "answerable to" or "liable to prosecution," "accountable." Paul pictures God both as the one offended and as the judge who weighs the evidence and pronounces the verdict.[48] The image, then, is of all humanity standing before God, accountable to him for willful and inexcusable violations of his will, awaiting the sentence of condemnation that their actions deserve.[49]

---

41. See the note on 2:12. Str-B (3.159) note that the rabbis sometimes use תּוֹרָה in just this sense. By contrast, Zahn and Gifford think that νόμος refers to the Mosaic law here.

42. Kuss; Cranfield; Watson, 129; Morison, *Exposition*, p. 139.

43. E.g., Käsemann.

44. Gk. ἐν having a metaphorical spatial sense, as in the similar ἐν νόμῳ in 2:12.

45. As, e.g., Murray.

46. Similar language is used in Job 5:16; Ps. 63:11; 107:42.

47. ὑπόδικος.

48. The person named in the dative case following ὑπόδικος can be either the one who has been wronged, or the judge before whom one appears (cf. LSJ; MM; C. Maurer, *TDNT* VIII, 557-58). We suggest that τῷ θεῷ here may indicate both.

49. See esp. Käsemann; Cranfield.

But how is it that Paul can use accusations addressed to Jews ("those in the law") to declare that all people are guilty? Some would limit the reference of "every mouth" to Jews,[50] but the parallelism with "the whole world" makes this unlikely. Probably Paul is using an implicit "from the greater to the lesser" argument: if Jews, God's chosen people, cannot be excluded from the scope of sin's tyranny, then it surely follows that Gentiles, who have no claim on God's favor, are also guilty.[51] We must remember that Paul's chief purpose throughout Rom. 1:18–3:20 is not to demonstrate that Gentiles are guilty and in need of God's righteousness — for this could be assumed — but that Jews bear the same burden and have the same need. It is for this reason that, while all people are included in the scope of vv. 19-20, there is particular reference to the Jews and their law.

20 This verse may give the reason why the whole world is accountable to God,[52] or it may serve to confirm this accountability.[53] The latter suggestion is best — Paul counters any Jewish evasion of v. 19 by explicitly denying that the law can offer any hope of defense. Paul alludes to the OT to make his point; for his words, while not a quotation, resemble Ps. 143:2b: "no one living is righteous before you."[54] Paul's most significant addition, of course, is his reference to the law: it is not "out of works of the law" that a person is justified. The meaning of this phrase, which also occurs in Rom. 3:28; Gal. 2:16; 3:2, 5, 10, has been the subject of considerable debate and influences significantly our understanding of Paul's doctrines of justification and of the law.

Interpreters of Paul have traditionally thought that "works of the law" refers to anything done in obedience to the law, particularly those "good works" that one might put forth as a reason why God should accept a person. These interpreters then viewed "works of the law" as a subset of the larger category "good works"; and they understood this verse, and others like it, to be refuting the idea that a person could gain a right standing with God by anything that that person did.[55] Alternatives to this interpretation of "works

---

50. Bengel; Morison, *Exposition*, p. 144.

51. See esp. Kuss; Cranfield.

52. Gk. διότι = "because" (Gifford).

53. διότι = "for," in the sense of ὅτι (BAGD; Cranfield).

54. The Greek of Ps. 143:2b (142:2b in the LXX) is οὐ δικαιωθήσεται ἐνώπιόν σου πᾶς ζῶν. Paul also alludes to this verse in the parallel Gal. 2:16. Contra Cranfield, the lack of an introductory formula, along with the significant differences between the Psalm verse and Paul's words, makes it unlikely that we should view the words as a quotation. Thus, in place of the LXX πᾶς ζῶν ("every living thing" [MT כָּל־חָי]), Paul has πᾶσα σάρξ ("all flesh"). "Flesh" was a common way of referring to human beings in the OT; and this makes it very improbable that we should find any negative nuance in Paul's use of σάρξ here (contra Dunn).

55. This general view is shared by virtually all the Reformers and became a hallmark of traditional Protestant interpretation.

of the law" have been advocated in the past.[56] But especially popular of late has been the idea that "works of the law" is Paul's way of referring to Jewish existence — to the Jews' special covenantal relationship with the Lord, a relationship that came to be expressed especially in the Jews' observance of those "works of the law," like circumcision, avoidance of certain food, and observance of special days, that marked them off from their Gentile environment.[57] If we interpret the phrase this way, Paul's point is that the covenant, as the Jews understood it, is inadequate to maintain them in right standing with the Lord. On this view, in other words, the problem Paul has with the Jews here does not have to do with their *performance* of the law but with their *possession* of it. Advocates of this view do not usually trace the inadequacy of the covenant to human inability; they think, rather, that Paul drew this conclusion because Christ's coming rendered obsolete the Jewish covenant and/or because the Jewish covenant focused too narrowly on the Jewish people to the exclusion of Gentiles.

I think, however, that this new interpretation of the phrase "works of

56. E.g., some have thought that "works of the law" denoted only the observance of the ritual or ceremonial law. This interpretation was advanced by Pelagius (cf. in loc.) and some others in the early church (cf. Schelke; M. F. Wiles, *The Divine Apostle: The Interpretation of St. Paul's Epistles in the Early Church* [Cambridge: Cambridge University, 1967], pp. 67-69 — against this interpretation, see esp. Calvin, *Institutes* 3.11.19). D. P. Fuller argued that "works of the law" denoted a legalistic approach to the law (cf. "Paul and 'The Works of the Law,' " *WTJ* 38 [1975-76], 31-33; note also Snodgrass, "Justification by Grace," p. 84 ["works done in the flesh"]).

57. Some decades ago, E. Lohmeyer came close to this interpretation (cf. "Gesetzeswerke," in *Probleme paulinischer Theologie* [Stuttgart: Kohlhammer, n.d.], pp. 33-73), but by far its most prominent advocate has been J. D. G. Dunn. He first proposed this interpretation in his "The New Perspective on Paul" (*BJRL* 65 [1983], 107-11) and has been advocating and refining it ever since (cf. "Works of the Law and the Curse of the Law [Gal. 3:10-14]," *NTS* 31 [1985], 528-29; his commentary on Romans; "Additional Note" to the reprint of "The New Perspective on Paul" in *Jesus, Paul, and the Law: Studies in Mark and Galatians* [Louisville: Westminster/John Knox, 1990], p. 210; *The Parting of the Ways between Christianity and Judaism and Their Significance for the Character of Christianity* (London: SCM, 1991), pp. 119-39; "Yet Once More — 'The Works of the Law': A Response," *JSNT* 46 [1992], 99-117 [he responds to Cranfield]; "Echoes of Intra-Jewish Polemic in Paul's Letter to the Galatians," *JBL* 112 [1993], 465-67). Significantly, Dunn has modified his view a bit over the years. His initial article came close to implying that "works of the law" meant only certain parts of the law (such as circumcision, food laws, and observance of days). In his latest essay ("Echoes," p. 466), however, he argues that the phrase refers more broadly to "acts of obedience required by the law of all faithful Jews, all members of the people with whom God had made the covenant at Sinai — the self-understanding and obligation accepted by practicing Jews that E. P. Sanders encapsulated quite effectively in the phrase 'covenantal nomism.' " (See also Dunn's admission that his first article might have left the wrong impression ["Additional Note," p. 210].) Many other authors have adopted Dunn's view; cf., e.g., Watson, 119, 129-30.

the law" is wrong. First, the new interpretation is closely related to a new approach to first-century Judaism. And, while this new view of Judaism has many attractive features, it is also ultimately inadequate (see the excursus following this section). To the extent, then, that the new approach to the meaning of "works of the law" is tied to this new view of Judaism, it must be questioned. Second, the linguistic basis for this new interpretation is weak. While the Greek phrase Paul uses here[58] is not attested before Paul, it has a close equivalent in several Hebrew phrases current in the Judaism of Paul's day.[59] These phrases, because of their Jewish context, of course refer to an obedience of the law set within an understanding of the Jewish covenant. But none of the phrases, in their contexts, suggests that they, in themselves, refer to the covenant as such. Each clearly refers to performance of the law. Third, the context does not favor a restricted or nuanced meaning. Paul emphasizes that what he is saying about the inadequacy of "works of the law" applies to all people (cf. "all flesh" — a reference in this context to Gentiles as well as Jews [cf. 3:9]). "Works of the law" cannot be, then, so interpreted as to restrict the principle to Jews only.[60] Another contextual factor is the apparent formal equivalence between "works of the law" here (and in 3:28) and the simple "works" in 4:2-6 (cf. also 9:32). This suggests that "works of the law" is one specific form of "works" generally — not a technical reference to "Jewish only" torah obedience. And this general equivalence is supported by the previous context. We would expect "works

---

58. τὰ ἔργα τοῦ νόμου.

59. See especially the phrases תורה מצשי ("works of the law") in 4QFlor 1:7 (= 4Q174), מצשין בתורה ("his works in the law") in 1QS 5:21; 6:18, and מקצת מַעֲשֵׂי הַתּוֹרָה ("some works of the law") in 4QMMT 3:29 (cf. Fitzmyer and, on 4QMMT, E. Qimron and J. Strugnell, "An Unpublished Letter from Qumran," in *Biblical Archaeology Today: Proceedings of the International Congress on Biblical Achaeology, Jerusalem, April 1984* [Jerusalem: Israel Exploration Society, 1985], pp. 400-407). Dunn ("Echoes," p. 167; "Yet Once More," pp. 103-4) notes these parallels but argues that the phrases in question denote, in practice, those "works" that distinguished Qumran community members from other Jews. But evidence for this restricted sense of the phrase is simply not forthcoming from the contexts where the phrases occur. They appear simply to denote those things that the law demands. Paul's phrase is probably equivalent to the rabbis' use of the simple "works" (מַעֲשִׂם) or "commandments" (מִצְוֹת) (cf. Str-B, 3.160-61, and N. A. Dahl, "Widersprüche in der Bibel: ein altes hermeneutisches Problem," *ST* 25 [1971], 13), Paul adding the phrase "of the law" because he could not assume the reference to the law in his context. Note also the phrase "works of the commandments" in *2 Apoc. Bar.* 57:2.

60. Cf. M. A. Seifrid, "Blind Alleys in the Controversy over the Paul of History," *TynBul* 45 (1994), 77-82. It is true that the Psalm verse Paul may be alluding to (MT 143:2b; LXX 142:2b) already contains a reference to "every living thing." But Paul does not simply take over this phrase automatically from the Psalm text; instead he changes the wording (Paul writes πᾶσα σάρξ instead of πᾶς ζῶν [cf. the Heb. כָּל־חָי]).

of the law" here to be something of a summary of the extended discussion of Jewish "doing" in chap. 2. But the context of chap. 2 makes it clear that this "doing" is not restricted to any particular kind of "works." In fact, Paul makes clear that the problem with Jewish works is essentially the same as the problem with Gentile works (cf. vv. 2-3, 22-23, 25, 27). Again, this makes it impossible to conclude that the problem with "works of the law" is narrowly Jewish.

"Works of the law," then, as most interpreters have recognized, refers simply to "things that are done in obedience to the law."[61] Paul uses the phrase "works of the law" instead of the simple "works" because he is particularly concerned in this context to deny to Jews an escape from the general sentence pronounced in v. 19.[62] But, since "works of the law" are simply what we might call "good works" defined in Jewish terms, the principle enunciated here has universal application; nothing a person does, whatever the object of obedience or the motivation of that obedience, can bring him or her into favor with God. It is just at this point that the significance of the meaning we have given "works of the law" emerges so clearly. Any restricted definition of "works of the law" *can* have the effect of opening the door to the possibility of justification by works — "good" deeds that are done in the right spirit, with God's enabling grace, or something of the sort. This, we are convinced, would be to misunderstand Paul at a vital point. The heart of his contention in this section of Romans is that *no one* is capable of doing *anything* to gain acceptance with God; this is

---

61. The genitive (τοῦ νόμου) in the phrase may, then, be objective — "works that fulfill the law" — or, perhaps more likely, a subjective genitive — "[the doing of] the works that the law requires" (see, e.g., C. E. B. Cranfield, " 'The Works of the Law' in the Epistle to the Romans," *JSNT* 43 [1991], 100; T. R. Schreiner, " 'Works of Law' in Paul," *NovT* 33 [1991], 235). For this general view of the phrase, see especially my " 'Law,' 'Works of the Law,' and Legalism," pp. 90-96. Cf. also, especially, Calvin; Schlatter; Cranfield (and his article " 'Works of the Law,' " pp. 89-101); Wilckens; Schmithals; Stuhlmacher; Fitzmyer; H. Hübner, "Was heisst bei Paulus 'Werke des Gesetzes'?" in *Glaube und Eschatologie. Festschrift für W. G. Kümmel zum 80. Geburtstag* (ed. E. Grässer and O. Merk; Tübingen: Mohr, 1985), pp. 123-33 (with particular reference to Gal. 2:16); Westerholm, 116-21; Schreiner, " 'Works of the Law,' " pp. 217-44; Davies, *Faith and Obedience,* pp. 115-27. The views of Käsemann and Schlier, while more nuanced, also probably belong here. D. A. Campbell, on the other hand, thinks that Paul formulates the phrase as a negative counterpart to "on the basis of faith" and that it accordingly has little specific meaning for him ("The Meaning of Πίστις and Νόμος in Paul: A Linguistic and Structural Perspective," *JBL* 111 [1992], 98-102).

62. Contra, e.g., Melanchthon, Haldane, and Morison (*Exposition,* pp. 155-57), who think that νόμος refers to divine law generally. While we agree with these expositors that the verse has ultimate application to all people, the reference to the law of Moses here is clear.

why for *everyone* faith in Christ is the only possible way to God. In this verse, Paul does not spell out the "logic" of *why* works cannot justify. But the context, where the principle that "doers of the law will be justified" has been enunciated (2:13), and where it has been shown that all are under the power of sin (3:9; cf. 3:10-18), suggests that it is because no one is able to do the law sufficiently well to gain favor with God[63] (see, further, the excursus on pp. 211-17).

The last part of v. 20 supports Paul's contention in the first part of the verse by setting forth what it is that the law does accomplish (as opposed to that which it cannot accomplish). The law does not justify; rather, "through"[64] it comes "knowledge of sin." Since "knowledge" in the Bible can sometimes designate personal experience of something (cf. 2 Cor. 5:21, where Christ is said not to have "known" sin), "knowledge of sin" might mean the actual experience of sinning. On this view, the law, because it encourages people to perform good works, entices them to seek to determine their own destiny and to "boast" in their accomplishments. Thus are people (and especially Jews) led by the law into sinning.[65] This conception, which is particularly associated with Bultmann and his followers, is a basic misrepresentation of Paul. He does not view the attempt to do the law as bad, nor is the doing of the law wrong. It is people's failure to do it that creates the problem.[66] "Knowledge of sin," on the other hand, does not simply mean that the law defines sin; rather, what is meant is that the law gives to people an understanding of "sin" (singular) as a power that holds everyone in bondage and brings guilt and condemnation.[67] The law presents people with the demand of God. In our constant failure to attain the goal of that demand, we recognize ourselves to be sinners and justly condemned for our failures.

---

63. Cf. esp. Wilckens and his article "Was heisst bei Paulus," pp. 77-109.

64. Gk. διά.

65. Bultmann, 1.264; Klein, "Sündenverständnis," p. 261; Schlier; Käsemann; Schmithals.

66. There have been many thorough criticisms of this view. Cf., e.g., Wilckens, "Was heisst bei Paulus"; Räisänen, 168-77.

67. Cf., e.g., Luz, 187; Fitzmyer, "Paul and the Law," p. 190; Cranfield; Nygren; Watson, 129. This interpretation does not rest on the alleged (e.g., Trench, *Synonyms*, p. 285 [on this verse], cf. Sullivan, "Epignosis," p. 407) more "intense" meaning of ἐπίγνωσις as opposed to γνῶσις. See the note on 1:28; in the present context, note the parallel between "knowing [ἐπιγινώσκω] the just decree of God" (1:32) and "knowing [γινώσκω] his will" (2:18).

EXCURSUS: PAUL, "WORKS OF THE LAW," AND FIRST-CENTURY JUDAISM

Two significant issues are raised by Paul's assertion in 3:20 that "no one is justified by works of the law."

The first is the question of the logic of this denial. Why can't "works of the law" justify? We might take our starting point in the juxtaposition of 2:13 — "doers of the law will be justified" — and 3:20 — "no one will be justified by works of the law." There appear to be only five ways of explaining this contrast. First, one could argue that 2:13 states only a hypothetical promise: only for the sake of argument does Paul suggest such a possibility. As I have noted in the exegesis of 2:13, this is unlikely. Second, one could find a salvation-historical distinction between the two: in the "old age," doing the law could justify, but in the "new age" it no longer can. Not only does this make Paul's argument in 2:13 irrelevant to his present readers (who are in the "new age"), but it contradicts the express denial of Paul that the law could justify (see Gal. 3:21). Third, one could argue that "justify" in 2:13 refers to the judgment, or to a "second justification," while "justify" in 3:20 relates to the initial entrance into salvation.[68] But, while there is some precedent in Judaism and in James for the use of "justify" to depict the judgment, evidence from Paul's usage for this meaning is lacking. Fourth, one could define "doing the law" and "works of the law" in different ways, so that the former means "fulfilling the law in Christ," or "obeying God as a response to grace" while the latter connotes simple doing of the law or doing it in a legalistic spirit. We have also found reason for rejecting this interpretation: lexical and contextual evidence does not justify any sort of distinction.

We are left, then, with the supposition that one must insert a step in the argument between the two statements, to the effect that "no one can do the law." Not only does this make the best sense of both statements in their contexts, but it is, in effect, the assertion that Paul inserts between the two verses: "all are under the power of sin . . . there is no one righteous, no, not one" (3:9-10). We should add that a view like Dunn's, according to which "works of the law" are defined as Jewish identity markers and do not justify because the covenant that they represent cannot justify simply moves the question back one step further: Why doesn't the covenant justify? Paul has shown why in 2:1–3:19: the law cannot be "done" to the extent necessary to secure justification through that

---

68. C. H. Cosgrove ("Justification in Paul: A Linguistic and Theological Reflection," *JBL* 106 [1987], 653-78) argues that the ἐκ following δικαιόω in 3:20 denotes the instrument through which justification takes place, while statements such as 2:10 and 2:13 indicate that works are "the evidential basis" for justification. But the phrase "evidential basis" conceals a crucial ambiguity — basis for justification or evidence of justification? — and it is questionable whether δικαιόω ἐκ can be defined as narrowly as this.

"law" covenant. It is far more likely, then, that this is the ultimate logic undergirding his denial that works of the law can justify here — a logic rooted not (or at least not only) in salvation history, or in concern about social barriers, but, more deeply, in the human condition itself.

The second issue, related to the first, has to do with the viewpoint that Paul is opposing with his statement. Traditionally, it has been understood as a denial that a person can "earn" salvation by doing anything: no "works," however "good" — even those done in obedience to God's holy law — can bring a person into relationship with God. It has, furthermore, usually been assumed that this thesis was directed against Jews in Paul's day who believed that, indeed, they could get into relationship with God by obedience to the law. Many modern interpreters (some of whom label this traditional view the "Lutheran orthodox" interpretation) question this explanation of the situation. i think, however, that, properly nuanced, the traditional view remains the best explanation of the Pauline polemic. The attentive reader will recognize in the commentary on texts such as 2:11 and 13 and 3:20 our general endorsement of this view. But here I would like to explore perhaps the most attractive counterposition and explain why I do not find it convincing.

We must begin with the work of E. P. Sanders. His monograph, *Paul and Palestinian Judaism* (1977), is the stimulus for most of the recent reconstructions of Paul's interaction with Judaism on the law. To understand his position, then, we must understand his basic thesis about Palestinian Judaism.

Sanders argues that Palestinian Judaism in Paul's day was characterized by a "pattern of religion" that he labels "covenantal nomism." In contrast to the "traditional" picture of Judaism as a religion that required works as a means of entry into salvation, this pattern of covenantal nomism features obedience to the law as the means to *maintain* the Jews' status in the covenant, a status that was freely granted to Jews through their election. Thus, obedience to the law was not the means of "getting in" but of "staying in." While this portrait is drawn on the basis of the surviving literature of early Palestinian Judaism, Sanders insists that, for lack of conflicting evidence, this must have been the common first-century Jewish belief.

If Sanders's view of first-century Judaism is adopted as accurate — and it has met with wide acceptance — then it is necessary to ask: "Why has Paul so often and so emphatically denied that 'works of the law' can justify"? If no one in first-century Judaism really believed that a person could be justified by doing the law, then why deny it? To this question Sanders in his original monograph gave no clear answer beyond asserting that Paul ruled the law out of court on the basis of his "exclusivist soteriology": because Christ was the only means of salvation, the law could not be. But others quickly rushed in to fill the void. Two basic approaches can be distinguished.

First are those who think that both Sanders's view of Judaism *and* the traditional understanding of Paul — that he implied that Jews sought justification through the law — are correct and that the consequence is that Paul either misunderstood or deliberately misrepresented Judaism for polemical purposes. Jews did not really believe that "a person could be justified by works of the law"; but Paul implies that they did as a result of an overreaction against his previous religion and with the purpose of distancing Christianity from Judaism.[69] We think so extreme a conclusion is unwarranted. Not only does it presume to judge Paul on the basis of questionable claims about what Jews believed in Paul's day (see below), but it also makes the unlikely assumption that Paul would misrepresent a position that some of the people he was trying to convince would know very well.

The second general attempt to explain Paul against the background of Sanders's interpretation of Judaism is found among scholars who think that Paul can be "reinterpreted" in such a way that his teaching meshes with Jewish "covenantal nomism." Several specific proposals that take this general tack have emerged. One, associated especially with J. Gager and L. Gaston, argues that virtually all Paul's negative statements about the law are directed against those who wanted to impose the law on Gentiles.[70] But the best-supported and most reasonable proposal is the one that J. D. G. Dunn has made prominent and which we touch on in the commentary on 3:20: that "works of the law" connotes Jewish obedience to the law in its function as establishing a boundary around the Jewish people, marking them off from the Gentile peoples around them. Jews did not see these works as bringing them into relationship with God but as maintaining their "national righteousness," their peculiar status as God's covenant people. Throughout Rom. 2–3, then, Paul argues against this presumption of "favored status," showing that Jews cannot rely on their supposed special relationship with God for salvation. "No one is justified by works of the law" means, then, that no Jew can expect to be justified through those works "by which a member of the covenant people identified himself as a Jew and maintained his status within the covenant."[71] What the Jews, need, then, is a more inclusive understanding of salvation history and of the law, by which Gentiles can be allowed to take their rightful place alongside Jews within God's covenant community.[72]

---

69. Several scholars find some degree of misrepresentation in Paul, but the clearest and strongest presentation is that of Räisänen.

70. See esp. J. G. Gager, *The Origins of Anti-Semitism: Attitudes toward Judaism in Pagan and Christian Antiquity* (New York: Oxford University Press, 1983); L. Gaston, *Paul and the Torah* (Vancouver: University of British Columbia, 1987), esp. pp. 15-34.

71. *Romans,* 1.158.

72. The first scholar, apparently, to advance this general idea was N. T. Wright (cf. "The Paul of History and the Apostle of Faith," *TynBul* 29 [1978], 61-88). Sanders himself, in his second monograph on the general topic, *Paul, the Law and the Jewish People* (1983), suggests that Paul's denial that "works of the law" could justify was directed

Despite its popularity, Dunn's proposal suffers from some serious drawbacks. First, while Rom. 2 certainly has a great deal to say about Jewish complacency because of a misunderstanding of the covenant, it must be questioned whether we can confine Paul's polemic to this one issue. Dunn consistently downplays the role that transgression of the law — not just adherence to certain ethnic identity markers — plays in Paul's argument. Again and again, Paul insists in 2:1-29 that it is not dependence on the law or circumcision as such that renders the Jews liable to judgment, but their *disobedience* of the law. Transgressions of the law are the *reason* why the Jews cannot presume on the covenant for salvation.[73] And these transgressions are said to involve the "same things" that Gentiles do (2:2-3) — clearly making it a matter not of "inner" Jewish issues but of sin against God generally. It is this larger and more basic problem of transgression of the law that informs Paul's conclusion to this section in 3:20: "no human being will be justified by works of the law." The "works" mentioned here must, as Dunn says, be the "works" Paul has spoken of in chap. 2.[74] But it is not circumcision — let alone other "identity markers" that are not even mentioned in Rom. 1–3 — that the Jew "does" in Rom. 2; it is, generally, what is demanded by the law, the "precepts" (v. 26; cf. vv. 22-23, 25, 27).[75] Therefore, 3:20 must deny not the adequacy of Jewish *identity* to justify, but the adequacy of Jewish *works* to justify. Belonging to the Jewish people does not justify because no Jew does the law sufficiently to give to that identity salvific power. It is this root *anthropological* issue — human inability — that informs 3:20, and justifies its application to the circumstance of any person.[76]

This, however, brings us back to the question: Against whom is the polemic in 3:20 directed? Two things can be said here.

First, as Sanders argues, Paul's denial that works of the law can justify may signify simply an attack on the covenant as understood by Jews. As Sanders points out, Jews regarded the *intention* to obey the commandments as sufficient to maintain one's covenant status.[77] Paul, however, insists that only what is

---

against the "covenantal nomism" of Palestinian Judaism: "The argument is that one need not be Jewish to be 'righteous' and is thus against the standard Jewish view that accepting and living by the law is a sign and condition of favored status" (p. 46).

73. See, e.g., Schreiner, " 'Works of the Law,' " pp. 226-28.

74. See his *Romans,* 1.158.

75. Significantly, B. W. Longenecker, who embraces Dunn's viewpoint, admits that in Rom. 2 Paul sets up a "straw man," arguing against a view that did not in fact exist (*Eschatology and the Covenant: A Comparison of 4 Ezra and Romans 1–11* [JSNTSup 57; Sheffield: JSOT, 1991], p. 279).

76. M. Silva ("The Law and Christianity: Dunn's New Synthesis," *WTJ* 53 [1991], 350-51) criticizes Dunn for an "all-or-nothing" approach that sets up an unjustifiable mutual exclusion between individual and corporate concerns in Paul.

77. Sanders, *Paul and Palestinian Judaism,* pp. 157-82.

actually done counts. This argument is an outright attack on the "covenantal nomism" that Sanders has sketched.[78] The denial of special status to the Jews is an implicit rejection of the election that was the foundation for "covenantal nomism,"[79] and coheres closely with the polemic of John the Baptist (cf. Matt. 3:7-10) and of Jesus.[80] How does this critical attitude toward the covenant cohere with the OT itself? As we have seen, Paul is close to the prophets in his criticism of those who rely on the covenant as an automatic protection from judgment. And, while he is more explicit, Paul's polemic against the Mosaic covenant is in keeping with the pessimistic attitude expressed toward that covenant in Deuteronomy (cf. chap. 32) and many of the prophets (e.g., Jer. 31:31-34). Paul stresses that the Abrahamic promise, to which one must respond with faith, and which is now fulfilled in Christ, is the true locus of salvation (Rom. 4). He therefore does not deny the promise of salvation given in the Scriptures to the Jews, but attaches it not to the Mosaic covenant, as did Judaism, but to the Abrahamic.[81] One could, at the least, make a very good case for finding Paul's interpretation of the OT to be more accurate than that of "covenantal nomism." "Works of the law" — those things done by Jews in obedience to the law by which they sought to maintain their covenant status — cannot justify because the covenant within which they performed those works was inadequate to bring justification. Jewish works, then, are no different from Gentile works, once the larger framework of the covenant — as usually understood in first-century Judaism — is eliminated.

But a second possibility should also be considered — that Palestinian Judaism was more "legalistic" than Sanders allows, and that Paul is also responding to Jews who did, in some sense, think to be justified by doing the law. Even in Sanders's proposal, works play such a prominent role that it is fair to speak of a "synergism" of faith and works that elevates works to a crucial salvific role. For, while works, according to Sanders, are not the means to "getting in," they are essential to "staying in." When, then, we consider the matter from the perspective of the final judgment — which we must in Jewish theology — it is clear that "works," even in Sanders's view, play a necessary and instrumental role in "salvation."[82] But this is what

---

78. As both Dunn and Wright ("Paul of History") emphasize.

79. Sanders, *Paul, the Law and the Jewish People,* p. 47.

80. Cf. D. C. Allison, Jr., "Jesus and the Covenant: A Response to E. P. Sanders," *JSNT* 29 (1987), 61-63.

81. Cf. M. D. Hooker, "Paul and Covenantal Nomism," in *Paul and Paulinism,* p. 51.

82. See esp. Seifrid, *Justification,* pp. 56-57, 71-81 (he finds a clear emphasis on the importance of works for eventual salvation in *Psalms of Solomon* and 1QS); Laato, *Paulus und das Judentum,* pp. 73-75, 195-211; Gundry, "Grace, Works, and Staying Saved," pp. 19-20, 35-36; Westerholm, 143-50; Byrne, 230; K. T. Cooper, "Paul and Rabbinic Soteriology," *WTJ* 44 (1982), 137-38.

Paul denies, by equating "initial" justification with the final verdict of salvation and by stressing faith *alone* as the necessary corollary to the grace of God. In effect, then, while not denying the role of faith, Jews were insisting on works as a means of justification. But this is just what Paul denies in 3:20, and why he distinguishes in principle between faith and works (see 3:27-28; 4:1-5).

Moreover, there is some question as to whether Sanders's reconstruction of first-century Judaism is to be accepted *in toto*.[83] While agreeing with Sanders that many interpreters have ignored the importance of election and covenant in Palestinian Judaism, and have been guilty, thereby, of caricaturing Jewish theology, I think that there is reason to conclude that Judaism was more "legalistic" than Sanders thinks. In passage after passage in his scrutiny of the Jewish literature, he dismisses a "legalistic" interpretation by arguing that the covenantal framework must be read into the text or that the passage is homiletical rather than theological in intent. But was the covenant as pervasive as Sanders thinks? Might not lack of reference in many Jewish works imply that it had been lost sight of in a more general reliance on Jewish identity?[84] And does not theology come into expression in homiletics? Indeed, is it not in more practically oriented texts that we discover what people *really* believed? Sanders may be guilty of underplaying a drift toward a more legalistic posture in first-century Judaism.[85] We must also reckon with the possibility that many "lay" Jews were more legalistic than the surviving literary remains of Judaism would suggest. Certainly the undeniable importance of the law in Judaism would naturally open the way to viewing doing the law in itself as salvific. The gap between the average believer's theological views and the informed views of religious leaders is often a wide one. If Christianity has been far from immune from legalism, is it likely to think that Judaism, at any stage

83. Note in this regard the warning of J. C. Beker: "We might wonder whether the work of Krister Stendahl and E. P. Sanders influences our treatment of Judaism so heavily these days that their important contributions are unduly exaggerated and — as it were — considered to be dogmatic, unassailable truth" ("Echoes and Intertextuality: On the Role of Scripture in Paul's Theology," in *Paul and the Scriptures of Israel* [ed. C. A. Evans and J. A. Sanders; JSNTSup 83; Sheffield: Sheffield Academic Press, 1993], p. 68).

84. J. Neusner raises a similar question about Sanders's treatment (cf. "The Use of the Later Rabbinic Evidence for the Study of Paul," in *Approaches to Ancient Judaism,* vol. 2 [ed. W. S. Green; Brown Judaic Studies 9; Chico, CA: Scholars Press, 1980], pp. 47-52) — and cf. Sanders's response in the same volume ("Puzzling Out Rabbinic Judaism," pp. 69-75).

85. G. B. Caird, Review of *Paul and Palestinian Judaism,* by E. P. Sanders, *JTS* 29 (1978), 539-40; D. A. Carson, *Divine Sovereignty and Human Responsibility* (Atlanta: Knox, 1981), pp. 86-95; Snodgrass, "Justification by Grace," p. 77.

of its development, was?[86] Finally, and, I think, most important, I am convinced that the teaching of Paul — and of Jesus and Matthew and Luke and Mark and Peter — cannot satisfactorily be explained without the assumption that some Jews, at least, had drifted from a biblical conception of the primacy and sufficiency of God's grace into a belief that accorded their own works done in obedience to the law as basic to their justification/salvation.

We conclude, then, that Paul criticizes Jews for thinking that the Mosaic covenant is adequate without that perfection in "works" without which any system of law must fail to bring one into relationship with God. The Jews become, as it were, representative of human beings generally. If the Jews, with the best law that one could have, could not find salvation through it, then *any* system of works is revealed as unable to conquer the power of sin. The "bottom line" in Paul's argument, then, is his conviction that sin creates for every person a situation of utterly helpless bondage. "Works of the law" are inadequate not because they are "works of *the law*" but, ultimately, because they are "works." This clearly removes the matter from the purely salvation-historical realm to the broader realm of anthropology. No person can gain a standing with God through works because no one is able to perform works to the degree needed to secure such a standing. This human inability to meet the demands of God is what lies at the heart of Rom. 3. On this point, at least, the Reformers understood Paul correctly.[87]

---

86. See, e.g., Seifrid, *Justification,* pp. 56-57; D. A. Hagner, "Paul's Quarrel with Judaism," in *Anti-Semitism and Early Christianity: Issues of Polemic and Faith* (ed. C. A. Evans and D. A. Hagner; Minneapolis: Fortress, 1993), pp. 138-39; idem, "Paul and Judaism. The Jewish Matrix of Early Christianity: Issues in the Current Debate," *Bulletin for Biblical Research* 3 (1993), 118-19; T. F. Best, "The Apostle Paul and E. P. Sanders: The Significance of Paul and Palestinian Judaism," *RestQ* 25 (1982), 72-73; Silva, "Dunn's New Synthesis," pp. 349-50. Sanders goes so far as to question whether "the notion of 'legalism' — an attitudinal sin which consists in self-assertion — goes back to the first century" ("Paul on the Law, his Opponents, and the Jewish People in Philippians 3 and 2 Corinthians 11," in *Paul and the Gospels,* vol. 1 of *Anti-Judaism in Early Christianity* [Studies in Christianity and Judaism 1; ed. P. Richardson; Waterloo, Ont.: Wilfrid Laurier University {Corporation for Studies in Religion}, 1986], pp. 78-79). Longenecker's suggestion (pp. 68-85) that Judaism probably featured at least two kinds of approaches — an "acting legalism" and a "reacting nomism" — has (despite Sanders's criticisms) much to be said for it. Scholars are giving more and more recognition to the diversity of first-century Judaism, to the point of speaking of "Judaisms" (e.g., J. Neusner, *Judaic Law from Jesus to the Mishnah* [South Florida Studies in the History of Judaism 84; Atlanta: Scholars Press, 1993], pp. 49-53; B. Longenecker, *Eschatology and the Covenant,* pp. 32-33). Note also the careful criticisms of Sanders in Laato, *Paulus und das Judentum,* pp. 38-82; cf. also Schreiner, *The Law and Its Fulfillment,* pp. 92-121.

87. Westerholm (pp. 221-22) comes to a similar conclusion.

B. JUSTIFICATION BY FAITH (3:21–4:25)

Romans 1:18–3:20, while important in its own right, is nevertheless preliminary to the main point that Paul wants to establish in this part of his letter: the availability of God's righteousness to all who respond in faith. This "good news," announced in 1:17, is now elaborated. The essential points are packed into 3:21-26, a passage that Luther called "the chief point, and the very central place of the Epistle, and of the whole Bible."[1] The remainder of the section develops one major element of this extraordinarily dense passage: faith as the only basis for justification. In 3:27-31, Paul highlights the exclusivity of faith (3:28) as he makes a number of points clearly directed to a Jewish viewpoint: faith excludes all boasting (3:27), provides for the inclusion of the Gentiles (3:29-30), and complements rather than nullifies the law (3:31). In chap. 4, each of these points is reiterated with respect to Abraham, as other elements are also drawn into the picture: the place of circumcision, the cruciality of grace, the promise, and the nature of faith. From this emphasis, we can surmise that Paul was well aware of the point at which his gospel was most often (and not only in Galatia) attacked and wanted to demonstrate as clearly as possible that faith was both the necessary and necessarily exclusive response of human beings to God's work of redemption.

1. Justification and the Righteousness of God (3:21-26)

21*But now, apart from the law, the righteousness of God has been made manifest, being witnessed to by the law and the prophets,* 22*the righteousness of God that is through faith in Jesus Christ for all*[2] *who believe. For there is no distinction,* 23*for all have sinned and are falling short of the glory of God,* 24*being justified freely by his grace through the redemption that is in Christ Jesus.* 25 *God set forth Jesus as a propitiatory sacrifice through faith,*[3] *in his blood, for a demonstration*

---

1. Margin of the Luther Bible, on 3:23ff.
2. Instead of εἰς πάντας, a significant block of MSS and early versions read εἰς πάντας καὶ ἐπὶ πάντας (the second corrector of ℵ, the secondary Alexandrian witness 33, the western uncials D, F, and G, and the majority text). While a few scholars have accepted the longer reading, regarding the omission of καὶ ἐπὶ πάντας as due to a scribe's eye accidentally picking up the second πάντας after he had copied the first (homoioteleuton) (e.g., Morison, *Exposition,* pp. 224-26; Nygren), the longer reading is suspect as a conflation of the widely supported εἰς πάντας (the papyrus P[40], the primary Alexandrian uncials ℵ [original hand], and B, the secondary Alexandrian C, 81, and 1739, and the uncials P and Ψ) and ἐπὶ πάντας (presumed by the Vulgate and two Church Fathers) (cf. Metzger, 508).
3. While NA[25] omitted the article before πίστεως (following the primary Alexandrian ℵ, the secondary Alexandrian C [original hand] and 1739, the western D [original

of his righteousness because of the passing over of sins committed beforehand 26in the forbearance of God, for a demonstration of his righteousness at the present time, in order that he might be just and the justifier of the person who has faith in Jesus.

In a passage that is loaded with key theological terms, the phrase "righteousness of God" *(dikaiosynē theou)* stands out. It occurs four times (vv. 21, 22, 25, 26 ["his righteousness" in the last two]), while the related verb "justify" *(dikaioō)* is found twice (vv. 24, 26) and the adjective "just" *(dikaios)* once (v. 26). After a section in which the need for this righteousness has been demonstrated in detail (1:18–3:20), Paul is now prepared to explain how the righteousness of God — his eschatological justifying activity — empowers the gospel to mediate salvation to sinful human beings (cf. 1:16-17). The passage falls into four parts. In the first, Paul reiterates (cf. 1:17) the revelation of God's righteousness and relates it to the OT (v. 21). The second section focuses on the way in which all human beings, equal in their sin, have equal access also to God's righteousness through faith (vv. 22-23). The source of God's righteousness in the gracious provision of Christ as an atoning sacrifice is the theme of the third part of the passage (vv. 24-25a). Finally, Paul shows how the atonement not only provides for the justification of sinners but also demonstrates the "just-ness" of God throughout the process (vv. 25b-26). In making this last point, we are presuming that "righteousness of God," which refers in vv. 21-22 to the justifying act of God, refers in vv. 25-26 to the "integrity" of God, his always acting in complete accordance with his own character.[4] Most contemporary exegetes and theologians reject this interpretation; but we are convinced that this shift in meaning is required by the data of the text, and, indeed, gives to the text its extraordinary power and significance. For, as James Denney says,

> There can be no gospel unless there is such a thing as a righteousness of God for the ungodly. But just as little can there be any gospel unless the integrity of God's character be maintained. The problem of the sinful world, the problem of all religion, the problem of God in dealing with a sinful race, is how to unite these two things. The Christian answer to the problem is given by Paul in the words: "Jesus Christ, whom God set forth a propitiation (or, in propitiatory power) in his blood."[5]

---

hand], F, and G), NA[27] and UBS[4] enclose the word in brackets (it is read in P[40], the primary Alexandrian B, the secondary Alexandrian C [third corrector], 33, and 81, in Ψ, and in the majority text). The difference in meaning is slight, the article, if read, probably being anaphoric (cf. πίστεως Ἰησοῦ Χριστοῦ in v. 22).

4. The jump from the one to the other is not as great as might at first appear, since always lurking in "righteousness" language is allusion to the character and person of God.

5. J. Denney, *The Death of Christ* (ed. R. V. G. Tasker; London: Tyndale, 1951), p. 98.

The occurrence in this passage of some words and concepts that are not typical of Paul's presentation of the gospel[6] suggests to many scholars that Paul is quoting an early Christian tradition.[7] This is possible, but it is more likely that Paul has himself written these verses in dependence on a certain Jewish-Christian interpretation of Jesus' death. This interpretation, which appears also in Heb. 9–10, viewed Jesus' death as the fulfillment of

6. E.g., ἱλαστήριον ("mercy seat," "propitiation"); πάρεσις ("passing over"); προτίθημι with the meaning "set forth"; δικαιοσύνη with reference to God's attribute of righteousness; reference to "redemption" as a past event and God's passing over past sins.

7. Additional reasons for this hypothesis are: (1) the awkward transition from vv. 23-24, or, if the fragment is seen to begin in v. 25, the relative pronoun introducing that verse, which can be compared to the introduction to other NT "hymnic" traditions; and (2) the apparently redundant duplication of the ἔνδειξις ("demonstration") clauses in vv. 25b-26a.

Several competing suggestions as to the extent and origin of the pre-Pauline fragment are extant.

(a) Bultmann thought that everything from δικαιούμενοι ("being justified") in v. 24 through τοῦ θεοῦ ("of God") in v. 26a was pre-Pauline, with Paul adding to it the phrases δωρεὰν τῇ αὐτοῦ χάριτι ("by his grace") in v. 24 and διὰ [τῆς] πίστεως ("though faith") in v. 25. E. Käsemann has sought to provide stronger evidence for this alternative by a novel interpretation of the way the tradition functions in the context. He suggests that the tradition Paul quotes set forth a conception of God's righteousness with which he disagreed and which he corrects by his addition of the phrase πρὸς τὴν ἔνδειξιν . . . ("for a demonstration") in v. 26b ("Zum Verständnis von Römer 3,24-26," in *Exegetische Versuche und Besinnungen I* [Göttingen: Vandenhoeck & Ruprecht, 1960], pp. 96-100; cf. also J. Reumann, "The Gospel of the Righteousness of God: Pauline Reinterpretation in Rom. 3:21-31," *Int* 20 [1966], pp. 432-52; R. P. Martin, *Reconciliation: A Study of Paul's Theology* [Atlanta: John Knox, 1981], pp. 81-89).

(b) The most popular alternative to this view — one that appears to be gaining ascendancy — holds that only vv. 25-26a are pre-Pauline. This tradition, it is suggested, is a Jewish-Christian one that was originally associated with the Eucharist (cf. esp. E. Lohse, *Märtyrer und Gottesknecht: Untersuchungen zur urchristlichen Verkündigung vom Sühntod Jesu Christi* [FRLANT 46; Göttingen: Vandenhoeck & Ruprecht, 1963], pp. 149-54; note also P. Stuhlmacher, "Recent Exegesis on Romans 3:24-26," in *Reconciliation, Law and Righteousness*, pp. 96-98; G. Friedrich, *Die Verkündigung des Todes Jesu im Neuen Testament* [Biblische Theologische Studien 6; Neukirchen/Vluyn: Neukirchener, 1982], pp. 57-58; Wengst, *Christologische Formeln*, pp. 87-88; B. F. Meyer, "The Pre-Pauline Formula in Rom. 3.25-26a," *NTS* 29 [1983], pp. 204-6; van der Minde, *Schrift und Tradition*, pp. 58-60).

(c) In addition to these fairly popular alternatives, it has been suggested that all of vv. 25-26 is pre-Pauline (D. Zeller, "Sühne und Langmut. Zur Traditionsgeschichte von Röm 3,24-26," *TP* 43 [1968], 64-75), or even that these verses are a post-Pauline interpolation (C. H. Talbert, "A Non-Pauline Fragment at Romans 3.24-26?" *JBL* 85 [1966], pp. 287-96; G. Fitzer, "Der Ort der Versöhnung nach Paulus," *ThZ* 22 [1966], 161-83; for a solid argument against this interpolation hypothesis, see Williams, *Jesus' Death*, pp. 7-10).

the Day of Atonement ritual.[8] Perhaps Paul used such a tradition at this point in Romans both because it suited his argument and because it created yet another point of contact with the Jewish Christians in Rome.

21 Paul signals the transition to a new phase of his exposition of the gospel with "but now."[9] The phrase could have a purely logical force — "but now here is the situation apart from the law"[10] — but is more likely to preserve its normal temporal meaning. As in 6:22, 7:6, 1 Cor. 15:20, Eph. 2:13, and Col. 1:22, "but now" marks the shift in Paul's focus from the old era of sin's domination to the new era of salvation.[11] This contrast between two eras in salvation history is one of Paul's most basic theological conceptions, providing the framework for many of his key ideas. Rom. 1:18–3:20 has sketched the spiritual state of those who belong to the old era: justly condemned, helpless in the power of sin, powerless to escape God's wrath. "But now" God has intervened to inaugurate a new era, and all who respond in faith — not only after the cross, but, as Rom. 4 will show, before it also — will be transferred into it from the old era. No wonder Lloyd-Jones can exclaim, "there are no more wonderful words in the whole of Scripture than just these two words 'But now.' "

8. In response to the arguments in favor of a set tradition here: (1) the presence of some rare words is at least partly due to the fact that Paul does not elsewhere discuss the exact theological concepts found here; (2) whether these concepts could or could not have been independently broached by Paul is very difficult to know; (3) abrupt transitions are, if anything, typical of Pauline style; (4) the apparent duplication of clauses in vv. 25b-26 is a problem on any view of the literary origins of the text. For these points and others, see R. Wonneberger, *Syntax und Exegese. Eine generative Theorie der griechischen Syntax und ihr Beitrag zur Auslegung des Neuen Testaments, dargestellt an 2. Korinther 5,2f und Römer 3,21-26* (BET 13; Frankfurt: Lang, 1972), pp. 202-77; N. H. Young, "Did St. Paul Compose Romans III.24f?" *AusBR* 22 (1974), 23-32; Cambier, *L'Evangile de Dieu,* pp. 73-79; Hultgren, *Paul's Gospel,* pp. 60-69; J. Piper, "The Demonstration of the Righteousness of God in Romans 3:25, 26," *JSNT* 7 (1980), 7-9; D. A. Campbell, *The Rhetoric of Righteousness in Romans 3:21-26* (JSNTSup 65; Sheffield: Sheffield Academic Press, 1992), pp. 45-57; Althaus; Schlier; Cranfield.

9. Gk. νυνὶ δέ. Hays contests the notion that a major break occurs at v. 21, noting that vv. 21-26 carry on the discussion of covenant faithfulness begun in 3:1-8 ("Psalm 143," p. 115; cf. also Viard). But we are not as convinced as Hays that "covenant faithfulness" is so prominent in either 3:1-8 or 3:21-26, and his view gives insufficient attention to the way 3:21 resumes 1:17.

10. E.g., Meyer.

11. Paul here views the transition from the standpoint of history, with the cross as the point of transition between old era and new. He can also apply this basic salvation-historical concept at the level of the individual, with conversion as the point of transition. See on this particularly Ridderbos, *Paul,* pp. 44-49, 52, 154, 161-66; Nygren, pp. 144-47, passim; and Luz, 168-69.

As "the wrath of God" dominated the old era (1:18), so "the righteousness of God" dominates the new. "Righteousness of God" means the same here as in Rom. 1:17: the justifying activity of God. From God's side, this includes his eschatological intervention to vindicate and deliver his people, in fulfillment of his promises. From the human side, it includes the status of acquittal acquired by the person so declared just.[12] In 1:17, Paul asserts that this "righteousness of God" is constantly revealed[13] through the preaching of the gospel. Here he simply asserts its presence as a dominating force in God's interaction with humanity.[14]

The relationship of this manifestation of God's righteousness to the OT is indicated in two prepositional phrases that together display the combination of continuity and discontinuity in salvation history that is characteristic of Romans. "Apart from the law" could go with "righteousness of God" (cf. KJV, "the righteousness of God without the law is manifested"),[15] but it makes better sense if taken with the verb "is manifested" (cf. NAB, "the righteousness of God has been manifested apart from the law").[16] Paul's purpose is to announce the way in which God's righteousness has been manifest rather than to contrast two kinds of righteousness.

What does Paul mean by this? In Rom. 2:1–3:20 Paul has made clear that the law has failed to rescue Jews from the power of sin because compliance with its demands to the extent necessary to secure justification has not been — and cannot be — forthcoming. "Apart from the law" might mean, then, "apart from doing the law": God's righteousness is now attained without any contribution from "works of the law."[17] While this may, indeed, be part of what Paul intends, it is questionable whether it goes far enough; for there is, as Paul will show in chap. 4, nothing really "new" about this: justification

---

12. Our reasons for adopting this interpretation are given in the exegesis of 1:17; see also the excursus following 1:17. The alternative explanations of δικαιοσύνη θεοῦ are the same here as at 1:17: the status of righteousness given by God (e.g., Cranfield), "the actuality of God's right to his creation as this reveals itself as saving power" (Käsemann; cf. Stuhlmacher, *Gerechtigkeit Gottes,* p. 91); similar to the previous view, God's saving righteousness, but against the background of Ps. 143 (Hays, "Psalm 143," pp. 114-15); God's faithfulness to the Abrahamic promise (Williams, "Righteousness of God," p. 276). Ziesler (*Righteousness,* p. 191) is correct to stress both divine action and human participation, but is wrong in thinking that an ethical dimension is present.

13. ἀποκαλύπτεται, an iterative present.

14. The verb is πεφανέρωται, with the perfect tense connoting a stative idea (on this interpretation of the perfect tense, see esp. Porter, *Verbal Aspect,* pp. 245-70) and the "but now" making it clear that Paul is thinking of the present time (= "stands manifest").

15. See also NIV and Hodge.

16. So, in effect, most English translations; cf., e.g., Godet.

17. Calvin; Nygren; Murray; Cranfield; Hübner, 127. Gifford takes νόμος to include any law, Morison (*Exposition,* p. 209) any divine instruction.

has always been by faith, apart from the law. Furthermore, it is not the manner in which God's righteousness is *received* that Paul is talking about here, but the manner in which it is *manifested* — the divine side of this "process" by which people are made right with God. This phrase, then, reiterates the salvation-historical shift denoted by "but now." In the new era inaugurated by Christ's death God has acted to deliver and vindicate his people "apart from" the law. It is not primarily the law as something for humans to do, but the law as a system, as a stage in God's unfolding plan, that is in view here. "Law" *(nomos),* then, refers to the "Mosaic covenant," that (temporary) administration set up between God and his people to regulate their lives and reveal their sin until the establishment of the promise in Christ.[18] One aspect of this covenant, of course, is those Jewish "identity markers," such as circumcision, the Sabbath, and food laws; Paul is certainly affirming, then, that the righteousness of God is now being manifested "outside the national and religious parameters set by the law."[19] But Paul's point cannot be confined to this. The reason these "identity markers" are no longer required is that the covenant of which they were a part has been made "obsolete" (cf. Heb. 8:7-13). It is this basic shift in salvation history that Paul alludes to here, and much of his discussion of the law in the rest of this letter (cf. 3:27-31; 4:15; 5:13, 20; 6:14; and especially chap. 7) is an attempt to explain this "apart from the law," while at the same time justifying his assertion that faith "establishes" the law (cf. 3:31; 8:4).

But Paul hastens to balance this discontinuity in salvation history with a reminder of its continuity. While God's justifying activity in the new age takes part outside the confines of the Old Covenant, the OT as a whole anticipates and predicts this new work of God: God's righteousness is "witnessed to[20] by the law and the prophets."[21]

---

18. Cf. Rom. 4:13-15; 5:20; and esp. Gal. 3:15–4:7.

19. Dunn.

20. Gk. μαρτυρουμένη. Only here does Paul use μαρτυρέω of the testimony of the OT to God's work in Christ (cf. Acts 10:43), but his meaning is clear enough.

21. The phrase νόμος καὶ προφηταί ("law and prophets") reflects a customary division of the OT into the Pentateuch and "everything else" — the entire OT is included (cf. also Matt. 5:17; 7:12; 11:13; 24:14; Luke 16:16; John 1:45; Acts 13:15; 24:14; 28:23; and 4 Macc. 18:10; cf. Str-B, 1.240). Wilckens suggests that "law and prophets" may represent the two "witnesses" required by Deut. 18:15, but the phrase is too stereotyped to make that likely. A third division, the "writings," was not yet widely used (although cf. Luke 22:44). What OT passages was Paul referring to? The most likely are those texts in Isaiah where "God's righteousness" is bound up with the eschatological deliverance of his people (46:13; 51:5, 6, 8). Perhaps, however, since "righteousness of God" is representative in Paul of the eschatological intervention of God in its fullness, we would be wrong to limit the OT texts that Paul refers to. For him, as for Jesus (cf. Matt. 5:17; 11:13), the entire OT anticipated and paved the way for the new age of fulfillment.

22a "Righteousness of God," repeated for clarity because of the distance from its first occurrence, is now considered from the "human" side of the transaction: it is "through[22] faith in Jesus Christ for all who believe." Picking up another key theme from 1:17, Paul highlights faith as the means by which God's justifying work becomes applicable to individuals. This, at least, is how this phrase has usually been interpreted (and cf. almost all modern English translations). But an alternative interpretation has been gaining favor. On this view, Paul asserts not that God's righteousness is attained "through faith *in* Jesus Christ," but "through the faith *of* Jesus Christ," or "through the faithfulness *shown by* Jesus Christ."[23] Advocates of this interpretation argue that it is the more likely linguistically[24] and that it makes better sense in the context. For this interpretation avoids the tautology involved in the traditional view, which has Paul asserting the importance of human faith twice: "faith in Jesus Christ," "for all who believe." On the other hand, the translation "through the faithfulness of Jesus Christ" results in a natural Pauline combination of divine initiative and human response.[25]

Subjective genitive

22. While Paul prefers to use ἐκ with πίστις to denote the means by which justification takes place (cf. 1:17), διά occurs frequently also (Rom. 3:25, 30; 2 Cor. 5:7; Gal. 2:16; 3:14, 26; Eph. 2:8; 3:12, 17; Phil. 3:9; Col. 2:12; 1 Thess. 3:7; 2 Tim. 3:15). Similarly, Paul usually denotes the object in which one places one's faith with ἐν, especially when the verb πιστεύω is used, but also with the noun πίστις (cf. Gal. 3:26; Eph. 1:15; Col. 1:4; 2 Tim. 3:15). But Paul most often uses the genitive following πίστις to denote the object of faith (Rom. 3:26; Gal. 2:16 [twice], 20; 3:22; Eph. 3:12; Phil. 3:9).

23. The difference involves the interpretation of the genitive Ἰησοῦ Χριστοῦ. The traditional interpretation assumes an objective genitive, while the alternative views it as possessive or subjective.

24. They note that in cases where πίστις is followed by the genitive of a noun denoting a person (or persons), the genitive is usually subjective or possessive. For example, πίστις Ἀβραάμ in Rom. 4:12 and 16 means "the faith exercised *by* Abraham"; an objective genitive, "faith in Abraham," is obviously impossible. This subjective rendering of the genitive when it follows πίστις is, it is argued, typical in Greek, and makes it a priori likely that Ἰησοῦ Χριστοῦ is also a subjective genitive.

25. The most thorough defense is L. T. Johnson, "Rom 3:21-26 and the Faith of Jesus," *CBQ* 44 (1982), 77-90. Cf. also T. F. Torrance, "One Aspect of the Biblical Conception of Faith," *ExpTim* 68 (1956-57), 111-14 (and the interchange between Torrance and C. F. D. Moule in the same volume, pp. 221-22); Longenecker, 149-50; G. Howard, " 'The Faith of Christ,' " *ExpTim* 85 (1973-74), 212-14; D. W. B. Robinson, " 'Faith of Jesus Christ' — A New Testament Debate," *RTR* 29 (1970), 71-81; Campbell, *Rhetoric,* pp. 58-69; R. B. Hays, "ΠΙΣΤΙΣ and Pauline Christology: What Is at Stake?" in *Society of Biblical Literature 1991 Seminar Papers* (ed. E. H. Lovering, Jr.; Atlanta; Scholars Press, 1991), pp. 714-29; Barth. S. K. Williams ("Again *Pistis Christou*," *CBQ* 49 [1987], 431-47) takes a slightly different tack, viewing the genitive as adjectival, and understanding the phrase to denote the "Christ faith," the faith actualized by Christ, and in which others come to participate. See also the interchange between R. Hays and J. D. G. Dunn in the papers of the SBL Pauline Theology Seminar in 1991.

Despite these arguments, the traditional interpretation of the phrase is preferable. The linguistic argument in favor of the alternative rendering is by no means compelling.[26] In addition, contextual considerations favor the objective genitive in Rom. 3:22. While the Greek word *pistis* can mean "faithfulness" (see 3:3), and Paul can trace our justification to the obedience of Christ (5:19), little in this section of Romans would lead us to expect a mention of Christ's "active obedience" as basic to our justification.[27] Moreover, *pistis* in Paul almost always means "faith"; very strong contextual features must be present if any other meaning is to be adopted.[28] But these are absent in 3:22. If, on the other hand, *pistis* is translated "faith," it is necessary to introduce some very dubious theology in order to speak meaningfully about "the faith exercised by Jesus Christ."[29] Finally, and most damaging to the hypothesis in either form, is the consistent use of *pistis* throughout 3:21–4:25 to designate the faith exercised by people in God, or Christ, as the sole means of justification. Only very strong reasons would justify giving to *pistis* any other meaning in this, the theological summary on which the rest of the section depends. The simple references to "faith" in 3:28 and 3:30 are abbreviations of the "faith in Christ/Jesus" that is enunciated in 3:22 and 26 (cf. v. 25).[30]

But if Paul mentions human faith in this phrase, why then does he add the phrase "for all who believe"? Comparison has been made with the combination "from faith for faith" in 1:17, but this is to appeal from the uncertain

26. A genitive following πίστις certainly need not be subjective. Most such genitives in the NT are, indeed, possessive or subjective, usually employing the personal pronoun (e.g., Rom. 1:8: ἡ πίστις ὑμῶν, "your faith"). But many are objective (with a divine name: Mark 11:22; Acts 3:16; Jas. 2:1; Rev. 2:13; 14:12; cf. also Col. 2:12; Phil. 1:27; 2 Thess. 2:13), while only a few are purely subjective (Rom. 3:3; 4:12, 16). Only context, then, can determine the force of the genitive.

27. Note that in vv. 24-26, on whatever interpretation we take, Paul refers not to Christ's "righteousness"/"faithfulness," but to God's.

28. In 3:3, e.g., the meaning "faithfulness" for πίστις is warranted by the parallel terms and by the fact that the reference is clearly to God's own πίστις. Note also that the phrase "faith of Abraham" in 4:12 and 16 does *not* mean Abraham's "faithfulness."

29. Specifically, one must interpret Jesus more as the "pattern" for our faith than as the object of our faith (see Williams, *"Pistis Christou,"* p. 434, and the monograph by R. B. Hays, *The Faith of Jesus Christ: An Investigation of the Narrative Substructure of Galatians 3:1–4:11* [SBLDS 56; Chico, CA: Scholars, 1983]). But this interpretation not only misreads key parts of Paul's letters but places too much emphasis on Christ as example in the atonement.

30. For these points and others, see esp. Murray, 1.363-74; J. D. G. Dunn, "Once More, ΠΙΣΤΙΣ ΧΡΙΣΤΟΥ," in *Society of Biblical Literature 1991 Seminar Papers,* pp. 730-44. A. Hultgren ("The Pistis Christou Formulation in Paul," *NovT* 22 [1980], 248-63) agrees that the objective genitive is primary in this and the other phrases in question, but suggests that it be combined with a genitive of quality: "the faith of the believer which comes forth as Christ is proclaimed in the gospel" (p. 257).

to the obscure (see the notes on 1:17). Paul's purpose is probably to highlight the universal availability of God's righteousness. This theme is not only one of the most conspicuous motifs of the epistle, but is explicitly mentioned in vv. 22b-23. God's righteousness is available only through faith in Christ — but it is available to *anyone* who has faith in Christ.

22b-23   Paul tells us in vv. 22b-23 why this righteousness is available to all, and why, also, all need this righteousness. "There is no distinction" summarizes a key element of Paul's presentation in 1:18–3:20, and is likely, therefore, to have special application to Jew and Gentile.[31] In v. 23, Paul elaborates this point. His "no distinction," as we would expect, has to do with the absence of any basic difference among people with respect to their standing before God. Jews may have the law and circumcision; Americans may lay claim to a great religious heritage; "good" people may point to their works of charity; but all this makes no essential difference to one's standing before the righteous and holy God. Paul reduces the argument of 1:18–3:20 to its essence in a justly famous statement of the condition of all people outside Christ: "all have sinned[32] and are falling short of the glory of God." The second verb states the consequences of the first: because all have sinned, all are falling short[33] of the glory of God. "Glory" in the Bible characteristically refers to the magnificent presence of the Lord, and the eternal state was often pictured as a time when God's people would experience and have a part in that "glory" (e.g., Isa. 35:2; Rom. 8:18; Phil. 3:21; 2 Thess. 2:14).[34] And just as this sharing in God's "glory" involves conformity to the "image of Christ" (Rom. 8:29-30; Phil. 3:21), so the absence of glory involves a declension from the "image of God" in which human beings were first made. "The future glory may be regarded as the restoration of the lost, original glory."[35] Paul, then, is indicating that all people fail to exhibit that "being-like-God" for which they were created; and the present

31. Cf. 10:12, where the same word — διαστολή ("distinction") — occurs.

32. Gk. ἥμαρτον. The aorist tense here could refer to the sin of all people "in and with" Adam in the past (cf. 5:12; see Lloyd-Jones; Dunn; Hughes, *True Image,* p. 130) but is more likely a "summary" aorist, gathering up the sins of people throughout the past into a single "moment" (Porter [*Verbal Aspect,* p. 222], disdaining the usual past-referring significance of the aorist tense, calls this verb "omnitemporal").

33. The verb Paul uses here, ὑστερέω, means, in the passive, "to lack" or, with a following genitive, as here, "come short of [something]" (BAGD); its present tense suggests that Paul thinks all people are regularly falling short of God's glory.

34. In classical Greek, δόξα means "opinion," and a few commentators (e.g., Calvin) suggest that it may have this general meaning here: people have fallen short of the "approbation" of God (cf. John 12:43). But the biblical concept of δόξα and Paul's usage point to a different meaning; see the note on 1:23.

35. Barrett. Cf. also Morison, *Exposition,* p. 242; Murray; Käsemann; Cranfield. Jewish texts speak specifically of Adam's having lost his "glory" through sin (cf. *Gen. Rab.* 12.6; *Apoc. Mos.* 21:6; see esp. Jervell, *Imago Dei,* pp. 180-83, passim).

tense of the verb, in combination with Rom. 8, shows that even Christians "fall short" of that goal until they are transformed in the last day by God.[36]

24 The connection between this verse and the previous verses is not clear. Those who think a pre-Pauline fragment begins here find in the difficult transition evidence for a shift from Paul's original dictation to the citation of a tradition. But whatever his dependence on tradition, Paul is himself composing the verses, and we need to determine what connection he intends. The participle "being justified"[37] is most naturally taken as a modifier of one or both of the finite verbs in v. 23: "sinned" and/or "falling short." If so, Paul's purpose in highlighting the gift character of justification in the participial clause would presumably be to provide evidence for the total religious impotence of humanity.[38] The objection to this interpretation is that it gives to a verse (24) that continues the main theme of the paragraph (justification/righteousness) a relatively subordinate role. Scholars suggest several other ways of relating this participle to its context,[39] but perhaps the best suggestion is Cranfield's. He argues that "being justified" is dependent on v. 23, to the extent that it has as its subject "all," but that it also picks up and continues the main theme of the paragraph from vv. 21-22a. With this we would agree, with the caveat that "all" in its connection with "being justified" indicates not universality ("everybody") but lack of particularity ("anybody"). Paul's stress on the gift character of justification in v. 24 illuminates from the positive side the "lack of distinction" in God's dealings (vv. 22b-23) even as it continues and explains the theme of "righteousness by faith" from v. 22a.

Paul uses the verb "justify" *(dikaioō)* for the first time in Romans to depict his distinctive understanding of Christian salvation. As Paul uses it in these contexts, the verb "justify" means not "to make righteous" (in an ethical sense) nor simply "to treat as righteous" (though one is really not righteous), but "to declare righteous." No "legal fiction," but a legal *reality* of the utmost significance, "to be justified" means to be acquitted by God from all "charges" that could be brought against a person because of his or her sins.[40]

---

36. Cranfield.

37. Gk. δικαιούμενοι.

38. Morison, *Exposition*, p. 245; Meyer; Wonneberger, *Syntax und Exegese,* pp. 250-51.

39. E.g., (1) δικαιούμενοι ("being justified") could have the sense of a finite verb, parallel, rather than subordinate, to ὑστεροῦνται and ἥμαρτον in v. 23 (cf. NIV: "All . . . fall short of the glory of God, and are justified freely"; Schlier); (2) the finite verbs of v. 23 could be subordinated to δικαιούμενοι (RSV: "Since all have sinned and fall short of the glory of God, they are justified by his grace"; Kuss); (3) vv. 22b-23 could be parenthetical, with δικαιούμενοι resuming the discussion of righteousness by faith in vv. 21-22a (S-H; Michel; Murray).

40. See, further, the excursus after 1:17.

This judicial verdict, for which one had to wait until the last judgment according to Jewish theology, is according to Paul rendered the moment a person believes. The act of justification is therefore properly "eschatological," as the ultimate verdict regarding a person's standing with God is brought back into our present reality.

Characteristic also of Paul's theology is his emphasis on the gift character of this justifying verdict; we are "justified freely[41] by his grace."[42] "Grace" is one of Paul's most significant theological terms.[43] He uses it typically not to describe a quality of God but the way in which God has acted in Christ: unconstrained by anything beyond his own will.[44] God's justifying verdict is totally unmerited. People have done, and can do, nothing to earn it. This belief is a "theological axiom" for Paul and is the basis for his conviction that justification can never be attained through works, or the law (cf. Rom. 4:3-5, 13-16; 11:6), but only through faith.[45] Once this is recognized, the connection between v. 22a and v. 24 is clarified; that justification is a matter of grace on God's side means that it must be a matter of faith on the human side. But the gracious nature of justification also answers to the dilemma of people who are under the power of sin (v. 23). As Pascal says, "Grace is indeed needed to turn a man into a saint; and he who doubts it does not know what a saint or a man is."[46]

41. Gk. δωρεάν, the abverbial form of δωρεά, which means "gift" (cf. 2 Cor. 9:15).

42. Those who view this verse as pre-Pauline in origin generally think that τῇ αὐτοῦ χάριτι ("by his grace") is Paul's addition to the tradition (e.g., Reumann, "The Gospel of the Righteousness of God," p. 442). But if, as we think, the verse is Paul's own formulation, the repetition should not surprise us, for it occurs elsewhere in Paul (Rom. 5:15, 17; Eph. 3:7).

43. In secular Greek, χάρις is "what delights," and is used with reference to things that bring joy (χαρά), especially gifts (where it occurs often with δωρεά). It can be used of the "favor" of the gods (in which case, however, the word lacks the specifically Pauline notion of "totally unmerited favor") and occurs frequently in the Hellenistic period to denote instances of a ruler's "favor." In the LXX, χάρις occurs over 190 times. Of those with a Hebrew equivalent (only about 70), most translate חֵן. This word has the special connotation of the "assistance" rendered to a weaker person by a stronger, and approaches more closely thereby the Pauline usage. Note, e.g., the ubiquitous phrase "to find grace [חֵן; χάρις] in the eyes of . . ." (Gen. 6:8; Exod. 33:12; Num. 11:15; Deut. 24:1). Still, the emphasis on the inherent quality of the person who finds favor distinguishes it from Paul's conception (cf. H. Conzelmann, W. Zimmerli, TDNT IX, 372-87; H.-H. Esser, NIDNTT II, 115-17).

44. Bultmann, 1.288-92; Ridderbos, Paul, pp. 173-74. Melanchthon notes, "the word gratia does not signify some quality in us, but rather the will or kindness of God itself toward us."

45. Cf. esp. D. J. Doughty, "The Priority of ΧΑΡΙΣ," NTS 19 (1972-73), 163-80.

46. Pensées, #508.

What gives this paragraph its unparalleled significance is the number of perspectives from which God's justification of sinners is considered. If "freely by his grace" indicates the mode of justification, as entirely free and unmerited, "through the redemption" illumines the costly means by which this acquitting verdict is rendered possible. "Redemption"[47] means, basically, "liberation through payment of a price." Thus, in the second and first centuries B.C., "redemption" often refers to the "ransoming" of prisoners of war, slaves, and condemned criminals.[48] If "redemption" has this connotation here, then Paul would be presenting Christ's death as a "ransom," a "payment" that takes the place of that penalty for sins "owed" by all people to God.[49] Though widely rejected today,[50] this interpretation of the significance of the word should be retained.[51] While it is not clear whether Paul was thinking specifi-

---

47. Gk. ἀπολύτρωσις is the compound form of λύτρωσις, the former predominating in the NT probably because of the penchant for compound forms in Hellenistic Greek (F. Büchsel, *TDNT* IV, 352). Chrysostom, on the other hand, regards ἀπολύτρωσις as an intensive form of λύτρωσις, implying the definitive nature of Christian redemption so that, as he puts it, "we might never again fall under the same slavery."

48. See the survey in Morris, *Apostolic Preaching,* pp. 22-26.

49. Morison, *Exposition,* p. 265; Hodge; Godet; S-H; Barrett; Michel; Murray; Ridderbos, *Paul,* pp. 193-94; Morris, *Apostolic Preaching,* pp. 37-38.

50. Critics of the traditional interpretation marshal several arguments. The one occurrence of ἀπολύτρωσις in the LXX does not clearly refer to a process of "ransoming" (Dan. 4:32 LXX). More important, the verb λυτρόω, from which ἀπολύτρωσις is derived, and which occurs 104 times, translates Hebrew words (mainly גאל and פדה) that usually mean simply "liberate," "set free" — no notion of a price paid for that liberation (a ransom) is generally present. The same omission of any "ransom" connotation is claimed to be true for the other occurrences of ἀπολύτρωσις in Paul (Rom. 8:23; 1 Cor. 1:30; Eph. 1:7, 14; 4:30; Col. 1:14) and the rest of the NT (Luke 21:28; Heb. 9:15; 11:35), as well as for other λυτρ- words (λυτρόω: Luke 24:21; Tit. 2:14; 1 Pet. 1:18; λύτρον: Mark 10:45 = Matt. 20:28; λύτρωσις: Luke 1:68; 2:38; Heb. 9:12; λυτρωτής: Acts 7:35). Accordingly, many argue that ἀπολύτρωσις in this verse means simply "act of liberation or emancipation," with no suggestion of the price at which the liberation was secured or the means by which it was effected (cf. esp. O. Procksch/F. Büchsel, *TDNT* IV, 329-35, 341-56; Hill, *Greek Words,* pp. 58-80; Black; Schlier).

51. L. Morris has shown that a price is often indicated as the basis for the "release" specified by λυτρόω in the LXX, and concludes that, while there was some movement away from an emphasis on price in the use of the word in Jewish Greek, the connotation of a "ransoming" was usually present. Certainly, a "ransom" is always implied with the word in secular Greek contemporary with the NT (*Apostolic Preaching,* pp. 9-26). The idea of "ransom" is maintained in Josephus's one use of ἀπολύτρωσις (*Ant.* 12.27) and of ἀπολυτρόω (*J.W.* 2.273), and in one of Philo's two uses of ἀπολύτρωσις (*Every Good Man Is Free* 114 — the word does not clearly refer to a "ransom" in *Prel. Stud.* 109, nor does the verb in *Allegorical Interpretation* 3.21). Even in the LXX use of λυτρόω, connotations of "cost" are usually present, even if a specific "price" is not clearly indicated (on this distinction, see I. H. Marshall, "The Development of the Concept of Redemption in

cally of slave manumissions when he applied the word to Christian salvation,[52] it is likely that Paul views sin as that power from which we need to be liberated (cf. 3:9).[53] If we ask further the question "To whom was the 'ransom' paid?" it is not clear that we need to answer it. The usage of the word makes it clear that there need be no specific person who "receives" the "payment." Certainly we are not to think of Christ's death as a payment of God made to Satan, a view that became very popular in the first centuries of the Christian church. A more biblical answer, and one that might be implied by v. 25, would be that God, the judge who must render just verdicts, is the recipient of the ransom. If so, an equal emphasis must be placed on the fact that God is also the originator of the liberating process.

As he does in Eph. 1:7 and Col. 1:14, Paul adds that this redemption is "in Christ Jesus." It is not clear whether Paul means by it that the liberation was accomplished by Christ at the cross or that the liberation occurs "in relation to" Christ, whenever sinners trust Christ.[54] Favoring the latter, however, is the connection of "redemption" with the forgiveness of sins in Eph. 1:7 and Col. 1:14, and 1 Cor. 1:30: "Christ was made . . . *our* redemption." While, then, the "price" connoted by the word "redemption" was "paid" at the cross in the blood of Christ, the redeeming work that the payment made possible is, like justification, applied to each person when he or she believes.

25 Although the Greek word for "whom" connects v. 25 to v. 24, the connection is so loose that v. 25 may be considered as beginning a new sentence. The focus shifts from human reception of God's justifying work to God's initiative in providing for it. Specifically, Paul now unfolds the nature and means of "the redemption that is in Christ Jesus," showing that this redemption takes place at the will and initiative of God the Father. While the

---

the New Testament," in *Reconciliation and Hope*, p. 153 n. 4). In the NT itself, λύτρον almost certainly means "ransom" in Mark 10:45 (= Matt. 20:28; cf. esp. A. Feuillet, "Le logion sur la rançon," *RSPT* 51 [1967], 365-402, and, more recently, P. Stuhlmacher, "Vicariously Giving His Life for Many, Mark 10:45 [Matt. 20:28]," *Reconciliation, Law and Righteousness,* pp. 16-29; he also defends the authenticity of the saying). The addition of "through his blood" to ἀπολύτρωσις in Eph. 1:7 spells out the "price" at which the liberation was accomplished. There is a similar emphasis on Christ's death as a sacrifice in this context (v. 25), and this, coupled with the presence in Paul's letters of statements such as "we were bought with a price" (1 Cor. 6:20; 7:23; cf. also Gal. 3:13-14), makes it likely that ἀπολύτρωσις includes the notion of Christ's death as a ransom.

52. Deissmann argued that he was (cf. *Light from the Ancient East. The New Testament Illustrated by Recently Discovered Texts of the Graeco-Roman World* [New York: George H. Doran, 1927], pp. 327-30), but see Ridderbos, *Paul*, p. 193.

53. See Campbell, *Rhetoric*, pp. 118-30, who argues that ἀπολύτρωσις denotes freedom from an enslaving power through substitution.

54. See, particularly, F. Büchsel, *TDNT* IV, 353-354; Schlier; K. Wennemer, "ΑΠΟΛΥΤΡΩΣΙΣ. Römer 3:24-25a," *SPCIC* 2.283-88.

persons of God the Father and God the Son must be kept distinct as we consider the process of redemption, it is a serious error to sever the two with respect to the will for redemption, as if the loving Christ had to take the initiative in placating the angry Father. God's love and wrath meet in the atonement, and neither can be denied or compromised if the full meaning of that event is to be properly appreciated. "Our own justification before God rests on the solid reality that the fulfilling of God's justice in Christ was at the same time the fulfilling of this love for us."[55]

The first five Greek words of v. 25 form the main clause of this new sentence, with the series of prepositional phrases and clauses in the rest of v. 25 and v. 26 dependent on it. The verb in this clause could be translated either "propose, plan" (cf. REB, "designed") or "display publicly" (NASB).[56] A good case can be made for the former,[57] but the latter fits better with the background and imagery of the concept Paul alludes to here (see below on *hilastērion*) and should probably be preferred.[58] Redemption is "in Christ" in that God "displayed him publicly," or "set him forth as a sacrifice" on the cross as a *hilastērion*. Nor should it be missed that it is God who thus takes the initiative in the process of redemption — not Christ, and certainly not human beings. As P. T. Forsyth remarks, "The prime doer in Christ's cross was God. Christ was God reconciling. He was God doing the very best for man, and not man doing his very best for God."[59]

What Paul means by designating Christ a *hilastērion* has been the subject of considerable debate.[60] When the use of *hilastērion*[61] in the Bible is considered,

---

55. Hughes, *True Image,* p. 360.

56. The verb is προέθετο, a middle form of the verb προτίθημι. Each of the two meanings noted above is common for this form of the verb (BAGD). The meaning "offer," in a sacrificial sense (cf. the TEV rendering, "God offered him"), is proposed for the verb in the active (cf. MM), but there is no evidence for this meaning in the middle.

57. Paul is the only NT author to use the verb, both times in the middle, and both having the meaning "plan, determine" (Rom. 1:13; Eph. 1:9). In addition, the cognate noun πρόθεσις is used fairly frequently in the NT with the meaning "purpose" (cf. Rom. 8:28; 9:11). Cf. esp. Cranfield; also Godet; A. Pluta, *Gottes Bundestreue. Ein Schlüsselbegriff in Röm 3,25a* (Bibelstudien 34; Stuttgart: Katholisches Bibelwerk, 1969), p. 59. Zeller ("Sühne und Langmut," pp. 57-58) suggests the meaning "predestining for the purpose of revelation."

58. The double accusative after the verb — ὅν, the direct object, and ἱλαστήριον, a predicative accusative — also favors this meaning. Note also the uses of the verb and its cognate noun with reference to the "showbread" of the altar (cf. Pss. 54:3; 86:14; 101:3), where the verb means "set before." See, e.g., S-H; Murray; Käsemann; Fitzmyer; Hultgren, *Paul's Gospel,* pp. 56-57.

59. *The Cruciality of the Cross* (2d ed.; London: Hodder and Stoughton, 1910), p. 17.

60. For the history of interpretation, see Hultgren, *Paul's Gospel,* pp. 47-72, and Pluta, *Gottes Bundestreue,* pp. 17ff.

61. Grammatically, the word is to be taken as the substantive of the adjective ἱλαστήριος (L. Morris, "The Meaning of ἱλαστήριον in Romans III.25," *NTS* 2 [1955-56],

a strong case can be made for taking the word as a reference to the OT "mercy seat,"[62] the cover over the ark where Yahweh appeared (Lev. 16:2), and on which sacrificial blood was poured. For this is what the word refers to in its one other NT occurrence (Heb. 9:5), as well as in 21 of its 27 LXX occurrences.[63] Particularly significant are the several occurrences of the word in the description in Lev. 16 of the "Day of Atonement" ritual. According to this text, the high priest is to enter the "Holy of Holies" once a year and sprinkle on the mercy seat (= LXX *hilastērion*) the blood of a sacrificial victim, thereby "making atonement."[64] In the OT and Jewish tradition, this "mercy seat" came to be applied generally to the place of atonement.[65] By referring to Christ as this "mercy seat," then, Paul would be inviting us to view Christ as the New Covenant equivalent, or antitype, to this Old Covenant "place of atonement," and, derivatively, to the ritual of atonement itself. What in the OT was hidden from public view behind the veil has now been "publicly displayed" as the OT ritual is fulfilled and brought to an end in Christ's "once-for-all" sacrifice. This interpretation, which has an ancient and respectable heritage,[66] has been gaining strength in recent years.[67] It is

---

34) rather than as a masculine noun ("propitiator" — cf. the reading *propitiatorem* in some MSS of the Latin Vulgate, and some Fathers [Cranfield mentions Ambrose, Ambrosiaster, Jerome, and Pelagius]) or as an adjective modifying ὄν (S-H; Morison, *Exposition,* pp. 279-305; Scott, *Christianity,* p. 68).

62. The English "mercy seat" comes from Tyndale's translation, which was in turn influenced by Luther's Germ. "Gnadenstuhl."

63. The underlying Hebrew word in these texts is כַּפֹּרֶת. All six of Philo's uses of the word also refer to the "mercy seat," but all occur in the context of biblical exposition (*On the Cherubim* 25; *Who Is the Heir?* 166; *On Flight and Finding* 100, 101; *On the Life of Moses* 2.95, 97).

64. The Greek verb is a cognate of ἱλαστήριον, ἐξιλάσκομαι (the Hebrew verb is כפר).

65. Cf. esp. B. Janowski, *Sühne als Heilsgeschehen. Studien zur Sühnetheologie der Priesterschrift und zur Wurzel KPR im Alten Orient und im Alten Testament* (WMANT 55; Neukirchen/Vluyn: Neukirchener, 1982), p. 361. Note also D. McC. L. Judisch, "Propitiation in the Language and Typology of the Old Testament," *Concordia Theological Quarterly* 48 (1984), 231; and, for later Judaism, Str-B, 3.175-78.

66. Origen; Theodoret; Luther; Calvin; Bengel.

67. The best arguments are given by Hultgren, *Paul's Gospel,* pp. 47-72, and Stuhlmacher, "Zur neueren Exegese," pp. 320-30 (ET, "Recent Exegesis"). Cf. also Pluta, *Gottes Bundestreue,* pp. 62-70; Meyer, "Pre-Pauline Formula," 206; T. W. Manson, "ἱλαστήριον," *JTS* 46 (1945), 1-10; L. Sabourin and S. Lyonnet, *Sin, Redemption and Sacrifice: A Biblical and Patristic Study* (AnBib 48; Rome: Biblical Institute Press, 1970), pp. 157-66; A. von Dobbeler, *Glaube als Teilhabe* (WUNT 2.22; Tübingen: Mohr, 1987), pp. 78-87; M. Newton, *The Concept of Purity at Qumran and in the Letters of Paul* (SNTSMS 53; Cambridge: Cambridge University, 1985), pp. 75-77; Davies, 237-42; Janowski, *Sühne als Heilsgeschehen,* pp. 350-54; Goppelt, *Theology,* 2.95-96; Campbell, *Rhetoric,* pp. 130-33 (not "mercy seat" as such, but reference to the Day of Atonement rite); Nygren; Gifford; Gaugler; Barrett; Bruce(?); Wilckens; Fitzmyer.

attractive because it gives to *hilastērion* a meaning that is derived from its "customary" biblical usage, and creates an analogy between a central OT ritual and Christ's death that is both theologically sound and hermeneutically striking.

To be sure, there are objections to taking *hilastērion* as a reference to the "mercy seat."[68] Some claim, for instance, that the imagery would have been foreign to the Gentile Christian church in Rome; and Paul would hardly have used imagery that he knew they would fail to understand.[69] However, arguments based on what the Gentile congregation in Rome would, or would not, have been familiar with are precarious. Paul's letters furnish abundant proof that he expected his Gentile readers to be fully conversant with the OT. Surely he could expect his Gentile readers in Rome to have some knowledge of the Day of Atonement ritual and the significance within it of *hilastērion.*[70]

68. The word ἱλαστήριον was used for other things than the mercy seat in the OT and is used widely in secular Greek with reference to memorials and sacrifices that are intended to propitiate the gods. Therefore, Deissmann's insistence that ἱλαστήριον does not *mean* "mercy seat" is correct ("ἱλαστήριος and ἱλαστήριον. Eine lexikalische Studie," *ZNW* 4 [1903], 207-8). The word specifies the function of the cover over the ark — in its first occurrence in the LXX, it is used adjectivally (Exod. 25:16) and thereafter always has the article when the mercy seat is denoted. The anarthrous state of ἱλαστήριον in Rom. 3:25 has, then, been cited as evidence against the translation "mercy seat" (e.g., Morris, "ἱλαστήριον," p. 40). But this argument has little weight since there would be good grammatical reasons for the omission of the article in Rom. 3:25 (e.g., the predicative function of ἱλαστήριον [cf. Stuhlmacher, "Recent Exegesis," p. 99]). Moreover, while ἱλαστήριον does not *mean* "mercy seat," it is used absolutely in 20 of its LXX occurrences to denote that object. More serious is the logical strain involved in linking Christ with a *place* of atonement; but perhaps the strain is no greater than in thinking of Christ as the new temple (John 2:19-21), as the rock that followed in the wilderness (1 Cor. 10:4), or as both High Priest and sacrifice at the same time (cf. Hebrews). Moreover, there is evidence that the word, or the mercy seat it designates, becomes a semitechnical way of designating the atonement itself. In this case, objections to the interpretation based on the literal function of the mercy seat fall to the ground.

69. Many of the contemporary advocates of this view avoid this difficulty by attributing the imagery to a pre-Pauline confession formulated in Jewish-Christian circles (e.g., Hultgren, *Paul's Gospel,* pp. 47-72; Stuhlmacher, "Recent Exegesis," pp. 99-100). But this is a move of questionable validity. Not only is the existence of a tradition uncertain (see the introduction to the section), but it is unlikely that Paul, were he using a tradition, would have quoted words from it that he knew, or suspected, would fail to communicate with his readers.

70. Cf. Stuhlmacher ("Apostle Paul's View of Righteousness," p. 83): "The Roman congregation was at home in the Old Testament Scriptures from the synagogue and from Christian worship. They were instructed in the traditions of their faith by Jewish-Christian missionaries." Thus Paul might well be using cultic imagery from a tradition with which the Christians in Rome would have been familiar. Note particularly the striking similarities between Paul's argument here and the argument of Heb. 9–10. These include verbal parallels — notably ἱλαστήριον, used only in Rom. 3:25 and Heb.

233

In fact, we do not find anything that would render the interpretation of *hilastērion* against the background of the OT mercy seat improbable. Before drawing conclusions, however, other alternatives must be considered.

While Deissmann has shown that *hilastērion* usually means "means of propitiation" in ordinary Greek,[71] C. H. Dodd has argued that the word in the LXX means "means of expiation," and he accordingly opts for this translation in Rom. 3:25. "Propitiation" has reference to the turning away of wrath, and the appeasement of the "wrath of the gods" by various means is a frequent theme in Greek literature. This theme Dodd finds totally absent in the Bible. The verb cognate to *hilastērion* in the LXX has as its object sin, not God. The idea conveyed by the word and its cognates is thus, Dodd argues, the "covering," or forgiving, of sins, not the appeasing of God's wrath.[72] Others, while not endorsing all Dodd's conclusions, agree that reference to God's wrath should be eliminated from the word, and translate generally "means of atonement,"[73] or "atoning," or "expiatory sacrifice."[74]

9:5 in the NT, and ἀπολύρωσις, found in Rom. 3:24 and Heb. 9:15 (cf. also λύτρωσις in 9:12) — but, more importantly, thematic parallels. Hebrews makes much of the inadequacy of the Old Covenant ritual — it "cannot perfect the conscience of the worshiper" (9:9), "can never take away sins" (10:11), and means, in its yearly repetition, a constant "remembrance of sins" (10:1-4). This inadequacy, according to Hebrews, is met in the "once-for-all" sacrifice of Christ (cf. 9:14: "the blood of Christ"), whose death "redeems [those who are called] from the transgressions under the first covenant" (9:15), brings the "forgiveness" of sins, as promised in the new covenant prophecy (10:17-18), so that there is now "at the end of the age" a "putting away" of sin (9:26). In the same way, according to Paul, God has set forth Christ "at the present time" as a sacrifice that satisfies the demands of God's justice in his "passing over sins in the past." In both passages, then, the focus is on the way God has provided in Christ as a sacrificial victim the basis for eternal redemption — a basis that was not provided through the OT cult. Moreover, Hebrews directs attention particularly to the Day of Atonement ritual (cf. 9:6). Not only, then, are we justified in suggesting that the passages move in a similar direction, but there is also further reason for thinking that Lev. 16 may be in the background of the Romans text.

71. Deissmann, "ἱλαστήριος," pp. 195-211.

72. Cf. also the use of the verb ἱλάσκεσθαι in Heb. 2:17; and ἱλασμός in 1 John 2:2; 4:10. C. H. Dodd, "ἱλάσκεσθαι, Its Cognates, Derivatives and Synonyms in the Septuagint," *JTS* 32 (1931), 352-60 (reprinted in *The Bible and the Greeks* [London: Hodder & Stoughton, 1935], pp. 82-95).

73. Lietzmann; Schlier; Friedrich, *Die Verkündigung des Todes Jesu,* pp. 65-67; Zeller, "Sühne und Langmut," pp. 56-58; V. Taylor, "Great Texts Reconsidered," *ExpTim* 50 (1938-39), 296.

74. Lohse, *Märtyrer und Gottesknecht,* pp. 150-52. Further reason for this interpretation is found in the alleged background of Paul's language in the traditions of the deaths of the Maccabean martyrs. Particularly significant is 4 Macc. 17:21b-22: ". . . [the martyrs] having become, as it were, a ransom [ἀντίψυχον] for the sin of our nation. And through the blood of those devout ones and their death as an expiation [τοῦ ἱλαστηρίου {τοῦ} θανάτου], divine Providence preserved Israel that previously had been afflicted." See Lohse, ibid.; cf. also Hill,

But Dodd is almost certainly wrong on this point. The OT frequently connects the "covering," or forgiving, of sins with the removal of God's wrath.[75] It is precisely the basic connotation of "propitiate" that led the translators of the LXX to use the *hilask-* words for the Hebrew words denoting the covering of sins.[76] This is not, however, to deny the connotation "expiation"; the OT cult serves to "wipe away" the guilt of sin at the same time as — and indeed, because — the wrath of God is being stayed.[77] When to the linguistic evidence we add the evidence of the context of Rom. 1–3, where the wrath of God is an overarching theme (1:18; cf. 2:5), the conclusion that *hilastērion* includes reference to the turning away of God's wrath is inescapable.

This propitiation is, of course, altogether different from pagan notions of propitiation. First, as we have seen, the biblical conception of the wrath of God is far removed from the pagan picture of a capricious and often vindictive deity. God's wrath is the inevitable and necessary reaction of absolute holiness to sin. Second, in contrast to the secular religious tradition, it is God himself who initiates the propitiatory offering. "In the heathen

---

Greek Words, pp. 41-48; Williams, *Jesus' Death,* pp. 40-41; J. S. Pobee, *Persecution and Martyrdom in the Theology of Paul* (JSNTSup 6; Sheffield: JSOT, 1985), pp. 61-63. W. J. Heard ("Maccabean Martyr Theology" [Ph.D. diss. University of Aberdeen, 1987], pp. 487-94) thinks the primary background is the Maccabean martyr traditions, but sees these as built, in turn, on texts like Lev. 16 (cf. also Dobbeler, *Glaube,* pp. 78-87). However, it is unlikely that Maccabean martyr theology has had any important influence on Paul's use of ἱλαστήριον; see particularly Stuhlmacher, "Recent Exegesis," pp. 100-102 (Lohse apparently reads 4 Macc. 17:22 according to the text of A, as τοῦ ἱλαστηρίου θανάτου; his interpretation is not as cogent, however, if the text of א, τοῦ ἱλαστηρίου τοῦ θανάτου, is read [see Ralhfs]). Despite claims to the contrary, these traditions have not exerted any strong influence on the NT. Paul's great indebtedness to the OT makes it more likely that the primary background for a word like ἱλαστήριον, which is used significantly in the OT, will be found there rather than in post-OT writings.

75. Cf. esp. Morris, *Apostolic Preaching,* pp. 136-56; R. R. Nicole, "C. H. Dodd and the Doctrine of Propitiation," *WTJ* 17 (1954-55), 117-57; Hill, *Greek Words,* pp. 23-41.

76. Cf. Williams, *Jesus' Death,* pp. 38-40. While there is little agreement about the etymology or meaning of the Hebrew root כפר, a good case can be made for finding some allusion to the notion of propitiation when it is used in conjunction with the cult. See the careful survey of usage by P. Garnet, "Atonement Constructions in the Old Testament and the Qumran Scrolls," *EvQ* 46 (1974), 131-63. He concludes that כפר relates particularly to the removal of the guilt, or punishment due sin, and that this inevitably involves a change in God's attitude toward the sinner, and hence propitiation. Janowski (*Sühne als Heilsgeschehen,* pp. 15-102) provides a complete evaluation of the etymological question. The notion of propitiation in ἱλαστήριον and its cognates is clearly present in the first-century Jewish author Josephus (cf. *War* 5.385; *Ant.* 6.124, 8.112, 10.59, 16.182; *Ag. Ap.* 1.308[?]).

77. Cf. N. H. Young, "C. H. Dodd, 'Hilaskesthai' and his Critics," *EvQ* 48 (1976), 67-78.

view expiation renders the gods willing to forgive; in the Biblical view expiation enables God, consistently with his holiness, to do what he was never unwilling to do. In the former view sacrifice changes the sentiment of the gods toward men; in the latter it affects the consistency of his procedure in relation to sin."[78]

Finally, we must decide whether Paul intends to present this wrath-averting sacrifice of Christ against the background of the typology of the mercy seat. Our main reason for hesitating to find allusion to the mercy seat is the lack of evidence for an early Christian or Jewish Greek tradition in which *hilastērion* was given the symbolic importance this interpretation suggests.[79] Nevertheless, in this, as in so many other areas, Paul may have been the theological innovator; and the lexical data, combined with the theological appropriateness of the image, make it likely that Paul intends such an allusion. Christ, Paul implies, now has the place that the "mercy seat" had in the Old Covenant: the center and focal point of God's provision of atonement for his people. Since this atonement takes place by means of Christ's death as a sacrifice, and the word *hilastērion* includes reference to propitiation, translations such as "means of propitiation"[80] and "propitiatory sacrifice"[81] are not inaccurate. But they may be too restrictive. "Mercy seat" would be all right if the broader theological connotations of the phrase were obvious; but, considering the breadth of the concept to which the term refers, the NIV and NRSV[82] "sacrifice of atonement" is as good as we can do.

In a piling up of prepositional phrases that are often seen as indicative of a confessional or hymnic style, Paul now expands on the significance and implications of God's setting forth Christ as the New Covenant "propitiatory." "Through faith" is not likely to modify "set forth," since faith was not the instrument through which God "set forth" Christ as *hilastērion*.[83] Rather, the phrase modifies *hilastērion* and indicates the means by which individuals appropriate the benefits of the sacrifice. It is

78. G. B. Stevens, *The Johannine Theology* (New York: Scribner's Sons, 1894), pp. 183-84.

79. While, e.g., both Philo and Hebrews use the word, they attach no special theological significance to it.

80. Morris, "ἱλαστήριον," pp. 36-37; Godet; C. M. Robeck, "What Is the Meaning of *hilastērion* in Rom 3,25?" *Studia Biblica et Theologica* 4 (1974), 21-36.

81. Hodge; Murray; Ridderbos, *Paul*, pp. 187-88.

82. Note particularly the change in the NRSV from the RSV "expiation."

83. Only if πίστις designates the "faithfulness" of Christ is this connection likely (cf. Pluta, *Gottes Bundestreue*, pp. 42-56; C. Cousar, *A Theology of the Cross: The Death of Jesus in the Pauline Letters* [Minneapolis: Augsburg/Fortress, 1990], pp. 57-58; Campbell, *Rhetoric*, pp. 58-69; Williams, *Jesus' Death*, p. 47 [as possible]), but this meaning is improbable (see the exegesis of v. 22).

harder to know whether "in his blood" indicates the object of "faith" — "faith in his blood" (cf. KJV),[84] modifies the verb "set forth" — "through his blood God has presented him,"[85] or modifies *hilastērion* — "a propitiation in blood" (note the reversal of terms in NASB: "a propitiation in his blood through faith").[86] But Paul never elsewhere makes Christ's blood an object of faith,[87] so the latter is preferable. "In his blood" singles out Christ's blood as the means by which God's wrath is propitiated.[88] As in several other texts where Christ's blood is the means through which salvation is secured (Rom. 5:9; Eph. 1:7; 2:13; Col. 1:20), the purpose is to designate Christ's death as a sacrifice.[89]

The third prepositional phrase in the series indicates the purpose for which God "set forth Christ as a sacrifice of atonement": "for[90] a demonstration[91] of his righteousness because of the passing over of sins committed beforehand in the forbearance of God." Just what Paul means by this phrase is disputed, the pivotal issue being the meaning of "his righteousness." Scholars have proposed many interpretations, but there are two general approaches. The first takes "righteousness" *(dikaiosynē)* to designate what we might call an aspect of God's character, whether this be his "justice" *(iustitia distributiva),* his impartiality and fairness, or his acting in accordance with his own character and for his own glory. The whole clause would, then, be interpreted along the lines of the following paraphrase: "in order to demonstrate [or show] that God is just, acting in accordance with his own character, [which was necessary] because he had passed over sins committed before, in

---

84. Calvin; Hodge; Morison, *Exposition,* p. 311.

85. Fitzmyer.

86. So most commentators; see, e.g., Godet; Barrett; Michel.

87. Paul can use ἐν after πίστις to denote the object of faith (Gal. 3:26; Eph. 1:15; Col. 1:4; 1 Tim. 3:13; 2 Tim. 1:13; 3:15), but it is not his usual construction.

88. The ἐν is probably instrumental.

89. Cf. Davies, 232-37; Morris, *Apostolic Preaching,* pp. 108-24.

90. Gk. εἰς, used here to introduce a purpose clause.

91. Gk. ἔνδειξις. This is a relatively rare word, not occurring in the LXX and only twice outside this passage in the NT. It is debated whether it means here "proving" (BAGD; Cranfield) or "showing" (cf. particularly W. G. Kümmel, "πάρεσις und ἔνδειξις. Ein Beitrag zum Verständnis der paulinischen Rechtfertigungslehre," ZTK 49 [1952], 161-62), but the emphasis should probably be placed on the latter in light of προέθετο. (Note also that, of Philo's 11 uses of ἔνδειξις, 10 refer to a public demonstration or indication. Piper ["Romans 3:25, 26," pp. 12-15] argues for the meaning "establish" in the light of v. 26c, but lexical support for this translation is lacking.) On the other hand, this "showing" is probably to be understood as a "demonstration" of something, as in Phil. 1:28 and 2 Cor. 8:24, so the notion of "proof" cannot be entirely eliminated. God's public display of Christ as ἱλαστήριον has, as at least one of its purposes, the demonstration that he is "righteous."

the time of his forbearance."[92] The second interpretation understands "righ-teousness" here to be God's saving, covenant faithfulness, which requires that the clause as a whole be translated something like "in order to manifest his saving faithfulness through his forgiving of sins committed before, in the time of his forbearance."[93] On the first view, this clause makes an important contribution to our understanding of the "internal" mechanism of the atone-ment, explaining the necessity of Christ's propitiating work in terms of the requirements of God's holy character. God's past restraint in punishing sins with the full measure of punishment they deserved calls into question his fair and impartial "justice," or holiness, creating the need for this justice to be "satisfied," a satisfaction rendered by the propitiatory sacrifice of Christ. On the second view, the clause ties God's work in Christ to his fulfilling of his covenant promises. God now fulfills those salvific promises by putting forth Christ as the means by which sins are forgiven. While the second view has been preferred by most contemporary scholars, there are sound reasons for adopting the first. Since the interpretation of "his righteousness" is so depen-dent on the meaning of other key words in the clause, we will begin with these words and come back to this phrase.

Especially critical is the interpretation of the prepositional phrase "be-cause of the passing over of sins committed beforehand." Those who argue that "his righteousness" refers to God's covenant faithfulness insist that this translation of the phrase is incorrect. It should, they claim, be rendered some-thing like "through [or for the sake of] the forgiveness of sins committed beforehand." The phrase would then express the means (or purpose) by which God has demonstrated his saving faithfulness: by acting to secure forgiveness for the sins committed under the Old Covenant.[94] But this rendering has insufficient lexical support. The word we translate "passing over" does not mean "forgiveness," but, when applied to legal charges or sins, "postpone-ment of punishment" ("pretermission") or "neglect" of prosecution.[95] Nor

---

92. This is what might be called the "traditional" view, particularly in Protestant exegesis. Cf. the particularly clear presentation of this view by Denney, *Death of Christ,* pp. 96-107, and the recent succinct exegetical defense of Piper, 115-30; idem, "Romans 3:25, 26," pp. 12-32. (Piper understands God's righteousness a bit differently than in the tradition, but his view certainly fits generally into the traditional Protestant view.)

93. The 1952 article of Kümmel, "πάρεσις und ἔνδειξις," pp. 154-67, paved the way for this interpretation. Cf. also Käsemann; Müller, *Gerechtigkeit Gottes,* pp. 109-11; Schlier; Wilckens; Dunn; Reumann, *Righteousness,* pp. 37-38; Stuhlmacher, "Recent Ex-egesis," p. 95; Campbell, *Rhetoric,* pp. 157-76.

94. Kümmel, "πάρεσις," pp. 155-64; cf. also Lietzmann; Käsemann.

95. See esp. Dionysius of Halicarnassus, *Ant. Rom.* 7.37 (and the comments of J. M. Creed, "ΠΑΡΕΣΙΣ in Dionysius of Halicarnassus and in St. Paul," *JTS* 41 [1940], 28-30), and παρίημι in Xenophon, *Eq. Mag.* 7.10; Josephus, *Ant.* 15.48; slightly different, yet still giving evidence of the meaning "pass over," is Sir. 23:2. See the discussion in

is it likely that the preposition *dia* can here be translated "through."[96] The preposition could have virtually a telic meaning ("with a view to"),[97] but this makes little sense with the word "passing over."[98] The translation "through [or for the purpose of] forgiveness of sins" must, then, be rejected as requiring strained and unusual meanings for too many words.[99] But this further makes it very difficult for "his righteousness" to refer to God's saving faithfulness. For it makes no sense for Paul to say that "passing over" former sins was the *reason* for God's demonstration of his saving faithfulness.

But what are these "former sins" to which Paul is referring? The phrase at the beginning of v. 26 points toward an answer. "In the forbearance of God" should be connected with "passing over," and in light of Paul's only other use of "forbearance" (Rom. 2:4),[100] it will refer to the period of time

---

Trench, *Synonyms,* pp. 114-17; Williams, *Jesus' Death,* pp. 23-25; and Michel). The word is rare, occurring only here in biblical Greek, once in Josephus, three times in Philo, and sporadically elsewhere. Moreover, many of its occurrences come in medical contexts, where the word means "paralysis" (cf. Philo, *On Rewards and Punishments* 143, 145; Hippocrates, *Epidēmai* 4.45; Aretaeus, *Peri Haimatōn* 1.7, 2.5; some of the church fathers accordingly use πάρεσις to mean the paralysis caused by sin [cf. Lampe, *Patristic Greek Lexicon,* p. 1033]) and are of minimal help in determining the meaning of the word in this very different kind of context. On the basis of the meaning of its verbal cognate, παρίημι ("neglect," "slacken"; cf. Luke 11:42; Heb. 12:12), and its use in several key texts, Trench concluded that πάρεσις means "suspension," "passing over" (*Synonyms,* pp. 114-19). It is therefore to be distinguished from ἄφεσις, which denotes "forgiveness," "remission" (cf. Eph. 1:7; Col. 1:14). Kümmel and others (e.g., R. Bultmann, *TDNT* I, 509-10) who translate πάρεσις with "forgiveness" do so on the basis of the alleged semantic overlap between the related verbs παρίημι and ἀφίημι (compare Luke 11:42 and Matt. 23:23). This overlap does not occur when ἀφίημι means "forgive," but only when it means "neglect" or "let go."

96. An instrumental translation of διά followed by an accusative, while possible in Hellenistic Greek, is so rare that compelling contextual reasons must be present if it is to be adopted. BDF (222) give only one instance of διά with accusative meaning "through" in the NT, and it is in a compound verb. Cf. H. G. Meecham, "Romans iii.25f, iv.25 — the Meaning of διά c. acc.," *ExpTim* 50 (1938-39), 564; Williams, *Jesus' Death,* pp. 20-23; Piper, "Romans 3:25, 26," pp. 29-30.

97. Calvin; Godet; Lietzmann; Wilckens; Fitzmyer; Talbert, "Non-Pauline Fragment," 290.

98. E.g., Paul would be unlikely to claim that God has displayed his righteousness "for the purpose of *passing over* sins."

99. As concludes Taylor, "Great Texts," pp. 299-300.

100. Gk. ἀνοχή. Williams (*Jesus' Death,* pp. 25-33), on the basis of certain OT and Jewish texts, takes ἀνοχή as a negative term, denoting God's failure to deal with the sins of Gentiles, allowing them rather to "pile up" and accumulate wrath. But there is insufficient evidence that this specialized aspect of God's "forbearance" is in view here. J. R. Mackay ("Romans iii.26," *ExpTim* 32 [1920-21], 329-30) and W. E. Wilson ("Romans iii.25, 26," *ExpTim* 27 [1917-18], 472-73) both suggest the translation "delay."

before the cross (cf. also Acts 14:16; 17:30). The sins "committed beforehand" will not, then, be sins committed before conversion, or baptism,[101] but before the new age of salvation. This does not mean that God failed to punish or "overlooked" sins committed before Christ; nor does it mean that God did not really "forgive" sins under the Old Covenant.[102] Paul's meaning is rather that God "postponed" the full penalty due sins in the Old Covenant, allowing sinners to stand before him without their having provided an adequate "satisfaction" of the demands of his holy justice (cf. Heb. 10:4).

In view of this, it is clear that "his righteousness" must have reference to some aspect of God's character that might have been called into question because of his treating sins in the past with less than full severity, and that has now been demonstrated in setting forth Christ as "the propitiatory." "God's righteousness" in v. 25 (and 26) must, then, mean something different than it does in vv. 21-22, where the process by which God justifies sinful people is designated.[103] Ridderbos thinks Paul refers to God's punitive righteousness,[104] Piper to God's acting always to uphold his glory,[105] but we prefer a more general reference to God's "consistency" in always acting in accordance with his own character.[106]

26 We have already dealt with the first phrase of this verse in conjunction with the last clause in v. 25. The next part of the verse seems unnecessarily to repeat what Paul has already said in v. 25: "for a demonstration[107] of his righteousness at the present time."[108] Some think that the phrase

---

101. Contra, e.g., Mundle, *Glaubensbegriff,* p. 88.

102. This was the position of the seventeenth-century Reformed theologian Cocceius and his followers — a position somewhat similar to the Roman Catholic *limbus patrum.* It stimulated a lively debate in the early seventeenth century (cf. Trench, *Synonyms,* pp. 115-16; Berkhof, *Systematic Theology,* pp. 267-68).

103. Contra, e.g., Gifford; Nygren.

104. *Paul,* pp. 167-68. Cf. also Pfleiderer, *Paulinism,* 1.94-95.

105. Pp. 127-30.

106. See the excursus after 1:17 for OT precedent for this meaning of God's "righteousness."

107. Gk. πρὸς τὴν ἔνδειξιν. The change from εἰς in v. 25 to πρός here is purely stylistic; they both indicate purpose.

108. Käsemann views this phrase, with the rest of v. 26, as Paul's "correction" of the tradition he quotes in vv. 24-26a. While that tradition manifested a Jewish-Christian view of God's righteousness as covenant faithfulness, Paul's addition broadens the conception to one of God's faithfulness to creation (cf. also Müller, *Gottes Gerechtigkeit,* pp. 109-11; Stuhlmacher ["Recent Exegesis," pp. 104-5] speaks more cautiously of Paul's "going beyond" the tradition rather than correcting it). This interpretation is, however, highly improbable. That Paul quotes a tradition in v. 25 is possible, if not certain; that he would quote a tradition with which he does not entirely agree is also possible — but only if he indicated very clearly his disagreement with it. This is where Käsemann's hypothesis is most vulnerable, for the "correction" he attributes to Paul is not at all evident.

expresses the ultimate purpose of vv. 25b-26a: God let sins go unpunished, in his forbearance, "with a view to" demonstrating his righteousness at the present time.[109] But it is better to take the clause as parallel to "for a demonstration . . ." in v. 25. It resumes the topic of the demonstration of God's righteousness after the intervening qualifiers and adds the important point that this demonstration has significance not only for the past but also for the present age.[110] A reference back to "but now" at the beginning of the paragraph is obvious, as Paul focuses again on the time after Christ's coming as the climactic, eschatological age of salvation history.

There are only two ways to make sense of the connection between the final clause of the verse and the preceding context. Either Paul is indicating the ultimate purpose or result[111] of the sentence he began in v. 25 — "God set forth Christ as a propitiation in order that [or with the result that] he is just and the justifier of the one who has faith in Jesus"[112] — or it explains the immediately preceding clause — "for a demonstration of his righteousness at the present time, in order that he might show that he is just and the justifier of the person who has faith in Jesus." Despite its somewhat weak support in the commentaries, this last rendering should be preferred, because it preserves what seems to be a natural connection between "the present time" and "justifying the one who has faith in Jesus."[113] On this view, the two purpose clauses in vv. 25 and 26 — both beginning "for a demonstration" — are parallel modifiers of "set forth," the former focusing on how the propitiatory sacrifice of Christ enabled God to maintain his righteous character in postponing punishment of sins in the past, the latter showing how this same sacrifice

---

109. E.g., S-H.

110. Cf. Hodge; Morison, *Exposition,* p. 339; Schlier; Cranfield. Cf. the phrase ἐν τῷ νῦν καιρῷ ("at the present time"); Paul refers to ὁ νῦν καιρός also in Rom. 8:18 and 11:5, both with reference to the "present age" as the time of sharing the sufferings of Christ and of Israel's hardening (cf. also ὁ νῦν αἰών in 1 Tim. 6:17; 2 Tim. 4:10; Tit. 2:12; and 2 Cor. 6:2).

111. This alternative gives the construction of εἰς with the infinitive (τὸ εἶναι) what many would argue is its usual meaning.

112. E.g., Morison, *Exposition,* p. 315.

113. The rendering is grammatically unobjectionable: it gives to εἰς with the infinitive a meaning the phrase has in almost 25 percent of its Pauline occurrences (see the additional note on 1:24). A few scholars, building on their reading of the genitive Ἰησοῦ Χριστοῦ in v. 22 as objective, think that τὸν ἐκ πίστεως Ἰησοῦ also denotes the person who rests on the "faithfulness shown by Jesus" (e.g., G. Howard, "Romans 3:21-31 and the Inclusion of the Gentiles," *HTR* 63 [1970], 229-31) or the person who shares the faith that Jesus had (e.g., Cousar, *Theology of the Cross,* p. 58). But our reasons for rejecting the subjective genitive in v. 22 are equally decisive against this reading. Paul only rarely uses Ἰησοῦς absolutely (see also Rom. 8:11; 1 Cor. 12:3; 2 Cor. 4:10-11; Gal. 6:17; Eph. 4:21; Phil. 2:10; 1 Thess. 1:10; 4:14), and his reason for doing so here is not clear.

preserved God's righteous character as he justifies those who, in this age of salvation, place their faith in Jesus. This being so, it is likely that "the justifier"[114] is not coordinate with "just"[115] — "just *and* justifying," nor instrumental to it — "just *by means of* justifying,"[116] but concessive — "just *even in* justifying."[117] Paul's point is that God can maintain his righteous character ("his righteousness" in vv. 25 and 26) even while he acts to justify sinful people ("God's righteousness" in vv. 21 and 22) because Christ, in his propitiatory sacrifice, provides full satisfaction of the demands of God's impartial, invariable justice.[118] To be sure, this way of viewing the atonement is out of fashion these days, frequently being dismissed as involving ideas completely foreign to the biblical teaching about God's sovereignty and love. But whatever the mistakes of Anselm of Canterbury, whose famous treatise *Cur Deus Homo* ("Why God Became Man") is widely regarded as the fountainhead of this approach, his emphasis on the divine character as incapable of dismissing sin lightly is a vital component in the biblical doctrine of God. Those who ignore or minimize the problem inherent in a holy God accepting sinners may well heed Anselm's own warning: "You have not yet considered the weight of sin."[119]

Luther called this paragraph "the chief point . . . of the whole Bible" (see the introduction to his paragraph) because it focuses on what Luther thought was the heart of the Bible: justification by faith. Luther believed that this "article" was vital: "if that article stands, the church stands; if it falls, the church falls."[120] Later Lutherans coined the slogan "the article by which the church stands or falls" to highlight the central role that they accorded this doctrine. In Luther's day, of course, "justification by faith" was a polemical thrust against a Roman Catholic teaching that insisted on the place of human cooperation in the grace of justification. Hence to the *sola fide* of the Reformers was added *sola gratia* — "by grace alone." With these phrases, the Reformers expressed their conviction that justification is, from first to last, a matter of God's own doing, to which human beings must respond but to which they can add nothing.

---

114. Gk. δικαιοῦντα.

115. Gk. δίκαιον.

116. Käsemann.

117. Morison, *Exposition,* p. 343; Cranfield.

118. See again, especially, Denney, *Death of Christ,* pp. 97-98; also Ridderbos, *Paul,* pp. 193-96; Morris, *Apostolic Preaching,* p. 257.

119. "Nondum considerasti quanti ponderis peccatum sit." On Anselm, see the comments of Weber, *Dogmatics,* 2.207-14 (a bit too negative?); McGrath, *Iustitia Dei,* 1.55-60.

120. Luther's Exposition of Ps. 130:4.

Despite important and welcome moves toward reconciliation between Protestants and Roman Catholics, the division between the two groups over justification remains. In an age that minimizes doctrine, there is a danger that this difference will be too easily swept under the carpet. But it is a significant one, affecting one's understanding of salvation, the sacraments, assurance, and other matters both doctrinal and practical.

The Reformation doctrine of justification by faith is also being challenged from other fronts these days. Chief among them, perhaps, is the tendency to read Paul's justification by faith as having primary focus on the inclusion of the Gentiles. The Reformers' justification by faith, referring to the acceptance before a holy God of a sinful individual through that individual's believing, becomes the acceptance of the Gentiles within the people of God through Christ's faithfulness or act of believing.[121] As I suggest in my comments on a number of passages (cf. 3:20, 3:22, and the excursuses after 1:17 and 3:20), I think this general tendency both exegetically indefensible and theologically dangerous. Our era is one that — quite rightly — manifests deep concern for social issues. Interpreting Paul's gospel in social terms (e.g., as having primary focus on the inclusion of Gentiles along with Jews in the people of God) is correspondingly very attractive. But for all Paul's very vital interest in the unity of the people of God, he is even more vitally concerned about the relationship of the individual Jew or Gentile to the Lord of history.

2. "By Faith Alone" (3:27–4:25)

In 3:27–4:25, Paul expounds the great theological thesis of 3:21-26. Or, to be more accurate, he expounds one key element in that thesis. For we hear no more in 3:27–4:25 about the atonement, or the demonstration of God's righteousness, or the provision for sins under the Old Covenant. Rather, Paul concentrates on the vital theme stated in v. 22: "the righteousness of God through faith in Jesus Christ to all who believe." Faith is the topic in every paragraph of this section of the letter, as Paul uses a series of antitheses to draw out the nature and implications of faith as the sole means of justification. Faith is contrasted with "works of the law" (3:28), "works" (4:1-8), circumcision (4:9-12), the law (4:13-16), and "sight" (4:17-22). With these contrasts Paul enunciates what has become a hallmark of the Reformation teaching: *sola fide* — that "faith alone" is the means by which a person can be brought into relationship with the God of the Bible. *Sola fide,* Paul argues in this

---

121. See, among many articles and monographs pursuing this general approach, H. Boers, *The Justification of the Gentiles: Paul's Letters to the Galatians and Romans* (Peabody, MA; Hendrickson, 1994); J. D. G. Dunn, "The Justice of God: A Renewed Perspective on Justification by Faith," *JTS* 43 (1992), 1-22.

section, is necessary in order to maintain *sola gratia:* "by grace alone." But it is also necessary in order to ensure that Gentiles have equal access with Jews to the one God. The inclusion of Gentiles in the people of God has been God's plan all along, as his dealings with Abraham demonstrate. The revelation of God's righteousness "apart from the law" (v. 21) has now opened up this possibility in a way that was not the case before. This concern with the inclusion of the Gentiles is thus also an important theme in this section; but, contrary to many contemporary scholars, who are reacting to what they perceive to be an excessive concern with the individual and his or her relationship to God in traditional theology, it is not the main theme. The inclusion of the Gentiles within the people of God continues to crop up — 3:29-30; 4:9-12, 16-17 — but only as one motif within the larger argument.

The antitheses in this section reveal its polemical thrust. Paul is once again "arguing" with a Jewish or Jewish-Christian viewpoint, contesting the importance of the law (3:27-28; 4:13-15), works (4:2-8), and circumcision (4:9-12). Indicative of this thrust is the return to the "dialogical" style of 2:1-5, 17-19; 3:1-8. On the other hand, in the balance that so characterizes Paul's presentation of his gospel in Romans, he is at pains to maintain continuity with the OT and with Judaism. Justification by faith is nothing more than what the OT itself teaches (chap. 4, passim); faith "establishes" the law (3:31); and even circumcision, while no longer the necessary sign of those who belong to God, is upheld as valid for Jews (4:11-12). These positive remarks about OT and Jewish institutions stand in marked contrast to the somewhat parallel passage in Galatians (chap. 3), where Paul's polemical concerns force him to take a more one-sided slant. In Romans, however, Paul is intent on showing how his gospel breaks the boundaries of the Old Covenant while at the same time standing in continuity with it; continuity within discontinuity is his theme. Such balance was necessary if the Romans were to understand and appreciate Paul's gospel as a message that meets the needs of all people.

While the preoccupation with Abraham in chap. 4 sets apart that chapter from the last paragraph of chap. 3, the two sections are closely related. In fact, an impressive degree of parallelism between the two is evident:[1]

---

1. The parallel between chap. 4 and 3:27-31 extends to key words:

καύχησις/-μα	3:27	4:2
ἔργα/-ζομαι	3:27, 28	4:2, 4, 5, 6
νόμος	3:27, 28, 30	4:13, 14, 15 (twice), 16
δικαιόω/-σύνη	3:28, 30	4:2, 3, 5 (twice), 6, 9, 11, 13, 22
λογίζομαι	3:28	4:3, 4, 5, 6, 8, 9, 10, 11, 22, 23, 24
πίστις/-ευω	3:27, 28, 30, 30, 31	4:3, 5 (twice), 9, 11 (twice), 12, 13, 14, 16 (twice), 17, 18 (twice), 20, 24

Boasting is excluded (3:27a)	Abraham has no right to boast (4:1-2)
. . . because one is justified by faith, not works of the law (3:27b-28)	. . . because Abraham was justified by faith, not works (4:3-8)
Circumcised and uncircumcised are united under the one God through faith (3:29-30)	Circumcised and uncircumcised are united as children of Abraham through faith (4:9-17)

Naturally, the much longer chap. 4 introduces a number of points not found in 3:27-31,[2] but the similarity in general theme and development is striking. We may, then, view 3:27-31 as the initial statement of the theme, with chap. 4 as its elucidation and elaboration.[3]

a. "By Faith Alone": Initial Statement (3:27-31)

27*Where then is boasting? It is excluded. Through what law? Of works? No, but through the law of faith.* 28*For[4] we reckon that a person is justified by faith apart from works of the law.* 29*Or is God the God of Jews only? Is he not also the God of Gentiles? Yes, he is God also of the Gentiles,* 30*since there is one God, who will justify the circumcision on the basis of faith and the uncircumcision through that faith.* 31*Do we then nullify the law through faith? By no means! Rather, we establish the law.*

2. Moxnes (*Theology in Conflict*, pp. 226-29) finds a further parallel, holding that 3:31 and 4:13-22 are similar: the law is "established" (3:31) when it is viewed as promise (4:13-22). But, as I argue in my exegesis, the meaning Moxnes attributes to 3:31 is unlikely.

3. See esp. R. A. Harrisville III, *The Figure of Abraham in the Epistles of St. Paul: In the Footsteps of Abraham* (San Francisco: Mellen, 1992), pp. 21-22. Stowers is more exact, classifying 3:27–4:2a as a dialogue between Paul and a Jewish "student," with 4:2b-25 as the "exemplum" (example from the life of a famous person) that validates the points of the dialogue (*Diatribe*, pp. 164-73).

4. Much of the Alexandrian text (ℵ, A, 81), the heart of the western text (original hand of D, F, G), and the uncial Ψ read γάρ, the basis for our translation "for." But some important MSS (the Alexandrian B, C, 33, and the second corrector of D; cf. also the majority text) read οὖν in its place. And this alternative is adopted by a number of scholars, who argue that it is more difficult, γάρ making for a more natural transition between vv. 27 and 28 (e.g., Morison, *Exposition*, pp. 369-78). But this is not clear; οὖν is used so often by Paul, and particularly in verses such as this, that a scribe could easily have substituted it for γάρ (cf. Alford; Bengel; Metzger, 509).

Paul moves quickly through several implications of and arguments for justification by faith. He begins by showing how justification by faith excludes any possibility of boasting on the part of Jews (vv. 27-28). The next two verses provide further reason for accepting the principle that justification must be by faith with no admixture of "works of the law"; only so can God truly be the God of Gentiles as well as Jews. Finally, in v. 31, Paul responds briefly to a Jewish objection to his stress on faith; no, he argues, faith does not nullify but "establishes" the law — enables it to be truly fulfilled. The style, as in 2:1-5, 17-29 and 3:1-8, reflects the diatribe method of argumentation, with its question-and-answer format. As in the earlier sections, it is difficult to say — and perhaps not all that important — whether we have here a "real" dialogue between Paul and a Jewish interlocutor,[5] or whether Paul himself is responsible for posing questions to himself as a means of making his points.[6]

27 The question "Where then is boasting?" with its answer "It is excluded"[7] draws an inference from vv. 21-26. "Boasting,"[8] of course, is a sin common to all people — it reflects the pride that is at the root of so much human sinfulness. But Paul is probably thinking here particularly of Jews and their boasting. This is suggested by his elaboration in terms of the "law" in vv. 27b-28, by his dialogical style — the "Jew" has been his dialogue partner earlier (cf. 2:17), and by the focus on Jew and Gentile in vv. 29-30. What is the nature of this boasting? and why is it wrong? One interpretation holds that Paul is thinking of the pride of the Jews in their special covenant relationship to God (cf. 2:17). Such pride, Paul would then be arguing, has now been ruled out by the revelation of God's righteousness apart from that covenant and its law.[9] There is considerable truth in this view, as is clear from the Jewish emphasis throughout these chapters and from Paul's stress that God has now revealed his righteousness "apart from the law" (3:27). But this "salvation-historical" explanation does not, in itself, go far enough. Paul's reason for

---

5. Stowers, *Diatribe,* pp. 164-65.

6. E.g., Wilckens, 1.244.

7. The verb is the aorist ἐξεκλείσθη. Some scholars have suggested that the aorist connotes a "decisive," once-for-all, rejection (e.g., Räisänen, 170); but this reflects the all-too-typical overloading of the meaning of the aorist tense in Greek.

8. Paul here uses the Greek word καύχησις, which he uses ten times in his letters (cf. also Rom. 15:17; 1 Cor. 15:31; 2 Cor. 1:12; 7:4, 14; 8:24; 11:10, 17; 1 Thess. 2:19); he also uses the related word καύχημα ten times (Rom. 4:2; 1 Cor. 5:6; 9:15, 16; 2 Cor. 1:14; 5:12; 9:3; Gal. 6:4; Phil. 1:26; 2:16). Based on their formation, we would expect the former to connote the act of boasting and the latter the cause of boasting. While this distinction is not always observed in Paul, καύχησις here certainly refers to the boasting itself. (On the meaning of "boasting" in Paul, see the comments on 2:17.)

9. Sanders, *Paul, the Law and the Jewish People,* p. 33; Räisänen, 170-71; Watson, 133; R. W. Thompson, "Paul's Double Critique of Jewish Boasting: A Study of Rom 3,27 in Its Context," *Bib* 67 (1986), 520-31; Wilckens; Dunn.

excluding boasting has to do with a contrast between faith and works (vv. 27b-28) — two kinds of human response to God (reasons for not limiting "works of the law" to Jewish covenant privileges will be given below). And this is confirmed by the parallel teaching about Abraham in chap. 4. The hypothetical basis for Abraham's boasting is not simply covenant "identity markers" but "works" in a general sense. Moreover, Paul's use of Abraham as a key example shows also that it is not just with the coming of Christ that boasting becomes wrong;[10] Abraham, many centuries before Christ, had no cause to boast either.

The root issue here, then, is not salvation-historical, but anthropological. It is not the Jew's pride in a covenant relationship with God, but the pride in accomplishments, the tendency for the Jew to think that his obedience to the law constituted some kind of claim on God, that Paul rejects.[11] This does not mean, however, that the very doing of the law was wrong because it involved sinful, boastful presumption.[12] There is nothing at all wrong with doing the law, according to Paul. The problem, rather, is when doing the law is regarded as an achievement on the basis of which a relationship with God could be established or maintained. This is wrong because justification can come only by faith: not only now that Christ has been revealed (vv. 21-24) — although this makes it even clearer — but in the past also (chap. 4). This is not to say, either, that all Jews were prone to such a "legalistic" attitude. Certainly, the centrality of the law in the Jewish religion rendered Jews very susceptible to such a tendency; but all people, being fallen, exhibit the same tendency: Greeks, boasting in their wisdom (cf. 1 Cor. 1:19-31); Americans, boasting in their "American way of life"; and all too many Christians, boasting in their "good deeds" instead of in the grace of God.

Paul's explanation for the exclusion of boasting, as we have seen, rests on a contrast between "works" and "faith" (v. 27b). What is striking about this contrast is that Paul formulates it with the help of the word "law" *(nomos)*: "Through what *nomos* [is boasting excluded]? [Through the *nomos*][13] of works? No, but through the *nomos* of faith." What is his purpose in using this word here? Paul's normal usage of *nomos* would suggest that he uses the word throughout the verse with reference to the law of Moses, the torah. Paul would then be contrasting two different ways of understanding, or using, the law of Moses: understood simply in terms of "works," it could lead to boasting; but

10. Contra, e.g., J. Lambrecht, "Why Is Boasting Excluded? A Note on Romans 3:27 and 4:2," *ETL* 61 (1985), 365-68.

11. E.g., Ridderbos, *Paul,* pp. 140-41; Westerholm, 170.

12. Contra, e.g., Bultmann, 1.242, 264; Hübner, 113-24.

13. The Greek here is simply τῶν ἔργων (see our translation above); but the words διὰ νόμου from the previous question are to be supplied.

understood in terms of "faith," it excludes all such boasting.[14] Advocates of this view sometimes point to the word we have translated "what?" as important support for their view. For the "literal" meaning of this word is "what kind of?" and this qualitative connotation supports the idea that Paul is asking here about contrasting qualities of the same law.[15] But the "literal" translation is, in fact, not clearly dominant in the NT, where the translation "what?" receives strong support.[16] On either translation, it is straining the wording to think that Paul is referring to two perspectives on the same law rather than to two different laws.

But an even more serious objection to this interpretation is the close relationship between the law of Moses and faith that it assumes. For such a positive relationship between these two contradicts both the movement of this passage and Paul's larger teaching about the law. In both 3:21-26 and 3:28, the faith that gains a standing with God is explicitly distanced from the Mosaic law ("apart from the law"; "apart from works of the law"). It is just this distance that gives rise to the question in v. 31: "Do we then nullify the law through faith?" This question does not make sense unless Paul has, in this context, fully separated "faith" from the law of Moses. And this same careful distinction between believing and "doing" (the law, works of the law) is

---

14. Advocates of this interpretation differ over the precise connotation of the phrase νόμου πίστεως: (1) "the law as it testifies to faith" (G. Friedrich, "Das Gesetz des Glaubens. Römer 3,27," in *Auf das Wort kommt es an. Gesammelte Aufsätze* [ed. J. H. Friedrich; Göttingen: Vandenhoeck & Ruprecht, 1978], pp. 107-22; C. T. Rhyne, *Faith Establishes the Law* [SBLDS 55; Chico, CA: Scholars Press, 1981], pp. 67-70; E. Lohse, "ὁ νόμος τοῦ πνεύματος τῆς ζωῆς. Exegetische Anmerkungen zu Röm 8.2," in *Neues Testament und christliche Existenz* [Tübingen: Mohr, 1973], p. 281); (2) "the law's demand for faith" (Cranfield); (3) "the law as viewed from the perspective of faith" (Hübner, 138-39; Dunn speaks of the law as "addressed to faith and fulfilled through faith"); (4) "the law as it is fulfilled in faith" (Wright, "Messiah and People of God," pp. 117-18; P. von der Osten-Sacken, *Römer 8 als Beispiel paulinischer Soteriologie* [FRLANT 112; Göttingen: Vandenhoeck & Ruprecht, 1975], pp. 245-46; idem, "Das paulinische Verständnis des Gesetzes im Spannungsfeld von Eschatologie und Geschichte," *EvT* 37 [1977], 549-87; E. Jüngel, *Paulus und Jesus. Ein Untersuchung zur Präzisierung der Frage nach dem Ursprung der Christologie* [Tübingen: Mohr, 1962], pp. 54-55; Wilckens). Gese and Stuhlmacher share a more nuanced view, according to which "the law of works" designates the "Sinai torah" and "the law of faith" the "Zion torah," the transformed, eschatological form of God's law for the messianic age (H. Gese, "The Law," in *Essays in Biblical Theology* [Minneapolis: Augsburg, 1981], pp. 60-92; Stuhlmacher, "The Law as a Topic of Biblical Theology," pp. 114-17, 126-28).

15. Cf. Friedrich, "Das Gesetz des Glaubens," p. 415.

16. The Greek word is ποῖος. While this word has a basic "qualitative" meaning — "what kind of?" — it frequently loses all qualitative force, being used as equivalent to τί (cf. BDF 298[3]). In fact, the majority of the 33 NT occurrences of ποῖος seem to have lost any qualitative meaning.

maintained throughout Romans (cf. 2:25-29; 3:20; 4:2-8; 9:31–10:8) and the Pauline writings (cf. esp. Gal. 3:12). An allusion to a connection — however it is viewed — between faith and the Mosaic law in v. 27 would run quite counter to this clear principial distinction. It is our faith, "apart from works of the law" (v. 28), that rules out of court any possibility of boasting — not a new way of looking at the law (cf. also the plain antitheses in 4:2-6 and 13-15).

A second interpretation is, then, to be preferred: that Paul is contrasting two different "laws." On this view, the word *nomos,* in both its actual occurrences in the verse, has a metaphorical sense: "principle," or "rule."[17] Some scholars think, then, that there is no direct allusion to the law of Moses at all here; Paul simply contrasts the "principles" of works and faith.[18] But Paul connects the Mosaic law and "works" too often in Romans (cf. 2:6-16, 25-27; 3:20) to make it possible to eliminate reference here to the torah. We take it, then, that *nomos* in Paul's question, while meant to have a general reference — "what 'rule' or 'system of demands' excludes boasting?" — would naturally bring to mind *the* law, the torah. Paul then adds the contrasting modifiers to make clear his point: no, it is not through the torah, that law which demands works, through which boasting is excluded; it is through the "rule" of faith, the "ordinance" or "demand" of God for faith as the basis for justification (v. 28).[19] Rather than being entirely metaphorical, then, Paul's use of *nomos*

17. A broader meaning of νόμος, in the sense of a "principle" or "order" or "rule," is well established in pre-Christian Greek. From the etymological meaning of νόμος, "that which is allotted, that which is proper," comes the meaning "any kind of existing or accepted norm, order, custom, usage or tradition" (cf. H. Kleinknecht, *TDNT* IV, 1023-24). While this broad meaning became largely subsumed under the more dominant legal usage in later times — a process accelerated in "Jewish Greek" by the use of νόμος to translate תּוֹרָה — the broader meaning of νόμος did not disappear. For instance, Josephus can speak of the "νόμοι of war," e.g., the "[unwritten] rules, or customs of warfare" (*J.W.* 5.123) or of the "law" of historical writing (*J.W.* 5.20). Similarly, Philo refers to the νόμοι, or "norms" of music (*On the Creation* 54, 70). These references, and others from roughly the same period, show that this "general" use of νόμος was very much a "live" meaning in first-century Greek — and especially among Greek-speaking Jews. See especially the thorough survey of H. Räisänen, "Sprachliches zum Spiel des Paulus mit ΝΟΜΟΣ," in *The Torah and Christ* (Publications of the Finnish Exegetical Society 45; Helsinki: Kirjapaino Raamattutalu, 1986), pp. 119-47. Paul probably uses the word with this meaning also in 7:21, 23-25; 8:2. And Winger (*By What Law?* 92) notes that a genitive modifier is one possible pointer to this metaphorical sense of νόμος.

18. Cambier, *L'Evangile de Dieu,* pp. 148-52; Alford; Godet; Hodge; S-H; Denney; Murray; Barrett; Kuss; Morris.

19. See esp. Räisänen, "Gesetz des Glaubens," pp. 101-17. Note also Fitzmyer, "Paul and the Law," pp. 186-87; W. Gutbrod, *TDNT* IV, 1071; F. Thielman, *Paul and the Law: A Contextual Approach* (Downers Grove: InterVarsity, 1994), pp. 182-84; Gifford; Lietzmann; Michel; Käsemann; Schlier.

embodies a "play on words," in which the characteristic demand of the Mosaic covenant — works — is contrasted with the basic demand of the New Covenant (and of the OT, broadly understood; cf. chap. 4) — faith.

Paul's point is that the narrow focus of most of his fellow Jews on the Mosaic law as the system within which their relationship to God was established gives rise to an implicit "boast" in human achievement; what a person does in obedience to the law becomes, in some sense and to varying degrees, critical to one's "righteousness." Once it is seen, however, that God's righteousness comes to people "apart from the law," there can be no more cause for any pride in human achievement.[20]

28 In this verse Paul explains[21] "the *nomos* of faith." It is a "rule" or "principle" pertaining to faith that "a person[22] is justified by faith[23] apart from works of the law." Paul here promulgates no new rule; the first person plural "we reckon" probably indicates that he assumes that his readers would join him in this assessment.[24] Paul's concern to meet Jewish views is evident in his addition "apart from works of the law." As in 3:20, what is meant is not certain kinds of works, or works viewed in a certain light, but anything a person does in obedience to the law and, by extrapolation, anything a person does. This being the case, Luther's famous addition of *sola* ("alone") to *fide* ("faith") — in which he was preceded by others, including Thomas Aquinas[25]

---

20. Dunn argues that the contrast in this verse is between a view of the law in terms of "works," with prominence thereby given to Jewish "identity markers," and looking at it in terms of faith, which opens it up to the Gentiles. But this underplays the fact that the law as a whole — not just certain "identity markers" — is particularly Jewish in its focus (see, e.g., S. Westerholm, Review of *'The Obedience of Faith': A Pauline Phrase in Historical Context,* by D. S. Garlington, *JBL* 112 [1993], 356). This was a viewpoint that Paul shared (cf., e.g., 2:12; 3:19) with the OT itself; cf. Ps. 147:19-20: "He declares His words to Jacob, His statutes and ordinances to Israel. He has not dealt thus with any nation; and as for his ordinances, they have not known them." If the barrier between Jew and Gentile is to be removed, it is not a new perspective about the law that must come, but the law itself, as a system, that must go. See also Laato, *Paulus und das Judentum,* pp. 229-40; Schreiner, "Works of the Law," pp. 234-38.

21. Assuming that the conjunction to be read here is γάρ, with an explanatory function.

22. Gk. ἄνθρωπος, which universalizes the statement (cf. also Gal. 2:16).

23. Gk. πίστει. This is the only place in which Paul uses πίστις in the dative with δικαιόω ("justify"), but it is no more than a stylistic variant of the more typical ἐκ πίστεως.

24. The Greek is λογιζόμεθα. Paul uses this word with various nuances, but it here refers to the "conviction" about God's way of justifying that Paul has been setting forth (cf. RSV: "we hold"). The plural form of the verb may be editorial, or it may include both Paul and other Christian teachers, but it probably embraces both Paul and his readers.

25. Others who added the "alone" here are, according to Fitzmyer, Origen, Theodoret, Hilary, Basil, Ambrosiaster, Chrysostom, Cyril of Alexandria, Bernard, and Theophylact.

— brings out the true sense intended by Paul. A serious erosion of the full significance of Paul's gospel occurs if we soften this antithesis; no works, whatever their nature or their motivation, can play any part in making a sinner right with God.

29-30   "Or"[26] introduces the alternative to the principle set forth in v. 28: if justification is by works of the law, then only those "in the law" can be justified, and God becomes the God of Jews only. Paul rejects this alternative with the question, "Is he not also the God[27] of Gentiles?" To this question Paul gives the answer already implied by the form of the question:[28] "Yes, he is God also of the Gentiles." In v. 30, Paul both explains why[29] God must be God of the Gentiles as well as of the Jews and draws an implication from that truth. The explanation comes in the main clause: "there is one God."[30] Paul takes one of the most basic of Jewish beliefs, monotheism, and turns it against Judaism. The "oneness" of God was confessed by the pious Jew every day: "the LORD our God is one LORD" (Deut. 6:4). Yet if this is so, then God must be God of the Gentiles; else they would be left with no god. To be sure, Jews also believed that God was God of the whole world. But the limitations they placed upon this concept illustrate the radicality of Paul's argument. For, in Judaism, God was the God of Gentiles only by virtue of his creative work, while only the Jews enjoy any meaningful relationship with God; this is expressed in later Jewish text: "I am God over all that came into the world, but I have joined my name only with you [Israel]; I am not called the God of the idolaters, but the God of Israel."[31] Only by accepting the torah could Gentiles hope to become related to God in the same way as Jews. In this paragraph, and in many other places in Romans, Paul makes clear that the torah no longer functions as the "dividing wall" between those who are outside and those who are inside the sphere of God's people.[32] In the

26. Gk. ἤ.

27. The Greek is simply οὐχὶ καὶ ἐθνῶν; as in the other two clauses in this verse, the word θεός ("God") must be supplied from the context — e.g., ἤ [θεὸς] Ἰουδαίων ὁ θεὸς μόνον; οὐχὶ [θεὸς] καὶ ἐθνῶν; ναὶ καὶ [θεὸς] ἐθνῶν.

28. The οὐχί implies that the question has a positive answer.

29. The εἴπερ introducing the verse has a slightly causal meaning: "since," "seeing that" (BAGD; Cranfield).

30. R. W. Thompson, however, thinks that Paul bases his argument not simply on the oneness of God, but on the "God who justifies the circumcision by faith and the uncircumcision by faith" ("The Inclusion of the Gentiles in Rom 3,27-30," *Bib* 69 [1988], 545-46).

31. *Exod. Rab.* 29 [88d].

32. Cf., on this, Dahl, 178-91; E. Grässer, " 'Ein einziger ist Gott' (Röm 3,30). Zum christologischen Gottesverständnis bei Paulus," in *'Ich will euer Gott werden.' Beispiele biblischen Redens von Gott* (SBS 100; Stuttgart: Katholisches Bibelwerk, 1981), pp. 203-5; Moxnes, *Theology in Conflict,* pp. 78-80.

OT, while the law was not the means of salvation, it did function to "mark out" the people of God; and in Judaism, it became an impenetrable barrier. But for Paul monotheism, as he has come to see it in Christ, means that there can be no such barrier; all must have equal access to God, and this can be guaranteed only if faith, not works in obedience to the Jewish law, is made the "entrance requirement."

Paul states this radical implication of monotheism in a relative clause: "who will justify[33] the circumcision on the basis of faith and the uncircumcision through that[34] faith." The variation in prepositions in Paul's description of the faith of the circumcised ("*ek* faith") and that of the uncircumcised ("*dia* faith") has stimulated the ingenuity of commentators for years.[35] But none of the suggested distinctions makes very good sense; the change in prepositions is probably simply a stylistic variation.[36]

31 The function of this verse in the context can be determined only after the meaning of Paul's assertion that "faith establishes the law" has been decided. This assertion comes in response to the question, raised by Paul himself ("we"), but undoubtedly reflecting an objection he had heard frequently as he preached to Jews: "Do we then nullify[37] the law through faith?" How would faith nullify

---

33. δικαιώσει, a future. It could be future in tense because Paul writes from the perspective of the beginning of the age of redemption (Morison, *Exposition,* p. 393), but it is more likely simply a logical future, with gnomic significance (Käsemann; Cranfield).

34. The article here (contrast anarthrous πίστεως in the first phrase) is anaphoric: Gentiles are justified by "the same" faith as are Jews (cf. N. Turner, *Grammatical Insights into the New Testament* [Edinburgh: T & T Clark, 1965], pp. 108-9).

35. Godet thinks that Paul may use ἐκ to connote the category of faith (as opposed to works), which would be appropriate for Jews, while διά simply marks out faith as the "way" by which Gentiles become justified (similar are the suggestions of Bengel and Cambier [*L'Evangile de Dieu,* pp. 156-57]). S-H suggest that Paul uses ἐκ to imply that the Jews' justification is "from the source of" faith, but with circumcision as the "attendant circumstances." Calvin thinks that Paul may intend irony: " 'If any wishes to have a difference made between the Gentile and the Jew, let him take this, — that the one obtains righteousness *by* faith and the other *through* faith.' " S. K. Stowers, understanding πίστις to refer to Christ's faithfulness, thinks that Paul consistently uses ἐκ with reference to the Jews and διά with reference to the Gentiles ("ΕΚ ΠΙΣΤΕΩΣ and ΔΙΑ ΠΙΣΤΕΩΣ in Romans 3:30," *JBL* 108 [1989], 665-74).

36. The stylistic explanation is at least as early as Augustine (*Spirit and Letter* 29.50 [*NPNF* 5.104-5]), and is the opinion of the great majority of modern scholars (see, most recently, Campbell, "Meaning of πίστις," pp. 93-96). It must be noted, however, that while rhetorical variations of ἐκ and ἀπό and of ἐν and διά are quite common in the NT, there is no clear example of such a variation between ἐκ and διά. In only two other verses do ἐκ and διά take the same object, and the prepositions have different meanings in both (Rom. 11:36; 2 Pet. 3:5).

37. Gk. καταργοῦμεν. καταργέω is a typically Pauline word that has various nuances (see the exegesis of 3:3). Here it might take on a specific meaning by virtue of

the law? Through Paul's emphasis on faith "alone," to the exclusion of "works of the law," in justification. The polemical situation forced Paul to harp on the inadequacy of works and the limited, and passing, importance of the Mosaic law; and this gave to his preaching an "anti-law" flavor. But, as on other occasions when Paul faces such an objection (cf. Rom. 7:7), he responds with a forthright denial: "By no means!" He then follows this up with a counterassertion: "Rather,[38] we establish the law." That Paul affirms here a continuing role for the law, despite its playing no part in justification, is clear. But what role Paul may intend for the law is disputed.

The main possibilities are three, according to whether Paul views the law as testifying, convicting, or commanding.

(1) The first is the most popular.[39] Its advocates point to 3:19 and 3:21 for evidence that Paul in this context uses "law" broadly as a reference to Scripture. And, in both 3:21 and chap. 4 (Gen. 15:6), Paul affirms just this "testifying" role of the law in relationship to his teaching of justification by faith. While, then, it is faith, not the law, that justifies, this stress on faith "establishes" the law by setting forth that to which the law bears witness. While a "testifying" role of the OT is plainly asserted in this context, this interpretation suffers from two major problems. First, the connection between v. 31b and chap. 4, on which so much rests, is questionable. Had this been the function of v. 31b, we would have expected chap. 4 to begin with "for"[40] rather than with "therefore." A second objection is more serious. That Paul sees in the OT a witness to his teaching about

---

its contrast with the verb ἵστημι ("establish"). For this contrasting pair of verbs is said to reflect the use of the Hebrew verbs בטל and קום in rabbinic exegetical discussions (Michel; Käsemann; Cranfield; Dunn). But the evidence for the exegetical application of the Hebrew words is weak, and so is the evidence for their equivalence with the Greek words used here (see esp. Hübner, 140-41; Rhyne, *Faith Establishes the Law,* p. 73; Fitzmyer). Probably, then, we need to interpret both words apart from this background, in which case καραργέω will mean something like "make of no account," "render purposeless."

38. Gk. ἀλλά.

39. The most detailed defense is that by Rhyne, *Faith Establishes the Law.* Cf. also, *inter alia,* Hübner, 137-44; E. Lohse, " 'Wir richten das Gesetz auf!' Glaube und Thora im Römerbrief," in *Treue zur Thora. Beiträge zur Mitte des christlich-jüdischen Gesprächs* (ed. P. von der Osten-Sacken; Berlin: Institute Kirche und Judentum, 1977), p. 65; O. Hofius, "Das Gesetz des Mose und das Gesetz Christi," *ZTK* 80 (1983), 279-80; Cambier, *L'Evangile,* pp. 160-62; Räisänen, 69-70 (as one meaning); Godet; Alford; Meyer; Lietzmann; Käsemann; Wilckens. Moxnes (*Theology in Conflict,* p. 229) holds a variation of this view, according to which Paul upholds the law as promise.

40. E.g., γάρ. The lack of a γάρ here distinguishes this context from the typical Pauline sequence in which an objection in the form of a question is met with a curt negative — usually μὴ γένοιτο — a counterassertion, and extended explanation (contra Rhyne, *Faith Establishes the Law,* pp. 34-61, who argues that 3:31ff. fit this pattern).

justification by faith is clear. But when denoting that function of the OT, he uses "the law and the prophets" (v. 21) or the "Scripture" (Gal. 3:8). Nowhere does he use "law" by itself to indicate this witnessing role of the OT. Even in Rom. 4, "law" is used in a negative sense and is not linked with the "witness" of Gen. 15:6. Perhaps most significant is 4:3, which introduces the quotation of this verse by asking, not "What does the 'law' say?" but "What does the Scripture say?" These points do not make it impossible that Paul refers here to the testifying role of the law — but they make it unlikely.[41]

(2) According to a second interpretation, the law is established in its role of condemning sinners and preparing the way for Christ.[42] This function of the law is also mentioned in the context (3:19) and receives extensive treatment in Gal. 3:15–4:7. While this view deserves more consideration than it has been given, it has against it the fact that "law" is not used with this reference in the immediately preceding verses. Yet it is these verses, 27-30, that spark the objection in v. 31.

(3) When the meaning of "law" in the immediate paragraph is considered, it is clear that it is the commanding aspect of the law that is prominent: "[law] of works" (v. 27); "works of the law" (v. 28). In fact, as we have noted, Paul normally uses "law" to denote the body of commands given by God through Moses.[43] And in other contexts where the continuing validity of the law is discussed, this is also the significance of "law" (cf. 7:7-12; 8:2-4; 13:8-10). This makes it likely that Paul argues here for the establishment of the Mosaic law in its commanding aspect. But in what sense is the law as demand established? (a) Does Paul mean that Christians are obliged to continue to obey the ("moral") demands of the law?[44] (b) Or does he anticipate 13:8-10, where the command to love is set forth as the "fulfillment" of the law?[45] (c) Or is he thinking of the way in which our faith in Christ provides for the full satisfaction of the demands of the law

---

41. For these objections and others, see Luz, 171-73; G. Klein, "Römer 4 und die Idee des Heilsgeschichte," in *Rekonstruction und Interpretation: Gesammelte Aufsätze zum Neuen Testament* (BEvT 50; Munich: Kaiser, 1969), pp. 166-67; J. Lambrecht and R. W. Thompson, *Justification by Faith: The Implications of Romans 3:27-31* (Zacchaeus Studies: New Testament; Wilmington, DE: Michael Glazier, 1989), pp. 45-50; Murray; Cranfield.

42. W. Feyerabend, "Über den Schluss des 3. Kapitels im Briefe an die Römer," *NKZ* 3 (1892), 409-20; A. J. Bandstra, *The Law and the Elements of the World* (Kampen: Kok, 1964), pp. 99-100; W. Grundmann, *TDNT* VII, 649; Watson, 134-35.

43. See the footnote on 2:12.

44. Cf. Murray.

45. Cf., e.g., Morison, *Exposition*, pp. 416-17; Lambrecht and Thompson, *Justification by Faith*, pp. 45-50.

(cf. 8:4)?[46] The brevity of Paul's assertion and the lack of any immediate explanation make a decision difficult. But the stress on *faith* as establishing the law suggests that it is law as fulfilled in and through our faith in Christ that Paul thinks of here. In 8:4, Paul will argue that those who are in Christ and who "walk according to the Spirit" have the law fulfilled "in them," in the sense that their relationship to Christ by faith fully meets the demands of God's law. While we cannot be certain, it is likely that Paul means essentially the same thing here: that Christian faith, far from shunting aside the demands of the law, provides (and for the first time!) the complete fulfillment of God's demand in his law.

b. "By Faith Alone": Elaboration with Respect to Abraham (4:1-25)

In this chapter, Paul appeals to Abraham to support his insistence that righteousness can be attained only through faith. But, as in 3:27-31, Paul's purpose is not only to establish the doctrine of justification by faith alone, but also, indeed especially, to draw out the implications of this *sola fide*. To accomplish these purposes, Paul "exposits" Gen. 15:6: "Abraham believed God, and it was reckoned to him as righteousness."[1] This text is quoted in v. 3 after Paul sets up his problem in terms of Abraham's "right" to boast (vv. 1-2). Thereafter, Paul quotes or alludes to this text in every paragraph of the chapter, using a series of antitheses to draw out its meaning and implications. In vv. 3-8, Paul shows that the "reckoning" of Abraham's faith for righteousness is an entirely gracious act that by its nature excludes any appeal to works. The contrast between circumci-

---

46. E.g., though with differences in detail, Luther, "Preface to Romans"; Haldane; Dugandzic, *Das 'Ja' Gottes in Christus,* pp. 172-77; Gaugler; Barth, *Shorter;* Luz, 171-72; W. Gutbrod, *TDNT* IV, 1076-77; P. von der Osten-Sacken, *Das Evangelium als Einheit von Verheißung und Gesetz. Grundzüge paulinischer Theologie, Evangelium und Tora: Aufsätze zu Paulus* (Munich: Kaiser, 1987), pp. 22-23, 25; Fitzmyer (he refers also to 13:8-10).

1. Many scholars label Rom. 4 a "midrash." As in a midrash, Paul not only concentrates on the exposition of a verse from Scripture (Gen. 15:6), but he also adduces a secondary text from outside the Pentateuch (Ps. 32:1-2; cf. vv. 7-8), which is linked to the primary text through a wordplay (λογίζομαι). Indeed, some scholars have gone so far as to suggest that Paul is building the chapter on a preexisting midrash (cf. esp. van der Minde, *Schrift und Tradition,* pp. 68-85; also Michel; P. Borgen, *Bread from Heaven* [NovTSup 10; Leiden: Brill, 1965], p. 49). However, while Paul makes extensive use of traditional themes, there is no evidence to justify the supposition of a traditional piece behind Rom. 4 (cf. Moxnes, *Theology in Conflict,* pp. 204-5). Whether we call the chapter a midrash or not will depend on the definition we give to that exceedingly slippery term. Certainly the chapter contains features reminiscent of Jewish midrashic techniques. But we would perhaps be wise to refrain from labeling the chapter a midrash until a firmer definition of the term is forthcoming.

sion and uncircumsion dominates vv. 9-12. Here Paul shows that the "reckoning" of Abraham's faith for righteousness took place before he was circumcised, thereby enabling him to become the "father" of both Jewish and Gentile believers. This same concern with the inclusive importance of Abraham is stressed in vv. 13-22, where Paul focuses on the promise that Abraham would be the father of "many nations," or "all the seed." The ruling contrast — though not so clearly sustained as those in the previous two paragraphs — is between "faith" and "law," with a minor contrast perhaps suggested in vv. 18-21 between faith and "sight." The quotation of Gen. 15:6 at the end of v. 22 brings Paul's exposition back to where it began in v. 3; the final three verses of the chapter apply the lessons Paul has drawn from his text to his Christian readers.[2]

As we noted in the introduction to 3:27–4:25, the parallels between them show that Paul in chap. 4 expands on the themes he introduced in 3:27-31. But why has Paul singled out Abraham as the reference point for this expansion? One reason is undoubtedly polemical. Abraham was revered by the Jews as their "father"[3] and his life and character were held up as models of God's ways with his people and of true piety. "Abraham was perfect in all his deeds with the Lord, and well-pleasing in righteousness all the days of his life" (*Jub.* 23:10); Abraham "did not sin against thee" (Pr. Man. 8); "no one has been found like him in glory" (Sir. 44:19).[4] In keeping with the nomistic focus of first-century Judaism, Abraham was held up particularly as a model of obedience to God. His righteousness and mediation of the promise were linked to this obedience, it even being argued that he had obeyed the law perfectly before it had been given.[5] Paul would naturally want to show his Roman readers that this understanding of Abraham, which his Jewish and Jewish-Christian opponents undoubtedly cited against his teaching (cf. Gal. 3–4), was not in accord with the OT. Through Paul's interpretation of Gen. 15:6, Abraham is wrested from the Jews as an exemplar of torah-obedience and made into an exemplar of faith. As a result, Abraham ceases to be for Paul the father of Jews exclusively but the father of all who believe. Käsemann's judgment is therefore justified: "The polemic which runs through the whole chapter shows that we are dealing here not with an extension or modification of the Jewish view, but with its contrast."[6]

---

2. Moxnes, *Theology in Conflict,* p. 41, has a similar outline.

3. Cf. Isa. 51:1-2; *m. Qidd.* 4.14.

4. See also 1 Macc. 2:52; *m. 'Abot* 5.3; Philo, *On Abraham* 52–54, passim; Josephus, *Ant.* 1.256; etc.

5. *m. Qidd.* 4.14; Sir. 44:19-21; cf. *2 Apoc. Bar.* 57:2. For surveys of Abraham in Jewish literature, see Moxnes, *Theology in Conflict,* pp. 125-69; G. Mayer, "Aspekte des Abrahambildes in der hellenistisch-jüdischen Literatur," *EvT* 32 (1972), 118-27; Harrisville, *Abraham,* pp. 47-135; Watson, 135-36; Str-B, 3.186-201.

6. "The Faith of Abraham in Romans 4," in *Perspectives,* p. 79. Cf. also Watson, 135-41.

But Paul is drawn to Abraham for more than polemical considerations. That Paul cites Abraham as an example for believers is clear. But Abraham is much more than an example. After all, the Jews focused as much as they did on Abraham because of the decisive role the OT gives to him in the formation of the people of Israel and in the transmission of the promise. Both Paul's insistence that justification is by faith alone and his concern for the full inclusion of the Gentiles in the people of God make it necessary for him to integrate Abraham theologically into his scheme.[7] At least, it was necessary if Paul's teaching was to have any claim to continuity with the OT. It is also evident that Paul considered this continuity to be essential — not just for polemical reasons, but for the sake of the gospel itself, which is the gospel of *God* (1:1) — "the God of Abraham, Isaac and Jacob."[8]

i. Faith and Works (4:1-8)

1*What then shall we say that Abraham, our forefather according to the flesh, has found?*[9] 2*For if Abraham was justified by works, he has*

7. Paul's interpretation of Abraham's significance in this chapter is fair to the teaching of Gen. 12–25 and shows little dependence on Jewish traditions (see Harrisville, *Abraham*).

8. The importance of continuity in salvation history for Paul in Rom. 4 has been stressed repeatedly by Wilckens in debate with G. Klein: Wilckens, "Die Recht-fertigung Abrahams nach Römer 4," in *Studien zur Theologie der alttestamentlichen Überlieferungen. Festschrift für Gerhard von Rad* (ed. R. Rendtorff and K. Koch; Neukirchen/Vluyn: Neukirchener, 1961), pp. 111-27 (reprinted in *Rechtfertigung*, pp. 33-49); Klein, "Römer 4"; Wilckens, "Zu Römer 3,21–4,25: Antwort an G. Klein," *EvT* 24 (1964), 586-610 (reprinted in *Rechtfertigung*, pp. 50-76); Klein, "Exegetische Probleme in Römer 3,21–4,25," in *Rekonstruction*, pp. 170-79; idem, "Heil und Geschichte"; Wilckens, 1.282-85). Klein denies any real "salvation history" in Rom. 4, since Abraham stands as an isolated individual, used by Paul polemically to counter Jewish claims. There is no continuity in history between Abraham and Christ/the Christian; we cannot speak of a "history" of salvation — Klein goes so far as to characterize Paul's argument in Rom. 4 as a "paganizing" of Israel's history. However, while it would certainly be improper to speak of a salvation history in the sense of an evolutionary development — and Klein is right to question the formulation "faith *in* history" that Wilckens uses — the promise theme binds Abraham and the Christian together in an overall scheme that can appropriately be labeled "salvation history" (cf. L. Goppelt, "Paulus und die Heilsgeschichte: Sclussfolgerungen aus Röm. IV und I Kor X.1-13," *NTS* 13 [1966-67], 31-42 [ET in *Int* 21 {1967}, 315-26]). A mediating position between Wilckens and Klein is taken by K. Berger, "Abraham in den paulinischen Hauptbriefen," *MTZ* 17 (1966), 75-77, and P. B. Likeng, "La paternité d'Abraham selon Rom. 4,1-25," *Revue Africaine de Theologie* 4 (1980), 153-86.

9. The middle part of v. 1 is found in four forms in the textual tradition:

1. εὑρηκέναι Ἀβραὰμ τὸν προπάτορα ἡμῶν — "has found Abraham our fore-

reason to boast, but not before God. 3For what does the Scripture say? "Abraham believed in God, and it was reckoned to him as righteousness."ᵃ 4Now for the one who works, the wages are not reckoned according to grace, but according to obligation. 5But to the one who does not work but believes on the one who justifies the ungodly, his faith is reckoned for righteousness. 6Just as also David pronounces a blessing on the person to whom God reckons righteousness apart from works:

*7Blessed are those whose lawless acts are forgiven
and whose sins are covered;
8blessed is the person whose sin the Lord does not reckon.ᵇ*

a. Gen. 15:6
b. Ps. 32:1-2

The argument of the paragraph unfolds in four stages. In vv. 1-2 Paul denies that Abraham is any exception to the principle laid down in 3:27-28: all boasting is excluded because justification is by faith. Verse 3 cites the scriptural evidence for Abraham's justification by faith. This reckoning of Abraham's faith for righteousness is shown in vv. 4-5 to be a gracious act of the "God who justifies the ungodly," thereby eliminating any place for "works" in the process. Finally, vv. 6-8 confirm the sovereign character of God's "reckoning," here defined in terms of forgiveness, with appeal to

---

father" (the Alexandrian MSS ℵ [original hand], A, C [original hand], and 81; the Byzantine second corrector of ℵ);

2. εὑρηκέναι Ἀβραὰμ τὸν πάτερα ἡμῶν — "has found Abraham our father" (the Alexandrian MS C [third corrector], the western MSS D, F, G, the uncial Ψ, the Byzantine first corrector of ℵ);

3. Ἀβραὰμ τὸν πάτερα ἡμῶν εὑρηκέναι — "Abraham our father has found" (the Alexandrian minuscule 33 and the majority text);

4. Ἀβραὰμ τὸν προπάτορα ἡμῶν — "Abraham our forefather" (the Alexandrian MS B; 1739 has πάτερα).

The presence of πάτερα in some MSS is a clear case of a more common word being substituted for a less common one; προπάτορα is almost certainly original. More significant is the possibility that εὑρηκέναι is not original (cf. option 4). It is omitted in the very important B; and the different placement of the word (cf. options 1, 2, and 3) may suggest that it was added to the text (Lightfoot; S-H). With this omission, we would translate v. 1 as in REB, "What, then, are we to say about Abraham, our ancestor by natural descent?" But it is more likely that εὑρήκεναι has been omitted from the original text, either accidentally, because of its similarity to the preceding ἐροῦμεν (Metzger, 509), or deliberately because of the awkwardness of the syntax. Godet argues for reading 3 because he thinks κατὰ σάρκα should be attached to the verb, but this connection is unlikely, and reading 1, with its stronger external support, should be adopted.

David's words in Ps. 32:1-2. Verses 4-5, which appeal to the gracious nature of God's dealings with his people as support for justification by faith apart from works, are the heart of this paragraph. In this sense, we may characterize 4:1-8 as a kind of "commentary" on 3:27-28.[10]

1 As so often in Romans, Paul uses a rhetorical question to introduce the next stage of his argument: "What then[11] shall we say that Abraham, our forefather[12] according to the flesh, has found?"[13] But just how does Paul's discussion of Abraham in chap. 4 advance his argument? As we saw in the commentary on 3:31, many scholars take this verse as the heading of chap. 4. On this view, Paul in chap. 4 would be explaining what he means by "we establish the law" in 3:31c: we uphold the testimony of the Pentateuch (Gen. 15:6), which also makes clear that a person is justified by faith (cf. 3:28).[14] However, we have argued that this reading of 3:31c is unlikely. It is better viewed as a quick riposte to the objection raised in v. 31a, and not as a "heading" or introduction to chap. 4. This being the case, the deliberative question in 4:1 will connect the chapter generally with the discussion in 3:27-31.[15] Paul in chap. 4 elaborates through the history of Abraham each of the key points he has made in 3:27-31.[16]

"According to the flesh" is attached by some expositors to the verb. Paul would then be asking what Abraham discovered "by his own [fleshly] exertions."[17] But the stress in the chapter on the expansion of Abraham's "fatherhood" to include the spiritual paternity of all believers (cf. vv. 12,

---

10. Berger, "Abraham," p. 65.

11. While οὖν frequently has inferential force ("therefore"), it marks a simple transition here ("then").

12. προπάτωρ, used only once in the LXX and only here in the NT, is a variant on the usual formula "Abraham our father."

13. This translation assumes that the infinitive εὑρηκέναι introduces a noun clause that specifies the content of the verb ἐροῦμεν ("we say"). This is more likely than the suggestion of Hays, who takes τί οὖν ἐροῦμεν as a separate question and "Abraham" as the object of εὑρηκέναι: "What then shall we say? Have we found Abraham (to be) our forefather according to the flesh?" ("Have we found?" pp. 76-98; cf., contra Hays, Harrisville, *Abraham,* p. 22). The somewhat awkward use of εὑρίσκω ("to find") in the question may be due to the LXX expression εὑρίσκειν ἔλεος [χάριν] ("to find mercy [grace]") — used with respect to Abraham in Gen. 18:3 (e.g., Cranfield; Dunn). But it is probably a case simply of εὑρίσκω meaning "find to be the case," "discover by experience" (cf. 7:10, 21). Paul asks his readers to contemplate with him what Abraham has found to be the case with respect to the matters he is discussing.

14. Cf., e.g., Rhyne, *Faith Establishes the Law,* pp. 75-76.

15. E.g., Murray; Cranfield; Dunn.

16. See the introduction to 3:27–4:25 for the parallels.

17. Jewett, *Anthropological Terms,* pp. 425-26; Hodge; Godet; Meyer; Stuhlmacher.

16-18) suggests rather that this phrase limits "our forefather." This limitation may involve physical as opposed to spiritual generation — "our [the Jews'] forefather 'according to natural physical generation.' "[18] But something of the usual pejorative sense of the phrase "according to the flesh" is probably to be found here as well: Abraham's "paternity" in relationship to Paul and other Jewish Christians ("we")[19] is limited not just by physical descent but also by a narrow, "old era" perspective.[20] For from a "new era" perspective, Abraham is the father of all believers, both Jewish and Gentile (cf. 4:11-12).

2 In this verse, Paul explains why[21] he has asked about Abraham's experience in v. 1.[22] The flow of thought may be paraphrased: "What shall we say about Abraham? *For* if we say he was justified by works, he has reason to boast, and my claim in 3:27-28 that all boasting is excluded is called into question." The question about Abraham's being justified by works is no idle one. As we have seen, the Jewish interpretation of Abraham stressed his works as the essence of his piety and the basis for his extraordinary, exemplary relationship to God. Paul's conditional sentence assumes the reality of this situation for the sake of argument — "if Abraham was justified by works"[23] — and draws out the consequence: he "has reason to boast."[24] Paul contests the conclusion in a brief rejoinder: "but not before God."[25] But does this rejoinder limit Abraham's boasting or reject it altogether? If the former, Paul would be implying that Abraham's boasting was limited to the sphere of his fellow human beings: before people Abraham has some reason for pride; but "before God" he has no reason to boast.[26] If Paul were speaking simply about Abraham's works, this would be a possible interpretation. But Paul is speaking of Abraham's works in relation to his justification.

---

18. E.g., Cranfield.

19. The ἡμῶν does not require that Paul be addressing Jewish Christians at this point (as Minear, 52-53, thinks); he may be speaking from the perspective of himself and other Jews or Jewish Christians, without including his readers.

20. Cf. Dunn, "Jesus — Flesh and Spirit," pp. 46-47.

21. Note the γάρ, "for."

22. Cf. Godet; Cranfield.

23. Paul uses εἰ with the indicative in a so-called "first-class" condition. Since Paul clearly rejects the possibility stated in this condition, Schmithals thinks that Paul here abandons the usual meaning of the conditional clause. But the "first-class" condition does not require that the condition be a real one — only that it be viewed as such for the sake of argument. On the nature of this conditional sentence, cf. further Lambrecht, "Why Is Boasting Excluded?" pp. 366-67.

24. "Reason to boast" translates καύχημα; cf. BAGD and the note on 3:27.

25. Gk. ἀλλ' οὐ πρὸς θεόν. The preposition πρός here means "as far as — is concerned, with reference to" (BAGD); its meaning here is probably influenced by the Hebrew לִפְנֵי.

26. E.g., Godet; S-H; Wilckens.

And since Paul rejects any possibility of justification by works (cf. vv. 3-5), it is more likely that Paul rejects Abraham's claim altogether: *all* boasting in this context, whether before God or people, must be ruled out. "But not before God," then, rejects the logic stated in the conditional sentence: when God's viewpoint is considered, Abraham has no right to boast at all.[27] The abrupt "but not before God" states in preliminary fashion the conclusion of Paul's argument, in which the protasis of the sentence ("if Abraham was justified by works") is disproved.[28]

3 Paul now explains[29] this "but not before God" by citing the scriptural teaching about Abraham's justification. The text that he cites, and which becomes the reference point for the rest of the chapter, is Gen. 15:6.[30] While Jewish authors had already seized on Gen. 15:6 as a particularly important text,[31] Paul has more than a polemical purpose in citing the verse. Not only is this the first time the word "believe"[32] occurs in Scripture, but it is connected with the attaining of righteousness — one of the very few times in the OT that this connection is made. And the verse, of course, describes Abraham — the "father" of Israel and recipient of God's promise. Paul therefore has very good reasons from within the OT itself to make this a banner verse for his gospel, as he does both here and in Gal. 3.

In Gen. 15:6, Abraham's "faith" is his complete trust in God with reference to God's promise that he would have a natural descendant (vv. 4-5). But since this promise is a renewal of the one that God made to Abraham in Gen. 12:1-3, the promise with reference to which Abraham believes in Yahweh

---

27. See, e.g., Calvin; Murray; Barrett; Cranfield.

28. Paul's rejection of Abraham's being "justified" by works raises a question about James's insistence that Abraham was, in fact, "justified by works" (ἐξ ἔργων ἐδικαιώθη) (2:21). While scholars have for centuries proposed all kinds of harmonizations, it is best to understand James to be using δικαιόω differently than is Paul. For Paul, "justification" is the initial acceptance of the "ungodly" by God (cf. v. 5). James, however, uses δικαιόω in a more traditional sense, of the ultimate judgment of God over the life of a person. Paul, then, is insisting that Abraham could not have achieved a right standing with God through works; James, that Abraham could not have maintained that status, or gone free in the final judgment, without works. See, further, Moo, *James,* pp. 110-12.

29. Cf. the γάρ, "for."

30. Paul's quotation is from the LXX, which varies from the MT in using a passive verb — ἐλογίσθη ("it was reckoned") — in place of the active verb of the Hebrew — וַיַּחְשְׁבֶהָ ("he [Yahweh] reckoned it [faith]"). This change leads the LXX to use εἰς with δικαιοσύνην ("righteousness") to indicate the predicative function of the word (cf. BDF 145[2]; for the use of the transitive deponent λογίζομαι in the passive, see Turner, 58). These grammatical differences, however, do not create a material change; the meaning is the same in both versions.

31. See Dunn; and cf. Jas. 2:22-23.

32. Heb. אָמַן.

includes the worldwide blessing promised in the earlier text.[33] Of considerable importance for Paul's use of the text is the meaning of God's "reckoning" Abraham's faith "for" righteousness. The language could suggest that his faith is considered as the "equivalent" of righteousness — that God sees Abraham's faith as itself a "righteous" act, well pleasing to him.[34] But if we compare other verses in which the same grammatical construction as is used in Gen. 15:6 occurs, we arrive at a different conclusion. These parallels suggest that the "reckoning" of Abraham's faith as righteousness means "to account to him a righteousness that does not inherently belong to him."[35] Abraham's response to God's promise leads God to "reckon" to him a "status" of righteousness. If this interpretation of Gen. 15:6 is correct, then Paul's application of the verse is both fair and appropriate. To be sure, the new connotations given the terms "faith" and "righteousness" as a result of Paul's christological focus cannot be ignored. But the essential point, that Abraham's relationship with God is established as an act of God's grace in response to Abraham's faith, is the same in both Genesis and Romans.[36] Here Paul distances himself emphatically from the typical interpretation. For Jewish interpreters often viewed Gen. 15:6 through the lens of Gen. 22, so that Abraham's "faith" became his obedience to God and was regarded as a "work" for which God owed Abraham a reward.[37] Paul's interpretation stands squarely against this tradition and is also a more faithful interpretation of the original.

33. Cf., e.g., J. Calvin, *Commentaries on the First Book of Moses, called Genesis* (Grand Rapids: Eerdmans, n.d.), p. 406; H. C. Leupold, *Exposition of Genesis* (Grand Rapids: Baker, 1942), p. 478. On the importance of the Abrahamic promise, see esp. W. C. Kaiser, Jr., *Toward an Old Testament Theology* (Grand Rapids: Zondervan, 1978), e.g., pp. 91-92.

34. Cf., e.g., Ziesler, *Righteousness,* pp. 181-85.

35. O. P. Robertson, "Genesis 15:6: New Covenant Exposition of an Old Covenant Text," *WTJ* 42 (1980), 265-66; cf. also H. H. Schmid, "Gerechtigkeit und Glaube. Genesis 15, 1-6 und sein biblisch-theologischer Kontext," *EvT* 40 (1980), 408; Calvin, *Genesis,* p. 405; Leupold, *Genesis,* p. 477; W. Brueggemann, *Genesis* (Atlanta: John Knox, 1982), pp. 144-46. The relevant construction is the use of the verb הָשַׁב followed by the preposition לְ. It describes the offering of sacrifices, which are "reckoned" to a person's benefit (cf. Lev. 7:18; Num. 18:27, 30 — this background is stressed by G. von Rad, "Die Anrechnung des Glaubens zur Gerechtigkeit," *TLZ* 76 [1951], cols. 129-32; K. Seybold, on the other hand, stresses a commercial background [*TDOT* V, 243]). Others refer to a status, or legal standing, which someone "reckons" to someone else. In 2 Sam. 19:20, e.g., Shimei, who confesses his sin, nevertheless asks David not to "credit his guilt against him" (אל־יַחֲשָׁב־לִי אֲדֹנִי עָוֹן). What Shimei is asking is that David "reckon" or "regard" him in a way that overlooks, or does not correspond to, the facts of the case. In Ps. 106:31, similarly, God's "reckoning" Phinehas as righteous (see Num. 25) is a declarative act, not an equivalent compensation or reward for merit (cf. also Gen. 31:15; Ps. 32:2).

36. Cf. Schmid, "Gerechtigkeit und Glaube," pp. 417-19; Ridderbos, *Paul,* p. 177.

37. Moxnes, *Theology in Conflict,* pp. 155-63; E. Käsemann, "The Faith of Abraham in Romans 4," *Perspectives on Paul,* p. 81.

4 In vv. 4-5, Paul draws two theological consequences from what is said about Abraham's justification in Gen. 15:6: (1) works have no part in justification; and (2) this is so because God's justifying verdict is not earned, but given freely. To be sure, Paul does not state things in just this way. His argument is more involved and even somewhat unclear. This is because he disrupts what would seem to be an intended parallelism between vv. 4 and 5 by shifting from the contrast between grace and obligation in v. 4 to a conclusion about justification in v. 5. Nevertheless, the two points isolated above emerge clearly enough.

The theological application of Gen. 15:6 that Paul makes in vv. 4-5 reveals his true interest in Abraham's justification and illustrates the hermeneutical principle he states in vv. 23-24: "the words 'it was reckoned to him' were written not for his sake alone, but for ours also." And it is particularly the nature of the "reckoning" that Paul is interested in. Verse 4 picks up this key word[38] from the quotation in v. 3, as Paul lays down a general principle about the "reckoning" or "accounting" of "wages"[39] to a worker. If a person "works," says Paul, the pay he or she receives in return is a matter of obligation, or fair compensation; the employer "owes" the worker a certain wage and is not giving it "freely," or "without compulsion."[40] This contrast, which is found in secular commercial language[41] as well as in the religious discussions of Judaism,[42] is never given its theological application in this context. But the implicit "theologic" of Paul is clear: since work means the reward is given by obligation, the reward of righteousness must not be dependent on work — for God is never obliged by his creatures; justification is a gift, freely bestowed, not a wage, justly earned. That God acts toward his creatures graciously — without compulsion or necessity — is one of Paul's nonnegotiable theological axioms. He uses it here to show that the faith that gained righteousness for Abraham was a faith that excluded works.[43] For many of us, accustomed by four centuries of Protestant theology to the Pauline "faith vs. works" contrast, this point might appear mundane. But it flew in the face of the dominant Jewish theology of the day, which joined faith and works closely together, resulting in a kind of synergism with respect to salvation.[44] Against this, Paul argues that the "reckoning" of faith

38. Gk. λογίζομαι.
39. Gk. μισθός.
40. Gk. κατὰ χάριν.
41. Cf. Thucydides, 2.40.4.
42. Cf. 4 Ezra 8:31-36; and, for further examples, Str-B, 3.201-2.
43. See esp. Doughty, "The Priority of ΧΑΡΙΣ," pp. 165-67. Cf., for a similar emphasis, B. Reicke, "Paul's Understanding of Righteousness," in *Soli Deo Gloria. New Testament Studies in Honor of William Childs Robinson* (ed. J. M. Richards; Richmond: John Knox, 1968), p. 46.
44. See Stuhlmacher; and the excursus after 3:20.

for righteousness — in Abraham's life, or in anyone else's — is a reckoning that is wholly of grace and must be, then, based on faith. Viewed in this light, Paul's point does not rest on an alleged Hebrew concept of reckoning;[45] nor is he arguing that grace is the necessary consequence of reckoning,[46] or of faith.[47] Grace is not the end point but the beginning of his logic; from the fact of grace comes the conclusion that the faith that justifies must be a faith that is "apart from" all works (cf. 3:28).

5 The transition from general principle to theological principle explains the contrast between "the one who works" in v. 4 and "the one who does not work" at the beginning of this verse. With this last clause Paul is not "canonizing laziness" (Morris); nor does he mean that a Christian need never produce "good works." As Calvin rightly emphasizes, Paul is the last theologian who would countenance a complacent Christian, unconcerned with the active putting into practice of one's faith. Rather, what Paul has in mind, in light of the contrast with "[the one who] believes on the one who justifies the ungodly," is the person who does not depend on her works for her standing before God.[48] "The one who justifies the ungodly"[49] is justly famous as a succinct and bold statement of Paul's conviction that our standing with God is wholly of God's free grace. To appreciate the boldness of this characterization, we must set it beside OT condemnations of human judges who "justify" the guilty (Isa. 5:23; Prov. 17:15), and especially with God's declaration in Exod. 23:7 that "I will not justify the wicked." What is involved, of course, is a new application of the word "justify." The OT texts refer to the declaration or recognition of an existing situation. But Paul has in mind a creative act, whereby the believer is freely given a new "status." What is highlighted by the phrase is the nature of God — loving, freely giving, and incapable of being put under obligation to any human being. It is the person who believes in *this* God, and who thereby in his belief renounces any claim on God that his good works might exert, whose "faith is reckoned for righteousness." Likewise, it becomes clear again that faith for Paul is something qualitatively distinct from any human-originated endeavor. *We* believe, but we can take no credit for it. As Jonathan Edwards puts it, the point of the verse is,

---

45. As, e.g., H. W. Heidland (*TDNT* IV, 290) thinks.
46. As, e.g., Barrett and Moxnes (*Theology in Conflict,* p. 110) conclude.
47. As Cranfield suggests.
48. See Hodge; Cranfield.
49. "Ungodly" translates the Greek word ἀσεβής, which denotes one who "refuses to worship" (cf. my comments on the cognate ἀσέβεια in 1:18). The term is therefore a strong one, as its other NT occurrences attest; cf. Rom. 5:8; 1 Tim. 1:9; 1 Pet. 4:18; 2 Pet. 2:5, 6; 3:7; Jude 4, 15.

. . . that God, in the act of justification, has no regard to anything in the
person justified, as godliness, or any goodness in him; but that immediately
before this act, God beholds him only as an ungodly creature; so that
godliness in the person to be justified is not so antecedent to his justification as to be the ground of it.[50]

Paul's purpose in vv. 4-5, then, is to show that the faith that justifies
is "faith alone," faith "apart from works." And, as Chrysostom remarks, it
is significant that this point is made with reference to Abraham:

For a person who had no works, to be justified by faith was nothing
unlikely. But for a person richly adorned with good deeds, not to be made
just from these, but from faith, this is the thing to cause wonder, and to
set the power of faith in a strong light.

6 Paul's concern to exclude "works" from justification surfaces again
in this verse: "Just as also David[51] pronounces[52] a blessing[53] on the person[54]
to whom God reckons[55] righteousness apart from works." Paul's addition of
the negative "apart from works" makes it likely that vv. 6-8 confirm vv. 4-5.[56]
But Paul probably also intends to add a further OT confirmation of his doctrine
of justification by faith (v. 3). If so, Paul may be imitating Jewish homiletical
practice by adding to his primary proof from the Pentateuch a secondary
witness from "the prophets and the writings."

50. "Justification by Faith Alone," *Works* 1.622. Dunn implies that such conclusions represent an overinterpretation of the text as a result of reading it through Lutheran
spectacles. But it needs to be said, first, that the spectacles are not peculiar to Lutheranism;
the same pair are worn by virtually all the heirs of the Reformation — from strict Reformed
to Methodist. But, second, and most important, we are convinced that Dunn's own dismissal
of these implications is the result of an overly narrow interpretation of Paul's interaction
with his Jewish contemporaries (see, further, the excursus after 3:20).
51. "David" appears in the title of Ps. 32; in addition, it was becoming customary
to associate him with the Psalter as a whole.
52. Gk. λέγει, which here means "speak about," "announce," "pronounce."
53. Gk. μακαρισμός. Paul is the only NT author to use this word (cf. also v. 9;
Gal. 4:15); he uses it here as the substantive corresponding to μακάριοι and μακάριος in
the quotation in vv. 7-8.
54. Gk. τοῦ ἀνθρώπου. The genitive indicates the person "with reference to"
whom or "over" whom the blessing is pronounced.
55. Paul's use of the middle form λογίζεται in an active sense with God as its
subject (in contrast to the passive ἐλογίσθη with faith as its subject as in v. 3) because he
is again anticipating the language of the quotation that follows. Nevertheless, as Murray
notes, the variation in Paul's language shows that he regards as materially equivalent the
expressions "it was reckoned to him for righteousness," "God reckoned righteousness to
him," and "God justified him."
56. See the introduction to these verses, καθάπερ καί, "just as also."

7-8 The words of David are taken from Ps. 32:1-2a.[57] One of the reasons why Paul quotes these verses is the presence in them of the key word "reckon." The practice of associating verses from the OT on the basis of verbal parallels was a common Jewish exegetical technique.[58] But unlike the extremely artificial connections between verses often established through this method by Jewish exegetes, Paul's association of Ps. 32:1-2 with Gen. 15:6 and his exposition of it is very much to the point. For the Psalm verses closely associate the forgiveness of sins (v. 1) with the Lord's "not reckoning" a person's sins against her (v. 2). In other words, it is not the "reckoning" of people's good works but God's act in *not* reckoning their sins against them that constitutes forgiveness. This perfectly accords with Paul's concern to portray justification as a free act of God that has no basis in a person's works. Two other implications follow from the association of these Psalm verses with Paul's exposition. First, it is clear that the forgiveness of sins is a basic component of justification. Second, Paul reveals again his strongly forensic understanding of justification. For he uses this quotation to compare justification to the non-accrediting or not "imputing" of sins to a person. This is an act that has nothing to do with moral transformation, but "changes" people only in the sense that their relationship to God is changed — they are "acquitted" rather than condemned.

ii. Faith and Circumcision (4:9-12)

9*Therefore, was this blessing given to the circumcised, or to the uncircumcised also? For we are saying, "Faith was reckoned to Abraham for righteousness."* 10*How, then, was it reckoned? When he was circumcised or when he was yet uncircumcised? It was not when he was circumcised but when he was uncircumcised.* 11*And he received circumcision as a sign, a seal of the righteousness of faith that was his when he was uncircumcised, in order that he might be the father of all those who believe while not circumcised — so that righteousness might also[1] be reckoned to them —* 12*and the father of the circumcised*

---

57. LXX 31:1-2a. Paul reproduces the LXX exactly, the LXX translation differing from the MT only on minor stylistic points.

58. The rabbis named it *gezerah shewa;* cf., on its use here, Jeremias, "Gedankenführung," pp. 271-72.

1. Many early and important witnesses (the primary Alexandrian uncials ℵ [original hand] and B, the secondary Alexandrian minuscules 81 and 1739, and the uncial Ψ) omit the adverbial καί ("also") in this clause. UBS[4] encloses the word in brackets, indicating that the decision is a difficult one but that the editors incline slightly to its inclusion (following the Alexandrian C, the western D, F, and G, and the majority text). The decision has minimal impact on the meaning of the verse.

— those who are not only circumcised but also walk in the steps of our father Abraham, who believed while still uncircumcised.

Quickly returning to his key text, Paul notes another significant aspect of the reckoning of Abraham's faith for righteousness — it took place before he was circumcised. This circumstance allows Paul to claim Abraham as the father of *all* believers, both circumcised and uncircumcised. Paul thereby makes clear that it is not necessary to be Jewish to become a member of the people of God. Faith *alone* — apart from works (4:3-8), apart from circumcision (4:9-12) — is sufficient to gain entrance into Abraham's spiritual "family." It becomes evident here that Abraham is much more than an "example" of faith. As the recipient and mediator of the promise, his experience becomes paradigmatic for his spiritual progeny.

9 Having used Ps. 32:1-2 to confirm and interpret Gen. 15:6, Paul now turns back to Gen. 15:6 to add a further dimension to his application of Ps. 32:1-2. The question that is raised is whether "the blessing" of forgiveness of sins, accomplished through the Lord's gracious "non-reckoning" of them against a person (cf. vv. 7-8), is applicable only "to[2] the circumcised,[3] or to the uncircumcised also."[4] The second sentence of the verse, in which Paul cites Gen. 15:6 again, does not explain the opening question,[5] nor does it gives its answer.[6] Rather, Paul here sets the stage for his answer by reminding his readers[7] of the OT text that speaks authoritatively about these matters.[8]

10 As in vv. 3-5, Paul focuses on the meaning and circumstances of the "reckoning" of Abraham's faith: "How, then, was it reckoned? When he

---

2. The Greek preposition is ἐπί. It might be that we are to assume here the verb λέγεται (e.g., "is this blessing 'pronounced over' the circumcised. . . ?"; cf. Fitzmyer). But the connection with Abraham that Paul has already considered makes it more likely that we should assume a verb such as δίδοται (e.g., "is this blessing bestowed upon the circumcised. . . ?").

3. As in 3:30, the abstract nouns περιτομή and ἀκροβυστία (lit., "circumcision" and "uncircumcision," respectively) refer here to representative circumcised and uncircumcised people.

4. A rabbinic interpretation of Ps. 32 held that the forgiveness David speaks of here was confined to Israel only (cf. *Pesiq. R.* 45, 185b). If such an interpretation were known to Paul, it would give special relevance to his question here.

5. As the γάρ ("for") might at first be thought to indicate; e.g., "I am asking this because we say. . . ."

6. E.g., "The answer is 'even upon the uncircumcision' because we say . . ." (cf. Cranfield). This reading would make v. 10 needlessly repetitive.

7. Hence the present tense of λέγομεν ("we are saying"); cf. λέγει in v. 6.

8. See, e.g., Meyer.

was[9] circumcised[10] or when he was yet uncircumcised?'' Paul's answer is clear and direct: "It was not when he was circumcised but when he was uncircumcised." Paul does not justify this answer, but the course of the argument in v. 11 makes clear that Paul has in mind the chronological progression of the Genesis narrative about Abraham. Abraham's faith "is reckoned for righteousness" when God promised him a son (Gen. 15); but it is not until much later — twenty-nine years, according to the rabbis — that he is circumcised (Gen. 17)

11 In the first part of this verse, Paul amplifies his answer at the end of v. 10 by showing the relationship between Abraham's justification by faith and his later circumcision.[11] What was the significance of Abraham's circumcision? It was, Paul claims, a "sign."[12] Paul tells us what this "sign" was in an appositive addition: "a seal of the righteousness of faith that was his[13] when he was uncircumcised." Genesis 17:11 calls circumcision a "sign of the covenant."[14] In light of the tendency among Paul's Jewish contemporaries to identify this covenant as the Mosaic covenant, Paul's decision to connect the signatory value of circumcision with "the righteousness of faith" (Gen. 15:6) is emphatic.[15] Everything in Abraham's experience with the Lord, Paul suggests, has its source in his justification by faith. While there are Jewish texts that characterize circumcision as a "seal," their late date makes it uncertain whether the description

9. The participle ὄντι is adjectival, modifying τῷ Ἀβραάμ, which is carried over by implication from the quotation in v. 9b.

10. Literally, "in the state of circumcision" (ἐν περιτομῇ).

11. Cf., e.g, Cranfield. This view of the sequence of thought is preferable to that of Barrett, who thinks that v. 11a is a parenthetical remark about the significance of circumcision, with the purpose clause in v. 11b (εἰς τὸ εἶναι . . .) dependent on v. 10b. But the indication that Abraham is the "father of the circumcision" in the continuation of the main purpose clause in v. 12 makes it more likely that the clause is dependent on a statement that includes reference to Abraham's circumcision. This statement comes in v. 11a.

12. περιτομῆς is an epexegetic genitive: "the sign that is circumcision."

13. "Which was his" is a paraphrase that attempts to bring out the force of the definite article τῆς. The article signifies the adjectival function of the phrase ἐν τῇ ἀκροβυστίᾳ ("in uncircumcision"), which probably modifies δικαιοσύνης ("righteousness") (see Cranfield, contra Godet, who takes it with πίστεως).

14. σημείῳ διαθήκης (אוֹת בְּרִית); and cf. Acts 7:8, "He gave to him [Abraham] a covenant of circumcision [διαθήκην περιτομῆς]." The rabbis occasionally used אוֹת ("sign") by itself to denote circumcision; and note *Jub.* 15:26, where circumcision is described as "a sign" that marks a person as belonging to the Lord. See, further, K. H. Rengstorf, *TDNT* VII, 258; Str-B, 4.32.

15. Cf. Käsemann; C. K. Barrett, *From First Adam to Last: A Study in Pauline Theology* (New York: Scribner's, 1962), p. 38. Rengstorff, on the other hand, thinks that a reference to the covenant is implied (ibid.).

was known in Paul's day.[16] In any case, Paul uses the word to denote something that "confirms" the truth or reality of something else, as in 1 Cor. 9:2, where Paul describes the Corinthian believers themselves as the "seal," the confirmation and authentication, of his apostleship. In like manner, Abraham's circumcision confirms his righteous status, a status that was his by virtue of his faith.[17] Circumcision, therefore, has no independent value. It cannot effect one's entrance into the people of God; nor does it even "mark" a person as belonging to God's people apart from a prior justifying act. Abraham was declared righteous while still uncircumcised. His later circumcision added nothing materially to that transaction; it simply signified and confirmed it.[18]

In verses 11b-12 we have one long purpose clause, with a result clause ("so that righteousness might also be reckoned to them") stuck inside it. In the major purpose clause, Paul depicts Abraham as the spiritual father of all believers, both Gentiles and Jews. It is dependent on v. 11a, although the two parts of the clause relate to different elements in 11a: because Abraham believed while uncircumcised, he is the father of all Gentile believers; because he believed and was *also* circumcised, he is qualified to be the father of all Jewish believers. As we have seen, Abraham is specially revered as the "father" of the Jewish nation (cf. 4:1); and with salvation practically confined to Israel, this meant that one could become Abraham's spiritual descendant only through incorporation into Israel — through birth, or, occasionally, through conversion.[19] Paul now claims Abraham and the inheritance that is

16. The texts are *b. Shabb.* 137b; *Exod. Rab.* 19 (81c); *Tg. Ket.* Cant. 3:8. Also significant is the allusion in *Barn.* 9:6. Michel, D. Flusser, and S. Safira ("Who Sanctified the Beloved in the Womb," *Immanuel* 11 [1980], 46-55) think the usage pre-dates the NT; G. Fitzer believes it is later (*TDNT* VII, 949).

17. The genitive τῆς πίστεως indicates source: "righteousness that has its source in faith."

18. From the middle of the second century, the word "seal" was used with reference to Christian baptism (cf. *Herm.; 1 Clem.*). Many scholars also think that the word has baptismal connotations in Eph. 1:13 and 4:30. This factor, coupled with the relationship drawn between circumcision and baptism elsewhere in the NT (cf. Col. 2:11-15), has led many expositors to suggest that Rom. 4:11 has at least indirect reference to Christian baptism (e.g., Wilckens; Käsemann [cautiously]). The evidence for this claim is, however, inconclusive. The Ephesians texts fall far short of a clear allusion to baptism, and reading back the imagery of later Christian writings into the NT with respect to the sacraments is a questionable methodology. Moreover, the connections established in texts like Col. 2:11-15 are between *spiritual* circumcision and baptism. We consider an allusion to baptism in this verse, then, as unproven and improbable (cf., e.g., Dunn).

19. Although proselytes were forbidden from calling Abraham "our father" (cf. Barrett, *From First Adam to Last,* p. 31).

his (cf. vv. 16-17), for anyone who believes. It is through faith, and not through incorporation into the nation of Israel, that one becomes Abraham's spiritual "child." Indeed, Abraham's Gentile "children" are mentioned first in the compound purpose clause. Paul at this point inserts a parenthetical remark in which he notes a consequence[20] of the belief of the Gentiles; they, like Abraham, have their faith reckoned to them for righteousness.

12 After the brief interruption at the end of v. 11, Paul now resumes his main purpose clause. Paul indicates that Abraham's receiving of circumcision had the purpose of qualifying him to be the "father of the circumcised — those who are not only circumcised but also walk in the steps of our father Abraham, who believed while still uncircumcised." But who comprises this category of "the circumcision"? A few expositors think the word might have a spiritual sense here, designating the Christian community as a whole (cf. Phil. 3:3).[21] But the context of Rom. 4 focuses too much on the distinction between Jews and Gentiles to make that likely. Others think that the long explanatory clause Paul adds to the word "circumcision" makes it clear that he has two groups in mind: both Jewish believers, "children" of Abraham as participants in the righteousness of faith, and Jews generally, who continue to be the beneficiaries of at least some of the promises God made to Abraham (see Rom. 9:5 and 11:28). Advocates of this view argue that the wording of the qualifying clause could point to a translation in which two separate groups are denoted: "not only to those who are 'of the circumcision' but also to those who follow in the footsteps of faith that our father Abraham had when uncircumcised."[22] But there are other elements of the wording that point to one group; and the context strongly suggests that Paul is referring to Jewish Christians: those of the circumcision "who[23] are not only circumcised but also walk in the steps of our father Abraham,[24] who believed while still uncircumcised."[25]

---

20. The infinitive εἰς τὸ λογισθῆναι probably indicates result rather than purpose (Käsemann; Cranfield; Wilckens; contra Godet; Michel; Barrett; Dunn; Turner, 143).

21. E.g., Cambier, *L'Evangile*, pp. 170-71.

22. The grammatical point that could favor this rendering is the presence of the article (τοῖς) before στοιχοῦσιν ("those who walk"). See, e.g., Käsemann; Fitzmyer. In a variation of this view, some think that the two groups are Jewish Christians and Gentile Christians (cf. J. Swetnam, "The Curious Crux at Romans 4,12," *Bib* 61 [1980], 110-15).

23. Gk. τοῖς; the article is plural (it refers to the singular noun περιτομῆς) because Paul is thinking of the sense in which he uses the latter word.

24. This translation is necessarily interpretive. Paul actually makes "faith" (πίστεως) the object of "walk in the footsteps," thus revealing both the metaphorical nature of the phrase and the emphasis Paul wants to put on faith.

25. As Cranfield points out, the placement of the first τοῖς is strange if Paul had intended to enumerate two separate groups. Had this been his intention, we would have

In addition to Gentiles who believe, Abraham's children are also comprised of Jews who believe. In keeping with the theme of the paragraph, Paul stresses again that the faith of Abraham that Jewish Christians imitate is a faith that was first exercised when Abraham was in an "uncircumcised state." Jews who follow their biblical paradigm will place the proper value on their circumcision: as a mark of a relationship they enjoy with the Lord through their faith rather than as a visa that will automatically insure their entrance into heaven.

iii. Faith, Promise, and the Law (4:13-22)

13*For it was not through the law that the promise was to Abraham or to his seed, that they should be the heirs of the world, but through the righteousness of faith.* 14*For if those who are of the law were heirs, faith would be emptied and the promise would be nullified.* 15*For the law produces wrath. And*[1] *where there is no law, neither is there transgression.*

16*Because of this, it is of faith, in order that it might be according to grace, so that the promise might be confirmed to all the seed, not to those who are of the law only, but also to those who are of the faith of Abraham, who is the father of us all.* 17*Even as it is written, "I have appointed you as the father of many nations,"*[a] *before the God in whom he believed, the God who gives life to the dead and calls those things that are not as though they were.* 18*Who against hope, on the basis of hope, believed, so that he became the father of many nations, according to what was said, "So shall your seed be."*[b] 19*And he did not weaken in faith when he observed*[2] *his own body, already*[3] *dead — being about*

---

expected the order οὐκ τοῖς ἐκ περιτομῆς μόνον ("not to those of the circumcision only"); cf. the order of words in v. 16b. Scholars who think that Paul is referring to only one group explain the second article as a careless "slip of the pen" on the part of Paul or Tertius, his scribe (S-H; Kuss; Cranfield; Wilckens), or as the mistake of an early scribe, who wrote τοῖς where Paul had αὐτοῖς ("to them") (Michel). It may be better, however, simply to acknowledge an unsual word order (cf. Moule, *Idiom Book,* p. 110 ["an intrusive article"]; Godet; Lightfoot).

1. The translation "and" reflects the reading δέ, supported strongly by the Alexandrian family (the original hand of ℵ, B, C, and 81). The alternative reading is γάρ ("for"), which musters support from the western family (D, F, G), one MS of the Alexandrian family (1739), and the majority text. There would have been good reason for γάρ to have replaced δέ since γάρ has been used three times in vv. 13-15a and v. 15b is naturally construed as an explanation of v. 15a.

2. Many witnesses (the western family [D, F, G], the majority text, the Alexandrian minuscule 33, and the uncial Ψ) include the negative particle οὐ in front of the verb κατενόησεν ("observe"). At first sight, this reading would seem to yield a significant

*a hundred years old — and the deadness of the mother Sarah. 20He
did not doubt the promise of God because of unbelief, but grew strong
in faith, giving glory to God, 21and being fully convinced that he was
able also to do what had been promised. 22Wherefore also[4] "it was
reckoned to him for righteousness."[c]*

    a. Gen. 17:5
    b. Gen. 15:5
    c. Gen. 15:6

Many expositors divide this passage into two paragraphs, putting a break after
v. 16 or v. 17. But while Paul's focus does shift at this point from a polemical
contrast between law and faith to a more positive portrayal of Abraham's faith,
the theme of the promise runs throughout vv. 13-22, binding them together
in an overall unity.[5] The noun "promise," which occurs for the first time here
in the letter,[6] is used four times in these verses, the verb "to promise" once.
In each case, the reference is to the promise given to Abraham, with Paul
emphasizing particularly how it was faith that secured what God had promised.
There is evidence that Paul has built his exposition on the foundation of a
traditional Jewish and Jewish-Christian interpretation of Abraham's faith. This
interpretation, whose general outline can be discerned in Philo, Acts 7, Heb.

---

difference in meaning. Yet this is not the case. If the particle is included, Paul would be
emphasizing that Abraham did not weaken in faith because he did not "consider," in the
sense of "let himself be influenced by," the physical circumstances. If it is omitted, on the
other hand, Paul would be saying that Abraham did not weaken in faith, even though he
"considered," in the sense of "took into account but dismissed," the physical evidence.
Since the omission of the word has slightly stronger external support (strong support from
the Alexandrian family [א, A, B, C, 81, and 1739]) and the addition of the particle is the
sort of "correction" that a scribe would naturally be tempted to make, οὐ should not be
read.

    3. The external support is almost evenly balanced on the question of whether to
read ἤδη before νενεκρωμένον ("dead"). The bulk of the Alexandrian family (א, A, C,
33, 81), the western D, the uncial Ψ, and the majority text include it; while two Alexandrian
witnesses (B and 1739) and two western uncials (F and G) omit it. NA[27] and UBS[4] include
the word in brackets. The UBS committee decided that external evidence favored inclusion,
while internal evidence went the other way, it being easier to understand how the word
would have been added than subtracted (Metzger, 510-11). A decision is difficult, but we
are inclined to accept it since it makes good sense with the perfect participle.

    4. The external evidence favors including the καί after διό — the majority of
witnesses include it (most of the Alexandrian family [א, A, C, 33, 81, and 1739], the
western D [first corrector], Ψ, and the majority text), and the combination of B, the Greek
text of D, and G, which omit it, is not a strong one. This makes a decision difficult, but
the tendency may well have been to omit an original καί as redundant.

    5. Cf. Moxnes, *Theology in Conflict,* p. 113.

    6. The verb προεπαγγέλλω, "promise beforehand," occurs in 1:2.

11, and *1 Clem.* 10, focuses particularly on the miracle-working power of God and the way Abraham (and Sarah) experienced this power by ignoring the "facts" of the situation and trusting rather in the promise of God.[7] However, while this theme is evident in vv. 17-21, the first part of Paul's exposition departs from the traditional interpretation with its polemical contrast between the law and faith and, to a lesser extent, with its inclusion of the Gentiles in the "seed" of Abraham. Paul's concern to claim Abraham as the spiritual ancestor of Christians is evident here again. Surfacing again also is his concern with grace and universalism, which Paul believes can be upheld only if faith rather than the law is the instrument by which what had been promised to Abraham is attained. Verses 13-22 continue, then, Paul's exposition of faith by way of contrasts: to "faith apart from works" (vv. 3-8) and "faith apart from circumcision" (vv. 9-12), we can add "faith apart from the law" (vv. 13-16) and "faith apart from sight" (vv. 17-21).

13 As the "for"[8] suggests, the paragraph beginning in v. 13 has an explanatory function — it explains why Paul made no mention of the law in tracing the spiritual descendants of Abraham (vv. 11-12). This omission, in light of the standard Jewish view that it was Abraham's fidelity to the law that secured God's blessing (see the introduction to 4:1-25) and that one could be Abraham's child only by taking on oneself "the yoke of the torah," requires explanation and defense. Paul makes his position clear in v. 13: it was not "through law"[9] but "through the righteousness of faith" "that the promise was to Abraham or to his seed, that they[10] should be the heirs of the world." "Law" refers, as the Jewish polemical context makes clear, to the Mosaic law.[11] In Gal. 3, Paul makes his case for the exclusion of the law from God's dealings with Abraham on the basis of simple chronology — the law, given four hundred and thirty years after the promise, cannot annul or substantially alter this previous agreement between God and Abraham (vv. 15-17). Some think that his argument is presumed here in Romans also.[12] But this is not

7. See, again, esp. Moxnes, *Theology in Conflict*, pp. 195-203.

8. Gk. γάρ.

9. Gk. διὰ νόμου. διά may indicate "attendant circumstances": the promise does not fall "within the domain of the law" (Barrett). But the customary instrumental sense is better, particularly if, as is likely, ἐπαγγελία ("promise") means not the act of promising, but "what was promised" (cf. *Pss. Sol.* 12:6; 1 John 2:25; cf. BAGD; Williams, "Righteousness of God," p. 279).

10. This translation reflects our understanding of this promise (see below) as collectively applying to all of Abraham's "seed."

11. The lack of an article before νόμου has led some expositors to think that Paul is thinking here of "law" in general, as a principle (e.g., S-H), but there are too many reasons for the omission of the article in Greek to justify such a verdict. In this case, the article may be lacking because of the preposition (Schlier; cf. Turner, 179, for the grammatical point).

12. E.g., Klein, "Römer 4," p. 158.

clear. Probably Paul has not used the chronological argument because he wants to apply his reasoning to Abraham's descendants as well as to Abraham. And, since most of Abraham's putative descendants lived after the giving of the Mosaic law, the chronological argument would obviously have no point.

"Not through the law" denies, then, that what had been promised to Abraham was attained by him or by his descendants through the law, for example, by their doing of the law.[13] Rom. 4 does not focus on the christological implications of "seed" that Paul brings out in Gal. 3.[14] The word here is purely collective, the reference being to all who are numbered among the "descendants" of Abraham (cf. also vv. 16, 18; 9:7-8). The clause "that they should be the heirs of the world" explains what the promise is.[15] This language does not exactly match any promise to Abraham found in the OT but succinctly summarizes the three key provisions of the promise as it unfolds in Genesis: that Abraham would have an immense number of descendants, embracing "many nations" (Gen. 12:2; 13:16; 15:5; 17:4-6, 16-20; 22:17), that he would possess "the land" (Gen. 13:15-17; 15:12-21; 17:8), and that he would be the medium of blessing to "all the peoples of the earth" (Gen. 12:3; 18:18; 22:18). Particularly noteworthy is the promise in Gen. 22:17b that Abraham's seed would "possess[16] the gate of their enemies." Later in the OT, there are indications that the promise of the land had come to embrace the entire world (cf. Isa. 55:3-5),[17] and many Jewish texts speak of Israel's inheritance in similar terms.[18] Against this background — to which we can add Jesus' beatitude, "Blessed are the gentle, for they shall inherit the earth"[19] — Paul probably refers generally to all that God promised his people.[20]

14 Paul now explains ("for"[21]) why the promise cannot be attained "through the law": "if[22] those who are of the law were heirs,[23] faith would be

---

13. Hence νόμου comes close to meaning "works of the law" (Leenhardt); but with the broad neutral meaning "anything done in obedience to the law" (see our comments on 3:20).

14. Contra P. L. Hammer, "A Comparison of ΚΛΗΡΟΝΟΜΙΑ in Paul and Ephesians," *JBL* 79 (1960), 271.

15. It is a substantival infinitive clause in apposition to ἐπαγγελία.

16. LXX κληρονομήσει.

17. Cf. T. McComiskey, *The Covenants of Promise* (Grand Rapids: Baker, 1985), pp. 34, 51-55.

18. Cf. Sir. 44:21; *Jub.* 22:14; 32:19; *2 Apoc. Bar.* 14:13; 51:3.

19. Although γή, not κόσμος, is used here.

20. See Moxnes, *Theology in Conflict*, pp. 247-49.

21. Gk. γάρ.

22. Gk. εἰ. The condition is a so-called "first-class" or "real" type, Paul using this form not because the condition is "real" — obviously it is not — but because he wants to show what the consequences would be if it *were* real.

23. For the sentence to make sense, κληρονόμοι ("heirs") must be predicative.

emptied[24] and the promise would be nullified."[25] "Those who are out of the law" is a literal and rather awkward translation of a phrase that appears to means something like "those who are basing their hope for the inheritance on the law."[26] The phrase does not, then, refer to Jews per se,[27] but to those who have nothing more than their status as Jews as a basis for inheriting the blessings promised to Abraham. For there are Jews who, living "in the sphere of the law,"[28] add to their Jewishness faith in Christ; and the righteousness before God they gain by that faith makes them, like Abraham, heirs of the promise. As "only" is appropriately added to "faith" in 3:28 to bring out the meaning, so also here we might paraphrase "if those who have only the law are heirs. . . ."

Why, if Jews as such were heirs, would faith and the promise be jeopardized? Paul might mean that the granting of the inheritance to Jews on the basis of their relationship to the law would empty the terms "faith" and "promise" of their essential theological meaning. One can hardly apply the word "promise" to something that a person has a "right" to; nor is faith, in the Pauline sense of absolute trust in God, an appropriate word to use for what is one's "birthright" or "wage."[29] However true this may be (cf. 4:4-5), the verbs Paul uses do not naturally suggest this interpretation.[30] In light of these verses, Paul probably means that the exercise of faith has failed to attain its end. Why are faith and the promise rendered futile if Jews apart from faith are the heirs? The reason that is suggested by the logic of Rom. 1–3 and by the explanation in v. 15 is the inherent impossibility of any person adhering to the law to the extent necessary to gain the inheritance. In other words, Paul is arguing: "If it is the case that the inheritance is to be based on adherence to the law, then there will be no heirs, because no fallen human being can adequately adhere to the law — and that means that faith is exercised in vain and the promise will never be fulfilled."[31]

24. Gk. κεκένωται, a perfect passive form of κενόω.

25. Gk. κατήργηται, a perfect passive form of καταργέω. Paul probably uses the perfect tense of both verbs in this apodosis to emphasize the state of affairs that would result from the condition being fulfilled.

26. The Greek is οἱ ἐκ νόμου.

27. Contra, e.g., Klein, "Römer 4," p. 158.

28. See the phrase ἐν τῷ νόμῳ ("in the law") in 2:12; 3:19.

29. See Barrett; Nygren.

30. In Paul, who is the only NT author to use the word, κενόω ("empty") means "deprive of power" (1 Cor. 1:17), "render vain or futile" (1 Cor. 9:15; 2 Cor. 9:3), or "make of no effect" (Phil. 2:7 — cf. M. Silva, *Philippians* [BECNT; Grand Rapids: Baker, 1992], p. 119). Perhaps most important, however, is Paul's use of κενός in 1 Cor. 15:14, where he tells the Corinthians that their faith is "in vain" if Christ has not been raised. καταργέω, while having a fairly broad range of meaning in Paul (see on 3:3), probably has a similar meaning here: the promise fails to take effect, is rendered null and void.

31. Calvin; cf. also Godet; Cranfield.

15 The first clause of this verse substantiates the conclusion drawn in v. 14 by showing what the law *does* — "produces[32] wrath" — as opposed to what it *cannot do* — secure the inheritance. Paul is countering the very positive, and sometimes even salvific, function given the law in Jewish theology. The second clause in the verse is a parenthetical explanation of the reason why the law produces wrath: "And[33] where there is no law, neither is there transgression." It is difficult to decide whether the clause is a statement about the Mosaic law specifically or a kind of "gnomic" statement about the nature and function of law, as "law."[34] In either case, the application is to the Mosaic law, which is clearly referred to in the first part of the verse. But what is the point of this statement? Murray thinks that Paul is justifying the universal infliction of God's wrath. According to him, Paul's logic goes like this:

God justly inflicts wrath for transgressions
Wherever there is "law," there is "transgression"
"Law" is universal (Paul here assuming what he argued in Rom. 2:12-16)
Therefore: God's infliction of wrath on all people is just

Another way of reading the clause, however, is to attribute to it the more limited purpose of explaining why the Mosaic law works wrath. Paul's logic would then be:

Violation of law turns "sin" into the more serious offense of "transgression," meriting God's wrath
God gave the law to the Jews
The Jews have transgressed the law (cf. 2:1-29; 3:9-19)
The law brought wrath to the Jews[35]

This second interpretation is the more likely. A statement about the negative results of the Mosaic law fits well in the context, since vv. 13-16 are dominated by the "not through the law" of v. 13a. An explanation of the causes of God's

32. Gk. κατεργάζεται. This compound verb often emphasizes the results of an action: "produce." This meaning is appropriate here. Rather than referring to the current infliction of God's wrath (Dunn), the present tense is probably gnomic, asserting what the law "generally," by its nature, does.

33. As we have noted, the original reading here is probably δέ. But this does not imperil the explanatory function of the clause, since δέ often introduces an explanation — cf. Rom. 1:13.

34. For the latter view, see, e.g., Winger, *By What Law?* p. 83.

35. See esp. Calvin; Godet; Denney; Nygren; Luz, 187-88.

wrath does not fit nearly as well and appears to be a needless repetition of the argument of Rom. 1:18–3:20. Moreover, Paul's use of the word "transgression" rather than "sin" suggests that he is not thinking of the general condition of sin that justifies the infliction of God's wrath, but the more specific situation that obtains wherever people are confronted with clearly defined, verbally transmitted laws and commands. For Paul does not use "transgression" as a synonym for "sin." "Transgression" denotes a specific kind of sin, the "passing beyond" the limits set by a definite, positive law or command.[36] While every "transgression" is also a "sin," not every "sin" is a "transgression." Paul, then, is not claiming that there is no "sin" where there is no law, but, in almost a "truism," that there is no deliberate disobedience of positive commands where there is no positive command to disobey. As Calvin puts it: "He who is not instructed by the written law, when he sins, is not guilty of so great a transgression as he is who knowingly breaks and transgresses the law of God." Paul's real point emerges in the application of this principle to the Mosaic law as an explanation of how it is that "the law works wrath." Before and outside the Mosaic law wrath certainly exists, for all people, being sinners, stand under God's sentence of condemnation (1:18). But the Mosaic law "produces" even more wrath; rather than rescuing people from the sentence of condemnation, it confirms their condemnation. For by stating clearly, and in great detail, exactly what God requires of people, the law renders people even more accountable to God than they were without the law.[37]

16 In vv. 14-15 Paul has elaborated the negative point in v. 13: the inheritance comes "not through the law." Now Paul turns to its positive antithesis: the inheritance is given "through the righteousness of faith." "Because of this"[38] may, then, refer back to the negative argument of vv. 14-15: "because of this" incapacity of the law to secure the promise, it must be by faith that it is attained.[39] However, the phrase "because of this" often looks ahead to a following clause in the NT,[40] and this makes good sense here. The antecedent of "this" will then be the purpose clause "in order that it might be according to grace." It is for that reason, that grace might be preserved, that "it is of faith."[41] But what is this "it," the implied subject of the verse? Probably, in light of v. 13, "the promised inheritance."[42] The intimate relation

36. The Greek word is παράβασις, which he uses elsewhere in 2:23; 5:14; Gal. 3:19; and 1 Tim. 2:14. See, on this issue, the survey by J. Schneider, *TDNT* V, 739.

37. A similar logic underlies 5:13-14 and 7:7-12.

38. Gk. διὰ τοῦτο.

39. Most commentators hold this view.

40. See the note on 5:12.

41. See esp. Cranfield and Schlier. Others refer διὰ τοῦτο back to v. 13 (Godet) or v. 14 (Barrett).

42. E.g., Käsemann.

in Paul's thought between faith and grace emerges again here. As Paul has shown in vv. 4-5, grace is the necessary corollary to faith, as "obligation" is to works. Thus, "God's plan was made to rest upon faith on man's side in order that on God's side it might be a matter of grace."[43] But there was, according to Paul, a still further purpose in God's provision of the inheritance through faith: "that[44] the promise might be confirmed to all the seed." The benefit denoted by this clause is, as Chrysostom notes, twofold: that the promise might be "firm"[45] — that it might come to fruition — and that the promise might be confirmed to *every* descendant of Abraham. Neither blessing would have come to pass if it had depended on human "works" or obedience to the law; but because faith grasps the absolutely sure promise of God, a promise that he has determined freely to give, the inheritance God has promised can become a reality, and a reality for anyone who believes.

Paul puts a particular spin on "all the seed" in two contrasting phrases: "not to those[46] who are of the law only, but also to those who are of the faith of Abraham." As is the case throughout Romans, and certainly in chap. 4, Paul's "universalism" is a "qualified" universalism that gives the Gentiles the same opportunity as Jews to respond to the gospel and to become part of the people whom God is calling out of the world in the last days. While Paul does not express himself extremely clearly, this inclusion of both Jew and Gentile in the "seed" of Abraham is what is in view in this last part of v. 16. "Those who are of the law only" could, especially in light of the contrast with "those who are of the faith of Abraham," refer to unbelieving Jews.[47] In this case, Paul would be asserting that Jews continue to be part of the "seed of Abraham," in a different way, however, from that in which Christians are the seed of Abraham. Such a point would not, if properly nuanced, be incompatible with Paul's thought (see Rom. 11:11-30). But it is perhaps unlikely that this is what he intends here. Paul has forcefully stated that the true descendants of Abraham are those who believe (vv. 11-12); and when he uses the word "seed" here, it must be with this spiritual meaning that he has given the word. Moreover, the phrase "out of faith" rules

---

43. Barrett.

44. Gk. εἰς τὸ εἶναι.

45. Gk. βεβαίαν.

46. In agreement with the word σπέρματι, the Greek here, and in the next clause, is singular: τῷ. But, recognizing the collective force of σπέρματι, a translation "according to the sense," in which the individuals who comprise the "seed" are denoted, is appropriate. So most modern English Bibles, which also usually translate σπέρματι "descendants."

47. F. Mussner, "Wer ist 'Der ganze Samen' in Röm 4,16?" in *Begegnung mit dem Wort. Festschrift für Heinrich Zimmermann* (ed. J. Zmijewski and E. Nellessen; BBB 53; Bonn: Peter Hanstein, 1980), pp. 213-17; L. Gaston, "Abraham and the Righteousness of God," *Horizons in Biblical Theology* 2 (1980), 58; Fitzmyer.

the entire verse and must be carried over to this latter part of it. The meaning, then, is that the promise is for the Jew who is part of the seed through faith.[48] "Out of the law" must mean something a bit different from what it does in v. 11, and designate Jews as such, "those who had the advantage of being under the Mosaic economy."[49] In light of the contrast indicated by "not only . . . but also," "those out of the faith of Abraham" are Gentile believers.[50] It is in this sense that Abraham is the "father of us all" — the spiritual forefather of all of "us" who are believers.

17 This verse is composed of two main clauses:

Even as it is written, "I have appointed you as the father of many nations"

before the God in whom he believed,[51] the one who gives life to the dead and calls those things that are not as though they were.

They can be related to one another and to the larger context in several ways. (1) The two clauses could follow one another in a straightforward, consecutive sequence, with the quotation from Gen. 17:5 confirming "who is the father of us *all*" at the end of v. 16, and the second clause being dependent on the first clause.[52] (2) The first clause could confirm "to all the seed" in the middle of v. 16, with the second clause again dependent on the first.[53] (3) According to most commentators, v. 17a depends on 16b, as in the first reading, but is somewhat parenthetical, with 17b taken with "father of us all" in v. 16b.[54] (4) Again, as in v. 1, the first clause may be attached to v. 16b, with the second

---

48. So most commentators, ancient and modern.

49. Murray.

50. Godet; Kuss; contra, e.g., Käsemann, who thinks the reference is to believers generally.

51. The beginning of this second clause is elliptical, κατέναντι οὗ ἐπίστευσεν θεοῦ standing for κατέναντι τοῦ θεοῦ ᾧ ἐπίστευσεν (such ellipsis is common in Greek; cf. BDF 294[5]). κατέναντι means "before," often with reference to place, but also figuratively, with reference to persons. In all three of the occurrences in Paul (cf. also 2 Cor. 2:17; 12:19), the word is used with reference to God, in probable dependence on the Hebrew לִפְנֵי.

52. Note the rendering of TEV: "as the Scripture says, 'I have made you father of many nations.' So the promise is good in the sight of God, in whom Abraham believed — the God who brings the dead to life and whose command brings into being what did not exist." See also REB; Käsemann. In a variation of this reading, Godet considers v. 16b to be a resumption of the main line of discussion from v. 12b, vv. 13-16a being an aside to deal with a Jewish objection.

53. Wilckens.

54. Note the NASB rendering: "(as it is written, 'A father of many nations have I made you') in the sight of Him whom he believed, even God, who gives life to the dead and calls into being that which does not exist." See also KJV; and, e.g., Calvin; Michel; Murray; Cranfield.

clause going as far back as "all the seed" in v. 16.[55] (5) Finally, one could construe the first clause according to any of these suggestions, with the second clause initiating a new paragraph.[56]

The connection between "father" in the quotation in v. 17a and "father" in v. 16b is so clear that we must take these clauses closely together, as is done in all the alternatives except the second. There is some truth in the last suggestion, for v. 17b does prepare the way for the exposition of Abraham's faith, with its application to Christians, in vv. 18-25. But the relative clause also looks backward — it functions as the pivot in Paul's argument.[57] But to what, exactly, does it look back? This is the most difficult problem, and the one that serves to differentiate the remaining three alternatives (1, 3, and 4). The connection is awkward in any case, because the preposition "before" does not naturally follow on any of the verbs found in the three immediately preceding clauses. But the connection that makes the most sense is with the immediately preceding clause (e.g., option 1). It adds little to Paul's point to note that the confirmation of the seed (v. 16a) or the spiritual fatherhood of Abraham (v. 16b) exists "in the sight of God," for, while true, it hardly needs to be said. On the other hand, to add to the quotation of a promise that is couched in the past tense — "I *have* made you the father of many nations" — a reminder of the nature of this God "in the presence of whom" the promise is given and accepted explains the certainty expressed in that past tense. God can promise Abraham — and Abraham can believe — that certain things not now existing *will* exist because God is the God who "gives life to the dead and calls those things that are not as though they were."

The quotation in v. 17a, from Gen. 17:5,[58] substantiates v. 16, the "many nations" including both Jews and Gentiles. The promise in Genesis probably has a similar intention, although whether it refers simply to physical ancestry or spiritual "fatherhood" also is not clear. Paul's further characterization of God in terms of his "making alive" and "calling" picks up widespread OT and Jewish teaching. God's power to give life is underscored in the OT (Deut. 32:39; 1 Sam. 2:6) and was featured in the important Jewish liturgy, the *Shemoneh Ezreh*, the "Eighteen Benedictions."[59] In light of the promise quoted in v. 17a, Paul is thinking to some extent of God's bringing life from the body of Abraham and the womb of Sarah.[60] The exposition of

---

55. Bruce.
56. Black.
57. Schlier.
58. Paul quotes the LXX exactly.
59. Str-B, 3.212.
60. See, e.g., Fitzmyer.

Abraham's faith that follows confirms this, as v. 19 notes the "deadness" of Abraham's body and the barrenness of Sarah as the visible evidence that Abraham's faith had to transcend. However, this characterization of God receives a further application in the context, vv. 24-25 defining as the object of Christian belief "the one who raised Jesus our Lord from the dead." Finally, it is possible, though perhaps unlikely, that Paul is also thinking of the application of these words to the rescue of Isaac from his near death (cf. Heb. 11:19).

It is more difficult to know what Paul intends by describing God as the one "who calls those things that are not as though they were." Our conclusion will depend on the meaning we give to "call." If it means, prosaically, "name" or "address," then Paul would be further alluding to the certainty of the fulfillment of God's promise to Abraham: although "the many nations" do not yet exist, God can address them as if they did.[61] Somewhat similar is the interpretation that takes "call" to mean "summon": God summons, calls up before Abraham's view, these nations that "are not" as if they were.[62] While each of these explanations fits the syntax and the context well, some interpreters discern a further reference. In the OT, the verb "call" refers to God's creative work (cf. Isa. 41:4; 48:13), and later Jewish authors perpetuate this usage, sometimes adding the idea that this creative "calling" involves a bringing into being things that were not.[63] It may be, then, this tradition of a *creatio ex nihilo* to which Paul alludes, with the purpose of reminding his readers of God's creative power generally.[64] Moreover, several texts apply this language to spiritual conversion, and sometimes, as here, with reference to God's giving life to the dead.[65] These parallels make it possible that Paul's description of God as "the one who calls into being things that are not" is a reminder that God "justifies the

---

61. Denney.

62. Godet; S-H; Murray's view is similar.

63. Cf., e.g., Philo, *On the Special Laws* 4.187: τὰ γὰρ μὴ ὄντα ἐκάλεσεν εἰς τὸ εἶναι; "for he called things that are not into being." There are many occurrences of substantially similar expressions in Philo; cf. also 2 Macc. 7:28; *2 Apoc. Bar.* 21:4; 48:8.

64. Barrett; Bruce; Cranfield. O. Hofius finds in Paul and in the Jewish tradition (especially 2 Macc. 7:28) a connection between creation *ex nihilo* and the eschatological resurrection of the dead ("Eine altjüdische Parallele zu Röm. IV.17b," *NTS* 18 [1971-72], 93-94).

65. See esp. *Jos. and As.* 8:9: "Lord, God of my father Israel, highest and most powerful God, who gives life to all things and calls from darkness into light, and from error into truth, and from death into life" (κύριε ὁ θεὸς τοῦ πατρός μου Ἰσραηλ, ὁ ὕψιστος καὶ δυνατὸς θεός, ὁ ζωοποιήσας τὰ πάντα καὶ καλέσας ἀπὸ τοῦ σκότους εἰς τὸ φῶς, καὶ ἀπὸ τῆς πλάνης εἰς τὴν ἀλήθειαν, καὶ ἀπὸ τοῦ θανάτου εἰς τὴν ζωήν). Cf. also *2 Clem.* 1:8.

ungodly" (v. 5): he creates out of the nothingness of people's empty, sinful lives a new, vibrant, spiritual life.[66]

There can be no doubt that Paul's language is quite close to this Jewish *creatio ex nihilo* tradition and that an allusion to either God's general creative power or his spiritual creative power would not be out of place in the context. However, if this were Paul's purpose, it is surprising that he speaks of God's calling things "as though" they existed; we would have expected him to say "calls things into being."[67] This leads us to conclude, somewhat hesitantly and reluctantly, that the clause cannot refer to God's creative power as such, whether general or spiritual. It is, then, the nature of God as "speaking of" or "summoning" that which does not yet exist as if it does that Paul must mean. And this interpretation fits the *immediate* context better than a reference to God's creative power, for it explains the assurance with which God can speak of the "many nations" that will be descended from Abraham.

18 As we have seen, a number of commentators hold that a new paragraph begins here.[68] However, while it is true that Paul shifts his focus a bit, spotlighting the positive characteristics of Abraham's faith in vv. 18-21, his attention is still on the promise: how Abraham responded to the promise — in faith — and how it was *that* faith which secured righteousness and what had been promised. The emphasis in v. 18 falls on the paradoxical description of Abraham's faith as "against hope, on the basis of hope."[69] No better explanation of the phrase can be found than Chrysostom's: "It was against man's hope, in hope which is of God." As Paul will explain in v. 19, Abraham had every reason, from a human point of view, to give up the attempt to produce a child through Sarah. His faith flew in the face of that hope which is founded on the evidence of reason and common sense — "hope" as we often use the word ("I hope to win the lottery"). Yet his faith was firmly based on the hope that springs from the promise of God. We note here that Abraham's faith is not described as a "leap into the dark," a completely baseless, almost irrational "decision" — as Christian faith is pictured by some

---

66. Käsemann; Wilckens; Schlier; Dunn. The most detailed defense of this view is given by Moxnes, who argues also that Paul applies this language to the Jews, to show that they are in the same position as Gentiles, requiring a conversion to become part of God's people (*Theology in Conflict,* pp. 241-50).

67. That is, in place of Paul's ὡς, we would have expected an εἰς τὸ εἶναι or simply εἰς. To be sure, ὡς can indicate result or purpose, but only rarely, and in constructions different from Paul's (LSJ and BAGD both list the consecutive and final uses of ὡς but note that they usually are found with the infinitive or subjunctive; none of the occurrences is close to the syntactical structure of Rom. 4:17b).

68. See the introduction to this section; note, e.g., Kuss.

69. Gk. παρ' ἐλπίδα ἐπ' ἐλπίδι. παρά could mean "beyond" here, but a more forceful point is made if it means "against" (BAGD).

"existentialist" theologians — but as a "leap" from the evidence of his senses into the security of God's word and promise.

As a consequence of his strong faith, Abraham "became the father of many nations."[70] Paul indicates that Abraham's clinging in faith to the divine promise resulted in the fulfillment of what he had been promised. Instead of Gen. 17:5, Paul quotes an earlier promise to Abraham, from Gen. 15:5. After inviting Abraham to contemplate the star-strewn desert sky, God promises him: "Thus shall your descendants be."[71] This suggests that, in Paul's mind, the "many nations" of which Abraham is the father are equivalent to the spiritual "seed" made up of believing Jews and Gentiles (see v. 16).

19 Verses 19-20 detail the way in which Abraham believed "against hope on the basis of hope." Almost all commentators make "weakening" subordinate to "observed," the normal relationship between a participle and finite verb. But Greek does allow for a reversal of these roles, with the finite verb expressing the subordinate thought, and this makes good sense in the present verse: "He did not weaken in faith[72] when he observed his own body."[73] The "against hope" aspect of Abraham's faith is accentuated, as Paul stresses that Abraham continued to believe God's promise to him even as he observed the physical condition that rendered the fulfillment of that promise so unlikely.

This physical evidence would certainly have given Abraham reason to doubt that he would produce offspring through Sarah. His own body was "already dead,"[74] in the sense that he was past the age when procreation was likely to occur — he was "about a hundred years old" (cf. also Heb. 11:12).[75]

---

70. This clause is introduced with an infinitival construction, εἰς τὸ γενέσθαι. This construction could specify (1) the content of Abraham's faith — "he believed that he would become the father of many nations" (Zahn; Michel); (2) the consequence of Abraham's faith — "he believed and as a result became the father of many nations" (NIV; NEB; JB; Käsemann; Cranfield); or (3) the purpose of his faith (with reference also, perhaps, to the purpose of God) — "he believed with the purpose that he might become the father of many nations" (NASB; Turner, 143; most earlier commentators and Murray; Dunn). The second of these interpretations is justified syntactically (see the additional note on 1:20) and is the most natural way to complete the verb.

71. Paul again quotes the LXX exactly (which is faithful to the MT).

72. Gk. τῇ πίστει. The dative is probably dative of respect: "did not weaken with respect to his faith."

73. Cf. RSV; TEV, JB; and, on the syntactical point, Zerwick, 263, 376.

74. "Dead" translates νενεκρωμένον, a perfect passive participle. Here, as is usually the case, the perfect tense connotes an existing state of affairs.

75. Paul's indication that Abraham was past the age of procreation creates difficulties for the notice in Gen. 25:1-2 that Abraham later bore six sons to another wife, Keturah. Augustine, noting the difficulty, suggested that only Sarah's barrenness stood in the way of Abraham's producing a child (*City of God* 16.28), but both this verse and Heb. 11:12 are clear in attributing physical disability to Abraham as well as Sarah. The best

Since Gen. 17:1 claims that Abraham was ninety-nine years old when the promise of offspring was renewed, Paul's is an acceptable approximation. But standing in the way of the fulfillment of the promise was not only Abraham's advanced age but the "deadness," the "barrenness," of Sarah, the woman predicted to be the mother of the child through whom Abraham's "seed" would come. Since the word "deadness"[76] is not the normal word for a woman's barrenness, Paul has deliberately chosen his language to make clear that Abraham's faith with respect to this promise was specifically faith in the "God who gives life to the dead" (v. 17b). In another way, also, our faith is to be like Abraham's, as Calvin eloquently notes:

> Let us also remember, that the condition of us all is the same with that of Abraham. All things around us are in opposition to the promises of God: He promises immortality; we are surrounded with mortality and corruption: he declares that he counts us just; we are covered with sins: He testifies that he is propitious and kind to us; outward judgments threaten his wrath. What then is to be done? We must with closed eyes pass by ourselves and all things connected with us, that nothing may hinder or prevent us from believing that God is true.

20 This verse resumes and expands on what we have identified as the main point of v. 19: "[Abraham] did not weaken when he considered. . . ."[77] The Greek phrase equivalent to "the promise of God"[78] comes first in the sentence for emphasis. When Paul says that Abraham did not "doubt . . . because of unbelief,"[79] he means not that Abraham never had

---

solution is to assume that the procreative power granted by God to Abraham was not confined to the birth of Isaac alone, but remained with him afterward also (Bengel; Calvin).

76. Gk. νέκρωσις.

77. If, however, "observe" is the main verb of v. 19, then v. 20 will express a thought adversative to it (cf. δέ, "but"): "he considered . . . but did not doubt the promise of God because of unbelief" (e.g., Godet).

78. The preposition εἰς that introduces this phrase means "with reference to" and depends on διεκρίθη ("doubt"). This gives a more natural sense than translating εἰς "looking unto" and attaching it more loosely to διεκρίθη; cf. Barrett's translation: "Looking rather to God's promise, he did not waver . . ." (cf. also Turner, 266). J. R. Mantey ("The Causal Use of ΕΙΣ in the New Testament," *JBL* 70 [1951], 46-47) suggests a causal use of εἰς here ("did not waver because of the promise"), but this meaning for εἰς is too rare — some would say it is nonexistent — to be applied to a text that makes sense with other, more accepted meanings.

79. τῇ ἀπιστίᾳ is probably a relatively rare example of the causal dative; although it could also be a dative of "sphere" — "he did not waver 'in' the attitude of disbelief." This "unbelief" might be better termed "dis-belief": as Michel says, "Unbelief is more than a negation of faith: what is meant is the refusal to believe, the renunciation of the promise of God that has been given" (ἀπιστία ist mehr als eine Negation von πίστις: gemeint ist die Absage an den Glauben, der Verzicht auf die angebotene Verheissung Gottes").

momentary hesitations, but that he avoided a deep-seated and permanent attitude of distrust and inconsistency in relationship to God and his promises.[80] Unlike the "double-souled" person who displays a deeply rooted division in his attitude toward God (Jas. 1:6-8), Abraham maintained a single-minded trust in the fulfillment of God's promise.[81]

In contrast to[82] Abraham's refusal to waver in disbelief, he "grew strong[83] in faith." This phrase might refer to the procreative power that Abraham attained through his faith.[84] But the natural contrast between "he did not weaken in faith" in v. 19a and this clause makes it probable that "faith" is the object rather than the means or cause of the "strengthening": it was Abraham's faith itself that grew stronger.[85] In what way did Abraham's faith "grow strong"? In the sense that anything gains strength in meeting and overcoming opposition — muscles when weights are raised; holiness when temptation is successfully resisted. So Abraham's faith gained strength from

---

80. διεκρίθη is the aorist passive deponent form (the Greek of the NT period is prone to use aorist passives for deponent verbs; cf. BDF 78) of the verb διακρίνω, which in the deponent form means "to be divided" or "to waver" (used as the opposite of faith also in 14:23; Matt. 21:21; Mark 11:23; Jas. 1:6). However, the suggestion that διακρίνω here must mean "decide that a thing is impossible" (F. C. Synge, "Not Doubt But Discriminate," *ExpTim* 89 [1977-78], 203-5) goes too far in this direction.

81. Paul's insistence that Abraham "did not waver because of unbelief" in the face of God's promise that he would foster offspring seems to be unjustified in light of Gen. 17:17, which says that Abraham, when told that Sarah would bear him a son, "fell on his face and laughed, and said in his heart 'Will a child be born to a man one hundred years old? And will Sarah, who is ninety years old, bear a child?' " The apparent conflict can be resolved in three main ways. (1) The reaction of Abraham in Gen. 17:17 may be understood as an "expression of wonder" at the promise rather than a reaction of disbelief (Calvin; and Philo suggests something like this [*Questions and Answers on Genesis* 3.55]). But Abraham's request immediately afterward that God might work through Ishmael, as well as the parallel with respect to Sarah in Gen. 18:12-15, makes this suggestion unlikely. (2) We might confine Paul's comment to the situation as described in Gen. 15 (Godet; Meyer). For it is a promise from Gen. 15:5 that is quoted in v. 18, where this immediate discussion begins. This is a more likely possibility and may well be right. But (3) we might also stress the meaning of the word διακρίνω as we have brought it out above and suggest that Paul is not denying the presence of some degree of doubt in Abraham's faith (for, after all, he was a sinful human) but is focusing on the heart attitude of Abraham toward God's promise.

82. Gk. ἀλλ'.

83. Gk. ἐνεδυναμώθη. The translation "grew strong" is preferable to treating it as a genuine passive — "he was strengthened [by God]" (Cranfield; Wilckens) — or as equivalent to a middle with reflexive force — "he strengthened himself" (suggested, though not adopted, by Godet).

84. Especially if τῇ πίστει is a causal or instrumental dative (BDF 196[1]; Turner, 242; Käsemann) — "he grew strong because of or through faith"; cf. S-H.

85. The dative, then, is probably a dative of reference (Barrett; Murray; Cranfield).

its victory over the hindrance created by the conflict between God's promise and the physical evidence. And in this strengthening of his faith, Abraham gave "glory[86] to God." In his faithful response to God's word, Abraham therefore accomplished what the idolaters of 1:21 failed to do.

21 The sentence begun in v. 20 is continued. As "giving glory to God" denotes the result of Abraham's growing strong in faith, "being fully convinced[87] that he was able also to do what had been promised" repeats and further describes what this "growing strong" means. It is Abraham's conviction that God is fully able to do whatever he promised that enabled his faith to overcome the obstacle of the tangible and visible "facts."

22 "Wherefore"[88] indicates that this verse draws a consequence or conclusion from the preceding verses. Paul certainly sees this as the conclusion of the immediately preceding verses, in which he has described Abraham's faith (vv. 18-21). And since these verses include aspects of the promise that are brought out in Gen. 17 and later, it would seem that Paul agrees to this extent with the Jewish tradition, that the faith Abraham exercised in Gen. 15:6 is explained and exemplified in the later career of the patriarch. But the verse may serve to conclude more than the immediate section. With a last reference to Gen. 15:6, Paul rounds off the discussion of that verse which has been the constant touchstone since v. 3. Now, in a sense, Paul's "historical" exposition is ended, and he can turn in application to his Christian readers.

iv. The Faith of Abraham and the Faith of the Christian (4:23-25)

23And it was not written for him only, that "it was reckoned to him," 24but also for us, to whom it was going to be reckoned, to those who believe in the one who raised Jesus our Lord from the dead, 25who was handed over because of our trespasses and raised for our justification.

While these three verses are related to vv. 18-22, they can be considered a separate paragraph because they draw conclusions from the entire exposition of vv. 3-22. Paul has, of course, applied his far-ranging exposition of Gen. 15:6 to Christians throughout the chapter, in both explicit and implicit ways.

---

86. Gk. δούς. The participle, though aorist, describes action coincidental with the verb it modifies. This happens far more often than some grammars suggest.

87. Gk. πληροφορηθείς, a participle that is coordinate with δούς at the end of v. 20. πληροφορέω is frequently a synonym of πληρόω ("fill, fulfill"; cf. Luke 1:1; 2 Tim. 4:5, 17), but in the papyri it can denote the "completion" of business transactions (MM). From these meanings, it takes on the nuance of "fill with certainty," "be fully persuaded." This is its meaning here, in Rom. 14:5, and (perhaps) in Col. 4:12.

88. Gk. διό.

But nowhere does he so solemnly and clearly state the application as he does here.

23   The conviction expressed in vv. 23-24 that what is written in Genesis about Abraham has relevance to the Christian believer has been the implicit assumption of the whole of chap. 4. There is a close relationship between vv. 23-24 and v. 22: "[It was the faith delineated in vv. 18-21 that] 'was reckoned' to Abraham for righteousness (22), but this 'it was reckoned' was written not for his sake only (23), but also for ours. . . ." Paul's conviction that the OT everywhere speaks to Christians is fundamental to his theology and preaching.[1] In the interests of avoiding hermeneutical foolishness, however, we must be quite clear in what way various parts and verses of the OT are relevant to the Christian. In the case of Gen. 15:6, the significance is clear and very direct. Christians share with Abraham the same basis for justification — faith — and the same God as the object of that faith. Paul cites only the words "it was reckoned to him" from Gen. 15:6 in v. 23, perhaps as a "shorthand" allusion to the verse, or perhaps because all along it has been Paul's concern to unfold the meaning of that "reckoning." It is *faith* that is "reckoned": a faith that is *apart from works, apart from circumcision, apart from the law, apart from sight* — and therefore a "reckoning" that is solely a matter of *grace*.

24   Paul chooses to describe Christians in two parallel clauses,[2] each of which brings out their connection with Abraham. First, Christians are those "to whom it was going to be[3] reckoned": that is, those people who experience in its eschatological fullness the righteousness that Abraham attained by faith. Second, Christians are "those who believe in the one who raised Jesus our Lord from the dead." It is typical for Paul to designate God as the one who raised Jesus from the dead (cf. 8:11; 10:9; 1 Cor. 6:14; 15:15; 2 Cor. 4:14), but it is somewhat unusual for him to designate God himself as the object of Christian faith. Undoubtedly he does so here to bring Christian faith into the closest possible relationship to Abraham's faith. Not only is our faith of the

---

1. See also, e.g., Rom. 15:4 and 1 Cor. 10:11.

2. The first is introduced with a relative pronoun (οἷς) dependent on ἡμᾶς ("us"); the second uses a substantival participle (τοῖς πιστεύουσιν) that is in apposition to οἷς (and/or ἡμᾶς).

3. It is not clear why Paul uses the word μέλλει ("going to be") here. He may be thinking of the "reckoning" of the future judgment, when justification will receive its final ratification (see 3:30 — e.g., Schlatter). But the concentration in 4:25 and 5:1ff. on the present, this-life, verdict of justification experienced by the believer suggests rather that the word has a logical rather than a temporal meaning: "every time the condition shall be fulfilled, the same imputation will certainly take place" (Godet; cf. also Cranfield; Wilckens). Paul looks at our justification from the standpoint of the promise to Abraham: Christians are those who eventually experienced the justification promised to him.

same nature as Abraham's; it ultimately has as its object the same God, "who gives life to the dead" (cf. v. 17b). And the connection is even closer. For Abraham's faith in God had to do not just with the miraculous creation of life where there was "deadness," but with the fulfillment of God's promise to bless the world through him. It is the God of the promise, the promise given to Abraham but ultimately fulfilled in Christ and Christians, in whom both Abraham and we believe. While, therefore, the locus of faith has shifted as the course of salvation history has filled out and made ever more clear the specific content of the promise, the ultimate object of faith has always been the same.

25 The last words of v. 24 have a rather solemn tone, and this is continued in v. 25. The two clauses of the verse exhibit a clear parallelism:

> who   was handed over   because of our trespasses[4]
> and   was raised   because of our justification[5]

Most commentators think that this parallelism betrays the presence of a pre-Pauline tradition.[6] This may well be the case, although it must be insisted that, if so, Paul has fully integrated the elements of the tradition into his exposition. But, whether traditional or not, the wording resembles that of the LXX of Isa. 53, particularly v. 12: "because of their sins he was handed over."[7] As is probably the case in Isaiah, and certainly in Paul (cf. 8:32), the passive "was handed over" is a "divine passive," God being the implied agent of the action. God the Father has himself taken the initiative in giving up his Son to and for sinful people (cf. 3:25: "God set forth Christ as a propitiation").

The second line of the formula — "who was raised because of our justification"[8] — may allude to Isa. 53 as well, for the LXX of v. 11 (which differs widely from the MT) speaks of the servant as "justifying the righ-

---

4. Gk. παραπτώματα. Paul uses παράπτωμα as an equivalent to ἁμαρτία ("sin") (cf. Eph. 2:1).

5. Gk.: ὃς   παρεδόθη   διὰ   τὰ παραπτώματα ἡμῶν
         καὶ   ἠγέρθη   διὰ   τὴν δικαίωσιν ἡμῶν.

6. See, e.g., Wengst, *Christologische Formeln,* pp. 101-3, for a discussion; Stuhlmacher, "Jesus' Resurrection and the View of Righteousness in the Pre-Pauline Mission Congregations," in *Reconciliation, Law and Righteousness,* pp. 55-56.

7. The Greek of Isaiah here is διὰ τὰς ἁμαρτίας αὐτῶν παρεδόθη. Jeremias suggests that there may be influence from the Aramaic targum of Isa. 53:5b — אתמסר בַּעֲוָיָתַנָא (*The Servant of God* [London: SCM, 1965], p. 89).

8. The Greek word for "justification" here is δικαίωσις instead of Paul's usual δικαιοσύνη. By form, δικαίωσις would suggest more of an emphasis on the process as opposed to the results of the action (BAGD). But any such distinctions here are precarious, since Paul might be quoting tradition.

teous."[9] But the allusion is not clear, since the meaning of the LXX is not the same as Paul's. The puzzling feature of the second line is the connection Paul suggests between Jesus' resurrection and our justification. Paul uses a preposition that normally means "because of"; and if we give it this meaning here, Paul will be suggesting that our justification was in some sense a cause of Jesus' resurrection. Godet, who argues for this meaning, suggests that Paul is teaching that Christ's death had definitively effected justification and that his resurrection was therefore the "necessary effect." Yet it is difficult to see why this would be so, and Paul has hitherto used "justification" with reference to the subjective appropriation through faith. Accordingly, we can give the preposition a "prospective" reference — "because of" in the sense of "because of the need to," "for the sake of": Christ was raised "for the sake of" our justification.[10] The problem with this interpretation is that it is difficult to give this meaning to the same preposition because it is used in the parallel first clause. Some attempt to find this meaning there also by suggesting that we add an inference: "he was handed over for the sake of [for the purpose of] *taking care of* transgressions."[11] But since maintaining the same meaning for this preposition in both lines requires questionable additions or interpretations of one line or the other, it is probably best to give the word a retrospective meaning in the first line and a prospective meaning in the second: "he has handed over *because of* our trespasses [e.g., because we are sinners], and was raised *for the sake of* our justification [e.g., in order to secure our justification]."

Finally, the theological implications of the formula need to be explored. Particularly striking, because unusual, is the connection made between Christ's resurrection and our justification. To be sure, it would be easy to make too much of this; the division of the lines may be purely for rhetorical effect, the whole formula saying no more than that Jesus' death and resurrection are basic to the believer's salvation.[12] There is some truth to this, as is clear from

9. δικαιῶσαι δίκαιον. Cf. A. Feuillet, "Les attaches bibliques des Antithèses pauliniennes dans la première partie de l'Epître aux Romains (1–8)," in *Mélanges bibliques en hommage au R. P. Béda Rigaux* (ed. A. Descamps and A. de Halleux; Gembloux: Duculot, 1970), pp. 332-33; Cranfield.

10. Gifford; Hodge; Murray. For this prospective use of διά, see Matt. 24:22; Mark 2:27; John 11:42; 12:30; 1 Cor. 11:9 and BDF 222; Turner, 267-68; Harris, "Prepositions," pp. 1183-84; A. Oepke, *TDNT* II, 69-70; Moule, *Idiom Book*, p. 55: "while the commonest sense [of διά with acc.] is *because of* (consecutive), some steps are traceable towards the final or prospective sense, *for the sake of* or *with a view to.*" (Modern Greek γιά is customarily used to state purpose.)

11. Cf. Turner, 268; D. M. Stanley, *Christ's Resurrection in Pauline Soteriology* (AnBib 13; Rome: Pontifical Biblical Institute, 1961), p. 172; and most commentators.

12. B. McNeil, "Raised for Our Justification," *ITQ* 42 (1975), 104-5; Kuss; Nygren; Fitzmyer.

the fact that Paul would obviously not want to separate Christ's death (the first line) from our justification (the second line). But when due allowance is made for rhetoric, we must still insist that Paul is affirming here a theological connection between Jesus' resurrection and our justification (cf. 5:10). As Jesus' death provides the necessary grounds on which God's justifying action can proceed, so his resurrection, by vindicating Christ and freeing him forever from the influence of sin (cf. 6:10), provides for the ongoing power over sins experienced by the believer in union with Christ.

III. THE ASSURANCE PROVIDED BY THE GOSPEL: THE HOPE OF SALVATION (5:1–8:39)

In this letter to the Romans, Paul explains and defends his gospel to a Christian community he has neither founded nor visited but which he hopes to enlist as supporters of an evangelistic campaign in the western Mediterranean. To accomplish this purpose, Paul writes a "tractate"-style letter with a careful and logical structure. After introducing himself as one "set aside for the gospel" and announcing his plans to bring that "good news" to Rome (1:1-15), Paul justifies his commitment to the gospel because it transmits "God's power that brings salvation" (1:16). And why does the gospel have such power? Because, Paul explains, it reveals God's justifying activity — and all who respond to that activity in faith become "just" before God (1:17). This teaching of "justification by faith," so basic to Paul's gospel, is the theme of the first major section of the letter (1:18–4:25). To explain why God has manifested this new justifying activity, and why it can be experienced only by faith, Paul shows that all people have rebelled against God and are helpless under the power of sin, unable of themselves to do anything to escape God's impartial judgment (1:18–3:20). But, expanding on 1:17, Paul shows how God's sacrifice of his Son has enabled him both to rescue people from this dilemma and to do it without violating his own holy justice (3:21-26). Again, though, Paul stresses that this new relationship with God is available only for those who believe — it cannot be attained by works, or by circumcision, or by the law (3:27–4:25). But, as these last negations reveal, Paul's exposition of the gospel has constant reference to Jewish viewpoints. In both major sections of 1:18–4:25, Paul shows how the revelation of God's righteousness erases distinctions between Jews and Gentiles: the Jew, like the Gentile, is under the power of sin (3:9); the Jew, like the Gentile, can be justified only by faith (3:28-30).

How does chap. 5 carry on Paul's argument? Since Paul continues to stress justification (5:1, 9, 16-19, 21) and only at 6:1 breaks the course of the argument with a rhetorical question about the Christian life, chap. 5 could be closely connected to 1:18–4:25, with chaps. 6–8 forming the second major section of the letter.[1] This has been a very popular way of outlining the letter, with 1:18–5:21 and 6–8 often being viewed as describing, respectively, "justification" and "sanctification."[2] Another way of looking at the matter is to place a major transition at the middle of the chapter, with 1:18–5:11 being dominated by the antithesis between sin and justification and 5:12–8:39 by the antithesis between life and death.[3] Each section would then go over similar ground, with an introductory section on sin (1:18–3:20; 5:12-21) and a concluding section on hope (5:1-11; 8:18-39).[4] Still others insist that the chapter is transitional and refrain from attaching it more to what precedes or to what follows.[5] But, as the heading to the section indicates, I think it better to place the transitional point between chaps. 4 and 5. To be sure, this whole question requires caution, lest we impose on the letter a rigidly logical, dogmatically oriented outline that Paul may never have intended. After all, he is writing a letter, not a systematic theology.[6] Nevertheless, while mindful of the danger of oversystematizing and of erecting barriers between sections so that the continuity of Paul's argument is lost,[7] Paul *is* arguing, and arguing *theologically;* therefore, it is quite appropriate to look for transitions in that argument. While we must not draw too heavy a line between chaps. 4 and 5, the progress of Paul's argument reveals a transition in topic at this point.[8]

1. The best recent defense of this structure is to be found in Wilckens (1.286-87) and Dunn (1.242-44; although he also speaks of chap. 5 as a "bridging" chapter; cf. also his "Paul's Epistle," pp. 2856-57). Cf. also Godet, 59, 231; Murray, 1.211-12; Ridderbos, 104-5, 124; Kuss, 1.199; Morris, 217; Hoppe, *Idee der Heilsgeschichte,* pp. 78-79; M. Wolter, *Rechtfertigung und zukünftiges Heil: Untersuchungen zu Röm 5,1-11* (BZNW 43; Berlin: de Gruyter, 1978), pp. 214-16.

2. E.g., Godet; Lagrange.

3. Cf. Melanchthon, who comments on 5:12, "now there follows, as it were, a new book" (pp. 131-32). See also A. Feuillet, "Le règne de la mort et le règne de la vie (Rom V, 12-21)," *RB* 77 (1970), 481-521; H. A. Lombard, "The Adam-Christ 'Typology' in Romans 5:12-21," *Neot* 15 (1981), 83.

4. Leenhardt, 131; cf. also F. Hahn, "Das Gesetzverständnis im Römer- und Galaterbrief," *ZNW* 67 (1976), 43.

5. Black, 81; Sanders, *Paul and Palestinian Judaism,* pp. 486-87; B. N. Kaye, *The Thought Structure of Romans with Special Reference to Chapter 6* (Austin, TX: Schola, 1979), pp. 1-13; P. M. McDonald ("Romans 5.1-11 as a Rhetorical Bridge," *JSNT* 40 [1990], 81-96) sees 5:1-11 as a bridge paragraph, in which Paul argues from an identity with his readers.

6. See especially the warnings of Beker, 66-69.

7. We are thinking particularly of A. Schweitzer's strict division of the argument of Rom. 1–8 into two "craters," one focusing on justification (1-5) and the other, the "main" crater, on "mysticism" *(Mysticism,* pp. 225-26, passim).

8. This division was advocated by Bengel, 61, and finds a large number of contemporary advocates. See esp. Nygren, 187-89; Cranfield, 1.252-54; Beker, 83-86;

Four main arguments combine to show that Paul intends a transition in the letter at 5:1. First, the opening phrase of the chapter, "having been justified by faith," summarizes the argument of 1:18–4:25 while preparing the way for a new topic that will build on it. Second, a shift in style at 5:1 is noticeable. 1:18–4:25 has a polemical tone — Paul is plainly *arguing* against a (mainly) Jewish viewpoint, sometimes addressing his opponent directly in the second person singular. But with 5:1, the first person plural begins to dominate, Paul including fellow Christians with him in a more "confessional" style: "*we* have peace," "access," "*we* rejoice," "Christ died for *us*," "*we* are now justified," "*we* have now received our reconciliation." While not as concentrated as in 5:1-11 (from which the quotations are taken), this style recurs throughout chaps. 5–8.[9] A third indication that a shift in focus occurs at 5:1 is the relative frequency of certain key words in chaps. 5–8 in comparison with 1:18–4:25. Particularly striking is the contrast between the 33 occurrences of "faith" and "believe" in 1:18–4:25 and the three uses in chaps. 5–8 (and two of the latter refer back to the argument in 1:18–4:25). On the opposite side, "life" and "to live," used only twice in the first section, occur 24 times in chaps. 5–8. No such clear contrast is present in "righteousness" words: there are 26 in 1:18–4:25 and 16 in chaps. 5–8. But a closer analysis reveals a significant difference. In the earlier section, the great majority of occurrences focus on justification as the status attained by the sinner through faith, while in chaps. 5–8 the connection with faith is rare, the words denoting the status of justification as the means to eternal life (5:12-21) or having a more "ethical" connotation as a description of the Christian obligation (6:15-23). While statistics are easily used (or abused!) to prove anything anyone wants, these figures concern key words in Paul's argument and signal a significant shift in focus.[10]

The fourth, and most important, argument for connecting chap. 5 more closely with what follows than with what precedes is that it provides a more convincing reading of what Paul is teaching in this part of the letter than any

---

P. Rolland, " 'Il est notre justice, notre vie, notre salut.' L'ordonnance des themes majeurs de l'Epître aux Romains," *Bib* 56 (1975), 394-404. There are, however, no grounds for thinking of these chapters as a separate composition (contra R. Scroggs, "Paul as Rhetorician: Two Homilies in Romans 1–11," in *Jews, Greeks and Christians: Religious Cultures in Late Antiquity. Essays in Honor of William David Davies* [ed. R. Hamerton-Kelly and R. Scroggs; SJLA 21; Leiden: Brill, 1976], pp. 271-98).

9. Paul uses first person plural verbs 13 times in Rom. 1–4, mainly editorially or as a stylistic device; in Rom. 5–8, however, there are 48 first person plural verbs. On this point, cf. particularly Beker, 78.

10. The argument from word frequency was used by Nygren, 187-89, and criticized by Feuillet ("La citation d'Habakuk," pp. 55-56).

alternative is able to give. As several scholars have noticed, key words found in 5:1-11 recur again in 8:18-39. Note the following:

	5:1-11	5:12–8:16	8:18-39
"love" (of God/Christ)	5:5, 8	—	8:35, 39
"justify"	5:1, 9	6:7	8:30 (twice), 33
"glory"	5:2	6:4	8:18, 21, 30 ("glorify")
"peace"	5:1	8:6	—
"hope"	5:2, 4, 5	—	8:20, 24 (four times), 25
"tribulation"	5:3 (twice)	—	8:35
"save"	5:9, 10	—	8:24
"endurance"	5:3, 4	—	8:25

Both 5:1-11 and 8:18-39 affirm, against the threat of tribulation and suffering, the certainty of the Christian's final salvation because of God's love, the work of Christ, and the ministry of the Holy Spirit.[11] This theme, the "hope of sharing in God's glory" (cf. 5:2 and 8:18, 30), "brackets" all of chaps. 5–8. Assurance of glory is, then, the overarching theme in this second major section of Romans.[12] The verdict of justification, which Jews relegated to the day of judgment, has, Paul proclaims, already been rendered over the person who believes in Jesus. But can that verdict, "hidden" to the senses, guarantee that one will be delivered from God's wrath when it is poured out in the judgment? Yes, affirms Paul. Nothing can stand in its way: not death (5:12-21), not sin (chap. 6), not the law (chap. 7) — nothing! (chap. 8). What God has begun, having justified and reconciled us, he will bring to a triumphant conclusion, and save us from wrath.

As 8:18-39 shares a common theme with 5:1-11, so 8:1-17 has much in common with 5:12-21 (see the introduction to chap. 8). And sandwiched between these passages is 6:1–7:25. Here Paul focuses on the situation of the Christian in this life — a situation of some tension and conflict because, while

11. See esp. Dahl, 82-91. Contra Wilckens (1.287) and Wolter, *Rechtfertigung,* pp. 209-10, the parallels are far more than superficial verbal ones.

12. With differing emphases, this overriding theme is also stressed by R. Bultmann, "Romans 7 and the Anthropology of Paul," in *Existence and Faith. The Shorter Writings of Rudolf Bultmann* (New York: Meridian, 1960), pp. 147-57; Dodd, 71; Viard, 124-25; Lloyd-Jones, 2-4; Wright, "Messiah and People of God," p. 162; B. Byrne, "Living Out the Righteousness of God: The Contribution of Rom. 6:1–8:13 to an Understanding of Paul's Ethical Presuppositions," *CBQ* 43 (1981), 557-58; B. Lindars, "Paul and the Law in Romans 5-8: An Actantial Analysis," in *Law and Religion: Essays on the Place of the Law in Israel and Early Christianity* (ed. B. Lindars; Cambridge: James Clarke, 1988), pp. 130, 140.

transferred through our justification into the new realm of God's kingdom, the powers of the old realm to which we no longer belong nevertheless continue to influence us. Temptations to sin, the sufferings that are a part of our sin-sick world, and the last enemy — the death of the body — must still be faced. But, proclaims Paul, the God who has provided for the beginning of spiritual life (justification) and the end (glorification) also provides for the period "between." In union with Christ, we have been delivered from the tyranny of sin (chap. 6) and the law (chap. 7). At the risk of oversimplifying a complex section and obscuring many other significant connections, we may view the *main development* of chaps. 5–8 as a "ring composition," or chiasm:

A.	5:1-11	— assurance of future glory
B.	5:12-21	— basis for this assurance in work of Christ
C.	6:1-23	— the problem of sin
C'.	7:1-25	— the problem of the law
B'.	8:1-17	— ground of assurance in the work of Christ, mediated by the Spirit
A'.	8:18-39	— assurance of future glory

In a certain sense, then, 6:1–7:25 is parenthetical to the main point of the section.[13] But there are many points of contact between this central section and both chaps. 5 and 8, and the topics that are treated in it are hardly incidental.[14] It is also important to see that the concern for Jewish/Gentile relationships, and the related topic of the Mosaic law, so basic to Paul's argument in chaps. 1–4, is by no means dropped. In the midst of his depiction of life in Christ, Paul keeps inserting comments about the law (5:13-14, 20; 6:14-15), climaxing in the chapter-long discussion in 7, and spilling over into 8 (vv. 1-4, 7, 15). Paul does not lose sight of the larger theological issue against which, and in relation to which, he hammers out his teaching in Romans. Indeed, Paul contributes in a major way to this motif by showing how many of those privileges and blessings the Jews thought were their own through the law have been "transferred" to the new covenant community that exists "in Christ."[15]

In chaps. 5–8, then, Paul invites the Christian to join with him in joyful

---

13. Dahl, 82-91; Byrne, "Living Out," pp. 562-63; Jeremias, "Gedankenführung," p. 270; R. Schnackenburg, "Die Adam-Christus-Typologie (Röm 5,12-21) als Voraussetzung für das Taufverständnis in Röm 6,1-14," in Lorenzi, *Battesimo e Giustizia,* pp. 39-41.

14. Käsemann, 159; Kaye, *Thought Structure,* pp. 14-20; Barrett, Discussion in *Battesimo e Giustizia,* p. 56.

15. Cf. esp. Wright, "Messiah and People of God," passim; and Dunn, 1.242-43, for this emphasis.

thanksgiving for what the gospel provides — a new life given to God's service in this life and a certain, glorious hope for the life to come. At the same time Paul is continuing his defense of the gospel. His opponents (probably Jewish, mainly) attacked his message as proclaiming no more than a legal fiction — a "declaration" of a relationship that cannot be proved and which effects no change — and requires no change! — in this life and which offers no security for the day of judgment. Quite the contrary, Paul affirms, the person who has experienced the gospel as the justifying activity of God (cf. 1:17) is assured of finding that gospel to be truly "God's power for salvation" (cf. 1:16) — power for dedicated Christian service in this life and for deliverance from all the forces of evil and of judgment in the next.[16]

A. THE HOPE OF GLORY (5:1-21)

1. From Justification to Salvation (5:1-11)

> 1*Having, therefore, been justified by faith, we have[17] peace with*

---

16. Several scholars suggest that 1:17 is the theme of 1:18–4:25 and 1:16 the theme of chaps. 5–8 (see the notes on 1:16-17). Caution about emphasizing the connection too strongly is in order, since, as U. Luz points out ("Zum Aufbau von Röm. 1-8," *TZ* 25 [1969], 161-81), there are few linguistic connections.

17. In a probable example of itacism (in which early scribes, hearing the text read, confused similar-sounding vowels [on which, see I. A. Moir, "Orthography and Theology: The Omicron-Omega Interchange in Romans 5:1 and Elsewhere," in *New Testament Textual Criticism: Its Significance for Exegesis. Essays in Honour of Bruce M. Metzger* {ed. E. J. Epp and G. D. Fee; Oxford: Clarendon, 1981}, pp. 179-83]), the manuscript tradition attests both the indicative ἔχομεν ("we have") and the (presumably) subjunctive ἔχωμεν ("let us have"). The subjunctive form has the stonger external attestation, being perhaps the original reading in the two most important Alexandrian uncials, ℵ and B (the early corrections make this uncertain), as well as in the secondary Alexandrian MSS A, C, 33, and 81, the western uncial D, and a part of the majority text. This reading was accepted by the majority of the Greek Fathers, who interpreted the exhortation as a command to cease from sin (cf. Schelkle and, e.g., Chrysostom). External evidence and scribal tendencies (it being easier to explain the change from a subjunctive to an indicative than vice versa) combine to make this reading very strong; and many modern commentators adopt it (Alford; S-H; Lightfoot; Kuss; Murray; Lagrange). It is then usually explained as an exhortation to "enjoy peace with God" or to "continue at peace" (cf. NEB; REB has changed).

Most modern translations and commentators, however, adopt the indicative ἔχομεν. While this reading does not have as strong external support as the subjunctive (correctors of ℵ and B, the Western MSS F and G, Ψ, the Alexandrian 1739, and part of the majority text), the context strongly favors a statement about what we have rather than an exhortation to enjoy what we have. To be sure, Paul can use ἔχωμεν in the sense "let

God through our Lord Jesus Christ, 2through whom also we have access[18] *into this grace in which we stand; and we boast in the hope of the glory of God. 3And not only this, but we boast also in our tribulations, knowing that tribulation produces endurance, 4and endurance a proven character, and proven character hope.*

5Now this hope will not put us to shame, because the love of God has been poured out into our hearts by the Holy Spirit who has been given to us. 6For while we were still weak, at just the right time,[19] *Christ died for godless people. 7For hardly ever will someone die for a righteous person; although for a good person one might dare to die. 8But God commends his own love for us, in that while we were still sinners Christ died for us.*

9Therefore how much more, having now been justified through his blood, will we be saved through him from wrath. 10For if, while we were enemies, we were reconciled to God through the death of his Son,

---

us experience" (cf. Rom. 15:4). But this meaning does not work well with the clearly objective "peace" (status of reconciliation); and other suggested glosses of ἔχωμεν lack lexical justification. The decision, then, lies in balancing the claims of external evidence and scribal probabilities on the one hand and Pauline usage and context on the other. Since the itacism involved makes a very early change from one to the other so easy (Lietzmann, indeed, suggests that Tertius, Paul's scribe, may have written ἔχωμεν after Paul had dictated ἔχομεν), preference should probably be given to internal considerations. We accept, therefore, and assume in the exposition, the indicative.

18. After ἐσχήκαμεν ("we have"), a number of good MSS (e.g., the original hand of ℵ [and its second corrector], C, Ψ, 33, 81, 1739; cf. also the majority text) read τῇ πίστει; and others (e.g., the first corrector of ℵ and A) ἐν τῇ πίστει. Several modern English versions assume the adoption of this variant (e.g., NIV; NASB; REB; and cf. most older commentators and, e.g., Fitzmyer). It makes perfect sense to think of faith as the means by which we gain an introduction into grace; but it is just this appropriateness that makes the reading suspect as a later addition. We should probably, therefore, follow B, D, F, and G, and omit the phrases.

19. The textual situation in v. 6 is confused. The following readings need to be considered:

1. εἴ γε Χριστὸς ὄντων ἡμῶν ἀσθενῶν ἔτι κατὰ καιρὸν ὑπὲρ ἀσεβῶν ἀπέθανεν (B; this reading is adopted by Alford and S-H);
2. εἰς τί γὰρ Χριστὸς . . . ἔτι . . . (F and G; Black adopts this reading);
3. ἔτι γὰρ Χριστὸς . . . [omit] . . . (the second corrector of D, Ψ, 33, 1739, and the majority text; Tholuck, Godet, and Meyer adopt it);
4. ἔτι γὰρ Χριστὸς . . . ἔτι . . . (ℵ, A, C [probably], D [original hand], 81; adopted by most commentators).

Of these, the last has the best claim to be original since it provides the best explanation for the existence of the other variants. The double ἔτι has led to attempts to remove the first (accidentally or deliberately) by replacing it with similar words, and the second by omission.

how much more, being reconciled, will we be saved through his life.
11And not only this, but we also boast in God through our Lord Jesus
Christ, through whom we have received this reconciliation.

In this paragraph, Paul invites us to join with him in celebrating the marvelous benefits conferred upon the justified believer: "the Apostle speaks as one who is extremely happy and full of joy" (Luther); "it is now the believer who is speaking — in fact we might almost say, singing" (Leenhardt). Paul highlights two blessings in particular: "peace with God" (or reconciliation) and hope. The former theme occurs at the beginning (vv. 1-2a) and end (v. 11) of the paragraph while the latter is the focus of vv. 2b-10. Some scholars single out reconciliation as the key theme of the paragraph,[20] while a greater number think that hope is the central concept.[21] Still others decline to make a choice and give the paragraph a general heading such as "the blessings of justification."[22] This last alternative is alone broad enough to encompass everything in the paragraph. Paul proclaims that Christians are not only "justified" — "acquitted" in a legal sense — but placed into an entirely new situation, both in the present ("reconciliation") and in the future ("sharing the glory of God").[23] Nevertheless, of these two topics, it is "hope" that comes to dominate the paragraph — in v. 10, for instance, Paul argues from reconciliation to hope. Moreover, it is the topic of "hope" and "glory" that Paul elaborates on in 5:12-21 and 8:14-39, while reconciliation is mentioned without further attention or description.

---

20. E.g., Martin, *Reconciliation,* p. 139. Estimations of the importance of reconciliation language in Paul's theology vary widely. Martin, e.g., finds reconciliation to lie at the center of Paul's thinking, and thinks it is the overarching theme of Rom. 5–16 (cf. also J. Dupont, *La Réconciliation dans le Théologie de Saint Paul* [ALBO 2.32; Bruges/Paris: Desclée, 1953], pp. 50-52). Käsemann, however, takes a very different view, dismissing reconciliation as a concept that has very little importance in Paul ("Some Thoughts on the Theme 'The Doctrine of Reconciliation in the New Testament'," in *The Future of Our Religious Past: Essays in Honor of Rudolf Bultmann* [ed. J. Robinson; London: SCM, 1971], pp. 51-64). To some extent, these differences reflect differing decisions over whether to include as Pauline Colossians and Ephesians, in both of which letters reconciliation plays a role. But even if both letters are Pauline (as we think they are), reconciliation can hardly be given a central place in Paul's theology. The language is too infrequent and the concepts too undeveloped for such a judgment. It is better to view reconciliation as one image, among many others, that is used to capture something of the meaning of God's act in Christ for us.

21. Godet, 186; Kuss, 1.207; Schlier, 139; Dunn, 1.246; Wolter, *Rechtfertigung,* p. 217; Hoppe, *Idee der Heilsgeschichte,* p. 69; Watson, 144.

22. E.g., S-H, 118; Murray, 1.158; Barrett, 101; Wilckens, 1.288.

23. Cf., e.g., H. Ridderbos, "The Earliest Confession of the Atonement in Paul," in *Reconciliation and Hope,* pp. 84-85.

The central thrust of the passage is summarized in v. 2b — "we boast in the hope of the glory of God" — and v. 5a — "hope will not put us to shame." The enumeration of present benefits in vv. 1-2a leads up to this climax in v. 2b. The paradoxical boasting in tribulations of vv. 3-4 is something of an excursus, although it contributes to the central theme by showing that even the sufferings of the Christian lead on to hope (v. 4b). Verses 5-8 set Christian hope on the unshakable foundation of the love of God revealed in the cross. The parallel "how much more" arguments of vv. 9-10 reveal Paul's concern to show the unbreakable connection between the Christian's present status ("justified," "reconciled") and his fate in the judgment ("saved from wrath"). Verse 11, finally, picks up the "boasting" theme from vv. 2b-3a, returning to the peaceful relationship with God the believer may enjoy in this life.[24] Paul invites believers to take joyful pride in what God has given them; and, especially, he wants us to have complete assurance that God will deliver us from the final outpouring of his wrath on the day of judgment.[25]

1 The opening phrase of Rom. 5 is transitional. "Therefore, having been justified by faith" not only sums up the central teaching of Rom. 1–4, but, dependent as it is on the first person plural verb following, presents it as a blessing experienced by the readers of the letter. By believing in Jesus Christ, the divine agent in God's climactic act of deliverance, Paul and the Roman Christians — and Christians of all ages and places — have been declared innocent of all charges justly brought against those who "sin and fall short of God's glory" (3:23). Paul presents this declaration of justification as a past act, a perspective that is maintained throughout chaps. 5–8.[26] While justification brings to the believer a new and permanent status, justification itself is a once-for-all act by which God acquits the sinner. But what is the exact nature of this new status? What are its implications for our present lives and for the

---

24. For careful analyses of the structure of this paragraph, see Wolter, *Rechtfertigung,* p. 221; G. Nebe, *'Hoffnung' bei Paulus: Elpis und ihre Synonyme im Zusammenhang der Eschatologie* (SUNT 16; Göttingen: Vandenhoeck & Ruprecht, 1983), p. 124; and esp. N. S. L. Fryer, "Reconciliation in Paul's Epistle to the Romans," *Neot* 15 (1981), 36-39.

25. Schmithals thinks that 5:1-11 is an interpolation, a Pauline fragment that an editor has revised and inserted into Romans at this point. For sufficient refutation of this unlikely hypothesis, see Wilckens, 1.287. Equally unlikely is the claim that vv. 5-6 might be an interpolation (as argued by L. E. Keck, "The Post-Pauline Interpretation of Jesus' Death in Rom. 5,6-7," in *Theologica Crucis — Signum Crucis* [ed. C. Andresen and G. Klein; Tübingen: Mohr, 1979], pp. 237-48).

26. See also 5:9; 8:30; and even, probably, 8:33 (on which see the exegesis). The aorist tense of the participle δικαιωθέντες does not, in itself, require a past reference. But the context (see esp. v. 9) suggests that it does; in fact, the aorist participle, when it precedes the verb it modifies, is usually past-referring.

future? It is these questions that Paul takes up in this paragraph, and in chaps. 5–8 as a whole.

The first implication of our justification is that "we have peace with God." "Peace" is a word that, like so many in Paul and in the NT, must be understood according to its use in the LXX, where it translates the wide-ranging Hebrew word *shalōm*. As a result, the word "peace"[27] moves beyond the largely negative signification of the word in secular Greek — "peace" as the cessation or absence of hostilities — to a more positive nuance — the well-being, prosperity, or salvation of the godly person. These are often expressly treated as the gifts of God, as in the well-known benediction, "The LORD lift up his countenance on you and give you peace" (Num. 6:26). But especially important for Paul's usage is the OT prophets' use of the term peace to characterize the salvation that God would bring to his people in the "last days."[28] This background defines for us what Paul means by "peace with God": not an inner sense of well-being, or "feeling at peace" (what we might call the "peace *of* God" [cf. Phil. 4:7]), but the outward situation of being in a relationship of peace *with*[29] God.[30] While the word is not used again in this paragraph, the language of "reconciliation" in vv. 10-11 picks up this concept. "Peace," or "reconciliation" with God, then, "frames" this paragraph. And, despite our emphasis on the "positive" dimensions of "peace" in the OT, we must recognize that Paul conceives this "peace with God" or "reconciliation" as created out of a situation of hostility; it was while we were "enemies" of God that he reconciled us (v. 10). We were weak, ungodly, sinners (vv. 6-8) when God in his love brought us into a new relationship of peace with him.

"Peace with God" comes through, and only through, "our Lord Jesus Christ." As the ultimate locus of God's atoning, wrath-averting work, Christ is the one through whom the believing sinner receives justification (Rom. 3:25-26). Since peace with God, or reconciliation, is one way of viewing the new relationship into which we have been put by God's justifying act in Christ,

---

27. Gk. εἰρήνη.

28. See, e.g., Ezekiel's prediction of "a covenant of peace" (Ezek. 34:25; cf. also Isa. 54:10; Jer. 37:26). "Peace" in some contexts is virtually equivalent to "salvation" — see Isa. 52:7, the first line of which is quoted by Paul in Rom. 10:15: "How lovely on the mountains are the feet of him who brings good news (εὐαγγελίζομαι), who announces peace (εἰρήνη) and brings good news of happiness, who announces salvation (σωτηρία), and says to Zion, 'Your God reigns!' " See, e.g., W. Foerster, *TDNT* II, 400-408.

29. Gk. πρός, used to denote a "friendly relationship" (cf. BDF 239 [5]).

30. The clearest parallels to this use of εἰρήνη in Paul come in Eph. 2 (see vv. 14, 15, 17); cf. also Rom. 2:10; 8:6; 14:17(?). Paul's plea that God might give his readers "peace" (Rom. 1:7; 1 Cor. 1:3; 2 Cor. 1:2; Gal. 1:3; Eph. 1:2; Phil. 1:2; Col. 1:2; 1 Thess. 1:1; 2 Thess. 1:2; 1 Tim. 1:2; 2 Tim. 1:2; Tit. 1:4; Phlm. 3) and his references to the "God of peace" (Rom. 15:33; 16:20; 2 Cor. 13:11; Eph. 6:15; Phil. 4:9; 1 Thess. 5:23; 2 Thess. 3:16) may also have some allusion to this concept.

it can no more be achieved apart from Christ than can justification itself. That all God has for us is to be found "in" or "through" Jesus Christ our Lord is a persistent motif in Rom. 5–8: peace with God comes "through our Lord Jesus Christ" (5:1); our boasting in God is "through our Lord Jesus Christ" (5:11); grace reigns through righteousness, resulting in eternal life "through Jesus Christ our Lord" (5:21); the gift of God bringing eternal life is "in Christ Jesus our Lord" (6:23); thanks for deliverance are due to God "through Jesus Christ our Lord" (7:25); the love of God, from which nothing can ever separate the believer is "in Christ Jesus our Lord" (8:39). When we consider that these phrases occur in only one other verse in Romans (15:30), and that every chapter in this part of the letter concludes on this note, a very definite focus on this matter is evident here. It is well known that Romans lacks any extended christological discussion per se, but Paul's repeated insistence in these chapters that all the believer experiences of God's blessings comes only through Christ develops a very significant christological focus in its own right. Christology, we might say, is not the topic of any part of Rom. 5–8, but it is the basis for everything in these chapters.

2 As it is "through Jesus Christ our Lord" that we enjoy peace with God, it is through him also that "we have[31] access into this grace in which we stand." It is very difficult to know whether we should follow the NASB in translating "introduction" or the majority of English translations (e.g., KJV, NRSV, NIV, REB, and NAB) and translate "access."[32] With the former translation, Paul would be focusing on the believer's initial entry into the presence of the Lord Christ;[33] with the latter, the attention is more on the believer's continuing ability to enjoy the presence of Christ. As my translation suggests, however, I think the context — in which Paul focuses on the blessings enjoyed by the believer as a result of being justified — favors the translation "access."[34] Rather than making "God" the object of "access," as we

---

31. While using the same verb as in v. 1 (ἔχω), Paul now uses the perfect tense (ἐσχήκαμεν; the present tense is used in v. 1). Moulton, 145, thinks that this is an "aoristic" perfect, referring to a past event; BDF (243[2]) think that is a normal perfect. As we have suggested elsewhere in this commentary, there is good reason for thinking that the Greek perfect usually connotes a state of affairs. Both ἔχομεν in v. 1 and ἐσχήκαμεν here, then, refer to present time, but the latter puts more emphasis on the continuing situation of the believer.

32. The Greek word in question is προσαγωγή. It does not occur in the LXX and only in Paul in the NT.

33. The word is sometimes used of a person's being conducted into the presence of royalty (cf. LSJ, p. 1500, who refer to Xenophon, Cyr. 7.5.45; cf., e.g., Dunn; Morris).

34. In favor of this translation also are Paul's two other uses of the word (Eph. 2:18 and 3:12), in which he appears to denote present, ongoing conditions (see, e.g., Godet; Murray; Käsemann; Kuss). On the other hand, the verb that is cognate to this word (προσάγω) is used in 1 Pet. 3:18 of Christ's work of "introducing" the believer into the

might have expected (see Eph. 2:18), Paul chooses "grace."[35] But it is not just to "grace" in general that we have access; but to "this grace in which we stand."[36] Paul has stressed at key points in his argument that all the believer has comes by grace (3:24; 4:16). Grace describes the free, unconstrained manner in which God acts toward his creatures (see also Rom. 11:5-6). Later in Rom. 5, Paul will use "grace" to denote the act of God in Christ (vv. 15, 17). Here, however, grace is used with a slightly different nuance, denoting not the manner in which God acts, or the gift that God gives, but the "state" or "realm" into which God's redeeming work transfers the believer. It is the realm in which "grace reigns" (5:21), a realm that is set in contrast to the realm or domain of the law (6:14, 15: the believer is not "under the law" but "under grace"; cf. also Gal. 5:4).[37] Without denying the presence of God's grace throughout human history, Paul, along with the rest of the NT (cf. John 1:17), so focuses on God's work in Christ as that act in which God's grace was decisively and finally realized that he can picture the new status of the believer as one in which grace is characteristic and dominant. While this state of grace includes our justification as a key element,[38] the notion goes beyond justification to all that is conveyed to us by God in Christ.

Included in that panoply of blessings is hope. As Paul in vv. 1-2a looks at the present situation of the Christian in light of the past, he now begins to contemplate that situation in light of the future.[39] This is the note that will dominate this paragraph, and "we boast in the hope of the glory of God"[40] is the key assertion in the passage. The word "boast" suggests here confidence

---

presence of God; and the preposition εἰς may favor this more dynamic concept (cf. S-H; Cranfield). Since the verb προσάγω occurs widely in the LXX to describe the "offering" of sacrifices, some scholars discern sacrificial allusions here in Romans (e.g., Wolter, *Rechtfertigung,* 126; Käsemann; Wilckens). But Dunn and Fitzmyer are probably right to question this connotation, since in the LXX it is always the sacrifice rather than the worshiper that is "offered."

35. Indeed, Stuart and Tholuck take "God" to be the understood object of προσαγωγήν, making εἰς τὴν χάριν ταύτην ("in this grace") depend on τῇ πίστει ("by faith"). But not only is τῇ πίστει textually uncertain (see the note on the translation), but this reading of the syntax is quite awkward.

36. The verb here is again a perfect (ἑστήκαμεν), but the perfect form of this verb, when it has an intransitive meaning, is used for the present tense.

37. See Beker, 264-65; H. Conzelmann, *TDNT* IX, 395. J. Nolland shows that "grace" was used occasionally in the LXX to denote "tangible power at work" ("Grace as Power," *NovT* 28 [1986], 26-31).

38. Bengel, Murray, Cranfield, and others confine "this grace in which we stand" to justification.

39. Cf. Wolter, *Rechtfertigung,* p. 127.

40. ἐλπίδι τῆς δόξης τοῦ θεοῦ is well rendered in the TEV: "the hope we have of sharing [objective genitive] God's [possessive genitive] glory."

and joy; perhaps we could render "we are joyfully confident of."[41] "Boasting" in human achievement is excluded by the gospel (3:27; cf. 4:2), but "boasting" because of the gracious provision of God in Christ is entirely appropriate. As in 3:23, "the glory of God" is that state of "God-like-ness" which has been lost because of sin, and which will be restored in the last day to every Christian (cf. 8:17, 18, 21, 30). A joyful confidence in this prospect, overcoming our (proper) frustration at our present failure to be all that God would want us to be, should be the mark of every believer.

3a As Paul in the parallel 8:18-30 contrasts the "glory that will be revealed in us" with "present sufferings" (v. 18), so he here turns quickly from our boasting in the hope of God's glory to our boasting in "tribulations." As Gifford puts it, "No sooner has the Apostle pointed to 'the glory of God,' as a light shining afar to cheer the believer on his course, than he thinks of the contrast between that bright distance and the darkness that lies around him here." It is probably to head off criticism of his teaching that Paul introduces the "problem" of suffering. For (particularly) Jewish objectors would be likely to question Paul sharply about his affirmation that the Christian is enjoying "peace with God" when that same Christian is facing illness, persecution, and difficulties of all kinds. Indeed, Christians themselves, then as today, were surely wondering about the reality of these blessings in the face of suffering. Characteristically, Paul takes an offensive posture. Not only do sufferings not overthrow the reality of these blessings, but they are themselves occasions for joyful boasting! The believer should boast "not only" in the hope of the glory of God "but also" in afflictions. This means not merely that we are to exult "in the midst of" afflictions but that we are to exult "in"[42] the afflictions themselves: that is, to view them as a basis for further confidence in our redeemed status.

What are these "afflictions"?[43] Some would confine them to those sufferings caused directly by the believer's profession of Christ. But Paul's

---

41. The Greek verb is καυχώμεθα. This verb is difficult to translate; some versions choose "we are rejoicing" (most), others "we are boasting" (JB), still others "we exult" (REB; NASB; note NJB: we "look forward exultantly"). Perhaps "rejoicing" is the best choice, but the following ἐπί also suggests the nuance of "taking confidence in" (only here in the NT is ἐπί used after καυχάομαι; although cf. LXX Ps. 48:6; Prov. 25:14).

42. Gk. ἐν, introducing the object in which we boast, as often in the NT.

43. The Greek word is θλίψις. Besides those places where θλίψις refers to the afflictions of God's eschatological judgment (Rom. 2:9; 2 Thess. 2:9), Paul uses the word of the sufferings experienced by himself and other apostles (e.g., Eph. 3:13; Col. 1:24), and by Christians generally. Sometimes these sufferings are closely related to, and perhaps caused by, one's relationship to Christ (cf. 1 Thess. 1:6). But in most cases the reference is to any "external pressure" (θλίβω means originally to "press") that may afflict the believer in this life, including "distress, persecution, famine, nakedness, peril, the sword" (Rom. 8:35).

use of the word "affliction(s)" makes any such restriction questionable. Indeed, in a certain sense, all sufferings are "on behalf of Christ." This is so because all the evil that the Christian experiences reflects the conflict between "this age," dominated by Satan, and "the age to come," to which the Christian has been transferred by faith. All suffering betrays the presence of the enemy and involves attacks on our relationship to Christ. If met with doubt in God's goodness and promise, or bitterness toward others, or despair and even resignation, these sufferings can bring spiritual defeat to the believer. But if met with the attitude of "confidence and rejoicing" that Paul encourages here, these sufferings will produce those valuable spiritual qualities that Paul lists in vv. 3b-4.

3b-4 The reason why the believer can "rejoice in afflictions" is that he or she "knows"[44] that affliction "produces[45] endurance," and endurance, in turn, "a tested character," and a tested character, in turn, hope. Sequences of this kind, in which suffering inaugurates a chain of linked virtues, are introduced as a stimulus to face difficulties with joy in two other NT texts (1 Pet. 1:6b-7; Jas. 1:2-4) and must have been popular in the early church — probably reflecting earlier Jewish exhortation.[46] As in Jas. 1:3, the first virtue in the list is "endurance," a word that denotes the spiritual fortitude that bears up under, and is, indeed, made even stronger by, suffering.[47] It suggests that "stick-to-itiveness" which is required if the word of God is to produce fruit in us (Luke 8:15) and that long-distance, marathoner's endurance which will enable us to run the race set before us right to the finish line (Heb. 12:1). "Endurance," in turn, will, if our attitude is right, produce a "tested character."[48] As a result of this tested character, finally, the Christian who responds to sufferings with the proper attitude will find, at the end of the line, that hope has been strengthened. Sufferings, rather than threatening or weakening our hope, as we might expect to be the case, will, instead, increase our certainty in that hope. Hope, like a muscle, will not be strong if it goes unused. It is in

---

44. The participle εἰδότες is causal.

45. The Greek verb is κατεργάζομαι; see the note on 1:27.

46. Cf. M. Dibelius, *A Commentary on the Epistle of James* (rev. H. Greeven; Hermeneia; Philadelphia: Fortress, 1976), pp. 74-76.

47. Gk. ὑπομονή. On Paul's use, see the note on 2:7; and for — respectively — the secular and biblical Greek use of the word, see F. M. Festugière, "Ὑπομονή dans la tradition grecque," *RSR* 21 (1931), 477-86; C. Spicq, "ΥΠΟΜΟΝΗ, Patientia," *RSPT* 19 (1930), 95-106.

48. Gk. δοκιμή. In Jas. 1:3 (cf. also 1:12) and 1 Pet. 1:7, the cognate δοκίμιος refers to the "testing" or "testedness" of faith, but no occurrence of δοκιμή before Paul has been found. However, on the basis of these cognates, and his usage of the word elsewhere (2 Cor. 2:9; 8:2; 9:13; 13:3; Phil. 2:22), the word must mean "tested character," the quality of "having been proved." The verb δοκιμάζω means "test," "approve."

suffering that we must exercise with deliberation and fortitude our hope, and the constant reaffirmation of hope in the midst of apparently "hopeless" circumstances will bring ever-deeper conviction of the reality and certainty of that for which we hope (see Rom. 4:18-19).

5 This verse makes clear that "hope" is the focal point of 5:1-11. It functions as a "hinge" in the paragraph (Godet), attached on the one side to v. 2b, which v. 5a reiterates and expands, and on the other side to vv. 6-10, which v. 5b introduces. We can rejoice in hope, knowing it will not disappoint us, because of the "amazing grace" of God's love (vv. 5b-8) and because of the decisive and final significance of what God has done for us in Christ (vv. 9-10).

The first part of v. 5 — "Now this hope will not put us to shame" — is reminiscent of OT passages that affirm that those who hope in God will not "be put to shame."[49] Christians need not fear that the judgment will "put them to shame," in the sense that the foundation on which they have built their lives and hope for eternal blessing should prove inadequate. The last clause of the verse is causal: Christians are confident that they will not be put to shame "because[50] the love of God has been poured out into our hearts by the Holy Spirit who has been given to us." Granted this purpose, and Paul's choice of the verb "pour out," it is certain that we should paraphrase "the love of God for us" rather than "our love for God."[51] The confidence we have for the day of judgment is not based only on our intellectual recognition of the fact of God's love, or even only on the demonstration of God's love on the cross (although that is important; cf. vv. 6-8), but also on the inner, subjective certainty that God does love us. This is the point Paul is making by affirming that God's love has been "poured out in our hearts through the Holy Spirit who was given to us." The verb "pour out"[52] connotes an abundant, "extravagant," effusion: "he does not say 'given' but 'shed abroad in our hearts,' so showing the profusion of it" (Chrysostom). Paul uses this same

---

49. Ps. 22:6; 25:3, 20; Isa. 28:16 (quoted in 9:33 and 10:11). καταισχύνει, so accented (as in UBS[4]), is a present form of the verb; but it could also be a future: καταισχυνεῖ. Since the passages mentioned above all focus on future judgment, the future reading makes better sense: "hope" — the hope of the glory of God — "will not put us to shame" (Michel [as possible]; Käsemann; contra, e.g., Godet; Cranfield; Dunn — in either case, as Schlier notes, Paul is thinking of the final judgment). The active form of the verb implies an object, which must, of course, be ἡμᾶς, "us" — Christians.

50. Causal ὅτι.

51. That is, the genitive τοῦ θεοῦ is subjective rather than objective. Augustine (*Spirit and Letter* 32 [*NPNF* 5.108]) and Luther, among a few others, have advocated the objective genitive, but most ancient (cf. Schelkle) and modern commentators have insisted on the subjective genitive. The context makes it unlikely that both genitive relationships are intended (contra, e.g., Zerwick, 38).

52. Gk. ἐκκέχυται, from ἐκχύνω, the Hellenistic Greek form of ἐκχέω.

verb to depict the "pouring out" of God's Spirit (Tit. 3:6; cf. Acts 2:17, quoting Joel 2:28-32). This raises the possibility that the "real" subject of "pour out" is the Holy Spirit, who witnesses to our hearts of the love of God.[53] But we must respect Paul's decision to make "the love of God" the subject of the verb.[54] Paul is asserting two things at once: that God's love has been poured into our hearts in the past, and that this love is now within us.[55] And this love is conveyed to our sensations by the Holy Spirit, who resides in every believer.[56]

For the first time in Romans, Paul speaks of God's love, a topic that is more prominent in Paul than we sometimes realize (cf. Morris). Paul stresses that God's love for us is active — it is a love that gives to us and takes possession of us (cf., e.g., 2 Cor. 5:14: "the love of Christ controls us"), and which can stand for all that God has done and will do for us (cf. 8:35: "Who shall separate us from the love of Christ?"). Paul's language reflects prophetic descriptions of the eschatological gift of God's Spirit as part of the inauguration of the New Covenant.[57] That covenant promises a new and permanent relationship between God and his people, a relationship in which our "sins are remembered no more" (Jer. 31:34) and in which we are given a hope that involves "being changed into Christ's likeness from one degree of glory to another" (2 Cor. 3:12-18).[58] What in the Old Covenant was (in some respects, at least) external has been internalized in the New Covenant. And it is this internal, subjective — yes, even emotional — sensation within the believer that God does indeed love us — love expressed and made vital in real, concrete actions on our behalf — that gives to us the assurance that "hope will not disappoint us."[59]

6 Verses 6-8 form a single argument that demonstrates the abundant and absolute nature of God's love for us. We may summarize Paul's argument (making explicit some points that are implicit) as follows:

53. E.g., Barrett.

54. Cranfield.

55. Hence the perfect ἐκκέχυται and the use of ἐν rather than εἰς.

56. Since the verb is used several times in the Revelation of the "pouring out" of God's wrath (Rev. 16:1-17), some think that Paul may be implicitly contrasting the situation of the person in the "old age," who suffers God's wrath (1:18), with that of the Christian, who experiences God's love (e.g., Nygren). But Paul's failure ever to use this verb to depict the infliction of the wrath of God makes this suggestion unlikely.

57. See, as noted above, Joel 2:28 (3:1 in the LXX); also Jer. 31:31-34; Ezek. 36:25-27.

58. On the relationship between this text and the New Covenant, and the importance of this concept in Paul, see esp. Deidun, 128.

59. Lloyd-Jones especially stresses the subjective element in the believer's assurance implied by texts like this one.

a. Human love, at its best, will motivate a person to give his or her life for a truly "good" person (v. 7);

b. Christ, sent by God, died, not for "righteous" people, or even for "good" people, but for rebellious and undeserving people (v. 6);

c. Therefore: God's love is far greater in its magnitude and dependability than even the greatest human love (v. 8).

This argument functions not only to provide evidence for the love of God (and especially its profusion ["poured out"]) by tracing that love we experience in our hearts to its source but also, in doing so, to substantiate the utter dependability of our hope (v. 5a).[60] Paul accentuates the unity of the argument in vv. 6-8 by ending each sentence (in the Greek text) with the verb "die."[61]

The first sentence in Paul's argument (v. 6) is syntactically complex, but clear enough in its meaning: "For while we were still weak, at just the right time, Christ died for godless people."[62] Paul makes clear the point he especially wants to convey here by characterizing the human beings Christ died for as both "godless" and "weak." "Godless" is a strong pejorative term in Paul (cf. Rom. 4:5); "weak" is not always as negative, but here designates that "total incapacity for good" which is characteristic of the unredeemed.[63] Paul thereby stresses that God's love came to us when we were utterly helpless.[64]

60. γάρ ("for"), then, introduces all of vv. 6-8, and not just v. 6.

61. Gk. ἀποθνήσκω; cf. Käsemann.

62. The syntax in the Greek is confusing because of the two occurrences of ἔτι, one at the beginning of the verse and one toward the middle. Both probably modify the subordinate, genitive absolute clause — ὄντων ἡμῶν ἀσθενῶν ("while we were weak") — the first occurring early in the sentence for emphasis (cf. Moule, *Idiom Book,* p. 166), the second being added for clarity (this is the interpetation presupposed by all major English translations). For a good defense of this interpretation, see G. Bornkamm, "Paulinische Anakolouthe," in *Das Ende des Gesetzes. Paulusstudien* (BEvT 16; Munich: Kaiser, 1966), p. 79.

63. See Godet. The Greek word is ἀσθενής. Paul's use of this term here is somewhat unexpected. He uses this word, along with its cognate noun (ἀσθενία) and verb (ἀσθενέω), to refer to physical illness (Phil. 2:26-27; Gal. 4:13; 1 Tim. 5:23; 2 Tim. 4:10; 1 Cor. 11:30), but more typically he uses the word to characterize the human inability that is an inevitable part of life — even redeemed life — on this earth (see esp. 1 Cor. 15:43: "it [the body] is sown in weakness, it is raised in power" and the many occurrences in 2 Cor. 11:21–13:9, where Paul contrasts his own "weakness" with the supposed "strength" of his boastful opponents). See for this perspective L. Fatum, "Die menschliche Schwäche im Römerbrief," *ST* 29 (1975), 31-52. But his proposal to give ἀσθενής a generally "neutral" meaning (pp. 39-41) takes insufficient account of the context. For here ἀσθενής is roughly synonymous with ἀσεβής ("ungodly") and ἁμαρτωλός ("sinner," though there may be a gradation [Dunn]) and must have a more negative connotation.

64. Cf. Meyer.

Paul's assumptions about the intimate relationship between God and Christ, as well as his concern to highlight the practical, concrete nature of God's love, surfaces in his argument that *Christ's* dying "for[65] us" demonstrates the love *"of God"* (v. 5; and note the reference to the Holy Spirit in v. 5b). Paul never thinks of God's love for us apart from the cross, and he never thinks of Christ's dying for us apart from the Father's giving of the Son (cf. Rom. 3:25). The most puzzling element in this verse is the prepositional phrase "at just the right time." The phrase probably modifies the main clause of the verse, "Christ died for godless people."[66] But what does Paul mean by saying that Christ died "at the appropriate time"?[67] He may mean that it was the "right" time in world history for the sending of Christ and the proclamation of the gospel.[68] Or he may be thinking of the time as "right" because it was the time when, had not Christ died, God's wrath would have been poured out.[69] Related to both these suggestions, but with better foundation in Paul's theology, is the interpretation that takes "right time" to mean the culminating, eschatological "time" of God's intervention in Christ (see Rom. 3:26; 8:18; 13:11).[70] This last suggestion, which is the best of the three, is yet open to the objection that Paul usually adds a qualifier to "time" when it has this meaning. Considering the context, it is best to give the phrase a less theological and more prosaic meaning, and take it as further emphasizing "still": "Christ died for the ungodly just *at that very time* when we were weak."[71]

7   The main point of this verse is clear enough. Paul accentuates the love of God manifested in the cross of Christ by reminding us that the pinnacle of human love is the giving of one's life for a person one is close to — a spouse, child, or combat buddy — whereas God sent his Son to die for people who hated

---

65. Gk. ὑπέρ. Paul frequently uses this preposition to designate Christ's death as vicarious — e.g., a death "for," or "on behalf of," others. Paul's choice of this preposition is sometimes thought to exclude the notion of Christ's death as a substitution for the sinner's own penalty — the preposition ἀντί being the word that would clearly convey a substitutionary concept (e.g., Meyer; Gifford). However, while the focus in ὑπέρ is on representation, the idea of substitution is not necessarily lost; many instances of ὑπέρ include both, and this is probably the case here (Robertson, 632; Moule, *Idiom Book,* p. 64; Hodge; and cf., on this issue generally, Harris, "Prepositions," pp. 1196-97). In any event, the nature of Christ's death "for" us cannot finally be understood apart from the clear NT teaching that his death is *for* us because it is death suffered *in our place* (Mark 10:45; Rom. 3:25; Gal. 3:13; 1 Tim 2:6).

66. See, e.g., Godet; Murray; Käsemann; contra Calvin, Wilckens, and Schlier, who take it with the clause "while we still weak."

67. The Greek word is καιρός. This word differs from χρόνος in possessing (often, though not always) a more specific or definite meaning: "point in time" or "appropriate season" (cf. Trench, *Synonyms,* pp. 209-12).

68. As some interpret Gal. 4:4, "the fullness of time [χρόνου]" (S-H).

69. Godet.

70. Murray.

71. Käsemann; Dunn.

him (v. 8).[72] But Paul's way of stating this point creates some confusion. For it is not clear what the relationship between the two clauses is — "hardly ever[73] will someone die[74] for a righteous person; although for a good person one might dare to die." Interpretations fall into two categories. On the one hand are those that do not make any important distinction between "righteous person" in the first sentence and "good person" in the second. If this is so, the second sentence could be the replacement for the first, Tertius, Paul's scribe, accidentally leaving in the first, "uncorrected," sentence.[75] Or it could clarify the first by "softening" the assertion that a person would "scarcely" die for anyone else.[76] In the second category are those interpretations that give to the second sentence a concessive force: "one would scarcely die for a righteous person, *although*[77] for a good person, one might, indeed, be willing to die." On this view, a "good person" would be one who has a stronger claim on one's emotions than the "righteous person" of the first clause. While the "righteous person" would be one who is just and upright in his dealings and would therefore have some claim on our respect, the "good person" would be one for whom we have a strong personal attachment and for whom, therefore, we would be more willing to die.[78] It is true that a distinction of this sort between "righteous" and "good" does not have much NT support.[79] But it does find some support in extrabiblical materials.[80]

72. The γάρ at the beginning of the verse, then, is explanatory, introducing the argument of vv. 7-8 as a whole.

73. Gk. μόλις. This adverb usually denotes the difficulty of accomplishing an action (cf. Luke 9:39; Acts 14:18; 27:7-8, 16; 1 Pet. 4:18), but here — its only Pauline occurrence — it probably indicates how rare the action is (cf. BAGD).

74. The future ἀποθανεῖται ("will die") is gnomic (BDR 349[1]).

75. Barrett; Käsemann.

76. Murray; Wilckens.

77. The Greek particle is γάρ, which would normally not have this kind of meaning. But this may be a case where the particle is repeated after the first clause with a similar force (cf. BAGD 1.c).

78. This is probably the most popular view (cf., e.g., Bengel, S-H). Cranfield argues a variation of this interpretation, taking τοῦ ἀγαθοῦ to designate a person's "benefactor" (the article acquiring an almost possessive force: "his benefactor"). Others understand τοῦ ἀγαθοῦ as a neuter, designating "the public good." Paul perhaps refers then especially to those martyrs who give their lives for "the public good" (e.g., Godet; Wolter, *Rechtfertigung*, pp. 174-75).

79. In the three places in the NT where the words are used together (Matt. 5:45; Luke 23:50; Rom. 7:12) no distinction is possible, nor does Paul's general usage of the terms reveal any marked distinction.

80. Irenaeus, e.g., claims that gnostics characterize the "God of the OT" as δίκαιος and the "God of the NT" as ἀγαθός (*Adv. Haer.* 1.27.1; cf. also Cicero, *De Officiis* 3.15 [Latin]). See, further, the examples collected by Lightfoot and S-H. F. Wisse ("The Righteous Man and the Good Man in Romans V.7," *NTS* 19 [1972-73], 91-93), finding no difference between δίκαιος and ἀγαθός, attaches v. 7a to v. 6 and v. 7b to v. 8, but the two parts of the verse are too obviously related to justify this separation.

8 In contrast to[81] the very best of human love is God's love; for he "commends[82] his own[83] love for us,[84] in that[85] while we were still sinners Christ died for us." Again we see the assumption that *God's* love is shown in *Christ's* death (cf. v. 6). We notice also that Paul finds a basic unity, even identity, between the love of God as it is shown in the objective, factual event of Christ's death on the cross and as it is experienced "in the heart" by the believer (v. 5b). An emotional feeling of God's love, in itself, is little comfort to the person who is lost, condemned, doomed for hell. But a cold, sober, historical interpretation that indeed God "loved the world" on the cross is of little benefit to a person until that love is experienced, is received, by faith in Christ. It is when these are properly experienced as two aspects of one great love, ultimately indivisible, that our assurance that "hope will not put us to shame" (v. 5a) will be strong and unshakable.

9 In vv. 9-10, Paul gathers together the main pieces of vv. 1-8 into a synthesis that reiterates and expands the central point of the paragraph as a whole: the certainty of Christian hope (vv. 2b, 5a). The two verses are parallel statements of the same point, as the following layout shows:

v. 9	v. 10
	if, while we were enemies,
having now been justified	we were reconciled to God
through his blood	through the death of his Son
how much more	how much more
	being reconciled
will we be saved	will we be saved
from wrath	
through him	through his life

The argument in each of the verses takes the form of a popular logical sequence, called by the rabbis *qal wayyōmer* ("light and heavy") and in the western tradition *a minori ad maius* ("from the minor to the major").[86] In

---

81. The verse is introduced with a δέ, a mild adversative here.

82. The Greek verb is συνίστημι, which means here, as in 3:5, "demonstrate," or "prove."

83. Emphatic ἑαυτοῦ.

84. Taking εἰς ἡμᾶς ("for us") with ἀγάπην ("love") rather than with συνίστησιν (cf. Cranfield; contra S-H).

85. Gk. ὅτι (cf. BDF 394).

86. Cf. Str-B, 3.223-26; and J. Bonsirven, *Exégèse rabbinique et exégèse paulinienne* (Bibliothèque de Théologie Historique; Paris: Beauchesne and Sons, 1939), pp. 83-88. Note the example in *m. 'Abot* 1:5: "talk not much with womankind. They said this of a man's own wife: how much more of his fellow's wife!"

this case, however, the "how much more" in Paul's transition suggests that the argument proceeds from the "major" to the "minor":[87] if God has already done the most difficult thing — reconcile and justify unworthy sinners — how much more can he be depended on to accomplish the "easier" thing — save from eschatological wrath those who have been brought into such relationship with him. In this double statement, Paul incorporates in the first member many of the elements of present Christian experience that he has touched on in vv. 1-8: "being justified by faith" (v. 1a; alluded to in v. 9a), "having peace with God" (v. 1b; picked up in the language of reconciliation in v. 10), having the love of God, revealed on the cross, in our hearts (vv. 5b-8; suggested by the stress on the death of *God's* Son in v. 10), having experienced all this when we were "ungodly," "weak," "sinners" (vv. 6-8; cf. v. 10a: "enemies"). Similarly, the second part of the argument restates and elaborates the "hope" of vv. 2b and 5a.

As in v. 1, "being justified"[88] alludes to the past declaration of acquittal pronounced over the sinner who believes in Christ. But the "now" adds the nuance of the continuing "just" status of those so acquitted. The means by which this justifying act takes place is Christ's blood.[89] As in 3:25, "blood" signifies Christ's death as a sacrifice for sins. These are the only two places in Romans in which "blood" has this sacrificial sense, and the other similarities between vv. 9-10 and 3:21-26 (justification, deliverance from wrath [alluded to with *hilastērion*]) suggest that Paul may here be drawing from that compact summary of the work of Christ.[90] The justified status conveyed to the believer on the basis of Christ's sacrificial death issues in salvation from wrath. The temporal element in the verse makes clear that wrath refers here to eschatological judgment (cf. 2:5). "We will be saved" is, then, a genuine temporal future. As he typically does, Paul uses salvation language to depict the final deliverance of the believer from sin, death, and judgment.[91] Salvation,

---

87. This point is stressed by Godet; Meyer; Wolter, *Rechtfertigung,* pp. 179-80. Bonsirven also points out that both "directions" of argument — from the major to the minor and from the minor to the major — are found in the rabbinic *qal wayyōmer* (*Exégèse rabbinique,* p. 85).

88. Gk. δικαιωθέντες, an aorist participle.

89. Gk. ἐν τῷ αἵματι. The ἐν is probably instrumental (BDF 195 [1{e}]; Moule, *Idiom Book,* p. 77), though it is also possible that the construction is a "Hebrism" (בְּ), meaning "at the cost of" (Fryer, "Reconciliation," p. 48).

90. Cf. H.-J. Findeis, *Versöhnung — Apostolat — Kirche. Eine exegetisch-theologische und rezeptionsgeschichtliche Studie zu den Versöhnungs-aussagen des Neuen Testaments (2 Kor, Röm, Kol, Eph)* (FzB 40; Würzburg: Echter, 1983), pp. 280-86.

91. This future-oriented use of σῴζω is quite usual in Paul. For while he sometimes uses the verb to denote the deliverance from the penalty of sin that comes at conversion (e.g., Rom. 8:24; Eph. 2:5, 8), he more often uses the word (and its cognates; cf. Rom. 13:11) to depict the final deliverance of the Christian from the power of sin, the evils of

accomplished in Christ and the believer's appropriation of Christ, is finally realized only in the last day. This double temporal conception is typical of NT teaching, which insists on the absolute and final nature of the believer's acceptance of salvation while also maintaining that salvation is not complete until the body is redeemed and glorified (cf. Rom. 8:23; Phil. 3:21). It is precisely the tension set up by this "already–not yet" perspective that gives rise to the need to proclaim the unbreakable connection between the believer's justification and his or her salvation from the wrath of God still to be poured out in the last day. Paul suggests the unbreakable connection between the two by insisting that, as initial salvation is "through his blood," so final salvation is also "through him." In light of the parallel phrase in v. 11, "in his life," Paul probably means by this the mediation of the risen Christ, who, through his resurrection, has been "appointed as Son-of-God-in-power" (cf. 1:4; 8:35).[92]

10   The parallelism between this verse and v. 9 renders the differences between them all the more significant. Perhaps the most interesting is the substitution of "reconciled" for "justified." Justification language is legal, law-court language, picturing the believer being declared innocent by the judge. Reconciliation language, on the other hand, comes from the world of personal relationships. "To reconcile" means to bring together, or make peace between, two estranged or hostile parties (cf. 1 Cor. 7:11).[93] The language of reconciliation is seldom used in other religions because the relationship between human beings and the deity is not conceived there in the personal categories for which the language is appropriate.[94] Reconciliation in Paul has two aspects, or "moments": the accomplishment of reconciliation through Christ on the cross (cf. 2 Cor. 5:19: "in Christ God was reconciling the world to himself")[95] and the acceptance of that completed work by the believer (cf. 2 Cor. 5:20b: "We beseech you on behalf of Christ, be reconciled to God").[96]

---

this life, and, especially, judgment (e.g., 1 Cor. 3:15; 5:5; Phil. 2:12). Paul pictures the Christian as *having been* saved, as *looking forward* to being saved, and even as *in the process of* being saved (cf. 2 Cor. 2:15; 2 Thess. 2:10).

92. Cf. Godet.

93. The two images are therefore complementary descriptions of the transformed relationship between human beings and God that takes place in Christ. The two are not simply equivalent (contra Barrett); nor is reconciliation a step beyond justification (Martin, *Reconciliation,* p. 151).

94. See F. Büchsel, *TDNT* I, 254.

95. See, e.g., Fryer ("Reconciliation," p. 56), Morris (*Apostolic Preaching,* pp. 198-99), and Ladd (*Theology,* pp. 450-56) for the importance of the objective aspect of reconciliation.

96. Paul uses the verb καταλλάσσω and the cognate noun καταλλαγή, both here and in 2 Cor. 5:18-20, to depict what has occurred in our relationship to God through the work of Christ; the related verb ἀποκαταλλάσσω occurs in Eph. 2:16; Col. 1:20, 22.

Naturally, while the focus can be on one of these moments or the other, the reconciling activity of God is ultimately one act; and in the present verse the complete process is in view. Paul makes explicit the hostile relationship implicit in the language of reconciliation: it was "while we were enemies" that we were reconciled to God. Paul may mean by this simply that we, rebellious sinners, are hostile toward God — violating his laws, putting other gods in his place.[97] But, as Paul has repeatedly affirmed in this letter (cf. 1:18; 3:25), God is also "hostile" toward us — our sins have justly incurred his wrath, which stands as a sentence over us (1:19-32), to be climactically carried out on the day of judgment (2:5). Probably, then, the "enmity" to which Paul refers here includes God's hostility toward human beings as well as human beings' hostility toward God.[98] Outside of Christ, people are in a situation of "enmity" with God; and in reconciliation, it is that status, or relationship, that changes: we go from being God's "enemies" to being his "children" (cf. Rom. 8:14-17).

As in v. 9 justification is accomplished "through" Christ's blood, so here reconciliation takes place "through[99] the death of [God's] Son." Similarly, "we will be saved," though not further defined, must have the same referent as the same verb in v. 9: salvation from the wrath of God on the day of judgment. The meaning of the phrase "through[100] his life" is not so clear. In light of Paul's frequent, and theologically significant, use of "in Christ" language in Rom. 5–8, he could intend to depict our salvation as occurring "in the sphere of" Christ, or his life.[101] On the other hand, it is unusual for Paul to use "in Christ" language with another noun intervening between the preposition and "Christ"; and the phrase seems to be parallel to "through him" in v. 9, where an instrumental meaning is certain. Probably, then, the phrase indicates that the new life won by Christ and in which believers share is the means by which they will be saved in the judgment.[102]

11 This verse wraps up the paragraph by rehearsing many of its key

97. See, e.g., Kuss, Käsemann, and Wilckens.

98. See, e.g., Godet; Michel; Dunn; Fitzmyer; Morris, *Apostolic Preaching,* p. 199. Others think that Paul refers only to God's hostility toward human beings (e.g., Haldane; Martin, *Reconciliation,* p. 144; Fryer, "Reconciliation," pp. 52-53; Wolter, *Rechtfertigung,* p. 86). Of Paul's nine uses of ἐχθρός, six are active (denoting the hostility of the subject toward others — cf. Rom. 12:20; 1 Cor. 15:25, 26; Gal. 4:16; Phil. 3:18; Col. 1:21), one is passive (2 Thess. 3:15), and two (Rom. 5:10 and 11:28) probably work both ways.

99. The Greek preposition here is, however, διά (in place of the ἐν in v. 9); but the two cannot be distinguished in meaning here (cf. Dunn; contra Martin, *Reconciliation,* p. 147).

100. Gk. ἐν.

101. S-H; Nygren.

102. Murray; Fryer, "Reconciliation," p. 50; and see the discussion in Moule, *Idiom Book,* pp. 194-95.

elements: "boasting/rejoicing" (cf. vv. 2-3); the present experience of reconciliation with God (vv. 1b, 10); and, most of all, the fact that this boasting,
and this reconciliation, are "through our Lord Jesus Christ" (vv. 1, 2, 6-8, 9,
10).[103] But the exact relationship of this verse to the rest of the paragraph is
dependent on decisions we must make about two syntactical issues. First is
the question of the point of comparison in the transitional phrase "and not
only this."[104] If Paul intends these words as a transition from the immediately
preceding verse, then the point of comparison could be "we will be saved"
— "and not only will we be saved, but . . . ."[105] — or "being reconciled" —
"and not only [are we those] who are reconciled, but [we are those] rejoicing."[106] On the other hand, Paul may want us to go further back into the
text for the implied connection: either to the last use of "rejoice" in v. 3 —
"and not only do we rejoice in afflictions, but we rejoice also in . . . ."[107] —
or, more generally, to the teaching of vv. 3-10 as a whole — "and not only
is all this true, but. . . ."[108] Since Paul elsewhere uses this transitional phrase
to pick up an immediately preceding statement,[109] it is more likely that Paul
wants us to supply something from v. 10; and "salvation" is more likely than
"reconciliation," since the latter occurs later in the verse.

The second issue has to do with the mood of the verb we have translated
"boast." It is a participle in Greek,[110] and it could well then be a subordinate
verb, with a main verb to be discovered. This main verb could be "we will
be saved" from v. 10.[111] But taking the participle as the main verb of the
sentence is grammatically unobjectionable[112] and makes for a smoother reading. We take it, then, that Paul in v. 11 is turning back from the future prospect
of the believer, with which he has been occupied in vv. 5-10, to the "boasting"
or "rejoicing"[113] that marks the reaction of the believer in this life to all that
God has done for him or her (cf. vv. 1-4) — rejoicing that everything God
gives us is "through our Lord Jesus Christ." But perhaps we should say,

103. Cf. Fryer, "Reconciliation," pp. 39, 53-54.
104. Gk. οὐ μόνον δέ; the "this" in our translation is an addition necessary to
make sense of the phrase in English.
105. Chrysostom; Cranfield.
106. Meyer; cf. JB.
107. Stuart.
108. Bengel; Michel; Käsemann; Dunn.
109. Rom. 5:3; 8:23; 9:10; 2 Cor. 7:7; 8:19; 1 Tim. 5:13.
110. καυχώμενοι.
111. See Godet. He presumes that another participle (σῳζόμενοι, "being saved")
must be read after οὐ μόνον δέ; he paraphrases: "much more certainly shall we be saved
(ver. 10) and that not only as saved, but as glorying in God."
112. Cf. Moulton, 224; Moule, *Idiom Book*, p. 179.
113. See our comments on v. 3 for the meaning of this verb.

313

"should mark" the reaction of the believer — for although Paul states our boasting as a fact, he undoubtedly wants to encourage any who are faltering or downhearted to contemplate again what he or she has in Christ — a new relationship with God ("justification," "peace with God," "reconciliation") that overcomes all present adversity ("rejoicing in afflictions") and that provides absolute security for the life to come ("rejoicing in the glory of God," "hope does not disappoint us," "saved from wrath"). And such contemplation can lead only to rejoicing. So Chrysostom: "And so the fact of his saving us, and saving us too when we were in such plight, and doing it by means of his only-begotten, and not merely by his only-begotten, but by his blood, weaves for us endless crowns to glory in."

2. The Reign of Grace and Life (5:12-21)

12*Because of this, just as sin came into the world through one man, and through sin death, and in this way death spread to all people, because all people sinned —* 13*for sin was in the world before the law, and sin is not reckoned where there is no law,* 14*but death reigned from Adam until Moses, even over those who did not sin in the likeness of the transgression of Adam, who is a type of the one to come.*

15*But the gift is not like the trespass. For if the many died through the trespass of the one, how much more has the grace of God and the gift in grace of the one man Jesus Christ abounded for the many.* 16*And the gift is not like the one who sinned. For the judicial verdict that resulted in condemnation was from one sin, but the gift that leads to justification came after many transgressions.* 17*For if death reigned through one man because of the transgression of one man, how much more will those who receive the abundance of grace and the gift of righteousness reign in life through the one man Jesus Christ.*

18*Therefore, as condemnation came to all people through the trespass of one man, so also did the righteousness that leads to life come to all people through the righteous act of one man.* 19*For just as through the disobedience of the one man were the many made sinners, so also through the obedience of the one will the many be made righteous.*

20*Now the law came in to increase the trespass. But where sin increased, grace increased all the more,* 21*in order that, just as sin reigned in death, so also grace might reign through righteousness leading to eternal life through Jesus Christ our Lord.*

In a passage that rivals 3:21-26 for theological importance, Paul paints with broad brush strokes a "bird's-eye" picture of the history of redemption. His canvas is human history, and the scope is universal. We hear nothing in this paragraph of "Jew" and "Gentile"; both are subsumed under the larger category "human being."[1] The perspective is corporate rather than individual. All people, Paul teaches, stand in relationship to one of two men, whose actions determine the eternal destiny of all who belong to them. Either one "belongs to" Adam and is under sentence of death because of his sin, or disobedience, or one belongs to Christ and is assured of eternal life because of his "righteous" act, or obedience. The actions of Adam and Christ, then, are similar in having "epochal" significance. But they are not equal in power, for Christ's act is able completely to overcome the effects of Adam's. Anyone who "receives the gift" that God offers in Christ finds security and joy in knowing that the reign of death has been completely and finally overcome by the reign of grace, righteousness, and eternal life (cf. vv. 17, 21).

The power of Christ's act of obedience to overcome Adam's act of disobedience is the great theme of this paragraph. We must not so narrowly focus on what this passage has to say about sin that we fail to do justice to this theme. It emerges in the "just as . . . so also" comparisons that are the backbone of the paragraph's structure (cf. vv. 12, 18, 19, 21); see also the "not as . . . so is" negative comparisons in vv. 15-17. In each case, Adam, his sin, and its consequences figure in the "just as" or "not as" clauses, while Christ, his act of righteousness, and its consequences occur in the "so also" or "so is" clauses.[2] The universal consequences of Adam's sin are the *assumption* of Paul's argument; the power of Christ's act to cancel those consequences is its *goal*.

What relationship does this argument bear to the rest of the letter? Opinions differ markedly, the paragraph being characterized, for instance, as "the logical centre of the Epistle" on the one hand[3] and "a digression" on the other.[4] As we indicated in the introduction to chaps. 5–8, 5:12-21 is sometimes connected more with what precedes and sometimes more with what follows. And there certainly are connections in both directions. Thus, the emphasis on the justification secured by Christ, in contrast to the condemnation introduced by Adam (vv. 18-19), harks back to the central theme of 1:18–4:25 — particularly to the critical tenet that justification is available "for all who believe" (3:22).[5] On the other hand, some of the concepts introduced in 5:12-21 — "grace," "death," and "sin" as reigning powers, the sin-producing effects of the law (vv. 13-14, 20), the corporate structures of "in

---

1. As Beker, 85, points out.

2. While the "so also" clause is not explicit in vv. 12-13, Paul's argument clearly assumes it (see the notes on v. 12).

3. Griffith Thomas; cf. Nygren, 207.

4. Denney, 627.

5. Cf. Godet, 202-3.

Adam" and "in Christ" — are precisely those that come to dominate chaps. 6–8.[6] We will not here reproduce those arguments that lead us to view all of chap. 5 as related more closely to chaps. 6–8 than to chaps. 1–4 (see the introduction to chaps. 5–8). What is necessary at this point is to establish the relationship between 5:12-21 and the previous course of Paul's argument. The main connection is with the teaching of assurance of final salvation in the immediately preceding paragraph (vv. 2b, 9-10). The passage shows why those who have been justified and reconciled can be so certain that they will be saved from wrath and share in "the glory of God": it is because Christ's act of obedience ensures eternal life for all those who are "in Christ." (See below, on v. 12, for alternatives and argument.)

The argument of the paragraph proceeds disjointedly because Paul begins in v. 12a a comparison ("just as" . . .) that he never completes. Instead, he becomes involved in expanding on the first part of his comparison — the sin of Adam (vv. 12d-14). At the end of v. 14, in affirming that Adam is a "type" of Christ, Paul hints at the completed comparison, but before stating it he institutes a series of contrasts between Adam and Christ (vv. 15-17). Finally, then, in two roughly parallel statements (vv. 18, 19), the full comparison is made. Verse 20 introduces the question of the law, for a Jewish believer might well object that Paul has omitted from his rapid survey of saving history the most important event of all: Sinai. Verse 21 then brings the text to a triumphant summary and conclusion. And the final note in this conclusion is again christological: "through Jesus Christ our Lord."[7]

12 The opening words of the paragraph, "because of this,"[8] suggest that what Paul is about to teach in 5:12-21 is the conclusion he is drawing from something he has argued earlier in the letter. But commentators disagree about what it is earlier in the letter that leads to the discussion of the contrasting "headships" of Adam and Christ. The following options are all found in the literature: the argument of the epistle thus far,[9] the believer's reconciliation (5:11),[10] the central role of Christ in salvation (5:9-10),[11] the idea that we will

---

6. Cf. P. Lengsfeld, *Adam et le Christ* (Théologie 71; Paris: Aubier, 1970), p. 78; E. Brandenburger, *Adam und Christus. Exegetisch-religionsgeschichtliche Untersuchungen zu Röm. 5:12-21 (1 Kor 15)* (WMANT 7; Neukirchen/Vluyn: Neukirchener, 1962), pp. 255-64.

7. Bornkamm, "Paulinische Anakoluthe," pp. 81-82, has an excellent summary of the structure of the paragraph.

8. Gk. διὰ τοῦτο; see further n. 17.

9. Godet; Dunn; F. G. Lafont, "Sur l'interprétation de Romains 5, 12-21," *RSR* 45 (1957), 511-12.

10. Meyer and Morris think that the certainty of life in Christ is the conclusion Paul draws from our reconciliation, while Cranfield argues that the reconciliation of believers (5:11) leads to the inference of Christ's relationship to all of humanity.

11. Michel.

be saved "in union" with Christ (5:10);[12] or the certainty of final salvation (cf. 5:1-11).[13] Of these, the last suggestion does most justice both to the contents of 5:1-11 and 12-21 and to the natural meaning of the phrase Paul uses. But we must question whether 5:12-21 reads most naturally as the *conclusion* of what Paul has already argued. The verses make better sense when viewed as the *basis* for what has just been said; specifically, based on content alone, 5:12-21 would seem to function very nicely as the ground, or reason, for the confidence in hope that Paul has stressed in 5:1-11. As linguistic justification for this reading, then, other commentators give "this" a prospective force — "we boast [v. 11] because of this: that whatever we have lost in Adam we have gained in Christ"[14] — or interpret the phrase as a very loose transition.[15] Neither of these alternatives is likely.[16] But what seems the natural relationship between the two paragraphs can be maintained if we take "because of" in the sense of a "final cause" (e.g., "for the sake of") and make the antecedent of "this" the promise of final salvation (vv. 9-10). The phrase "because of this" can function this way,[17] and its suitability to the context leads us to adopt it as the most likely

12. Lloyd-Jones.

13. S. L. Johnson, "Romans 5:12 — An Exercise in Exegesis and Theology," in *New Dimensions in New Testament Study,* pp. 300-301.

14. E.g., Griffith Thomas; Nygren.

15. Lietzmann; Lagrange; Schlier; R. Bultmann, "Adam und Christus nach Römer 5," in *Exegetica. Aufsätze zur Erforschung des Neuen Testaments* (ed. E. Dinkler; Tübingen: Mohr, 1967 [= *ZNW* 50 {1959}, 145-65]), p. 433.

16. τοῦτο only rarely looks ahead; and the distance between καυχώμενοι and διὰ τοῦτο renders this interpretation even more unlikely. Nowhere else does Paul use διὰ τοῦτο as a loose transition. In fact, there are no clear examples of such a use in the NT.

17. διά often has this kind of telic force (cf. the note on 4:25), and the phrase διὰ τοῦτο states a "final cause" or purpose in several verses (cf. 2 Cor. 13:10; Col. 1:9[?]; 2 Thess. 2:11; 1 Tim. 1:16; 2 Tim. 2:10[?]; Phlm. 15). Some claim that the phrase has this meaning only when a ἵνα clause follows (Thayer, *Lexicon,* p. 134; Zerwick, 112), but there are at least two NT verses in which διὰ τοῦτο states "final cause" without an accompanying ἵνα clause (John 12:27; 1 Cor. 4:17). (The "final cause" in John 12:27 is unexpressed, but must be something like "to undergo the experiences of 'this hour'". In 1 Cor. 4:17, the final cause is inferred from v. 16: "It is for this reason [viz., to help you to become imitators of me] that I am sending [have sent?] Timothy to you.") If, as we have argued, 5:12-21 harks back particularly to vv. 9-10, this interpretation is natural here because of the future tenses in those verses. When the antecedent of τοῦτο is a future condition, or promise, "because of this [τοῦτο]" naturally comes to have a final sense: "because of this promise," e.g., "because of the need to make this promise come to pass," or "for the sake of bringing this promise to pass."

διὰ τοῦτο occurs a total of 63 times in the NT, with the following meanings:

(1) διά as causal and τοῦτο retrospective, e.g., "because of what has just been said . . ." (Matt. 6:25; 12:27, 31; 13:52 [?]; 14:2; 18:23[?]; 21:43; 24:44[?];

meaning here. We would then paraphrase the transition at 5:12 as follows: "in order to accomplish this [namely, that God has promised to save all those who are justified and reconciled through Christ], there exists a life-giving union between Christ and his own that is similar to, but more powerful than, the death-producing union between Adam and all his own."

The internal structure of v. 12 is unclear. When it comes toward the beginning of a sentence, *hōsper,* "just as,"[18] normally introduces the protasis of a comparative sentence. We would expect, in other words, to find a "so also" clause to complete the sentence. Some scholars have identified such a "so also" clause in this verse or the next, but their identifications are not very plausible.[19]

Mark 6:14; 11:24; Luke 11:19, 49; 12:22; 14:20; John 6:65; 7:22; 9:23; 13:11; 15:19; 16:15; 19:11; Acts 2:26; Rom. 1:26; 13:6; 15:9; 1 Cor. 11:10[?], 30; 2 Cor. 4:1; 7:13; Eph. 1:15; 5:17; 6:13; Col. 1:9; 1 Thess. 3:5, 7; Heb. 1:9; 2:1; 9:15; 1 John 4:5; 3 John 10; Rev. 7:15; 12:12; 18:8);

2. διά as causal and τοῦτο as prospective, e.g., "because of what is about to be said, namely that . . ." (Matt. 13:13; Mark 12:2; John 5:16, 18; 10:17; 12:18, 39[?]; 1 Thess. 2:13; 1 John 3:1);

3. διά denoting final cause and τοῦτο as prospective, e.g., "for this reason, namely, with the purpose that . . ." (usually with a ἵνα clause following; Matt. 23:34; Rom. 4:16; 2 Cor. 13:10; 2 Thess. 2:11; 1 Tim. 1:16; 2 Tim. 2:10[?]; Phlm. 15);

4. διά denoting final cause and τοῦτο as retrospective, e.g., "in order to accomplish what we have just said . . ." (John 1:31; 1 Cor. 4:17).

A survey of one-fourth of the more than 350 LXX occurrences revealed that almost all fit in category 1 (we surveyed Genesis, Judges, and the Psalms; the only possible exceptions were Judg. 11:8[B]; Isa. 26:14; 37:33).

18. Gk. ὥσπερ, repeated in vv. 19 and 21, where it is completed with οὕτως καί.

19. Since the apodosis of this kind of sentence is often introduced with οὕτως ("so also"), the most obvious possibility is to make v. 12c-d the apodosis; thus: "(a) just as sin entered the world through one man, (b) and through sin death, (c) so also death spread to all people, (d) because all people sinned" (Barrett; Lenski; J. T. Kirby, "The Syntax of Romans 5.12: A Rhetorical Approach," *NTS* 33 [1987], 283-86). But when οὕτως has this function in the NT, it is either used alone (Matt. 13:40; 24:27, 37; Luke 17:24; Rom. 6:19) or with καί *following* (John 5:21, 26; Rom. 5:19, 21; 6:4; 11:30; 1 Cor. 11:12; 15:22; 16:1; Gal. 4:29; Jas. 2:26). The order found in v. 12 — καὶ οὕτως — never occurs to complete a comparison and is a most unnatural way to do so. Another alternative, then, is to find the completed comparison somewhere else: in v. 14b ("just as sin entered through one man . . . so Adam is the type of the one to come"; cf. Calvin; S-H), in v. 15c ("just as sin entered through one man . . . so the grace of God and the gift in grace abounded to the many through the one man Jesus Christ"; cf. B. Englezakis, "Rom 5,12-15 and the Pauline Teaching on the Lord's Death: Some Observations," *Bib* 58 [1977], 232), or in v. 18b ("just as sin entered through one man . . . so also through the righteousness of the One, there is righteousness of life for all men"; cf. Godet; Hodge). But the first suggestion does not produce a natural comparison, while the other two occur only after the first member of the comparison has been reintroduced.

Most scholars therefore conclude that Paul starts a comparison in this verse that he does not (grammatically) finish.[20] Having introduced his comparison with reference to Adam and his sin, Paul becomes "sidetracked" on this point and abandons the comparison, only to reintroduce and complete it later in the text. It is not until vv. 18-19 that the comparison is fully made, although vv. 15-17 hint at it. It is difficult to know whether the "break" in the construction occurs between v. 12b and v. 12c,[21] between v. 12c and v. 12d, or after v. 12.[22]

The first clause attributes the entrance of sin into the world to "one man." This "man" is, of course, Adam, whose very name means "man."[23] Reference to "sin" in the singular is characteristic of Rom. 5:12–8:13.[24] Throughout these verses, Paul attributes to "sin" a very active role: it "reigns" (5:20; cf. 6:13, 14), can be "obeyed" (6:16-17), pays wages (6:23), seizes opportunity (7:8, 11), "deceives," and "kills" (7:11, 13). In a word, he personifies sin, picturing it as a power that holds sway in the world outside Christ, bringing disaster and death on all humanity.[25] Through this personification, Paul shows that individual acts of sin constitute a principle, or "network," of sin that is so pervasive and dominant that the person's destiny is determined by those actions (see also on 3:8). In the present instance, then, the "sin" that enters the world is more than an individual sin; it is the bridgehead that paves the way for "sinning" as a condition of humanity.[26] The fact that Paul attributes to Adam this sin is significant since he certainly knows from Genesis that the woman, Eve, sinned first (cf. 2 Cor. 11:3; 1 Tim. 2:14). Already we see that Adam is being given a status in salvation history that is not tied only to temporal priority.

Paul's claim that "sin came into the world through one man" would have been nothing new to anyone who knew his or her OT or Jewish tradition.

---

20. What grammarians call an anacolouthon.

21. E.g., S-H; M. C. de Boers, "The Defeat of Death. Paul's Apocalyptic Eschatology in 1 Corinthians 15 and Romans 5:12-21" (Ph.D. diss., Union Theological Seminary, 1983), p. 240.

22. Most commentators and translations (this is the significance of the "dash" mark at the end of v. 12 in the NRSV; NAB; NASB; NIV).

23. Heb. אָדָם.

24. Over 65 percent of all Paul's uses of ἁμαρτία (42 of 64) occur in this passage, and all are in the singular.

25. But it is not clear that Paul *personalizes* sin, viewing it as a "demon" that exists prior to, and independent of, personal acts of rebellion against God (cf. Kaye, *Thought Structure,* pp. 34-57; Godet; and the discussion of this issue in Lorenzi, *Battesimo e giustizia,* pp. 60-71; contra, e.g., Scott, *Christianity,* pp. 46-47; Laato, *Paulus und das Judentum,* p. 95).

26. Taking κόσμος, "world," to be the world of humanity (cf. "all people" in v. 12c, and the repeated "many" and "all" in vv. 15-19); cf. e.g., Cranfield; contra, e.g., Kuss, who refers to 8:18ff.

Nor would his second assertion in this verse: "and through sin death [came into the world]."[27] For the unbreakable connection between sin and death, made clear in Gen. 2–3, was a staple of Jewish theology.[28] But what does Paul mean by death here?[29] He may refer to physical death only, since "death" in v. 14 seems to have this meaning.[30] But the passage goes on to contrast death with eternal life (v. 21). Moreover, in vv. 16 and 18 Paul uses "condemnation" in the same way that he uses death here. These points suggest that Paul may refer here to "spiritual" death: the estrangement from God that is a result of sin and that, if not healed through Christ, will lead to "eternal" death.[31] In fact, however, we are not forced to make a choice between these options. Paul frequently uses "death" and related words to designate a "physico-spiritual entity" — "total death," the penalty incurred for sin.[32] Here, then, Paul may focus on physical death as the evidence, the outward manifestation of this total death;[33] or, better, he may simply have in mind this death in both its physical and spiritual aspects.[34]

As v. 12b depicts the *entrance* of death as the consequence of sin, v. 12c makes explicit that this death has *spread* to every single person.[35] The exact relationship of this clause to its context depends on what exactly the adverb "in this way" *(houtōs)*[36] means. If it is not correlative with "just as" (which we have seen reason to doubt), there are three possibilities. (1) It may pick up v. 12a-b as the general condition in which sin and death spread to all people: Adam having introduced sin into the world, and with it death, it was in these circumstances that death spread and all sinned.[37] But it would be unusual for the word to mean simply "in these circumstances." (2) *Houtōs* might pick up the reference to "the one man": as one man was responsible

---

27. We must supply εἰς τὸν κόσμον εἰσῆλθεν from the first clause.

28. See, particularly, A. J. M. Wedderburn, "The Theological Structure of Romans V.12," *NTS* 19 (1972-73), pp. 339-42.

29. Gk. θάνατος. The noun occurs five times in the passage, the cognate verb twice.

30. E.g., J. Freundorfer, *Erbsünde und Erbtod beim Apostel Paulus. Eine religionsgeschichtliche und exegetische Untersuchung über Römerbrief 5,12-21* (NTAbh 13; Münster: Aschendorff, 1927), pp. 227-30; Godet; S-H; Murray; Harrison.

31. This was important for Pelagius's conception (or lack thereof) of original sin (cf. Schelkle).

32. See esp. Beker, 224; T. Barrosse, "Death and Sin in Saint Paul's Epistle to the Romans," *CBQ* 15 (1953), 449-55; Cambier, *L'Evangile,* pp. 227-29.

33. E.g., Kuss; Morris.

34. So most commentators.

35. The Greek verb is διῆλθεν, in which the διά has distributive force (S-H; Cranfield; Käsemann [BAGD, however, suggest the simple meaning "come"]).

36. Gk. οὕτως.

37. Stuart; cf. Godet.

for the *entrance* of sin and death (v. 12a), so, "in this [same] way," was one man responsible for the *spread* of death.[38] Defenders of this interpretation point to the emphatic position of "through one man"[39] and to the form of the comparison in vv. 18 and 19, where Adam's sin is said to be the cause of the condemnation of all people. But it may be significant that Paul in v. 12 — unlike in vv. 18-19 — speaks not of "the sin of one man," but of "sin" entering through one man. This suggests that Paul's focus is not at this point on the corporate significance of Adam's act but on his role as the instrument through whom sin and death were unleashed in the world. (3) With the majority of commentators, then, we think that "in this way" draws a comparison between the manner in which death came into the world — through sin — and the manner in which death spread to everyone — also through sin.[40] Verse 12 then is a neatly balanced chiasm:

> A   sin (12a) produces
> B   death (12b);
> B   all die (12c)
> A   because all sin (12d).

If this reading of the structure of the verse is right, then v. 12d has the purpose of showing that death is universal because sin is universal: "all sinned." This means, in turn, that we are giving the opening words of this last clause *(eph' hō)*[41] a causal meaning. This is the meaning adopted by most commentators and by almost all English translations. But it is not the only possible rendering. Perhaps the most famous alternative is the translation "in whom," adopted by Augustine and by a few others. For, assuming that "the one man" is the antecedent of the pronoun, we have then an explicit statement of "original sin": "in Adam all sinned."[42] But this interpretation, and others

---

38. See, with some difference in detail, Bengel; Gifford; Ridderbos, *Paul,* p. 96.

39. The phrase (δι' ἑνὸς ἀνθρώπου) comes first in its clause.

40. On this view, οὕτως could be either retrospective — "in the manner indicated in 12a-b sin spread to everyone" (e.g., Stevens, *Pauline Theology,* p. 127; Murray; and probably a majority of the commentators) — or prospective — "in the manner indicated in 12d ['in that all sinned'] death spread to everyone" (e.g., Lyonnet, *Les Etapes,* pp. 93-94). In either case, the point is that, as death *came into* the world through sin, so death *spread* to everyone "in the same way" — by sinning. A variation in this view is to take οὕτως as consecutive: "sin entered the world through one man, and death through sin; *and so* death spread to everyone, because everyone sinned" (cf. RSV; Freundorfer, *Erbsünde,* pp. 230-31; Hodge; Wilckens; Cranfield; cf. BAGD [under 1.b] for this meaning of οὕτως).

41. Gk. ἐφ' ᾧ.

42. Cf. Augustine, *Against Two Epistles of the Pelagians* 4.4.7 (*PL* 44, col. 614). Augustine was here explicitly following Ambrosiaster. The Vulgate translation *in quo* could

that rest on a similar grammatical basis,[43] are unlikely. For the two words in the Greek phrase probably function together as a conjunction.[44] The phrase may then mean "from which it follows,"[45] "with the result that,"[46] "inasmuch as,"[47] or "because."[48] The last suggestion is by far the most popular among modern scholars, although the evidence in its favor is not nearly as strong as some suggest. Nevertheless, this is the meaning the phrase almost certainly has in 2 Cor. 5:4, and probably also in Phil. 3:12 (it almost certainly does not in Phil. 4:10), and it is the meaning that fits best in the context here.

Paul, then, has shown that the entrance of death into the world through the sin of Adam has led to death for all people; and all people die, Paul asserts, because all people "sinned." In a sense, then, Paul's concern in this verse, and throughout the passage, is not with "original sin," but with "original

---

also have helped this interpretation, although some think even this phrase could mean "because of."

43. Augustine assumed that the relative pronoun in the phrase (ᾧ) had independent pronominal force ("which," or "whom"). Others who take the same approach are: (1) Cambier, who thinks that "one man" is the antecedent of ᾧ and gives ἐπί a causal meaning: "because of one man, all sinned" (J. Cambier, "Péchés des hommes et péché d'Adam en Rom. V.12," *NTS* 11 [1964-65], 246-54; idem, *L'Evangile*, pp. 237-50; similar are the views of Turner, *Grammatical Insights*, pp. 116-18; W. Manson, "Notes on the Argument of Romans (Chapters 1–8)," in *New Testament Essays: Studies in Honour of T. W. Manson* [ed. A. J. B. Higgins; Manchester: Manchester University, 1952], p. 159); (2) E. Stauffer, who thinks that θάνατος is the antecedent — "in the direction of death all sinned," e.g., death was the result of all sinning (*New Testament Theology* [New York: Macmillan, 1955], p. 270; cf. the similar suggestion of R. Jacob, "La véritable solidarité humaine selon Romains 5,12-21," in *La culpabilité fondamentale. Péché originel et anthropologie moderne* [ed. P. Guilluy; Gembloux: Duculot, 1975], pp. 26-33); (3) F. W. Danker, who thinks that "law" might be the antecedent (cf. νόμος in v. 13) — "it was on the legal basis [of the law] that all sinned" ("Romans V.12 and Sin under Law," *NTS* 14 [1967-68], 424-39); or (4) Zahn, who finds the antecedent in the preceding context generally — "in which circumstances all sinned."

44. In Paul's three other uses of the phrase (2 Cor. 5:4; Phil. 3:12; 4:10), the relative pronoun does not have independent pronominal force, but reflects an abbreviation of τούτῳ ὅτι; the phrase as a whole, would mean, literally translated, "upon this, that" (cf., e.g., Harris, "Prepositions," pp. 1194-95; BDF 294[4]).

45. Black.

46. J. A. Fitzmyer, "The Consecutive Meaning of EΦ' Ω in Romans 5.12," *NTS* 39 (1993), 321-39.

47. Cf. esp. S. Lyonnet, "Le sens de ἐφ' ᾧ en Rom 5,12 et l'exégèse des pères grecs," *Bib* 36 (1955), 436-56.

48. Most of the Greek Fathers gave the phrase this meaning; and cf., e.g., BDF 235(2) (though note the question mark); Turner, 272; Moule, *Idiom Book,* p. 50. Note also the examples cited by Meyer. As Wedderburn ("Theological Structure," p. 350) points out, even Lyonnet's interpretation comes to mean virtually "because" in a clause — such as Rom. 5:12d — with a verb that refers to past time.

death."[49] Paul says nothing explicitly about *how* the sin of one man, Adam, has resulted in death for everyone; nor has he made clear the connection — if any — between Adam's sin (v. 12a) and the sin of all people (v. 12d). What he *has* made clear is that the causal nexus between sin and death, exhibited in the case of Adam, has repeated itself in the case of every human being. No one, Paul makes clear, escapes the reign of death because no one escapes the power of sin.

But we cannot stop here. For the fact that Paul in this verse asserts the universality of sin (v. 12d) after mentioning the responsibility of Adam in unleashing sin in the world forces us to ask the question: What is the relationship between Adam's sin and ours? Or, to put it another way, why do all people, without exception, sin? This question is made even more insistent by Paul's focus on the sin of Adam as the reason for universal condemnation in vv. 18-19. How is it that the sin of Adam led to the condemnation of all people? These questions force us to look more carefully at just what Paul means in v. 12d when he asserts that "all sinned."[50]

At first sight, this question would appear easy to answer. Paul certainly uses the verb "sin" regularly to denote voluntary sinful acts committed by individuals; and this is what most commentators think this same word, in the same tense as is used here (the aorist), designates in Rom. 3:23: that all people, "in their own persons," commit sins. Probably a majority of contemporary scholars interpret v. 12d, then, to assert that the death of each person (v. 12c) is directly caused by that person's own, individual sinning. The question is then how this "individual" explanation of death is to be squared with the "corporate" explanation of the universality of death in v. 12a-b and, with even greater emphasis, vv. 15-19. In other words, how can we logically relate the assertions "each person dies because *each person* sins [in the course of history]" and "*one man's* trespass led to condemnation for all people" (v. 18a)?[51]

---

49. See, e.g., Dunn.

50. Gk. πάντες ἥμαρτον. Some would argue that such a question is out-of-bounds for the commentator on Romans, since it raises systematic theological issues that are not rightly within the province of exegesis. To be sure, we would do wrong to insist that Paul provide answers for our questions that he never thought of or that he speak to us in the categories of later dogmatic theology. But: (1) resolution of tensions within a text are part of the exegete's job — we cannot simply pass over the question of the relationship of v. 12 and vv. 18-19 at the logical level; (2) interpretation must be appropriate to the kind of document it has to do with; and in Romans, we believe, we have not only a first-century religious document, but Holy Scripture — demanding to be read in light of the whole message of Scripture and in terms of the (theological) categories that are integral to it. See, on the whole point in relation to 5:12, esp. Johnson, "Romans 5:12."

51. One alternative is simply to deny any real relationship between Adam's sin and the sin of all people. We sin, "as Adam did," or in imitation of Adam, but there is nothing in Adam's sin that makes it *necessary* that we sin. This interpretation, which is

First, we could be content to posit an unresolved "tension" between the individual and the corporate emphasis.[52] Paul in v. 12 asserts that all people die because they sin on their own account; and in vv. 18-19 he claims that they die because of Adam's sin. Paul does not resolve these two perspectives; and we do wrong to try to force a resolution that Paul himself never made.[53] A systematic

---

usually called "Pelagian" after the fourth-century theologian who made it famous (see his commentary on Romans and Schelkle, 175-76), is not very widely held in our day. The reason is that the text so clearly makes the sin of Adam to be, in some sense, the *cause* of universal condemnation (see particularly vv. 18-19). Moreover, while not strictly a criticism of the "Pelagian" view, it must be pointed out that this interpretation fails to explain why it is that, as Paul makes clear, *everyone* does, in fact, sin. Surely there must be *something* inherent in "being human" that causes everyone, without exception, to decide to worship idols rather than the true God (cf. 1:22-23).

52. Cf. particularly Wedderburn, "Theological Structure," pp. 338-39; K. M. Fischer, "Adam und Christus. Überlegungen zu einem religionsgeschichtlichen Problem," in *Altes Testament-Frühjudentum-Gnosis* (ed. K.-W. Tröger; Gütersloh: Mohn, 1980), pp. 284-98; Cambier, "Péchés des hommes," pp. 219-22; Scroggs, *Last Adam,* pp. xxi-xxii. Advocates of this view (see again Wedderburn) find confirmation for this view in the fact that contemporary Judaism evidenced a similar tension between individual and Adamic responsibility for sin and death. Note, e.g., how the Syriac *Apocalypse of Baruch* can assert, on the one hand, "when Adam sinned a death was decreed against those who were to be born" (23:4) and "What did you [Adam] do to all who were born after you?" (48:42) and, on the other hand, "Adam is, therefore, not the cause, except only for himself, but each of us has become our own Adam" (54:19). Similarly, note 54:15: "although Adam sinned first and has brought death upon all who were not in his own time, yet each of them who has been born from him has prepared for himself the coming torments." Note also *Bib. Ant.* 13:8, 9. Still other Jewish texts attributed sin and death to the devil; e.g., "by the envy of the devil death entered into the world [θάνατος εἰσῆλθεν εἰς τὸν κόσμον], and those who have part with him experience it" (Wis. 2:24, which some [e.g., Cambier, "Péchés des hommes," p. 230] think has influenced Paul). And some put the blame on Eve (Sir. 25:24; on which see J. Levison, "Is Eve to Blame? A Contextual Analysis of Sirach 25:24," *CBQ* 47 [1985], 617-23). On the Jewish conception of sin and death, see esp. Davies, 32-49; Schoeps, 188-89; Scroggs, *The Last Adam,* pp. 17-58; Str-B, 3.227-29.

53. On one variation of this view, Paul is said to have used a "gnostic"-oriented deterministic tradition in v. 12a-c — a tradition that he "corrects" with the emphasis on individual responsibility in v. 12d (cf. esp. Brandenburger, *Adam und Christus,* pp. 157, 175-78; Bultmann, 1.174; G. Schunack, *Das hermeneutische Problem des Todes im Horizont von Römer 5 untersucht* [HUTh 7; Tübingen: Mohr, 1967], pp. 244-47). Often coupled with this perspective is the idea that Paul's description of Adam must be treated as a "myth": "we are not 'in Adam' substantially, but in so far as we take over his act in our own. The mythical idea of representation is thus limited to the truth that I can no longer break out of sin through decision and action. I always already have the fall behind me" (Conzelman, *Theology,* p. 197; cf. also, e.g., P. Grelot, *Péché originel et rédemption examinés à partir de l'Epître aux Romains. Essai théologique* [Paris: Desclée, 1973]. W. Pannenberg [*Anthropology in Theological Perspective* {Philadelphia: Westminster, 1985}], p. 129] follows J. Müller [*Die christliche Lehre von der Sünde*] in advocating a supra-

theologian may have to find a resolution; but we exegetes need not insist that Paul in this text assumes or teaches one. Now it is certainly the case that we can err by insisting that a text give us answers to all our questions about a topic or (still worse) by foisting on a biblical author theological categories that do not fit that author's teaching. But we can also fail to do our job as exegetes by failing to pursue reasonable harmonizations that the author may assume or intend. So we think it is legitimate to ask whether Paul suggests any resolution of the tension between individual and Adamic responsibility for sin in this text.

One popular explanation holds that Paul assumes a "middle term" in the connection between Adam's sin and the condemnation of all human beings: a corrupted human nature.[54] V. 12d refers, indeed, to sins committed by individuals in the course of history — but as the necessary result of a corrupt nature inherited from Adam. Death, then, is due immediately to the sinning of each individual but ultimately to the sin of Adam; for it was Adam's sin that corrupted human nature and made individual sinning an inevitability.[55] This view has much in its favor: it retains the "normal"

---

historical, mythical fall into sin). But there is every reason to think that Paul read Gen. 2–3 as a historical account of real people, and no reason at all for us to think we must "demythologize" what Paul took to be real. Indeed, it is difficult to see how Paul's argument in Rom. 5:12-21 hangs together if we regard Adam as mythical. For Adam and Christ are too closely compared in this passage to think that one could be "mythical" and the other "historical." We must be honest and admit that if Adam's sin is not "real," then any argument based on the presumption that it is must fall to the ground (see, e.g., D. A. Carson, "Adam in the Epistles of Paul," in *In the Beginning. . . . A Symposium on the Bible and Creation* [ed. N. M. de S. Cameron; Glasgow: The Biblical Creation Society, 1980], pp. 28-43). As to the suggested "religions-history" background, dependence of Paul on a gnostic-influenced tradition is unlikely; everything Paul says can be explained in terms of his new Christian convictions against the background of the OT and Judaism (see esp. Wedderburn, "Theological Structure," pp. 348-54; idem, "Adam in Paul's Letter to the Romans," p. 424; Lengsfeld, *Adam et le Christ,* pp. 78-114; A. Sand, "Sünde, Gesetz und Tod zum Menschenbild des Apostels Paulus," in *Zum Problem der Erbsünde. Theologische und philosophische Versuche* [ed. N. Lohfink et al.; Essen: Ludgerus, 1981], pp. 73-85).

54. Indeed, some scholars (e.g., Luther and Calvin) think that "all sinned" in v. 12 means just that: all people exist "in a state of sin." According to them, Paul is not basing the universal reign of death on individual acts of sin, but on sinful human nature. (Note, however, that Calvin's comment on p. 210 of his commentary, and his discussion in the *Institutes* [2.1.5-8] appear to presume original guilt in some sense). However, there is little evidence that the verb ἁμαρτάνω can denote the possession of a sin nature, and the view is little defended in our day.

55. Representative is the succinct summary of the early seventeeth-century theologian Johannes Wollebius: "as person has infected nature, so in turn the nature has infected persons" (quoted in Heppe, *Reformed Dogmatics,* p. 314); cf. also Chrysostom; Stuart; Denney; Gore; S-H; Cranfield. While sometimes called "mediate imputation," the attribution is not strictly correct. "Mediate imputation," associated particularly with the Reformed theologian Placcaeus (1596-1655), holds that the guilt of Adam's sin is imputed to his descendants not directly (at

meaning of "sin" in v. 12 while explaining at the same time how Paul could assert that Adam's sin brings condemnation upon all (vv. 18-19). It also explains why all people act contrary to the will of God: there is a fatal, God-resisting, "bent" in all people, inherited from Adam (Adam as fallen, not as created). For this reason alone, most theologians have assumed the necessity for some such view of the effects of Adam's sin. Nevertheless, we may question whether this is what Paul means in v. 12d. The most serious objection is that this interpretation requires us to supply the crucial "middle term" in the argument — Adam's having and passing on a corrupt nature. For in each case where Adam's sin and the death of all are related, the relationship is stated directly: "many died through one man's trespass" (v. 15a); "the judgment following one trespass brought condemnation" (v. 16b); "because of the trespass of one man, death reigned" (v. 17a); "one man's trespass led to condemnation for all men" (v. 18a). Only v. 19a — "by one man's disobedience many were made sinners" — could possibly allude to such a notion, but this is probably not what is intended here either (see below on that verse). On the view we are examining, these statements must be expanded to mean "one man's trespass *resulted in the corruption of human nature, which caused all people to sin, and so* brought condemnation on all men." While it is possible that Paul would want us to assume these additions, he has given us little basis for doing so.

If, then, we are to read v. 12d in light of vv. 18-19 — and, since the comparative clauses in these verses repeat the substance of v. 12, this seems to be a legitimate procedure — "all sinned" must be given some kind of "corporate" meaning: "sinning" not as voluntary acts of sin in "one's own person," but sinning "in and with" Adam. This is not to adopt the translation "in Adam" rejected above. The point is rather that the sin here attributed to the "all" is to be understood, in the light of vv. 12a-c and 15-19, as a sin that in some manner is identical to the sin committed by Adam. Paul can therefore say both "all die because all sin" and "all die because Adam sinned" with no hint of conflict because the sin of Adam *is* the sin of all. All people, therefore, stand condemned "in Adam," guilty by reason of the sin all committed "in him." This interpretation is defended by a great number of exegetes and theologians.[56] It maintains the close connection

---

the Fall) but through inborn corruption (cf. J. Murray, *The Imputation of Adam's Sin* [Grand Rapids: Eerdmans, 1959], pp. 42-64; also Johnson, "Romans 5:12," pp. 311-13).

56. For the best defenses of this view, see Freundorfer, *Erbsünde,* pp. 240-55; Murray, *Imputation,* pp. 7-21, 64-70; Hodge, pp. 148-55. It was first clearly taught (apparently) by Ambrosiaster (cf. Schelkle, pp. 162-78). A detailed historical survey (up to 1925) is found in Freundorfer, *Erbsünde,* pp. 105-214; a clear and concise setting forth of the major views is given by A. A. Hoekema, *Created in God's Image* (Grand Rapids: Eerdmans, 1986), pp. 154-67.

between Adam's sin and the condemnation of all that is required by vv. 15-19, a connection suggested also by 1 Cor. 15:22 — "in Adam all die."[57] And a sin committed before individual consciousness also explains how Paul could consider all people as "by nature children of wrath" (Eph. 2:3).[58] The major problem with this view is, of course, whether it is the most natural way to read v. 12d. While Paul does not make explicit a connection with Adam's sin in this clause, the parallel created by Paul ("and in this way") between the entrance into the world of sin and death (v. 12a-b) and the spread of death to all people (v. 12c) makes it possible to argue that the causes of these phenomena — the sin of "the one man" and the sin of "all" — are also closely related.

We must admit that the case for interpreting "all sinned" in v. 12d as meaning "all people sinned in and with Adam" rests almost entirely on the juxtaposition of v. 12 with vv. 18-19. And maybe we should not force this combination when Paul himself did not explicitly do so. But one further point inclines us to think that Paul may, indeed, have been thinking along these lines: the popularity of conceptions of corporate solidarity in the Jewish world of Paul's day. This notion, rooted in the OT,[59] held that actions of certain individuals could have a "representative" character, being regarded as, in some sense, the actions of many other individuals at the same time.[60] I think that there is good reason to suppose that Paul adopted such a concept as a fruitful way of explaining the significance in salvation history of both Adam

---

57. As Freundorfer points out (*Erbsünde,* p. 243), Paul's clear teaching about "original death" would seem to require a corresponding teaching of "original sin."

58. Two other arguments frequently used to support this view are not entirely convincing. First, it is often said that the parallel between Adam and Christ requires that, if Christ's righteousness is imputed to us directly, so must Adam's death be imputed directly to us. However, it can be argued from the other side that, just as the imputation of Christ's righteousness is mediated by a human act — faith — so also must the imputation of death. The point in both cases is that the analogy should not be made to "walk on all fours." It is further frequently maintained that an "in Adam" view of v. 12d is required if it is to be true that "all" sinned, since otherwise children and others not morally responsible would be excluded. While this argument has some merit, Paul may want *here* to describe only the situation of responsible adults.

59. The classic biblical evidence for such a notion comes from Josh. 7, where a sin committed by one individual, Achan, is also said to be "Israel's sin" (vv. 1, 11), and the reason why God's anger "burns against Israel" (v. 1).

60. H. W. Robinson (*Corporate Personality in Ancient Israel* [rpt.; Philadelphia: Fortress, 1980]) is one of the key proponents of the importance of solidarity in "Hebrew" thinking. Robinson and others certainly go too far in speaking of corporate *personality* (cf. J. W. Rogerson, "The Hebrew Conception of Corporate Personality: A Reexamination," *JTS* 21 [1970], 1-16), but the importance of "corporate" categories for the OT and Jewish thinking is generally accepted.

and Christ.[61] For Paul, Adam, like Christ, was a corporate figure, whose sin could be regarded at the same time as the sin of all his descendants.[62]

61. See esp. Ridderbos, *Paul,* pp. 53-64; R. Shedd, *Man in Community: A Study of St. Paul's Application of the Old Testament and Early Jewish Conceptions of Human Society* (Grand Rapids: Eerdmans, 1964); Barrett, *From First Adam to Last,* pp. 4-5; and, on 5:12 specifically, E. Best, *One Body in Christ* (London: SPCK, 1955), pp. 36-38; S.-H. Quek, "Adam and Christ according to Paul," in *Pauline Studies,* pp. 72-73; G. C. Berkouwer, *Sin* (Grand Rapids: Eerdmans, 1971), pp. 424-545; W. Barclay, "Romans 5:12-21," *ExpTim* 70 (1958-59), 173-75; Bruce.

Can we go any further in pinning down the nature of this "corporate" relationship? In the history of interpretation, two suggestions have been particularly popular. (1) The "realist" interpretation. On this view, our relationship to Adam is "real" in the sense that we are all biologically descended from Adam. "The totality of human nature" was concentrated in Adam; his sin can, then, be said to be the sin of everyone. See esp. Shedd; A. H. Strong, *Systematic Theology* (Valley Forge, PA: Judson, 1907), pp. 593-637; Hughes, *True Image,* pp. 131-32. Many Roman Catholic expositors, following Augustine (cf. *Against Two Letters of the Pelagians* 4.4.7 [*NPNF* 5.41-49]) also emphasize the reality of physical union (cf. Prat, *Theology,* 1.220-21, 235; A.-M. Dubarle, *The Biblical Doctrine of Original Sin* [New York: Herder and Herder, 1964], pp. 144-66, 171), although they generally stress propagation as the mechanism by which Adam's sin and guilt are transferred to his descendants. (2) Many Reformed theologians offer a "representative," or "federal," explanation. Without denying the fact of realistic union with Adam, advocates of this approach insist that Adam's sin was "imputed" to all directly by virtue of his being appointed by God as our representative. Thus, when he sinned, we sinned; when he fell, we fell; and we die because we have been accounted as having sinned in and with him. See, e.g., Murray, *Imputation,* pp. 27-41; Johnson, "Romans 5:12," pp. 307-14. A decision between these two is difficult. On the one hand, the "realist" view can appeal to explicit biblical teaching — cf. Heb. 7:10: Levi was "in the loins of" Abraham — and perhaps offers a better response to the question of "fairness." On the other hand, viewing Adam as the divinely appointed "head" or "representative" of the human race provides a better parallel with our relationship to the "Second Adam" — both Adam and Christ would then be viewed as "inclusive" representatives whose actions can be considered as the actions also of those who belong to them. Perhaps, indeed, Paul has not provided us with enough data to make a definite decision; and we should probably be content with the conclusion that Paul affirms the reality of a solidarity of all humanity with Adam in his sin without being able to explain the exact nature of that union.

62. The Jewish text that comes closest to Paul's conception is 4 Ezra 7:118: "O Adam, what have you done? For though it was you who sinned, the fall was not yours alone, but ours also who are your descendants." It must be said, however, that the idea of a corporate sinning of all in Adam is never made explicit in Judaism. At a later date, indeed, the rabbis tended to stress individual responsibility for sin (cf. A. P. Hayman, "The Fall, Freewill and Human Responsibility in Rabbinic Judaism," *SJT* 37 [1984], 13-22). Indeed, Paul's pessimistic view of human beings trapped under sin's power played a key role in establishing differences between his theology and that of Judaism generally (see esp. Laato, *Paulus und das Judentum*). On the other hand, Paul gives no evidence of being influenced by some of the Jewish traditions about Adam as "primal man" or "anthropos." As Käsemann puts it, Paul is interested in the function rather than the "substance" of Adam.

One last point needs to be addressed: the question of fairness. The German theologian W. Pannenberg puts is bluntly: "It is impossible for me to be held jointly responsible as though I were a joint cause for an act that another did many generations ago and in a situation radically different from mine."[63] Various theological and philosophical constructs can offer more or less help in answering this question, but no explanation ultimately removes the problem. "Original sin" remains an "offense to reason."[64] On the other hand, some such doctrine is necessary to explain the fact of universal sin and evil. Pascal, in a famous passage, put it like this:

> Original sin is foolishness to men, but it is admitted to be such. You must not then reproach me for the want of reason in this doctrine, since I admit it to be without reason. But this foolishness is wiser than all the wisdom of men. For without this, what can we say that man is? His whole state depends on this imperceptible point. And how should it be perceived by his reason, since it is a thing against reason, and since reason, far from finding it out by her own ways, is averse to it when it is presented to her?[65]

The folly, degradation, and hatred that are the chief characteristics of human history demand an explanation. Why do people so consistently turn from good to evil of all kinds? Paul affirms in this passage that human solidarity in the sin of Adam is the explanation — and whether we explain this solidarity in terms of sinning in and with Adam or because of a corrupt nature inherited from him does not matter at this point. On any view, this, the biblical, explanation for universal human sinfulness, appears to explain the data of history and experience as well as, or better than, any rival theory.

13 Paul has already within v. 12 begun to disrupt his comparison between Adam and Christ with a series of "run-on" clauses; now, he abandons his sentence altogether. (English versions signal this abandonment of the sentence with a dash at the end of v. 12.) Paul apparently thinks that something he has said in v. 12 requires immediate elaboration[66] in a kind of "aside." But what is the purpose of this "aside," which takes up vv. 13-14? There are two main possibilities.

---

63. *Anthropology,* p. 124; cf. also C. W. Carter, "Harmartiology: Evil, the Marrer of God's Creative Purpose and Work," in *A Contemporary Wesleyan Theology* (ed. C. W. Carter; 2 vols.; Grand Rapids: Zondervan, 1983), 1.267: ". . . guilt stems from a culpable act traceable to the unethical conduct of a morally reponsible person."

64. *Offense to Reason* is the title of Bernard Ramm's recent study of the doctrine (San Francisco: Harper & Row, 1985).

65. *Pensées* #445.

66. Note the γάρ, "for."

(1) The first, ably defended by Cranfield, views vv. 13-14 as a reinforcement of v. 12a-c. Paul's assertion of the universality of sin and death in this part of v. 12 is open to the objection, on the basis of Jewish beliefs, that there can be no sin, and hence no death, apart from the law. To meet this objection, Paul makes clear that even without the law to define sin sharply (v. 13b), both sin (v. 13a) and death (v. 14) were present and powerful.[67] This interpretation places all the emphasis on the assertions of vv. 13a and 14 and relegates v. 13b to the status of a rather negligible aside. But it is just in doing this that the interpretation is open to criticism. For the "but"[68] at the beginning of v. 14 presumes a sharp contrast with something that precedes, and this can only be with what Paul has said in v. 13b: "sin is not 'reckoned' where there is no law; *nevertheless* death reigned. . . ." Rather than being an aside, then, v. 13b is integral to Paul's argument.

(2) Advocates of the second main interpretation of these verses focus just on this contrast between vv. 13b and 14. They think that Paul raises conflicting points in vv. 13b and 14a in order to stimulate his audience to draw an inference. The conflict arises because Paul asserts that sin is not "reckoned" — interpreted to mean "deemed worthy of death" — except on the basis of transgression of the law. Yet he has also shown in v. 12 that all people — even those who are not, it appears, "under the law" — have died. What, then, did Paul want his readers to conclude from this apparent contradiction? Again, there are two main possibilities.

(a) Paul may want his readers to see that "law" is universal. All people die, and die because their sins are imputed to them; therefore, in light of v. 13b, all people must be faced with God's law in some form (cf. 2:14-15).[69] However, as Godet puts it, the assumption that Paul is referring to the "unwritten law" here is "at once too essential and too unfamiliar to the minds of his readers to be passed over in silence as self-evident." Moreover, this view fails to do justice to the phrase, "even over those who did not sin in the likeness of the transgression of Adam." Paul's use of "transgression,"[70] a term that he always associates with disobedience of an express commandment, shows that he refers to people who were not subject to the "law" that he speaks about in these verses. They were people who, unlike Adam, sinned without violating an express command of God to them.

(b) Paul may want his readers to understand that only the corporate

---

67. See also, especially, Calvin; Alford; Stuart; Dunn; Brandenburger, *Adam und Christus,* pp. 180-205; and, with variations, M. G. Kline, "Gospel until the Law: Rom 5:13-14 and the Old Covenant," *JETS* 34 (1991), 433-46.

68. Gk. ἀλλά.

69. E.g., Danker, "Romans V.12," pp. 430-31.

70. Gk. παράβασις; see the note on 4:15.

sinning of all people "in and with" Adam can explain the universality of death. Paul's reference to the time from Adam until Moses (v. 14a) implies that the "law" he refers to in these verses is the law of Moses. Now obviously people who lived before Moses did not have God's law in this specific, concrete form. How then would they "transgress" and so be judged worthy of death? Only because they had sinned when Adam sinned and because, therefore, Adam's transgression was considered their transgression also.[71]

This last interpretation explains Paul's language best, but it suffers from a serious theological objection: Can we suppose, in light of 1:18–3:20 (note especially 1:32) — not to mention Gen. 6 — that Paul would have regarded the sins of people before Moses as not meriting condemnation?[72] Certainly Paul argues that the coming of the law made sin a more serious thing, more "worthy" of death (cf. 3:20; 4:15; 5:20; 7:7-12); but he does not think it changed innocence into guilt.[73] This objection has given rise to the widespread assumption that "those who did not sin in likeness of the transgression of Adam" must be a reference to infants and perhaps other mentally handicapped people — it is the death of those who could not be considered to have sinned in their own persons that can be explained only by recourse to their sinning in Adam.[74] But this limitation is unlikely in view of the express mention of the period of time between Adam and Moses as well as the addition of "in the likeness of the transgression of Adam" to the phrase "those who did not sin." This points to people who *did* consciously, personally sin, but did not sin "in the same way" that Adam did — by violating an express commandment, carrying with it the sanction of death.[75] In another attempt to overcome this theological difficulty, some argue that Paul, while not wanting to deny that all sins justly merit death, highlights Adam's sin as the key.[76] If

---

71. Specifics of interpretation differ widely, but see esp. Chrysostom; Bengel; Godet (he takes the death referred to as physical only); Tholuck; Dubarle, *Original Sin*, pp. 157-66; Freundorfer, *Erbsünde*, pp. 247-54; Espy, "Robust Conscience," pp. 165-70; H. Preisker, *TDNT* II, 516-17.

72. Cf. Westerholm, 180.

73. See esp. Stuart for a clear statement of this objection. Some, indeed, go so far as to argue that Paul here holds that people before Adam died only because of Adam's sin (e.g., Dahl, 91; Espy, "Paul's Robust Conscience," pp. 169-70, 183-84), but this view cannot be reconciled with Paul's teaching in Rom. 1–3. (Sanders, in fact, finds at this point an inconsistency between Rom. 2 and 5 [*Paul, the Law and the Jewish People*, pp. 35-36].)

74. E.g., Melanchthon; Shedd; Murray.

75. As we noted in commenting on v. 12, Paul does not seem even to be considering in these verses the special issues created for the doctrine of universal sin and judgment by mentally restricted human beings.

76. E.g., Bengel; Tholuck.

this is acknowledged, however, it is difficult to see how the argument holds together. For "sin is not reckoned" would not, then, mean "sin is not worthy of death," and this destroys the contrast with v. 14.

Each of the two usual views of the text suffers, then, from a serious objection, making a choice between the two difficult. But it is easier to overcome the syntactical objections to the first — that Paul is focusing on the *fact* of universal death — than the theological objection to the second — that he is focusing on a (corporate) *explanation* of universal death. And perhaps the syntactical objection to the first can at least be softened by treating v. 13b not as an "aside" summarizing the standard Jewish teaching, but as a reminder of Paul's own teaching about the negative effects of the law on the sinful condition of humanity. Since this teaching could suggest that people can be penalized for their sins only if they are "under the law," Paul insists that, on the contrary, death reigned even over those who did not sin by violating a specific law of God. In vv. 13-14, then, Paul is reasserting the universality of death in the face of an objection to the effect that his own emphasis on the law as bringing wrath (4:15) would imply the absence of death in the absence of torah.

With this overall perspective in mind, we can now turn to the details of the text. "Before the law"[77] refers to the time before the giving of the Mosaic law to Israel; "sin was in the world" repeats v. 12a. "And sin is not reckoned where there is no law" expresses Paul's view that sin can be charged explicitly and in detail to each person's account only when that person has consciously and knowingly disobeyed a direct command that prohibits that sin.[78]

---

77. Gk. ἄχρι νόμου. The lack of an article creates no difficulty for a reference to the Mosaic law (see the note on 2:12). Although the article may be lacking because of the preposition (BDF 258[2] point out that in prepositional phrases in Romans, νόμος is without the article 14 out of 23 times), it may also be that there is a certain qualitative emphasis: Mosaic law *qua* law.

78. The key word is ἐλλογεῖται, "is reckoned" (it is in the present tense, in contrast to the imperfect in v. 13a and the aorist in v. 14a, because Paul is stating a general principle). The verb ἐλλογέω occurs only here and in Phlm. 18 in the NT and never in the LXX. It is taken from the world of commerce and suggests the careful, specific, rendering of accounts necessary in bookkeeping (cf. H. Preisker, *TDNT* II, 516-17; MM). The Reformers understood this "reckoning" as the subjective recognition of sins: one cannot recognize one's sinfulness without a law to define sin (e.g., Luther, Calvin; cf. also Stuart). But, while this function of the law has some place in Paul's thinking (cf. 3:20; 7:7), the juxtaposition between sin not being reckoned with the imposition — not the realization — of death in v. 14 makes this interpetation unlikely. At the other extreme are those who take ἐλλογεῖται to refer to the imputation of sin as leading to death. This interpretation is, as we have seen, unlikely if Paul has in mind the Mosaic law, or, indeed, any positive written law, since he clearly regards all sin as

14 Though sins were not "charged up separately" as in the case of Adam and Israel — both confronted with direct "law" — still, "death reigned[79] from Adam until Moses." "Death" refers clearly to physical death, but not to physical death alone;[80] as in v. 12, spiritual death, condemnation, is also involved. By using the image of death "reigning," Paul emphasizes that death was both universal and inescapable. "Those who did not sin in the likeness of the transgression of Adam" might be a different group than those who lived between Adam and Moses.[81] But it is more likely that the clause is a further identification of those who lived during this time period.[82] With this description, Paul brings out the characteristic of these people that is essential to his argument: the "law-less" context of their sin. They lived before God gave specific commandments to the people and they could not then, sin, as Adam did, by "transgressing."[83]

Having gone far enough astray, Paul resumes the main course of his argument in the last phrase of v. 14: "who is a type of the one to come."[84] The word "type" denotes those OT persons, institutions, or events that have

---

"worthy of death." As we suggested in the interpretation above, Paul is probably referring to the greater degree of responsibility for and punishment of sin in a context where one is obliged to a positive law (see the notes on 4:15; and note similar assertions in 5:20; 7:7-12; Gal. 3:19; and 1 Cor. 15:56). See, for this general approach, Cranfield; Griffith Thomas; Lloyd-Jones; E. Jüngel, "Das Gesetz zwischen Adam und Christus: Eine theologische Studie zu Röm 5,12-21," *ZTK* 60 (1963), 54; Westerholm, 180-81. G. Friedrich suggests the connotation of "entrust to the heavenly accounting book" ("Ἁμαρτία οὐκ ἐλλογεῖται. Röm 5,13," *TLZ* 77 [1952], 523-28; cf. also Laato, *Paulus und das Judentum,* pp. 133-35).

79. Gk. ἐβασίλευσεν, a "constantive" aorist.

80. Contra, e.g., Godet.

81. See, e.g., Murray, who takes the καί as coordinating and thinks Paul refers to infants.

82. The καί, therefore, is epexegetic ("even"), as most English versions take it.

83. Paul uses the expression τοὺς μὴ ἁμαρτήσαντας ἐπὶ τῷ ὁμοιώματι τῆς παραβάσεως Ἀδάμ. ἐπί might go with ἐβασίλευσεν ("reign"), introducing the basis on which death reigned (cf., e.g., Chrysostom; V. P. Branick, "The Sinful Flesh of the Son of God (Rom 8:3). A Key Image of Pauline Theology," *CBQ* 47 [1985], 258-59). But it is more likely to go with the immediately preceding phrase, "those who did not sin," with the meaning "after," in the sense of a pattern or standard (Thayer, *Lexicon,* p. 233). ὁμοίωμα, a theologically important term in Paul (see the notes on 6:5), means here "copy," "likeness," in the sense of that which is not identical to, but resembles in some important way, that with which it is compared. It would be misinterpreting the point of the comparison to suggest that this statement makes impossible the view that all people sinned in Adam. Paul is speaking of the personal sins of the people involved and comparing them with the personal sin of Adam; whether all people may have participated in Adam's personal sin is simply not in view.

84. Indeed, some think that this phrase completes the comparison that Paul began in v. 12 (cf. ὥσπερ); but, as I have argued above, this is unlikely.

a divinely intended function of prefiguring the eschatological age inaugurated by Christ — hence the word "typology."[85] It is in this sense that Adam is a "type" of Christ; the universal impact of his one act prefigures the universal impact of Christ's act. "The one to come"[86] may reflect the contemporary Jewish designation of the Messiah as "the coming one,"[87] and the future tense is probably used because Paul is viewing Christ's work from the perspective of Adam.[88]

15 Paul explains the typological relationship between Adam and Christ in vv. 15-21. The similarity between the two consists in the fact that an act of each is considered to have determinative significance for those who "belong" to each. This "structural" similarity between Adam's relationship to his "descendants" and Christ's to his underlies all of vv. 15-21. But vv. 15-17 reveal that this parallelism in structural relationship does not extend to the nature of the two acts and their consequences. These three verses present two basic contrasts between the work of Adam and of Christ. Paul introduces each contrast with the phrase "is not like"[89] (vv. 15a, 16a) and follows it with an elaboration (vv. 15b and 16b-17) using the phrase "how much more."[90] The first contrast is one of *degree:* the work of Christ, being a manifestation of grace, is greater in every way than that of Adam (v. 15). The second contrast is (mainly) one of *consequence:* Adam's act brought condemnation (v. 16b) and death (v. 17a); Christ's brought righteousness (v. 16b) and life (v. 17b).

Verse 15 begins with a "but" because Paul is now qualifying the

---

85. τύπος means originally the impression made by striking something, and comes, thereby, to designate a form, pattern, or example. Paul uses the word in 1 Cor. 10:6 to designate the OT people of God as "types" for the Corinthian believers. On the meaning of the word and the nature of typology, see esp. L. Goppelt, *Typos: Die typologische Deutung des Alten Testaments im Neuen* (BFCT 43; Darmstadt: Wissenschaftliche Buchgesellschaft, 1969); R. Davidson, *Typology in Scripture. A Study of Hermeneutical Typos Structures* (Andrews University Seminary Doctoral Dissertations 2; Berrien Springs, MI: Andrews University Press, 1981) (pp. 297-316 on 5:14).

86. Gk. τοῦ μέλλοντος.

87. Lightfoot; cf., e.g., Matt. 11:3.

88. Godet. It is unnecessarily complicated to think that the name "Adam" must be understood with the participle — "the Adam who is to come" (cf. 1 Cor. 15:45; cf., e.g., Schlier) or that "the one to come" refers to Moses (this is the view of Scroggs, *Last Adam,* pp. 80-81).

89. Gk. οὐχ ὡς.

90. Note the γάρ in vv. 15b, 16b, and 17. A few expositors have argued that vv. 15a and 16a are questions that assume a positive answer, in which case these verses state a comparison rather than a contrast (cf. Griffith Thomas; C. C. Caragounis, "Romans 5:15-16 in the Context of 5:12-21: Contrast or Comparison?" *NTS* 31 [1985], 142-48).

typological relationship between Adam and Christ he enunciated in v. 14b. He first states the difference: "the gift is[91] not like the trespass." Paul uses yet a third term to describe Adam's representative act: "trespass," or "false step." He probably shifts to this term to create a phonetic parallel with the key word in the verse: *charisma*, "gift."[92] In light of "gift of righteousness" in v. 17 and verses such as 6:23, this "gift" could be the righteous status that God gives to people,[93] but the contrast with "trespass" points to an act of Christ rather than the effects of that act. This is confirmed by v. 16, where the gift *leads to* "righteousness." In this verse, then, "gift" denotes not the gift given to the believer (as is usually the case in Paul), but the act of Christ himself considered as a "work of grace."[94] Paul chooses this unusual way of designating the work of Christ to accentuate its gracious character and its power: Christ's act, being a work of God's grace (*charis*), is far more potent than Adam's act.[95]

Paul explains the difference between Adam's trespass and Christ's act of grace in the last part of the verse: "for if the many died through the trespass of the one, how much more has the grace of God and the gift[96] in

---

91. The word ἐστιν is assumed in v. 15a: ἀλλὰ [ἐστιν] οὐχ ὡς τὸ παράπτωμα, οὕτως καὶ τὸ χάρισμα. We might paraphrase: "but it is not in the case of the trespass, as it is in the case of the gift."

92. Gk. παράπτωμα (cf. ἀμαρτία ["sin"] in v. 12 and παράβασις ["transgression"] in v. 14; cf. also vv. 17 and 18). See Dunn. The word παράπτωμα is relatively rare in Paul (16 occurrences; in Romans, outside this paragraph, 4:25 and 11:11, 12) but is essentially synonymous with ἀμαρτία (note the interchange in v. 20). (See W. Michaelis, *TDNT* VI, 171-73. Trench suggests a difference in meaning between the two terms at places in the NT [*Synonyms*, pp. 245-47], but his case is not persuasive.) παράπτωμα does not allude to the concept of law-breaking inherent in Paul's use of παράβασις (e.g., Godet; Cranfield; contra Cambier, *L'Evangile*, p. 289; Barrett; Wilckens). But this does not mean that it denotes any less serious an offense than does ἀμαρτία or παράβασις (contra, e.g., Godet, who argues from etymology).

93. E.g., Cranfield.

94. Cf. Meyer; Gifford.

95. See esp. Doughty, "The Priority of Grace," pp. 173-75.

96. The extraordinary concentration of "gift" words in this apodosis — χάρις ("grace"), δωρεά ("gift"), ἐν χάριτι ("in grace") — reveals the stress that Paul wants to put on this point but creates syntactical questions as well. First, is ἡ χάρις τοῦ θεοῦ καὶ ἡ δωρεά a hendiadys ("the gracious gift of God") or do χάρις and δωρεά each have separate importance — "the grace of God *and* the gift"? With the repetition of the article, the latter is more likely. What, then, is the difference between the two? Stuart suggests that χάρις is the general "gift" available to all, while ἡ δωρεά denotes the actual benefits granted only to believers. But it is unlikely that we can distinguish them in extent, since they are coordinated as subjects of "abound to the many." More likely, "grace" denotes the motive or manner in which God works, while "the gift" is the specific manifestation of this grace — the righteous status and life conferred on "the many."

grace[97] of the one man Jesus Christ abounded for the many." In the protasis ("if . . .") of this sentence, Paul states the relationship between Adam's sin and the spiritual plight of all people that he has hinted at in v. 12: the transgression of "the one" brought death to "the many."[98] Most scholars (probably) think that Paul in this passage uses "the many" equivalently to "all" (cf. v. 18).[99] It is true that "the many" can at times refer to "all" those belonging to whatever group may be under discussion. But the claim that it usually does so is exaggerated.[100] "The many" refers simply to a great number; how inclusive that number might be can be determined only by context. In the protasis of this verse, "the many" clearly includes all people; for Paul has already said that "all died" with reference to the sin of Adam (v. 12). But in the apodosis ("how much more . . .") "the many" must be qualified by Paul's insistence in v. 17 that only those who "receive" the gift benefit from Christ's act. Here it refers to "a great number" of people (but

97. The prepositional phrase ἐν χάριτι κτλ. may modify ἡ δωρεά ("the gift which comes through the grace of the one man Jesus Christ" [e.g., S-H; Cranfield; and most English translations]) or ἐπερίσσευσεν ("the gift has abounded through the grace of the one man Jesus Christ to the many" [Meyer; Lafont, "Romains 5,15-21," p. 483]). While a good argument for the latter is the parallelism thereby attained with the protasis (ἐν χάριτι corresponding to τῷ παραπτώματι), the protasis and apodosis of the sentence are not syntactically parallel anyway, and word order would slightly favor the former rendering. On this reading, ἐν is probably instrumental: the gift . . . which has come *through* the grace of the one man Jesus Christ. As with χάρισμα in v. 15a, χάρις in this last clause designates Christ's work as an act of grace.

98. The dative τῷ παραπτώματι could be causal ("because of the trespass of the one the many died"), referential ("in conjunction with the trespass of the one the many died"), or instrumental ("through the trespass of the one the many died"). We prefer the last. A related issue is the significance of the aorist tense of ἀπέθανον ("died"). It need not, of course, mean that Paul views the infliction of death as a "one-time" event; he simply portrays the condemnation of all people as a comprehensive whole. However, if Paul had thought of death as a penalty inflicted on each individual when he sins, we might have expected the imperfect or the present tense. This point gains force from the observation that Paul in this passage always presents the effects of Adam's act as a completed fact, while the effects of Christ's act are always viewed as continuing or future (cf. vv. 17, 19, 21). The aorist tense of ἀπέθανον may, then, suggest that the sentence of death imposed on all people took place immediately in conjunction with the trespass of Adam.

99. See esp. J. Jeremias, *TDNT* VI, 536-41. He argues that the use of οἱ πολλοί inclusively (= "all") is rooted in the OT (esp. Isa. 53) and is extremely common in the NT.

100. In Paul, e.g., the clear majority of the occurrences of [oἱ] πολλοί are restrictive, designating "many" or "most" but not "all" (cf. 1 Cor. 9:19; 10:5; 15:6; 2 Cor. 2:6, 17; 4:15; 6:10; Phil. 1:14 [all articular]; Rom. 16:2; 1 Cor. 1:26 [twice]; 11:30; 16:9; 2 Cor. 11:18; Gal. 3:16; Phil. 3:18; Tit. 1:10). Although a number of these could have an inclusive reference, Jeremias's claim (*TDNT* VI, 540) that "οἱ πολλοί is always used inclusively" in the NT except in Matt. 24:12 and 2 Cor. 2:17 cannot stand. Places where Paul uses πολλοί inclusively but where the context limits the group intended are Rom. 12:5 and 1 Cor. 10:17.

not all of them) or to "all who respond to the gift of grace." For them, Paul claims, the enjoyment of the gift and grace of God will be even more certain[101] than the death that came to all in Adam. Condemnation through Adam is inescapable, and Paul says nothing that would diminish the horrible reality of this judgment under which all people stand. But alongside condemnation there is the grace of God. And since it is precisely God's grace with which we have to do, there is an "abounding plus" (Murray), a superabundance connected with God's gift in Christ that has the power not only to cancel the effects of Adam's work but to create, positively, life and peace. Adam's "trespass" is the quintessence of human *activity,* an act for which a strict accounting must be due (cf. 4:1-6); but Christ's act is precisely a "gift," a matter of God's initiative, of his "unmerited favor" in which people are passive and which can, accordingly, never be earned, but only "received" (cf. v. 17).[102]

16 Paul announces a second contrast between the act of Adam and that of Christ in v. 16a and then explains it in vv. 16b and 17. The first sentence in the verse is extremely compact in Greek, a literal translation being "and the gift is not like the one who sinned."[103] Since "the one who sinned" does not make an adequate contrast with "the gift," we have to assume the point of contrast from the context; and perhaps the "condemnation" from the following verse is the best alternative. We might then paraphrase, "and the gift is not like the condemnation that came through the one who sinned."[104]

---

101. The phrase πολλῷ μᾶλλον ("how much more"), used to introduce the apodosis (the "then" clause) of the sentence, may have a qualitative force — "how much more abundantly will the grace of God . . . abound to the many" (Alford) — but, in keeping with its use in 5:10-11 (see the note there), it is more likely to have simple logical significance — "how much more [certainly] will the grace of God . . . abound to the many" (Meyer).

102. Cf. again, especially, Doughty, "The Priority of Grace," pp. 174-75; also H. Weder, "Gesetz und Sünde: Gedanken zu einem Qualitativen Sprung im Denken des Paulus," *NTS* 31 (1985), 364-71.

103. The Gk. is καὶ οὐχ ὡς δι' ἑνὸς ἁμαρτήσαντος τὸ δώρημα. The only element that we assume in our translation is the copulative verb (in this case ἐστιν), which is quite regular in Greek. Our literal rendering is close to that of the KJV.

104. See esp. Wilckens. The main clause is then καὶ οὐχ [ἐστιν] . . . τὸ δώρημα, with δώρημα, like δωρεά in v. 15, referring to the righteousness, or life, given to "the many" through Christ's act and ἁμαρτήσαντος being an adjectival participle, modifying ἑνός. There are two main alternatives to this rendering: (1) assume the neutral concept of "effect" or "result" as the point of contrast with "gift" (so most English translations; cf. NIV, "the gift of God is not like the result of one man's sin"); (2) take δώρημα to refer to Christ's "gracious act," with Adam's act as the assumed contrast (cf. NJB: "there is no comparison between the gift and the offence of the one man"). (For a complete list of alternatives and fuller discussion, see esp. Meyer.) The advantage of our rendering is that it provides the most natural basis for the expansion in v. 16b, which focuses on two aspects in which Adam's act differs from Christ's: number of sins taken into account, and outcome.

As he did in v. 15, Paul goes on to elaborate this contrast: "For the judicial verdict[105] that resulted in condemnation was from one sin,[106] but[107] the gift that leads to justification[108] came after[109] many transgressions." Paul, in fact, has two contrasts in mind: (1) the contrast between the results of Adam's act and Christ's — condemnation versus justification — and (2) the number of sins taken into account — the judicial verdict associated with Adam was based on one sin; the decree of justification that came through Christ came after an untold number of sins. Not only, then, are the results of the actions of Adam and Christ diametrically opposed; but the graciousness of God's work in Christ becomes all the more evident when one considers the number of sins taken into consideration in each respective action: "That one single misdeed should be answered by judgment, this is perfectly understandable: that the accumulated sins and guilt of all the ages should be answered by God's free gift, this is the miracle of miracles, utterly beyond human comprehension."[110]

105. Gk. κρίμα. This word usually in Paul means simply "judgment," and often the actual execution of the penalty (cf. Rom. 2:2, 3; 3:8; 1 Cor. 11:29, 34), but, applied here to the immediate result of Adam's sin, and differentiated from κατάκριμα ("condemnation"), probably means "judicial verdict," the sentence of judgment (BAGD).

106. Gk. ἐξ ἑνός. The numerical pronoun could refer to Adam (as the KJV rendering, "by one," seems to imply; and cf. Godet; Käsemann), but, in light of the rest of the sentence, almost certainly refers to the sin of Adam (so all major modern English translations; cf. Barrett).

107. Gk. δέ, corresponding to the μέν in the first clause.

108. The Greek word here is δικαίωμα, which by etymology (because of its suffix -μα) denotes the result of the action of "making right," and can mean, thus, "judgment," "ordinance," or "decree." This latter meaning, especially with reference to the commandments of God, is the most common in the LXX and NT (cf. Luke 1:6; Rom. 1:32; 2:26; 8:4; Heb. 9:1, 10). As with many words ending in -μα, however, δικαίωμα also came to refer to the action itself, a "righteous activity" or "deed" (cf. 1 Sam. 3:28; Rev. 15:18; 19:8; and [probably] 5:18). M. Hooker argues that the word should be taken in its accepted meaning of "act of making right," or vindication, the reference being to God's vindicating Christ in raising him from the dead and thereby providing for our being vindicated, or "made right" in him (M. D. Hooker, "Interchange and Atonement," *BJRL* 60 [1978], 465-66). Probably, however, δικαίωμα means "justification," or, perhaps, the righteous status that results from God's justifying action (BAGD; Barrett; Cranfield; Dunn). This meaning seems to be required by the contrast with κατάκριμα and by the words that are parallel to it in the text — δικαίωσιν ζωῆς ("righteousness of life" [v. 18]), δίκαιοι κατασταθήσονται ("constituted righteous" [v. 19]). Presumably, then, Paul uses δικαίωμα here for rhetorical effect, continuing the series of words ending in -μα: παράπτωμα, χάρισμα, δώρημα, κρίμα, and κατάκριμα.

109. Gk. ἐκ. In the first part of the sentence, ἐκ (ἐξ) denotes basis: the judicial verdict resulting in condemnation came "on the basis of" one sin. Here, however, the preposition has a temporal reference or, perhaps, indicates the situation "out of which" the justification came.

110. Cranfield.

17 Rather than an explanation, or further proof of v. 16a, parallel to v. 16b, v. 17 elaborates the contrast between the "condemnation" and the "justification" in v. 16b.[111] At the same time, v. 17 reiterates the argument of v. 15b, as is clear from the parallels in structure — "if . . . how much more" — and language — "the trespass of the one," "death," "grace," "gift," "abound." In fact, v. 17 is the summary and climax of Paul's delineation of the contrasting effects of the parallel redemptive-historical acts of the two "men."[112] The parallel, as Paul stresses throughout this paragraph, is that, in each case, a critical spiritual condition has been introduced into human history "through"[113] the act of "one man." This emphasis on the "one man Adam" and his sin as the instrument by which death exercises its rule reveals again the concern of Paul to tie the fate of all people in some direct way with the sin of Adam. Paul's purpose is not, however, to leave us depressed and hopeless in the face of this tragic and inescapable fact of human existence. Quite the contrary, he wants to cheer and encourage us by showing that the same connection between the act of one man and the fate of all that obtained in the case of "the one man" Adam also obtained in the case of another act of another "man," and that the act of this second "man" brings consequences even more glorious than those of the first man were deleterious. There is on the side of Christ's act an "abundance"[114] that leads Paul to put the two parts of the sentence not in a relationship of simple comparison — "as . . . so also" — but in a relationship of degree — "how much more." As in v. 15, the "abundance" is due to, or "consists of," God's grace and his gift, the result of that grace.[115] This gift is specified to be "righteousness,"[116] here clearly the status of a new relationship with God. It is because it is *God* working freely in the act of Christ that that act possesses the power to more than reverse the effects of Adam's human decision.

Paul breaks the parallelism of the sentence in another significant way: while the result of Adam's act is the subject in the first clause — "death reigned through the one"[117] — it is human beings who are the subject in the second — "those who receive the abundance of grace and the gift of righ-

---

111. Meyer.

112. Käsemann.

113. As in v. 15, τῷ παραπτώματι in v. 17a is instrumental, corresponding to the διά with reference to Christ at the end of the verse.

114. Gk. περισσείαν; cf. ἐπερίσσευσεν in v. 15b.

115. Taking both τῆς χάριτος and τῆς δωρεᾶς as epexegetic.

116. Gk. τῆς δικαιοσύνης, another epexegetic genitive.

117. Since ἑνός at the beginning of the verse refers to Adam, the ἑνός ("one") here probably does also (Murray; Käsemann). The aorist ἐβασίλευσεν may be ingressive — "death took up its reign" (Z-G, 471) — but is probably constantive, embracing the whole period of death's reign.

teousness." This change underscores an important difference between the reigns of death and life. The former has the character of fate; while, as v. 12 has shown, not unrelated to our own act of sin, death is — originally — not a consciously chosen destiny. The reign of life, on the other hand, is experienced through choice and personal decision; it is for those who "receive" the gift.[118] The importance of this qualification can hardly be overemphasized. For it reminds us — lest we have forgotten Rom. 1–4! — that righteousness and life are for those who *respond* to God's grace in Christ and that they are *only* for those who respond. What appears at first sight to be a universalism on both sides of the Adam/Christ parallel is here, then, importantly qualified (see further the discussion of v. 18).[119] Because Paul uses a future verb[120] to depict the reigning of those who receive the gift, most think that the reference must be to the eschatological future. But, without denying that this is involved, and may even be the primary emphasis, it may be that this "reigning in life" begins with the reception of the gift of righteousness.[121]

18 Paul now summarizes[122] his basic argument in this paragraph, finally stating the full comparison between Adam and Christ that he began in v. 12, parenthetically remarked on in vv. 13-14, and elaborated on in vv. 15-17.[123] After the negative comparisons of vv. 15, 16a, and 16b, and the qualitative contrasts ("how much more") in vv. 15b and 17, Paul returns to the simple comparative structure of v. 12. This comparative structure is the basic building block of vv. 18-21, Paul using it three times to state the parallel between Adam and Christ: "as . . . so" (v. 18); "just as . . . so" (v. 19); "just as . . . so" (v. 21). Verse 20, like vv. 13-14, breaks into the sequence with a comment about the role of the Mosaic law in the general salvation-historical scheme of Adam and Christ.

Paul again expresses himself in v. 18 elliptically, leaving important elements to be supplied by the reader.[124] Probably we should translate something like "as condemnation came to all people through the trespass of one

---

118. Cf. esp. R. Bultmann, "Adam und Christus," p. 437; Nygren.

119. See Kuss.

120. Gk. βασιλεύσουσιν.

121. The future tense may be, in other words, something of a "logical" future; future not so much in time as Paul writes but future from the standpoint of the reign of death in Adam (Murray).

122. Note the strong summary combination ἄρα οὖν.

123. Cf. Schmithals, who calls vv. 18-19 the "high point" of the paragraph.

124. Paul enhances the comparison by making the two parts of the verse syntactically parallel:

ἄρα οὖν
ὡς   δι' ἑνὸς παραπτώματος εἰς πάντας ἀνθρώπους εἰς κατάκριμα,
οὕτως καὶ δι' ἑνὸς δικαιώματος εἰς πάντας ἀνθρώπους εἰς δικαίωσιν ζωῆς.

man,[125] so also did the righteousness that leads to life[126] come to all people through the righteous act[127] of one man."[128] Paul again asserts that Adam's

125. ἑνός, both here and in the second clause, particularly because they lack the article (contrast vv. 15 and 17), is frequently taken adjectivally: "one trespass" (NASB, NIV — cf., e.g., Godet; S-H; Murray). But the contast with πάντας ἀνθρώπους ("all people") is stronger if we take ἑνός with pronominal force, referring to Adam and Christ, respectively — "one man's trespass"/"one man's act of righteousness" (NRSV) — and this reading is thereby to be preferred (Bengel; Cranfield; Käsemann; Wilckens).

126. "Righteousness that leads to life" translates δικαίωσιν ζωῆς. Two matters call for comment. (1) While δικαίωσις is not the usual word for "justification," Paul has used it in this sense in Rom. 4:25 (its only other NT occurrence); and, since the suffixes -σις and -συνη (cf. δικαιοσύνη) have a similar function (cf. BDF 109), it is likely that δικαίωσις here means simply "justification," right standing before God. (2) The genitive ζωῆς may be epexegetic (Turner, 214; Zerwick, 45), but, in light of the distinction between "justification" and "life" made in v. 21, it is more likely to be a genitive "of result": "justification that leads to life" (e.g., S-H; Murray; Cranfield). While rigid distinctions cannot be made, and what distinctions are made certainly cannot be applied everywhere, Paul, in this paragraph, uses justification to describe the status of the believer in this age, while "life" is confined to the eschatological future (cf. Lafont, "Romains 5,15-21," p. 498). As in 5:9-10, which, I have argued, is the basic "text" for the exposition in vv. 12-21, Paul insists that the justification now enjoyed by the believer will infallibly result in salvation from wrath in the last day — "life."

127. Gk. δικαιώματος. In light of the fact that this word is used in v. 16 to refer to justification, it is not surprising to find that many commentators insist that this must be its meaning here also: it was through the "one sentence of justification," or "the sentence of justification procured by the one man," that righteousness of life is "for" all people (e.g., Godet; S-H; Morris). But there are two reasons to prefer the translation "righteous act," as a reference to Christ's "obedience" (cf. v. 19). First, if, as we think likely, ἑνός refers to Christ, it is awkward to speak of justification or a sentence of justification as being "of Christ." Second, and more important, the strict parallelism between the first and second clauses suggests that, as παράπτωμα refers to something Adam did, so δικαίωμα will refer to something Christ did. While giving the same word two different meanings within the space of three verses may appear dubious, it is, in fact, the meaning in v. 16 that is unusual, the word being chosen there, as we have argued, for rhetorical considerations. The meaning "righteous act" for δικαίωμα is well established (in addition to the verses cited above [on v. 16], reference is usually made to Aristotle, *Rh.* 1.13.1 — where δικαίωμα is contrasted with ἀδίκημα — and Bar. 2:19), and the context — always of paramount consideration for the meaning of a word — makes this sense the more natural one here (BAGD; Murray; Cranfield; Käsemann; Dunn).

128. Other commentators think that we should add nothing to the verse, Paul intending it to be a kind of exclamation: "so then as through one trespass, unto all men, to condemnation, so also through one justificatory sentence, unto all men, to justification of life" (the translation is Gifford's). At the other extreme are those who think that we should supply both subjects and verbs; cf., e.g., the KJV: "Therefore, as by the offence of one *judgment came* upon all men to condemnation; even so by the righteousness of one *the free gift came* upon all men unto justification of life" (and cf., e.g., Murray). This is certainly a possible rendering since the subjects in question are picked up from the previous

trespass has been instrumental in leading to the "condemnation" of all people.[129] In keeping with the alternatives we explored for the interpretation of v. 12d, some take this instrumental connection to be mediate — Adam's "trespass"–human sinning–"condemnation" of all[130] — and others immediate — Adam's "trespass"–"condemnation" of all. While the text does not rule out the former, we think the latter, in light of the parallel with Christ and the lack of explicit mention of an intermediate stage, to be more likely (cf. the discussion on 5:12d).

In the last paragraph we have spoken of "justification leading to life" as applicable to believers. But does not Paul's explicit statement that this justification leading to life is "for all people" call into question the propriety of so confining justification only to some people? Indeed, this verse simply makes explicit what seems to be the logic of the paragraph as a whole, as Paul has repeatedly used the same terminology of those who are affected by Christ's act as he has of those who are affected by Adam's. And if, as is clear, Adam's act has brought condemnation to all, without exception, must we not conclude that Christ's act has brought justification and life for all? A growing number of scholars argue that this is exactly what Paul intends to say here. Recently, for instance, A. Hultgren has urged that the universal statements in this passage must be taken seriously, as descriptive of a "justification of humanity" that will be revealed at the judgment. Some people are justified by faith in this life, but those who do not accept the offer of God in this life are nevertheless assured of being justified at the judgment.[131]

Such universalistic thinking is, naturally, very appealing — who *likes* the idea that many people will be consigned to the eternal punishment of hell? But if, as seems clear, many texts plainly teach the reality of such punishment for those who do not embrace Christ by faith in this life (cf., e.g., 2 Thess. 1:8-9; Rom. 2:12; and the argument of 1:18–3:20), those who advocate such a viewpoint are guilty of picking and choosing their evidence. But can we reconcile the plain universalistic statements of this verse with these other texts that speak of the reality of hell? Some deny that we can, suggesting that we face a paradox on this point that God will resolve

---

context. Nevertheless, adding both subjects and verbs overloads the verse a bit, and I prefer to add verbs only: "as through the trespass of one man *there resulted* condemnation for everyone, so also through the righteous act of one man *there resulted* justication of life for everyone" (e.g., Godet). The notion of result is inherent in the εἰς that precedes, respectively, κατάκριμα and δικαίωσιν ζωῆς.

129. See also vv. 15-17.

130. See, e.g., Meyer; Denney.

131. A. J. Hultgren, *Christ and His Benefits: Christology and Redemption in the New Testament* (Philadelphia: Fortress, 1987), pp. 54-55; cf. also his *Paul's Gospel*, pp. 82-124.

someday.[132] Others argue that what is universal in v. 18b is not the actual justification accomplished in the lives of individuals, but the *basis* for this justification in the work of Christ. Christ has won for all "the sentence of justification" and this is now offered freely to all who will "receive the gift."[133] Nevertheless, whatever one's view on "limited atonement" might be (and the view just outlined is obviously incompatible with this doctrine), it is questionable whether Paul's language can be taken in this way. For one thing, Paul always uses "justification" language of the status actually conferred on the individual, never of the atonement won on the cross itself (cf. particularly the careful distinctions in Rom. 3:21-26). Second, it is doubtful whether Paul is describing simply an "offer" made to people through the work of Christ; certainly in the parallel in the first part of the verse, the condemnation actually embraces all people. But perhaps the biggest objection to this view is that it misses the point for which Paul is arguing in this passage. This point is that there can be an assurance of justification and life, on one side, that is just as strong and certain as the assurance of condemnation on the other. Paul wants to show, not how Christ has made *available* righteousness and life for all, but how Christ has secured the benefits of that righteousness for all who belong to him.

In this last phrase, we touch on what is the most likely explanation of Paul's language in this verse. Throughout the passage, Paul's concern to maintain parallelism between Adam and Christ has led him to choose terms that will clearly express this. In vv. 15 and 19, he uses "the many"; here he uses "all people." But in each case, Paul's point is not so much that the groups affected by Christ and Adam, respectively, are coextensive, but that Christ affects those who are his just as certainly as Adam does those who are his. When we ask who belongs to, or is "in," Adam and Christ, respectively, Paul makes his answer clear: every person, without exception, is "in Adam" (cf. vv. 12d-14); but only those who "receive the gift" (v. 17; "those who believe," according to Rom. 1:16–5:11) are "in Christ."[134] That

---

132. Cf. Barrett. Cranfield, following Barth (cf. *Christ and Adam. Man and Humanity in Romans 5* [New York: Collier, 1962], pp. 108-9), opens the door more widely to unqualified universalism. M. C. Boring ("The Language of Universal Salvation in Paul," *JBL* 105 [1986], 269-92) uses the idea of "language games" to explain the difference between "particularist" and "universal" statements in Paul. The "language game" concept is helpful, but, contra Boring, we must still strive for logical consistency on the "propositional" level.

133. Cf., although with differences in specifics, Melanchthon; Prat, *Theology,* 1.219; Denney; Godet; Stuart; Lenski; Meyer; Gifford; G. R. Beasley-Murray, *Baptism in the New Testament* (Grand Rapids: Eerdmans, 1962), pp. 136-37; Hughes, *True Image,* pp. 174-75.

134. Cf., e.g, Murray; Ridderbos, *Paul,* pp. 340-41; Morris. Cf. Augustine, *On Nature and Grace* 41.48: the "all" in v. 18b means that all who are justified are justified in Christ (*NPNF* 5.137-38).

"all"[135] does not always mean "every single human being" is clear from many passages, it often being clearly limited in context (cf., e.g., Rom. 8:32; 12:17, 18; 14:2; 16:19), so this suggestion has no linguistic barrier. In the present verse, the scope of "all people" in the two parts of the verse is distinguished in the context, Paul making it clear, both by his silence and by the logic of vv. 12-14, that there is no limitation whatsoever on the number of those who are involved in Adam's sin, while the deliberately worded v. 17, along with the persistent stress on faith as the means of achieving righteousness in 1:16–4:25, makes it equally clear that only certain people derive the benefits from Christ's act of righteousness.

19 In case we have missed his main point, Paul reiterates it in this verse, using the same basic structure as in v. 18 but different language.[136] In contrast to the "all people" of v. 18, Paul denotes those who are affected by the acts of Adam and Christ by "the many" (as in v. 15).[137] Two other differences are more important, suggesting that v. 19 is not just the repetition of v. 18, but its elaboration.

(1) Paul calls Adam's destiny-determining action an "act of disobedience"[138] rather than simply a "sin" (v. 12) or "trespass" (vv. 15, 17, 18). The characterization is, of course, a fair one since Adam and Eve had been explicitly told not to eat the fruit of the tree. In keeping with the careful contrasts that Paul has used throughout the passage, then, Christ's work is characterized as "an act of obedience."[139] Paul may be thinking of the "active obedience" of Christ, his lifelong commitment to "do his Father's will" and so fulfill the demands of the law.[140] But Paul's focus seems rather to be on Jesus' death as the ultimate act of obedience. This is suggested by the parallel with Adam's (one) act of disobedience, Phil. 2:8 — Jesus "became obedient unto death, even the death of the cross" — and the consistent connection Paul makes between justification and Jesus' death.[141]

(2) As Paul chooses different language to characterize the era-initiating

---

135. Gk. πᾶς.

136. In place of the combination ὡς . . . οὕτως of v. 18, Paul in v. 19 uses ὥσπερ . . . οὕτως. But the meaning is the same. A few commentators think that v. 19 might give the basis for v. 18, in the sense that the two destinies of condemnation and justification of v. 18 are seen to be based on two conditions in which people are put, "sinners" and "righteous" (e.g., Stuart).

137. Paul also adds ἀνθρώπου to each occurrence of ἑνός, making explicit what I argued was implicit in v. 18: that the adjective refers to the person rather than to the act.

138. Gk. παρακοή.

139. Gk. ὑπακοή.

140. E.g., Godet; R. N. Longenecker, "The Obedience of Christ in the Theology of the Early Church," in *Reconciliation and Hope*, p. 145.

141. See, e.g., Meyer; Dunn.

acts of Adam and Christ, so he also uses different language to describe the results of their respective acts. Rather than states, or destinies (death/life, condemnation/justification), Paul now describes these results in more "personal" categories: through Adam, the many "were made sinners"; through Christ, they "will be made[142] righteous [people]."[143] Debate surrounds the exact meaning of the verb Paul uses here. Some argue that it means nothing more than "make." But this translation misses the forensic flavor of the word. It often means "appoint," and probably refers here to the fact that people are "inaugurated into" the state of sin/righteousness.[144] Paul is insisting that people were really "made" sinners through Adam's act of disobedience just as they are really "made righteous" through Christ's obedience.[145] This "making righteous," however, must be interpreted in the light of Paul's typical forensic categories. To be "righteous" does not mean to be morally upright, but to be judged acquitted, cleared of all charges, in the heavenly judgment. Through Christ's obedient act, people become *really* righteous; but "righteous" itself is a legal, not a moral, term in this context.[146] Since this "being made righteous" is put in the future tense, Paul may have regard for the final

142. The future verb καταστασθήσονται might be a "real" future, looking to the last day as the time when sinners will be "made righteous" (e.g., Kuss; Schlier). But it is better to take it as a "logical" future since Paul consistently looks at justification as something enjoyed in this life in these verses (cf. esp. Fitzmyer; and cf. Lagrange).

143. Paul may allude here to Isa. 53:11c, which speaks of the servant of the Lord "making many righteous" (trans. of the Heb.; LXX differs; cf. J. Jeremias, *TDNT* VI, 543).

144. The verb is καθίστημι. In the NT, it means "bring, conduct" (Acts 17:15), "appoint" (seven times in the Gospels; four times in Acts; three times in Hebrews; Tit. 1:5) or "make," "constitute" (Jas. 3:6; 4:4; 2 Pet. 1:8). On the legal connotations of the verb, see MM. Some commentators (e.g., Zahn; Hodge; Shedd) may go too far in stressing the forensic force of the word to the neglect of the actual state of affairs it seems always to suggest (see A. Oepke, *TDNT* III, 445).

145. This does not necessarily mean, however, that people become sinners only by actually sinning in their own persons. People can be "made" sinners in the sense that God considers them to be such by regarding Adam's act as, at the same time, their act (cf. esp. Murray). It seems fair, then (against, e.g., Prat, *Theology*, 1.217-18), to speak of "imputation" here (Lafont ["Romans 5,15-21," p. 493] suggests a reference both to sin in Adam and personal sinning). This particular understanding of the word is in keeping with the legal connotations that the term often has (see above), and it alone matches the second use of the verb in the verse. For, while some suggest that, as people are "made" righteous by believing, so they are "made" sinners by sinning, the substitution of a different term in the second member — "believing" — destroys the analogy. To maintain strict parallelism, we would have to argue rather that, as people are made sinners by sinning, they are made righteous by being righteous, or doing righteous things. Yet this interpretation is obviously impossible; people are made righteous only by the righteousness of Christ and their faith in Christ, not by *being* righteous.

146. Godet; contra, e.g., Stuart, who takes it as purely ethical, and Ziesler, *Righteousness*, p. 199, who sees both forensic and ethical elements.

declaration of justification at the judgment.[147] It is more likely, however, in light of vv. 17 and 18, that Paul uses the future tense because he has in view the continual, discrete acts of "making righteous" that occur as people believe.[148]

In both parts of the verse, then, we are dealing with a real, though "forensic," situation: people actually become sinners in solidarity with Adam — by God's decision; people actually become "righteous" in solidarity with Christ — again, by God's decision. But there is one important difference, plainly hinted at in the emphasis on "grace" throughout vv. 15-17: while our solidarity with Adam in condemnation is due to our solidarity with him in "sinning," our solidarity with Christ in righteousness is *not* because we have acted righteously in and with Christ. While Rom. 6 suggests that we were in some sense "in Christ" when he "obeyed even unto death," that obedience is never accounted to us as our own. In other words, while we *deserve* condemnation — for "all have sinned" — we are *freely given* righteousness and life. It is this gratuitous element on the side of Christ's work that enables Paul to celebrate the "how much more" of our "reigning" in life (v. 17) and that gives to every believer absolute assurance for the life to come.

20 The division of humankind into two groups, determined by solidarity with the two divinely appointed representative-corporate figures of Adam and Christ, is simple and straightforward. But, it may be objected, is not this scheme overly simple? Can the centuries of salvation history recorded in the pages of the OT be so blithely ignored? Specifically, how about the law of Moses, which occupies so central a place in the life of God's people, Israel? Such questions would naturally occur to the reader of the OT, but they must have been particularly urgent in light of the discord between Jew and Gentile in the church at Rome and elsewhere in the early church. Many Jews accorded to the law of Moses great theological, even, at times, salvific, importance. It is, then, no wonder that Paul feels it necessary to interject a comment about the role of the Mosaic law in salvation history.

The "law,"[149] Paul asserts, "came in beside." The verb Paul uses here[150] often has a negative connotation; the only other occurrence in the NT is in Gal. 2:4, where Paul applies it to Judaizers, who have "sneaked in" to spy out the freedom of the Gentile Christians. However, it would be going too far to think that Paul pictures the God-given Mosaic law as "slipping in" with an evil purpose. On the other hand, the word should not be given a

---

147. E.g., Godet; Käsemann; Michel; de Boers, "The Defeat of Death," pp. 253-54 (who refers to 1 Cor. 15:21-22 as parallel).

148. S-H; Murray; Brandenburger, *Adam und Christus,* p. 234.

149. Anarthrous νόμος, but clearly the Mosaic law.

150. παρεισέρχομαι.

completely neutral significance either.[151] Negative connotations dominate in the use of this verb during the NT period (cf. BAGD), and Paul seems purposely to have chosen it in order to "relativize" the role of the law in salvation history. It has been "added" (cf. Gal. 3:19), introduced into a situation in which sin already holds sway, and has no power fundamentally to alter that situation.

Nevertheless, the law came with a purpose.[152] But its purpose, Paul affirms, was not to change the situation created by Adam, but to make it worse. The law "has increased" the trespass — not erased, or eased, or neutralized it, as many Jews, and perhaps some Jewish Christians, may have argued. But in what sense has the law "increased the trespass"?

(1) Some refer to the idea of "forbidden fruits": by forbidding certain activities, the law makes these very activities attractive to depraved people, leading to an increase in sinning.[153] But if this had been Paul's main point, we would have expected the plural "trespasses" rather than the singular. This same objection can be made against the view that the multiplication of commandments in the law, by defining more activities that are "sinful," so increases the trespass.[154]

(2) As part of his distinctive understanding of Pauline anthropology, Bultmann suggests that the law increases sin by encouraging people to find their "security" in obeying it. By holding out the prospect of "life," the law deceives people into becoming preoccupied with it. Paradoxically, then, according to Bultmann, the very attempt to obey the law betrays a sinful attempt to establish one's own righteousness.[155] The suggestion that Paul faults people for the attempt to obey the law, however, is not true to Paul's theology of the law; it is not trying to obey, but failing to obey, that is the problem (cf. Rom. 3:10-20; 7:7-25). This so-called "nomistic" interpretation of Paul's critique of the law must be rejected.[156]

(3) A third interpretation takes Paul's language subjectively: the law brings a new understanding to the sinner that he or she stands condemned

---

151. See Dunn; contra Cranfield.

152. This clause is occasionally taken to indicate result (BDR 391[11]; Chrysostom; Stuart; Lenski; Black), but there is no reason to abandon the usual final (purpose) meaning of ἵνα (cf., e.g., Moule, *Idiom Book,* 143). Undoubtedly, the law has had the consequence of "increasing the trespass," but Paul is considering the situation from the perspective of God's purpose: if it has had this consequence, it is because this was God's intention in giving the law.

153. E.g., Augustine, *Spirit and Letter* 4.6 (*NPNF* 5.85).

154. Godet.

155. Cf., e.g., *Theology,* 1.264.

156. See the critique of Bultmann's view in Ridderbos, *Paul,* pp. 145-46; Schreiner, " 'Works of Law,' " pp. 238-41; see also the notes on 7:5.

before God.[157] While Paul may on occasion allude to this function of the law (cf. 3:20; 7:7-13), it does not fit well in this context, where the increase of the trespass is juxtaposed with an increase in grace (v. 20b), implying that Paul is thinking of the objective status of the sinner before God.[158]

(4) Finally, then, in accordance with our interpretation of 4:15 and 5:14, we understand Paul to be asserting that God's purpose (or one of his purposes) in giving the law of Moses to Israel was to "intensify" the seriousness of sin. The word "trespass"[159] alludes to the sin of Adam (cf. vv. 15, 17, 18), but considered in its corporate dimension as "power." The fact and power of "sin" introduced into the world by Adam has not been decreased by the law, but given a new dimension as rebellion against the revealed, detailed will of God; sin has become "transgression" (cf. our comments on 4:15 and 5:14 [on "transgression"]).[160] That this interpretation is on the right track is confirmed by (though not proven by) the parallel text, Gal. 3:19: "the law was added in order to create[161] transgressions," and by Rom. 7:13. Hence, as Bornkamm summarizes, "The law has therefore no epoch-making significance, but has only the function of actualizing and radicalizing the crisis of Adamitic human existence."[162] Since Paul has used "trespass" of the sin of Adam in this context, we may say that the law has the function of turning those it addresses into "their own Adam": as a sinner who "transgresses" known "law" (cf. v. 14).[163] Against Jewish tendencies to attribute virtually salvific meaning to the law, Paul dethrones the law by ranging it on the side of Adam and sin.

But this negative purpose in the law is not, of course, God's final word. The law remains God's law, a gift given to Israel with an *ultimately* positive salvation-historical role. In showing sin to be "utterly sinful" (Rom. 7:13), the law reveals the desperate situation of people apart from grace. But, as Paul has emphasized throughout this paragraph, God's grace is more than

---

157. E.g., Calvin; Tholuck.

158. See Räisänen, 144.

159. Gk. παράπτωμα.

160. Cf. esp. Cranfield; Wilckens; Beker, 243-45; Luz, 202-3; F. Thielman, *Paul and the Law: A Contextual Approach* (Downers Grove: InterVarsity, 1994), p. 192.

161. Gk. χάριν; on this translation, see, e.g., Luz, 186-89; F. F. Bruce, *The Epistle to the Galatians* (NIGTC; Grand Rapids: Eerdmans, 1982), p. 175.

162. "Es hat also keine epochemachende Bedeutung, sondern nur die Funktion, die Krisis des adamitischen Menschseins zu aktualisieren und zu radikalisieren" ("Anakalouthe," pp. 88-89).

163. Cf. V. P. Furnish, *Theology and Ethics in Paul* (Nashville: Abingdon, 1968), p. 140. N. T. Wright ("Adam in Pauline Christology," *Society of Biblical Literature 1983 Seminar Papers* [Chico, CA: Scholars Press, 1983], pp. 359-89; rewritten in *The Climax of the Covenant* [Edinburgh: T & T Clark, 1991], pp. 18-40) draws attention to the many parallels between Adam and Israel in Jewish literature.

sufficient to overcome the increase in the power and seriousness of sin brought by the law. For in that very place where[164] sin[165] "increased,"[166] grace "super-increased."[167] Paul's purview is salvation history, considered in its broadest dimensions, and his point is simply that the law's negative purpose in radicalizing the power of sin has been more than fully met by the provisions of God's grace. However deep in the power of sin Israel may have sunk, God's grace was deeper yet. How many times, after reminding Israel of her blatant, repeated sin, do the prophets yet proclaim the willingness of God to forgive; indeed, his settled purpose to bless his people, in spite of themselves. In Christ, of course, we find the fulfillment of the promise of God's "super-abounding" grace.

21 This verse gives the purpose[168] of the superabounding of grace in v. 20b and also brings Paul's comparison and contrast between Adam and Christ to its climax. He thus returns for one last time to the language of comparison that dominates this discussion — "just as . . . so also" — and picks up some of the key terms he has used on both sides of the solidarity spheres: the reign of sin and death and the reign of grace through righteousness, leading to life. But Paul relates sin and death differently than he had done earlier; now, he says, sin reigned "in death." This "in"[169] might indicate accompaniment — "sin reigned with death"[170] — instrument — "sin reigned through death"[171] — or sphere — "sin reigned in the 'dominion' of death."[172] Of these alternatives, the second can claim the parallel in the second part of the verse — where grace reigns "through" righteousness — but the terms are not consonant; sin is not to grace as death is to righteousness. The first alternative is possible, but we have good reason to prefer the third. Paul often thinks in terms of "spheres" or "dominions," and the language of "reigning" is particularly well suited to this idea. Death has its own dominion: humanity as determined, and dominated, by Adam. And in this dominion, sin is in

---

164. οὗ ("where") might have a general reference — "wherever sin increased" — but probably refers to Israel (Godet; Cranfield; Dunn). But there is no reason to think that Paul is alluding specifically to the sin of Israel in rejecting the Messiah (contra Godet and Cranfield).

165. Gk. ἁμαρτία. Paul perhaps shifts from παράπτωμα to this word because he is thinking again especially of sin as a salvation-historical "power" (see the note on v. 12).

166. Gk. ἐπλεόνασεν.

167. Gk. ὑπερεπερίσσευσεν; cf. the use of this verb and its cognate noun in vv. 15 and 17.

168. Gk. ἵνα.

169. Gk. ἐν.

170. Cranfield.

171. Meyer.

172. Käsemann.

control. But those who "receive the gift" (v. 17) enjoy a transfer from this domain to another, the domain of righteousness, in which grace reigns and where life is the eventual outcome. Again, we see how Paul can highlight the importance of grace by giving it an active role, and how he pictures righteousness as the "gateway" to eternal life. And all of this, Paul reminds us in conclusion, is "through Jesus Christ our Lord" — ending this marvelous paragraph on the same christological theme as the preceding one (5:11).

B. FREEDOM FROM BONDAGE TO SIN (6:1-23)

Paul has shown how God's gracious act in Christ, when appropriated by faith, puts people into a new relationship with God and assures them that they will be saved from wrath in the last day. What has this to do with life in this present age? Anything? Everything, Paul asserts in Rom. 6. Christ's death "on our behalf" (cf. 5:6-8) frees us not only from the *penalty* of sin but from the *power* of sin also. Justification — acquittal from the guilt of sin — and sanctification — deliverance from "sinning" — must never be confused, but neither can they be separated. The Westminster Larger Catechism puts it like this: Question: "Wherein do justification and sanctification differ?" Answer: "Although sanctification be inseparably joined with justification, yet they differ, in that God in justification imputeth the righteousness of Christ; in sanctification his Spirit infuseth grace, and enableth to the exercise thereof; in the former, sin is pardoned; in the other, it is subdued."

Subduing the power of sin is the topic of Rom. 6. Paul hints at this theme by using the word "sin" in the singular throughout the chapter. As in 5:12-21 (and cf. 3:9), Paul pictures sin as a power or master that exercises unbreakable control over all who are "in Adam" (cf. the notes on v. 12). Sin's tyranny is broken, however, for the person who is "in Christ." Rom. 6 is thus permeated with the imagery of slavery, mastery, and freedom: those crucified with Christ should no longer "serve" sin (v. 6), should not let sin "rule" them because they have been "set free" from sin and been "enslaved" to God, or to righteousness (vv. 17-22): sin no longer "rules over" the believer (v. 14a).

From this quick summary, it is evident that one basic theme — the Christian's freedom from sin's tyranny or lordship — dominates the entire chapter. At two points, however, something of a "break" in the argument occurs. The first comes at v. 12, where imperatives begin replacing the indicatives of vv. 1-11. This shift, along with the similarity between vv. 13 and 19 (both using the imperative "present"[1]), might suggest that we should divide

---

1. Gk. παρίστημι.

the chapter into two parts, vv. 1-11 and 12-23.[2] But indicative and imperative are mixed throughout the chapter, and vv. 12ff. should be attached to vv. 1-11.[3] A more obvious break occurs at v. 15: we can hardly overlook the pause in the argument signaled by "what then?" and the following question, which reproduces v. 1 so closely. But it is only a shift of emphasis in the argument, and not the beginning of a new one.[4] Both paragraphs, vv. 1-14 and 15-23, look at the Christian's transfer from the realm of sin to that of righteousness. But the first focuses on the negative — release from sin — and the second on the positive — dedication to righteousness. Verses 15-23 elaborate on the theme of vv. 1-14, using the slavery imagery introduced in v. 6 to draw out the nature and consequences of the believer's transfer from the realm of sin to that of righteousness and life.

Because Paul's teaching in this chapter and in the next comes largely in response to questions (6:1, 15; 7:7, 13), these two chapters could be considered an excursus, in which Paul takes up objections to his teaching in chap. 5 and, perhaps, earlier in the letter.[5] Lending support to this supposition is the way chap. 8 resumes so many of the same themes that dominate chap. 5 (see the introduction to chaps. 5–8). Nevertheless, it is a mistake to regard chaps. 6 and 7 as "excursuses." Paul's overriding purpose in this part of the letter is to show that the justified believer can be confident that he or she will be "definitively" saved on the last day. No mere legal fiction, justification transfers the believer into the new age of redemption, where, joined with Christ, he or she lives under the reign of grace and looks confidently to the outcome of that reign, eternal life. This teaching, which dominates chap. 5, shows that union with Christ frees the believer from death. But what about sin and the law, both of which are also prominent in chap. 5 as two other "powers" of the old age? Chapters 6 and 7 deal with these, as Paul shows that union with Christ also frees the believer from the tyranny of sin and from the regime of the law. Far from being "excursuses," then, these chapters are fundamental to Paul's demonstration that the believer's justification unleashes the "power of God for salvation."

In 5:12-21, Paul has sketched in broad and impersonal language two "realms": that of sin and death, founded by Adam; and that of righteousness

---

2. Lagrange; Käsemann, 172; Murray, 1.226; Black, 90; Dunn, 1.305-6.

3. So most commentators: e.g., S-H, 167; Godet, 235; Michel, 199; Schlier, 205; Cranfield, 1.321.

4. This is emphasized by J. Kürzinger, "ΤΥΠΟΣ ΔΙΔΑΧΗΣ und der Sinn von Röm 6,17f," *Bib* 39 (1958), 156-57. Cf. also R. C. Tannehill, *Dying and Rising with Christ: A Study in Pauline Theology* (BZNW 32; Berlin: Töpelmann, 1966), p. 8.

5. E.g., J. Knox, *Chapters in a Life of Paul* (Nashville: Abingdon, 1950), p. 49. Schmithals (*Römerbrief,* pp. 18-21) views 6:1–7:16 as the excursus and Byrne ("Living Out," pp. 562-63) 6:1–8:13 (an "ethical excursus").

and life, founded by Christ. All people belong in one of these realms or the other; and they are now in the one or the other because God has viewed them as participating in the founding acts of these realms: the sin of Adam and the "obedience" of Christ (cf. vv. 12, 18-19). Since, in terms of salvation history, the realm of Christ has been instituted after that of Adam, we can also speak in temporal categories and call the realm of Adam the "old age" or "aeon" and that of Christ the "new age" or "aeon." This concept is a basic premise of much of what Paul has to say in Rom. 6, 7, and 8 (see also the section on "Theme" in the introduction). For he now "personalizes" this "two-realm" or "two-age" conception by proclaiming that believers are "transferred" from the one realm to the other and by showing how this transfer creates a new relationship to sin (chap. 6) and the law (chap. 7).[6] We are using the word "realm" because it captures well the emphasis in these chapters that the transfer from Adam to Christ, from old age to new, involves particularly a change in masters. Thus Paul presents the Christian as one who has moved from the "reign" of sin and death to that of righteousness and life (5:21); from the servitude, or "lordship," of sin to that of righteousness and God (6:6, 14, 17-22); from being "under the power of" the law to being "under the power of" grace (6:14, 15); from service "in oldness of letter" to service "in newness of Spirit" (7:6); from the "law," or "compelling power," of sin leading to death to that of the Spirit who brings life (8:2). By using this imagery of a transfer of realms, or "dominions," with its associations of power and rulership, Paul makes clear that the new status enjoyed by the believer (justification) brings with it a new influence and power that both has led and must lead to a new way of life (sanctification).

This "must" is very important. For, as decisive and final as is this transfer into a new realm, it would be a bad misinterpretation of Paul to think that the believer is thereby removed from all contact or influence with the old realm of sin. While belonging to a new realm, the believer brings with him into it many of the impulses, habits, and tendencies of the old life, a constant threat to putting into actual practice the realities of our new realm status. It is this "eschatological reservation" — the fact that not until the resurrection and transformation of the body will the believer be severed from all contact with the old Adamic dominion — that explains the "indicative/imperative" combinations that are so characteristic of these chapters: "sin will not rule over you"/"do not let sin reign" (6:13-14); "you are not in the flesh"/"do not live according to the flesh" (8:9, 12).[7]

6. Cf., e.g., Käsemann, 159; Osten-Sacken, *Römer 8*, pp. 174-75.
7. See esp. Dunn, 1.301-2, on this eschatological context of Paul's imperative.

1. *"Dead to Sin" through Union with Christ (6:1-14)*

1*What, then, shall we say? Should we remain in sin, in order that grace might increase? 2By no means! We who have died to sin, how can we yet live in it? 3Or are you ignorant of the fact that as many as were baptized into Christ Jesus have been baptized into his death? 4Therefore,[8] we were buried together with him through baptism unto death, in order that, just as Christ was raised from the dead by the glory of the Father, so we, too, might walk in newness of life. 5For if we have become joined with the likeness of his death, we will also be joined with the likeness of his resurrection.*

6*We know this: that our old man was crucified with Christ, so that the body of sin might be rendered powerless, with the purpose that we should no longer serve sin. 7For the one who dies has been justified from sin. 8But[9] if we have died with Christ, we believe that we shall also live with him, 9knowing that Christ, having been raised from the dead, will no longer die; death no longer has lordship over him. 10For the death that he died, he died to sin once for all; and the life that he lives, he lives for God. 11In the same way, then, you also consider yourselves to be dead to sin and alive to God in Christ Jesus.[10]*

12*Do not, therefore, let sin reign in your mortal body, in order to obey its passions.[11] 13And do not present your members as weapons*

---

8. This assumes that οὖν, attested in all but one (1506) Greek MS, is the correct reading, rather than γάρ, presumed in OL and by Origen.

9. The important early papyrus P[46] and the secondary western uncials F and G read γάρ, "for"; but the support is too slight to render this reading a serious consideration.

10. After Χριστῷ Ἰησοῦ, a significant number of MSS (including P[94] [?], the primary Alexandrian uncial ℵ, the secondary Alexandrian witnesses C, 33, 81, and 1739, and the majority text) add τῷ κυρίῳ ἡμῶν, "our Lord" (cf. KJV). But this addition is surely a secondary assimilation to the phraseology of verses such as 5:1, 21 and, especially, 6:23.

11. Three variants of the last words of the verse are found in the MS tradition:

1. ταῖς ἐπιθυμίαις αὐτοῦ, "its [the body's] passions" — with strong Alexandrian support (the primary witnesses ℵ and B and the secondary MSS A, C [original hand], 81, and 1739; and cf. also P[94]);
2. αὐτῇ, "it" (e.g., sin) — with mainly western support (D, F, G; although cf. also P[46]);
3. αὐτῇ ἐν ταῖς ἐπιθυμίαις αὐτοῦ, "it [sin] in its [the body's] passions" — with support from the third corrector of C (a secondary Alexandrian MS), 33 (secondary Alexandrian), Ψ, and the majority text.

Gundry (p. 40) argues that αὐτῇ is original, it being changed because of its distance from ἁμαρτία, its antecedent. But the external evidence rather decisively supports the first alternative, with the third being a rather obvious conflation of the other two (cf. Cranfield).

of unrighteousness for sin, but present yourselves to God as those who are living and your members as weapons of righteousness for God. 14For sin will no longer have lordship over you, for you are not under law but under grace.

Paul uses the language of "realm transfer" to show how inconceivable is the suggestion that a believer should "remain in sin" in order to accentuate grace (vv. 1-2a). We Christians, Paul affirms, have "died to sin" (v. 2b); we have been taken out from under its tyranny in a transfer so radical and decisive that the language of death and new life can be used of it. In vv. 3-4 Paul shows how this transfer has taken place: we "died to sin" in baptism (which Paul uses to summarize our conversion to Christ and our initiation into his body; see below). For this "conversion-initiation," in joining us with Christ, joins us with Christ's death — and, as Paul will show in vv. 9-10, Christ's death was itself a "death to sin." 12 So close is this association with Christ's death that we may be said to have been "buried with him." Burial both sets the seal on death and prepares for that which is to follow: living a new life patterned after the resurrection of Christ. Many commentators view vv. 5-7 and 8-10 as two roughly parallel elaborations of this basic teaching. 13 But it is better to connect v. 5 closely with v. 4, since it makes explicit the connection between our being with Christ in death and our being with him in life that is assumed in v. 4b. Verses 6-7 then resume and explain further the "death" side of our union with Christ (vv. 4a and 5a), while vv. 8-10 focus on the "life" side of that union (vv. 4b and 5b). 14 Verse 11 is the hinge of the paragraph. It summons believers to regard themselves in the way that Paul has described in vv. 2-10: as dead to sin and alive to God. That this "regarding" is no mere mental state is made clear in vv. 12-14. The declaration and promise of God

---

12. We may summarize the basic logic of the paragraph as follows:

Christ died to sin (vv. 8-10)
We died with Christ (vv. 3-7)
Therefore: we died to sin (v. 2)

(I want to express my thanks to Dan Bailey for helping me sort out the logical flow of this text.)

13. Cf., e.g., the discussion in Michel, 200-201. Advocates of this outline stress the syntactical parallelism between vv. 5-7 and 8-10. Both begin with a conditional sentence that argues from the past fact of dying with Christ to the future certainty of resurrection with him (vv. 5, 8), are followed by an explanation of the significance of the death mentioned in the form of a participial clause using a verb meaning "know" (vv. 6, 9), and conclude with a further explanation (cf. γάρ) of the previous verse.

14. Cf., e.g., Lagrange; Wilckens.

that sin no longer is the Christian's "lord" (v. 14a) must be "activated"; we must not let sin rule us (v. 12), but give ourselves in service to God (v. 13).

The theology of this paragraph is both profound and controversial. What makes for the controversy are the related questions of the meaning and importance of baptism (vv. 3-4) and the relationship between baptism and the "with Christ" language that is so characteristic of the paragraph (cf. vv. 4, 5, 6, 8). I will explore these questions in some detail in the notes that follow, but a quick survey of the "lay of the land" as I see it may be helpful. First, it is clear that Paul refers in vv. 3-4 to water baptism; but baptism is not the theme of the paragraph nor is it Paul's purpose to exposit his theology of baptism. Baptism, rather, functions as shorthand for the conversion experience as a whole. As such, it is the instrument (note the "through" in v. 4) by which we are put into relationship with the death and burial of Christ. It is not, then, that baptism is a symbol of dying and rising with Christ; nor is it that baptism is the place at which we die and rise with Christ. Dying and rising with Christ refers to the participation of the believer in the redemptive events themselves; and the ultimate basis for Paul's appeal in this chapter is not what happened when we were baptized, but what happened when Christ died and rose again. That death of his to sin is also our death to sin (vv. 2, 6, 9-10); and that resurrection of his to new life, in which we will "participate" in the future (vv. 5b and 8b), is even now working to enable us to "walk in newness of life" (vv. 4b, 11).

1 "What, then, shall we say?"[15] takes us back to the lively question-and-answer style that Paul has employed earlier in the letter (cf. 3:1-9, 27-31; 4:1-12). Rather than being part of a longer question (as in 4:1), "What, then, shall we say?" here stands independently, introducing a second question: "Should we remain in sin in order that grace might increase?" This question is raised in response to Paul's assertion in 5:20b that "where sin abounded, grace abounded all the more."[16] This half-verse is a joyful proclamation of the triumph of God's grace in salvation history; even in the era of the law, when sin was rendered more serious than ever before, God did not abandon his people or his purpose. He showered blessings upon them, undeservedly, and persisted in his plan to bring redemption through the Messiah. But the statement of historical fact that grace increased in precisely the "place" where sin was increasing is in the question of 6:1b turned into a statement of general principle, as if God is somehow bound to bestow more grace while we remain willfully in "the state of sin."[17] It is as if the

---

15. Gk. Τί οὖν ἐροῦμεν;

16. Aletti (*Comment Dieu est-il juste?* 38-48) suggests that 5:20-21 announces the propositions that Paul expounds in chaps. 6 and 7.

17. This is the meaning of the singular τῇ ἁμαρτίᾳ.

knowledge that their father had forgiven them in the past would lead children to do wrong with abandon precisely so as to enjoy more forgiveness. Only a foolish parent would tolerate such a situation, and God's grace must not be interpreted in these terms.

Who, we might ask, is putting such a question to Paul? Particularly if these questions reflect a "diatribe" style whose locus is in the debate, Paul may be quoting an opponent of his — perhaps a Jew,[18] or Judaizer.[19] But as I have argued earlier (see, particularly, on 3:1-8), Paul's question-and-answer style in Romans is pedagogical rather than polemical in orientation. Because of this, and because he is obviously concerned throughout the chapter not just with intellectual objections to his view but with the obedience and lifestyle of Christians, it is better to think that Paul himself poses this question in order to draw out the implications of the Christian's experience of grace.[20] Undoubtedly, as 3:8 indicates, detractors of Paul's gospel were criticizing him on just this point; and it has historically been the case that critics of Christianity have objected that free grace undercuts morality. Particularly, in light of the negative reference to the law in 5:20b, we can imagine this question being raised by a Jew: If the law does not have the authority to quell sin, how can grace do it? Will not the "reign of grace" simply encourage sinning without the law to curb it?

In response, essentially, Paul argues that the law could never curb sinning; and the reign of grace, far from encouraging sin, is the only means by which sin can truly be defeated.[21] But, as is also true both historically and in our own day, Christians are by no means immune from the temptation to slip from a celebration of grace to an abuse of grace, to be complacent about sin because, after all, God is gracious and will forgive. In practice at least, we echo the French skeptic Voltaire: "God will forgive; that is his 'business' [*métier*]." (Similarly, W. H. Auden: "I like committing crimes. God likes forgiving them. Really the world is admirably arranged."[22]) While, therefore, the objection was one that Paul must have heard from opponents of the gospel, he himself raises it here in order to show Christians that the gospel of grace, properly interpreted, leads not to licentiousness but to righteousness (now understood as godly living).

2 With his familiar "By no means!"[23] Paul emphatically denies that the Christian should sin in order to secure more grace, and explains himself

18. Michel.

19. Wilckens.

20. Bornkamm, "Baptism and New Life in Paul: Romans 6," in *Early Christian Experience* (London: SCM, 1969), pp. 72-73; Cranfield; Dunn; Fitzmyer.

21. Dunn.

22. *For the Time Being* (London: Faber and Faber, 1958), p. 116.

23. Gk. μὴ γένοιτο.

in a rhetorical question: "We who[24] have died to sin, how can we yet live in it?" The Christian's death "to sin" is the main point of Rom. 6. But what does this death "to sin" mean? Grammatically, the "to" probably carries the idea of "disadvantage": the believer has died "to the detriment of sin."[25] And Paul uses the verb "die" because (1) it creates an immediate tie with the death of Christ, central to the believer's own "death to sin"; and (2) it connotes a decisive and final break in one's state of being. The idea, then, is of a decisive separation from sin.[26] This separation could be a separation from the penalty due because of sin,[27] but the context demonstrates that Paul is talking not about the penalty, but about the power, of sin (cf. v. 6b: "that we should no longer serve sin"; v. 14a: "sin shall no longer have lordship over you"). It is better, then, to view the separation as a separation from the "rule" or "realm" of sin, sin being personified, as throughout this chapter, as a power that rules over the person outside Christ.

When did this "death to sin" take place? In light of the stress on participation in the redemptive events of Christ's death, burial, and resurrection that follows (vv. 4-6), one could argue that the Christian died to sin when, on Golgotha, he or she died with Christ.[28] But v. 3 connects death to sin specifically with baptism, and the "yet" in the second part of the verse suggests that the believer's death to sin transfers him or her from a condition

---

24. The indefinite relative pronoun οἵτινες is often equivalent in the NT to the simple relative pronoun (ὅς), but it is used deliberately here with a "qualitative" nuance: "we who are of such a nature that . . ." (Moule, *Idiom Book*, pp. 123-25).

25. English "to," used in all modern English translations, represents the dative case in Greek (τῇ ἁμαρτίᾳ), which often has the idea of something done "to one's disadvantage." Most scholars think the dative here is that of "disadvantage" *(incommodi)* (cf. esp. C. F. D. Moule, "Death 'to Sin', 'to Law,' and 'to the World': A Note on Certain Datives," in *Mélanges bibliques en hommage au R. P. Béda Rigaux* [ed. A. Descamps and A. de Halleux; Gembloux: Duculot, 1970], pp. 367-75), although some prefer a more general "reference" idea (e.g., BDF 188; Robertson, 539; W. Thüsing, *Per Christum in Deum* [NTAbh 1; Münster: Aschendorff, 1965], pp. 79-81).

The dative after the verb ἀποθνῄσκω ("die") is unusual, occurring only five times in Paul: vv. 2 and 10, Rom. 14:7 and 8 ("no one dies to himself [ἑαυτῷ]"; "we die to the Lord [τῷ κυρίῳ]"), and Gal. 2:19 ("I have died to the law [νόμῳ]"). Somewhat parallel are Gal. 6:14b — "the world is crucified to me [ἐμοὶ κόσμος ἐσταύρωται], and I to the world"; Rom. 7:4 — "you have been put to death to the law [ἐθανατώθητε τῷ νόμῳ]"; Rom. 7:6 — "dying [to that] in which [ἀποθανόντες {ἐκείνῳ} ἐν ᾧ] we were bound"; and Rom. 6:11 — "dead to sin [νεκροὺς τῇ ἁμαρτίᾳ]." Eph. 2:1, 5, and Col. 2:13 ("dead in trespasses"; νεκροὺς [τοῖς] παραπτώμασιν) are similar in construction but obviously different in meaning, with "dead" meaning spiritually dead.

26. Note the use of the ablatival ἀπό in the parallel Col. 2:20: "you have died with Christ *from* the elements of the world."

27. E.g., Haldane.

28. Ribberbos, *Paul*, p. 206.

that has been consciously experienced. For these reasons, it is better to think of the "death to sin" as occurring in conjunction with the believer's (conversion-)baptism.[29] But it is necessary to explore further the logical force of Paul's "how . . . yet." Turned into a statement, which is the logical equivalent of the rhetorical question, it may be taken in two different ways: (1) "We Christians should realize that we must not live in sin" (a "moral" appeal); or (2) "We Christians are no longer able to live in sin" (a "theological" assertion). In other words, is "living in sin" a possibility to be avoided, or an impossibility to be recognized?

Everything depends on the meaning we give to the phrase "living in sin." If by this Paul means committing sins, or living at times *as if* sin still reigned, then the first alternative is certainly a possibility. For, to go no further, it is clear from the imperatives in vv. 11-14 that Paul considers sin a continuing and ever-present threat to the Christian. On the other hand, if "living in sin" means existing "in the sphere of" and so "under the lordship" of sin, then the second alternative must be correct; for Paul makes clear that the deliverance from sin's lordship is a past, unchangeable occurrence (vv. 6, 14, 17-22). The balance between these two is a fine one, but the first appears to be closer to the truth. "Living in sin" is best taken as describing a "lifestyle" of sin — a habitual practice of sin, such that one's life could be said to be characterized by that sin rather than by the righteousness God requires. Such habitual sin, "remaining in sin" (v. 1), "living in sin" (v. 2), is not possible, as a constant situation, for the one who has truly experienced the transfer out from under the domain, or tyranny, of sin. Sin's power is broken for the believer, and this *must* be evident in practice (see also Jas. 2:14-26; and perhaps 1 John 3:6, 9). Yet the nature of Christian existence is such that the believer can, at times, live in a way that is inconsistent with the reality of what God has made him in Christ.[30] It is not sin, but the believer, who has "died," and sin, as Wesley puts it, "remains" even though it does not "reign."[31] Therefore, while "living in sin" is incompatible with Christian existence and impossible for the Christian as a constant condition, it remains a real threat. It is this threat that Paul warns us about in v. 2.

Having said this, however, we must not ignore the importance of the "indicative" "we have died to sin." It is only because we have been delivered from sin's power by God's act in Christ that we can be expected to cease obeying sin as a master. The imperative "Thou shalt" would be a futile and

---

29. See, e.g., Beasley-Murray, *Baptism,* p. 140.

30. In a pardonable exaggeration, one scholar calls sin "the impossible possibility" (Beker, 215-18).

31. From his sermon "On the Repentance of Believers," quoted in *Compendium of Wesley's Theology,* p. 179.

frustrating demand without the "Thou hast" of the indicative.[32] Living a life pleasing to God flows from the real experience of liberation from sin's domain secured by God for us in Christ (note the passive forms of the verbs in vv. 6, 17, and 22). "Justification by faith and sanctification by struggle," as Griffith Thomas puts it, is the view held by many Christians; but Paul asserts in this passage the inseparability of justification and sanctification as provided for equally in Christ.

3 Death to sin, Paul argues in v. 3, is part and parcel of becoming a Christian. For baptism involves us with the death of Christ, a death that itself is a death to sin (as Paul will argue in vv. 8-10). By introducing this teaching with the phrase "or are you ignorant,"[33] Paul signifies that what he is saying has a basis in what the Roman Christians already know about baptism and Christian experience.[34] Paul's reference is to the Roman Christians' water baptism as their outward initiation into Christian existence. To be sure, a few scholars have denied any reference to water baptism here, arguing that "baptize" means "immerse" in a metaphorical sense,[35] or that Paul refers to "baptism in the Spirit,"[36] or that he uses "baptize" as a metaphor for incorporation into the body of Christ.[37] But, without discounting the possibility of allusions to one or more of these ideas, a reference to water baptism is primary. By the date of Romans, "baptize" had become almost a technical expression for the rite of Christian initiation by water,[38] and this is surely the meaning the Roman Christians would have given the word.

Paul, then, argues from the Roman Christians' familiarity with Christian baptism to make his point: "as many as were baptized into Christ Jesus have been baptized into his death." But why does Paul qualify baptism with

---

32. Althaus.

33. Gk. ἤ ἀγνοεῖτε; cf. also 7:1.

34. It is difficult, and perhaps unnecessary, to determine precisely how much of what Paul says in vv. 3-6 the believers in Rome already knew. Probably Beasley-Murray is right: while no single element of what Paul says would have been completely novel, the significance of each is "deepened" in Paul's teaching (*Baptism*, p. 128; cf. also A. J. M. Wedderburn, "Hellenistic Christian Traditions in Romans 6?" *NTS* 29 [1983], 345-46, and, in greater detail, idem, *Baptism and Resurrection: Studies in Pauline Theology against its Graeco-Roman Background* [WUNT 44; Tübingen: Mohr, 1987], pp. 41-69).

35. This idea is suggested by Morris, although he does not exclude reference to water baptism.

36. See, e.g., Lloyd-Jones.

37. J. D. G. Dunn, "Salvation Proclaimed: VI. Romans 6:1-11: Dead and Alive," *ExpTim* 93 (1982), 361.

38. Paul uses the verb βαπτίζω eleven other times, and — in our estimation — all but one (1 Cor. 10:2 — and it is probably used in analogy to Christian water baptism) denote Christian water baptism (cf. also 1 Cor. 1:13, 14, 15, 16 [twice], 17; 12:13 [debated, but I think it belongs here]; 15:29 [twice]; Gal. 3:27).

the phrase "into Christ Jesus?"[39] (1) Many scholars think that this phrase is an abbreviated form of the more familiar "into the name of [the Lord] Christ Jesus." Paul would simply be making it clear that he is talking about Christian baptism — our baptism makes us Christ's disciples.[40] (2) Other interpreters claim that the context, in which our incorporation into Christ is so prominent, favors a spatial meaning: we were baptized "into union with Christ."[41] Two arguments favor this second view. First, the closest parallel to the language here is Gal. 3:27, with strongly suggests a spatial sense: "For as many of you as were baptized *into* Christ, have put on Christ."[42] Second, being "buried with Christ in baptism" (v. 4a) is a conclusion ("therefore") drawn from v. 3. But it is difficult to account for this sequence unless v. 3 has already alluded in some way to the concept of a union *with* Christ. Paul, then, argues that Christian baptism, by joining the believer with Christ Jesus, also joins him or her with the death of Christ.[43]

39. Gk. εἰς Χριστὸν Ἰησοῦν.

40. The phrase εἰς τὸ ὄνομα follows the verb βαπτίζω in Matt. 28:19 ("the Father and the Son and the Holy Spirit"); Acts 8:16 and 19:5 ("the Lord Jesus"); 1 Cor. 1:13, 15 ("Paul"/"mine"). For this view, see esp. Beasley-Murray, *Baptism*, pp. 128-29; Barrett; P. Siber, *Mit Christus Leben. Eine Studie zur paulinischen Auferstehungshoffnung* (ATANT 61; Zürich: Theologischer, 1971), pp. 206-7 (and on the formula, see L. Hartman, " 'Into the Name of Jesus': A Suggestion Concerning the Earliest Meaning of the Phrase," *NTS* 20 [1974], 432-40). A similar interpretation holds that εἰς has referential sense: we were baptized "with reference to" Christ Jesus; see Godet; Cranfield; B. N. Kaye, "βαπτίζειν εἰς with Special Reference to Romans 6," *Studia Evangelica* 6 (ed. E. A. Livingstone; Berlin: Akademie, 1969), p. 59.

41. So, e.g., S-H; Murray; Dunn; Best, *One Body,* pp. 56-57; Ridderbos, *Paul,* pp. 401-3; A. Oepke, *TDNT* I, 539; Tannehill, *Dying and Rising,* pp. 22-24; M. Bouttier, *En Christ. Étude d'exégèse et de théologie pauliniennes* (Paris: University of France, 1962), pp. 36-38; Wedderburn, *Baptism,* pp. 54-60. The phrase could be considered a shortened form of the "in the name of" formula even with a spatial meaning. Wedderburn (*Baptism,* pp. 54-60) appeals to Str-B (1.1054), who cite *b. Yebam.* 45b for evidence that the formula "wash in the name of" can signify a being bound to the person in whose name one is washed.

42. The only other occurrences of εἰς after βαπτίζω in the NT have a local/physical sense (Mark 1:9 ["into the Jordan"]) or indicate purpose/result (Matt. 3:11 and Acts 2:38 ["forgiveness of sins"]; 1 Cor. 12:13 ["in order to become one body"]). 1 Corinthians 10:2 ("they all were baptized into Moses [εἰς Μωϋσῆν]") is very difficult, but it perhaps indicates "into relationship with Moses" as their leader. P.-E. Langevin ("Le baptême dans la mort-résurrection. Exégèse de Rm 6,1-5," *Sciences Ecclésiastiques* 17 [1965], 45) combines the spatial with a final meaning: baptized "with a view to being incorporated into Christ" (Dunn's paraphrase is similar).

43. Some object that the spatial meaning of εἰς Χριστὸν Ἰησοῦν in the first clause does not work in the second (εἰς τὸν θάνατον αὐτοῦ). But (1) the two need not have the same meaning; and (2) a spatial rendering of the second clause works quite well: we have been brought into intimate union with Christ's death (by sharing it and its effects).

4 In this verse, Paul draws a conclusion[44] from the believer's incorporation into the death of Christ. If we have died "with" Christ through baptism, Paul reasons, then we have also been buried with him "through baptism [which is] unto [his[45]] death."[46] And this burial not only marks the end of the old life but is also part of the transition to a new life, in which the believer is now called to "walk." This clause raises three interrelated and controversial issues: why has Paul introduced the image of burial, what is the meaning of the Christian's being "with" Christ, and how does baptism mediate this being with Christ?

A bewildering number of answers to these questions has been given, but the most important can be grouped into three general approaches.

(1) Many evangelical scholars understand "burial with Christ" as a metaphor for the believer's complete break with the old life and view baptism as a symbolic picture of the transfer from the old life to the new. Immersion represents death to the old life, submersion the "burial" — the seal of death — of that old life, and emersion the rising to new life. In this way baptism pictures what has taken place in the believer's life through conversion. As A. H. Strong puts it, "Baptism symbolizes the previous entrance of the believer into the communion of Christ's death and resurrection."[47] Despite the popularity of this view, it does not, by itself, provide a sufficient explanation for the verse. The problem is with the prepositions in the first clause. Paul makes baptism the *means* by which we are buried with Christ (*dia* baptism), not the *place* in which we are buried with him.[48] Indeed, although

---

44. Cf. Gk. οὖν, "therefore."

45. The "death" to which Paul refers is, in light of v. 3b, the death of Christ rather than "death" generally (contra, e.g., Godet).

46. In the first prepositional phrase following συνετάφημεν ("we were buried"), διὰ τοῦ βατίσματος, the article is anaphoric, picking up the reference to baptism in v. 3 (hence the "this" in our paraphrase above). The second prepositonal phrase, εἰς τὸν θάνατον, could modify the verb: "we were buried so as to share his death" (cf. TEV; see also Zahn; Lagrange; B. Frid, "Römer 6:4-5: εἰς τὸν θάνατον und τῷ ὁμοιώματι τοῦ θανάτου αὐτοῦ als Schlüssel zu Duktus und Gedankengang in Röm 6,1-11," *BZ* 30 [1986], 190-91). But it is better taken with the immediately preceding noun, βαπτίσματος (cf. REB; NJB; and see, e.g., Godet; Murray; Cranfield; Käsemann; the lack of an article before εἰς is no bar to this interpretation; NT Greek frequently omits articles before attributive prepositional phrases [cf. BDF 272]).

47. *Systematic Theology,* p. 940. Cf. also W. F. Flemington, *The New Testament Doctrine of Baptism* (London: SPCK, 1957), p. 59; Bruce; J. D. G. Dunn, *Unity and Diversity in the New Testament: An Inquiry into the Character of Earliest Christianity* (Philadelphia: Westminster, 1977), pp. 158-59 (although he confines the symbolism of baptism to burial and death, and he appears less certain of this view in his commentary).

48. As, e.g., an ἐν might suggest. Even in Col. 2:12, where ἐν is used in a similar statement — συνταφέντες αὐτῷ ἐν τῷ βαπτισμῷ — the preposition is probably instrumental.

the interpretation can be traced to a fairly early date in the history of the church,[49] there is no evidence in Rom. 6, or in the NT elsewhere, that the actual physical movements — immersion and emersion — involved in baptism were accorded symbolical significance. The focus in Rom. 6, certainly, is not on the *ritual* of baptism, but the simple *event* of baptism.[50] Therefore, while not ruling out the possibility of a secondary allusion to the symbolism of the baptismal rite,[51] we conclude that this cannot be the main reason why the Christian's burial with Christ is introduced. A second preposition also creates difficulties for a purely symbolic view: "with" *(syn).*[52] While the force of *syn* with verbs of action can vary,[53] it is questionable whether its normal meaning of accompaniment can be stretched so far as to embrace the idea of a being buried (in our lives) *as* Christ was buried in his.

(2) A second way of relating burial with Christ to baptism is, as in the first view, to take "burial" as a metaphor for the believer's complete break with the old life but to understand baptism as the mediator of that break.[54]

49. Cf. Tertullian, *On Baptism,* chap. 3; as it is put in *The Apostolic Constitutions and Canon* (4th cent.): ἡ κατάδυσις τὸ συναποθανεῖν, ἡ ἀνάδυσις τὸ συναναστῆναι: "The immersion is dying with him, the emersion is rising with him."

50. Cf., e.g., H. Frankemölle, *Das Taufverständnis des Paulus: Taufe, Tod und Auferstehung nach Röm 6* (SBS 47; Stuttgart: Katholisches, 1970), p. 56; R. Schnackenburg, "Todes- und Lebensgemeinschaft mit Christus. Neue Studien zu Röm 6,1-11," *MTZ* 6 (1955), 39-41; Langevin, "Baptême," pp. 38-55.

51. Cf., e.g., Beasley-Murray, *Baptism,* p. 133; Barrett.

52. The preposition is attached to the verb τάφω, "bury."

53. See the excursus following this section.

54. Cf., e.g., Stuart; Scott, *Christianity,* pp. 117-18. Many also suggest the symbolism of immersion and emersion as a secondary factor — e.g., S-H. Most proponents of this view think that "baptism," the instrument by which this burial is accomplished, refers to water baptism (e.g., J. D. G. Dunn, *Baptism in the Holy Spirit* [SBT 15; London: SCM, 1970], pp. 140-42), but a few prefer to take the word metaphorically, as a reference to "spiritual" baptism, or conversion (Lloyd-Jones; Griffith Thomas [?]). Still others suggest that Paul's conception is related to ideas of union with a dying and rising god that were popular in Hellenistic "mystery religions." These "mystery religions," a group of religions very popular in the Hellenistic world, featured secret initiations and promised their adherents "salvation," often by participation in a cultic act that was held to bring the initiate into union with a god. Under the impulse of the history-of-religions movement early in this century, many scholars attributed various doctrines of Paul to dependence on these religions (the best known are W. Bousset, *Kyrios Christos* [2d ed.; Göttingen: Vandenhoeck & Ruprecht, 1921; ET Nashville: Abingdon, 1970] and R. Reitzenstein, *Die hellenistischen Mysterienreligionen nach ihren Grundgedanken und Wirkung* [3d ed.; Leipzig: B. G. Teubner, 1927; ET *Hellenistic Mystery Religions: Their Basic Ideas and Significance* {Pittsburgh: Pickwick, 1978}]). But direct dependence of Paul on these religions is now widely discounted (for Rom. 6, see esp. G. Wagner, *Pauline Baptism and the Pagan Mysteries* [London: Oliver & Boyd, 1967]; Davies, 88-98). More popular is the view that Paul's Hellenistic churches interpreted their experience of Christ in the light of these

This interpretation compares favorably to the first in giving "through baptism" an instrumental sense, but we find the same problem as in the first with the understanding of the *syn* ("with") compound. Again, the "with Christ" must be taken to mean "as Christ, so we": as Christ was buried, so sealing his death to the old age, so we are "buried," sealing our death to the old age. We must say again that such a conception does not do justice to Paul's conception of what it means for the believer to be, or do things, "with Christ." Others try to do greater justice to this *syn* language by applying it to the general relationship between the believer and Christ; baptism brings us into union with Christ, so that we experience a baptism like his.[55] But Paul says not that we have been *joined* with Christ, but that we have been *buried* with him.

(3) We come then to the third and, I would argue, correct approach. "Burial with Christ" is a description of the participation of the believer in Christ's own burial, a participation that is mediated by baptism. Paul's point, as Beasley-Murray puts it, "is not that the believer in baptism is laid in his own grave, but that through that action he is set alongside Christ Jesus in his."[56] This approach interprets *dia* naturally and explains *syn* in a way that accords both with the normal meaning of the word and with Paul's larger conception of "with Christ." But what is the exact nature, or time, of this believer's being "buried with Christ"?

Since it is through baptism that we are buried with Christ, we might think of Christ's burial (and death and resurrection also; cf. v. 5) as being present in baptism. Baptism is then a sacrament that is efficacious because there is in it — as, it is argued, in the Eucharist — a "real presence" of Christ.[57] While there are elements in this text that could support this view (see the notes on v. 5), it suffers from two fatal objections. First, it is questionable whether Paul's insistence on the "once-for-all" nature of Christ's death

---

religions and that Paul's teaching demonstrates points of contact with, and corrections of, this existing tradition (cf., e.g., N. Gäumann, *Taufe und Ethik. Studien zu Römer 6* [BEvT 47; Munich: Kaiser, 1967], pp. 37-49; Käsemann, 160-62; G. M. M. Pelser, "The Objective Reality of the Renewal of Life in Romans 6:1-11," *Neot* 15 [1981], 108-9). In this light, it is often thought that Paul is alluding to this kind of tradition when he introduces his teaching in v. 3 with "or are you ignorant?" However, even this indirect influence is not very clear, at least in Rom. 6:1-6 (cf. particularly Wedderburn, *Baptism,* pp. 90-163). The very concept that is seen as the closest parallel between the mysteries and Paul's teaching — σὺν Χριστῷ — is probably rooted in Paul's own conception of Christ rather than in the mysteries (Siber, *Mit Christus Leben,* pp. 191-213; Wedderburn, *Baptism,* pp. 50-52). The mystical and repeated "dying and rising" of a mystery religion adherent with a nature god like Osiris or Attis has little to do with Paul's focus on the Christian's participation in the historical events of Christ's life.

55. E.g., S-H.
56. *Baptism,* p. 130.
57. Cf., e.g., Kuss; J. Schneider, *TDNT* V, 195.

and resurrection (cf. v. 10) allows for them to be understood as present in, or repeated in, the act of baptism. While freely admitting that the death, burial, and resurrection of Christ are eschatological events whose significance transcends time, I think it is going too far to say that these events, *as events,* are "timeless." The second objection is that, by locating death, burial, and resurrection with Christ in baptism, a significance is given to baptism that does not fit the argument of Rom. 6 and that cannot be accommodated within Paul's general conception of what it means to be "with Christ." Thus, after mentioning baptism in vv. 3-4, Paul drops the subject, never to resume it in this chapter.[58] Even in vv. 3-4, baptism is introduced not to explain *how* we were buried with Christ but to demonstrate *that* we were buried with Christ. And the subsidiary role of baptism in our union with Christ is confirmed by the fact that Paul can elsewhere claim a "being with Christ" that is not related to baptism (cf. Gal. 2:19-20; Eph. 2:5-6).

Baptism, then, is not the place, or time, at which we are buried with Christ, but the instrument *(dia)* through which we are buried with him. It might, then, be an obvious conclusion that the "time" of our burial with Christ was the time of his own burial: that, when Christ died, was buried, and resurrected, we were "in him" and so participated in these events "with" him. Support for this conception can be found in the aorist passive verbs used throughout this passage, the reference to Christ's own form of death, crucifixion, as that in which we participate (v. 6), and the simple logic that runs "if we died with Christ, and he died 'once' (v. 10), on Calvary, then our dying 'with' him must also have taken place on Calvary." Moreover, it is very natural to apply to our relationship with Christ the same kind of "inclusive" relationship that Paul has just indicated to be the case with Adam (5:12-21).[59]

Each of these points has merit. But before concluding that A.D. 30 was the "time" of our burial with Christ, we must consider some other factors. First, vv. 2, 14, and 17-22 suggest that the transition from the old life to the new has taken place in the conscious experience of the believer. Second, the reference to baptism likewise draws attention to the lifetime of the believer.[60] Third, many of Paul's "with Christ" statements include reference to the life experience of the individual. Since, then, the text does not allow us to focus on the cross *or* our own experience as the "time" of our being buried with

---

58. To be sure, some scholars find allusions to baptism in many other verses of Rom. 6 (cf., e.g., U. Schnelle, *Gerechtigkeit und Christusgegenwart. Vorpaulinische und paulinische Tauftheologie* [Göttinger Theologische Arbeiten 24; Göttingen: Vandenhoeck & Ruprecht, 1983], pp: 85-87, 145-61), but none of them is likely (cf., e.g., Dunn; Kaye, *Thought Structure,* pp. 58-65; Wedderburn, *Baptism,* pp. 49-50; Siber, *Mit Christus Leben,* pp. 217-27).

59. Cf. Haldane.

60. Murray.

Christ, we are forced to the conclusion that we are dealing with a category that transcends time.[61] Our dying, being buried, and being resurrected with Christ are experiences that transfer us from the old age to the new. But the transition from old age to new, while applied to individuals at their conversion, has been accomplished through the redemptive work of Christ on Good Friday and Easter. Paul's *syn* refers to a "redemptive-historical" "withness" whose locus is *both* the cross and resurrection and Christ — where the "shift" in ages took place historically — *and* the conversion of every believer — when this "shift" in ages becomes applicable to the individual.

On the view we have adopted, Paul alludes to our burial with Christ because it was included in the basic kerygma that recited the key salvific events — "Christ died for our sins according to the Scriptures, he was buried, he was raised on the third day in accordance with the Scriptures" (1 Cor. 15:3-4).[62] But burial was probably included in this simple summary because burial confirmed the reality of death, and the purpose for mentioning the believer's participation in it both here and in Col. 2:12 is the same: our death with Christ to the old age of sin is final and definitive.[63] More than this, the mention of burial makes for a fitting antithesis to the "newness of life" which is the sequel to our burial with Christ.[64]

Why, finally, does Paul make baptism the means by which the believer becomes identified with these kerygmatic events? Schweitzer saw baptism as a rite that accomplished incorporation with Christ automatically, as part of the "mystical" or participationist concept that he found to be dominant in Rom. 5–8. He admitted that this concept conflicts with the "juridical" justification by faith concept of Rom. 1–4, but dismissed the latter as a "subsidiary" viewpoint of importance only in controversy with Jews.[65] But we cannot put Paul's "juridical" and "participationist" language into separate compartments, and any explanation of the role of baptism in Rom. 6 must come to grips with the obvious centrality in Paul of faith as the means by which our relationship to Christ is appropriated. This is one of the reasons that some scholars dismiss any reference to water baptism in these verses. However, as we have seen, a reference to water baptism cannot be eliminated in v. 3, and the same is true in v. 4.[66]

---

61. Schlatter.
62. Cf. Gifford.
63. See, e.g., Cranfield.
64. Stuart; Schlatter.
65. *Paul and His Interpreters,* pp. 225-26.
66. Paul uses the noun βάπτισμα, a rare word (it may be of Christian creation; cf. J. Ysebart, *Greek Baptismal Terminology: Its Origin and Early Development* [Graecitas Christianorum Primaeva, 1; Nijmegen: Dekker & van de Vegt, 1962], pp. 51-53) that always includes reference to a baptism in water (usually of John's baptism: cf. Matt. 3:7;

How, then, can we preserve the cruciality of faith at the same time as we do justice to the mediatorial role of baptism in this text? Here the suggestion of J. Dunn is helpful. He points out that the early church conceived of faith, the gift of the Spirit, and water baptism as components of one unified experience, which he calls "conversion-initiation."[67] Just as faith is always assumed to lead to baptism, so baptism always assumes faith for its validity.[68] In vv. 3-4, then, we can assume that baptism stands for the whole conversion-initiation experience, presupposing faith and the gift of the Spirit. What, we might ask, of the Christian who has not been baptized? While Paul never dealt with this question — and his first reaction would undoubtedly have been "Why hasn't he been baptized?" — we must assume from the fact that faith is emblazoned in every chapter of Romans while baptism is mentioned in only two verses that genuine faith, even if it has not been "sealed" in baptism, is sufficient for salvation.

The main point of v. 4 is not, however, our being with Christ, or baptism, but the new life to which these events are to lead. It is the purpose[69] of our burial with Christ that "we might walk[70] in newness of life." "Newness of life" is a life empowered by the realities of the new age — including especially God's Spirit (Rom. 7:6) — and a life that should reflect the values of that new age.[71] This connection between the "indicative" of our incorpora-

---

21:15; Mark 1:4; 10:38, 39 [while a reference to water baptism in Mark 10:38 and 39 is not immediately clear, there is probably allusion to Jesus' own baptism by John [cf. D. J. Moo, *The Old Testament in the Gospel Passion Narratives* {Sheffield: Almond, 1983}, pp. 116-20]); 11:30; Luke 3:3; 7:29; 12:50; 20:4; Acts 1:22; 10:37; 13:24; 18:25; 19:3, 4; of Christian baptism in Rom. 6:4; Eph. 4:5; 1 Pet. 3:21).

67. *Baptism,* pp. 145, etc.; cf. also D. A. Tappeiner, "Hermeneutics, the Analogy of Faith and New Testament Sacramental Realism," *EvQ* 49 (1977), 40-52.

68. Cf. also Scott, *Christianity,* p. 114; Flemington, *Baptism,* p. 81; and esp. Beasley-Murray, *Baptism,* pp. 272-73.

69. Gk. ἵνα.

70. περιπατήσωμεν, an aorist subjunctive of περιπατέω. This verb, as in its 31 other occurrences in Paul, designates manner of life or "lifestyle." This application of the verb, unknown in classical Greek, is taken from the LXX and Jewish usage, where הלך is used in this sense (H. Seesemann, *TDNT* V, 944-45). The context suggests that the aorist might signal an ingressive idea: "that we might take up a new way of walking" (Robertson, 850).

71. Nygren. Paul always uses the words καινότης and καινός with reference to the "new age" of salvation that has come with the inauguration of the New Covenant (cf. καινότης in Rom. 7:6; καινός in 1 Cor. 11:25; 2 Cor. 3:6; 5:17; Gal. 6:15; Eph. 2:15; 4:24). The genitive ζωῆς might be a genitive of quality, with ζωῆς rather than καινότητι the "ruling" word — "new life" (Turner, 213); or an epexegetic genitive — "newness, that is, life" (e.g., Murray); but, in light of what we have said about the meaning of καινότητι, it is probably an objective genitive — "the newness [the new age] that leads to, or confers, life."

tion into Christ and the "imperative" of Christian living is the heart of Rom. 6. But Paul does more than announce that this living in the new age is the purpose of our identification with Christ in baptism; he also compares it to the resurrection of Christ: "*just as* Christ was raised from the dead by the glory of the Father,[72] *so, too.* . . ."[73] But the context suggests that more than comparison is intended. While Paul in this paragraph does not, as in Col. 2:12 and Eph. 2:6, plainly speak of the Christian's participation in the resurrection of Christ as already "realized" (see the notes on 6:5 and 6:8), he nevertheless makes it clear that the believer is, in this life, already benefiting from the power and influence of that resurrection; see especially 6:11, where believers are called to consider themselves "alive to God" in a fashion parallel to Christ's resurrection (vv. 8-10), and 6:12, where believers are called those who are "alive from the dead." In light of these considerations, "just as . . . so also" probably here has a causal flavor: "because Christ has been raised, we can and should walk in newness of life." Paul, in other words, grounds the believer's present participation in life in the spiritual power of Christ's resurrection.[74]

Christians, then, are both empowered and summoned to live a new kind of life by virtue of their participation in the death, burial, and resurrection of Christ. This is put effectively and powerfully by Calvin:

> By these words [vv. 3-5] he not only exhorts us to follow Christ as if he had said that we are admonished through baptism to die to our desires by the example of Christ's death, and to be aroused to righteousness by the example of his resurrection, but he also takes hold of something far higher; namely, that through baptism Christ makes us sharers in his death, that we may be engrafted in it. And, just as the twig draws substance and nourishment from the root to which it is grafted, so those who receive baptism with right faith truly feel the effective working of Christ's death in the mortification of their flesh, together with the working of his resurrection in the vivification of the Spirit.[75]

---

72. By noting that Christ was raised "through the glory of the Father" (διὰ τῆς δόξης τοῦ πατρός), Paul, while alluding to the "power" of God (cf. John 11:23 and 11:40), is also implying that this power is specifically the power of the new age (Bornkamm, "Baptism and New Life," p. 74). Even now believers participate in this glory (cf. 2 Cor. 3:16) as they look toward the final manifestation of glory in connection with the transformation of the body (Phil. 3:21).

73. As Fitzmyer notes, this comparison reminds us of the logic that dominates Rom. 5:12-21.

74. Beasley-Murray, *Baptism*, pp. 138-39; M. J. Harris, *Raised Immortal: Resurrection and Immortality in the New Testament* (Grand Rapids: Eerdmans, 1983), pp. 103-4.

75. *Institutes* 4.15.5.

5 Verse 5 affirms what has been implied in v. 4b: the participation of the believer in the resurrection of Christ. The verse takes the form of a conditional sentence, in which the protasis (the "if" clause) states what is already known — the believer's connection[76] with Christ's death — as the basis for the conclusion drawn in the apodosis (the "then" clause): that this connection with Christ in death assures participation in his resurrection.[77] Complicating Paul's assertion, however, is his use of the phrase "the *form* of [Christ's] death." Two issues must be resolved.

First, what is the syntactical function of the phrase? Many scholars think that "likeness of his death" is the *means* by which the believer is united with Christ or, more generally, the *location* at which this union takes place. See, for instance, the rendering in the NAB: "if we have grown into union with him *through a death like his* [my italics]."[78] But this is not the most natural reading of the syntax. It is preferable to take "likeness of his death" as the object with which we are "joined"; cf. our translation: "we have become united *with* the likeness of his death."[79]

Second, what does Paul refer to with the phrase? The decisive issue is the meaning of the Greek word *homoiōma*. Two basic meanings are possible.

(1) *Homoiōma* can refer to something that resembles something else:

76. Paul expresses this connection with the word σύμφυτοι (continuing the series of words compounded with σύν that convey so much of the theology of this paragraph). The verb on which this word is built, συμφύω, means "make to grow together," "join," "unite," "become assimilated" (LSJ). Many stress the horticultural application of the word, and compare the metaphor to Jesus' teaching about the vine and the branches (e.g., Murray). But, however apropos the comparison with John 15 might be — and there are similarities — the word σύμφυτος is used in too many contexts other than the horticultural to justify any degree of probability about this being the association of the word here (cf. W. Grundmann, *TDNT* VII, 786; Käsemann; Cranfield). We should translate simply "joined" or "united."

77. The εἰ introducing the protasis then, as often (BDF 372 [1]), introduces a "factual" condition.

78. On this view, we are to supply an αὐτῷ ("[with] him") as the implicit object of σύμφυτοι ("joined"), with τῷ ὁμοιώματι being an instrumental or locative dative. See, e.g., Godet; Lagrange; Michel; Langevin, "Baptême," p. 58. Another option is to understand τοῦ θανάτου αὐτοῦ as the object of both σύμφυτοι and τῷ ὁμοιώματι, yielding the translation "through the image of his death we have become joined with his death" (cf. Barrett; Schnelle, *Gerechtigkeit und Christusgegenwart*, p. 82). But it is awkward to construe θανάτου with both words and unnatural to have the genitive depend on σύμφυτοι (Turner, 220).

79. With a dative already present to function as the object of σύμφυτοι — τῷ ὁμοιώματι — the addition of αὐτῷ is unnecessary. σύμφυτοι can certainly express a union between things different in nature (e.g., people and "the likeness of his death"; cf. Kuss), and v. 4a shows that Paul in this context thinks of believers as united not only with Christ but also with events of his life. This reading of the syntax has the support of most recent interpreters; cf., for a full defense, F. A. Morgan, "Romans 6:5a: United to a Death like Christ's," *ETL* 59 (1983), 273-76.

a "copy" or "image."[80] Many scholars argue that this "something" here relates to baptism, in the sense, perhaps, of the "copy" or "image" of Christ's death that is present in baptism (cf. vv. 3-4).[81] But this interpretation suffers from two serious drawbacks. First, "likeness of his death" makes sense as a reference to baptism only if it refers to the means by which we are joined to Christ. But I have argued that this is not the most likely reading of the syntax. Second, the movement of Paul's thought in this passage is away from baptism. Other scholars who argue that *homoiōma* here means "image" assert that Paul is referring to the Christian's own death to sin, a "copy" of Christ's death (which was itself a "death to sin," v. 10).[82] But the language "become joined with" is overly strong if the "union" is with our own death to sin.[83]

(2) *Homoiōma* can also mean "form," in the sense of the outer appearance, or shape, of the reality itself.[84] "Likeness of his death" may, then, simply

80. Rare in classical Greek, ὁμοίωμα occurs about 40 times in the LXX. There it usually means "likeness" or "copy," in the sense of something that looks like, but is not identical to, something else. Thus its two most frequent references are to idols, considered as "copies" or "representations" of gods (cf., e.g., Exod. 20:4; Deut. 4:16-25; 2 Chron. 4:3; Ps. 106:20; Isa. 40:18-19), and to the "figures" that Ezekiel sees in his visions (e.g., 1:4-26). See the surveys in H. W. Bartsch, "Die theologische Bedeutung des Begriffes ΟΜΟΙΩΜΑ im Neuen Testament," in *Entmythologisierende Auslegung* (Theologische Forschung 26; Hamburg: Evangelischer, 1962), pp. 160-67; J. Schneider, *TDNT* V, 191; Morgan, "Romans 6:5a," p. 282; V. P. Branick, "The Sinful Flesh of the Son of God (Rom 8:3): A Key Image of Pauline Theology," *CBQ* 47 (1985), 248-50. Branick quotes the study of U. Vanni (unavailable to me), whose conclusion is that the basic meaning of ὁμοίωμα is the "perceptible expression of a reality."

81. See, e.g., Barrett; Schlier; Kuss; Fitzmyer.

82. See esp. Morgan, "Romans 6:5a," pp. 267-302. Note also Godet; Gifford; Calvin; J. Gewiess, "Das Abbild des Todes Christi (Röm 6,5)," *Historisches Jahrbuch* 77 (1958), 341-44; Frid, "Römer 6:4-5," pp. 196-97. Morgan claims that this interpretation was the most popular through the nineteenth century (p. 278).

83. W. Schrage, understanding ὁμοίωμα to mean that which is like Christ's death, takes it to refer to the church as the body of Christ ("Ist die Kirche das 'Abbild seines Todes'? Zu Röm 6,5," in *Kirche. Festschrift für Günther Bornkamm zum 75. Geburtstag* [ed. D. Lührmann and G. Strecker; Tübingen: Mohr, 1980], pp. 205-19). But his reasoning is not convincing, and the context simply gives too little support to the notion.

84. Cf. Deut. 4:12: "The LORD spoke to you out of the fire. You heard the sound of the words, but saw no form [ὁμοίωμα]" (contra Morgan ["Romans 6:5a," p. 282], who argues that ὁμοίωμα always means "likeness" in the LXX). Outside Rev. 9:7 (where it means "form," "appearance"), ὁμοίωμα is used only by Paul in the NT. One of his uses of the word refers, as in the LXX, to idolatry (Rom. 1:23), but the meaning of each of the other four (Rom. 5:14; 6:5; 8:3; Phil. 2:7) is hotly debated. In Rom. 5:14, as we have seen, ὁμοίωμα means "likeness"; the sins of those before the giving of the law were not "like" the sin of Adam. In both 8:3 and Phil. 2:7, on the other hand, ὁμοίωμα connotes a deeper identity between the two items being compared. Christ was not just "like" human beings; he really was a human being (Phil. 2:7). Similarly, it can be argued that Christ was not

be the death of Christ itself.[85] Substantiation for this can be found in the parallel v. 8, where Paul speaks simply of "dying with Christ." However, while I think this interpretation is on the right track, Paul's use of *homoiōma* still suggests that he wants to portray Christ's death in a particular light. Some think that Paul uses it to designate Christ's death as the death that is sacramentally present in baptism.[86] But, again, this ignores the plain teaching of v. 4 that baptism mediates our union with Christ — it does not "contain" it.[87] A better alternative, then, begins with the recognition that, as we have seen, the believer's death and burial "with Christ" is a redemptive-historical association that cannot be precisely defined in terms of time or nature. *Homoiōma,* while not differentiating the death to which we are joined from Christ's, nevertheless qualifies it in its particular redemptive-historical "form."[88] Further, by speaking of the "form" of Christ's death, Paul may also be reminding us that our "dying with Christ" initiates a "conformity" with Jesus' death that is to have a continuing effect on our existence.[89] Reference to this ongoing conformity to the death of Christ explains the perfect tense of the verb Paul uses:[90] we have been joined to the "form" of Christ's death and are constantly being (and need to be) "conformed" to it. We may, then, paraphrase: "we (at 'conversion-initiation') were united with the death of Christ in its redemptive-historical significance, and are now, thus, in the state of 'conformity' to *that death.*"

The "but also"[91] introducing the second part of the verse stresses the certainty that our union with "the form of Christ's death" will mean union with the form of Christ's resurrection.[92] But what are we to make of the future

---

simply "similar" to "sinful flesh" but actually took on "sinful flesh" (without himself, however, sinning) (Rom. 8:3; cf., e.g., Branick, "Sinful Flesh," pp. 251-61). Nevertheless, it must be said that in both these verses — the latter particularly — ὁμοίωμα may suggest an element of difference (see, further, our notes on 8:3).

85. Bornkamm, "Baptism and New Life," p. 77.

86. Schlier; Kuss; J. Schneider, *TDNT* V, 195.

87. So, e.g., Frankemölle, *Taufverständnis,* pp. 65-70.

88. See, though with differences, Ridderbos, *Paul,* pp. 406-7; Käsemann; Wilckens; Frankemölle, *Taufverständnis,* pp. 65-70; Thüsing, *Per Christum in Deum,* pp. 135-38; Siber, *Mit Christus Leben,* p. 220. Note also the suggestion of Bartsch ("Die theologische Bedeutung des Begriffes OMOIΩMA," pp. 167-69) that Paul uses ὁμοίωμα to stress the "faith" aspect of the reality depicted.

89. Cf. Phil. 3:10, "being conformed [present, continual] to his death"; Rom. 8:17, "if we suffer with him, we shall also be glorified with him." See, for this idea, Tannehill, *Dying and Rising,* pp. 38-39; Cranfield; Wedderburn, *Baptism,* p. 47 n. 7.

90. Gk. γεγόναμεν.

91. Gk. ἀλλὰ καί.

92. Cf. BDF 448(5). The second clause is elliptical, but we are almost certainly to supply σύμφυτοι τῷ ὁμοιώματι from the first clause (so, e.g., Cranfield; others, however, want to supply only σύμφυτοι [e.g., Chrysostom; Zahn; Alford]).

verb "we will be"?[93] Paul may put the matter this way because being "joined to the form of Christ's resurrection" follows logically upon "being joined to the form of his death." In this case, the reference could be to the already realized "spiritual" resurrection of believers "with Christ" (as in Col. 2:12 and Eph. 2:6),[94] or to the imperative of living in the "form" and power of Christ's resurrection life in the present.[95] Either of these options is possible, considering the fact that Paul himself infers in this text that believers in this life live in the resurrection power of Christ (vv. 4b, 11, 13). However, I believe the scales are tilted slightly to a true future here by v. 8, which asserts a similar point but with a construction that is more difficult to read as a "logical" future.[96] With most interpreters, then, I take it that Paul is referring to the physical resurrection of believers "with Christ" (cf. 2 Cor. 4:14) — to that time when God will transform our earthly bodies, "making them conformed to the body of his [Christ's] glory."[97]

This does not mean, however, that all allusions to the present are eliminated. For, even as union with the "form" of Christ's death at baptism-conversion works forward to the moral life, so the union with the "form" of Christ's resurrection at death or the parousia works backward. It is in this sense that the believer can be said to have been "raised with Christ" and to be living in the power of that resurrected life. Perhaps, then, as our union with Christ's death cannot be fixed to any one moment, so we should view our union with Christ's resurrection as similarly atemporal. But, while the spiritual effects of resurrection are felt now, we must not commit the mistake of some in the early church (cf. 2 Tim. 2:18) and spiritualize the resurrection. We await a real, physical resurrection, and this physicality destroys the parallel at this point with our "dying with Christ." The futurity of our resurrection reminds us that complete victory over sin will be won only in that day; until then, we live under the imperative of making the life of Jesus manifest in the way we live (cf. 2 Cor. 4:10).

---

93. Gk. ἐσόμεθα.

94. Cf., e.g., Prat, *Theology,* 1.224; Zahn; Harrison; Fitzmyer; Frid, "Römer 6:4-5," pp. 198-99. Porter (*Verbal Aspect,* pp. 422-23) claims that the future tense here is probably not temporal.

95. E.g., Godet; Cranfield.

96. E.g., πιστεύομεν ὅτι καὶ συζήσομεν αὐτῷ, "we believe that we shall also live with him."

97. Philippians 3:20, where the similarity in wording to our verse should be noted: σύμμορφον τῷ σώματι τῆς δόξης αὐτοῦ. Many who take this view consider that the references to a past resurrection of believers with Christ in Colossians and Ephesians indicate a post-Pauline "departure" from Paul's careful eschatological "tension." But, while Colossians and Ephesians emhasize more than Rom. 6 a "realized eschatology," this is not a movement away from Paul but is Paul's own application of one side of his eschatology to a specific situation.

6 Many interpreters connect v. 6 very closely to v. 5. They think that Paul in v. 6 explains why conformity with Christ's death leads to conformity with his resurrection; see, for example, NASB: "For if we have become united with him in the likeness of his death, certainly we shall be also in the likeness of his resurrection, knowing this. . . ."[98] But I think that a minor break occurs between vv. 5 and 6. Verses 6-7 restate and elaborate the meaning of the believer's death with Christ, taught in vv. 4a and 5a. Verses 8-10, then, focus on the relationship between death with Christ and life with him that is the substance of the other part of these verses (4b, 5b).[99] Paul is summarizing: "We know this: that[100] our old man was crucified with Christ, so that the body of sin might be rendered powerless, with the purpose that we should no longer serve sin."[101]

The verb "crucified with" picks up and brings to a climax the "death"-side of the "union with Christ" motif of vv. 3-5. Like "buried with him" in v. 4 and "united with the form of his death" in v. 5, "crucified with Christ" refers not to our own burial and death but to our participation in Christ's crucifixion.[102] What is meant is not the believer's duty to put away sin, but the act of God whereby, in response to our faith, he considers us to have died the same death Christ died. Again, the "moment" of our being "crucified with Christ" cannot be fixed, either at the cross[103] or at conversion-baptism.[104] The "redemptive-historical" participation of the believer in the crucifixion of Christ is such that temporal categories cannot helpfully be applied to it.[105] The image of crucifixion is chosen not because Paul wants to suggest that our "dying with Christ" is a preliminary action that the believer must complete

---

98. The participle γινώσκοντες is then seen as causal (cf. Robertson, 1128). See, e.g., Gifford.

99. See Wilckens. γινώσκοντες, then, is but loosely related to the preceding, functioning virtually as a finite verb — "we know" (cf. NRSV, NIV, TEV, REB; Burton, 449, 450 labels this kind of participle "attendant circumstance").

100. τοῦτο ("this") is prospective, its antecedent being the ὅτι ("that") clause that follows. What Paul describes in this verse, then, is not "known" through experience (contra, e.g., Hodge), or reflection on that experience (contra, e.g., Gifford), but through Paul's own words that follow. It is, again, possible that Paul alludes here to traditional teaching (Käsemann), but the distinctly Pauline "with Christ" motif in the verse shows that any such dependence is limited at best.

101. Note the addition of καί in codex B, perhaps an early indication in this direction.

102. Cf. also Gal. 2:19, Paul's only other use of the verb συσταυρόω. The Gospels use the verb in the prosaic sense of those who were physically crucified with Christ (Mark 15:32; Matt. 27:44; John 19:32).

103. Ridderbos (cf. *Paul,* p. 63) is the most consistent advocate for this interpretation.

104. See Cranfield.

105. See the discussion on v. 4; and Dunn.

by daily "dying to sin,"[106] but because Christ's death took the form of crucifixion. The believer who is "crucified with Christ" is as definitely and finally "dead" as a result of this action as was Christ himself after his crucifixion (as Paul stresses in v. 10: the death Christ died he died "once for all"). Of course, we must remember what this death means. This is no more a physical, or ontological, death than is our burial with Christ (v. 4) or our "dying to sin" (v. 2). Paul's language throughout is forensic, or positional; by God's act, we have been placed in a new position. This position is real, for what exists in God's sight is surely (ultimately) real, and it carries definite consequences for day-to-day living. But it is status, or power structure, that Paul is talking about here. Just as Christ's crucifixion meant his release from the realm of sin (6:10), the law (Gal. 4:4) and death (v. 9; Phil. 2:7-8), so our crucifixion with Christ means our release from the realm of sin (this verse), the law (6:14; 7:4), and death (8:1-11).

But Paul does not claim that "we" have been crucified with Christ; it is "our old man"[107] who has been so definitively put to death. There has been considerable misunderstanding of this phrase, which, with its counterpart "the new man," occurs also in Eph. 4:22-24 and Col. 3:9-11 (cf. also Eph. 2:15 and 4:13). Many popular discussions of Paul's doctrine of the Christian life argue, or assume, that Paul distinguishes with these phrases between two parts or "natures" of a person. With this interpretation as the premise, it is then debated whether the "old nature" is replaced with the "new nature" at conversion, or whether the "new nature" is added to the "old nature." But the assumption that "old man" and "new man" refer to parts, or natures, of a person is incorrect. Rather, they designate the person as a whole, considered in relation to the corporate structure to which he or she belongs. "Old man" and "new man" are not, then, ontological, but relational or positional in orientation. They do not, at least in the first place, speak of a change in nature, but of a change in relationship. "Our old man" is not our Adamic, or sin "nature" that is judged and dethroned on the cross,[108] and to which is added in the believer another "nature," "the new man." Rather, the "old man" is what we were "in Adam" — the "man" of the old age, who lives under the tyranny of sin and death.[109] As J. R. W. Stott puts it, "what was crucified

---

106. Contra, e.g., Godet; Cranfield.

107. Gk. ὁ παλαιὸς ἡμῶν ἄνθρωπος.

108. E.g., Calvin; William Ames, *The Marrow of Theology* (rpt.; Pittsburgh: Pilgrim, 1968), p. 171: "the corrupted part which remains in the sanctified."

109. J. Murray, *Principles of Conduct* (Grand Rapids: Eerdmans, 1957), pp. 211-19, has a very helpful discussion, although his conception differs slightly from ours. Cf. also Beasley-Murray, *Baptism*, p. 134; Frankemölle, *Taufverständnis*, pp. 74-76; Barrett, *From First to Last Adam*, pp. 98-99.

with Christ was not a part of me called my old nature, but the whole of me as I was before I was converted."[110]

Behind the contrast between "old man" and "new man" is the contrast between Adam and Christ, the "first man" and the "last" (1 Cor. 15:45; cf. Rom. 5:15, "the one man Jesus Christ").[111] Those, then, who are "in Adam" belong to and exist as "the old man"; those who are "in Christ" belong to and exist as "the new man." In other words, these phrases denote the solidarity of people with the "heads" of the two contrasting ages of salvation history.[112] It is only by interpreting "old man" and "new man" in this manner that we are able to integrate two apparently conflicting viewpoints in Paul. On the one hand, this verse and Col. 3:9-11 make clear that the believer has ceased to be "old man" and has become "new man." On the other hand, Paul in Eph. 4:22-24 commands Christians to "put off the old man" and "put on the new man." Attempts to reconcile these have often taken the form either of taking the "crucifixion" of the old man to be only a preliminary judgment (see above) or of denying that Paul is giving commands in Eph. 4:22-24.[113] Neither approach is exegetically sound.[114] If, however, these phrases look at the person as one who belongs to the old age or the new, respectively, then this conflict is easily resolved. For Paul makes it clear that the believer has been transferred from the old age of sin and death to the new age of righteousness and life (Rom. 6:6 and Col. 3:9-11) just as he indicates that the "powers" of that old age continue to influence the believer and must be continually resisted — hence the imperatives of Eph. 4:22-24. At the heart of

110. J. R. W. Stott, *Men Made New: An Exposition of Romans 5–8* (London: Inter-Varsity, 1966), p. 45.

111. Ridderbos, *Paul,* pp. 62-64.

112. Paul can therefore use the phrases with a corporate meaning. This seems to be the case in both Col. 3:10-11 — "the new man" includes Greek and Jew, circumcision and uncircumcision, etc. — and Eph. 2:15 — Jews and Greeks are united into "one new man." Some, indeed, have thought that "the old man" in Rom. 6:6 is corporate, and that Paul is depicting the crucifixion with Christ of "the corporate unity," in which believers have been included (Ridderbos, *Paul,* pp. 62-64; Tannehill, *Dying and Rising,* pp. 24-30). However, while the phrase always has undoubted corporate associations — in the sense that "the old man" is what he is by virtue of belonging to Adam — "old man" in this verse refers to the individual. The ἡμῶν ("our"), while not requiring this, suggests it, as does the reference to "body" in the next phrase (see esp. Wilckens; Dunn). Furthermore, as we have seen, the "moment" of conversion-baptism cannot be eliminated from the "with" language of Paul in this text, and this demands an individual interpretation.

113. Cf., e.g., Murray, *Principles of Conduct,* pp. 214-18.

114. Murray (see the previous note) and others take the infinitives ἀποθέσθαι and ἐνδύσασθαι in Eph. 4:22-24 as equivalent to indicatives. But their dependence on the verb ἐδιδάχθητε (v. 21) makes an imperatival rendering more likely (cf., e.g., F. F. Bruce, *The Epistles to the Colossians, to Philemon and to the Ephesians* [NICNT; Grand Rapids: Eerdmans, 1984], pp. 358-59n).

the contrast between "old man" and "new man" is the eschatological tension between the inauguration of the new age in the life of the believer — he or she belongs to the "new creation" (2 Cor. 5:17) — and the culmination of that new age in "glorification with Christ" (8:17). What we *were* "in Adam" is no more; but, until heaven, the temptation to *live* in Adam always remains.

This participation of our old man in the crucifixion of Christ has the purpose[115] of "rendering powerless[116] the body of sin." The "body" to which Paul refers is naturally often understood to refer to the physical body.[117] If so, the qualification "of sin" would not mean that the body is inherently sinful (a Greek notion rejected by the Bible) but that the body is particularly susceptible to, and easily dominated by, sin.[118] But Paul also uses the word *sōma* to refer to the whole person, with an emphasis on that person's interaction with the world.[119] This interpretation seems to fit this verse well. What must be "rendered impotent" if *I* am to be freed from sin (v. 6c) is not just my physical body but myself in all my sin-prone faculties. There is little evidence that Paul conceived of the physical body as the source or reigning seat of sin.

115. Gk. ἵνα.

116. καταργηθῇ, from the verb καταργέω (on which, see the note on Rom. 3:3). Some translate the word here "destroyed" (e.g., Murray), but Paul's use of this verb in similar salvation-historical contexts (cf. Rom. 3:31; 4:14; 7:2, 6; Gal. 3:17; 5:4; Eph. 2:15) suggests rather the connotation of a power whose influence is taken away; see esp. Bandstra, *The Law and the Elements of the World*, pp. 77-81; Kaye, *Thought Structure*, p. 77; G. Delling, *TDNT* I, 453; Dunn.

117. See esp. Gundry, 29-31; Jewett, *Paul's Anthropological Terms*, pp. 291-92; Murray; Godet; Morris. Beker (pp. 287-89) takes "the body of sin" to be the person of the old age and "mortal body" the person of the new age, but Paul does not suggest such a change of "bodies."

118. A few interpreters have suggested that σῶμα might mean "mass" or "organism," the genitive τῆς ἁμαρτίας being epexegetic ("the mass consisting of sin"; cf. Calvin; Hodge; D. E. H. Whiteley, *The Theology of St. Paul* [Philadelphia: Fortress, 1972], p. 42). This view should not be dismissed as quickly as it sometimes is because it explains several things: the lack of a possessive pronoun in the clause ("*our* old man was crucified . . . so that *the* body of sin . . . with the purpose that *we* should not serve sin"), the singular σῶμα, and the fact that this σῶμα is the subject of the passive verb "be destroyed" or "rendered impotent." Nevertheless, this view suffers from the fatal defect of insufficient lexical support. The text would have to offer more reasons than these to substantiate so rare (for the NT) a use of the word.

119. This understanding of σῶμα in Paul is associated especially with Bultmann (cf. 1.192-203); note also — though with modifications — Ladd, *Theology*, pp. 464-66; Ridderbos, *Paul*, pp. 115-17; E. Schweizer, *TDNT* VII, 1064-66. Gundry has registered some valid objections to this "aspectival" approach to σῶμα (cf. his *Sōma*), and there is no doubt that Bultmann and others have gone too far in eliminating reference to the physical body in Paul's use of the term. But the frequent parallels between σῶμα and words denoting the whole person in Paul (cf. 6:12-13) constitute good reason to interpret σῶμα more broadly in many instances.

However, we should not go so far as to say simply that "body of sin" means "man in his fallenness."[120] Paul chooses *sōma* to connote the person as the instrument of contact with the world, a choice especially appropriate in a context that speaks of crucifixion. It is that "aspect" of the person which "acts" in the world and which can be directed by something else: either by that person's new, "higher nature" or by "sin."[121] Here, then, Paul wants to say that our capacities to interact with the world around us have been rescued from the domination of sin.[122]

Paul's point, then, is that the real, though forensic, inclusion of the believer with Christ in his crucifixion means that our solidarity with, and dominance by, Adam, through whom we are bound to the nexus of sin and death, has ended. And the purpose of this was that the body as a helpless tool of sin might be definitively defeated. What this means for the Christian life, though inherent in what Paul has already said, is spelled out in the concluding clause: "that we should no longer serve[123] sin."

7 This verse explains[124] the connection between death ("crucified with Christ") and freedom from sin ("no longer serve sin") that is the main point of v. 6. Precisely how it does so is, however, debated. On one view, "he who dies" is "the one who has died [with Christ]" and "has been justified"[125] has its usual Pauline sense, "acquit from the penalty of sin." On this, the "theological" interpretation, Paul is pointing to justification through participation in Christ's death as the basis for the freedom from sin enjoyed by the believer.[126] But there are difficulties in taking "justify" in this sense here. Paul does not connect *our* dying with our justification anywhere else. To avoid this problem, it has been suggested that "the one who dies" is Christ, who through his death secured

---

120. As Cranfield suggests.

121. Ridderbos, *Paul,* p. 117; Harris, *Raised Immortal,* p. 120. In this respect, Gundry's objections (pp. 186-88) to Bultmann's always confining σῶμα to the status of "object" are valid.

122. Käsemann.

123. Gk. τοῦ δουλεύειν. The infinitive could be epexegetic, expanding and restating the previous clause (BDF 400[8]; Turner, 141); consecutive — "with the result that we are no longer servants of sin"; or final — "with the purpose that we should no longer serve sin" (so most commentators). A decision is not easy because Paul's uses of the articular genitive infinitive fall into no clear pattern (see the note on 1:24), but the final alternative perhaps should be preferred.

124. Cf. the Gk. γάρ.

125. Gk. δεδικαίωται.

126. Best, *One Body,* p. 44; Reumann, *Righteousness,* p. 81; Cranfield; Fitzmyer. K. G. Kuhn refers to *Sipre Num.* #112 (on 15:31), which speaks of death as making atonement ("Rm 6,7," *ZNW* 30 [1931], 305-10), but Scroggs points out that this idea was not widespread ("Romans VI.7. Ο ΓΑΡ ΑΠΟΘΑΝΩΝ ΔΕΔΙΚΑΙΩΤΑΙ ΑΠΟ ΤΗΣ ΑΜΑΡΤΙΑΣ," *NTS* 10 [1963-64], 104-8).

justification for himself and others.[127] But this introduces a shift in subject for which the context has not prepared us.[128] For these reasons, it is likely that "justified from sin" means "set free from [the power of] sin."[129] "The one who dies" could still refer to "the one who has died with Christ,"[130] but this would make v. 7 virtually repeat v. 6. It is more likely, then, that Paul is citing a general maxim, to the effect that "death severs the hold of sin on a person."[131] Paul's readers may have been familiar with similar sayings, known to us from the rabbinic writings.[132] His purpose, then, is not to prove v. 6 but to illustrate his theological point by reference to a general truth.

8 Paul now reiterates the tie between dying with Christ and being raised with Christ that he established in v. 5: "But if[133] we have died with Christ, we believe that we shall also live with him." He does this in order to draw out the significance of that connection as seen in the light of the nature of Christ's own death and resurrection (vv. 9-10). The future form "we shall live" sparks the same debate as does the future "we will be [united with his resurrection]" in v. 5b. Is Paul thinking (mainly) of the resurrection of believers "with Christ" at death or the parousia[134] or of the believer's present enjoyment of new life with Christ?[135] The undeniable assumption of the passage (cf. vv. 4b, 11, 13) that the Christian has, as a result of "baptismal-conversion death," new life with Christ points to the second alternative. But the future tense is not the most natural if this were Paul's point, and the fact that this "life with Christ" is an object of belief ("we believe") also fits better with a reference to what we have been promised than with what we already possess. But this future life of resurrection casts its shadow into the believer's present experience, and it is clear from the sequel that Paul wants us to see the present implications of this promise of future resurrection life.

127. Though with differences, see Scroggs, "Romans VI.7," pp. 104-8; C. Kearns, "The Interpretation of Romans 6,7," *SPCIC* 1.301-7; Wilckens.

128. Moreover, while Acts 13:38 might give reason to consider the combination δικαιόω and ἀπό one that Paul could use in speaking of "justification," it is found nowhere else in Paul.

129. See, e.g., BAGD; Käsemann. The combination δικαιόω ἀπό has this general meaning in Sir. 26:29 and *T. Sim.* 6:1. (δικαιόω also occurs with ἀπό in Matt. 11:19 = Luke 7:35, but δικαιόω means "vindicate" here.)

130. E.g., Murray.

131. See, e.g., Godet; Michel; Käsemann.

132. *b. Shabb.* 151b, *Bar.:* "when a man is dead he is freed from fulfilling the law" (cf. Str-B, 3.232).

133. As in v. 5, Paul uses εἰ with "the indicative of logical reasoning" (BDF 373 [2b]); we might paraphrase: "since it is true that we died with Christ, we believe that we will also live with him."

134. Cf. 2 Cor. 4:14; Phil. 3:21; 1 Thess. 4:17; 2 Tim. 2:11; for this view, see, e.g., Thüsing, *Per Christum in Deum,* p. 70; Käsemann.

135. Cf. v. 4b; cf. Col. 2:13; Eph. 2:5-6; see, e.g., Murray; Cranfield.

9 The faith that we will share Christ's resurrection is grounded in what we know:[136] "Christ, having been raised from the dead, will no longer die; death no longer has lordship over him." Unlike Lazarus's "resurrection" (better, "revivification"), which did not spare him from another physical death, Christ's resurrection meant a decisive and final break with death and all its power. For his resurrection was the anticipation of the general resurrection — he is the "first fruits" of those that rise (1 Cor. 15:23). As such, his resurrection spelled the beginning of the new age of redemption, in which sin and death are being vanquished (cf. 1:4). But Paul's focus in this verse is on the significance of Christ's resurrection for Christ himself.[137] Christ's resurrection means that *he* "no longer" dies; "death no longer has lordship[138] over *him.*" This language shows again that Paul is viewing matters from the perspective of the two ages of salvation history. Christ, in coming to earth incarnate, came under the influence of the powers of the old age: sin (cf. v. 10), the law (cf. Gal. 4:4), and death. Because of this Paul can say that Christ is no longer under the lordship of death. Just as the general resurrection will bring "death" to an end (Rev. 20:11-15), so Christ's resurrection ends the power of death over himself, as well as anticipating the defeat of death in all those who belong to him. So, as those who are identified with Christ, we can be confident of sharing in that defeat of death when we "live with him" (v. 8b).

10 The immediate purpose of this verse is to furnish further proof for the last statement of v. 9 — "death no longer has lordship over him." But in doing so, Paul also provides an important link in his chain of reasoning in this passage. We "die to sin" (v. 2) when we die "with Christ" (vv. 3-6) because "the death[139] that he died, he died to sin once for all." What is striking

---

136. εἰδότες at the beginning of the verse is clearly a causal participle: "because we know" (cf. NIV; TEV).

137. While the resurrection of Christ in this verse has significance for Christ himself, that significance is better not described as his "justification" (contra, e.g., R. B. Gaffin, *The Centrality of the Resurrection* [Grand Rapids: Baker, 1978], pp. 115-16, 129-31; Byrne, "Living Out," p. 573). Paul reserves that language for the acquittal of one who needs to be acquitted because of his sins. While Christ was subject to the power of sin, he had no need for release from the guilt of sin. As far as we can see, Paul never uses "justification" language of Christ personally; 1 Tim. 3:16, Christ "was justified [ἐδικαιώθη] in, or by, the Spirit," is no exception because δικαιόω here means "vindicate," not "justify."

138. Gk. κυριεύει, a verb from the common title of Christ, κύριος, "Lord." Str-B, 3.232-33, compare the use of שָׁלֵט in passages that speak of the "angel of death" (e.g., *Mek. Exod.* 20,19; *Exod. Rab.* 41).

139. Paul writes in a compact style, using at this point in the Greek simply a relative pronoun as the object of the verb. It may characterize the "dying" — e.g., "whereas he died" (Moule, *Idiom Book,* p. 131) — or, as we have translated, restate the verbal idea for emphasis in an abbreviated cognate construction. Thus we take Paul's ὃ ἀπέθανεν to stand for τὴν θάνατον ὃν ἀπέθανεν (BDF 152; Robertson, 471; and most commentators).

about this verse is that Paul uses the same language to describe Christ's relationship to sin as he has done to describe the Christian's: dying "to sin."[140] Despite the similarity in language, many think that the concepts must be different; for Christ, being sinless, had no need to be freed from sin, as Christians do. Therefore, Christ's death must be "to sin" in the sense that "He affected sin by his dying," for in his death he bore the penalty of the sins of others.[141]

While, however, it is true that Christ did not need to be freed from sin's power in the same way that we need to be, a close parallel between the situation of Christ and of the Christian can be maintained if we remember that Paul is continuing to speak of sin as a "ruling power." Just as death once had "authority" over Christ because of his full identification with sinful people in the "old age," so that other ruling power of the old age, sin, could be said to have had "authority" over Christ. As a "man of the old age," he was subject to the power of sin — with the critical difference that he never succumbed to its power and actually sinned. When these salvation-historical perspectives are given their due place, we are able to give "die to sin" the same meaning here as it had in v. 2: a separation or freedom from the rule of sin.[142] And this transfer into a new state was for Christ final and definitive: "once for all."[143] The finality of Christ's separation from the power of sin shows why death can no longer rule over him — for is not death the product of sin (Rom. 6:23, etc.)?

But, as he has done throughout the passage, Paul sees death as the gateway to life; thus Christ, having died to sin, "lives for God." The life Christ now lives,[144] he lives for the glory of God.[145] Paul does not imply that Christ ever lived without seeking the will and glory of God first of all. But his resurrection has given him new power to carry out God's will and purpose. And the main reason Paul mentions Christ's "living to God" is to set up the comparison between Christ and the Christian that he will draw in v. 11.

140. Dative τῇ ἁμαρτίᾳ; cf. v. 2.

141. The quotation is from Cranfield. Cf. also Haldane; Calvin; Osten-Sacken, *Römer 8,* pp. 178-79; Kaye, *Thought Structure,* pp. 51-52; Hultgren, *Christ and his Benefits,* p. 51.

142. Cf., e.g, Lietzmann; Lagrange; Murray; Frankemölle, *Taufverständnis,* pp. 78-79.

143. Gk. ἐφάπαξ, used by Paul here, in 1 Cor. 15:6, and in Heb. 7:27; 9:12; 10:10. Cf. also ἅπαξ in 2 Cor. 11:25; Phil. 4:16; 1 Thess. 2:18; 1 Pet. 3:18; Jude 3, 5; and eight times in Hebrews.

144. Paul uses the same construction, with the relative pronoun, at the beginning of this clause as he did at the beginning of the verse (see the note there on the construction).

145. If, as in v. 2, we take the dative τῇ ἁμαρτίᾳ in the first part of the verse as a "dative of disadvantage," τῷ θεῷ will be a dative "of advantage." See a similar contrasting parallel with the same verbs in Rom. 14:7-8.

11 The introductory words, "in the same way also" indicate that Paul is now drawing a comparison — a comparison between the death and life of Christ and the attitude Christians are to adopt toward themselves. But Paul also states in this verse a summarizing inference from the teaching of the paragraph as a whole.[146] As the death Christ died was a death "to sin" (v. 10), so Christians who have died with Christ (vv. 4a, 5a, 6, 8a) must now regard themselves as being those who are "dead to sin."[147] And as Christ's "once-for-all" death led on to resurrection and new life "in God's service" (vv. 4b, 9-10), so Christians who participate in that resurrection life (vv. 4b, 5b, 8b) must regard themselves as those who are "alive to God."[148] Paul uses a present imperative, urging us constantly to view ourselves in this light. As always in Paul, the indicative grounds the imperative. In union with Christ we *have been made* dead to sin and alive to God; it remains for us to appropriate (v. 11) and apply (vv. 12-13) what God has done for us. As Thielicke puts it, "The imperative does not refer to the dying. Over this we have no control, since Jesus Christ has died for us and we only receive the gift of his dying and are drawn into it. The object of the imperative is that we should take this death into account, take it seriously, and thus make the gift become a gift in which we participate."[149] The last phrase of the verse reminds us that this new state is possible only in union with Christ: we are alive to God only "in Christ Jesus."[150] Being "dead to sin" and "alive to God" is a

---

146. See BAGD for this meaning of οὕτως ("so then") here; and cf. Cranfield.

147. Gk. νεκροὺς τῇ ἁμαρτίᾳ.

148. Gk. ζῶντας τῷ θεῷ.

149. H. Thielicke, *Theological Ethics,* vol. 1: *Foundations* (Grand Rapids: Eerdmans, 1966), p. 85.

150. This is only the second verse in Romans in which Paul's distinctive "in Christ" formula appears (cf. 3:24; note also 6:23; 8:1, 2, 39; 9:1; 14:14; 15:17; 16:2, 3, 7, 8, 9, 10, 11, 12a, 12b, 13, 22). While it is probably fair to call Paul's "in Christ" something of a formula, it is a formula that he uses with great flexibility. Modern study of the phrase was set on its course by Deissmann, who understood the ἐν in the phrase as a locative dative and interpreted Christ as a kind of "medium" or "ether" in which the Christian lives. This "mystical" approach to the phrase, while considerably popular in the "religions-history" school, is now widely discounted (for the history of research, see Bouttier, *En Christ,* pp. 5-22; F. Neugebauer, *In Christus* (ΕΝ ΧΡΙΣΤΩΙ). *Eine Untersuchung zum paulinischen Glaubensverständnis* [Göttingen: Vandenhoeck & Ruprecht, 1961], pp. 18-33). Replacing it have been several other models: a sacramental approach (communion mediated through a cultic experience); an ecclesiastical approach (incorporation into the church as the body of Christ); and a strictly forensic approach ("in Christ" as speaking of the "historical" and "indicative" fact that Christians have had their destinies determined by Christ; cf. esp. Neugebauer, *In Christus*). However, not all Paul's "in Christ" phrases have necessarily the same meaning (cf. the outline in A. Oepke, *TDNT* II, 541, and the chart in Bouttier, *En Christ,* p. 133). Grammatically, the ἐν in the phrase can have different functions; thus, while many are, in some sense, "local," others appear to be instrumental (cf.

state achieved only in union with Christ, who himself died to sin and is alive to God.[151] In this context, "in Christ" must be seen in light of the persistent "with Christ" language of vv. 4-10. Both phrases connote that the believer has experienced what has taken place with our representative, Christ. While the "with" language is more suitable to actions (dying, being buried, being raised), the "in" language fits better the continuing relationship of "deadness" to sin and "aliveness" to God of which this verse speaks. Only "in relation to," "as joined to," Christ — by faith — can the new life of victory over sin become a reality.

12 Moving from thought to action, Paul now spells out just what it will mean for the believer to "consider" him- or herself to be "dead to sin and alive to God" (v. 11). He uses two prohibitions (vv. 12 and 13a) and one command (v. 13b) to make his point. The first prohibition — "do not let sin reign" — is matched by the promise at the end of this small unit of verses that "sin will not have lordship over you" (v. 14a). Without this promise, which recapitulates a main emphasis of vv. 1-11, the imperative would be futile. One may as well tell a drowning person simply to swim to shore as tell a person who is under sin's mastery not to let sin reign. Many interpreters think that the form of imperative verb that Paul uses here (present tense) implies that he is calling on his readers to "*stop* letting sin reign."[152] And this could make good sense in the context, as Paul urges Christians to "put into action" the new power over sin that he has described in vv. 1-11: "now that you have realized that you have been delivered from sin's power, *stop*

A. J. M. Wedderburn, "Some Observations on Paul's Use of the Phrases 'in Christ' and 'with Christ,' " *JSNT* 25 [1985], 83-90). While grammar must not be ignored, Paul's "in Christ" conception can ultimately be explained only in light of general theological considerations.

It is Paul's conception of "salvation history" that best explains the general meaning of his "in Christ" language. The "informing" theology is Paul's understanding of Christ as the representative head of the new age, or realm, who incorporates within himself all who belong to that new age. For us to be "in Christ" means, then, to belong to Christ as our representative, so that the decisions applied to him apply also to us (cf., e.g., Ridderbos, *Paul,* pp. 57-62; Beker, 272-73; A. Oepke, *TDNT* II, 541-43). Cf. 1 Cor. 15:22, especially: "as in Adam all die, so in Christ shall all be made alive" (note also 2 Cor. 5:14-17). Usually, then, ἐν has a spatial sense ("in" Christ as inclusive person) but also, to a greater or lesser extent from text to text, an instrumental force (what we do is done "through" Christ, or "in and through Christ" — what Beker [272] calls a "participatory-instrumental" meaning). In addition, we must not so emphasize the forensic (as Neugebauer does; cf. Tannehill, *Dying and Rising,* p. 19; Käsemann, 220-23) that we lose sight of the element of ongoing personal relationship, which is, albeit in an unfortunate direction, captured in Deissmann's "mystical" approach.

151. Cf. Byrne, "Living Out," p. 563; Thüsing, *Per Christum in Deum,* pp. 73-77.
152. Cf., e.g., Turner, 76; Godet; Cranfield; Fitzmyer. The Greek is μὴ βασιλευέτω.

letting it have power over you." But the grammatical basis for this interpretation is not strong,[153] and I question whether Paul would want to imply that the Roman Christians are now letting sin reign over them (cf. 15:14-15). I consider it more likely that Paul is issuing here a general prohibition. Having urged Christians (on the basis of vv. 1-10) "constantly to consider" themselves as dead to sin (v. 11), he now commands them to make it their practice never to let sin hold sway over them.[154]

Specifically, Paul urges his readers not to let sin reign "in your mortal

153. The notion that the use of the present tense in prohibitions suggests the need to stop doing an action in which one is already engaged is widespread (cf., e.g., Turner, ibid.). But a number of grammarians have argued, correctly, that this nuance is not inherent in the tense and often reads more into NT texts where the construction appears than is warranted (cf. esp. J. Louw, "On Greek Prohibitions," *Acta Classica* 2 [1959], 43-57 [he here summarizes the fruit of his doctoral dissertation on the topic]; note also Porter, *Verbal Aspect,* pp. 351-52; B. Fanning, *Verbal Aspect in New Testament Greek* [Oxford: Clarendon, 1990], pp. 335-37). Of Paul's 51 uses of μή with the present imperative, 16 pretty clearly cannot have the nuance "stop [doing]" (cf. 1 Cor. 10:28; 2 Cor. 6:14; Gal. 5:1; Eph. 4:26; 5:7, 11, 17, 18; Eph. 6:4; Phil. 4:6; Col. 3:9, 19, 21; 1 Thess. 5:19, 20; 2 Thess. 3:15). Probably only if contextual factors indicate should we find this idea (e.g., note 1 Tim. 5:23, μηκέτι ὑδροπότει, "*no longer* drink [only] water").

154. Grammarians debate the significance of the tenses when used in commands in prohibitions; and it must be admitted that there are many places in the NT where no clear pattern emerges (cf. Moule, *Idiom Book,* pp. 20-21). Among recent proposals, three (all of which advocate an "aspectual" approach to the tense of the Greek verb) might be noted. Porter (*Verbal Aspect,* pp. 351-52) suggests that the aorist tense is used when the author chooses to view the command as a whole, while the present tense, being "more heavily marked," is used "to specify" the command, treating it as in progress or (in prohibitions) to deny that it is in progress. He thinks therefore that Paul draws special attention to the (present) prohibitions in vv. 12 and 13a, while the (aorist) command in v. 13b assumes what the Romans already know (*Verbal Aspect,* p. 357). K. L. McKay ("Time and Aspect in New Testament Greek," *NovT* 34 [1992], 209-28) also thinks the aorist "urges an activity as a whole action" while the present (the "imperfective") "urges it as an ongoing process." He also, however, thinks that μή with the present imperative often prohibits an activity in progress. B. Fanning (*Verbal Aspect,* pp. 326-32) distinguishes between "specific" and "general" commands, the aorist usually used for the former and the present for the latter. In prohibitions, the present tense can signify that an action in progress is to cease, but it can also mean "make it your practice not to do."

The lack of agreement among the grammarians on this point urges great caution in imposing any one scheme on the text, a caution confirmed by my own conclusion that none of these schemes (or any other I have found) seems able with any degree of comprehensiveness to account for Paul's use of the tenses in commands. Negatively, Porter's suggestion that the present often carries emphasis does not seem to work very often; and his suggestion that in this text the present prohibitions in vv. 12 and 13a are emphatic while the positive command in v. 13b assumes what the Romans already know (*Verbal Aspect,* p. 357) turns the natural flow of the text on its head. But there does seem to be some reason to think that Paul often uses the present to connote durative action.

body." "Body" (*sōma*) may be the physical body;[155] but it is probably, as in 6:6, the whole person, viewed in terms of the person's interaction with the world.[156] As Nygren puts it, "the arena of the battle is in the world." The battle is a spiritual one, but it is fought, and won or lost, in the daily decisions the believer makes about how to use his body. In characterizing the body as "mortal," Paul is reminding us that the same body that has been severed from its servitude to sin (6:6) is nevertheless a body that still participates in the weakness, suffering, and dissolution of this age.[157] Until we are fully "redeemed" (8:23) and "put on immortality" (1 Cor. 15:53), we will continue to be subject to the influences of this age; and the believer must not let these influences hold sway. The Christian is no longer "body of sin" (6:6) or "body of death" (7:24), but he or she is still "mortal body."[158]

"The mortal body" is, then, the believer's form of existence in this world, which still has part in "this age." It is because of this, and not because of anything inherent in the body — whether limited to the corporeal or not — that Paul can in the last clause of this verse relate the body so closely to sin: "in order to obey its [the body's][159] passions."[160] Paul can use "passions" with a neutral meaning (cf. Phil. 1:23; 1 Thess. 2:17), but here the word refers to desires that are in conflict with the will of God.[161] If "body" has the general meaning we have suggested, these "passions" would include not only the physical lusts and appetites but also those desires that reside in the mind and will: the desire to have our own way, the desire to possess what other people have (cf. 7:7-8), the desire to have dominance over others. The whole clause relates to the general sense of the verb "reign" rather than to the prohibition "let [sin] not reign" as such and probably expresses result.[162] We might

155. Gundry, 29-31; Jewett, *Anthropological Terms,* pp. 293-94; Godet; Murray. In favor of this identification is the adjective θνητός ("mortal"), the reference to "its passions" later in the verse, and "members" in v. 13.

156. See, e.g., Calvin; Käsemann; Cranfield. In favor of this broader meaning are the parallel between "body" here and "yourselves" in v. 13 and the fact that sin certainly influences more than just the physical side of people.

157. In every place where Paul uses θνητός, this is its connotation (8:11; 1 Cor. 15:53, 54; 2 Cor. 4:11; 5:4).

158. Schlier.

159. We assume the reading ταῖς ἐπιθυμίαις αὐτοῦ (see the note on the translation above). The antecedent of αὐτοῦ must be σώματι, αὐτοῦ being either a genitive of possession — "the body's passions" — or of source — "the passions that come from the body."

160. Cf. Gundry, 40.

161. This is the usual meaning of ἐπιθυμία in Paul; cf. 1:24; 7:7, 8; 13:14; Gal. 5:16, 24; Eph. 2:3; 4:22; Col. 3:5; 1 Thess. 4:5; 1 Tim. 6:9; 2 Tim. 2:22; 3:6; 4:3.

162. Robertson, 1090 (probable). On εἰς τό with the infinitive in Paul, see the note on 1:20.

paraphrase: "Do no let sin's reign — which leads to obedience to the body's sinful passions — occupy your lives."[163]

13 The imperatives of this verse unfold in more specific and practical terms the general command "not to let sin reign" (v. 12).[164] Paul has moved from the general "you" (v. 11) to the more definite "body" (v. 12) to the even more definite "members."[165] If "body" in v. 12 means "person in contact with the world" instead of "physical body," then "members" also will mean "natural capacities" rather than limbs, or parts, of the body.[166] Paul's command is that Christians "not present" these members as "weapons of unrighteousness." The prohibition "do not present" is, like "do not let sin reign" in v. 12, in the present tense; and, as in v. 12, Paul is probably suggesting that this prohibition is one that remains in force throughout the Christian life. Now that we understand ourselves to be "dead to sin, alive to God" (v. 11), we must constantly avoid using our abilities and resources in the service of sin. The words Paul chooses here fit well with his focus throughout this passage on the concepts of rulership and domination. Our natural capacities are "weapons"[167] that we are not to "offer in service"[168] to the tyrant sin.[169] Since sin is no longer our "ruler" (v. 14a), we must stop letting it "reign" over us (v. 12), and stop serving it as if it were our rightful sovereign (v. 13a). Those natural capacities and abilities that God has given us are

163. Note the somewhat parallel Gal. 5:16: "Do not complete the passion of the flesh [ἐπιθυμίαν σαρκός]." But the Galatians text differs in that this prohibition is preceded by the command, "Walk by the Spirit." Paul takes a different tack in Romans, leaving the vital ministry of the Spirit for discussion in chap. 8.

164. Hence the transitional word οὖν, "therefore."

165. Gk. μέλη. Cf. J. Horst, *TDNT* IV, 561.

166. Käsemann; Cranfield; contra Godet. This broader meaning of μέλη is supported by texts such as 7:5 and 7:23, where "members" is closely associated with "flesh" (σάρξ); for flesh in these contexts is not physical flesh but the fallen person as a whole.

167. ὅπλα may have the general meaning "instruments," or "tools" (cf. F. S. Malan, "Bound to do Right," *Neot* 15 [1981], 123), but Pauline usage suggests the more specific military meaning "weapons" (cf. Rom. 13:12; 2 Cor. 6:7; 10:4; the only other NT usage is in John 18:3, where it means "weapons" literally); cf. Lagrange; Dunn; K. G. Kuhn, *TDNT* V, 294. The heavily armored Greek foot soldier was called a ὁπλίτης.

168. Paul's prohibition uses the verb παρίστημι, which, being used again in v. 19, is central to this second part of Rom. 6. Some think, in light of ὅπλα ("weapons"), that its military associations are preeminent here (e.g., Käsemann, who refers to Polybius, *Hist.* 3.109.9). But the verb is used in the LXX with reference to the service offered to a king or ruler (cf., e.g., 1 Kings 10:8: the Queen of Sheba counts as blessed those who "serve" or "minister" [παρεστηκότες] before King Solomon; cf. G. Bertram and B. Reicke, *TDNT* V, 838, 839). παριστάνετε will not, then, have the passive meaning "yield," or even "present," but the more active and concrete meaning "give in service to" (Malan, "Bound to Do Right," p. 124; Godet).

169. τῇ ἁμαρτίᾳ is, then, again personified as a power.

weapons that must no longer be put in the service of the master from whom we have been freed.[170]

The renunciation of our service to sin is to be followed immediately by our enlisting in the service of a new master: God. Matching the negative "do not present your members for sin" is the positive "present yourselves[171] to God." This positive command, in contrast to the prohibitions in vv. 12 and 13a, is in the aorist tense.[172] Some commentators think that Paul therefore pictures this "presenting" as a "once-for-all" action,[173] or as ingressive ("start presenting"),[174] or as urgent.[175] But the aorist tense in itself does not indicate such nuances;[176] and nothing in the context here clearly suggests any of them. In fact, the aorist imperative often lacks any special force, being used simply to command that an action take place — without regard for the duration, urgency, or frequency of the action. This is probably the case here. However, we may surmise that, as the negative *not* presenting ourselves to sin is constantly necessary, so is the positive giving ourselves in service to God, our rightful ruler.

As Paul will make clear in vv. 16ff., there can be no "neutral" position between service of God and service of sin. By characterizing those whom he commands "as those alive from the dead," Paul reminds us that this presenting of ourselves to God can take place only because[177] of the new state we find ourselves in as a result of our union with Christ in his death and resurrection (see

---

170. Probably, then, ἀδικίας is an objective genitive, suggesting purpose — "weapons for the purpose of unrighteousness" (BDF 168; Cranfield) — rather than a genitive of quality — "unrighteous weapons" (Michel; Kuss).

171. The use of ἑαυτούς here suggests, as we have seen, that μέλη (v. 13a) and σῶμα (v. 12) should not be confined to the physical "part" of the person. (The third person reflexive pronoun is frequently used for the second person in *Koinē* Greek [cf. Turner, 42].)

172. Gk. παραστήσατε.

173. E.g., Gifford; Murray.

174. BDF 337(1); Turner, 76; Fanning, *Verbal Aspect,* p. 357.

175. S-H; Godet; A. B. du Toit, "Dikaiosyne in Röm. 6. Beobachtungen zur ethischen Dimension der paulinischen Gerechtigkeitsauffassung," *ZTK* 76 (1979), 274-75. Porter argues that the aorist, being "less heavily marked" than the present, is less important, stating something that the Romans already know (*Verbal Aspect,* p. 357). But it is impossible to think that the Romans would have known that they were to offer themselves to God (v. 13b) without knowing also that they needed to resist sin's reign (v. 12) and to keep their members from sin (v. 13a). Porter's suggestion, in fact, reverses the natural emphases of the text.

176. Cf., e.g., Zerwick, 240-69; F. Stagg, "The Abused Aorist," *JBL* 91 (1972), 222-31; McKay, "Aspect"; Porter, *Verbal Aspect,* pp. 336-52.

177. ὡσεί means not "as if you were" but "as you really are" (Longenecker, 178) and, while formally a comparison, has something of a causal nuance: "present yourselves to God, since you are alive from the dead" (Michel).

v. 11). Since "being alive" is obviously the state of the believer in this life, the reference must be to the rescue from the state of death that takes place when the believer becomes united with Christ. The bodily resurrection lies ahead, but there has already taken place a "spiritual" resurrection (cf. Col. 2:12; Eph. 2:6)[178] that introduces the believer into a new life, a life "in God's service."[179]

Paul adds one last characterization of believers, completing the contrasting parallel with the first part of the verse. What we are to offer to God are "your members as weapons of righteousness." The "members" that were once used as "weapons" in the service of sin and for unrighteous purposes are now to be used as weapons in God's service,[180] for righteous purposes.[181] "Righteousness," used here for the first time since 5:21, probably does not have a forensic meaning (status of righteousness) but a moral meaning: behavior pleasing to God.[182] To be sure, while not the same, these two "righ-

---

178. See Beker, 224. Wedderburn (*Baptism*, pp. 44-45) contests the idea that the clause assumes a spiritual resurrection.

179. The significance of the dative τῷ θεῷ (dative of advantage).

180. τῷ θεῷ is probably to be connected with ὅπλα, "weapons" (Godet) rather than with the distant παραστήσατε.

181. Like ἀδικίας, δικαιοσύνης probably denotes the object, or purpose, of the weapons.

182. Cf., e.g., Ridderbos, *Paul,* p. 262; Schnelle, *Gerechtigkeit und Christusgegenwart,* p. 86; and most commentators. This meaning for the word is, of course, well attested in both the LXX and the NT (cf., e.g., Matt. 3:15; 6:33; Jas. 1:20; Eph. 4:24; 5:9; Phil. 1:11[?]; 1 Tim. 6:11; 2 Tim. 2:22; 3:16; 4:8; Tit. 3:5[?]). The most important consideration favoring this meaning is the context. Note, e.g., v. 16: ὑπακοῆς εἰς δικαιοσύνην ("obedience leading to righteousness") and the contrast between "righteousness" and "unrighteousness" (here), "sin" (vv. 16[?], 18, and 20), and "uncleanness" and "lawlessness" in v. 19.

Our conclusion that δικαιοσύνη means something basically different in this chapter than it does in the earlier chapters of Romans is denied by those who associate the idea of God's power with the word. In Rom. 6, like "sin," righteousness is conceived as a power to which one submits (cf. vv. 18, 19) and is thus paralleled with God (compare vv. 18 and 22). In this manner, righteousness as God's power for salvation (chaps. 1–5) can be essentially identified with righteousness as that power to which we are now joined (cf. particularly Käsemann; note also, though with variations in precise formulation, Dunn; Roberts, "Righteousness," pp. 20-21; du Toit, "Dikaiosyne in Röm. 6," pp. 263-90; Reumann, *Righteousness,* pp. 81-84). However, while it is true that Paul personifies righteousness and casts it in the role of a "power" from which one can be "free" (v. 20) or enslaved, the word never loses its reference to concrete activity (this is the case also with sin, as we argued earlier [see the notes on 5:12]; cf. Ziesler, *Righteousness,* p. 201; Hübner, 132). This is especially clear in v. 19, where the contrast with "uncleanness and ever-increasing lawlessness" requires that righteousness, while summarizing and personified, connote specific acts in the world. And while it could be argued that it is preferable to maintain a single meaning for righteousness throughout Romans, the distinct contrast in the linguistic associations of righteousness between chaps. 1–5 and chap. 6 points to a difference in meaning. Thus, e.g., in chaps. 1–5, righteousness has a "gift-character" to which man can contribute nothing (cf. 4:5); but in 6:16 righteousness is the result of obedience.

teousnesses" are inextricably bound, for it is only the righteousness attained "before God" that introduces the sinner into a new state from which he is able to be obedient to the righteousness of life that God demands.

14   After the imperatives of vv. 11-13, this short paragraph concludes with a return to the indicative. "For sin will no longer have lordship over you" grounds the specific commands of vv. 12-13[183] while summarizing the keynote of the chapter. "Sin" is again personified as power.[184] Commentators have thought that Paul's future tense verb — "will no longer have lordship"[185] — implies that he is giving a command ("sin must not be your lord"),[186] a promise for the future ("sin will one day have no control over you"),[187] or a conditional promise ("*if* you stop letting sin reign, it will have no mastery over you").[188] But these words are to be understood as a promise that is valid for every believer at the present time: "sin shall certainly not be your Lord — now or ever!"

To put a stop to the reign of sin — to stop engaging in those sins that have too often become so habitual that we cannot imagine *not* doing them — is a daunting responsibility. We feel that we must fail. But Paul then reminds us of just what we have become in Jesus Christ: "dead to sin, alive to God." There has already taken place in the life of the believer a "change of lordship" (Paul could hardly use the verb *kyrieuō* without thinking of the real *kyrios* of the Christian), and it is in the assurance of the continuance of this new state that the believer can go forth boldly and confidently to wage war against sin.

This promise is confirmed[189] by the assurance that "you are not under law but under grace." That the law is so suddenly brought onto the scene at the end of this paragraph reveals the extent to which Paul's presentation of his gospel in this letter never moves too far from the salvation-historical question of Old Covenant and New, Jew and Gentile. This allusion is one of a series of interjections about the negative effects of the law in salvation history (cf. 3:19-20, 21, 27-28; 4:13-15; 5:13-14, 20) that culminate in chap. 7. These texts — especially 5:20 and 7:1-6 — furnish the context in which the enigmatic and much-debated phrase "not under the law" must be interpreted. As in all these references, *nomos* here must be the Mosaic law, the

---

183. Cf. the γάρ, "for."

184. The lack of the article with ἁμαρτία perhaps lends a qualitative note (e.g., "sin qua sin").

185. Gk. κυριεύσει.

186. O'Neill; Fitzmyer.

187. E.g., Lloyd-Jones.

188. E.g., Dodd; cf. Luther's gloss: " 'For sin will have no dominion over you,' unless you want it to."

189. Another γάρ.

torah.[190] And, while most of the (Gentile-) Christians in Rome have never lived "under the law," the situation of the Jews under the Mosaic law, as we will see in 7:4, is used by Paul as representative of the situation and need of all people.

Interpreting 6:14b against the background of these other texts also makes it unlikely that Paul could be referring here to a "legalistic" abuse of the law — making it a means of salvation[191] — or to the "social dimension" of the law — the Jewish tendency to turn the law into their own, private "national guardian angel."[192] For it is clear that Paul is speaking in these passages of the law *as God gave it,* and thus of the intended function of the law in salvation history — not to a human misunderstanding. Such interpretations as these illegitimately "soften" the salvation-historical contrasts that are endemic to Paul's presentation of the gospel as a new and climactic work of God in history.

Since Paul presents the Mosaic law as a force that brought condemnation of sin (cf. 4:15; implicitly in 5:13-14; 7:4), it may be that he is thinking here specifically of the condemning effect of the law. To be "under the law" means to be subject to the curse of the law that comes because of the inevitable failure to accomplish the law (cf. 3:19-20; Gal. 3:10-14) — to be under "the covenant of works," as the Puritans often put it.[193] But confining the phrase

---

190. Contra, e.g., Hodge; Murray; and Barrett, who think it refers here to "law" in general. The omission of the article is no problem for this interpretation, for the presence or absence of the article is of little help in determining the meaning of νόμος in Paul (see the note on 2:12). Both νόμος and χάρις ("grace") owe their anarthrous states to stylistic considerations (cf. Robertson, 793 and BDF 252, who refer to the omission of the article as stylistic in "closely related pairs of substantives"), and perhaps to their function as objects of ὑπό (BDF 255; Godet suggests that the words may have qualitative force, but this is unlikely).

191. This legalistic interpretation is argued by, e.g., Stuart; Cranfield (as part of the meaning); Hübner, 134-35; C. F. D. Moule, "Obligation in the Ethic of Paul," in *Christian History and Interpretation: Studies Presented to John Knox* (ed. W. R. Farmer, C. F. D. Moule, and R. R. Niebuhr; Cambridge: Cambridge University, 1967), pp. 394-95.

192. See esp. Dunn.

193. Calvin; Melanchthon; Cranfield; Murray, *Principles of Conduct,* pp. 187-88; Stalder, *Werk des Geistes,* p. 279. Some of the Reformers (see Melanchthon on this verse) and many of the Puritans made the distinction between the law as a "covenant of works" and the law in terms of commandment; the believer is free from the former but bound to the latter. See, e.g., John Ball, *A Treatise of the Covenant of Grace* (London, 1645), p. 15; Samuel Bolton, *The True Bounds of Christian Freedom* (London, 1645; rpt., Banner of Truth, 1964), p. 28; John Cotton, *A Treatise of the Covenant of Grace* (3d ed.; London, 1671), p. 87; and see the discussion in J. von Rohr, *The Covenant of Grace in Puritan Thought* (AAR Studies in Religion 45; Atlanta: Scholars Press, 1986), p. 110.

only to the notion of condemnation fails to grasp the salvation-historical contrast that Paul sets up here.[194]

Several bits of evidence suggest that Paul is thinking of "law" and "grace" as contrasting salvation-historical "powers." (1) The contrast between being "under the law" and "under grace" fits naturally into the "transfer of realm" language that so characterizes Rom. 5:12–8:39. (2) Paul has used "under" (sin) in 3:9 to characterize the situation of people "under the power of" sin, and the prominence of slavery imagery in Rom. 6 suggests that the preposition has the same connotation here. "Law" and "grace" are viewed as "realms" or "powers." (3) Paul's other uses of the phrase "under the law" all denote the objective situation of "subject to the rule of the Mosaic law."[195] As in John 1:17, then, "law" and "grace" contrast the old age of bondage and "tutelage" (cf. Gal. 3:25) with the new age of freedom and "sonship" (cf. Gal. 4:1-7; Rom. 8:14-17).

"Under law," then, is another way of characterizing "the old realm." This explains why Paul can make release from the law a reason for the Christian's freedom from the power of sin: as he has repeatedly stated, the Mosaic law has had a definite sin-producing and sin-intensifying function: it has brought "knowledge of sin" (3:20), "wrath" (4:15), "transgression" (5:13-14), and an increase in the severity of sin (5:20). The law, as Paul puts it in 1 Cor. 15:56, is "the power of sin." This means, however, that there can be no final liberation from the power of sin without a corresponding liberation from the power and lordship of the law. To be "under law" is to be subject to the constraining and sin-strengthening regime of the old age; to be "under grace" is to be subject to the new age in which freedom from the power of sin is available.[196] The contrast of "grace" and "law" here picks up their juxtaposition in the last passage where they were both mentioned together: 5:20-21. Since this text stimulates Paul's teaching in 6:1-14, it is not at all

194. Two other reasons for thinking that "under law" means more than under the condemnation of the law are: (1) "not being under condemnation" does not explain why "sin will no longer have lordship over you" (v. 14a) — being "justified" gives, in itself, no basis for freedom from the *power* of sin; and (2) Paul uses ὑπὸ νόμον elsewhere in places where "under condemnation" can hardly be the meaning: Gal. 4:4, referring to Christ's status on earth; 1 Cor. 9:20, referring to his own decision to live like Jews in order to win them to Christ (1 Cor. 9:20); and Gal. 4:21, referring to what the Galatians were seeking to do (the phrase also occurs in Gal. 3:23; 4:5; 5:18).

195. See the references in the previous note; and cf. the discussion in Westerholm, "Letter and Spirit," pp. 242-43; D. J. Moo, "The Law of Moses or the Law of Christ," in *Continuity and Discontinuity: Perspectives on the Relationship between the Old and New Testaments. Essays in Honor of S. Lewis Johnson, Jr.* (ed. J. S. Feinberg; Westchester, IL: Crossway, 1988), pp. 210-17.

196. For this emphasis, see particularly Luther; Nygren; Ridderbos, *Paul*, p. 148; on "grace" as a power, see our comments on 5:2.

surprising that he returns to this issue at its end. The paragraph that began with the question "Should we remain in sin in order that grace may increase?" ends with the glad tidings that we are under grace in order that sin may be overcome.

Three caveats are, however, necessary.

(1) The nature of Paul's salvation-historical scheme is such that, as we have seen, a neat transfer into straightforward temporal categories is impossible. People before the coming of Christ, while still "bound" to the law, could nevertheless escape its condemning power (e.g., Abraham, David — chap. 4). Moreover, people after the coming of Christ can still be subject to its rule. While, then, it is fair to speak of all of Israel between Moses and Christ as being "under the law" (cf. especially Gal. 3-4) — insofar as it was the "ruling" authority of that "dispensation" — we must at the same time recognize that people during that time could escape the condemnatory "rule" of that law by faith in the God who had made promises to Abraham.

(2) We must be careful to distinguish the Mosaic law from the other "powers" of the old age in one vital respect; unlike sin, the flesh, and death, the law is not an intrinsically negative force, as Paul will explain at length in chap. 7.

(3) Finally, we must respect the degree to which Paul is here thinking of the Mosaic law as a *system* or *body*.[197] Therefore, while there is no doubt that release from the commanding force of the Mosaic law is included in not being "under law" — for this is Paul's usual focus with *nomos;* and cf. 1 Cor. 9:20 — we must be careful about drawing conclusions from this that would be too sweeping. We are justified in considering the Christian to be free from the commandments of the Mosaic law insofar as they are part of that system, and perhaps in the sense that whatever commandments are applicable to us come with a new empowering through the "indicative" of God's grace in Christ.[198] But we cannot conclude from this verse that the believer has no obligation to any of the individual commandments of that law — insofar, we may say, as they may be isolated from the "system." Still less does this verse allow the conclusion that Christians are no longer subject to "law" or "commandments" at all — for *nomos* here means *Mosaic* law, not "law" as such.

Romans 6 is the classic biblical text on the importance of relating the "indicative" of what God has done for us with the "imperative" of what we are to do. Paul stresses that we must actualize in daily experience the freedom

---

197. T. R. Schreiner rightly stresses this point ("The Abolition and the Fulfillment of the Law in Paul," *JSNT* 35 [1989], pp. 54-59).

198. Cf. Deidun, 204-10.

from sin's lordship (cf. v. 14a) that is ours "in Christ Jesus." State is to become reality; we are "to become what we are" — or, with due recognition of the continuing work of God in our lives, we might say "become what you are becoming."[199] Balance on this point is essential. "Indicative" and "imperative" must be neither divided nor confused. If divided, with "justification" and "sanctification" put into separate compartments, we can forget that true holiness of life comes only as the outworking and realization of the life of Christ in us. This leads to a "moralism" or "legalism" in which the believer "goes it on his own," thinking that holiness will be attained through sheer effort, or ever more elaborate programs, or ever-increasing numbers of rules. But if indicative and imperative are confused, with "justification" and "sanctification" collapsed together into one, we can neglect the fact that the outworking of the life of Christ in us is made *our* responsibility. This neglect leads to an unconcern with holiness of life, or to a "God-does-it-all" attitude in which the believer thinks to become holy through a kind of spiritual osmosis.[200] Paul makes it clear, by the sequence in this paragraph, that we can live a holy life only as we appropriate the benefits of our union with Christ. But he also makes it clear, because there *is* a sequence, that living the holy life is distinct from (but not separate from) what we have attained by our union with Christ and that holiness of life can be stifled if we fail continually to appropriate and put to work the new life God has given us. Jeremiah Bourroughs, a seventeenth-century Puritan, put it like this: ". . . from him [Christ] as from a fountain, sanctification flows into the souls of the Saints: their sanctification comes not so much from their struggling, and endeavors, and vows, and resolutions, as it comes flowing to them from their union with him."[201] Or, as Thielicke puts it, we saints must not close our mouths to this fountain of sanctification, but continue to drink from it.[202]

EXCURSUS: PAUL'S "WITH CHRIST" CONCEPTION

Paul's use of σύν to describe the relation between Christ and the Christian is an important and controversial aspect of his Christology and soteriology. Paul

199. Dunn; Deidun, 239-43.

200. On this point, see esp. O. Weber, *Foundations of Dogmatics* (2 vols.; Grand Rapids: Eerdmans, 1983), 2.289-339; Thielicke, *Foundations,* pp. 84-92; Ridderbos, *Paul,* pp. 253-58; Furnish, *Theology and Ethics,* pp. 225-27; Murray, *Principles of Conduct,* pp. 202-28; Deidun, 239-43.

201. *Saints' Treasury* 46, quoted in E. F. Kevan, *The Grace of Law: A Study of Puritan Theology* (rpt.; Grand Rapids: Baker, 1976), p. 236.

202. *Foundations,* p. 93.

brings Christ and believers together with the preposition σύν 32 times; they can be put into nine categories:

1. The believer's "dying with" (σύν-ἀποθνῄσκω) Christ (Rom. 6:8; Col. 2:20; 2 Tim. 2:11; cf. Rom. 6:5);
2. The believer's "being crucified with" (συσταυρόω) Christ (Rom. 6:6; Gal. 2:20a);
3. The believer's being "buried" with" (συντάφω) Christ (Rom. 6:4; Col. 2:12);
4. The believer's being "raised with" (συνεγείρω) Christ in the past (Col. 2:12[1]; Col. 3:1; Eph. 2:6);
5. The believer's "coming to life with" (συνζωοποιέω) Christ (Col. 2:13; Eph. 2:5);
6. The believer's being "seated with" (συγκαθίζω) Christ in "the heavenlies" (Eph. 2:6);
7. The believer's being "with" Christ (various verbs) in this life (Rom. 8:17a, 17b, 29; Phil. 3:10; Col. 3:3; 2 Cor. 13:4b[2]);
8. The believer's eventual deliverance "with" Christ (various verbs) (Rom. 6:5b, 8b; 8:17b, 32b; 2 Cor. 4:14; Phil. 3:21; Col. 3:4; 1 Thess. 4:14b; 5:10b; 2 Tim. 2:11b[3]);
9. The believer's being "with" Christ after death/parousia (1 Thess. 4:17; Phil. 1:23).

We note that the greatest number of occurrences are eschatological; and many interpreters think that Paul has taken his "with Christ" concept from apocalyptic. These references would therefore be the earliest stratum of tradition, with a movement over time to use the language of earlier phases of the believer's experience until the allegedly post-Pauline "realized" eschatology of Colossians and Ephesians is reached.[4] But it is also quite possible that Paul is himself the originator of the conception.[5] We have no reason to think that the idea of a past spiritual resurrection of believers with Christ is

---

1. The verse is controversial, but we take the ᾧ to have βαπτισμῷ ("baptism") as its antecedent (cf. J. B. Lightfoot, *St. Paul's Epistles to the Colosssians and to Philemon* [London: Macmillan, 1879], p. 185; Beasley-Murray, *Baptism*, pp. 153-54).

2. The reference here could be to the Christian's future resurrection or heavenly existence, but in context it probably refers to Paul's strength with respect to his impending visit to Corinth (cf. P. E. Hughes, *Paul's Second Epistle to the Corinthians* [NICNT; Grand Rapids: Eerdmans, 1962], p. 479).

3. If συζήσομεν is durative, this reference could be put in the next category.

4. See, e.g., E. Schweizer, "Dying and Rising with Christ," *NTS* 14 (1967-68), 1-14; Beker, 274-75.

5. See Siber, *Mit Christus Leben,* pp. 191-213; Wedderburn, *Baptism,* pp. 50-52.

post-Pauline; the idea is clearly assumed in Rom. 6:1-11.[6] Paul's σὺν Χριστῷ language must certainly be related to his more common ἐν Χριστῷ language. But it is probably overly simple to think that the former relates to the Christian's past and future while the latter describes present experience (see category 7 above).[7]

　　More germane to our purposes is the meaning of the phrase in Paul. In the NT, σύν, when used with verbs (either independently or in compound form), usually indicates accompaniment in a temporal sense. But a temporal "withness" cannot be insisted on in all the σὺν Χριστῷ references, as Rom. 8:17 and 2 Cor. 4:14 make clear. It is also clear that the actions brought together in Paul's "with" compounds need not be identical; our past resurrection with Christ is obviously spiritual, whereas Christ's has a primarily physical meaning.

　　What does this "withness" indicate, then? We must not insist that every occurrence have precisely the same significance. As Tannehill points out, σὺν Χριστῷ is not a formula but a motif.[8] Often the ideas of correspondence ("as Christ, so we") and/or causality ("because Christ, so we")[9] are present. But Paul would not have chosen to use the preposition σύν if this were all that was meant.[10] Although the temporal is not always present, the idea of *participation* or *association* does seem to be basic to the expressions. In other words, Paul's "with Christ" language cannot be reduced to the ideas of "modeling" or "repetition." In order to go further, we must move beyond grammar. As J. A. T. Robinson says, Paul "clearly feels the manifest inadequacy of language to convey the unique 'withness' that Christians have in Christ."[11]

　　The theological concept that grounds and motivates the "with Christ" language of Paul is his understanding of Christ as a representative, even inclusive, figure.[12] Rom. 5:12-21 has established that Christ's "obedience"/"act of righteousness" affects all who belong to him. Davies (102-4) refers in this regard to the Jewish teaching that every generation was to consider itself as having taken part in the Exodus (e.g., *m. Pesaḥ*. 10). As Tannehill notes, it is but a "short step" to the inference that Christ's death is

6. See Harris, *Raised Immortal,* pp. 103-4.

7. Contra Bouttier, *En Christ,* p. 53.

8. *Dying and Rising,* p. 6.

9. See Stevens, *The Pauline Theology,* pp. 33-36, for an emphasis on causality.

10. W. Grundmann, *TDNT* VII, 782.

11. *The Body: A Study in Pauline Theology* (SBT 5; London: SCM, 1952), p. 60.

12. See especially, though with differences in detail, Ridderbos, *Paul,* pp. 57-62; Tannehill, *Dying and Rising,* passim; Beasley-Murray, *Baptism,* pp. 132-38; Davies, 101-8; Thüsing, *Per Christum in Deum,* pp. 74-75; Best, *One Body,* pp. 55-57; Wedderburn, *Baptism,* pp. 343-48; idem, "Some Observations," pp. 83-97.

a corporate or inclusive act, so that his death is at the same time the death of all those who are "in" him.[13] And Paul takes just this step in 2 Cor. 5:14: "One died on behalf of all; therefore all died." The death of Christ is also the death of all whom he represents.[14] But we must be careful just how we understand this inclusiveness.

First, we must question whether Paul thinks of this inclusion with Christ's death as taking place before one's coming to Christ in faith. Although many scholars speak as if this were the case,[15] there are reasons for doubt. To begin with, as we have already seen, several of Paul's "with Christ" expressions connect actions of Christ and of the believer that *cannot* have taken place simultaneously (cf. Rom. 8:17; 2 Cor. 4:14). Then, several other actions that believers are said to "do" with Christ appear to designate actions that have taken place in their own experience; for example, both Col. 2:13 and Eph. 2:5 speak of a "coming to life with Christ" out of the state of being "dead in tresspasses." The Colossians text further connects this coming to life with faith and the forgiveness of sins. In these texts, and almost certainly in others also, our inclusion in Christ's acts takes the form of a being "caught up into" these acts, rather than an appropriation of an already existing relationship. It is, indeed, at this point that the parallel between Adam and Christ, so often appealed to in this regard, breaks down. For although we think it likely that Paul views all people as having sinned when Adam sinned, it is not the case that he thinks of all people as having "obeyed" when Christ obeyed. If this were so, it would destroy the gracious, vicarious nature of Christ's death.[16]

This same difference between the representative nature of Adam and Christ raises questions about using Paul's "with Christ" statements to justify speaking of Christ as a representative of humanity.[17] For Paul's "with Christ" statements refer not to potential benefits but to actual accomplishments. In Rom. 6, for example, those who die and are buried with Christ are apparently only those who have been baptized (v. 3) — and surely only Christians have been set free from sin's power.

On the other hand, as we have seen, σύν cannot convey less than "participation"; and Christ's death and resurrection are historical, datable,

13. *Dying and Rising,* p. 27.
14. On 2 Cor. 5:14, see Hughes, *Second Corinthians,* pp. 193-96.
15. E.g., Ridderbos, *Paul,* p. 207.
16. See Käsemann, 165-66.
17. For some scholars who speak in this way, see, e.g., J. D. G. Dunn, "Paul's Understanding of the Death of Jesus," in *Reconciliation and Hope,* pp. 126-37; Leenhardt, 155; Beasley-Murray, *Baptism,* pp. 136-37. O. Cullmann goes so far as to speak of "two baptisms" with reference to Rom. 6 (*Baptism in the New Testament* [SBT; London: SCM, 1950], pp. 23-40).

and unrepeatable events. For these reasons, we must conclude with Murray that Paul intentionally brings together into a relationship that cannot be precisely defined the once-for-all redemptive events and the application or realization of these events in the experience of individuals.[18] We must insist again, however, that this does not mean a repetition of Christ's death and resurrection in the lives of believers; nor does it mean that those events are "timeless." Rather, we find here the inevitable temporal tension between the salvation-historical accomplishment of redemption and its application in the lives of people. The transition from the old era to the new effected on the cross is realized individually in a dying and being raised "with" Christ.

A second caution has to do with the nature of this union with Christ. Even though it has been popular to call this union a "mystical" one,[19] this language is best avoided as suggesting an ontological or natural union. In the case of both Adam and Christ, the union between them and those whom they represent is primarily — and in Christ's case perhaps exclusively — forensic. Because he is our representative, the judgment or decision that has fallen on Christ falls also on those who come to belong to him.[20] Seen in this light, the "participationist" language of Paul is at the service of, and determined by, his forensic or "judicial" conception of the work of Christ.[21] There is no conflict between these two Pauline conceptions.[22] We must also avoid absolutizing any one of Paul's many ways of conceiving our relationship to Christ: for example, "we in Christ," "Christ in us," and "Christ for us." Each of these says something important about what God has done for us in Christ and how he has done it, but none should be taken ontologically. Only when this happens do inevitable difficulties arise in working out the logical relationship among them.

18. *Principles of Conduct,* pp. 208-11; cf. Siber, *Mit Christus Leben,* pp. 222-24; Bornkamm, "Baptism and New Life," pp. 74-76; Whiteley, *Theology,* p. 169; Calvin, 221; Wilckens, 2.24; L. B. Smedes, *All Things Made New: A Theology of Man's Union with Christ* (Grand Rapids: Eerdmans, 1970), pp. 142-48.

19. E.g., S-H, 153; and, with far greater detail and elaboration, Schweizer, *Mysticism.*

20. See esp. Wedderburn, "Some Observations," pp. 90-91 (also his *Baptism,* pp. 343-48), who calls attention to Gal. 3:9, where Gentile believers are said to be blessed "with Abraham." Somewhat similar is H. Halter, *Taufe and Ethos. Paulinischen Kriterien für das Proprium christlicher Moral* (Freiburger Theologische Studien 106; Freiburg/Basel/Vienna: Herder, 1977), pp. 43-50.

21. So Käsemann, 165; contra, e.g., Sanders, *Paul and Palestinian Judaism,* pp. 463-68.

22. See further on this, Ridderbos, *Paul,* p. 169; Byrne, "Living Out," pp. 571-73; Kim, *Origin of Paul's Gospel,* pp. 306-7; Gäumann, *Taufe und Ethik,* pp. 134-62.

2. Freed from Sin's Power to Serve Righteousness (6:15-23)

15*What then? Shall we sin because we are not under the law but under grace? By no means!* 16*Do you not know that to whom you present yourselves as slaves for obedience, you are slaves to whom you obey, whether sin leading to death or obedience leading to righteousness?* 17*But thanks be to God because you were slaves of sin, but you have obeyed from the heart that pattern of teaching to which you were handed over.* 18*Having been set free from sin, you have been enslaved to righteousness.* 19*(I am speaking in a human way because of the weakness of your flesh.)*

For just as you presented your members as slaves to uncleanness and to lawlessness leading to lawlessness, so now present your members as slaves to righteousness leading to sanctification.

20*For when you were slaves of sin, you were free with respect to righteousness.* 21*What fruit did you have then? Fruit of which you are now ashamed, for the end of these things is death.* 22*But now, having been set free from sin and enslaved to God, you have your fruit leading to sanctification, and the end is eternal life.* 23*For the wages of sin is death, but the gift of God is eternal life in Christ Jesus our Lord.*

In 6:1-14, Paul responds to an objection that the very abundance of God's grace in Christ encourages sin by arguing that Christ, in fact, sets believers free from sin. In 6:15-23, Paul responds to a similar objection by emphasizing the "flip side" of this freedom from sin: slavery to God and to righteousness. Slave imagery dominates this paragraph.[1] Paul also uses the language of freedom but less often.[2] Thus, it is not "freedom" that is the topic of this paragraph but "slavery."[3]

This emphasis on the Christian's slavery — which Paul admits is not the whole picture; cf. v. 19a — is necessary in order to show that the freedom of the Christian "from sin" is not a freedom "to sin." Between the dangers of legalism and licentiousness Paul steers a careful course. He makes it clear that Christians are free from the binding power of the Mosaic law while at the same time stressing that Christians are "under obligation" to obey their

---

1. Paul uses δοῦλος ("slave") and δουλόω ("enslave") eight times and in every verse except 15, 21, and 23; and the related words ὑπακοή ("obedience") and ὑπακούω ("obey") occur three times.

2. ἐλεύθερος ("free") and ἐλευθερόω ("set free") occur, together, only three times; and two of these refer back to the teaching of 6:1-14.

3. Cf. esp. Kaye, *Thought Structure,* p. 117. On the concept of slavery in this passage, see L. Schottroff, "Die Schreckensherrschaft der Sünde und die Befreiung durch Christus nach dem Römerbrief des Paulus," *EvT* 39 (1979), 497-510.

new "master" — God, or righteousness.[4] Against those who would insist on the necessity of the law as a force to curb and restrain sin, Paul proclaims the release of Christians from the power of the law as a necessary step in overthrowing the reign of sin (v. 14; cf. 7:1-6). And against those who would pervert this new freedom into an excuse for sinning, Paul insists that even "under grace" there are obligations of obedience that must be taken seriously. For, as Paul makes clear, there is no such thing as human "autonomy," a freedom from all outside powers and influences. Either people are under the power of sin, or they are under the power of God. The question is not, then, whether one will have a master, but which master one will serve. Serving sin, Paul shows, leads to death; serving God, to life.

The passage begins, as does 6:1-14, with a rhetorical question that picks up the substance of something Paul has just said (v. 15). Paul's initial response (v. 16) is a reminder that our actions have serious consequences, in that those actions serve to bind us to different powers — "sin" and "obedience" — and lead to very different results — "death" or "righteousness." In vv. 17-18 and 20-23, Paul uses his customary "once . . . but now" device to contrast his readers' pre-Christian existence with their Christian experience. "Once" they were slaves of sin, doing shameful things that led to death; "now" they are slaves of God and of righteousness, and do things that lead to holiness and life. This "indicative" frames the "imperative" of v. 19: "just as" we once gave ourselves over to those powers to which we were formerly enslaved, "so now" we are to give ourselves over to those powers to which we are now enslaved.

15 Paul opens this paragraph exactly as he did the previous one:

brief interjection: "What then?";
rhetorical question: "Shall we sin[5] because we are not under the law but under grace?";
strong negation of the question: "May it never be!";
lengthy explanation (vv. 16-23).

---

4. See Nygren.

5. The aorist ἁμαρτήσωμεν may signify another difference between 6:1 and 6:15 since the former uses the present ἐπιμένωμεν τῇ ἁμαρτίᾳ, "should we remain in sin?" Thus, while 6:1 asks about "remaining in the state of sin," 6:15, it could be argued, asks about something more specific: "should we commit a sin?" (cf. Turner, 72; McKay, "Aspect," p. 222; Robertson, 850, claims, in commenting on 6:1 and 15, that "the point lies chiefly in the difference in tense"). However, the legitimacy of pressing the distinction in the tenses in this way is questionable. The present tense in 6:1 is almost required by the verb ἐπιμένω; and the aorist in 6:15 need not refer to a particular case or instance of sin, but simply to sinning in a simple, undefined sense. Probably, then, no substantial difference can be attributed to the different tenses (cf. Kuss).

Even the content of the rhetorical questions is similar. In both vv. 1 and 15 Paul asks whether the grace of God should lead to sin. However, in 6:1 it is a question of sinning *in order to gain more* grace, while in 6:15 it is a question of sinning *because of* grace. The reference in 6:15 is obviously to 6:14b, where Paul proclaims that the believer is not "under the law" but "under grace." Those who are joined to Christ by faith live in the new age where grace, not the law of Moses, reigns. This being the case, believers' conduct is not directly regulated by the law. Under Jewish premises, such a "law-less" situation would be assumed to foster sin. Christians would be no better than "Gentile sinners" (cf. Gal. 2:15).[6] But Paul sees in God's grace not only a liberating power but a constraining one as well: the constraint of a willing obedience that comes from a renewed heart and mind and, ultimately (cf. Gal. 5:17-24; Rom. 8:4-9), the impulse and leading of God's Spirit.

16 "Do you not know"[7] introduces, as is customary in Paul, a fact that he assumes is known to his readers. In this case, the fact is one with which his readers would have been familiar even before their conversion: habitually "presenting" oneself to something or someone makes one a slave of that something or someone.[8] For people in the ancient world would often sell themselves into slavery as a way of avoiding financial disaster.[9] It is not completely clear whether Paul means by this that habitual obedience *manifests* a condition of slavery or that habitual obedience *constitutes* or *leads to* a condition of slavery.[10] In light of the context, where the verb "present" again occurs in the imperative (v. 19; and cf. v. 13), the latter, with its implicit exhortation, is more likely. Christians, who have been set free from sin by their union with Christ, must recognize that, were they constantly to yield to the voice of temptation, they would effectively become slaves of sin again. The Lord Jesus made the same point: "Every person who is committing sin is a slave to sin" (John 8:34). Without taking anything away from the reality of the transfer from one master to another, then, Paul wants to make clear that "slavery" is ultimately not just a "legal" status but a living experience. Christians, who *are* no longer slaves of sin, must no longer *live* as slaves of sin.

The last part of the verse has the purpose of convincing Christians of the seriousness of this practical obedience by making it clear that there are two, and only two, options open to every person and that these options carry

---

6. Cf. Dunn.

7. Gk. οὐκ οἴδατε.

8. Note the present tense παριστάνετε, which has a durative connotation here.

9. See, e.g., W. A. Meeks, *The First Urban Christians: The Social World of the Apostle Paul* (New Haven: Yale University, 1983), pp. 20-23.

10. See the discussion in Kaye, *Thought Structure*, p. 113 (though he comes to the opposite conclusion from ours).

serious consequences. Either[11] one is a slave of sin[12] or a slave of "obedience." Paul makes it clear in this "either . . . or" that there is no "possibility of neutrality" (Käsemann). One is never "free" from a master, and those non-Christians who think that they are "free" are under an illusion created and sustained by Satan. The choice with which people are faced is not "Should I retain my freedom or give it up and submit to God?" but "Should I serve sin or should I serve God?" But Paul is writing to Christians, and we, too, must not forget that to sin is to submit ourselves as slaves to sin.

In this contrast, it is surprising to find sin and obedience rather than sin and God (cf. v. 22) or sin and righteousness (cf. vv. 18, 20) as the competing "masters." "Obedience" here obviously has a positive meaning, as opposed to the neutral meaning earlier in the verse ("slaves for obedience"). Some interpreters think that "obedience" refers mainly to the act of believing rather than to moral activity. Support for this is found in the formula "the obedience of faith" (cf. 1:5), and in the following verse where, it is claimed, "obedience" may also mean basically "accept in faith."[13] But this interpretation moves too far from the meaning of "obedience" earlier in the verse and does not square with Paul's obvious interest in this passage with concrete behavior. Paul is out to emphasize the significance of obedience in the Christian life, in a context where such an emphasis is necessary to counter a false libertinism. The freedom of the Christian is not freedom to do what one wants, but freedom to obey God — willingly, joyfully, naturally. "Obedience," says Calvin, "is the mother of true knowledge of God."[14]

In order to underscore further the seriousness of the choice between these masters, Paul specifies the consequences[15] of the respective "slaveries": death and righteousness. "Death" may include reference to physical death and present spiritual death, but in this context it means mainly "eternal" death: the final and eternal exclusion from God's presence that is the ultimate result of sin. Since it is contrasted with death, "righteousness" could refer to "final" justification: that ultimate acquittal from sins and introduction to eternal life that come to the believer in the last day.[16] And this interpretation is bolstered

---

11. Paul uses the construction ἤτοι . . . ἤ to denote this "either . . . or" relationship. Although this is the only place in the NT where the combination occurs, there is no reason to think a special emphasis is thereby intended (contra Gifford).

12. The genitive case of ἁμαρτίας ("sin") and ὑπακοῆς ("obedience") shows that these words depend on δοῦλοι ("slaves") rather than on παριστάνετε ("present").

13. Godet; Käsemann.

14. *Institutes* 1.6.2.

15. This is the function of the εἰς in each phrase.

16. Stuart; Meyer; Cranfield; Dunn(?); O. Pfleiderer, *Paulinism: A Contribution to the History of Primitive Christian Theology* (2 vols.; London: Williams and Norgate, 1891), 1.180-81; Sanders, *Paul and Palestinian Judaism,* p. 494.

by the fact that "eternal life" appears to occupy a parallel place to righteousness in vv. 22 and 23. However, Paul never clearly uses the word "righteousness" to refer to this eschatological verdict (Gal. 5:5 is the only possible exception; cf. "justify" in 2:13), and in Romans thus far, "righteousness" is not equivalent to "life" but is the means to "life" (cf. 5:21). Since righteousness is the result of obedience, it could designate initial justification only if obedience were interpreted as "the obedience of faith." But, as we have seen, this is unlikely. Another option is to view righteousness more comprehensively, either as encompassing both moral living and final vindication,[17] or, in keeping with the inclusive interpretation of the "Käsemann" school, as the "power" in which the justified believer lives.[18] But, in light of vv. 13, 17-20, the best option is to understand righteousness to refer to "moral" righteousness, conduct pleasing to God.[19] The objection that this does not make a natural contrast with "death" is not a telling one, since the contrast "sin" and "obedience" has already disrupted a precise antithesis.

17 Paul now dispels any idea that Christians stand in a situation of neutrality with respect to the master they are to serve. This verse and the following one reveal Paul's conviction that they have already made the decision to follow a new master. For Paul gives "thanks to God"[20] for the transfer of spiritual allegiance that they have manifested. Once, Paul says, "you were slaves of sin";[21] but now "you have obeyed that pattern of teaching to which you were handed over."[22] "You have obeyed" points to the time of conversion, when the Roman Christians first bowed the knee to Jesus the Lord. The word therefore includes reference to faith[23] but must not be confined to it. As we argued in commenting on "the obedience of faith" in 1:5, Paul views faith in Christ and commitment to him as Lord as inseparable and mutually interpreting. Here, then, the focus is on the initial commitment of the Roman Christians

---

17. Murray. Roberts, who thinks θάνατος refers to the "state of lostness," takes δικαιοσύνη to mean "the state or condition of having been put right with God" ("Righteousness," p. 20).

18. G. Schrenk, *TDNT* II, 209 (although cf. p. 210); Reumann, *Righteousness*, p. 83; Käsemann.

19. See Godet; and the note on v. 13.

20. Gk. χάρις τῷ θεῷ. The construction is elliptical, the verb ἔστω ("let it be") being assumed. χάρις here means "thanks" or "gratitude" (BAGD).

21. The context requires that the clause ἦτε δοῦλοι τῆς ἁμαρτίας have a concessive force: "although you were slaves of sin"; note almost all the modern English translations.

22. The syntax of this clause is complicated, but it is best to view τύπον διδαχῆς as the object of ὑπηκούσατε, its case being accusative — rather than the dative that the verb ὑπακούω normally requires — because of attraction to the case of the relative pronoun (ὅν). Putting things in a more natural word sequence, then, we would have ὑπηκούσατε τύπον διδαχῆς εἰς ὃν παρεδόθητε. Cf. Robertson, 719; Godet.

23. Note the parallel between obedience and faith in 10:16.

to Christ as Lord, including both their "faith" in him and their submission to him. Paul uses "obey" because he wants to underscore the aspect of submission to Christ as Lord of life that is part of becoming a Christian.

It is probably for this same reason that Paul chooses so unusual a way of describing the object of their obedience: "that pattern of teaching to which you were handed over."[24] The verb "hand over" might connote the transfer of a slave from one master to another — an image appropriate to this paragraph.[25] But perhaps more relevant in conjunction with a word like "teaching" are those places where, in probable dependence on Jewish concepts, Paul uses "hand over" to refer to the transmission of the early Christian teaching or tradition (cf. 1 Cor. 11:2, 23; 15:3).[26] In this verse, however, it is not the teaching that is handed down to believers but the believers who are handed over to the teaching. This unusual way of putting the matter is intentional; Paul wants to make clear that becoming a Christian means being placed under the authority of Christian "teaching," that expression of God's will for NT believers. The new convert's "obedience" to this teaching is the outgrowth of God's action[27] in "handing us over" to that teaching when we were converted.

But why does Paul say "pattern [typos] of teaching" rather than just "teaching"? Many interpreters think that Paul alludes to a "rule" or "pattern"[28] of early Christian teaching.[29] There is good reason to think that this is the case, but he may also want to suggest a contrast with another "pattern" of teaching. Godet thinks Paul contrasts his own "gospel" with the pattern

24. So unusual is the construction that a few interpreters have (quite unnecessarily) concluded that the verse is a later addition to Paul's text; cf. Bultmann, who calls it a "stupid insertion" ("stupiden Zwischensatz"; cf. "Glossen," p. 283); cf. also Furnish, *Theology and Ethics,* pp. 197-98; Gäumann, *Taufe und Ethik,* pp. 94-96; Schmithals. R. A. J. Gagnon ("Heart of Wax and a Teaching That Stamps: ΤΥΠΟΣ ΔΙΔΑΧΗΣ (Rom 6:17b) Once More," *JBL* 112 [1994], 671-73) effectively criticizes these theories.

25. Cf. J. Kürzinger, "ΤΥΠΟΣ ΔΙΔΑΧΗΣ und der Sinn von Röm 6,17f.," *Bib* 39 (1958), 163-64; F. W. Beare, "On the Interpretation of Romans VI.17," *NTS* 5 (1958-59), 207.

26. The Greek verb is the same; cf. Stuhlmacher.

27. Note the passive verb παρεδόθητε.

28. τύπος originally meant "the impression made by a blow" and then came to have a variety of meanings (L. Goppelt, *TDNT* VIII, 246-47). One of these was "form, pattern," which seems to fit best in this context.

29. Cf. J. Moffatt, "The Interpretation of Romans 6:17-18," *JBL* 48 (1929), 237; Fitzmyer; Stuhlmacher. Many suggest that this code may have been associated with baptism. An allusion to a pre-Christian teaching is unlikely (contra M. Trimaille, "Encore de «typos Didachès» de Romains 6,17," in *La Vie de la Parole: De l'Ancien au Nouveau Testament: Etudes d'exégèse et d'herméneutique bibliques offertes à Pierre Grelot* [ed. Departement des Etudes Bibliques de l'Institut Catholique de Paris; Paris: Desclée, 1987], pp. 267-80).

of teaching that the Romans had already heard. But a more likely contrast is that between the "form" of Christian teaching and the "form" of Jewish teaching.[30] Paul would then imply that Christians, while no longer "under the [Mosaic] law," are nevertheless bound by an authoritative code of teaching. And Paul may have an additional reason for using *typos*. Most of the Pauline occurrences of this word refer to believers as "examples" to other believers.[31] In these verses, *typos* includes the active connotation of a pattern that "molds" others. Similarly, in this verse, it is likely that *typos* includes the idea that Christian teaching "molds" and "forms" those who have been handed over to it.[32]

18 This brief verse recapitulates the "indicative" of the believer's transfer from the old realm to the new that was the central teaching of 6:1-14 and that was hinted at in v. 17a. For the first time, however, Paul uses the language of "freedom" to describe the believer's new status with respect to sin. In a world in which "freedom" has taken on all kinds of historical and social baggage, we must remember that Paul's concept of freedom is not that of autonomous self-direction but of deliverance from those enslaving powers that would prevent the human being from becoming what God intended.[33] It is only by doing God's will and thus knowing his truth that we can be "free indeed" (John 8:31-36). This is why, without paradox, Christian freedom is at the same time a kind of "slavery." Being bound to God and his will enables the person to become "free" — to be what God wants that person to be.[34] As a Puritan Confession of Faith puts it, "The liberty which Christ hath purchased for believers under the gospel consists in their yielding obedience unto him, not out of slavish fear, but a child-like love, and willing mind."[35]

As in vv. 2, 6, and 11-14, "sin" is the power from which believers are set free in Christ. Now for the first time, however, Paul follows through on his "transfer" language and makes clear that freedom from the power of sin means servitude to a new power. Addressing the Roman Christians, and

---

30. Kaye, *Thought Structure,* p. 131; Käsemann. Cf. 2:20, where one of the Jews' possessions is "the form [μόρφωσιν] of knowledge and truth in the law."

31. Phil. 3:17; 1 Thess. 1:7; 2 Thess. 3:9; 1 Tim. 4:12; Tit. 2:7. J. D. G. Dunn ("Paul's Knowledge of the Jesus Tradition: The Evidence of Romans," in *Christus Bezeugen: Für Wolfgang Trilling* [ed. K. Kertelge, T. Holtz, and C.-P. März; Freiburg/Basel/Vienna: Herder, 1990], pp. 196-97), noting this personal focus in Paul's use of the term, suggests that he refers to Christ himself.

32. Beare, "Romans VI.17," pp. 209-10; Goppelt, *TDNT* VIII, 250; Cranfield.

33. Paul uses the language of "freedom" mainly to indicate the Christian's "freedom from" the various powers of the old age — sin (6:18, 22), the law (7:3; and frequently in Galatians, though implicitly), and death (8:2).

34. J. Blunck, *NIDNTT* I, 717-20; cf., in Paul, Gal. 5:13-14.

35. Quoted by Kevan, *Grace of Law,* p. 249.

referring, as with "you obeyed" in v. 17, to their conversion, Paul reminds them that "you have been enslaved to righteousness."[36] The passive verb draws attention again here (as in vv. 17 and 22) to the initiative of God. "Righteousness," as the antithesis to sin, has a clearly "ethical" dimension. The contrast with "sin" and the use of the verb "enslave" suggest also that this "right conduct" is conceived as a "power" that exercises authority over the believer (see the notes on 6:13). The Christian is not just called to do right in a vacuum but to do right out of a new and powerful relationship that has already been established.

19 The first sentence of this verse is not explicitly linked to what precedes.[37] We may therefore take the verse either with v. 18[38] or with v. 19b.[39] But we need not make a choice. The sentence is a parenthetical explanation of why Paul is using slavery imagery to depict the Christian and so is related both to v. 18 ("you were enslaved") and v. 19b ("slaves").[40]

Paul's claim that he is speaking "in a human way"[41] may have a neutral[42] or a negative[43] significance, depending on how we interpret "because of the weakness of your flesh."[44] Three different interpretations are possible: (1) "because of the difficulty you have as human beings in understanding things"[45] (2) "because of your insensitivity to spiritual things caused by the continuing influence of your fallen natures";[46] (3) "because of the temptation to live independently that is typical of your human nature."[47] The first two are similar in viewing the problem as basically "intellectual" — Paul writes *as* he does to help them understand — while the third sees the problem to be basically "moral" — Paul writes *what* he does because his readers need to hear it. Paul's wording suggests that it is his manner of speaking that he refers to, so we should prefer one of the first two options.[48] Of these two, the first

---

36. Gk. ἐδουλώθητε τῇ δικαιοσύνῃ.

37. This is a fairly unusual situation in Greek, which the grammarians call asyndeton.

38. So most commentators.

39. Chrysostom; Barrett; Schmithals.

40. Wilckens. Eliminating the sentence as a gloss (cf. W. H. Hagen, "Two Deutero-Pauline Glosses in Romans 6," *ExpTim* 92 [1981], 364-67) is unwarranted.

41. Gk. ἀνθρώπινον, an accusative neuter form of the adjective ἀνθρώπινος used as an adverb. The word means "human" in a rather neutral sense (Acts 17:25; 1 Cor. 2:13; 4:3; 10:13; Jas. 3:7; 1 Pet. 2:13).

42. Cf. κατὰ ἄνθρωπον in Gal. 3:15.

43. Cf. κατὰ ἄνθρωπον in Rom. 3:5 and 1 Cor. 9:8.

44. Or "your weakness of flesh," if, as Michel argues, ὑμῶν governs the entire phrase.

45. Most clearly, Barrett.

46. Cf., e.g., Cranfield.

47. E.g., Käsemann.

48. Cf. the term ἀνθρώπινον.

is too weak and the second too strong. Both "weakness"[49] and "flesh"[50] depict what it is to be human apart from God and his Spirit. As such, they are not always strictly negative, but neither are they simply "neutral." Here Paul's point would appear to be that human nature produces a weakness in understanding that can be overcome in this life only by the use of (imperfect) analogies. However, Paul is not withdrawing or "apologizing" for his slavery imagery.[51] Indeed, he goes right ahead and uses it twice more in this passage with the same application (vv. 19, 22). It is just that Paul recognizes that his language could be interpreted to mean that Christian experience bears the same marks of degradation, fear, and confinement that were typical of secular slavery. But, while shorn of these characteristics, life in the new realm of righteousness and life does mean that a person is given over to a master who requires absolute and unquestioned obedience; and to make this point, the image of slavery is quite appropriate.[52]

The last part of v. 19 is very similar to v. 13. Both use the verb "give oneself as a servant,"[53] both use "members" to emphasize the need for Christians to obey God with all their capacities, and both contrast the pre-Christian with the Christian master that is to be served. But, whereas v. 13 made this contrast with a double imperative — "do not present . . . present" — Paul in this verse employs a comparison: "just as you presented . . . so now present." He thus makes clear that Christians should serve righteousness with all the single-minded dedication that characterized their pre-Christian service of such "idols" as self, money, lust, pleasure, and power. Would that we would pursue holiness with the zeal that so many of us pursued these other, incomparably less worthy goals!

Paul makes explicit the idea of service inherent in the verb "present" by describing our "members" as "slaves."[54] In the pre-Christian state, these members were given in slavery to "uncleanness and to lawlessness[55] leading to[56] lawlessness." The repetition of "lawlessness" is unexpected; perhaps Paul adds it to create rhetorical parallelism with the contrasting set of "masters" (i.e., "leading to sanctification" at the end of the verse). Paul means that the service of

49. Cf. Rom. 8:26 and the note on 5:6.
50. Cf. 1:3; 4:1; 7:5; 8:4-9; and the note on 1:3.
51. Contra Cranfield.
52. Cf. Murray; Käsemann.
53. The Greek verb is παρίστημι; see the notes on v. 13 for this meaning.
54. Gk. δοῦλα. Since the word is neuter plural, it must be a predicate adjectival modifier of μέλη; "as slaves" (Moule, *Idiom Book,* p. 97).
55. Gk. τῇ ἀκαθαρσίᾳ καὶ τῇ ἀνομίᾳ. Both words are general terms for sinful behavior, and Paul probably intends no strict difference in their meaning here (for the former, see 1:24; for the latter, 4:7). The repetition of the article probably serves to draw attention to the two different descriptions.
56. Gk. εἰς.

"uncleanness" and "lawlessness" leads on to ever increasing lawlessness. In contrast, service of righteousness[57] "leads to sanctification." "Sanctification"[58] may refer to the state of "holiness," as the end product of a life of living in service of righteousness.[59] But most of Paul's uses of this word have an active connotation: the *process* of "becoming holy."[60] This is probably the case here also.[61] Committing ourselves as slaves to doing what is right before God ("righteousness") results in living that is increasingly God-centered and world-renouncing.

20 The imperative "present yourselves as slaves to righteousness" in v. 19b is the center of the paragraph. But this command does not, and cannot, stand in isolation. We can, and must, serve righteousness because God has freed us from sin and made us slaves to righteousness. The "imperative" grows out of, and reflects, the "indicative." In order to maintain this careful balance, Paul "frames" the command in v. 19b with reminders of our new status in Christ (vv. 17-18, 20-23). Therefore the "for"[62] in this verse introduces vv. 20-23 as the ground of the command in v. 19b. As in v. 18, Paul reminds his Christian readers that they were formerly slaves of sin. But instead of immediately completing the temporal sequence with a description of their present Christian status, he pauses to remind them of an implication of their past lives. Non-Christians often pride themselves on possessing a "freedom" appropriate to autonomous human beings and deride Christians for giving that up — becoming "subhuman" — in obedience to a "god." And Paul admits that those apart from Christ have a certain "freedom."[63] But it is a freedom

---

57. In antithetical parallelism with "uncleanness" and "lawlessness," δικαιοσύνη, as in 6:13 and 6:18, refers to the "right conduct" demanded by God.

58. Gk. ἁγιασμός. This word is one of a series of words from the same root that Paul uses to describe Christian existence (cf. also ἅγιος ["holy, saint"], ἁγιάζω ["sanctify"], ἁγιωσύνη ["holiness"]). Their use in Paul and in the NT is rooted in the LXX, where they are used to translate words from the קדשׁ group. They depict the Christian as one who has been singled out, separated from the world, and dedicated to God (a "saint"). But "holiness," while achieved in one sense (cf. 1 Cor. 6:11; Eph. 5:26), is a way of living, or a state, that it is the Christian's duty yet to achieve (cf. 1 Thess. 4:3; 5:23; 2 Thess. 2:13). See, e.g., the convenient summary in O. Procksch, *TDNT* I, 105-15.

59. E.g., Godet; Murray. Although the suffix of the word (-μος) ideally identifies a noun as a noun of action, many Greek words with this suffix came to have a static meaning.

60. Cf. 1 Thess. 4:3, 4, 7 (contrast with "uncleanness"); 1 Tim. 2:15 — 1 Cor. 1:30 and 2 Thess. 2:13 are not clear.

61. Cf., e.g., S-H; Cranfield; Ziesler, *Righteousness,* p. 202. The -μος ending of the noun often identifies a noun as having this "active" quality.

62. Gk. γάρ.

63. On the concept of freedom here, and throughout the paragraph, see F. S. Jones, *"Freiheit" in den Briefen der Apostels Paulus. Eine historische, exegetische und religionsgeschichtliche Studie* (Göttinger Theologische Arbeiten 34; Göttingen: Vandenhoeck & Ruprecht, 1987), esp. pp. 113-14.

"with respect to"[64] one thing only: "righteousness." As throughout this paragraph, "righteousness" is "ethical" righteousness, as is clear from the connection between this verse and the next. For in stating that this "freedom from righteousness" issues in shameful deeds, Paul implies that the righteousness he describes here has to do with our actions rather than our status. As "slaves to sin," people are "free" from the power and influence of the conduct that pleases God; they are deaf to God's righteous demands and incapable of responding to them even were they to hear and respect them. For Paul makes it clear that those outside Christ, to varying degrees, can recognize right and wrong (cf. Rom. 1:18-32; 2:14-15); but the power to do the right and turn from the wrong is not present. "All are under sin" (3:9) and therefore incapable of doing God's will.

21 This verse continues Paul's characterization of the pre-Christian situation of his readers: "then" matches the "when" in v. 20. There are two ways in which the verse could be punctuated:

1. "Therefore, what fruit did you have then, of which you are now ashamed? For the end of these is death."[65]
2. "Therefore, what fruit did you have then? That of which[66] you are now ashamed. For the end of these is death."[67]

If we adopt the first reading, the answer to the question is unexpressed but assumed to be negative, while the last clause is then an explanation of that assumed negative. One important consideration cited in its support is that the word "fruit"[68] can be given the "positive" reference — "actions pleasing to God" — that it has everywhere else in Paul.[69] But this argument has little weight.[70] There is little else in favor of the first alternative, and a good reason

---

64. τῇ δικαιοσύνῃ is probably a dative of respect (Moule, *Idiom Book,* p. 46). Turner (238), however, classifies it as a dative of disadvantage, and Robertson (523) as locative.

65. Cf. the UBS[3] *Greek New Testament;* most English versions (e.g., KJV; NRSV; NIV; NASB; TEV; NAB); and many commentators (e.g., S-H; Murray).

66. Gk. ἐφ' οἷς. This phrase is short for ἐκεῖνα ἐφ' οἷς, the ἐπί indicating the basis for the "shame" (BAGD). Paul uses the plural οἷς because καρπός is distributive.

67. Cf. UBS[4] and NA[27]; NEB; NJB; and many commentators (e.g., Godet; Michel; Cranfield; Dunn).

68. Gk. καρπός.

69. Cf. Rom. 1:13; 6:22; 15:28; 1 Cor. 9:7; Gal. 5:22; Eph. 5:9; Phil. 1:11, 22; 4:17; 2 Tim. 2:6.

70. In three of the verses (1 Cor. 9:7; Phil. 1:22; and 2 Tim. 2:6) καρπός has a more "neutral" than positive meaning, and passages such as Matt. 7:16-20 (e.g., v. 16: "by their καρπῶν you will know them") show that the NT uses the word of both good and evil actions.

to adopt the second. This is the clear parallelism between vv. 21 and 22 that is created if v. 21 is punctuated with a question mark after "then":

	Status	Result	Outcome
v. 21:	"then": slaves of sin, free from righteousness	"fruit" bringing shame	death
v. 22:	"now": free from sin, slaves of God	"fruit" bringing sanctification	eternal life

Paul highlights the negative nature of the "freedom" enjoyed by Christians in their past by showing that the "fruit" of which they are now ashamed resulted from that freedom. "Fruit" is used in the NT to describe both concrete actions and general character traits. Both are in view here. This attitude of shame on the part of believers toward the "products" of their pre-Christian lives is, as Calvin suggests, positive: "He only then is imbued with the principles of Christian philosophy, who has well learnt to be really displeased with himself, and to be confounded with shame for his own wretchedness."

As confirmation ("for")[71] of the shameful character of pre-Christian "fruit," Paul reminds his readers of the "end" or "outcome"[72] of them: "death." In contrast with "eternal life" (v. 22), "death" refers particularly to what we usually call "eternal death": the eternal separation from God in hell that begins after death.[73]

22 "But now" answers to "when" at the beginning of v. 20, as Paul contrasts his readers' present situation as believers with their pre-Christian past. As we noted above, the descriptions of these two situations are parallel. Once "slaves of sin" and "free with respect to righteousness" (v. 20), Christians have been "set free from sin" and "enslaved to God."[74] In this, the last of the antitheses in this chapter, Paul confronts us with the ultimate "powers" that dominate the two respective "ages" of salvation history: sin and God. Behind believers' subservience to "grace" (vv. 14, 15), "obedience" (v. 16), "pattern of teaching" (v. 17), and "righteousness" (vv. 18, 19), and embracing them all, is their ultimate allegiance to God.

But Paul's focus in this verse, expressed in its main clause, is on the results of that past "transfer" for his readers' present experience: "you have your fruit leading to sanctification." The "fruit" of which they are now

---

71. Gk. γάρ.

72. Gk. τέλος; for the meaning of the word, see the notes on 10:4.

73. Cf. Barrosse, "Death and Sin," pp. 441-42.

74. Both participles, ἐλευθερωθέντες ("set free") and δουλωθέντες ("enslaved"), are aorist, depicting this new subservience as a status already attained in the past.

ashamed has been replaced with fruit that "yields a harvest"[75] of sanctification.[76] And the final outcome of this "fruit leading to sanctification"[77] is
"eternal life." "Life," while it begins for the believer at the moment of
conversion (cf. 6:4 and 8:6), is not granted in its full and final form until "that
which is mortal is swallowed up by life" (2 Cor. 5:4).[78]

23 This verse not only explains the contrasting "outcomes" of death
and life specified in vv. 22-23 but also brings the entire chapter to a fitting
climax. As in v. 22, "sin" and God are contrasted as the rival "powers" that
determine the destinies of each individual. Paul fittingly describes the (eternal)
"death" that those under the power of sin experience with the word
"wages."[79] He thereby implies that the penalty sin exacts is *merited,* in
contrast to the "eternal life" from God, which is a "free gift."[80] It is therefore
very appropriate that this verse, and this chapter, should end with the note of
christological inclusion: "in Christ Jesus our Lord." It is not clear whether
this modifies only "eternal life" — "eternal life in Christ Jesus our Lord" —
or the entire clause — it is "in Christ Jesus our Lord" that God gives the gift
of eternal life. But in light of the all-embracing importance of this being "in
Christ," the latter is preferable. We may summarize the verse by noting, with
Lloyd-Jones, its three contrasts: the master that is served — sin versus God;
the outcome of that service — death versus eternal life; and the means by
which this outcome is attained — a "wage" earned versus a gift received.

75. The preposition εἰς connotes result or purpose.

76. Gk. ἁγιασμόν; as in v. 19, it refers to the process of "becoming holy."

77. We assume that καρπόν — rather than ἁγιασμόν or "slavery to God" — is
the implied genitive after τέλος.

78. Particularly when modified by αἰώνιος ("eternal"), ζωή has this eschatological
connotation (cf. Rom. 2:7; 5:21; 6:23; Gal. 6:8; 1 Tim. 1:16; 6:12; Tit. 1:2; 3:7). While
possessing temporal reference — "un-ending" — αἰώνιος ultimately transcends time, suggesting that the "life" Christians enjoy takes part in the eternity that is the nature of God
and divine things (cf. H. Sasse, *TDNT* I, 209).

79. Gk. ὀψώνια, from ὀψώνιον. The word has the general meaning "provisions"
(C. C. Caragounis, "ΟΨΩΝΙΟΝ: A Reconsideration of Its Meaning," *NovT* 16 [1974],
35-57) but refers usually to money paid for services rendered. It can be applied to almost
any sphere of life (MM cite a papyrus in which it refers to a child's "allowance"), but it
is used particularly often of the pay given to soldiers (LSJ). ὀψώνιον has this reference in
all three of its LXX uses (1 Esdr. 4:56; 1 Macc. 3:28 and 14:32) and in two of the three
other NT occurrences (Luke 3:14; 1 Cor. 9:7; 2 Cor. 11:8 is not specific). In light of this,
it is probable that the word here would convey military associations: Paul pictures "sin"
as a commanding general paying a wage to its "soldiers."

80. Gk. χάρισμα. A few interpreters have suggested that Paul uses χάρισμα here
with reference to the "bounty" *(donativum)* given to the army at the accession of Roman
emperors (e.g., Tertullian, *Res.* 47; Zahn; Black). But there is no good linguistic basis for
the identification. Paul has already used the word in Rom. 5:15 and 16 to describe the
gracious gift secured by "the one man Jesus Christ" for all who belong to him.

C. FREEDOM FROM BONDAGE TO THE LAW (7:1-25)

Romans 7 is one of the most famous chapters in the Bible. Scholars, preachers, and laypeople alike are fascinated by Paul's vivid description of human struggle and frustration in vv. 7-25. Along with this fascination has come vigorous debate over the identity of the person depicted in these verses — unregenerate Paul, regenerate Paul, the back-sliding Christian, and the like. These various identifications have in turn given rise to — or, often, been dictated by — significantly different theologies of sanctification. However, for all our legitimate interest in these questions, we must start our interpretation of this chapter on the right foot by insisting that anthropology — the identity and situation of the "I" of vv. 7-25 — is a subordinate issue in Rom. 7.

The main topic is the Mosaic law. Paul makes two basic points. First, using the analogy of marriage, Paul argues that a person's bondage to the law must be severed in order that he or she may be put into a new relationship with Christ (7:1-6). This, the "positive" teaching of the chapter, gives rise to questions about the origin and nature of the law. These Paul answers in 7:7-25, where he shows that the law is from God, but that it has nevertheless become the unwitting tool of sin, being used to confirm and imprison in death. Despite its divine origin, the law can neither justify nor sanctify. "What the law could not do because it was weakened by the flesh" (8:3a) succinctly sums up this second major point in Rom. 7.

How does this teaching about the Mosaic law fit into the development of the letter? Three points of contact can be discerned. First, and most generally, Rom. 7 provides the extensive treatment and explanation of the negative effects of the Mosaic law that Paul has briefly mentioned several times in the letter (cf. 3:19-20, 27-28; 4:13-15; 5:13-14, 20). Second, 7:1-6 repeats with respect to the law many of the same points that were made in Rom. 6 with respect to sin. As in chap. 6 the believer has "died to sin" (v. 2), and thus been "freed from it" (vv. 18, 22) so that it no longer "rules" (v. 14a), so in 7:1-6 the believer has been "put to death to the law" (v. 4) and thus been "freed from it" (v. 6) so that it no longer "rules" (v. 1). And as in chap. 6 this freedom from sin also means "serving" righteousness, or God, so that "fruit" pleasing to God may be produced (vv. 18-22), so in 7:1-6 freedom from the law means being joined to Christ in a new "service" so that "fruit" pleasing to God may be forthcoming (vv. 4-6).[1] These parallels suggest to some expositors that 7:1-6 should be included with 6:15-23 in a discrete section in which Paul gives two parallel responses to the suggestion that

---

1. Cf. R. Schnackenburg, "Römer 7 im Zusammenhang des Römerbriefes," in *Jesus und Paulus*, p. 291; Luz, "Aufbau," p. 170.

Christians under the age of grace can sin with impunity.[2] While other factors indicate that the dividing line between sections should be drawn at 7:1 rather than at 6:15, it is clear that 7:1-6 continues the stress of 6:15-23 on the necessary ethical implications of the believer's transfer into the new realm of grace. The third point of contact between Rom. 7 and the preceding context is with the assertion of vv. 14 and 15 that the believer is no longer "under the law." Indeed, this statement is the immediate occasion for the chapter, as Paul explains what it means no longer to be "under the law," how this transfer from the law's dominion has been accomplished, and why it was necessary.

1. Released from the Law, Joined to Christ (7:1-6)

> 1*Or are you ignorant, brothers and sisters — for I am speaking to those who know the law — that the law rules over a person only as long as he or she lives? 2For the woman who is married is bound by the law to her husband as long as he lives. But if her husband dies, she is released from the law relating to her husband. 3Therefore, while her husband lives she will be called an adulteress if she becomes joined to another man. But if her husband dies, she is free from the law, so that she is not an adulteress if she is joined to another man. 4Therefore, my brothers and sisters, you also have been put to death to the law through the body of Christ, so that you might be joined to another, to the one who has been raised from the dead, in order that we might bear fruit for God.*
>
> 5*For when we were in the flesh, sinful passions that were through the law were working in our members, with the result that we were bearing fruit for death. 6But now we have been released from the law, dying[3] to that in which we were held captive, so that we might serve in newness of the Spirit and not in oldness of the letter.*

As we have seen, this paragraph contains the main point that Paul wants to make in this chapter. It has four parts. In v. 1, the general principle on which the teaching of the paragraph is based is given: death severs one's bondage to the law. This is the case in marriage, where the death of a spouse sets the other spouse "free from" the law that brands a second marriage as adulterous (vv. 2-3). This general principle is applied to Christian experience in v. 4,

2. E.g., Morris, 260. Myers suggests a chiastic arrangement in which 6:16-23 develops "under grace" and 7:1-6 "not under the law" in 6:15 ("Chiastic Arrangement," pp. 40-41).

3. The KJV translation, "we are delivered from the law, *that being dead* wherein we were held" assumes ἀποθανόντος, which Beza introduced into the *Textus Receptus* without MS support, based only on what he thought Chrysostom was reading (Gifford).

which is the key verse in the paragraph; Christians, in dying with Christ, have suffered a death that severs their bondage to the law and that makes possible their new relationship with Jesus Christ. Then, in vv. 5-6, Paul shows the need for, and results of, this "transfer of masters" by contrasting the situation of people "in the flesh," in whose case the law aids and abets sin, with the situation of people who are released from the law and serve in "newness of Spirit."

1 "Or are you ignorant"[4] occurs only here and in 6:3 in the Pauline corpus, another (though minor) point of contact between these chapters. Like Paul's more customary formula "do you not know?" (6:15), it introduces teaching with which Paul assumes his readers are familiar. The phrase implies that Paul is elaborating on a point he has just made. Meyer insists that this point must be found in the immediately preceding words (6:23), but the focus on the law that now begins makes it almost certain that Paul is harking back to his assertion in 6:14b (cf. v. 15) that Christians are not "under law." Paul makes this assertion almost in passing, and it cries out for elaboration — which he now gives.

Before he enters into his teaching, however, Paul addresses his readers: "brothers,"[5] "those who know the law." Some think that this address signals a shift in his audience, from the church as a whole to a specific group within the Roman Christian community: Jewish Christians, who "know" the Mosaic law.[6] But a narrowing of the audience is unlikely in light of Paul's wording[7] and when considering the clear connection between this passage and earlier texts in the letter. Others think that Paul characterizes his entire audience but that the reference to the law shows that this audience must have been a Jewish-Christian one.[8] But this conclusion conflicts with clear indications that Paul's audience in Romans was a mainly Gentile one (see 1:5-7, 13-15; and cf. the Introduction). Paul may, then, use the word "law" *(nomos)* here to refer to Roman law[9] or to law in its most general sense.[10] This interpretation is certainly compatible with Paul's intention in vv. 1-3 to formulate a general principle. On the other hand, Paul never elsewhere uses *nomos* to refer to secular law, and he certainly uses the word in 6:14, 15 and in most of chap. 7 with reference to the Mosaic law. This does not require, however, that his readers be Jewish Christians. Many of the Gentile Christians in Rome were

---

4. Gk. ἦ ἀγνοεῖτε.

5. Gk. ἀδελφοί. This is the first time since 1:13 that Paul has so addressed the Romans.

6. See, e.g., Minear, 62, 64.

7. Zahn notes that, had Paul intended to narrow his focus, we would perhaps have expected him to have written τοῖς ὑμῖν γινώσκουσιν νόμον.

8. See, e.g., Zahn.

9. E.g., Käsemann.

10. S-H.

probably "god-fearers," or synagogue worshipers, before coming to Christ.[11] In any case, new converts would have been exposed to the OT and the law early in their Christian instruction.[12] It is almost certain, then, that Paul here refers to the Mosaic law,[13] but no implications about the ethnic background of his audience can be derived from the fact.

What these converts know is a general principle: "that the law rules over[14] a person only as long as he or she lives." This principle is similar to a maxim of the rabbis: "if a person is dead, he is free from the Torah and the fulfilling of the commandments."[15] Paul may be citing this principle,[16] although the relative dates call for caution, and the principle is of such a nature that it could have parallels in almost any culture.

2-3 Paul illustrates this general principle with an allusion to the marriage relationship. Perhaps alluding to the Mosaic law, Paul notes that "the woman who is married[17] is bound by the law[18] to her husband as long as he lives." But if her husband dies, she is "released from[19] the law relating to her husband."[20] In v. 3, Paul spells out the implications[21] of this situation: as long as her husband lives, the woman "will be called"[22] an adulteress if

---

11. Cf. Dunn; Schmithals, *Theologische Anthropologie*, p. 24. See, for more detail, the discussion of audience in the introduction.

12. Texts such as Gal. 4:21 and 1 Cor. 10:1 show that Paul assumes knowledge of the OT among his Gentile converts.

13. Cf., e.g., Godet; Murray; Cranfield; Wilckens; Dunn; Fitzmyer. Michel suggests a reference both to the Mosaic law and to a general knowledge of judicial procedure; Hodge to the Mosaic law, but as a revelation of general moral law. The anarthrous state of νόμος does not support this view, for Paul demonstrates no consistent relationship between the meaning of νόμος and its articular state. And the second occurrence of νόμος in the verse, which must refer to the same thing as the first, is articular.

14. Gk. κυριεύει: note the parallel with 6:14a.

15. *b. Shabb.* 30a, *Shabb.* 151b *bar.*

16. Cf. esp. Str-B, 3.232; Schoeps, 171, 192; W. Diezinger, "Unter toten Freigewerden: Eine Untersuchung zu Röm. III–VIII," *NovT* 5 (1962), 271-74.

17. Gk. ὕπανδρος γυνή. The word ὕπανδρος means, literally, "under a husband" (continuing Paul's use of the preposition ὑπό to indicate a relationship of bondage); cf. the Heb. תַּחַת־אִישׁ (cf. Num. 5:29, etc.).

18. Gk. νόμῳ, an instrumental dative.

19. The Gk. κατήργηται ἀπό means "separated from" (cf. Gal. 5:4; also *Acts of Jn.* 84:10-20; Origen, *Comm.* on Eph. 2:15; and Macarius, *Logos B* 12.1-6 and 3.15 [I am indebted to Gerald Peterman, "Paul and the Law in Romans 7:1-6" {M.A. thesis, Trinity Evangelical Divinity School, 1988}, for these references]).

20. The genitive τοῦ ἀνδρός after τοῦ νόμου is probably objective: "the law directed towards the hubsand" (Turner, 212).

21. Note the ἄρα οὖν.

22. χρηματίσει, a gnomic future, used "to express that which is to be expected under certain circumstances" (BDF 349 [1]).

she is to "be joined to" (i.e., marry[23]) another man.[24] On the other hand, were her husband to die, she would be "free from the law." This "law" refers back to "the law relating to her husband" in v. 2, but Paul may have chosen to use an unqualified reference in order to set up his application more effectively. Since her husband's death frees her from the law, the woman will not be labeled an adulteress if she marries again.[25]

Paul's point is clear enough; but problems arise when we seek to relate the point to the conclusion in v. 4. If we assume that the details of the illustration in vv. 2-3 are parallel to the application in v. 4, then the "first husband" must represent the law, the "second husband" Christ, and the woman the Christian. Why, then, does Paul have the first husband dying in the illustration and the Christian (= the woman) in the application? In order to maintain an "allegorical" interpretation of vv. 2-3 while explaining this apparent discrepancy, interpreters have resorted to a number of alternatives. The most likely takes the wife in the illustration as the "true self," the first husband as the "old man," and the second husband as Christ.[26] But this explanation, and others of its kind that maintain an allegorical relationship between vv. 2-3 and v. 4, must import concepts into the text that are not there. Probably, then, Paul does not intend us to find significance in the details of vv. 2-3. Thus many recent interpreters conclude, arguing that vv. 2-3 make a single point — death severs relationship to the law. The verses illustrate v. 1 as a preparation for v. 4.[27]

We think that this conclusion is basically sound; but it may go too far in minimizing some of the striking parallels between vv. 2-3 and v. 4: the use

---

23. The Greek phrase γίνομαι ἀνδρί means "be married to" in the LXX, where it translates הָיָה לְ (Lev. 22:12; Deut. 24:2; Hos. 3:3; cf. Fitzmyer). One of the reasons Paul may use it here is in order to create a verbal parallel with the situation of the Christian and Christ (cf. v. 4).

24. These verses are sometimes cited to prove that remarriage on any basis other than the death of one's spouse is adulterous. Whether this is the biblical teaching or not, these verses at any rate are probably not relevant to the issue. Paul is not teaching about remarriage but citing a simple example to prove a point. In such a situation, one often generalizes to what is usually true in order to simplify the analogy. Since Paul does not mention divorce, we can assume that the remarriage of the woman has taken place without a divorce of any kind; and any such remarriage is, of course, adulterous. Further, any body of law that Paul may be citing — Roman or OT (cf. Deut. 25:1-4) — allows for remarriage on grounds other than the death of the spouse. His readers, who "know the law" (v. 1), would certainly recognize this possibility without it in any way spoiling the effectiveness of Paul's analogy.

25. The clause introduced with τοῦ μὴ εἶναι is probably consecutive rather than telic (see Robertson, 1002; contra, e.g., Gifford).

26. E.g., Godet, S-H.

27. Cf., e.g., Murray; Kuss; Käsemann; Cranfield; Fitzmyer.

of "join to" to express the relationship, respectively, of wife and husband (vv. 2-3) and of the Christian and Christ (v. 4), and the emphasis on the new union that follows "death." Not only, then, does Paul in vv. 2-3 illustrate the general principle that "a death frees one from the law" (v. 1); he also sets up the theological application in v. 4 by citing an example — marriage — in which severance from the law enables one to enter into a new relationship.[28]

4 In this verse, the center of the paragraph, Paul states an inference[29] drawn from vv. 1-3. This inference depends not only on the principle stated in v. 1 but also on the illustration and expansion of that principle in vv. 2-3.[30] We might paraphrase: "Recognizing the validity of the principle that 'death severs one's bondage to the law,' you believers can understand that, like this woman, you have through a death been severed from your bondage to the law and been enabled to be joined to another." "You have been put to death to the law" is reminiscent of the main point of chap. 6: "we have died to sin" (cf. vv. 2 and 11).[31] What does this mean?

Since this verse is materially and contextually related to 6:14b, "you have been put to death to the law" will describe that act which results in not being "under law." Therefore, those who interpret "not being under the law" to mean "not being under the condemnation pronounced by the law," usually interpret "being put to death to the law" to mean "delivered from the law insofar as it has the power to condemn." Calvin's interpretation is representative and becomes virtually the "orthodox" view in Reformed theology. He distinguishes sharply between the law in its "office," "which was peculiar to the dispensation of Moses," and the law as "rule of life." The first, which includes specifically the demand of the law for perfection of obedience, leading to condemnation for the inevitable failure to attain this standard, is, as Paul asserts here, abrogated for the Christian; but the second "office" of the law remains in force.[32] Some scholars add to this "freedom from con-

---

28. Cf. esp. J. A. Little, "Paul's Use of Analogy: A Structural Analysis of Romans 7:1-6," *CBQ* 46 (1984), 82-90. Little argues for a third theological application from vv. 2-3: that the law exercises a valid function during the time of its dominion.

29. Cf. ὥστε, "so that," "therefore." Paul often uses this conjunction to introduce the application of his theological argument.

30. This is shown by the καί, "also," following ὥστε.

31. The shift from the active ἀπεθάνομεν ("we died") in 6:2 to the passive ἐθανατώθητε ("you were put to death"), while putting more stress on the divine initiative — "you have been made to die [by God]" — does not affect the basic syntax or meaning. As in 6:2, then, the dative (here τῷ νόμῳ) will denote that the death occurs "to the disadvantage" of the law, and the meaning will be that the Christian has been delivered from the mastery, or power, of the law.

32. In addition to his commentary, see also the *Institutes* 2.11.9. A similar distinction is made by, *inter alia,* Melanchthon (*Loci Communes:* the believer is free from the moral law "quoad justificationem et condemnationem, non quoad obedientium [with

demnation" the idea of a setting free from the perversion of the law into an instrument of securing justification,[33] and a few confine Paul's intention to this idea alone.[34]

But reference to deliverance from such a misunderstanding of the law is unlikely, for Paul regards the law as a force that exercises "legitimate" authority over its subjects (vv. 1-3). Moreover, if "misunderstanding" the law was the root problem, God would certainly not have had to resort to so drastic a step as the death of his Son to free us from its "rule."[35] On the other hand, reference to condemnation must be included. The context connects being bound to the law with existence "in the flesh" (vv. 5-6), and with sin's power to bring death (vv. 7-12; and note the reference to condemnation in 8:1). But we should not confine the meaning to condemnation alone. Throughout chaps. 5–8, Paul focuses not so much on the condemnation that comes when the law is disobeyed — "the curse of the law" (Gal. 3:13) — as on the failure of the law to deal with the problem of sin — "the inability of the law" (cf. 8:3a). Thus, in vv. 5-6, where Paul elaborates v. 4, the law is presented as not only failing to deal with sin but as actually *stimulating* sin in the person who is "bound" to it. That law which Jews, not unnaturally, considered a great bulwark against sin is actually, according to Paul, an instrument that sin has used to produce more sin (vv. 5, 8) and to make the sin problem even worse than it was without the law (vv. 9-11, 13). This suggests that, as in 6:14, Paul in 7:4 is viewing the law as a "power" of the "old age" to which the person apart from Christ is bound. The underlying conception is again salvation-historical, as is suggested also by the use of the "letter"/"Spirit" contrast in v. 6. Just as, then, the believer "dies to sin" in order to "live for God" (chap. 6), so he or she is "put to death to the law" in order to be joined to Christ. Both images depict the transfer of the believer from the old realm to the new. As long as sin "reigns," God and righteousness cannot; and neither, as long as the law "reigns," can Christ and the Spirit.

It is this deliverance from the power, or "binding authority," of the law that Paul describes in this verse. In being released from the law in this

---

respect to justification and condemnation, but not obedience]"), most of the Puritans (cf. J. S. Coolidge, *The Puritan Renaissance in England: Puritanism and the Bible* [Oxford: Clarendon, 1970], pp. 103-4), and Wesley (cf. H. Lindström, *Wesley and Sanctification* [Wilmore, KY: Asbury, n.d.], pp. 78-81). Cf. also P. Fairbairn, *The Revelation of Law in Scripture* (rpt.; Grand Rapids: Zondervan, 1957), pp. 429-30; Scott, *Christianity,* pp. 41-42; Longenecker, 145.

33. Cranfield (on 7:6); D. R. de Lacey, "The Sabbath/Sunday Question and the Law in the Pauline Corpus," in *From Sabbath to Lord's Day* (ed. D. A. Carson; Grand Rapids: Zondervan, 1982), p. 169.

34. E.g., Stuart.

35. Cf. Räisänen, 46-47; Sanders, *Paul, the Law and the Jewish People,* p. 99.

sense, the believer is, naturally, freed from the condemning power of the law. But we introduce categories that are foreign to Paul — at least at this point — by distinguishing between the law in its condemning power and the law as a "rule of life." Paul plainly teaches here a deliverance from the "binding force" of the law as a whole. But, to recapitulate what we have said on 6:14, this must be carefully qualified. First, we must remember that Paul is not here speaking of the OT as a whole, but of the Mosaic law. And, second, he is speaking of the Mosaic law as a *system* or body. This means that it would be premature to conclude from this text that the law can play no role at all in the life of the believer.[36] For to be "dead to the law," as we have seen, means to be delivered from the "power-sphere" of the law. It does not necessarily mean that the believer "has nothing more to do with the law." Thus, positively, as a "witness" (1:2; 3:21) the law continues to teach the believer much that is indispensable about God's holiness and the holiness he expects of his people. Moreover, while this verse implies that the believer is not directly under the authority of the law — thus excluding any "third use of the law" in the traditional sense[37] — this is not to say that individual commandments from that law may not be re-applied as "new covenant law" (see, further, on 8:4 and 13:8-10). Finally, the law of which Paul speaks here is the *Mosaic* law, not "law" in the Lutheran sense of "anything that commands us." Paul affirms here that the believer is no longer under the authority of the Mosaic law, not that he or she is under no law at all. In fact, Paul himself makes clear that the believer is still "under law" in the broader sense — still obligated to certain commandments (see Gal. 6:2; 1 Cor. 7:19; 9:20-22).[38]

---

36. As argued, e.g., by Räisänen, 46-47, and Westerholm, 198-205. For the opposite view, see esp. Schreiner, "Abolition and Fulfillment," pp. 52-59.

37. The "third use of the law" refers to the role of the law as a positive authoritative guide to the Christian life (cf. the idea of the law as "rule of life" cited above from Calvin). Great care is needed in defining exactly what is meant by this "authority," and one must observe many nuances (cf., e.g, Weber, *Foundations of Dogmatics* 2.394-97). Most scholars do not think that Luther has a third use of the law, as usually defined (cf., e.g., G. Ebeling, "On the Doctrine of the *Triplex Usus Legis* in the Theology of the Reformation," in *Word and Faith,* pp. 62-64; H. Bornkamm, *Luther and the Old Testament* [Philadelphia: Fortress, 1969], pp. 124-28; W. Joest, *Gesetz und Freiheit: Das Problem des 'Tertius Usus Legis' bei Luther und die neutestamentliche Paränese* [Göttingen: Vandenhoeck & Ruprecht, 1961], pp. 129-33; perhaps the most extreme expression of Luther's views on this matter is in his "How Christians Should Regard Moses" [1525]; cf. *LW* 35.162-71). But a "third use of the law" is adumbrated in Zwingli (cf. G. W. Locher, "The Characteristic Features of Zwingli's Theology in Comparison with Luther and Calvin," in *Zwingli's Thought: New Perspectives* [Studies in the History of Christian Thought 25; Leiden: Brill, 1981], pp. 197-99), is clear in Calvin — for whom the "third use" is the "chief use" — and in Melanchthon (*Loci Communes* 7; cf. also the Formula of Concord, Art. 6), and is generally taught in "Reformed" theology.

38. On this, see especially the monograph of Deidun, *New Covenant Morality in Paul.*

In a passage somewhat parallel to this one, Paul says of himself that he "died to the law in order that he might live for God" (Gal. 2:19). In that context (cf. v. 15: "we who are Jews by birth"), Paul is describing his experience as a Jewish convert to Christianity and, as in this paragraph, showing that he had to be released from the binding authority of the law if he were to be able to please God. We can understand how a Jew who became a Christian would "die to the law," for the Jew would have grown up under the authority of that law. But how could it be said of Gentile converts that they would need to "die to the law"? In order to evade this problem, some expositors suggest that the "law" in 7:4 is moral law generally[39] or that the "brothers" whom Paul addresses in this passage are exclusively Jewish Christians.[40] But neither solution is acceptable.[41] While Paul never makes the matter clear, we suggest that Paul views the Jewish experience with the Mosaic law as paradigmatic for the experience of all people with "law."[42] Israel stands in redemptive history as a kind of "test case," and its relationship with *the* law is *ipso facto* applicable to the relationship of all people with that "law" which God has revealed to them (cf. 2:14-15). In 7:4, then, while being "put to death to the law" is strictly applicable only to Jewish Christians, Paul can affirm the same thing of the whole Roman community because the experience of Israel with the Mosaic law is, in a transferred sense, also their experience. And, of course, Paul also wants to make clear that, in the new era, in which righteousness is revealed "apart from the law" (cf. 3:21), Gentiles have no need to come under the law to become full-fledged members of the people of God.

The instrument[43] by which by the believer is put to death to the law is "the body of Christ." A few interpreters have thought that Paul might be using this phrase with the collective sense it has in, for example, 1 Cor. 12: believers are put to death to the law by belonging to the church, the body of Christ.[44] But Paul has laid no groundwork in Romans for this application; he must be referring to the physical body of Christ, put to death on the cross for

39. E.g., Hodge.

40. E.g., Bandstra, *The Law and the Elements of the World,* p. 140; Lagrange, 163.

41. The flow of thought requires that the νόμος here must be the same as the νόμος of v. 5 and vv. 7ff., and this is clearly the Mosaic law (cf. the quotation in v. 7). Moreover, as we noted on v. 1, Paul's audience cannot be confined to any one part of the Roman Christian community — a community that included a significant number of Gentiles.

42. Cf., for similar suggestions, Ebeling, "The Doctrine of the Law," pp. 275-80; T. L. Donaldson, "The 'Curse of the Law' and the Inclusion of the Gentiles: Galatians 3:13-14," *NTS* 32 (1986), 104-6; J. Blank, "Gesetz und Geist," in Lorenzi, *The Law of the Spirit,* 83; Westerholm, 192-95.

43. Note Gk. διά.

44. Robinson, *The Body,* p. 47; Tannehill, *Dying and Rising,* p. 46; Dodd.

us.[45] The purpose for which believers have been put to death to the law is "so that you might be joined to another." The phrase echoes the language of v. 3: as death separated the woman from her first husband so that she could be "joined to another," so the believer has been separated by death from the law in order to be "joined to" Christ.[46] This new relationship, Paul implies, will be a never-ending one. For the "other" to which the Christian is joined is "the one who has been raised from the dead" — never to die again (cf. 6:9-10).[47] This theologically dense verse ends on the practical note that is basic to Paul's concern in this section: "in order that we might bear fruit for God." Our new relationship with Christ enables us — and requires us — to produce those character traits, thoughts, and actions that will be "for God's glory."[48]

5 With his now-familiar "when . . . now" (vv. 5-6) contrast between the pre-Christian and Christian situations, Paul explains[49] why it is necessary that believers be freed from the domain of the law. In describing the person outside of Christ as being "in the flesh [*sarx*]," Paul means, in effect, that the non-Christian is "enveloped in," and hence controlled by, narrowly human, this-worldly principles and values.[50] We must again understand Paul's language against the background of his salvation-historical framework. Paul pictures *sarx* as another "power" of the old age, set in opposition to the Spirit — with which *sarx* is always contrasted in chaps. 7–8.[51] As both Rom. 8:9 and the "when" in this verse make clear, this situation is an objective one in which all non-Christians find themselves and from which all Christians are delivered in Christ.

45. See, e.g., Gundry, 239-40; Jewett, *Paul's Anthropological Terms,* pp. 299-300. Probably, as in chap. 6, Paul looks at Christ's death as a "corporate" event in which believers share. Christ's death on the cross was also the believer's death, a death "to the law" as well as "to sin" (Barrett). On the other hand, to read into this text connotations of baptism from 6:1-3 (as, e.g., Wilckens does) is not justified (Dunn).

46. Gk. γίνομαι + dative in each case.

47. Bruce.

48. A way of paraphrasing the meaning of the dative of advantage, τῷ θεῷ. Many commentators have discerned in the image of "fruit-bearing" a continuation of the marriage analogy: good works are the offspring produced by the believer's union with Christ (Bengel; Godet; S-H; Barrett; Fitzmyer). But this is pressing the analogy too far, especially since vv. 2-3 have not mentioned children at all (Lightfoot; Denney).

49. The γάρ in v. 5 thus introduces vv. 5-6 together as the explanation of v. 4.

50. On the theological and ethical significance of σάρξ in Paul, see the note on 1:3.

51. "Flesh," in this sense, is not part of the person, nor even exactly an impulse or "nature" within the person — for this reason the NIV translation "sinful nature" for σάρξ throughout Rom. 7–8 is very misleading (cf. Dunn; and note the NIV marginal reading) — but a "power-sphere" in which a person lives. See the discussion in Fee, *God's Empowering Presence,* pp. 816-22.

Existence in the domain of the flesh is determined by the three other "powers" of the old age: sin, the law, and death. In a sequence that is determinative for the direction of his argument in vv. 7ff., Paul brings these three together, claiming that "sinful passions[52] that[53] were through the law were working in our members, with the result that we were bearing fruit for death." In asserting that "sinful passions" are "through the law," Paul reaffirms the close connection between sin and the law that he has touched on before (3:20; 4:15; 5:20). Here, however, he appears to go further and speaks of the law as not just revealing sin (3:20) or as turning sin into transgression (5:20), but as actually producing sin itself.[54]

We can understand this concept in two different ways. First, there is Bultmann's so-called "nomistic" view, according to which the "passions" in view are the desires of people to establish their own righteousness. In holding out the prospect of life (v. 10), the law encourages people to obey the commandments as a means of attaining this life and leads them thereby into boastful pride and sinful independence of God and his grace.[55] While, however, Paul castigates his Jewish brethren for pursuing righteousness through the law (cf., e.g., 10:1-8), he does not teach that the law itself encourages such a pursuit. It is unlikely that he would accuse the law of

---

52. Gk. τὰ παθήματα τῶν ἁμαρτιῶν, lit. "the passions of sins." This phrase may, in light of ταῖς ἐπιθυμίαις αὐτοῦ in 6:12, mean "passions that arise from sins" (genitive of source; cf. Schlatter), but the plural ἁμαρτιῶν makes this unlikely. Just because of this plural — unusual in chaps. 5–8 — others think that ἁμαρτιῶν might be an objective genitive: "the passions that produce sins" (Godet; Bandstra, *The Law and the Elements of the World,* p. 127). But it is unlikely that Paul distinguishes "passions" and "sins" as two separate stages, so ἁμαρτιῶν is probably a genitive of quality: "sinful passions" (Murray; Käsemann). πάθημα usually means "sufferings" in both pre-NT and NT Greek (cf. 8:18; 2 Cor. 1:5, 6, 7; Phil. 3:10; Col. 1:24; 2 Tim. 3:11; Hebrews [3 times] and 1 Peter [4 times]), but it is used both here and in Gal. 5:24 as equivalent to πάθος, meaning "passion" or "desire." Perhaps it is because "passions" need not be negative that Paul adds ἁμαρτιῶν. Schlatter has suggested that Paul uses the unusual word πάθημα to connote that the "passions" in question are aroused from without, but this depends overmuch on the etymology of the word.

53. The definite article τά ties the following prepositional phrase to the word παθήματα.

54. Cf. Sanders, *Paul, the Law and the Jewish People,* pp. 84-85. Indeed, some deny this kind of connection between sins and the law, interpreting the phrase to mean simply that sins were "made apparent" through the law (e.g., Chrysostom). But the lack of any mediating word or phrase between παθήματα and διά makes this unlikely; what Paul seems to mean is that "sinful passions" were actually aroused "by means of" the law.

55. Bultmann, "Romans 7," pp. 154-55; cf. also his *Theology,* 1.246, 248; Jewett, *Paul's Anthropological Terms,* pp. 145-49; Furnish, *Theology and Ethics,* pp. 141-42.

provoking these desires. Moreover, the "sinful passions" of this verse are interpreted in v. 7 as the "desire" *that the law forbids*.[56] We must, then, reject this "nomistic" explanation in favor of the second explanation: that the "sinful passions" are those desires to disobey God and his law that are, paradoxically, exacerbated by the law itself. As Paul explains more fully in 7:7-11, the law, in setting forth God's standard, arouses sins by stimulating human beings' innate rebelliousness against God. In addition — although this idea is not so evident in this verse — the law increases the seriousness of sin by branding sinful failure as violation of God's positive decree.

Although Paul has departed from his usual use of the singular "sin," the remainder of this verse shows that he continues to characterize sin/sins as an active force: the sinful passions aroused by the law were continually "working"[57] in the "members"[58] of the Roman Christians before their conversion. And death — in all its dimensions — was the result.[59]

6 Because Paul's focus is on the law, he "postpones" what would be the expected contrast between being "in the flesh" and being "in the Spirit" until chap. 8 in order to emphasize once again the Christian's deliverance from the law (v. 6) and to explore the implications of his teaching for the law itself (vv. 7-25): "But now we have been released from[60] the law, dying to that in which we were held captive."[61] "That in which" the non-Christian is

---

56. Cf., for these criticisms and others, Ridderbos, *Paul,* pp. 145-46; Beker, 239-40; Althaus; Wright, "Messiah and People of God," pp. 147-48; H. Räisänen, "Legalism and Salvation by the Law: Paul's Portrayal of the Jewish Religion as a Historical and Theological Problem," in *Die Paulinische Literatur und Theologie* (ed. S. Pedersen; Teoloiske Studien 7; Århus: Aros, 1980), pp. 69-71; idem, "Zum Gebrauch von ΕΠΙΘΥΜΙΑ und ΕΠΙΘΥΜΕΙΝ bei Paulus," *ST* 33 (1979), 85-99. See also the notes on 5:20 and 7:15.

57. The verb ἐνηργεῖτο (middle and intransitive) is imperfect in tense, emphasizing the constant activity of sin.

58. Gk. τοῖς μέλεσιν; as in 6:13 and 19, our emotional and cognitive as well as physical faculties.

59. The εἰς τό with infinitive construction here could indicate a purpose (BAGD; Godet), but it is more likely to be consecutive (Kuss; Cranfield): the "working" of the passions has as its consequence the producing of activities leading to, or worthy of, death (on Paul's use of εἰς with the infinitive, see the additional note on 1:20).

60. Gk. κατηργήθημεν ἀπό. See the note on 7:2 for the meaning of καταργέω + ἀπό.

61. Gk. ἀποθανόντες ἐν ᾧ κατειχόμεθα. This participial clause modifies the verb, explaining in language taken from v. 4 how the believer's release from the law has taken place. The clause is elliptical and must be filled out by inserting the word ἐκείνῳ after ἀποθανόντες (although Lightfoot takes κατειχόμεθα independently and attaches ἀπὸ τοῦ νόμου to ἀποθανόντες). And see BAGD for the meaning of κατέχω in the passive.

"held captive" is, as the parallel with v. 4 makes clear, the law.[62] Believers, however, have been set free from this "regime" of the law.[63]

While, however, still preoccupied with the law, Paul knows where he wants to go eventually in his argument, and so he announces it in the last part of this verse: "so that we might serve in newness of the Spirit[64] and not in oldness of letter."[65] This is the second time in Romans that Paul has used the letter/Spirit contrast (cf. 2:27-29). As in this earlier text, the antithesis is not between the misunderstanding or misuse of the law and the Spirit,[66] nor even, at least basically, between the outer demand and the inner disposition to obey,[67] but between the Old Covenant and the New, the old age and the new.[68] The essence of the old, or Mosaic, covenant, is the law as an "external," written demand of God. "Serving" in the old state created by the "letter" meant not,

62. See, e.g., W. G. Kümmel, *Römer 7 und die Bekehrung des Paulus* (UNT 17; Leipzig: J. C. Hinrichs, 1929), p. 42; Cranfield; contra, e.g., Griffith Thomas and Lagrange, who think Paul refers to the flesh, and Zahn, Denney, and Lenski, who refer generally to the old pre-Christian circumstances. Note the parallels between this verse and Paul's teaching about the law in Gal. 3:22, 23.

63. As we argued at 7:4, the language used by Paul does not permit a restriction to a discharge from the condemnation pronounced by the law (as Cranfield suggests).

64. Gk. καινότητι πνεύματος. The genitive here, and in the contrasting phrase παλαιότητι γράμματος could be epexegetic — "newness, that is, the Spirit"; "oldness, that is, the letter" (e.g., Cranfield) — but is probably source, or subjective: "the new state determined by the Spirit"; "the old state determined by the letter."

65. Older commentators insist that ὥστε followed by the infinitive must mean "contemplated result" (e.g., S-H), but it is not clear that NT Greek is so strict in its categories. Since it depends on a verb depicting past action (κατηργήθημεν, "we were released"), it is more likely that the ὥστε clause denotes actual result: believers are now actually serving "in newness of Spirit and not in oldness of letter" (see Robertson, 1091, for a list of texts in which ὥστε with infinitive denotes actual result).

66. E.g., Cranfield; Dunn.

67. Godet; Huby.

68. Cf. Käsemann; J. Kremer, " 'Denn der Buchstabe tötet, der Geist aber macht lebendig.' Methodologische und hermeneutische Erwägungen zu 2 Kor 3,6b," in *Begegnung mit dem Wort (für Heinrich Zimmermann)* (ed. J. Zmijewski and E. Nellessen; BBB 53; Bonn: Peter Hanstein, 1980), pp. 220-29; Westerholm, "Letter and Spirit," pp. 238-39. In 2:27 γράμμα denoted the law of Moses as a simple possession of the Jew, and in 2:29 πνεῦμα, in contrast, the sphere in which true, "inward" circumcision takes place. The only other place in which Paul contrasts γράμμα and πνεῦμα is 2 Cor. 3:6, where γράμμα again depicts the law of Moses as the "letters" carved on tablets, and πνεῦμα as the Holy Spirit. In this text the contrast is explicitly one between "old" and "new" covenants. These parallels (and 2 Cor. 3:5-18 has a significant number of similarities to 7:6; cf. B. Schneider, "The Meaning of St. Paul's Antithesis 'The Letter and the Spirit,' " *CBQ* 15 [1953], 203) suggest that this antithesis is present here also. Note also that γράμμα and πνεῦμα reproduce the "when . . . now" contrast between vv. 5-6 and that the παλαι-/καινο- contrast in Paul is always a salvation-historical one (cf. 2 Cor. 3:6, 14; 5:17; Eph. 4:22-24).

as the Jews thought, a curbing of sin, but a stimulating of the power of sin — and "death" is the end-product of sin (v. 5). Now, though, the believer, released from bondage to the law, can serve in the new condition created by God's Spirit, a condition that brings life (2 Cor. 3:6) and fruit pleasing to God (cf. 6:22-23). Before Paul goes on to develop the nature of "serving in the Spirit" (Rom. 8), he pauses to explain further the condition of "serving in oldness of letter," and of being "in the flesh" where the law arouses sinful passions (7:7-25).

Before going on to this text, however, we might pause to comment further on this matter of "bondage to the law" in the OT era. Fairbairn argues for a subjective interpretation of "being bound to the law," as applying only to those in the OT who did not find justification by faith.[69] But this illegitimately eliminates the necessarily objective contrast between Old Covenant and New, old age and new.[70] I have dealt with this problem before, noting that Paul's salvation-historical contrasts must not be applied with temporal precision. In particular, it is clear that Paul is often thinking only of the situation now that Christ has come: a situation in which there can no longer be a true "saint" who has not exercised explicit faith in Christ and become a partaker of the New Covenant. From *this* perspective, Paul's contrasts are absolute — either one is bound to the law, and hence in the old, outdated covenant that produces only condemnation; or one has "died to that law" and been transferred into the new age of the Spirit and life. It is only when we ask the question about the status of OT saints — a question that was probably not in Paul's mind at the time — that a problem arises.

Nevertheless, it is clear that OT saints, while not suffering all the penalties incurred through the law, were bound to that law in a way that NT saints are not. Their status is somewhat anomalous, as they participate in the same salvation that we experience — through faith in conjunction with the promise — yet experience also that "oldness" and sense of bondage which was inescapable for even the OT saints. To be sure, these saints could, and did, delight in God's law (e.g., Ps. 119). But even so strong a defender of the continuity of the covenants as Calvin recognized the inevitability of some degree of "bondage" under the Old Covenant that could be taken away only by the coming of Christ:

69. Fairbairn, *Revelation of Law,* pp. 429-30.

70. It is just this objective status of being bound to the law that Dunn consistently underplays by suggesting that the problem with the law was mainly one of Jewish misuse of the law as a "most favored nation" treaty. This may have been part of the problem, but there is an objective "inability" of the law that plays a much larger role in Paul's teaching on this subject than Dunn has allowed.

[W]e shall deny that they [the patriarchs] were so endowed with the spirit of freedom and assurance as not in some degree to experience the fear and bondage arising from the law. For, however much they enjoyed the privilege that they had received through the grace of the gospel, they were still subject to the same bonds and burdens of ceremonial observances as the common people. . . . Hence, they are rightly said, in contrast to us, to have been under the testament of bondage and fear, when we consider that common dispensation by which the Lord at that time dealt with the Israelites.[71]

2. The History and Experience of Jews under the Law (7:7-25)

In 7:1-6 Paul teaches that people must be released from the bondage of the Mosaic law in order to be joined to Christ because life under the law brings forth only sin and death. This paragraph brings to a climax the negative assessment of the law that is such a persistent motif in Rom. 1–6 and thereby also raises with renewed urgency perhaps the most serious theological issue with which Paul (and early Christianity generally) had to grapple: How can *God's* law have become so negative a force in the history of salvation? How could the law be both "good" and an instrument of sin and death? This dilemma can, of course, be avoided if the divine origin of the law is denied, and this is the route followed by Marcion in the second century. But the rejection of the OT and a great deal of the NT required by this simple and superficially attractive cutting of the theological Gordian knot exposes this solution as the heresy it is. And despite Marcion's appeal to Paul, it is certainly not Paul's solution. This he makes clear in 7:7-25.

The law, Paul affirms, is "God's law" (v. 22) and is "good" (vv. 12, 17), "holy" (v. 12), "just" (v. 12), and "spiritual" (v. 14). How, then, could the law come to have so deleterious an effect? How could the good law of God "work wrath" (4:15), "increase the trespass" (5:20), and "arouse sinful passions" (7:5)? This Paul seeks to explain in 7:7-25, pointing to sin as the culprit that has used the law as a "bridgehead" to produce more sin and death (7:7-12) and to the individual "carnal" person, whose own weakness and internal division allows sin to gain the mastery, despite the "goodness" of the law (7:13-25). Romans 7:7-25, therefore, has two specific purposes: to vindicate the law from any suggestion that it is, in itself, "sinful" or evil; and to show how, despite this, the law has come to be a negative force in the history of salvation.

Both major sections of 7:7-25 (7-12; 13-25) follow the dialogical style with which we have become so familiar in Romans: question — emphatic rejection ("by no means!") — explanation. Paul uses this format in a variety

---

71. *Institutes* 2.11.9. We would dissent from Calvin here only in not confining the source of this bondage to the ceremonial law.

of ways in Romans, but in this case it marks the whole section as something of an excursus. The main line of development proceeds from 7:6b — "serving in newness of Spirit" — to chap. 8, with its focus on the Spirit in the new age (e.g., Barrett). To be sure, there are points of contact between 7:7-25 and chap. 8 (cf. Käsemann). But these are confined to the first few verses of chap. 8 and are in the nature of "counterfoils" to the positive development of Paul's teaching. In labeling 7:7-25 a parenthesis, we must also stress that we mean by this not that 7:7-25 is an unimportant aside but that it is a detour from the main road of Paul's argument. No one could dispute the importance of 7:7-25 for Paul's theology of the law and of human nature.

We may divide this section into two major parts, v. 13 being a "bridge" between the two. In 7:7-12 Paul uses a narrative to show how sin has used the law to bring death. Verses 14-25, on the other hand, use present tense verbs to describe the constant battle between the "mind," which agrees with God's law, and the "flesh," or the "members," which succumb to "the law of sin." The result, then, is that the law of God, which aroused sin, is impotent to break the power of sin.

Thus far I have described the teaching of Rom. 7:7-25 without identifying the "I" *(egō)* who figures so prominently in these verses. This is deliberate, for we must insist again that the central topic of these verses is not human nature, or anthropology, but the Mosaic law. Because this is the case, the most important teaching of the section is the same however the "I" is identified. The law, God's good, holy, and spiritual gift, has been turned into an instrument of sin because of the "fleshiness" of people. It is therefore unable to deliver a person from the power of sin, and people who look to it for such deliverance will only experience frustration and ultimate condemnation. Having said this, however, the identification of the "I" in this passage is not an insignificant matter. It affects, to some extent, the way we understand Paul's presentation of the law, but, even more, the way we understand the Christian life. And certainly the identification of this "I" affects dramatically the interpretation of individual verses.

In the history of interpretation, four main identifications of the *egō* in this passage have been proposed. Not all of these identifications are maintained for the entire passage, and many (perhaps most) scholars now combine one or more of these identifications in their interpretation of the chapter. It might be more accurate, then, to speak of four "directions" in interpretation. In describing these directions, I will include an "expanded paraphrase" of vv. 9-10a because these verses are crucial for the correct identification of this *egō*.[1]

---

1. In what follows, I present the basic interpretations and the main reasons why I have chosen the interpretation that I have. Many points are left for the detailed notes that follow, and many of the points included below are dealt with in more detail later.

1. *The autobiographical direction.* The average Christian is — understandably! — likely to ask, "What is all the fuss about?" Doesn't Paul use "I"? Who else except Paul would it be? Most interpreters throughout the history of the church have agreed and concluded that Paul uses *egō* simply because he is depicting his own experience. Most, however, would quickly add that he describes his experience not because it is unique but because it is typical — the experience of "every person." Those who defend an autobiographical interpretation differ over what experience in Paul's life he may be describing in vv. 7-12.[2] The following are the main possibilities:

a. The awakening of the sinful impulse at the time of Paul's "coming of age," or "bar mitzvah": "I was living without understanding the real power of sin at one time, but when I became responsible for the commandment, sin sprang to life and I perceived myself to be under condemnation"[3] (or "perceived myself to be unable to throw off sin's power"[4]).

b. The realization of condemnation just previous to Paul's conversion: "I thought myself to be 'alive' in the days when, as a self-satisfied Pharisee, I thought I was fulfilling the law. But when the Spirit began to make clear to me the real, inward, meaning of God's law, I saw that I was far short of its demands and was, in fact, under condemnation."[5]

In vv. 14-25, then, defenders of the autobiographical view think that Paul is describing his experience as a Jew under the law, his immediate postconversion struggle with the law, or his continuing struggle to obey the law as a Christian. (See, further, the introduction to vv. 14-25.)

2. *The Adamic direction.* While few have thought that Paul describes the experience of Adam throughout the section, many, from the earliest days of the church, have thought that vv. 7-12 can be applied directly only to Adam. "I was fully alive [spiritually] before the 'law' not to eat of the fruit of the tree came. But when that commandment was given, sin [through the serpent] sprang to life and brought upon me spiritual condemnation." Most contemporary interpreters, while not thinking that vv. 7-11 describe only Adam, think

---

2. A few advocates of the autobiographical approach (e.g., Zahn, 341-44; Denney, 640; J. D. G. Dunn, "Rom. 7,14-25 in the Theology of Paul," *TZ* 31 [1975], 201) think that Paul is not narrating any specific experience but his general situation.

3. A. Deissmann, *Paul: A Study in Social and Religious History* (2d ed.; New York: Harper & Row, 1927), p. 91; Davies, 24-25. (In this and the following entries, only the best or most representative treatments for each view are given.)

4. R. H. Gundry, "The Moral Frustration of Paul before his Conversion: Sexual Lust in Romans 7:7-25," in *Hagner and Harris,* pp. 232-33.

5. Augustine, *Against Two Letters of the Pelagians* 1.9 (*NPNF* 5.382-83) (although Augustine appears to allow for elements of other views listed here also [cf. Wilckens, 2.103-4]); Calvin, 255; Hodge, 224; Murray, 1.251; Bandstra, *The Law and the Elements of the World,* p. 137.

that reference to Adam is present and prominent.[6] Interpretations of vv. 14-25 by proponents of this view differ widely, but perhaps the most attractive is that of Longenecker. He argues that after using the idea of corporate solidarity with Adam in vv. 7-13 — "I in Adam" — Paul goes on in vv. 14-25 to describe the continuing effects of that solidarity — "Adam in me."[7]

3. *The Israel direction.* Since Chrysostom, some interpreters have understood the *egō* in at least parts of 7:7-25 (usually vv. 8-10 especially) to be a representation of the people of Israel. "We [the nation Israel] were, relatively-speaking, spiritually 'alive' before the giving of the law at Sinai. But when that law was given, it gave sin its opportunity to create transgression and so to deepen and radicalize our spiritual lostness."[8] Most of these interpreters, then, think that Paul in vv. 14-25 describes the continuing situation of Jews under the Mosaic law. This is often called the "salvation-historical" view.

4. *The existential direction.* Convinced that vv. 7-12 cannot be identified with any particular person or experience, many interpreters identify the *egō* in 7:7-25 as nobody in particular and everybody in general. Paul, they argue, is using figurative language to describe the confrontation between a "person," *qua* person, and the demand of God.[9] Paraphrase of vv. 9-10a in this case is both impossible and inappropriate.

In assessing these views, three issues are key: the potential lexical range of *egō;* the identification of the "law" depicted in the chapter; and the

---

6. This view was held by several church fathers, including Theodoret (and cf. Schelkle). Cf. also Feine, *Das gesetzesfreie Evangelium,* pp. 131-46; S. Lyonnet, "L'histoire du salut selon le chapitre vii de l'épître aux Romains," *Bib* 43 (1962), 117-51; idem, " 'Tu ne convoiteras pas' (Rom. 7.7)," in *Neotestamentica et Patristica: Eine Freundesgabe, Herrn Professor Dr. Oscar Cullmann zu seinem 60. Geburtstag überreicht* (NovTSup 6; Leiden: Brill, 1962), pp. 158-64; Longenecker, 88-95; F. Bussini, *L'homme pécheur devant Dieu. Théologie et anthropologie* (Paris: Cerf, 1978), pp. 115-31; Käsemann, 196-97; Dunn, 1.378-86; Stuhlmacher, 106-7.

7. Longenecker, 88-95; cf. also Laato, *Paulus und das Judentum,* pp. 137-84.

8. Because this view is rather rare, I am giving it a full listing: Chrysostom; Hugo Grotius (according to Kümmel [*Römer 7,* p. 85]); E. Stauffer, *TDNT* II, 358-62; G. Schrenk, *TDNT* II, 550-51; van Dülmen, *Theologie des Gesetzes,* pp. 109-10; J. Lambrecht, "Man before and without Christ: Romans 7 and Pauline Anthropology," *Louvain Studies* 5 (1974), 18-33; Wright, "Messiah and People of God," pp. 93-96, 145-48; idem, *Climax of the Covenant,* pp. 197-98; M. W. Karlberg, "Israel's History Personified: Romans 7:7-13 in Relation to Paul's Teaching on the 'Old Man,'" *TrinJ* 7 (1986), 68-69; and, less clearly, Ridderbos; P. Benoit, "La Loi et la Croix d'après Saint Paul (Rom. 7:7–8:4)," *RB* 47 (1938), 483-87; Berkhof, *Christian Faith,* p. 260; Whiteley, *Theology,* pp. 51-53.

9. Kümmel, *Römer 7,* e.g., pp. 124, 132; G. Bornkamm, "Sin, Law and Death: An Exegetical Study of Romans 7," in *Early Christian Experience,* pp. 83-94; Brandenburger, *Adam und Christus,* pp. 210-16; Kuss; Fitzmyer, 463-66; Patte, *Paul's Faith,* pp. 266-77 (from a psychoanalytic point of view).

experience described by Paul in vv. 9-10a. When these are considered, we will find that, while elements of all four of these interpretations are present, a combination of views 1 and 3 yields the best explanation of the text. Paul is describing his own, and other Jews', experience with the law of Moses: how that law came to the Jewish people and brought to them, not "life," but "death" (vv. 7-12); and how that law failed, because of the reign of the flesh, to deliver Jews from the power of sin (vv. 13-25).

Since the ground-breaking study of Kümmel, it has been widely assumed that *egō* (or the first person singular verb) could be used as a rhetorical device, without any personal reference being intended at all. And Kümmel is certainly right.[10] But this use of *egō* is not frequent in Paul[11] and almost always occurs in conditional or hypothetical statements — a far cry from the sustained narrative and descriptive use in 7:7-25. When Paul's use of *egō* is considered — due allowance being made for the influence of Jewish and Greek rhetorical patterns — it is impossible to remove autobiographical elements from *egō* in Rom. 7:7-25.[12]

10. See, e.g., Rom. 3:7: "But if the truth of God through my [ἐμῷ] lie abounds to his glory, why am I [κἀγώ] still being judged as a sinner?"

11. Of 73 occurrences of the first person singular pronoun in Paul outside Rom. 7, 59 are clearly personal, while ten occur in quotations with clearly personal reference. The same is true, relatively, of first person singular verbs in Paul.

12. Kümmel, as the title of his monograph indicates, is motivated partly by the desire to show that Rom. 7 cannot be used to construct a biography of Paul's conversion. He therefore musters evidence to show that ancient writers could use the first person pronoun as a "Stilform," without including reference to the speaker or writer. However, as Theissen points out, it would be more helpful to distinguish three possible meanings of "I": the "personal," which depicts one's own experience as unique or individual; the "typical," which depicts one's experiences but as representative of that of others; and the "fictive," where no personal reference at all is intended (*Psychologische Aspekte paulinischer Theologie* [FRLANT 131; Göttingen: Vandenhoeck & Ruprecht, 1983], p. 194). There are places in Greek literature and the NT where a "fictive" ἐγώ occurs, but they always occur in an explicitly hypothetical construction (Rom. 3:5 [first person plural], 7; 1 Cor. 11:31-32; 13:1-3; 14:11; Gal. 2:18; Philo, *On Dreams* 1.176), a deliberative style (1 Cor. 6:15; 10:29-30; 14:15 [plural]; Demosthenes, *Kata Philippou* 3.9.17; Ps-Xenophon, *Re Publica Athen.* 1.11 and 2.11), or a quotation (1 Cor. 6:12). These are very different from 7:7-25, both in style and in length. Since Kümmel's work, others have found a "rhetorical" "I" in the DSS, particularly 1QH 1:21-23; 3:24-26; 1QS 11:9-10 (e.g., K. G. Kuhn, "New Light on Temptation, Sin and Flesh in the New Testament," in *The Scrolls and the New Testament* [ed. K. Stendahl; New York: Harper & Row, 1957], p. 102; Longenecker, 88-89). But while rhetorical, the "I" in these passages is not "fictive" because the writer includes himself or herself in his description (H. Bardtke, "Considerations sur les cantiques de Qumran (1)," *RB* 63 [1956], 220-33; S. Holm-Nielsen, *Hodayot: Psalms from Qumran* [Acta Theologica Danica 2; Aarhus: Universitetsforlaget, 1960], p. 75). Stowers (*Diatribe*, pp. 136, 232) finds the closest parallels to Rom. 7 in the

As we have noted, the topic of Rom. 7 is the law; and not just "law" in general, but the *Mosaic* law. This is clear both from Paul's general usage of *nomos* and from the context. For Paul, the law is basically the torah, the body of instruction and commandments given to the people of Israel through Moses at Sinai. This law is the focus of this chapter, which is linked, through 6:14, to 5:20a, where Paul asserts that "the law came in beside"; and this "coming in beside" refers to the giving of the law through Moses (cf. 5:13-14; Gal. 3:19). Moreover, the commandment quoted in v. 7 as representative of the law is from the Decalogue (see, further, the notes on v. 7).

While acknowledging that Paul's focus is on the Mosaic law, some interpreters nevertheless think that he widens his purview as the chapter proceeds so that he is eventually describing "God's law" in any form — written and unwritten.[13] There is some basis for this view, but it is not finally acceptable; except for several "non-legal" occurrences in vv. 21-23, *nomos* continues throughout the chapter to denote the Mosaic law (except in v. 21; see the notes on 7:21 and 22). Expansion to the situation of all people comes not through a broadening of the reference to "law," but through the paradigmatic significance of Israel's experience with the Mosaic law. While Paul directly describes only this experience in this chapter, it has application to all people because what is true of Israel under God's law through Moses is true *ipso facto* of all people under "law" (cf. 2:14-15 and the notes on 7:4).

If Rom. 7 is about the Mosaic law, two conclusions follow. First, it is unlikely that Paul describes in vv. 7-12 the situation of "everybody" — because "everybody" has not been given the Mosaic law — and still more unlikely that he describes the experience of Adam — because Paul insists that the law was given through Moses (cf. 5:13-14), "four hundred and thirty years" after Abraham (Gal. 3:17). To be sure, some argue that Paul,

---

Discourses of Epictetus (1.10.7; 1.29.9-10; 3.26.29; 4.7.26-31), but here again the pronoun includes the author and the passages are short.

Pauline usage, coupled with the weakness of the alleged parallels to Rom. 7 in a "purely rhetorical" sense, are leading more and more scholars to insist that, whatever the ἐγώ in Rom. 7 represents, or whatever events may lie in the background, some reference to Paul himself must be included. See esp. Theissen, *Pyschologische Aspekte,* pp. 194-204. Cf. also D. H. Campbell, "The Identity of ἐγώ in Romans 7,7-25," *Studia Biblia* III (JSNTSup 3; Sheffield: JSOT, 1980), pp. 59-60; A. F. Segal, "Romans 7 and Jewish Dietary Law," *SR* 15 (1986), 361-62; J. Lambrecht, *The Wretched "I" and Its Liberation: Paul in Romans 7 and 8* (Louvain Theological and Pastoral Monographs 14; Louvain: Peters/Grand Rapids: Eerdmans, 1992), pp. 73-91; Dunn, "Rom. 7,14-25," p. 261; Beker, 240-43; Gundry, "Moral Frustration," pp. 229-30.

13. A. Feuillet, "Loi de Dieu, loi du Christ et loi de l'esprit d'après les Epîtres pauliniennes: Les rapports de ces trois lois avec la Loi Mosaique," *NovT* 22 (1980), 32-42; Lindars, "Paul and the Law," pp. 129-40; Feine, *Das gesetzesfreie Evangelium,* pp. 158-60; Deidun, 196-99; Hodge, 222; Lagrange, 165; Kuss, 2.457; Barrett, 140.

depending on Jewish traditions, could view Adam as bound by the torah;[14] but this is unlikely.[15] In light of these considerations, while there may be allusion to Adam's situation in vv. 7-11 — in that the situation depicted parallels Adam's — I cannot think that Paul is *describing* events in the Garden of Eden.

But there is a second, positive, conclusion to be drawn from the fact that Rom. 7 is about the Mosaic law. This is that "the coming of the commandment" in v. 9 is most naturally taken as a reference to the giving of the law at Sinai. Before we pursue this conclusion, we must discuss the third point: the narrative sequence in vv. 9-10a.

This sequence provides the strongest evidence for the "Adamic" view. For who else in the history of the race could say "I was alive apart from the law" and it was only "when the commandment came" — and I disobeyed — that "I died?" Everyone after Adam and Eve is born as a sinner, "dead" in trespasses and sins (Eph. 2:1); and to all of us disobeying the law does not bring, but confirms, death. This point, of course, assumes that "I was alive" and "I died" refer, respectively, to eternal life and eternal death, or condemnation. But, while there is legitimate question about "I was alive" (see the notes on 7:9), "I died," because of the connections in the passage, must refer to the same "death" that is spoken of in vv. 5 and 13. And this is clearly "total death," the condemnation that comes as a penalty for sin.[16] It is this consideration that is most damaging to the identification of *egō* as either Paul or the people of Israel. Paul "died" spiritually long before his coming to maturity or his alleged pre-conversion "awakening," and the people of Israel were certainly under condemnation before the giving of the law (see 5:13-14). Yet, as we have seen, the Adamic view suffers from what we think is an even more serious objection: the theologically incongruous attribution to Adam of responsibility for the Mosaic law. Because of this, I prefer to understand "I died" in a theological, but relative, sense: "though 'I' had sinned, and was

---

14. Cf. one of the Aramaic paraphrases of the OT, *Targum Neofiti* I, on Gen. 2:15-16: "And the Lord God took man and caused him to dwell in the Garden of Eden, in order to keep the Law and to follow his commandments" (quoted by Stuhlmacher, "Paul's Understanding," p. 98). On this, see esp. Lyonnet, "Tu ne convoiteras pas," pp. 158-64, who adduces more evidence for the tradition from the Targums and rabbinic literature.

15. Not only is there nothing in Paul to suggest that Adam was given the (Mosaic) law (Adam's sin is "like" the sin of people under the law only in being a violation of a specific commandment [5:14]), but it also runs counter to what is a point of crucial theological significance for Paul: that the law is not the primary locus for the fulfillment of God's purposes — as most Jews and many "Judaizers" believed — but that it has a subordinate role, coming long *after* the establishment of God's salvific promise to Abraham and his heirs (cf. Gal. 3:15-26).

16. Cf. Kümmel, *Römer 7*, p. 124.

condemned before the law came, the coming of the commandment gave sin greater power and destructiveness than ever before, making me fully and personally responsible for my sin. The coming of the law brought to me, then, not life but death ('I died')."[17]

If these points are valid, Paul could be describing either his own personal confrontation with the law or that of the people of Israel generally. The latter is preferable for two reasons. First, to make the language apply to Paul personally, "without the law" and "when the commandment came" (v. 9) must both be interpreted subjectively: "without being conscious of the [real demands of the] law" and "when I became responsible for, or aware of, the commandment." Not only should we avoid, if possible, a subjective application of Paul's apparently objective language, but it is difficult to fit such an experience into what we know, or can surmise, of Paul's own experience. For there is little evidence that a Jewish child was ever considered to have so little responsibility for the law as to be said to be "without the law" (assumed by view 1a above).[18] And, despite its popularity, there is even less evidence that Paul before his conversion was brought to a deeper consciousness of his sinfulness (assumed by view 1b).[19]

A second factor favoring reference to Israel as a whole is the similarity between the sequence of vv. 9-10a and Paul's persistent teaching about how the giving of the Mosaic law made the situation of Israel worse, not better. The law, Paul has affirmed, "brings wrath" (4:15), turns sin into transgression (5:14; cf. Gal. 3:19), and "increases the trespass" (5:20a). The prominence of this "salvation-historical" sequence in Paul makes it likely that in vv. 9-10 he is using a vivid narrative style to describe this sequence from a more "personal" angle.

We have reason, then, to think that Paul alludes to the giving of the law to the people of Israel in vv. 9-10. But could he use *egō* to represent the nation? This is possible, in light of the use of "I" to stand for Jerusalem,

17. See also Benoit, "La loi et la croix," p. 487.

18. While the rabbis attest to some degree of increase in responsibility for the law as the child grows (cf. *m. 'Abot* 5:21), they also insist that the Jewish child is fully responsible for the law (cf. Kümmel, *Römer 7*, pp. 81-83; Longenecker, 91-92). The institution of the *bar mitzvah* at age 13 is medieval (S. Safrai, "Home and Family," in *The Jewish People in the First Century* [ed. S. Safrai and M. Stern; CRINT 1; 2 vols.; Philadelphia: Fortress, 1976], 2.771).

19. Philippians 3:2-11 implies that Paul was quite satisfied with his "righteousness of the law" until he "exchanged" that righteousness for "the righteousness of faith that Christ gives," and this is confirmed by the unexpected and sudden nature of Paul's conversion as it is described in Acts (cf. 9:3-6; 22:6-11; 26:12-18). From all indications (cf. Acts 9; Phil. 3:3-11), Paul's reevaluation of the law came only *after* and as a result of his conversion. See esp. Longenecker, 86-105.

or the nation of Israel, in some OT passages.[20] But perhaps more likely, in light of the undeniable autobiographical elements in vv. 14-25, is that Paul uses *egō* to describe himself — and, by extension, other Jews — in solidarity with the experiences of his people. We know that the individual Jew had a lively sense of "corporate" identity with his people's history. Most famous in this regard, of course, is the Passover ritual, in which each Jew confesses that he or she was a slave in Egypt and was redeemed through the events of the Passover.[21] In like manner, I suggest that Paul in vv. 7-11 is describing his own involvement, as a member of the people Israel, with the giving of the law to his people at Sinai.[22] In vv. 14-25, then, Paul describes what the coming of the law meant for himself and other Jews. And since this situation was one consciously experienced by Paul, autobiographical elements are more strongly in evidence in vv. 14-25 than in vv. 7-11.

We conclude, then, that *egō* denotes Paul himself but that the events depicted in these verses were not all experienced personally and consciously by the Apostle. It is in this sense that we argue for a combination of the autobiographical view with the view that identifies *egō* with Israel. *Egō* is not Israel, but *egō* is Paul in solidarity with Israel.[23]

a. The Coming of the Law (7:7-12)

7*What then shall we say? Is the law sin? By no means! But I would not have known sin except through the law. For I would not have known covetousness if the law had not said, "You shall not covet."*a 8*But sin, taking opportunity through the commandment, produced in me all kinds of coveting. For apart from the law sin is dead.* 9*And I was alive apart from the law at one time; but when the commandment came, sin sprang to life again,* 10*and I died. And the commandment that was unto life proved to be unto death.* 11*For sin, taking opportunity through the commandment, deceived me, and through it killed me.* 12*Therefore, the law is holy, and the commandment is holy and just and good.*

a. Exod. 20:17; Deut. 5:21

---

20. Cf. Jer. 10:19-22; Mic. 7:7-10; Lam. 1:9-22; 2:20-22; and cf. *Pss. Sol.* 1:1-2, 6. Cf. Luz, 159; Wilckens, 2.77-78.

21. Cf. *m. Pesaḥ.* 10. For discussion, see Davies, 102-4.

22. R. B. Sloan, "Paul and the Law: Why the Law Cannot Save," *NovT* 33 (1991), 55-56, argues for more of an analogical relationship between Paul and Israel: both had found that devotion to the law led to spiritual downfall.

23. For elaboration of almost all these points, see D. J. Moo, "Israel and Paul in Romans 7.7-12," *NTS* 32 (1986), 122-35.

This paragraph has two purposes: to exonerate the law from the charge that it is sinful and to delineate more carefully the true relationship among sin, the law, and death. Paul takes care of the first of these purposes at both "ends" of the paragraph: in v. 7a, with the rhetorical question followed by his characteristic strong negative, and in v. 12, with a closing assertion. Between these, Paul cares for his other main purpose. He admits that, though the law is not "sin," it does have a close relationship to sin. For the law brings recognition of sin and even stimulates sinning (vv. 7b-8). In fact, alluding, as we have seen, to his and other Jews' solidarity with the people of Israel at Sinai, he argues that the coming of the law brought a "radicalizing" of the sentence of condemnation (vv. 9-10a). Strangely, then, the very commandment that was "unto life" became the instrument of death (v. 10b). Verse 11 summarizes: sin has used the law as a "bridgehead" to deceive and to condemn.

7 "What then shall we say?"[24] brings us back to the dialogical style of 6:1-23. As there, the question raised here reflects a criticism of Paul's gospel that he must often have heard. If Paul teaches that the law "increases the trespass" (5:20) and "arouses sinful passions" (7:5), he must believe that the law is by its nature evil and sinful. Should Paul hold such a view, he would effectively destroy any continuity between the law and his gospel, between the OT and the NT, between Moses and Christ. Indeed, many Jews and Jewish Christians accused Paul of holding just such an opinion. Paul is undoubtedly aware that such charges against him have reached the ears of the Roman Christians; so, to prepare the way for his visit and the enlistment of the Romans in his missionary efforts, he seeks here to dispel any such apprehensions.[25] "Is the law sin? By no means!"

But Paul's rejection of the equation between the law and sin does not mean that he is taking back what he has said earlier (e.g., 5:20; 7:5) — the law *has* become allied with sin. This relationship he reaffirms and further explains in what follows. The "but"[26] that introduces this discussion is therefore not strictly adversative — "no, the law is not sin; on the contrary . . ."[27] — but restrictive — "no, the law is not sin, although it is true that. . . ."[28] Although the law is not itself sin, the law and sin do have a definite relationship. Specifically, according to v. 7b, the law brings "knowledge" of sin. Paul first states this relationship in a general assertion — "I would not have known sin except through the law" — then adduces a

---

24. Gk. τί οὖν ἐροῦμεν; cf. also 3:5; 4:1; 6:1; 8:31; 9:14, 30.

25. See esp. Stuhlmacher, who stresses the polemical thrust of Romans throughout his exposition.

26. Gk. ἀλλά.

27. See, e.g., Wilckens.

28. See, e.g., Denney.

specific example — "I would not have known[29] covetousness if the law had not said, 'You shall not covet.' "

But what kind of "knowing" is this? Perhaps the most obvious possibility is that Paul is talking about the law as *defining* sin: through the law, the revelation of the righteous standard of God, "I" come to know that certain acts are sinful, that, for example, my inner desire to "possess" is nothing but a "coveting" that is prohibited by God.[30] This is no doubt true, but Paul implies earlier that such knowledge is available even to those who do not have the (Mosaic) law (1:32; 2:14-16). The context, in which Paul stresses that the law reveals sin to be "sin" and renders sin "utterly sinful" (v. 13), suggests a stronger nuance: that through the law "I" come to "understand" or "recognize" the real nature and power of sin. The law, by branding "sin" as transgression (cf. 4:15; 5:13-14) and bringing wrath and death (4:15; 7:8-11, 13), unmasks sin in its true colors.[31] But we should probably go further, and

29. In both sentences, the verb "to know" is in the indicative mood — ἔγνων; ᾔδειν. Because of the εἰ μή ("if not") construction that follows in each case, both are probably "unreal" indicatives, justifying our rendering "I would not have known" (Turner, 92; E. Fuchs, *Die Freiheit des Glaubens. Römer 5–8 auslegt* [BEvT 14; Munich: Kaiser, 1949], p. 55; contra, e.g., S-H, who take both as "real" indicatives, or Godet, who takes the first as "real" and the second as "unreal"). Whether there is significance in the change of tense is not so clear. The aorist ἔγνων simply states the fact of knowing, but the "imperfect" ᾔδειν (actually pluperfect in form, but οἶδα is deponent in its tense formation) may suggest the continuing nature of this "knowing": "I would not have known, nor would I now know, sin except through the law" (Cranfield; Dunn). But this point cannot be pressed because οἶδα has no aorist form that Paul could have used. There is probably, then, no difference in nuance (Godet; Barrett).

Nor is it likely that the change in verbs signals a difference in meaning. In classical Greek, οἶδα and γινώσκω are generally distinguished, the former meaning "to perceive, know intuitively," and the latter "come to understand through experience." If this distinction is preserved here, the first sentence would connote "an intimate, experimental acquaintance" with sin, the second "simple knowledge that there was such a thing as lust" (e.g., S-H). But the context would lead us to expect, if anything, just the reverse emphasis: a general statement regarding the way the law brings "knowledge" of sin, followed by an example of "coming to know and experience" a specific sin (in fact, this is essentially what Gifford implies). In point of fact, οἶδα and γινώσκω do not always retain their "classical" meanings in the NT; cf. the studies of D. W. Burdick, "οἶδα and γινώσκω in the Pauline Epistles," in *New Dimensions in New Testament Study,* pp. 344-56; M. Silva, "The Pauline Style as Lexical Choice: ΓΙΝΩ-ΣΚΕΙΝ and Related Verbs," in *Pauline Studies,* pp. 184-207. Other distinctions are possible (cf., e.g., Porter, *Verbal Aspect,* pp. 281-87 [following McKay]), but the context in this case makes it difficult to posit any difference in meaning between the two (cf. Burdick, "οἶδα," p. 351; Cranfield).

30. See, e.g., Calvin; Benoit, "La loi et la croix," p. 487 n. 4.

31. E.g., Cranfield. Both οἶδα and γινώσκω can indicate such "understanding" (for οἶδα, cf., e.g., Rom. 13:11; and for γινώσκω 7:15; 11:34 — and cf. BAGD).

conceive this "understanding" of sin not in a purely noetic way but in terms of actual experience: through the law, "I" have come to experience sin for what it really is. Through the law sin "worked in me" all kinds of sinful desires (v. 8), and through the law sin "came to life" and brought death (vv. 9-11). It is through this actual experience of sin, then, that "I" come to understand the real "sinfulness" of sin.[32]

Paul's choice of the commandment he cites in v. 7c, "You shall not covet, or desire" is often thought to reflect his personal history. Gundry, for instance, emphasizing the sexual connotations of "desire," argues that Paul describes his own awakening to sexual lust as an adolescent.[33] However, Pauline usage dictates a broader meaning of "desire," encompassing illicit desires of every kind.[34] In fact, Paul's citation is almost certainly an abbreviated version of the tenth commandment of the Decalogue (Exod. 20:17; Deut. 5:21).[35] It may still be, of course, that Paul cites this commandment

32. In arguing this interpretation of "knowing," however, I do not want to shift the focus from the primarily noetic meaning of the verbs. This is done by those who take "knowing" in the "Hebrew" sense of "practical" knowledge, and think that Paul is describing how the law leads "me" into actual sinning. Certainly both γινώσκω (cf. 1:21; 1 Cor. 8:3; Gal. 4:9; Phil. 3:10) and οἶδα (1 Cor. 2:2; Gal. 4:8; 1 Thess. 4:4, 5; 5:12; 2 Thess. 1:8; Tit. 1:16) can, like the Hebrew ידע, mean "experience," "be in relation with," and 2 Cor. 5:21 shows that Paul could use the construction γινώσκω ἁμαρτίαν to mean "commit sin" (Kümmel, *Römer 7*, p. 45; Bultmann, 1.264; Bornkamm, "Sin, Law and Death," p. 102; Ridderbos, *Paul*, p. 151; Gaugler; Schlier). However, οἶδα and γινώσκω connote "experience" — as opposed to "know by experience" — only rarely in Paul. And, while Paul certainly accuses the law of increasing sin (5:20 and 7:5), he does not teach — indeed, he explicitly denies (5:13-14) — that sin is possible only where the law is present. Yet here he says that he would not have "known sin" except through the law. (This difficulty can be avoided only by arguing that the sin Paul has in view is only the sin "against grace," the "nomistic" attempt to use the law as a means of acquiring righteousness [e.g., Bultmann, 1.265]. But "sin" cannot be restricted to so narrow a conception in this context [see on 7:5].) In addition, "coming to know" sin here probably means the same as ἐπίγνωσις ἁμαρτίας in 3:20, where there is no idea of the law "producing" sin.

33. "Moral Frustration," pp. 232-33.

34. The Greek verb is ἐπιθυμέω, which Paul nowhere else uses to describe sexual desire as such (13:9; 1 Cor. 10:6; Gal. 5:17; 1 Tim. 3:1). And only three of his seventeen uses of the cognate noun ἐπιθυμία outside this context focus on sexual desire (1:24; 2 Tim. 2:22; 3:6).

35. Cf. also *Pesiq. R.* 21 (107a) (fourth cent.) (Schoeps, 191). S. Lyonnet ("Tu ne convoiteras pas") and others argue that Paul here refers to the commandment given to Adam and Eve rather than to the Mosaic law. He notes that "desire" without object is found in *Tg. Neof.* Exod. 10:17, that *Tg. Neof.* likewise uses the root חמד (whose Hebrew equivalent is sometimes translated with ἐπιθυμέω in LXX) in Gen. 3:6, and that *b. Shabb.* 145b-146a says that "desire" was injected in Eve by the serpent. But the first reference proves no more than that, as argued above, there was a tendency to absolutize "coveting," while the other two are tangential to the issue. In fact, Lyonnet furnishes no evidence that Jews ever interpreted the Paradise commandment as a prohibition of "coveting." ἐπιθυμέω

because he himself had experienced the full force of the law through it. But this is certainly not the only explanation. The citation of the prohibition of coveting in general (without naming the objects of the coveting) has Jewish antecedents, where it stands as a representative summation of the Mosaic law.[36] This, rather than any personal reasons (for which there is no evidence elsewhere), may be why Paul cites this commandment.[37]

8 The first sentence in v. 8 elaborates v. 7c. Not only has the commandment "Do not covet" brought "me" to see the true nature of "desire," but[38] sin has taken advantage of the "opportunity"[39] afforded "through the commandment"[40] to produce[41] "all kinds of coveting" in me. The law is not

---

and its cognates do not even appear in Gen. 1–3 — but they are used in Ps. 106:14 with reference to the generation of Israel in the wilderness (cf. J. G. Strelan, "A Note on the Old Testament Background of Romans 7:7," *Lutheran Theological Journal* 15 [1981], 23-25).

36. See Philo, *Decalogue,* 142-43, 173; 4 Macc. 2:6. Jewish writers could do this because they tended to view "coveting" as the root of all sins (cf. Jas. 1:15; *Life of Adam and Eve,* 19; Philo, *Special Laws* 4.84-94; and see F. Büchsel, *TDNT* III, 169).

37. J. A. Ziesler argues yet another reason why Paul cites the tenth commandment: by focusing on a prohibition of attitude, Paul is able to conclude that people are totally incapable of doing the law. Such a conclusion would have been impossible if Paul had selected a prohibition of an action as his illustration ("The Role of the Tenth Commandment in Romans 7," *JSNT* 33 [1988], 41-56). However, this is to misread Paul's argument in 7:15-23. His point is not that all Jews disobey all the commandments, or that every Jew feels himself or herself to be in bondage, but that every Jew fails to satisfy the demands of God's law and, to some extent, senses that this is the case. This being so, Paul's selection of the tenth commandment is a fair test because it does have to do with that aspect of God's law — the inner attitude — which most clearly reveals the Jews' failure to live by that law.

38. Gk. δέ.

39. Gk. ἀφορμή (cf. also v. 11). This word perfectly conveys the role that Paul assigns to the law in these verses. It refers often to the "base of operations," or "bridgehead," required for successful military operations. Unfortunately, we cannot be sure that this nuance clings to the word here since it is used in many different contexts (see the other NT uses: 2 Cor. 5:12; 11:12 [twice]; Gal. 5:13; 1 Tim. 5:14; Luke 11:54 [v.l.]) (LSJ; MM). But the idea, generally, of "occasion" or "starting point" still makes the point very well.

40. This phrase, διὰ τῆς ἐντολῆς in the Greek, could modify κατειργάσατο: "sin, seizing its opportunity, worked all kinds of coveting in me through the commandment" (e.g., S-H; Murray; Cranfield; Dunn). The phrase διὰ αὐτῆς in the parallel v. 11 could favor this reading since it repeats ἀφορμή and modifies the main verb. But the word ἀφορμή cries out for a modifier, and it is better (with almost all English translations) to attach διὰ τῆς ἐντολῆς to this word (cf., e.g., Wilckens; Kümmel, *Römer 7,* p. 44).

41. Paul uses the verb κατεργάζομαι, a compound form of ἐργάζομαι. The preposition often gives the verb an emphatic flavor: "produce," "accomplish" (see, further, on 7:15).

"sin," nor the originator of sin, but the occasion or operating base that sin has used to accomplish its evil and deadly purpose. Paul again personifies sin, picturing it as a "power" that works actively and purposefully (cf. Gen. 4:7). Paul uses "commandment" instead of "law" (*nomos;* cf. v. 7) because he is referring to the single commandment he cited in v. 7,[42] but the commandment represents the Mosaic law as a whole.[43] Paradoxically, what sin produces by taking advantage of the commandment is just what the commandment prohibited: "all kinds of coveting."[44]

But how is it that the law can give sin the occasion to stir up all these desires? To some extent, the old adage about "forbidden fruits" can explain what Paul means: people, told not to do something, immediately conclude that there must be something "fun" about it and are motivated all the more, or even perhaps for the first time, to do it.[45] Ancient moralists noted this phenomenon, and we are all familiar with it; witness the result of a parent telling her child, "Now do not go outside and jump in that mud puddle!"

Paul, however, probably applies this conception in a more distinctly theological way: Israel, confronted in God's law with limitations imposed by its rightful sovereign, was stimulated by that very limitation to rebellion.[46] It was only after the Israelites had heard the commandment not to make any idols for themselves (Exod. 20:4) that they had Aaron fashion a golden calf for them to worship (Exod. 32). In just this way the law, abused by the sinful tendency already resident in every person, has been instrumental in stimulating all kinds of sinful tendencies.

The last sentence of the verse initiates a sequence of clauses (vv. 8b-10a) in which Paul explains[47] the way in which the law has become the "occasion" for the activity of sin. Paul constructs this sequence in a chiastic

---

42. Paul does not use the singular νόμος to refer to individual laws.

43. See also the shift from νόμος to ἐντολή in v. 9; Kümmel, *Römer 7*, p. 56.

44. Gk. πᾶσαν ἐπιθυμίαν. As in v. 7, ἐπιθυμία means sinful "desire," "covetousness" (RSV) — "lust" not being a good translation because we tend to confine the word to sexual desire. The lack of any object after ἐπιθυμία — as with ἐπιθυμέω in v. 7 — shows that Paul's focus is on the sinful propensity to "covet" per se; and the addition of the word πᾶσαν lends a qualitative nuance: "every manner of coveting." Whatever human beings might see and want selfishly for themselves is included: prominence, wealth, power, possessions. Perhaps, indeed, we should include in this list that illicit desire which is at the root of all others — the desire to "be like God," to usurp the place of the Creator.

45. E.g., Godet.

46. See, e.g., Barrett; Cranfield.

47. Cf. the γάρ, "for."

pattern, in which he portrays "dead" sin coming to "life" at the same moment as the "living" "I" "dies":

"Apart from the Law"	"When the Commandment came"
"sin is *dead*" (v. 8c)	"sin sprang to *life* again" (v. 9b)
"I was *alive*" (v. 9a)	"I *died*" (v. 10a)

I have argued above that this sequence portrays the effect of the coming of the Mosaic law for the people of Israel and that *egō* ("I"), while referring to Paul, refers to him in solidarity with the Jewish people and therefore with the experience of the coming of the law at Sinai. While what is narrated in vv. 7-8a may, therefore, have been experienced by Paul personally, what is narrated in these clauses was experienced by him only through his involvement with the history of his people.

Accordingly, "apart from the law" will not mean "before I became aware of the true meaning, or real force, of the law" (as in the autobiographical view) or "before the law was given to Adam in the Garden" (an interval of time for which the Genesis account does not, in any case, appear to allow[48]), but, as in 5:13, "before the Mosaic law existed." In the years before Sinai, Paul asserts, sin was "dead" to Israel. That sin was "dead" does not mean that it did not exist but that it was not as "active" or "powerful" before the law as after.[49]

9 In this time, "apart from the law," the *egō* was "living." Only if *egō* designates Adam can this verb be given full theological meaning — "spiritual" life — but we have seen that the identification of *egō* with Adam is unlikely. Therefore "was living" must be given a milder meaning: either a relative theological sense — compared to the seriousness of "my" situation after the law, I was "living" before it[50] — or a purely prosaic meaning — "I was existing." The former interpretation has in its favor the fact that "I was living" stands in contrast to "I died," which has clear theological meaning. But the prosaic interpretation is not impossible since Paul rarely uses the verb "live" with any theological force.[51] In either case, this clause will depict the situation of Israel before the giving of the law at Sinai — when sins were not yet "being reckoned" (5:13).

Paul describes the giving of the Mosaic law with the word "commandment" under the influence of the paradigmatic significance of the tenth com-

---

48. Cf., e.g., Gundry, "Moral Frustration," p. 231.

49. For νεκρός meaning "inactive," see Jas. 2:26; and, for the conception, see Rom. 4:15; 5:13-14; and esp. 5:20 and 7:5.

50. E.g., Benoit, "La loi et la croix," p. 487; Schlatter; Cranfield. Contra, e.g., Barrosse, "Death and Sin," pp. 443-44.

51. In Romans, only 1:17; 6:13; 8:13; 10:5[?].

mandment cited in v. 7. "When this commandment came"[52] "sin sprang to life again."[53]

10 Even as sin gained new life, however, *egō* "died." As we have seen earlier, proponents of the autobiographical interpretation generally think that Paul is describing his realization that he stood condemned,[54] although a few think he refers to the situation of helplessness under the power of sin that ensued with "the coming of the commandment."[55] "I was living" in v. 9 is interpreted accordingly, as meaning a living without an awareness of the seriousness of sin and its consequences. This interpretation is possible, but there is nothing in the context to suggest it. Throughout Rom. 7, "die" and "death" refer to an objective reality, never to a subjective realization (cf. vv. 2, 3, 4, 5, 10, 11, 13, 24). And this verse is directly related to vv. 5 and 13, making it difficult to think that the "death" mentioned there is any different from the one described here. Accordingly, "I died" will describe that situation according to which the law, by turning "sin" into "transgression," confirms, personalizes, and radicalizes the spiritual death in which all find themselves since Adam. Israel, in this sense, "died" when the law was given to it.

In saying this, Paul undoubtedly has in mind the tendency among some Jews to accord to the Mosaic law life-giving power.[56] What Paul says in these verses confronts such notions head-on: the law has not restrained but stimulated "evil desire" (vv. 7-8a); the law has not led to life but to "death" (vv. 8b-10a). Direct allusion to Adam is, as I have argued, unlikely; but the parallels between Adam and Israel in Jewish literature,[57] as well as 5:13-14, would

52. The genitive absolute construction, ἐλθούσης τῆς ἐντολῆς, probably has a temporal force.

53. The Greek verb is ἀναζάω. The prefix ἀνα may have lost its true force, in which case we could translate simply "sin sprang to life" (Käsemann; Cranfield). But the only other occurrence of this verb in the NT (Luke 15:24) preserves the "again" nuance of the preposition, and this is probably the case here also. After lying relatively "dormant" since working through the Paradise commandment, sin "sprang back to renewed vigor" with the coming of the Mosaic commandment (cf. Lambrecht, "Romans 7," p. 24; Wright, "Messiah and People of God," p. 151).

54. E.g., Calvin; Gifford; S-H.

55. Dodd; Lloyd-Jones; Gundry, "Moral Frustration," pp. 232-33.

56. In one tradition, e.g., the giving of the law was said to have provided Israel with the chance to choose life; when they turned from the law, in the incident of the golden calf, they lost that opportunity for life. Another tradition has it that Israel's "lust," though not the Gentiles', was taken away at Sinai; cf., e.g., *b. Qidd.* 30b: "Even so did the Holy One, blessed be he, speak unto Israel: 'My children, I created the evil desire but I [also] created the torah as its antidote; if you occupy yourselves with the torah, you will not be delivered into its hand.'" See, e.g., E. E. Urbach, *The Sages: Their Concepts and Beliefs* (2 vols.; Jerusalem: Magnes, 1979), 2.425-28; Str-B, 3.237; Moore, *Judaism*, 1.491.

57. See the notes on 5:12.

suggest that the experience of Israel with the law depicted here is parallel to and, to some extent, recapitulates the experience of Adam with the commandment of God in the Garden.

It is in light of the traditions quoted above that we are to understand Paul's qualifying the "commandment" with "unto life."[58] Again, this is often applied, by advocates of the Adamic interpetation, to the Paradise commandment[59] or to that commandment as representative of God's law generally.[60] But we will have to understand "commandment" again here to be referring to the Mosaic law. And it is likely that this description of the law reflects the purpose that it was considered to have among many of his Jewish contemporaries.[61] But the notion that the law has life-giving potential is asserted in the OT itself. While God never intended the law to be a means of salvation, the law did come with promises of life for obedience (cf. Lev. 18:5 [?] [cf. Rom. 10:5]; Ps. 19:7-10; Ezek. 20:11; Luke 20:28). From these verses, it seems fair to conclude that the law would have given life *had it been perfectly obeyed.* In this sense the law "promises life," even though God did not give it with this intention — for he, of course, knew that the power of sin made it impossible for any human being to fulfill the law and so attain the promised life.[62] Thus, although the commandment was "unto life," this same commandment[63] "proved to be"[64] a cause of death for Israel.

11 Paul now returns to the language of v. 8a. Again he claims that sin has used the commandment as a bridgehead[65] and through that bridgehead has brought evil to the *egō.* In v. 8, however, Paul spoke of the law as instrumental in creating sinful impulses; here he shows it to have been used

---

58. Gk. εἰς ζωήν, where εἰς has a telic force: "the commandment intended to bring life."

59. Cf., e.g., O. Hofius, "Das Gesetz des Mose und das Gesetz Christi," *ZTK* 80 (1983), 270.

60. E.g., Stuhlmacher, "Paul's Understanding of the Law," pp. 98-99.

61. Cf., e.g., *t. Shabb.* 15.17: "The commands were given only that men should live through them, not that men should die through them"; Sir. 17:11: "He bestowed knowledge upon them, and allotted to them the law of life [νόμον ζωῆς]"; *m. 'Abot* 6:7; *Pss. Sol.* 14:2; Bar. 3:9; and the discussion in Urbach, *The Sages,* 1.424-26, and Schoeps, 175.

62. Lloyd-Jones; Morris; and esp. Westerholm, 144-50; D. J. Moo, "The Law of Christ as the Fulfillment of the Law of Moses: A Modified Lutheran View," in *The Law, the Gospel, and the Modern Christian: Five Views* (ed. W. Strickland; Grand Rapids: Zondervan, 1993), pp. 324-27.

63. Paul repeats reference to the commandment with the demonstrative pronoun αὕτη, "this," thereby accentuating the paradox that "this" law, the law "intended for life," has instead brought death (cf. Dunn).

64. Gk. εὑρέθη; cf. BAGD on this meaning.

65. As in v. 8, we take διὰ τῆς ἐντολῆς with ἀφορμὴν λαβοῦσα.

to "deceive" and "kill." Many scholars pounce on Paul's use of the verb "deceive" here as the clearest objective indication that he is thinking of the experience of Adam in the Garden.[66] They think that Paul is putting sin in the role of the serpent, which springs to life to use the commandment as a means of deceiving the first human pair and bringing upon them spiritual disaster. These interpreters may be right to see allusion to the paratypical "temptation" experience; but the reference is not at all clear.[67] In keeping with Paul's intention throughout this passage, the direct reference must certainly be to the law's function within Israel. Probably Paul thinks of the way that the "promise of life" held out by the law "deceived" Israel into thinking that it could attain life through it.[68] But the attempts of Israel to find life through the law brought only death — not because obeying the law itself is sinful, or worthy of death, but because the law could not be fulfilled. This is the burden of vv. 14-25: that the Jews found themselves under the "law of sin" because, while honoring the law, they could not practice it. So sin, through the law, "killed" Israel. But although this happened in accordance with the intention of God (cf. 5:20 and Gal. 3:19-26), the ultimate intention this served was positive: that, being "bound under sin," Israel might learn to look to God and his promise of a Messiah for life and salvation.

12 Having shown that the law is the innocent "cats paw" of sin, Paul can now return and complete the point with which he began the paragraph. "Is the law sin? Of course not! [v. 7a]. . . . The law is holy, and the commandment is holy and just and good." Paul introduces this verse[69] as the inference to be drawn from the true role of the law in the history that he has sketched in vv. 7b-11. Paul brings together as essentially parallel terms "law" and "commandment"; both refer to the Mosaic law, the former as a body, the latter in terms of the specific commandment that Paul has cited in v. 7 as representative of the whole.[70] In calling the law "holy," Paul is not describing its demand for holiness[71] but its origin — it was given by the one who is in

---

66. Paul uses the verb ἐξαπατέω in 2 Cor. 11:13 and 1 Tim. 2:14 to describe Eve's "deception" (LXX Exod. 3:15 uses the simplex, ἀπατέω).

67. Paul uses the verb ἐξαπατέω three other times (Rom. 16:18; 1 Cor. 3:18; 2 Thess. 2:3) without any allusion to the Garden of Eden narrative, and it is, of course, Eve, not Adam, who is deceived according to Genesis (a point Paul makes in 1 Tim. 2:14).

68. Bornkamm, "Sin, Law and Death," pp. 91-92; Bultmann, 1.248.

69. See the ὥστε, "so then." Paul also uses the particle μέν ("on the one hand"), which would normally require a balancing δέ ("on the other hand") clause. Paul never supplies such a clause, perhaps hinting at an implicit contrast with sin: "the law, in contrast to sin (vv. 7b-11) . . ." (Cranfield; Dunn).

70. Cf. Calvin; contra, e.g., Theodoret, who thinks νόμος refers to the Mosaic law and ἐντολή to the Paradise commandment.

71. Godet.

his nature "holy." Again, the description "just" may allude to the function of the law, in that it prescribes "just" conduct, or perhaps to the nature of the law, as demanding no more than what is "right." But the context encourages us to view "just" in accordance with the legal connotation this word group often has in Paul: the law, being holy, "cannot be charged with anything wrong."[72] "Good," finally, also denotes the nature of the law, attributing to it that "goodness" which is characteristic, ultimately, of God alone (cf. Mark 10:18).

Although it is the experience of Israel with the Mosaic law that Paul describes in vv. 7-12, their experience, as we have seen, is symptomatic of that of all people who, in various ways, are confronted with God's "law." Thus the failure and "death" of Israel should serve to remind all of us that salvation can never be earned by doing the "law," but only by casting ourselves on the grace and mercy of God in Christ. Augustine says, "God commands what we cannot do that we may know what we ought to seek from him."[73] And Calvin: "In the precepts of the law, God is but the rewarder of perfect righteousness, which all of us lack, and conversely, the severe judge of evil deeds. But in Christ his face shines, full of grace and gentleness, even upon us poor and unworthy sinners."[74] The experience of Israel with the law should also remind Christians never to return to the law — whether the Mosaic or any other list of "rules" — as a source of spiritual vigor and growth.

b. Life under the Law (7:13-25)

13*Therefore, did the good become death in me? By no means! But sin, in order that it might be manifest as sin, through the good produced death in me, in order that sin might become exceedingly sinful through the commandment.*

14*For we know*[1] *that the law is spiritual; but I am fleshly, sold under sin.* 15*For what I am producing I do not know. For it is not what I will, this I am practicing, but what I am hating, this I am doing.* 16*Now, if*

---

72. Calvin.

73. *On Grace and Free Will* 16.32.

74. *Institutes* 2.7.8.

1. My translation assumes the reading of the first person plural οἴδαμεν, apparently found in the vast majority of MSS (some doubt exists because of the lack of consistent spacing and accentuation in most early MSS). But a few MSS, among them the secondary Alexandrian minuscule 33, read οἶδα μεν, "on the one hand, I know." While the first singular reading would bring this verb into conformity with the others in vv. 14-25 and is therefore preferred by some (e.g., Zahn; Wilckens), it is suspect, as the "easier" reading, for that same reason.

I am doing what I do not will, I agree with the law, that it is good.
17But now it is no longer I who am producing it but sin dwelling in
me. 18For I know that the good does not dwell in me, that is, in my
flesh. For the willing of the good is present with me, but the producing
of the good is not.2 19For I am not doing the good I will, but the evil
I am not willing I am practicing. 20But if what I3 am not willing, this
I am doing, it is no longer I producing it, but sin dwelling in me.

21Therefore, I find this law: when I will to do the good, evil is present
there with me. 22For I rejoice in the law of God4 according to the inner
person, 23but I see another law in my members, fighting against the
law of my mind and holding me captive in the law of sin that is in my
members. 24Wretched person that I am! Who will deliver me from the
body of this death? 25Thanks be to God5 through Jesus Christ our
Lord. Now, then, I in my mind am serving the law of God, but in my
flesh the law of sin.

As we approach this controversial paragraph, we must keep in mind that Paul's
focus is still on the Mosaic law. And what Paul says about the Mosaic law
comes to much the same thing, whatever we decide about the identity and
spiritual condition of the person whose situation is depicted in these verses.

2. In the text read by NA[27] and UBS[4], v. 18b has only one finite verb, παράκειται
(this reading has the support of almost all of the Alexandrian family [א, A, B, C, 81, 1739]).
But the western text (D, F, G) and the majority text (along with the Alexandrian 33 and
the uncial Ψ) read, in place of οὖ alone at the end of the verse, οὐχ εὑρίσκω, "I do not
find," making this the verb that governs τὸ δὲ κατεργάζεσθαι τὸ καλόν. But this reading
is suspect as an assimilation to v. 21, since scribes may well have considered the ending
of v. 18b in the accepted text as abrupt and awkward (Lietzmann). Note also that a few
MSS "correct" the text by adding the verb γινώσκω.

3. Some MSS include ἐγώ and others omit it, but it makes no difference for the
meaning.

4. The primary Alexandrian uncial B has νοός ("of my mind") in place of θεοῦ.

5. There are four variants to χάρις δὲ τῷ θεῷ ("but thanks be to God"):

1. χάρις τῷ θεῷ ("thanks be to God") — the primary Alexandrian uncial B;
2. ἡ χάρις τοῦ θεοῦ ("the grace of God") — the western uncial D;
3. ἡ χάρις τοῦ κυρίου ("the grace of the Lord") — the secondary western uncials
   F and G;
4. εὐχαριστῶ τῷ θεῷ ("I am giving thanks to God") — the primary Alexandrian
   א (original hand) and A, the secondary Alexandrian 1739, and the majority
   text; hence the KJV, "I thank God."

Lietzmann makes a strong case for the first variant, arguing that all the others can
be explained as corrections or scribal errors for the accepted reading. Two and three are
syntactically easier, while four may have arisen from mistaken duplication of τω
(ΧΑΡΙΣΤΩΤΩΘΕΩ), to which the prefix ευ- was added to make sense of it.

The law, Paul insists again, is *God's* law (cf. vv. 22, 25), "spiritual" (v. 14a), "good" (v. 16). Yet, because "I" am unable to do what the good law requires (vv. 15-20, 21), "I" find myself to be a "prisoner" of sin (v. 23), a situation from which only God in Christ can deliver me (v. 24; cf. 8:1-4). In these verses Paul shows again that the Mosaic law is impotent to rescue people from their sin. For the law informs us of our duties before God, but it does not give us the ability to fulfill those duties. As good as God's law is, it encounters people when they are already "fleshly" (v. 14b), indwelt by sin (vv. 17, 20). From this situation the law does not, and cannot, rescue us; on the contrary, it reveals the depth of the division in our beings, between willing and doing, the "mind" and the "flesh" (vv. 15-20, 25). Paul's essential teaching about the inability of the Mosaic law to rescue sinful people from spiritual bondage is the same whether that bondage is the condition of the unregenerate person — who cannot be saved through the law — or that of the regenerate person — who cannot be sanctified and ultimately delivered from the influence of sin through the law. I emphasize this point both in order to get started in my exegesis with the right perspective and in order to relieve undecided exegetes of some degree of strain. One can preach this paragraph, in its *basic* intention, without even making a definite identification of the *egō*.

Few of us, however, would be satisfied to leave this question unanswered — and even fewer congregations will be satisfied with sermons that fail to deal with the matter! And rightly so. For, while not substantially affecting the main point of the text, our identification of the person whose struggle Paul depicts in this text does have an impact on several theological and practical issues. One of the most important of these is the nature of the Christian life. Should we expect Christian existence to be characterized by the sort of severe struggle described here? Or is this struggle one from which we believers have been rescued by Christ (chap. 8)? Can a Christian suffer the experience described here if he or she fails to live by the Spirit? It is partly because expositors of Rom. 7 exegete this text with an eye on these larger issues that they have divided so sharply over its interpretation. And it may be generally said that the interpretation of few passages has been more influenced by one's broad theological perspective, experience, and sheer a priori assumptions than Rom. 7:14-25.[6]

Most of the early church fathers thought that these verses described an unregenerate person.[7] This was Augustine's early view, but, partly as a

---

6. Cf. T. de Krujf, "The Perspective of Romans 7," in *Miscellanea Neotestamentica* (ed. T. Baarda, A. J. F. Klijn, and W. C. van Unnik; NovTSup 48; Leiden: Brill, 1978), p. 127.

7. See the surveys of the Fathers in Schelkle, 242-48. Kuss (2.462-85) has a thorough survey of the entire history of interpretation.

result of his battle with Pelagius over (among other things) the freedom of the will, he changed his opinion and decided that the person depicted in these verses was a Christian.[8] This interpretation was adopted by almost all the Reformers.[9] None gave it more theological significance than Luther, who saw in these verses the classic statement of his view of the believer as "at the same time a justified person and a sinner" *(simul iustus et peccator)*. Justification, being an entirely forensic declaration of the believer's status "before God" *(coram Deo)*, does not remove from the believer the presence and influence of sin. Thus, even the child of God, as long as he is in the earthly body, will struggle with sin and fail to do God's will. The interpretation of vv. 14-25 in terms of "normal" Christian experience was typical of Lutheran and Reformed theology right into the twentieth century and is still widespread.

A different approach was taken by those theologians, usually called "pietists," who at the end of the seventeenth century reacted against what they perceived as "dead orthodoxy" in the churches of the Reformation. Thinking perhaps that the "normal" Christian view of this paragraph opened the door too widely to a complacent Christian lifestyle, men like A. H. Francke and J. Bengel ascribed the experience depicted in this paragraph to one who is only "halfway" to true Christian experience — under conviction but not yet "reborn."[10] Similar concerns led Wesley to conclude that vv. 14-25 depict the experience of the unregenerate.[11] The nineteenth century saw a bewildering welter of viewpoints, while scholarly study in the twentieth century has been dominated by the 1929 monograph of W. G. Kümmel. He sought to demonstrate that *egō* in Rom. 7 is a rhetorical figure of speech and need not have any autobiographical reference. Paul is not, therefore, rehearsing his own experience in this chapter, and vv. 14-25 describe an unregenerate person, under the law, from a Christian persective. This interpretation, endorsed and embellished by Bultmann, was for years almost the "orthodox" view in scholarship. On the other hand, Christians in general have shown far less inclination toward this viewpoint. Indeed, the last thirty years have witnessed considerable criticism of the interpretation inaugurated by Kümmel among

8. See especially his *Retractions* 1.23.1 and 2.1.1 (ET in *The Fathers of the Church*, vol. 60 [Washington: Catholic University of America, 1968], pp. 101-4); *Against Two Letters of the Pelagians* 1.10-11 (cf. *NPNF* 5.383-85).

9. Cf., e.g., Luther, 327 (and cf. H. Deuser, "Glaubenserfahrung und Anthropologie. Röm 7,14-25 und Luthers These: totum genus humanum carnem esse," *EvT* 39 [1979], 409-31); Calvin, 264-75; Melanchthon, 160-62. Kümmel (*Römer 7*, p. 88) notes only Bucer and Musculus as dissenters from this interpretation among the early Reformers.

10. Francke, e.g., identified the individual as one who is baptized but not reborn (cf. Wilckens, 2.110-11), Bengel as one in the transition from the state of law to the state of grace (pp. 91-92).

11. Wesley, 543-44.

scholars as well. Many are insisting that autobiographical elements cannot be eliminated from Rom. 7, and the interpretation of *egō* in vv. 14-25 in terms of "normal" Christian experience is enjoying a resurgence.

The diversity in interpretation that we have just sketched is due not only to differing theological agendas and concerns; the exegetical data do not all point in one direction. Much will depend on the particular perspective from which one approaches the passage and which arguments are given greater weight. Interpreting Rom. 7 is like fitting pieces of a puzzle together when one is not sure of the final outline; the best interpretation is the one that is able to fit the most pieces together in the most natural way. Because of this, it is inconclusive, and even misleading, to cite several arguments in favor of one's own view and conclude that the issue has been settled. The best interpretation will be the one that is able to do most justice to all the data of the text within the immediate and larger Pauline context. In order to keep my discussion here within reasonable bounds, I will mention at this point the major viewpoints, the key arguments for each viewpoint, and my own brief evaluation and conclusion. I will leave to the verse-by-verse notes thorough evaluation of the arguments given here as well as discussion of additional arguments.

The most important reasons for thinking the experience depicted in vv. 14-25 is that of an *unregenerate* person are the following:

1. The strong connection of *egō* with "the flesh" (vv. 14, 18, and 25) suggests that Paul is elaborating on the unregenerate condition mentioned in 7:5: being "in the flesh."
2. *Egō* throughout this passage struggles "on his/her own" (cf. "I myself" in v. 25), without the aid of the Holy Spirit.
3. *Egō* is "under the power of sin" (v. 14b), a state from which every believer is released (6:2, 6, 11, 18-22).
4. As the unsuccessful struggle of vv. 15-20 shows, *egō* is a "prisoner of the law of sin" (v. 23). Yet Rom. 8:2 proclaims that believers have been set free from this same "law of sin (and death)."
5. While Paul makes clear that believers will continue to struggle with sin (cf., e.g., 6:12-13; 13:12-14; Gal. 5:17), what is depicted in 7:14-25 is not just a struggle with sin but a defeat by sin. This is a more negative view of the Christian life than can be accommodated within Paul's theology.
6. The *egō* in these verses struggles with the need to obey the Mosaic law; yet Paul has already proclaimed the release of the believer from the dictates of the law (6:14; 7:4-6).

For those who find these arguments decisive, vv. 14-25 describe the struggle of the person outside Christ to do "what is good," a struggle that is doomed to failure because it is fought without the power of God that alone is able to break the power of sin. Deliverance from this situation comes with the converting, regenerating work of God in Christ, who transfers the believer from the realm of "sin and death" to the realm of "the Spirit of life" (v. 24b; 8:2). Within this general "unregenerate" interpretation are various subdivisions. Some think that the text portrays Paul's own experience under the law.[12] Others think that Paul is describing Jews under the law generally, or even all people confronted with "the law of God."[13] There is further disagreement over the extent to which the description reflects the conscious experience of those "under the law" and the extent to which Paul portrays the pre-Christian past from a Christian perspective.

The most important reasons for thinking that the experience depicted in 7:14-25 must be that of a *regenerate* person are the following:

1. *Egō* must refer to Paul himelf, and the shift from the past tenses of vv. 7-13 to the present tenses of vv. 14-25 can be explained only if Paul is describing in these latter verses his present experience as a Christian.
2. Only the regenerate truly "delight in God's law" (v. 22), seek to obey it (vv. 15-20), and "serve" it (v. 25); the unregenerate do not "seek after God" (3:11) and cannot "submit to the law of God" (8:7).
3. Whereas the "mind" of people outside of Christ is universally presented by Paul as opposed to God and his will (cf. Rom. 1:28; Eph. 4:17; Col. 2:18; 1 Tim. 6:5; 2 Tim. 3:8; Tit. 2:15), the "mind" of *egō* in this text is a positive medium, by which *egō* "serves the law of God" (vv. 22, 25).
4. *Egō* must be a Christian because only a Christian possesses the "inner person";[14] cf. Paul's only other two uses of the phrase in 2 Cor. 4:16; Eph. 3:16.
5. The passage concludes, *after* Paul's mention of the deliverance wrought by God in Christ, with a reiteration of the divided state of the *egō* (vv. 24-25). This shows that the division and struggle of the *egō* that Paul

12. E.g., Chrysostom, Homily 13; Godet 292-93; Gundry, "Moral Frustration," pp. 228-45.

13. Among the many defenses of this view, some of the best are Kümmel, *Römer 7;* Bornkamm, "Sin, Law and Death," pp. 87-104; E. Fuchs, "Existentiale Interpretation von Römer 7,7-12 und 21-23," *ZTK* 59 (1962), 285-314; K. Kertelge, "Exegetische Überlegungen zum Verständnis der paulinischen Anthropologie nach Römer 7," *ZNW* 62 (1971), 105-14; Lambrecht, "Romans 7," pp. 18-33; B. L. Martin, "Some Reflections on the Identity of *ego* in Rom. 7:14-25," *SJT* 34 (1979), 39-47; Käsemann, 199-212; Kuss, 2.457-58.

14. Gk. ὁ ἔσω ἄνθρωπος.

depicts in these verses is that of the person already saved by God in Christ.

If these arguments are found to be decisive, then vv. 14-25 will describe an important aspect of "normal" Christian experience: the continuing battle with sin that will never be won as long as the believer, through his or her body, is related to this age. The new age may have dawned, but the believer, until death or the parousia, remains tied to the old age and its powers of sin, the flesh, and the law. Deliverance will come only when God intervenes to transform the "body of death" (vv. 24b-25a; 8:10-11) into the body conformed to the glorious body of Christ (Phil. 3:20-21).[15]

Considering the apparently strong arguments that can be mustered for each of these views, it is not surprising that a variety of compromise viewpoints has been proposed. As we noted, some of the pietists saw in this passage the cry of a person under conviction of sin but not yet regenerate, and this view continues to be held.[16] It has the advantage of being able to explain how the *egō* can will the good and be concerned with God's law at the same time as that willing results in utter defeat. Another compromise view, better represented in popular than in scholarly literature, is that the *egō* in vv. 14-25, while regenerate, is a new, or immature, believer seeking to live the Christian life in his or her own power. Such a Christian, it is said, must "leave Romans 7 and get into Romans 8." Various other compromise interpretations are found. One of the more attractive of these holds that *egō* in vv. 14-25 describes "Adam in me," the sin-prone "nature" that is to be found in any person, Christian or non-Christian.[17]

Our conclusion, already indicated in the exegesis of 7:7-12, is that vv. 14-25 describe the situation of an unregenerate person. Specifically, I think

---

15. Some of the best defenses of this view are: Nygren, 284-97; Cranfield, 1.344-47; Dunn, 1.387-89, 403-12; idem, "Rom. 7,14-25," pp. 257-73; Murray, 1.256-59; Morris, 284-88; Barrett, 151-53; Campbell, "Identity of ἐγώ," pp. 57-64; J. I. Packer, "The 'Wretched Man' in Romans 7," *Studia Evangelica,* 2.621-27.

16. A thorough presentation is given by Lloyd-Jones, 229-57; cf. also Bandstra, *The Law and the Elements of the World,* pp. 134-49; D. M. Davies, "Free from the Law: An Exposition of the Seventh Chapter of Romans," *Int* 7 (1953), 156-62; Davies, 23-26.

17. Although with differences, see Longenecker, 109-16; C. L. Mitton, "Romans VII Reconsidered," *ExpTim* 65 (1953), 78-81, 99-102, 132-35; D. Wenham, "The Christian Life: A Life of Tension? A Consideration of the Nature of Christian Experience in Paul," in *Pauline Studies,* pp. 80-94; R. Y.-K. Fung, "The Impotence of the Law: Toward a Fresh Understanding of Romans 7:14-25," in *Scripture, Tradition and Interpretation* (ed. W. W. Gasque and W. S. LaSor; Grand Rapids: Eerdmans, 1978), pp. 34-48; Bruce, *Paul,* p. 198. Probably to be placed here also is Seifrid's Luther-like exposition of the section in terms of the sinful propensity within the believer (*Justification,* pp. 228-44; idem, "The Subject of Rom 7:14-25," *NovT* 34 [1992], 313-33).

that Paul is looking back, from his Christian understanding, to the situation of himself, and other Jews like him, living under the law of Moses. Of course, Paul is not giving us a full picture of that situation; he is concentrating on the negatives because this is what he must do to prove how useless the law was to deliver Jews from their bondage to sin. We might say, then, that Rom. 7:14-25 describes from a personal viewpoint the stage in salvation history that Paul delineates objectively in Gal. 3:19–4:3.

As I have argued above, Paul in Rom. 7 uses *egō* to represent himself, but himself in solidarity with the Jewish people. Because of this solidarity, Paul can put himself in the shoes of those who received the law at Sinai (vv. 8b-10a). Now, in vv. 14-25, he portrays his own condition as a Jew under the law, but, more importantly, the condition of all Jews under the law. Paul speaks as a "representative" Jew, detailing his past in order to reveal the weakness of the law and the source of that weakness: the human being, the *egō*. The more personal and emotional flavor of vv. 14-25 in comparison with vv. 7-13 is due to the fact that Paul was not, of course, personally present at Sinai when the law was given — but he has personally experienced the struggle and defeat that he describes in vv. 14-25.

The plausiblity of this interpretation can be gauged only when we have finished the exegesis of this paragraph and seen how all the pieces of the puzzle fit together. But — without implying that this has settled the matter — I should mention here the factors that have tipped the scales in favor of this particular view.

Decisive for me are two sets of contrasts. The first is between the description of the *egō* as "sold under sin" (v. 14b) and Paul's assertion that the believer — *every* believer — has been "set free from sin" (6:18, 22). The second contrast is that between the state of the *egō*, "imprisoned by the law [or power] of sin" (v. 23), and the believer, who has been "set free from the law of sin and death" (8:2). Each of these expressions depicts an objective status, and it is difficult to see how they can all be applied to the same person in the same spiritual condition without doing violence to Paul's language. In chaps. 6 and 8, respectively, Paul makes it clear that "being free from under sin" and "being free from the law of sin and death" are conditions that are true for every Christian. If one is a Christian, then these things are true; if one is not, then they are not true. This means that the situation depicted in vv. 14-25 cannot be that of the "normal" Christian, nor of an immature Christian. Nor can it describe the condition of *any* person living by the law because the Christian who is mistakenly living according to the law is yet a Christian and is therefore *not* "under sin" or a "prisoner of the law of sin." Other points are significant also — the lack of mention of the Spirit, the links with 7:5 and 6:14, and the connections between vv. 7-12 and 13-25 — but I think these arguments are the most important. I do not deny that advocates of other views can marshal good arguments of their own. But when all the data have been weighed, I think that the balance tilts toward the interpretation of the *egō* in these verses as unregenerate.

This conclusion does not mean that Christians do not struggle with sin. Paul makes it abundantly clear, both explicitly — for instance, Gal. 6:1 — and implicitly — by the amount of time he spends scolding Christians in his letters! — that believers are not delivered from the influence of sin. While "transferred" into the new realm, ruled by Christ and righteousness, believers are still prone to obey those past masters, sin and the flesh. I do not, then, deny that Christians struggle with sin — I deny only that this passage describes that struggle. For, while the believer continues to be influenced by both "realms," Paul makes it clear that he *belongs* to the new realm. In identification with Christ, he has *died* to sin (6:2), been taken out of the enveloping power of the flesh (8:9), been made a slave of God (6:22). Either these assertions or the force of what Paul says about the *egō* in vv. 14-25 must be watered down to make them "fit" together. Dunn, for instance, takes the first alternative when he claims that vv. 14-25 depict the regenerate person "in his belongingness to the epoch of Adam";[18] Cranfield, the second, arguing that vv. 14 and 23 describe the believer's "continuing sinfulness."[19]

Some expositors become more specific in their identification and think that Paul is describing an unregenerate Jew who is under conviction of sin. But it is unlikely that we can be so specific. For vv. 13-25 explain the situation that resulted from the event depicted in vv. 7-12; and this means that, as vv. 7-12 describe the impact of the giving of the law on Israel generally, so vv. 14-25 must describe the situation of the people of Israel generally under that law. These conditions are true for all Jews under the law, not just for those who are under conviction of sin. At the other extreme, I question whether the text can be applied directly to all unregenerate people, under "the law" in one form or another. True, vv. 14-25 speak to the situation of all non-Christians in the sense that the situation of Israel under the law is paradigmatic for the situation of all people confronted with divine law (see the introduction to 7:7-25), and this gives warrant for the Christian expositor to apply this text to non-Christians generally. But, as the salvation-historical sequence in vv. 7-12 makes clear, Paul's focus throughout this text is on the situation of the

18. 1.388. Dunn argues that the strong claims of the believer's "freedom" from sin, the law, and the flesh that begin chaps. 6, 7, and 8 are "qualified" with more "ambivalent" statements later in the same chapters (1.302-3, passim). But I question whether the imperatives that come at the end of these chapters "qualify" the indicatives at the beginning: present another side, yes; but "qualify"? Dunn's view appears to take too much from the decisive salvation-historical shift that takes place when a person believes in Christ.

19. 1.358.

Jewish people under the Mosaic law. And this helps to explain how Paul can be so positive about *egō*'s regard for the law — Jews did, indeed, "rejoice in God's law," and Paul never suggests that this was anything but a genuine and proper regard for the law.[20] Paul faults Jews not for having insufficient regard for the law, but for misunderstanding its ultimate intention (Rom. 10:1-4) and failing to obey it (Rom. 2:17-29).

More difficult is to decide exactly what perspective Paul is taking in describing this condition of the Jew under the law, and especially in his graphic depiction of the conflict in the *egō*'s willing and doing. Many deny that *egō* here is autobiographical because Paul gives no hint elsewhere of this kind of struggle before his conversion. Some, indeed, go so far as to view the struggle described in vv. 15-20 as a "trans-subjective" existential conflict between the *egō*'s desire for "life" and the resulting failure to attain it. On this view, the struggle is not a conscious one at all (see, further, the notes on v. 15). But we have seen reason to think that Paul's *egō* in this passage must include himself, and this paragraph adds further reasons for that conclusion. Paul's emotional cry in v. 24 — "wretched person that I am!" — certainly implies that he identifies with the situation he has been describing, and it would be straining credulity to think that he would not himself have experienced the situation that he is attributing to Jews generally under the law.[21]

What, then, of the apparent conflict between the despairing struggle in this paragraph and the complacent self-satisfaction of Phil. 3:2-11? In Phil. 3, Paul is describing his *status* from a Jewish perspective; in Rom. 7, his *experience* from a Christian perspective. With respect to the Pharisaic definition of righteousness, "the righteousness of the law," Paul says in Phil. 3, I was "blameless." But this status of righteousness by Jewish standards does not rule out some degree of frustration in not fulfilling the divine standard, particularly since in Rom. 7 Paul is to some extent looking back at this failure to meet God's demands from his new, Christian understanding of those demands — much as a new convert will be able to look back at his pre-Christian existence and find there the inner conflict, frustration, and despair that perhaps were not as clear at the time.[22] Particularly in vv. 21-23, Paul is characterizing his pre-Christian situation from his

20. Note Paul's claims about his own pre-Christian attitude in Phil. 3:2-11.

21. Cf. Kim, *Origin of Paul's Gospel,* p. 53; Beker, 240-43; Espy, "Robust Conscience," pp. 102-6; Räisänen, 232-33.

22. Reference in this respect has been made to the parallel with Luther's differing descriptions of his life as a monk. In 1533 he wrote: "I was a good monk, and kept strictly to my order. . . . All my companions who knew me would bear witness to that" (cf. Phil. 3, "blameless with respect to the righteousness of the law"); in 1519 he said, "However irreproachable my life as a monk, I felt myself, in the presence of God, to be a sinner with a most unquiet conscience" (cf. Rom. 7:15-21).

present Christian perspective. While, therefore, there is no evidence that Paul's frustration at failing to fulfill the law was excessive with respect to other Jews, or that this frustration was instrumental in his conversion, there seems to be every reason to believe that he would have sensed, as Peter did, that the law was a "yoke that neither our fathers nor we have been able to bear" (Acts 15:10).

Paul's characterization of the situation of Jews under the law in this paragraph describes, in personal terms, the state that resulted from the event he has narrated in vv. 7-13. This goes some way toward explaining the shift from past to present tense verbs; Paul first narrates past events, then depicts the continuing status of those who were involved in those events.[23] But, in describing this continuing state of affairs, this paragraph also fills in a crucial gap that Paul has left in his argument in vv. 7-12.[24] How was it possible for sin to use the law to bring death to "me"? Is "sin" a power, outside a person, that can arbitrarily bring to pass so disastrous a state of affairs? Not at all, Paul affirms in vv. 14-20, for sin dwells "in me." "I" am ultimately at fault; certainly not the law, not even sin. It is "me" and my "carnality," my helplessness under sin, that enables sin to do what it does. "Sin" has invaded my existence and made me a divided person, willing to do what God wants but failing to do it.

This subjective characterization of the divided situation of the Jew under the law is followed by a more objective characterization in vv. 21-23. Here Paul uses the word *nomos* with great rhetorical skill to depict the opposing forces that control the non-Christian: the *nomos* of God, the Mosaic law, with which "my" mind agrees; and the *nomos* of sin, the power of sin, that controls my body and prevents me from carrying out what my "mind," in agreement with the law of God, wills. The *nomos* of sin wins this battle: "I" am a prisoner of that *nomos*. In personal identification with his own past, as he now views it, Paul decries his wretched, helpless state and cries for deliverance (v. 24). Here Paul can forbear no longer and interjects thanksgiving for the deliverance that has come (v. 25a). Finally, he returns to summarize the divided state of the Jew under the law, serving "two masters" — the *nomos* of God and yet also the *nomos* of sin (v. 25b).

13 Many interpreters attach this verse to vv. 7-12 since it summarizes the three main points that Paul has made in that paragraph: the law is good; sin is made "manifest" through the law; and sin works through the law to produce death.[25] Like v. 7, however, this verse contains a question

---

23. E.g, Wilckens, 2.85.
24. Cf. Räisänen, 142-43.
25. See, e.g., Theissen, *Psychologischer Aspekte,* pp. 188-89; Godet; Käsemann; Fitzmyer.

and a brief answer, which is then explained in vv. 14-25. Therefore, other interpreters take the verse with what follows.[26] These conflicting considerations suggest that v. 13 is a bridge between the two main parts of Paul's discussion, summarizing the teaching of vv. 7-12 as the starting point for vv. 14-25.

The question Paul asks here restates the basic objection of v. 7. How could "that which is good" (= the commandment/law of v. 12) become the source of death? Does not the intimate involvement of the law in securing the death of *egō* reveal again its true nefarious nature? As in v. 7, Paul strongly repudiates any such idea: "By no means!"[27] But hasn't Paul already answered this question? In a sense he has, and the explanation he gives in this verse does not really go beyond what he has already said about the relationship of sin, the law, and death in vv. 7-11. However, Paul's return to the matter suggests that he is not yet fully satisfied with the answer he has given. Accordingly, he moves forward in vv. 14-25 to explain in detail the role of another key player in this drama: *egō*.

"But"[28] introduces Paul's counterassertion and is probably here (contrast v. 7) fully adversative: "this death is not at all the fault of the law; on the contrary, it is sin that is responsible." The syntax of the sentence that follows is convoluted but should probably be resolved along the lines assumed in our translation: "sin, in order that it might be manifest as sin, through the good produced death in me, in order that sin might become exceedingly sinful through the commandment."[29] Continuing his main theme from vv. 7-11, Paul places full responsibility for the death of *egō* on sin, absolving the law from blame by making it an instrument ("through the good")[30] used by sin. The two purpose[31] clauses state the divine and ultimately positive purpose behind sin's destructive use of the law. The first restates the revelatory role of the law that Paul described in v. 7; in bringing death, sin has "been made manifest" for what it really is — "sin." The

26. E.g., Osten-Sacken, *Römer 8,* p. 201; Watson, 155; Morris; Cranfield.

27. Gk. μὴ γένοιτο.

28. Gk. ἀλλά.

29. The main problem is that the sentence lacks a main verb. My translation assumes that we should supply a finite stative verb before the participle κατεργαζομένη ("producing") and make it the main verb of the sentence: "was producing" (e.g., Barrett; Cranfield). Other interpreters, however, carry over the verb γίνομαι ("become") from the question (τὸ ἀγαθὸν ἐμοὶ ἐγένετο θάνατος;): "But sin *became* death to me, in order that it might appear to be sin, by producing [κατεργαζομένη] death in me through the good, in order that sin . . ." (alternatively, κατεργαζομένη could be taken with what follows: ". . . that it might appear to be sin, working death in me through the good in order that sin . . ." [cf. NASB{?}; Godet]).

30. διὰ τοῦ ἀγαθοῦ; compare the διά phrases in vv. 8 and 11.

31. Each is introduced with ἵνα.

second purpose clause elaborates the first. Sin is revealed "as sin" in that the "commandment" causes sin to become "exceedingly sinful."[32] What Paul means, in light of Rom. 4:15, 5:13-14, and 5:20, is that the "good" commandment of God, by strictly defining sin, turns sin into conscious and willful rebellion against God. Sin is always bad; but it becomes worse — even more "sinful" — when it involves deliberate violation of God's good will for his people. The law, by making sin even worse than before, reveals sin in its true colors.

14 Paul now explains[33] how it is that "sin" has been able to "work death in 'me' through that which is good" (v. 13). This could happen, Paul asserts, because, while the law is indeed good and "spiritual," "I" am "fleshly." Verses 15-25 justify and develop this statement about himself, concluding from his tragic inability to put into practice what he knows to be right (vv. 15-21) that he is controlled by an alien and negative force — "the law of sin" (vv. 22-23). It is because of his captivity to the power of sin that the law can become the instrument of death.

Throughout these verses Paul continues to write in the first person singular, as he portrays his own — typical — experience as a Jew under the law. Yet in v. 14a he breaks this pattern with a first person plural, "we know." This serves to draw the readers of the letter into the argument. Paul implies that these readers — who "know the law" (7:1) — would already agree that the law is "spiritual." This militates against Dunn's suggestion that Paul is beginning to assert here the new attitude toward the law possible under the reign of Christ. Clearly, as well, it is not the Roman Christians whom Paul must convince about the divine origin and "goodness" of the law. Rather, it is Paul's own "orthodoxy" on this issue that has been called into question — probably by opponents of Paul who have reached Rome. In calling the law "spiritual," Paul is asserting its divine origin.[34] While the OT abounds in similar assertions of the holy origin and character of the law (cf., e.g., Ps. 19:7-11), it is never called "spiritual." Paul has chosen this word in order to set up the strongest possible contrast between the "spiritual" law and the "fleshly" *egō*.

In calling himself "fleshly," Paul may mean no more than that he is human, subject to the frailty of all human beings, whether Christian or

---

32. Gk. καθ' ὑπερβολὴν ἁμαρτωλός.

33. Hence the γάρ, "for."

34. The Greek word is πνευματικός, which Paul uses in 1 Cor. 10:3, 4 with a similar meaning; note the rabbinic assertion that canonical books are spoken "through the Holy Spirit" [*t. Yad.* 2:14]; cf. Str-B, 3.238; and, for the the interpretation of this clause in the Greek fathers, W. Keuck, "Das 'geistliche Gesetz.' Röm 7,14a in der Auslegung der griechischen Väter," in *Wort Gottes in der Zeit (Festschrift für K. H. Schelkle)* (ed. H. Feld and J. Nolte; Düsseldorf: Patmos, 1973), pp. 215-35.

not.[35] But the contrast with "spiritual" points to a more negative meaning. As in 1 Cor. 3:1-3, where "fleshly" is contrasted with "spiritual," "fleshly" means "carnal," subject to, and under the influence of, "this world."[36] Since "fleshly" in 1 Cor. 3:1 is applied to Christians, it is clear that this adjective itself does not require that the *ego* be unregenerate. Nevertheless, we cannot overlook the fact that v. 5, which anticipates the argument of 7:7-25, describes the non-Christian state as being "in the flesh."

But it is the additional description, "sold under sin," that clinches the argument for a description of a non-Christian here. Cranfield is representative of those who argue that this language can appropriately be applied to the Christian, inasmuch as the Christian continues to be sinful, and can therefore be said to be "under the power of sin."[37] However, while it is true that Christians are still very much influenced by sin, and will, perhaps, never finally overcome sin's influence in this life, Paul appears to say more than that here. His language points to a condition of slavery under sin's power.[38] And I question whether Rom. 6 allows us to say that the Christian is "under the power of sin" in this sense. In fact, Paul is saying just the reverse in that chapter; Christians have "died to the power of sin" (v. 2) and are therefore no longer "slaves of sin" (vv. 18, 22). However much it is true, as chap. 6 also asserts, that this freedom from sin's power must be lived out, appropriated, and put into action, and that Christians will sometimes fail to do this (cf., e.g., 1 Cor. 3:1-3), that freedom from sin's power is absolute and irreversible (cf. 6:8-10). Yet v. 14b asserts, in what certainly appears to be an objective assessment of status, that this *ego* has been sold so as now to be "under sin." Earlier in Romans (3:9), Paul summarizes his teaching about people outside of Christ by asserting that they are all "under sin." Christ delivers the believer from this condition, but the *ego* here in Rom. 7 confesses that he is still in that condition.

---

35. Cf. σάρξ, "flesh" in vv. 18 and 25 and "in the flesh" in Gal. 2:20. See, e.g., Nygren; Gundry, 137-39. The Gk. σάρκινος, with its -νος ending, would naturally mean "composed of flesh," as, so it appears, in 2 Cor. 3:3 (contrasted with λίθινος, "made of stone").

36. Note that σάρκινος is here also parallel to σάρκικος.

37. Cf. also Haldane; Murray; Espy, "Robust Conscience," p. 173.

38. The Greek is πεπραμένος ὑπὸ τὴν ἁμαρτίαν. The participle comes from the verb πιπράσκω, which means "sell," and often — though certainly not always — of the selling of slaves; eleven of its 24 LXX occurrences have this reference, and it is so used in Matt. 18:25. The ὑπό suggests that, in being sold, ἐγώ has been placed "under the authority of" sin. Because of this, and because Paul has just been using slavery imagery (6:6, 16-22; 7:6), allusions to slavery here are probable. The perfect πεπραμένος may allude to the sin of Adam as the occasion when all people became subject to the bondage of sin (e.g., Haldane) but probably simply indicates the state in which ἐγώ finds himself.

15 In one of the most famous passages of the epistle, Paul now graphically portrays his failure to do what he wills. The conflict between "willing"[39] and "doing"[40] dominates the narration of this conflict (vv. 15-20) and the inference Paul draws from it (v. 21). What Paul wills is that "good" required by God's law; the "evil" that he does, which he hates and does not acknowledge, is, then, a collective term for those things prohibited and in conflict with God's law.[41] As I have argued above, the conflict Paul depicts

39. Gk. θέλω, used seven times.

40. Paul uses three different Greek words in this context: ποιέω, πράσσω, and κατεργάζομαι. In the translation, we have distinguished the three, translating ποιέω as "do," πράσσω as "practice," and κατεργάζομαι as "produce." Yet it is not clear that Paul intends any difference in meaning among them. In accordance with their usage in secular Greek, some scholars argue that ποιέω is the more colorless of the three and that κατεργάζομαι stresses the outcome of what is "done" or "produced." A distinction between ποιέω and πράσσω is more difficult to establish, although some think that πράσσω stresses more the habitual nature of what is done (Espy, "Robust Conscience," pp. 184-85), or the moral consequences of one's actions (e.g., S-H), or the incompleteness of the action (Cranfield). But Paul does not always use these words with any difference in meaning. In 1:32; 2:3; 13:4; and 1 Thess. 4:10-11, ποιέω and πράσσω appear to mean the same thing; in 1 Cor. 5:2-3, πράσσω and κατεργάζομαι; and in 1:27-28 and Phil. 2:12, 14, ποιέω and κατεργάζομαι. These instances of considerable, if not complete, overlap in meaning, along with the very number of suggestions for distinguishing the words in this context, suggest that there may not be any important difference in meaning among the three here (H. Braun, *TDNT* VI, 478; Kuss). Certainly it is virtually impossible to think that ποιέω and πράσσω have different meanings (cf. vv. 15b, 19). On the other hand, it is possible that κατεργάζομαι has a slightly stronger connotation than the others — "produce" (Zahn).

41. R. Bultmann has a very different interpretation of the essential conflict in these verses. He claims that what Paul portrays is not a conscious conflict between a willing to do what is right and the actual doing what is wrong, but between a "trans-subjective propensity of human nature," the "desire" of human beings to secure their own existence by using "law" to find life and their failure to do so. "Man, called to selfhood, tries to live out of his own strength and thus loses his self — his 'life' — and rushes into death. This is the domination of sin: All man's doing is directed against his true intention — viz., to achieve life" (Bultmann, 1.246; cf. also his "Romans 7 and the Anthropology of Paul," pp. 174-75; Bornkamm, "Sin, the Law and Death," pp. 96-97; Käsemann, 202; Furnish, *Theology and Ethics,* pp. 141-43). Bultmann argues in favor of this interpretation that it is natural to supply as objects of the verbs in these verses the terms "death" and "life" that have occurred in vv. 7-13, and that, generally, this view fits better with Paul's basic critique of the law.

We have found reason at several points to criticize this so-called "nomistic" interpretation of Paul's critique of the law (see the notes on 5:20 and 7:5), and the specific reasons given for this interpretation in this context are unconvincing also. There is no reason to supply the word "life" as the object of "willing," nor "death" as the object of "producing." It is the law and its demands that are defined as "the good" in the context (vv. 13, 14, 16; cf. 8:2-4, 7); and "the evil" must be, as its opposite, that which is prohibited by the law. Furthermore, the issue in Rom. 7 is not the "boasting" or "self-righteousness"

here, leading to defeat (v. 23) and despair (v. 24), is a conflict he experienced as a Jew under the Mosaic law. To what extent Paul was conscious of this conflict and his failure *at the time* of that conflict is difficult to ascertain.

Undoubtedly his perspective as a Christian enables him to see that conflict more clearly and more radically than he did at the time. This helps explain why Paul can be so pessimistic about Jewish failure to keep the law. Surely Paul knew that he, along with other Jews, succeeded in keeping many of the commandments and infringed only a small percentage of the whole. It is this knowledge, coupled with his pre-Christian, Jewish interpretation of "righteousness," that enables Paul to claim that he was "blameless according to the righteousness of the law" (Phil. 3:6). But, as a Christian, Paul has a new perspective on God's law. He now sees it as a unity, an expression of God's will for his people that, when broken in any part, is broken in the whole.[42] That which Paul "willed" to do was keep the law; and it is just this, in the light shed on God and his law by Christ, that he failed as a Jew to do. The fact that Paul is describing the experience of the Jew under the Mosaic law does not mean, of course, that the conflict described here is peculiar to the Jew. All non-Christians are in a similar situation, and many — probably most — Christians can find in this description of nagging failure to do what is good an all-too-accurate reflection of their own experience. But, without denying the similarity, I must say again that the conflict Paul describes here is indicative of a slavery to the power of sin as a way of life (v. 14b) that is *not* typical, nor even possible, for the Christian.

Verses 15-20 are related to v. 14 in two ways. First, they show how, in willing to do the good the law demands, Paul attests to the divine origin of the law (v. 16). Second, and more important for Paul's purpose, the conflict between willing and doing reveals that he is indeed "fleshly," and under sin's power; for only the presence of such an alien influence — "sin dwelling in my flesh" (vv. 17b-18a) — can explain his radical failure to do what he wills. Recognizing the close parallelism between vv. 15-16 and vv. 19-20, some expositors divide vv. 15-20 into two parts, each of which explains a different part of v. 14 — vv. 15-16 the "spirituality" of the law (cf. v. 16b — "the law is good") and vv. 17-20 the "fleshiness" of *ego*.[43] But no such neat division is possible, for the paragraph is pervaded throughout by the conflict between

---

that Bultmann's view supposes, but the problem of transgressions: people not doing what the law requires and finding themselves subject to condemnation because of it. See, e.g., Althaus, 47-49; Ridderbos, *Paul,* pp. 145-46; Wright, "Messiah and People of God," pp. 147-48; Beker, 239.

42. See the singular δικαίωμα ("righteous requirement") in 8:4 and Jas. 2:9-12.

43. E.g., Osten-Sacken, *Römer 8,* p. 202. Espy ("Robust Conscience," p. 172) thinks that vv. 15-17 explain "fleshly" and vv. 18-20 "sold under sin," and Dunn takes vv. 15-17 and 18-23 as two parallel sections (1.377).

willing to do the right (e.g., what the law demands) and the failure to put it into practice.

With these overall perspectives established, we can turn to the specifics of the text. Paul begins with a general assertion that he does not "know," or, better, "approve,"[44] what he "does." In v. 15b, Paul explains in what sense he does not "approve" what he is doing: "For it is not what I will,[45] this I am practicing, but what I am hating, this I am doing." Paul's confession is similar to others found in the ancient world, the most famous being that in Ovid's *Metamorphoses* 7.21: "I see and approve the better course, but I follow the worse."[46]

16 The fact that he does not do what he purposes to do means that he "agrees"[47] with those who say — as Paul has done in vv. 12, 13, and 14 — that the law is good. Assumed in Paul's argument is that what he wills to do (v. 15b) is what the law demands. And because he does not do what the law demands, it could be concluded that he rejects the law as a moral guide. But Paul wants to draw the opposite conclusion; the very fact that he has a will that conflicts with the evil actually done shows that there is a part of this person — the "part" that has to do with the will — that acknowledges the just demands of God's law.

17 "But now . . . no longer" is logical, not temporal; it states what must "now," in light of the argument of vv. 15-16, "no longer" be considered true. And what is no longer true, Paul says, is that he can be considered the one who is "doing" these actions that he deplores. At first sight, Paul would appear to be saying something unlikely and, indeed, dangerous: that he is not responsible for his actions. But this is not what he means. His point is that his failure to put into action what he wills to do shows that there is something

---

44. γινώσκω could retain its purely cognitive meaning, in the sense that Paul does not "perceive" the real nature of what he is doing (Chrysostom). But it is more likely that the word means (as in, e.g., Matt. 7:23; 25:12) "acknowledge, approve" (BAGD; Cranfield).

45. θέλω means not "wish" or "desire," but "will," "purpose to accomplish" (BAGD; cf., e.g., Phil. 2:13).

46. Cf. also Epictetus, *Discourses* 2.26.4. Some scholars deny any real parallelism between these sayings and what Paul says here (e.g., Bultmann, 1.248 [because of his existential interpretation]; Cranfield [because he sees the conflict as one between the Spirit-filled believer and God's law] [Cranfield's persistent reading into this passage references to the Holy Spirit — when, of course, none at all appears — is rather perplexing.]). To be sure, Paul is speaking of the failure to follow the law of God, not a general morality; and his analysis of the human problem goes far deeper than those of these pagans. But as an assessment of the basic "human" condition apart from Christ, Ovid's and Paul's statements are substantially the same: a will to do the good does not (Paul would say "cannot") overcome the human propensity to do what is evil.

47. σύμφημι, a rare word, only here in biblical Greek.

besides himself involved in the situation. If we had only to do with him, in the sense of that part of him which agrees with God's law and wills to do it, we would not be able to explain why he consistently does what he does not want to do. No, Paul reasons, there must be another "actor" in the drama, another factor that interferes with his performance of what he wants to do. This other factor is indwelling sin. Sin is not a power that operates "outside" the person, making him do its bidding; sin is something resident in the very being, "dwelling"[48] within the person, ruling over him or her like a master over a slave (v. 14b).[49]

Because of this power of "sin dwelling in me," Paul is frustrated in carrying out what he knows to be God's good will. Paul does not, then, transfer responsibility for doing wrong from the individual Jew to an outside influence; he fixes that responsibility on that power *within* the person which leads that person to do what is wrong. Because of our involvement in the sin of Adam, "sin" has become resident in all people; and those outside Christ — such as the Jew under the law, as Paul once was — cannot ultimately resist sin's power. Thus they are unable to do the good that God requires of them (cf. 3:9-18; 8:7-8).

18   The assertion in v. 17 that indwelling sin is finally responsible for Paul's tragic failure to do God's will is the center of vv. 15-20. Verses 15-16 have led up to it; vv. 18-20 expand on it.[50] Verse 18a is closely related to v. 17b, continuing with the language of "dwelling in me." Paul has just said that "sin dwells in me"; now he restates this same basic point from the negative side: "good[51] does not dwell in me." Not "good," but "sin," has taken control of him, and is determining his actions. But Paul adds a very important qualification to this statement: "that is, in my flesh." Those who find in this passage a description of Christian experience think this phrase qualifies the statement that "good does not dwell in me" by leaving room for the Holy Spirit. On this view, "flesh" could mean "the whole fallen human nature" (Cranfield; cf. Nygren). Others, however, who think that Paul is describing an unregenerate situation, take the "that is" clause as a definition

---

48. Gk. οἰκοῦσα.

49. Paul's idea of "indwelling sin" and the flesh in this passage (cf. vv. 18, 25) may owe a lot to the rabbinic concept of the "evil desire" (*yēṣer hārāʿ*) — that tendency toward the evil which the rabbis taught exists in every person (see esp. Davies, 19-27). In contrast to the rabbis, Paul claims that deliverance from the domination of this "evil desire" comes not through the law or through the power of the "good desire" (*yēṣer haṭṭôb),* but through God's grace in Christ.

50. The similarity in these texts is one point that leads Schmithals to the curious notion that 7:17–8:39 is an independent Pauline tractate (pp. 228-32).

51. "The good" (ἀγαθόν) is an abbreviated way of saying "the will, or the power, to do the good."

of "me," rather than as a qualification: "nothing good dwells in me, I who am a person fallen and alienated from God."[52]

Both these views take "flesh" in its typical Pauline "ethical" meaning, and v. 14b can lend support to this conclusion. But the word is more likely to have a simple material meaning here. This is suggested by v. 25, where "flesh" is contrasted with "mind," and by v. 23, where the "other law," "the law of sin," is said to be "in my members."[53] While Paul's anthropology is essentially "monistic" rather than dualistic — that is, he usually regards people as wholes, in relationship to other things, instead of, as the Greeks did, as divided into two distinct "parts," body (or flesh) and soul (or spirit, or mind) — there is an undeniable element of anthropological dualism as well.[54] This dualism is probably more to the fore in this passage than anywhere else in Paul.[55] This is deliberate; Paul wants to reveal the "dividedness" of Jews under the law as a way of explaining how sincere respect for that law could be combined with failure to perform it. It is not that Paul is viewing the "flesh" as inherently evil, or as necessarily leading to evil,[56] but that he considers the material body to be that "part" of the person which is particularly susceptible to sin, and which in the non-Christian falls under the dominion of sin. On this view, "that is, in my flesh" qualifies the absolute assertion that "good does not dwell in me." For "good," the will to do the good, is, as Paul has already asserted, part of the *egō* (Lietzmann).

Verse 18b reasserts the conflict between "willing" and "doing" as a way of demonstrating the extent to which the "flesh" has fallen under the control of sin. "The willing of the good is present[57] with me, but the producing of good is not." We should make clear that, in attributing this "performing" to the sphere of the material body (v. 18a), Paul does not mean to suggest that the mind and will of the non-Christian is pure and only the body corrupted. As the whole context, and the fact that the "will" is unable to carry out its desires, makes clear, Paul is drawing a dichotomy between a certain element within the "mind" or "will" of the non-Christian and the "rest" of that non-Christian — the flesh. His point is that the Jew under the law, and, by extension, other non-Christians, do have a genuine striving to do what is right, as defined by God (cf. also 2:14-15). But this striving after the right, because of the unbroken power of sin, can never so "take over" the mind and will that it can effectively and consistently direct the body to do what is good.

---

52. Käsemann; Wilckens; Sand, *Der Begriff 'Sarx'*, pp. 190-91.
53. Pfleiderer, *Paulinism*, 1.49; S-H; Gundry, 137; E. Schweizer, *TDNT* VII, 133-34.
54. See esp. Gundry.
55. Cf. E. Schweizer, *TDNT* VII, 133-34.
56. Contra Pfleiderer, *Paulinism*, 1.47-67.
57. Gk. παράκειται, "be at hand," "lies near." The word occurs only in this verse and in v. 21 in biblical Greek.

19 This verse repeats the substance of v. 15b, with the difference that the "good" that is willed and the "evil" that is done are made explicit.[58]

20 Paul continues to go over the same ground, making sure that his point gets across. In this verse, he brings together a clause from v. 16b and v. 17b in a new combination, but he does not go beyond what he has already said there.

21 On the basis of the unsuccessful struggle to do the good demanded by the Mosaic law, Paul now draws a conclusion: "Therefore,[59] I find this law: when I will to do the good, evil is present there with me."[60] Consistency would suggest that the "law" *(nomos)* Paul refers to here is the Mosaic law, in accordance with his usual use of the term and its meaning throughout 7:4-20. We would then translate "I find, with respect to the law, that. . . ."[61] But it makes better sense to give *nomos* here its well-established meaning "principle."[62]

22 Verses 22-23 belong together antithetically, as Paul once again contrasts the conflicting tendencies toward the Mosaic law within himself:

58. The fact that ποιέω is used of the "doing" of "good" and πράσσω of the doing of evil — just the reverse of v. 15b — demonstrates not that Paul intends a subtle difference in meaning (as Godet suggests), but that the two are synonymous in this text.

59. Gk. ἄρα οὖν.

60. The placement of the ὅτι in this sentence renders its syntax awkward and unclear. The key issue is what to do with the participle τῷ θέλοντι. It could (1) be a dative of advantage dependent on εὑρίσκω — "I find the law [to be], that for me who wants to do the good, evil lies close at hand" (e.g., Chrysostom; Wilckens); (2) an appositional modifier of ἐμοί in the last clause — cf. NASB: "I find then the principle that evil is present in me, the one who wishes to do good"; or (3) a temporal clause dependent on the last clause — "I find, then, this law: that when I want to do the good, evil lies close at hand" (e.g., Godet; Michel; Kuss; Cranfield). While the first alternative sticks closest to the word order, it fails to state the problem, as Paul has revealed it in vv. 15-20, as clearly as the other two. Both these others require that the τῷ θέλοντι clause be part of the sentence introduced by ὅτι, but this reversal of order is not unknown in Greek (cf. BDF 408, 476). Of the two, the latter is the better because of the presence of ἐμοί in both clauses.

61. E.g., τὸν νόμον would be an accusative of respect. See, e.g., Denney; Chrysostom; Theodoret; Schlatter; Moule; Wilckens (though his treatment is somewhat confusing); Dunn; K. Snodgrass, "Spheres of Influence: A Possible Solution for the Problem of Paul and the Law," *JSNT* 32 (1988), 105; Wright, *Climax,* p. 198.

62. See esp. Godet; Kuss; Käsemann; Cranfield. This meaning is related to the most basic sense of νόμος, "what is laid down, required" (see the note on 2:12). Two points favor this interpretation. (1) The accusative τὸν νόμον is more naturally taken as direct object of εὑρίσκω ("I find"), with ὅτι used to introduce the "content" of that νόμον. But if this is the case, νόμος cannot refer to the Mosaic law. (2) Paul speaks, for the first time in the context, of the Mosaic law as "the law of God" in v. 22, suggesting that the qualifier is needed to differentiate this νόμος from some other νόμος. Nor should we identify the νόμος here with the ἕτερον νόμον of v. 23 (contra, e.g., W. Gutbrod, *TDNT* IV, 1071; Gifford; S-H; Murray; Cranfield; Morris); for this "other law" appears in v. 23 as if it is introduced there for the first time.

genuine, deep-seated delight in that law and acceptance of it in "the mind"; unrelieved and successful resistance to the demands of that law in "the members." These verses, then, restate in objective terms the conflict that Paul has subjectively described in vv. 15-20. His immediate purpose is to explain[63] the "rule" he has discovered with respect to himself in v. 21.

He begins with the positive side: "I rejoice[64] in the law of God according to the inner person." "The law of God" is again the Mosaic law, the torah, to which Paul as a Jew was devoted.[65] One of the strongest arguments in favor of identifying the *ego* in this passage with the Christian is that only those regenerated by God's Spirit can truly "delight in" God's law. There is weight to this argument; but it is not conclusive. Leaving aside the question of the propriety of calling OT saints (who certainly delighted in God's law — cf., e.g., Pss. 19 and 119) regenerate Christians, we have abundant evidence that Jews in Paul's day professed a delight in God's law, and passages such as Rom. 10:2 — "for I bear witness that they [Israel] have a zeal for God" — show that Paul regarded that delight as genuine. Certainly these people did not fully understand, and did not fully obey, the law — but neither do Christians. This is not to deny that many Jews paid only lip-service to the law and could certainly not be said to "delight in the law of God according to the inner person." But Paul, reflecting his own experience, focuses in this passage on a "pious" Jew — one who took his religion seriously and sought to do what was required of him. Taking as his example the "best" in the non-Christian world, Paul reveals the utter helplessness of the person apart from Christ who has nothing but his "works" on which to rely for salvation.

63. Note the γάρ.

64. Gk. συνήδομαι, a biblical Greek *hapax*, means "rejoice together with" and has a variety of extended meanings, such as "congratulate," or even "sympathize with" (LSJ; MM). While the context may suggest that we translate "agree with" (Michel), lexical justification for this translation is lacking. With the dative, the meaning "rejoice in," "take delight in" (with the implication of agreement with — cf. BAGD: "[joyfully] agree with") is to be preferred (LSJ; Cranfield).

65. Particularly because νόμος is qualified by τοῦ θεοῦ ("of God"), some interpreters think that Paul refers to the "will of God" generally, his "law" in its various forms: torah for Israel, the "law of nature" and the conscience to the Gentiles, and even, perhaps, the "law of Christ" to Christians (Feuillet, "Loi de Dieu," pp. 33-42; Deidun, 199, 203; Kuss). There is some slight justification for this lexically since the negative ἄνομος θεοῦ in 1 Cor. 9:21 appears to mean "without being under the law of God in any form," and Paul's only other use of (ὁ) νόμος (τοῦ) θεοῦ (Rom. 8:7) may also have a general meaning. But these occurrences are too few to establish a pattern, and the continuity of Paul's argument, as well as our identication of ἐγώ with Paul *as a Jew*, strongly favors viewing νόμος here again as the Mosaic law (e.g., Michel). Paul adds τοῦ θεοῦ in order to make clear that he is speaking here of the "good," "spiritual" law given by God (vv. 12, 13, 14, 16) rather than the νόμος he cites in v. 21 or the ἕτερον νόμον he describes in v. 23.

But advocates of the Christian interpretation of these verses insist that the last phrase in the verse settles the matter. "Inner person"[66] occurs only twice elsewhere in Paul, and both times the reference is undoubtedly to a Christian (2 Cor. 4:16; Eph. 3:16). But this does not mean that the phrase is a "technical" designation for a Christian. In other words, a phrase, or word, may be used to describe a Christian without that phrase or word necessarily denoting what is distinctive to Christians. This seems to be the case with "inner person."[67] This phrase was used in secular Greek to denote "man . . . according to his Godward, immortal side."[68] In this sense, "inner person" must be distinguished from "new person" (cf. 6:6) — which does have a clearly soteriological meaning.[69] Certainly, the context of Rom. 7 favors an anthropological interpretation. Throughout this passage, Paul has used words to contrast the "outer," or bodily, aspect of the person with the "inner," or mental, or spiritual, aspect of the person: "flesh" (vv. 18, 25) and "members" (v. 23) on the one hand and "mind" (vv. 23, 25) on the other. And these words, as we have seen, correspond to the two contrasting activities of "willing" and "doing" (vv. 15-21). In this context, it is much more likely that "inner person" has its well-attested anthropological meaning than a questionable soteriological meaning.

23 Now comes the negative objective evaluation of the condition of *egō*. Ranged against his delight in God's law is "another law," "in my members," "fighting against the law of my mind and holding me captive in the law of sin that is in my members."[70] The three occurrences of *nomos* ("law") in this verse, coming after the debated occurrences of the same word in vv. 21 and 22, provide fertile ground for exegetical debate — particularly when the equally debated occurrences of *nomos* in 8:2 are brought into the picture. We have two main options.

(1) Steadily gaining adherents in the last few decades has been the view that all the occurrences of *nomos* in 7:22-25 (as well as those in 8:2)

---

66. Gk. ἔσω ἄνθρωπος.

67. In 2 Cor. 4:16, "inner person" is used in contrast to ἔξω ἡμῶν ἄνθρωπος, "our outer person." In this context, this "outer person," which is "wasting away," denotes the outward, weak, and mortal "frame," or "flesh" (cf. v. 11) of the person. This suggests that the two phrases are not soteriological but anthropological — that they do not denote spiritual, but physical, realities. In this sense, it could be said that all people possess both an "outer person" and an "inner person"; the difference for the Christian is that his or her "inner person" is being "renewed." No more does Eph. 3:16 prove that "inner person" is a technical soteriological expression. Paul prays that the Ephesians may be strengthened "in the inner person," and this could well be another way of designating that "spirit" which all people possess.

68. J. Jeremias, *TDNT* I, 365.

69. Cf. Gundry, 135-37.

70. μέλη, in this context — contrasted with νοῦς — has physical connotations (cf. 6:12, 13).

refer to the Mosaic law, or (for those who interpret "law of God" in v. 22 broadly) to the law of God generally. Paul, it is argued, has throughout this context been detailing the "duality" of the law: "good," "holy," "just," "spiritual," and "for life," yet the stimulator of sin, an "imprisoning" force, and an instrument of death. It is this duality that Paul, it is alleged, now brings to a climax in these verses by contrasting the law as it comes from God (v. 22), and with which the "mind" agrees ("the law of my mind"), with that same law as it is twisted by sin ("the law of sin"). The distinction, on this view, is not between two different laws but between the different operations and effects of the same law. It is, on the one hand, the law that, because of the flesh, arouses sin and brings death (cf. 8:2) — "the law of sin"; but it is also God's law, with which the mind agrees — "the law of my mind" — the law that is "unto life" (v. 10) and, through the Spirit, can produce that life (8:2).[71]

However, there are serious objections to this view, both exegetical and theological. The greatest exegetical difficulty is Paul's qualification of the *nomos* in v. 23a as "another": if Paul had intended to refer in v. 23a to the same law as in v. 22, even if viewed from a different perspective, or with a different function, or even as "renewed and transformed," he would not have called it "another" or "different" law.[72] Another difficulty with this view is that it entails a shift from the perspective of vv. 15-21. In these verses, the chief protagonists are the *egō* that agrees with God's law and the *egō,* defined as "sin dwelling in the flesh," that prevents *egō* from carrying out that law. Yet if "another law"/"law of sin" in v. 23 is the law of God, then the chief protagonists in vv. 22-25 are both God's law. To put it another way: what is "in the flesh/members" according to v. 18 is "sin," not the law. The Mosaic law is ranged on the side of the will but not on the side of the flesh, in the sense that it indwells or compels the flesh to sin. And this brings us to the main theological difficulty. If "the other law"/"the law of sin" is identified as the Mosaic law, Paul would be giving to the Mosaic law just the active role in creating his predicament that he has been

71. Cf., e.g., Lohse, "ὁ νόμος τοῦ πνεύματος," pp. 285-86; Hahn, "Gesetzverständnis," p. 46; B. Reicke, "Paulus über das Gesetz," *TZ* 41 (1985), 242-44; Wright, "Messiah and People of God," p. 153; idem, *Climax,* p. 199; Osten-Sacken, *Römer 8,* pp. 210-11; Wilckens; Dunn; Snodgrass, "Spheres of Influence," pp. 106-7; Schmithals, *Theologische Anthropologie,* pp. 67, 84-85; Moule, "Justification," pp. 177-87 (hesitantly; see now his "retraction" in "Jesus, Judaism and Paul," in *Tradition and Interpretation in the New Testament: Essays in Honor of E. Earle Ellis* [ed. G. F. Hawthorne and O. Betz; Grand Rapids: Eerdmans, 1987], p. 48).

72. ἕτερος does not always (in distinction from ἄλλος) mean "another *of a different kind*" in NT Greek, but it always means "another," distinguishing two separate entities. The only possible exceptions are Gal. 1:6 and 2 Cor. 11:4. But even here the "other gospel," etc., while in some sense related to the gospel that Paul preaches, is — and this is Paul's point — *not* his gospel. While claiming to be the same, it is, in fact, different — disastrously so.

at pains to deny throughout this context. While the Mosaic law has been used by sin, it never, even when so used, ceases to be God's good, holy, spiritual law (cf. vv. 7-13). It is sin using the law, or the failure of *egō* to do the law, that is the problem, never the law in itself.

(2) For these reasons, I believe that "the other law" is not God's law in any form, but an "authority" or "demand" that is like, but opposed to, the Mosaic law.[73] As in 3:27, Paul plays on the word *nomos* to create a rhetorically effective antithesis: "I, in my inner being, delight in and accept the authority of the Mosaic law; but I see a competing 'authority,' operating in my members."[74] What, then, of the other two "laws" in v. 23 — "the law of my mind" and "the law of sin"? That the former is closely related to "the law of God" and the latter to the "other law" is clear. Some consider these to be the subjective counterparts to the two external, objective "laws": "the law of my mind" the inner moral monitor that responds to, and appropriates, God's law; "the law of sin" the individual's natural propensity to sin, or concupiscence, that answers to the demand and call of sin.[75] It is, however, simpler to take "law of my mind" and "law of sin" as two further and more specific designations of the "law of God" and the "other law," respectively.[76] The Mosaic law is that law with which the mind agrees, that "I" confess to be good and seek to obey (vv. 15-20 — and note v. 25, where *egō* claims to serve the law of God "with the mind"), while the "other law" is nothing more than that authority or demand of sin which works through, and becomes resident in, my "members" (cf. vv. 17b-18a: sin dwelling in the flesh).

Thus sin, working in and through the flesh, makes demands on and gains authority over *egō;* thus Paul calls it "the law of sin." Using military language, Paul describes this "law of sin" as "waging war"[77] against "the law of my mind." "Mind" refers to the reasoning side of a person.[78] Paul makes clear that this "reason" of people apart from Christ is perverted and darkened, preventing them from thinking correctly about God and the world.[79]

---

73. In addition to most of the commentaries, see esp. Winger, *By What Law?* 186-88; Lindars, "Paul and the Law," pp. 136-39; Deidun, 199-200; W. Gutbrod, *TDNT* IV, 1071; R. Bergmeier, "Röm 7,7-25a (8,2): Der Mensch — der Gesetz — Gott — Paulus — die Exegese im Widerspruch?" *KD* 31 (1985), 168-70.

74. A similar rhetorical contrast of the law of God with the "law" of evil occurs in *T. Naph.* 2:6: "As a person's strength, so also is his work; . . . as is his soul, so also is his thought, whether on the Law of the Lord or on the law of Beliar" (cf. Bergmeier, "Röm 7,7-25a," p. 170).

75. E.g., Calvin; Godet.

76. See, e.g., Cranfield.

77. Gk. ἀντιστρατευόμενον; the verb is a NT *hapax*.

78. The Greek is νοῦς. The word occurs only seven times in the LXX, but it is frequent in Greek generally. On its meaning, see esp. E. Würthwein, *TDNT* IV, 952-53.

79. Cf. 1:28; Eph. 4:17; Col. 2:18.

Here, however, Paul implies that the mind is an ally of God's law; many therefore conclude that Paul must be describing a Christian, with a "renewed" mind able to respond favorably to God's will.[80] But this does not follow. Granted that the mind of people apart from Christ is tragically and fatally flawed, it does not follow that the mind cannot understand and respond to God at all. All that Paul is saying is that the "reason" or "will" of the non-Christian is capable of approving the demands of God in his law. Especially if, as we have argued, Paul is speaking of his own experience under the law as typical of others, this capability cannot be denied (cf. 1:32; 2:14-15).

Continuing the military metaphor, Paul claims that the result of the battle between "the law of sin" and "the law of my mind" is an unqualified victory for the former: "I" have become a "captive to the law of sin." That the struggle between the law of God, the mind, and the will, on the one hand, and the "law of sin," the flesh/members, and what is done, on the other, has so negative an outcome is an important reason for thinking that Paul must be describing the experience of a non-Christian. The believer, while he or she may, and will, struggle with sin, commit sins, and even be continually overcome by a particular, individual sin, has been freed from sin's power (chap. 6; 8:2) and could therefore hardly be said to be "held captive in the 'power' or 'authority' of sin."

24 Paul has now concluded the description of his pre-Christian situation, as a Jew who reverences the Mosaic law but finds that the power of sin is too strong to enable him to comply with the demands of that law. As he has put it in v. 14b, "I am fleshly, sold under sin." No wonder, then, that he decries his condition and calls out for deliverance: "Wretched[81] person that I am! Who will deliver me from the body of this death?" Certainly the Christian who is sensitive to his or her failure to meet God's demands experiences a sense of frustration and misery at that failure (cf. 8:23); but Paul's language here is stronger than would be appropriate for that sense of failure.[82] Nor is it fair to say that this cry of despair is contrived and "theatrical" if Paul is not describing his own present feelings. First, as I have argued, Paul is describing an experience he has, to some extent at least, shared. Second, Paul well knows that this very condition characterizes most of his "kinfolk according to the flesh" as he writes. Third, however, we must recognize that, while this cry is uttered by a Jew under

---

80. Cf. 12:2; 1 Cor. 2:16; Eph. 2:3.

81. Gk. ταλαίπωρος, a strong term. It and its cognates are used several times in the LXX and the NT of the "misery" or "distress" that will come with the judgment of God (cf. Isa. 47:11; Jer. 6:7; 15:8; 20:8; 51:56; Amos 5:9; Mic. 2:4; Joel 1:15; Zeph. 1:15; Jas. 5:1; Rev. 3:17[?]).

82. Contra, e.g., Cranfield.

the law, it is written by a Jew who in Christ has discovered just how "wretched" his past condition really was; and this Christian insight undoubtedly colors the narrative.

Paul's cry for deliverance from "the body of this death"[83] might express his longing, as a Christian, for physical resurrection (cf. 8:10)[84] or his desire, as a non-Christian, for rescue from spiritual frustration and condemnation. In light of Paul's use of "death" language throughout this chapter, and especially in v. 13, which is the immediate launching pad for vv. 14-25, I think the latter is preferable. Paul has been showing how *egō*, through, and despite, the law, has been brought into condemnation because of the reigning power of sin. Here, in the personal plea that brings to a climax the narrative of vv. 7-23, the condition from which deliverance is sought can be nothing but the condition Paul has depicted in these verses: the status of the person under sentence of spiritual death, condemned, bound for hell.[85]

25 Paul immediately supplies the answer to the plea of v. 24b: "Thanks be to God through Jesus Christ our Lord." Yet the chapter does not end on this triumphant note but returns to a final description of *egō* in conflict, as this has been delineated in vv. 15-23. This sequence is one of the most oft-cited arguments in favor of the view that Paul is describing Christian experience in 7:14-25. For Paul's renewed confession of struggle, *after* the thanksgiving for deliverance, suggests that the "divided" *egō* is precisely that *egō* which knows that deliverance comes through God's work in Christ. Without, however, denying the force of the argument, I do not think that it is decisive.[86] On any reading

---

83. Or "this body of death." It is not easy to decide whether τούτου modifies τοῦ σώματος (NRSV; NIV; NJB; TEV; and cf., e.g., Zerwick, 41; Cranfield) or τοῦ θανάτου (KJV; NASB; and cf., e.g., Turner, 214; Robertson, 497). Paul has referred in the context both to "death" (vv. 10, 11, 13) and to words describing the body ("flesh" in v. 18; "members" in v. 23). Since, however, the references to the body occur in the immediate context, τούτου is probably better attached to σώματος.

84. E.g., Murray; R. Banks, "Romans 7:25a: An Eschatological Thanksgiving?" *AusBR* 26 (1978), 34-42; Dunn, "Rom. 7,14-25," pp. 263-64. Cranfield, however, suggests that Paul, the Christian, is bemoaning his failure to satisfy God's righteous demands, and is crying out for rescue from his "human nature in its condition of occupation by sin."

85. E.g., Godet; Wilckens; Gundry, "Moral Frustration," p. 239. We might also ask whether, if a Christian were speaking, the question would have been *"who* will rescue me?" A Christian, longingly anticipating his or her final deliverance from the sins and woes of this life, would not have been expected to ask about the identity of the deliverer.

86. A neat way of avoiding the problem is to remove v. 25b from the text as a gloss (Bultmann, "Glossen," pp. 278-79; Käsemann; Osten-Sacken, *Römer 8,* p. 146; Kuss; Schmithals) or to rearrange the order of the sentences (vv. 23-25b-24-25a) (Dodd). But there is no textual justification for either, and such expedients are little more than desperate attempts to make the text say what we think it *ought* to say, when we should be figuring out what it *does* say.

of the passage, v. 25a is anticipatory of a victory yet to come: on the regenerate view, anticipatory of the final deliverance from the "mortal body" depicted in 8:10, 23; on the unregenerate view, anticipatory of deliverance from sin and death depicted in 8:2-4. On the unregenerate view, it must be assumed that Paul, the Christian, has at this point interjected his own thanksgiving.[87] And perhaps it could be argued that the use of the plural ("our") rather than the "I" style of the surrounding context signals the presence of such an interjection.

"Now, then," introduces v. 25b as a summarizing recapitulation of the "dividedness" of the *egō* that Paul has portrayed in vv. 15-23. For the first time in this context, Paul contrasts his two responses, or situations, in terms of "serving," but the other terms reflect the language Paul has already used: serving "the law of God" (v. 22) "with the mind" (cf. v. 23) versus serving "the law of sin" (v. 23) "with the flesh"[88] (v. 14b, 18). Some interpreters think that the emphatic "I myself"[89] means "I, by myself [without the help of the Spirit]," but there is no reason to see such a nuance. The emphatic pronoun is used to stress that, when all allowance has been made for the different "parts" and "directions" of this *egō,* as they have been delineated in vv. 15-23, there remains *one* person, who is caught in the conflict between mental assent to God's word and practical failure to do it.

While Paul is not, in my opinion, depicting a Christian situation in this paragraph, there are important theological applications for the Christian. First, we are reminded of our past — unable to do God's will, frustrated perhaps at our failure — so that we may praise God for his deliverance with deeper understanding and greater joy. Second, we are warned that the Mosaic law, and, hence, all law, is unable to deliver us from the power of sin; the multiplication of "rules" and "commands," so much a tendency in some Christian circles, will be more likely to drive us deeper into frustration than to improve the quality of our walk with Christ.

D. ASSURANCE OF ETERNAL LIFE IN THE SPIRIT (8:1-30)

The inner sanctuary within the cathedral of Christian faith; the tree of life in the midst of the Garden of Eden; the highest peak in a range of mountains — such are some of the metaphors used by interpreters who extol chap. 8 as the

---

87. Stuhlmacher appeals to OT laments for an "abrupt" thanksgiving, referring to Psalms 22 and 69. Unfortunately, in neither Psalm does the speaker return to the lament after the thanksgiving.

88. σάρξ will here again have a material rather than an ethical meaning, and both σάρχι and νοΐ are instrumental datives.

89. Gk. emphasizing pronoun, αὐτός.

greatest passage within what so many consider to be the greatest book in Scripture.[1] While the varied riches of God's Word make any such comparisons precarious, Rom. 8 deserves to be put in the front rank for its rich and comprehensive portrayal of what it means to be a Christian. Prominent in this description is the work of the Holy Spirit.

The word *pneuma* occurs 21 times in Rom. 8, and all but two (those in vv. 15a and 16b) refer to the Holy Spirit.[2] This means that the Spirit is mentioned in this chapter almost once every two verses, while its closest competitor, 1 Cor. 12, mentions the Spirit a little over once every three verses. Nevertheless, despite the prominence of the Holy Spirit, Rom. 8 is not really *about* the Spirit. For one thing, the Spirit is not equally prominent throughout, being mentioned 15 times in vv. 1-17 but only four times in vv. 18-39. For another, Paul's focus is not so much on the Spirit as such, but on what the Spirit *does*. And perhaps this is the best way to learn about the Spirit. For, as important as it may be to define the nature of the Holy Spirit and his relation to Christ and the Father, the Spirit is best known in his ministry on behalf of Christians. It is those blessings and privileges conferred on believers by the Spirit that are the theme of this chapter.

If we were to sum up these blessings is a single word, that word would be *assurance.* From "no condemnation" at the beginning (v. 1) to "no separation" at the end (v. 39) (Godet), Paul passes in review those gifts and graces that together assure the Christian that his relationship with God is secure and settled. The chapter contains no sharp breaks,[3] but four major sections emerge.

(1) In vv. 1-13, the key word is *life.* "The Spirit of life" (v. 2) confers life both in the present — through liberating the believer from both the penalty (justification) and power (sanctification) of sin — and in the future — by raising the "mortal body" from the dead. Yet this life is not attained without the believer's active participation in the Spirit's progressive work of "mortification" (vv. 12-13).

(2) The Spirit is also the "Spirit of adoption," conferring on us the status of God's own dearly loved children and making us aware of that status at the same time (vv. 14-17).

(3) In the last verse of the second section, Paul makes the transition into the theme of hope, which dominates the last part of Rom. 8. To be a child of God means to be his heir (v. 17) — and an heir must wait for the full realization of what has been promised. So believers in this age of warfare

---

1. The second of these comparisons is attributed to the Puritan divine Thomas Draxe (cf. W. Haller, *The Rise of Puritanism* [Philadelphia: University of Pennsylvania, 1938], p. 87).

2. Many interpreters deny that πνεῦμα in v. 10b refers to the Holy Spirit; but I argue below that it does.

3. This is repeatedly emphasized by Osten-Sacken, *Römer 8,* e.g., p. 132.

between the kingdom of God and the kingdom of Satan suffer and groan —
but their groans are not the despairing cries of the hopeless. Rather, they are
the impatient yearnings of those who have been saved in hope and hunger for
that "glory" which has been promised them (vv. 18-30).

(4) Paul celebrates this comforting expectation in vv. 31-39, a hymn
of triumph that caps off and applies the exposition of Christian privileges
given in vv. 1-30, as well as bringing to a conclusion the exposition of chaps.
5–8 generally.

How does this portrait of the new life and hope of the believer relate
to what has come before in Romans? The "therefore" at the beginning of the
chapter indicates that Paul is drawing a conclusion. What immediately follows
is the assertion that "there is now no condemnation for those who are in Christ
Jesus" (v. 1). This language forges a link with Rom. 5:12-21: the word "condemnation"[4] occurs only here and in 5:16 and 18 in the NT, and "in Christ
Jesus" succinctly summarizes the relationship of believers to Christ that is
developed in that great paragraph. Nor do these parallels stand alone. In both
5:12-21 and 8:1-13 Paul assures the believer of the reality and finality of life
in Christ, and shows how this life is the product of righteousness (cf. 5:17,
18, 21; 8:10).[5] We are justified, then, in thinking that 8:1-13 or, probably,
8:1-17, restates and elaborates 5:12-21. This restatement is made with particular respect to the threats of sin and the law (cf. v. 2: "the law of sin and
death") that occupied Paul in chaps. 6 and 7, and, as we have seen, with a
new focus on the ministry of the Spirit. Since the second part of Rom. 8 is
closely related to 5:1-11 (see the introduction to 5:1-11), the result is a "ring
composition" in which 8:18-39 picks up 5:1-11, as 8:1-17 does 5:12-21.[6]

This scheme captures the main development of Paul's discussion but
does not tell the whole story. For there are other connections between Rom.
8 and the rest of the epistle that must not be overlooked. A connection with
what has immediately preceded at the end of Rom. 7 is unlikely.[7] But, in
keeping with Paul's habit in Romans of touching on topics that are to be
developed later, the reference to "newness of Spirit" in 7:6b anticipates and
prepares for the concentrated focus on the Spirit in chap. 8.[8] Further, we cannot
ignore the way in which 8:2-4 sketches the solution to the dilemma of *egō* in
7:7-25. God's work in Christ, mediated by the Spirit, is what overcomes the
inability of the law, weakened as it is by the flesh (v. 3a), and liberates the

4. Gk. κατάκριμα.
5. Cf., e.g., Osten-Sacken, *Römer 8,* p. 175; Myers, "Chiastic Inversion," pp.
42-43; Fitzmyer.
6. See the discussion and outline in the introduction to chaps. 5–8.
7. Contra, e.g., S-H, 190, and Denney, 644, who connect 8:1 with v. 25a and
Meyer, 2.40, who connects 8:1 with v. 25b.
8. See, e.g., Godet, 294; Cranfield, 1.372; Fitzmyer, 481; and many others.

believer from "the law of sin and death" (v. 2). While not to be ignored, however, neither 7:6b nor 7:7-25 is to be seen as the main jumping-off point for chap. 8. Both are subordinate connections taken up within Paul's reiteration of the theme of Christian assurance and eschatological victory. Further, while Rom. 8 does, in some ways, summarize and bring to a climax the discussion of the entire epistle to this point,[9] the particular connection with chap. 5 that I have sketched cannot be ignored. Like a snowball rolling downhill, Rom. 8 picks up many of the earlier themes of the letter as it reiterates and expands on the assurance of eschatological life that the believer has in Christ.

1. The Spirit of Life (8:1-13)

1*Now, therefore, there is no condemnation for those who are in Christ Jesus.*[10] 2*For the law of the Spirit of life has, through Christ Jesus, set you*[11] *free from the law of sin and death.* 3*For what the law could not do, in that it was weakened by the flesh, God did: by sending his own Son in the form of sinful flesh and concerning sin he condemned sin in the flesh,* 4*in order that the righteous requirement of the law might be fulfilled in us, who walk not according to the flesh but according to the Spirit.*

5*For those who are according to the flesh have their minds set on the things of the flesh, while those who are according to the Spirit have their minds set on the things of the Spirit.* 6*For the mind of the flesh*

---

9. See, e.g., Hodge, 248-49.

10. The addition after "Christ Jesus" in the KJV translation, "who walk not after the flesh, but after the Spirit," reflects a variant reading found in the majority text and also in a few other MSS (the second [Byzantine] corrector of ℵ, the second corrector of the western D, and [possibly] the secondary Alexandrian 33; a few other MSS have only the Greek equivalent of "who do not walk after the flesh" [the Alexandrian A, the first corrector of the western D, Ψ]). These words have been added at some point in the scribal transmission of Romans in assimilation to v. 4.

11. Whether to read σε ("you") or με ("me") here is difficult to decide. External support for the two is fairly even, the combination of the primary Alexandrian witnesses ℵ and B (note also F, G, and 1739) in favor of σε perhaps outweighing the secondary Alexandrian A, the western D, and the majority text, which read με (a few MSS, including Ψ, read ὑμᾶς). As far as internal evidence goes, an original σε may have been changed to με under the influence of the first person singular in 7:7-25, or been omitted by haplograpy after ἠλευθέρωσεν and then replaced with με. Alternatively, an original με may have been changed to σε as a result of dittography after ἠλευθέρωσεν. UBS[2] read με, whereas UBS[3,4] and NA[26, 27] read σε. But the strong combination of ℵ and B and allowance for the influence of Rom. 7 tilt the scales pretty strongly in favor of σε (so, e.g., Fee, *God's Empowering Presence*, p. 519 n. 134; Kuss; Gaugler; Cranfield; contra, e.g., Godet; Gifford; Meyer — Barrett suggests that we follow Origen in omitting an object altogther).

470

is death, but the mind of the Spirit is life and peace, 7because the mind of the flesh is hostile toward God, for it does not submit to the law of God, for it cannot do so. 8Now those who are in the flesh cannot please God. 9But you are not in the flesh but in the Spirit, if the Spirit of God dwells in you. And if someone does not have the Spirit of Christ, that person does not belong to Christ. 10But if Christ is in you, the body is dead because of sin, but the Spirit is life because of righteousness. 11And if the Spirit of the one who raised Jesus from the dead dwells in you, the one who raised Christ from the dead will also give life to your mortal bodies through his Spirit12 who is dwelling in you.

12Therefore, brothers, we are debtors, not to the flesh, to live according to the flesh — 13for if you are living according to the flesh, you will die. But if by the Spirit you are putting to death the practices of the body, you will live.

In this first paragraph of Rom. 8, Paul reasserts the triumphant conclusion of 5:12-21: that for those who are "in Christ" eternal life replaces the condemnation and death that were the lot of everybody in Adam. But this reassertion of the believer's assurance of life takes a new form, being modeled from the material with which Paul has been working in chaps. 6–7. The Spirit now plays the dominant role, as Paul returns to his preparatory reference to "serving in newness of Spirit" in 7:6b. And the "powers" against which the Spirit is ranged in these verses are those "authorities" of the old age that have been portrayed in the two previous chapters. The Spirit battles against and conquers the hostility and power of the flesh (vv. 5b-9; cf. 7:5, 14, 18, 25), rescues the believer from captivity to sin and death, both "spiritual" and "physical" (v. 2; for sin, see v. 3 and chap. 6; for death, see vv. 6, 10-11, 13 and 6:12, 13, 16, 21, 23; 7:5, 9-11, 13, 24), and, accomplishing what the law itself could not do (v. 3a; cf. 7:7-25), enables the law,

---

12. "Through the Spirit" reflects the genitive reading τοῦ ἐνοικοῦντος . . . πνεύματος, found in ℵ (primary Alexandrian), A, C, and 81 (secondary Alexandrian). The alternative, "because of the Spirit," reflects the accusative reading τὸ ἐνοικοῦν . . . πνεῦμα, found in B (primary Alexandrian), 33 and 1739 (secondary Alexandrian), D, F, and G (western), Ψ, and the majority text. External evidence is evenly divided and both readings, as implied by the comments of Maximus in the seventh century, are very early. Early Fathers generally insisted on the genitive reading to ensure the divinity and personality of the Spirit (Gifford). But this, of course, raises the suspicion that orthodox scribes may have changed an original accusative to the genitive (Meyer; cf. also Godet; E. Schweizer, *TDNT* VI, 422). Or a scribe may have changed an original accusative reading to the genitive because the latter is more customary in the NT (Fee, *God's Empowering Presence,* pp. 543, 553). Nevertheless, the context favors the genitive: note that in v. 10 Paul has called the Spirit "life" and made this assertion causally dependent on righteousness (see, e.g., Harris, *Raised Immortal,* pp. 145-46; and especially the discussion in Lietzmann).

for the first time, to be "fulfilled." Thus Paul weaves together various threads from chaps. 6–7 in a new argument for the assurance of eternal life that the believer may have in Christ.

Most commentators put a major break in the flow of Paul's argument after v. 11.[13] But the break is better placed after v. 13.[14] The antithesis between "flesh" and "Spirit" that is central to vv. 4b-9a becomes a matter of application and exhortation in vv. 12-13, and these latter verses should therefore be considered part of the same basic block of material. In addition to this, the central theme of vv. 1-11 is continued right through v. 13. This theme is "life." The "no condemnation" that heads this paragraph is grounded in the reality of the believer's transfer from death to life. In vv. 2-4, this transfer emanates from "the Spirit of life," who applies to the believer the benefits won by Christ on the cross, thereby enabling the fulfillment of the law's just demand. Verses 5-9 teach that the flesh is necessarily in opposition to God, turning every person into a rebel against God and his law and reaping death in consequence. This explains why it is only by "being in the Spirit" (v. 9) and "walking according to the Spirit" (v. 4b) that life and peace can be had. And the life that the Spirit gives is by no means ended by the grave, for the presence of the Spirit guarantees that the bodies of believers will be raised from physical death (vv. 10-11). Verses 12-13 cap off this proclamation of life in Christ by reminding us that God's gift of eternal life does not cancel the complementary truth that only by progressing in holiness will that eternal life be attained.

1 The combination "therefore, now"[15] is an emphatic one, marking what follows as a significant conclusion. As we have seen, these verses pick up various themes from chaps. 6–7 to restate the assuring message of 5:12-21 that Christ has secured eternal life for all who belong to him. The "now" alludes to the new era of salvation history inaugurated by Christ's death and resurrection (see also 3:21; 5:9; 6:19, 22; 7:6). "For those who are in Christ Jesus," this era is marked by the wonderful announcement that "there is no condemnation." Many interpreters, noting that Paul focuses in this context on the new life in Christ (vv. 5-13), think that "no condemnation" includes the breaking of sin's power in all its aspects.[16] It is, of course, important that we not separate the destruction of sin's power from the removal of its penalty. But the judicial flavor of the word "condemnation" strongly suggests that Paul is here thinking only of the believer's deliverance from the penalty that

13. E.g., Godet, 295; Michel, 248; Käsemann, 212; Cranfield, 1.372; Dunn, 1.414-15.

14. See, e.g., Byrne, "Living Out," p. 580; Wilckens, 2.120; Lagrange, 200; Fitzmyer, 480.

15. Gk. ἄρα νῦν.

16. E.g., Godet; Harrison.

sin exacts.[17] Like "death," a parallel term (cf. 5:16 and 17; 5:18 and 21; and 8:1 and 6), "condemnation" designates the state of "lostness," of estrangement from God that, apart from Christ, every person will experience for eternity. Those "in Christ Jesus" are removed from this state — and removed forever from it, as the emphatic "no"[18] indicates. No more will condemnation of any kind be a threat (cf. 8:34). How can this happen for those "in Christ"? Because those in Christ experience the benefits of Christ's death "for us": "He was *for us* in the place of condemnation; we are *in him* where all condemnation has spent its force" (cf. 2 Cor. 5:21).[19] Paul's judicial "for us" language and his "participationist" "in him" language combine in perfect harmony.

2 The "for"[20] indicates that this verse is the ground of the "no condemnation in Christ" announced in v. 1. A liberation has taken place through the Holy Spirit, and this liberation is the basis on which the person "in Christ" is forever saved from condemnation. In describing this liberation, Paul uses the word *nomos* to characterize both "sides" of the situation: "the *nomos* of the Spirit of life has, through Christ Jesus,[21] set you free from the *nomos* of sin and death." Why does he do so?

(1) *Nomos* in both parts of the verse might refer to the Mosaic law. Paul would then be suggesting that the Mosaic law has a dual role. In the context of the "flesh," it is misunderstood as nothing more than a series of demands. As such, the law becomes an instrument of sin, leading to death (7:5, 7-13). However, in the context of the Spirit, the law is experienced in all its fuller and truer nature — as promise, and thus as calling for faith. It can then become an instrument of righteousness leading to life (cf. 7:10 —

---

17. Cf., e.g., Gundry, "Grace, Works, and Staying Saved," pp. 31-32. Murray argues against the narrowly forensic meaning of the word because he thinks this would create the theologically incorrect teaching that justification (v. 1) depends on sanctification (v. 2). But I argue below that v. 2 includes more than sanctification. κατάκριμα often designates the punishment that follows the "sentence," rather than the sentence itself — the fine, imprisonment, or execution rather than the judge's verdict (BAGD; MM; Bruce). But Paul does not use the word so narrowly, for in 5:16 and 18 κατάκριμα is the antithesis to justification, summing up the penal effects of Adam's disobedience.

18. Gk. οὐδέν, lit., "not one."

19. M. L. Loane, *The Hope of Glory: An Exposition of the Eighth Chapter in the Epistle to the Romans* (London: Hodder and Stoughton, 1968), p. 15.

20. Gk. γάρ.

21. ἐν Χριστῷ Ἰησοῦ could go with τῆς ζωῆς ("life which is in Christ Jesus"; cf. Zahn; Michel; Lagrange; Feuillet, "Loi de Dieu," pp. 57-58), with ὁ νόμος ("the law which is in Christ Jesus"; cf. e.g., Godet), or with the entire phrase (Kuss). But it makes best sense to take it with the verb and give the preposition an instrumental force (cf. S-H; Cranfield; Robertson, 784; Wedderburn, "Some Observations," p. 89; Fee, *God's Empowering Presence,* pp. 523-24).

473

the commandment is "unto life"). In support of this interpretation are (a) the undoubted preference of Paul to use *nomos* to refer to the Mosaic law and (b) the fact that this dual understanding of the law is, allegedly, present in the immediately preceding paragraph (see 7:22-23, 25b). On this view, then, Paul is teaching that the Spirit for the first time puts the law of God in its proper focus and context, and enables it thereby to free the sinner from the narrow and death-dealing misuse of the law.[22]

(2) *Nomos* in both parts of the verse might have a figurative meaning, contrasting the "principle," "authority," or "power" of sin and death with the "principle," "authority," or "power" of the Spirit.[23] As we have seen (see the note on 3:27), *nomos* can mean "binding authority" or "power," so this translation is lexically acceptable. And this interpretation is clearly preferable to the first.

The first occurrence of *nomos,* at least, cannot refer to the Mosaic law. The immediate context stresses the incapacity of the law to do what v. 2 describes. It was God acting through his Son who accomplished "what the law could not do" (v. 3). To make the Mosaic law the liberating agent in v. 2 would be to make v. 2 contradict v. 3. But, more seriously, giving the law this kind of role would contradict a central and oft-repeated tenet of Paul's theology. Throughout his letters, and not least in Romans, Paul pictures the Mosaic law as ranged on the opposite side of the Spirit, righteousness, and life. God's righteousness has come "apart from the law" (3:21; cf. Gal. 2:15–3:14); the promise can be attained only through faith and *not* through the law (4:12-15; cf. Gal. 3:15-18); the believer must be "released from" the law through union with Christ in order to produce fruit pleasing to God (7:4-6; cf. Gal. 2:19-20). To be sure, Paul affirms that the law is *God's* law and that it was given with a positive purpose within the overall plan of salvation (7:7-13; cf. Gal. 3:19–4:5). But this purpose is not the liberation of the believer from a misunder-

22. Cf. Lohse, "ὁ νόμος τοῦ πνεύματος," pp. 279-87; P. von der Osten-Sacken, "Befreiung durch das Gesetz," in *Richte unsere Füsse auf den Weg des Friedens* (ed. A. Baudis et al.; Munich: Kaiser, 1979), pp. 349-55; idem, "Verständnis," pp. 13-21; E. Reinmuth, *Geist und Gesetz: Studien zu Voraussetzungen und Inhalt der paulinischen Paränese* (Theologische Arbeiten 44; Berlin: Evangelische, 1985), pp. 68-69; Jüngel, *Paulus und Jesus,* pp. 54-55; Byrne, 92 n. 47; Barth, *Shorter;* Wilckens; Dunn; Reicke, "Paulus über das Gesetz," p. 256; Snodgrass, "Spheres of Influence," p. 99; E. J. Schnabel, *Law and Wisdom from Ben Sira to Paul* (WUNT 2.16; Tübingen: Mohr, 1985), p. 288.

23. This is the majority view among commentators; cf. e.g., Chrysostom; Melanchthon; Godet; Michel; Cranfield; Fitzmyer; and note also van Dülmen, *Gesetz,* p. 120; Deidun, 194-202; Räisänen, "Das 'Gesetz des Glaubens'," pp. 113-16; Winger, *By What Law?* p. 195; L. E. Keck, "The Law and 'The Law of Sin and Death' (Rom 8:1-4): Reflections on the Spirit and Ethics in Paul," in *The Divine Helmsman: Studies on God's Control of Human Events, presented to Lou H. Silberman* (ed. J. L. Crenshaw and S. Sandmel; New York: KTAV, 1980), pp. 41-57; Fee, *God's Empowering Presence,* pp. 523-24.

standing or misuse of the law, or from the power of sin and death. The Pauline pattern, enunciated in v. 3, is clear: the impotence of the law has been met not with a new empowering of the law but with God's gracious activity in Jesus Christ.[24] As Chrysostom put it, "The other [the Mosaic law] was merely given by the Spirit, but this [the law of the Spirit] even furnishes those that receive it with the Spirit in large measure." To these points may be added the incongruity, however the qualifying genitives be construed and the concept paraphrased, of the *nomos* liberating the believer from the same *nomos*. Nor does appeal to the context help; as I have argued, it is unlikely that Paul in 7:21-25 refers to a dual role of the Mosaic law.

The "*nomos* of the Spirit" cannot, then, refer to the Mosaic law. It may, however, allude to the "law written on the heart" (cf. Jer. 31:31-34), the "law" of the New Covenant that, according to the parallel text in Ezek. 36:24-32, is closely related to the Spirit.[25] But it is not clear that the "law" in Jeremiah is anything but an internalized Mosaic law; and it is not, in any case, the liberating power of the new age. This also rules out any notion of "the law of the Spirit" being a new, Christian ethical standard that takes the place of the law of Moses (as some interpret "the law of Christ" [Gal. 6:2]). Paul's use of *nomos* here may be rhetorically dependent on his customary use of *nomos*,[26] but he does not use it in order to suggest that the Spirit is, or conveys, a norm that functions like, or can be substituted for, the Mosaic law. Others think the *nomos* is the gospel, the new "rule" of which the Spirit is the author.[27] This is possible, but the other texts in which Paul uses *nomos* in a "nonlegal" manner (cf. 3:27; 9:31-32), and especially the immediate context (7:21-25), point rather to *nomos* meaning "power," or "binding authority," with the following genitive specifying that authority or power. Paul always uses *nomos* with this meaning in contexts where he has been talking about the Mosaic law. This suggests an intentional play on the word, as Paul implicitly contrasts the law of Moses with a different "law," in this case the " 'law' of the Spirit who confers life."[28] The actor in the situation is, then, the Spirit

---

24. For these points, see esp. Räisänen, "Das 'Gesetz des Glaubens'," pp. 113-16. This issue is discussed thoroughly in *Battesimo e Giustizia* (ed. Lorenzi), pp. 177-201. Moule, who at one time entertained the idea that this first νόμος meant the Mosaic law (cf. "Justification," *Battesimo e Giustizia*, pp. 177-87), has now rejected this interpretation ("Paul and Judaism," p. 48).

25. See esp. Lyonnet, *Les Etages*, pp. 163-66; Feuillet, "Loi de Dieu," pp. 58-61. The view of Gese ("Law," pp. 68-90) and Stuhlmacher (e.g., "Law as a Topic," pp. 126-27), that the reference here is to the eschatological "Zion" torah, is similar.

26. Fitzmyer, "Paul and the Law," p. 187.

27. Bengel; Hodge.

28. See, e.g., Fee, *God's Empowering Presence*, pp. 523-24. We are taking τοῦ πνεύματος as an epexegetic genitive and τῆς ζωῆς as an objective genitive (cf. Cranfield).

himself. It is God's Spirit, coming to the believer with power and authority, who brings liberation from the powers of the old age and from the condemnation that is the lot of all who are imprisoned by those powers.

More difficult to decide is whether the second *nomos* in the verse designates the Mosaic law or whether it, too, means "binding authority" or "power." In favor of the former is the fact that *nomos* in v. 3a refers to the Mosaic law; and certainly Paul's discussion in 7:7-25 would justify describing the Mosaic law as, in some sense, a "law of sin and death" (cf. also 1 Cor. 15:56). Though given by God, the law of Moses comes to sinful, "fleshly" people, for whom that law therefore becomes an instrument of sin and death.[29] While this interpretation fits both the context and Paul's theology, another factor tilts the scales slightly in favor of rendering this second *nomos* also as "binding authority" or "power." This factor is the occurrence of the almost identical phrase, "the *nomos* of sin," in 7:23, where, because it is called "the other law," in distinction from the Mosaic law (v. 22), it must mean the "authority" or "power" of sin. That these similar phrases mean the same thing is suggested also by the material relationship between 7:23 and 8:2; we can hardly miss the fact that the "liberation" of 8:2 is the answer to the "imprisonment" of 7:23.[30] We might, then, paraphrase this second phrase, "the binding authority of sin that leads to death."[31] The real contrast in the verse is then between the Spirit on the one hand and sin and death on the other. As sin and death are those powers that rule the old age (cf. chaps. 6–7), so the Spirit and the eschatological life conferred by the Spirit are those powers that rule the new age.[32]

But what is the nature of the liberation Paul depicts here? Since v. 1, as I have argued, has to do with justification, the liberation of v. 2 may also be restricted to the believer's being freed from the penalty of sin.[33] Others,

29. Haldane; Hodge; Barrett.

30. E.g., Deidun, 201.

31. The genitive τῆς ἁμαρτίας will then, like τοῦ πνεύματος, be epexegetic. τοῦ θανάτου could conceivably be dependent on ἀπό — "from the law of sin and from death" (Stuart). Syntactically, the question is whether the second genitive in a tandem genitive phrase, the first of whose members depends on an earlier genitive, will also depend on that earlier genitive, or whether it will be parallel to that earlier genitive. By means of Project GRAM-CORD, twenty-six similar syntactical contructions within the NT were found (cf. Matt. 16:6, 11, 12; Luke 3:1, 2; 5:17; 6:17; 21:25; John 1:44; 11:1; Acts 3:12; 6:9; 11:30; 12:11; Rom. 2:4; 2 Cor. 6:7; 7:1; 1 Tim. 4:5; Tit. 2:13; 3:5; Heb. 4:12; 9:12; 1 Pet. 1:23; 3:3; 2 Pet. 3:2; Rev. 22:1). In 21 of these, the second genitive clearly depended on the earlier genitive; this was true for three of the four in which, as in Rom. 8:2, all three genitives were articular. This makes it very likely that τοῦ θανάτου depends on νόμου rather than on ἀπό. In this case, τοῦ θανάτου is probably, in light of, e.g., 6:23, objective: "the power exercised by sin that leads to death."

32. Beker (256-57) points out that Paul uses a "liberation symbolism" that employs the notion of a change in power structures.

33. E.g., Haldane.

however, while not excluding justification, think that v. 2 is focusing more on sanctification; for "the law of sin," it is argued, is the internal, regulating power of sin.[34] But the liberation here is not just from "the law of sin," but from "the law of sin and death." And this expanded phrase appears to be deliberately chosen in order to summarize the total situation of the sinner as Paul has described it in chaps. 6 and 7: helpless under sin's power, doomed thereby to death and condemnation.[35] This being the case, we cannot restrict the application of v. 2 to either "justification" or "sanctification"; indeed, the very introduction of these terms at this point in Paul's discussion may unnecessarily complicate matters. "No condemnation" is the banner triumphantly flying over all those who are "in Christ" (v. 1) only because "in Christ" we have been set free by the Spirit from that realm, ruled by sin, in which condemnation (= death) is one's ineluctable fate. Verse 2, we might say, is speaking directly about neither justification nor sanctification but about that "realm transfer" that is the presupposition of both. As such, it significantly advances the discussion of chaps. 5–7 by introducing the Spirit as a key agent of liberation from the old realm of sin and death.

3 Nevertheless, as the "in Christ Jesus" in v. 2 — and in v. 1 — has already indicated, the Spirit's liberating work takes place only within the situation created by Christ. Verse 3 spells this out, showing that the Spirit can liberate the believer from sin and death only because in Christ and his cross God has already "condemned" sin. Believers are no longer "condemned" (v. 1) because in Christ sin has been "condemned": "For what the law could not do,[36] in that it was weakened by the flesh, God did: by sending his own Son in the form of sinful flesh and concerning sin he condemned sin in the flesh."[37]

---

34. See Calvin; Murray.

35. Cf. Fitzmyer, "Paul and the Law," p. 193.

36. Gk. τὸ ἀδύνατον τοῦ νόμου; whether ἀδύνατον is active ("what the law was incapable of doing") or passive ("what was impossible for the law") makes little difference to Paul's meaning (cf. Fitzmyer; most of the ancient commentators understand the word to be active; most contemporary commentators as passive). In either case, Paul is highlighting the inability of the law to accomplish that which God, in sending his Son, did accomplish.

37. The syntactical structure of the verse is unclear — specifically, how the opening clause τὸ . . . ἀδύνατον τοῦ νόμου ἐν ᾧ ἠσθένει διὰ τῆς σαρκός, relates to the main clause. This has been taken as a nominative absolute, "this [the liberation of v. 2] being impossible for the law" (Alford, Gifford), or as an accusative absolute, in apposition either to the main verb ("what was impossible for the law . . . God condemned sin"; cf. Cranfield), or to the sentence as a whole (S-H). But the best solution, which is represented in most English translations, is to posit an anacolouthon, a "broken construction." As he began his sentence, Paul intended to use as his main verb ἐποίησεν ("he did"), or something equivalent to it, thus establishing a direct contrast between "what the law could not do" and what "God *did*." Due, perhaps, to the number of prepositional modifiers, Paul does not complete this contrast. Instead, he moves immediately to the means by which God has

Nomos is now clearly the Mosaic law, and the clause succinctly states the most important point Paul makes about this law in the epistle — that it has proved incapable of rescuing people from the domain of sin and death (cf. 3:19; 3:28; 4:12-15; 7:7-25). But the law should not be criticized for this — for in a phrase that echoes 7:14b ("I am fleshly"), Paul reminds us that the law has failed only because "it was weakened by the flesh." Nor should we think of the flesh as frustrating the intentions of the law, for the law was never given as a means to secure righteousness.[38]

"Flesh," as in 7:5, is not the flesh of our bodies, or the bodies themselves, but the "this-worldly" orientation that all people share. It is this power that the law cannot break; indeed, as Paul has made clear, the law serves to strengthen the power of sin (cf. 5:20; 7:5). Luther uses a very appropriate analogy to make the point:

> It is as with a sick man who wants to drink some wine because he foolishly thinks that his health will return if he does so. Now if the doctor, without any criticism of the wine, should say to him: "It is impossible for the wine to cure you, it will only make you sicker," the doctor is not condemning the wine but only the foolish trust of the sick man in it. For he needs other medicine to get well, so that he then can drink his wine. Thus also our corrupt nature needs another kind of medicine than the Law, by which it can arrive at good health so that it can fulfill the Law (Scholium on 8:3).

In light of this criticism of the law in Romans, and the focus on liberation from sin and death in v. 2, "what the law could not do" is not to condemn sin (e.g., Godet), but to break sin's power — or, to put it positively, to secure eschatological life.[39]

It is God himself who has done what the law could not do, and he has done it through the sending[40] of "his own Son."[41] In most references to the

---

accomplished what the law could not do: "sending his own Son . . . he condemned sin in the flesh." The best way to convey the meaning Paul intended, then, will be to supply the missing verb, as is done, e.g., by RSV: "For God has done what the law, weakened by the flesh, could not do: sending his own Son in the likeness of sinful flesh and for sin, he condemned sin in the flesh" (see esp. Michel and Barrett).

38. Stalder, *Werk des Geistes,* pp. 398-99.

39. Hodge; Barrett; Osten-Sacken, *Römer 8,* pp. 147-48; Byrne, 92-93.

40. Such a reference to the "sending" (πέμψας) of Christ is unusual in Paul, the closest parallels being Gal. 4:4 — "God sent forth [ἐξαπέστειλεν] his Son" — and Phil. 2:7c — "becoming in the likeness [ὁμοιώματι] of human beings." The similarities among these verses (ὁμοίωμα, of course, occurs later in this verse, and the context of Gal. 4:4 has much in common with 8:3-17), along with the far more frequent reference to the "sending" of the Son in John's writings, have led to the supposition that Paul may here be dependent on a tradition. See, e.g., E. Schweizer, "Zum traditionsgeschichtlichen Hintergrund der

"sending" of the Son the focus is on the incarnation. But the sacrificial allusions later in this verse show that, without eliminating allusion to the incarnation, Paul's application of the language is broader, with a particular focus on the redemptive death of the Son (cf. also Gal. 4:4).[42] Paul's description of the way in which God sent the Son contributes to this sacrificial focus. "In the form of sinful flesh" emphasizes the full participation of the Son in the human condition.[43] Like the phrases "born from a woman, born under the law" in Gal. 4:4, it shows that the Son possesses the necessary requirement to act as our substitute. But why does Paul say that Christ came in "the *homoiōma* of sinful flesh"? Certainly, in light of "in the flesh" later in this very verse, Paul cannot mean that Christ had only the "appearance" of flesh.[44] Moreover, the word *homoiōma* here probably has the nuance of "form" rather than "likeness" or "copy." In other words, the word does not suggest superficial or outward similarity, but inward and real participation or "expression." It may be, then, that Paul wants simply to say that Christ really took on "sinful flesh."[45] But this may be going too far in the other direction. Paul uses *homoiōma* here for a reason; and it is probably, as in 6:5 and 5:14, to introduce a note of distinction. The use of the term implies some kind of reservation about identifying Christ with "*sinful* flesh."[46] Paul is walking a fine line here. On the one hand, he wants to insist that Christ fully entered into the human condition, became "in-fleshed" *(in-carnis),* and, as such, exposed himself to the power of sin (cf. 6:8-10). On the other hand, he must avoid suggesting

---

'Sendungsformel' Gal 4,4f. Rm 8,3f. Joh 3,16f. 1 Joh 4,9," *ZNW* 57 (1966), 199-200; Käsemann, 216. This is possible, but the evidence is inconclusive.

41. Note the emphatic ἑαυτοῦ ("his own"); and cf. 8:32, τοῦ ἰδίου υἱοῦ.

42. Contra, e.g., Whiteley (*Theology of Saint Paul,* p. 100), who minimizes sacrificial allusions and says that 8:3 is "primarily incarnational."

43. Byrne, 95.

44. This essentially docetic interpretation was advocated by Marcion.

45. See, e.g., Branick, "Sinful Flesh," pp. 248-61; F. M. Gillmann, "Another Look at Romans 8:3: 'In the Likeness of Sinful Flesh,'" *CBQ* 49 (1987), 598-600 (although she rightly criticizes Branick's interpretation of the lexical data).

46. See esp. Kuss and Cranfield. Some interpreters (e.g., the majority of the church fathers [cf. Schelkle]; Gaugler; Barrett; Stevens, *Pauline Theology,* pp. 209-11) think, specifically, that Paul is guarding against the idea that Christ had committed sin (a notion he rejects; cf., e.g., 2 Cor. 5:21). A deeper theological implication has been spotted by many, particularly among those (such as Reformed dogmaticians) who stress original sin. According to this view, Paul implies something about the nature of the incarnation itself: that Christ, although taking on real, human flesh, did not take on "sinful," or "fallen," human flesh. For had he done so, Christ would have been subject to the penalties of original sin and thus disqualified from vicariously taking upon himself the penalty due our sin. See, on the Reformed tradition, Calvin, *Institutes* 2.13.4, and the quotations in Heppe, *Reformed Dogmatics,* pp. 426-27. Cf. also, e.g., Murray.

that Christ so participated in this realm that he became imprisoned "in the flesh" (cf. the negative use of this phrase in 7:5 and 8:8, 9) and became, thus, so subject to sin that he could be personally guilty of it. *Homoiōma* rights the balances that the addition of "sinful" to "flesh" might have tipped a bit too far in one direction.

Sacrificial allusions are probably also present in the next phrase, "concerning sin." Paul might mean no more than that Christ's mission generally "had to do" with sin.[47] But the phrase so frequently means "sin offering" in the LXX[48] that it is likely to mean that there too: God sent his own Son "to be a sin offering."[49] This brings us to the end of the subordinate material and, finally, to the (grammatical) main clause: God, in sending his Son, "condemned sin in the flesh."[50] "In the flesh" naturally implies the humanity of Christ, but it also alludes to that sphere of human weakness into which Christ entered to accomplish his work. The flesh that made the law ineffective in dealing with sin was conquered from within.

But what does Paul mean when he says that God *condemned* sin in the flesh"? Putting together the natural meaning of the term[51] with the context, we can conclude that what Paul must mean is a judicial action that was accomplished through the sacrifice of Christ on the cross and that had as its object that "the just requirement of the law be fulfilled" in Christians (v. 4a). The focus on sacrifice means that Paul is probably not referring to the "overpowering" of sin through Christ's incarnation (Lagrange) or to the "living condemnation of sin" represented in Christ's sinless life (Godet). Also ex-

---

47. Cf. esp. T. C. G. Thorton, "The Meaning of καὶ περὶ ἁμαρτίας in Romans viii.3," *JTS* n.s. 22 (1971), 515-17. See also, e.g., Whiteley, *Theology of Saint Paul,* p. 136; Gifford; Godet; Murray; Cranfield.

48. 44 of 54 LXX occurrences of περὶ ἁμαρτίας refer to sacrifice; the phrase translates חַטָּאָה, חַטָּאת, and אָשָׁם. Three of the eight NT occurrences also have this meaning (Heb. 10:6, 8; 13:11).

49. See esp. N. T. Wright, "The Meaning of περὶ ἁμαρτίας in Romans 8:3," in *Studia Biblica 1978, III,* pp. 453-59. Also, e.g., Michel; Dunn, "Jesus' Death," p. 132; Gundry, "Grace, Works and Staying Saved," p. 31 n. 83. The phrase should probably be taken with πέμψας ("sending") rather than with κατέκρινεν ("condemn").

50. ἐν τῇ σαρκί goes with κατέκρινεν, not ἁμαρτίαν (e.g., "condemned the sin that was in the flesh"). See Robertson, 784.

51. κατακρίνω is a judicial term. It usually denotes the act of "passing sentence" (e.g., Mark 14:64: "they all condemned him to be worthy of death") but sometimes, particularly when God is the subject, includes both the "passing of sentence" and the actual execution of that sentence (Rom. 14:23 [?]; 1 Cor. 11:32; 2 Pet. 2:6; cf. F. Büchsel, *TDNT* III, 951). In an extension from this first meaning, the word can also connote "condemn by showing someone to be in the wrong in comparison with oneself" (cf. Matt. 12:41, 42; Luke 11:31, 32; Heb. 11:7). The word almost always has a personal object: people are condemned.

cluded is the popular interpretation according to which Paul means that God in Christ "broke the power of" sin.[52] While it fits the context, and may be an implication of what Paul is saying, this view illegitimately eliminates the judicial connotations of "condemn." The interpretation that best meets the criteria above sees the condemnation of sin to consist in God's executing his judgment on sin in the atoning death of his Son. As our substitute, Christ "was made sin for us" (2 Cor. 5:21) and suffered the wrath of God, the judgment of God upon that sin (cf. *hilastērion* in Rom. 3:25; Gal. 3:13).[53] In his doing so, of course, we may say that sin's power was broken, in the sense that Paul pictures sin as a power that holds people in its clutches and brings condemnation to them. In executing the full sentence of condemnation against sin, God effectively removed sin's ability to "dictate terms" for those who are "in Christ" (v. 2). The condemnation that our sins deserve has been poured out on Christ, our sin-bearer; that is why "there is now no condemnation for those who are in Christ Jesus" (v. 1).

4   Verse 4 states the purpose[54] for which God has condemned sin in the flesh: "that the righteous requirement of the law might be fulfilled in us." What Paul means by this depends a great deal on how we interpret the word we have translated "righteous requirement." Based on its meaning[55] and use earlier in Romans, it could mean either (1) "just decree," "ordinance that decrees punishment" (cf. 1:32); (2) "righteousness" (see 5:16 and our notes there); or (3) "just requirement," the reference being either to the behavior required by the law (2:26) or to the righteousness demanded by the law. The first would fit the context very nicely; the sentence of judgment executed on sin in Christ (v. 3) "fulfills" that "decree of the law" which demands death for sin (cf. 3:19).[56] However, it has against it the positive flavor of Paul's

---

52. See, e.g., Alford, Stuart, Murray, Cranfield.

53. Haldane; Hodge; Denney; Byrne, 95. Theissen argues that this text, Gal. 3:13-14, and 2 Cor. 5:21 share a similar soteriological symbolism, in which Christ as redeemer takes on our "Unheil" so that we can have salvation ("Soteriologische Symbolik," p. 290).

54. Note the Gk. ἵνα.

55. The Greek term is δικαίωμα. As its suffix -μα would suggest, it refers to the consequence of "establishing right" (δικαιόω), and therefore is used in secular Greek to mean legal claim or document, judicial sentence or punishment, and statute or ordinance (cf. G. Schrenk, *TDNT* II, 219-21). This last meaning is particularly frequent in the LXX, where the plural δικαιώματα occurs over one hundred times to designate (especially cultic or social) "statutes" or "ordinances" of God's law (usually translating חֹק, חֻקָּה, or מִשְׁפָּט [e.g., Deut. 4:1; 5:1; 29 times in Ps. 119]). In most cases, the word occurs in the plural, although the singular is used to denote specific commandments (cf. Exod. 21:31; Num. 15:16). The NT follows the LXX in using the plural to designate OT laws (Luke 1:6; Heb. 9:1, 10; and Rom. 2:26).

56. Benoit, "La loi et la croix," pp. 498-99.

language in the rest of the verse: "fulfilled in us, who walk not according to the flesh but according to the Spirit."[57] The second is unlikely because the meaning of "righteousness" for this term in 5:16 is very much dependent on the rhetorical contrast in that context. Probably, then, especially in light of the qualification "of the law," Paul uses the word with its usual LXX meaning, "right or just requirement." But what is this "just requirement"? And how is it accomplished?

Since Paul singles out the command to love as the "fulfillment" and "summary" of the law (cf. 13:8-10 and Gal. 5:14), the "just requirement" or "legal claim" of the law may well be love, and its fulfillment a consistent lifestyle of love on the part of Spirit-led Christians.[58] Besides, however, the fact that Paul has done nothing to prepare his Roman readers for this application, the language "in us" is inappropriate as a way of indicating Christians' acts of love (contrast the active formulation in 13:8).[59] We must, then, give the phrase its simplest and broadest meaning: the summary (note the singular, as opposed to the plural of 2:26) of what the law demands of God's people. Through God's breaking of the power of sin (v. 3), the "right requirement" of the law is accomplished by those who "walk according to the Spirit." To quote Augustine's famous formulation, "Law was given that grace might be sought, grace was given that the law might be fulfilled."[60]

But we still must pin down the nature of this "fulfillment." Some think that Christians, participants in the New Covenant, with the "law written on the heart" and the Spirit empowering within, fulfill the demand of the law by righteous living.[61] However, while it is true that God's act in Christ has as

57. Cf. Byrne, 93-94 n. 53.

58. S. Lyonnet, "Le Nouveau Testament à lumière de l'Ancien. A propos de Rom 8,2-4," *NRT* 87 (1965), 582-84; Bandstra, *The Law and the Elements of the World,* pp. 107-8; H. M. W. van de Sandt, "Research into Rom. 8,4a: The Legal Claim of the Law," and "An Explanation of Rom. 8,4a," *Bijdragen* 37 (1976), 252-69 and 361-78; R. W. Thompson, "How Is the Law Fulfilled in Us? An Interpretation of Rom. 8:4," *Louvain Studies* 11 (1986), 32-33; Lambrecht and Thompson, *Justification by Faith,* pp. 62-63.

59. Other suggestions for a specific referent include Ziesler's ("The Just Requirement of the Law [Romans 8:4]," *AusBR* 35 [1987], 77-82), that the "righteous requirement" is the prohibition of coveting (cf. 7:7), and Cranfield's, that the reference is to faith. But the former is too far removed from this context, and the idea that Paul would think of faith as the basic demand of the law rests, I believe, on a misinterpretation of several texts (see the comments on 2:25-26 and 3:27 especially). As Paul has made clear, it is "works" or "doing" that is the law's basic demand (see 2:13; compare 2:25, "obeying the law," with 2:26, "keeping the precepts of the law"; 3:20 and 28 ["works of the law"]).

60. *On the Spirit and the Letter* 19.

61. See esp. Deidun, 77; also Murray; Cranfield; Morris; Ridderbos, *Paul,* pp. 280-88; Schreiner, "Abolition and Fulfillment," pp. 60-61; idem, *The Law and Its Fulfillment,* pp. 150-54; Thielmann, *Plight to Solution,* pp. 88-89; Fee, *God's Empowering Presence,* pp.

one of its intents that we produce "fruit" (cf. 6:15-23; 7:4), and that the law cannot be cavalierly dismissed as of no significance to the Christian life, we do not think that this is what Paul is saying here.

Two points may be made. First, the passive verb "might *be* fulfilled" points not to something that we are to do but to something that is done in and for us.[62] Second, the always imperfect obedience of the law by Christians does not satisfy what is demanded by the logic of this text. The fulfilling of the "just decree of the law" must answer to that inability of the law with which Paul began this sentence (v. 3a). As we have seen, "what the law could not do" is to free people from "the law of sin and death" — to procure righteousness and life. And it could not do this because "the flesh" prevented people from obeying its precepts (see 8:7 and 7:14-25). The removal of this barrier consists not in the actions of believers, for our obedience always falls short of that perfect obedience required by the law. As Calvin puts it, "the faithful, while they sojourn in this world, never make such a proficiency, as that the justification of the law becomes in them full or complete. This [v. 4a] then must be applied to forgiveness; for when the obedience of Christ is accepted for us, the law is satisfied, so that we are counted just."

If, then, the inability of the law is to be overcome without an arbitrary cancellation of the law, it can happen only through a perfect obedience of the law's demands (cf. 2:13 and our comments there). This, of course, is exactly what Jesus Christ has done. As our substitute, he satisfied the righteous requirement of the law, living a life of perfect submission to God. In laying upon him the condemnation due all of us (v. 3b; cf. v. 1), God also made it possible for the righteous obedience that Christ had earned to be transferred to us. Verses 3-4 then fit into a pattern in Paul's presentation of the work of Christ that has been called an "interchange" — Christ becomes what we are so that we might become what Christ is.[63] In this sense, then, we may interpret "the righteous requirement of the

---

534-37. The phrase ἐν ὑμῖν could then have an instrumental force — "by us" (cf. Lambrecht and Thompson, *Justification by Faith*, pp. 64-70) — or a locative sense (see, e.g., Fee). By turning the singular δικαίωμα into an English plural ("righteous requirement," "Law's requirements," "righteous demands") NIV, NJB, and TEV suggest this interpretation.

62. Paul consistently uses the verb πληρόω with reference not to a human being "doing" the law in concrete existence, but with reference to the climactic, eschatological completion of the law first made possible in Christ (cf. also Rom. 13:8, 10 [πλήρωμα]; Gal. 5:14).

63. Cf. M. D. Hooker, "Interchange in Christ," *JTS* n.s. 22 (1971), 349-61; idem, "Interchange and Atonement," p. 469, and, on this verse, Byrne, 92-95; Dunn, "Jesus' Death," p. 137. Notable examples of this pattern in Paul are: he "became a curse" to redeem us from "the curse of the law" (Gal. 3:13); was "born under the law" to redeem those who were "under the law" (Gal. 4:4-5). But the closest parallel to Rom. 8:3-4 is perhaps the clearest "interchange" text, 2 Cor. 5:21: "Him who knew no sin, he [God] made to be sin that we might become the righteousness of God in him."

law" to be the demand of the law for perfect obedience, or for righteousness.[64] And the law's just demand is fulfilled in Christians not through their own acts of obedience but through their incorporation into Christ.[65] He fulfilled the law; and, in him, believers also fulfill the law — perfectly, so that they may be pronounced "righteous," free from "condemnation" (v. 1). It is in this way that Paul's stress on faith "establishes the law" (3:31), for, in grasping Christ by faith, people are accounted as really having "done the law." Indeed, as Paul makes clear in this letter, it is *only* through faith in Christ that the law can really be accomplished.[66]

If this interpretation of the first part of v. 4 is correct, then the participial clause modifying "us" is not instrumental — "the just decree of the law is fulfilled in us *by* our walking not according to the flesh but according to the Spirit"[67] — but descriptive, characterizing those in whom the just decree of

64. Note Wright's suggestion (*Climax,* pp. 203, 211) that δικαίωμα refers to the "covenant decree" that those do the things of the law shall live by them.

65. Melanchthon; Nygren; Barrett; Stuhlmacher; Fitzmyer; Byrne, 93-94; idem, "Living Out the Righteousness of God," pp. 568-69; Wilckens; Keck, "The Law of Sin and Death," p. 53; Deidun, 72-75; Beker, 105-7, 186.

66. This verse, then, gives little support for the "third use of the law" as tradition-ally defined. For, if we are right, Paul is claiming not that Christians must live under the law as a "rule for the new life" (Ridderbos, *Paul,* p. 281; cf. his discussion on pp. 279-81 and note Bandstra, *The Law and the Elements of the World,* pp. 183-89), but that Christians have, in Christ, fully satisfied the demands of the law. Whether or not it is incumbent on Christians to obey the Mosaic law — or, as is usually meant, parts ("the moral law") of the Mosaic law — is not said in this verse.

Certainly this verse implies — as does, e.g., 8:7 — that satisfaction of God's "eternal moral demands" is necessary for righteousness to be obtained (cf. 2:13). But Paul's point is not that the demands of the Mosaic law as such must be met, but that the "just requirement" expressed in that law must be met. It is God's law in this broader sense that Paul makes applicable to all people (perhaps in 8:7; cf. especially the distinctions in 1 Cor. 9:20-22), not the Mosaic law per se. It is this basic demand of God that Christ has met on the cross, and, as I have argued, Paul in 8:4 is showing that it is by our appropriation of Christ that we meet this demand — not in our obedience to the law, whether Mosaic or not. Without confining the point to this alone, I suggest that it is this new "indicative" that is at the heart of the new covenant (cf. Jer. 31:31-34; Ezek. 36:26-27; and cf. Deidun, 37, 204-5). God enables the fulfillment of his "law," his just demand on his creatures, by acting himself in his Spirit to provide for that fulfillment. "Writing the law on the heart" means, I take it, that God's demand will no longer be imposed on his people from without, in the Mosaic form of "tablets," "that which is written" (γράμμα), but that it will, under the New Covenant, be put within God's people, through the Spirit's work of transformation and renewal. The essence of that demand does not change, but its "form," or "means of expression," does. Nothing, then, is said in this text about the Mosaic law being the demand under which Christians in this age must live. And, that being so, no conflict with 6:14 and other like passages exists (contra, e.g., Räisänen, 114-17; Sanders, *Paul, the Law and the Jewish People,* pp. 98-101, who find a key "tension" in Paul's thinking on this point).

67. For this interpretation, see, e.g., Cranfield.

the law is fulfilled as "those *who* walk not according to the flesh but according to the Spirit."[68] The reference to Christian behavior in this phrase[69] shows that Paul does not separate the "fulfillment" of the law from the lifestyle of Christians. But, this does not mean that Christian behavior is how the law is fulfilled — a conclusion that is incompatible with the considerations adduced in the last paragraph. Rather, Christian behavior is the necessary mark of those in whom this fulfillment takes place. God not only provides in Christ the full completion of the law's demands for the believer, but he also sends the Spirit into the hearts of believers to empower a new obedience to his demands. Christians now are directed by the Spirit and not by the flesh.[70] As I have noted elsewhere (see on 7:5 and the introduction to chap. 8), flesh and Spirit stand over against each other not as parts of a person (an anthropological dualism),[71] nor even as impulses or powers within a person, but as the powers, or dominating features, of the two "realms" of salvation history. "To walk according to the flesh," then, is to have one's life determined and directed by the values of "this world," of the world in rebellion against God.[72] It is a lifestyle that is purely "human" in its orientation.[73] To "walk according to the Spirit," on the other hand, is to live under the control, and according to the values, of the "new age," created and dominated by God's Spirit as his eschatological gift.

5 In vv. 5-13, Paul continues to use this opposition between flesh and Spirit to expand on the life that is given to believers in and through God's Spirit. He begins by asserting again the unbreakable connection between Spirit and life on the one hand and flesh and death on the other (vv. 5-8). His purpose here is more on the negative side, as he elaborates particularly on the "weakness of the flesh" (v. 3a; cf. 7:14-25). Paul then (vv. 9-11) turns to a more positive point, as he expresses his confidence that the Romans themselves are firmly on the "Spirit" side of this contrast (cf. vv. 3b-4).[74] In the concluding verses of this section (vv. 12-13), however, Paul reminds his readers that the life-giving power of God's Spirit is finally effective only in those who continue to let the Spirit change their lives.

The antithesis between flesh and Spirit stated in v. 4b in terms of

---

68. Turner, 285; Keck, "The Law of Sin and Death," p. 52; Stalder, *Werk des Geistes,* p. 406; Deidun, 75.

69. The verb περιπατέω ("walk") is one of Paul's favorites to depict the daily behavior, or moral direction, of the believer (see the notes on 6:4).

70. The preposition κατά probably has the connotation "directed by."

71. On this point, see particularly Stacey, *Pauline View of Man,* pp. 174-78.

72. Cf., e.g., Sand, *Der Begriff 'Sarx',* p. 279.

73. See the interchange between being "fleshly" (σαρκικοί) and walking "according to man" (κατὰ ἄνθρωπον) in 1 Cor. 3:3.

74. See Wright, *Climax,* pp. 200-201, for the relationship of vv. 5-11 to vv. 3-4.

"walking according to" is pursued in vv. 5-9 with several different expressions:

> v. 5a: "being according to the flesh/according to the Spirit"
> v. 5b: "thinking the things of the flesh/of the Spirit"
> v. 6: "the mind of the flesh/Spirit"
> vv. 8-9: "being in the flesh/in the Spirit"

To begin at the end of the sequence: what Paul says in vv. 8-9 makes clear that the contrast between "being in the flesh" and "being in the Spirit" is a contrast between non-Christian and Christian. As in 7:5, Paul uses "in" to connote the idea of "realm," with flesh and Spirit denoting those "powers" that dominate the two realms of salvation history. To become a Christian means to be transferred from the realm dominated by the flesh to the realm dominated by the Spirit. The "mind" *(phronēma)* of the flesh/Spirit (v. 6) will then denote the mind-set or attitude that characterizes those who belong to these two respective realms, with "thinking" *(phronousin)* the things of the flesh/Spirit (v. 5b) a rhetorical equivalent. Finally, considering the connection between vv. 4b and 5, "being according to the flesh/Spirit" and "walking according to the flesh/Spirit" may mean roughly the same thing: the "lifestyle" or daily conduct of a person.[75] But the logic of Paul's argument suggests rather that "being according to the flesh" in v. 5 is the same as "being in the flesh" in v. 8: that is, a "positional" rather than a "behavioral" concept.

Paul's purpose in pursuing this series of contrasts is not "paraenetic"; that is, he is not warning Christians about two different possibilities they face in order to encourage them to live according to the Spirit.[76] Paul certainly does this, and in language similar to the language here (cf. Gal. 5:16-26). But, as we have noted, "being in the flesh" (v. 8) is *not* a possibility for the believer; and when we add to this the lack of any imperatives and the general, third person, language of the paragraph, we are warranted in concluding that Paul's interest here is descriptive rather than hortatory.[77] In some sense, then, it is fair to say that Paul is contrasting two groups of people: the converted and the unconverted.[78] But Paul's main purpose is to highlight the radical differences between the flesh and the Spirit as a means of showing why only those who "walk/think/are" after the Spirit can have eschatological life.[79] This is the connection between vv. 1-4 and vv. 5-8. Life, eschatological life, is con-

---

75. Cranfield.
76. Contra, e.g., Michel.
77. Cf. Deidun, 77; Fee, *God's Empowering Presence,* p. 539.
78. Lietzmann; cf. Schmithals, *Theologische Anthropologie,* pp. 86-87.
79. Stalder, *Werk des Geistes,* pp. 418-19.

ferred only on those who "walk according to the Spirit" (cf. v. 4b). "For"[80] those who are "according to the flesh" can never escape death (v. 6); the flesh prevents people from obeying God's law (v. 7) or from pleasing him (v. 8). It is the Spirit, "the Spirit of life" (v. 2), who reverses this situation, making it possible, through Christ, for believers to "fulfill the law" (v. 4) and to be delivered from condemnation (v. 1). In vv. 9-11 Paul draws out these life-giving consequences of the Spirit. To begin with, however, he notes the basic tendencies of both the flesh and the Spirit (vv. 5-6), and then develops the negative side of the situation in vv. 7-8: the natural situation of the person in this world — life in the flesh — as a situation of death. These verses thus recapitulate the main themes of chap. 7.

In vv. 5-6, Paul uses a logical progression to contrast the ends to which the flesh and the Spirit lead. In this progression Paul uses the language of "thinking" as the "middle term" to connect existence determined by flesh or Spirit ("those who are according to flesh/Spirit") with the contrasting destinies of death on the one hand and life and peace on the other. Both words, "think" in v. 5 and "mind" in v. 6, come from the same Greek root, a root that connotes not a purely mental process but, more broadly, the general direction of the will, encompassing "all the faculties of the soul — reason, understanding, and affections."[81]

6 The "for"[82] is neither causal nor explanatory, but continuative.[83] The "mind" of the flesh/Spirit, the attitude characterized and determined by the flesh/Spirit,[84] is simply the substantival equivalent of thinking "the things of the flesh/Spirit" (v. 5b). The accent falls on what results from these contrasting mind-sets. Those who have the mind-set of the flesh, who, we might say, have a strictly "this-worldly" attitude, experience death. As throughout Rom. 5–8, this is death in its broadest aspect, certainly including eschatological condemnation (see vv. 1-4), but not confined to that. "Death" reigns in this life over all those who are outside Christ (cf. 5:12, 15, 21). Likewise,

---

80. The γάρ in v. 5. Instead of introducing an explanation of the antithesis between flesh and Spirit in v. 4b (e.g., Lagrange), it introduces the whole following argument, in which Paul develops the reasons why the flesh brings death and the Spirit life.

81. Calvin. The two words are distinctively Pauline; 23 of the 26 NT occurrences of φρονέω are Paul's, and all four of the NT occurrences of φρόνημα are his. Cranfield, comparing similar phrases in Greek literature outside the NT, suggests that φρονοῦσιν τὰ τῆς σάρκος/τοῦ πνεύματος means "to take the side of the flesh/Spirit." But this would force a distinction in meaning between this phrase and τὸ φρόνημα τῆς σάρκος/τοῦ πνεύματος in v. 6, disrupting the natural flow of Paul's argument. It is better, therefore, to translate "regard things with an attitude characteristic of the flesh/Spirit," taking the genitives as descriptive.

82. Gk. γάρ.

83. NRSV and NIV appropriately leave it untranslated; cf. Kuss; BAGD.

84. As in v. 5, the genitives τῆς σάρκος and τοῦ πνεύματος are probably descriptive.

"life" and "peace" denote that state of freedom from "the law of sin and death" that begins for the believer in this life, albeit in less than its final and definitive form.[85] The words do not denote a subjective state of mind (e.g., "peace of mind and heart") but the objective reality of the salvation into which the believer, who has "the mind of the Spirit," has entered.[86] The "peace" here is that "peace with God" given through justification (see 5:1; cf. also 14:17), the state that is in contrast to the non-Christian's "enmity toward God" (see v. 7).

7-8 Verses 7-8 explain why[87] the mind-set of the flesh must lead to death. As shorthand for the principle and power of the godless world, "flesh" and the mind-set characteristic of it are necessarily hostile to God and all his purposes. No neutrality is possible; without the Spirit's mind-set, found only through union with Christ (see vv. 9-10), people can only order their lives in a way that is hostile to God and that will incur his wrath. The second part of v. 7 and v. 8 explain[88] this hostility to God. The "mind-set produced by the flesh" does not, and cannot, submit to God's law. Those "in the flesh" — the "natural" person apart from Christ — cannot please God. In light of vv. 3-4 (and chap. 7), we might expect "law of God" to refer to the Mosaic law.[89] On the other hand, this may be one of those verses in which Paul uses *nomos* to depict the demand of God generally rather than any particular expression of that demand.[90] In either case, we may draw two important implications from these statements.

First, the "law of God" remains a standard by which the conduct of unbelievers can be measured and condemned. Believers are no longer "under the law" (Rom. 6:14, 15), subject to its binding authority (7:4); but unbelievers are subject still to this power of the "old age." Second, Paul's assessment of persons apart from Christ may justly be summed up in the theological categories of "total depravity" and "total inability." "Total depravity" does not mean that all people are as evil as they possibly could be — that all people

---

85. This calls into question Siber's observation (*Mit Christus Leben*, p. 85) that Paul refrains from saying in this passage that the Christian is now "alive."

86. E.g., Käsemann; contra Gifford; Dodd.

87. διότι has causal force — "because" (BAGD).

88. Explanatory γάρ.

89. Support for this interpretation can be found in the notion held by some "covenant" theologians (e.g., Gomarus [1594]) that the Mosaic law "restated" the Adamic "covenant of works"; cf. G. Schrenk, *Gottesreich und Bund im älteren Protestantismus vornehmlich bei Johannes Cocceius, zugleich ein Beitrag zur Geschichte des Pietismus und des heilsgeschichtlichen Theologie* (Gütersloh: Mohn, 1923), pp. 63-64. Cf. also the discussion in M. Karlberg, "The Mosaic Covenant and the Concept of Works in Reformed Hermeneutics: A Historical-Critical Analysis with Particular Attention to Early Covenant Eschatology" (Th.D. diss., Westminster Theological Seminary, 1980).

90. See, e.g., Feuillet, "Loi de Dieu," p. 42.

commit every possible sin — nor does it deny that there is knowledge of the good within each person. What is meant rather is that every person apart from Christ is thoroughly in the grip of the power of sin, and that this power extends to all the person's faculties. This Paul has enunciated clearly by accusing all non-Christians of having a "mind-set," a total life-direction, that is innately hostile to God (v. 7). All people, by nature derived from Adam, are incurably "bent" toward their own good rather than the good of others or of God. The various sins to which we are attracted — desire for riches, or station in life, or power, or sexual pleasure — are but different symptoms of this same sickness, this idolatrous bent toward self-gratification.[91] Once again, we must remember that Paul is not here using "flesh" as we often do, to denote sexual sin specifically. To be "in the flesh," or "carnal," or "fleshly," includes, in the sense Paul is using flesh here, all sins. The person who is preoccupied with his or her own success in business, at the expense of others and of God, is just as much dominated by the flesh as the person who commits adultery. Both persons are manifesting, in different ways, that destructive, self-centered rebellion against God and his law which can be overcome only by the power of God's Spirit in Christ. Verse 8, on the other hand, plainly shows that no person can rescue himself from this condition. As long as that person is "in the flesh" — and only the Spirit can rescue us from this envelopment in the flesh — he or she is "totally unable" to please God.

9 Paul signals a change in direction with the adversative "but."[92] From the situation of those apart from Christ, Paul turns his attention to the Roman Christians, whom he now begins addressing directly: "those 'in the flesh' can never please God; *but you*[93] are not in the flesh, but in the Spirit. . . ." As we noted earlier, the contrast between being "in the flesh" and "in the Spirit" is a contrast between belonging to the old age of sin and death and belonging to the new age of righteousness and life. So characteristic of these respective "ages" or "realms" are flesh and Spirit that the person belonging to one or the other can be said to be "in" them. In this sense, then, no Christian can be "in the flesh"; and all Christians are, by definition, "in the Spirit." We miss Paul's intention if we think of being "in the flesh" here as the condition of mortality that continues to characterize even believers (Nygren), or as the moral weakness and proneness to sin that, more lamentably, we still possess (Dunn). For the rest of the verse makes absolutely clear that (1) to be a Christian is to be indwelt by God's Spirit; and (2) to be indwelt by God's Spirit means to be "in the Spirit" and *not* "in the flesh." Paul's language is "positional": he is depicting the believer's status in Christ, secured for him

91. See esp. Luther; contra, e.g., Stuart.
92. Gk. δέ.
93. Emphatic ὑμεῖς.

or her at conversion.[94] Paul certainly views the Christian as, in some sense, affected by both realms of salvation history. But it is probably overstating the matter to say that the believer is situated "between" these two ages or realms (as does, e.g., Nygren). For this formulation misses the decisive past transfer of the believer into the new age of life and peace that Paul is celebrating in these chapters. Subject to physical decay and death, prone to sin, tempted to let the flesh take control of us again we may be — but, to do justice to Paul, we must insist that the believer is freed from "the law of sin and death" (8:2; cf. 5:12-21), "dead to sin's power" (6:1-23), and no longer "in the flesh."

To be sure, a condition is placed on this being "in the Spirit": having the Spirit of God dwelling in the person. But, as 1 Cor. 3:16 shows — addressed to the "carnal" (cf. 3:1-3) Corinthian Christians, no less! — Paul believes that every Christian is indwelt by the Spirit of God. Indeed, this is just what Paul affirms in the last part of the verse, where he denies that the person who does not have the "Spirit of Christ" can make any claim to being a Christian at all. In other words, for Paul, possession of the Spirit goes hand-in-hand with being a Christian. However much we may need to grow in our relationship to the Spirit; however much we may be graciously given fresh and invigorating experiences of God's Spirit, from the moment of conversion on, the Holy Spirit is a settled resident within.[95] That Paul in the same verse can speak of the believer as "in the Spirit" and the Spirit as being "in" the believer reveals the metaphorical nature of his language. In the one case, the Spirit is pictured as entering into and taking control of the person's life; in the other, the believer is pictured as living in that realm in which the Spirit rules, guides, and determines one's destiny.

The conditional language Paul uses here ("if" . . . "if"[96]) could mean that he is not convinced that all his readers are truly indwelt by the Spirit.[97] Since, however, both words can be translated "since," Paul may, on the other hand, be assuming the reality of his readers' Christian experience.[98] The context in this case strongly suggests that Paul is, indeed, assuming the reality of the Christian experience of his readers.[99] Here (see vv. 15-16), and

94. See Ridderbos, *Paul,* p. 221.

95. Paul uses the verb οἰκέω, "dwell," which implies a settled residence (see also John 14:17; cf. Str-B, 3.239; Dunn); contrast the "dwelling" of sin in the non-Christian (7:17, 20).

96. εἴπερ and εἰ, respectively.

97. Dunn.

98. Cranfield; Kuss.

99. The issue cannot be settled lexically, for the degree to which the reality of the condition stated by εἴπερ and εἰ is assumed can be determined only from context. εἴπερ means "if indeed," "if after all" [BDF 454{2}]; in Rom. 3:30 and 2 Thess. 1:6, the reality of the condition is supposed, but this is not clearly the case in Rom. 8:17; 1 Cor. 8:5; 15:15.

throughout the letter (see, e.g., 1:8; 15:14), Paul addresses the Romans as believers; and the shift from the general third person in vv. 7-8 to the second plural of direct address in v. 9 (and note the shift back to the third person in v. 9b!) reveals Paul's attitude about his readers.

10 Paul now contrasts the situation he has just described in v. 9b[100] at the same time as he resumes the main thread of his teaching from v. 9a. Significantly, Paul now speaks of "Christ" being in the Roman Christians, whereas in v. 9 it was "the Spirit of God" who was said to be dwelling in believers. What this means is not that Christ and the Spirit are equated or interchangeable, but that Christ and the Spirit are so closely related in communicating to believers the benefits of salvation that Paul can move from one to the other almost unconsciously. Again, it is clear that the believer who by faith has come to be joined with Christ (see Rom. 6:1-11) has not only Christ but also the Spirit resident within. The indwelling Spirit and the indwelling Christ are distinguishable but inseparable. Moreover, the quick and unstudied movement from "Spirit of God" (v. 9a) to "Spirit of Christ" (v. 9b) to "Christ" (v. 10a) to "Spirit" (vv. 10b-11) reveals the "practical trinitarianism" that already characterizes the NT. Note also, once more, the flexibility of Paul's theological metaphors. The union of the believer with Christ, our representative head (cf. 5:12-21), can be conveyed both by the language of the believer being "in" Christ and of Christ being "in" the believer.[101]

Paul spells out the benefits secured for the believer by the indwelling Christ in two parallel clauses: "the body is dead because of sin"; and "the Spirit is life because of righteousness." In the first clause, "body" *(sōma)* might refer to the "person" as a whole, dead "with reference to" sin, in the sense of Rom. 6 — that is, that the person has "died to," been freed from, the dominion of sin.[102] But it is better to think of the body's "deadness" here as a negative condition, the state of condemnation — a condition that has come about "because of sin."[103] And the "body" is probably the physical body specifically, its deadness consisting in the penalty of physical death that must still be experienced by the believer.[104]

---

100. Hence the δέ, "but."

101. No clear difference in meaning between the two phrases can be discerned, although the "Christ in you" language is far less frequent in Paul (here and in 2 Cor. 13:5; Gal. 2:20; 4:19; Eph. 3:17; Col. 1:27). Both phrases stress the believer's intimate union with, and domination by, Christ.

102. So most church fathers (according to Schelkle); and, e.g., Kuss; Käsemann; Wilckens.

103. When Paul teaches that the believer is "dead *to* sin," he always uses the dative case; and the preposition διά, which normally has a causal meaning, would be a singularly poor choice to convey this sense.

104. An important point in favor of this interpretation is that Paul refers to resurrection as the solution to this "deadness" in v. 11. See esp. Gundry, 38; Harris, *Raised*

Adopting this interpretation, we will then give the first clause a concessive thrust — "*although* the body is 'subject to death' because of sin . . ." — and the main point will come in the second clause. Here again, there is considerable difference of opinion over the meaning of the clause. Many English versions (cf., e.g., RSV, NIV, NASB) translate *pneuma* in an anthropological sense: "your spirit is alive because of righteousness."[105] However, although the undeniably anthropological meaning of "body" favors this view, it is better to understand *pneuma* as a reference to the Holy Spirit (note NRSV [in contrast to RSV], REB, TEV).[106] *Pneuma*, as we have seen, consistently refers to the Holy Spirit in Rom. 8, and it certainly does so in v. 11, which explains v. 10b. Moreover, identifying *pneuma* as the Holy Spirit makes better sense of the other words in the clause.[107] Paul is teaching that the believer, although still bound to an earthly, mortal body, has residing within him or her the Spirit, the power of new spiritual life, which conveys both that "life," in the sense of deliverance from condemnation enjoyed now and the future resurrection life that will bring transformation to the body itself. All this takes place "because of righteousness," this "righteousness" being that "imputed righteousness" which leads to life (see 5:21).[108]

11 In a fourth consecutive conditional sentence, Paul caps off his rehearsal of the life given in and by the Spirit with an affirmation of the Spirit's instrumentality in securing bodily transformation. Appropriate to this point, the Spirit is now designated as "the Spirit of the one who raised Jesus from the

---

Immortal, pp. 145-46. Dunn, however, thinks that σῶμα is a corporate concept here: "the embodiment which characterizes all human existence in this age." "Death" (νεκρός) includes both mortality and the present hold of sin on the believer (he refers to 7:24). But if our understanding of 7:24 is correct, the phrases are not comparable: "the body of this death" is the unredeemed person still subject to the full penalties of sin, while the body in this verse belongs to the Christian. (Note also the distinction drawn by Beker [288] between "the body of sin" (6:6), which belongs to the era of sin, and "the mortal body," which carries over into the era of the Spirit.) For Christ dwells individually in each believer (v. 10a — ἐν ὑμῖν: "in each one of you"); cf. the plural τὰ θνητὰ σώματα ὑμῶν ("our mortal bodies") in v. 11. νεκρόν, then, refers to the mortality of the body. Note also that διὰ ἁμαρτίαν, denoting the reason for the deadness of the body, can be applied to the Christian only in this sense; for the Christian is no longer subject to the penalties of sin in any other way — cf. "no condemnation" in v. 1 (see, e.g., S-H; Michel; Cranfield; Dunn; Schmithals, *Theologische Anthropologie,* pp. 110-12).

105. See Godet; S-H; Wilckens; Fitzmyer.

106. See Chrysostom; Calvin; Michel; Barrett; Murray; Cranfield; Dunn; Byrne, "Living Out," p. 571; Gundry, 46; Fee, *God's Empowering Presence,* pp. 550-51; and the discussion in Harrison. The weight of recent scholarship is moving toward this interpretation.

107. The anthropological rendering requires that we take the noun ζωή as an adjective ("living") and add a possessive idea ("your") that is not in the text.

108. Cf., e.g., Cranfield; Schmithals, *Theologische Anthropologie,* pp. 110-12.

dead." The reference, of course, is to God the Father (see Col. 2:12; Rom. 6:4), but the focus is on the Spirit. Since reference to resurrection is so plain in the first part of the sentence, "will make alive" must also refer to future bodily transformation[109] — through resurrection for dead believers — rather than, for instance, to spiritual vivification in justification,[110] or to the "mortification" of sin in the Christian life.[111] Paul certainly stresses the certainty and unbrokenness of life, a theme that is prominent in the rest of the chapter,[112] but the future is genuinely temporal. The cause-and-effect relationship between Christ's resurrection and the believer's, made so plain in Rom. 6:5 (cf. 8:17), lies behind Paul's affirmation that God will give life to "our mortal bodies" just as he raised Christ from the dead. And in keeping with Paul's focus throughout this part of Rom. 8, it is the Spirit who is the instrument by whom God raises the body of the Christian.[113] As in v. 9, the *indwelling* of the Spirit suggests that the Spirit has "made his home" in the believer; and since the Spirit is "life" (v. 10b; cf. v. 2: "the Spirit of life"), his presence cannot but result in life for that body which he inhabits. The Spirit's life-giving power is not circumscribed by the mortality of the body but overcomes and transforms that mortality into the immortality of eternal life in a resurrected body.

12   Although many commentators think v. 12 commences a new paragraph,[114] we prefer to attach vv. 12-13 to vv. 1-11. In vv. 5-11 Paul has delineated the contrary natures and tendencies of the two great powers of salvation history: flesh and Spirit. He has put the Roman Christians — and, by implication, all Christians — on the side of the Spirit, and has drawn out the consequences of that relationship: life, in the full theological sense of the word, life that will transcend and overcome physical death itself. Now, with the emphatic inferential "now, therefore,"[115] Paul shows that there are consequences of this new relationship for the day-to-day life of the believer. Specifically, Paul claims, "we" — Christians generally — have no more "obligation" to the flesh, "to live according to it,"[116] to follow its dictates or obey its will.

---

109. Harris, *Raised Immortal,* p. 145; cf. also, e.g., Cranfield. It is doubtful whether the distinction made by Godet between ἐγείρω ("raise"), used with reference to Jesus, and ζῳοποιέω, used for believers ("a stronger act"), is warranted.

110. Lietzmann; Stuart.

111. Calvin.

112. See esp. Byrne, 96.

113. I assume here the reading of the genitive, τοῦ ἐνοικοῦντος αὐτοῦ πνεύματος (see the note on the translation above).

114. See the introduction to this section.

115. Gk. ἄρα οὖν; cf. also 7:25.

116. The infinitive τοῦ ζῆν may be consecutive — "debtors to the flesh with the result that we live by it" (BDF 400[1]) — but is probably epexegetic — "debtors to the flesh, so as to live by it" (Moulton, 217; cf. the additional note on 1:24).

Once more, we note that flesh refers not only to our physical, or "animal," appetites (e.g., for food, or drink, or sex); nor does it refer even to a "nature" within us (as the NIV rendering "sinful nature" can imply). "Flesh" sums up what we often call "the world": all that is characteristic of this life in its rebellion against God. It is to this "power" of the old age that we are no longer "obliged" to render obedience. Against Dunn, this does not imply that believers "belong to the realm of the flesh, inescapably"; rather, it means that our (definitive) rescue from "the realm of the flesh" (see 7:5 and 8:9) has not removed us from contact with, and influence from, the flesh. Still "embodied" (see 8:10 and v. 13), we have in this life a continuing relationship to that old realm of sin and death — but we no longer "belong" to it. Like freed slaves who might, out of habit, obey their old masters even after being released — "legally" and "positionally" — from them, so we Christians can still listen to and heed the voice of that old master of ours, the flesh.

13 Paul abandons the syntactical structure he had used in v. 12[117] in order to warn his readers (note the shift to second plural — "you") that if they continue to live[118] by the dictates of the flesh they will certainly die.[119] This death is not, of course, physical death, for it would hardly make sense to make physical death, the fate of *all* who do not live until the Lord's return — believers and unbelievers alike — the penalty only for those who live according to the flesh. What is meant is death in its fullest theological sense: eternal separation from God as the penalty for sin. We must not eviscerate this warning; Paul clearly affirms that his readers will be damned if they continue to follow the dictates of the flesh. As Murray puts it, "The believer's once-for-all death to the law of sin does not free him from the necessity of mortifying sin in his members; it makes it *necessary* and *possible* for him to do so."

On this point Calvinists and Arminians are agreed. The difference lies elsewhere. The Arminian believes that a regenerate believer may, indeed, fall back into a "fleshly" lifestyle so that the threat of this verse becomes real. But the Calvinist believes that the truly regenerate believer, while often committing "fleshly" acts, will be infallibly prevented from living a fleshly lifestyle by the Spirit within. I believe that the strength of the assurances Paul has given to justified believers throughout these chapters (see especially

---

117. The placement of οὐ after the verb in v. 12 shows that Paul planned on continuing his sentence with something like ἀλλὰ τῷ πνεύματι τοῦ κατὰ πνεῦμα ζῆν ("but [we are debtors] to the Spirit, to live according to the Spirit").

118. ζῆτε is a durative present.

119. μέλλετε, lit. "about to," focuses attention on the certainty of death and so strengthens the warning.

5:9-10, 21; 8:1-4, 10-11), along with the finality of justification itself, favors the "Calvinist" interpretation. But such an interpretation in no way mitigates the seriousness of the warning that Paul gives here. In a way that we cannot finally synthesize in a neat logical arrangement, Paul insists that what God has done for us in Christ is the sole and final grounds for our eternal life at the same time as he insists on the indispensability of holy living as the precondition for attaining that life.[120] Neither the "indicative" — what God has done for us in Christ — nor the "imperative" — what we are commanded to do — can be eliminated. Nor can they be severed from one another; they are inextricably connected. The point of that connection in this passage is the Spirit. The same Spirit that "set us free from the law of sin and death" has taken up residence within us, producing in us that "mind-set" which tends toward the doing of God's will and resists the ways of the flesh.

In the same way as "die" signifies "theological" death, so the life promised to those who "put to death[121] the practices of the body" in the second sentence of the verse denotes spiritual life (as in vv. 10 and 11). Paul's use of the phrase "the practices of the body" to depict sin is troublesome; for he seems to violate his careful distinction between "flesh" — in its "ethical" sense, as the evil influence of this world — and "body" — the "neutral" body, or person, interacting with the world, capable of serving God, the object not of destruction but of transformation. Some[122] think that this is a case in which Paul does, in fact, use body as equivalent to flesh.[123] But it may be better to retain the usual meaning of body and find the pejorative connotation in an implicit carryover from flesh at the beginning of the verse: "deeds worked out through the body under the influence of the flesh."[124]

While the Christian is made responsible for this "mortification" of sins, he or she accomplishes this only "through the Spirit."[125] Holiness of life, then, is achieved neither by our own unaided effort — the error of "moralism" or "legalism" — nor by the Spirit apart from our participation — as some who insist that the key to holy living is "surrender" or "let go and let

---

120. This problem is basic to Reformed theology. See a particularly interesting discussion of the issue as handled by different Puritan divines in Coolidge, *Puritan Renaissance,* pp. 101-13.

121. Gk. θανατοῦτε, an unusual word for this concept in Paul, has undoubtedly been chosen to match the conclusion of the preceding sentence: *you* will not "die" if you cause your *sin* to "die."

122. E.g., Cranfield.

123. A few MSS even "correct" to σάρξ.

124. Gundry, 39; cf. also Deidun, 98; Jewett, *Paul's Anthropological Terms,* pp. 157-60.

125. πνεύματι, a dative of agent.

God" would have it — but by our constant living out the "life" placed within us by the Spirit who has taken up residence within.[126] We face here another finely nuanced balance that must not be tipped too far in one direction or the other. Human activity in the process of sanctification is clearly necessary; but that activity is never apart from, nor finally distinct from, the activity of God's Spirit. Deidun puts it like this: the Christian imperative "demands the Christian's continuing 'yes' to an activity which does not originate in himself, but which is nevertheless already real and actual in the core of his being."[127]

2. The Spirit of Adoption (8:14-17)

> 14For as many as are led by the Spirit of God, these are sons of God. 15For you did not receive a spirit of slavery again unto fear, but you received the Spirit of adoption, in whom we cry "Abba, Father!" 16The Spirit himself bears witness with our spirit that we are the children of God. 17And if we are children, we are also heirs: heirs of God and fellow heirs with Christ — if, indeed, we suffer with him so that we might be glorified with him.

If "life" is the ruling idea in vv. 1-13, being "sons" (v. 14; cf. "sonship/adoption" in v. 15) or "children" (vv. 16, 17) of God dominates vv. 14-17. The way these verses focus on this concept justifies their being treated as a separate unit of thought.[1] Nevertheless, the connections between this paragraph and what precedes and follows are particularly close. On the one hand, being sons of God explains further why those who are placed under the dominion of the Spirit experience eschatological life (v. 14, in relation to v. 13). On the other hand, being children of God also places believers squarely in the "already–not yet" tension created by their belonging to the new realm of righteousness at the same time as they continue to live in the midst of the old realm of sin and death. In a word, being a "child" of God means to be an "heir" of God also, and thereby one who must look to the future for the full enjoyment of "sonship" (v. 17, in relation to vv. 18-30).[2] These points carry the basic thrust of the paragraph, with vv. 15-16 a somewhat parenthetical elaboration and justification of the assertion

---

126. See the fine, practical discussion in Lloyd-Jones, pp. 91-147; on the Puritans' careful balance on this point, see Kevan, *The Grace of Law,* pp. 221-23.

127. P. 80; cf. the whole discussion of this passage on pp. 75-80.

1. The concept of sons/children of God comes up again in vv. 19, 21, and 23, but incidentally. This makes it impossible to view the concept as central to the chapter as a whole (as does J. J. J. van Rensburg, "The Children of God in Romans 8," *Neot* 15 [1981], 159-61).

2. Osten-Sacken (*Römer 8,* pp. 143-44) is among those who think that vv. 14-30 are one large unit of thought, focused on the eschatological existence of the "sons of God."

that those led by the Spirit are sons of God.[3] This paragraph, then, carries forward Paul's theme of assurance in three ways: (1) it gives further reason for the triumphant proclamation that believers who have God's Spirit will "live"; (2) it adds to the growing list another important description — "sons of God" — of believers as God's people, the heirs of God's promises; and (3) it provides yet further justification for Paul's categorical assertion that "there is now no condemnation for those who are in Christ Jesus" (v. 1).[4]

The movement of thought in this paragraph is very similar to that of Gal. 4:1-7.[5] In both texts, Paul affirms that believers are transformed from slaves to

3. See, e.g., Lagrange; Ridderbos, *Paul,* p. 201.

4. See Lloyd-Jones.

5. Note the striking parallels between Gal. 4:3b-7 and certain parts of Rom. 8:2-17:

Gal. 4:3b: ὑπὸ τὰ στοιχεῖα τοῦ κόσμου ἤμεθα δεδουλωμένοι ("we were enslaved under the elemental spirits of the world")

Rom. 8:2b: ἠλευθέρωσέν σε ἀπὸ τοῦ νόμου τῆς ἁμαρτίας καὶ τοῦ θανάτου (". . . set you free from the law of sin and death")

Gal. 4:4a: ὅτε δὲ ἦλθεν τὸ πλήρωμα τοῦ χρόνου ("when the fullness of time came")

Gal. 4:4b: ἐξαπέστειλεν ὁ θεὸς τὸν υἱὸν αὐτοῦ, γενόμενον ἐκ γυναικός, γενόμενον ὑπὸ νόμου ("God sent forth his Son, born of a woman, born under the law")

Rom. 8:3b: ὁ θεὸς τὸν ἑαυτοῦ υἱὸν πέμψας ἐν ὁμοιώματι σαρκὸς ἁμαρτίας ("God sent his own Son in the likeness of sinful flesh")

Gal. 4:5a: ἵνα τοὺς ὑπὸ νόμον ἐξαγοράσῃ ("in order to redeem those under the law")

Rom. 8:3c: καὶ περὶ ἁμαρτίας κατέκρινεν τὴν ἁμαρτίαν ἐν τῇ σαρκί ("and as a sin offering, he condemned sin in the flesh"),

Gal. 4:5b: ἵνα τὴν υἱοθεσίαν ἀπολάβωμεν ("in order that we might receive adoption")

Rom. 8:15b: ἀλλὰ ἐλάβετε πνεῦμα υἱοθεσίας ("but you received the Spirit of adoption")

Gal. 4:6: ὅτι δέ ἐστε υἱοί, ἐξαπέστειλεν ὁ θεὸς τὸ πνεῦμα τοῦ υἱοῦ αὐτοῦ εἰς καρδίας ἡμῶν κρᾶζον: αββα ὁ πατήρ ("because you are sons, God has sent forth his Spirit into your hearts, crying, 'Abba, Father' ")

Rom. 8:15c: ἐν ᾧ κράζομεν: αββα ὁ πατήρ ("in which we cry, 'Abba, Father' "); cf. 9b: πνεῦμα θεοῦ οἰκεῖ ἐν ὑμῖν ("the Spirit of God dwells in you")

Gal. 4:7a: ὥστε οὐκέτι εἶ δοῦλος ἀλλὰ υἱός ("so that you are no longer a slave, but a son")

Rom. 8:15a: οὐ γὰρ ἐλάβετε πνεῦμα δουλείας πάλιν εἰς φόβον ("for you did not receive the Spirit of slavery again unto fear")

Gal. 4:7b: εἰ δὲ υἱός, καὶ κληρονόμος διὰ θεοῦ ("and if a son, then also an heir through God")

Rom. 8:17a: εἰ δὲ τέκνα, καὶ κληρονόμοι ("and if children, then also heirs")

These parallels might point to the use of a pre-Pauline tradition or a fixed Pauline

sons of God through the redeeming sacrifice of Christ, "sent" as one like us. In both, this new status is called "adoption" and is tied to the indwelling Spirit, the Spirit who makes us deeply aware that we now belong to God as his dearly loved children (cf. "Abba"). And in both, being God's children leads to our being his heirs. We have to do here with what must have been an important way of conceptualizing what Paul understands a Christian to be. As the Galatians passage suggests, this conceptualization may have grown out of the question of the identity of Israel. But in both Galatians and Romans, Paul makes clear that the slave/son/heir language can be applied more generally to the status of all people within his salvation-historical scheme. Before the cross, the people of Israel, "under the law," lived as "minors," little better than slaves; in a similar way, Gentiles were enslaved under the "elementary principles of the world" (Gal. 4:9), subject to the "spirit of bondage" (Rom. 8:15). Those who accept Christ, however, whether Jew or Gentile, receive the Holy Spirit and become both "sons" and "heirs" of God.

14 As I suggested above, the "for"[6] shows that this verse explains and justifies the conclusion that Paul has just reached in v. 13: that putting to death the misdeeds of the body through the power of the Spirit will bring eschatological life. The imperatival accent of v. 13, which, in itself, could mislead the reader into thinking that life could be gained through works, is immediately qualified in an "indicative" direction. This is signaled by the passive "as many as[7] *are led.*"[8] To be "led by the Spirit" probably means not to be *guided* by the Holy Spirit[9] but, as in Gal. 5:18, to have the direction of one's life as a whole determined by the Spirit.[10] The phrase is thus a way of summarizing the various descriptions of the life of the Spirit that Paul has used in vv. 4-9.[11] Paul may well

---

creed (e.g., Bindemann, *Die Hoffnung der Schöpfung,* pp. 35-38; Siber, *Mit Christus Leben,* pp. 135-38). It may be more likely, however, that Paul has used in both Gal. 4 and Rom. 8 elements of a common preaching or teaching pattern. In Rom. 8, obviously, this pattern is woven into the larger fabric of Paul's argument in the chapter.

6. Gk. γάρ.

7. Gk. ὅσοι. This pronoun can have an "exclusive" meaning — "only those who" — but, in light of the fact that Paul develops only the positive side of v. 13 without taking the warning of v. 13a any further, an "inclusive" sense — "all those who" — is preferable (Cranfield; cf. also Stalder, *Werk des Geistes,* p. 470).

8. Gk. ἄγονται.

9. As a majority of interpreters in the ancient church took it (see I. de la Potterie, "Le chrétien conduit par l'Esprit dans son cheminement eschatologique (Rom 8,14)," in Lorenzi, *The Law of the Spirit,* pp. 210-15).

10. See, e.g., Byrne, 98.

11. De la Potterie's suggestion ("Le chrétien," pp. 216-38) that the phrase describes the Christian's path to eschatological fulfillment in imitation of the OT description of the people of God being led into the promised land is intriguing, but it lacks clear lexical support in the NT and LXX.

want to include in this "being led" an "inner compulsion" and the involvement of the emotions, but the context and the parallel in Gal. 5:18 make it unlikely that the idea is specifically "ecstatic" or "charismatic."[12] The active "you put to death through the Spirit" of v. 13 is one aspect of the passive "being led by the Spirit," pointing again to the inextricable relationship between "indicative" and "imperative" in Paul's teaching about the Christian life.[13]

The result of this Spirit-dominated existence is being "sons of God": the one necessarily includes the other. Despite Gal. 4:6, Paul probably does not mean that the Spirit is the agent by which we are made sons of God. Verses 15-16 suggest, rather, that "being led by the Spirit" is a "distinguishing sign" of being a son of God.[14] The phrase "son of God" is used in the OT and Judaism to denote Israel as the people whom God has called to be "his own";[15] correspondingly, Yahweh is pictured as Israel's "father."[16] The plural "sons of God" is less often applied to the people of Israel, but it occurs often enough to make it likely that this is the source for Paul's use of the phrase.[17] If this is so, then the connection between vv. 13 and 14 becomes even clearer; the "sonship" attested to by God's Spirit brings life because "life" is inherent in belonging to God's people, the people of promise.[18] But we must not overlook a source for this "sonship" idea even more intimately related to Paul's theology — the unique sonship of Christ. Note, in this context, Rom. 8:29 — God's ultimate purpose is that believers be "conformed to the image of his Son" — and the reference to Jesus as God's Son in v. 3. The next verse, where Paul attributes to Christians the "Abba" address to God that was peculiarly Jesus' own, confirms that this dimension is very much present here.

15 Before moving on to the last element in the sequence that forms the backbone of this paragraph — Spirit–sonship–heir — Paul pauses to explain a bit more the relationship between the first two in the chain.[19] Paul's description of the Spirit's work in conferring sonship forms one the most beautiful pictures of the believer's joy and security anywhere in Scripture. The heart of v. 15 is an

---

12. Cf. 1 Cor. 12:2-3; contra, e.g., Käsemann and Dunn, who cite Hellenistic parallels.

13. See Murray.

14. Morris; cf. Murray.

15. Cf. esp. Exod. 4:22; Jer. 3:19; 31:9; Hos. 11:1; and, e.g., Sir. 36:12; 4 Ezra 6:58.

16. E.g., Deut. 32:6; Isa. 64:8; *Jub.* 1:25.

17. Cf., e.g., Deut. 14:1; Isa. 43:6; Hos. 2:1 (LXX) (quoted in Rom. 9:26); Wis. 5:5; *T. Mos.* 10:3; *2 Apoc. Bar.* 13:9. See esp. Byrne, 9-70; note also G. Fohrer and E. Schweizer, *TDNT* VIII, 347-60.

18. Byrne, 98.

19. Hence the γάρ.

antithesis between two "spirits": the "spirit of slavery," which believers have *not* received, and the "spirit of adoption," which we *have*.[20] What are these "spirits"? A few interpreters think that both refer to the human spirit, in the sense of an inner attitude or disposition, with "received" being interpreted rhetorically.[21] But, in light of the manifest connection between the Holy Spirit and the believer's sonship in v. 14 and v. 23 — not to mention Gal 4:6: "God sent forth the Spirit of his Son into our hearts" — the "Spirit of adoption" must refer to the Holy Spirit. Because of this, many expositors conclude that the "Spirit of slavery" must also designate the Holy Spirit. Many of the Puritans (followed by Lloyd-Jones) saw a reference here to the sense of "slavery" created by the working of God's law in the heart of the person under conviction by God's Spirit.[22] Others take a less individualistic and more salvation-historical tack, viewing "Spirit of slavery" as the Spirit's work in the old age under the law.[23]

Certainly there is support for such a conception in Paul, since he claims that the law is "spiritual" (7:14) and yet argues that it has brought, or confirmed, bondage to sin (7:23). In Gal. 4:1-7 the idea of slavery is specifically tied to the situation of being "under the law" (see also the contrast in Heb. 12:18-24, cited by Calvin). But it may be questioned whether Paul would speak of this effect of the law as brought about by God's Spirit, in light of the contrast between "letter" and "Spirit" in 7:6 and 2 Cor. 3:6-18. This makes it unlikely that "spirit of slavery" refers directly to the Holy Spirit. Paul may, then, refer to the human spirit, enslaved to sin;[24] but more likely he uses the word rhetorically, as a hypothetical antithesis to the "Spirit of adoption": "the Spirit that you have received is *not* a 'spirit of bondage' but a Spirit of adoption."[25]

With this interpretation, "again" will modify "unto fear": the Spirit that believers have received does not bring about "again" that anxiety and fear of judgment which they suffered in their pre-Christian state (compare Gal. 4:8-10). Since Paul has pictured the law as bringing awareness of sin and the corresponding penalty of condemnation (see 3:20; 7:7-13), he probably alludes to the ministry of the law. Contrasted with this inner sense of dread before God, the righteous judge, is the sense of peace and security before

20. The Greek is, respectively, πνεῦμα δουλείας and πνεῦμα υἱοθεσίας.

21. E.g., Gifford; Lagrange.

22. Cf. Kevan, *Grace of Law*, pp. 88-89.

23. Chrysostom; Luther; Calvin; Wilckens; Dunn; J.-M. Cambier, "Le Liberté du spirituel dans Rom. 8.12-17," in *Paul and Paulinism*, p. 211. Some of the fathers of the church (e.g., Irenaeus) used this verse to prove, against Marcion, that the Holy Spirit was operative in both testaments (cf. Schelkle).

24. E.g., Haldane; S-H.

25. See the parallel in 1 Cor. 2:12 and 2 Tim. 1:7. Cf. Godet; Murray; Barrett; Cranfield; Stalder, *Werk des Geistes*, pp. 480-81; Byrne, 99.

God, our heavenly Father, that is produced by God's Spirit in the heart of Christians. Paul could hardly have chosen a better term than "adoption" to characterize this peace and security. The word denoted the Greek, and particularly Roman, legal institution whereby one can "adopt" a child and confer on that child all the legal rights and privileges that would ordinarily accrue to a natural child.[26] However, while the institution is a Greco-Roman one,[27] the underlying concept is rooted in the OT and Judaism. "Adoption" is one of the privileges of Israel (Rom. 9:4), and Israel, as we have seen, is regularly characterized as God's "son" or "sons" in the OT and Judaism (see the notes on v. 14). Once again, then, Paul has taken a term that depicts Israel's unique status as God's people and "transferred" it to Christians.[28]

Since adoption, according to 8:23, takes place when the body is redeemed, some interpret "Spirit of adoption" here in the sense of "the Spirit that anticipates, or pledges, our adoption."[29] But this flies in the face of the immediate context, in which the stress is on the present enjoyment of our status as God's children.[30] We should, then, attribute the apparent contradiction between this verse and 8:23 to the "already–not yet" tension of the Christian's eschatological status: "already" truly "adopted" into God's family, with all its benefits and privileges, but "not yet" recipients of the "inheritance," by which we will be conformed to the glorious image of God's own Son (see 8:29).[31] Since in Gal. 4:5-6 the Spirit's testimony of our being God's sons *follows,* and is the result of, God's having adopted us as sons; since vv. 15b-16

26. See esp. F. Lyall, "Roman Law in the Writings of Paul — Adoption," *JBL* 88 (1969), 458-66; idem, *Slaves, Citizens, Sons: Legal Metaphors in the Epistles* (Grand Rapids: Zondervan, 1984), pp. 67-99. Scholars debate whether the term υἱοθεσία, as Paul uses it, denotes the *act* of adoption (see, e.g., Cranfield) or the *status* of "sonship" (Byrne, 215). In Rom. 9:4, status appears to be the focus, and probably also in Gal 4:5 (since we "receive" it); and the contrast with δουλείας ("slavery") may tip the scales in this direction here. But in 8:23 the stress seems to be on the act of adopting and, since the word almost invariably has this meaning outside the NT (Scott, *Adoption,* pp. 3-57), this is probably Paul's main focus (Paul also uses the word in Eph. 1:5, but it cannot be certain whether "act" or "status" is primary).

27. That Paul alludes to the Greco-Roman institution is certain since the term υἱοθεσία does not occur in the LXX or in Hellenistic Jewish authors; nor was the legal practice of adoption officially recognized among Jews. See again, e.g., Lyall, "Roman Law," pp. 458-66.

28. Paul thereby stimulates the agonizing questions of 9:1-6; cf. Dunn and, on the larger idea, Ridderbos, *Paul,* pp. 197-98; cf. esp. Byrne, passim (cf. the summary on pp. 215-19); and Scott, *Adoption,* pp. 61-117. 2 Sam. 7, with its reference to the divine adoption of the king, is a central OT text.

29. Barrett; Byrne, 100.

30. Note especially the present tense of κράζομεν ("we are crying") in the latter part of this verse.

31. Cf. Rensburg, "Children of God," p. 166.

focus on the Spirit's ministry of making us aware of our status as sons; and since the image naturally suggests God the Father as the "adopter," we may be right to take "Spirit of adoption" in the sense of "the Spirit who confirms adoption" rather than "the Spirit who brings about adoption." But this may be overly subtle; and since the Spirit is presented as the Father's agent in conferring "life" (see v. 11), it may be better to think of the Spirit as the agent through whom the believer's sonship is both bestowed and confirmed.

As the spirit that we have *not* received, the "spirit of slavery," would produce a sense of "fear" before God, so the Spirit of adoption that we *have* received causes to well up within us a comforting conviction that we are God's own children. The Spirit not only bestows "adoption" on us; he also makes us aware of this new relationship: "we have not only the status, but the heart of sons."[32] The NRSV takes the last part of v. 15 with v. 16 — "When we cry, 'Abba! Father!' it is that very Spirit bearing witness . . ." — but it is better to follow most English translations and commentators and attach these words to what precedes: "in whom we cry, 'Abba, Father!' "[33] In using the verb "crying out," Paul stresses that our awareness of God as Father comes not from rational consideration nor from external testimony alone but from a truth deeply felt and intensely experienced.[34] If some Christians err in basing their assurance of salvation on feelings alone, many others err in basing it on facts and arguments alone. Indeed, what Paul says here calls into question whether one can have a genuine experience of God's Spirit of adoption without its affecting the emotions.

In crying out "Abba, Father," the believer not only gives voice to his or her consciousness of belonging to God as his child but also to having a status comparable to that of Jesus himself. The Aramaic *abba* was the term Jesus himself used in addressing his Father, and its preservation in the Greek Gospel of Mark

---

32. Denney.

33. See, e.g., Cranfield.

34. What exactly Paul means by χράζω is debated. Since the word is used frequently in the Gospels of those who "cry out" under the influence of demons, and since Paul has been speaking of the believer as, in a sense, "possessed" by the Spirit, it may be that the allusion is to an "ecstatic" acclamation (Käsemann; Kuss; Dunn). If so, of course, we must be careful to distance the idea here from the type of "ecstatic" utterances associated with some of the Hellenistic "mystery" religions; for Paul is quite clear in attributing this "cry" to us, not to the Spirit (although see Gal. 4:6), and clearly implies in v. 16 that this "cry" is the product not of mindless possession but of conscious under-standing. Others, however, compare the notion here to the frequent references in the Psalms to people who "cry out" to God in prayer (G. Schrenk, *TDNT* V, 1006; W. Grundmann, *TDNT* III, 902-3; Cranfield), and still others to the "solemn declaratory word" of a herald (see Rom. 9:27) (Leenhardt). But, stripped of its non-Christian religious baggage, the first alternative offers the best interpretation. In any case, we miss the connotations of the word if we neglect its allusion to the emotions.

(14:36) and in the Greek-speaking Pauline churches attests to the fact that it was remembered and treasured as distinctive and meaningful. In ascribing to Christians indwelt by the Spirit the use of this same term in addressing God, Paul shows that Christians have a relationship to God that is like (though, of course, not exactly like) Christ's own relationship to the Father. In "adopting" us, God has taken no half measures; we have been made full members of the family and partakers of all the privileges belonging to members of that family.[35] Luther's comments on the believer's use of this word "Abba" are worth reproducing:

> This is but a little word, and yet notwithstanding it comprehendeth all things. The mouth speaketh not, but the affection of the heart speaketh after this manner. Although I be oppressed with anguish and terror on every side, and seem to be forsaken and utterly cast away from thy presence, yet am I thy child, and thou art my Father for Christ's sake: I am beloved because of the Beloved. Wherefore this little word, Father, conceived effectually in the heart, passeth all the eloquence of Demosthenes, Cicero, and of the most eloquent rhetoricians that ever were in the world.[36]

16 This verse is not connected syntactically to v. 15, but its function, clearly enough, is to explain how it is that "receiving the Spirit of adoption" enables *us* to cry out "Abba, Father!" The Holy Spirit is not only instrumental in *making* us God's children; he also makes us *aware* that we are God's children. While the first occurrence of *pneuma* denotes the Holy Spirit, the second, modified as it is by "our," refers to the human "spirit."[37] This is, then, the only occurrence of *pneuma* in Rom. 8 that does not refer to the Holy Spirit.[38] Paul

---

35. Many expositors have argued that the Aramaic אַבָּא was unknown among Jews as an address to God and suggested the speech of a little child ("Daddy"). Yet the Hebrew equivalent of Aram. *abba* has turned up in prayers to God at Qumran (cf. Fitzmyer), and the use of *abba* is not restricted to little children (see, e.g., E. Haenchen, *Der Weg Jesu* [Berlin: Töpelmann, 1966], pp. 492-94; J. Barr, " 'Abba, Father' and the Familiarity of Jesus' Speech," *Theology* 91 [1988], 173-79; idem, " 'Abba isn't 'Daddy,' " *JTS* 39 [1988], 28-47; note, however, the criticism of Barr in Fee, *God's Empowering Presence*, pp. 410-12).

36. From Luther's commentary on Galatians, quoted in Bruce.

37. When Paul speaks of the human πνεῦμα — and he does not do so often; only in 1:9 elsewhere in Romans and about 20 other places in his letters — he focuses on the "inner" dimension of the person (see the opposition with σάρξ ["flesh"] in 1 Cor. 5:5; 2 Cor. 7:1, and Col. 2:5, and with σῶμα ["body"] in 1 Cor. 5:3; 7:34, and 1 Thess. 5:23 [in the last verse, with ψυχή {"soul"} also]). It may be going too far, however, to speak of "spirit" as "the Godward side of man" (Stacey, *The Pauline View of Man*, p. 137), for Paul's usage is more neutral than that (see Ridderbos, *Paul*, pp. 120-21).

38. As I argued above, even the πνεῦμα δουλείας ("spirit of slavery") in v. 15a refers, *via negationis*, to the Holy Spirit.

refers to the human spirit here because he wants to stress that the witness of "the Spirit himself"[39] about our adoption as sons affects the deepest and innermost part of our beings. It is because of this that we cry so sincerely and spontaneously, "Abba, Father!" Indeed, taking the verb Paul uses here to mean "bear witness with,"[40] Paul involves our own spirit in the very process of testifying to us that we are "children of God."[41]

17 This verse is transitional, connecting Paul's description of the adoption as children that believers enjoy at the present time (vv. 14-16) with his moving portrait of the culmination and full benefits of that adoption that await the believer in the future (vv. 18-30).[42] Paul uses the concept "inheritance" to introduce his qualification of our adoption in terms of its future aspects. In many ways this concept is a natural one; a child who has been adopted into a family, while truly a part of that family, does not (usually) receive all the benefits of that adoption until a later time. In both Gal. 4:1-7 and in this text, Paul uses this idea to emphasize the necessarily incomplete nature of those privileges inherent in the believer's adoption into God's family.

39. Paul adds the emphatic pronoun αὐτό to πνεῦμα perhaps to stress the distinction from the human πνεῦμα.

40. The verb is συμμαρτυρέω, and the question is whether the συν that forms the prefix carries its usual sense of accompaniment — "bear witness *with*" — or whether it has simply intensive force — "bears witness *to*" (BAGD note first-century-B.C. examples of the word with this meaning). The verb has this latter meaning in its only two other NT occurrences (see Rom. 2:15 and 9:1), and many scholars naturally prefer this meaning (e.g., H. Strathmann, *TDNT* IV, 508-9; Cranfield; Wilckens; Morris; and cf. REB). On the other hand, a papyrus document from the second century shows that the word was still used to mean "bear witness with" (MM), and this additional nuance makes excellent sense in a context where two "spirits" are prominent (Stalder, *Werk des Geistes,* p. 484; S-H; Murray). God's Spirit joins in bearing "joint" witness with our spirit; see Gal. 4:6, where the Holy Spirit is said to "cry, 'Abba, Father.'" It may even be that Paul wants to add certainty to the situation by adducing more than one witness (cf. Deut. 19:15 and the Roman law that required multiple witnesses for an adoption to be "legal" [cf. Bruce, *Galatians,* pp. 199-200]).

41. Gk. τέκνα θεοῦ. Paul's shift to this phrase from υἱοὶ θεοῦ (v. 14; cf. υἱοθεσία in v. 15) is no more than a stylistic variant (contra, e.g., Alford; Godet). Although Paul never uses τέκνον of Christ, τέκνον and υἱός are used to almost the same extent to describe Christians or the people of God (τέκνον in Rom. 8:16, 17, 21; 9:7, 8 [3 times]; Gal. 4:28; Phil. 2:15; υἱός in Rom. 8:14, 19; 9:26; Gal. 3:7, 26; 4:6, 7 [twice]), and the flow of Paul's argument in these verses makes any distinction impossible.

42. Since this verse touches on key themes from what follows, a few commentators (e.g., Cranfield) think v. 17 is the beginning of this new paragraph. But, recognizing Paul's habit in Romans of ending a paragraph by sounding notes that will be developed later on (see Dunn), it is better to follow most commentators by making this verse the conclusion to the previous section.

But there is a deeper, theological, purpose behind Paul's use of the "inheritance" idea. While the concept of inheritance was well known in Roman law (and this background undoubtedly contributes to Paul's use of the imagery),[43] the language of inheritance is also very prominent in the OT and Judaism. In the OT, the "inheritance" is particularly the land, promised to Abraham and his "seed," a promise that is renewed after the disaster of the Exile.[44] In later Judaism, however, the "inheritance" did not always maintain a distinctive spatial focus and came to be used to describe eschatological life.[45] Paul follows in this line by awarding the "inheritance" promised to Abraham to all those who have faith (see Rom. 4:13-15). As he puts it in Galatians, it is Christ who is "the seed of Abraham" and heir to all that has been promised to Abraham; thus, it is those who are "in Christ" who also become the seed of Abraham and heirs of the promise (3:16-18, 29). All this informs Paul's description of believers in this verse as both "children" and "heirs." Christians are God's people of the new age, "children of God," and, as such, also the recipients of what God has promised to his people.[46]

Christians are, then, "heirs of God" — meaning probably not that Christians inherit God himself,[47] but that they inherit "what God has promised."[48] In immediately adding "fellow heirs with Christ," Paul is not correcting the first description but filling it out by reminding us that Christians inherit the blessings of God's kingdom only through, and in, Christ.[49] We, "the sons of God," are such by virtue of our belonging to *the* Son of God; and we are heirs of God only by virtue of our union with the one who is *the* heir of all God's promises (see Mark 12:1-12; Gal. 3:18-19; Heb.1:2).

But, in a typical NT preservation of the "eschatological reservation," Paul adds that this glorious inheritance is attained only through suffering (cf. the similar transition in 5:1-4). Because we are one with Christ, we are his fellow heirs, assured of being "glorified with him." But, at the same time, this oneness means that we must follow Christ's own road to glory, "suffering with him" (cf. also Phil. 1:29; 3:10; 2 Cor. 1:5). Both the present tense of the verb and the continuation of the thought in v. 18 show that this

43. See Lyall, *Slaves,* pp. 102-3.

44. Compare, e.g., Gen. 15:7 with 17:8; Deut. 30:5; Num. 34:2; with, e.g., Isa. 60:21; Ezek. 36:8-12.

45. See, e.g., *Pss. Sol.* 14:10; *1 Enoch* 40:9; 4 Macc. 18:3; cf. W. Foerster, *TDNT* III, 776-81; Byrne, 68-69.

46. Byrne, 101-2, passim; Ridderbos, *Paul,* p. 203; Tannehill, *Dying and Rising,* p. 110; Dunn.

47. E.g., θεοῦ as objective genitive (cf. Murray; Cranfield).

48. This assumes that θεοῦ is a source or subjective genitive.

49. Byrne, 101-2.

suffering is not identical to that "dying with Christ" which takes place at conversion. Rather, the suffering Paul speaks of here refers to the daily anxieties, tensions, and persecutions that are the lot of those who follow the one who was "reckoned with the transgressors" (Luke 22:37). Paul makes clear that this suffering is the condition for the inheritance; we will be "glorified with" Christ (only) *if*[50] we "suffer with him."[51] Participation in Christ's glory can come only through participation in his suffering.[52] What Paul is doing is setting forth an unbreakable "law of the kingdom" according to which glory can come only by way of suffering. For the glory of the kingdom of God is attained only through participation in Christ, and belonging to Christ cannot but bring our participation in the sufferings of Christ. Just as, then, Christ has suffered and entered into his glory (1 Pet. 1:11), so Christians, "fellow heirs with Christ," suffer during this present time in order to join Christ in glory.

3. The Spirit of Glory (8:18-30)

18*For I consider that the sufferings of the present time are not worth comparing with the glory that shall be revealed to us.*

19*For the eager expectation of the creation is awaiting the revelation of the sons of God.* 20*For the creation was subjected to frustration, not of its own will, but because of the one who subjected it, in hope* 21*that*[1] *the creation itself would also be set free from the bondage to decay*

---

50. Gk. εἴπερ. Some interpreters argue that this word states an assumed condition — "*since* we are suffering with him" (e.g., Siber, *Mit Christus Leben,* pp. 139-40; Cranfield). But, as in v. 9, this may be an overinterpretation of the word. It is better to view εἴπερ as stating a real condition, with emphasis, perhaps, on the condition ("if it is indeed true").

51. The ἵνα ("in order that") that Paul uses to connect our suffering with Christ and our being glorified with him does not indicate the purpose *we* have in suffering with Christ but the objective goal, or outcome, of the sufferings as set forth by God (Siber, *Mit Christus Leben,* p. 140; Lagrange).

52. See, e.g., Käsemann; Dunn.

1. We follow NA[27] and UBS[4] in reading ὅτι in place of διότι. Both readings have solid external support, in both early and genealogically diverse MSS — ὅτι in the early papyrus P[46], in the Alexandrian family (A, B, C, 33, 81, 1739), in the uncial Ψ, and in the majority text; and διότι in the Alexandrian (ℵ) and western (D, F, G) families. Both can be explained on the basis of orthographic factors also: διότι could have arisen as a result of dittography after ἐλπίδι, ὅτι as a result of haplography in the same way. While it could be argued that διότι should be read because ὅτι would be the more natural word after ἐλπίδι (cf. Cranfield), the stronger external support for ὅτι and the more natural reading it gives to the text make ὅτι the preferable reading (cf. Metzger, 517).

into the freedom of the glory of the children of God. 22*For we know that the whole creation groans together and suffers birth pangs together up to the present time.* 23*And not only this, but also we ourselves, having the first fruits of the Spirit, groan in ourselves, awaiting adoption,² the redemption of our bodies.* 24*For we were saved with hope. But hope that is seen is not hope. For who hopes for what one sees?³ *25*But if we hope for what we do not see, we await it with endurance.*

26*In the same way, the Spirit also comes to the aid of our weakness. For we do not know what we are to pray as it is necessary, but the Spirit himself intercedes⁴ in groans that words cannot express.* 27*And he who searches hearts knows what is the mind of the Spirit, for he intercedes for the saints in accordance with the will of God.*

2. A few, mainly western MSS (D, F, G, and P⁴⁶, which has western tendencies) omit υἱοθεσίαν, reading (apparently) τὴν ἀπολύτρωσιν τοῦ σώματος ἡμῶν as the object of ἀπεκδεχόμενοι: e.g., "awaiting the redemption of the body" (cf. P. Benoit, " 'Nous gémissons, attendant le déliverance de notre corps' (Rom. VIII,23)," *RSR* 39 [1951-52], 267-80). The theological difficulty of υἱοθεσίαν here (see the notes on the verse) probably led to its omission.

3. The last few words of v. 24 present difficulties of text, punctuation, and accent. The following are the main alternatives:

1. ὃ γὰρ βλέπει τις, τί [καὶ] ἐλπίζει; ("for that which one sees, why does he [also] hope?"; cf. NA²⁵, KJV, NASB) — the second [Byzantine] corrector of ℵ, B (first corrector), and C and the western D, F, and G;

2. ὃ γὰρ βλέπει, τίς ἐλπίζει; ("for what one sees, who hopes [for]?"; cf. NIV, NRSV) — P⁴⁶ and the primary Alexandrian B (original hand);

3. ὃ γὰρ βλέπει, τις ἐλπίζει ("for what one sees, one hopes") — the textual basis for this is the same as for 2; the difference is accentuation;

4. ὃ γὰρ βλέπει τίς καὶ ὑπομένει; ("for what one sees, who also endures?") — the primary Alexandrian ℵ (original hand);

5. ὃ γὰρ βλέπει τις, τί καὶ ὑπομένει; ("for what someone sees, why does he also endure [for] it?"; cf. NEB: "why should a man endure and wait for what he already sees?") — the secondary Alexandrian uncial A.

While reading #5 has enjoyed considerable popularity, as being the "most difficult reading" (cf., e.g., Lietzmann; Käsemann; Schmidt), the verb ὑπομένει is suspect of assimilation from v. 25; and the progress of Paul's logic in v. 25 appears to demand ἐλπίζει in v. 24b (Cranfield); and these considerations eliminate #4 also. The third makes little sense, so the choice must be made between the first two. The first has slightly stronger external support and fits acceptably into Paul's line of argument (cf. Lipsius; Zahn). It is, however, suspect as being an expansion of the more cryptic shorter reading, #1 (Metzger, 517), and the second should therefore probably be read (Wilckens; Cranfield; and H. R. Balz, *Heilsvertrauen und Weltenfahrung: Strukturen des paulinischen Eschatologie nach Römer 8,18-39* [BEvT 59; Munich: Kaiser, 1971], pp. 61-62n).

4. A few MSS (the second [Byzantine] corrector of ℵ, C, and 33, as well as the independent Ψ) add ὑπὲρ ἡμῶν ("on our behalf") after ὑπερεντυγχάνει ("intercede").

28*And we know that all things work together[5] for good for those who love God, for those who are called according to his purpose. 29For those whom he foreknew, he also predestined to be conformed to the image of his Son, so that he might be the firstborn among many brothers. 30And those whom he predestined, these also he called; and those whom he called, these also he justified; and those whom he justified, these also he glorified.*

This passage develops the reference to suffering and glory in v. 17b, continues the overall theme of assurance that dominates chap. 8, and brings us back full circle to the opening paragraph (5:1-11) of this major section of the letter.

Although "glory" is mentioned only three times in vv. 18-30, it is the overarching theme of this passage. Occurring at both the beginning (v. 18 — "the glory that shall be revealed in us") and at the end (v. 30 — "these he glorified"), this concept frames these verses, furnishing us with an important indicator of Paul's central concern. This "inclusio," the noticeable shift at v. 17b from the Christian's present status to his future inheritance, and the parallels between vv. 17-30 and 5:1-11 (on which see below) show that vv. 18-30 comprise a coherent unit of thought, whose focus is eschatological glory.[6] Paul enlists several other concepts in his elaboration of this glory: "freedom" (v. 21), "the redemption of the body" (v. 23), and, most important, "sonship" (vv. 19, 23, 29).[7] The causal connection suggested in v. 17b between suffering and glory — "if we suffer with Christ *in order to be* glorified with him" — is not developed in vv. 18-30. To be sure, "suffering" — of both creation (vv. 19-22) and of Christians (vv. 18, 23, 26 ["weakness"]) — is still present, but Paul is not so much interested in its relationship

---

5. Four important MSS (the very early P[46], the primary Alexandrian witness B, and the secondary Alexandrian witnesses A and 81) read ὁ θεός ("God") after the verb συνεργεῖ. If these words are part of the text, then one difficulty in this verse would be cleared up: Paul is saying that "*God* works all things together for good" (see, e.g., S-H; F. Pack, "A Study of Romans 8:28," *RestQ* 22 [1979], 53). Probably, however, we should follow the majority of MSS and reject this reading, for it looks suspiciously like an attempt to clarify a difficult text (see, e.g., C. D. Osburn, "The Interpretation of Romans 8:28," *WTJ* 44 [1982], 109; Metzger, 518; and see, on the variant generally, J. M. Ross, "Panta synergei, Rom. VIII.28," *ThZ* 34 [1978], 84-85).

6. Alternative paragraph identifications are: (1) vv. 14-30 (e.g., Osten-Sacken, *Römer 8*, pp. 137-39); (2) vv. 18-27 (e.g., Bindemann, *Hoffnung der Schöpfung*, p. 67); or (3) vv. 18-25 (cf. Nebe, *'Hoffnung' bei Paulus*, p. 93).

7. Because the notion of sonship occurs in every subparagraph of the text and picks up the central topic of vv. 14-17, many think it is the topic of the paragraph (cf. esp. Byrne, 104, 115). "Sonship" is important, but it is better viewed as a key element in the Christian's glory rather than as the topic of the paragraph in its own right.

to glory[8] as he is in their sequence. He assumes the fact of suffering as the dark backdrop against which the glorious future promised to the Christian shines with bright intensity.

In vv. 1-17, Paul has focused on the Spirit as the agent through whom believers are granted life and sonship. "No condemnation" can be proclaimed over the Christian (v. 1) because he or she has been transferred from death to life and made God's own child. But the problem that Paul had already broached in vv. 10-11 is insistently raised by v. 17b: How can the Christian maintain hope for eternal life in the face of sufferings and death? How can those who have been set free "from the law of sin and death" die? How can God's very own, dearly loved children suffer? Do not these contradict, or at least call into question, the reality of Paul's "there is now no condemnation for those who are in Christ Jesus"? The exposition of the future glory to be enjoyed by the believer is necessary to answer this objection. In a sense, what Paul is saying in vv. 18-30 is that the Christian must go the way of his Lord. As for Jesus glory only followed suffering, so for the Christian (cf. v. 17c). The life we now definitively enjoy is, nonetheless, incomplete or, better, inchoate — present but not yet fully worked out. "Flesh and blood cannot inherit the kingdom of God" (1 Cor. 15:50), and only when the "mortal body" is transformed will the life that we now have be visible and final (v. 23; cf. vv. 10-11).

It is this transformation of the body that brings to fruition our sonship (v. 23). Only then will our sonship be "revealed" (v. 19), and will we be fully conformed to the image of God's Son (v. 29). We may, perhaps, draw here a loose parallel with Jesus' own sonship, for it was only at the time of his resurrection that he became "Son-of-God-in-power" (1:4). All this is summed up in Paul's words in v. 24a: "we were saved in hope": "saved" — a past, definitive action; "in hope" — the state in which we now live, waiting with anticipation and assurance for the culmination of God's plan for us and the world.[9] And, while the Spirit is not mentioned nearly as often in vv. 18-30 as in vv. 1-17, it is just in bridging this gap between our present status and our future deliverance that the Spirit plays the crucial role. For the Spirit is the "first fruits" — the pledge, or first installment, of God's gifts to us that both anticipates and guarantees the gift of glory yet to come (v. 23). The Spirit connects our "already" with our "not yet," making "the hope of glory," though unseen, as certain as if it were already ours — which, in a sense, it is (cf. "glorified" in v. 30).

Finally, vv. 18-30 (with vv. 31-39) remind the attentive reader of the

---

8. Cf. Schmithals, *Theologische Anthropologie,* p. 139; contra, e.g., Siber, *Mit Christus Leben,* p. 142.

9. The centrality of this half-verse is stressed by J. Cambier, "L'espérance et le salut dans Rom. 8,24," in *Message et Mission. Recuiel commémoratif du Xe anniversaire de la Faculté de Théologie* (Louvain/Paris: Nauwelaerts, 1968), pp. 77-107.

themes with which Paul opened this great section of his letter to the Romans. In both 5:1-11 and this text, Paul demonstrates the unbreakable connection between the Christian's present status — "justified by faith" (5:1, 9, 10; 8:30); "set free from the law of sin and death" (8:2); "children of God" (vv. 14-17) — and her enjoyment of the blessings of God's eternal kingdom — "saved from wrath" (5:9b); "glorified" (8:18, 19, 30). Sufferings, though real, unavoidable, and painful, cannot break this connection (5:3-4; 8:18, 23); for the Spirit is active to instill within us a deep sense of God's love as the basis for our hope (5:6) and to act as God's pledge that he will continue to work on our behalf (8:23; cf. 26-27). (For additional details, see the introduction to Rom. 5–8.) There are, of course, important differences in these texts: 8:18-30 delineates in more detail this "hope of glory" than does 5:1-11, and sets the issue against a more "cosmic" background. But the basic message is very much the same.

Several key words, or concepts, serve to bind vv. 18-30 together. In addition to "glory" (vv. 18, 21; cf. "glorify" in v. 30), these are "groaning" (vv. 22, 23, 26), "hope" (vv. 20, 24-25), "await, wait for" (vv. 19, 23, 25), and, as we have seen, "sonship" (vv. 19, 21, 23, 29). Some have suggested divisions of the paragraph based on one or more of these words — particularly the threefold groaning of the creation (vv. 19-22), the Christian (vv. 23-25), and the Spirit (vv. 26-27 [-30])[10] — but none is very obvious. If we go by literary markers, the most obvious breaks occur at v. 26 ("likewise"]) and v. 28 ("we know").[11] And these markers correspond to the logical flow of the passage. Verse 18, and particularly the last phrase of v. 18 — "the glory that shall be revealed in us" — states the theme of the section as a whole. Verses 19-25, whose key words are "wait for" (vv. 19, 23, and 25) and "hope" (vv. 20, 24-25), develop particularly the note of futurity implicit in the word "to be revealed." Paul wants Christians to realize that they, along with the subhuman creation, are in the position of waiting and hoping for the culmination of God's plan and purposes. There is, Paul is arguing, a necessary and appropriate sense of "incompleteness" in our Christian experience and a consequent eager longing for that incompleteness to be overcome. But, cautions Paul at the end of this subparagraph, this yearning for our final redemption should be characterized by "patient fortitude." The final two subparagraphs describe those works of God that help us to maintain this attitude. First, during this present stage of incompleteness, or "weakness," the Spirit helps us to pray that prayer which God infallibly hears and answers (vv. 26-27). And, second, God himself is working in accordance with his fixed and eternal purpose to bring all things touching our lives to a triumphant conclusion — the "good" (v. 28), conformity to the person of Christ (v. 29), and, coming back to the overall theme, "glory" (v. 30).

10. E.g., Balz, *Heilsvertrauen,* p. 33.
11. See, e.g., Gifford, 154; NA[26].

18 The "for"[12] introduces this verse and, indeed, the entire paragraph that follows, as an elaboration of the sequence of suffering and glory attributed to believers in v. 17b. Viewed from a perspective that holds this world to be a "closed system," suffering is a harsh and final reality that can never be explained nor transcended. "All is trouble, adversity, and suffering!" cries Sue Fawley, summarizing Thomas Hardy's own judgment in his most pessimistic novel, *Jude the Obscure.*[13] But a Christian views the suffering of this life in a larger, world-transcending context that, while not alleviating its present intensity, transcends it with the confident expectation that suffering is not the final word. "The present and visible can be understood only in the light of the future and invisible" (Leenhardt). Thus, Paul can "consider[14] that the sufferings of the present time are not worth comparing with[15] the glory that shall be revealed to us." We must, Paul suggests, weigh suffering in the balance with the glory that is the final state of every believer; and so "weighty," so transcendently wonderful, is this glory that suffering flies in the air as if it had no weight at all. "For this slight momentary affliction is preparing us for an eternal weight of glory beyond all comparison" (2 Cor. 4:17).

These "sufferings of the present time" are not only those "trials" that are endured directly because of confession of Christ — for instance, persecution — but encompass the whole gamut of suffering, including things such as illness, bereavement, hunger, financial reverses, and death itself. To be sure, Paul has spoken of our suffering in v. 17 as "suffering with Christ." But there is a sense in which all the suffering of Christians is "with Christ," inasmuch as Christ was himself subject, by virtue of his coming "in the form of sinful flesh," to the manifold sufferings of this world in rebellion against God. The word Paul uses here[16] refers to "sufferings" in any form; and certainly the "travail" of creation, with which the sufferings of Christians are compared (vv. 19-22), cannot be restricted to sufferings "on behalf of Christ."[17] And the qualification "of the

---

12. Gk. γάρ.

13. New York: New American Library, 1961 (= 1895), p. 327.

14. Gk. λογίζομαι. Paul often uses the word with the connotation of "realize from the standpoint of faith"; cf. Rom. 2:3; 3:28; 6:11; 14:14; 1 Cor. 4:1; 2 Cor. 10:7, 11; 11:5; Phil. 3:13; 4:8. See H. W. Heidland, *TDNT* IV, 288.

15. The construction is οὐκ ἄξια . . . πρός ("not worthy . . . to be compared with"), where πρός has the classical notion of comparison (BDF 239[8]).

16. πάθημα, which Paul has used in 7:5 with the rare meaning "illicit passion." Paul uses πάθημα to denote sufferings in 2 Cor. 1:5, 6, 7, where the parallel is "all our afflictions"; in Phil. 3:10, which speaks of conformity to Christ's sufferings and mentions his death specifically; in Col. 1:24, where Paul mentions his "afflictions" for the sake of believers (including the various things he lists in 2 Cor. 11:23-28?); and in 2 Tim. 3:11, in which the παθήματα may denote, in distinction from διωγμοίς, illness (cf. Gal. 4:13). See the discussion in W. Michaelis, *TDNT* V, 931-34.

17. Lenski.

present time" links these sufferings with the old age of salvation history, conquered in Christ but remaining as the arena in which the Christian must live out his or her new life.[18]

Paul was certainly not the only ancient author to contrast present sufferings and future glory; see, for example, *2 Apoc. Bar.* 15:8: "For this world is to them [the righteous] a struggle and an effort and much trouble. And that accordingly which will come, a crown with great glory." But, since the Christian's glory is a partaking of Christ's own glory ("glorified with him"), Paul puts more stress than does Judaism on the righteous person's *participation* in this glory.[19] In light of this focus on certainty, and since Paul conceives the Christian's glory to be something that has, in some sense, already been determined (8:30), we are probably justified in seeing in "to be revealed" the nuance of a manifestation of that which already exists. "Glory," like salvation in 1 Pet. 1:4-5, can be conceived as a state that is "reserved for us," a state that Christ, our forerunner, has already entered. This is not, then, to say that the Christian already possesses this glory,[20] but that the last day, by bringing the believer into the scope of the glory of God,[21] will manifest the decision that has already been made on our behalf.[22]

18. The Greek is τοῦ νῦν καιροῦ. See the use of καιρός in Rom. 11:5(?), 1 Cor. 7:29, and 2 Cor. 6:2, where in each case it is equivalent to αἰών: the whole phrase is synonymous with "the present evil age" (ὁ αἰῶνος ὁ ἐνεστῶς πονηρός, Gal. 1:4; cf., e.g., Gaugler; Hendriksen).

19. G. Kittel, *TDNT* II, 250. Paul may allude to the certainty of this glory with the unusually worded phrase τὴν μέλλουσαν δόξαν ἀποκαλυφθῆναι εἰς ἡμᾶς — "the glory about to be revealed in us" (τὴν δόξαν μέλλουσαν ἀποκαλυφθῆναι would be expected). This may be simply a stereotyped phrase, "the coming glory" (Turner, 350; cf. also the note in Moule, *Idiom Book,* pp. 169-70; and note a similar phenomenon in Gal. 3:23), though 1 Pet. 5:1 — τῆς μελλούσης ἀποκαλύπτεσθαι δόξης, "the about-to-be-revealed glory" — makes this doubtful. The μέλλουσαν might, then, be part of a periphrasis for a future tense (e.g., Cranfield); or it might stress the imminence of the revelation of this glory (e.g., Käsemann), or its certainty (e.g., S-H). A survey of Paul's use of μέλλω in periphrastic constructions is inconclusive (certainty appears to be stressed in 4:24; 8:13; 1 Thess. 3:4; 2 Tim. 4:1; simple futurity in Gal. 3:23 and 1 Tim. 1:16; and several of these could connote imminence). Perhaps, considering Paul's focus in this paragraph, a nuance of certainty is the best alternative.

20. As Chrysostom, followed by Cranfield, suggests.

21. Paul speaks of this glory as being revealed εἰς ἡμᾶς, a phrase difficult to render into English. The dynamic meaning of ἀποκαλύπτω, combined with the fact that Paul does not normally use εἰς with the meaning of ἐν ("in"; cf. Turner, 256; Zerwick, 106-10), suggests that we should probably not translate "to be revealed *in* us" (KJV, NIV; cf. Robertson, 535). However, the main alternative translation, "to be revealed *to* us" (NRSV, NASB, TEV), is not much better, for it suggests the idea, normally conveyed by the dative, that believers are simply the recipients of revelation (see, e.g., Matt. 16:17; 1 Cor. 2:10). Paul's choice of εἰς (this is the only place in the NT where εἰς follows ἀποκαλύπτω) suggests that the glory reaches out and includes us in its scope (cf. Michel). Perhaps the NEB captures it best: "which is in store for us."

22. See Dunn. ἀποκαλύπτω, as in 1:17 and 18 (see the notes there), refers not to

19 Verses 19-25 support in some way what Paul has said in v. 18.[23] But in what way? Is Paul explaining and demonstrating the suffering he has mentioned;[24] giving reasons for the patient endurance commanded by implication in v. 18;[25] supporting the certainty of the future manifestation of glory;[26] or giving evidence of the transcendent greatness of the glory?[27] None of these suggestions does justice to the focus of these verses, which is on the longing anticipation of future transformation shared by both the creation and Christians. In these verses, therefore, Paul supports and develops "to be revealed" in v. 18 by showing that both creation and Christians (1) suffer at present from a sense of incompleteness and even frustration; and (2) eagerly yearn for a culminating transformation.

Paul begins with the yearning of creation: "For the eager expectation of the creation is awaiting[28] the revelation of the sons of God." The word "eager expectation" suggests the picture of a person craning his or her neck to see what is coming.[29] Paul further enhances the idea of anticipation by using a common literary device: "eager expectation," the grammatical subject, is put in place of the real subject, "creation." But what does Paul include in this "creation"?[30] Noting the naturally broad meaning of the word, and Paul's addition of "the whole" in v. 22, some interpreters argue that Paul must mean the entire created universe — human beings, animals, plants, and so on.[31] Others, however, insist

---

intellectual perception but to an activity, a manifestation, or coming to pass in this world of God's purpose.

23. The γάρ in v. 19 has a causal force.

24. Godet.

25. Murray.

26. Meyer; Gifford.

27. Alford.

28. The Greek verb is ἀποδέχομαι, a linking word in this paragraph (cf. vv. 23, 25; cf. also 1 Cor. 1:7; Gal. 5:5; Phil. 3:20; 1 Pet. 3:20).

29. The Greek word is ἀποκαραδοκία, from κάρα, "head" + δέχομαι, "stretch," with the prefix ἀπο- perhaps meaning "away from." See Phillips's paraphrase: "the creation is on tiptoe . . ."). The word is extant only in Christian literature (in the NT only here and in Phil. 1:20), although the cognate verb occurs elsewhere (e.g., Josephus, *J.W.* 3.264). G. Bertram ("ἀποκαραδοκία," *ZNW* 49 [1958], 264-70) finds a note of anxiety in the word, but this is improbable (cf. D. R. Denton, "Ἀποκαραδοκία," *ZNW* 73 [1982], 138-40).

30. Gk. κτίσις. This word means "act of creating" (perhaps Rom. 1:20) or, more often, "that which has been created," either in an individual sense — "creature" (Rom. 8:39; 2 Cor. 5:17; Gal. 6:15; Col. 1:23) — or in the most general sense — the "creation" (Mark 10:6; 13:19; Rom. 1:25; Col. 1:15; Heb. 4:13; 9:11; 2 Pet. 3:4; Rev. 3:14; in 1 Pet. 2:13, it has the unusual meaning "authority" — cf. BAGD). The meaning "creation," broadly defined, is required here.

31. Many would, however, exclude spiritual beings, and many also think that the focus is on the subhuman part of creation. See, e.g., W. Foerster, *TDNT* III, 1031; Balz, *Heilsvertrauen*, pp. 47-48; Käsemann.

that the distinctly personal activities Paul attributes to the creation ("anticipating," "set free," "groaning") show that he has only the human part of creation in view (cf. Col. 1:23) — either all humankind (Augustine) or unbelievers only.[32] However, while we may agree with Schlatter that the transition from v. 22 to v. 23 — "we ourselves" — plainly excludes believers from the scope of creation in vv. 19-22, Paul's insistence in v. 20 that the "vanity" to which this creation was subjected was not of its own choice appears to exclude all people, not just believers. With the majority of modern commentators, then, I think that creation here denotes the "subhuman" creation.[33] Like the psalmists and prophets who pictured hills, meadows, and valleys "shouting and singing together for joy" (Ps. 65:12-13) and the earth "mourning" (Isa. 24:4; Jer. 4:28; 12:4), Paul personifies the subhuman creation in order to convey to his readers a sense of the cosmic significance of both humanity's fall into sin and believers' restoration to glory.[34]

32. Schlatter; N. Walter, "Gottes Zorn und das 'Harren der Kreatur': Zur Korrespondenz zwischen Römer 1,18-32 und 8,19-22," in *Christus Bezeugen: Für Wolfgang Trilling* (ed. K. Kertelge, T. Holtz, and C.-P. März; Freiburg/Basel/Vienna: Herder, 1990), pp. 220-23.

33. κτίσις occurs with this meaning in Wisdom of Solomon: 2:6; 5:17(?); 16:24; 19:6. While the early Fathers exhibit no consensus on this point (cf. Schelkle), many adopted this interpretation (see Cranfield). Among the moderns, see especially Godet; Zahn; Kuss; and Cranfield.

34. Scholars have speculated about other sources for Paul's use of the creation motif here, with particular attention being given to apocalyptic motifs. The cosmological picture of hope as a "new creation," especially prominent in the latter parts of Isaiah, became a key element in apocalyptic eschatology (see the survey in P. Stuhlmacher, "Erwägungen zum ontologische Charakter des καινὴ κτίσις bei Paulus," *EvT* 27 [1967], 10-20). Many texts speak of a renewal of the earth, a new creation, etc., that will characterize the "age to come" (cf. *1 Enoch* 45:5; 51:4-5; 72:1; *2 Apoc. Bar.* 29; 32:6; 44:12; 57:2; *Jub.* 1:29; 4:26). But the most famous text is 4 Ezra 7, for here, in addition to the hope of a renewed earth "in the days of the Messiah" (vv. 29, 75), the present corruption of the world is linked to the sin of human beings:

> For I made the world for their sake, and when Adam transgressed my statutes, what had been made was judged. And so the entrances of this world were made narrow and sorrowful and toilsome; they are few and evil, full of dangers and involved in great hardships. But the entrances to the greater world are broad and safe, and really yield the fruit of immortality. Therefore unless the living pass through the difficult and vain experiences, they can never receive these things that have been reserved for them. (vv. 11-14)

Does Paul depend on these motifs, perhaps even incorporating into vv. 18-30 preexisting apocalyptic material (see esp. H. Paulsen, *Überlieferung und Auslegung in Römer 8* [WMANT 43; Neukirchener/Vluyn: Neukirchener, 1974]; Osten-Sacken, *Römer 8*, pp. 78-101)? Paul probably knows of these traditions but gives little indication of dependence on them. Certainly the paragraph contains "apocalyptic motifs," but wholesale dependence on intertestamental Jewish traditions is not demonstrable (see, e.g., Bindemann,

The "revelation of the sons of God" that creation keenly anticipates is the "unveiling" of the true nature of Christians. Paul has already made clear that Christians are already "sons of God" (vv. 14-17). But, experiencing suffering (v. 18) and weakness (v. 26) like all other people, Christians do not in this life "appear" much like sons of God. The last day will publicly manifest our real status.[35] Nevertheless, since this "being revealed" as God's sons takes place only through a further act of God — causing his glory to reach out and embrace us (v. 18), transforming the body (v. 23) — we are justified in attaching a degree of dynamic activity to "revelation" here also. The "revelation" of which Paul speaks is not *only* a disclosure of what we have always been but also a dynamic process by which the status we now have in preliminary form and in hiddenness will be brought to its final stage and made publicly evident.

20   In this verse and in v. 21 (which make up one sentence in Greek) Paul explains what many of his readers would naturally be wondering: Why must the creation be eagerly anticipating the revelation of the sons of God? The reason, Paul says, is that the subhuman creation itself is not what it should be, or what God intended it to be. It has "been subjected to "frustration.""[36] In light of Paul's obvious reference to the Gen. 3 narrative — Murray labels these verses "Paul's commentary on Gen. 3:17, 18" — the word probably denotes the "frustration" occasioned by creation's being unable to attain the ends for which it was made.[37] Humanity's fall into sin marred the "goodness" of God's creation, and creation has ever since been in a state of "frustration."[38]

But creation's frustration, Paul reminds us, came "not of its own will, but because of the one who subjected it." The "one who subjected it" has been identified with (1) Adam, whose sin brought death and decay into the world (cf. Rom. 5:12);[39] (2) Satan, whose temptation led to the Fall;[40] and

---

Hoffnung der Schöpfung, pp. 24-29). Nor is the more specific proposal of O. Christoffersson (*The Earnest Expectation of the Creature: The Flood-Tradition as Matrix of Romans 8:18-27* [CBNT 23; Stockholm: Almquist & Wiksell, 1990]), that Paul was indebted to the intertestamental Jewish "flood tradition," acceptable.

35. The NT writers, drawing from Jewish apocalyptic, often use ἀποκάλυψις and its cognates with this nuance.

36. τῇ ματαιότητι. ματαιότης occurs only here and in Eph. 4:17 and 2 Pet. 2:18 in the NT, although several cognates are found. Some interpreters think that it may connote the "vanity" that the author of Ecclesiastes deplores (32 of the 47 LXX occurrences of the word are in this book) — the "emptiness" or "absurdity" of things in general.

37. Cf., e.g., S-H, Murray, Cranfield.

38. Bruce thinks that Paul might also see this subjection in terms of the rule of evil spiritual forces over the cosmos (the cognate μάταιος refers to idolatry in Rom. 1:20), but this idea is not clear.

39. E.g., G. W. H. Lampe, "The New Testament Doctrine of Ktisis," *SJT* 17 (1964), 458; Balz, *Heilsvertrauen,* p. 41; Chrysostom; Godet (and Satan also); Zahn; Schlier.

40. Cf., e.g., Godet (with reference also to Adam).

(3) God, who decreed the curse as a judgment on sin (Gen. 3:17).[41] Reference to Adam, however, is unlikely; as Bengel says, "Adam rendered the creature obnoxious to vanity, but he did not *subject* it." Nor did Satan, whatever his role in the Fall, "subject" creation. Paul must be referring to God, who alone had the right and the power to condemn all of creation to frustration because of human sin.[42] But this decree of God was not without its positive side, for it was issued "in hope."[43] Paul probably has in mind the *protoevangelium* — the promise of God, given in conjunction with the curse, that "he [the seed of the woman] will bruise your [the serpent's] head" (cf. Rom. 16:20). The creation, then, though subjected to frustration as a result of human sin, has never been without hope; for the very decree of subjection was given in the context of hope. As Byrne puts it, this phrase is the "pivot" of Paul's argument in vv. 19-22,[44] because he now moves from explanation of the reason why creation should need to be looking ahead in hope to the nature of that hope and its relationship to the "revelation of the sons of God" (v. 19).

21 In this verse, Paul specifies the content of the hope that he mentioned at the end of v. 20:[45] "[the hope that] the creation itself[46] would be set free from the bondage to decay into the freedom of the glory of the children

---

41. Most commentators; e.g., S-H; Käsemann; Michel; Cranfield; Fitzmyer.

42. The aorist passive ὑπετάγη, "was subjected," also points in this direction, since it probably denotes an action of God. Note also Ps. 8:6, quoted by Paul in 1 Cor. 15:27: "He [God] has subjected [ὑπέταξεν] all things under his [man's] feet." The main objection to this interpretation is grammatical: Paul uses διά with the accusative, which suggests that the person indicated is not the agent of the subjection — as God is — but the reason for it. But this may be a case in which διά with the accusative means the same as διά with the genitive (cf. John 6:57; BAGD; BDF 223[3]), or Paul may be choosing to emphasize God's decree as the cause of the subjection; in either case, this grammatical point cannot overcome the strength of the lexical and theological arguments.

43. Gk. ἐφ' ἐλπίδι; the translation "in" for ἐπί is justified because the preposition denotes the "condition" in which the action took place (Turner, 272). Since οὐχ ἑκοῦσα ("not of its own will") is balanced by ἀλλὰ διὰ τὸν ὑποτάξαντα ("but because of the one who subjected it"), it is better to construe ἐφ' ἐλπίδι with ὑπετάγη (e.g., "it was subjected in hope") than with ὑποτάξαντα (e.g., "because of the one who subjected it in hope").

44. P. 106.

45. If we adopt the reading διότι (see the note on the textual variant in the translation above), v. 21 will give the reason why Paul can attribute hope to the creation (cf. KJV); for, while διότι can mean "that" (BAGD, MM) in Hellenistic Greek, this meaning for the word is not otherwise attested in the NT (Cranfield). However, while the call is a close one, we should probably read ὅτι instead of διότι. In this case, while a causal meaning is still possible, it is more likely that ὅτι functions to introduce a noun clause (see Phil. 1:20).

46. The combination of καί — which means "even" here — and the emphasizing pronoun αὐτή ("itself") conveys a sense of wonder: "Why, even the creation itself is going to be set free!"

of God." Creation, helplessly enslaved to the decay[47] that rules this world after the Fall, exists in the hope that it will be set free to participate in the eschatological glory to be enjoyed by God's children. Paul describes this glory in terms of freedom; we might paraphrase, "the freedom that is associated with the state of glory to which the children of God are destined."[48] The repetition of the "freedom" idea here — "set free . . . into[49] the freedom" — suggests that it is only with and because of the glory of God's children that creation experiences its own full and final deliverance (Chrysostom). As in v. 19, then, the hope of the creation is related to, and even contingent upon, the glory to be given Christians.[50] We might also note that the idea of creation "being set free" strongly suggests that the ultimate destiny of creation is not annihilation but transformation. When will this transformation take place? If one adopts a premillennial structure of eschatology (see Rev. 20:4-6), then it is tempting to apply the language Paul uses here to that period of time. But we cannot be certain that Paul has the millennium in mind because there is some evidence that the language he uses could also apply to the eternal state (see, e.g., the description of "the new heaven and new earth" in Rev. 21:1–22:7).

47. Gk. τῆς δουλείας τῆς φθορᾶς. φθορά can denote "destruction" (cf. Gal. 6:8 for eschatological condemnation), but, with reference here to the subhuman creation, probably refers rather to "decay," combining the ideas of both mutability and corruption (cf. Col. 2:22; 1 Cor. 15:42, 50). The genitive has been explained as subjective — "the state of slavery that comes from decay" (Cranfield), qualitative — "slavery characterized by decay" (noted as a possibility by Turner, 213), and epexegetic — "the slavery that is decay" (Lenski, Murray); but, in light of the meaning of the words, it is probably objective — "slavery to decay" (BAGD [p. 858]; Byrne, 107).

48. The Greek features an accumulation of genitives that is very typical of Paul: τὴν ἐλευθερίαν τῆς δόξης τῶν τέκνων τοῦ θεοῦ. The last two are almost certainly loosely "possessive" — the glory (or, the glorious freedom; see below) "belongs to" the children who, in turn, "belong to" God (this last is often classified more narrowly as a "genitive of relationship"). The first genitive, τῆς δόξης, is often taken as a genitive of quality — "glorious freedom" (Moule, *Idiom Book,* p. 175; cf. KJV, RSV, NIV, TEV) — but is probably loosely possessive — "the freedom that belongs to, is associated with, the state of glory" (Alford; Byrne, 107; Phil. 3:21, "the body that belongs to the state of humiliation/state of glory" [= τὸ σῶμα τῆς ταπεινώσεως/τῆς δόξης], is similar).

49. Gk. εἰς, in contrast to ἀπό, expresses the goal of creation's being set free (Bengel).

50. While Paul obviously says some important things in this paragraph about the renewal of creation, his focus is consistently on anthropology (see esp. J. Baumgarten, *Paulus und die Apokalyptic: Die Auslegung apokalyptischer Überlieferungen in den echten Paulusbriefen* [WMANT 44; Neukirchen/Vluyn: Neukirchener, 1975], pp. 175-78, passim; Bindemann, *Hoffung des Schöpfung;* A. Vögtle, "Röm 8, 19-22: eine schöpfungstheologie oder anthropologisch-soteriologische Aussage?" in *Mélanges bibliques in hommage au Béda Rigaux,* pp. 351-66).

22 This verse, concluding the subparagraph on the hope of the creation, comes back to the theme with which the paragraph began (v. 19): the longing of creation for deliverance. "We know,"[51] Paul says, "that the whole creation[52] groans together and suffers birth pangs together up to the present time."[53] Paul uses the simple verb "groan" in 8:23, and in 2 Cor. 5:2 and 4, to depict the "groans of eschatological anticipation."[54] And, while neither the verb "suffer birth pangs together" nor the simple "suffer birth pangs" is used elsewhere in the NT in this sense,[55] the noun form of this verb is used in Mark 13:8 (= Matt. 24:8) to depict the times of distress preceding the end. Indeed, the image is a natural one, for the difficulties and trials of this age are, for Christians and the creation, fraught with the knowledge that they will ultimately issue in victory and joy. Our Lord makes this application in John 16:20b-22, as he addresses the disciples:

> You will be sorrowful, but your sorrow will turn into joy. When a woman is in travail she has sorrow, because her hour has come; but when she is delivered of the child, she no longer remembers the anguish, for joy that a child is born into the world. So you have sorrow now, but I will see you again and your hearts will rejoice, and no one will take your joy from you.

The "with" idea in both verbs means not that creation is groaning and in birth pangs with believers,[56] but that the various parts of the creation are groaning together, are in birth pangs together, uttering a "symphony of sighs" (Phillips).

23 In vv. 19-22, Paul has described the yearning anticipation of creation for deliverance and tied that deliverance to the "glory to be revealed"

---

51. Paul generally uses οἴδαμεν γὰρ ὅτι ("for we know that") to introduce a commonly recognized truth (see also 2:2; 3:19; 7:14; 8:28), and it may be that he sees the violence and disasters in nature as evidence of the "yearning" he speaks of in this verse.

52. Gk. πᾶσα ἡ κτίσις. While the "rule" that πᾶς with an articular noun means "the whole of" — as opposed to its use with an anarthrous noun, in which it has a distributive force ("every, each") — is not always followed in biblical Greek (cf. F. C. Conybeare and St. George Stock, *A Grammar of Septuagint Greek* [Grand Rapids: Zondervan, 1980 {= 1905}], ¶63), it is observed here: not "each creation" but "the whole of creation."

53. Gk. ἄχρι τοῦ νῦν. Some scholars give this phrase theological force — "the decisive moment when God's purposes are fulfilled" (Barrett; see also Käsemann, Dunn) — but it probably has simple temporal meaning, as in Phil. 1:5, Paul's only other use of the phrase (Wilckens).

54. The verb Paul uses in v. 22 is συστενάζω, which occurs nowhere else in the NT.

55. Again, the compound verb συνωδίνω occurs only here; the simple form ὠδίνω in Gal. 4:19, 27; Rev. 12:2.

56. E.g., Tholuck.

to believers. Now he shows how believers share this same eager hope. The transition from creation to Christian is made via the idea of "groaning"; not only is the creation "groaning together," but "we ourselves, having the first fruits of the Spirit, groan in ourselves,[57] awaiting adoption, the redemption of our bodies." By saying that Christians "groan in themselves," Paul suggests that these groans are not verbal utterances but inward, nonverbal "sighs," indicative of a certain attitude.[58] This attitude does not involve anxiety about whether we will finally experience the deliverance God has promised — for Paul allows of no doubts on that score (cf. vv. 28-30) — but frustration at the remaining moral and physical infirmities that are inevitably a part of this period between justification and glorification (see 2 Cor. 5:2, 4) and longing for the end of this state of "weakness."[59]

Paul defines those who experience this frustrated longing for final deliverance as those "who have the first fruits of the Spirit." The word "first fruits" signifies a ministry of the Spirit that is very characteristic in Paul. The word alludes to both the *beginning* of a process and the unbreakable *connec-*

---

57. στενάζομεν is the main verb in the verse, and both the αὐτοί after ἀλλὰ καί at the beginning of the verse and the αὐτοί following ἡμεῖς καί go with this verb. The apparent reason for this awkward repetition of αὐτοί is that Paul decided in mid-stream to introduce a participial qualifier of the main verb, and the clause is long enough that he felt it necessary to repeat the emphatic pronoun when he came back again to the main clause.

58. Murray, Cranfield, Dunn; contra, e.g., Käsemann.

59. The verb στενάζω and its cognate, στεναγμός, occur infrequently in the NT, but more often in the LXX. They are used characteristically of the "groaning" occasioned by oppression, and often of entreaty to God for deliverance from oppression. In the NT, στενάζω refers to the same frustrated longing for deliverance in 2 Cor. 5:2 as in this verse (cf. the compound συστενάζω in v. 22); Mark 7:34, though not entirely clear, probably refers to a prayer of strong entreaty. In both Heb. 13:17 and Jas. 5:9, it denotes "groaning" in the sense of "complaining." The noun στεναγμός occurs elsewhere in the NT only in Acts 7:34, in a quotation of Exod. 3:7. In the LXX, στεναγμός refers to the groaning occasioned by pain (e.g., childbearing — Gen. 3:16; cf. Isa. 35:10, 51:11; Jer. 45:3), but more often, in a more metaphorical sense, the "groaning" under oppression; cf., e.g., Lam. 1:22; Ezek. 24:17.

But even more characteristic are texts in which "groans" are cries to God of the righteous person who is being oppressed, cries that suggest both the expression of pain and a plea for deliverance. Ps. 38:9 is typical: after complaining of physical and spiritual agony, David says, "LORD, all my longing is known to thee, my sighing (ὁ στεναγμός μου) is not hidden from thee" (see also Exod. 2:24; 6:5; Judg. 2:18; Pss. 6:6; 12:5; 31:10; 79:11; 102:20). στενάζω is used less often with reference to prayer in this way, although cf. Job 24:12 and Tob. 3:1 (in codex ℵ): καὶ περίλυπος γενόμενος τῇ ψυχῇ καὶ στενάξας ἔκλαυσα καὶ ἠρξάμην προσεύχεσθαι μετὰ στεναγμῶν ("Then in my grief I wept, and I cried out, *groaning,* and began to pray with *groans* . . ."). Paul, therefore, has chosen a word that very aptly conveys both the sense of frustrated longing occasioned by the continuing pressures of "this age" and the sense of entreaty to God for deliverance from that situation.

tion between its beginning and the end.[60] As applied to the Spirit, then, the word connotes both that God's eschatological redemptive work has begun and that this redemptive work will surely be brought to its intended culmination. The Spirit, in this sense, is both the "first installment" of salvation and the "down payment" or "pledge" that guarantees the remaining stages of that salvation.[61]

But does Paul want to say that Christians groan *because* we possess the Spirit as "first fruits"[62] or that we groan *even though* we have the Spirit as "first fruits"?[63] Both make good sense in this context and fit Paul's theology of the Spirit. However, the fact that Paul refers to "the first fruits of the Spirit" rather than simply the Spirit shows that he is thinking of the Spirit's role in anticipating and pledging the completion of salvation rather than as the agent of present blessing. This being so, a causal interpretation of the participle is to be preferred: it is *because* we possess the Spirit as the first installment and pledge of our complete salvation that we groan, yearning for the fulfillment of that salvation to take place. The Spirit, then, functions to join inseparably together the two sides of the "already–not yet" eschatological tension in which we are caught. "Already," through the indwelling presence of God's Spirit, we have been transferred into the new age of blessing and salvation; but the very fact that the Spirit is only the "first fruits" makes us sadly conscious that we have "not yet" severed all ties to the old age of sin and death.[64] A healthy balance is necessary in the Christian life, in which our joy at the many blessings we already possess should be set beside our frustration at our failures and our intense yearning for that day when we will fail no more — when "we shall be like him."

---

60. ἀπαρχή has a sacrificial flavor in the LXX, where it is used most often to describe those "first fruits" of the harvest that were to be offered to the Lord and to his priests (see, e.g., Num. 5:9; Deut. 18:4; 2 Chr. 31:5-6). But these allusions are not clearly present in the NT, where ἀπαρχή is used in a natural metaphorical way (contra, e.g., Dunn) to describe a "first stage" of something — Christians as the first converts in a particular area (Rom. 16:5; 1 Cor. 16:15), or as the first stage in God's redemptive work generally (Jas. 1:18; Rev. 14:4; 2 Thess. 2:13? [v.l.]); Christ as the first to be raised from the dead (1 Cor. 15:20 and 23; cf. also the purely illustrative use in Rom. 11:16).

61. As used here, ἀπαρχή has basically the same meaning as ἀρραβών, "pledge," in 2 Cor. 1:22; 5:5; Eph. 1:14 (cf. Fitzmyer). In light of these parallels, it is far better to understand the genitive τοῦ πνεύματος as epexegetic — "the first fruits which is the Spirit" (with most commentators) — than as partitive — "the first bestowal of the Spirit" (cf. Gifford; Stuart; Meyer; Murray).

62. ἔχοντες having a causal nuance (cf., e.g., Bengel; Kuss; Dunn).

63. ἔχοντες as concessive (e.g., Godet; Wilckens).

64. This function of the Spirit is stressed by Dunn, *Jesus and the Spirit,* p. 310, and Beker, 279; The rabbis, on the other hand, relegated the Spirit mainly to the past and the future (cf. Davies, 208-17).

Paul's description of the climax of salvation for which we are eagerly awaiting[65] furthers this sense of eschatological tension. For the "adoption" that, in vv. 14-17, we were said already to possess is here made the object of our hope. As we noted at v. 15, some seek to relieve the tension thus created by making only the "Spirit of adoption," not the adoption itself, a present possession of the Christian, but Paul clearly goes further than that in vv. 14-17. Christians, at the moment of justification, are adopted into God's family; but this adoption is incomplete and partial until we are finally made like *the* Son of God himself (v. 29).[66] This final element in our adoption is "the redemption of our bodies."[67] "Redemption" shares with "adoption" and many other terms in Paul the "already–not yet" tension that pervades his theology, for the redemption can be pictured both as past[68] and as future.[69] As Paul has hinted in v. 10, it is not until the body has been transformed that redemption can be said to be complete; in this life, our bodies share in that "frustration" which characterizes this world as a whole (cf. 20).[70]

24 Paul's purpose in the last two verses of this subsection (vv. 19-25) is to make it clear that this need for expectant waiting is not surprising. For, as creation was subjected to frustration "in hope" (v. 20), so Christians, though saved, are nevertheless also saved "with hope" — and hope, by its very nature, means that expectant and patient waiting is going to be necessary. The juxtaposition of the assertion of past experience — "we were saved"[71] — and its qualification "with hope"[72] is one more expression of the eschato-

---

65. Gk. ἀπεκδεχόμενοι, a key word in this paragraph (cf. vv. 19 and 25).

66. See 1 John 3:2: "Beloved, we are God's children now; it does not yet appear what we shall be, but we know that when he appears we shall be like him, for we shall see him as he is."

67. Gk. τὴν ἀπολύτρωσιν τοῦ σώματος ἡμῶν. The genitive, in light of the biblical stress on the permanence of "bodily" life through resurrection and transformation, must be objective — it is the body that is redeemed — rather than ablatival — "redemption *from* the body" (contra Lietzmann).

68. Eph. 1:7; Col. 1:14; cf. Rom. 3:24 and 1 Cor. 1:30.

69. Eph. 1:14; 4:30.

70. Bruce.

71. Paul uses the aorist ἐσώθημεν. It is somewhat unusual for Paul to use the σῴζω word group of a past experience (although see Eph. 2:5, 8; 2 Tim. 1:9; Tit. 3:5), but there is nothing inconsistent in his doing so. While final salvation from God's wrath will not take place until the last day (see 5:9, 10), deliverance in principle from that wrath *has* already taken place when we were justified by faith.

72. Gk. τῇ ἐλπίδι. The dative has been variously explained. The most likely alternatives are (1) instrumental: "through hope" (Robertson, 531-33; Schlatter; cf. KJV, TEV); (2) dative of advantage: "for hope" (Lenski); (3) modal: "in hope" (most commentators; e.g., Bengel; S-H; Käsemann; Cranfield; and cf. Turner, 241; Byrne, 110; NIV, NASB, NRSV); and (4) associative: "with hope." (The JB rendering "we must be content to hope that we shall be saved," treating the aorist ἐσώθημεν as if it were a future, is

logical tension of Christian existence. Hope, Paul is saying, has been associated with our experience of salvation from the beginning. Always our salvation, while definitively secured for us at conversion, has had an element of incompleteness, in which the forward look is necessary. The last part of the verse is a rather obvious explanation of the very nature of "hope" — it involves looking in confidence for that which one cannot see. Paul uses the word "hope" in both an objective sense — that for which we hope — and a subjective sense — our attitude of hope. Here, by modifying hope with the phrase "that is seen," he shows that he is thinking of the former meaning. That "glory to be revealed," which is the focus of our hope, is not visible; and the frustrations and difficulties of life can sometimes all but erase the image of that glory for us. But hope would not be what it is if we could see it, for "who hopes for what one sees?"

25 Paul rounds off this subsection with a return to its central theme: the need, in this age of salvation history, for "earnest waiting."[73] In the "if" clause, Paul resumes the point he made in v. 24b and draws a conclusion from it: hoping for what one does not see means that we must wait for it with "patient fortitude."[74] While this emphasis on what is not seen may be nothing more than a reiteration of what hope, by its nature, is, the logic of this verse may imply that Paul is thinking more distinctly theologically about the matter. For, as Paul puts it in 2 Cor. 4:18b, "the things that are seen are transient, but the things that are unseen are eternal" (cf. also Heb. 11). If this thought lies behind what Paul is saying here, then the logic of this verse is strengthened; we Christians can wait expectantly and with fortitude for the "hope" to manifest itself precisely because that for which we hope is "unseen" and thereby part of the eternal and sure purposes of God.[75] The attitude of "patient endurance" is one that is frequently required of Christians undergoing trials[76] and as they await the climax of God's salvation for them.[77] The word suggests the connotation of "bearing up" under intense pressure. This is the virtue required by Christians as we eagerly await "the hope of the glory of God."

26 In vv. 24-25, Paul has argued that the nature and solidity of our Christian hope enable us to wait for its culmination with fortitude. Now, he

---

without warrant.) Of these, the third or fourth is to be preferred, for Paul nowhere suggests that hope is a means of salvation; and, despite the weight of commentators in favor of a modal rendering, the associative may be best: "we were saved, with hope as the ever present companion of this salvation."

73. Once again, he uses the verb ἀπεκδέχομαι (cf. vv. 19, 23).

74. Gk. δι' ὑπομονῆς. The διά indicates manner (Turner, 267).

75. See esp. Barth.

76. Rom. 5:3-4; Jas. 1:3, 4; 5:11; Rev. 13:10; 14:12.

77. Luke 21:19; 1 Thess. 1:3; Heb. 10:36.

says, "in the same way [as this hope sustains us], the Spirit also comes to our aid."[78] To be sure, this is not the only way that v. 26 might be connected to its context. Especially popular, for instance, is the view that "in the same way" compares the groaning of the Christian (v. 23) with the "groaning" of the Spirit.[79] But the "groans" of the Spirit come rather late in v. 26 for this to be the point of comparison; and, while there is an obvious literary parallelism between the "groaning" of creation (v. 22), the Christian, and the Spirit, the groaning of the Spirit is very different in its nature and purpose from the other two "groanings."

The word we have translated "come to the aid of" connotes "joining *with* to help," "bearing a burden along with."[80] The Spirit joins with us in bearing the burdens imposed by our "weakness." This weakness may be specific — inability in prayer or external sufferings (v. 18) — but is probably general: the "totality of the human condition" (Dunn), the "creatureliness" that characterizes even the child of God in this period of overlap between the old age and the new.[81] This condition means that we believers do not know "what we are to pray as it is necessary."[82] The wording of the clause indicates that it is not the manner, or style, of prayer that Paul has in view[83] but the content, or object, of prayer — what we are to pray *for*.[84] Some think that the context suggests a restriction of this prayer to entreaties for the realization of God's glory,[85] but Paul's language is too

78. See, e.g., Haldane; Stuart; Murray; Harrisville; Harrison.

79. E.g., Godet; S-H; Cranfield; Dunn.

80. The verb is συναντιλαμβάνομαι. It occurs only three (or four) times in the LXX. In both Exod. 18:22 and Num. 11:17, it translates the Hebrew וְנָשְׂאוּ אִתְּךָ, where the people appointed to assist Moses are said to "bear the burden with you." The *with* idea, clearly present here, is probably also to be found in Ps. 89:21, where the Lord promises that his hand "will be established with" (תִּכּוֹן עִמּוֹ) David. (The verb is v.l. in Ps. 88:22.) The only NT occurrence of the verb is in Luke 10:40, where Martha requests that Jesus command her sister to "join with her in helping" (ἵνα μοι συνταντιλάβηται). To be sure, in all these occurrences, the person to whose aid one comes is denoted with the dative, while in Rom. 8:26 the situation in which the aid is needed is stated in the dative. But, as Balz suggests, the object of the implied "with" is "hidden" in the ἡμῶν (*Heilsvertrauen*, pp. 71-72); it is justified, then, to retain the original force of the preposition (see also Harrison).

81. See esp. K. Niederwimmer, "Das Gebet des Geistes, Röm. 8, 26f." *ThZ* 20 (1964), 257-59; Barth; Cranfield.

82. Gk. τὸ . . . τί προσευξώμεθα καθὸ δεῖ. The article preceding the clause shows that the whole phrase is the object of the verb οἴδαμεν ("we know"): "the 'what-we-are-to-pray-as-it-is-necessary' we do not know."

83. Contra, e.g., Lagrange.

84. See, e.g., P. O'Brien, "Romans 8:26, 27. A Revolutionary Approach to Prayer?" *RTR* 46 (1987), 67.

85. Byrne, 112; Niederwimmer, "Das Gebet des Geistes," p. 254.

general for that; and surely we know enough to pray for that glory, however much specific knowledge of it we may lack. Again, there is no good reason to restrict this knowledge to some special circumstance. What Paul apparently has in mind is that inability to discern clearly God's will in the many things for which we pray; note that the "as it is necessary" of this verse is paralleled by "according to God," that is, "according to his will," of v. 27. *All* our praying is conditioned by our continuing "weakness" and means that — except perhaps on rare occasions — our petitions must be qualified by "if it is in accordance with your will."[86] This does not, of course, mean that we should not strive to understand the will of God for the circumstances we face, or that we are in the wrong to make definite requests to God; but it does mean that we cannot presume to identify our petitions with the will of God.

This inability to know what to pray for cannot be overcome in this life, for it is part of "our weakness," the inescapable condition imposed on us by our place in salvation history. Therefore, Paul does not command us to eradicate this ignorance by diligent searching for God's will or by special revelation.[87] Instead, Paul points us to the Spirit of God, who overcomes this weakness by his own intercession.

What, however, is the nature of this intercession? Specifically, is it an intercession that comes about through our praying, aided by the Spirit? Or is it an intercession that is accomplished solely by the Holy Spirit on our behalf? One clue to the meaning may be found in the term we have translated "that words cannot express" *(alalētois)*. This word, found only here in biblical Greek, means, as its etymology implies, "unspoken," "wordless." But does it mean here specifically "ineffable," incapable of being expressed in human language,[88] in which case the "groans" may well be audible though inarticulate?[89] Or does it mean simply "unspoken," never rising to the audible level at all?[90] If the former is correct, then the "groans" are probably the believer's own, inspired and directed by the Spirit. Paul's reference may then be to those times when, in the perplexity of our ignorance, we call out to God in "content-less" groans — whether expressed out loud or kept to ourselves.[91]

However, others who ascribe the groans to believers think that Paul is

---

86. See esp. Barth and Cranfield on this; against, e.g., Käsemann.

87. Contra, e.g., Zahn, who arrives at this conclusion by the unlikely connection of καθὸ δεῖ with οἴδαμεν — "we do not know as we should."

88. Compare the "unspeakable words" (ἄρρητα ῥήματα) that Paul heard in his heavenly vision (2 Cor. 12:4).

89. Michel; Käsemann; Wilckens; Morris.

90. Cranfield; Hendriksen.

91. See Morris.

referring to glossolalia — the "speaking in tongues" of 1 Cor. 12–14.[92] Like tongues, these "groans" are a "prayer language," inspired by the Spirit, and taking the form of utterances that cannot be put in the language of earth. But this identification is unlikely. The gift of tongues is clearly restricted by Paul to *some* believers only (cf. 1 Cor. 12:30), but the "groans" here are means of intercession that come to the aid of all believers.[93]

Furthermore, and to return to our original point, the word *alalētois* probably means "unspoken" rather than "ineffable"; and this makes it almost impossible to identify the "groans" with glossolalia; for tongues, of course, are verbalized if not understandable.[94] Moreover, it is likely that the groans are not the believer's but the Spirit's.[95] While we cannot, then, be absolutely sure (and we have no clear biblical parallels to go by), it is preferable to understand these "groans" as the Spirit's own "language of prayer," a ministry

92. See, particularly, Käsemann in his commentary and, more fully, in his article, "The Cry for Liberty in the Worship of the Church," in *Perspectives on Paul,* pp. 122-37. This view is hinted at also by Chrysostom (who confines the phenomenon to the apostolic days) and defended by Balz, *Heilsvertrauen,* pp. 80-92; and Fee, *God's Empowering Presence,* pp. 577-86.

Käsemann's interpretation is part of a larger understanding of the setting and purpose of Rom. 8. He thinks that much of what Paul says is directed against what he calls "enthusiasts": Hellenistic Christians who overemphasize the presence of salvation and its spectacular phenomena at the expense of the necessary "weakness" that is part of this age of salvation. Paul, then, while maintaining the truth of the Christian's present status and the glory that will come, wants also to show that this glory arises only out of the sufferings and ambiguities of this age. By putting tongues — a highly prized phenomenon of the ecstatics — in the context of suffering and weakness, Paul is effectively reinterpreting its significance. But there is little evidence for an "anti-ecstatic" posture in Rom. 8 (Bindemann, *Die Hoffnung der Schöpfung,* pp. 78-79); and, even if it were present, Paul's purpose, as Käsemann sees it, would be so subtle as to be missed (Wedderburn, "Romans 8:26," p. 371).

93. In addition to many others, see J. Schniewind, "Das Seufzen des Geistes, Röm 8.26, 27," in *Nachgelassene Reden und Aufsätze* (Berlin: Töpelmann, 1952), p. 82; C. C. Mitchell, "The Holy Spirit's Intercessory Ministry," *BSac* 139 (1982), 230-42.

94. See A. J. M. Wedderburn, "Romans 8:26 — Towards a Theology of Glossolalia," *SJT* 28 (1975), 372-73.

95. If Paul had meant to identify the groanings as believers', we would perhaps have expected a ἡμῶν ("ours") after the phrase to make this clear; without it, we are led to expect that the groanings are to be attributed to the one who is interceding — the Spirit. To be sure, Paul could identify the groans as the Spirit's and still view them as coming to expression through the believer — for the divine/human interplay in such matters escapes logical precision (Leenhardt); but v. 27 makes even this degree of involvement of the Christian difficult. For in this continuation of the thought of v. 26, all attention is focused on the Spirit; it is his "mind" that God understands and responds to, and it is he who intercedes "on our behalf" (see esp. Niederwimmer, "Das Gebet des Geistes," pp. 263-64; Hendriksen).

of intercession that takes place in our hearts (cf. v. 27) in a manner imperceptible to us. This means, of course, that "groans" is used metaphorically. But vv. 22 and 23, with their references to the "groans" of creation and the "groans" of Christians "in" themselves, has prepared us for such a meaning. I take it that Paul is saying, then, that our failure to know God's will and consequent inability to petition God specifically and assuredly is met by God's Spirit, who himself expresses to God those intercessory petitions that perfectly match the will of God. When we do not know what to pray for — yes, even when we pray for things that are not best for us[96] — we need not despair, for we can depend on the Spirit's ministry of perfect intercession "on our behalf." Here is one potent source for that "patient fortitude" with which we are to await our glory (v. 25); that our failure to understand God's purposes and plans, to see "the beginning from the end," does not mean that effective, powerful prayer for our specific needs is absent.[97]

27 Verse 27 continues[98] Paul's discussion of the intercession of the Spirit and focuses on the effectiveness of this intercession. The reason for this effectiveness is the perfect accord that exists between God, "the one who searches[99] hearts," and "the mind of the Spirit."[100] God, who sees into the

---

96. While stated in exaggerated fashion, Luther's observation on this point contains more than a germ of truth: "It is not a bad but a very good sign if the opposite of what we pray for appears to happen. Just as it is not a good sign if our prayers eventuate in the fulfillment of all we ask for. This is so because the counsel and will of God far excel our counsel and will."

97. The background for the idea of the intercession of the Spirit has often been found in Hellenistic or gnostic conceptions; but — if a background beyond Paul's own understanding of and experience of the Spirit is necessary (see Dunn on this) — Paul's teaching more probably arises from OT and Jewish (especially apocalyptic) notions of angelic and other intercessors. See esp. E. A. Obeng, "The Origins of the Spirit Intercession Motif in Romans 8:26," *NTS* 32 (1986), 621-32; Bindemann, *Die Hoffnung der Schöpfung*, pp. 78-79.

98. Cf. the δέ, probably a weak "and" here.

99. Gk. ἐραυνῶν. Although the verb ἐραυνάω is not used in the LXX to depict God (indeed, the word does not occur at all in the LXX), Paul's language brings to mind the frequent designation of God as the one who "knows" or "judges" the hearts or "inner thoughts" of people (cf. 1 Sam. 16:7; 1 Kings 8:39; Pss. 7:9; 17:3, etc.; note also Acts 1:24; 15:8, and the use of ἐραυνάω in Rev. 2:23 of the Son of God, who "searches mind and heart").

100. Gk. τὸ φρόνημα τοῦ πνεύματος. This phrase could mean, in light of the use of φρόνημα in vv. 6-7, "what the [human] spirit sets its mind on" (G. MacRae, "A Note on Romans 8:26-27," *HTR* 73 [1980], 229-30), or "the [human] mind formed by the Spirit." But the context suggests that the genitive is possessive and that Paul refers to the Spirit's own "mind" or "intention" (e.g., Schniewind, "Seufzen," p. 83). And the τί (e.g., "*what* is the mind of the Spirit") implies that φρόνημα has something of a verbal force: "what the Spirit sets his mind on," "what the Spirit intends."

inner being of people, where the indwelling Spirit's ministry of intercession takes place, "knows," "acknowledges," and responds to those "intentions" of the Spirit that are expressed in his prayers on our behalf.

The second clause of the verse is usually taken as explicative: God "knows" what the Spirit intends, in that, or "for,"[101] the Spirit intercedes in accordance with God's will for the saints. But the emphatic position of "in accordance with [the will of] God"[102] suggests that Paul is rather giving a reason for the first statement. God knows what the Spirit intends, and there is perfect harmony between the two, *because* it is in accordance with God's will that the Spirit intercedes for the saints.[103] There is one in heaven, the Son of God, who "intercedes on our behalf," defending us from all charges that might be brought against us, guaranteeing salvation in the day of judgment (8:34). But there is also, Paul asserts in these verses, an intercessor "in the heart," the Spirit of God, who effectively prays to the Father on our behalf throughout the difficulties and uncertainties of our lives here on earth.

28 This verse may be in adversative relationship to what comes before it — "we groan, we do not know how to pray, *but* God is working . . ."[104] — but is probably continuative: in this time of suffering and expectation (vv. 18-25) the Spirit helps us by interceding for us (vv. 26-27) *and,* by God's providence, "all things work together for good."[105] This sentiment is one that has parallels in both pagan and Jewish literature,[106] and Paul may presume that his readers "know" this to be true because they are familiar with these sayings. It is more likely, however, that Paul assumes they know this because they have come to know God in Christ and experienced the fullness of his grace in their lives.

The translation and interpretation of the sentence are disputed. The first difficulty is the subject. There are three main possibilities.

(1) God. Some MSS contain the word; but even if it is not original,[107] God could still be presumed to be the subject of the verb, since the immediately preceding clause contains the word ("to those who love God"). If we do this, then "all things"[108] could be either the direct object of the verb — "God

---

101. Gk. ὅτι.

102. The equivalent Greek phrase, κατὰ θεόν, comes first in the clause. It is fair to paraphrase "according to God's will."

103. Schniewind, "Seufzen," p. 86; Haldane, Käsemann, Wilckens.

104. See, e.g., Godet.

105. The Greek particle is δέ.

106. Note the oft-quoted saying of Rabbi Aqiba: "All the Almighty does, he does for good" (*b. Ber.* 60b; cf. Str-B, 3.255-56 for further references).

107. It is probably not; see the note in the translation above.

108. Gk. πάντα.

causes all things to work together for good" (NASB)[109] — or a reference to the sphere in which the assertion is true[110] — "in all things God works for the good" (NIV; cf. also NRSV, TEV). The problem with the first rendering is that the verb "works together" does not usually take a direct object.[111] The second rendering, then, is preferable,[112] but it, too, has its difficulties.[113]

(2) Another possibility, then, is to assume that "works together" has the same subject as all the main verbs in vv. 26-27 — the Spirit (cf. REB: "he [the Spirit] cooperates for good with those who love God").[114] But the subject of the verbs that follow in vv. 29-30 is clearly "God," and the close relationship between these verses and v. 28 makes it likely that Paul has moved away from his focus on the Spirit already in v. 28.

(3) This leaves, then, what may be the most straightforward reading of the clause: "all things work together for good" (KJV, NIV margin).[115] If, however, we adopt this translation, it is important to insist that "all things" do not tend toward good in and of themselves, as if Paul held to a "naively optimistic" interpretation of history (Dodd's objection to this rendering). Rather, it is the sovereign guidance of God that is presumed as the undergirding and directing force behind all the events of life. This being so, it does not finally matter all that much whether we translate "all things work together for good" or "God is working in and through all things for good."

---

109. See S-H; Morris.

110. E.g., πάντα would be an accusative of respect.

111. Although BDF (148 [1]) point out the tendency of some intransitive verbs, like ἐνεργέω, to take on transitive meanings, there is little evidence that this has occurred with συνεργέω (see Ross, "Rom. VIII.28," pp. 83-84; Cranfield).

112. For full defenses, see esp. Ross, "Rom. VIII.28"; Pack, "Romans 8:28"; Osburn, "Romans 8:28"; Byrne, 113-14.

113. First, though not impossible, construing πάντα in the sense of "in all things" or "with respect to all things" would not be the first choice of translation (see Cranfield). Second, more seriously, the sequence "for those who love God, God works" is awkward; we would not expect the object of the participle to become the subject of the main verb (Black).

114. See esp. J. P. Wilson, "Romans viii.28: Text and Interpretation," *ExpTim* 60 (1948-49), 110-11; M. Black, "The Interpretation of Romans 8:28," in *Neotestamentica et Patristica (for O. Cullmann)* (NovTSup 6; Leiden: Brill, 1962), pp. 166-72; Fee, *God's Empowering Presence,* pp. 588-90.

115. See Godet; Barrett; Murray; Käsemann; Fitzmyer; B. Mayer, *Unter Gottes Heilsratschluss: Prädestinationsaussagen bei Paulus* (FzB 15; Würzburg: Echter, 1974), pp. 139-142; and esp. Cranfield, in most detail in his article "Romans 8:28," *SJT* 19 (1966), 204-15. On this rendering, πάντα is, of course, the subject of the verb (singular because of the neuter plural subject), συνεργεῖ has its usual intransitive meaning, and εἰς ἀγαθόν denotes the goal toward which the activity is directed. The one syntactical difficulty is that the verb συνεργέω normally takes a personal subject (Osburn, "Romans 8:28," p. 102); but, on the whole, it is the best alternative.

A second difficulty in the verse is the scope of "all things." We would expect that Paul has particularly in mind the "sufferings of the present time" (v. 18; cf. vv. 35-37), but the scope should probably not be restricted. Anything that is a part of this life — even our sins — can, by God's grace, contribute toward "good."[116] A third issue is the precise meaning of the main verb. Should we render, with most English translations, "works *together*" or simply "work," in the sense of "help, assist"? If we adopt the former,[117] then Paul might think of all things "working with" the believer" for good,[118] or of all things "working together, with one another" (interacting and converging together) for good,[119] or of God "working with" the believer in all things to produce good. However, we think the second, simpler, translation to be preferable: all things work for good on behalf of believers.[120] In any case, the uncertainty about the word should make us cautious about concluding that it is only in the *interaction* of "all things" that good comes.

A fourth difficulty in the verse is the meaning of the "good."[121] Many interpreters insist that it has a very specific meaning in this context: eschatological glory.[122] The "good," these scholars argue, is "defined" in vv. 29-30 as consisting in our ultimate conformity — in heaven — to the image of Christ and the glory that will then be ours. While, however, Paul's focus is on this completion of our salvation, we should probably include in the word those "good" things in this life that contribute to that final salvation and sustain us on the path to that salvation.[123] Certainly Paul does not mean that the evil experienced by believers in this life will always be reversed, turned into "good." For many things that we suffer will contribute to our "good" only by refining our faith and strengthening our hope. In any case, we must be careful to define "good" in God's terms, not ours. The idea that this verse

---

116. Haldane; Cranfield.

117. In favor of this rendering is the fact that the συν- in the verb συνεργέω usually retains its natural meaning of "withness" (cf. the other NT occurrences, 1 Cor. 6:16; 2 Cor. 6:1; Jas. 2:22 [Mark 16:20] and one of the two LXX occurrences, 1 Esdr. 7:2).

118. Godet.

119. Gifford; Murray.

120. There are many places where συνεργέω loses its "with" connotation and means simply "help, assist someone to obtain something" — the person or thing assisted being in the dative (see LSJ; BAGD; 1 Macc. 12:1[?]; *T. Iss.* 3.8; *T. Gad* 4:7, etc.). See, e.g., Käsemann; Cranfield; Dunn.

121. Paul's use of the word ἀγαθός offers no help, for he uses it consistently to mean moral good (its opposite, often stated, being κακός ["bad, evil"]), a meaning that is not appropriate here.

122. In the OT, "good" or "good things" is sometimes used to denote the blessings of the coming age (e.g., Isa. 32:42; 52:7 [quoted in Rom. 10:15]; Jer. 8:15; and cf. Sir. 39:25, 27). See W. Grundmann, *TDNT* I, 14; Schlier.

123. See Zahn; Gifford.

promises the believer material wealth or physical well-being, for instance, betrays a typically Western perversion of "good" into an exclusively material interpretation. God may well use trials in these areas to produce what he considers a much higher "good": a stronger faith, a more certain hope (cf. 5:3-4). But the promise to us is that there is nothing in this world that is not intended by God to assist us on our earthly pilgrimage and to bring us safely and certainly to the glorious destination of that pilgrimage.

We have now exposited the main clause of the verse; it remains to look at the subordinate clauses. These are two parallel descriptions of those for whom "all things work for good." First, they are "those who love God." Paul speaks only rarely of Christians "loving" God,[124] but the expression is widely used in the OT and Jewish literature to describe God's people. "Loving God" is therefore a qualification for the enjoyment of the promise of this verse,[125] but it is a qualification met by all who belong to Christ. In other words, Paul does not intend to suggest that the promise "all things work for good" ceases to have validity for a Christian who is not loving God enough. "Loving God" sums up the basic inner direction of *all* Christians — but *only* of Christians.

The second description of those to whom this promise applies looks at our relationship to God from its other, divine, side. While we must not play one of these descriptions off against the other — for both are important — it is nevertheless clear, from vv. 29-30, that this second clause contains the real reason why Christians can know that "all things work for good." We might paraphrase: "we know that all things are working for good for those of us who love God; and we know this is so because we who love God are also those who have been summoned by God to enter into relationship with him, a summons that is in accordance with God's purpose to mold us into the image of Christ and to glorify us." "Those who are called," then, describes Christians not as the recipients of an invitation that was up to them to accept or reject, but as the objects of God's effectual summoning of them to become the recipients of his grace.[126]

---

124. 1 Cor. 2:9; 8:3; cf. Eph. 6:24, "those who love our Lord Jesus Christ."

125. Mayer (*Prädestinationsaussagen,* pp. 142-49) notes that the OT (and esp. Deuteronomy) links love of God with God's bestowal of "good things" on his people (cf. esp. Deut. 10:12-15).

126. Some have argued that "those who are called" (τοῖς . . . κλητοῖς οὖσιν) designates, at least in principle, all people, "called" to a relationship with Christ through the preaching of the gospel and through God's inward work of grace (Chrysostom; Godet). However, while Jesus sometimes spoke of what we might refer to as a "general" call (cf. Matt. 22:14: "many are called, but few are chosen"), Paul always uses the verb καλέω and the noun κλητοί, when they have God as the subject of the action, of God's effective summons by which people are brought into relationship with himself. κλητοί designates Christians in Rom. 1:6, 7; 1 Cor. 1:1, 2, 24; Jude 1; Rev. 17:14; the only other NT

This calling takes place "in accordance with and on the basis of[127] God's purpose."[128] The majority of early interpreters took this to be a human purpose,[129] but Augustine was surely right in insisting that it is God's purpose that is intended.[130] Paul adds "according to [God's] purpose" to "those who are called" to indicate that God's summons of believers was issued with a particular purpose, or plan, in mind — that believers should become like Christ and share in his glory. And it is because this is God's plan for us who are called and who, thereby, love God, that we can be certain that all things will contribute toward "good" — the realization of this plan in each of our cases.

29   Verses 29-30 may support v. 28 as a whole,[131] or, specifically, the promise that "all things work for good,"[132] but a better immediate connection is with the word "purpose."[133] In these verses Paul spells out the "purpose," or "plan," of God. At the same time, however, he also states the ultimate ground for the promise of v. 28 and for the assurance that has been his theme throughout this chapter. The realization of God's "purpose" in individual believers is the bedrock of "the hope of glory."[134]

Paul exposits God's plan in four parallel clauses, in which Paul repeats key verbs as a way of connecting them closely together.[135] He thereby creates what has been called a "golden chain" and has furnished theologians throughout the history of the church with rich material for the construction of a doctrine of soteriology — particularly for its earliest (predestination) and

---

occurrence is Matt. 22:14, mentioned above. For καλέω with God as subject in Paul, see Rom. 4:17; 9:12, 24, 25, 26; 1 Cor. 1:9; 7:15, 17, 18 (twice), 20, 21, 22 (twice), 24; Gal. 1:6, 15; 5:8, 13; Eph. 4:1, 4; Col. 3:15; 1 Thess. 2:12; 4:7; 5:24; 2 Thess. 2:14; 1 Tim. 6:12; 2 Tim. 1:9. The flurry of occurrences in 1 Cor. 7:15-22 reveals that, for Paul, "to be called by God" is equivalent to "having become a Christian." See, on this whole issue, Klein, "Paul's Use of *Kalein*"; Prat, *Theology,* 1.241.

127. The preposition is κατά; the paraphrase is Mayer's (*Prädestinationsaussagen,* p. 151).

128. Gk. πρόθεσιν. The NT follows the LXX in using this word to denote the "presentation" loaves of the cult (Matt. 12:4 = Mark 2:26 = Luke 6:4; Heb. 9:2), but it means here "purpose," or "design."

129. See, e.g., Chrysostom; Origen; Theodoret.

130. Paul connects this πρόθεσις of God with his salvific actions in four other key texts (Rom. 9:11; Eph. 1:11; 3:11; 2 Tim. 1:9; the only other Pauline occurrence is of human "design," or "direction," in 2 Tim. 3:10).

131. Cranfield.

132. S-H.

133. Murray. The connecting word is ὅτι, which we take to be explanatory ("namely," "e.g.") rather than causal ("because").

134. See Byrne, 114.

135. The parallelism in this series of verbs has led some to think that Paul may be quoting a liturgical piece, into which he inserts v. 29b in order to tailor the piece to its context (cf., e.g., Michel; Käsemann).

latest (perseverance) stages. While such application is entirely justified, we must remember that (1) Paul does not intend to give a complete picture of his, still less of NT, soteriology; and (2) these verses have a definite role to play in the argument of this chapter.

The first of the verbs is the most controversial. "Foreknow," as its etymology in both Greek and English suggests, usually means "to know ahead of time."[136] See Acts 26:5, where Paul says that the Jews *"knew before* now, for a long time, if they wished to testify, that I had lived according to the strictest party of our religion." This being the commonest meaning of the verb, it is not surprising that many interpreters think it must mean this here also. Since, however, it would be a needless truism to say that God "knows" (about) Christians ahead of time, the verb would have to suggest that God "foresees" something peculiar to believers — perhaps their moral fitness (so many patristic theologians) or (which is far more likely, if this is what the verb means) their faith.[137] In this manner the human response of faith is made the object of God's "foreknowledge"; and this foreknowledge, in turn, is the basis for predestination: for "whom he foreknew, he predestined."[138]

But I consider it unlikely that this is the correct interpretation. (1) The NT usage of the verb and its cognate noun[139] does not conform to the general pattern of usage. In the six occurrences of these words in the NT, only two mean "know beforehand" (Acts 26:5, cited above, and 2 Pet. 3:17); the three others besides the occurrence in this text, all of which have God as their subject, mean not "know before" — in the sense of intellectual knowledge, or cognition — but "enter into relationship with before" or "choose, or determine, before" (Rom. 11:2; 1 Pet. 1:20; Acts 2:23; 1 Pet. 1:2).[140] (2) That the verb here contains this peculiarly biblical sense of "know" is suggested by the fact that it has a simple personal object. Paul does not say that God knew anything *about* us but that he knew *us*, and this is reminiscent of the

136. The Gk. word is προ-["before"]γινώσκω.

137. E.g., Pelagius; Alford; Meyer; Lenski; Godet.

138. For a simple, straightforward presentation, see J. Cottrell, "Conditional Election," in *Grace Unlimited* (ed. C. Pinnock; Minneapolis: Bethany, 1975), pp. 57-62.

139. προγνῶσις.

140. While somewhat strange against the background of broad Greek usage, this meaning flows naturally from the use of γινώσκω in the LXX to translate the Heb. ידע when it denotes intimate relationship. This OT relational sense of ידע is too well known and widely accepted to require argument. Some outstanding examples are Gen. 18:19 — "for I have 'known' [RSV, NIV, "chosen"] him [Abraham]"; Jer. 1:5 — "Before I formed you in the womb I 'knew' you" [where "know" is paralleled by "consecrate" and "appoint"]; Amos 3:2 — "You [Israel] only have I 'known' [NIV "chosen"] of all the families of the earth." For discussion and more examples, see R. Bultmann, *TDNT* I, 697-98; E. D. Schmitz, *NIDNTT* II, 395-96. The verb προγινώσκω itself does not occur in the LXX.

OT sense of "know."[141] (3) Moreover, it is only *some* individuals — those who, having been "foreknown," were also "predestined," "called," "justified," and "glorified" — who are the objects of this activity; and this shows that an action applicable only to Christians must be denoted by the verb. If, then, the word means "know intimately," "have regard for,"[142] this must be a knowledge or love that is unique to believers and that leads to their being predestined. This being the case, the difference between "know or love beforehand" and "choose beforehand" virtually ceases to exist.[143] What, then, is the meaning of this "beforehand"? While it is of course true that God's actions, in and of themselves, are not bound to created "time,"[144] it is also clear that the "before" can have no other function than to set the divine action in the conceptual framework of what we call "time." The "before" of God's "choosing," then, could relate to the time at which we come to "love God" (v. 28),[145] but 1 Pet. 1:20 and Eph. 1:4 suggest rather that Paul would place this choosing of us "before the foundation of the world."[146]

With this first verb, then, Paul highlights the divine initiative in the outworking of God's purpose. This does not entail any minimizing of the importance of the human response of faith that has received so much attention in chaps. 1–4.[147] But this "before" does make it difficult to conceive of faith as the *ground* of this "choosing." As Murray puts it, what is involved is "not the foresight of difference but the foresight that makes difference to exist, not a foresight that recognizes existence but the foreknowledge that determines existence." But what, or whom, precisely, has God "foreknown" in this way? The answer of many contemporary exegetes and theologians is "the church." What is "foreknown," or "elected," is not the individual but Christ, and the church as "in Christ."[148] But whatever might be said about this interpretation elsewhere, it does not fit these verses very well. Not only is nothing said here about "in Christ" or the church, but the purpose of Paul is to assure individual believers — not the church as a whole — that God is working for *their* "good" and will glorify *them*.

While this first verb generates much of the discussion, it is the second verb in the verse that Paul emphasizes. "Foreknowing" is simply the step that

---

141. Murray.

142. E.g., S-H; I. H. Marshall, *Kept by the Power of God: A Study of Perseverance and Falling Away* (Minneapolis: Bethany, 1969), p. 102.

143. Murray.

144. Cf., e.g., Weber, *Foundations of Dogmatics,* 2.446, 460-65.

145. Marshall, *Kept by the Power,* p. 102; Leenhardt.

146. Cranfield.

147. Cf. Stevens, *Pauline Theology,* p. 120.

148. This view is associated particularly with Karl Barth (see *CD* II/2). On this text, see esp. R. Shank, *Elect in the Son: A Study of the Doctrine of Election* (Springfield, MA: Westcott, 1970), pp. 45-55, 154-55; Ridderbos, *Paul,* pp. 350-51.

leads to what Paul is really concerned to stress: God's "foreordaining," or "predestining,"[149] to conformity with the image of his Son. This second verb takes a step beyond the first by focusing attention on the purpose of God's electing grace.[150] And the way in which Paul disrupts his careful parallelism in the last part of v. 29 to develop this idea reveals the importance it had for him. The "destination" toward which believers have been set in motion is that we might "be conformed to the image of [God's] Son." The language Paul uses here reminds us of his central "with Christ" theology and suggests a (negative) comparison with Adam.[151] Now it is God's purpose to imprint on all those who belong to Christ the "image" of the "second Adam."[152]

When does this "being conformed" take place? In light of v. 17b — "suffer with Christ in order to be glorified with him" — Paul may think of the believer as destined from his conversion onward to "conform" to Christ's pattern of suffering followed by glory.[153] Hodge is representative of those who argue for an even broader reference: conformity to God's will, exemplified by Christ, in this life and glory in the life to come.[154] But the closest

149. The verb is προορίζω. The simple verb ὁρίζω means "appoint," "determine" (see on 1:4); προ-ορίζω then means "pre-determine" or "pre-destine" (the Vulgate translates *praedestinavit*). In the NT, it has as its objects the crucifixion (Acts 4:28), the "wisdom" now manifested in Christ (1 Cor. 2:7), and believers (Eph. 1:5, 11; and here). Once more, the "before" will mean "before the foundation of the world" (cf. Eph. 1:4-5).

150. R. Muller notes that some Puritans (e.g., William Perkins) distinguished between "foreknowing" as "eternal" election and "predestining" as election "in time" (cf. *Christ and the Decree: Christology and Predestination in Reformed Theology from Calvin to Perkins* [Grand Rapids: Baker, 1988], p. 165).

151. The Greek is συμμόρφους τῆς εἰκόνος τοῦ υἱοῦ αὐτοῦ. συμμόρφους picks up the "with Christ" dimension of Christian experience that was last found in 8:17b. The word is used by Paul in Phil. 3:21 in a similar way, and even in a similar syntactical structure: "who [Christ] will transform the body [belonging to] our [state of] humiliation, making it conformed [σύμμορφον] to the body [belonging to] his [state] of glory." Paul adds the word εἰκών (seemingly redundant because of the idea of "form" found in σύμμορφος [e.g., μορφή]) (1) to emphasize the idea of "pattern" or "imprint" — Christians are "fitted into" the "pattern of existence" that Christ has established and modeled — and (2) to invite comparison with Adam: Adam, created in God's "image" (LXX εἰκών) has tragically "transformed" that image into one that is "earthly," sin-marred; and this image is what is now imprinted on all who were descended from him. This sense of εἰκών is to the fore in those texts in which Christ (2 Cor. 4:4; Col. 1:15) or the Christian community (Col. 3:10) are said to be "in the image of God" (cf. J. Kürzinger, "συμμόρφους τῆς εἰκόνος τοῦ υἱοῦ αὐτοῦ (Röm 8,29)," *BZ* 2 [1958], 294-99; Thüsing, *Per Christum in Deum*, pp. 122-25).

152. This idea is explicit in 1 Cor. 15:49; cf. esp. Dunn and Hughes, *True Image*, p. 27, who takes the genitive υἱοῦ as epexegetic: "the image, that is, which is his Son."

153. Nygren; Wilckens.

154. Note that in 2 Cor. 3:18 Paul attributes the transforming into the Lord's image to the present time.

parallels, Phil. 3:21 and 1 Cor. 15:49, are both eschatological; and eschatology is Paul's focus in this paragraph.[155] This makes it more likely that Paul thinks here of God's predestining us to future glory, that glory which Christ already enjoys.[156] The last clause of the verse tends to confirm this interpretation: "so that[157] he [Christ] might be the firstborn among many brothers." For the idea of Christ as "firstborn" reminds us of Christ's place as the "first fruits" of those who are raised (1 Cor. 15:20; cf. vv. 10-11).[158] It is as Christians have their bodies resurrected and transformed that they join Christ in his glory and that the purpose of God, to make Christ the "firstborn" of many to follow, is accomplished.

30 Paul resumes his "chain" of verbs by repeating the one with which the chain was "broken": "predestined." Forming the next link is the verb "he called," which denotes God's effectual summoning into relationship with him.[159] The exact correspondence between those who are the objects of predestining and those who experience this calling is emphasized by the demonstrative pronoun "these"[160]: "it was precisely those who were predestined who also[161] were called." This leaves little room for the suggestion that the links in this chain are not firmly attached to one another, as if some who were "foreknown" and "predestined" would not be "called," "justified," and "glorified."[162]

The next link in the chain brings us back to the central theme of chaps. 1–4: justification. As we recall Paul's repeated stress on faith in those chapters, we do well to remember that Paul's focus in these verses on the divine side of salvation in no way mitigates the importance of human response. It is, indeed, God who "justifies"; but it is the person who believes who is so justified.

With the final verb in the chain, Paul has come back to his starting point in this paragraph and to the paragraph's central theme: glory. This verb is in the same tense as the others in the series.[163] What makes this interesting

---

155. "Glory to be revealed" (v. 18); "awaiting adoption" (v. 23); "hope" (vv. 24-25); "glory" again (v. 30).

156. Byrne, 117-18; Thüsing, *Per Christum in Deum,* pp. 122-25; S-H; Murray; Dunn; Scott, *Adoption,* pp. 245-47; Volf, *Paul and Perseverance,* pp. 9-11.

157. The Greek uses εἰς with the infinitive (τὸ εἶναι); the construction is probably telic (Burton, 409).

158. Note also Ps. 89:28, where it is said that God will adopt the (Davidic) Messiah as his "firstborn" Son.

159. See the note on κλητοίς in v. 28.

160. Gk. τούτους.

161. Gk. καί.

162. Cf. Volf, *Paul and Perseverance,* pp. 12-14; contra, e.g., Wesley.

163. It is an aorist, ἐδόξασεν.

is that the action denoted by this verb is (from the standpoint of believers) in the future,[164] while the other actions are past. Most interpreters conclude, probably rightly, that Paul is looking at the believer's glorification from the standpoint of God, who has already decreed that it should take place.[165] While not yet experienced, the divine decision to glorify those who have been justified has already been made; the issue has been settled.[166] Here Paul touches on the ultimate source of the assurance that Christians enjoy, and with it he brings to a triumphant climax his celebration of the "no condemnation" that applies to every person in Christ.

Scholars are fond of using the inelegant phrase "already . . . not yet" to decribe an essential dimension of NT teaching: while "already" redeemed, justified, reconciled to God, and so on, the believer has "not yet" been glorified, released from temptation and suffering, and the like. Nowhere in the NT is this tension as clear as in this paragraph; and nowhere is the solution to that tension more clearly expressed. God's intention, Paul emphasizes, is to bring to glory every person who has been justified by faith in Jesus Christ. Our assurance of ultimate victory rests on this promise of God to us. But Paul, ever the realist, knows that that ultimate victory may lie many years ahead — years that might be filled with pain, anxiety, distress, and disaster. Thus he also encourages us by reminding us that God sends his Spirit into the heart of everyone he justifies. The Spirit brings power and comfort to the believer in the midst of suffering; and he brings assurance in the midst of doubt. Christians who are unduly anxious about their relationship to the Lord are failing to let the Spirit exercise that ministry. It is by committing ourselves

164. See, e.g., vv. 17, 18, 19; Phil. 3:21; Rom. 5:2. Contra, e.g., Zahn and Marshall (*Kept by the Power of God*, pp. 102-3), who think that Paul must be referring to that glory which the Christian is already experiencing (cf. 2 Cor. 3:18).

165. See, e.g., Augustine, *On Rebuke and Grace* 11.23 (*NPNF* 5.480-81); Turrettin; Alford; Michel; Cranfield; Byrne, 121-22 (Godet takes it in this sense but as a reference to the glorification of Christ, in which believers participate). Close to this is the idea that the tense, like the Hebrew "perfect," has a proleptic force; Paul is so certain that the glorification will take place that he writes as if it already had (Haldane; Murray). Still others suggest that Paul is writing from the standpoint of the eschatological completion of salvation (Wilckens). We must, of course, be careful about making temporal categories too important in interpreting the Greek tenses, and it may be that Paul uses the aorist simply to state the "completion" of the action without regard to time (Gifford; cf. Robertson, 837; Porter, *Verbal Aspect*, p. 237).

166. Some respond that Paul is only looking at what God has determined; whether a particular individual actually experiences these things depends on his or her perseverance in faith (cf., e.g., Godet; S-H). However, while the "condition" of faith is, of course, assumed, it must be questioned whether it is of such a nature as to "cancel" the divine decisions here presented.

anew to the life of devotion — prayer, Scripture reading, Christian fellowship — that we enable the Spirit to have this ministry of assurance in our hearts.

E. THE BELIEVER'S SECURITY CELEBRATED (8:31-39)

> 31*What then shall we say in view of these things? If God is for us, who is against us?* 32*He who did not even spare his own Son, but handed him over for all of us — how will he not also freely give us all things with him?* 33*Who will bring any charge against God's elect? God is the one who justifies;* 34*who is the one condemning? Christ Jesus*[1] *is the one who died and, more, was raised, who is also at the right hand of God, who also is interceding for us.*
>
> 35*Who will separate us from the love of Christ?*[2] *Will tribulation, or distress, or persecution, or famine, or nakedness, or peril, or the sword?* 36*Even as it is written, "For your sake we are being put to death all day long; we are considered as sheep for slaughter."*[a] 37*But in all these things we are more than conquerors through the one who loved us.* 38*For I am persuaded that neither death nor life, neither angels nor rulers, neither present things nor things to come, neither powers,*[3] 39*nor height, nor depth, nor any created thing will be able to separate us from the love of God in Christ Jesus our Lord.*

a. Ps. 44:23

This beautiful and familiar celebration of the believer's security in Christ comes in response to Paul's rehearsal of the blessings that have been granted to the believer through the gospel. Since Paul has been enumerating these blessings from virtually the first verses of the letter, this paragraph could be

1. One of the most important MSS (the primary Alexandrian B), along with several others (the secondary Alexandrian 1739; the western D) and the majority text, omit Ἰησοῦς. The tendency of scribes to add divine names supports this omission. On the other hand, Ἰησοῦς has strong external support (the primary Alexandrian ℵ, the secondary Alexandrian A, C, 33, and 81, the western F and G, and the uncial Ψ), and the double name fits the solemn style of this paragraph (see also v. 39).

2. The reading θεοῦ ("God") in place of Χριστοῦ (cf. the secondary Alexandrian uncial ℵ) is almost certainly an assimilation to v. 39, particularly in light of the reading in B — θεοῦ τῆς ἐν Χριστῷ Ἰησοῦ ("God in Christ Jesus").

3. οὔτε ἐξουσίαι ("neither authorities") is added in some MSS both before οὔτε ἀρχαί (the western uncial D) and after (the secondary Alexandrian uncial C), in imitation of the familar conjunction of these terms (cf. Eph. 3:10; Col. 1:16; 2:15); and other MSS rearrange the order of ἐνεστῶτα, μέλλοντα, and δυνάμεις. But the accepted text has strong support.

the climax of the letter up to this point.[4] At the other extreme, "these things" in v. 31 could refer only to those blessings enumerated in the immediately preceding verses (28, or 29-30).[5] But the similarity between the language and contents of this passage and Rom. 5 suggests rather that this paragraph, while responding immediately to what Paul has been saying in chap. 8, and especially 8:18-30,[6] is intended to cap Paul's many-sided discussion of Christian assurance in chaps. 5–8 as a whole.[7] Thus, we hear again, as in 5:1-11, of the love of God in Christ for us and the assurance that that brings to us; of the certainty of final vindication because of the justifying verdict of God; and of how these great forces render ultimately impotent and unimportant the tribulations of this life.

The elevated style of this paragraph, with its rhetorical questions, plethora of relative pronouns and unusual vocabulary, has suggested to many that Paul may be quoting from a liturgical tradition.[8] This is, of course, possible, although the way in which the paragraph so naturally picks up themes that are present elsewhere in Rom. 5–8 suggests rather that the style reflects Paul's own emotions as he looks back over the abundance of the Christian's privileges. Various subdivisions of the paragraph have been suggested,[9] but I think it is simplest and most natural to divide the paragraph into two parts: vv. 31-34 and vv. 35-39.[10] The first is dominated by judicial imagery — "on our behalf," "hand over," "bring any charge," "justify," "condemn," "intercede." God being "for us" means that the verdict he has already rendered in justification stands as a perfect guarantee of vindication in the judgment. In vv. 35-39, Paul expands the picture by adding to our assurance for the "last day" assurance for all the days in between. Not only is the believer guaranteed ultimate vindication; he or she is also promised victory over all the forces of this world. And the basis for this many-faceted assurance is the love of God

---

4. Cf., e.g., Godet, 329; Cranfield, 1.434; Stuhlmacher, 138.

5. Meyer, 2.97; Gifford, 161.

6. Cf. Murray, 1.322.

7. See esp. Käsemann, 246; Osten-Sacken, *Römer 8,* pp. 55-60; P. Fiedler, "Röm 8:31-39 als Brennpunkt paulinischer Frohbotschaft," *ZNW* 68 (1977), 29-30. A. H. Snyman ("Style and the Rhetorical Situation of Romans 8.31-39," *NTS* 34 [1988], 218-31) agrees, noting that an emotional appeal to readers at the end of an argument conforms to ancient rhetorical practice. Schmithals (pp. 305-6) thinks these verses respond to a discrete treatise in 7:17–8:30.

8. See especially the discussions and suggestions in Osten-Sacken, *Römer 8,* pp. 20-47; G. Schille, "Die Liebe Gottes in Christus. Beobachtungen zu Rm 8 31-39," *ZNW* 59 (1968), 230-44.

9. E.g., (1) vv. 31-33a, 33b-34a, 34b-39 (Bengel, 111); (2) vv. 31-32, 33-34, 35-39 (Käsemann, 246); (3) vv. 31-32, 33-34, 35-37, 38-39 (Michel, 279; Cranfield, 1.434).

10. See Balz, *Heilsvertrauen,* pp. 117-18, for a similar suggestion.

for us in Christ; God's, or Christ's, love is the motif of this paragraph, mentioned three times (vv. 35, 37, 39; cf. Rom. 5:5-8).

31 As we have seen, Paul uses the rhetorical question "What, then, shall we say?" frequently in Romans to advance his argument. Here, however, as in 3:1 and 4:1 (and cf. the variant in 9:19), these words do not stand alone but are part of a substantive question: "What shall we say in view of[11] these things?" "These things," as I suggested above, should not be confined to what Paul has just said in vv. 28-30, or even in chap. 8 as a whole, but embrace all the blessings ascribed to Christians in chaps. 5–8. All this Paul sums up in the simple statement, "if God be for us." The preposition I translate "for" could also be translated "on behalf of."[12] Paul uses it frequently to depict the vicarious work of Christ (cf. especially 5:6-8); here it suggests that God is "on our side," that he is working "for" us. If this be so, Paul asks, "who[13] is against us?" Obviously, Paul does not mean that nobody will, in fact, oppose us; as Paul knows from his own experience (to which he alludes in v. 35), opposition to believers is both varied and intense. What Paul is suggesting by this rhetorical question is that nobody — and no "thing" — can ultimately harm, or stand in the way of, the one whom God is "for." This is how Chrysostom put it:

> Yet those that be against us, so far are they from thwarting us at all, that even without their will they become to us the causes of crowns, and procurers of countless blessings, in that God's wisdom turneth their plots unto our salvation and glory. See how really no one is against us!

32 The lack of connecting conjunction between this verse and v. 31[14] is typical of this paragraph, lending it a solemn and elevated style. But the implicit connection is with "for us": God being "for us" has its deepest demonstration in his giving his own Son for us,[15] a demonstration that should leave us in no doubt about his commitment to be "for us" right up to, and including, the end. The argument of this verse — God's giving his Son as a guarantee of his future blessings — is very close to 5:8-9[16] and

---

11. Gk. πρός; for this meaning, see Moule, *Idiom Book*, p. 53.

12. Gk. ὑπέρ.

13. Some interpreters think that Paul might have someone specific in mind here: e.g., the Jews, who question the right of Gentiles to be included as full members of the people of God (Fraikin, "Rhetorical Function of the Jews," p. 100). But the breadth of the enumerations in vv. 35 and 38-39 suggests a general reference.

14. E.g., asyndeton.

15. The emphatic nature of this assertion is heightened by Paul's use of γε, "even," an intensive particle here (BAGD) that adds a "sweetness full of exultation" (Bengel) to the awesome fact that God "indeed" gave his own Son for us.

16. Cf. Beker, 363.

is another example of the way in which the last part of chap. 8 comes back to the basic themes with which this section of the letter began. Calling Christ God's "own"[17] Son distinguishes him from those many "adopted" sons that have come into God's family by faith (8:14-16); but it may also suggest a parallel with Abraham's giving of his "beloved" son Isaac (Gen. 22).[18] Rather than "sparing" his Son, God "handed him over,"[19] a verb that reminds us of the initiative of God in the crucifixion.[20] The addition of "all" to "us" stresses that it is for *all* believers ("you" in this context) that God has given his Son (note, however, that the text does not say "*only* for all you believers").

Verse 32 is a kind of conditional sentence, with "God handing over his Son" being the "if" clause and "how will he not also freely give[21] us all things" the "then" clause. But by introducing the second with "how," Paul suggests how inconceivable it would be for this "then" clause to remain unfulfilled: "If God has, indeed, given his Son for us, how can anyone doubt that he will not also[22]

17. Gk. ἴδιος.

18. I believe that Paul may well intend an allusion to the Isaac incident since the negative statement that God "did not spare (ἐφείσατο) his own Son" is reminiscent of Gen. 22:12 and 16, where God commends Abraham for not "sparing" (the same verb is used in the LXX as is used here) his beloved son (cf. also A. F. Segal, " 'He who did not spare his own Son . . .': Jesus, Paul and the Aqedah," in *From Jesus to Paul: Studies in Honour of Francis Wright Beare* [ed. P. Richardson and J. C. Hurd; Waterloo, Ont.: Wilfrid Laurier University, 1984], pp. 169-84; contra, e.g., D. R. Schwartz, "Two Pauline Allusions to the Redemptive Mechanism of the Crucifixion," *JBL* 102 [1983], 264-66, who argues that 1 Sam. 21:1-14, not Gen. 22, is alluded to). But allusion to the Jewish legend of the "Aqedah," in which atoning significance was accorded to Abraham's action, is not only improbable but well-nigh impossible — as, e.g., Fitzmyer points out, this tradition dates from the Amoraic (post–A.D. 200) period. On the tradition, see esp. G. Vermes, *Scripture and Tradition in Judaism: Haggadic Studies* (SPB 4; Leiden: Brill, 1961). Supporting an allusion to the Aqedah is, e.g, Schoeps, 141-49. P. R. Davies and B. D. Chilton ("The Aqedah: A Revised Tradition History," *CBQ* 40 [1978], 514-46), Barrett (*From First Adam to Last,* pp. 27-30), and R. Le Déaut ("La presentation targumique du sacrifice d'Isaac et la soteriologie paulinienne," *SPCIC,* 2.563-74) contest any allusion to the tradition.

19. The verb is παραδίδωμι, which is prominent especially in the Gospel passion predictions, and is picked up from LXX Isa. 53, where it is used three times to describe the "handing over" of the suffering Servant (see D. J. Moo, *The Old Testament in the Gospel Passion Narratives* [Sheffield: Almond, 1983], pp. 92-98). Paul also uses the word frequently with reference to Jesus' death — sometimes, as here, of the Father's "handing him over" to death (cf. the passive in 4:25 and 1 Cor. 11:23[?]), and at other times of the Son's own "giving of himself" to death (Gal. 2:20; Eph. 5:2, 25).

20. Murray quotes Octavius Winslow: "Who delivered up Jesus to die? Not Judas, for money; not Pilate, for fear; not the Jews, for envy — but the Father, for love!"

21. The Greek verb is χαρίζομαι.

22. Gk. καί. On the translation, see Godet.

freely give us all things along with him?"[23] How broad is the scope of the "all things" that God so graciously bestows on us? Paul could be alluding to our share in Christ's sovereignty over creation.[24] But it is not clear that these ideas play a role in our present passage. Certainly Paul's focus is on those things necessary for our salvation;[25] but, as with "the good" in v. 28, we should not restrict the meaning to salvation as such but include all those blessings — spiritual and material — that we require on the path toward that final salvation.[26] "Why be dubious about the chattels, when you have the Lord?" (Chrysostom).

33 There are at least six possible ways to punctuate this verse and the next;[27] but the best alternative is the one that emerges most clearly in the NASB: "Who will bring a charge against God's elect? God is the one who justifies; who is the one who condemns? Christ Jesus is he who died, yes, rather, who was raised, who is at the right hand of God, who also intercedes for us."[28] "Bring a charge"[29] is the first of the explicitly judicial terms in this context.[30] The future tense of the verb focuses attention on the last judgment: Who will stand and accuse us at that time? To be sure, Satan, the

---

23. σὺν Χριστῷ ("with Christ") might allude to the fact that our receiving "all things" (the "inheritance"; cf. v. 17b) takes place in "union with Christ" (Michel). But it is probably intended more prosaically: "along with Christ, God's Son, whom God has already 'handed over' for us, God will surely give us 'all things.' "

24. Cf. Ps. 8:6 and 110:1, quoted by Paul in 1 Cor. 15:25-28. Cf. Dunn.

25. Bengel.

26. Hendriksen.

27. The main possibilities are:

1. To make every clause in vv. 33-34 a distinct question (seven in all).
2. To find two questions in each of the two verses:
   "Who shall bring a charge . . . ?; Is not God justifying?
   Who condemns? Is not Christ Jesus . . . for us?" (Barrett)
3. As in 2, with the second sentence made a statement (RSV).
4. "Could anyone accuse. . . ?
   When God acquits, could anyone condemn?
   Could Christ Jesus?
   No! He not only died for us . . ." (JB)
5. "Who will bring any charge . . . ? It is God who justifies.
   Who is he that condemns? Christ Jesus . . . for us." (NIV)

28. See also NA[27], UBS[4], and most commentators. The advantages of this punctuation are: (1) by taking only those sentences that begin with interrogative particles as questions, it maintains the vivid question-answer style used throughout the paragraph; and (2) by using a semicolon after "justifies" (a high point after δικαιῶν in the Greek text), it joins together two clauses that, by virtue of the natural contrast between "justify" and "condemn," appear to belong together.

29. Gk. ἐγκαλέω. Apart from this verse, it occurs six times in Acts with reference to various facets of Paul's trials (19:38, 40; 23:29, 38; 26:2, 7).

30. Although παραδίδωμι (v. 32) may have judicial overtones.

"accuser," may seek to do so; so may our enemies and, perhaps most persuasively of all, our own sins. But no accusation will be effective because it is against God's "elect" that the accusation is being made; and, as Paul has shown in vv. 28-30, those who are God's "elect ones" by virtue of his calling and purpose are assured of glory. In a sense, then, this manner of designating Christians in the question itself is the only answer required.[31] But it is natural to view the following sentence as a further basis for the ultimate failure of any accusations against us: it is *God* who is justifying.[32]

34 That "who is the one condemning?"[33] is not a fresh, independent question but a "follow-up" on the discussion in v. 33, is suggested by the fact that "condemn" and "justify" are natural contrasts. This question is, then, to be seen as an additional rhetorical response to the statement in v. 33b that it is God who justifies. The sentence beginning "Christ Jesus" consists of four clauses, the first two using participles in a way similar to vv. 33b-34a, the last two being relative clauses describing further aspects of Christ's work. The sentence as a whole can be construed as a response to the question "who will condemn?" — "no one [implied]; for Christ Jesus . . ."[34] — or as a preparation for v. 35 — Christ Jesus has done these things for us; who, then, will separate us from the love of Christ?[35] The continued use of judicial images in the sentence — especially Christ's intercession — favors the former alternative. The enumeration of actions accomplished by, and through, Christ occurs in ascending order, with the emphasis falling on the last in the series. Not only has Jesus died to secure our justification — "more than that"[36] he has "been raised" and has also ascended to the right hand of God, so that he may intercede for us, ensuring that the justifying verdict for which he died is applied to us in the judgment. The language of Jesus being at "the right hand of God"[37] is taken from Ps. 110:1,

---

31. Cranfield.

32. The present tense of δικαιῶν is taken by Dunn to suggest that justification is an "on-going, sustaining" activity. But the present could be a reference to the future — "God is the one who will justify" (Michel, Black) — or, more likely, is "gnomic," in a kind of titular sense. God's "justifying," as virtually everywhere else in Paul, is a verdict rendered at the moment of conversion, but — and this is Paul's point here — an irrevocable verdict that must, therefore, render impotent any accusations against us at the judgment (cf. 5:9-10 and the allusion to Isa. 50:7-9).

33. It is impossible to know whether κατακρινων ("condemning") should be accented κατακρίνων (present tense; cf. S-H) or κατακρινῶν (future tense; cf. ἐγκαλέσει in v. 33; Cranfield). (Most of the important witnesses to the text do not, of course, have accents [cf. the apparatus of NA[27]].) In either case, the reference will be to the judgment (if present tense, κατακρίνων will, like δικαιῶν, be gnomic).

34. Cf. NJB.

35. Cf. REB; Gifford; Meyer; S-H; Murray.

36. Gk. μᾶλλον.

37. Gk. ἐν δεξιᾷ τοῦ θεοῦ. The unusual situation of an articular genitive noun

one of the most often quoted OT verses in the NT.[38] The language is, of course, metaphorical, indicating that Jesus has been elevated to the position of "vice-regent" in God's governance of the universe. But it is not with the universe, but with Christians, that Paul is concerned here. Because Christ lives and has ascended, he is able to "intercede" for us, acting as our High Priest in the very presence of God.[39]

35 The question that begins and sets the tone for the next five verses is formally parallel to those in vv. 33 and 34; but, materially, it makes a new start. Left behind is the forensic image of "God for us"; begun is the more personal and relational emphasis on the love of God in Christ for us. Not, of course, that these images are contradictory, or even to be put in separate compartments. As 5:6-10 makes absolutely clear, it is in the "giving of his Son" "for us" that God's love is preeminently shown; and God's love for us is not simply an "emotion" but his gracious action on our behalf. But, perhaps because he has just delineated the work of Christ for us, Paul in this verse speaks not, as in v. 39, of the love of God but of the love of Christ.[40]

The "who" in this opening question embraces any conceivable "opponent," whether personal or impersonal.[41] The list of difficulties that follows requires little comment, except to note that all the items except the last are found also in 2 Cor. 11:26-27 and 12:10, where Paul lists some of those hazards he himself has encountered in his apostolic labors. All these, then, Paul himself has experienced, and he has been able to prove for himself that they are quite incapable of disrupting his relationship with the love of Christ. And the last — the "sword," death by execution — Paul was to find overcome for him in the love of Christ at the end of his life.

36 This verse is something of an interruption in the flow of thought, and one that is typical for Paul. For he is constantly concerned to show that

---

dependent on an anarthrous noun may reflect the Hebrew "construct" state (cf. Turner, 179-80).

38. See Jesus' own application of this verse to himself in Matt. 22:24 and parallels and also Matt. 26:64; Acts 2:33-34; 5:31; 7:55, 56; Eph. 1:20; Col. 3:1; Heb. 1:3, 13; 8:1; 10:12; 12:2; 1 Pet. 3:22.

39. See, of course, Hebrews (esp. 7:25); cf. O. Bauernfeind, *TDNT* VIII, 243. In Rom. 11:2, ἐντυγχάνω means "make a complaint" (cf. also Acts 15:24); but here, and in Heb. 7:25, the verb refers to Christ's high-priestly ministry of intercession on behalf of his own.

40. That Paul means "the love Christ has for us" (subjective genitive) and not "the love we have for Christ" (objective genitive) is obvious from the context.

41. Some, however, have seen significance in the fact that a masculine or feminine interrogative particle — τίς — is "filled out" with a series of "things" (cf. Calvin). But τίς has probably been chosen simply for stylistic reasons: it maintains a parallel with vv. 33 and 34.

the sufferings experienced by Christians should occasion no surprise (see a similar interruption in Phil. 1:29). Here Paul cites Ps. 44:22 (LXX 43:22)[42] to show, as Calvin puts it, that "it is no new thing for the Lord to permit his saints to be undeservedly exposed to the cruelty of the ungodly."

37 The "but"[43] connects this verse with v. 35. Paul assumes a negative answer to the question of v. 35 and here proceeds to go even further: not only are such things as enumerated in that verse unable to separate us from Christ's love, *but,* on the contrary, we are "more than conquerors" with respect to them. "More than conquerors" is a felicitous rendering, going back to the Geneva Bible, of the intensive verb Paul uses here.[44] If more than simple emphasis is intended, perhaps Paul wants to emphasize that believers not only "conquer" such adversities; under the providential hand of God, they even work toward our "good" (v. 28).[45] But the victory is not ours, for it is only "through the one who loved us"[46] that it happens.

38 The assurance expressed in v. 37 is now grounded[47] in a more personal testimony of Paul's own. Paul stands completely convinced[48] that nothing at all will be able to separate believers from the love of God in Christ. The enumeration of possible threats to this security unfolds mainly in obvious pairs: "death and life," "angels and rulers," "things present and things to come," "height and depth." Only the word "powers"[49] disrupts the sequence of pairs, leading some to suggest it originally appeared after "rulers," with which it is often joined in the NT.[50] But there is no textual evidence for this displacement, and we must conclude that Paul has not arranged his sequence as carefully as some critics would have wanted him to.

"Death" probably comes first in the list because it picks up the reference to "being put to death" in the quotation (v. 36). While this might suggest

42. Paul introduces the quotation with his typical formula, καθὼς γέγραπται, "even as it is written" (cf. 1:17; 2:24; 3:4, 10; 4:17; 9:13, 29, 33; 10:15; 11:8, 26; 15:3, 9, 21). The text of the quotation follows the LXX (43:22, which accurately renders the MT), the only difference being a minor orthographic one (in place of Paul's ἕνεκεν, the LXX has ἕνεκα). The appropriateness of the quotation is suggested by the fact that the rabbis applied the verse to the death of martyrs (Str-B, 3.259-60).

43. Gk. ἀλλά.

44. ὑπερνικάω. The verb is rare but attested — though sometimes in a different sense — before Paul.

45. Hendriksen.

46. The substantive participle ἀγαπήσαντος ("who loved") must, in light of v. 35, refer to Christ; and the aorist tense focuses our attention on the love manifested on the cross (see, again, 5:6-8).

47. Cf. the Gk. γάρ.

48. The perfect πέπεισμαι has an "intensive present" focus; cf. Robertson, 895.

49. Gk. δυνάμεις.

50. See Denney.

that Paul has specifically martyrdom in mind,[51] it is more likely that he is thinking of physical death in any form. Similarly, while "life" has been taken to mean the distractions and cares of this life[52] or the sufferings of this life,[53] it is preferable to regard Paul as using the term in a rather "unreflective" way, as a natural contrast to "death" and without any specific aspect of life in mind. We must avoid introducing more precision in Paul's choice of terms than his evident rhetorical purpose would justify.[54] The first pair of terms, then, refers in the most general way to the two possible states of existence.[55] The second pair of terms, "angels and rulers," embraces the spirit world. While there are places where Paul uses "angel" to refer to any "spirit" being, whether good or evil,[56] he usually uses the word to denote the "good" angels, and this is probably his intention here also.[57] "Rulers" is never used with "angels" elsewhere in Paul. Paul can use "ruler" to denote a secular authority,[58] but more often he uses it to denote powers or authorities of the spirit world, sometimes those of an evil nature (Eph. 6:12; Col. 2:15) but also in a general way that makes it difficult to know whether evil, or evil and good, spirit "rulers" generally are meant.[59] If "angels" refers to "good" angels, it is natural to think that "rulers" denotes evil spiritual powers,[60] but the lexical evidence makes it impossible to be sure.

Having touched on the modes of human existence and the spirit world, Paul now includes the temporal dimension in his enumeration of those "powers" that are unable to separate the believer from God's love. These "things present" and "things to come" are sometimes also taken as references to spiritual beings,[61] but evidence is lacking for such an identification. Paul's point is rather that the believer need have no fear that either present or future circumstances and events will call into question his relationship to God in Christ. The last term in this verse, "powers," is the only one in the list (except, of course, for the last, summarizing item) that occurs by itself. Since Paul

51. Godet.

52. Godet.

53. Dunn.

54. Kuss.

55. Note that this same pair occurs also in 1 Cor. 3:22 — along with the pair ἐνεστῶτα εἴτε μέλλοντα ("things present or things to come") — in Paul's description of life's conditions.

56. Gk. ἄγγελος; cf. 1 Cor. 4:9; 6:3[?]; 13:1.

57. Godet; Murray.

58. This is the usual meaning of ἀρχή in the LXX, and Paul uses it with this reference in Tit. 3:1. Cf. G. Delling, *TDNT* I, 481. Delling notes that an occurrence of ἀρχή approaching the spirit world context of Paul is found in Dan. 7:27.

59. Cf. 1 Cor. 15:24; Eph. 1:21; 3:10; Col. 1:16; 2:10.

60. Cf. Godet; Murray.

61. E.g., Wilckens.

uses the word to denote miracles,[62] he may mean that nothing of such a nature — performed perhaps by Satan — can threaten our security as believers. But the occurrence of "powers" with "rulers" to denote spiritual beings suggests rather that some kind of spiritual forces are denoted here.[63] Why the word occurs on its own is impossible to know.

39 The final pair of terms — "height" and "depth" — is the most controversial. There are two main possibilities. First, since these terms, or terms like them, were used in astronomical contexts to denote the celestial space below and above the horizon, and, derivatively, celestial powers,[64] Paul may be referring to spiritual beings.[65] However, neither term occurs elsewhere in the NT with this meaning,[66] and the imagery in some of the texts where the terms occur — especially Eph. 3:18 — suggests that Paul is using the terms in a simple "spatial" sense. According to this, the second main interpretation, the terms are intended to embrace the entire universe: either those things above the heavens and beneath the earth,[67] heaven and earth itself,[68] or, perhaps most likely, heaven and hell.[69]

Lest a picky reader think that Paul has omitted something that could threaten the believer's security in Christ, Paul concludes with the comprehensive "any created thing."[70] Are even the responsible decisions of Christians themselves included in this last phrase? Calvinists usually think so, and conclude that Paul clearly teaches here the eternal security of believers.[71] Others, however, argue that Paul, by implication, focuses on only those forces that lie outside the believer's own free and responsible choices; and that what Paul says here and in this paragraph does not, then, preclude the possibility

62. 1 Cor. 12:10, 28-29; 2 Cor. 12:12.

63. Cranfield. Cf. 1 Cor. 15:24; Eph. 1:21.

64. BAGD.

65. E.g., Käsemann.

66. ὕψωμα ("height") occurs elsewhere only in 2 Cor. 10:5; βάθος ("depth") in Matt. 13:5 par.; Rom. 11:33; 1 Cor. 2:10; 2 Cor. 8:2; Eph. 3:18.

67. Many of the Fathers.

68. Hodge.

69. Cranfield. See esp. Ps. 139:8 (though with a different application): "If I ascend to heaven, thou art there! If I make my bed in Sheol, thou art there!"

70. Gk. τις κτίσις ἑτέρα. Insisting that κτίσις must mean "creation" and that ἑτέρα implies that this creation is "completely different," Godet takes Paul to mean that not even another "universe," should it exist, would be able to separate the Christian from God's love (cf. also S-H). But κτίσις frequently means "creature" rather than "creation" (BAGD) and ἕτερος is not so carefully distinguished from ἄλλος in the NT so as to justify the "wholly different" connotation. It is much simpler, and more natural, to think that Paul intends this last reference as a "catch-all," embracing anything that one might think has been omitted from the previous list.

71. See, e.g., Hodge; Volf, *Paul and Perseverance*, pp. 57-58n.

that a believer might decide to separate himself from the love of God in Christ.[72] While we must not press Paul's language beyond what he intends, we think that the broad "who" in v. 35 and the phrase here more naturally would include even the believer herself within the scope of those things that cannot separate us from Christ.

The subparagraph ends on the note with which it began: the impossibility that the believer can be "separated" from the divine love. The fact that this love is identified specifically as "the love of Christ" in v. 35 and "the love of God" here only shows again how much Paul joined (without equating) God and Christ in the experience of the believer. But even here, this love of God for us[73] is "in Christ Jesus our Lord." For it is in giving "his own Son" that God's love is above all made known to us, and only in relation to Christ do we experience the love of God for us. As we have noted repeatedly, the absence from Romans of an extended passage on Christology per se should not blind us to the centrality of Christology in the letter. Here again, as at the conclusion of chaps. 5, 6, and 7 (cf. v. 25a), Paul reiterates the supreme significance of Christ for all that he is teaching.

IV. THE DEFENSE OF THE GOSPEL: THE PROBLEM OF ISRAEL (9:1–11:36)

Paul's celebration of God's faithfulness and love in 8:31-39 is a fitting end to his theological exposition. We might now expect Paul to solidify and apply his theology in a series of exhortations of the kind that often conclude his letters. But these exhortations do not begin until chap. 12. What fills the gap between the end of chap. 8 and the beginning of chap. 12 is Paul's anguished wrestling with the problem of Israel's unbelief. Is this section, then, a detour from the main line of Paul's argument in Romans, an excursus that disrupts the natural flow of the letter?[1] Not at all. Rom. 9–11 is an important and integral part of the letter.

---

72. See, e.g., Godet; S-H.

73. The genitive τοῦ θεοῦ is again here (cf. v. 35) subjective.

1. Many scholars have come to just this conclusion. Augustine, e.g., thought that Paul added these chapters to illustrate and expand on his teaching of predestination (for a discussion of Augustine's view in comparison with those of Origen and Chrysostom, see P. Gorday, *Principles of Patristic Exegesis: Romans 9–11 in Origen, John Chrysostom, and Augustine* [Studies in the Bible and Early Christianity 4; New York/Toronto: Edwin Mellen, 1983], esp. pp. 1-3, 190-91, 232-33). Dodd thinks that Paul has inserted in chaps. 9–11 a pre-existing sermon (149-50). See also Kuss (3.664-65) and S-H, who claim that after chap. 8 "Paul has now finished his main argument" (p. 225; cf. also Denney, who

Those who relegate chaps. 9–11 to the periphery of Romans have misunderstood the purpose of Rom. 9–11, or of the letter, or of both. As we showed in the introduction, Paul's presentation and defense of "his" gospel to the Roman Christians occurs against the backdrop of controversy over the relationship between Judaism and the church. Paul, the "apostle to the Gentiles," found himself at the center of this debate. A decade of struggle to preserve the integrity and freedom of the gospel from a fatal mixture with the Jewish torah lies behind him; a critical encounter with Jews and Jewish Christians suspicious of him because of his outspoken stance in this very struggle lies immediately ahead (cf. Rom. 15:30-33). And the Roman Christians themselves are caught up in this issue, divided over the degree to which, as Christians, they are to retain the Jewish heritage of their faith.

Once we recognize the importance of this Jewish motif in Romans, we can give Rom. 9–11 its appropriate place in the letter. In these chapters Paul is not simply using Israel to illustrate a theological point, such as predestination[2] or the righteousness of God.[3] He is talking about Israel herself, as he wrestles with the implications of the gospel for God's "chosen people" of the OT.[4] Paul frames chaps. 9–11 with allusions to the key tension he is seeking to resolve: the Jews, recipients of so many privileges (9:4-5), are not experiencing the salvation offered in Christ (implied in 9:1-3); they are the objects of God's electing love, yet, from the standpoint of the gospel, they

---

finds a psychological, but no logical link between chaps. 1–8 and 9–11 [p. 655]). F. Refoulé makes, but does not clearly advocate, a more radical suggestion: that chaps. 9–11 may have been added to Romans by a disciple of Paul's ("Unité de l'Épitre aux Romains et histoire du salut," *RSPT* 71 [1987], 219-42).

2. As, e.g., Augustine thought (see the previous note). See also G. Maier, *Mensch und freier Wille nach den jüdischen Religionsparteien zwischen Ben Sira und Paulus* (WUNT 12; Tübingen: Mohr, 1971), pp. 399-400; E. Dinkler, "The Historical and the Eschatological Israel in Romans Chapters 9–11: A Contribution to the Problem of Predestination and Individual Responsibility," *JR* 36 (1956), 109. As Gorday has pointed out, making predestination the theme of Rom. 9–11 virtually forces it into the status of an appendix to the letter (*Principles,* pp. 232-33).

3. See, e.g., Käsemann, 253-56; Müller, *Gottes Gerechtigkeit,* p. 47. God's righteousness, with its closely related theme of human justification, is a crucial doctrine in Romans and one that lies at the heart of the gospel, the theme of Romans. And it continues to be crucial in Rom. 9–11 (see 9:30–10:13 and the related language of 9:10-12 and 11:5-7). Yet, unless God's righteousness be defined more broadly than it should be (see the excursus after 1:17), it cannot stand as the theme of Rom. 9–11.

Barth's interpretation of Rom. 9–11 is somewhat similar, in that he sees Israel as standing for the church, the religion of human beings that stands in opposition to the "wholly other" divine power of the gospel (see, e.g., his *Romans,* pp. 330-34, 337, 347-48).

4. See, e.g., Murray, 2.xii-xv; Dunn, 2.520; Schlier, 282; N. Walter, "Zur Interpretation von Römer 9–11," *ZTK* 81 (1984), 172.

are "enemies" (11:28). Paul's aim is to resolve this tension.[5] The tension arises from the *historical* circumstance that the majority of Jews have rejected the gospel. Why is this, if indeed the gospel is "first of all" for Jews (cf. 1:16)? But the tension has *theological* roots also. Paul's own explanation of the gospel in chaps. 1–8 is partly responsible for this theological tension. He has denied that Jews are guaranteed salvation through the Mosaic covenant (chap. 2, especially). What, then, becomes of their OT status as "God's chosen people"? Magnifying the problem is Paul's repeated insistence that what once apparently belonged to, or was promised to, Israel now belongs to believers in Jesus Christ, whether Jew or Gentile. Christians are Abraham's heirs (chap. 4), God's adopted children (8:14-17), possessors of the Spirit (chap. 8), and heirs of God's own glory (5:2; 8:18-30). If Jewish rejection of the gospel creates the problem Paul grapples with in Rom. 9–11, Gentile acceptance of that same gospel exacerbates it.[6] It seems that Israel has not only been disinherited but replaced. Paul earlier categorically but briefly rejected the conclusion that his teaching implied the cancellation of all the Jews' advantages (3:1-4). Now he elaborates.

5. A few outspoken scholars have recently challenged the traditional view of this tension. Especially identified with this revised interpretation are J. Gager and L. Gaston. They argue that Paul does not think that Israel stands under God's condemnation. Texts such as 9:4-5, 11:1-2, and 11:26, they claim, show that Paul thought that Israel was still enjoying salvation through her own covenant with God, rooted in the OT and the torah. For what, then, did Paul criticize Israel? And why did he lament her situation (e.g., 9:1-3)? Because the Jews had refused to acknowledge that God's grace was now being extended to the Gentiles. See esp. Gaston, "Israel's Misstep in the Eyes of Paul," in *Paul and the Torah*, pp. 135-50 (rpt. in Donfried, 309-26); idem, "Israel's Enemies in Pauline Theology," *NTS* 28 (1982), 400-23; Gager, *Anti-Semitism*, esp. pp. 197-212; cf. also P. van Buren, "Paul, The Church and Israel: Romans 9–11," *The Princeton Seminary Bulletin* 11 (1990), 10-11; B. Klappert, "Traktat für Israel: Die paulinische Verhältnisbestimmung von Israel und Kirche als Kriterium neutestamentlicher Sachaussagen über die Juden," in *Jüdische Existenz und die Erneuerung der christlichen Theologie: Versuch der Bilanz des christlich-jüdischen Dialogs für die Systematiche Theologie* (ed. M. Stöhr; Abhandlungen zum christlich-jüdischen Dialog 11; Munich: Kaiser, 1981), pp. 73-76; S. G. Hall, III, *Christian Anti-Semitism and Paul's Theology* (Minneapolis: Fortress, 1993), pp. 88-93, 113-27.

An adequate response to this proposal would require an extensive discussion of many texts. Suffice to say here that this view fails (1) to justify the strength of Paul's lament about Israel; (2) to explain adequately the many texts in which Paul faults Israel for a failure to believe; (3) to reckon with Paul's expressed conviction that faith in the gospel of Jesus Christ is the way to salvation for both Jew and Gentile (1:16; 10:11-13). For more thorough criticisms, see esp. E. E. Johnson, *The Function of Apocalyptic and Wisdom Traditions in Romans 9–11* (SBLDS 109; Atlanta: Scholars Press, 1989), pp. 176-205; Thielman, *From Plight to Solution*, pp. 123-32; Kaylor, *Paul's Covenant Community*, pp. 184-88; Segal, *Paul the Convert*, pp. 129-33.

6. See, e.g., Johnson, *Function*, pp. 141-44.

Of course, Paul could have cut the Gordian knot by simply claiming that the church had taken over Israel's position and leaving it at that. But what, then, would become of the continuity between the OT and the gospel? For the Jewish claim to privileged status arises not simply from a self-generated nationalistic fervor; it is rooted in the OT: "The LORD your God has chosen you out of all the peoples on the face of the earth to be his people" (Deut. 7:6b).[7] Paul could not jettison these promises, for to do so would be to jettison the gospel. The gospel is "the gospel of God" (1:1), and the God of whom Paul speaks is none other than the God who has spoken and acted in Israel's history. Paul must, then, demonstrate that the God who chose and made promises to Israel is the same God who has opened the doors of salvation "to all who believe." To do so, Paul must prove that God has done nothing in the gospel that is inconsistent with his word of promise to Israel; that the gospel he preaches is not the negation but the affirmation of God's plan revealed in the OT (see, e.g., 1:2; 3:21).[8] It is for this reason that Paul quotes the OT so often in Rom. 9–11 (almost a third of all Paul's quotations are found in these chapters[9]): he is seeking to demonstrate "the congruity between God's word in Scripture and God's word in Paul's gospel."[10] At the same time, then, Paul is demonstrating that God is con-

---

7. E.g., B. Corley, "The Jews, the Future, and God (Romans 9–11)," *SJT* 19 (1976), 48-49.

8. As Beker says, ". . . the gospel to the Gentiles has no foundation and no legitimacy unless it confirms the faithfulness of God to his promises to Israel" (p. 332).

9. Koch, 21-23. He counts 89 Pauline quotations, with 27 in Rom. 9–11. Stanley (*Paul and the Language of Scripture*), on the other hand, includes 74 quotations in his study, but he does not include Ephesians and the Pastoral Epistles, which would add at least six more. He finds 24 in Rom. 9–11. In addition to these, of course, are many allusions to OT texts. Moreover, Paul's references to the OT in these chapters do not simply illustrate points established independently; the OT itself often sets the agenda, establishes the themes, and moves the argument along (see, e.g., J. W. Aageson, "Scripture and Structure in the Development of the Argument in Romans 9–11," *CBQ* 48 [1986], 265-89; B. Chilton, "Romans 9–11 as Scriptural Interpretation and Dialogue with Judaism," *Ex Auditu* 4 [1988], 27-31). Paul's extensive use of the OT in these chapters has frequently led scholars to suggest that they form a "midrash," or that Paul in engaged in midrashic activity. If midrash be defined broadly — e.g., Jewish appropriation and contemporarizing of Scripture — then the appellation is accurate though not very helpful. If it is defined in terms of the sort of scriptural commmentary found in the classic rabbinic *midrashim* — as it probably should be — then the term is not applicable to Rom. 9–11 (see Chilton, "Romans 9–11," pp. 31-32; Ellis says that Paul here "employs the ancient midrashic form of commentary," but he immediately adds: "but his incisive manner and compact, integrated treatment [are] quite at odds with the rabbinic system" [*Paul's Use of the Old Testament,* p. 46]).

10. Hays, 64; Watson, 160-62.

sistent, faithfully fulfilling all his promises — whether they are found in the OT or the NT (cf. 9:6a).[11]

Romams 9–11, therefore, is an integral part of Paul's letter to the Romans.[12] These chapters contribute to Paul's exposition of the gospel by showing that it provides fully for God's promises to Israel, when those promises are rightly understood. The appropriateness of Rom. 9–11 within the letter is revealed also in the many specific textual and thematic contacts with chaps. 1–8.[13] But the very number of these contacts suggests that chaps. 9–11 form a distinct argument, relating generally to the argument of chaps. 1–8 without being tied to any one text or theme.[14] However, to call Rom. 9–11 the climax or center of the letter is going too far.[15] Such an evaluation often arises from a desire to

---

11. Among those who make this theme primary in Rom. 9–11 are Morris, "Theme," p. 260; Luz, 19-22; R. Schmitt, *Gottesgerechtigkeit — Heilsgeschichte — Israel in der Theologie des Paulus* (Europäische Hochschulschriften 23.240; Frankfurt: Peter Lang, 1984), pp. 72-75; Corley, "The Jews," pp. 42-56; H. Hübner, *Gottes Ich und Israel: Zum Schriftgebrauch des Paulus in Römer 9–11* (FRLANT 136; Göttingen: Vandenhoeck & Ruprecht, 1984), p. 16; S. Hafemann, "The Salvation of Israel in Romans 11:25-32: A Response to Krister Stendahl," *Ex Auditu* 4 (1988), 43-44; Walter, "Römer 9–11," p. 172; Wilckens, 2.181-83.

12. Donfried claims that the integral relationship between chaps. 9–11 and the letter as a whole is a matter of general scholarly consensus (p. lxx).

13. Particularly popular are the suggestions that chaps. 9–11 continue the discussion of 3:1-8 (e.g., E. Brandenburger, "Paulinische Schriftauslegung in der Kontroverse um das Verheißungswort Gottes (Röm 9)," *ZTK* 82 [1985], 3-5; Myers, "Chiastic Inversion," p. 45; Schlier, 283) or that they respond to Paul's strong affirmations of the church's election and privileges in chap. 8 (e.g., Byrne, 127-29; Volf, *Paul and Perseverance,* pp. 161-62; N. Elliot, *The Rhetoric of Romans: Argumentative Constraint and Strategy and Paul's "Dialogue with Judaism"* [JSNTSup 45; Sheffield: JSOT, 1990], pp. 261-63; Luz, 19-22). For a complete list and full discussion of these contacts, see H.-M. Lübking, *Paulus und Israel im Römerbrief. Eine Untersuchung zu Römer 9–11* (Europäische Hochschulschriften 23.260; Frankfurt: Peter Lang, 1986), pp. 21-51.

14. W. G. Kümmel, "Die Probleme von Römer 9–11 in der gegenwärtigen Forschungslage," in Lorenzi, *Israelfrage,* p. 15; Aletti, *Comment Dieu est-il juste?* pp. 150-55, 201-2; Aune, "Romans," pp. 294-95 [pagination from Donfried ed. of art.]; Schlier, 282-83; J. Becker, *Paulus: Der Apostel der Völker* (Tübingen: Mohr, 1989), p. 362; H. Räisänen, "Paul, God, and Israel: Romans 9–11 in Recent Research," in *The Social World of Formative Christianity and Judaism: Essays in Tribute of Howard Clark Kee* (ed. J. Neusner, P. Borgen, E. S. Fredrichs, and R. Horsley; Philadelphia, Fortress, 1988), pp. 179-80. This general relationship to chaps. 1–8 renders unlikely the supposition that chaps. 9–11 were originally attached to chaps. 1–4 as a separate homily (contra Scroggs, "Paul as Rhetorician," pp. 271-98).

15. F. C. Baur contested the "dogmatic" interpretation of Romans then (mid-eighteenth century) so dominant in Protestant scholarship, with its focus on justification by faith in chaps. 1–8. He argued for a historical interpretation of the letter, focused on the debates between Jews and Christians and with 9–11 the "germ and centre" of the letter (*Paul the Apostle,* 1.315-41 (315). See also Stendahl, *Paul,* p. 4; Beker, 87; Wright, *Climax of the Covenant,* p. 236; Fitzmyer, 541 ("the climax of the doctrinal section"). Noack,

minimize the importance of the individual's relationship to God in chaps. 1–8. But the individual's standing before God is the center of Paul's gospel, which offers salvation only on the basis of a personal response (1:16). If some earlier expositors of Paul were too preoccupied with his teaching about the individual's relationship to God at the expense of his emphasis on the corporate relationship between Jews and Gentiles, many contemporary scholars are making the opposite mistake. Individual and corporate perspectives are intertwined in Paul. His claim that individual Jews are sinners, in danger of God's wrath (2:1–3:20), requires him to deal with the status of the people Israel.

In these chapters Paul continues to use the dialogical style that is so characteristic of Romans. He uses rhetorical questions to move his argument along (9:14, 30; 10:8, 14-15a, 18, 19; 11:1, 7, 11) and in 9:19-23 engages in a dialogue with a fictional respondent. These are argumentative devices and do not necessarily provide us with any information about the "real" addressees of Paul's argument in these chapters. However, Paul's address of Gentile Christians in 11:13-32 is in a different category. This must be read as an indication of Paul's intended audience at this point in his discussion[16] and demonstrates that one of Paul's purposes in Rom. 9–11 is the rebuke of Gentile arrogance (in Rome and elsewhere) toward Jews and Jewish Christians.[17] But does it require that this be Paul's only intended audience throughout these chapters? We do not think so. Paul's vehement affirmation of concern for his Jewish kinfolk, as well as his careful scriptural defense of the exclusion of many Jews from the messianic salvation, suggests strongly that he also writes to convince Jewish Christians of the truth of his gospel.[18] As he has throughout the letter, then, Paul in Rom. 9–11 writes to both Gentile and Jewish Christians, both of whom are represented, as we have seen, in the church at Rome.[19] Paul's complex theologizing in chaps.

---

while not arguing that Rom. 9–11 is the center of the letter, links it with 1:1-17; 3:9-20, 27-31; and chap. 4 as part of the main "current" of the letter ("Current and Backwater," pp. 164-65).

16. Contra, e.g., Aletti, *Comment Dieu est-il juste?* pp. 200-202, who thinks that these references are simply a rhetorical device. Cf. also those who think that Paul's audience throughout Rom. 9–11 is Jewish-Christian (A. B. Bruce, *St. Paul's Conception of Christianity* [New York: Charles Scribner's Sons, 1911], pp. 97-98; Räisänen, "Paul, God, and Israel," p. 181; Watson, 160-61; R. E. Brown and J. P. Meier, *Antioch and Rome: New Testament Cradles of Catholic Christianity* [New York: Paulist, 1983], pp. 119-20).

17. Almost all scholars identify Gentiles as at least a significant part of Paul's audience.

18. Brandenburger, "Paulinische Schriftauslegung," pp. 6-9; Wilckens, 2.189-90; Räisänen, "Paul, God, and Israel," pp. 180-81.

19. E.g., Schmithals, 324-25; Walter, "Römer 9–11," pp. 187-89. C. A. Evans notes that Paul therefore conforms to the model of the "true prophet": giving hope to the people even as he rebukes them for their sin and presumption ("Paul and the Hermeneutics of 'True Prophecy': A Study of Romans 9–11," *Bib* 65 [1984], 560-70).

9–11 has a very practical purpose: to unite the squabbling Roman Christians behind his vision of the gospel and its implications for the relationship of Jew and Gentile. As so often in Romans, Paul's approach is balanced. He insists, against the presumption of many Gentiles in the community, that the gospel does not signal the abandonment of Israel (chap. 11, especially).[20] But he also makes clear that Jews and Jewish Christians who think that they have an inalienable salvific birthright are in error (chaps. 9 and 10, especially). Paul therefore criticizes extremists from both sides, paving the way for his plea for reconciliation in chaps. 14–15.[21]

Tied though these chapters are to the immediate needs and problems of both Paul and the Roman Christians, we should not miss the larger and enduring theological issue that they address. Israel's unbelief of the gospel is a matter of significance not only to the Roman Christians, or to first-century Christians generally, but to all Christians.[22] For it raises the question of the continuity of salvation history: Does the gospel presented in the NT genuinely "fulfill" the OT and stand, thus, as its natural completion? Or is the gospel a betrayal of the OT, with no claim therefore to come from the same God who elected and made promises to Israel? We need to hear Paul's careful and balanced answer to these questions. He teaches that the gospel is the natural continuation of OT salvation history — against an incipient "Marcionism" that would sever the gospel from the OT and Judaism. But at the same time, he teaches that the gospel is also the fulfillment of salvation history — against the Judaizing tendency to view the gospel in terms of the torah.

The body of Rom. 9–11 is framed by an opening personal lament (9:1-5) and a closing doxology (11:33-36). The intervening material can be divided into four basic sections. The first (9:6-29) opens with a positive assertion — "It is not as though the word of God had failed" — that states a possible implication from what Paul has written in vv. 1-5. This assertion is taken by many to be the thesis that Paul defends throughout Rom. 9–11. While it is true that Paul is concerned to show the compatibility of his understanding

20. As Seifrid (*Justification,* pp. 245-48) notes, Paul's rhetorical stance is from the perspective of the Gentile Christians. In contrast to chap. 2, where Paul addresses the Jew directly, in chaps. 9–11 he usually addresses them in the third person (9:3-5, 27, 31-32; 10:1-3, 14-19, 21; 11:11-24, 28, 30-31).

21. See, e.g., Wedderburn, *Reasons,* 87-91. In this regard, Dahl (p. 141) notes that Rom. 9–11 is very closely tied to the "epistolary situation" of Romans.

22. E.g., J. Munck: "The unbelief of the Jews is not merely a missionary problem that concerned the earliest mission to the Jews but a fundamental problem for all Christian thought in the earliest church. Israel's unbelief is a difficulty for all Christians, both Jewish and Gentile" (*Christ and Israel: An Interpretation of Romans 9–11* [Philadelphia: Fortress, 1967], pp. 34-35).

of the gospel and the OT throughout these chapters, those who view each of the main units of Rom. 9–11 as parallel defenses of this statement may be guilty of imposing a neat "outline" format on Paul that he never intended.[23] Paul's argument proceeds in a more "linear" fashion, with each new section building on, or responding to, points in the previous section (or sections).[24] Suggesting such a progressive form of argument is the fact that each of the three remaining units in Paul's argument is introduced with a rhetorical question that ties it to what has preceded. We may then summarize the movement of Paul's argument as follows:

9:1-5 — Introduction of the issue Paul seeks to resolve: the Jews' failure to embrace the gospel (vv. 1-3) calls into question the value of the privileges and promises God has given them (vv. 4-5).

9:6-29 — Defense of the proposition in v. 6a — "the word of God has not failed." Paul argues that God's word never promised salvation to all the biological descendants of Abraham (9:6b-13). Salvation is never a birthright, even for Jews, but always a gift of God's electing love (vv. 14-23), a gift he is free to bestow on Gentiles as well as Jews (vv. 24-29).

9:30–10:21 — Connected to 9:6b-29 (and esp. vv. 25-29) with the rhetorical question "What then shall we say?" Paul uses his understanding of the gospel to explain the surprising turn in salvation history, as Jews are cast aside while Gentiles stream into the kingdom.

11:1-10 — Connected to 9:30–10:21 (esp. vv. 20-21) and indirectly to 9:6b-29 with the rhetorical question "I ask, then. . . ." Paul summarizes the situation of Israel as he has outlined in the previous two sections and prepares for the next section by affirming the continuation of Israel's election.

11:11-32 — Connected to 11:1-10 (esp. v. 7a) with the rhetorical question "I ask then. . . ." Paul argues that Israel's current hardened state is neither an end in itself nor is it permanent. God is using Israel's casting aside in a salvific process that reaches out to Gentiles and will include Israel once again.[25]

11:33-36 — Response to the teaching of Rom. 9–11 with extolling of God's transcendent plan and doxology.

---

23. Cf., e.g., Bruce, 174. Note Beker's warnings about imposing an "architectonic" structure on Romans generally (pp. 64-69).

24. Readers of Romans should be familiar with this style of argument, in which an initial positive assertion of a theme is followed by a series of elaborations and clarifications introduced with questions. Compare 2:1-29 with 3:1-8; 3:21-26 with 3:27-31; 4:1-25; 5:1-21 with 6:1-14, 15-23; and 7:1-6 with 7:7-12, 13-25.

25. Note also that each of these sections concludes with a series of OT quotations, or a mixed OT quotation (9:25-29; 10:18-21; 11:8-10; 11:26b-27).

A. INTRODUCTION: THE TENSION BETWEEN GOD'S PROMISES AND ISRAEL'S PLIGHT (9:1-5)

> 1*I am speaking the truth in Christ, I am not lying, as my conscience bears witness to me through the Holy Spirit,* 2*for I have great pain and ceaseless anguish in my heart.* 3*For I could pray that I might be accursed from Christ for the sake of my fellow Jews, my kindred according to the flesh,* 4*who are Israelites, and whose are the adoption, and the glory, and the covenants,*[1] *and the giving of the law, and the worship, and the promises,* 5*whose are the fathers, and from whom, according to the flesh, is the Messiah, who is over all, God blessed forever. Amen.*

Paul signals a break in his argument by the abrupt transition from chap. 8 to chap. 9. No conjunction or particle connects the two chapters, and the tone shifts dramatically from celebration (8:31-39) to lamentation (9:1-3).[2] Paul begins his exposition of the gospel and Israel with an impassioned assertion of his own concern for his "kindred according to the flesh" (vv. 1-3). Implied by this concern, as the word "accursed" in v. 3 makes especially clear, is a circumstance well known among the Roman Christians: the great majority of the Jewish people have not responded in faith to the gospel. But Paul's concern is not the result only of a natural love for his own people; nor is it directed only to their salvation. As the rehearsal of Israel's privileges in vv. 4-5 makes clear, Paul is also concerned that Israel's unbelief has ruptured the continuous course of salvation history: the people promised so many blessings have, it seems, been disinherited. It will be Paul's task to show that this is not the case.

1 Paul draws his readers' attention to what he is about to say by forcefully proclaiming his sincerity. He emphasizes the point by putting it

---

1. In place of the plural αἱ διαθῆκαι, two early and important MSS (P[46] and B, the latter a primary witness of the Alexandrian text), as well as the western tradition (D, F, G), read the singular ἡ διαθήκη. This combination of Alexandrian and western witnesses is a strong one; and a scribe may have changed an original singular into a plural to match αἱ ἐπαγγελίαι at the end of the verse. But it is perhaps more likely that an original plural has been changed into a singular to bring it in line with customary NT usage (cf., e.g., Wilckens, 2.188).

2. This is not to deny connections between chaps. 8 and 9 in both vocabulary and subject matter: e.g., the theme of election (compare 8:26-30 and 9:6b-23), with its key words πρόθεσις (8:28; 9:11) and κλητός/καλέω (8:28, 30; 9:7, 11, 24, 26); the issue of "sonship"/adoption (cf. υἱοθεσία in 8:15, 23; cf. 9:4; τέκνα in 8:16, 17, 21; cf. 9:7, 8; υἱός in 8:14, 19; cf. 9:9, 26); and the hope for eschatological glory (cf. δόξα in 8:18, 21 [cf. 30]; cf. 9:4, 23).

both positively — "I am speaking the truth" — and negatively — "I am not lying."[3] And he adds conviction to his assertions by joining to each a reference to the Christian reality from which he speaks. The truth that Paul speaks (the word for truth in the Greek comes first for emphasis), he speaks "in Christ," "as one united with Christ."[4] Moreover, his assertion that he does not lie is confirmed to him[5] by the witness of his conscience. "Conscience" in Paul is an inborn faculty that monitors a person's conformity to a moral standard.[6] The word thus has much the same meaning as it has in modern usage, when we speak, for instance, of having "a good conscience" or "a bad conscience." Paul assures the Romans that he has a good, or "clear," conscience about the truthfulness of what he is about to tell them. But one's conscience is only as good as the moral standards that it monitors. Hence Paul reminds the Romans that, as a believer with a "renewed mind" (12:1-2), his conscience testifies "by means of" the Holy Spirit.[7]

Why has Paul stressed so strongly the truth of his concern for Israel (v. 2)? Almost certainly because he knew that his passionate and well-known defense of the law-free Gentile mission had earned him the reputation — in Rome, as elsewhere — of being anti-Jewish.[8] To the Jewish Christians in the church Paul therefore wants to make clear that his focus on the Gentile mission has by no means meant the abandonment of his concern for, and, indeed, plans for, the salvation of their fellow Jews. But he also wants to dispel any notion that he might have joined with the Gentile Christians in Rome in their sinful disdain for the Jewish people (cf. 11:13-24).

3. The lack of a conjunction to connect these clauses lends Paul's assertions a "solemn emphasis" (Dunn). For a similar sequence, see 1 Tim. 2:7.

4. S-H. They add, "St. Paul has just described that union with Christ which will make any form of sin impossible; cf. viii. 1, 10; and the reference to this union gives solemnity to an assertion for which it will be difficult to obtain full credence."

5. The Greek word συμμαρτυρούσης (a genitive participle, connected with συνειδήσεως in a genitive absolute construction) could mean (as in 8:16) "witness with": "my conscience witnesses along with me." But the idea of Paul's conscience witnessing along with himself to the Romans is a difficult one. Probably, then, συμμαρτυρέω here, as in 2:15 (also with συνείδησις), means simply "witness to" (Dunn; Schlier; contra, e.g., Cranfield; Godet).

6. See 2:15; 11:5; 1 Cor. 8:7, 10, 12; 10:25, 27, 28, 29 (twice); 2 Cor. 1:12; 4:2; 5:11; 1 Tim. 1:5, 19; 3:9; 4:2; 2 Tim. 1:3; Tit. 1:15; see, further, the notes on 2:15.

7. The Greek preposition ἐν before πνεύματι ἁγίῳ could be local, in a metaphorical sense (Kuss: Paul's consience testifies *within* the realm of the Holy Spirit) or, perhaps more likely, instrumental — the conscience testifies to Paul *through* the Holy Spirit (cf. NRSV). Reference to both Christ and the Holy Spirit could be Paul's attempt to meet the biblical requirement of "two or three witnesses" to establish lawful testimony (Deut. 17:6; 19:15; cf. 2 Cor. 13:1).

8. See, e.g., Kühl; Barrett; Black; contra Cranfield.

2 The rhetorically effective doubled expressions[9] of v. 1 ("I am speaking the truth"/"I am not lying"; "in Christ"/"in the Holy Spirit") continue in v. 2: "great pain"/"ceaseless anguish."[10] Paul's grief over the spiritual state of Israel (cf. v. 3) is similar to laments over Israel's sinful or fallen state in the OT prophets.[11] In these texts, lament over Israel's fallen condition generally gives way to expressions of hope for her future. Without, then, calling into question the reality of Paul's grief, we can see how naturally his lament fits into the subject that he develops in these chapters.

3 Paul now gives the reason[12] for his sorrow: the condemnation under which so many of his fellow Jews stand by reason of their refusal to embrace the gospel. To be sure, he does not state this as his cause for concern in so many words. But that no less than eternal condemnation is the issue is plain from his expressed wish to be "accursed" and "cut off from Christ [or the Messiah[13]]" for the sake of his fellow Jews. "Accursed" translates the Gk. *anathema*, which, transliterated, has entered ecclesiastical English to denote a person who is excommunicated. Paul, however, applies the word to the underlying spiritual reality of which the church's excommunication is but the response: eternal damnation.[14] Paul's

---

9. See Michel.

10. The repetition, then, is a matter of style rather than meaning: no clear difference in sense between "pain" and "anguish" can be established. Contra, e.g., Godet and S-H, who argue that λύπη ("pain") connotes an inner feeling of grief while ὀδύνη ("anguish") refers to the result, or outward expression, of grief. But no solid evidence backs up such a distinction in meaning. ὀδύνη occurs only one other time in the NT (1 Tim. 6:10; cf. v.l. in Matt. 24:8); in the LXX it is a variant reading for λύπη in Gen. 44:31 and Tob. 3:10; and the two are used together, with no apparent difference in meaning, in Prov. 31:6; Isa. 35:10; 51:11. It is unlikely, however, contra Dunn, that Paul's use of the two terms owes anything to these two texts in Isaiah.

11. See, e.g., Jer. 4:19; 14:17; Lamentations; Dan. 9:3; note also *2 Apoc. Bar.* 14:8-9; 35:3; *T. Jud.* 23:1; 4 Ezra 8:16; 10:24, 39; *Par. Jer.* 4:10; 6:17. On this theme, see, e.g., Schlier; F. Refoulé, ". . . *Et ainsi tout Israël sera sauvé: Romans 11,25-32* (LD 117; Paris: Cerf, 1984), pp. 86-88. Johnson has shown that many of the themes and motifs of Rom. 9–11 are remiscent of Jewish apocalyptic (*Function*, pp. 124-31).

12. Gk. γάρ.

13. The definite article with Χριστοῦ, especially in this context (vv. 4-5), gives to the word a titular sense: not "Christ," but "*the* Christ," the Messiah (see, e.g., Dunn).

14. Cf. 1 Cor. 12:3; 16:22; Gal. 1:8, 9. Paul picks up the word ἀνάθεμα from the LXX, where it translates Heb. חֵרֶם, "something set apart for God." That which is so set apart may be, in a positive sense, an offering in devotion to God (e.g., Lev. 27:28; Jud. 16:19). But, more often, it has the negative sense of something destined to destruction as an offering to God (e.g., the city of Jericho and the plunder of the Caananite cities is called "anathema" [Josh. 6:17, 18; 7:1, 11-13; 22:20; 1 Chr. 2:7]). The rabbis later used חֵרֶם to denote excommunication (Str-B, 3.260). Besides the four Pauline occurrences cited above, ἀνάθεμα is found only twice elsewhere in the NT, both with a positive or neutral meaning (Acts 23:14; Luke 21:5 [where the texts vary between the spelling ἀνάθεμα and ἀνάθημα; cf. BAGD]).

willingness to suffer such a fate himself makes sense only if those on behalf of whom he offers himself stand under that curse themselves.[15]

Paul's prayer[16] that he become *anathema* for the sake of his fellow Jews strikingly demonstrates his love for his own people. But it also creates a difficulty: Would Paul actually have prayed that he be eternally damned so that others could be saved? A few scholars, noting that Paul uses a Greek tense that usually denotes past action (the imperfect), think that Paul is describing only what "he used to pray."[17] But this is both contextually unlikely and grammatically unnecessary.[18] I prefer, in agreement with most English translations, to ascribe a hypothetical nuance to the imperfect tense; as Cranfield paraphrases, "I would pray (were it permissible for me so to pray and if the fulfillment of such a prayer could benefit them)."[19] Paul's willingness to suffer on behalf of Israel may reflect certain ideas in his own heritage. He would know the stories of the Maccabean martyrs, whose deaths were sometimes thought to have atoning value for the nation of Israel as a whole.[20] Closer to Paul's situation, however, and more likely to have influenced him, is the example of Moses, who, after the Golden Calf incident, prayed that God would forgive the people of Israel and asked that his own name be blotted out of "the book" if God chose not to forgive (Exod.

---

15. See, e.g., H. Räisänen, "Römer 9–11: Analyse eines geistigen Ringens," *ANRW* 25.4.2891-2938. This point must be asserted against those who argue that Paul never questioned the salvation of Jews through their own covenant (see esp. Gaston, "Israel's Enemies," pp. 411-18).

16. NRSV, KJV, NIV, and NASB translate the verb εὔχομαι here as "wish" (see also Godet; Kuss; Schlier; Käsemann). But all other NT occurrences of the word denote a wish expressed to God (Acts 26:29; 27:29; 2 Cor. 13:7, 9; Jas. 5:16; 3 John 2) and, therefore, for all intents and purposes, a prayer (see REB; NEB; Michel; Cranfield; Wilckens).

17. Haldane; Hays, 62, 206.

18. While the imperfect tense that Paul uses here often denotes past action, it is not, strictly speaking, a past action tense. Only context can make clear that a action denoted by the imperfect takes place in the past, and the context here speaks against a past reference. See Porter, *Verbal Aspect,* pp. 208-11; he thinks ηὐχόμην is "timeless" (p. 210).

19. Cranfield; cf. Fitzmyer; G. P. Wiles, *Paul's Intercessory Prayers: The Significance of the Intercessory Prayer Passages in the Letters of St. Paul* (SNTSMS 24; Cambridge: Cambridge University, 1974), pp. 256-57. The NT imperfect tense, doing duty at this point for the optative, can denote a present-time action that is potential or attempted but never carried out. Several grammarians find this idea in Rom. 9:3: Robertson, 886; Turner, 65; BDF 359(2); Z-G, 478; K. L. McKay, "Time and Aspect in New Testament Greek," *NovT* 34 (1992), 213; idem, *A New Syntax of the Verb in New Testament Greek: An Aspectual Approach* (Studies in Biblical Greek: New York: Lang, 1994), 10.3.1-2.

20. See esp. 4 Macc. 6:28-29; 17:20-22.

32:30-32).[21] Allusions to Moses' history and person elsewhere in Rom. 9–11 (e.g., 9:14-18; 10:19; 11:13-14) make it likely that Paul does see Moses as, to some extent, his own model. As Moses, the leader of God's people, offered himself for the sake of his people, so Paul offers himself.[22] In keeping with this substitutionary concept, the preposition translated "for the sake of" probably includes the connotation "in place of."[23] It is by taking the place of his "kindred according to the flesh" under the curse of God that Paul will be able to act "for their sake," and thus save his fellow Jews (see 10:1).[24] The unbelieving Jews for whom Paul grieves are his "kindred" in the sphere of human relationships — "the flesh" (for Paul's use of this word, see the notes on 1:3 and 7:5; and see 11:14, where "my flesh" refers to unbelieving Jews).[25] Paul applies "kindred" to his fellow Jews to demonstrate the degree of his continuing identification with, loyalty to, and concern for them. "Apostle to the Gentiles" he may be; but a Jew he remained.

4 In vv. 4-5, Paul enumerates some of the divine privileges given to

21. Most commentators note the parallel; see especially, however, Munck, 305-6; idem, *Christ and Israel,* p. 29. P. Bratsiotis suggests that LXX Esth. 4:17 may also have influenced Paul's language and conception ("Eine exegetische Notiz zu Röm. IX.3 und X.1," *NovT* 5 [1962], 299-300).

22. J. Munck, especially, has taken the parallel between Paul and Moses even further, arguing that Paul viewed himself as a crucial figure in salvation history, comparable to Moses (see esp. *Paul*). But Munck has overemphasized the degree to which Paul sees himself as personally significant in the conversion of Israel at the end of history (see 11:14).

23. Gk. ὑπέρ often implies that the way in which one acts "on behalf of" someone is by taking his or her place (see BAGD).

24. The word I translate "fellow Jews" is the Gk. ἀδελφοί, "brothers" (cf. most other English translations). Paul adds the phrase "my kindred according to the flesh" to make clear that he is not using "brothers" in his usual spiritual sense (e.g., fellow Christians), but in a physical sense (M. Crawford, "Election and Ethnicity: Paul's View of Israel in Romans 9:1:1-13," *JSNT* 50 [1993], 35-38; Fitzmyer). Cranfield, however, claims that Paul's application of the word ἀδελφοί to unbelieving Jews means that he "recognizes them still, in spite of their unbelief, as fellow-members of the people of God" and "within the elect community" (cf. K.-W. Niebuhr, *Heidenapostel aus Israel* [Tübingen: Mohr, 1992], p. 163). Lexically, Cranfield is on solid ground, for 130 of Paul's 133 other uses of ἀδελφός clearly mean "fellow Christian" (the exceptions are 1 Cor. 9:5 and Gal. 1:19, where a blood relationship is denoted). Paul also furnishes some theological ground for this interpretation; as 11:1-2 makes clear, Paul continues to view Israel as an "elect people." But it is important to distinguish between this general (and nonsalvific) corporate election of Israel and the salvific individual election of 9:6-29 and 11:5-7. Nevertheless, it is possible that Paul is using ἀδελφός here to mean simply "fellow countryman" (BAGD; cf. Acts 2:29; 3:17, 22; 7:2, 23, 25-26).

25. Paul's addition of κατὰ σάρκα to συγγενῶν may signal that the latter word also has a spiritual connotation in Paul (see the notes on Rom. 16:7, 11, 21) and must therefore also be qualified to make clear its physical sense here (W. Michaelis, *TDNT* VII, 741).

his "kindred according to the flesh."[26] This suggests that Paul's willingness to sacrifice himself for unbelieving Israel (v. 3) arises not only from love for his own people but also from love for the truthfulness of God's word. Paul's concern is not just that so many of his own people seem doomed to hell; it is also that their fate seems incompatible with the many privileges and promises granted to Israel by God in the OT. Thus Paul's listing of Israel's blessings prepares the way for the question that is central to this whole section: Has God's word failed (v. 6a)? But, more than this, it also suggests, albeit very indirectly, one of the answers to that question. For the blessings Paul lists relate not only to Israel's glorious past that she has forever forfeited; some of them, at least, relate also to Israel's present state and are pregnant with potential future significance (especially, "adoption," "promises," and "patriarchs"). While, then, Paul's inventory of Jewish privileges has as its main purpose the explanation of his willingness to sacrifice himself for his people, it also hints at why that sacrifice will not be necessary: God "has not rejected his people whom he foreknew" (11:2).

We are justified in suggesting a causal relationship between vv. 4-5 and v. 3: "I have great sorrow for my fellow Jews and could even pray that I might be condemned so that they could be saved *because* they are. . . ."[27] Paul's list of Jewish privileges reflects a careful organization.[28] The first term, "Israelites," stands in its own clause and is the heading for the whole series. There follow three clauses, each connected to Israelites with the relative pronoun "whose":

v. 4b, "whose are[29] the adoption . . . and the promises";

v. 5a, "whose are the patriarchs";

v. 5b-c, "and from whom . . . forever."

Paul's selection of the term "Israelites" to head this list is significant. For, in contrast to the colorless, politically and nationally oriented title

---

26. Paul appears to begin such a list in 3:2 (cf. πρῶτον) without completing it. Since Paul often in Romans introduces briefly themes that he treats in detail later in the letter, we may view this list, along with the larger discussion in chaps. 9–11, as the continuation and expansion of that earlier digression.

27. The indefinite relative pronoun that connects v. 3 with v. 4, οἵτινες, has here, as it often does elsewhere, a causal flavor (cf., e.g., Calvin).

28. This arrangement, coupled with the fact that some of the terms are unusual for Paul, or bear meanings not customary in Paul, has led some scholars to think that Paul may be quoting from a Hellenistic Jewish tradition (e.g., Byrne, 82-84; Michel). Piper, on the other hand, thinks that it may be a composition of Paul's that he had used before (p. 47).

29. All three clauses lack a verb; to be supplied, from the first clause in the verse, is εἰσιν, "they are."

560

"Jew," "Israelite" connotes the special religious position of members of the Jewish people.[30] It is therefore no accident that Paul in Rom. 9–11 generally abandons the word "Jew," which has figured so prominently in chaps. 1–8,[31] in favor of the terms "Israelites" and "Israel."[32] Paul is no longer looking at the Jews from the perspective of the Gentiles and in their relationship to the Gentiles but from the perspective of salvation history and in their relationship to God and his promises to them. The appellation "Israelites," then, is no mere political or nationalistic designation but a religiously significant and honorific title. And despite the refusal of most of the Israelites to accept God's gift of salvation in Christ, this title has not been revoked.[33] Here is set up the tension that Paul seeks to resolve in these chapters.[34]

The first of the clauses that unfolds the significance of the word "Israelites" lists six privileges. The Greek suggests an arrangement in two series

---

30. Ἰσραηλίτης (used 27 times in the LXX and also spelled Ἰσραηλείτης and Ἰσραηλεῖτις) denotes one who belongs to Israel, the name given by God to Jacob (Gen. 32:28; 35:10) and applied to his offspring (e.g., Gen. 32:32; 46:8). It therefore suggests a people chosen by God to belong to him in a special way and to be the vessels of his plan of salvation for the world. Ἰουδαῖος (Heb. יְהוּדִי) originally denoted a person of the tribe of Judah, or of the southern kingdom generally. But after the Exile, when Judah was all that was left of historical Israel, the name was applied to any member of the Israelite nation (see especially, e.g., Nehemiah and Esther; and cf. the note on 2:17).

The tendency of some intertestamental books to use "Israelite" or "Israel" when speaking from the standpoint of the people's special religious position and "Jew" when speaking from the standpoint of the people's national or political status is instructive (e.g., in 1 Maccabees "Jew" is used consistently in letters written to foreign nations or which are about political matters [e.g., chaps. 8, 10, 11]; "Israel" is used of the people's religious status and distinction from the other nations). Similarly, Philo uses "Israel" and "Israelite" in the two treatises in which he defends the rights and privileges of the Jews [Flaccus and Laws]). The rabbis also preferred "Israel" and "Israelites" to "Jew." (See, on this subject, K. G. Kuhn, TDNT III, 359-65.) This evidence cannot be pushed too far because it does not hold for all intertestamental books (e.g., Sirach, Judith, Tobit, Psalms of Solomon) and because stylistic choice may sometimes play a role (Ἰουδαῖος being preferred to Ἰσραηλίτης for the plural; Ἰσραήλ, naturally, being used for the people collectively). Still, we have enough evidence to conclude that Paul's shift in terms is significant.

31. 1:16; 2:9, 10, 17, 28, 29; 3:1, 9, 29; neither "Israel" nor "Israelites" occurs at all.

32. 9:6 (twice), 27 (twice), 31; 10:19, 21; 11:1, 2, 7, 25, 26; "Jew" occurs only twice (9:24 and 10:12), and in each place in explicit contrast to Gentiles.

33. Note the present εἰσιν, "they are."

34. Refoulé's application of this title to believing Jews only, the "remnant" (Tout Israel, pp. 167-77), too facilely resolves this tension and ignores the connection between vv. 3 and 4 (cf., e.g., J. M. Osterreicher, "Israel's Misstep and Her Rise: The Dialectic of God's Saving Design in Romans 9–11," in SPCIC 1.319).

561

of three.[35] The first prerogative is also the most striking. "Adoption,"[36] Paul has just informed us, is the Spirit-conferred status of all those who have been justified by faith in Christ (8:15, 23; cf. Gal. 4:5 and Eph. 1:5). Paul's attribution of this blessing to the Israelites, most of whom are unbelieving (cf. v. 3), is surprising — particularly since the word is not used in the OT or in Judaism.[37] Some interpreters think this indicates that Paul is affirming that the people of Israel remain God's children in just the way that the church is God's people. There are, according to these scholars, two "separate but equal" peoples of God, both saved and destined for glory: the church, those who become God's children through faith in his Son, and Israel, those who are God's children by virtue of God's covenant through Moses.[38] But this view is incompatible both with what Paul has said earlier in this letter (e.g., 2:1-29; 3:9-20) and with what he will say later in this same section (e.g., 9:6b-13; 9:30–10:8). Moreover, if Israel remains within the sphere of salvation, we cannot explain Paul's anguish in the preceding verses.

Clearly, then, Israel's "adoption" here must mean something different than the adoption of Christians in chap. 8. The term is Paul's way of summing up the OT teaching about Israel as "God's son."[39] The privilege is one that adheres to the nation as a whole, branding the people as set aside by God from other peoples for blessing and service.[40] God's "adoption" of Christians gives to every believer in Christ all the rights and privileges that are included within new covenant blessings. God's adoption of Israel, on the other hand, conveys to that nation all the rights and privileges included within the Old Covenant. These blessings, as Paul indicated earlier (2:17–3:8) and as he will reiterate again in the next paragraph (vv. 6-13), do not include salvation for every single Israelite. Nevertheless, Paul's choice of the term "adoption" is a deliberate attempt (after 8:15, 23) to highlight the continuing regard that God has for Israel, despite her widespread unbelief. It may therefore hint at the new and ultimate work of God among the people Israel that Paul predicts in 11:25-28.[41]

---

35. Paul begins each triad with two feminine singular nouns, completing it with a feminine plural noun:

υἱοθεσία . . . δόξα . . . διαθῆκαι
νομοθεσία . . . λατρεία . . . ἐπαγγελίαι.

36. Gk. υἱοθεσία.

37. See the exegesis of 8:15 for the background and meaning of the word.

38. This theological position, labeled "bi-covenantal" theology, has become particularly influential in the last twenty years. For more detailed interaction with the position, see the discussion on 11:26.

39. E.g., Exod. 4:22-23; Deut. 14:1-2; Isa. 63:16; 64:8; Jer. 31:9; Hos. 11:1; Mal. 1:6; 2:10.

40. Fitzmyer.

41. For this approach, see esp. F. Dreyfuss, "Le passé et le présent d'Israel (Rom 9:1-5; 11:1-24)," in Lorenzi, *Israelfrage*, pp. 132-39; Piper, 16-18; Byrne, 127-40.

The second privilege that adheres to the Israelites is "the glory." It is difficult to know whether this term, like "adoption," is picked up from chap. 8 and refers therefore to eschatological blessing (e.g., 5:2; 8:17, 18, 21, 30),[42] or whether it is historically oriented to the manifestation of God's presence with the Israelites in the OT — "the splendour of the divine presence" (NEB).[43] But these are not mutually exclusive alternatives. Granted the other items in this list, "glory" probably refers basically to God's presence with the people of Israel; but the very fact that Paul raises the question that he does here suggests that it is the ultimate continuation of that presence (into the eschaton) that is the issue.

Paul's use of the plural "covenants" is unusual, the singular being much more frequent in both OT and NT. He could be referring to (1) the covenants with Abraham and the other patriarchs,[44] (2) the several ratifications of the Mosaic covenant,[45] (3) the several covenants mentioned throughout the OT (with Noah, Abraham, the people of Israel at Sinai, and David [e.g., 2 Sam. 23:5]),[46] or (4) all the biblical covenants, including the New Covenant (Jer. 31:31-34; cf. 11:26-27).[47] The third option is best, since intertestamental passages that use the plural "covenants" refer generally to all the covenants that God had made with the "fathers" (Sir. 44:12, 18; Wis. 18:22; 2 Macc. 8:15). Paul uses the plural "covenants" in the same sense in Eph. 2:12, where he refers to "the covenants of promise" that mark Israel as God's special people and from which, therefore, Gentiles were alienated.

Paul begins his second triad of Israelite privileges with mention of the "giving of the law." The word Paul uses can refer both to the act of giving

---

42. E.g., Piper, 18-19.

43. See, e.g., Michel; Kuss; Cranfield; Fitzmyer. The OT often speaks of the appearance of "the glory of the Lord," especially in the temple and on significant occasions, such as the giving of the law at Sinai (e.g., Exod. 16:7, 10; 24:16; 40:34-35; Lev. 9:6, 23; Num. 14:10, 21; 16:19, 42; 1 Kings 8:11; Ezek. 1:28). The use of the simple term, without the addition of a divine name, is unusual (there is no clear OT example, and Str-B find no parallel in the rabbis [3.262]), but it may be the product of Paul's desire for stylistic parallelism (ἡ υἱοθεσία/ἡ δόξα; cf. Dunn).

44. See Gen. 17 especially; also Gen. 6, 9, and 15 and the references to the "covenant" with the forefathers; e.g., Deut. 4:31; 7:12 (Kuss; Dunn).

45. Barrett. There were three such ratifications, as the rabbis saw it: at Sinai (Exod. 19:5-6), on the plains of Moab (Deut. 29–31), and at Mounts Ebal and Gerizim (Josh. 8:30-35) (Str-B, 3.262).

46. Cranfield.

47. E.g., H. L. Ellison, *The Mystery of Israel: An Exposition of Romans 9–11* (Grand Rapids: Eerdmans, 1966), pp. 36-37; Piper, 19-20; L. Cerfaux, "Le privilège d'Israel selon S. Paul," *ETL* 17 (1940), 13-16; E. J. Epp, "Jewish-Gentile Continuity in Paul — Torah and/or Faith?" *HTR* 79 (1986) 83. The suggestion of C. Roetzel, that δια-θῆκαι refers here to the "ordinances" and "oaths" that God gave to the people ("Διαθῆκαι in Romans 9,4," *Bib* 51 [1970], 377-90), is unlikely.

a law or to the results of that act, the law or "legislation." Many scholars adopt the second definition here (see NEB, "the law"; NIV, "the receiving of the law").[48] But the first definition has better lexical support and fits Paul's argument better: he wants to focus on the law as given to Israel by God, not on its negative effects on the people as a result of the power of sin.[49] "Worship" could refer broadly to Israel's worship of God wherever and however that was carried out.[50] But it is more likely to focus more narrowly on the Israelite sacrificial system.[51] The importance of the temple cult and the worship associated with it is seen in one of the most famous statements of the Mishnah: "By three things is the world sustained: by the Law, by the [Temple-] service, and by deeds of loving-kindness" (*m. 'Abot* 1:2). "The promises" conclude Paul's initial list of prerogatives enjoyed by the Israelites. Paul's characteristic emphasis on the promises given to Abraham and the other patriarchs suggests that these are the promises that he here has in mind.[52]

5 Paul highlights the last two Jewish privileges in his list by giving to each a separate clause. The first is a final privilege "belonging to" the Israelites: "the fathers," or "the patriarchs."[53] Descent from the patriarchs is valuable because God gave promises to Abraham, Isaac, and Jacob that were valid both for them and for their descendants. The meaning and extent of these promises are the linchpin in Paul's interpretation of salvation history; see 9:6b-13; 11:15; and especially 11:28, which forms with this verse an

---

48. They note occurrences of the word with this meaning in Jewish literature roughly contemporary to Paul (e.g., 2 Macc. 6:23; 4 Macc. 5:35; 17:16; *Ep. Arist.* 15; Philo, *On Abraham* 5; *On the Cherubim* 87) and argue that Paul has used this rare word (it occurs only here in the NT and the canonical OT), rather than the familiar νόμος, to match in form the other words in his series (see W. Gutbrod, *TDNT* IV, 1089; Piper, 20-21; Hodge; Wilckens; Cranfield; Fitzmyer).

49. See the argument earlier in the letter, e.g., 3:19-20; 4:15; 7:7-25. All three occurrences of words cognate to νομοθεσία in the Greek Bible connote law-*giving* (νομοθετέω in Heb. 7:11 and 8:6 and νομοθέτης in Ps. 9:21; cf. *GEL* 33.339-40), as do many of the occurrences in Jewish Greek literature at the time (e.g., Josephus, *Ag. Ap.* 2.170; *Ant.* 3.287; 12.37; Philo, *On the Life of Moses* 2.2). See, for this conclusion, e.g., Munck, *Christ and Israel,* p. 32; Epp, "Jewish-Gentile Continuity," p. 89; Luz, 272; Käsemann; Kuss; Meyer; Schmidt.

50. Cranfield.

51. All nine of the LXX occurrences of λατρεία (translating עֲבוֹדָה) and three of its other four NT occurrences (John 16:2; Heb. 9:1, 6]) have this denotation. See H. Strathmann, *TDNT* IV, 59-62; Käsemann. Note also Paul's use of this term and its cognates to denote Christian worship, in juxtaposition to the OT/sacrificial worship.

52. Cf. "the promises given to the patriarchs" in 15:8; the plural ἐπαγγελίαι refers to the promise(s) to Abraham and the patriarchs also in Gal. 3:16, 21.

53. Gk. οἱ πατέρες denotes the patriarchs of the Israelite nation and perhaps the generation of those who were redeemed from Egyptian slavery (see 11:28; cf. Exod. 3:15; 1 Kings 8:58; Josephus, *Ant.* 13.297).

"inclusio" surrounding Paul's discussion in these chapters. Much of what Paul says in Rom. 9–11 is an attempt to explain just what the Israelites legitimately can expect to inherit from their founding fathers.

The last privilege mentioned by Paul not only occupies its own clause but is introduced in a different construction. Rather than "belonging" to the Israelites, the Messiah "is from"[54] them. The shift is significant, suggesting, as do vv. 2-3, that the Israelites, for all the privileges they enjoy, have not, as a group, come into genuine relationship with God's Messiah and the salvation that he has brought.[55] As Paul qualified the meaning of his own relationship to the Jewish people ("kindred according to the flesh," v. 3), so he now qualifies in the same way the descent of the Messiah from the Israelites. The Messiah, Paul is pointing out, comes from the people of Israel "only in respect to that relationship which is strictly and narrowly human."[56] "Flesh," then, while it is basically "neutral" in meaning here, carries with it that nuance of "this-worldliness," with implicit contrast with "the world to come," which is rarely absent from the word in Paul's usage.[57]

This prepositional phrase implies that what Paul has said of the Messiah so far, while true, is incomplete. Does Paul explicitly complete the picture by denoting in the last part of v. 5 another aspect of Messiah's person: his deity? Exegetes and theologians since the inception of the church have been sharply divided over this question. The issue is one of punctuation and therefore of interpretation, for Greek manuscripts of the NT rarely contain punctuation marks and the marks that are found tend to be sporadic and irregular. At least eight different possibilities for the punctuation of the last part of the verse have been suggested, but they can be reduced to two basic choices.[58]

---

54. Gk. ἐξ ὧν.

55. Kuss.

56. The neuter article τό before κατὰ σάρκα does not agree with Χριστός, stressing the limitation expressed in the prepositional phrase (BDF 266[2]).

57. See the note on 1:3.

58. In addition to the four punctuation options considered in the text above, an emendation of the text has been suggested: the transposition of ὁ and ὧν, leading to the translation "from whom is Christ, whose is [also] the one who is over all things, God blessed forever." This conjecture was mentioned, though not adopted, by the seventeenth-century Socinian theologian J. Szlichting (see Cranfield). It has more recently been defended by H. W. Bartsch ("Röm. 9,5 und 1 Clem. 32,4. Eine notwendige Konjektur im Römerbrief," *TZ* 21 [1965], 401-9), is adopted by Ziesler, and considered possible by Dodd. A slightly different conjecture was proposed by W. L. Lorimer, "Romans IX.3-5," *NTS* 13 (1966-67), 385-86. However, not only is there no textual evidence for this reading, but it faces several serious objections (see esp. B. M. Metzger, "The Punctuation of Rom. 9:5," in *Christ and Spirit in the New Testament: In Honour of Charles Francis Digby Moule* [ed. B. Lindars and S. Smalley; Cambridge: Cambridge University, 1973], pp. 99-100). The most serious, perhaps, is the lack of a καί after σάρκα: in our paraphrase above, the "and" in brackets is required to make sense

(1) A comma could be placed after "flesh," meaning that the words following the comma would modify "Messiah."[59] The words following "Messiah" can then be punctuated in two different ways:

a. ". . . from them, according to the flesh, comes the Messiah, who is over all, God blessed forever. Amen" (NRSV; cf. also KJV; JB; NASB).
b. ". . . from them is traced the human ancestry of Christ, who is God over all, forever praised! Amen" (NIV).[60]

(2) The second general approach to the punctuation of these words places a period after "Messiah" and takes what follows as an independent ascription of praise to God.[61] Again, two possible translations result, depending on the punctuation adopted within the clause.

a. ". . . of their race, according to the flesh, is the Christ. God who is over all be blessed for ever. Amen" (RSV; cf. also NEB; TEV).
b. ". . . from them, in natural descent, sprang the Messiah. May God, supreme over all, be blessed for ever! Amen" (NEB; cf. also TEV).[62]

The christological implications of this issue are great, for if the first alternative is adopted, Paul here calls Jesus "God," and Rom. 9:5 becomes one of the most important "proof-texts" for the deity of Christ. Such evidence from Greek manuscripts that we possess favors slightly the second view.[63] Most of the church fathers, on the other hand, favor the first interpretation.[64]

---

of the passage but has no basis in the Greek text. O'Neill, in keeping with his idiosyncratic approach, treats the last part of v. 5 as a gloss.

59. This punctuation is adopted in the latest versions of the two standard Greek New Testaments: NA[27] and UBS[4].

60. The difference between these translations arises from different assumptions about the place of a comma in the last part of the verse. The former option puts it between πάντων and θεός, while the latter puts it between θεός and εὐλογητός.

61. Previous editions of both NA (the 25th ed.) and UBS (the 2nd ed.) punctuated the text in this way.

62. The former rendering assumes no further punctuation at all, while the latter assumes commas on either side of θεός.

63. See particularly Metzger, "Rom 9:5," pp. 97-99.

64. Metzger cites Irenaeus, Tertullian, Hippolytus, Novatian, Cyprian, Athanasius, Epiphanius, Basil, Gregory of Nyssa, Chrysostom, Theodoret, Augustine, Jerome, Cyril of Alexandria, and Oecumenius. Only Diodore of Tarsus and Photius held the opposite view ("Rom 9:5," pp. 102-3; cf. also Schelkle). An anti-Arian motive is likely responsible to some degree for the popularity of the dominant view (cf. O. Kuss, "Zu Römer 9,5," in *Rechtfertigung* (*Festschrift für Ernst Käsemann*) [ed. J. Friedrich, W. Pohlmann, and P. Stuhlmacher; Tübingen: Mohr, 1976], pp. 291-303), but the evidence cannot simply be dismissed.

Ancient translations almost all take "God" as a designation of Christ;[65] modern translations, as we have seen, are divided, as are modern commentators.[66] Despite this difference of opinion, arguments in favor of taking "God" as an appellation of "Messiah" greatly outweigh those that support the alternative.

Favoring a comma after "Messiah" (and thus the first option) are several stylistic arguments. First, the words "the one who is"[67] are most naturally taken as a relative clause modifying a word in the previous context (see the similar construction in 1 Cor. 11:31). Second, Paul's doxologies are never independent but always are tied closely to the preceding context.[68] Third, independent blessings of God in the Bible, with only one exception (Ps. 67:19), place the word "blessed"[69] in the first position. Here, however, the Greek word for "blessed" occurs after "God," suggesting that the blessing must be tied to the previous context. As Metzger points out, it is "altogether incredible that Paul, whose ear must have been perfectly familiar with this constantly recurring formula of praise, should in this solitary instance have departed from established usage."[70] Fourth, as suggested above, the qualifying phrase "according to the flesh" implies an antithesis; and Paul usually supplies the antithetical element in such cases, rather than allowing the reader simply to assume it. In other words, we would expect, after a description of what the Messiah is from a "fleshly" or "this-worldly" standpoint, a description of what he is from a "spiritual" or "otherworldly" standpoint; see especially Rom. 1:3-4.

Proponents of the other interpretation, the placing of a period after "Messiah," admit the force of these arguments but insist that they are outweighed by theological and contextual considerations. The theological issue

65. Metzger, "Rom 9:5," pp. 100-101.

66. In favor of taking θεός with Χριστός: Calvin; Haldane; Stuart; Hodge; Liddon; Shedd; Zahn; Gifford; S-H; Denney; Moule; Schlatter; Leenhardt; Huby; Althaus; Nygren; Lagrange; Sickenberger; Lenski; Schmidt; Best; Bruce; Schlier; Cranfield; Fitzmyer. See also J. Morison, *Exposition of the Ninth Chapter of the Epistle to the Romans* (London: Hodder and Stoughton, 1888), pp. 45-51; Munck, *Christ and Israel,* pp. 32-33; Cullmann, *Christology,* pp. 312-13; Wright, *Climax of the Covenant,* p. 237. In addition to the article by Metzger, see especially, for a thorough and careful argument in favor of this view, M. J. Harris, *Jesus as "God": Theos as a Christological Term in the New Testament* (Grand Rapids: Baker, 1992), pp. 144-72.

Understanding θεός as independent of Χριστός are Meyer; Lietzmann; Kuss; Gaugler; Wilckens; Käsemann; Dunn; Zeller; Stuhlmacher; Schmithals. For a history of interpretation, see Kuss, 3.679-96.

67. Gk. ὁ ὤν.

68. See 1:25; 11:36; 2 Cor. 11:31; Gal. 1:5; 2 Tim. 4:18.

69. Gk. εὐλογητός; Heb. בָּרוּק.

70. "Rom. 9:5," p. 107.

boils down to the insistence that Paul does not elsewhere call Jesus "God" and that, considering his Jewish monotheistic background, it is very unlikely that he would have done so. But this objection cannot stand. First, Paul almost certainly does call Jesus "God" in one other text (Tit. 2:13).[71] Second, the exalted language Paul uses to describe Jesus[72] as well as the activities Paul ascribes to him[73] clearly attest Paul's belief in the full deity of Christ. The argument from context is that it would be inconceivable for Paul to describe Christ as God in a passage in which he is trying to create common ground with his unbelieving "kindred." However, as we have noted, Paul's shift in construction when introducing the Messiah implies already a certain "distance" between unbelieving Jews and the reality of Jesus the Messiah. And this fits naturally into Paul's overall perspective, accenting his grief at Jewish unbelief by highlighting the divine status of the Messiah whom his fellow Jews have rejected.

Connecting "God" to "Christ" is therefore exegetically preferable, theologically unobjectionable, and contextually appropriate. Paul here calls the Messiah, Jesus, "God," attributing to him full divine status. The frequent association of God with "blessed" makes it likely that these should be kept together, and the whole taken in apposition to "the one who is over all": "Christ, who is supreme over all things, God blessed forever" (thus, essentially, option 1.a above).[74]

B. DEFINING THE PROMISE (1): GOD'S SOVEREIGN ELECTION (9:6-29)

According to the typical Jewish understanding of Paul's day, salvation history had taken an unexpected turn. Most of the people of Israel to whom the promises of salvation had been given refused to recognize the fulfillment of those promises. At the same time Gentiles, who were considered to be excluded from the covenant, were embracing the one in whom those promises had come to fruition. Paul insists, however, that this turn of events, though unexpected, does not violate the integrity of God's word and his promises. Paul justifies that claim by showing what God's word itself says about becoming a member of God's true spiritual people.[1] If the OT teaches that

---

71. See Harris, *Jesus as God,* pp. 174-85, and his earlier article, "Titus 2:13 and the Deity of Christ," in *Pauline Studies,* pp. 262-77.

72. E.g., "Lord"; cf. on 10:13; "in the form of God" (Phil. 2:6).

73. E.g., creation (Col. 1:16); dispensing of grace (Rom. 1:7); forgiving of sins (Col. 3:13); and judging sins (1 Cor. 4:4-5; 2 Cor. 5:10; 2 Thess. 1:7-9).

74. See esp. Harris, *Jesus as God,* pp. 163-70, 172; also, e.g., S-H; Cranfield.

1. The qualification "true spiritual" is needed because Paul recognizes that national

belonging to physical Israel in itself makes a person a member of God's true spiritual people, then Paul's gospel is in jeopardy. For were this the case, the gospel, proclaiming that only those who believe in Jesus Christ can be saved (cf. 3:20-26), would contradict the OT and be cut off from its indispensable historical roots. Paul therefore argues in vv. 6b-29 that belonging to God's true spiritual people has always been based on God's gracious and sovereign call and not on ethnic identity. Therefore, God is free to "narrow" the apparent boundaries of election by choosing only some Jews to be saved (vv. 6-13; 27-29).[2] He is also free to "expand" the dimensions of his people by choosing Gentiles (vv. 24-26).[3]

God's "calling" of a spiritual "people" is therefore the topic of the passage, a topic Paul characteristically highlights at both the beginning (v. 7) and end (vv. 27-29) of the section.[4] Verses 6-13 and 24-29 contain the brunt of Paul's argument, while vv. 14-23 form an excursus in which Paul deals with certain questions that his teaching about the freedom of God in election raises.[5] Throughout, Paul argues from Scripture,[6] seeking

---

Israel remains, in a different sense, the people of God (see 11:1-2 and 9:6b). Contra Watson (pp. 164, 228), Paul does not in 9:6ff. argue that the privileges named in 9:4-5 have been forfeited; he is beginning to show in what way they still apply.

2. As Michel (p. 298) points out, Paul is engaged here in a discussion of the Jewish doctrine of election. Mainstream Jewish teaching held that all Jews were elected to salvation by virtue of their inclusion in that people with whom God had entered into covenant relationship. Only by apostatizing did the Jew forfeit that salvation (see on the subject E. P. Sanders, *Judaism: Practice and Belief, 63 BCE–66 CE* [Philadelphia: TPI, 1992], pp. 272-75). The implication of vv. 6-23, then, that salvation for Jews as well as Gentiles depends on God's call and *not* on Jewish identity contradicts Jewish theology (cf., e.g., Byrne, 133-34; A. F. Segal, "Paul's Experience and Romans 9–11," *Princeton Seminary Bulletin* 1 [1990], 57; contra, e.g., Johnson, *Function,* pp. 147-48).

3. See Ziesler, 234, for this conception.

4. Two of the key words of the paragraph occur in the OT quotations in these verses (Gen. 21:12 and Isa. 1:9): καλέω ("call"; cf. also vv. 12, 24, 25, 26 and ἐκλογή ["election"] in v. 11) and σπέρμα (cf. also v. 8 and the related terms υἱός, "son" [vv. 9, 26, 27], and τέκνον, "child" [vv. 7 and 8]). The two quotations thus form an inclusio (see, e.g., Hays, 65; P. E. Dinter, "The Remnant of Israel and the Stone of Stumbling in Zion according to Paul (Romans 9–11)" [Ph.D. diss., Union Theological Seminary, 1980], pp. 10-22). Dunn (2.537) discerns a more detailed chiastic structure, according to which vv. 6-9 go with vv. 26-29 (λόγος, Ἰσραήλ, κληθήσεται, σπέρμα, τέκνα), vv. 10-13 with vv. 24-25 (καλέω, ἀγαπάω), and vv. 14-18 with vv. 19-23 (ἐλεέω-θέλων, θέλων-ἐλεέω). For a similar proposal, see J.-N. Aletti, "L'argumentation paulinienne en Rm 9," *Bib* 68 (1987), 42-43.

5. Note that all occurrences of the terms I isolated in the previous note are clustered in vv. 6-13 and 24-29.

6. The heavy use of Scripture in 9:6-29 leads many scholars to call the section a midrash (see esp. W. R. Stegner, "Romans 9.6-29 — a Midrash," *JSNT* 22 [1984], 37-52; E. E. Ellis compares it to the rabbinic *yelammedenu rabbenu* ["let our master teach us"]

to convince both his Jewish and Gentile Christian readers in Rome that his viewpoint is rooted in the OT.[7]

1. The Israel within Israel (9:6-13)

> 6Now it is not that the word of God has failed. For not all those who are of Israel, these are Israel. 7Neither is it the case that all of Abraham's children are his seed; but, "In Isaac your seed shall be called."[a] 8That is, it is not the children of the flesh, these are the children of God, but the children of the promise who are reckoned as seed. 9For this is the word of the promise: "About this time I will come and Sarah shall have a son."[b]
>
> 10And not only this, but also Rebecca, when she conceived children in one act of intercourse with Isaac, our ancestor — 11for her sons, not yet having been born or done anything good or evil, in order that the purpose of God according to election might remain, 12not out of works but out of the one who calls — it was said to her, "The greater shall serve the lesser."[c] 13Just as it is written,

> Jacob I loved,
> but Esau I hated.[d]

a. Gen. 21:12
b. Gen. 18:10, 14
c. Gen. 25:23
d. Mal. 1:2-3

Paul's distinction between a broader, ethnic, Israel and a narrower, "spiritual," Israel (v. 6b) is his basic defense of the proposition that "the word of God

---

midrashic form; "Biblical Interpretation in the New Testament Church," in *Mikra: Text, Translation, Reading and Interpretation of the Hebrew Bible in Ancient Judaism and Early Christianity* [ed. M. J. Mulder; CRINT 2.1; Philadelphia: Fortress, 1988], p. 708 n. 73). The appropriateness of this designation depends on what one means by "midrash." That Paul uses techniques similar to ones found in rabbinic midrashim is clear. But the differences between the more strictly "commentary" form of the rabbinic midrashim and 9:6-29 render the application of the term "midrash" to Paul's exposition inappropriate (see, e.g., Koch, 226-27; Räisänen, "Römer 9–11," pp. 2897-98).

7. Rather than being directed, then, to any particular group within the Roman church (e.g., the mainly Jewish "weak in faith" [Minear, 72-75] or Jewish Christians generally [Watson, 167]), 9:6b-29 is of relevance to the whole community: Jewish Christians who may still retain too much "nationalism" in their conception of the basis for belonging to God's people as well as Gentile Christians who, whether they had experience with the synagogue or not (many may have been "God-fearers"; cf. Schmithals, 339 and the Introduction), would need to understand how the gospel confirmed the OT.

has not failed." He justifies the distinction in two parallel arguments (vv. 7-9 and 10-13).[8] In each, Paul quotes the OT twice to contrast two brothers. God's choice of Isaac rather than Ishmael and Jacob rather than Esau reveals a pattern in God's creation of his spiritual people that Paul applies to the problem of widespread Jewish unbelief in his own day. For these stories about the founders of the Jewish people demonstrate that the reason why some were included in the people of God and others were not was that God freely chose some and did not choose others. Physical descent, these stories show, was not the crucial qualification. In the same way, Paul implies, belonging to the New Covenant people of God is based on God's free choice and is not a birthright. Thus it should be no surprise, and certainly no threat to the integrity of God's word, if many Jews have failed to trust Christ and to be saved.

In summarizing the paragraph in this way, we take issue with an increasingly large number of scholars who are convinced that Paul in this paragraph, and in the succeeding ones (9:14-18, 19-23), is implying nothing about the salvation of individuals.[9] Rather, they urge, Paul is describing the way in which God has used some individuals rather than others in the further-ance of his plan: salvation-historical roles, not eternal destinies, is the issue. Moreover, as the quotation of Mal. 1:3 in v. 13 suggests, Paul may not be thinking of individuals at all, but of peoples: Israel (Isaac), Edom (Esau), and Egypt (Pharaoh in v. 17). These scholars have a point: the OT verses Paul cites do not clearly refer to the eternal destiny of the individuals concerned. Yet three points suggest that Paul, however he understands the original mean-ing of these texts,[10] applies them here to the issue of individual salvation.[11]

(1) His argument requires such an application. Paul must explain why some Israelites in his own day are being saved and why others are not (vv.

8. See Wilckens, 2.191.

9. A pioneering work in this direction was W. Beyschlag, *Die paulinische Theo-dicee, Römer 9–11* (2d ed.; Halle: Eugen Strien, n.d.). Advocates of this general interpreta-tion disagree over the extent to which Paul is focusing on individuals or peoples, but agree that no reference to the eternal destiny of individuals is present. See, *inter alia,* W. W. Klein, *The New Chosen People: A Corporate View of Election* (Grand Rapids: Zondervan, 1990), pp. 173, 197-98; Zahn, 446-48; Lagrange, 231; S-H, 245; Gaugler, 2.34-37; Munck, *Christ and Israel,* p. 42; Ellison, *Mystery,* p. 43.

10. Commentators take three basic positions on Paul's appropriation of these OT texts. (1) Paul sticks to their original meaning and applies them only to salvation-historical roles. (2) Paul disregards the original sense of the OT texts and sees them as containing "types" of God's salvific methods (e.g., Käsemann, 264). (3) Paul legitimately uses principles derived from OT texts that speak of God's formation of his people Israel to show how God operates to call out his true spiritual people. We adopt this third alternative; see also Piper, 45-54.

11. For these points, see esp. Piper. Similar points are made by T. R. Schreiner, "Does Romans 9 Teach Individual Election unto Salvation? Some Exegetical and Theo-logical Reflections," *JETS* 36 (1993), 25-40.

3-5); to justify his assertion that only some from "among Israel" are truly Israel (v. 6b). A discussion of the roles of individuals or peoples in salvation history simply does not meet the point Paul needs to make.

(2) Key words in the paragraph — "children of God" (v. 8), "descendants" (vv. 7 and 8), "counted" (v. 8), "children of promise" (v. 8) "name" or "call" (vv. 7, 12), and "not of works" (v. 12) — are consistently applied by Paul elsewhere to the salvation of individuals (see the exegesis below for details).

(3) The continuation of vv. 6b-13 in vv. 24-29 shows that Paul's point is to demonstrate how God has called *individuals* from among both Jews and Gentiles to be his people and that those Jews who are called (the "Israel" within Israel of vv. 6b-13) constitute the "remnant" that will be "saved" (v. 27).

6 The first half of v. 6 is the transition between the introduction and the "body" of Paul's exposition in chaps. 9–11. Paul makes clear that the problem of Israel is at the same time the problem of God's word and, ultimately, of God himself. For God has adopted Israel, revealed himself to her, bound her to him with his covenants, and given her his law, the temple service, and his promises. Do these now mean nothing? Has God revoked these blessings and gone back on his word to Israel? Many Christians, both Jewish and Gentile, in Rome and elsewhere, must have thought that this was the logical implication of Paul's radical critique of the Jewish assumption of guaranteed salvation (cf., e.g., Rom. 2). And, if God had indeed reneged on his earlier word, the consequences were dire for more than Jews. For how could Christians trust such a God to fulfill his promises to them?

Thus Paul must affirm that "it is not that[12] the word of God has failed."[13] "The word of God" might refer specifically to the gospel.[14] Paul would then be defending his gospel against the charge that its failure to bring Israel to salvation at the present time invalidates it.[15] But the sequence of

---

12. This translation, along with the similar "it is not as though" (NRSV; NIV; RSV) or "it is impossible that" (NEB), assumes that οὐχ οἷον δὲ ὅτι is a mixture of two constructions: οὐχ οἷον ("by no means") and οὐχ ὅτι (with the ellipsis of ἐστιν: "it is not as if"). Cf. BAGD, 562; Turner, 47 and 298.

13. Gk. ἐκπέπτωκεν, from ἐκπίπτω. This verb means "fall," "fall away from" (in a physical sense: Acts 12:7; 27:17, 26, 29, 32; Jas. 1:11; 1 Pet. 1:24; in a metaphorical sense: Gal. 5:4; 2 Pet. 3:17). But it can also mean "fail," "become weakened" (see Sir. 34:7; 1 Cor. 13:8 [v.l.]), and this is its meaning here.

14. Paul uses ὁ λόγος τοῦ θεοῦ to depict the message of the gospel in 1 Cor. 14:36; 2 Cor. 2:17; 4:2; Col. 1:25; 1 Thess. 1:8; 2:13; 1 Tim. 4:5; 2 Tim. 2:9; Tit. 2:5. Cf. also ὁ λόγος τοῦ Χριστοῦ in Col. 3:16 and ὁ λόγος τοῦ κυρίου in 1 Thess. 1:8; 2 Thess. 3:1.

15. E. Güttgemanns, "Heilsgeschichte bei Paulus oder Dynamik des Evangeliums? Zur structurellen Relevanz von Röm 9–11 für die Theologie des Römerbriefs," *Studia Linguistica Neotestamentica* (BEvT 60; Munich: Kaiser, 1971), pp. 40-41; R. D. Kotansky, "A Note on Romans 9:6: *Ho Logos Tou Theou* as the Proclamation of the Gospel," *Studia Biblica et Theologica* 7 (1977), 24-30.

thought requires that the "word of God" mentioned in v. 6 is that word which contains the privileges just listed (vv. 4-5) and to which Paul makes reference throughout this chapter. Moreover, "the word of God" here is somewhat parallel to "the oracles of God" in 3:2. Therefore "the word of God" is God's OT word,[16] with particular reference to his promises to Israel.[17]

Paul now introduces his first justification for the denial that Israel's unbelief nullifies God's promises to Israel, a justification that gets to the heart of the matter: Who constitutes the "Israel" to whom God's promises of salvation have been given? The standard view among Paul's Jewish contemporaries was that this Israel was made up of all those physically descended from Jacob, the heir of Abraham and Isaac, who was himself named "Israel." Only those who had refused their inheritance by outright apostasy would be excluded from this Israel to whom the promises belonged. Paul does not deny that ethnic Israel remains God's people, in some sense (cf. 9:4-5; 11:1-2, 28). But he denies that this corporate election of Israel means the salvation of all Israelites; and he insists that salvation has never been *based* on ethnic descent (see 2:1-29; 4:1-16). Therefore the people of Israel cannot look to their birthright as a guarantee of salvation. This is the point that Paul makes by asserting that "all those who belong to Israel[18] (in a physical sense) do not belong to Israel (in a spiritual sense)."[19]

What does Paul mean by this "spiritual Israel"? He may be referring to the church, the messianic community composed of both Jews and Gentiles.[20] Paul has already in Romans claimed that Abraham's true descendants

---

16. See, e.g., Zahn; Schmitt, *Gottesgerechtigkeit,* pp. 201-2 n.

17. The focus on God's promises is stressed by, e.g., Godet; Murray; Käsemann; Dunn.

18. Gk. οἱ ἐξ Ἰσραήλ. The phrase could mean "those descended from Israel [e.g., Jacob]" (ἐκ indicating derivation; see Schlatter; Michel) but probably means "the ones who belong to Israel," e.g., "Israelites" (BAGD, 235; cf. NRSV). L. Gaston, on the other hand, argues that the phrase means "those who are outside Israel," e.g., Gentiles and Jewish apostates ("Israel's Enemies," pp. 412-13). But this is an unusual meaning for ἐκ. Gaston's translation stems from his opinion that Paul does not in Rom. 9 disenfranchise ethnic Israel — a view that is exegetically indefensible (see the notes on 9:3).

19. Most English translations assume that οὐ goes with πάντες οἱ ἐξ Ἰσραήλ: "Not all who are of Israel are Israel" (see, e.g., NRSV). But it is preferable grammatically to take οὐ with οὗτοι Ἰσραήλ: "all who are of Israel, these are not Israel" (See Piper, 47-48; Dunn).

20. Beyschlag, *Theodicee,* p. 32; E. Dinkler, "Prädestination bei Paulus — Exegetische Bemerkungen zum Römerbrief," in *Signum Crucis: Aufsätze zum Neuen Testament und zur christlichen Archäologie* (Tübingen: Mohr, 1967), pp. 249-50 (in a later addition to the article, however, he retracts this opinion; cf. p. 267); G. Klein, "Präliminarien zum Thema 'Paulus und die Juden'," in *Rechtfertigung,* pp. 235-36; D. Sänger, "Rettung der Heiden und Erwählung Israels. Einige vorläufige Erwägungen zu Römer 11,25-27," *KD* 32 (1986), 106; Volf, *Paul and Perseverance,* pp. 163-64; Johnson, *Function,* p. 140; Wright, *Climax of the Covenant,* p. 238; Schmidt; Schmithals.

are composed of *all* who believe (4:1-16; cf. Gal. 4:28, where Paul calls Christians "children of promise, like Isaac"). He can elsewhere claim that Christians are "the circumcision" (Phil. 3:3) and uses the title "Israel" to denote the church (Gal. 6:16).[21] These texts show that Paul was quite capable of transferring language and titles applied to God's Old Covenant people Israel to his New Covenant people, the church. Moreover, in v. 24, which resumes the topic of vv. 6-13, Paul emphasizes the inclusion of Gentiles in the new people of God.

These points make it quite possible that Paul includes Gentile Christians in his second reference to "Israel" in v. 6. But we must finally reject this interpretation. (1) Verses 1-5 establish the parameters within which Paul's language of Israel in Rom. 9–11 must be interpreted, and these verses focus on ethnic Israel. Throughout these chapters, Paul carefully distinguishes between Israel and the Jews on the one hand and the Gentiles on the other. Only where clear contextual pointers are present can the ethnic focus of Israel be abandoned. (2) Paul explains v. 6b in vv. 7-13 with examples of God's selection of his people from *within* ethnic Israel. (3) Verses 27-29, which, as we have seen, relate closely to vv. 6-13, feature OT quotations that focus on the idea of the remnant — again, a group existing within ethnic Israel. The "true Israel" in v. 6b, therefore, denotes a smaller, spiritual body *within* ethnic Israel rather than a spiritual entity that overlaps with ethnic Israel. Paul is not saying "it is not *only* those who are of Israel that are Israel," but "it is not *all* those who are of Israel that are Israel."

7 Paul supports this distinction between ethnic and spiritual Israel and explains its basis in vv. 7-13. His argument falls into two sections, vv. 7-9 and vv. 10-13, in each of which he cites and comments on Scripture to prove his point.

---

21. The referent of the phrase τὸν Ἰσραήλ τοῦ θεοῦ ("the Israel of God") in Gal. 6:16 is much debated. It might refer to a group distinct from those denoted earlier in the verse by the phrase ὅσοι τῷ κανόνι τούτῳ στοιχήσουσιν ("as many as adhere to this rule"). Since this latter phrase presumably includes all Christians, Paul would then be denoting Jews, or perhaps Jewish Christians, with the phrase "Israel of God" (see, e.g., G. Schrenk, "Der Segenwunsch nach der Kampfepistel," *Judaica* 6 [1950], 170-90; P. Richardson, *Israel in the Apostolic Church* [SNTSMS 10; Cambridge: Cambridge University, 1969], pp. 74-84 [Richardson argues that "Israel" was not applied to the church until the post-NT period]). But the syntax of the verse makes it more likely that "Israel of God" is epexegetic of αὐτούς, which in turn finds its antecedent in the phrase "as many as adhere to this rule." This means that "Israel of God" refers to the church as a whole (see N. A. Dahl, "Der Name Israel: Zur Auslegung von Gal 6,16," *Judaica* 6 [1950], 161-70; Longenecker, *Galatians,* pp. 297-99). Note also Paul's reference in 1 Cor. 10:18 to "Israel according to the flesh," implying the existence of an "Israel according to the Spirit" (Ridderbos, *Paul,* p. 336 n. 30). The first explicit and unquestioned application of Israel to the church comes in Justin Martyr (*Dialogue* 11.5).

Paul begins where anyone seeking to define "Israel" must begin: with Abraham. God's call of and promises to Abraham were the basis for both physical and spiritual Israel.[22] Jews therefore looked to their descent from Abraham as the source of their spiritual benefits: they were the "children" or "seed"[23] of Abraham.[24] It is this assumption that Paul calls into question: "Not all of Abraham's children are his seed."[25] To be a child of Abraham in a physical sense, Paul is saying, is not necessarily to be his descendant in a spiritual sense. Salvation is not a Jewish birthright.

Paul finds support for the distinction between physical and spiritual descent from Abraham in Gen. 21:12: "In Isaac your seed[26] shall be called."[27] These words of God to Abraham come in response to his reluctance to follow Sarah's advice to banish his son Ishmael and Ishmael's mother Hagar. They remind Abraham of a crucial distinction between his two sons. The "calling" of descendants "in" Isaac therefore involves more than the promise of physical offspring.[28] For God promised that he would give many descendants to Ishmael

22. Gen. 12:1-3; 15:1-5, 18-21; 17:1-8, 15-16, 19-21; 18:18-19; 22:17-18.

23. Gk. σπέρμα, a collective singular noun (e.g., "descendants").

24. See Matt. 3:9 = Luke 3:8; Luke 13:16; 16:24, 30; 19:9; Acts 13:26; Rom. 4:1, 12; 2 Cor. 11:22; Gal. 3:7, 29; Heb. 2:16; Jas. 2:21; and esp. John 8:33-58. Jews believed that one could forfeit one's spiritual benefits by deliberate apostasy (refusal even to attempt to keep the law).

25. This translation (cf. also, e.g., NRSV) takes ὅτι with οὐδ' as the introduction to the whole sentence ("neither [is it the case] that"), parallel to οὐχ [οἷον δὲ] ὅτι in v. 6a, and understands σπέρμα, "seed," as the "narrower" and spiritually significant term of the predicate. The alternative is to take ὅτι with εἰσὶν σπέρμα Ἀβραάμ, giving it a causal sense, and to view τέκνα as the spiritually significant word: "Nor because they are his descendants are they all Abraham's children" (NIV). In favor of the latter is the word order in the parallel vv. 6b and 7 (οὐ or οὐδέ + the more inclusive term with the narrower designation last; see Byrne, 130 n. 201; Cranfield; Fitzmyer). But σπέρμα is the theologically significant term in vv. 7b and 8 — a connotation the term has elsewhere in Paul (see, in connection with Abraham, Rom. 4:13, 16, 18; Gal. 3:16, 19, 29; two other occurrences are more physical in their focus: Rom. 11:1; 2 Cor. 11:22). Since the interpretation that gives σπέρμα the same force in v. 7a is grammatically unobjectionable, it should be preferred (Barrett; Dunn; M. Rese, "Israel und Kirche in Römer 9," NTS 34 [1988], 209-10; Hays, 65, 206).

26. Because σπέρμα is singular, some commentators (e.g., Meyer; Murray) think that the reference is to Isaac as the "true seed" of Abraham. But σπέρμα is clearly collective in the first part of the verse, and this sense probably carries over into the quotation.

27. Paul's quotation agrees exactly with the LXX, and it, in turn, is a literal translation of the MT: בְּיִצְחָק יִקָּרֵא לְךָ זָרַע. The text is quoted in the same form in Heb. 11:18. The awkward κληθήσεταί σοι ("be called to you") is due to the retention in Greek of the Hebrew construction.

28. The Greek for "be called" is κληθήσεται (from καλέω, "call"). It could here mean no more than "shall be," so that we could paraphrase "in (through) Isaac you are to have your descendants" (BAGD; the Hebrew idiom is similar [see BDB]). Cranfield's suggested translation of the term, "be named," "be recognized as," moves in the same

as well as to Isaac (Gen. 17:20; 21:23). The advantage of Isaac lies rather in the spiritual realm: it is with Isaac, and not Ishmael, that God promises to establish his covenant (Gen. 17:21).[29] It is from among Isaac's descendants — not Ishmael's — that God will call individuals to become part of his covenant people.

8 Verse 7 in itself provides little support for Paul's assertion in v. 6b that "not all those who are of Israel belong to [spiritual] Israel." To claim that covenant blessings descended only through the line of Isaac was no more than what all Jews acknowledged — indeed, insisted on. But it is the conclusion Paul draws from his quotation in v. 7b that distances Paul's view from that of his Jewish compatriots and buttresses his assertion in v. 6b.[30] The opening phrase of v. 8 resembles a formula used by some Jews to introduce interpretations of Scripture, suggesting that v. 8 is Paul's "commentary" on his quotation of Gen. 21:12.[31] This commentary contrasts the "children of the flesh" with "the children of promise,"[32] and asserts that only the latter can be truly considered "the children of God." The immediate reference is to Ishmael — tied to Abraham only by natural descent ("the flesh")[33] — and Isaac — tied to Abraham by both natural descent *and* God's promise.

---

direction [cf. also Godet]). But the theological significance of the term καλέω in this passage suggests rather that Paul wants us to see in it at least overtones of the notion of God's sovereign, creative summons to spiritual blessing: "through Isaac shall God call individuals to participate in the benefits of the covenant" (Michel; S-H; Byrne, 131; Kuss; Lübking, *Paulus und Israel,* pp. 62-63; cf. also Dunn).

29. Some commentators (e.g., Cranfield; Morris) seek to minimize the spiritual implications of God's choice of Isaac rather than Ishmael by noting that God blesses Ishmael (Gen. 17:20; cf. 21:20), promises to give him many descendants and to make of him a great nation (Gen. 16:10; 17:20; 21:13, 18), and causes him to receive the "sign of the covenant," circumcision (Gen. 17:23). But the text Paul quotes focuses, as we have seen, on the clear distinction drawn in Genesis between Isaac and Ishmael in terms of the covenant. Isaac is the heir who receives and through whom are transmitted the spiritual blessings of the covenant.

30. See, e.g., Kuss; Byrne, 132. As Segal notes, Paul distinguishes here between God's promise and election in a way impossible for a Pharisaic Jew, for whom election and ancestry cohered (*Paul the Convert,* p. 277).

31. Gk. τοῦτ' ἔστιν, which may reflect the formula פִּשְׁרוֹ, "its interpretation [is]," used frequently in the Dead Sea Scrolls (see, e.g., Ellis, "Biblical Interpretation," p. 696). Piper (p. 49), on the other hand, argues that v. 8 interprets all of vv. 6b-7.

32. The genitives in both phrases (τῆς σαρκός; τῆς ἐπαγγελίας) may be descriptive ("children characterized by flesh"/children characterized by promise"; cf. BDF 165; Wilckens), but are probably generally possessive: "children who belong to the flesh"/"children who belong to the promise."

33. Leenhardt and Morris suggest that "of the flesh" refers to the human-oriented decisions and expediency that led to Ishmael's birth. But the context suggests rather that Paul is thinking of the purely physical relationship between Abraham and Ishmael (cf. NIV: "natural children"; Cranfield).

It is possible that Paul intends his commentary to apply only to those salvation-historical privileges enjoyed by Isaac and his descendants. But that Paul intends something more than this is evident from the principial nature of Paul's assertion (note the present "are reckoned") and from his choice of vocabulary. "Children of God" in Paul always denotes people who belong to God and thus partake of his salvation (Rom. 8:16, 17, 21; Eph. 5:1; Phil. 2:5). The phrase "reckoned as" likewise translates a Greek phrase that Paul elsewhere uses only when referring to Gen. 15:6, a text that Paul quotes to prove that Abraham's faith brought him into righteous relationship with God (Rom. 4:3, 5, 22; Gal. 3:6).[34] And the reference to "promise," while applicable immediately to the promise expressed in Gen. 21:12, also harks back to the argument of Rom. 4 (cf. vv. 13, 14, 16, 20), where Paul discusses the means by which God brings people into relationship with himself.[35] Thus God's words to Abraham in Gen. 21:12, according to Paul, imply a principle according to which God acts in bestowing his covenantal blessings; as N. T. Wright puts it, "what counts is grace, not race."[36] And the language Paul uses to express that principle implies that he includes within those covenantal blessings the new life experienced by believers in Christ.

9   Paul now explains[37] his use of the word "promise" to describe Isaac (and others like him) in his commentary on Gen. 21:12 (v. 8).[38] Isaac, though like Ishmael a natural son of Abraham, was born in unusual circumstances as a direct act of God in fulfillment of his promise. The promise that Abraham and Sarah, despite their advanced age and the latter's barrenness,

---

34. Gk. λογίζομαι εἰς. Paul's use of λογίζομαι shows that membership in the people of God is based solely on God's will (see, e.g., Müller, *Gottes Gerechtigkeit,* pp. 90-91).

35. Paul chooses language that reminds the reader inevitably of his argument about participation in God's righteousness in Rom. 4; see Dunn; Byrne, 132; Brandenburger, "Schriftauslegung," pp. 33-35. Note also Gal. 4:22-23: ". . . it is written that Abraham had two sons, one by a slave woman and the other by a free woman. One, the child of the slave, was born according to the flesh [κατὰ σάρκα]; the other, the child of the free woman, was born through the promise [δι᾽ ἐπαγγελίας]."

36. Wright, *Climax of the Covenant,* p. 238. Some scholars find a contradiction between Paul's denial that being "children of God" is based on natural descent and the attribution of "adoption" to Israel as a whole in vv. 4-5. But the conflict is resolved once we keep two points in mind. First, as I have argued earlier, the "adoption" of v. 4 involves general salvation-historical privileges, whereas "children of God" here implies a salvific relationship. Second, Paul's point in v. 8 is not to deny that God cannot take racial descent into account in his free reckoning of the promise, but to deny that race "forces God's hand."

37. Gk. γάρ.

38. Ἐπαγγελίας is thrown to the front of the sentence for emphasis: "Of the nature of promise is this word."

would have a child is first made in Gen. 17:15-16 and then reiterated in 18:10 and 14. Paul's quotation appears to be a loose paraphrase of one or both of the latter two verses.[39] Paul emphasizes again God's initiative in creating his covenant people: not by natural generation but by God's supernatural intervention is the promise to Abraham fulfilled.[40]

10 In vv. 10-13 Paul moves down one patriarchal generation to develop further his distinction between an ethnic and a spiritual Israel (v. 6b). In fact, God's choice of Jacob rather than Esau illustrates particularly clearly the principle of "grace rather than race" developed in vv. 7-9.[41] Three particulars in the scriptural story about God's choice of Jacob over Esau provide Paul with powerful support for his insistence that covenant participation comes only as the result of God's call. First, Jacob and Esau shared the same father and mother. This silences the objector who might argue that Isaac was preferred over Ishmael simply because they had different mothers. Second, God promised that Jacob would be preeminent before the twins were born, implying (as I will argue) that it was God's will alone, and not natural capacity, religious devotion, or even faith that determined their respective destinies. Third, Jacob's being the younger of the two makes it even more clear that normal human preferences had nothing to do with God's choice.[42]

39. The first part of Paul's quotation parallels Gen. 18:10 (κατὰ τὸν καιρὸν τοῦτον εἰς ὥρας, καὶ ἕξει υἱὸν Σαρρα ἡ γυνή σου), while the latter part follows Gen. 18:14 (εἰς τὸν καιρὸν τοῦτον ἀναστρέψω πρὸς σε εἰς ὥρας, καὶ ἔσται τῇ Σάρρᾳ υἱός). Most scholars think that Paul has therefore used both verses (Stanley, however, dissents, arguing that Paul refers only to v. 14 [*Paul and the Language of Scripture*, p. 104].) Paul's ἐλεύσομαι, on the other hand, differs from the LXX rendering in both verses as well as from the MT (אָשׁוּב; "I will return"). Some think that Paul's choice may have a theological motivation (e.g., Byrne, 133), but it may be no more than a substitution made necessary by the removal of the quotation from its context.

40. The first person singular verb, "I will come" (Gk. ἐλεύσομαι) focuses on God's intervention, reflecting a motif found throughout this passage (see also vv. 13, 15, 17, 24). See particularly Hübner, *Gottes Ich und Israel*, pp. 24-31.

41. While the argument is different, the movement of thought in 4 Ezra 3:13-16 shows that Paul is utilizing a common Jewish motif:

> And when they were committing iniquity before thee, thou didst choose for thyself one of them, whose name was Abraham; and thou didst love him, and to him only didst thou reveal the end of the times, secretly by night. Thou didst make with him an everlasting covenant, and promise him that thou wouldst never forsake his descendants; and thou gavest to him Isaac, and to Isaac thou gavest Jacob and Esau. And thou didst set apart Jacob for thyself, but Esau thou didst reject; and Jacob became a great multitude. (RSV; Luz [pp. 64-65] drew my attention to this text)

42. For these points, see particularly Murray.

The transitional phrase "and not only this"[43] makes clear that vv. 10-13 take the argument of vv. 7-9 one step further. Since Paul highlighted Sarah's role in giving birth to the heir of the covenant promises in v. 9b, it is natural that the next step of this argument focuses on the matriarch of the next generation: Rebecca. Paul sees an important similarity between Sarah and Rebecca.[44] The point of comparison is obvious: Rebecca, like Sarah, was barren; Rebecca's barrenness, like Sarah's, was overcome by divine intervention (Gen. 25:21); and, especially important for Paul's argument, Rebecca's son, like Sarah's, was called by God to become the heir of the covenant promises (see v. 12). In addition, both of the sons who so inherited the covenant promises had a rival. But it is at this point that a critical difference in the two situations exists: Isaac's rival was but a half-brother, the son of a different woman, while Jacob's rival was his own twin. It is this difference to which Paul is probably alluding in v. 10b. Most translations (e.g., NRSV; NIV; NASB) suggest that Paul is simply referring to the birth of both Jacob and Esau from the same father, "our ancestor Isaac."[45] This point fails, however, to advance Paul's argument, for the essential situation is then no different than it was in the case of Isaac and Ishmael, who were both children of Abraham. It is therefore attractive to interpret Paul's Greek as a reference to the one act of conception that produced the twins Jacob and Esau (see our translation above).[46] Paul would then be highlighting the utter lack of natural distinguishing

43. Gk. οὐ μόνον δέ. This is a general transitional phrase in Paul (see also Rom. 5:3, 11; 8:23; 2 Cor. 8:19; note BDF 379), making it unnecessary to insert any particular subject (e.g., Sarah; cf. Meyer).

44. Note the "also" in our translation, corresponding to Gk. καί. There is, however, no verb in the Greek to go with the nominative 'Ρεβέκκα. One alternative is to assume an ellipsis, with a verb needing to be supplied; cf., e.g., Godet, who suggests ἐπάθη: "she [Rebecca] had to undergo the same lot." Most English versions translate in a similar way, although it is not clear whether they are assuming this reading of the syntax or simply choosing a helpful English paraphrase of the idea. A more likely explanation of the syntax takes 'Ρεβέκκα as a pendant nominative, with v. 12b (αὐτῇ) picking up the main line of thought again: "And as for Rebecca . . . it was said to her . . ."; see, e.g., KJV; RSV; Z-G, 479; Käsemann.

45. Paul calls Isaac "our ancestor" not because he is writing to Jewish Christians but because he is identifying at this point with his "kindred according to the flesh" (v. 3) (see, e.g., S-H).

46. The Greek is ἐξ ἑνὸς κοίτην ἔχουσα. κοίτη, meaning originally "bed" (cf. Luke 11:7), came to refer especially to the "marriage bed" (e.g., Heb. 13:4) and hence to sexual intercourse (Lev. 15:21-26; Wis. 3:13, 16; Rom. 13:13; see BAGD). It can also refer to the semen itself (Lev. 15:16-17, 32; 18:20; 22:4; Num. 5:20; on κοίτη as a semantic loanword, see M. Silva, "New Lexical Semitisms?" ZNW 69 [1978], 255), and this may be its meaning here (cf. BAGD; Cranfield; Michel; Dunn). Despite the fact that this is a relatively rare meaning of κοίτη (even in the LXX only Num. 5:20 uses the word absolutely; in the other occurrences, there is a phrase, κοίτη σπέρματος), the ἐξ may suggest that it is what Paul intends: Rebecca "had semen out of one"; i.e., Rebecca conceived both sons through one seminal emission.

characteristics separating Jacob and Esau. Born of the same mother, sharing the same father, and conceived at the same point in time, neither of the twins had a better claim to the divine promise as a birthright than the other.

11 This verse interrupts the flow of Paul's argument, leaving v. 10 syntactically incomplete. The sense (but not the syntax) of v. 10 finds its continuation in v. 12b: "it was said to her [that is, Rebecca, "when she conceived"; v. 10] that 'The greater shall serve the lesser.' "[47] The beginning of v. 11 describes the circumstances in which this prophetic word was spoken to Rebecca: "when they [Jacob and Esau] had not yet been born or done anything good or evil." The purpose clause in v. 11b and its further modifier in v. 12a then belong together as a parenthesis, explaining why it was that this word about her children was spoken to Rebecca when it was.[48] The awkwardness of the syntax reflects Paul's concern to emphasize that there was nothing within the persons of Jacob and Esau that could have been the basis for God's choice of the one over the other.

This is evident, Paul points out, from the situation in which God's promise about Jacob's primacy (v. 12b) was uttered. For it was before Jacob and Esau were born[49] and before, therefore, they had done anything, whether good or evil, that God predicted to Rebecca that "The greater shall serve the lesser." This lack of any human reason for differentiation between Jacob and Esau, which Paul reiterates in other terms at the beginning of v. 12, is the basis for the purpose clause in v. 11b — "so that God's purpose according to election might remain." For God's purpose in election is established not simply by virtue of God's prediction of Jacob's prominence over Esau, but by the fact that this prediction was made apart from any basis in the personal circumstances of Jacob and Esau. "Purpose"[50] is one of those many words that connect Paul's argument here with his teaching about the children of God in 8:18-39 (for this, see the introduction to chaps. 9–11). In 8:28, it denotes the "plan" or "design" according to which God calls people to belong to him, a plan whose steps Paul unfolds in vv. 29-30. Here, similarly, the word denotes a predetermined[51] plan that God would use to bring covenant blessings

---

47. The antecedent of αὐτῇ in v. 12b is Ῥεβέκκα in v. 10.

48. For this way of understanding the syntax, see, e.g., Cranfield; Dunn; and see NRSV and NIV. The γάρ opening v. 11 therefore picks up the implication that lies behind v. 10b: "[there was nothing to discrimate Jacob from Esau], *for* they had not even been born or done anything good or evil when God said to Rebecca . . ." (see S-H).

49. Gk. γεννηθέντων, as well as the parallel πραξάντων, are genitive absolutes, with the implied subject υἱών (αὐτῆς). Dunn thinks that πράσσω may convey a "more general sense" than ποιέω and thus emphasize the τι, but a distinction between πράσσω and ποιέω in Paul is difficult to maintain (see the notes on 7:15).

50. Gk. πρόθεσις.

51. As *GEL* (30.63) notes, the προ- prefix emphasizes advance planning.

to a people, Israel, and eventually to the world.[52] Paul's use of the word "election" to characterize this plan reflects his purpose in this part of Rom. 9: to demonstrate that God's plan has unfolded in the OT by a series of free "choices" that he has made.[53] Isaac was chosen; Ishmael was not. Jacob was chosen; Esau was not. By these choices God has seen to it that his plan to bring into existence a people who would be his "peculiar possession" would "remain."[54] If God's plan depended on the vagaries of sinful human beings for its continuance, then, indeed, God's "word" would have fallen to the ground long ago (see v. 6a). But God's purpose in history is fulfilled because he himself "elects" people to be part of that purpose.

12 The first part of this verse repeats and generalizes what Paul said in v. 11a about the circumstances in which God's promise pertaining to Rebecca's sons was given. God's choice of Jacob over Esau came before either had "done anything good or evil"; therefore, Paul now concludes, this choice must not have been based on works but on God's call. The connection between v. 12a and v. 11a

---

52. Maier (*Mensch,* pp. 359-60) suggests that the word may reflect the Hebrew מַחֲשָׁבָה as used in the DSS; cf., e.g., 1QS 3:15-16a: ". . . From the God of Knowledge comes all that is and shall be. Before they existed He established their whole *design,* and when, as ordained for them, they come into being, it is in accord with His glorious *design* that they accomplish their task without change." See also the Heb. עֵצָה in texts such as Isa. 25:1; Job 38:2; 42:3 (Michel).

53. ἐκλογή, "election," is used in the NT elsewhere by Paul only in 1 Thess. 1:4; Rom. 11:5, 7, 28 (other NT occurrences are Acts 9:15 and 2 Pet. 1:10; it is not used in the LXX). The word can refer to the act of "electing" (1 Thess. 1:4; Rom. 11:5, 28) or to those who are elected (Rom. 11:7). Two other words from the same root are important for Paul: ἐκλέγομαι, "choose" (1 Cor. 1:27 [twice], 28; Eph. 1:4); ἐκλεκτός, "one chosen" (Rom. 8:33; 16:13; Col. 3:12; 1 Tim. 5:21; 2 Tim. 2:10; Tit. 1:1). Outside of Rom. 9–11, Paul always uses these terms of Christians (with the exception of 1 Tim. 5:21, where the reference is to angels). Maier (*Mensch,* p. 360) notes that the word ἐκλογή was used in some Jewish works to describe what he considers the typically Pharisaic concern to leave room in God's governance of the world for human free will; note, e.g., *Pss. Sol.* 8:4: "Our works (are) in the *choosing* and power of our souls, to do right and wrong in the works of our hands, and in your righteousness you oversee human beings" (cf. also *Pss. Sol.* 18:5; *Ep. Arist.* 33; Josephus, *J.W.* 2.165; *Ant.* 8.24). He plausibly argues that Paul in texts like this is deliberately criticizing too strong an emphasis in this direction.

The relationship between πρόθεσις and κατ' ἐκλογήν is debated (only here does Paul use the two terms together: note, however, Rom. 8:28: τοῖς κατὰ πρόθεσιν κλητοῖς). Some think that the latter term simply defines πρόθεσις: God's "electing purpose" (Kuss). Others think that "election" may express the basis for the purpose: "the purpose that is based on and carries out God's election" (see Murray [though cautiously]). But it is more natural to take κατ' ἐκλογήν to express the means by which God's πρόθεσις is carried out: "the plan that is implemented through a process of election" (e.g., Käsemann).

54. Gk. μένω, which here means "abide; stand firm"; for a parallel use note Ps. 33 (LXX 32):11: "The counsel of the LORD stands [μένει] forever" (cf. also Prov. 19:21; Isa. 14:24; 40:8; 2 Cor. 3:11; 7:9; Heb. 7:24; 12:27; 1 Pet. 1:23, 25; see Cranfield).

makes clear that "works" has general reference to human activity and cannot be restricted to any particular category of "works."[55] At the same time, this new assertion advances Paul's argument by making it clear that the temporal relationship between Jacob's and Esau's works and God's choice mirrors a causal relationship as well: God's choice not only came *before* they had done anything but also was not *based on* anything they had done. The particular phrase Paul uses here — "[not] on the basis of works"[56] — is prominent in Paul's discussion of Abraham's justification in Rom. 4 (cf. vv. 2-8). The use of this phrase, along with the general way in which Paul states the matter, suggests that he has more in mind here than the situation of Jacob and Esau per se. As Paul in v. 8 drew from the history of Isaac and Ishmael a principle about the way God bestows his covenant blessings, so he now derives another principle about the basis for God's election from the history of Isaac's sons.[57]

Contrasted with "works" as the basis for God's election is "the one who calls."[58] Highlighted again is the activity of the God of creation and history whose own word powerfully and irresistibly brings about what he chooses.[59] Earlier in Romans Paul sets "works" in contrast with another kind of human response — faith (e.g., 4:2-8). Some commentators suggest that this antithesis is implicit here also, and that Paul's denial that God's election is based on works does not mean that he would exclude faith as a basis for

55. Contra Dunn, who argues that ἐξ ἔργων is shorthand for ἐξ ἔργων τοῦ νόμου ("works of the law"), interpreted in his distinctive approach to mean "faithfulness to the law." Quite apart from our questions about Dunn's interpretation of the phrase "works of the law" (for which see our notes on 3:20), there is no good reason to find reference to the phrase here. Not only is it problematic to think that Paul would have thought of the law in conjunction with Jacob and Esau (for Paul elsewhere insists that the law was given long after the time of the patriarchs [Gal. 3:17]), but he clearly intends this phrase to be a generalized summary of v. 11a, where the reference is to any acts, whether good or evil. As I have argued elsewhere, "works of the law" is simply a subset of the more general "works"; and it is gratuitous to read the former into the latter (" 'Law,' 'Works of the Law' and Legalism in Paul," pp. 90-99; cf. also Cranfield, " 'Works of the Law,' " p. 97).

56. Gk. [οὐκ] ἐξ ἔργων.

57. In stating the principle this way, we are assuming that οὐκ ἐξ ἔργων ἀλλ᾽ ἐκ τοῦ καλοῦντος qualifies the word ἐκλογήν, or perhaps the whole phrase ἡ κατ᾽ ἐκλογήν πρόθεσις; see TEV: ". . . so God's choice was based on his call, and not on anything they had done." Grammatically, the clause could also go with μένῃ (e.g., Meyer) or ἐρρέθη in v. 12b (cf., e.g., the Vulgate: "non ex operibus, sed ex vocante dictum est ei . . ."; Kuss). But the meaning is essentially the same.

58. Gk. τοῦ καλοῦντος, a substantival participle.

59. As we noted earlier (see the notes on 8:28), Paul always uses the word "call" (καλέω), when God is its subject, of "an effective summons by which people are brought into relationship with himself." God's "call" here, then, is not an invitation (contra, e.g., Morison, *Exposition,* pp. 69-70). As we noted above (see the introduction to 9:6-29), καλέω is a key word in this section (see also vv. 24-25).

election.[60] But the contrast between human activity and God's activity suggests rather that Paul wants to base election in what God does and not in anything that the human being does.[61] Surely, if Paul had assumed that faith was the basis for God's election, he would have pointed this out when he raised the question in v. 14 about the fairness of God's election. All he would have needed to say at that point was "of course God is not unjust in choosing Jacob and rejected Esau, for his choosing took into account the faith of one and the unbelief of the other." Paul's silence on this point is telling. While, therefore, the phrase "not by works" does not in itself exclude faith as a basis for God's election (for Paul carefully distinguishes works and faith), I believe "on the basis of the God who calls" does.[62]

The point that Paul has been qualifying throughout vv. 10a-12a is now

60. See, e.g., Pelagius. See also Godet; S-H; Nygren; Morison, *Exposition,* pp. 269-70. For a fuller description of this typically Arminian approach to Paul's teaching on election here, see J. W. Cottrell, "Conditional Election," pp. 51-73. Wesley argues that Paul's point here is simply that God has the right to accept and reject any that he chooses; but the apostle is not here indicating the bases on which God might make that choice (pp. 556-58; cf. also Stevens, *Pauline Theology,* pp. 118-19). Many of the early Fathers of the church went much farther in attaching God's election to human response, arguing that Paul here is excluding only *past* works from election; foreseen works may still be a basis for God's choice (Schelkle mentions Chrysostom, Photius, and Theodoret). Paul's exclusion of "works" from God's election is probably directed against a certain segment of early Jewish theology; cf., e.g., Philo, *Allegorical Interpretation of the Laws* 3.88:

> Once again, of Jacob and Esau, when still in the womb, God declares that the one is a ruler and leader and master, but that Esau is a subject and slave. For God the Maker of living beings knoweth well the different pieces of his own handiwork, even before He has thoroughly chiselled and consummated them, and the faculties which they are to display at a later time, in a word their deeds [τὰ ἔργα] and experiences. And so when Rebecca, the soul that waits on God, goes to inquire of God, He tells her in reply, "Two nations are in thy womb, and two peoples shall be separated from thy belly, and one people shall be above the other people, and the elder shall serve the younger"; cf. Dunn.

61. As Hübner, *Gottes Ich und Israel,* pp. 24-25, notes, the contrast here is different from the contrast between faith and works that Paul has earlier used. See also Räisänen, "Paul, God, and Israel," p. 182.

62. Augustine, who at one point in his life allowed for foreseen faith as a basis for God's election (see *Propositions, ad loc.*), later, as a result of the Pelagian controversy, denied that God's election was based on anything in the human being (*Ad Simplicianum* 1.2.5-22); see W. S. Babcock, "Augustine's Interpretation of Romans (A.D. 394-396)," *Augustinian Studies* 10 (1979), 55-74; P. Fredriksen, "Augustine's Early Interpretation of Paul" (Ph.D. diss., Princeton University, 1979), pp. 268-73. See also Calvin; Murray; Käsemann; Kuss; Piper, 35-38; F. W. Maier, *Israel in der Heilsgeschichte nach Röm. 9–11* (Biblische Zeitfragen, 12.11/12; Münster: Aschendorff, 1929), pp. 410-14; Beyschlag, *Theodicee,* pp. 35-36. Fitzmyer claims that the text does not allow us to conclude what the basis for God's calling might have been.

finally expressed: "She [Rebecca] was told, 'The greater shall serve the lesser' " (Gen. 25:23b).[63] As Paul has already made clear, God makes this prediction about the relationship between Esau (the elder) and Jacob (the younger) after the twins are conceived but before they are born.

13 Paul's quotation of Mal. 1:2-3, introduced with one of Paul's favorite formulas ("just as it is written"[64]), restates v. 12b and expands on it by making clear that the contrasting destinies of Jacob and Esau were not simply seen in advance by God but were also caused by him.[65] Jacob's preeminence was the result of God's love for him; Esau's servitude was the result of God's "hate" for him.[66] What Paul means by this depends on the referents of the names "Jacob" and "Esau." For, in addition to denoting individual persons, both names are also used in the OT to designate the peoples, or nations, descended from each of them. As the father of the twelve men who gave their names to the "tribes" of Israel, Jacob was given by God himself the name "Israel" (Gen. 32:28). Correspondingly, then, "Jacob" can refer to the nation of Israel.[67] In the same way, Esau gives his name to the people of Edom who are his descendants.[68] That Paul may be using the names in this way is strongly suggested by the contexts from which he takes his quotations in vv. 12b and 13. Immediately before the prediction quoted by Paul in v. 12b come these words: " 'Two nations are in your womb, and two peoples born of you shall be divided' " (Gen. 25:23a). And it is clear from what comes after Mal. 1:2b-3a that the prophet is using the names Jacob and Esau to stand for the countries of Israel and Edom (see vv. 3b-5). God's "love" of Jacob will then refer to God's election of the people Israel, not of individuals; and his "hatred" of Esau, correspondingly, will denote his rejection of the nation of Edom. As a corollary of this corporate interpretation, it is then

63. Paul's quotation follows the LXX exactly, which explains the unusual use of μείζων and ἐλάσσων to denote the relative ages of individuals. For the LXX translates the Hebrew literally (וְרַב יַעֲבֹד צָעִיר), bringing into the Greek words the sense that the Hebrew words can possess. It should be noted, however, that the Greek words can be used of relative age outside the LXX (see BAGD, 497).

64. Gk. καθὼς γέγραπται.

65. Cranfield. He rightly dismisses the more nuanced interpretations according to which v. 13 provides the basis for the prediction in v. 12b (Jacob's preeminence the result of God's "love" for him — see Murray) or illustrates from history the truth of v. 12b (Jacob's preeminence seen in the history of Israel — see S-H).

66. Paul's quotation differs from the LXX is reversing the order of the first three words (LXX has ἠγάπησα τὸν Ἰακωβ). Paul's change, if conscious, is probably stylistic; he brings the first clause into exact parallel with the second (article-object-verb).

67. Cf., e.g., Num. 23:7; Ps. 14:7; Isa. 41:8; note esp. Isa. 59:20, quoted in Rom. 11:26.

68. Gen. 36:8: "Esau is Edom" (cf. vv. 1 and 43); note also Deut. 2:4, 5, 8, 12, 22, 29; Jer. 49:8, 10; Obadiah, passim.

further alleged that election here must not be election to salvation but election to a special and honored role in salvation history: "it is election to privilege that is in mind, not eternal salvation."[69]

Advocates of the corporate interpretation of these verses make a strong case. In the OT God's election is primarily his "calling out" of a people "for his own name": Israel. And, as the OT itself makes clear, this election of a people does not in itself guarantee eternal life for every Israelite person. We would expect Paul to be thinking of "election" here in the same terms, an expectation that seems to be confirmed by the OT texts that Paul quotes. Nevertheless, for all its strong points, I think that a corporate and salvation-historical interpretation of vv. 10-13 does not ultimately satisfy the data of the text. In addition to the general points I made in the introduction to this section, the following points are especially relevant to vv. 10-13.

First, Paul suggests that he is thinking of Jacob and Esau as individuals in vv. 10b-11a when he mentions their conception, birth, and "works" — language that is not easily applied to nations.[70] Second, several of Paul's key words and phrases in this passage are words he generally uses elsewhere with reference to the attaining of salvation; and, significantly, they occur with this sense in texts closely related to this one: "election" (see esp. 11:5, 7[71]); "call" (see esp. 8:28); and "[not] of works" (see esp. Rom. 4:2-8 and 11:6). These words are therefore difficult to apply to nations or peoples, for Paul clearly does not believe that peoples or nations — not even Israel — are chosen and called by God for salvation apart from their works. Third, as we noted earlier (see the introduction to 9:6b-13), a description here of how God calls nations to participate in the historical manifestation of his salvific acts runs counter to Paul's purpose in this paragraph. In order to justify his assertion in v. 6b that not all those who belong to "physical" Israel belong also to "spiritual" Israel, and thus to vindicate God's faithfulness (v. 6a), he must show that the OT justifies a discrimination within physical Israel in terms of the enjoyment of salvation. An assertion in these verses to the effect that God has "chosen" Israel rather than Edom for a positive role in the unfolding of the plan of salvation would not contribute to this argument at all.

For these reasons I believe that Paul is thinking mainly of Jacob and Esau as individuals rather than as nations and in terms of their own personal

---

69. Morris. See also, *inter alia,* Morison, *Exposition,* pp. 72-73; Bruce; Beyschlag, *Theodicee,* pp. 35-42; Klein, *New Chosen People,* p. 173; Müller, *Gottes Gerechtigkeit,* pp. 75-77; Prat, *Theology,* 1.252; Ellison, *Mystery,* pp. 48-49; Cranfield; Fitzmyer; W. S. Campbell, "The Freedom and Faithfulness of God in Relation to Israel," *JSNT* 13 (1981), 39; Huby; Leenhardt.

70. See Dunn.

71. This word is, however, used in a broader sense in 11:28. But 9:10-13 is more closely related to 11:1-11 than to 11:28.

relationship to the promise of God rather than of their roles in carrying out God's plan. The nations denoted by these names, we must remember, have come into existence in and through the individuals who first bore those names. In a context in which Paul begins speaking rather clearly about the individuals rather than the nations, we should not be surprised that he would apply a text that spoke of the nations to the individuals who founded and, in a sense "embodied" them. It is not the issue of how God uses different individuals or nations in accomplishing his purposes that is Paul's concern, but which individuals, and on what basis, belong to God's covenant people. This matter of "belonging to God's covenant people" is the bridge that connects Paul's appeal to the patriarchs to his own concerns. Paul appeals to OT history to establish a principle about the way in which God brings into being his own people.[72] What it means to belong to the New Covenant people may not be exactly the same as what it means to belong to the Old Covenant people; in this regard, for instance, Paul is not clearly asserting that Jacob and Isaac were saved while Esau and Ishmael were not.[73] But he is arguing that God in his own day is bringing into being a covenant people in the same way that he did in the days of the patriarchs: by choosing some and rejecting others.[74] So, Paul will make clear later in this text, some Jews are called by God to be part of his people (vv. 24-29), while others have, for the time being at least, been rejected.[75]

This brings us back to our original question: What does Paul mean by

72. See Luz, 70-72; Rese, "Israel und Kirche," p. 212; Koch, 302-5; Brandenburger, "Schriftauslegung," pp. 13-15. Käsemann, 204, thinks that Paul views Jacob and Esau as "types." But this puts too much emphasis on comparison between Jacob and Esau on the one hand and Jewish Christians and Jews on the other. Paul's attention is on the way Jacob and Esau illustrate the nature of God's electing activity.

73. As J. Jocz points out, Jews, reflecting OT teaching, believe that they are chosen because they belong to a particular nation; most Christians, including, I would argue, Paul, believe that one belongs to a particular people, the church, because one is chosen (J. Jocz, *The Jewish People and Jesus Christ: The Relationship between Church and Synagogue* [3d ed.; Grand Rapids: Baker, 1979], p. 312). This point, of course, assumes that election to salvation in the NT is individual rather than corporate (contra, e.g., Barth, *CD* 2/2; Klein, *Chosen People;* for the problems involved in the corporate election view in the NT, see Schreiner, "Romans 9," pp. 35-37).

Although Esau is excluded from future reward in some rabbinic texts (Str-B, 3.269), Heb. 12:16, in which the readers are warned not to "become like Esau, an immoral and godless person," would seem to suggest that at least one NT author took the same viewpoint. The OT, likewise, takes a less than positive view of Esau's spiritual state (see Gen. 25:29-34; 26:35). In view of this, Cranfield's emphasis on God's "merciful care" for Esau (2.480) would seem to be misplaced.

74. See especially here Calvin.

75. Hübner is right, then, to insist that the distinction here between Jacob and Esau reflects the divided state of Israel in Paul's own day (*Gottes Ich und Israel,* pp. 27-28).

asserting that God "loved" Jacob but "hated"[76] Esau? The connection of this quotation with v. 12 suggests that God's love is the same as his election: God chose Jacob to inherit the blessings promised first to Abraham. God's "hatred" of Esau is more difficult to interpret because Paul does not furnish us at this point with contextual clues. Some understand Paul to mean only that God loved Esau less than he loved Jacob.[77] He blessed both, but Jacob was used in a more positive and basic way in the furtherance of God's plans. But a better approach is to define "hatred" here by its opposite, "love." If God's love of Jacob consists in his choosing Jacob to be the "seed" who would inherit the blessings promised to Abraham, then God's hatred of Esau is best understood to refer to God's decision not to bestow this privilege on Esau.[78] It might best be translated "reject."[79] "Love" and "hate" are not here, then, emotions that God feels but actions that he carries out. In an apparent paradox that troubles Paul (cf. 9:14 and 19 following) as well as many Christians, God loves "the whole world" at the same time as he withholds his love in action, or election, from some.

Before leaving this paragraph, we must put some of the issues it raises in a larger context. As the attentive reader will realize, I have argued that this passage gives strong exegetical support to a traditional Calvinistic interpretation of God's election: God chooses those who will be saved on the basis of his own will and not on the basis of anything — works or faith, whether foreseen or not — in those human beings so chosen. Attempts to avoid this theological conclusion, whether by leaving room for human faith in v. 12 or by restricting the issue to the roles of nations in salvation history, are, I think, unsuccessful. But if we exclude faith as a basis for God's choice here, what becomes of Paul's strenuous defense of faith as the means of justification in Rom. 3:21–4:25 and again in the following section of the letter, 9:30–10:21? It is precisely in an attempt to do justice to these texts that many interpreters

---

76. Gk. ἐμίσησα.

77. This interpretation finds in the contrast of "love" and "hate" a Semitism in which the two contrasting elements are not directly opposed but put in a relative relationship with one another. Examples of love and hate in such a relative contrast are Gen. 29:30-33; Deut. 21:15; Matt. 6:24; John 12:25; see also Luke 14:26. See Tholuck; Shedd; Hodge; Fitzmyer.

78. Paul's stress on the divine decision in this rejection could again be polemical: *Biblical Antiquities,* e.g., quotes Mal. 1:2b-3a this way: "God loved Jacob, but he hated Esau because of his deeds" (32:5).

79. As R. L. Smith points out, "love" and "hate" in Mal. 1:2-3 reflect the covenant: God has chosen Jacob and "not chosen," or rejected, Esau (*Micah-Malachi* [WBC; Waco, TX: Word, 1984], p. 305). Cf. also Calvin; Cranfield; Schlier; Michel; Käsemann. Only here in the NT is God said to hate anyone; in the OT, see Ps. 5:6; 11:5; Jer. 12:8. God's hatred of sinners is mentioned in intertestamental wisdom books (e.g., Wis. 14:9-10; Sir. 12:6; 27:24), but these lack the covenantal flavor of Malachi and Paul.

insist on finding room for faith in this text also: God's choice, they argue, is a choice to bestow his salvation on those who believe. Faith, then, in this traditional Arminian perspective, becomes the basis for God's choice.

I can only reiterate that the introduction into this text of *any* basis for God's election outside God himself defies both the language and the logic of what Paul has written. The only logical possibility, then, would seem to be to reverse the relationship between God's choosing and faith; as Augustine stated it: "God does not choose us because we believe, but that we may believe."[80] This way of putting the matter seems generally to be justified by this passage and by the teaching of Scripture elsewhere. But it comes perilously close to trivializing human faith: something that many texts in Romans and in the rest of the NT simply will not allow us to do. We need, perhaps, to be more cautious in our formulations and to insist on the absolute cruciality and meaningfulness of the human decision to believe at the same time as we rightly make God's choosing of us ultimately basic. Such a double emphasis may strain the boundaries of logic (it does not, I trust, break them!) or remain unsatisfyingly complex, but it may have the virtue of reflecting Scripture's own balanced perspective.[81]

At stake in all this, as Paul makes clear in 11:5-7, a text that takes up the argument of these verses, is the grace of God. As we have seen (see the notes on 3:24 and 4:5), Paul rules out any human claim on God as a violation of his grace. Perhaps, as my Arminian friends and colleagues insist, foreseen faith, as the product of "prevenient" grace, need be no threat to God's freedom and grace. But by making the human decision to believe the crucial point of distinction between those who are saved and those who are not, and thus making God's election a response to human choice, this perspective seems to me to minimize Paul's insistence that election to salvation is itself an act of God's grace (cf. 11:5): a decision he makes freely and without the compulsion of any influence outside himself.

2. Objections Answered: The Freedom and Purpose of God (9:14-23)

14*What then shall we say? There is no unrighteousness with God, is there? By no means!* 15*For to Moses he says, "I will have mercy on whomever I have mercy, and I will have compassion on whomever I*

---

80. *Predestination of the Saints* 17.34.

81. For the understanding of the relationship between God's sovereignty and human responsibility that underlies this approach, see J. Feinberg, "God Ordains All Things," in *Predestination and Free Will* (ed. D. and R. Basinger; Downers Grove, IL: InterVarsity, 1986), pp. 17-43; Carson, *Divine Sovereignty,* cf. pp. 201-22. Michel (p. 341) and Dinkler ("Predestination," pp. 256-57) argue God's election and human believing cannot be put into a logical relationship to one another.

have compassion."[a] 16Therefore it is not a matter of the person who wills or the person who runs, but of the God who shows mercy. 17For the Scripture says to Pharaoh, "For this very reason I have raised you up, so that I might demonstrate through you my power and so that my name might be proclaimed in all the earth."[b] 18Therefore he has mercy on whomever he wishes, and he hardens whomever he wishes.

19You will then say to me, "Why then[1] does he still find fault? For who resists his will?" 20On the contrary, O man,[2] who are you to answer back to God? "That which is molded does not say to the molder, 'Why did you make me in this way?' does it?"[c] 21Or does the potter not have authority over the clay, to make from the same lump both a vessel for honor and a vessel for dishonor? 22But what if God, wishing to demonstrate his wrath and to make known his power, bore with much patience vessels of wrath, prepared for destruction, 23and[3] in order to make known the riches of his glory to vessels of mercy, whom he prepared beforehand for glory?

    a. Exod. 33:19b
    b. Exod. 9:16
    c. Isa. 29:16

These verses are a detour from the main road of Paul's argument. Paul takes this detour because he knows that his insistence on God's initiative in determining who should be saved and who rejected (see vv. 10-13 especially) will meet with questions and even objections. Appropriately, therefore, Paul reverts to the diatribe style, with its question-and-answer format and references to a

---

1. This translation reflects the Gk. οὖν, found in P[46], the primary Alexandrian MS B, and the western uncials D, F, and G. It is omitted in the other primary Alexandrian uncial, ℵ, the secondary Alexandrian uncial A, Ψ, and the majority text. Cranfield supports the omission, arguing that a copyist may have added it to match similar expressions (2.489 n. 4). But the combination of P[46], B, and the western tradition is a strong one; and it is equally probable that a copyist omitted an original οὖν to avoid repeating it so soon after v. 19a.

2. This translation follows the majority of the Alexandrian tradition (the original hand of ℵ, A, [B], 81, 1739, and a few other MSS) in reading ὦ ἄνθρωπε, μενοῦνγε. Other alternatives are (1) to place μενοῦνγε in the first position (cf. the second corrector of ℵ and the western uncial D, Ψ, and the majority text; cf. Käsemann, 269) or to omit it (as does the early papyrus P[46], the original hand of D, and the later western tradition [F, G]). But both are probably secondary attempts to clarify a difficult text, the position of μενοῦνγε after a vocative being unusual (cf. Wilckens, 2.201).

3. The syntactical problems presented by these verses have resulted in the omission of καί, "and," in a few MSS (the primary Alexandrian uncial B being the most important; cf. also several minuscules, including 1739[mg]). The difficulty of the word is a strong case for its inclusion (Dunn, 2.550).

dialogue partner, that he has utilized earlier in the letter (see 2:1–3:8; 3:27-31; 6–7). While Paul himself formulates these questions in order to carry on his argument, they undoubtedly represent objections that Paul has heard frequently during his ministry.[4] Indeed, these questions state the inevitable human response to an insistence on the sovereignty of God in salvation: if God decides apart from anything in the human being whom he will choose and whom he will reject (v. 13), how can he still be "righteous" (v. 14) — and how can he blame people if they reject him (v. 19)?

Paul responds to the first question with citations of and comments on Scripture (vv. 15-18) and to the second with a series of rhetorical questions (vv. 20-23). These responses are not what we might expect. Paul does not attempt to show how God's choice of human beings for salvation fits with their own "choosing" of God in faith. Quite the contrary: rather than compromising the apparent absolute and unqualified nature of God's election, he reasserts it in even stronger terms. God not only has mercy on whomever he wants, he also hardens whomever he wants (v. 18). God's freedom to act in this way, Paul suggests, while directed toward a definite end (vv. 22-23), is the freedom of the Creator toward his creatures, and cannot be qualified (vv. 20-21). Many commentators are troubled by Paul's apparent disregard for human choice and responsibility. Dodd criticizes the argument here as "a false step."[5] O'Neill goes further, claiming the teaching is "thoroughly immoral,"[6] and follows a number of the church fathers in ascribing the offending verses to someone other than Paul.[7] These criticisms are sometimes the product of a false assumption: that Paul's justification of the ways of God in his treatment of human beings (his "theodicy") must meet the standard set by our own assumptions and standards of logic. Paul's approach is quite different. He considers his theodicy to be successful if it justifies God's acts against the standards of his revelation in Scripture (vv. 15-18) and his character as Creator (vv. 20-23). In other words, the standard by which God must be judged is

---

4. The questions in the text are raised by Paul himself (especially clear in v. 14b, with the use of μή to signal an expected negative answer to the question). But they undoubtedly reflect actual accusations brought against Paul (see, e.g., Wilckens, 2.199), perhaps by Jews or Jewish Christians who held the popular Pharisaic conception of a cooperation between God and human beings in salvation (see esp. Maier, *Mensch*).

5. Dodd, 157; he further characterizes vv. 19-21 as "the weakest point in the whole epistle" (p. 159).

6. His comment is on v. 18 specifically (p. 158).

7. O'Neill thinks vv. 14-23 are a later interpolation, while many of the Fathers considered at least vv. 14-19 to be Paul's quotation of his opponents' viewpoint (see Schelkle [341-43], who names Origen, Diodorus, Theodore of Mopsuestia, and Chrysostom; Pelagius attributed vv. 15-19 to an objector). Erasmus early in his career held a similar view (see J. B. Payne, "Erasmus on Romans 9:6-24," in *The Bible in the Sixteenth Century* [ed. D. C. Steinmetz; Durham, NC: Duke University, 1990], pp. 119-35).

nothing less and nothing more than God himself.[8] Judged by this standard, Paul contends, God is indeed "just." Paul does not provide a logically compelling resolution of the two strands of his teaching — God, by his own sovereign choice, elects human beings to salvation; human beings, by a responsible choice of their will, must believe in order to be saved. But criticism of the apostle on this score is unfair. It is unfair, first, because Paul can accomplish his purpose — showing God to be just — without such a resolution. And it is unfair, second, because no resolution of this perennial paradox seems possible this side of heaven.

14 The opening question — "What then shall we say?" — is typical of the questions Paul uses at several points in Romans to advance his argument.[9] At some points such questions introduce clarifications of Paul's teaching (e.g., 6:1; 7:7). Here, however, it introduces a defense of his teaching, for the following question embodies an accusation: if God on the basis of nothing but his own choice (v. 12) determines who is to be saved and who rejected (v. 13), then there is "unrighteousness with God."[10] The criticism Paul raises is that, in choosing and rejecting individuals apart from their own merits or faith, God has acted "against what is right" (Gk. *adikia*). The standard assumed for "what is right" might be general considerations of justice, in which case the objector might be accusing Paul of attributing to God a way of acting that is "unfair" or "partial."[11] But the word "unrighteousness" comes from a Greek word group that is used in both the OT and in Paul with reference to God's faithfulness to his promises and to his covenant with Israel. Paul may, then, be reflecting a specifically Jewish objection to the effect that God's choosing and rejecting whomever he wants is incompatible with their understanding of his promises to Israel.[12] However, as I have argued earlier, Paul also uses "righteousness" language to refer to God's faithfulness to his own person and character.[13] And the course of Paul's argument suggests that, in Paul's answer at least, it is ultimately this standard, revealed in Scripture and

---

8. See Munck: ". . . the difference between Paul and his Jewish adversaries lies in his refusal to measure God by human standards" (*Christ and Israel,* p. 44). Müller notes that Greek theodicies usually dealt with God's "righteousness" in the context of a general norm of "fairness," while Paul answers the question of God's ἀδικία with an assertion of God's ἐξουσία ("authority") (*Gottes Gerechtigkeit,* pp. 84-85).

9. Gk. τί οὖν ἐροῦμεν; see 6:1; 7:7. He uses the same expression in 9:30 and a similar one in 3:5 and 4:1; see also 3:3, 9; 6:15; 11:7.

10. The Gk. παρὰ [τῷ θεῷ] may reflect the Heb. עַם (Str-B, 3.79-80; Michel). See, however, BAGD (610) for the possibility of a native Greek explanation.

11. E.g., Murray; Käsemann; Zeller.

12. See, e.g., Beyschlag, *Theodicee,* pp. 43-45; Maier, *Mensch,* p. 367; Viard; Wilckens; Dunn.

13. See the excursus after 1:17.

in creation, against which God's acts must be measured.[14] But this is to anticipate. At this point, Paul simply rejects the charge about God's unrighteousness with his characteristic "By no means!"[15]

15 The "for"[16] introducing this verse shows that Paul is not content simply to reject the accusation that God is unrighteous: he will also explain why that rejection is justified. The first part of Paul's explanation uses Scripture to show that God's unconstrained decision to choose Jacob and reject Esau was no isolated case but reflects God's very nature (vv. 15 and 17). Continuing the trend of this passage (see vv. 7, 9, 12, and 13), Paul cites OT texts in which God himself speaks. Such texts constitute the most important evidence we can have about God's essence and ways of acting.[17]

Paul's first citation is from Exod. 33:19b.[18] In the Exodus context, Moses requests that the Lord show him his glory. The Lord replies by promising to cause all his "goodness" to pass in front of Moses and to proclaim to him his name, "the LORD." Then follow the words that Paul here cites. Justifiably, Paul finds in God's words to Moses a revelation of one of God's basic characteristics: his freedom to bestow mercy on whomever he chooses. It is against this ultimate standard, not the penultimate standard of God's covenant with Israel, that God's "righteousness" must be measured.[19] Paul's reference to Moses reinforces the point, for it is to the mediator of the covenant himself that God reveals his freedom in mercy.[20]

16 Paul now spells out the conclusion ("therefore"[21]) he wants to draw from his quotation: "it is not a matter of the person who wills or the

---

14. Slight (though negative) support for this interpretation may be found in the fact that the LXX uses ἀδικία with reference to God only three times (Deut. 32:4; 2 Chron. 19:7; Ps. 91:16 [LXX]). We might have expected more occurrences if the word had the covenantal connotations that the other interpretation assumes. (Paul uses the word with reference to God only here.) My own view is similar to that of Piper, 70-73.

15. Gk. μὴ γένοιτο. The form of Paul's question, using the Greek particle μή, already assumes this negative response (see the translation above).

16. Gk. γάρ.

17. See, again, esp. Hübner, *Gottes Ich und Israel.*

18. The text agrees with the LXX exactly (the Hebrew underlying the text explains the unusual transitive use of οἰκτηρέω; see BDF 148[2]). Godet thinks that there may be a difference in meaning between ἐλεέω and οἰκτιρέω (heart attitude versus outward expression), but the words are probably synonymous here.

19. See esp. Piper, 55-68, for development of the connection between God's "righteousness" and the revelation of his "name" and "glory" in Exod. 33:19. Paul will in due course show that God is faithful to his covenant with Israel as well (see esp. chap. 11).

20. It is Moses' role as mediator of the Old Covenant, then, and not as examplar of works (contra Maier, *Israel in der Heilsgeschichte,* pp. 417-19; Byrne, 134), that accounts for his name being mentioned here.

21. Gk. ἄρα οὖν.

person who runs, but of the God who shows mercy." The sentence reads like a general principle (note the present tenses of the verbs). But to what does the principle apply? Our translation preserves the ambiguity of the original in not making clear the subject of the sentence ("it"). We might substitute "salvation"[22] or "God's purpose in election" (cf. v. 11b),[23] but the connection with v. 15 suggests rather "God's bestowal of mercy."[24] In keeping with a popular view of this passage as a whole, many commentators think that the "mercy" involved here is God's mercy in choosing different persons or nations in the outworking of his historical plan.[25] But, as we have seen earlier (see esp. the notes on v. 13), Paul's use of OT examples of God's choosing and rejecting develop a principle that he applies to the salvation of individual Jews and Gentiles in his own day (see 9:3, 6a, 22-23, 24).[26] Here, the principle Paul formulates moves beyond the positive assertion of v. 15 — God's bestowal of mercy has its origin in his own will to be merciful — to its negative corollary — God's mercy does not, then, depend[27] on human "willing" or "running." The former denotes one's inner desire, purpose, or readiness to do something[28]; the latter the actual execution of that desire.[29] Together, then, they "sum up the totality of man's capacity."[30]

17 In vv. 15-16 Paul reiterates and expands the positive side of God's sovereignty in election that he alluded to in vv. 10-13 ("Jacob I have loved"). Now Paul will do the same with respect to the "negative" side ("Esau I have rejected"). Verses 17-18 parallel vv. 15-16: Paul begins by citing Scripture and then states a principle drawn from it (note, as in v. 16, the "therefore"

22. Hodge.
23. Z-G, 480.
24. E.g., S-H; Kuss; Cranfield.
25. E.g., Leenhardt.
26. See, e.g., Kuss; Käsemann; Murray; and esp. Piper, 137.
27. The genitive participial phrases are best classified as genitives of "source": "God's bestowal of mercy does not 'come from' a person's willing or running, but 'comes from' the God who shows mercy."
28. Gk. θέλω; Paul often contrasts the word with "doing"; see esp. Phil. 2:13; Rom. 7:15-20.
29. Paul's metaphorical use of "run" (Gk. τρέχω) may come from the sphere of Greco-Roman athletics (Wilckens; see 1 Cor. 9:24, 26; other Pauline references: Gal. 2:2; 5:7; Phil. 2:16; 2 Thess. 3:1) or, more likely, from Jewish references to "walking" or "running" (see Ps. 119:32) according to the will of God (see B. Noack, "Celui qui court (Rom. IX,16)," *ST* 24 [1970], 113-116; Maier, *Mensch*, pp. 368-70; Piper, 132-33; Dunn). The possible Jewish background does not, however, mean that Paul is referring *only* to the doing of the law (contra Viard). All "doing" must be intended, including, of course, human works that God foresees (contra many of the Fathers of the church: see Schelkle).
30. Dunn.

in v. 18). The "for"[31] introducing v. 17 may, then, function as does its counterpart in v. 15 and indicate that vv. 17-18 contain a second reason to reject the accusation that God is unjust.[32]

14 Is God unjust?
15 A [No], because *(gar)* it says *(legei)* . . .
16 Therefore *(ara oun)* . . .
17 B [No], because *(gar)* Scripture says *(legei)*
18 Therefore *(ara oun)* . . .

It is also possible, however, that the "for" connects vv. 17-18 to v. 16, as a further illustration of God's sovereign freedom in bestowing mercy.[33] However, vv. 17-18 can hardly be an explanation of God's mercy in v. 16 since the "hardening" that Paul illustrates in v. 17 is, according to v. 18, antithetical to "mercy." Verses 17-18 probably relate mainly to v. 14, although there may be a secondary connection with v. 16 as Paul develops from another side the primacy of God's will that v. 16 implies.[34]

As in v. 15, Paul introduces the OT quotation with the verb "says" and specifies the person to whom the text is addressed ("to Pharaoh"; cf. "to Moses" in v. 15).[35] The words are again from Exodus, from the Lord's instructions to Moses about what he is to say to Pharaoh on the sixth occasion that Moses and Aaron are told to go before the Egyptian ruler to demand the release of the people of Israel (9:16). Paul's wording, "I have raised you up,"[36] differs from both the standard Greek LXX text and the Hebrew MT.[37] Various explanations for the differences have been offered,[38] but it seems

31. Gk. γάρ.

32. E.g., Cranfield.

33. Achtemeier; Dunn.

34. See Piper, 138-39.

35. Hübner notes a difference as well: the subject of the verb λέγει in v. 15 is presumably God, while in v. 17 the subject is ἡ γραφή (*Gottes Ich und Israel,* p. 45). Contra Hübner, however, the difference is probably inconsequential.

36. Gk. ἐξήγειρα.

37. The MT reads: וְאוּלָם בַּעֲבוּר זֹאת הֶעֱמַדְתִּיךָ בַּעֲבוּר הַרְאֹתְךָ אֶת כֹּחִי וּלְמַעַן סַפֵּר שְׁמִי בְּכָל הָאָרֶץ; the LXX: καὶ ἕνεκεν τούτου διετηρήθης, ἵνα ἐνδείξωμαι ἐν σοὶ τὴν ἰσχύν μου, καὶ ὅπως διαγγελῇ τὸ ὄνομά μου ἐν πάσῃ τῇ γῇ. Two of Paul's differences from the LXX are minor and probably are due to Paul's own stylistic preferences: his use of εἰς αὐτὸ τοῦτο in place of ἕνεκεν τούτου and his δύναμιν in place of ἰσχύν (Koch, 141).

38. Some (e.g., Michel) think that Paul may be conforming more closely to the Hebrew: the MT הֶעֱמַדְתִּיךָ, a hiphil form from the root עמד, may mean "cause to stand" (or, perhaps, "maintain"; cf. BDB). Others suggest that Paul may be dependent on a variant Greek text (Stanley, *Paul and the Language of Scripture,* pp. 107-8).

reasonable to conclude that Paul has deliberately accentuated God's initiative in the process.[39] The verb "raise up" probably, then, has the connotation "appoint to a significant role in salvation history."[40] Of particular importance in the quotation is the purpose of God's raising Pharaoh up: "so that I might demonstrate through you[41] my power and so that my name might be proclaimed in all the earth." Indeed, this purpose clause is probably the reason that Paul has cited this particular text since its lack of explicit reference to Pharaoh's "hardening" makes it less suitable than others as a preparation for Paul's conclusion in v. 18.[42] Paul wants to make clear that even God's "negative" actions, such as the hardening of Pharaoh, serve a positive purpose (a point Paul will develop further in vv. 22-23). And this positive purpose is the greatest imaginable: the demonstration of God's power[43] and the wider proclamation of God's name. In Pharaoh's day, the plagues on the land of Egypt and the deliverance of Israel through the "Sea of Reeds," made necessary by Pharaoh's hardened heart, accomplished this purpose (see Josh. 2:10). In Paul's day, he implies, the hardening that has come upon a "part of Israel" (see 11:5-7, 25) has likewise led to the name of God being "proclaimed in all the earth" through the mission to the Gentiles.[44]

18 Anyone who knows the Exodus story would understand that God "raised up" Pharaoh with a negative rather than a positive purpose. By

39. Kuss; Cranfield; Lagrange.

40. See Zech. 11:16; Hab. 1:6; Jer. 50:41 (LXX 27:41); cf. Murray. Others have suggested the connotation of "cause to come into existence" (*GEL* 13.83 [as one possibility]) or "incite, arouse [to hardness]" (G. K. Beale, "An Exegetical and Theological Consideration of the Hardening of Pharaoh's Heart in Exodus 4–14 and Romans 9," *TrinJ* 5 [1984], 151). The verb occurs elsewhere in the NT only in 1 Cor. 6:14, with reference to the physical resurrection of dead Christians (it is a v.l. in Mark 6:45).

41. I am giving ἐν an instrumental sense. This word corresponds to the LXX but differs from the MT, where the corresponding second person singular pronoun is the object of the verb: "that I might show *to* you" (הֶרְאֹתְךָ).

42. H. Räisänen, *The Idea of Divine Hardening: A Comparative Study of the Notion of Divine Hardening, Leading Astray and Inciting to Evil in the Bible and Qur'an* (Publications of the Finnish Exegetical Society 25; Helsinki: n.p., 1972), p. 81. Paul's use of the emphatic εἰς αὐτὸ τοῦτο (BDF paraphrase "just this [and nothing else]"; 290[6]) accentuates the purpose clause.

43. The debate over whether this power is God's saving power (Cranfield; Dunn) or his power in judgment (Käsemann) is probably misguided. While salvation is certainly the overriding concern in both Exodus and here in Rom. 9, judgment on God's enemies is certainly included as well.

44. I consider it likely, therefore, that Paul sees a similarity between Pharaoh and unbelieving Israel (with, e.g., Barth, *Shorter;* Cranfield; Byrne, 135; Räisänen, "Paul, God, and Israel," 182-83). A parallel, however, between Pharaoh as oppressor of Israel and unbelieving Jews as persecutors of the church (asserted by Munck, *Christ and Israel,* pp. 47-48) is without foundation in Rom. 9–11.

resisting God's will to deliver his people from bondage, Pharaoh caused that deliverance to assume a more spectacular aspect than it would have otherwise. Pharaoh's resistance to God's purpose is caused, according to Exod. 4–14, by his "hardness" of heart. It is this concept that connects vv. 17 and 18, as Paul now states a principle of God's acting that Pharaoh's experience serves to illustrate: God hardens "whomever he wishes." But Paul expands the principle to reiterate God's freedom in bestowing mercy as well. This shows that v. 18 embodies a conclusion drawn from all of vv. 15-17. As God's self-revelation to Moses demonstrates that he is a God who freely bestows mercy on "whomever he wishes," so God's words to Pharaoh reveal that he is at the same time a God who hardens "whomever he wishes."

I have argued that Paul intends his assertion of the freedom of God in showing mercy to apply to the salvation of individuals (see v. 16). This must certainly be true here also. But does the other part of the principle, God's hardening, also have such an application? The term "harden" (Gk. *sklērynō*) occurs 14 times in Exod. 4–14, where it has the connotation "make spiritually insensitive."[45] Many scholars, noting that Pharaoh's role in Exodus is purely salvation-historical and that reference to his own final spiritual condition is foreign to the context, insist that Paul applies God's hardening only to the processes of history. God prevents some people, or nations, from understanding his work and message in order to further his plan of salvation; no implications for the ultimate destiny of the individuals concerned are present.[46] However, this limitation of Paul's language to the sphere of historical process, which we have seen to be unlikely in earlier texts (vv. 12-13, 16), is particularly difficult here. In addition to the points I have made earlier with reference to Paul's purpose in this section as a whole, we may note the following.

First, structural and linguistic considerations show that v. 18 is closely related to vv. 22-23, where the "vessels of mercy, destined to glory" are contrasted with "vessels of wrath, prepared for destruction." As God's mercy leads to the enjoyment of glory, God's hardening brings wrath and destruction. Second, the word group "harden" is consistently used in Scripture to depict a spiritual condition that renders one unreceptive and disobedient to God and his word.[47] Third, while the Greek word is a different one, most scholars

45. In secular Greek, σκληρύνω is usually used in medical contexts, with reference to the hardness of bones, and so on (cf. K. L. and M. A. Schmidt, *TDNT* V, 1030).

46. See, e.g., Gaugler; Cranfield; Munck, *Christ and Israel*, 44-45; L. J. Kuyper, "The Hardening of Heart according to Biblical Perspective," *SJT* 27 (1974), 459-74.

47. Outside Exod. 4–14, σκληρύνω occurs 23 times in the LXX. Eight of these are not relevant to our discussion since they do not refer to persons (Gen. 49:7; Judg. 4:24; 2 Kgdms. 19:44; 4 Kgdms. 2:10; 2 Chron. 10:4; 36:13; Ps. 89:6; 1 Macc. 2:30). Of the 15 remaining texts, 13 refer to a spiritual condition that leads people to fail to revere God, obey his laws, and the like (Deut. 10:16; 4 Kgdms. 17:14; 2 Chron. 30:8;

recognize that Paul's references to Israel's "hardening" in Rom. 11:7 and 25 are parallel to the hardening here.[48] Yet the hardening in Rom. 11 is a condition that excludes people from salvation.[49] Fourth, it is even possible that the references to Pharaoh's hardening in Exodus carry implications for his own spiritual state and destiny.[50]

God's hardening, then, is an action that renders a person insensitive to God and his word and that, if not reversed, culminates in eternal damnation. We have seen that Paul has insisted that God bestows his mercy on his own initiative, apart from anything that a person is or does (v. 16). The strict parallelism in this verse suggests that the same is true of God's hardening: as he has mercy on "whomever he wishes," so he hardens "whomever he wishes." However, many scholars deny that this is the case. They point particularly to Exod. 4–14, where the first reference to God's hardening of Pharaoh (9:12) comes only after references to Pharaoh's hardening of his own heart (8:11, 28).[51] This background implies, these scholars argue, that Paul would think of God's hardening as a

---

Neh. 9:16, 17, 29; Ps. 94:8; Jer. 7:25; 17:19; 19:15; 1 Esdr. 1:48). Note esp. Isa. 63:17: "Why have you led us astray, LORD, from your way, why have you hardened our hearts so that we do not fear you?" Paul does not use σκληρύνω elsewhere, but he uses a cognate word in Rom. 2:5, where he accuses people (and especially Jews) of storing up wrath for themselves by their "hard" (σκληρότητα) and impenitent hearts. Luke uses σκληρύνω for those who refused to obey the word of the Lord and publicly maligned "the Way" (Acts 19:9). The only other occurrences of σκληρύνω in the NT come in Hebrews, where the author applies the warning of Ps. 94:8 to his readers: "Do not harden your hearts" (3:8, 13, 15; 4:7). Note also σκληροκαρδία in Matt. 19:8; Mark 10:5 and σκληροτράχηλος in Acts 7:51.

48. The Greek word in Rom. 11:7 is πωρόω and in 11:25 πώρωσις. See, e.g., K. L. and M. A. Schmidt, *TDNT* V, 1030: σκληρύνω has "exactly the same sense as πωρόω." This word and its cognate πώρωσις also refer to a person's spiritual obduracy throughout the NT (Mark 3:5; 6:52; 8:17; John 12:40; 2 Cor. 3:14; Eph. 4:18). For a brief lexical analysis of the words, see K. L. Schmidt, "Die Verstockung des Menschen durch Gott: Eine lexikologische und biblisch-theologische Studie," *TZ* 1 (1945), 1-17.

49. In v. 7, the "rest" who are hardened are contrasted with the remnant who have obtained righteousness (see 9:30-31), while in v. 25 it is the removal of Israel's "hardening" that prepares the way for her salvation.

50. See Beale, "Hardening of Pharaoh's Heart," pp. 151-54.

51. The LXX does not use σκληρύνω in 8:11 and 28, but the concept is the same, and it is likely that Paul would have viewed all the references to hardening in this context together, whatever the Greek or Hebrew word involved. In all, there are three relevant Hebrew words (חזק [4:21; 7:13, 22; 8:15; 9:12, 35; 10:20, 27; 11:10; 14:4, 8, 17]; כבד [7:14; 8:11, 28; 9:7, 34; 10:1]; and קשה [7:3; 13:15]) and three Greek words (σληρύνω [4:21; 7:22; 8:15; 9:12, 35; 10:1, 20, 27; 11:10; 13:15; 14:4, 8, 17]; κατισχύω [7:13]; and βαρύνω [7:14; 8:11, 28; 9:7, 34]). Some OT scholars think that the different words for hardening may reflect different sources; see, e.g., R. R. Wilson, "The Hardening of Pharaoh's Heart," *CBQ* 41 (1979), 18-36.

response to a person's prior decision to harden himself or herself.[52] God's hardening may then be likened to his "handing over" of sinners to the sin that they had already chosen for themselves (see Rom. 1:24, 26, 28). Yet the assumption that Paul expects his readers to see behind God's hardening a prior self-hardening on the part of the individual is questionable.

First, Exod. 4–14 does not clearly indicate that Pharaoh's hardening of his own heart was the basis for God's hardening; in fact, it may well imply that Pharaoh's hardening of his own heart was the result of God's prior act of hardening.[53] Second, Paul's "whomever he wishes" shows that God's decision to harden is his alone to make and is not constrained by any consideration having to do with a person's status or actions. Third, if Paul had in fact wanted his readers to assume that God's hardening was based on a person's self-hardening, we would have expected him to make this clear in response to the objection in v. 19. What more natural response to the objection that God is unfair in "finding fault" with a person than to make clear that God's hardening is based on a person's own prior action?[54]

The "hardening" Paul portrays here, then, is a sovereign act of God that is not *caused* by anything in those individuals who are hardened.[55] And 9:22-23 and 11:7 suggest that the outcome of hardening is damnation. It seems, then, that this text, in its context, provides important exegetical support for the controversial doctrine of "double predestination": just as God decides, on the basis of nothing but his own sovereign pleasure, to bestow his grace and so save some individuals, so he also decides, on the basis of nothing but his own sovereign pleasure, to pass over others and so to damn them.[56] Many

52. See, e.g., Chrysostom; Morison, *Exposition,* 134-47; Lenski; Morris; Leenhardt; Godet; Brunner; Klein, *New Chosen People,* pp. 166-67; Fitzmyer.

53. Before Pharaoh is said to harden his own heart, God twice predicts that he would harden Pharaoh's heart (4:21 and 7:3), and there are also five references, in the passive voice, to Pharaoh's heart being hardened (7:13, 14, 22; 8:11, 15). The understood subject of these passive verbs is probably God. See esp. Piper, 139-52; Beale, "Hardening of Pharaoh's Heart," pp. 129-54.

54. See, e.g., Augustine, *Letters* 194.8.35 (*PL* 33.886); Calvin, *Institutes* 22.3.8. For the general argument of this paragraph see esp. Piper, 152-59. As Dunn puts it, "to look for reasons for God's hardening in Pharaoh's 'evil disposition' or previous self-hardening . . . is a rationalizing expediency" (2.555). It is interesting that the rabbis later criticized the "minim" (e.g., Jewish Christians) for using Exod. 10:1 — "I [the LORD] have hardened his [Pharaoh's] heart" — in stressing too strongly God's sovereignty with respect to evil (*Exod. Rab.* 13; cf. Str-B, 3.269).

55. For a similar conclusion, see Calvin; Meyer; Michel; Murray; Käsemann; Kuss; Maier, *Mensch,* pp. 368-72; Beale, "Hardening of Pharaoh's Heart," pp. 151-54; Räisänen, "Paul, God, and Israel," pp. 182-83; Luz, 74-78; Piper, 156-60.

56. The doctrine of double predestination has its roots in Augustine and was taught by some early medieval theologians (Gottschalk [b. 805] is one of the best known

scholars argue, however, that God's hardening of an individual is not final. They note that Romans clearly teaches that Israel's hardening will one day be reversed (see 11:25).[57] But this objection fails to make the vital distinction between the individual and corporate perspectives. In Rom. 11 Paul is arguing about the position of Israel as a nation in the plan of God: how God called that people (11:2), hardened much of it (11:7), and will eventually remove that hardening so as to save it (11:26). Here, however, Paul is speaking about the work of God in individuals. And vv. 22-23, where Paul expands on the idea of both God's mercy and his hardening, suggest that the division between those individuals who receive mercy and those who are hardened is basic and final.

No doctrine stimulates more negative reaction and consternation than this one. Some degree of such reaction is probably inevitable, for it flies in the face of our own common perceptions of both human freedom and God's justice. And vv. 19-23 show that Paul was himself very familiar with this reaction. Yet, without pretending that it solves all our problems, we must recognize that God's hardening is an act directed against human beings who are already in rebellion against God's righteous rule.[58] God's hardening does not, then, *cause* spiritual insensitivity to the things of God; it maintains people in the state of sin that already characterizes them. This does not mean, as I have argued above, that God's decision about whom to harden is based on a particular degree of sinfulness within certain human beings; he hardens "whomever he chooses." But it is imperative that we maintain side-by-side the complementary truths that (1) God hardens whomever he chooses; (2) human beings, because of sin, are responsible for their ultimate condemnation. Thus, God's bestowing of mercy and his hardening are not equivalent

---

and most controversial). But it was given its classic expression in the theology of Calvin (see the *Institutes* 3.21.5; 22.11; 23.1-14; 24.12-17) and (even more forthrightly) in the teaching of his theological descendants (for a survey, see Heppe, *Reformed Dogmatics,* pp. 156-62).

57. Morris, 362; Dunn, 2.555; G. Schrenk, *Die Weissagung über Israel im Neuen Testament* (Zürich: Gotthelf, 1951), pp. 30-33; O. Hofius, "Das Evangelium und Israel: Erwägungen zu Römer 9–11," *ZTK* 83 (1986), 300-306. There is some truth, then, in Whiteley's contention that Paul here teaches a predestination *to sin* rather than a predestination *to damnation* (*Theology,* pp. 96-97).

58. See, e.g, Calvin, *Institutes* 3.23.3: "But if all whom the Lord predestines to death are by condition of nature subject to the judgment of death, of what injustice toward themselves may they complain?" It must be said, however, that Calvin's view on this issue is not altogether clear. The "sublapsarian" view (God's election follows — in logical, *not* temporal order — human beings' fall into sin) became the dominant Reformed position, as opposed to the "supralapsarian" view (God's election precedes human beings' fall into sin [or God's decree permitting the Fall]); cf. Heppe, *Reformed Dogmatics,* pp. 157-62.

acts. God's mercy is given to those who do not deserve it; his hardening affects those who have already by their sin deserved condemnation.[59]

19 The diatribe style becomes more pronounced in this next paragraph (vv. 19-23). Paul explicitly quotes his interlocutor — "You will then say to me" — and answers the objections raised in the questions of v. 19b with a series of rhetorical questions of his own (vv. 20a, 21, 22-23). Paul's sharp response to the questions of v. 19 suggest that the interlocutor here is an opponent and not just a "dialogue partner."[60] The objector wonders how God can "still" — that is, assuming the truth of Paul's teaching in v. 18 — "find fault"[61] with people. For, "who resists[62] his will?"[63] Embodied in these questions is the objection that God's sovereign act of hardening (v. 18b) jeopardizes the clear biblical teaching about the justice of God's judgment on

---

59. See Augustine, *On Grace and Free Will*, chap. 43 (*NPNF* 5.463); and, especially clearly, Murray, 2.29-30.

60. We need not identify a specific opponent since the questions raised in v. 19b and c are natural human responses to Paul's teaching. But Michel and Dunn are probably right to suggest that Paul may be thinking especially of Jewish objections. Early Judaism was torn by debates over the relationship between divine sovereignty and human free will. Indeed, Josephus, in a famous passage, uses this issue to distinguish the main Jewish "parties":

> Now at this time there were three schools of thought among the Jews, which held different opinions concerning human affairs; the first being that of the Pharisees, the second that of the Sadducees, and the third that of the Essenes. As for the Pharisees, they say that certain events are the work of Fate, but not all; as to other events, it depends upon ourselves whether they shall take place or not. The sect of the Essenes, however, declares that Fate is mistress of all things, and that nothing befalls men unless it be in accordance with her decree. But the Sadducees do away with Fate, holding that there is no such thing and that human actions are not achieved in accordance with her decree, but that all things lie within our own power, so that we ourselves are responsible for our well-being, while we suffer misfortune through our own thoughtlessness. (*Ant.* 13.171-73; cf. also *J.W.* 2.119-66)

Paul's "opponent" may then be a Pharisaic Jew who criticizes Paul's doctrine for not leaving enough room for human free will (see especially, for this view, and on the whole subject, Maier, *Mensch*).

61. The Greek verb is μέμφομαι, used in the LXX only in Sir. 11:7; 41:7; 2 Macc. 2:7 and in the NT elsewhere only in Heb. 8:8 (it is a v.l. in Mark 7:2). An alternative translation here is "complain" (see Josephus, *Ant.* 2.63; cf. BAGD); but "find fault" makes better sense in this context.

62. Gk. ἀνθέστηκεν, a perfect form of the verb ἀνθίστημι. The perfect tense has no past-referring significance here; it is a "gnomic" perfect, used like the present tense to state a general truth (Kuss; Schlier; Fitzmyer).

63. The translation in many English versions, "Who *can* resist his will?" (RSV; NRSV; TEV; NEB; REB) is without warrant (see Cranfield).

people who resist him (see, in Romans itself, 1:19-23). For only if people are responsible for their own actions can God's judgment be truly just. Yet Paul's teaching about the sovereignty of God in hardening appears to remove such responsibility. Before analyzing what Paul does say in response to this objection, we do well to note what he does *not* say. He makes no reference to human works or human faith (whether foreseen or not) as the basis for God's act of hardening (as so many of Paul's "defenders" have done).[64] Nor does he defuse the issue by confining God's hardening only to matters of salvation history; quite the contrary, vv. 22-23 make more explicit than ever that Paul is dealing with questions of eternal destiny. In fact, Paul never offers — here or anywhere else — a "logical" solution to the tension between divine sovereignty and human responsibility that he creates. That he affirms the latter is, of course, clear; and we must never forget that Paul will go on in 9:30–10:21 to attribute the Jews' condemnation to their own willful failure to believe. Paul is content to hold the truths of God's absolute sovereignty — in both election and in hardening — and of full human responsibility without reconciling them.[65] We would do well to emulate his approach.

20   The adversative "on the contrary"[66] contrasts the objection implicit in the second question of v. 19 — it is "wrong" of God to "find fault" if he himself is the cause of a person's behavior — with Paul's viewpoint. "O man" need not have a derogatory sense, since this address occurs in dialogues similar to Paul's as a polite address.[67] But the present context, which emphasizes the gulf between human beings and God (v. 21; and note the contrast between "man" at the beginning of v. 20 and "God" at its end), shows that Paul chooses the term to accentuate the subordinate, creaturely status of the objector[68]: "who are *you*[69] to answer back to God?"

Paul quotes Isa. 29:16 to remind the objector of the dependent and

64. Note Augustine's comments on v. 14: "For after he had set forth something amazing concerning persons not yet born, and then confronted himself with the question; 'What then? Is there injustice with God?' here was the place for him to answer that God foreknew the merits of every man. Still he does not say this but takes refuge in God's judgments and mercy" (*Letters* 194.8.35 [*PL* 33.886]; cf. also Calvin, *Institutes* 3.22.8; P. K. Jewett, *Election and Predestination* [Grand Rapids: Eerdmans, 1985], pp. 71-72).

65. See Stevens, *Pauline Theology*, pp. 110-15.

66. Gk. μενοῦνγε (on this reading and the word order, see the note on the translation above). The word can have an intensifying meaning — "indeed," "to be sure"; probably in Phil. 3:8 — and some adopt this translation here (including many church fathers [Schelkle; cf. also Godet]). But the context here requires its well-established adversative meaning (cf. Luke 11:28 [v.l.]; Rom. 10:18; see BAGD; BDF 450; Moule, *Idiom Book*, 163; S-H; Wilckens; Fitzmyer).

67. Barrett paraphrases "my dear sir."

68. See, e.g., Cranfield; Dunn.

69. Gk. σύ, emphatic by both inclusion and position.

subordinate position of the human being in respect to God.[70] Human beings are in no more of a position to "answer back" to God than a vase is to criticize its molder for making it in a certain way. Paul is not here denying the validity of that kind of questioning of God which arises from sincere desire to understand God's ways and an honest willingness to accept whatever answer God might give. It is the attitude of the creature presuming to judge the ways of the creator — to "answer back"[71] — that Paul implicitly rebukes.

21 Paul continues to use the imagery of the potter and his clay to reinforce the point of v. 20. His rhetorical question asserts the right[72] of the potter to make out of the same "lump" of clay both a vessel "for honor"[73] and one "for dishonor."[74] While Isa. 29:16 and (probably) 45:9 have furnished the immediate source of Paul's language, the metaphorical application of the potter and the clay is quite widespread in both the OT and Judaism.[75] Scholars have argued that one text or another is key to Paul's imagery here and draw conclusions about Paul's meaning accordingly.

Noting that several of the OT texts involved (Isa. 45:9; Jer. 18:6-10) focus on Israel as a nation, some scholars think that Paul is arguing for God's right to use the people of Israel "for dishonor" — in other words, to use the nation in a negative way in salvation history.[76] The idea that Paul is focusing on God's use of what he makes rather than on the making itself is suggested also, it is argued, by the probable allusion to Wis. 15:7[77] and by the clear

---

70. The first six words — μὴ ἐρεῖ τὸ πλάσμα τῷ πλάσαντι — match the LXX of Isa. 29:16a exactly. The rest of the verse may reflect Isa. 45:9b — LXX μὴ ἐρεῖ ὁ πηλὸς τῷ κεραμεῖ, Τί ποιεῖς, ὅτι οὐκ ἐργάζῃ οὐδὲ ἔχεις χεῖρας; "The clay will not say to the potter, will it, 'Why have you made me?' for you do not work, neither do you have hands?" (e.g., Kuss; Schlier; Dunn). Johnson, however, thinks Paul may be thinking of Wis. 12:12 (*Function,* 132-33).

71. Gk. ἀνταποκρίνομαι, a term that suggests the nuance of contention. See, e.g., its only other NT occurrence: the Pharisees, wanting to condemn Jesus for his Sabbath healing but confronted with Jesus' provoking question, "were not able to *answer back* to these things" (Luke 14:6; cf. also Job 16:8; BAGD; Dunn).

72. Gk. ἐξουσίαν.

73. Gk. εἰς τιμήν.

74. Gk. εἰς ἀτιμίαν.

75. See esp. Job 10:9; 38:14; Isa. 29:16; 45:9-10; 64:7; Jer. 18:1-6; Sir. 33:13; Wis. 15:7; *T. Naph.* 2:2, 4; 1QS 11:22.

76. E.g., Munck, *Christ and Israel,* p. 58; Godet. Hays (p. 66) thinks that the key text is Jer. 18 and that Paul therefore implies, as does the Jeremiah text, that God is working with his vessels to reshape them. While hardened for the moment, therefore, the Jews have the opportunity to repent and be reestablished as the people of God.

77. "For when a potter [κεραμεύς] kneads the soft earth and laboriously molds [πλάσσει] each vessel for our service, he fashions out of the same clay [πηλοῦ] both the vessels [σκεύη] that serve clean uses and those for contrary uses, making all in like manner; but which shall be the use of each of these the worker in clay decides."

parallel between this text and 2 Tim. 2:20.[78] On this general approach, then, the verse is asserting God's right to use nations, or individuals, for different purposes in his unfolding plan of salvation.[79] Some — such as Ishmael, Esau, Pharaoh, and the hardened Jews — have a negative or "dishonorable" role to play in the purposes of God in history. Others — such as Isaac, Jacob, and believing Jews and Gentiles — have a positive role.

Other scholars, however, note that many of the OT and Jewish texts that compare God to a potter focus on God as Creator — a point that Paul underscores by using the verb *plassō*.[80] Further, the contrast between "honor" and "dishonor" is said to match the contrast between "glory" and "wrath," or "destruction," in vv. 22-23.[81] On this reading, Paul is asserting God's right to make from the mass of humanity (the "lump") some persons who are destined to inherit salvation and others who are destined for wrath and con-demnation.[82]

Certainty about which OT and Jewish texts Paul may have in mind is impossible to attain and probably immaterial: Paul's imagery is probably distilled generally from many of them without being specifically dependent on any one of them.[83] This means that our exegetical conclusions must be guided by Paul's own use of the metaphor, and not by any specific contexts in which the metaphor appears. We have seen that Paul is applying his teaching to the issue of the present spiritual condition and eternal destiny of unbelieving Jews (and believing Jews and Gentiles). This makes it likely that Paul is thinking here also of the eternal destinies of individuals.

---

78. "In a great house there are not only vessels [σκεύη] of gold and silver but also of wood and earthenware, and some for noble use [ἃ μὲν εἰς τιμήν], some for ignoble [ἃ δὲ εἰς ἀτιμίαν]."

79. See, e.g., Gifford; Morris; Cranfield; Leenhardt; Beyschlag, *Theodicee,* pp. 55-56; H. H. Rowley, *The Biblical Doctrine of Election* (London: Lutterworth, 1950), pp. 40-42.

80. This verb is used in the creation account (Gen. 2:7) and in many other texts referring to God as Creator (Job 10:8-9; Ps. 33:15; 2 Macc. 7:23; Josephus, *Ant.* 1.32, 34; cf. Dunn, 2.556). Paul's only other use of the verb is in reference to creation (1 Tim. 2:13). Müller (over-?)stresses the importance of creation ideas in this context (*Gottes Gerechtig-keit,* pp. 28-29).

81. τιμή is used as a synonym of glory in Rom. 2:7, 10, while ἀτιμία is used as the opposite of glory in 1 Cor. 15:43. On the other hand, Paul never elsewhere uses ἀτιμία of eternal destiny. And the closest verbal parallel to this language is in 2 Tim. 2:20 (σκεύη, εἰς τιμήν, εἰς ἀτιμίαν), which does not speak of eternal destiny.

82. See esp. Piper, 174-83; Hodge; Murray.

83. See esp. Cranfield. Thus, e.g., the vocabulary of v. 21 is closest to Wis. 15:7 (they share the Greek words κεραμεύς, πηλός, and πλάσσω), but the respective contexts (the text in Wisdom focuses on the foolishness of idolatry) are quite distinct (see Piper, 176-77).

22 The *de* introducing this verse is often given a slight adversative force ("but"; cf. NEB; REB) and taken to imply some distinction between the image of the potter (vv. 20-21) and its application to the ways of God (vv. 22-23).[84] But this seems overly subtle; Paul appears to use *de* with simple transitional force as he moves from the illustration to its application (cf. TEV: "And the same is true of what God has done").[85] The exact meaning of this application depends on our understanding of the structure of the following verses. There are two main difficulties. The first is that Paul begins a conditional sentence in v. 22 ("But if . . .") without indicating clearly where he finishes it (e.g., the apodosis of the sentence is not evident). Various solutions have been offered, but most recent commentaries agree that vv. 22-23 are a protasis that does not have an explicit apodosis.[86] Paul is inviting his readers to complete the thought from the context.[87] Many English versions suggest something of this sort by translating "what if" (KJV; NIV; RSV; NRSV; NASB), or, as we may paraphrase, "what if God has acted in this way? who will question God's authority [cf. v. 21] to do so?"

The second difficulty is two-pronged: What is the force of the participle "wishing" *(thelōn)* in v. 22a, and how does the clause this participle introduces relate to the purpose clause in v. 23 (*kai hina,* "and in order to . . .")? Commentators again propose several alternatives, but two are especially worth considering.

(1) The participle "wishing" might be concessive. In this case, the

---

84. S-H; Leenhardt; Cranfield; Dunn.

85. Meyer; Murray; Stevens, *Pauline Theology,* pp. 116-18.

86. See, e.g., Murray; Cranfield; Wilckens; Dunn. There are two other main alternatives:

1. Make v. 22 the protasis and v. 23 the apodosis (G. Stählin, *TDNT* V, 426; Nygren; F. Siegert, *Argumentation bei Paulus: gezeigt an Röm 9–11* [WUNT 34; Tübingen: Mohr, 1985], pp. 132-33): "But *if* (εἰ) God, because he wished (θέλων) to manifest (ἐνδείξασθαι) his wrath and to make known (γνωρίσαι) his power, bore (ἤνεγκεν) with much patience the vessels of wrath prepared for destruction, *then* [he did it] also in order to make known (ἵνα γνωρίσῃ) the riches of his glory to vessels of mercy which he prepared beforehand for glory." καί can introduce an apodosis (BDF 442[7]); but v. 23 is a weak and unnatural conclusion to v. 22 (Piper, 187).

2. Make vv. 22-24 the protasis, with the apodosis unexpressed (Stuart; Huby; Kuss; Godet; Zeller; idem, *Juden und Heiden,* pp. 203-8; Maier, *Israel in der Heilsgeschichte,* p. 428 [the latter three see vv. 22 and 23-24 as two separate protases]). The relative pronoun beginning v. 24 might seem to favor a close connection between vv. 23 and 24, but (as we will argue on v. 24 below) it is better to find a break between the verses.

87. Such a construction is not unusual in Greek (cf. LSJ, 481) and is found in the NT (Luke 19:42; John 6:62; Acts 23:9).

infinitives in v. 22a that depend on this participle would express what God wanted but did not actually do, while v. 23 would state God's ultimate purpose in bearing with vessels of wrath:

> "But (what) if God,
>> *although* he wished
>>> [1] to manifest his wrath and
>>> [2] to make known his power,
>> bore with much patience the vessels of wrath prepared for destruction, and [*kai*] [bore with them] in order to make known the riches of his glory to vessels of mercy that he prepared beforehand for glory. . . ."[88]

(2) The participle "wishing" might be causal. In this case, the two infinitives in v. 22a that depend on this participle would be essentially parallel to the purpose clause in v. 23, all three summarizing God's purpose in bearing patiently with the vessels of wrath:

> "But (what) if God,
>> *because* he wished
>>> [1] to manifest his wrath and
>>> [2] to make known his power,
>> bore with much patience the vessels of wrath prepared for destruction,
>>> [3] [doing this because he wished] also [*kai*] to make known the riches of his glory to vessels of mercy that he prepared beforehand for glory. . . ."[89]

A decision between these options is difficult. The former has in its favor the different placement and construction of the purpose statement in v. 22a as opposed to the one in v. 23a. But the second interpretation fits the context better since it achieves a more natural parallel with vv. 17-18. In the case both of Pharaoh and of the vessels of wrath, God withholds his final judgment so that he can more spectacularly display his glory. For this reason, I favor slightly the second interpretation. I will summarize my conclusions on the structure of these verses in a paraphrase: "What objection can you make if it is in fact the case that God has tolerated with great patience vessels of wrath prepared for destruction when you realize that his purpose in doing so has been to demonstrate his wrath, make known his power, and — espe-

---

88. S-H; Leenhardt; Meyer; Lenski; Prat, *Theology,* 1.257; Fitzmyer; cf. NASB.
89. Calvin; Murray; Cranfield; Wilckens; Zeller; Byrne, 136; Luz, 242-45; Piper, 188; Müller, *Gottes Gerechtigkeit,* pp. 31-32; cf. KJV. Dunn thinks the participle may be simply descriptive.

cially[90] — to make known the riches of his glory to vessels of mercy, prepared beforehand for glory?"

In v. 22, then, Paul is reiterating the point that he made with respect to God's dealings with Pharaoh in v. 17: God works with those who are not in positive relationship with him to display in greater degree his own nature and power. The Exodus background makes it clear how God's raising up of Pharaoh contributed to the widespread publication of his power and name: Pharaoh's obduracy required God to work miracle after miracle in order to secure his purpose. But how has God's patient toleration[91] of the vessels of wrath served the purpose of manifesting his wrath and power? On two other occasions Paul ascribes "patience" (makrothymia) to God, and both assume a positive purpose for that patience: allowing an opportunity for repentance (Rom. 2:4; 1 Tim. 1:16). Paul may then be thinking of the display of God's wrath and power as a historical process with both a negative and a positive side: God's patience in withholding final judgment has enabled him to demonstrate his anger at sin through the processes of history (see, perhaps, 1:18) and at the same time to make known the saving power of the gospel to more and more people.[92] However, Paul may here be viewing the revelation of God's wrath and power as taking place at the final judgment (as he often does; see, e.g., Rom. 2:5). In this case, the purpose of God's patience here would be to allow the rebellion of his creation to gain force and intensity so that his consequent victory is all the more glorious and also (and perhaps primarily) to give opportunity for him to bestow his mercy on those whom he has chosen for his own (v. 23).[93] This interpretation fits better with the causal meaning of the participle "wishing" in v. 22a (see above). In addition, it accords better with the sharp contrast Paul draws in these verses between the vessels of wrath and the vessels of mercy. This contrast would be unfairly diminished, I think, if we were to assume that the vessels of wrath could have the same ultimate destiny as the vessels of mercy. We must remember at this point that God, in strict justice, could have executed his sentence of condemnation on the entire human race immediately after the Fall. It is only because of God's great patience that he has waited to bring down his wrath on a rebellious world so that he can finish his wise and loving plan.

90. The καί introducing v. 23 and the separation of the purpose clause in the verse from the infinitives of purpose in v. 22 gives v. 23 a particular emphasis (Dunn).

91. The verb φέρω (ἤνεγκεν is the second aorist of φέρω) has the meaning here of "endure," "put up with"; see Josephus, Ant. 7.372; 17.342; Heb. 12:20; 13:13; cf. BAGD). ἐν πολλῇ μακροθυμίᾳ is adverbial: God has "very patiently" put up with vessels of wrath.

92. δύναμις ("power") is connected to the gospel in the letter's thesis statement (1:16).

93. Several Jewish texts attest a concept similar to this: see esp. 4 Ezra 7:72-74; 2 Macc. 6:12-14; Wis. 15; Pss. Sol. 13; 1QH 15:14-20. Defenders of this view include Calvin; Kuss; Wilckens; Piper, 190-92.

But what of the objects of God's patience endurance, the "vessels of wrath"? Is God's patience also for the purpose that they might come to repentance?[94] Much depends on our interpretation of the participle "prepared" that describes the vessels of wrath. For Paul does not tell us who has done the "preparing." Many commentators argue that the parallel with vv. 17-18 — where God "raises up" Pharaoh and hardens — and with v. 23 — where the subject of "prepared beforehand" must be God — make clear that God is the agent of this "preparing."[95] The phrase "prepared for destruction" would then refer to God's act of reprobation whereby he destines the vessels of wrath to eternal destruction.[96] However, others argue that it is the difference between Paul's description of the vessels of mercy in v. 23 and the vessels of wrath here that is significant. In contrast to the active participle "prepared beforehand" in v. 23, Paul here uses a middle/passive participle that does not clearly bring God into the picture.[97] But the parallel with vv. 17-18 suggests strongly that the agent of "prepared" is indeed God: Paul considers the "vessels on whom God's wrath rests"[98] as prepared by God himself for eternal condemnation.

94. See, e.g., Chrysostom; Leenhardt; Harrison; Cranfield; Dunn; Maier, *Israel in der Heilsgeschichte,* p. 431; M. J. Farrelly, *Predestination, Grace and Free Will* (Westminster, MD: Newman, 1964), pp. 54-60.

95. See, e.g., Calvin; Hodge; Käsemann; Meyer; Michel; Kuss; Pfleiderer, *Paulinism,* 1.245-50; Piper, 194; Räisänen, *Hardening,* p. 82; Watson, 162-64. Maier (*Mensch,* p. 381) points to 1QH 15:12-22, where the Hebrew word כון (which translates καταρτίζω three times in the LXX) is used to denote divine ordination. A few who assume that God is the agent of the participle think that Paul is speaking of historical roles rather than eternal destiny (e.g., Beyschlag, *Theodicee,* pp. 60-69; Munck, *Christ and Israel,* p. 69).

96. The word ἀπώλεια, "destruction," is always used by Paul with reference to final condemnation: Phil. 1:28; 3:19; 2 Thess. 2:3 (probably); 1 Tim. 6:9 (probably); and see the cognate verb ἀπόλλυμι in Rom. 2:12; 1 Cor. 1:18; 2 Cor. 2:15; 4:3. That the word connotes the eternal fate of the individual is especially clear from the contrasts with salvation in Phil. 1:28; 1 Cor. 1:18; and 2 Cor. 2:15.

97. Scholars who adopt this interpretation view the participle as (1) a passive, with Satan (Lenski) or their own sins (Chrysostom; Haldane; Godet; Morris) or "their own impenitence" (Wesley) as the implied agent; (2) middle, with the idea of "fitted themselves" (Prat, *Theology,* 1.257); or (3) a simple adjective (Tholuck; Lagrange; Harrison).

98. The genitive ὀργῆς is probably a qualitative genitive (BDF 165; Turner, 213) rather than an objective genitive ("vessels destined for wrath"; cf. Hodge; Murray). Rom. 1:18 makes it clear that God's wrath is even now resting on these individuals; contra, e.g., S-H, who translate "vessels which deserve God's anger." Paul uses the word σκεῦος in its well-attested meaning, "person," especially the body of the person (cf. Acts 9:15; 2 Cor. 4:7; 1 Thess. 4:4 [?]). Taking the phrase to mean "agents who effect God's wrath" (e.g. Munck, *Christ and Israel,* pp. 67-68; A. T. Hanson, "Vessels of Wrath or Instruments of Wrath? Romans IX.22-3," *JTS* 32 [1981], 433-43) founders on the clear parallelism between this phrase and "vessels of mercy" in v. 23: those vessels are not agents of God's mercy.

23 As I have argued above, this verse expresses a third, and climactic, purpose of God's patient endurance of the vessels of wrath. God has withheld the final judgment that could rightfully fall on his rebellious creatures at any time not only because he wanted to display more gloriously his wrath and power (v. 22a) but also, and especially, because he wanted to "make known his glorious riches[99] to vessels on whom his mercy rests,[100] vessels whom God has prepared beforehand for glory." God's ultimate purpose in his decree of hardening is mercy. But his mercy is in this context clearly discriminating rather than universal: some receive mercy (v. 18), those "vessels" of mercy whom God chooses (vv. 15-16); others, vessels of wrath, are hardened (v. 18). Therefore we must not allow the preeminence of God's purpose in bestowing mercy *on some* to cancel out the reality and finality of his wrath *on others*. Paul is clear here, as he is elsewhere: some people receive God's mercy and are saved, while others do not receive that mercy and so are eternally condemned.[101] And as those who do not receive that mercy refuse to do so ultimately because God himself hardens them, so those who experience that mercy with its outcome, glory, do so because God himself "prepared them beforehand."[102] "Prepared beforehand," then, refers to the same thing as the word "predestine" in 8:29: a decision of God in eternity past to bestow his mercy on certain individuals whom he in his sovereign design has chosen.[103]

Verses 14-23, while something of a parenthesis in Paul's argument, contribute significantly to our understanding of Paul's teaching in this chapter and to our

99. It is tempting to give the genitive τῆς δόξης a qualitative nuance — "glorious riches" — but the importance of the concept "glory" in Paul (see esp. Rom. 2:7, 10; 3:23; 5:2; 8:17, 18, 30) and in this context (v. 23b) requires that we preserve its independent significance. Perhaps the genitive is epexegetic or partitive: "riches, that is, glory," or "riches, consisting especially in glory." The phrase may have been standard in worship settings especially (see Eph. 1:18; Col. 1:27 ["riches in glory" in Phil. 4:19]).

100. Like ὀργῆς in the comparable phrase σκεύη ὀργῆς in v. 22, ἐλέους will be a genitive of quality.

101. This must be emphasized against, e.g., Barth (*Shorter,* 116-23), Cranfield (see, e.g., 2.496-97), and Dunn (2.559-61), who argue that God's mercy is the "bottom line" of the entire discussion and suggest, therefore, that Paul is implying that there will in the end be no "vessels of wrath"; all will eventually be recipients of God's mercy and thus saved. While Paul certainly highlights in this passage the mercy of God, and even gives it a certain preeminence in God's purposes (v. 23), he also carefully distinguishes between those who receive that mercy and others who do not; in fact, every occurrence of the word "mercy" is clearly restricted to some individuals as opposed to others (vv. 15-16, 18, 23). These scholars, of course, rely heavily on what they see to be the climax of Rom. 9–11: the assertion that God will eventually "have mercy on everyone" (11:32). But this is not a statement of universalism (see my exegesis) and cannot therefore be used to introduce this note into 9:6-29.

102. The verb is προετοιμάζω; cf. also Eph. 2:10.

103. See, e.g., Käsemann; Murray.

conception of God. In the face of the accusation that his stress on the initiative of God in determining who would be his people turns God into an unjust tyrant, Paul retreats not one step. On the contrary, he goes on the offensive and strengthens his teaching about the unconstrained freedom of God in making choices that determine people's lives. Paul also makes even clearer that the choices he is talking about have to do not just with historical roles but with eternal destinies. This text, then, gives further support (see Rom. 8:28-30) to the doctrine of unconditional election. It also supports, although more ambiguously, the doctrine of reprobation. Paul teaches that God has brought upon certain people whom he chooses on the basis of nothing but his own will a condition of spiritual stupor, a condition that leads to eternal condemnation.

Allusion in this part of the chapter to unbelieving Israel is muted but clear. So many Jews have failed to embrace the gospel because God has so willed it: as with Pharaoh, God has hardened them, and they are now vessels on whom God's wrath rests.

3. God's Calling of a New People: Israel and the Gentiles (9:24-29)

24[Whom] God has called us, not only from among Jews but also from among Gentiles, 25as it says also in Hosea:

"I will call that which is not my people 'my people,'
and that which is not loved 'my beloved';
26and it will be that in the place where it was said to them,
'You are not my people,'
there they shall be called sons of the living God."a

27But Isaiah cries out concerning Israel:

"If the number of the sons of Israel should be as the sand of the
sea, the remnant will be saved.
28For the Lord will perform his word on the earth, completing it
and cutting it short."b1

29And it is just as Isaiah foretold:

1. A considerable number of MSS add here words taken from Isa. 10:23: ἐν δικαιοσύνη ὅτι λόγον συντετμημένον, "in righteousness, for [the Lord will perform his word] that has been cut off" (the second [Byzantine] corrector of ℵ, the western uncials D, F, and G, Ψ, and the majority text); a few other MSS add only ἐν δικαιοσύνην (a few minuscules, including 81). The longer text might have been accidentaly omitted by haplography (note the similarity between συτέμνων and συντετμήμενον; cf. Meyer, 2.100), but it is more likely that an early scribe assimilated Paul's quote to the LXX, thereby also smoothing out the syntax. As is often the case, then, the early Alexandrian text (ℵ [original hand] and B) preserves the primitive text.

"If the Lord of hosts had not left for us a seed,
we would have become like Sodom and been made like
*Gomorrah."*c

a. Hos. 2:23; 1:10b
b. Isa. 10:22-23
c. Isa. 1:9

These verses return, after the excursus in vv. 14-23, to the theme of vv. 6-13: God's call is the sole basis for inclusion in the true people of God. Thus we encounter here again the characteristic vocabulary of that earlier paragraph: "sons of God" (v. 26; cf. v. 8); "seed" (v. 29; cf. vv. 7 and 8); and, especially, "call" (vv. 24 and 26; cf. vv. 7 and 12). Another similarity is Paul's constant appeal to the OT for substantiation of his teaching. In vv. 6-13 Paul mined the patriarchal stories for his citations; now he turns to the prophets. It is probably Paul's intention to cite the OT in 9:6b-29 in the order of the canon, moving from the patriarchal narratives (vv. 7-13) to the events of the exodus (vv. 14-18) to the time of the prophets (vv. 21, 24-29). Paul also changes his style of scriptural citation: whereas he has in the earlier paragraphs interspersed OT quotations with his own commentary, he now quotes in rapid sequence a series of quotations (vv. 25-29) to confirm his initial thesis statement (v. 24).

While vv. 24-29 pick up the theme of vv. 6b-13, they also move beyond what Paul has said in vv. 6b-13. For Paul now explicitly includes Gentiles among those whom God is sovereignly calling to be part of his people. God's people are constituted by his call and not by natural descent. Paul now takes this point to its logical and (from the perspective of first-century Judaism) radical conclusion: physical descent from Abraham not only does not guarantee inclusion in the true people of God; it is not even necessary. Verses 14-23, despite their somewhat parenthetical nature, have prepared the way for this conclusion by highlighting so intensely God's absolute freedom to bestow his mercy on whomever he chooses. Verses 24-29, therefore, bring Paul's defense of God's faithfulness to his word to its climax. The small number of Jews who have responded to the gospel fits with the prophetic insistence that only a remnant of the people of Israel would be saved. And the inclusion of Gentiles within the eschatological people of God, while not so clearly predicted in the OT, conforms to God's character and actions as presented in the Scriptures.

24 The opening words of this verse are difficult syntactically and raise questions about the relationship between vv. 22-23 and 24. We may view v. 24 as the continuation of the sentence begun in vv. 22-23[2] or as a new

2. See NIV; NRSV; NASB. The syntax may then be explained in two ways. (1) The antecedent of the relative pronoun (οὕς) may be σκεύη ἐλέους ("vessels of mercy"), with ἡμᾶς ("us") in apposition to it (the case of the relative pronoun being masculine rather

sentence that continues in v. 25. Clearly those called in v. 24 are to be identified with the "vessels of mercy" in v. 23, and some connection between vv. 22-23 and 24 must be retained. In fact, we find in vv. 23b-24 a sequence similar to that of Rom. 8:30a, as God's "call" follows his act of predestination. Still, Paul's word order suggests what Dunn calls "a pause for breath" here, and it seems best to view v. 24 as beginning a new sentence (and, indeed, a new paragraph).[3] The sequence in vv. 23b-24 from God's "preparing beforehand" vessels of mercy and his calling of them into relationship with himself[4] is similar to that in 8:30: "those whom he predestined, he also called." But Paul's focus here is not on the antecedents of God's calling or on its nature, but on its scope: God summons into relationship with himself Gentiles as well as Jews. This is the point Paul supports with the OT quotations that follow.

25-26   These quotations are chiastically related to the final words of v. 24[5]:

A	God calls Jews	v. 24
B	God calls Gentiles	v. 24
B′	OT confirmation of God's call of Gentiles	vv. 25-26
A′	OT confirmation of God's call of Jews	vv. 27-29

Paul's OT support for the calling of Gentiles comes from "the book of Hosea."[6] He quotes freely from Hos. 2:23 (MT and LXX 2:25) in v. 25 and

---

than neuter [as its antecedent σκεύη would normally require] because of assimilation to ἡμᾶς): "vessels of mercy prepared beforehand for glory whom God has also called, namely us, [called] not only from among Jews but also from among Gentiles" (see Cranfield, 2.497-98; Morris, 369; Kuss, 3.733; Wilckens, 2.205). (2) ἡμᾶς might be in apposition to σκεύη, with οὕς introducing a relative clause dependent on ἡμᾶς: "vessels of mercy prepared beforehand for glory, namely us, whom God has also called not only from among Jews but also from among Gentiles" (Moule, *Idiom Book,* 168; Barrett, 189).

3. See the punctuation of NA[27]; REB; TEV; Dunn, 2.570; Käsemann, 273; Schlier, 303. Favoring this reading is (1) the double object (οὕς, ἡμᾶς) of the verb ἐκάλεσεν ("called"), which is difficult to explain if v. 24 is a relative clause dependent on σκεύη (option 1 in the preceding footnote); and (2) the placement of οὕς at the beginning of the sentence, which is awkward if ἡμᾶς later in the verse is its antecedent (see option 2 in the previous footnote). The closest Pauline syntactical parallel to v. 24 is 1 Cor. 12:28, which is an independent sentence: Καὶ οὕς μὲν ἔθετο ὁ θεὸς ἐν τῇ ἐκκλησίᾳ πρῶτον ἀπο-στόλους. . . . Here also we have the relative pronoun, placed near the beginning of the sentence as one of two objects of the verb (although it must be admitted that the differing placement of καί might affect the validity of the parallel).

4. For this meaning of καλέω, see the notes on 8:28. The meaning "invite" (see, e.g., Morison, *Exposition,* pp. 159-60) misses the nuance of creative power that the word has in Paul.

5. E.g., Dinter, "Remnant of Israel," pp. 109-10.

6. Gk. ἐν τῷ Ὡσηέ, "in Hosea," matches a rabbinic introductory formula (e.g., *Midr. Qoh.* 13b; cf. Str-B, 3.272; and BDF 219[1]), although there is no instance of the

then verbatim from the LXX version of Hos. 1:10a (MT and LXX 2:1b) in v. 26. Paul changes the sequence of the verses, reverses the order of the two clauses he cites from 2:23, and uses wording different from both the LXX and MT.

> Hos. 2:23b-d: "And I will have pity on 'not-pitied,' and I will say to 'Not my people,' 'You are my people'; and he shall say, 'You are my God.'"
>
> Paul: "I will *call* that which is not my people 'my people,' and that which I have not loved 'my beloved'";
>
> Hos. 1:10: "Yet the number of the sons of Israel shall be like the sand of the sea, which cannot be measured or numbered; and in the place where it was said to them, 'You are not my people,' it shall be said to them, 'Sons of the living God.'"
>
> Paul: "and it will be that in the place where it was said to them, 'You are not my people,' there they shall be called sons of the living God."

These differences have given rise to the suggestion that Paul has taken these quotations with, perhaps, the others in this series, from a catena already in existence.[7] But this is unlikely.[8] One of the key differences is Paul's use of the verb "I will call" in place of the more generic verb, "I will say," of both the Hebrew and Greek. This is almost certainly Paul's own change since it matches exactly the point for which he adduces the quotations (cf. "call" in v. 24).[9] By reversing the order of the clauses in his quotation of Hos. 2:23, Paul is able to put this verb at the beginning of his composite quotation from Hosea. The same

---

name of one of the books of the minor prophets (which were usually grouped together as one entity) being used in this way. C. Burchard suggests "in the Hosea-part of the Twelve-prophet book" ("Römer 9:25: ἐν τῷ Ὡσηέ," *ZNW* 76 [1985], 131).

7. E.g., Michel; Wilckens.

8. See Koch, 104-5, 166-67; Stanley, *Paul and the Language of Scripture,* pp. 109-13; Käsemann; Dunn. A similar application of Hos. 2:23 in 1 Pet. 2:10 to *Gentile* Christians suggests, however, that the text may have been a standard "proof-text" in early Christianity (see C. H. Dodd, *According to the Scriptures: The Sub-structure of New Testament Theology* [London: James Nisbet, 1952], p. 75).

9. Another difference between Paul's quotation and the majority LXX tradition is his use of the verb ἀγαπάω ("love") in v. 25b rather than ἐλεέω ("have mercy"). A reason for Paul to want to make this substitution is difficult to find, especially since he has focused so much attention on the concept of mercy in the previous context. It is possible, then, that Paul found the use of ἀγαπάω in his text (MS B reads this verb). Lindars, on the other hand, thinks that Paul has made his own independent translation from the Hebrew (*New Testament Apologetic: The Doctrinal Significance of the New Testament Quotations* [London: SCM, 1961], p. 243).

verb comes at the end of the quotation — "they shall be called sons of the living God" — indicating clearly where Paul's stress lies.

But a potentially more serious instance of what seems to be arbitrary hermeneutics on Paul's part is his application of these Hosea texts to the calling of Gentiles. For the prophet Hosea is predicting a renewal of God's mercy toward the rebellious northern tribes of Israel: those whom God rejected and named *lō-ruhamah,* "not pitied," and *lō-ami,* "not my people" (the symbolic names given to Hosea's children [1:6-9]) are again shown mercy and adopted again as God's people. The problem disappears if Hosea is including the Gentiles in his prophecy;[10] but this is unlikely. Others avoid the difficulty by arguing that Paul applies these passages to the calling of the Jews rather than the Gentiles.[11] But the explicit reference to Israel in the introduction to the Isaiah quotations in v. 27 suggests that Paul views the Hosea quotations as related to the calling of the Gentiles. Others think that Paul may imply an analogy: God's calling of Gentiles operates on the same principle as God's promised renewal of the ten northern tribes.[12] But Paul requires more than an analogy to establish from Scripture justification for God's calling of Gentiles to be his people. Therefore we must conclude that this text reflects a hermeneutical supposition for which we find evidence elsewhere in Paul and in the NT: that OT predictions of a renewed Israel find their fulfillment in the church.[13] Moreover, Paul's use of these texts may further his effort to break down the boundaries between the Jews and other peoples that were so basic to Jewish thinking.

The geographical references in Paul's quotation of Hos. 1:10 — "in the place where . . . ," "there" — are puzzling. In Hosea, these probably refer to the land of Israel's exile: "in the place" where God said to the exiled Jews, "You are not my people" he will intervene to take them to himself once

---

10. See Calvin.

11. Zahn; J. A. Battle, Jr., "Paul's Use of the Old Testament in Romans 9:25-26," *Grace Theological Journal* 2 (1981), 115-29.

12. See, e.g., S. L. Johnson, "Evidence from Romans 9–11," in *A Case for Premillennialism: A New Consensus* (ed. D. K. Campbell and J. L. Townsend; Chicago: Moody, 1992), pp. 207-10; Aletti, *Comment Dieu est-il juste?* pp. 219-22. Hafemann suggests that Paul's use of ὡς ("as") in the introductory formula may signal the presence of such an analogy ("The Salvation of Israel in Romans 11:25-32," 47). See also Morison, *Exposition,* pp. 161-62; Godet.

13. See, e.g., H. K. LaRondelle, *The Israel of God in Prophecy: Principles of Prophetic Interpretation* (Berrien Springs, MI: Andrews University, 1983), pp. 98-108; Kuss; Dunn, 2.572; Ellis, "Old Testament," p. 122; Hübner, *Gottes Ich und Israel,* pp. 56-57. It is not that Paul's convictions about Christ have blinded him to the meaning of the OT text (contra Hays, 67), but that God's final revelation in Christ gives to him a new hermeneutical key by which to interpret and apply the OT. Schoeps (p. 240) notes that some rabbis applied these Hosea texts to the conversion of proselytes (cf. *Pesiq. R.* 87b).

again.[14] If Paul finds any particular meaning in the language (rather than simply preserving it as part of the text he quotes[15]), he probably intends a similar application but this time with reference to the Gentiles: it is in the land of exile, the dispersion, that God will call out a people for himself.[16]

27-28 If Hosea speaks allusively to the situation of the Gentiles, Isaiah quite directly "cries out[17] concerning[18] Israel." Paul quotes in vv. 27-28 from Isa. 10:22-23. His text is substantially that of the LXX, with only two exceptions worth noting.[19] First, while the subject of the verb in the first clause in the LXX (and the MT) is "the people Israel," Paul has "the number of the sons of Israel."[20] This exact phrase occurs in Hos. 1:10 (the verse Paul has just cited), so Paul's paraphrase is a clever way to emphasize his juxtaposition of these two texts. Second, in v. 28 Paul omits several words found in the LXX of Isa. 10:22b-23a. It may be that Paul's Greek text did not have these words;[21] or Paul may have omitted them because they were not integral to the point he wanted to draw from the text.

Paul's purpose in citing what Isaiah "cries out concerning Israel" is not simply, or even mainly, to cite OT support for God's calling of Jews to be his

14. C. F. Keil, *Minor Prophets,* vol. 10 of *Commentary on the Old Testament,* by C. F. Keil and F. Delitzsch (rpt.; Grand Rapids: Eerdmans, n.d.), p. 46.

15. As, e.g., Fitzmyer argues.

16. See, e.g., Black; Godet. Munck has popularized the view that Paul looks for an imminent gathering of the Gentiles to Jerusalem as a signal for the final regathering of Israel. He thinks that Paul is here identifying Jerusalem as the place of the Gentiles' calling (pp. 306-7; *Christ and Israel,* pp. 72-73). But Munck's thesis cannot be maintained (see Käsemann, 274, and the notes on 11:12). The significance Paul may attach to the geographical references depends a great deal on whether he found the word ἐκεῖ in his text (it is read in A) or not (it is omitted in B and Q and by Ziegler in his Göttingen LXX edition).

17. Gk. κράζει. The verb connotes intensity and urgency (Dunn).

18. Gk. ὑπέρ. Hays wants to retain here the usual meaning of the preposition: Isaiah cries out "on behalf of" Israel (p. 68). But this is more likely one of those many places where ὑπέρ trespasses on the linguistic territory of περί, "concerning" (Moule, *Idiom Book,* 65).

19. Minor differences are: (1) Paul's use of ὑπόλειμμα in place of the LXX κατάλειμμα. The words are synonymous (see V. Herntrich, *TDNT* IV, 195), so the change is insignificant. (2) Paul's wording of the end of Isa. 10:23 (v. 28) differs from the LXX, which has ποιήσει ὁ θεὸς ἐν τῇ οἰκουμένῃ ὅλῃ. Paul's language may be due to assimilation to Isa. 28:22: . . . ἃ ποιήσει ἐπὶ πᾶσαν τὴν γῆν. Paul's attention could easily have been drawn to this verse, since it shares with Isa. 10:23 the pair of verbs συντελέω and συντέμνω and comes from a section that Paul quotes in the immediate context (see v. 33).

20. Gk. ὁ ἀριθμὸς τῶν υἱῶν Ἰσραήλ. The Hosea text continues with the word ὡς ἡ ἄμμος τῆς θαλάσσης, "as the sand of the sea" (see the quotation in the text above). The presence of these same words in Isa. 10:22 was probably a factor in bringing these texts together in Paul's mind. See Aageson, "Scripture and Structure," p. 273; B. Lindars, "The Old Testament and Universalism in Paul," *BJRL* 69 (1987), 515-16.

21. Koch, 82-83.

people — a point that hardly required such substantiation. Rather, his purpose is to establish the truth that God is calling his "vessels of mercy" *from among* Jews. He thereby ends this section on the note with which it began (vv. 6b-13): the OT itself shows that God chooses only some from among national Israel to be his true spiritual Israel. It is in this way that Paul reconciles the promises of God to Israel and the small number of Jewish Christians (see v. 6a).[22] To establish the truth of God's selectivity from within Israel, Paul cites texts from Isaiah that describe the important OT concept of the "remnant." Characteristic especially of the prophets, the remnant doctrine contains both a word of judgment and a word of hope.[23] The judgment consists in the fact that, though "the number of the sons of Israel be as the sand of the sea" *only* "a remnant will be saved." In contrast to the smug self-assurance that the Lord's covenant with Israel insured both the political integrity and spiritual vitality of the people as a whole, the Lord through his prophets announces doom for the people as a whole. In the Hebrew text, this note of judgment is sounded at the end of v. 22 and v. 23: "Destruction has been decreed, overwhelming and righteous. The LORD, the LORD almighty, will carry out the destruction decreed upon the whole land" (NIV). The LXX paraphrases here, however, and it is not therefore clear what Paul means when he takes over its wording. But the idea of judgment, plain in the Hebrew text, is probably intended by Paul also: God will carry out his word [of judgment]; and it is a word that he will carry out "completely"[24] and "decisively."[25] For Paul also, then, the remnant doctrine confirms his word of judgment to Israel: it is "not all who are of Israel who are truly Israel" (v. 6b).[26]

22. See Koch, 279-80.

23. On the OT remnant concept see particularly G. F. Hasel, *The Remnant: The History and Theology of the Remnant Idea from Genesis to Isaiah* (Andrews University Monographs 5; Berrien Springs, MI: Andrews University, 1972). R. E. Clements notes that Isa. 7:3-9 is a foundational remnant text in Isaiah, and that it stresses explicitly the centrality of faith (v. 9). He suggests that Paul may have this text in mind throughout his application of the remnant concept (" 'A Remnant Chosen by Grace' [Romans 11.5]," in *Pauline Studies,* 108-18).

24. Gk. συντελῶν.

25. Gk. συντέμνων. συντελῶν certainly has the idea of "completion," but the meaning of συντέμνων is difficult. This is the only NT occurrence of the verb, and it is used only seven times in the LXX. It means to "cut off" or "shorten." Some interpreters think that its implied object here is "time," so that the point is the speedy execution of God's decree (see NIV; NASB; Morris). Others suggest that Israel is the implied object: God will execute his word by "cutting off" Israel (e.g., reducing her to a remnant) (Calvin; Wilckens; Dunn [?]). But it seems better to take as the object of both participles the word λόγον. If we do so, then the idea of "cutting off the word" probably refers to its decisive execution (see NRSV; S-H; Cranfield; G. Delling, *TDNT* VIII, 64). This is close in meaning to the Hebrew as well.

26. Stressing the judgmental note in Paul's use of this text are Koch, 145-49; Hübner, *Gottes Ich und Israel*, p. 57; Käsemann; Wilckens.

The note of hope in the prophetic remnant doctrine consists in God's promise that, despite the widespread disobedience of his people, "a remnant *will* be saved."[27] God's promise to preserve a remnant signals his continuing faithfulness to his people, however faithless they may have been. That Paul wants us to hear this note in the remnant doctrine also is clear both from the connection between these quotations and v. 24 and from his development of the remnant teaching in chap. 11, where the existence of a remnant (11:1-10), he suggests, is laden with hope for the future of Israel (see esp. 11:16a).[28]

29 Paul's catena of quotations ends with a further word of prediction from Isaiah. Paul cites Isa. 1:9 exactly according to the LXX, which faithfully renders the MT. What undoubtedly drew Paul's attention to this text was the word "seed" *(sperma),* which was so key in vv. 7-9. While, however, the tone in vv. 7-9 was mainly negative (among all the descendants only those whom God "reckons" as seed will be saved), here it is positive: God's "leaving" a seed means that he will not allow Israel's rebellion to bring her to the annihilation experienced by Sodom and Gomorrah. This concluding note of hope paves the way for Rom. 11.

C. UNDERSTANDING ISRAEL'S PLIGHT: CHRIST AS THE CLIMAX OF SALVATION HISTORY (9:30–10:21)

At first glance it seems natural to follow the chapter divisions in isolating the next major stage of Paul's argument. With 11:1, Paul certainly moves on to a new topic. And the same would seem to be true in 10:1, with its direct address to the readers — "brothers and sisters" — and its expression of concern for Israel, reminding us of the beginning of chap. 9.[1] But our first glance is in this case misleading; a more fundamental break comes at 9:30. (1) The question "What then shall we say?" often marks a new argument in Romans.[2] (2) Paul signals a shift in focus by a shift in vocabulary. The words "righ-

---

27. Hasel notes the presence of both salvation and judgment in Isa. 10:22-23 (*The Remnant,* pp. 330-31); cf. also V. Herntrich, *TDNT* IV, 198.

28. Stressing the positive note of hope in Paul's application of Isaiah are Richardson, *Israel,* p. 133; F. Mußner, " 'Ganz Israel wird gerettet werden' (Röm 11,26). Versuch einer Auslegung," *Kairos* 18 (1976), 245-46; Dinter, "Remnant of Israel," pp. 109-10; Hays, 68; Elliot, *Rhetoric of Romans,* p. 266; J.-N. Aletti, "L'argumentation paulinienne en Rm 9," *Bib* 68 (1987), 50-52; Dunn; Ziesler.

1. See Siegert, *Argumentation bei Paulus,* pp. 115-16; Klappert "Traktat," pp. 72-73; Gifford, 182; Viard, 222-23; Lenski, 634.

2. See 4:1; 6:1; 7:7; 8:31; 9:14.

3. δικαιοσύνη: 9:30, 31; 10:3, 4, 5, 6.

teousness"[3] and "faith"/"believe"[4] are central to the argument of 9:30–10:21 — yet they are almost entirely missing from 9:1-29 and 11:1-36.[5] (3) The integrity of 9:30–10:21 is further seen in the similarity of its beginning and ending. In both 9:30-32 and 10:20-21 Paul contrasts the surprising inclusion of Gentiles in the people of God with the exclusion of Israel.[6]

The rhetorical question "What then shall we say?" signifies that 9:30–10:21 (like 9:14-23) takes up an issue raised by the main line of Paul's teaching in 9:6-13, 24-29. As 9:30b-31 reveal, this issue is the surprising turn of salvation history Paul has sketched in 9:24-29: Gentiles, once "not a people," are now entering into the people of God; Israel, blessed and given so many privileges, is failing to act on her privileges and experience salvation in Christ.[7] As Paul has already explained, this situation is due to the sovereign determination of God. But in 9:30–10:21, he argues that it is also the result of human response.[8] The manifestation of God's eschatological righteousness in Christ has been met by Gentiles with faith, by Israel (generally) with disobedience and unbelief. But Gentile inclusion continues (as in 9:6-29) to be the subordinate note, as Paul continues to explore the problem of Israel's exclusion.[9]

4. πίστις/πιστεύω: 9:30, 32, 33; 10:4, 6, 8, 9, 10, 11, 14, 16, 17.

5. "Righteousness" does not occur in 9:1-29 or 11:1-36 at all; "faith" in 11:20 only.

6. These texts thus form an inclusio, bracketing the argument of 9:30–10:21; see esp. Dunn, 2.579; Aletti, "L'argumentation paulinniene," pp. 42-43; R. Badenas, *Christ the End of the Law: Romans 10:4 in Pauline Perspective* (JSNTSup 10; Sheffield: JSOT, 1985), p. 97; Johnson, *Function*, p. 159; R. H. Bell, *Provoked to Jealousy: The Origin and Purpose of the Jealousy Motif in Romans 9–11* (WUNT 2.63; Tübingen: Mohr, 1994), pp. 82, 154. Several other scholars view 9:30-33 as transitional: Schmitt, *Gottesgerechtigkeit*, p. 88; Schmithals, 365; Schlier, 305; Wilckens, 2.210-11; Michel, 319; Fitzmyer, 576.

7. Most commentators note the connection with 9:24-29; cf., e.g., Dunn, 2.577; also Müller, *Gottes Gerechtigkeit*, pp. 37-38; Osten-Sacken, "Römer 9–11," p. 301.

8. Scholars debate the theological ramifications of the emphases in these two sections. Some argue that Paul in 9:30–10:21 explains the basis on which God makes his decision about human beings: those who believe he calls to salvation; those who reject the gospel he "hardens" (note, e.g., Melanchthon: "Here he [Paul] expressly sets down the cause of reprobation, namely, because they are not willing to believe the Gospel" [p. 193]). Others, however, claim that human response (9:30–10:21) is simply the result of God's prior decision (9:24-29) (e.g., Maier, *Mensch*, p. 385; T. R. Schreiner, "Israel's Failure to Attain Righteousness in Romans 9:30–10:3," *TrinJ* 12 [1991], 211). As I have argued in assessing the implications of 9:16, I believe that the latter is closer to the truth. Nevertheless, Paul is content here to set the two down side-by-side without attempting a reconciliation (Kuss, 3.743).

9. Contra those who want to make the inclusion of the Gentiles as important as, or more important than, Israel and her failure in 9:30–10:21 (some representatives of this view are M. Barth, *The People of God* [JSNTSup 5; Sheffield: JSOT, 1983], p. 39; M. Theobald, "Kirche und Israel nach Röm 9–11," *Kairos* 29 [1987], 11-12; Gaston, "Israel's Enemies," p. 418; Johnson, *Function*, pp. 151-59; Zeller, *Juden und Heiden*, pp.

This new section, 9:30–10:21, is therefore something of an excursus from Paul's main argument in chaps. 9–11. That argument, as we have seen, seeks to reconcile the privileges granted to Israel in the OT with the plight of Israel that has resulted from her (general) refusal to believe the gospel. In 9:30–10:21, Paul pauses in his argument to explore the latter point: Israel's plight as a result of the gospel.[10] He shows (1) that Israel's situation is the result of her failure to recognize in the gospel and in the Jesus proclaimed in the gospel the culmination of salvation history (9:30–10:13); and (2) that Israel's failure to recognize this is inexcusable, because the OT itself points to this culmination (10:14-21 especially).

Paul signifies the first of these concerns by reverting in these verses to the language of the gospel that dominated 1:16-17; 3:21–4:25. Every component of Paul's "definition" of the gospel in the theme of the letter (1:16-17) is taken up in 9:30–10:21: "gospel" (see 10:15, 16); "salvation"/"save" (see 10:1, 9, 10, 13); "all" (10:4, 11, 12, 13); "Jew and Greek" (10:12); "faith" (passim); and "the righteousness of God" (10:3).[11] Matching and often directly related to Paul's gospel language are quotations of the OT (11 in 25 verses). In this is found Paul's second key concern: to show that the gospel, as outlined in 1:18–4:25, is in continuity with the OT. Paul shows that the law (10:6-8, 19), the prophets (9:32b-33; 10:15-16, 20-21), and the writings (10:18) all bear witness to "the message of faith," the gospel that Paul is preaching. Israel is zealous but ignorant: she has not understood that the gospel of Christ brings salvation history to its climax. And *she should have understood,* for the OT witnesses clearly to the gospel. Paul neatly summarizes this theme in his conflated quotation from Isaiah in 9:33: Israel has stumbled over the stone that God himself has "set in Zion."

1. Israel, the Gentiles, and the Righteousness of God (9:30–10:13)

The key word in this passage is "righteousness" *(dikaiosynē),* which occurs ten (or 11; see the variant reading in 10:3) times. Throughout this passage,

---

122-26). Still other scholars focus on other themes as key in the section: "righteousness by faith" (Munck, *Christ and Israel,* pp. 78-79; Luz, 30); the temporary and anomalous situation of Israel's rejection (Klappert, "Traktat," pp. 76-79). But these are minor motifs; it is Israel's failure, as traditionally recognized, that is the theme of 9:30–10:21 (see, e.g., Godet, 367; S-H, 277; Käsemann, 276; e.g., Barrett, "Fall and Responsibility," pp. 99-104; Lübking, *Paulus und Israel,* pp. 79, 92-93; Dunn, 2.577).

10. As Dahl says, chap. 10 "is not a part of Paul's answer to the question of whether or not God has repudiated his promises to Israel. The chapter is a delayed explanation of the factors which caused him to raise that question" ("Future of Israel," p. 148). Others think that 9:30–10:21 is parenthetical: Klappert, "Traktat," pp. 80-81; Hays, 25.

11. Dunn (2.577) also stresses this point.

Paul returns (after using the term to refer to moral righteousness in chaps. 6–8) to the forensic meaning of righteousness that he established in chaps. 1–4: the "right" standing with God that is the product of God's justifying work in Christ. Earlier in the letter Paul devoted considerable time to showing that a person could experience this right standing with God only through faith (1:17; 3:21–4:25). He now uses this cardinal gospel truth to explain why so many Gentiles, previously excluded from God's covenant concern, are being saved, while most Jews, the recipients of God's blessing and promises, find themselves estranged from God. Paul uses three roughly parallel contrasts between two kinds of righteousness to make his point:

(1) "the righteousness based on faith" versus "the law of righteousness" (9:30-31);

(2) "the righteousness of God" versus "their own righteousness" (10:3);

(3) "the righteousness based on the law" versus "the righteousness based on faith" (10:5-6).

Gentiles are being included in God's true spiritual people because they are experiencing the former, positive, kind of righteousness, a righteousness that is now available to anyone who believes (10:4b, 11-13). Most Jews, on the other hand, are finding themselves outside this true people of God because they are wrongly preoccupied with the other, false, kind of righteousness. They have persisted in seeking to work out their relationship with God through the law (9:31; 10:3, 5) and the works it demands (9:32a; 10:5). They have therefore missed the climax of salvation history, "stumbling" over Jesus Christ (9:32b-33), the embodiment of God's righteousness (10:3), climax of the law (10:4), and focus of God's word of grace in the new age of redemptive history (10:6-8).[12]

The threefold contrast between two kinds of righteousness stands at the heart of each paragraph in this section: 9:30-33; 10:1-4; 10:5-13. The integrity of this section is further marked by an inclusio: Paul both begins

---

12. In this passage, Paul's criticism of the Jews with respect to the law is mainly salvation-historical: they have failed to see that its era has come to an end. (Contrast Paul's earlier treatment of the Jews [2:1–3:20], which focuses on their inability to fulfill the law because he is there looking at the situation before Christ; cf. Wilckens, 2.102.) But this is not Paul's only basis for criticism of the Jews in these verses (contra, e.g., Sanders, *Paul, the Law and the Jewish People,* pp. 37-38). Paul also makes clear that Israel's failure to perceive the shift of salvation history in Christ is bound up with her myopic preoccupation with the law and its works. Criticism of the Jews for "legalism," the attempt to secure a relationship with God through doing the law, is part and parcel of this text (cf. Schreiner, "Israel's Failure," 215-20; Laato, *Paulus und das Judentum,* pp. 250-54; Bell, *Provoked to Jealousy,* pp. 187-91).

(9:30) and ends (10:11-13) with teaching about the inclusion of Gentiles. Note also the quotation of Isa. 28:16 in both 9:33 and 10:12.

a. The Righteousness of God and the "Law of Righteousness" (9:30-33)

30*What then shall we say? That Gentiles who do not pursue righteousness attained righteousness, righteousness that is based on faith.* 31*But Israel, pursuing a law of righteousness, did not achieve that law.*[13] 32*For what reason? Because it was not on the basis of faith but as if it were on the basis of works.*[14] *Israel stumbled over the stone of stumbling,* 33*as it is written,*

Behold, I am placing in Zion a stone of stumbling
and a rock of offense; and the one who believes[15] *on it*
will not be put to shame.[a]

a. Isa. 28:16 and 8:14

In this paragraph Paul uses a critical feature of the gospel — the indispensability of faith in attaining a right relationship with God (cf. 3:27–4:25 especially) — to explain the current state of affairs in salvation history. It is by their faith that Gentiles have attained a righteous status with God (v. 30); and it is because of their lack of faith that Israel has failed to attain the righteousness that the law demanded (vv. 31-32a). By means of a composite quotation from Isa. 8:14 and 28:16, Paul shows that Israel's failure is ultimately christological: by failing to believe in him, he has become for Israel the cause of her downfall (vv. 32b-33).

This paragraph bears an importance out of proportion to its length. It announces the themes that Paul will develop in the rest of chap. 10,[16] and its

13. The majority text, along with the second corrector of the primary Alexandrian uncial ℵ and the uncial Ψ, clarifies the relationship between νόμον and the earlier phrase νόμον δικαιοσύνης by adding δικαιοσύνης here. A few commentators (e.g., Meyer, 2.109; Godet, 368) think the longer reading may be original. But it is probably a scribal assimilation to the earlier phrase. The difficulty of the verse (see the commentary) has also led Schmiedel to conjecture that the original reading was δικαιοσύνην instead of νόμον.

14. The common Pauline antithesis of "faith" and "works of the law" has led to the addition of the word νόμου after ἔργων in some MSS (the majority text, the second [Byzantine] corrector of the uncial ℵ, the western uncial D, Ψ, and the minuscules 33 and 81).

15. The addition of the word πᾶς in a number of MSS (the majority text, Ψ, 33, and 1739) is due to assimilation to 10:11, where this clause is quoted again.

16. See, e.g., Kuss, 3.743; Cranfield, 2.504-5, who views 9:30-33 as a summary statement that is expanded and clarified in chap. 10. Note also Käsemann, 276; Wilckens, 2.211.

interpretation will therefore set the direction for our understanding of many of the debated points in that chapter — especially the nature of Israel's failure with respect to the law.

30 The question "What then shall we say?" need not suggest that Paul is responding to the objection of an opponent.[17] Rather, Paul uses it as a rhetorical device to introduce an implication of his teaching in 9:6b-29 (and esp. vv. 24-29): "Therefore, in light of God's calling of Gentiles and of only some Jews, what do we find now to be the case?"[18] Verses 30-32a give the answer to this question,[19] which is then expanded in 9:32b–10:21. Paul's response comes in two coordinate and parallel clauses, the first focusing on Gentiles (v. 30b) and the second on Israel (v. 31).[20] Paul describes Gentiles, as a class,[21] as "not seeking righteousness." The fact — as Paul well knows — that many Gentiles in his day were earnest and diligent in their pursuit of moral "uprightness" is one indication that the "righteousness" Paul speaks of here is not moral righteousness but forensic righteousness: a right standing before God. How have Gentiles attained this status when they were not even seeking it?[22] First, as Paul explains in an appositive phrase,

---

17. As Michel thinks.

18. Paul uses this question — τί οὖν ἐροῦμεν — or a similar one — τί οὖν — nine times in Romans. In six, Paul uses the question to introduce teaching that responds to a possible objection to what he has been saying (3:5, 6; 6:1, 15; 7:7; 9:14). In the other three, the question introduces a summary or amplification of his teaching (8:31; 9:30: 11:7). On this text, see Käsemann.

19. Since the questions τί οὖν and τί οὖν ἐροῦμεν are usually followed by another question in Romans, it is possible to take vv. 30b-31 as a question: "Should we then say that Gentiles who are not pursuing righteousness attained righteousness . . . while Israel. . . ?" (Fitzmyer). But the διὰ τί; at the beginning of v. 32, raising another question, makes this very difficult. All major English translations and almost all commentators take vv. 30b-31 as a statement.

20. The ὅτι introducing the sentence assumes the repetition of the verb ἐροῦμεν from the question: "We shall say that. . . ."

21. The lack of an article with ἔθνη conveys a qualitative nuance, the emphasis being not on the number of Gentiles but on their identity as Gentiles (in opposition to Israel; v. 31).

22. The pair "seek"/"attain" — διώκω/καταλαμβάνω — is found also in Phil. 3:12-14: "But I [Paul] am pursuing if I might attain." See also Gen. 31:23; Exod. 15:9; Deut. 19:6; Josh. 2:5 (with καταδιώκω); 1 Kgdms. 30:8 (with καταδιώκω); 4 Kgdms. 25:5; Ps. 7:5 (LXX 6) (with καταδιώκω); Lam. 1:3; Sir. 11:10; 27:8. Many scholars think that Paul may be using the image of a race here and in vv. 31-32a (especially emphasized by Badenas, *Christ the End of the Law,* p. 101; cf. τρέχω in 9:16). But the words are used too broadly to justify this conclusion (cf. Dunn). The combination "pursue righteousness" (διώκοντες . . . δίκαιον) is found in Isa. 51:1. A couple of scholars think that Isa. 51:1-7 has had a decisive influence on Paul's wording and teaching in vv. 30-33 (Hübner, *Gottes Ich und Israel,* pp. 63-65; Gaston, *Paul and the Torah,* pp. 126-27). However, while Isaiah exercises a profound influence on Paul throughout chaps. 9–11, it is unclear that Paul has this text in mind here.

the righteousness that Gentiles have attained is a righteousness "that comes by faith." And faith, as Paul has made clear earlier in the letter (1:16; 3:28-29) and will emphasize again (10:11-13), is a response that any person, Jew or Gentile, can make. But, second, Paul undoubtedly wants us to see the Gentiles' attainment of a righteous status with God without their having sought it as a specific and important example of the principle that he has enunciated in his previous argument: belonging to the people of God "is not a matter of the person who wills or the person who runs, but of the God who shows mercy" (9:16).[23]

31-32a The situation of Israel, Paul emphasizes, exhibits a complete contrast[24] to that of the Gentiles he has described in v. 30. The Gentiles, who were "not pursuing,"[25] have "attained";[26] Israel, which *was* "pursuing,"[27] has not "arrived at its goal."[28] The deliberate parallelism between the verses would lead us to expect that Paul would make "righteousness" the goal of Israel's pursuit. Instead, however, we find in v. 31 the phrase "law of righteousness" *(nomon dikaiosynēs)*. This phrase has become a storm center of debate, not only because its meaning is inherently unclear[29] but also because it has been a focal point in recent discussion about Paul's teaching on the law. Three main interpretations have emerged.

(1) *Nomos* might mean "principle" or "rule," with *dikaiosynēs* as an epexegetic genitive: "the principle which is righteousness."[30] The effect of giving *nomos* this purely formal meaning is to put all the weight on the word righteousness. Paul's criticism of Israel here, then, would be that she pursued a worthy goal — righteousness — in the wrong way, "not on the basis of faith but

---

23. See, e.g., Maier, *Mensch,* p. 385; Schreiner, "Israel's Failure," p. 211; Michel.

24. The δέ is adversative.

25. Gk. μὴ διώκοντα.

26. Gk. κατέλαβεν.

27. Gk. διώκων.

28. Gk. οὐκ ἔφθασεν. The verb φθάνω can mean "come first," and Badenas (*Christ the End of the Law,* p. 104) argues for that meaning here (cf. also Thielman, *From Plight to Solution,* pp. 112-13). The point, then, according to Badenas, is not that Israel has been disqualified from the race but simply that she has not "come first"; she has been overtaken by the Gentiles. But the linguistic basis for this interpretation is shaky. While φθάνω does mean "come first," "precede," once in Paul (1 Thess. 4:15), in all other NT occurrences, it means "attain," "arrive at" (Matt. 12:28; Luke 11:20; 2 Cor. 10:14; Phil. 3:16). The situation is the same in the LXX. Moreover, when φθάνω means "come first," it almost always has a personal object (as in 1 Thess. 4:15); when followed by a preposition, as is the case in Rom. 9:31, it means attain to, arrive at. See G. Fitzer, *TDNT* IX, 88-92.

29. Sanders goes so far as to call it "an almost incomprehensible combination of words" (*Paul, the Law and the Jewish People,* p. 42). The unusualness of the phrase has led to various suggestions for textual surgery, beginning with some early scribes (see n. 13). Schmiedel conjectured that δικαιοσύνην originally stood in place of νόμον δικαιοσύνης; O'Neill wants to omit δικαιοσύνης as a later addition.

30. S-H; Murray.

as if it were on the basis of works" (v. 32a), and so did not attain that goal. This view has more in its favor than many contemporary scholars have recognized. As we will see, there are sound reasons for thinking that righteousness remains a key concept throughout vv. 31 and 32a. Paul has earlier in Romans used *nomos* followed by a genitive in a formal sense (Rom. 3:27; 7:23; 8:2 — for which see the commentary). But we have also argued that in each of these cases *nomos* takes on such a "formal" sense only through a rhetorical contrast with the law of Moses. Such a contrast is not present here, and this renders the interpretation of *nomos* in terms of a "principle" or "order" unlikely.

(2) *Nomos* probably, then, has reference to the OT Scriptures. But in what sense? A number of scholars in recent years have taken the word in a "canonical" sense, to refer to the revelatory dimension of the OT, or the Pentateuch or the Mosaic covenant broadly conceived.[31] They usually then interpret the whole phrase in light of Rom. 3:21, where Paul asserts that the righteousness of God is "witnessed to by the law and the prophets." Paul would then be criticizing Israel for pursuing a worthy goal, the "law that testifies to righteousness," by the wrong means: as if that law could be fulfilled by works and the righteousness it points to thereby secured. If, on the other hand, Israel had recognized the call to faith found in "the law," she would have attained that law.

This view suffers also from grave objections. First, the language of "pursuing" and "attaining" seems ill-chosen to describe Israel's approach to, or attitude toward, the revelatory aspects of the OT.[32] Second, we have little, if any, basis for thinking that Paul would view *nomos* as a witness to righteousness by faith.[33] Third, rather than the positive nuance that advocates of this view find in the phrase, Paul's use of *nomos* in association with the word *dikaiosynē* or its cognates points in the opposite direction. Such phrases always have a negative connotation.[34] This is true also, I will argue, for the phrase

31. See Rhyne, *Faith Establishes the Law,* pp. 99-101; idem, *"Nomos Dikaiosynes* and the Meaning of Romans 10:4," *CBQ* 47 (1985), 486-99; Badenas, *Christ the End of the Law,* pp. 104-5; Cranfield.

32. See Westerholm, 127.

33. In Rom. 3:21 it is significant that Paul attributes the testifying function of the OT to "the law and the prophets," and not to "the law." In the same verse, Paul asserts that God's righteousness has been made manifest "apart from the law." The law as a witness to righteousness by faith is often seen also in Rom. 3:31, in conjunction with chap. 4 (see esp. Rhyne, *Faith Establishes the Law*). But I have argued that this is a false interpretation of these verses.

34. Rom. 3:21, 28; 4:13; Gal. 2:16, 21; 3:11, 21; 5:4; Phil. 3:6, 9. Badenas claims that Paul's four uses of νόμος in 9:30–10:13 are all "in construction with δικαιοσύνη, not in opposition to it" (*Christ the End of the Law,* p. 104). But 9:31 (two occurrences) is the text in doubt; 10:4, however we translate τέλος, assigns δικαιοσύνη to Christ as the "τέλος of the law," and not to the law; and 10:5, while bringing δικαιοσύνη and "law" together, does so only to criticize the whole concept (see 10:6).

"righteousness based on the law" in 10:5, an important text because it appears to be parallel to "law of righteousness" in v. 31. The consistently negative nuance of the association of righteousness and *nomos* in Paul renders it improbable that *nomon dikaiosynēs* is used positively as an appropriate goal for Israel to pursue.

(3) We conclude, therefore, that Paul uses *nomos* here in his usual sense, "law of Moses," the commands that God gave to the people of Israel through Moses at Sinai. With this meaning of *nomos,* and taking account of the apparently parallel phrase "righteousness based on the law" (10:5), it is tempting to reverse the terms in the phrase *nomon dikaiosynēs* in interpretation: "righteousness of the law" (cf. RSV; NJB).[35] Such a reversal is grammatically possible, and its effect of making "righteousness" the key term in the verse fits very well with the context and with Paul's customary language. For, first, the parallelism with v. 30 shows that Paul wants to contrast the success of Gentiles and the failure of Israel. But this contrast is more effective if the two groups were pursuing the same goal: righteousness. Second, as we noted in the introduction to 9:30–10:13, Paul's teaching this section is built on three successive and apparently parallel contrasts (9:30-31; 10:3, 5-6). Since both other contrasts are between two kinds of righteousness, we would expect the same to be true in vv. 30-31. And, third, Pauline usage would suggest that the contrast in v. 32 between "on the basis of faith" and "on the basis of works" relates to the attaining of righteousness.[36]

These arguments carry weight. But a reversal of the terms "righteousness" and "law" is not acceptable. If Paul had intended us to read the phrase this way, he would surely have not gone on to use the word "law" by itself as the object that Israel failed to attain later in the verse.[37]

---

35. Calvin; Shedd; O. Hofius, " 'All Israel Will Be Saved': Divine Salvation and Israel's Deliverance in Romans 9–11," *Princeton Seminary Bulletin* 1 (1990), 24-25.

36. The Greek is, respectively, ἐκ πίστεως and ἐξ ἔργων. See Rom. 3:20, 28; Gal. 2:16; 3:2, 5, 10-11 (all contrasting ἐκ πιστέως or a similar phrase with ἐξ ἔργων νόμου as a basis for righteousness or a similar concept). See also Rom. 4:2-3 (Abraham was not justified by works [ἐξ ἔργων], but by believing); Rom. 9:12 (God's purpose of election stands, not being based on works [οὐκ ἐξ ἔργων] but on the one who calls); Eph. 2:8-9 (we are saved by grace through faith and not on the basis of works [οὐκ ἐξ ἔργων]); 2 Tim. 1:9 (God saved us not according to our works [οὐ κατὰ τὰ ἔργα ἡμῶν] but according to his own purpose and grace); Tit. 3:5 (God saved us not on the basis of works [οὐκ ἐξ ἔργων] . . . but according to his mercy).

37. We would have to assume that νόμον at the end of the verse means "principle": Israel, pursuing a righteousness of the law, did not attain to that principle (cf., e.g., Calvin; Hodge; Zahn; Hofius, " 'All Israel Will Be Saved,' " p. 25). But such a shift of meaning in the word νόμος in the same verse is very difficult to accept. See Cranfield, "Some Notes on Romans 9:30-33," in *Jesus und Paulus. Festschrift für Werner Georg Kümmel zum 70. Geburtstag* (ed. E. E. Ellis and E. Grässer; 2d ed.; Göttingen: Vandenhoeck & Ruprecht, 1978), 36-37.

If, then, we take *nomos* to denote the Mosaic law and keep the usual relationship of the terms in the genitive construction, what does the phrase mean? Paul connects righteousness language and the word *nomos* absolutely in only two other verses in Romans: 2:13 and 10:5.[38] In both, Paul pictures righteousness as that which could be gained from the law through "doing." These parallels suggest that we should understand the phrase to mean "the law whose object is righteousness":[39] the law "promises" righteousness when its demands are met.[40] It is this "law that promises righteousness" that must then be carried over as the object of "attain" at the end of v. 31 and of the implied verb "pursue" in v. 32a.[41] "Law," therefore, remains the topic of

38. In Rom. 3:21 and 10:4, νόμος and δικαιοσύνη occur, but they are not connected in any case.

The phrase νόμος δικαιοσύνης occurs only once in the LXX, in Wis. 2:11. The author is taunting the godless: "Let our strength be the law of righteousness, for that which is weak is convicted of being useless." Pace Dunn, it is not likely that this occurrence helps explain Paul's phrase. Elsewhere in the LXX, νόμος is followed by a genitive 115 times. In the majority (89), the word in the genitive refers to the giver or mediator of the law: "law of God," "law of the Lord," laws of the Medes and Persians," and the like. In 20 others, the word in the genitive denotes the issue that a specific law is directed toward; e.g., "the law concerning the Passover" (Exod. 12:43). Of the remaining six, only Wis. 2:11 (see above) and Sir. 17:11 and 45:5, where the phrase is νόμον ζωῆς, "law that gives life," might shed light on Rom. 9:31. And the Wisdom text almost certainly involves a genitive of description ("righteous law"). Cf. Mal. 2:6: νόμος ἀληθείας, "truthful law"; Neh. 9:13: νόμους ἀληθείας, "truthful laws"; Sir. 39:8: νόμῳ διαθήκης κυρίου, "the law that belongs to the covenant of the Lord."

39. See also Rom. 7:10: ἡ ἐντολὴ ἡ εἰς ζωήν, "the commandment which is intended to give life." Most commentators assume that δικαιοσύνης is an objective genitive, though they define the exact relationship between righteousness and law differently. However, Meyer and Barrett take δικαιοσύνης as a qualitative genitive (the former translating "justifying law" and the latter "the law purporting to give righteousness"), while J. Toews calls it a "subjective" genitive but translates (referring to Zahn) "law characterized by righteousness" ("The Law in Paul's Letter to the Romans: A Study of Romans 9:30–10:13" [Ph.D. diss., Northwestern University, 1977], pp. 117-18, 132).

40. See Lietzmann; Michel; Schlier; Westerholm, 127; B. L. Martin, *Christ and the Law in Paul* (NovTSup 62; Leiden: Brill, 1989), pp. 137-38; Schreiner, "Israel's Failure," p. 212; Wilckens; Barrett, "Fall and Responsibility," p. 108; cf. Meyer's translation, "justifying law."

41. See particularly Cranfield. Various other suggestions for the syntax of vv. 31a-32b have been made. (1) Many scholars suggest that the object we should supply in v. 32a is "righteousness" (Hodge; Morris; Ziesler; Meyer, "Romans 10:4," p. 63. Sanders, thinking that the logic of Paul's argument demands that he be speaking about righteousness here, goes so far as to suggest that Paul adds νόμος simply "to make a balanced phrase" [*Paul, the Law and the Jewish People*, p. 42]). While there is reason to think that the concept of righteousness is very much in the forefront of Paul's thinking here, the prominence of "law" in v. 31 (esp. v. 31b) does not allow us to make this substitution. (2) Wilckens wants to bring over into Paul's response in v. 32a the verb ἔφθασεν, "arrived," rather

Paul's teaching throughout this verse and a half, but law conceived as a means to righteousness. As a result, the term "righteousness" also remains very much in the forefront of Paul's thinking throughout.[42] We may paraphrase: "Israel, pursuing a law that promised righteousness, did not attain that law. For what reason did Israel not attain the law that promises righteousness? Because Israel pursued that law that promises righteousness not on the basis of faith but as if[43] it could have been attained on the basis of works."

Paul therefore explains in v. 32a why Israel's pursuit of this "law for righteousness" failed: because she sought to "fulfill" that law by works rather than by faith. Now Paul has nothing in principle against Israel's seeking to do the law; he elsewhere makes clear that the law legitimately demands works.[44] Why then does he appear to condemn it here? For two reasons.

The first and probably primary reason why Paul condemns Israel's pursuit of "the law of righteousness" becomes clear when we take into account the christological emphasis of vv. 32b-33: Israel's failure came because she

---

than ἐδίωκεν, "pursued"; but the question assumes this verb, and a different one must be assumed in Paul's answer. (3) Schreiner suggests that the object of οὐκ ἔφθασεν in v. 31b is righteousness, εἰς νόμον being an accusative of reference ("Israel's Failure," p. 213); but εἰς is a regular way to complete the verb φθάνω. (4) T. D. Gordon thinks that the subject of v. 32a is "the law": "the law is not based on faith but, as it were, on works" ("Why Israel Did Not Obtain Torah-Righteousness: A Translation Note on Rom 9:32," *WTJ* 54 [1992], 163-66). Gordon's suggestion is intriguing, considering the parallel with Gal. 3:12a, but has difficulty accounting for the ὡς.

42. Many scholars in their interpretations assume this without arguing it (e.g., Schmidt; Fitzmyer); see, however, Siegert, *Argumentation bei Paulus,* pp. 141-42.

43. The ὡς before ἐξ ἔργων gives a "subjective idea" to the phrase (S-H, who refer to 2 Cor. 2:17; 11:17 and Phlm. 14). The subjectivity here arises from the false perception of the way in which the law could truly be "achieved" and its promise of righteousness activated.

44. Several recent "revisionist" approaches to Paul and the law have seized on 9:31-32 as evidence that the strict dichotomy between "doing" and the law on the one hand and believing and Christ, on the other, so typical of traditional Protestant interpretation, must be jettisoned (see, e.g., D. P. Fuller, *Gospel and Law: Contrast or Continuum? The Hermeneutics of Dispensationalism and Covenant Theology* [Grand Rapids: Eerdmans, 1980], pp. 71-79; Cranfield, 2.509-10). Here, they argue, Paul claims that the law is to be believed. But I do not think that this is what Paul is saying. His point is not that Israel should have believed the law. Rather, he is claiming that their pursuit of the law with respect to the righteousness that it promised should have been carried out on the basis of faith. Israel should have realized that the law could never be truly reached through works; that human sin would always prevent its promise to justify those who do it (cf. 2:13) from being fulfilled. What Paul says here, then, does not contradict his clear teaching elsewhere, to the effect that the law and believing operate in two separate spheres (see esp. Gal. 3:12a: "the law is not 'of faith' [ἐκ πίστεως]"). For a more detailed treatment of this point, see Westerholm, 127-30; Moo, "The Law of Christ as the Fulfillment of the Law of Moses," pp. 328-33.

"stumbled over" Christ, refusing to put faith in him. Here Paul suggests that it was not only the *manner* of Israel's pursuit of "the law of righteousness" that was misguided[45]; her very choice of a goal was wrong also: "[The Jews] not only deceive themselves as to the goal, but on the pathway on which they set out they come to a fall."[46] Israel has chosen to keep her focus on the law, seeking to find righteousness through it, when Christ, the culmination of that law and the only source of righteousness, has already come (see 10:4).[47] For it is only in Christ that the demand of the law is fully met; and only, therefore, by accepting him in faith that a person can find the righteousness that the law promises (Rom. 3:31; 8:4).[48]

Second, as we have seen, Paul's point is not simply that Israel was pursuing the law; she was pursuing the law *in terms of its promise of righteousness*. Yet Paul has been at pains earlier in the letter to demonstrate that the law's promise of righteousness (2:13) could never be activated in practice (3:20) because of human sin (3:9). Surely, although Paul does not here make it explicit, we must fill out Paul's logic with this earlier clear and sustained argument. Israel has failed to achieve a law that could confer righteousness because she could not produce those works that would be necessary to meet the law's demands and so secure the righteousness it promises.[49]

45. That Paul is condemning *only* the manner of Israel's pursuit is frequently stated. See, e.g., Rhyne, *Faith Establishes the Law*, p. 101; Badenas, *Christ the End of the Law*, p. 105; Cranfield, "Some Notes," pp. 39-40; Morris, 375; Fuller, *Gospel and Law*, p. 71.

46. Käsemann, 278; cf. also Gundry, "Grace," pp. 16-17; Ziesler, 253-54; Roberts, "Righteousness in Romans," p. 19.

47. Those scholars who argue that Paul is condemning Israel for failing to recognize the shift in salvation history that has come with Christ have, therefore, identified an important strand in Paul's teaching here (see 9:32b-33; 10:3-4; see esp. Sanders, *Paul, the Law and the Jewish People*, p. 37; Räisänen, 53-54; F. Refoulé, "Note sur Romains IX,30-33," *RB* 92 [1985], 161-86). But they are wrong when they suggest that this is Paul's only point of critique. Paul is insistent that the righteousness to which the law pointed had never been available through works done in obedience to the law (see esp. Gal. 2:21; 3:21; Rom. 4:2-3, 13). Pursuing the law that promises righteousness as if it could be fulfilled through works has always been wrong.

48. See again Westerholm, 129.

49. Many scholars deny that human inability to fulfill the law has any place in Paul's logic here (e.g., Sanders, *Paul, the Law and the Jewish People*, p. 42; Rhyne, *Faith Establishes the Law*, 101; Badenas, *Christ the End of the Law*, p. 101; Dunn, 2.593). For the view I adopt above, see, e.g., Westerholm, 129; Martin, *Christ and the Law*, pp. 137-38; Thielman, *From Plight to Solution*, p. 113; Gundry, "Grace," pp. 16-17; Schreiner, "Israel's Failure," p. 217.

Dunn, arguing that "works" must mean here "works of the law" in the sense he has defined them elsewhere, ascribes Israel's failure not to an inability to do works but to too great an emphasis on them. By looking at the law narrowly in terms of "the boundary markers" (= works) of the covenant, Israel has not understood the law and its larger promise

32a-33   The exclusivity of Christ is the premise of Paul's next point. For Christ is that "stone" which God has placed in Zion: the foundation for the new people of God; the keystone in the plan of salvation.[50] Yet rather than building on that stone, putting their faith in it, Israel has stumbled over it. Paul does not explicitly connect his assertion that Israel has "stumbled over the stone of stumbling" in v. 32b, with its scriptural support in v. 33, to vv. 31-32a.[51] It is clear, nevertheless, that they are related; but how? Has Israel's inappropriate focus on the law led her to stumble over Christ, the stone God has placed in Zion? Or has Israel's failure to place her faith in Christ led her to focus too exclusively on the law? At the risk of being accused of "having one's cake and eating it too," I answer: both. On the one hand, Paul argues that Israel has missed Christ, the culmination of the plan of God, because she has focused too narrowly on the law. Israel is like a person walking a path, whose eyes are so narrowly focused downward on the path itself that she trips over a stone in the middle of that path. On the other hand, Israel's failure to perceive in Christ the end and goal of the path she has been walking leads her to continue on that path after it had served its purpose.[52]

The "stone" imagery Paul uses in v. 32b comes from two passages in Isaiah, as the quotation in v. 33 reveals. Paul's quotation is a conflation of two texts that both speak about a "stone": Isa. 28:16 and 8:14. The former text reads: "Therefore thus says the Lord GOD, See, I am laying in Zion a foundation stone, a tested stone, a precious cornerstone, a sure foundation:

---

of righteousness for all who believe (2.581-83, 592-93; for a similar approach, see Wright, *Climax of the Covenant*, p. 240). I have elsewhere registered my disagreement with Dunn's interpretation of "works of the law" and his reading Paul's "works" as if it were "works of the law" (see the excursus after 3:20 especially). In addition to this problem, I question whether the language of "pursuing" and "attaining" that Paul uses here is conducive to Dunn's interpretation. For Dunn seems to see the issue as one of Israel's understanding and its implications for the inclusion of the Gentiles; while Paul suggests that the problem was that Israel herself had not attained to the law's fulfillment and so herself missed the righteousness that it promised.

50. A few scholars think that the "stone" over which Israel stumbles might be the law (Meyer, "Romans 10:4," p. 64; Barrett, "Fall and Responsibility," pp. 111-12; Gaston, *Paul and the Torah*, p. 129), or the law and Christ together (Wright, *Climax of the Covenant*, p. 244). But the evidence from the early Christian use of the text, as well as 10:11, where Paul clearly identifies the stone with Christ (contra Dinter, "Remnant of Israel," pp. 114-25, who thinks the stone there is "the message of faith"), points to a christological focus here.

51. A few commentators (e.g., Godet) think that v. 32 should be punctuated with a comma after ἔργων, so that the ὅτι would depend on προσέκοψαν: "because they pursued not on the basis of faith but as if it were on the basis of works, they stumbled. . . ." But we should probably put a full stop after ἔργων, with προσέκοψαν starting a new sentence, one that is not connected to the preceding by any conjunction or particle (e.g., asyndeton).

52. See Cranfield.

'One who trusts will not panic' " (NRSV). It is unclear what we should identify as the "stone" that Isaiah prophesies will be the foundation for Israel's hopes;[53] but some Jews before Paul's day were already apparently identifying the stone with the Messiah.[54] Isa. 8:14, on the other hand, is a prediction of judgment on Israel, warning that they would stumble and fall over the Lord himself: "He [the LORD of hosts; cf. v. 13] will become a sanctuary, a stone one strikes against; for both houses of Israel he will become a rock one stumbles over — a trap and a snare for the inhabitants of Jerusalem" (NRSV).[55] Since these same passages are quoted together in 1 Pet. 2:6-8, it is likely that early Christians before Paul's time had already combined them in a "stone *testimonium*."[56] However, the particular way they are conflated

53. For a survey of possibilities, see J. N. Oswalt, *The Book of Isaiah, Chapters 1–39* (NICOT; Grand Rapids: Eerdmans, 1986), p. 518. Oswalt himself identifies the stone of the prophecy broadly with ". . . the whole complex of ideas relating to the Lord's revelation of his faithfulness and the call to reciprocate with the same kind of faithfulness toward him."

54. See 1QH 6:26-27; 1QS 8:7; the targum (quoted in Cranfield); cf. Str-B, 3.276; J. Jeremias, *TDNT* IV, 272-73. See, however, the caution in Fitzmyer.

Paul's quotation does not agree exactly with either the LXX or the MT. Differences with the LXX are the verb τίθημι (not clearly based on the MT; LXX ἐμβαλῶ), ἐν Σιών (agreeing with the MT; LXX εἰς τὰ θεμέλια Σιων), and the future indicative καταισχυν-θήσεται (LXX has the aorist subjunctive καταισχυνθῇ). This last verb and its object is the main point of difference with the MT: Paul and the LXX both have καταισχύνω, "be ashamed," followed by ἐπ’ αὐτῷ, "on it [or him]"; MT has simply יָחִישׁ, which might be translated "will not panic," "will not be in haste," or "will not be still" (the derivation of the verb is debated; cf. J. D. W. Watts, *Isaiah 1–33* [WBC; Waco, TX: Word, 1985], 367-68). Paul's wording is, then, mainly LXX, but similarities with the wording in 1 Pet. 2:6 (cf. esp. τίθημι, which never in the LXX translates the Hebrew word used here) suggest that Paul may be relying on a Greek version of the text circulating among the early Christians (see Koch, 161-62; Stanley, *Paul and the Language of Scripture,* pp. 120-21).

55. Paul's wording of the phrase from 8:14 agrees neither with the LXX nor the MT, but is identical (except for a change of case) with 1 Pet. 2:8 (it also shows some similarities with the versions of Aquila, Symmachus, and Theodotion). Again, this suggests that Paul is drawing his reference from an early Christian tradition (see again, e.g., Koch, 59-60; Stanley, *Paul and the Language of Scripture,* pp. 123-24; and Dodd, *According to the Scriptures,* p. 43).

56. See, e.g., Lindars, *New Testament Apologetic,* pp. 177-79. D. Flusser thinks that the conflated quotation originated in an Essene homily (cf. 1QS 8:4-10) ("From the Essenes to Romans 9:24-33," in *Judaism and the Origins of Christianity* [Jerusalem: Magnes, 1988], pp. 75-87). Michel, however, thinks that 1 Peter may be dependent on Romans (*Paulus,* pp. 40-42). A third "stone" passage, Ps. 118:22, is quoted in Matt. 21:42 and parallels and may have been a third member of the "stone testimonia" (see the study by K. R. Snodgrass, "The Christological Stone Testimonia in the New Testament" [Ph.D. diss., University of St. Andrews, 1973]). Some scholars, more often in the past, have seen in this conflation evidence of an early "testimony book," a written collection of OT proof-texts circulating among early Christians (see Luz, 96-97). Most scholars are now inclined to attribute such conflations to oral tradition (e.g., Käsemann, 279).

here is probably Paul's own work. By replacing the middle of Isa. 28:16 with a phrase from Isa. 8:14, he brings out the negative point about Israel's fall that is his main point in this context. At the same time, by including the reference to Isa. 28:16, he lays the foundation for the positive exposition of Christ as a "stone" that he will develop in chap. 10 (see esp. v. 11).[57] The quotation concluding chap. 10, therefore, provides a significant christological basis for Paul's continuing discussion of Israel's failure and the Gentiles' inclusion in chap. 10. At the same time, it contributes significantly to Paul's concern to demonstrate that Israel's exclusion from God's people as a result of the gospel does not constitute a departure from the OT. Quite the contrary, Paul here implies: Israel's stumbling over Christ was predicted in the OT.[58]

b. The Righteousness of God and "Their Own Righteousness" (10:1-4)

1Brothers and sisters, the desire of my heart and my prayer to God on their behalf[1] is for their salvation. 2For I testify about them that they have zeal for God, but it is not according to knowledge. 3For, being ignorant about the righteousness of God and seeking to establish their own,[2] they have not submitted to the righteousness of God. 4For Christ is the culmination of the law, so that there might be righteousness for everyone who believes.

This paragraph unfolds in a series of logical steps, each related to the former with the conjunction gar, "for." Paul begins by reasserting his deep concern

---

57. See Dinter, "Israel as Remnant," p. 159; Müller, Gottes Gerechtigkeit, pp. 36-37; D. A. Oss, "The Interpretation of the 'Stone' Passages by Peter and Paul: A Comparative Study," JETS 32 (1989), 181-200.

58. See, e.g., Käsemann.

1. The majority text replaces the pronoun αὐτῶν with τοῦ Ἰσραήλ and adds the verb ἐστιν, while several other MSS (the second [Byzantine] corrector of ℵ, Ψ, and several minuscules, including 33) retain αὐτῶν and add ἐστιν. But the shorter text should certainly be preferred here, attested by the strong combination of P46, the primary Alexandrian uncials ℵ (original hand) and B (cf. also A and 1739), and the western bilinguals (D, F, and G).

2. Some early and important MSS (such as the papyrus P46 and the primary Alexandrian uncial ℵ; cf. also Ψ, the later western uncials F and G, and the majority text) include the word δικαιοσύνην here. The word might be original, scribes having omitted it as being unnecessarily repetitious (Meyer, 170). But it is more likely that scribes added the word to clarify τὴν ἰδίαν (Lietzmann, 91; S-H, 283; Käsemann, 281). We should probably follow that part of the Alexandrian tradition (A, B, 81, 1739) that omits the word, especially since it is accompanied by the witness of the western uncials D and P.

for the salvation of his "kindred according to the flesh" (cf. 9:1-3). Assumed in this expression of concern is, of course, the fact that most of his fellow Jews are not finding salvation. It is this assumption that is the basis for v. 2, as Paul explains why Jews have not found salvation: their commendable zeal for the Lord has not been matched by a comparable degree of knowledge. What have the Jews not understood? In a word, righteousness. As Paul shows in v. 3, the Jews have not recognized the manifestation of God's righteousness in Christ and have sought rather to establish their own, based on the doing of the law (cf. 9:32 and 10:5). That this is truly a serious misunderstanding is demonstrated in v. 4: Christ has brought the law to its culmination; it is in him that righteousness is now available, and for anyone who believes.

Verse 4 is justly famous as one of the most succinct yet significant theological assertions in all of the Pauline letters. Yet v. 3, with its explanation of Israel's failure in terms of a contrast between two kinds of righteousness, is the conceptual center of the paragraph. It therefore matches the similar contrast that Paul features in 9:30-31 and 10:5-6.

1 The address "brothers and sisters," as elsewhere in Romans,[3] signals a transition. In this case, however, the transition is not from one topic to another but from one aspect of a topic to another. Paul has given a brief explanation of Israel's failure to find inclusion in the eschatological people of God; now he will expand further on this explanation. At the same time, Paul's direct address of his mainly Gentile Christian readers serves to underline his sincerity and the importance of what he says in v. 1. He wants his predominantly Gentile Christian readers to know that he takes no delight or satisfaction from Israel's fall. Quite the contrary, on his part,[4] Paul remains passionately committed to the salvation of the Jews. His commitment rests in the desire, or will,[5] of his most inmost person, the heart; and it comes to expression in his prayer of petition[6] on behalf of Israel,[7] that they might

---

3. Gk. ἀδελφοί. Cf. 1:13; 7:1, 4; 8:12; 11:25; 12:1; 15:14, 30; 16:17.

4. BDF (447[4]) point out that Paul's use of the particle μέν without a correlative δέ has classical parallels, judging by which Paul would here be saying "so far as it depends on my desire."

5. Gk. εὐδοκία. The word often means "good will" (Phil. 1:15), and some commentators adopt that meaning here (Godet; S-H; Murray; Barrett). But it can also mean "favor" (Eph. 1:5, 9) or "will" (2 Thess. 1:11; Phil. 2:13 [possibly]), and that meaning fits better this context (see BAGD; G. Schrenk, *TDNT* II, 746; Michel; Cranfield; Dunn; Wilckens; Fitzmyer).

6. Gk. δέησις.

7. ὑπὲρ αὐτῶν probably depends on δέησις (see Godet; Cranfield; Dunn), although it could be part of the predicate; e.g., "my prayer to God is 'in their favor' " (cf. Barrett; Käsemann).

experience the salvation that has been made available in the gospel.[8] As Murray points out, the juxtaposition of this heartfelt prayer for Israel's salvation almost immediately after Paul's teaching about the ultimate determinancy of the will of God in salvation (9:6b-29) carries an important reminder: "We violate the order of human thought and trespass the boundary between God's prerogative and man's when the truth of God's sovereign counsel constrains despair or abandonment of concern for the eternal interests of men."[9]

2 "Zeal" emerged as an especially commendable characteristic in the intertestamental period, when the very existence of the Jewish faith was threatened by foreign enemies and internal unconcern.[10] It is also uniformly praised in the NT.[11] Paul's "testimony" about Israel begins, then, on a positive note: they have a praiseworthy devotion to God. The problem with Israel and the reason why Paul must continue to pray for their salvation is that, like the pre-Christian Paul (see Acts 22:3; Phil. 3:6), their zeal is not driven by "knowledge."[12] As v. 3 makes clear, what is involved is a discernment of the plan of God that enables one to recognize what God is doing in the world and to respond accordingly.

3 God's plan has reached its climax in the gospel of Jesus Christ (1:2-4). And at the heart of the gospel Paul has placed the revelation of the righteousness of God (see 1:16-17). It is natural, therefore, for Paul to characterize the Jews' lack of understanding (v. 2b) as consisting in their ignorance of "the righteousness of God."[13] This does not mean that the Jews did not understand that God was a righteous God. For, as the parallel phrases in 9:31

8. As I pointed out in the introduction to chaps. 9–11, this verse is one of the clearest indicators that Paul does indeed treat Israel as a whole in these chapters as separate from God and his people, under condemnation. Contra, e.g., van Buren, who thinks that Paul is praying here only that Israel might be saved from their blindness (*A Theology of the Jewish-Christian Reality,* p. 148).

9. Murray. However, Leenhardt's claim (endorsed by Dunn) that this prayer contradicts a strongly predestinarian reading of chap. 9 misses the almost paradoxical biblical interplay of divine sovereignty and human prayer (and evangelism) in salvation. On this whole topic, see esp. J. I. Packer, *Evangelism and the Sovereignty of God* (Downers Grove, IL: Inter-Varsity, 1961).

10. See especially the famous words of Mattathias, calling his fellow Jews to rebellion against the edict of Antiochus against the Jewish faith: "Let every one who is zealous for the law and supports the covenant come out with me!" (1 Macc. 2:27, RSV); cf. also, e.g., Jud. 9:4; Sir. 45:23-24 (lauding Phinehas [Num. 25]); Josephus, *Ant.* 12.271. That this zeal has a nationalistic element in the intertestamental period is, of course, clear. But there is no hint in this text that Paul thinks of Israel's zeal as "too nationalistically centered" (contra Dunn).

11. Cf. John 2:17; Acts 22:3; 2 Cor. 11:2; Phil. 3:6.

12. Gk. ἐπίγνωσιν. This word connotes a practical as opposed to a theoretical knowledge. See our note on 1:28; note also Godet; Käsemann; Michel; Wilckens.

13. Verse 3 therefore explains (cf. γάρ) the last phrase in v. 2: οὐ κατ᾽ ἐπίγνωσιν.

and 10:6 suggest, "the righteousness of God" here denotes the dynamic activity of God whereby he brings people into relationship with himself.[14] This "justifying" activity of God is manifested in Christ (3:21) and proclaimed in the gospel (1:17). The Jews' ignorance, therefore, involves their failing to understand that God has fulfilled his promise to reveal his saving activity in Jesus Christ.[15]

"The righteousness of God," in this sense, as I argued earlier, embraces on one side God's activity of "declaring right" and on the other the status of "being right" with God that people receive when they respond in faith to that activity.[16] Paul's language in this verse implies the presence of both these concepts. The nuance of divine activity is evident in the language of the last clause of the verse: the Jews "have not submitted to the righteousness of God." Paul's use of the verb "submit"[17] shows that the righteousness of God is an active force to which one must humbly and obediently subordinate oneself.[18] Another way to put the matter would be to say that the Jews have not responded to God's righteousness in faith.[19] So close a relationship does Paul establish between the righteousness of God and faith that one cannot

14. For this conception of "the righteousness of God," see the notes on 1:17 and the excursus following those notes. Those who make a different decision about "righteousness of God" in these other texts naturally come to different conclusions here: a status of righteousness that has its source in God (Godet; Murray; Cranfield); "der eschatologischen Verwicklung des Rechtes Gottes an der Welt" (Müller, *Gottes Gerechtigkeit,* p. 72; cf. also Stuhlmacher, *Gerechtigkeit Gottes,* pp. 92-93, 98-99); God's own saving faithfulness (Wilckens; Williams, "The 'Righteousness of God' in Romans," p. 283); God's power/gift (Käsemann).

15. For the translation of ἀγνοέω here by "disregard," see BAGD. Paul uses this verb in a similar sense in Rom. 2:4; 1 Cor. 14:38. Note also 2 Cor. 6:9, where ἀγνοέω is the opposite of ἐπιγινώσκω.

16. See again our notes on 1:17 and the excursus after that verse; cf. also Stuhlmacher, " 'The End of the Law,' " pp. 151-52.

17. Gk. ὑποτάσσω.

18. Paul uses ὑποτάσσω of a submission to something besides another person only in Rom. 8:7 (the unbeliever toward the law of God) and 8:20 (creation toward "frustration"). On ὑποτάσσω, see further the notes on 13:1. The aorist is constantive, summing up the rejection of the gospel by many Jews since the cross and resurrection. The confusion of middle and passive in Hellenistic Greek, and especially with this verb, makes it possible to understand the passive ὑπετάγησαν as a reflexive middle, "subjected themselves" (cf. Moulton, 163; KJV; NASB; REB; TEV); but it is not necessary.

19. See also, for the general idea here, *2 Apoc. Bar.* 54:5: "[You] reveal the secrets to those who are spotless, to those who subjected themselves to you and your Law in faith." A few scholars have argued that the aorist ὑπετάγησαν makes reference specifically to Israel's historical rejection of the Messiah (e.g., Cranfield). But Paul probably has in mind rather the continual rejection of Christ on the part of Jews (the aorist being constantive, with past reference). Whether Paul also thinks of the pre-Christian history of Israel's rejection of God (e.g., Hübner, *Gottes Ich und Israel,* pp. 92-93) is not clear, especially in light of Paul's teaching about the revelation of God's righteousness in Christ.

mention the former without thinking of the latter. And that Israel's "not submitting" is equivalent to their not having faith is evident from the parallel texts in this passage (9:32a; cf. v. 33b; 10:5-6). But the second participial clause in the verse — "seeking to establish their own righteousness" — suggests that "righteousness of God" includes also the nuance of "righteous status." "Their own"[20] must have a generally possessive sense and the righteousness "they" possess accordingly the notion of status. As its opposite, therefore, "the righteousness of God" must also include the idea of a status of righteousness conferred by God.

"Their own righteousness" can be understood in two different ways. If we give "their own" a distributive sense — "each of their own" — Paul will be referring to the attempt of individual Jews to establish a relationship with God through their own efforts.[21] However, if we give "their own" a corporate sense — "Israel's own" — Paul would presumably be referring to Israel's misunderstanding of righteousness as something that applied to Israel alone.[22] With the former meaning, Paul is scolding the Jews for *self*-righteousness — the attempt to establish a relationship with God based on one's own works. On the latter view, Paul is scolding them from for *national* righteousness — the attempt to confine a relationship with God to Israel to the detriment of all other nations. The "national righteousness" view can find some support in Paul's stress in vv. 4b and 9-13 on the universal dimensions of God's righteousness in Christ: against Israel's attempt to keep righteousness to themselves, Paul proclaims the availability of righteousness *"for all"* in Christ. But the more immediate contrast to "their own righteousness" is "God's righteousness." This suggests that "their own," like the contrasting term, "God's," is not simply possessive, but has the nuance of source. And this, in turn, favors an individualizing rather than a corporate interpretation: a righ-

---

20. Gk. τὴν ἰδίαν.

21. See, e.g., Augustine, "On Grace and Free Will," chap. 24 (*NPNF* 5); Cremer, *Die paulinische Rechtfertigungslehre,* pp. 301-2; Calvin; Godet; S-H; Murray; Michel; Barrett; Cranfield; Käsemann; Wilckens; Hofius, " 'All Israel Will Be Saved,' " p. 26; Westerholm, 114-16; Schreiner, "Israel's Failure," 215-18.

22. See esp. Sanders, *Paul, the Law and the Jewish People,* pp. 44-45; idem, "Paul on the Law, his Opponents, and the Jewish People in Philippians 3 and 2 Corinthians 11," in *Paul and the Gospels* (Anti-Judaism in Early Christianity, Studies in Christianity and Judaism 1; ed. P. Richardson; Waterloo, Ont.: Wilfrid Laurier University [Corporation for Studies in Religion]), 1986), 78-88; F. Refoulé, "Romains X,4. encoure une fois," *RB* 91 (1984), 339-40; Longenecker, *Eschatology and the Covenant,* p. 219; R. Liebers, *Das Gesetz als Evangelium. Untersuchungen zur Gesetzeskritik des Paulus* (ATANT 75; Zürich: Theologischer, 1989), pp. 55-58. Gager, in keeping with the interpretation of Paul's criticism of Jews that he and Gaston espouse, argues that Israel's failure here is a failure to recognize Paul's gospel to and about Gentiles (*Origins of Anti-Semitism,* pp. 249-50).

teousness that comes from one's own efforts. Three additional considerations also favor this view.

First, this meaning of "their own righteousness" stands in continuity with OT references to "one's own" righteousness. Particularly significant is the Lord's reminder to Israel in Deut. 9:4-6 that it was not because of "their own" righteousness that they were about to occupy the promised land but because of the Lord's gracious choice of Israel to be his own possession.[23] Second, interpreting "their own righteousness" as "self-righteousness" suits the context best since the parallel references to righteousness in 9:31-32a and 10:5 have roughly this same meaning.[24] Third, the only other time Paul contrasts "God's righteousness" and a righteousness of "one's own," he qualifies the former as "based on faith" and the latter as "based on the law" (Phil. 3:6-9). This suggests that Paul thinks of "one's own" righteousness as a righteousness tied to human effort rather than a righteousness confined to Israel.[25]

23. Thielman, *From Plight to Solution,* p. 113. Deut. 9 is significant not only because of its prominence in Deuteronomy but also because Paul alludes to this same section of Scripture in 10:6 (see H.-J. Eckstein, " 'Nahe ist dir das Wort': Exegetische Erwägungen zu Röm 10[8]," *ZNW* 79 [1988], 209). The notion of "one's own righteousness" occurs also in Isa. 64:5; Ezek. 14:14; 18:22, 24, 26; 33:12, 13, 18.

24. The phrases parallel to "establishing their own righteousness" in this context are "pursuing the law of righteousness . . . as if out of works" (9:31-32a) and "the righteousness that is based on the law" (10:5). Both refer to establishing a relationship with God based on works and a doing of the law, and are set in contrast with references to faith. Since "not submitting" to God's righteousness in v. 3 includes a failure to believe, this fundamental faith-works contrast is likely to be seen here again (Westerholm, 114-16; Gundry, "Grace, Works, and Staying Saved," p. 18; Laato, *Paulus und das Judentum,* pp. 250-54). There is admittedly a degree of circularity to this argument: Dunn argues that both these parallel phrases denote a concept similar to the one he is arguing for in 10:3. I argue, however, for a different interpretation of these phrases; and, if my interpretation is accepted, the point above stands.

25. In Phil. 3:6-9, Paul recounts his decision, upon becoming a Christian, to exchange δικαιοσύνην τὴν ἐν νόμῳ ("a righteousness that is in the law") (v. 6)/ἐμὴν δικαιοσύνην τὴν ἐκ νόμου ("a righteousness of my own, based on the law") (v. 9) for τὴν ἐκ νόμου δικαιοσύνην ἐπὶ τῇ πίστει ("the righteousness from God, based on faith)." Some scholars deny the parallel (e.g., Müller, *Gottes Gerechtigkeit,* pp. 72-74; Badenas, *Christ the End of the Law,* pp. 244-45 n. 193), but for no good reason (note, e.g., that "zeal for God" in Rom. 10:3 finds a parallel in Paul's description of himself as "according to zeal, persecuting the church"). In Phil. 3, Paul presents "his own" righteousness not as a contrast with a righteousness that is "intended for others," "not confined to Israel"; he presents it as a contrast with a righteousness that comes as a gift from God in response to faith. See esp. Seifrid, *Justification,* pp. 174-75. He argues that Paul's "my own righteousness, based on the law" is a result *both* of his Jewish heritage *and* his active obedience. Contra, e.g., Sanders, then, Paul's "own righteousness" is not simply a neutral or positive possession that was exchanged for a "better" one, the righteousness from God (*Paul, the*

The Jews failed to "submit" to God's righteousness not only because they did not recognize God's righteousness when it arrived but also because they were too narrowly focused on seeking a righteousness in connection with their obedience to the law.[26]

4 This verse, containing one of the most famous of all of Paul's theological "slogans," grounds (cf. "for," *gar*) what Paul has said about the Jews in v. 3. Specifically, he shows that the Jews' pursuit of a righteousness of their own, based on the law, is wrong because Christ has brought the law to its culmination and thereby made righteousness available to everyone who believes. We must now justify this reading of the verse by looking at (1) the meaning of the word "law"; (2) the syntactical relationship between the first part of the verse and the second; and (3) the meaning of the word *telos* (which I have translated "culmination").

(1) Scholars have argued for four different meanings of the word *nomos* in this verse: "law" in general, in whatever form;[27] "OT revelation" broadly;[28] "legalism";[29] and Mosaic law. The first and second of these interpretations are unlikely since neither meaning is found in the immediate context. The third, on the other hand, as I have argued elsewhere,[30] is unattested in Paul and cannot be accepted here. With the great majority of scholars, therefore, I conclude that *nomos* refers in this verse, as usually in Paul, to the Mosaic law.

(2) Verse 4 contains an assertion — "Christ is the *telos* of the law"[31] — and a prepositional phrase — "*eis* righteousness for everyone who believes." How are we to connect the prepositional phrase to the assertion? A

Law and the Jewish People, p. 140). Rather, in a combination typical of Pharisaic piety, Paul sees his pre-Christian righteousness as involving, though perhaps not "based on," his own performance. See esp. v. 3, which introduces the whole text with a contrast between "boasting in Christ Jesus" and "putting confidence in the flesh." It is this synergism that Paul as a Christian rejects in favor of the "altogether extrinsic" righteousness given by God through faith. For similar emphases, see Silva, *Philippians,* pp. 176, 186; P. T. O'Brien, *The Epistle to the Philippians* (NIGTC; Grand Rapids: Eerdmans, 1991), pp. 380, 395-96; Gundry, "Grace, Works and Staying Saved," p. 14.

26. This interpretation assumes that both adverbial participles, ἀγνοοῦντες and ζητοῦντες, are causal. This would imply that the Jews' attempt to establish their own righteousness was not only the *result* of their failure to submit to God's righteousness in Christ (contra those, such as Sanders, who think that Paul is criticizing the Jews here simply for failing to recognize the shift in salvation history).

27. Gifford; Denney.

28. W. S. Campbell, "Christ the End of the Law: Romans 10:4," in *Studia Biblica III,* p. 75; Badenas, *Christ the End of the Law,* pp. 113-14.

29. See esp. Bultmann, "Christ, the End of the Law," p. 54; Moule, "Obligation in the Ethic of Paul," p. 402.

30. See the notes on 2:12 and 6:14.

31. The Greek would also allow us to translate "the τέλος of the law is Christ," but this does not fit Paul's argument nearly as well (cf. Fitzmyer).

number of scholars argue that it should be connected directly to the word "law." Paul would then be claiming that Christ is the *telos* of the law *in its relationship to righteousness,* or *as a means of righteousness* ("for everyone who believes" would then be attached to the statement as a whole); see NASB: "For Christ is the end of the law for righteousness to everyone who believes" (KJV is similar). Most who construe the syntax in this way also think that *telos* means "end," "termination." They therefore conclude that Paul is proclaiming here the end of the (false) understanding of the law as a means of securing righteousness with God[32] or the end of Israel's misunderstanding of the law and its righteousness as confined to Israel.[33] But the syntax does not favor attaching the prepositional phrase directly to the word "law."[34] It is much more likely that the prepositional phrase introduced by *eis* functions as a purpose or result clause attached to the assertion as a whole: "Christ is the *telos* of the law, with the result that there is (or with the purpose that there

---

32. Hodge: Christ ends the law as "a covenant prescribing the condition of life"; cf. Morris; Murray; Zeller; Zahn; Althaus; Longenecker, 145-47; Williams, "The 'Righteousness of God' in Romans," p. 284. It is important to note that most of these scholars explicitly add that what is implied by this is not that the law was ever truly the means of achieving righteousness (see esp. Murray); what Christ has ended, many of them make clear, is all attempt at achieving righteousness through the law.

33. Dunn, 2.590-91, 596-97; cf. also his " 'Righteousness from the Law' and 'Righteousness from Faith': Paul's Interpretation of Scripture in Romans 10:1-10," in *Tradition and Interpretation in the New Testament,* p. 222.

34. In classical Greek, adnominal prepositional phrases (prepositional phrases that modify substantives) were usually identified by an article. This still occurs in the NT (e.g., ἡ ἐντολὴ ἡ εἰς ζωήν, "the leading-to-life commandment" [Rom. 7:10]), but it is no longer the usual construction. Therefore it is only by word order and context that one can in the NT determine what a prepositional phrase modifies. Of the almost 1800 occurrences of εἰς in the NT, only 77 (by my rough count) are adnominal. In 56 of these these 77 cases, the prepositional phrase occurs immediately before or after the substantive it modifies: e.g., τὸ φρόνημα τῆς σαρκὸς ἔχθρα εἰς θεόν, "the mind of the flesh [is] hostile to God" (Rom. 8:7). In the 22 remaining cases, the substantive is separated by its modifying εἰς phrase by a verb (twice: Acts 24:15; Rom. 16:19a), by a prepositional phrase (4 times: Rom. 3:22; 2 Cor. 2:16a; 2:16b; Phlm. 6), by a dependent dative (3 times: Rom. 5:2 [v.l.]; Eph. 5:2; Col. 1:25), by a dependent genitive (12 times: Mark 1:4; Luke 3:3; Rom. 6:22; 15:16; 16:5; 2 Cor. 9:13a; Eph. 1:19; 4:12a; 4:12b; Phil. 1:5; 2 Thess. 1:3), or by a prepositional phrase + dependent genitive (once: 1 Thess. 5:18; the remaining occurrence, Rom. 13:14, is difficult to classify). In none of these examples, however, do we find the situation that proponents of an adnominal interpretation of εἰς in Rom. 10:4 must suppose: εἰς being dependent on a noun (νόμου) from which it is separated by the subject of the sentence (Χριστός). For a similar conclusion, based on the occurrence of εἰς in Pauline sentences with the verb εἰμι, see M. A. Seifrid, "Paul's Approach to the Old Testament in Rom 10:6-8," *TrinJ* 6 (1985), 8-9. Cf. also Räisänen, 55 n. 59; Cranfield, 2.519-20 n. 2.

might be) righteousness for everyone who believes"[35] (so, essentially, most modern English translations).

(3) This leaves the question of the meaning of the word *telos*. All major English versions translate this word "end." But this translation contains a crucial ambiguity: does "end" mean (1) "termination," as in the sentence "The end of the class finally came!" or (2) "goal," as in the sentence, "The end of government is the welfare of the people"; or (3) "result," as in the sentence "She did not foresee the end of her actions." Each of these meanings is possible for the Greek word *telos*,[36] and each is attested in Paul.[37] If we accept the first meaning, Paul's point will be a purely temporal one: the coming of Christ means that, in some manner, the period of the law's significance and/or authority is at an end.[38] If we choose either the second or the third meaning, however, Paul will be presenting the law and Christ in a dynamic relationship, with the law in some sense directed toward, or pointing forward, to Christ.[39]

35. The use of εἰς to introduce what becomes, in effect, purpose or result clauses is found about 25 times in the NT. See, e.g., Rom. 3:25: ὃν προέθετο ὁ θεὸς ἱλαστήριον διὰ [τῆς] πίστεως ἐν τῷ αὐτοῦ αἵματι εἰς ἔνδειξιν τῆς δικαιοσύνης αὐτοῦ: "whom God publicly displayed as a place of atonement, to be received by faith, in his blood, *in order to demonstrate his righteousness*. . . ." If εἰς, then, introduces a purpose or result statement, παντὶ τῷ πιστεύοντι must be taken with εἰς δικαιοσύνην. This would rule out attempts to read παντὶ τῷ πιστεύοντι as if it were a qualifier of the main assertion: e.g., "Christ is the τέλος of the law *only for those who believe*." Cf. Mussner, who argues that, since Christ is "the end of the law" only for believers, Paul keeps open the possibility that the law may still be in force for unbelieving Jews (" 'Christus [ist] des Gesetzes Ende zur Gerechtigkeit für jeden, der glaubt' [Röm 10,4]," in *Paulus — Apostat oder Apostel? Jüdische und Christliche Antworten* [Regensburg: Pustet, 1977], p. 37).

36. Among the definitions in LSJ are: "consummation," "outcome," "supreme power," "office," "decision," "service," "offerings," "dues," "expenditure," "maturity," "end," "cessation," "attainment," "goal," "ideal," and "purpose."

37. (1) "Termination": "Then shall come τὸ τέλος, when he shall hand over the kingdom to God the Father . . ." (1 Cor. 15:24); (2) "Goal": "The τέλος of the commandment is love from a pure heart . . ." (1 Tim. 1:5); (3) "Result": "The τέλος of these things [sinful actions] is death" (Rom. 6:21).

38. All major English versions translate "end." While this English word has a considerable spectrum of meaning, a temporal sense is the most obvious. Scholars who advocate a mainly temporal translation are (in addition to those listed in n. 33 above): Godet; Käsemann; Meyer; Lietzmann; van Dülmen, *Theologie des Gesetzes,* p. 126; Luz, 139-57; Lagrange; Schmidt; Gaugler; Nygren; Michel; Schmithals; Schlier; Martin, *Christ and the Law,* pp. 129-34; Mussner, "Christus," 37; Ziesler, *Righteousness,* p. 206; Sanders, *Paul, the Law and the Jewish People,* p. 40; Räisänen, 53-56; Kim, *Origin of Paul's Gospel,* pp. 307-8; O. Hofius, "Das Gesetz des Mose und das Gesetz Christi," *ZTK* 80 (1983), 276-77. It should be noted, however, that these scholars often come to quite different conclusions about what exactly it is that Christ has "ended."

39. Since the law comes from God, it is proper to assume that the sense in which the law will be directed toward Christ will be teleological in nature; that is, there will be

Neither lexical nor contextual data point unambiguously toward one or the other of these two main options. R. Badenas has shown that *telos* usually means "goal" or "intent" (a teleological sense) in nonbiblical Greek.[40] But in both the LXX and the NT the temporal meaning ("closing part," "termination") of *telos* dominates.[41] The context uses language of pursuing and attaining with

---

an underlying sense of purpose rather than simply result. This sense of purpose is understood in at least three different ways. (1) Christ as the "fulfillment" of the law. This view was popular with the church fathers, many of whom paraphrased τέλος with the Greek words τελείωσις, πλήρωμα, or the Latin *perfectio;* see Schelkle; Cranfield. Cf., in modern times, Barth, *People of God,* p. 39; P. von der Osten-Sacken, *Die Heiligkeit der Tora: Studien zum Gesetz bei Paulus* (Munich: Kaiser, 1989), pp. 250-56; cf. also M. N. A. Bockmuehl, *Revelation and Mystery in Ancient Judaism and Pauline Christianity* (WUNT 2.36; Tübingen: Mohr, 1990), pp. 150-53 ("prophetic fulfillment" or "consummation"). (2) Christ as the "substance," "inner meaning," or "true content" of the law. (3) Christ as the "goal" or "aim" of the law. The difference between 2 and 3 is slight and not always clearly indicated by scholars, but it is nevertheless significant. On the second interpretation, Paul is asserting something about the true meaning of the OT, with the assumption that Jews all along should have seen Christ "in" the law. The third is more historically focused, the idea being that the Jews should now recognize in Christ the goal to which the law was pointing. For the second view, see Chrysostom; Calvin; Cranfield. For a general defense of the translation "goal," see Bengel; Fitzmyer; F. Flückiger, "Christus, des Gesetzes τέλος," *TZ* 11 (1955), 153-57; Bring, "Paul and the Old Testament," p. 47; Meyer, "Romans 10:4," pp. 65-66; Rhyne, *Faith Establishes the Law,* p. 104; idem, *"Nomos Dikaiosynes,"* pp. 492-94; Badenas, *Christ the End of the Law,* pp. 114-15; Jewett, "The Law," pp. 349-54; Osten-Sacken, "Verständnis," pp. 33-36; Fuller, *Gospel and Law,* pp. 84-86; W. C. Kaiser, "The Law as God's Gracious Guidance for the Promotion of Holiness," in *The Law, the Gospel and the Modern Christian,* pp. 185-88; Aletti, *Comment Dieu est-il juste?* 114-18.

40. *Christ the End of the Law,* pp. 38-80.

41. τέλος occurs approximately 155 times in the LXX. In 110 of these τέλος occurs as the object of the preposition εἰς. This construction indicates completeness — right up to "the end" — usually with respect to time (e.g., Hab. 1:4: "because of this the law is slackened and judgment *never* [εἰς τέλος] goes forth") but occasionally with respect to the quality of the action (e.g., Amos 9:8b: "However, it is the case that I will not *utterly* [εἰς τέλος] destroy the house of Jacob, says the LORD"). It also occurs in the heading of 56 Psalms, with uncertain meaning. Of the approximately 45 other occurrences, τέλος refers to a "tribute" 10 times, while the others are almost all to be translated "end": the "end" of a period of time, or the "end" of human beings, or the "end" of matters. Few, if any, occurrences are clearly teleological in meaning. In the NT, τέλος occurs 40 times. The set phrase εἰς [τὸ] τέλος occurs only three times, two with a quantitative sense ("completely," "thoroughly" — Luke 18:5; John 13:1 [probably]) and one with a temporal sense ("finally" — 1 Thess. 2:16 [probably]). Three times the word denotes "tribute," or taxes (Matt. 17:25 [plural]; Rom. 13:7a; 137b). In 17 cases, τέλος denotes the "last point" in a series of events (e.g., Matt. 10:22: "the person who endures to the end [εἰς τέλος] will be saved"; cf. also Matt. 24:6, 13, 14; Mark 13:7, 13; Luke 21:9; 1 Cor. 1:8; 10:11 [plural]; 15:24; 2 Cor. 1:13; 1 Pet. 3:8; 4:7; Heb. 3:14; 6:11; Rev. 2:26 — 2 Cor. 3:13 is debated but

reference to the law (9:31-32a); and this might lead us to expect that Paul would now present Christ as the true "goal" of the law, that goal that Israel sought but could not attain. In the same way, Paul's use of OT texts to describe Christ and the righteousness he has brought (9:32b-33; 10:6-8, 11, 13) might indicate that Paul is thinking of Christ as the true meaning or intent of the law. However, there is much in both the immediate and wider context to favor a temporal translation. The relationship between v. 4 and v. 3 shows that Paul wants to stress the discontinuity between Christ and the law. The Jews' striving for a righteousness of "their own," based on the law (v. 3), is wrong (among other reasons) because ("for" [*gar*]) Christ has brought an end to the law and to the era of which it was the center. This is the same point that Paul has made in Rom. 3:21: God's righteousness has been made manifest "apart from the law."[42] Indeed, the salvation-historical disjunction between the era of the law and the era of Christ is one that is basic to Paul's teaching in Romans (see also 6:14, 15; 7:1-6). Moreover, while Paul certainly emphasizes in this passage the continuity between the OT generally and Christ and the righteousness he has brought (e.g., 9:32b-33; 10:6-8, 11, 13), he consistently emphasizes the discontinuity between Christ and the *law* (9:30-32a; 10:3; 10:5-8).

---

probably belongs in this category). τέλος means "termination" in five other verses (e.g., Mark 3:26: "[his house] will not be able to stand, but will have an end [τέλος]"; cf. also Luke 1:33; Heb. 7:3; Rev. 21:6; 22:13). In nine other texts, τέλος refers to a "result" or "outcome" (e.g., Matt. 26:58: Peter followed Jesus and his arresters into the courtyard, "in order to see the outcome [τέλος] [of these matters]"; Rom. 6:21: "the result or outcome [τέλος] of these things [sinful behavior] is death"; cf. also Rom. 6:22; 2 Cor. 11:15; Phil. 3:19; Heb. 6:8; Jas. 5:11; 1 Pet. 1:9; 4:17). In Luke 22:37, τέλος comes closest to the meaning "fulfillment," "consummation." Only in 1 Tim. 1:5 does τέλος have a probably teleological meaning ("the goal [τέλος] of the commandment is love . . ."). For similar surveys see BAGD; G. Delling, *TDNT* VIII, 54-56; Schreiner, "Paul's View of the Law," pp. 117-19. Badenas (*Christ the End of the Law,* pp. 71-76) finds more teleological occurrences, but only by counting occurrences where the word means "result" or "outcome" in this category. Yet, properly speaking, only if purpose is clearly intended is it appropriate to use the word "teleology."

42. The parallels between Rom. 10:3-4 and Rom. 3:20-23 are impressive:

3:20-23	10:3-4
[works of] the law cannot confer righteousness	Jews have not attained their own righteousness
God's righteousness has been manifested apart from the law	Christ is the end of the law
righteousness is for all who believe	righteousness is for all who believe

Badenas, arguing for a teleological interpretation of τέλος, cites the phrase "witnessed to by the law and the prophets" as the parallel to Rom. 10:4 (*Christ the End of the Law,* p. 141). But "apart from the law," because it, like Rom. 10:4, uses the word νόμος absolutely, is the closer parallel.

These considerations require that *telos* have a temporal nuance: with the coming of Christ the authority of the law of Moses is, in some basic sense, at an end. At the same time, a teleological nuance is also present. This is suggested not only by the contextual factors mentioned above but also by the fact that similar NT uses of *telos* generally preserve some sense of direction or goal. In other words, the "end" that *telos* usually denotes is an end that is the natural or inevitable result of something else.[43] The analogy of a race course (which many scholars think *telos* is meant to convey) is helpful: the finish line is both the "termination" of the race (the race is over when it is reached) and the "goal" of the race (the race is run for the sake of reaching the finish line). Likewise, we suggest, Paul is implying that Christ is the "end" of the law (he brings its era to a close) and its "goal" (he is what the law anticipated and pointed toward).[44] The English word "end" perfectly captures this nuance; but, if it is thought that it implies too temporal a meaning, we might also use the words "culmination," "consummation," or "climax."

As Christ consummates one era of salvation history, so he inaugurates a new one. In this new era, God's eschatological righteousness is available to those who *believe;* and it is available to *everyone* who believes. Both emphases are important and reflect one of the most basic themes of the letter (cf. 1:16; 3:22, 28-30; 4:16-17). Because the Jews have not understood that Christ has brought the law to its culmination, they have not responded in faith to Christ; and they have therefore missed the righteousness of God, available only in Christ on the basis of faith. At the same time, Christ, by ending the era of the law, during which God was dealing mainly with Israel, has made righteousness

43. When τέλος is followed by the genitive in the NT (as here), the genitive indicates either (1) the whole, of which the τέλος is a part (partitive genitive; cf. 1 Pet. 4:7; 1 Cor. 10:11); (2) the person bringing the τέλος about (subjective genitive; cf. Jas. 5:11); or (3) the thing or person that is brought to an end (objective genitive; cf. Rom. 6:21; 2 Cor. 3:13; Phil. 3:19; 1 Tim. 1:5; Heb. 7:3; 1 Pet. 1:9; 4:17). Rom. 10:4 must be put in this last category; and in most of these texts (with the probable exception of Heb. 7:3 and possible exception of 2 Cor. 3:13) the "end" to which the person or thing is brought is the culmination of a process, not simply a termination.

44. Among those who combine the notions of "end" or "goal" in various ways in their interpretation of τέλος in Rom. 10:4 are Bruce; Barrett; Kuss; Wilckens; Dunn; Bandstra, *The Law and the Elements of the World,* pp. 105-6; Drane, *Paul,* 133; Furnish, *Theology and Ethics in Paul,* 158-61; Siegert, *Argumentation bei Paulus,* p. 149; Seifrid, "Paul's Approach," pp. 6-10; idem, *Justification,* p. 248; Schnabel, *Law and Wisdom,* pp. 291-92.

Badenas objects to this interpretation on the grounds that it posits an improbable "double meaning" for τέλος (*Christ the End of the Law,* p. 147; cf. also Räisänen, 53). But I am not arguing for a "double meaning" for the word; I am arguing that the *single* meaning of the Greek word here combines nuances of the English words "end" and "goal."

more readily available for Gentiles.[45] Verse 4 is, then, the hinge on which the entire section 9:30–10:13 turns. It justifies Paul's claim that the Jews, by their preoccupation with the law, have missed God's righteousness (9:30–10:3): for righteousness is now found only in Christ and only through faith in Christ, the one who has brought the law to its climax and thereby ended its reign. It also announces the theme that Paul will expound in 10:5-13: righteousness by faith in Christ for all who believe.[46]

Two theological reflections on this much quoted verse are in order before we leave it. First, while I have argued that Paul is teaching that Christ brought an "end" to the law, it is important to clarify what this means and, perhaps, more important, what it does *not* mean. Paul is thinking in this verse in his usual category of salvation history. He is picturing the Mosaic law as the center of an epoch in God's dealings with human beings that has now come to an end. The believer's relationship to God is mediated in and through Christ, and the Mosaic law is no longer basic to that relationship. But Paul is *not* saying that Christ has ended all "law"; the believer remains bound to God's law as it now is mediated in and through Christ (see Gal. 6:2; 1 Cor. 9:19-21). Nor is he saying that the Mosaic law is no longer part of God's revelation or of no more use to the believer. The Mosaic law, like all of Scripture, is "profitable" for the believer (2 Tim. 3:16) and must continue to be read, pondered, and responded to by the faithful believer.

Second, we find in Paul's teaching about Christ as the culmination of the law another evidence of the beautiful unity of the NT message. For what Paul says here is almost exactly what Jesus claims in one of his most famous theological pronouncements: "Do not think that I have come to abolish the law and the prophets. I have not come to abolish them, but to fulfill them" (Matt. 5:17).[47] Each text pictures Christ as the promised culmination of the OT law. And together they sound a note of balance in the Christian's approach to the OT and its law that is vital to maintain. On the one hand, both Jesus and Paul warn us about undervaluing the degree to which Christ now embodies and mediates to us what the OT law was teaching and doing. Our relationship with God is now found in Christ, not through the law; and our day-to-day

---

45. Dunn stresses this universal note in his interpretation of the Jews' failure: they have confined righteousness to themselves (v. 3) because they did not understand that Christ has opened it up for all (v. 4). I do not want to dismiss this idea entirely — although it is not the main point of the verse — but I do think that the universal focus at the end of v. 4 is looking ahead (to vv. 6-13) more than it is looking backward.

46. Michel, 327.

47. See my "Jesus and the Authority of the Mosaic Law," pp. 17-28, for the view that Jesus in Matt. 5:17 identifies his teaching as that which the law of Moses was pointing forward to.

behavior is to be guided primarily by the teaching of Christ and his apostles rather than by the law. On the other hand, Jesus and Paul also caution us against severing Christ from the law. For he is its fulfillment and consummation and he cannot be understood or appreciated unless he is seen in light of the preparatory period of which the law was the center.[48]

c. Gospel and Law (10:5-13)

5*For Moses writes about the righteousness that is based on the law:*[1] *"The person who does these things will live in them."*[a] [2] 6*But the*

48. For a further exploration of these themes, see my "The Law of Christ as the Fulfillment of the Law of Moses." Note also the differing views on this controversial theological issue found in that volume's other essays.

1. An important textual variant affects the sense of this verse (though, strangely, UBS[4] has dropped any reference to it!). There are two main possibilities: (1) ὅτι τὴν δικαιοσύνην τὴν ἐκ [τοῦ] νόμου. The effect of this is to make τὴν δικαιοσύνην . . . the object of the substantival participle ὁ ποιήσας in the quotation of Lev. 18:5 (most of the same MSS therefore also omit the word αὐτά; see the next note). See NASB: "For Moses writes that the man who practices the righteousness which is based on law shall live by that righteousness" (cf. also RSV). This reading is found in the primary Alexandrian uncial א, the secondary Alexandrian uncial A, the original text of the western D, and a number of important minuscules (e.g., 33, 81, 1739). It is adopted in the text of NA[25] and defended by a significant number of scholars (S-H, 286; Murray, 2.46; Käsemann, 285; Schlatter, 312; Cranfield, 2.520-21; Wilckens, 2.224; Bandstra, *The Law and the Elements of the World,* 103; Rhyne, *Faith Establishes the Law,* pp. 104-5; Badenas, *Christ the End of the Law,* pp. 118-19). (2) τὴν δικαιοσύνην ἐκ [τοῦ] νόμου ὅτι. With the ὅτι following the phrase, τὴν δικαιοσύνην ἐκ [τοῦ] νόμου will be an accusative of respect: "For Moses writes *with respect to the righteousness of the law,* that . . ." (see most English versions). This reading is to be preferred (it is adopted in NA[27] and UBS[4]). It has strong and diverse external support, with the early papyrus P[46], the important Alexandrian uncial B, part of the western tradition (the second corrector of D and G), Ψ, and the majority text. And it is easy to understand why a scribe might have moved ὅτι to a position before τὴν δικαιοσύνην in order to ease the syntactical abruptness of the accusative. It has against it, however, the suspicion of being a secondary assimilation to Gal. 3:12b, where Paul also quotes Lev. 18:5. But this consideration is not strong enough to overcome the evidence in the other direction. For a defense of the reading adopted here, see esp. A. Lindemann, "Die Gerechtigkeit aus dem Gesetz: Erwägungen zur Auslegung und zur Textgeschichte von Römer 10[5]," *ZNW* 73 (1982), 234-37; Metzger, 524-25; also Koch, 293-94; Meyer, 2.170; Godet, 376-77; Zahn, 477; Kuss, 3.754-55; Black, 143; Dunn, 2.599; Morris, 381; Fitzmyer, 589.

2. Most of those MSS that make τὴν δικαιοσύνην . . . the object of ὁ ποιήσας . . . ἄνθρωπος (see the previous note) naturally omit αὐτά; but if we adopt the reading I have argued for, then the αὐτά should probably be retained (though cf. Godet, 377). There is also a variant at the end of the verse, with some MSS (e.g., the two primary Alexandrian uncials, א [original hand] and B, the secondary Alexandrian uncial A, and several important minuscules) reading αὐτῇ ("in it," that is, righteousness), while others (e.g., the papyrus

righteousness based on faith speaks in this manner: "Do not say in your heart, 'Who will ascend into heaven?'" (That is, to bring Christ down.) 7Or "'Who will descend into the abyss?'" (That is, to bring Christ up from the dead.) 8But what does it say? "The word is near you, in your mouth and in your heart":[b] *that is, the word of faith that we are preaching. 9For if you confess with your mouth that Jesus is Lord and believe in your heart that God raised him from the dead, you will be saved. 10For with the heart one believes for righteousness, and with the mouth one confesses for salvation. 11For the Scripture says, "No one who believes on him will be put to shame."*[c] *12For there is no distinction between the Jew and the Greek, for the same Lord is Lord of all, bestowing his riches on all who call upon him. 13For "everyone who calls on the name of the Lord will be saved."*[d]

a. Lev. 18:5b
b. Deut. 9:4; 30:12-14
c. Isa. 28:16
d. Joel 2:32a

Central to the Reformers' teaching about salvation was their distinction between "law" and "gospel." "Law" is whatever God commands us to do; "gospel" is what God in his grace gives to us. The Reformers uniformly insisted that human depravity made it impossible for a person to be saved by doing what God commands; only by humbly accepting, in faith, the "good news" of God's work on our behalf could a person be saved. This theological "law"/"gospel" antithesis is at the heart of this paragraph, as Paul contrasts the righteousness that is based on "doing" the law (v. 5) with the righteousness that is based on faith (vv. 6-13). Significantly, Paul finds this distinction in the OT itself, manifesting his concern to prove that the gospel that has proved a stumbling block for so many Jews and a foundation stone for so many Gentiles is in continuity with the OT. In the earlier two paragraphs (9:30-33; 10:1-4) where Paul contrasted two kinds of righteousness, he was especially interested in explaining the plight of unbelieving Jews. The Gentiles' involvement was mentioned only briefly (9:30) or allusively (10:4b: "for all who believe"). In 10:5-13, however, Paul's focus shifts and he now gives special attention to the way in which the revelation of God's righteousness, the

---

P[46], the second corrector of ℵ, and D) have αὐτοῖς ("in them," that is, the commandments, the implied antecedent of αὐτά). Making τὴν δικαιοσύνην the object of ὁ ποιήσας . . . ἄνθρωπος naturally favors the former reading, and it is therefore presumed by NASB and RSV. While this reading is possible even if τὴν δικαιοσύνην is placed before the ὅτι (see, again, Godet), it is somewhat awkward and should probably be regarded as an assimilation that arose to accommodate the secondary variant.

righteousness that is based on faith, opens the door wide to the inclusion of Gentiles. This focus becomes especially evident at the end of this paragraph (vv. 11-13). Paul thereby creates an *inclusio,* with concern for the Gentiles' acceptance both beginning (9:30) and ending this section.

Verses 5-13 exposit the final words of v. 4: "so that there might be righteousness for everyone who believes."[3] Paul begins by anchoring the connection between righteousness and faith in Scripture (vv. 5-8). His appeal to Scripture here suggests that, for all his interest in the Gentiles, he still has Israel very much in mind. For it is particularly the Jews who need to understand that the righteousness of the law that they are seeking is a righteousness based on "doing" (v. 5, quoting Lev. 18:5). Such a righteousness, as Paul has already shown (9:31-32a; 10:3), is a phantom righteousness, for it cannot bring a person into relationship with a holy God. If the Jews would only see the message of the OT as Paul sees it, they would recognize that the OT itself proclaims the indispensability of faith — the very message that Paul and the other apostles are preaching (vv. 6-8, quoting Deut. 9:4 and 30:12-14). Verses 9-10 are transitional. They highlight the point that Paul has discovered in Deut. 30: a person experiences righteousness and salvation simply by believing the message. Since salvation is therefore not bound to the law but to faith, "anyone" can believe and be saved (vv. 11-13, quoting Isa. 28:16 and Joel 2:32). Thus the way is opened for Gentiles. At the same time, we should not diminish the genuine "universalism" Paul teaches here: if the way is opened for Gentiles, it is certainly not closed to Jews. They, especially, should recognize from their own Scriptures the importance of submitting to God's new work in Christ in humble faith.

5 The "for"[4] at the beginning of this verse connects v. 5, or vv. 5ff., to v. 4. But what is the nature of this connection? We can only answer this question once we have established the meaning of the phrase "the righteousness based on the law," which, Paul claims, "Moses writes about."[5] There are three main possibilities.

(1) "The righteousness based on the law" might be the same as the righteousness made available in Christ through faith (vv. 4b and 6a). Verse 5 is then in positive relationship to v. 4, and vv. 5 and 6 are not antithetical but

---

3. See particularly the fine analysis of Rhyne, *Faith Establishes the Law,* pp. 110-11; cf. also Maier, *Israel in der Heilsgeschichte,* p. 467; Godet, 376; Käsemann, 284; Aletti, *Comment Dieu est-il juste?* 122-24.

4. Gk. γάρ.

5. With the text we have adopted (see the translation and the relevant notes), τὴν δικαιοσύνην τὴν ἐκ νόμου is an accusative of respect dependent on γράφει (Z-G, 482; see also NRSV; NIV; REB; TEV). This is the only place where Paul uses the present tense of γράφω to introduce an OT quotation; the emphasis is on the current applicability of the quotation.

complementary. The "righteousness of the law" is nothing but the righteousness of faith, for, rightly understood, the law itself calls for faith: "the person who does the law," mentioned in the quotation from Lev. 18:5, is the person who submits to the law's deepest demand, "circumcises his heart," and trusts in the Lord.[6] Advocates of this view generally think that *telos* in v. 4a means "inner meaning" or "goal" and that vv. 5-8 provide a practical demonstration of that truth. For it is faith in Christ (v. 6) that is the true meaning of the law's requirement.

But such a complementary relationship between vv. 5 and 6 is not likely. Twice already in this passage Paul has contrasted two kinds of righteousness: "the righteousness based on faith" with "the law of righteousness" (9:30-31); "the righteousness of God" with "their own righteousness" (10:3). We are led to expect that the two righteousnesses of vv. 5 and 6 will likewise be contrasted. Confirming this expectation is the fact that v. 5 highlights "doing" and v. 6 faith. Faith and believing on the one hand and works and doing on the other are one of the most pervasive contrasts in the Pauline letters. For him to place them in a complementary relationship here would be for him to discard one of the most important building blocks in his theology.[7] A final indicator that vv. 5 and 6 are in contrast rather than in continuity is Phil. 3:6-9. This is the only other passage in Paul in which "righteousness based on the law" and "righteousness based on faith" are both found; and they are set in direct contrast to one another.

(2) A second interpretation of "righteousness based on the law" posits a mild contrast between it and "the righteousness based on faith." Advocates of this approach identify "the one who does these things" as Christ. By doing the law perfectly, he activates the promise of life found in Lev. 18:5 and makes that life available for all who believe (vv. 6-13).[8] Again, therefore, Paul provides evidence that Christ is indeed the "aim" of the law.

6. G. E. Howard, "Christ the End of the Law: The Meaning of Romans 10:4ff.," *JBL* 88 (1969), 333-36; Fuller, *Gospel and Law,* pp. 66-68; Flückiger, "Christus, des Gesetzes τέλος," pp. 153-57; R. Bring, *Christus und das Gesetz* (Leiden: Brill, 1969), p. 54; Toews, "The Law," pp. 252-62, 282-83; Badenas, *Christ the End of the Law,* pp. 120-25; Wright, *Climax of the Covenant,* p. 245; Kaiser, "The Law as God's Gracious Guidance," p. 184. The text that places ὅτι after γράφει, omits αὐτά, and reads αὐτῇ in place of αὐτοῖς is more congenial to this interpretation; e.g., "Moses writes that the one who does the righteousness of the law will live by it." It is therefore adopted by many (though not all) of the scholars who hold this view.

7. See Dahl (p. 106): "Paul's entire exegesis depends on the presupposition that faith and works of the Law exclude each other, that the Mosaic Law and faith in Christ cannot simultaneously express the proper way for man to relate to God." See, further, our notes on 2:25 and 3:27.

8. Bandstra, *The Law and the Elements of the World,* pp. 103-5; Cranfield; Campbell, "Christ the End of the Law," pp. 77-78; Barth, *People of God,* p. 39; Dinter, "The Remnant of Israel," pp. 139-41; cf. also Hendriksen, although he sees a contrast between vv. 5 and 6.

Christ's satisfaction of the law's requirements as a basis for securing righteousness for those who are his is a Pauline concept (see 3:31 and 8:4); but there is no good basis in the text to introduce it here. Moreover, accepting this interpretation would put Paul's application of Lev. 18:5 here in conflict with his application of the same text in Gal. 3:12. And, while not impossible, a difference between the two would be unlikely because the texts have a great deal in common.[9]

(3) "The righteousness based on the law," then, is a *negative* conception, in direct contrast to "the righteousness based on faith" (v. 6).[10] It is that "right standing with God,"[11] bound up with the law and one's own works, that Israel had pursued but not attained (cf. 9:31-32a; 10:3) and which Paul discarded in favor of the "righteousness from God" (Phil. 3:9). Such an antithetical understanding of vv. 5-6 could be intended to illustrate the way in which Christ "brings to an end" the law (v. 4a). But the focus on righteousness and faith in vv. 6ff. suggests rather that for Paul the connection is with v. 4b: "so that there might be righteousness for all who believe."[12] The "for" in v. 5 therefore introduces all of vv. 5-8 (or 5-13) as an elaboration of the connection between righteousness and faith and its significance. Verses 6 and following give a positive argument for this connection; v. 5 a negative one.

Before we can understand what this negative point is, we need to know how Paul's quotation of Lev. 18:5 contributes to the argument. In its context, Lev. 18:5 summons Israel to obedience to the commandments of the Lord as a means of prolonging her enjoyment of the blessings of God in the promised

---

9. As Strobel points out, the similarities between Rom. 10:1-8 and Rom. 1:16-17 on the one hand, and Gal. 3:11-12 and Rom. 1:16-17 on the other (both quoting Hab. 2:4) suggest that all three texts move in the same orbit of thinking (*Untersuchungen zum eschatologischen Verzögerungproblem,* pp. 190-92).

10. This is the view of the majority of scholars. See esp. J. S. Vos, "Die hermeneutische Antinomie bei Paulus (Galater 3.11-12; Römer 10.5-10)," *NTS* 38 (1992), 258-60; Dunn, "Romans 10," pp. 218-19; Rhyne, *Faith Establishes the Law,* p. 105. Sanders (*Paul, the Law and the Jewish People,* p. 63 n. 132) entertains the idea, which Lindemann adopts ("Gesetz aus dem Gesetzes," pp. 239-42), that "righteousness out of the law" is a neutral concept: a genuine and, as far as it goes, valuable possession, but one that does not save (and these modern scholars were anticipated by several ancient ones, among them Origen, Diodorus, and Ambrosiaster [see Schelkle]). This is an attractive hypothesis but does not fit well with the obviously negative connotation that the parallel expressions "law for righteousness" (9:31) and "their own righteousness" (10:3) have.

11. "Righteousness" (δικαιοσύνη) will here, as in 9:30-31; 10:3b, 4b, denote the judicial conception of status, the result of God's act of justifying.

12. Other scholars (e.g., Käsemann) think that vv. 5-8 ground Paul's assertion in v 4a, understood in the sense that Christ has "abrogated" the law.

land.[13] The verse is not speaking about the attainment of eternal life; and Paul clearly does not believe that the OT teaches that righteousness is based on the law (see Rom. 4). Paul is *not,* therefore, claiming that Christ has replaced the old way of salvation — by obedience to the law — with a new one — by faith in Christ.[14] But Paul does think that the law embodies, in its very nature, the principle that perfect obedience to it would confer eternal life (see 2:13 and 7:10). It may be this principle that Paul intends to enunciate here via the words of Lev. 18:5.[15]

However, we think that Paul's point is a more nuanced one. His purpose in quoting Lev. 18:5 is succinctly to summarize what for him is the essence of the law: blessing is contingent on obedience.[16] It is the one who

13. Lev. 18:1-30 is a unit. It begins with a general exhortation to the Israelites to follow the statutes and ordinances of the law of God rather than the customs and practices of Egypt from which they came or of Canaan to which they are going (vv. 1-5). There follows a series of specific aspects of that law of God (vv. 6-23), and the section concludes with a further exhortation to obedience and a warning of judgment should they fail (vv. 24-30). In this context, Lev. 18:5 must be saying more than that a man who does the commandments will live "in" them; e.g., live out his life in the sphere of the law (taking the בְּ of the Hebrew text and the ἐν of the LXX as a locative of sphere; this view is argued by W. C. Kaiser, Jr., "Leviticus and Paul: 'Do this and you shall live' (eternally?)," *JETS* 14 [1971], 19-28; cf. also B. A. Levine, *Leviticus* [The JPS Torah Commentary; Philadelphia: Jewish Publication Society, 1989], p. 119). The context points rather to "life" being the reward for obedience: it is the opposite of the expulsion from the land on the part of the nation and the expulsion from Israel on the part of the individual that the end of the chapter warns will be the judgment for disobedience (see vv. 28, 29; cf., e.g., G. Wenham, *A Commentary on Leviticus* [NICOT; Grand Rapids: Eerdmans, 1979], p. 253; R. K. Harrison, *Leviticus* [TOTC; Grand Rapids: Eerdmans, 1980], p. 185). Elsewhere in the Pentateuch also, "life" denotes the reward God gives to his people for obedience of the law (e.g., Deut. 30:15, 19). This life consists in material prosperity, deliverance from enemies, and peace and longevity in the land that the Lord is giving the people (Lev. 26:3-13; Deut. 28:1-14). Lev. 18:5 is warning that the continuance of this "life" that God has already initiated for the people depends on their faithful observance of the law (this is a repeated refrain in Deuteronomy; cf. 4:1-2, 40; 5:33; 6:1-3; 7:12-16; 8:1).

14. That this is what Paul is teaching seems to be suggested by, e.g., Meyer, 2.174.

15. Leviticus 18:5 was interpreted as a promise of eternal life by some Jewish authors (see Targums Onkelos and Pseudo-Jonathan; *b. Sanh.* 58b; *Sipra Lev.* 337a; cf. Str-B, 3.278). The idea that Paul sees in Lev. 18:5 a (hypothetical) promise of life to the doer becomes almost standard in the Reformed and Lutheran traditions. See, e.g., Calvin; Hodge; Haldane; Alford; Wilckens and idem, "Gesetzesverständnis," pp. 165-72; Westerholm, 134-35; Gundry, "Grace, Works and Staying Saved," pp. 24-25; Hübner, 19-20 (on Gal. 3:12); Ridderbos, *Paul,* p. 134; Hofius, " 'All Israel Will Be Saved,' " pp. 22-23. Cf. also Refoulé, "Romans X,4," pp. 346-50, who, however, thinks that Paul views the promise as still applicable to the Jewish remnant.

16. This appears to be Paul's point in quoting Lev. 18:5 in Gal. 3:12 also (cf. Longenecker, *Galatians,* p. 120). Paul has predecessors in using Lev. 18:5 as a "slogan,"

does the works required by the law[17] who must find life through[18] them. The emphasis lies on the word "doing" and not on the promise of "life."[19] Paul states this principle here as a warning. The Jew who refuses to submit to the righteousness of God in Christ, ignoring the fact that the law has come to its culmination in Christ and seeking to establish a relationship with God through the law, must be content in seeking that relationship through "doing."[20] Yet human doing, imperfect as even the most sincere striving must be, is always inadequate to bring a person into relationship with God — as Paul has shown in Rom. 1:18–3:20.[21] Throughout salvation history, faith and doing, "gospel" and "law" have run along side-by-side. Each is important in our relationship with God. But, as it fatal to ignore one or the other, it is equally fatal to mix them or to use them for the wrong ends. The OT Israelite who sought to base his or her relationship with God on the law rather than on God's gracious election in and through the Abrahamic promise arrangement made this mistake. Similarly, Paul suggests, many Jews in his day are making the same mistake: concentrating on the law to the exclusion

---

for the text appears to be quoted frequently in Jewish literature. See Neh. 9:29: ". . . Yet they acted presumptuously and did not obey your commandments, but sinned against your ordinances, *by the observance of which a person shall live*"; Ezek. 20:13 (cf. also v. 21): ". . . they did not observe my statutes but rejected my ordinances, *by whose observance everyone shall live* . . ." (both NRSV); CD 3:14-16: ". . . He unfolded before them His holy Sabbaths and his glorious feasts, the testimonies of His righteousness and the ways of His truth, and the desires of His will *which a man must do in order to live*"; cf. also *b. Sanh.* 59b.

17. The αὐτά and αὐτοῖς in Paul's quotation are without an antecedent. The LXX, which Paul is following (LXX turns the relative clause of the Hebrew [אֲשֶׁר יַעֲשֶׂה אֹתָם הָאָדָם יְחַי, "which, by doing them, a man shall live"] into an independent statement), has the αὐτοῖς, but not the αὐτά. Its antecedent is τὰ προστάγματα and τὰ κρίματα, "the decrees" and "the ordinances." Paul therefore probably intends the reader to identify the antecedent from the OT context, or to infer that the plural pronouns refer generally to those things that the law commands.

18. The ἐν is instrumental.

19. Schmithals.

20. For a view similar to this one, see Melanchthon; Fairbairn, *Revelation of Law,* p. 446; W. Gutbrod, *TDNT* IV, 1072; Lindemann, "Gerechtigkeit aus dem Gesetzes," pp. 242-46; Eckstein, " 'Nahe ist dir das Wort,' " pp. 204-6; Martin, *Christ and the Law,* pp. 139-40; Godet; Murray 2.249-51; Harrison; Dahl, 148; Aletti, *Comment Dieu est-il juste?* 124-27. Dunn again sees in Paul's quotation of Lev. 18:5 an expression of Jewish covenantal zeal that restricts God's righteousness to Israel ("Romans 10," p. 223; cf. also Longenecker, *Eschatology and the Covenant,* pp. 220-21).

21. That Paul here disparages "doing" because of its inability, due to the power of sin, to confer righteousness is the natural conclusion from his argument in Rom. 1:18–3:20 (cf., e.g., Chrysostom; Kuss). Others, however, think that Paul simply opposes doing in principle, as antithetical to faith (e.g., Koch, 291-95).

of God's gracious provision in Christ, the "climax" of the law, for their relationship with the Lord.[22]

6 Verse 6 is connected to v. 5 with the Greek word *de.* Our interpretation of v. 5 requires that we give the word an adversative meaning: "Moses writes about the righteousness based on the law (v. 5) . . . *but* the righteousness based on faith speaks in this manner. . . ."[23] By attributing to the righteousness based on faith the ability to "speak," Paul follows the biblical pattern of personifying activities and concepts that are closely related to God.[24] The "righteousness based on faith" is active and powerful because it is also "the righteousness of God" (see v. 3) — in contrast to the righteousness based on the law that Moses wrote about.[25] Paul relates what this righteousness based on faith "says" in vv. 6b-8, using language drawn from Deuteronomy. The introductory warning, "Do not say in your heart," is taken from Deut. 9:4. Paul's quotation of this clause is not haphazard; he wants his readers to associate these words with the context from which they

22. See the idea of "the bare law" in Calvin (e.g., *Institutes* 2.7.2; 2.11.7).

23. An adversative meaning for δέ is, of course, quite normal. Some advocates of a complementary relationship between vv. 5 and 6 have, however, argued that the combination γάρ . . . δέ (vv. 5 and 6) makes it more likely that δέ here means "and" (Howard, "Christ the End of the Law," pp. 331-32; Badenas, *Christ the End of the Law,* p. 123; Kaiser, "The Law as God's Guidance," p. 184). But there are two fatal weaknesses in this argument. First, γάρ . . . δέ is not a correlative pair in Greek, and it is artificial therefore to isolate places where they occur together as if they have a standard meaning. Second, however, even if the words are examined in this artificial combination, the results are just the reverse of what Howard and the others claim. In Rom. 1–8, e.g., this sequence occurs 22 times: in three δέ is continuative (4:15; 7:8-9; 8:24); in four explanatory ("that is," "now"; 1:11-12; 2:1b-2; 6:7-8; 5:13); and in 15 contrastive (2:25; 5:7-8, 10-11, 16; 6:10, 23; 7:2, 14, 18b, 22-23; 8:5, 6, 13, 22-23, 24-25).

24. Wisdom (Prov. 8:21ff., etc.); the Word (Isa. 55:10-11). For similar personifications of "righteousness," see Ps. 85:10-13; Isa. 45:8 (as Dunn notes, this last verse might be significant for Paul since he has perhaps alluded to Isa. 45:9 in 9:20-21).

25. It is argued that two further points of contrast are to be found in the introductory formulas in vv. 5a and 6a: that γράφει in v. 5 carries a negative nuance in comparison with λέγω in v. 6 (Käsemann relates the contrast to Paul's γράμμα/πνεῦμα antithesis [p. 284]; cf. also Schlatter; Michel; Dunn; Schlier; Fitzmyer); and that the reference to Moses in v. 5a implies that the principle being cited applies only to the old era, now superseded in Christ (Dunn, "Romans 10," pp. 218-19; Longenecker, *Eschatology and the Covenant,* pp. 222-23). Neither contrast, however, is clear (see Eckstein, " 'Nahe ist dir das Wort,' " pp. 207-8). Paul uses both γράφω and λέγω frequently in introductions to OT quotations (for λέγω, see, in Romans alone: 4:3, 6; 9:15, 17, 25; 10:11, 16, 18, 19, 20, 21; 11:2, 4, 9; 15:10, 12; γράφω is also, of course, common, although this is the only place that Paul uses the present tense of the verb in an introductory formula), and it is unlikely that we should see any contrast in the shift of verbs here (cf. Wilckens, 2.226). And, while Paul can associate Moses with the old era (cf. 5:14; 2 Cor. 3:7-15 esp.), he can also simply view him as an author of inspired Scripture (as in 10:19).

are drawn.[26] For in Deut. 9:4-6 Moses warns the people of Israel that when they have taken possession of the land God is bringing them to, they must not think that they have earned it because of "their own righteousness." Paul therefore adds implicit biblical support to his criticism of the Israel of his day for its pursuit of their own righteousness (see v. 5).

After this fragment of Deut. 9:4, Paul then adds directly to it a clause from Deut. 30:12: "Who will ascend into heaven?"[27] He then adds an explanatory phrase, claiming that the object of this ascent into heaven is "to bring Christ down." If Paul's attribution of Deut. 9:4 to the righteousness based on faith is particularly apropos, the same cannot be said about his use of this clause from Deut. 30:11-14. For Deut. 30:11-14 is about God's law:

> Surely, this commandment[28] that I am commanding you today is not too hard for you, nor is it too far away. [12]It is not in heaven, that you should say, *"Who will go up to heaven for us, and get it for us so that we may hear it and observe it?"* [13]Neither is it beyond the sea, that you should say, *"Who will cross to the other side of the sea for us, and get it for us so that we may hear it and observe it?"* [14]No, *the word is very near to you; it is in your mouth and in your heart* for you to observe. (NRSV; the fragments Paul quotes are in italics)

Moses' purpose is to prevent the Israelites from evading responsibility for doing the will of God by pleading that they do not know it. In God's laws, mediated through Moses and set forth in Deuteronomy, God has made his will for his people known to them. How, then, can Paul take a passage that is about the law of God and find in it the voice of righteousness by *faith?* And how, in his explanatory comments, can he claim that what the text is talking about is not the commandment but Christ?

Some scholars are content simply to accuse Paul of arbitrary exegesis: he has no warrant for the application of Deut. 30 other than his general conviction that the OT everywhere testifies of Christ.[29] Other scholars have overcome this apparent hermeneutical problem by arguing that Paul is not

---

26. The association would be an easy one because only here and in the closely related 8:17 do the words Paul uses — μὴ εἴπῃς ἐν τῇ καρδίᾳ σου — occur in the LXX (see also Deut. 18:17; Jer. 13:22). See, e.g., Hays, 78-79; Leenhardt; Cranfield; Michel; Dunn.

27. Gk. τίς ἀναβήσεται εἰς τὸν οὐρανόν. Paul follows the LXX (which accurately translates the MT closely, only omitting the first person plural dative (of advantage) pronoun, ὑμῖν, which comes between ἀναβήσεται and εἰς.

28. The singular "commandment" refers not to a single commandment, but to the law as a whole (see Deut. 11:22; 19:9, etc.).

29. Dodd, speaking of Paul's application of the language of Deut. 30 to Christ, calls the interpretation "fanciful."

quoting Deut. 30; he is only using biblical language to express his meaning.[30] But this solution will not work: v. 6a looks like the introduction to a quotation; the number of verbal similarities between Deut. 30:12-14 and vv. 6b-8 suggests that Paul intends us to recognize and make use of the context; and the three "that is" explanations imply that Paul is here applying a text he is quoting. Can we, then, find a hermeneutical rationale for Paul's application of this text?

One possibility would be to find in Deut. 30:11-14 a continuation of the prophecy in Deut. 30:1-10 about God's restoration of Israel after the Exile. It is at this time, when God himself circumcises the hearts of his people (v. 6), that he will bring his word near to Israel (v. 14). Paul would therefore legitimately be applying Lev. 18:5 to the Old Covenant and Deut. 30:11-14 to the New, when God writes his law on the hearts of his people (Jer. 31:31-34).[31] While an attractive alternative, this way of explaining Paul's use of Deut. 30:12-14 cannot be accepted: at v. 11 in this chapter, there is a clear transition from the prophecy of future restoration in vv. 1-10 to the situation of Israel as she prepares to enter the promised land.[32] Another possibility, then, is to find in intertestamental traditions a bridge between the text of Deut. 30 and Paul's application of it. Specifically, scholars posit an identification of Christ with the figure of wisdom. They reconstruct the process in three steps: (1) law and wisdom were frequently associated in intertestamental Judaism; (2) one intertestamental text, Bar. 3:29-30, describes wisdom with some of the same language from Deut. 30 that Paul uses here; (3) Paul often associates Christ with the figure of wisdom.[33] But Paul's reliance on the Baruch text is not

---

30. S-H; Hodge; Zahn; Denney; Fitzmyer; Hübner, *Gottes Ich und Israel*, pp. 86-91; Longenecker, *Biblical Exegesis*, pp. 121-23.

31. Thielman, *From Plight to Solution*, pp. 113-14; W. Strickland, "The Inauguration of the Law of Christ with the Gospel," in *The Law, the Gospel, and the Modern Christian*, p. 250; cf. J. H. Sailhamer, *The Pentateuch as Narrative* (Grand Rapids: Zondervan, 1992), pp. 473-74.

32. Deuteronomy 30:11-14 returns to the theme of 29:29, as Moses lays the basis for his appeal to the Israelites to obey the law that God gave the people (vv. 11-15). The future time orientation of vv. 1-10, with its *waw* + perfect verbs, is dropped in v. 11. See S. R. Driver, *A Critical and Exegetical Commentary on Deuteronomy* (ICC; New York: Charles Scribner's Sons, 1916), pp. 330-31.

33. This position is most fully worked out by M. J. Suggs, " 'The Word is Near You': Romans 10:6-10 within the Purpose of the Letter," in *Christian History and Interpretation*, pp. 289-312. Many scholars find this background to be at least part of the explanation for Paul's application; see Kim, *Origin of Paul's Gospel*, pp. 130-31; Schnabel, *Law and Wisdom*, pp. 248-49; Hays, 78-81; Koch, 153-60. Johnson (*Function*, pp. 133-37) thinks that there is contact with Baruch but that Paul simply identifies wisdom with the gospel. Bar. 3:29-30 reads: τίς ἀνέβη εἰς τὸν οὐρανὸν καὶ ἔλαβεν αὐτὴν καὶ κατεβίβασεν αὐτὴν ἐκ τῶν νεφελῶν; τίς διέβη πέραν τῆς θαλάσσης καὶ εὗρεν αὐτὴν καὶ οἴσει αὐτὴν χρυσίου ἐκλεκτοῦ;: "Who went up

clear;[34] and the association of Christ with wisdom is perhaps not as widespread nor as important to Paul's Christology as some have made it.

The best explanation for Paul's use of the Deut. 30 text is to think that he finds in this passage an expression of the grace of God in establishing a relationship with his people.[35] As God brought his word near to Israel so they might know and obey him, so God now brings his word "near" to both Jews and Gentiles that they might know him through his Son Jesus Christ and respond in faith and obedience. Because Christ, rather than the law, is now the focus of God's revelatory word (see 10:4), Paul can "replace" the commandment of Deut. 30:11-14 with Christ. Paul's application of Deut. 30:12-14, then, is of course not a straightforward exegesis of the passage. But it is a valid application of the principle of that passage in the context of the development of salvation history. The grace of God that underlies the Mosaic covenant is operative now in the New Covenant; and, just as Israel could not plead the excuse that she did not know God's will, so now, Paul says, neither Jew nor Gentile can plead ignorance of God's revelation in Jesus Christ.

---

into heaven and received her [wisdom] and brought her down from the clouds? Who travelled beyond the sea and found her and will buy her for precious gold?" Note the association of wisdom with "the commandment of life" in 3:9.

34. As Seifrid points out, Paul's text is closer to Deuteronomy than to Baruch ("Paul's Approach," pp. 20-23). Moreover, the language of ascending to heaven and crossing the sea (or going down into the abyss) became somewhat proverbial (see *Jub.* 24:31; 4 Ezra 4:8; *b. B. Meṣ.* 59b).

35. For similar approaches, see Calvin; Godet; Murray; Cranfield; Seifrid, "Paul's Approach," pp. 35-37; D. O. Via, "A Structuralist Approach to Paul's Old Testament Hermeneutic," *Int* 28 (1974), 215-18. Paul's application of the text to "righteousness by faith" would be aided by the similarity in language between Deut. 30:14 (the "near" word) and texts in Isaiah that speak of God bringing "near" his righteousness and that were probably basic for Paul's understanding of the righteousness of God (46:13; 51:5; see Eckstein, "'Nahe ist dir das Wort,'" pp. 217-19). Paul stands in an interpretive tradition in his innovative application of Deut. 30:12-14; Philo, e.g., applied the text to the search for "the good" (*Posterity and Exile of Cain* 84-85; *Change of Names* 236-37; *Rewards and Punishments* 80; *Virtues* 183; cf. Dunn, 2.604).

Another influence on Paul in choosing this text to describe the righteousness by faith may have been his knowledge of the larger context of Deuteronomy, with its call for a heartfelt obedience, including love for the Lord and the circumcision of the heart (see, in the immediate context of the text Paul quotes, 30:6 and 20; cf. S. Lyonnet, "Saint Paul et l'exégèse juive de son temps: a propos de Romains 10:6-8," in *Mélanges bibliques rédigés en l'honneur de André Robert* [Paris: Bloud & Gay, 1957], pp. 496-501). But, granted Paul's fundamental antithesis (reiterated in this text) between "faith" and "doing," it is unlikely that Paul wants us to identify true doing of the law with faith (contra, e.g., Flückiger, "Christus, des Gesetzes τέλος," p. 154; Fuller, *Gospel and Law,* pp. 85-87; Wright, *Climax of the Covenant,* pp. 122-24; Badenas, *Christ the End of the Law,* pp. 129-30). Nor does Paul identify the commandment with Christ; for he explicitly identifies the "word" of Deuteronomy with the apostolic message (v. 8; cf. Dunn).

As Paul therefore uses Lev. 18:5 to summarize the essence of "the law," so he quotes Deut. 30:12-14 to encapsulate "the gospel." Throughout salvation history, these two "words" from the Lord have operated side-by-side: God making his demand of his people on the one hand and providing in his grace for their deliverance on the other.[36] Viewed against this larger scriptural background, Paul's contrast of Lev. 18:5 and Deut. 30:12-14 does not violate their root theological significance; nor does it call into question the unity of Scripture. Rather, he is reminding the Jews of his day that righteousness before the Lord can never come from the law, involving as it does human effort, but from the gospel of God's grace.

In the OT, the language of "ascending into heaven" becomes almost proverbial for a task impossible for human beings to perform.[37] In Deut. 30, this impossible task is the bringing of God's commandment to his people. Paul, however, eliminates any reference to the commandment and applies the language to Christ. Paul's use of the phrase "that is"[38] to introduce his application may signal his intention to provide a "pesher" interpretation.[39] This method of exegesis, characteristic of the Qumran community, applies details of the biblical text to contemporary events and persons in a "this [the contemporary event or person] is that [what the OT author wrote about]" format. But the phrase "that is" does not clearly signal the Qumran "pesher" technique;[40] nor is it evident that Paul views his explanations of Deuteronomy as an exegesis of the "real" meaning of the text.[41] More likely, Paul uses these explanatory comments to suggest a contemporary application of the significance of the Deuteronomy text

36. The contrast between Lev. 18:5 and Deut. 30:12-14 is not simply, then, a salvation-historical one, as if the latter text was valid only for the old Mosaic era and the former for the new (contra, e.g., Dunn, "Romans 10," p. 225; Longenecker, *Eschatology and the Covenant,* pp. 222-23; M. A. Getty, "An Apocalyptic Perspective on Rom 10:4," *HBT* 4-5 [1982-83], 108-16).

37. See Isa. 14:13; Amos 9:2; Ps. 139:8; Prov. 30:4; and cf. J. Heller, "Himmel- und Höllenfahrt nach Römer 10, 6-7," *EvT* 32 (1972), 481-82.

38. Gk. τοῦτ' ἔστιν.

39. See, e.g., Michel; Cranfield; Wilckens. In the DSS (particularly in 1QpHab and 1QpNah), a portion of the OT text is quoted and its interpretation is then introduced with the word פִּשְׁרוֹ, "its interpretation [is]." For "pesher" exegesis, see, e.g., L. H. Silbermann, "Unriddling the Riddle: A Study in the Structure and Language of Habakkuk Pesher (1QpHab)," *RevQ* 3 (1961-62), 323-64; Moo, *Old Testament,* pp. 69-75.

40. The Greek phrase τοῦτ' ἔστιν is widely used in the LXX, Philo, and the NT to introduce an explanation; there is little reason to think that it deliberately echoes the DSS *pišrô* (see esp. Seifrid, "Paul's Approach," pp. 29-34; Dunn suggests that Paul's formula combines Jewish and Greek styles). The phrase then introduces the epexegetic infinitival clause Χριστὸν καταγαγεῖν as Paul's explanation (or application) of the word ἀναβήσεται in the quotation (see S-H; Meyer and Godet offer different and less natural explanations of the syntax).

41. Koch (pp. 229-30) notes the differences between Paul's method of interpretation here and "pesher."

in the light of the movement of salvation history. Viewed in the light of what God has done in and through his Son, "going into heaven" takes on a new and more literal significance. As the Israelite did not need to "ascend into heaven" to find God's commandment, so, Paul suggests, there is no need to ascend into heaven to "bring down Christ." For in the incarnation, the Messiah, God's Son, has been truly "brought down" already.[42] God, from his side, has acted to make himself and his will for his people known; his people now have no excuse for not responding.

7 The particle "or"[43] connects the following quotation from Deut. 30 with the previous one, both being dependent on the introductory "Do not say in your heart." In this second quotation of language from Deut. 30 we find a significant difference between Paul's wording and the original: for Deuteronomy's "Who will go across the sea?" Paul has "Who will descend into the abyss?" This difference has led some scholars to think that Paul may here be quoting Ps. 107:26 rather than Deut. 30:13.[44] But this is unlikely since Paul's language is generally parallel to that of Deuteronomy and since it is sandwiched between two other references to Deut. 30. In fact, the "sea" and the "abyss" were somewhat interchangeable concepts in the OT and in Judaism;[45] and some Aramaic paraphrases of the Deut. 30:13 used the language of the abyss.[46] Therefore, Paul could very easily change the horizontal

---

42. Most church fathers (see Schelkle) and many modern commentators (e.g., S-H; Murray; Barrett; Nygren; Fitzmyer) rightly see in Paul's language here an allusion to the incarnation. The sequence "come down" (v. 6) and "go up" (v. 7) reflects the common early Christian kerymatic sequence of Christ's incarnation and resurrection (see Phil. 2:6-11; 1 Tim. 3:16; and cf. E. Schweizer, "Zur Herkunft der Präexistenzvorstellung bei Paulus," *EvT* 19 [1959], 67-68). Some commentators, however, think that "bringing Christ down" alludes to Christ's ascension (e.g., Godet; Michel; Käsemann; Dunn).

43. Gk. ἤ.

44. See, e.g., Kuss; Fitzmyer. Ps. 107:26 refers to those whom God has redeemed from trouble (cf. v. 2): "They mounted up to heaven, they went down to the depths (LXX: καταβαίνουσιν ἕως τῶν ἀβύσσων); their courage melted away in their calamity."

45. In the LXX, ἄβυσσος almost always translates תְּהוֹם, which usually refers to the deep places of the sea (BDB), but which in later Judaism was also used of the depths of the earth and the place where evil spirits are confined (J. Jeremias, *TDNT* I, 9). On the equivalence of the terms, see esp. Heller, "Himmel- und Höllenfahrt," p. 482; Michel, *Paulus,* p. 60; on similar rabbinic traditions, see A. M. Goldberg, "Torah aus der Unterwelt? Eine Bemerkung zu Röm 10,6-7," *BZ* 14 (1970), 127-31. In the NT, "abyss" refers to the place where (evil) spirits dwell and are confined (Luke 8:31; Rev. 9:1-2, 11; 11:7; 17:8; 20:1, 3).

46. *Targum Neofiti* reads: "Neither is the Law beyond the Great Sea that one may say: Would that we had one like the prophet Jonah who would descend into the depths of the Great Sea and bring it up for us . . . (the translation is from M. McNamara, *The New Testament and the Palestinian Targum to the Pentateuch* [AnBib 27; Rome: Pontifical Biblical Institute, 1966], pp. 370-78). The "Fragment" targum is similar (see Lyonnet,

imagery of the crossing of the sea in Deut. 30:13 to the conceptually similar vertical imagery of descent into the underworld. His purpose for making such a change was to facilitate his christological application. As he could use the fact of the incarnation to suggest the foolishness of "going into heaven" to bring Christ down, so now he can use the fact of the resurrection to deny any need to "go down to the abyss" to bring Christ up from "the realm of the dead."[47]

8 The introductory formula "But what does it say?" reiterates the initial introduction to the series of quotations from Deut. 30 in v. 6a — the subject of the verb being, then, "the righteousness based on faith." Paul uses the adversative "but" because he now tells us what the righteousness based on faith *does* say, in contrast to what it warns us not to say (vv. 6-7). This positive assertion about the nature of the righteousness based on faith is therefore the key point that Paul wants to get across through his use of Deut. 30.[48] What is this point? That the message about the righteousness of faith, preached by Paul and the other apostles, is, like the law of God, accessible and understandable: "the word is near you, in your mouth and in your heart."[49] The word in Deuteronomy takes the form of a word of command; here in Romans, that word of God is "the word of faith that we are preaching." But both words have in common that God has brought them "near." Yet there is in the gospel that Paul and the other apostles are preaching an added sense in which the word is "near." For not only does the gospel proclaim and embody the fulfillment of God's promise to bring his righteousness "near" to his people; it also provides for the writing of God's law on the heart, in fulfillment of the New Covenant prophecy.[50] In Christ, the culmination of the law, God's word is near in a way that it has never been before. And all that is now required of human beings is the

---

"Saint Paul et le exégèse juive," pp. 501-5). It may also be significant for Paul's application of the language to the resurrection of Christ that Jonah 2:3-10 uses both מַיִם, "sea," and תְּהוֹם, "abyss," in parallel of the prophet's experience in the belly of the great fish (see Matt. 12:40).

47. Gk. ἐκ νεκρῶν; see the comments on 1:4. It may be that Paul is in this verse assuming the tradition of Christ's "descent into Hades" between the time of his death and his resurrection (so, e.g., Käsemann and many other commentators). On the other hand, this may read too much into the appearance of the word "abyss" in the quotation, since that word was, to some degree, "forced" on Paul by the OT tradition he is using.

48. Eckstein, " 'Nahe ist dir das Wort,' " p. 214.

49. Paul's wording is very close to the LXX, which reads σου ἐγγύς τὸ ῥῆμα σφόδρα ἐν τῷ στόματί σου καὶ ἐν τῇ καρδίᾳ σου (and the LXX faithfully renders the MT). Paul again quotes selectively, omitting the words "and in your hands, to do it" that complete the sentence in Deut. 30:14. He is thereby able to cite this language from Deuteronomy as a generalized reference to God's word.

50. Cf. Käsemann.

response of faith. For the gospel is "the word of faith": a message[51] that calls for faith.[52]

9 The word that connects v. 9 to v. 8 *(hoti)* could be translated either "that" or "because." If we translate it with "that," v. 9 would specify the content of "the word of faith" that Paul and the other apostles are preaching.[53] If, however, we translate it "because," v. 9 would explain how it is that "the word is near you."[54] The latter alternative should probably be adopted because it would be awkward to have two "content" clauses in a row (e.g., "that is the word of faith . . . ," "that if you confess . . ."). Paul is therefore explaining the "nearness" of the word of faith, the gospel, by emphasizing that it demands only a simple response and that, when responded to, it mediates God's salvation. This simple response, surprisingly in light of Paul's stress on faith in this context, is a twofold one: "if you confess with[55] your mouth" and "if you believe in your heart." Both the presence of these two conditions and the order in which they occur are due to Paul's desire to show how his "word of faith" precisely matches the description of the word in Deut. 30:14, as being "in your mouth" and "in your heart."[56] Paul's rhetorical purpose at this point should make us cautious about finding great significance in the reference to confession here, as if Paul were making oral confession a second requirement for salvation. Belief in the heart is clearly the crucial requirement, as Paul makes clear even in this context (9:30; 10:4, 11). Confession is the outward manifestation of this critical inner response.[57]

51. Paul, because of his dependence on the LXX of Deut. 30:13, uses the (for him) unusual ῥῆμα. Here the term denotes the gospel (BAGD).

52. The genitive τῆς πίστεως is objective — "the word that calls for faith" (cf. Meyer; S-H; Murray; Cranfield). Some commentators think that "faith" here might have the concrete sense of "the faith which is believed" *(fides quae creditur;* cf. Käsemann; Fitzmyer), but this is unlikely. Both πίστις and πιστεύω refer throughout this context to the act of believing rather than to the message that one is to believe.

53. See NIV: " 'The word is near you; it is in your mouth and in your heart,' that is, the word of faith we are proclaiming: That if you confess . . .' "; cf. Barrett; Käsemann.

54. NRSV: " 'The word is near you, on your lips and in your heart' (that is, the word of faith that we proclaim); because if you confess . . .; cf. Kuss; Cranfield.

55. The ἐν is instrumental.

56. Cf. Cranfield. Other scholars think that the order of the clauses, at least, might reflect Paul's use here of an early Christian confession, perhaps associated with baptism (e.g., P.-E. Langevin, "Sur le christologie de Romains 10,1-13," *Théologique et Philoso-phique* 35 [1979], 39-42; Käsemann; Wilckens).

57. Paul uses the "confession" word-group (ὁμολογέω and ὁμολογία) rarely. In 1 Tim. 6:12-13, confession is a public attestation of one's faith (cf. also Tit. 1:16, where the confession is verbal only); in 2 Cor. 9:13, the confession is one's Christian profession, to which the Corinthians are called to be obedient. On "confession" in the NT, see, further, V. H. Neufeld, *The Earliest Christian Confessions* (NTTS 5; Grand Rapids: Eerdmans, 1963). A double accusative (κύριον Ἰησοῦν) after ὁμολογέω is not unusual (BDF 157[2]).

657

The content of what we are to confess and to believe reflects basic early Christian proclamation. The acclamation of Jesus as Lord is a very early and very central element of Christian confession;[58] as is the conviction that God raised Jesus from the dead.[59] Paul's focus here on Christ's resurrection is not, of course, intended to detract from his death or from other aspects of his work; as Calvin explains, the resurrection alone is "often set before us as the assurance of our salvation, not to draw away our attention from his death, but because it bears witness to the efficacy and fruit of his death."[60] Paul may also focus on our belief in the resurrection as a final answer to the question "Who will ascend into the abyss? (That is, to bring Christ up)" in v. 7. The gospel, then, is "near" to us because it requires only what our own hearts and mouths can do; and when we respond, it brings near to us God's salvation.[61]

10 Verse 10 provides corroboration of the connection between confession and faith on the one hand and salvation on the other: "For with the heart one believes for righteousness, and with the mouth one confesses for salvation."[62] This general way of stating the matter prepares the way for Paul's universalizing application in vv. 11-13. Verse 10 is, then, transitional. Paul again writes rhetorically: the wording of the two parallel clauses follows the same order; and each clause reiterates one of the conditions of v. 9, but in reverse order (thus forming a chiasm). This evident rhetorical interest suggests

58. See Phil. 2:11; 1 Cor. 12:3; cf. Neufeld, *Confessions,* pp. 43-47. The μαράνα θά — "our Lord, come!" — of 1 Cor. 16:22, in particular, points to an early date for this confession since it preserves the Aramaic that was spoken by the first Jewish Christians. This confession in Jesus as Lord carried with it significant overtones, for it would inevitably associate Jesus closely with God, the "Lord." See, e.g., Langevin, "Romains 10,1-13," pp. 51-53; and, further, the note on v. 13; contra, e.g., Dunn, who unduly minimizes its significance.

59. See 4:24; 8:11; Gal. 1:1; 1 Cor. 6:14; 15:4, 12, 20; 2 Cor. 4:14; 1 Thess. 1:10; Col. 2:12; Eph. 1:20; Acts 3:15; 4:10; 10:40; 1 Pet. 1:21. On both these early Christian "words," see W. Führer, " 'Herr ist Jesus.' Die Rezeption der urchristlichen Kyrios-Akklamation durch Paulus; Römer 10:9," *KD* 33 (1987), 139-42.

60. Calvin.

61. σωθήσῃ, "you will be saved," might be a genuine temporal future, denoting final rescue from sin and death at the last day (see Barrett; Dunn). But it makes better sense in this context to view it simply as a relative or "logical" future — salvation being the result of, and therefore future to, confessing and believing — with its absolute time undetermined (see the notes on 6:5 and Porter, *Verbal Aspect,* pp. 421-23).

62. The two verbs in the verse (πιστεύεται and ὁμολογεῖται) are third person singular passive. It is possible to supply as the subjects of these verbs the objects of the comparable verbs in v. 9: "that Jesus is Lord is believed," "that God raised him from the dead is confessed." But this is awkward; it is better to think that Paul uses the passive to connote an impersonal nuance: "one believes," "one confesses." He thereby gives to the verse a summary and principial character (see Barrett).

that Paul would not want us to find any difference in the meanings of "righteousness" and "salvation" here.[63] Each expresses in a general way the new relationship with God that is the result of believing "with the heart" and confessing "with the mouth."[64]

11 Paul's quotation of Isa. 28:16 in this verse has two purposes. First, it provides further scriptural support for his critical connection of faith and salvation. For "not being put to shame" refers to deliverance at the time of judgment.[65] Second, by adding the word "no one"[66] at the beginning of the quotation, Paul is able to cite the text to support his contention that the salvation now made available in Christ is for anyone who believes. This verse therefore finally picks up the element of universality in 10:4b: "for *everyone* who believes."

12 Paul unpacks the universality inherent in "everyone" in this verse. As so often in Romans, Paul is particularly concerned with the equal footing given to both Jews and Gentiles by the gospel. As there is "no distinction" between the two groups of people in sin and judgment (3:23), so there is "no distinction" between them as far as the Lord who rules over them or in the grace that the Lord offers to them. Paul has earlier in the letter shown that the confession that there is only one God leads naturally to the conclusion that God must rule both Jews and Gentiles (3:29-30). His insistence here that "the same Lord is Lord of all,"[67] might be making the same point, in which case we would understand "Lord" to refer to God the Father.[68] But "Lord" *(kyrios)* in v. 9 refers to Jesus, and Christ is also the implicit antecedent of "him" in whom people believe in v. 11. Moreover, Paul's language here probably echoes again an early Christian acclamation of Jesus as "Lord of all."[69] The "Lord" here will then be

---

63. Dunn; Cranfield. Both scholars, however, think the words refer to deliverance at the last day; this, however, is not clear (see the note on v. 9). Murray, on the other hand, sees some distinction between righteousness and salvation here; Godet thinks that righteousness is a benefit conferred in this life, with salvation referring to eschatological deliverance. As Dunn notes, the collocation of "faith," "righteousness," and "salvation" reminds us again of the theme of the letter (1:16-17).

64. καρδίᾳ and στόματι, each placed first in its respective clause for emphasis, are instrumental datives.

65. See, e.g., Isa. 50:7b-8a: "I know that I shall not be put to shame; he who vindicates me is near" (NRSV); cf. R. Bultmann, *TDNT* I, 189; 5:5.

66. Gk. πᾶς.

67. Gk. ὁ γὰρ αὐτὸς κύριος πάντων. We are required to supply the verb "to be" and to repeat κύριος after the verb as predicate. πάντων in this context will refer to persons (Langevin, "Romains 10,1-13," pp. 50-51).

68. Ziesler; Gaston, *Paul and the Torah,* p. 131.

69. See Acts 10:36; cf. 1 Cor. 12:5; Eph. 4:5. J. Dupont argues that the tradition of Jesus as "Lord of all" might have arisen on the basis of Joel 2:28 (LXX 3:5) ("'Le Seigneur de tous' [Ac 10:36; Rm 10:12]: Arrière-fond scripturaire d'une formule christologique," in *Tradition and Interpretation,* pp. 229-36).

Jesus.[70] As Lord, Jesus not only demands allegiance from all; he graciously showers his "riches" on all who "call upon him." Paul frequently uses the language of "wealth" to connote the unlimited resources of God[71] that he makes available to his people in and through his Son.[72] Often, these riches are defined in terms of God's grace or mercy (2:4; Eph. 1:7; 2:7), and this is certainly Paul's intention here as well. "Call upon" with a personal object is used in secular Greek for asking someone for assistance, and especially of asking God, or the gods, for help or intervention.[73] But "calling on the Lord" is also quite common in the LXX and Jewish literature,[74] and was taken over by the early Christians with reference both to God the Father and to Christ.[75]

13 Paul brings to a close this paragraph with an implicit quotation from Joel 2:32 (LXX 3:5). The catchword "call upon" is clearly the link between the context and the quotation, which was important in early Christian preaching.[76] But perhaps even more important for Paul was its emphasis on the universal availability of salvation. The quotation brings together two crucial terms from this context: "everyone" (cf. vv. 4, 11, 12) and "salvation" (cf. vv. 1, 9, 10). In the OT, of course, the one on whom people called for salvation was Yahweh; Paul reflects the high view of Christ common among the early church by identifying this one with Jesus Christ, the Lord.[77]

70. E.g., Kuss; Dunn; Fitzmyer.

71. Rom. 2:4; 9:23; 11:33; Eph. 3:16.

72. 1 Cor. 1:5; 2 Cor. 8:9; Eph. 1:7; 2:7; 3:8; Phil. 4:19; Col. 1:27. The Greek words are πλοῦτος and πλουτέω; cf. also πλουτίζω in 1 Cor. 1:5; 2 Cor. 6:10; 9:11.

73. BAGD.

74. E.g., Deut. 4:7; Isa. 55:6; 2 Macc. 3:22; Jud. 16:2.

75. See, respectively, Acts 9:14; 2 Tim. 2:22[?]; 1 Pet. 1:17 and Acts 9:21; 22:16; 1 Cor. 1:2. Some commentators (e.g., Cranfield) think that Paul might be referring to calling on Christ in prayer here, but that is unlikely; NT usage (see above) suggests rather an appeal to Christ for mercy and favor.

76. Acts 2:17-21, 39; cf. Mark 13:24 and parallels; Rev. 6:12. Paul might also have been influenced in the choice of this text by the verses immediately preceding it (vv. 26-27), which speak of the day when God's people would not be "put to shame"; see the quotation of Isa. 28:16 in v. 11 (Lindars, "Old Testament and Universalism," 520-21).

77. The significance of NT quotations that use the title κύριος of Christ are debated because it is apparently the case that pre-Christian MSS of the LXX did not use this Greek word to translate the tetragram (reproductions of the Hebrew script were used). But there is good evidence that Greek-speaking Jews before the time of Christ were already at least orally substituting the Greek word κύριος for the tetragram. The NT application of texts that identify Christ with "the Lord" therefore suggest that the early Christians viewed Christ as in some sense equivalent to Yahweh. On this issue, see esp. J. A. Fitzmyer, "The Semitic Background of the New Testament *kyrios* Title," in *A Wandering Aramean: Collected Aramaic Essays* (SBLDS 25; Missoula, MT: Scholars Press, 1979), 115-42; also Koch, 84-88. A few scholars argue that Paul intends the κύριος in the quotation to refer to God the Father rather than to Christ (G. Howard, "The Tetragram and the New Testa-

2. Israel's Accountability (10:14-21)

14Therefore, how shall they call on one in whom they have not believed? And how shall they believe in whom they have not heard? And how shall they hear without a preacher? 15And how shall they preach unless they are sent? Just as it is written, "How timely are the feet[1] of those who bring good news!"[a]

16But not all have obeyed the gospel. For Isaiah says, "Lord, who has believed our report?"[b] 17Therefore, faith comes from hearing, and hearing is through the word of Christ.[2] 18But I say, have they not heard? Indeed they have:

Into all the earth their voice has gone forth,
their words unto the ends of the inhabited world.[c]
19But I say, has not Israel known? Moses first says,
I will make you jealous with what is not a nation, with
a nation that is without understanding, I will make you angry.[d]

20And Isaiah also boldly says,

I will be found by those who are not seeking me, I will make
myself manifest to those who are not asking for me.[e]

21But about Israel he says,

All the day long I have held out my hands to a people
who are disobedient and obstinate.[f]

a. Isa. 52:7
b. Isa. 53:1
c. Ps. 19:4

---

ment," *JBL* 96 [1977], 63-83; Gaston, *Paul and the Torah*, p. 131), but the flow of the context makes this almost impossible.

1. A number of MSS (the second corrector of ℵ, Ψ, the western uncials D, F, and G, 33, and the majority text) add here the phrase τῶν εὐαγγελιζομένων εἰρήνην, "of those who preach good news of peace." The words are a corruption seeking to conform Paul's quotation more closely to the LXX (see, e.g., S-H, 297; Cranfield, 2.534-35 n. 4; Fitzmyer, 597-98; contra, e.g., Godet, 386).

2. Instead of Χριστοῦ, some MSS (the primary Alexandrian uncial ℵ [first corrector], the secondary Alexandrian uncial A, Ψ, the western uncial D [first corrector], 33, and the majority text) have Θεοῦ. Howard ("Tetragram," pp. 78-79) argues for the latter, but Χριστοῦ has early and diverse support (the combination of the early uncial P46, the strength of the Alexandrian text [ℵ {original hand}, B, 1739; cf. also C and 81], and the western D [original hand]) and makes better sense in the context (cf. vv. 8-9). An early copyist has substituted the more customary ῥῆμα Θεοῦ (five times in the NT; ῥῆμα Χριστοῦ only here). See Metzger, 525; Dunn, 2.619; Fitzmyer, 598-99.

d. Deut. 32:21
e. Isa. 65:1
f. Isa. 65:2

Verse 14, with its "therefore"[3] followed by a question, marks the beginning of a new unit of thought.[4] The immediate point of contact is with the word "call upon" in the quotation of Joel 2:28 in v. 13. That quotation asserts that salvation is a matter of calling on the Lord. In vv. 14ff., Paul asks whether such calling on the name of the Lord is really possible. He begins by analyzing the conditions that are necessary for such calling on the Lord in a series of rhetorical questions (vv. 14-15a). He then makes clear that every condition — except one — has been met. First, the gospel, "the word of faith" (cf. v. 8), has been preached (v. 15; cf. v. 14c). Second, that message of the gospel, "the word of Christ" has been heard; indeed, the voices of its messengers have been heard throughout the inhabited world (v. 18; cf. vv. 14b and 17). Not only has the gospel been made known; it has, to at least some extent, been understood (vv. 19-20). What is the missing ingredient? Faith. For calling on the name of the Lord is another way of saying "believe"; and it is this humble acceptance for oneself of the gospel that is missing (v. 16). Verse 16 is therefore the center of this paragraph and expresses its main point.

But of whom is Paul speaking in this paragraph? He explicitly identifies "Israel" as the object of his criticism in v. 19. But up to that point, Paul has used indefinite third person plural verbs, making it likely that at least in vv. 14-15, and perhaps in all of vv. 14-18, he is thinking of people generally.[5] However, there are also indications that Paul is thinking of Israel particularly in this paragraph.[6] The third person plural verbs in v. 14 take the reader back inevitably to the last use of such verbs in chap. 10, in Paul's indictment of the Jews for their ignorance of, and failure to submit to, God's righteousness in vv. 2-3.[7] Verses 14-21 seem to continue that indictment, as Paul removes

3. Gk. οὖν.
4. See S-H, 294, who refer as parallels to 9:14, 30; 11:1, 11. All modern English versions and almost all commentators take this view. A few scholars, however, have argued for a break between vv. 10 and 11 (Hodge, 344), vv. 11 and 12 (Godet, 384), vv. 15 and 16 (Denney, 672), or vv. 16 and 17 (Aletti, *Comment Dieu est-il juste?* 119-20).
5. See, e.g., Denney, 672; Käsemann, 294; Black, 147; Wilckens, 2.228; Murray, 2.60; Dunn, 2.620; Munck, *Christ and Israel,* pp. 91-92; Bell, *Provoked to Jealousy,* pp. 83-87. Some commentators think, in light of the universalism of v. 13, that Paul might have Gentiles specifically in mind (e.g., Calvin, 396; Haldane, 512; Hodge, 346-47; Watson, 166-67; Gaston, *Paul and the Torah,* pp. 131-32; cf. Dunn, 2.620).
6. See Chrysostom, Homily 18 (p. 478); Godet, 385; S-H, 295; Lagrange, 259; Michel, 333; Schmidt, 180; Gaugler, 2.143; Zeller, 188; Kuss, 3.771-72; Cranfield, 2.533; Schlier, 316; Morris, 389.
7. See Chrysostom, Homily 18 (p. 478).

any possible excuse that the Jews might have for their failure to respond to God's offer of righteousness in Christ. Probably, then, Paul writes generally in vv. 14-18 about the relationship of all people to the message of the gospel while at the same time thinking especially of the application of these points to Israel. His point, then, is that Israel cannot plead ignorance: God has made his purposes clear in both the OT (note the six OT quotations in vv. 14-21) and the worldwide proclamation of the gospel. So the fault rests with Israel: she has been "disobedient and obstinate" (v. 21; cf. v. 16).

14-15   Verse 14 and the first part of v. 15 contain a series of four parallel rhetorical questions, each beginning with the interrogative "how."[8] By repeating the verb from the end of one question at the beginning of the next, Paul creates a connected chain of steps that must be followed if a person is to be saved (v. 13).[9] Paul in v. 13 has asserted a universally applicable principle: that salvation is granted to all who call on the Lord. But people cannot call on the Lord if they do not believe in him.[10] They cannot believe in him if they do not hear the word that proclaims Christ.[11] And that word will not be heard unless someone preaches it. But a preacher is nothing more than a herald, a person entrusted by another with a message. Thus preaching, finally, cannot transpire unless someone sends the preachers.

The quotation of Isa. 52:7[12] at the end of v. 15 serves two functions.

---

8. Gk. πῶς.

9. BDF 493(3) comment on the rhetorical nature of this repetition.

10. The Greek uses the preposition εἰς with πιστεύω. This construction, which is extremely common in John and 1 John, is rare in Paul (see Gal. 2:16; Phil. 1:29; Col. 2:5 has the substantive πίστος with εἰς).

11. Paul uses the genitive of the relative pronoun (οὗ) with the verb ἤκουσαν. Since this verb normally takes the genitive to denote the person who is heard (as opposed to the thing that is heard, which is usually denoted with the accusative), commentators suggest that Paul thinks of the preacher himself (Käsemann) or Christ (Godet) as the person who is heard. But the context (see vv. 15, 16, 17) seems to require a reference to the "word," the gospel. Therefore Paul may use the genitive to suggest that Christ is the one who is heard in the message of the gospel (e.g., S-H; Murray; Cranfield; Dunn).

12. Paul's wording differs from both the MT and the LXX in omitting any reference to the preaching of peace (although cf. the textual variant), but it is generally closer to the MT (מַה־נָּאווּ עַל־הֶהָרִים רַגְלֵי מְבַשֵּׂר מַשְׁמִיעַ שָׁלוֹם מְבַשֵּׂר טוֹב; "How beautiful upon the mountains are the feet of the messenger who announces peace, who brings good news . . ." [NRSV]) than to the LXX (ὡς ὥρα ἐπὶ τῶν ὀρέων, ὡς πόδες εὐαγγελιζομένου ἀκοὴν εἰρήνης, ὡς εὐαγγελιζόμενος ἀγαθά . . .). Paul may therefore be dependent on the Hebrew, or on a non-LXX Greek text (for the latter options, see Koch, 66-69; Stanley, *Paul and the Language of Scripture,* pp. 135-37). Allusion to Nah. 2:1 is also possible. Paul's use of the plural τῶν εὐαγγελιζομένων (in contrast to both MT and LXX) manifests his desire to make the text applicable to the multitude of Christian preachers. It is somewhat surprising, however, that Paul does not go on to quote the next part of the verse, which refers to the "message of salvation." Stuhlmacher suggests that Paul might be dependent

First, it provides scriptural confirmation of the necessary role of preaching. Second, however, it implicitly suggests that the last condition for salvation listed by Paul in vv. 14-15a has been met: God has sent preachers.[13] Significant for this latter point is the use of the verb "preach good news" in the Isaiah text. Paul's use of this passage would inevitably suggest an allusion to the preaching of the gospel by himself and other "authorized messengers" sent out by God (e.g., apostles) — especially since the passage was widely viewed as prophetic of the messianic age.[14] It is also possible that the Greek word *hōraioi* should be translated "timely," rather than "beautiful,"[15] lending further support to the eschatological focus on the apostolic preaching.

16 In this verse Paul identifies the link in the chain of requirements leading to salvation that is missing for so many people: faith (cf. v. 14a).[16] While Paul has been speaking generally of all people in vv. 14-15, here he probably focuses especially on Jews.[17] The verse therefore is central to Paul's argument in vv. 14-21 and, indeed, in 9:30–10:21, reasserting as it does Paul's basic accusation of his Jewish brothers and sisters (see also 9:32 and 10:3).[18] The "not all"[19] is a litotes: "only a few."[20] One of the reasons Paul chooses to put the matter this way is to echo the "remnant" theology he has introduced in 9:6b (cf. also 9:27): "not all those who belong to Israel are Israel."[21] Paul's identification of the break in the chain of vv. 14-15a seems a bit premature, since in vv. 18-21 he continues to do what he began in v. 15b, identifying

---

on the teaching of Jesus for his use of Isa. 52:7 (see Mark 1:14-15; Matt. 11:2-6; P. Stuhlmacher, "Jesustradition im Römerbrief? Eine Skizze," *TBei* 14 [1983], 248-49).

13. See esp. Cranfield, contra, e.g., Dunn, who thinks the quotation simply substantiates the need of preaching.

14. Str-B, 3.282-83; cf. also 11QMelch 15-19.

15. See BAGD; *GEL* 67.3; Käsemann; Dunn. In Greek generally, the meaning "timely," "in appropriate season" for ὡραῖος dominates (LSJ), although elsewhere in the NT it means "beautiful" (see Matt. 23:27; Acts 3:2, 10). The relevant Hebrew word in Isa. 52:7, נָאווּ, can mean either "beautiful" or "timely" (BDB).

16. Cranfield also argues that v. 16 asserts the lack of one of the conditions in the chain of vv. 14-15. Dunn, however, argues that v. 16 asserts the general failure of that chain of events in the case of the Jews. S-H, on the other hand, think that v. 16a states an objection to v. 15 to the effect that disobedience to the gospel reveals that that gospel must not be divinely ordained; v. 16b would then be Paul's response. But this is not the most natural way to take the verse.

17. This is suggested by the use of Isa. 53:1 in John 12:38, along with Paul's use of Isa. 53 elsewhere (cf. esp. Rom. 15:21); see esp. Bell, *Provoked to Jealousy*, pp. 90-92.

18. Cf. Käsemann.

19. Gk. οὐ πάντες.

20. BDR 495(2). Others argue that οὐ πάντες is not a figure of speech but picks up directly the πᾶς in v. 13: "everyone who calls on the name of the Lord will be saved" — but "not all" obey (Michel; Dunn).

21. Munck, *Christ and Israel*, pp. 92-93.

links in the chain that are in place.[22] But Paul could not resist the natural contrast between the truth of the publication of the good news (v. 15b) and the Jews' tragic reaction to it. Surprisingly, Paul characterizes this reaction as "disobedience" rather than unbelief. But Paul has linked faith and obedience since the beginning of the letter (see 1:5, "the obedience of faith"), and he is especially concerned in this context to show that Israel's situation is the result not simply of a relatively passive unbelief, but of a definite and culpable refusal to respond to God's gracious initiative (see 10:3 and 21).

Nevertheless, Paul considers Israel's disobedience and unbelief as two sides of the same coin, as the quotation from Isa. 53:1 in v. 16b makes clear: "Lord, who has *believed* our report?"[23] As he does on three other occasions in Rom. 9–11 (see also 9:27, 29; 10:20), Paul names Isaiah as the biblical author.

17 This verse seems awkwardly placed. The introductory "therefore"[24] and its content suggest that it is a conclusion drawn from the chain of salvation requirements in vv. 14-15a. Some scholars therefore think the verse is out of place[25] or even that it was a later addition to the text of Romans.[26] These desperate measures are not, however, necessary. As we have seen, the identification of the one point in the chain at which Israel has fallen short in v. 16 is premature, interrupting Paul's assertion of those points that have found fulfillment. What Paul says in v. 17 is therefore a necessary transition back into this topic. It picks up immediately the connection between "believing" and "hearing/report" that the quotation of Isa. 53:1 in v. 16b assumes and restates the second step in the series of salvation requirements: faith comes as a result of "hearing" (cf. v. 14b).[27] The last part of v. 17 then

22. Kuss.

23. Paul reproduces the LXX exactly, which accurately translates the MT; the only difference is that κύριε has no counterpart in the Hebrew. The quotation of this same text in John 12:38 suggests that it may have been a common early Christian "testimonium" used to explain and justify in Scripture the Jews' unbelief (Dodd, *According to the Scriptures*, p. 39). Perhaps Paul also sees the text as particularly appropriate since it closely follows Isa. 52:7, which he has just quoted in v. 15b.

24. Gk. ἄρα.

25. E.g., Barrett.

26. Bultmann, "Glossen," p. 280; Schmithals.

27. See, e.g., Cranfield; Morris; Wilckens; Munck, *Christ and Israel*, pp. 93-94. On the transitional nature of v. 17, see Käsemann; Aageson, "Scripture and Structure," p. 278.

ἀκοή in the quotation of Isa. 53:1 in v. 16b means "that which is heard," "report" (so almost all commentators, though see Godet). This could suggest that in v. 17 also ἀκοή means "report"; cf. NRSV: "So faith comes from *what is heard,* and *what is heard* comes through the word of Christ" (BAGD; Meyer; Kuss; Michel; Eckstein, " 'Nahe ist dir das Wort,' " p. 220). But it is more likely that ἀκοή in this verse has the active meaning "act

restates and expands on the third step in that sequence (v. 14c): hearing, the kind of hearing that can lead to faith, can only happen if there is a definite salvific word from God that is proclaimed.[28] That word through which God is now proclaiming the availability of eschatological salvation and which can awaken faith in those who hear it is "the word of Christ": the message whose content is the lordship and resurrection of Christ (see 10:8-9).[29]

18 Verse 17 has focused attention on the critical step of "hearing" in the sequence of steps leading to salvation. Paul now goes back to this step and asks "have they not heard?" Probably here again (as in vv. 14-15) Paul is speaking generally about all people but with special reference to Jews.[30] Paul puts his question in a form that makes it legitimate to paraphrase it with an assertion: people have heard.[31] In keeping with his concern throughout this paragraph and Rom. 9–11 generally, Paul substantiates this assertion with an appeal to Scripture: "Indeed,"[32] Paul says, they have heard, for Ps. 19:4 asserts that "their voice has gone out into all the earth, their words unto the ends of the inhabited world."[33] Paul's use of this text raises two questions. First, what is Paul's purpose in using a passage that extols God's revelation in nature (as Ps. 19:1-6 does) in this context? The implied object of the verb "heard" in Paul's question must be "the word of Christ"; "their voice" and "their words" in the Psalm verse must then refer to the voices and words of Christian preachers (see vv. 14-16). Paul is not,

---

of hearing" (so most English translations; cf. S-H; Barrett; Murray; Dunn; Cranfield). This meaning is preferable because (1) it matches the verb ἀκούω in vv. 14 and 18, verses that are closely related to this verse; and (2) ἀκοή must be distinct from ῥῆμα, which refers to the concrete message. Paul uses ἀκοή seven times outside this context; four probably refer to the "act" or organ of hearing (1 Cor. 12:17 [twice]; 2 Tim. 4:3, 4), while the other three are disputed (Gal. 3:2, 5; 1 Thess. 2:13).

28. Paul asserts that faith is "based on" (ἐξ) hearing, whereas hearing is "through" (διά) the word of Christ. Some commentators find significance in the shift from the one preposition to the other; e.g., Lenski thinks the former denotes that hearing is the *source* of faith while the latter implies that hearing is *mediated by* Christ's word. But the distinction seems artificial; the two are probably used interchangeably to denote source.

29. A few commentators take the genitive Χριστοῦ as a subjective genitive: "the word commissioned by Christ" (Kuss) or "proclaimed by Christ" (Munck, *Christ and Israel*, p. 94). But the obvious relationship between this phrase and vv. 8-9 (note the relatively rare ῥῆμα) suggests rather an objective genitive: "the word that proclaims Christ" (S-H).

30. Contra, e.g., Calvin, who applies it to the Gentiles.

31. The question is put in a negative form: οὐκ ἤκουσαν and introduced with another negative particle (μή), implying that the question should be answered in the negative: "it is not the case, then, that they have 'not heard,' is it?" See Turner, 283.

32. μενοῦνγε here means "truly," "indeed" (cf. BDF 450[4]), and not (as in 9:20), "on the contrary" (as, e.g., Käsemann thinks).

33. Paul's wording exactly follows the majority MSS tradition of the LXX; and the LXX accurately renders the MT.

then, simply using the text according to its original meaning.[34] His application probably rests on a general analogy: as God's word of general revelation has been proclaimed all over the earth, so God's word of special revelation, in the gospel, has been spread all over the earth.[35] His intention is not to interpret the verse of the Psalm, but to use its language, with the "echoes" of God's revelation that it awakes, to assert the universal preaching of the gospel.[36]

But this brings us to our second question: How could Paul assert, in A.D. 57, that the gospel has been proclaimed "to the whole earth"? Two implicit qualifications of Paul's language are frequently noted. First, as the word *oikoumenē* in the second line of the quotation might suggest, Paul may be thinking in terms of the Roman Empire of his day rather than of the entire globe.[37] Second, Paul's focus might be corporate rather than individualistic: he asserts not that the gospel has been preached to every person but to every nation, and especially to both Jews and Gentiles.[38] Both these considerations may well be relevant. But perhaps it would be simpler to think that Paul engages in hyperbole, using the language of the Psalm to assert that very many people by the time Paul writes Romans have had opportunity to hear.[39] It cannot be lack of opportunity, then, that explains why so few Jews have come to experience the salvation God offers in Christ.

19 The repetition of the opening words of v. 18 — "but I say" — marks out v. 19 as a second step in Paul's argument that began in v. 18. There he showed that it was not lack of opportunity to hear that prevented Jews from being saved. Now he takes a step further and, abandoning the opening sequence of steps, probes deeper into the nature of the Jews' "hearing." Specifically, he raises and rejects the possibility that this hearing was a merely superficial hearing, not accompanied by genuine understanding. No, Paul affirms, Israel has "known."[40]

34. Contra, e.g., Ellison (*Mystery of Israel,* 69-71).

35. See Calvin.

36. See particularly Hays, 175. The view that Paul is here simply using the language of the Psalm verse without intending to "quote" it has some truth. Note, e.g., the lack of an introductory formula, in contrast to the clear introductions when the OT is quoted in vv. 16, 19, 20, and 21; see, for this view, many of the Greek Fathers (Schelkle); Godet; Dunn; Fitzmyer. However, as Hays rightly emphasizes, Paul's use of the language from the Psalm has the purpose of drawing the reader's attention to that text; it creates an "echo" of Scripture.

37. See Schmithals; Wilckens.

38. Munck, *Christ and Israel,* pp. 95-99; Morris.

39. Comparison should be made with Col. 1:23, where Paul claims that the gospel has been preached "to every creature under heaven."

40. As in v. 18, Paul uses a negative question preceded by a particle signaling a negative answer — μὴ Ἰσραὴλ οὐκ ἔγνω;. Hofius, indeed, argues that the context requires that we overlook the normal force of the μή and construe the question as expecting a positive answer: "Israel has not known, has she?" ("Das Evangelium und Israel," p. 298 n. 5). But his argument from context is not strong enough to force us to abandon the normal meaning of the syntax.

Paul explicitly uses the word "Israel" to make clear for the first time his "real" subject in this paragraph. At the same time, the use of the word adds emphasis to his point: Can it really be that *Israel,* the recipient of God's numerous and detailed prophecies about his plans and purposes, does not "know"?[41] What it was that Israel "knows," as the subsequent context suggests, is that God could very well act in such a way that the preaching of Christ would result in the inclusion of the Gentiles and in judgment upon Israel (see the OT quotations in vv. 19b-21). This Israel knows from her own Scriptures; her "ignorance," then (v. 3), consists in her willful refusal to recognize the fulfillment of these texts in the revelation of God's righteousness in Christ. Israel, Paul suggests, "sees, but does not perceive; hears, but does not comprehend" (Isa. 6:9; cf. Mark 4:12 and pars.; John 12:40; Acts 28:26-27).

Paul quotes Deut. 32:21b as the first step ("Moses *first*[42] says") in his demonstration from Scripture of what Israel knew.[43] The verse is part of Moses' "song" to Israel, in which he rehearses the history of God's gracious acts on Israel's behalf and Israel's stubborn and sinful response to those acts. The words Paul quotes state God's "equivalent" response to Israel's idolatry: because Israel has made God jealous with "what is no god" (v. 21a), God will make Israel "jealous"[44] with what is "no people." The phrase "no people" was probably the catch phrase that drew Paul's attention to this text, since he quotes the Hosea prophecy about those "not my people" becoming the people of God in 9:25-26.[45] Paul sees in the words a prophecy of the mission to the Gentiles:[46] the inclusion of Gentiles in the new people of God stimulates the Jews to jealousy and causes Israel to respond in wrath against this movement in salvation history. From their own Scriptures, then, Israel should have recognized that God was at work in the gospel.

---

41. S-H; Cranfield.

42. πρῶτος here may have comparative force (= πρότερος, i.e., "former") but probably highlights Moses as the "first" in a long line of the witnesses to the truth Paul is communicating (Murray; Kuss; Dunn; Wilckens). The alternative punctuation, which would take πρῶτος with what precedes — "Did not Israel know first?" — is to be rejected (cf. Cranfield).

43. Paul's wording differs from the majority LXX MSS tradition (cf. also the MT) in using second person plural objects of the verbs — ὑμᾶς — in place of third person plural objects — αὐτούς. Paul probably introduces this change himself, in order to highlight the "personal" way in which God (cf. ἐγώ) addresses his people (Hübner, *Gottes Ich und Israel,* p. 97; Stanley, *Paul and the Language of Scripture,* pp. 143-44).

44. The verb is παραζηλόω, which can have a range of meanings. Crucial for Paul's use of the term in Rom. 10–11 are (1) "provoke to jealous anger" (in this verse); and (2) "provoke to jealous emulation" (cf. 11:11, 14). See Bell, *Provoked to Jealousy,* pp. 24-42. Bell further suggests that Deut. 32 was an important source for Paul's theological argument in Rom. 9–11.

45. Bruce.

46. E.g., Cranfield; Käsemann; Bell, *Provoked to Jealousy,* pp. 95-104.

668

20 But it is not only the "law" that anticipates the gospel and Israel's negative reaction to it; the "prophets" bear witness to the same truth. In fact, Paul suggests, the prophetic text testifies even more clearly to these points: "Isaiah boldly[47] says, 'I will be found by those who are not seeking me, I will make myself manifest to those who are not asking for me.' "[48] Paul quotes from Isa. 65:1, a verse that in its context refers to God's making himself known to the people of Israel.[49] As he did with Hos. 1:10 and 2:23 in 9:25-26, Paul takes OT texts that speak of Israel and applies them, on the principle of analogy, to the Gentiles. Paul's application of this text to the Gentiles could be based on the language of "those who did not seek me." The wording of the quotation therefore brings us back to where this whole passage began: Gentiles, who were not pursuing righteousness, have attained a right relationship with God (9:30).

21 Having applied Isa. 65:1 in v. 20 to the Gentiles, Paul now applies Isa. 65:2 to Israel,[50] an application that matches the original meaning of the text.[51] The passage stresses both God's constant offer of grace to his people and their stubborn resistance to that grace. But which is uppermost? God's continuing gracious concern for Israel?[52] Or Israel's disobedience?[53] The question that this verse sparks in 11:1 might suggest that the latter is closer to the truth. But we should probably not choose between the two. Both the

---

47. Gk. ἀποτολμᾷ, "with boldness." The word is used only here in the Greek Bible.

48. Paul, in relationship to the LXX, transposes the verbs, but otherwise, except for orthographic variants, quotes the LXX accurately. The LXX is an accurate enough rendering of the MT, but it may miss the force of the niphal verbs, thus assisting Paul in his use of the text.

49. This is the majority view among OT commentators. This majority thinks that the verbs in the MT are "tolerative niphals," to be translated "I allowed myself to be sought," "I was ready to be found," and that the last phrase in the verse should be translated "a nation that did not call on my name" (cf., e.g., NRSV). A few commentators, however, think that this last phrase should be translated "a nation not called by my name" and that the verse therefore refers to Gentiles (cf. KJV; J. A. Alexander, *Commentary on the Prophecies of Isaiah* [rpt.; 2 vols. in 1; Grand Rapids: Zondervan, 1953], 2.437-38; A. MacRae, "Paul's Use of Isaiah 65:1," in *The Law and the Prophets: Old Testament Studies Prepared in Honor of Oswald Thompson Allis* [ed. J. H. Skilton; Philadelphia: Presbyterian and Reformed, 1974], pp. 369-76).

50. This is the third quotation in these last verses of chap. 10 that returns to the emphasis on God's own speaking. πρός probably therefore, instead of meaning "concerning" or "with reference to" (so most English translations) has the force of a dative: God says *to* Israel (KJV).

51. Paul again probably quotes the LXX: the only difference between his wording and the LXX is that he moves the phrase ὅλην τὴν ἡμέραν to the beginning of the sentence.

52. E.g., Cranfield; Volf, *Paul and Perseverance,* pp. 166-67.

53. Godet; Michel.

grace of God in revealing himself and in reaching out to Israel and Israel's refusal to respond to that grace are important for Paul's argument.

D. SUMMARY: ISRAEL, THE "ELECT," AND THE "HARDENED" (11:1-10)

1*I say, therefore: God has not rejected his people,[1] has he? By no means! For even I am an Israelite, of the seed of Abraham, of the tribe of Benjamin. 2God has not rejected his people, whom he foreknew. Or do you not know what the Scripture says in the section about Elijah, how he appeals to God against Israel?*

3*Lord, they have killed your prophets, they have torn down your altars, and I alone am left, and they are seeking my life.*[a]

4*But what does the divine answer say to him?*

I have left for myself seven thousand men who have not bowed the knee to Baal.[b]

5*In this manner, therefore, there has also come into being at the present time a remnant, based on the election of grace. 6And if by grace, it is no longer on the basis of works; for otherwise, grace would no longer be grace.*[2]

7*What then? What Israel is seeking, this she has not attained; but the elect have attained it. But the rest have been hardened, 8even as it is written,*

1. The important early papyrus P[46] and two generally inferior western uncials (F and G) read the phrase τὴν κληρονομίαν, "the inheritance," in place of τὸν λαόν, "the people." This reading seems to be a western assimilation to the second half of Ps. 94:14 — "he will not forsake his inheritance [LXX κληρονομίαν]" — the first half of which Paul alludes to in this question and in v. 2a (Metzger, 526; Cranfield, 2.543).

2. With some minor differences among themselves, the second corrector of the uncial ℵ and uncial B (primary witnesses to the Alexandrian text), Ψ, 33, and many other minuscules and ancient translations add at the end of this verse εἰ δὲ ἐξ ἔργων, οὐκέτι ἐστὶ χάρις, ἐπεὶ τὸ ἔργον οὐκέτι ἐστὶν ἔργον — "and if on the basis of works, no longer is it grace, for otherwise work is no longer work" (one minuscule and a MS of an ancient translation add only the words from ἐπεί to the end). The presence of these words in the Textus Receptus led to their being translated in the KJV. But the different variants of the addition and the difficulty of finding a reason for its omission in the bulk of the MSS tradition make it certain that the shorter reading is original (Metzger, 526).

*God has given them a spirit of stupor, eyes that do not see and ears that do not hear, until the present day.*c

9*And David says,*

Let their table become for them a snare and a trap and a stumbling block and a retribution.
10*Let their eyes be darkened so that they do not see and cause their backs to be bent continually.*d

a. 1 Kings 19:10, 14
b. 1 Kings 19:18
c. Deut. 29:3; Isa. 29:10
d. Ps. 69:22-23

A single basic theme can be traced throughout 11:1-32, stated at the beginning and at the end of the section: "God has not rejected his people, whom he foreknew" (v. 2a); "from the standpoint of election they [Israelites] are beloved because of the patriarchs." At the same time, Paul provides clear evidence that an important transition in his argument takes place at 11:11, and I prefer therefore to view 11:1-10 and 11:11-32 as separate literary units.[3] Each of these units is introduced the same way: "Therefore, I say,"[4] followed by a question expecting a negative answer,[5] which is reinforced with the emphatic response "by no means."[6] Each also displays the ending typical of the other major literary units in chaps. 9–11: a mixed quotation, or series of quotations, from the OT (cf. 9:25-29; 10:19-21; 11:26b-27).

As he does so often in Romans, Paul uses a rhetorical question to introduce this next stage of his argument: "I say, therefore: God has not rejected his people, has he?" Paul raises this question because of what he has just said about Israel in 10:21: they are a "disobedient and contrary people." But this accusation summarizes Paul's main point in the whole section 9:30–10:21. At the same time, Paul's answer to his initial rhetorical question picks up important themes from 9:6-29 also. As he did there, Paul here divides Israel into two groups: a "remnant," enjoying the blessings of salvation and existing

---

3. See, e.g., Hafemann, "Salvation of Israel," pp. 45-46; Michel, 337, 343; Schmithals, 394. For a good presentation of the alternative view that finds in 11:1-32 a basic literary unit, see M. Rese, "Die Rettung der Juden nach Römer 11," in *L'Apôtre Paul: personnalité, style et conception du ministère* (ed. A. Vanhoye; BETL 73; Leuven: Leuven University, 1986), p. 424. This position is the usual one; see, e.g., Godet, 391; Käsemann, 298; Cranfield, 2.542; Wilckens, 2.235; Kuss, 3.782-83.

4. Gk. λέγω οὖν.

5. Signaled in Greek by the particle μή.

6. Gk. μὴ γένοιτο. While he recognizes this parallel, Schmeller (*Paulus und die "Diatribe,"* p. 286) argues that the two transitions are not equal in significance.

by virtue of God's gracious election (vv. 5-6; cf. 9:6b-13; 15-16, 18a, 22-23, 27-29), and "the rest," hardened by God in spiritual obduracy (vv. 7b-10; cf. 9:13b, 16-17, 18b, 22-23).[7] In this section, therefore, and especially in vv. 7-10, Paul gathers together the threads of his teaching about Israel to this point. Despite the refusal of most Jews to recognize in Christ the culmination of salvation history (9:2-3; 9:30–10:21) — a refusal that mirrors God's own act of hardening — God continues, in faithfulness to his word (9:4-5, 6a), to treat Israel as a whole as his people, manifesting his continuing concern for them in the preservation of a remnant of true believers. At the same time, 11:1-10 lays the foundations for what Paul will teach about Israel's future in 11:11-32. For the concept of the remnant, used negatively in 9:27-29 — *only* a remnant will be saved — serves a positive purpose in the movement from 11:1-10 to 11:11-32 — there *is* a remnant, a pledge of God's continuing faithfulness to Israel and the promises he has made to her. 11:1-10, therefore, functions as a transition between Paul's discussion of Israel's past and present (9:6–10:21) and her future (11:11-32).[8]

The paragraph unfolds in three sections. The rhetorical question and Paul's answer to it (vv. 1-2a) introduce its main thesis: God has not rejected his people. Paul defends this thesis in vv. 2b-6 with his remnant teaching. Verses 7-10 respond to the implications of this situation with a reprisal of Paul's understanding of Israel's present situation, with particular emphasis on the hardening of many Jews.

1 The verb "I say" in the rhetorical introduction to this section forges a link with 10:14-21, where Paul twice uses the same verb to signal transitions in his argument (vv. 18 and 19). At the same time, the "therefore" shows that Paul now draws an implication from what he has said there. Or, to be more accurate, Paul denies an implication that his readers might have drawn from the previous section. He does so by using a rhetorical pattern very typical of Romans: a question expecting a negative answer — "God has not rejected his people, has he?"[9] — followed by the strong negative response "By no means!"[10] The question is certainly a natural one. Israel's refusal to acknowledge Jesus Christ, the culmination of salvation history (10:4) and sole mediator of God's righteous-

---

7. See, e.g., Munck, *Christ and Israel,* pp. 105-6; Zeller, 191. As we noted at that point, Paul's teaching about election and hardening in 9:6b-29, while manifesting at many points a historical focus, has at the same time clear reference to the situation of Israel in his own day (see particularly 9:24-29). Therefore, while Paul is more explicit about this application to his own situation in 11:1-10, it does not materially move beyond what is already rather plain in chap. 9.

8. Lübking, *Paulus und Israel,* p. 143; Dunn, 2.633.

9. The question is introduced by the Greek particle μή, indicating that it expects a negative answer.

10. See also 3:4, 5-6; 9:14; 11:11; with a neutral question: 3:31; 6:2, 15; 7:7, 13.

ness (10:5-13), would seem to mean that she could no longer claim to be "God's people." But, as in 3:1, where Paul raises a similar question, Paul refuses to admit the "logical" conclusion. Despite her disobedience, Israel remains "the people of God" — in what sense, Paul will explain in the rest of the chapter.

As he did also at the beginning of his discussion of Israel ("my kindred according to the flesh," 9:3), Paul now again reminds his readers of his identification with Israel: "even I am an Israelite, of the seed of Abraham, of the tribe of Benjamin."[11] Paul may refer to his Jewish identity to explain his *motivation* in rejecting the notion that God might have rejected Israel so vehemently: as a Jew who still identified with his people, he could hardly countenance God's abandonment of Israel.[12] However, the "for"[13] introducing the sentence is more likely to introduce a *reason* for Paul's denial. Cranfield thinks that Paul refers to himself in his role of apostle to the Gentiles, a role that God chose a Jew to fill precisely in order to suggest his continuing commitment to the people as a whole.[14] But the importance of the remnant concept in this context (vv. 2b-6) makes it more likely that Paul intends here to associate himself with this entity. Paul himself, as a Jewish Christian, is living evidence that God has not abandoned his people Israel.[15] Jews, like

11. On "Israelite," see 9:4. Paul's addition of "seed of Abraham" is natural in light of the importance given this designation in 4:16-18 and 9:7-9, 29 (cf. also 2 Cor. 11:22). Why he mentions his descent from Benjamin (cf. also Phil. 3:5) is not so clear. Some commentators (e.g., Käsemann; Michel; Barth, *People of God*, p. 82 n. 3) appeal to rabbinic traditions about the tribe of Benjamin: that it was the first to cross the "Sea of Reeds" (e.g., *Mek. Exod.* 14:22 [37^b]), or that its restoration would be the sign of the renewal of all Israel. But the date of the traditions is not certain, and it is unlikely that Paul intends us to find such subtle allusions in his reference. He probably mentions his tribal ancestry simply to reinforce his Jewishness (cf. Phil. 3:5; Calvin; Jeremias shows that many Jews in the time of Paul knew of and boasted about their tribal identity [*Jerusalem in the Time of Jesus* {Philadelphia: Fortress, 1969}, pp. 275-83]).

12. E.g., S-H; Dunn; D. Johnson, "The Structure and Meaning of Romans 11," *CBQ* 46 (1984), 94.

13. Gk. γάρ.

14. Cf. also Gaugler. G. Schrenk likewise focuses on Paul's identity as an apostle, suggesting that Paul sees himself in a role similar to that of the OT prophets, who viewed their own calling as a pledge of God's faithfulness to the people (*TDNT* IV, 211). Gaston, pursuing his thesis that Paul's polemic against Jews had to do only with their refusal to go along with the extension of God's blessing to the Gentiles, suggests that Paul thinks of himself here as one engaged in the mission to the Gentiles and that the remnant mentioned later is made up of those Jews similarly involved in this mission ("Israel's Enemies," p. 142). But even if Gaston were right on v. 1b, there is no reason to carry the idea over into vv. 5-6.

15. E.g., Barrett; Godet; Käsemann; Wilckens; K.-W. Niebuhr, *Heidenapostel aus Israel* (WUNT 62; Tübingen: Mohr, 1992), pp. 169-71. As Kuss comments, Paul's way of referring to himself (χαί . . . ἐγώ; "even I") suggests that the majority of his readers were Gentile Christians.

Paul, are continuing to be saved and to experience the blessings God promised to his people.

2 Paul asserts positively what he denied in v. 1a: "God has not rejected his people." The wording reflects Ps. 94:14 and 1 Sam. 12:22.[16] The relative clause Paul adds to this assertion — "whom he foreknew" — does not simply define "his people" but adds a reason for the assertion. For the "know" in the verb "foreknow" refers to God's election: as Amos puts it, "You [people of Israel] only have I known of all the families of the earth" (3:2a).[17] The temporal prefix, "fore-" *(pro-),* indicates further that God's choosing of Israel took place before any action or status on the part of Israel that might have qualified her for God's choice. How could God reject a people whom he in a gracious act of choice had made his own? As Paul has made clear earlier in the letter (3:3-4), human sinfulness and disobedience cannot cancel his pledged word.

Who are the recipients of this gracious choice of God's? If the clause "whom he foreknew" is restrictive, Paul would be asserting only that God had not rejected a certain body of elect persons from within Israel.[18] This view has the benefit of bringing strict consistency into Paul's use of the verb "foreknow": in both this verse and in 8:29, it would refer to God's choosing individuals for salvation. And Paul certainly argues for an election to salvation of individuals within the larger body of national Israel (9:6-29). But the context demands that Paul here be speaking of God's election of the people as a whole.[19] For it is this national entity whose status is called into question by what Paul has said in 9:30–10:21 and about whom Paul then asks in v. 1. Furthermore, v. 28, which appears to reassert the point Paul makes here in v. 2, ascribes election to Israel as a nation also. Paul, then, uses the verb "foreknow" to indicate God's election, the purpose of that election being

---

16. The LXX of both reads οὐκ ἀπώσεται κύριος τὸν λαὸν αὐτοῦ (Ps. 93:14). Paul's dependence on these LXX texts explains his use of the verb ἀπωθέω, "push aside, reject," which is rare in the NT (cf. also Acts 7:27, 39; 13:46; 1 Tim. 1:9). He changes the future ἀπώσεται to the aorist ἀπώσατο because he is thinking of the situation of Israel's rejection of Christ that he has just depicted. (The shift from κύριος to θεός may reflect Paul's general preference to use κύριος of Jesus.) Paul may have had his attention drawn to Ps. 94:14 partly by the "echo" of his remnant theme created by the use of ἐγκαταλείπω in the second line of the Psalm verse (the verb is used in Rom. 9:29 [= Isa. 1:9]; cf. Hays, 69).

17. On προγινώσκω, see 8:29.

18. Cf. Calvin; Hodge; Haldane; Refoulé, *Tout Israël,* pp. 147-54; Dreyfuss, "Le passé et le présent de l'Israel," pp. 142-44; F. Davidson, *Pauline Predestination* (London: Tyndale, 1946), p. 17. Many of the church fathers restricted the reference to those whose faith God foresees (Schelkle).

19. So most commentators. See esp. S-H; Murray; Cranfield; note also Volf, *Paul and Perseverance,* 169-70; Hafemann, "Salvation of Israel," p. 50.

determined by the context. In 8:29, where all those "foreknown" are also justified and glorified, the election is clearly to salvation. In this verse, however, Paul reflects the common OT and Jewish corporate sense of election, according to which God's choosing of the nation Israel guarantees blessings and benefits (as well as responsibility; note the continuation of Amos 3:2, cited above) to the people as a whole but does not guarantee salvation for every single Israelite (see again the argument of 9:6-29).[20]

Paul has already hinted at his reason for denying the notion that God has rejected his people Israel: in his own person, an Israelite who is saved by faith in Christ, he gives evidence of God's continuing concern for Israel (v. 1a). Paul now makes explicit this line of reasoning and broadens it by reference to the concept of a remnant. He first provides biblical support for the concept. "Or do you not know" implies that Paul thinks his readers will be familiar with "the Scripture"[21] and its implications that he is about to cite. Paul identifies the passage with a formula similar to ones found in Jewish literature: "in the section about Elijah."[22] He further specifies the text as the one in which "Elijah appeals[23] to God against Israel."

3-4 The passage to which Paul refers is the story of King Ahab's attack on the prophets of Yahweh (1 Kings 19:1-18). After learning of Ahab's slaughter of the prophets, Jezebel threatens her nemesis Elijah with the same fate (vv. 1-2). Elijah then flees to the wilderness, where he bemoans his fate (vv. 3-14) and where the Lord comforts him with the assurance that he is

---

20. For the distinction between a general election of Israel as a nation and a specific election to salvation of individual Israelites, and others, see, e.g., Calvin, *Institutes,* 3.21.5-7; Murray, 2.67-68; Hofius, " 'All Israel Will Be Saved,' " p. 32. As Dunn notes, therefore, Paul does not question the fact of Israel's election, but its mode and implications (2.540). In doing so, Paul falls in line with other Jews of his day (especially the covenanters at Qumran and apocalyptic writers) who wrestled with the meaning of Israel's election in view of widespread (at least perceived) apostasy and persecution. This combination of a special election of individuals within, and alongside, a larger corporate election of Israel does better justice to the exegetical data than the view that Paul knows only a corporate election (for which view see, e.g., T. C. Vriezen, *Die Erwählung Israels nach dem Alten Testament* [ATANT 24; Zürich: Zwingli, 1953], pp. 109-15; Ridderbos, *Paul,* pp. 341-54; Klein, *Chosen People*).

21. ἡ γραφή could refer to the specific text Paul is about to cite (BAGD; Dunn) or to the Scripture generally.

22. Gk. ἐν Ἠλίᾳ; cf. Mark 12:26 (Luke 20:37), ἐπὶ τοῦ βάτου, "[in the section of the Book of Moses] about the bush." For rabbinic parallels, see Str-B, 3.288; S-H.

23. "Appeals" translates the verb ἐντυγχάνω, which means "petition, intercede." The intercession is usually a positive plea on behalf of someone, as in Rom. 8:27 (the Spirit's intercession "on behalf of" [ὑπέρ] the saints) and 8:34 (Christ's intercession "on behalf of" [ὑπέρ] Christians). Here, however, the petition of Elijah is not "on behalf of" Israel, but "against" (κατά) them (cf. also 1 Macc. 8:32; 10:61, 63; 11:25; BAGD; Dunn).

675

working out his plan for Israel and the surrounding nations (vv. 15-18). From this passage, Paul quotes Elijah's lament about being left alone after the slaughter of the prophets (v. 3 — 1 Kings 19:10 and 14) and the Lord's concluding reassurance to Elijah: "I have left for myself seven thousand men[24] who have not bowed the knee to Baal"[25] (v. 4 — 1 Kings 19:18b). Paul tailors the texts to suit his purpose without, however, changing their meaning.[26] He also supplies a suitable introduction to each citation, adding the vocative "Lord" in v. 3 to make clear to whom Elijah's words are addressed and using the rhetorical question "But what does the divine answer[27] say to him?" in v. 4 to announce the Lord's reply to Elijah.

The 1 Kings passage, which is one of the seminal "remnant" texts in the OT,[28] suits Paul's purpose admirably, with its contrast between the

---

24. Scholars have found symbolic significance in the number seven thousand, alleging that it represents an "apocalyptic completeness" (Michel; cf. also Cranfield). It is doubtful, however, that Paul intends any symbolic allusions: he takes the number from his text and makes nothing of it.

25. Paul (differing from the majority LXX tradition) uses the feminine article τῇ with the name Βάαλ. This reflects the Jewish practice of avoiding the name Baal by substituting for it the word בֹּשֶׁת, "shame," whose Greek counterpart is the feminine noun αἰσχύνη (see, e.g., Moule, *Idiom Book,* p. 183).

26. The LXX of 1 Kings (3 Kgdms.) 19:10b reads: τὰ θυσιαστήριά σου κατέσκαψαν καὶ τοὺς προφήτας σου ἀπέκτειναν ἐν ρομφαίᾳ, καὶ ὑπολέλειμμαι ἐγὼ μονώτατος, καὶ ζητοῦσι τὴν ψυχήν μου λαβεῖν αὐτήν. Verse 14b is identical, except that it substitutes καθεῖλαν for κατέσκαψαν. Paul's quotation reverses the order of "altars" and "prophets" (because killing the prophets had more contemporary relevance? — cf. Acts 7:51-52; 2 Thess. 2:15; see S-H), and shortens the rest. Paul may quote from memory (Cranfield; Dunn), he may be following a Greek text earlier than the LXX (Stanley, *Paul and the Language of Scripture,* pp. 150-58), or he may simply abbreviate deliberately. In LXX 1 Kings (3 Kgdms.) 19:18b, the relevant part of the divine reply to Elijah reads καταλείψεις ἐν Ισραηλ ἑπτὰ χιλιάδας ἀνδρῶν, πάντα γόνατα, ἃ οὐκ ὤκλασαν γόνυ [omitted in A and some other MSS] τῷ Βααλ. Paul abbreviates, eliminating some of the awkwardness in this overly literal Greek rendering, adds the reflexive pronoun ἐμαυτῷ to strengthen the point, and changes the tense of the initial verb from future to aorist, reflecting his own perspective (see also v. 2a). C. D. Stanley thinks that Paul might be dependent on a translation of this part of Kingdoms earlier than the majority LXX MSS ("The Significance of Romans 11:3-4 for the Text History of the LXX Book of Kingdoms," *JBL* 112 [1993], 43-54).

27. Gk. χρηματισμός, "authoritative divine answer," "oracle" (only here in the NT; but see 2 Macc. 2:4; and note the verb χρηματίζω in Matt. 2:12, 22; Luke 2:26; Acts 10:22; 11:26; Rom. 7:3; Heb. 8:5; 11:7; 12:25). The word need not mean "oracle"; it is used in a papyrus of the decision of a magistrate (*NewDocs,* 1.77; 4.176). This general usage calls into question Hanson's claim that Paul chooses the term to stress the oracular nature of the utterance (A. Hanson, "The Oracle in Romans XI.4," *NTS* 19 [1973], 300-302).

28. See Hasel, *Remnant,* p. 391. The texts Paul cites use two key "remnant" terms: καταλείπω and ὑπολείπω (note λεῖμμα in v. 5 and ὑπόλειμμα in 9:27 [quoting Isa. 10:22]).

apparent hopeless state of Israel and God's assurance of his continuing care for the people through his preservation of a remnant of true believers. It is possible that Paul also finds a parallel between Elijah and himself: each is a key salvation-historical figure, is confronted with the apparent downfall of spiritual Israel, but finds new hope in God's preservation of a remnant of true believers.[29] For God's preservation of a remnant is not only evidence of his present faithfulness to Israel; it is also a pledge of hope for the future of the people.[30]

5 Paul now makes the comparison between Elijah's situation and his own explicit. As God had "left[31] for himself" a solid body of faithful worshipers in Elijah's time, so "at the present time," the time of eschatological fulfillment,[32] he has brought into existence[33] a "remnant."[34] No more than the defection of Israelites to the worship of Baal in Elijah's time could the widespread Jewish indifference to the fulfillment of God's promises in Paul's day invalidate God's faithfulness to Israel and thereby cause his word to "fall" (cf. 9:6a). But, Paul is quick to add — reminding us of the principle that he developed at great length in 9:6-29 — this remnant has come into being as the result of God's gracious election.[35] There surfaces here again the careful balance that Paul preserves throughout Romans when dealing with Israel. He affirms the continuing significance of Israel in the stage of salvation history that the gospel has inaugurated. But he denies that this continuing significance owes anything to Israel's intrinsic merit or to her achievement in obeying the law (note a similar balance in 2:17–3:8; 9:1-29; 11:17-32). Jews are no

29. Cf. Munck, *Christ and Israel,* p. 109; Käsemann; Dunn; Hafemann, "Salvation of Israel," p. 49. Müller, *Gottes Gerechtigkeit,* pp. 44-45, thinks the Elijah *redivivus* myth might lie behind Paul's reference.

30. See, e.g., Mic. 7:18-19: "Who is a God like you, pardoning iniquity and passing over the transgression of the remnant of your possession? He does not retain his anger forever, because he delights in showing clemency. He will again have compassion upon us; he will tread our iniquities under foot. You will cast all our sins into the depths of the sea"; cf. also Ezra 9:7-15; Sir. 47:22; 1QH 6:6-8; 1QM 14:8-9; Johnson, *Function,* pp. 93-94; Zeller, 191-92.

31. Gk. κατέλιπον, from καταλείπω.

32. Gk. ἐν τῷ νῦν καιρῷ. The combination of νῦν and καιρός occurs five other times in Paul, four of them denoting the eschatological age of fulfillment (cf. 3:26; 8:18; 2 Cor. 6:2 [twice]).

33. The perfect tense of the verb γέγονεν may convey the notion of an existing condition resulting from a past action (e.g., Dunn). On the other hand, the tense could have a simple "stative" significance (cf. Porter, *Verbal Aspect,* p. 265).

34. Gk. λεῖμμα, cognate to καταλείπω.

35. Gk. κατ᾽ ἐκλογὴν χάριτος. On ἐκλογή, see the note on 9:11. The preposition κατά is virtually causal here: the remnant has come into being "because of" God's election (cf. BAGD, 407). χάριτος is probably a genitive of description: "an election characterized by grace"; "a gracious election."

different from Gentiles at this point: only by God's gracious intervention can they be transformed from sinners doomed to die into righteous people destined for eternal life (cf. 3:9, 23-24; 5:12-21).[36]

6 The polemical force of "based on the election of grace" becomes clearer in this verse, as Paul explains just what such a *gracious* election entails. The principle of grace is antithetical to that of "works"; if God has elected the individuals who make up the remnant "by grace,"[37] it follows that he could not have elected them on the basis of works. The word "works"[38] refers to anything that human beings do. Since Paul's focus is on the basis for the election of Israel, it is quite likely that he would think of these human actions as done specifically in obedience to the Mosaic law. But, as I have insisted before, it is not the fact that these works are "torah"-works that prevents them from being a basis for election.[39] As Paul's references to the "works" of Abraham (4:2-8) and Jacob and Esau (9:10-13) suggest, his problem with "works" lies not in the fact that they are "torah"-works but in the fact that they are *human* works. Paul's polemic, while focused on Israel because of his particular situation, is applicable to all human beings and finds its ultimate basis in the human condition.[40] Because of their sin but also simply because of their creaturely status, people can make no claim on God.

"For if it were otherwise,"[41] if human beings could by their works secure the blessing of God (as Paul points out in the second part of the verse), grace would "no longer"[42] be grace. For grace demands that God be perfectly free to bestow his favor on whomever he chooses. But if God's election were based on what human beings do, his freedom would be violated and he would no longer be acting in grace. For Paul, however, the gracious character of

36. The clearly salvific significance of the election here shows that Paul is thinking not of God's election of Israel as a nation (as, e.g., Godet and Dunn think), but of the election of individuals to salvation (cf. Murray).

37. χάριτι is probably a dative of manner.

38. Gk. ἔργα.

39. It is not necessarily wrong, therefore, to suggest that the term "works" here might connote the idea "works of the law" (Dunn). Where Dunn goes wrong is in insisting on too narrow a connotation for the term (works Jews do with a view toward affirming their national identity as God's covenant people), thereby foisting on this verse an overly restricted meaning.

40. See further our notes on 3:20, 4:3-5, and 9:10-13.

41. Gk. ἐπεί, meaning here "for otherwise" (BAGD, 284; Turner, 318).

42. οὐκέτι in both occurrences in this verse has a logical ("it is therefore not the case that") rather than a temporal meaning (e.g., Michel; Cranfield; Dunn; contra Wilckens, who thinks that Paul might imply some temporal distinction between the old age and "the age of grace" [(6:14)]).

God's activity is a theological axiom, automatically ruling out any idea that would conflict with it.[43]

7 The rhetorical question "What then?" marks the beginning of the last section in this paragraph. Here Paul takes up an implication of his teaching about the remnant in vv. 2b-6.[44] Paul has asserted that the existence of a remnant, Jews who are Christians, demonstrates that God has not rejected his people. In 9:26-29, Paul uses the remnant concept with a negative nuance: though all Jews are "Israelites" (9:4), it is *only* "the remnant that will be saved." In 11:2b-6, however, Paul cites the remnant with a positive purpose: the continuing validity of God's election of Israel is manifested in the fact that there *is* a remnant. Nevertheless, the very notion of a remnant who are receiving the blessings of God's election implies that many other Israelites are not. It is to this group that Paul draws particular attention in vv. 7-10.

Paul begins generally with a summing up of the situation of Israel as he has outlined it thus far in chaps. 9–11.[45] He distinguishes three entities: Israel as a corporate whole, the elect, and the hardened. As a corporate entity, Israel has "not attained"[46] what she "was seeking."[47] Paul here repeats in

---

43. Note the similar argument in Rom. 4:3-5. As Morris observes, Paul's teaching here clearly rules out the popular patristic view that God's election is based on his foreknowledge of human works. Many modern scholars, however, will insist that God's grace in election is by no means compromised if that election is based on foreseen faith (e.g., Godet, 395). To be sure, Paul distinguishes "works" from faith throughout Romans, and so his denial that election is based on works need not mean that it cannot be based on faith. But Paul's conception of God's grace (see particularly 4:3-5) would seem to rule out anything outside God's own free will as a basis for his actions. To make election ultimately dependent on the human decision to believe violates Paul's notion of the grace of God. To put it another way, God's grace is for Paul not simply the ultimate cause of salvation (cf. Chrysostom's comment on vv. 5-6: "And if by grace, it will be said, how came we all not to be saved? Because ye would not. For grace, though it be grace, saves the willing, not those who will not have it . . ."). God's grace is the efficient cause of salvation, human faith being not its basis but its result.

44. Most commentators think that Paul here takes up the implications of vv. 1-6 as a whole (e.g., S-H; Murray; Cranfield). But the connection is probably with the teaching about the remnant specifically.

45. Verse 7 has therefore an important summary role. It blends the predestinatory focus of 9:6-29 — "elect," "hardened" — with the human responsibility perspective of 9:30–10:21 — "sought," "did not attain" — to sum up Paul's discussion of Israel to this point in chaps. 9–11.

46. The Greek verb is ἐπιτυγχάνω. In its other NT occurrences (Heb. 6:5; 11:33; Jas. 4:2), it is followed by the genitive. But an accusative object with the verb is well attested (BAGD).

47. The Greek verb, ἐπιζητεῖ, is in the present tense. Most commentators think that Paul chooses the tense because Israel in his day was continuing to seek this righteous status (e.g., Godet; K. L. McKay, "Time and Aspect in New Testament Greek," *NovT* 34 [1992], 209-28 [responding to Porter]). But Porter, following aspect theory, thinks that the tense is timeless and that Paul has chosen the present to accentuate the verb (*Verbal Aspect,*

similar terms what he said about Israel as a whole in 9:31: "Israel, pursuing a law of righteousness, did not attain that law." This parallel allows us to fill in the missing object of the verbs in this assertion: it was "righteousness," a right standing with God, that Israel sought but failed to attain. What Israel as a whole did not attain, however, "the elect"[48] did. Here again Paul echoes his earlier teaching, where he contrasted Israel's failure to attain righteousness (9:31) with the Gentiles' success in doing so (9:30). This earlier contrast leads many commentators to assume that in this verse also "the elect" are composed of Gentiles, or perhaps Gentiles and Jews (all the elect) together.[49] But the context favors a restriction to Jews here since Paul's concern seems to be to distinguish two groups *within* Israel.[50]

Contrasted, then, with "the elect," who have by virtue of God's gracious choice attained a right standing with him, are "the rest," who have been "hardened." Despite a change in verbs in the Greek, the hardening Paul speaks of here is the same as that which he has described in 9:18: a spiritual insensitivity that prevents people from responding to God or to his message of salvation.[51] And since in both 9:18 and in the following verse Paul ascribes this hardening to God, it is clear that God is also the implied agent of the passive verb in this verse: "the rest have been hardened (by God)."[52] Calvin

---

p. 197). The prefix ἐπι- may add emphasis to the verbal idea (e.g., Morris; cf. NIV: "sought so earnestly"), but the tendency in Hellenistic Greek for compound verbs to lose their intensive force renders this uncertain. Dunn is certainly correct, however, to deny the negative nuance, "strive after," suggested by BAGD.

48. The Greek word ἐκλογή is an abstract term that usually connotes activity — "(God's) electing act" — but is used here with a concrete sense — "those elected by God." The term thus draws attention to the divine initiative in the election (e.g., Cranfield).

49. E.g., Dunn.

50. Nygren; Wilckens.

51. As most recognize, the verb Paul uses in 9:18 — σκληρύνω — and the one he uses here — πωρόω — are synonymous in this context. πωρόω is relatively rare in biblical Greek (Job 17:7; Prov. 10:20 [v.l.]; Mark 6:52; 8:17; John 12:40; 2 Cor. 3:14; cf. also πώρωσις in Mark 3:5; Rom. 11:25; Eph. 4:18). It is used especially often in secular Greek of medical phenomena: the forming of a "stone" (e.g., in the bladder) or the hardening that takes place when broken bones are knit together (cf. K. L. and M. A. Schmidt, *TDNT* V, 1025-26). All the NT occurrences are metaphorical, referring to a situation of spiritual obduracy. In most it is the heart that is the object of the hardening, while in 2 Cor. 3:14 it is the mind. Contra J. A. Robinson (*St. Paul's Epistle to the Ephesians* [2d ed.; London: James Clarke, n.d.], pp. 264-74), and despite the tendency in the MSS tradition to confuse the two, πωρόω and πηρόω ("cause to be blind") were not synonyms in the NT period (cf. S-H; Cranfield).

52. As most commentators recognize. S-H and Morris, however, are among those who demur. Chrysostom, followed by many others, insists that the basis on which God hardens some and not others is human sin. However, while God hardens sinners, it is stretching this text, and counter to 9:17-23, to argue that human sin is the cause of God's hardening. (See my comments on 9:18.)

understood this hardening as a pretemporal decree of God by which he destined some to eternal damnation.[53] And Reformed theologians have usually followed Calvin's lead, finding in this verse support for the doctrine of reprobation. As I noted in my comments on 9:18, this conclusion is often denied because Paul suggests in 11:11ff. that God's hardening need not be a permanent condition: a day is coming when God will remove his hardening from Israel (cf. v. 25).[54] But, in contrast to vv. 7b-10, Paul is in vv. 11-32 clearly thinking about Israel from a corporate perspective. The hardening of Israel as a national group, Paul argues, is temporary; but this says nothing about the permanence of his hardening of individuals within Israel. And we have seen reason to conclude (see the notes on 9:22-23) that God's hardening permanently binds people in the sin that they have chosen for themselves.[55]

8 In vv. 8-10 Paul supports his reference to hardening with two OT quotations. He follows Jewish precedent in using each of the three main divisions of the Hebrew canon: the "law" (Deut. 29:4), the prophets (Isa. 29:10), and the "writings" (Ps. 69:22-23).[56]

The quotation in v. 8, introduced with Paul's typical formula, "even as it is written," takes most of its wording and its basic structure from Deut. 29:4.[57] This verse comes from one of Moses' final exhortations to the people of Israel before they crossed the Jordan to take possession of the promised land. Moses reminds them of the great acts of God on their behalf but recognizes that they cannot fully appreciate what the Lord has done for

53. Calvin.

54. E.g., Hendriksen; Dunn; Ridderbos, *Paul,* pp. 345-46.

55. This is not to say that God chooses which people to harden based on the sin or failure to believe of those individuals (contra, e.g., many of the church fathers [cf. Schelkle]; S-H — "they have been hardened because they failed"; Morris; Leenhardt; Klein, *New Chosen People,* p. 175). It is rather that God's hardening is to be seen as affecting individuals who are already sinners. Paul keeps God's hardening of people and their own refusal to believe in tension (e.g., Barrett; Michel).

56. K. Müller compares Paul's string of citations to the rabbinic "Haraz" style (*Anstoss und Gericht: Eine Studie zum jüdischen Hintergrund des paulinischen Skandalon-Begriffs* [SANT 19; Munich: Kösel, 1969], pp. 19-21). See also, e.g., Schmithals.

57. LXX Deut. 29:3. Paul uses the words underlined: καὶ οὐκ ἔδωκεν κύριος ὁ θεὸς ὑμῖν καρδίαν εἰδέναι καὶ ὀφθαλμοὺς βλέπειν καὶ ὦτα ἀκούειν ἕως τῆς ἡμέρας ταύτης (the LXX accurately translates the MT). The form in which Paul cites this text, as well as his addition to it of elements from Isa. 29:10, seems to be Paul's own creation (cf. even Stanley, *Paul and the Language of Scripture,* pp. 158-59, who is generally reluctant to attribute Paul's variations from the LXX to the apostle; cf. also Koch, 170-71). It should be noted that Paul changes the simple infinitives of the LXX into articular infinitives. This change is difficult to account for, the construction not occurring in any of the OT texts that influenced Paul. Paul's infinitival constructions are difficult to classify, but they are probably adjectival: God has given the people "not seeing" eyes and "not hearing" ears. BDF (400[2]) explain them as consecutive: "such eyes that they."

681

them, for "the LORD has not given you a mind to understand, or eyes to see, or ears to hear." Paul changes the original negative statement — "the LORD has not given" — into a positive one — "God has given." This change suits better the purpose for which Paul cites the verse, for he is supporting the notion of a positive act of hardening on God's part (v. 7b). But Paul is probably also influenced in making this change by another OT text from which he takes some of the wording of his quotation. The phrase "spirit of stupor"[58] comes from Isa. 29:10: "For the LORD has poured upon you a spirit of deep sleep, he has closed your eyes, you prophets, and covered your heads, you seers." Paul's attention was probably drawn to this verse by both the similarity in content with Deut. 29:4 and by the verbal parallel, involving "eyes" that are blinded to the reality of spiritual things.[59] In addition, the text comes in a passage that supplies many NT references and quotations.[60]

9-10 The second quotation comes from another passage that has played a prominent role in helping early Christians understand Jesus, Ps. 69.[61] This interpretive tradition, according to which David's own sentiments in the psalm are applied to Jesus, makes it natural for Paul to apply to the enemies of Jesus Christ what David says about his own enemies. Paul's attention was probably drawn to these verses also by their reference to "darkened eyes," a verbal link to Deut. 29:4 and Isa. 29:10. Verses 22-23 in the psalm introduce David's prayer that the Lord might bring disaster on those who are persecuting him: "Let their table be a trap for them, a snare for their allies. Let their eyes be darkened so that they cannot see, and make their loins tremble continu-

---

58. The Greek word for "stupor," κατάνυξις, is very rare, occurring only here in the NT and only in Isa. 29:10 and 60:3 in the LXX. It is probably derived from the verb κατανύσσω, "stab, gouge, prick," hence, be pricked to the point of stupefaction (Cranfield). In this phrase, Paul uses the accusative πνεῦμα, in agreement with some MSS (e.g., Alexandrinus) of the LXX, but against the majority of LXX MSS, which read the dative πνεύματι. But the accusative in these LXX MSS is probably an assimilation to the text of Rom. 11:8.

59. While Paul does not clearly allude to the text, it is quite likely that undergirding his use of these texts is Isa. 6:9-10 (see, e.g., Lindars, "Old Testament and Universalism," p. 523). This became the standard early Christian "proof-text" to explain the spiritual obduracy of the Jews (Mark 4:12 and pars.; John 12:40; Acts 28:26) and has important verbal ("eyes that do not see," "ears that do not hear") and conceptual ("hardening"; the verb in LXX Isa. is παχύνομαι, a synonym of πωρόω) parallels with Paul's quotation (note also the link between Deut. 29:4 and Isa. 6:10 in their reference to the heart).

60. See, e.g., Paul's quotation of Isa. 28:16 in 9:33; cf. Lindars, *New Testament Apologetic,* p. 164.

61. Quotations and probable allusions to this psalm occur in Mark 3:21; 15:23 and pars.; Luke 13:35; John 2:17; 15:25; Acts 1:20; Rom. 15:3; Phil. 4:3; Rev. 3:5; 16:1.

ally."[62] What David prayed would happen to his persecutors, Paul suggests, God has brought upon those Jews who have resisted the gospel. Paul probably did not intend to apply the details in the quotation to the Jews of his own day.[63] Thus it is fruitless to inquire about what the "table" might stand for,[64] or what "bending the backs" might connote.[65]

E. DEFINING THE PROMISE (2):
THE FUTURE OF ISRAEL (11:11-32)

With a rhetorical question parallel to the one in v. 1, Paul moves into the next — and final — stage of his discussion of Israel and the gospel. As he has summarized the matter in vv. 7-10, the gospel has divided Israel into two parts: a "remnant," who through the electing grace of God has attained the righteousness revealed in the gospel, and "the rest," hardened by God in their sin and excluded from this righteousness. Paul now asks whether this situation is permanent. His answer? It is not. For the "rejection" of Israel as a whole is not God's last word to Israel. This rejection, Paul argues, is but the first step in an unfolding process. Its second step is of special relevance to the Gentiles: Israel's repudiation of the blessings naturally belonging to her has caused them to be diverted into another, wider, channel, in which they are are now flowing to the whole world. But this is not the end of the story. For this flood of blessings will one day be turned again toward Israel. At the climax of this age, her hardening will be removed, and the present tiny remnant of Jewish believers will be expanded to include a much greater number of Jews obedient to the gospel. And so, as Paul puts it in his famous assertion, "all Israel will be saved."[1] Israel's rejection is neither total (11:1-10) nor final (11:11-32).

---

62. Paul follows the LXX closely. His only changes are the omission of one phrase (ἐνώπιον αὐτῶν after ἡ τράπεζα αὐτῶν), his addition of the phrase καὶ εἰς θήραν, and his transposition of the phrases καὶ εἰς ἀνταπόδμα and καὶ εἰς σκάνδαλον. The LXX follows the MT closely except in the last clause.

63. See, e.g., Cranfield.

64. The most popular suggestions are: (1) an allusion to the sacrificial cult of the Jews (Müller, *Anstoss und Gericht*, pp. 23-27; Käsemann; Godet; Wilckens; Dunn); (2) an allusion to the close table fellowship that typified especially Pharisaic Judaism (Michel), with special reference, perhaps, to food laws, which were a matter of debate in the Roman community (chaps. 14–15; Minear, 78-79); (3) an allusion to the Jewish dependence on the law (S-H; Morris).

65. Some think the figure suggests the oppression of slavery; others of grief.

1. See the exegetical notes on that verse for substantiation of the end-time event that brings that promise to its fruition. Gifford (191-92) and Wright (*Climax of the Covenant*, p. 247) are representative of many who think that Paul's purpose in vv. 11-24 is only to assert the continuing *possibility* of salvation for Jews. But it does not seem likely

The three-stage process by which God's blessing oscillates between Israel and the Gentiles is at the heart of this entire section,[2] as the following summary reveals:

vv. 11-12: "trespass of Israel" — "salvation for the Gentiles" — "their fullness"

v. 15: "their rejection" — "reconciliation of the world" — "their acceptance"

vv. 17-23: "natural branches" broken off — "wild shoots" grafted in — "natural branches" grafted back in

vv. 25-26: "Hardening of Israel" — "fullness of Gentiles" — "all Israel will be saved" (?)

vv. 30-31: Disobedience of Israel — Mercy for Gentiles — Mercy to Israel

The presence of this pattern throughout these verses points to the underlying unity of this section.[3] However, it falls into three clearly distinguishable

---

that the Gentiles in Rome seriously believed that Jews could not be saved; and Paul's language suggests that Israel's salvation is more than a possibility.

2. As many scholars note (e.g., Dunn, 2.655), Paul's scheme is to some extent at least an adaption of the OT/Jewish "eschatological pilgrimage" theme. According to this tradition, Israel's restoration to glory in the end times would stimulate Gentiles to offer themselves and their gifts in the service of Yahweh. See, perhaps most clearly, *Pss. Sol.* 17:26-46:

> He will gather a holy people [v. 26]. . . . He will have Gentile nations serving him under his yoke, and he will glorify the Lord in (a place) prominent (above) the whole earth. And he will purge Jerusalem (and make it) holy as it was even from the beginning, (for) nations to come from the ends of the earth to see his glory, to bring as gifts her children who had been driven out, and to see the glory of the Lord with which God has glorified her [vv. 30-31].

(See also Isa. 2:2-3a; 56:6-7; 60:1-7; Tob. 13:11-13; 14:6-7; *T. Zeb.* 9:8; *T. Benj.* 9:2; *Sib. Or.* 3.767-95.) Paul, in light of his new understanding of events from the gospel, reverses the order of events and "spiritualizes" the process: instead of Gentiles coming to worship Yahweh in Jerusalem as a result of Israel's restoration, Israel is saved in response to the extension of salvation to the Gentiles. T. L. Donaldson (" 'Riches for the Gentiles' [Rom. 11:12]: Israel's Rejection and Paul's Gentile Mission," *JBL* 112 [1993], 92) questions the significance of the tradition for Paul, noting that Paul does not quote any of the standard OT pilgrimage texts. But Paul's quotation of Isa. 59:20-21 comes from the immediate context of one of the most important of the texts (Isa. 60:1-7); Donaldson's scepticism is unwarranted.

3. Contra, e.g., Schmeller (*Paulus und die "Diatribe,"* p. 286) and Aletti, *Comment Dieu est-il juste?* pp. 181-82), who put a major break between 11:24 and 25; and Johnson ("Structure and Meaning," p. 92), who divides chap. 11 into three major units, vv. 1-16, 17-32, and 33-36.

paragraphs: vv. 11-15, vv. 16-24, and vv. 25-32. In each of these paragraphs Paul directly addresses Gentile Christians: cf. v. 13, "I am speaking to you Gentiles," and the continuation of this address with the second person singular in vv. 17-24 and the second person plural in vv. 25-32. This address reveals the specific hortatory purpose of Paul's sketch of salvation history: to stifle the tendency among Gentile Christians to "boast over" Jews and Jewish Christians (cf. vv. 18 and 25; note also 14:3).[4] Paul knew that Gentile Christians in Rome were engaging in such inappropriate bragging; and the need to curb this sinful pride was one of his main motivations in writing chaps. 9–11 and, indeed, the letter as a whole.[5] But, in keeping with the nature of Romans, Paul also knew that the problem he was tackling here was endemic in the early Christian church. For the problem was an understandable outgrowth of the shift of salvation history that had taken place. The Gentiles' rejoicing at being *included* with Jews in God's people would all too easily lead to boasting that they had *replaced* the Jews as the people of God. Sorry to say, such an assumption is still rampant in the Christian church: witness the typical contrast "Jew"/"Christian." Paul therefore warns us, as he warned the first-century Gentile Christians in Rome: don't assume that Gentile preponderance in the church means that God has abandoned his people Israel. God has brought salvation to the Gentiles without violating any of his promises to Israel and without retracting his election of Israel as a corporate whole: an election that, like all God's gifts, is "irrevocable" (v. 29).

1. God's Purpose in Israel's Rejection (11:11-15)

11*I say therefore, they have not stumbled so as to fall, have they? By no means! But through their trespass salvation has come to the Gentiles, in order to make them jealous.* 12*Now if their trespass means riches for the world and their defeat means riches for the Gentiles, how much more will their fullness mean?*

13*Now I am speaking to you Gentiles. Therefore, in so far as I am apostle to the Gentiles, I glorify my ministry,* 14*if, in some way, I might stimulate my kinspeople to jealousy and save some of them.*

4. Paul's turn from argument to exhortation may help explain the sudden falloff in OT quotations (the only quotation comes in vv. 26b-27). It must be emphasized, however, that hardly a verse goes by without an allusion to the OT.

5. Some scholars (e.g., Schmeller, *Paulus und die "Diatribe,"* pp. 324-27 and Lübking, *Paulus und Israel,* pp. 105-8) minimize any reference to the Roman church, arguing that Paul's use of the second person is simply stylistic. But the evidence of 14:1–15:13 points to a concern on Paul's part for a situation in the Roman community. (Although, as I argue above, Paul writes with the consciousness that he is addressing a problem by no means confined to Rome.)

15For if their rejection means the reconciliation of the world, what will their acceptance mean, if not life from the dead?

The opening question shows that Paul wants to deny an inference that his readers might draw from what he has just said. According to most commentators, this potential inference is that God's hardening of the "remainder"[6] (v. 7b) of Israel is permanent. Paul corrects this possible misunderstanding by denying that these hardened Jews have fallen into irretrievable spiritual ruin.[7] But the antecedent to the third person possessive pronouns in v. 12 — "their"[8] — must be Israel as a whole and not the hardened "remainder" only. And the continuity between vv. 11 and 12 demands that the implied subject of the third person plural verbs in v. 11 be the same: Israel as a whole.[9] Paul's question in v. 11, therefore, is not related to vv. 7b-10 but to v. 7a, which restates a key point that Paul has made earlier: Israel (as a whole) has not attained the righteousness that it was seeking (see esp. 9:31-32; also 10:3, 21). The issue in vv. 11ff. is therefore not "Can the hardened within Israel still be saved?" but "Can Israel as a whole still be saved?" As the contrast with the Gentiles throughout vv. 11-32 suggests, Paul is thinking mainly in terms of corporate bodies, not in terms of individuals within those bodies.

The structure of this paragraph follows a familiar model: rhetorical question, emphatic denial (v. 11a), and explanation (vv. 11b-15). The explanation uses the pattern of oscillation between Israel and the Gentiles that is basic to this whole section (see above). Paul introduces this sequence in v. 11b and then develops it fully in v. 12. After a parenthetical remark about his own ministry (vv. 13-14), Paul repeats the sequence in different terms in v. 15.

11 The opening of this paragraph parallels the opening of vv. 1-10 exactly: "I say therefore,"[10] a rhetorical question expecting a negative answer,[11] followed by emphatic rejection: "By no means!"[12] Paul's question, as we have seen, picks up his summary assertion about Israel as a whole in v. 7a: "They [Israelites generally] have not stumbled so as to fall, have they?" Israel's "stumbling"[13] refers to her rejection of Christ and the righteousness

6. Gk. οἱ λοιποί.

7. E.g., S-H, 320; Kuss, 3.793; Schlier, 327; Cranfield, 2.554-55.

8. Gk. αὐτῶν.

9. Calvin, 421; Barrett, 212; Michel, 343; Hafemann, "Salvation of Israel," p. 50; Bell, *Provoked to Jealousy,* p. 115.

10. Gk. λέγω οὖν.

11. As the μή indicates.

12. Gk. μὴ γένοιτο.

13. The Greek word is πταίω, which is used elsewhere to refer to sinning (cf. Jas. 2:10; 3:2; in 2 Pet. 1:10, its only other NT occurrence, it probably means "be ruined, lost" [BAGD]). Paul may use this term here because it can connote the image of stumbling over

of God offered through him (9:31-33; 10:3), while "fall" denotes irretrievable spiritual ruin.[14] The relation between these two verbs is not clear. The Greek word connecting them can denote either purpose or result.[15] If it denotes purpose, Paul is asking whether it was God's intention that Israel's stumbling should lead to her fall;[16] if result, whether it has actually been the case that Israel's stumbling has led to her fall.[17] As so often in the NT, the two are difficult to distinguish here — if Israel's stumbling has not resulted in her downfall, it is because God did not intend that it do so.

In contrast ("but"[18]) to the inference that Israel's rejection of Christ has forever excluded her from any special place in God's purposes is the actual situation: Israel's sin is the starting point of a process that will lead back to blessing for Israel. The middle stage of this process involves the Gentiles. It is "because of"[19] Israel's "trespass"[20] that salvation has come[21] to the Gentiles. Paul probably has in mind the way in which he and other preachers of the gospel would turn to the Gentiles after being spurned by the Jews.[22] But the salvation

---

an obstacle that Paul used earlier to characterize Israel's failure (cf. προσκόπτω in 9:32) (cf. Michel; Dunn).

14. The word is the common πίπτω, generally used with simple physical connotation in the NT. But the notion of spiritual ruin is present in three of Paul's other uses of the term (Rom. 11:22; 14:4; 1 Cor. 10:12) and in Heb. 4:11. See also Isa. 24:20: "The earth staggers like a drunkard, it sways like a hut; its transgression lies heavy upon it, and it falls [LXX πίπτω] and will not rise again" (cited by S-H).

15. Gk. ἵνα. Some scholars in the past have insisted that the word always retains its telic force; but a number of "weakened" senses, including result, are now widely recognized (BAGD; Turner, 100-105; Moule, *Idiom Book,* pp. 142-46).

16. Kuss; Käsemann; Schlier. Murray puts a special spin on this interpretation by suggesting that Paul is asking whether the stumbling of the hardened "remainder" of Israel has had as its primary divine intention their final ruin. In other words, the stumbling of those hardened has led to their ruin; but this was not God's (only) purpose in their stumbling. Similar is the interpretation of Augustine in his Romans exposition.

17. Godet; S-H; Cranfield; Dunn(?). Michel (p. 344) wants to allow for both.

18. Gk. ἀλλά.

19. The dative τῷ . . . παραπτώματι is a case in which the common instrumental meaning has moved over into a causal sense (e.g., Cranfield; Wilckens; Zeller, *Juden und Heiden,* pp. 211-12).

20. Gk. παράπτωμα. Paul uses the term 16 times, but particularly significant are the six occurrences of the term in Rom. 5:15-21 to describe the sin of Adam and his heirs. Because of this Munck suggests that Paul may pick the word up from Gentile Christians who were accusing Israel of committing a sin as heinous and final as Adam's (*Christ and Israel,* p. 118). But this is farfetched.

21. Dunn (cf. Barrett) argues that Paul's usual future perspective on salvation would favor the translation "is coming." But the logic of the verse seems to require a past reference: most commentators argue that we must supply a verb like γέγονεν, "has come" (e.g., Schlier).

22. See Acts 13:44-47; 14:1-3; 18:4-7; 19:8-10; 28:23-29. Cf., e.g., Wilckens. Reference to Jewish responsibility for the crucifixion (Barth, *Shorter;* Cranfield) is unlikely.

of Gentiles leads in turn back to Israel. Borrowing the concept from Deut. 32:21, which he quoted in 10:19, Paul indicates that one of the purposes of the salvation of the Gentiles is to stimulate Israel to jealousy.[23] Paul apparently thinks that the Jews, as they see the Gentiles enjoying the messianic blessings promised first of all to them, will want those blessings for themselves.

12 Paul now elaborates on the process he has introduced in v. 11b, using the familiar "how much more" logic (see 5:9, 10, 15, 17) to contrast the benefits of Israel's rejection of Christ with the blessing that will come with Israel's "fullness." His purpose is thus to accentuate the importance of this final stage in the process. And, as his way of referring to Israel reveals — *their* trespass, *their* dimunition, *their* fullness — he seems already to have in mind Gentile readers.[24] Paul wants Gentile Christians to recognize the significance for themselves of Israel's restoration to divine favor.

The first part of the verse (the "if" clause) repeats the first two steps Paul outlined in v. 11b. Paul speaks again of Israel's "trespass," but characterizes it a second time with the term *hēttēma*. This rare word is sometimes given a qualitative meaning — KJV: "diminishing" — in order to preserve a more effective contrast with the word *plērōma*, which, it is argued, must be translated "full number."[25] But *hēttēma* seems to have a basically quantitative nuance, denoting a "defeat" or "loss,"[26] and this sense also fits the context well: Israel's trespass in rejecting Christ has been for her a signal spiritual defeat.[27] But Israel's loss has been the Gentiles' gain: her trespass has meant "riches[28] for the world";

23. Both the LXX of Deut. 32:21 and Paul use παραζηλόω, a comparatively rare word (seven occurrences in the LXX; four in the NT, all in Paul). Unlike its more common root verb verb ζηλόω, which can denote either a positive "zeal" for the Lord or a negative "jealousy" of others, παραζηλόω in the Bible always denotes "jealousy": either God's jealousy for his people (1 Cor. 10:22; 3 Kgdms. 19:22; Ps. 77:58) or a person's jealousy of others (Ps. 36:1, 7, 8; Sir. 30:3). Only in Deut. 32:21 and here does the word suggest that human jealousy might be a positive thing. See, further, the note on 10:19. Bell (*Provoked to Jealousy,* pp. 112-13) thinks that the significant role Paul gives here to the Gentiles stimulating Jews to jealousy is derived from Deut. 32.

24. Cf. Cranfield.

25. E.g., Godet; Barrett; Wilckens.

26. The word is derived from ἡττᾶσθαι, which means "be less, be weaker, be defeated," and in its only other two known occurrences it denotes a "defeat": Isa. 31:8 (οἱ δὲ νεανίσκοι ἔσονται εἰς ἥττημα: "the young men shall be [led] into defeat"; cf. ἡττάομαι in v. 9) and 1 Cor. 6:7 (ἤδη μὲν [οὖν] ὅλως ἥττημα ὑμῖν ἐστιν ὅτι κρίματα ἔχετε μεθ' ἑαυτῶν: "Indeed, already it is wholly a defeat for you, because you have judgments with one another"). See BAGD; Cranfield.

27. So most modern translations and commentators (e.g., S-H; Michel; Murray; Käsemann; Kuss; Cranfield; Fitzmyer; cf. also Bell, *Provoked to Jealousy,* p. 114).

28. Gk. πλοῦτος, here indicating the richness of spiritual blessing. Paul frequently uses the word to refer to the riches of God's grace and mercy (cf. Rom. 2:4; 9:23; 11:33; Eph. 1:7, 18; 2:7; 3:8, 16; Phil. 4:17; Col. 1:27).

her defeat "riches for the Gentiles."[29] Yet the logic of Paul's sentence implies that the blessing that will come to the Gentiles at the time of Israel's "fullness" will be much greater.[30] What is implicit here is made explicit in v. 15, where Paul identifies this blessing as "life from the dead."

But what specifically does Paul mean when he speaks of "their [the Jews'] fullness"? The Greek word is *plērōma,* and it denotes "full measure," "completeness."[31] Like *hēttēma,* the "fullness" denoted by *plērōma* is sometimes understood in a qualitative sense — "fulfillment," "completeness" (cf. NASB) — and sometimes a quantitative sense — "full number" (cf. TEV: "the complete number of Jews"). With a qualitative connotation, *plērōma,* as the opposite of Israel's "trespass" and "defeat," would refer to her "completion," the full restoration to Israel of the blessings of the kingdom that she is now, as a corporate entity, missing.[32] If, on the other hand, we give a quantitative sense to *plērōma,* Paul's reference would be to the "full number" of Jews. The implication in this case would be that to the present remnant there will be added a much greater number of Jewish believers so as to "fill up" the number of Jews destined for salvation.[33] Unlike *hēttēma, plērōma* is found with a quantitative meaning,[34] and the parallel occurrence of the word in v. 25 — "when the *plērōma* of the Gentiles comes in" — strongly favors a numerical sense: "the full number of Jews." However, occurrences of *plērōma* with a straightforward numerical

---

29. The parallelism demonstrates that "world" (κόσμος) means, as in typical Jewish fashion, the Gentile world (Str-B, 2.191).

30. Murray.

31. Greek words ending in -μα usually denote the result of an action; in this case, πλήρωμα would denote the outcome of the action denoted by the corresponding verb πληρόω, "fill," "fulfill." πλήρωμα would thus mean "full measure," "completeness." (See J. B. Lightfoot, *Saint Paul's Epistles to the Colossians and to Philemon* [rpt. ed.; Grand Rapids: Zondervan, 1959], pp. 257-60.) However, there is evidence that πλήρωμα, like many other Greek words ending in -μα, has broadened its meaning to include an active sense, with application both to the concrete — "that which fills" — and the abstract — "filling," "fulfilling" (cf. BAGD; Robinson, *Ephesians,* pp. 255-59; G. Delling *TDNT* VI, 298-302).

32. Lietzmann; Hodge; Murray; Lenski; Hendriksen; F. Hahn, "Zum Verständnis von Römer 11.26a: '. . . und so wird ganz Israel gerettet werden'," in *Paul and Paulinism* p. 229. Lietzmann argues that πλήρωμα means the same here as does πλήρωσις in 13:10, Paul choosing the word with the -μα ending to match παράπτωμα and ἥττημα.

33. Godet; Meyer; S-H; Cranfield; Barrett; Käsemann; Wilckens; Fitzmyer; Kuss; Volf, *Paul and Perserverance,* p. 173; R. Stuhlmann, *Das eschatologische Maß im Neuen Testament* (FRLANT 132; Göttingen: Vandenhoeck & Ruprecht, 1983), pp. 185-87.

34. BAGD cite Herodotus 8.43, 45; Aristotle, *Politics* 2.3.22; Aelius Aristides 13 (p. 262 D); G. Delling (*TDNT* VI, 298-302) adds Philo, *Special Laws* 1.272.

sense are rare, and entirely absent in biblical Greek elsewhere.[35] Perhaps, however, we need not choose between the qualitative and quantitative options. While *plērōma* probably has a qualitative denotation — "fullness" — the context and the parallel with v. 25 suggest that this "fullness" is attained through a numerical process. Paul would then be suggesting that the present "defeat" of Israel, in which Israel is numerically reduced to a small remnant, will be reversed by the addition of far greater numbers of true believers: this will be Israel's destined "fullness."[36]

13 In vv. 11b-12 Paul has justified his denial of the idea that Israel might be permanently excluded from the plan of God. He does so by arguing that Israel's present spiritual "defeat" will give way to a "fullness" of spiritual blessing once again. And this renewed state of blessing will be brought about through the medium of the Gentiles' salvation. It is this role played by the salvation of the Gentiles in Israel's future blessing that is the jumping off point for Paul's remarks about his own ministry in vv. 13-14.[37] Paul points out that the role played by Gentiles in the ultimate blessing of Israel means that his own ministry, largely devoted to the Gentiles, has nevertheless a significant indirect impact on Israel. These verses are something of an aside,

35. πλήρωμα occurs 15 times in the LXX, all but one translating a form of the Hebrew verb מלא, "fill." Most (11) involve the stereotyped phrase ἡ γῆ [or ἡ θάλασσα] καὶ τὸ πλήρωμα αὐτῆς, "the earth [or the sea] and its fullness" (1 Chron. 16:32; Ps. 23:1; 49:12; 88:12; 95:11; 97:7; Jer. 8:16; 29:2; Ezek. 12:19; 19:7; 30:12), where πλήρωμα has the active meaning "that which fills [it; e.g., the earth or the sea]." The other four have a passive nuance (two occurrences each in Eccl. 4:6 and Cant. 5:12). Two of the NT occurrences refer to a "patch," the sense apparently being that a patch "fills up" the hole in a garment (Matt. 9:16 = Mark 2:21). Two others have a quantitative sense, "that which fills up" a given container (Mark 6:43; 8:20). John uses the term once to refer to the "fullness" or "abundance" of Christ (John 1:16); five of Paul's uses of the word, in which he refers to the πλήρωμα of Christ or of God, are much debated but generally similar (Eph. 1:23; 3:19; 4:13; Col. 1:19; 2:9). Paul also uses the word to mean "abundance" in Rom. 15:29 and appropriates the typical LXX phrase in his quotation of Ps. 24:1 (LXX 23:1) in 1 Cor. 10:26. In Rom. 13:10, πλήρωμα probably has the active nuance "fulfilling." The closest Paul comes to a numerical connotation for the term is in his references to the "bringing to completion" of time in a salvation-historical perspective (Gal. 4:4; Eph. 1:10). But these are also probably qualitative: with Christ's coming, the "completion," the "full measure" of time has been reached.

36. A few commentators (e.g., Lenski; Hendriksen) suggest that Israel's "fullness" is something that she has already attained in Paul's day. But this flies in the face of Paul's pessimism about Israel's present status. As the following verses will show (cf. esp. 17-24), Paul presents Israel's "fullness" as a future occurrence.

37. Wilckens notes correctly that v. 12 expands on the first part of the process Paul has outlined in v. 11b — Israel's trespass bringing salvation for the Gentiles — while vv. 13-14 expand on the second part — "to make them jealous."

690

a parenthesis that anticipates the hortatory direction that Paul takes his argument in vv. 17-24.[38]

Verse 13a — "Now I am speaking to you Gentiles" — reveals Paul's concern to apply what he is saying in this passage to the Gentile Christian majority in the church at Rome.[39] In vv. 13-14 he is specifically concerned to correct any misapprehension among the Gentile Christians about the implications for Israel in his concentration on Gentiles in his ministry. For we can understand how Gentile Christians might appeal to Paul himself, "the apostle to the Gentiles,"[40] as further reason to disdain Jews and Jewish Christians. "You see," they might argue, "Paul himself, though a Jew, has given up on his own people and is devoting all his efforts to us, the Gentiles." True, Paul responds, in accordance with God's particular call on my life,[41] I have spent most of time ministering to Gentiles. But contrary to what you might expect,[42] to the degree that[43] I am apostle to the Gentiles, I "glorify my ministry" — I take pride in it and work very hard at it — [44] with the hope that it will indirectly serve to bring Jewish people into the kingdom of God (cf. v. 14).[45]

38. See, e.g., S-H; Kuss; Cranfield. Godet, however, denies any parenthetical element. Accepting a weakly attested variant reading in v. 13 (γάρ in place of δέ), he argues that Paul in vv. 13-15 is explaining how his ministry will help to bring about the great blessing for Gentiles at which he hints at the end of v. 12. Meyer's view is similar.

39. As most commentators recognize, this address suggests that the majority of the Christians at Rome were Gentiles, since Paul does not say "I am speaking to those of you who are Gentiles." See, e.g., Godet; S-H; Kuss; Dunn.

40. It is very difficult to know what conclusions to draw from the anarthrous ἐθνῶν ἀπόστολος. Since definite predicate nouns that follow the verb tend to have the article (part of "Colwell's rule"; cf. Turner, 183), the phrase is probably indefinite, and we should probably translate "an apostle to the Gentiles," or, better, simply "apostle to the Gentiles." However, caution is called for because the rule does not apply to proper nouns, and ἐθνῶν ἀπόστολος may be something of a title.

41. See Acts 9:15; 22:21; 26:17-18; Rom. 1:5; 15:16, 18; Gal. 1:16; 2:1-11; Eph. 3:1, 6, 8; 1 Thess. 2:15-16; 1 Tim. 2:7; 2 Tim. 4:17.

42. This is probably the force of the particle μέν (cf. Cranfield), which here occurs, as it does elsewhere in Paul, without a corresponding δέ.

43. The Greek phrase ἐφ᾽ ὅσον can mean "for as long as" (see Matt. 9:15; 2 Pet. 1:13), but here, as in Matt. 25:40, 45, it means "to the degree that," "in so far as" (BAGD, 289; MM, 461). Perhaps Paul introduces this limitation because, while particularly known for his ministry among Gentiles, he did also devote time and energy to Jewish ministry (as the Book of Acts makes clear). Contra Godet, it is unlikely that Paul wants to distinguish his attitude as apostle to the Gentiles from his attitude as a Jew.

44. This paraphrase captures the most likely connotation of δοξάζω ("glorify") here (cf. esp. Dunn). It is quite unlikely that Paul refers here to his prayers of thanksgiving (contra Michel).

45. Paul is not, of course, saying that this is the only reason he engages in that ministry, nor even that it is the most important reason for it. His purpose here is the limited one of showing that this is *one* of the motivations in his work.

14 Paul's hope[46] that his preaching to Gentiles will have a positive impact on Jews is based on the "jealousy" theme that he introduced in v. 11b. As God uses Paul's preaching to bring more and more Gentiles to salvation,[47] Paul hopes that Jews, his own "flesh and blood,"[48] will become jealous and seek for themselves the blessings of this salvation. In these verses Paul reveals his sense of being a significant figure in salvation history. As "apostle to the Gentiles," he has a critical — and controversial — role to play in the unfolding plan of God for the nations and for Israel. But Paul's modesty in the last part of v. 14 shows that we must not overestimate the importance that he assigned to his own ministry.[49] By limiting the hoped-for fruits of his ministry to "some of them" (e.g., Jews), Paul suggests that he does not see himself (as some imagine) as the figure whom God will use to bring Israel to its destined "fullness."[50]

15 This verse "takes up v. 12 and establishes vv. 13f."[51] The latter relationship is indicated by the "for"[52] at the beginning of the verse: Paul earnestly seeks to stimulate Israel to jealousy and save "some of" his fellow Jews (vv. 13-14), "for" Israel's return to divine favor will mean unprecedented blessing for the world (v. 15). At the same time, v. 15 restates the process that Paul has introduced in vv. 11b-12. This restatement, however, uses a different syntactical and logical structure — the "if . . . how much more" sequence of v. 12 gives way to an "if . . . what" sequence in v. 15 — and different terminology. This different terminology brings two emphases in comparison with vv. 11b-12. First, whereas the earlier text implied, by means of the "jealousy" motif, the importance of human response, v. 15 stresses God's initiative in the process. Second, the final and climactic stage of the process, only hinted at in v. 12, is now spelled out: "life from the dead."

---

46. The construction εἴ πως indicates hesitant expectation: "in the hope that, perhaps . . ." (Z-G, 484; BDF 175). The verbs dependent on εἰ, παραζηλώσω, and σώσω, could be either future indicatives or aorist subjunctives.

47. When Paul says "that *I* might save some of them," he means that it would be through his preaching that God would bring salvation.

48. The Gk. τὴν σάρκα μου, "my flesh," picks up a Hebrew expression in which "flesh" denotes one's kindred (see LXX Gen. 37:27; Lev. 18:6; 25:49; et al.; cf. BAGD).

49. Contra those scholars who argue that Paul views himself as a critical eschatological figure, whose preaching of the gospel to the Gentiles will trigger the end-time conversion of Israel (cf. esp. Munck, *Paul*, pp. 275-79; Käsemann; cf. the notes on v. 25).

50. See, e.g., Cranfield; Morris. Käsemann and others would respond by arguing that Paul's way of putting the matter is simply "diplomatic caution." They would also note that the expression "some of them" need not indicate a small number (cf. Rom. 3:3; Munck, *Paul*, pp. 45-46). But the contrast in this context with "fullness" in v. 12 is too obvious to ignore.

51. Käsemann; cf. also S-H; Murray; Wilckens.

52. Gk. γάρ.

Paul's focus on God's superintendence of the process is indicated first in the phrase "their rejection." The word translated "rejection" means "a throwing away" or "loss."[53] It could refer here to the Jews' "loss" of salvation or to their "throwing away," or "rejection," of salvation or of the Lord himself.[54] But two points favor the rendering "their [the Jews'] rejection [by God]."[55] First, Paul uses the word "acceptance" in the second half of the verse as a direct contrast to "rejection." And, while the word Paul uses here does not occur anywhere else in the NT, Paul uses a verb related to it in Rom. 14:3 and 15:7 to refer to God's and Christ's "accepting" of believers.[56] This strongly suggests that "acceptance" refers to "God's acceptance of the Jews"[57]; "rejection," by contrast, would refer to "God's rejection of the Jews." A second reason for adopting this rendering is the emphasis Paul places throughout this section on God's responsibility for Israel's present spiritual obduracy. "God has given them a spirit of stupor" (v. 8); they have been "cut off [by God]" (v. 17).

Echoing vv. 11b and 12, Paul indicates that God's rejection of the Jews has meant "the reconciliation of the world." "Reconciliation," as in Rom. 5:11 (and note the corresponding verb in 5:10), refers to God's act of bringing sinners into a peaceful relationship with himself.[58] Paul is again speaking in corporate categories; the "reconciliation of the world" does not mean that

---

53. Gk. ἀποβολή. See BAGD and note Acts 27:22, the only other occurrence of the word in the NT: ἀποβολὴ γὰρ ψυχῆς οὐδεμία ἔσται ἐξ ὑμῶν πλὴν τοῦ πλοίου: "for there shall be the *loss* of not one life from among you — except the boat [shall be lost]." The word is not found in the LXX; cf., however, Josephus, *Ant.* 3.314: ἔσεσθαι δὲ τὴν τούτων ἀποβολὴν οὐχ ἅπαξ ἀλλὰ πολλάκις: "but there shall be the loss of these things [cities and temple] not once, but many times."

54. On this view, αὐτῶν will be a subjective genitive: "the throwing away done *by* them." Cf. Fitzmyer; Donaldson, " 'Riches for the Gentiles,' " p. 93 n. 50.

55. This interpretation assumes that αὐτῶν is an objective genitive and that the understood subject of the action is God: "the rejection of the Jews by God." It is widely supported; see, e.g., BAGD; Godet; S-H; Michel; Murray; Kuss; Cranfield; Wilckens; Dunn; Hofius, "Das Evangelium und Israel," p. 307.

56. The verb is προσλαμβάνω; the word Paul uses here is πρόσλημψις. In the LXX, this word occurs only in a gloss to Sir. 10:20, the relevant phrase being προσλημψέως ἀρχὴ φόβος κυρίου: "the beginning of *acceptance* is the fear of the Lord."

57. See, e.g., Martin, *Reconciliation,* p. 134. Fitzmyer and Donaldson (" 'Riches for the Gentiles,' " p. 93 n. 50), consistent with their interpretation of ἀποβολή, think that the reference is to the Jews' acceptance of God.

58. As I noted in my comments on 5:10, reconciliation has two "moments": the cross, where Christ's death provides the objective grounds of reconciliation, and conversion, when the benefits of that death result in actual reconciliation for the believer. Paul probably has the latter "moment" in view here, although Cranfield argues for the former. It is unlikely that the reconciliation here is that between Jews and Gentiles (contra, e.g., Barrett; Dunn [he thinks this is one element of the meaning]).

every human being has been saved. As in v. 12, "world" refers to the Gentiles, and Paul's point is that Israel's rejection has made it possible for Gentiles, as a group, to experience Christ's reconciling work.

If, then, Paul argues, God's "casting away" of Israel has led to this extension to Gentiles of God's salvation, what will be the result of God's taking Israel to himself again?[59] Nothing less than "life from the dead."[60] Debate over the meaning of this phrase has been intense; nothing in chap. 11 except "All Israel will be saved" in v. 26 has sparked more disagreement. The logic of the verse shows that it must refer to a blessing even greater or more climactic than the extension of reconciliation to the Gentiles. For Paul argues from the lesser to the greater: if something negative like Israel's rejection means that Gentiles are being reconciled to God, how much greater must be the result of something positive like Israel's acceptance? Opinions about what this greater blessing might be fall into two general categories.

(1) We can interpret "life from the dead" literally, understanding the phrase to refer to the general resurrection that will take place after the return of Christ in glory, or to the blessed life that will follow that resurrection.[61]

(2) We can interpret "life from the dead" metaphorically, as a way of referring to a great and unprecedented blessing, whether this be a spiritual quickening of the whole world[62] or the spiritual "coming back to life" of Israel.[63]

---

59. Paul does not directly say that it is Israel that will be accepted. But the article with πρόσλημψις probably has possessive force, conveying the sense of the pronoun αὐτῶν in parallel expression in the first part of the verse.

60. Gk. ζωὴ ἐκ νεκρῶν.

61. See esp. 1 Cor. 15:22-24; also Matt. 25:31-46; Rom. 6:6(?), 8(?); 8:11, 23; Phil. 3:10-11; 1 Thess. 4:16; Rev. 20:4-6. This was the view adopted by most of the early Greek fathers (e.g., Origen, Theodore of Mopsuestia, Ephraem, Chrysostom, Theodoret; cf. Schelkle), and by many Puritans (cf. I. H. Murray, *The Puritan Hope: A Study in Revival and the Interpretation of Prophecy* [London: Banner of Truth, 1971], pp. 66-72). See also Lietzmann; Meyer; Zahn; Lagrange; S-H; Barrett; Bruce; Black; Käsemann; Schmidt; Schlier; Cranfield; Dunn; Zeller; Munck, *Christ and Israel,* pp. 126-27; W. D. Davies, "Paul and the Gentiles: A Suggestion Concerning Romans 11.13-24," in *Jewish and Pauline Studies* (Philadelphia: Fortress, 1984), p. 132; Martin, *Reconciliation,* pp. 133-34; Beker, 153; Refoulé, *Tout Israël,* pp. 251-55; Volf, *Paul and Perseverance,* pp. 173-74; Johnson, *Function,* p. 128; Bell, *Provoked to Jealousy,* pp. 116-18.

62. Advocates of this view often suggest as a parallel the phrase about the prodigal son's return in Luke 15:24: "This my son was dead (νεκρός) and has come to life (ἀνέζησεν)." Most of the later Greek fathers took this view (cf. Schelkle); see esp. Murray; also Gifford; Stuart; Godet; Denney; Morris; Haldane; Lenski; Huby; Viard; Ladd, *Theology,* p. 562; Zeller, *Juden und Heiden,* pp. 239-44.

63. Reference in this case is often made to Ezekiel's vision of the "dry bones" (chap. 37). See Calvin; Fitzmyer; Ziesler; Wright, *Climax of the Covenant,* p. 248; D. Judant, *Les deux Israël: essai sur le mystère du salut d'Israël selon l'économie des deux Testaments* (Paris: Cerf, 1960), pp. 182-91.

Three considerations favor the former. First, while the actual phrase "life from the dead" never occurs elsewhere in the Bible, the phrase "from the dead" is found 47 times in the NT; and every occurrence except one comes in a phrase referring to the resurrection. To be sure, the one exception is an important one, for it involves the closest parallel in Paul to the phrase he uses here, "those who are alive out of the dead"[64] (Rom. 6:13). This phrase refers to Christians who are spiritually "living," having been brought out of a state of death. However, it is important to note that Paul prefaces the phrase with the word "as."[65] By thereby adding an explicit indicator that he is giving the phrase a metaphorical nuance, he seems to bear witness indirectly to the normal literal force of the words. It is also argued that, had Paul wanted to refer to resurrection here, he would have explicitly used that word; see, for example, "resurrection of the dead"[66] in 1 Cor. 15:12. There is some point to this objection; it is likely therefore that "life from the dead" refers to the new life that comes after resurrection rather than to resurrection itself.[67]

A second reason to prefer a literal rendering of this phrase arises from a consideration of Paul's other descriptions of the process that he depicts here in v. 15. These descriptions suggest that "life from the dead" must be an event distinct from Israel's restoration, involving the whole world, and occurring at the very end of history. The logic of v. 12 implies that the event that follows the "fullness" of Israel will have, like Israel's "trespass," an impact on the (Gentile) world. And vv. 25-26 suggest that the salvation of Israel comes only after God has brought into the kingdom all the Gentiles destined to be saved. No room is therefore left for a spiritual quickening of the world; all that remains is the consummation.[68]

A third factor favoring a reference to the end of history is the apocalyptic worldview that lies behind Paul's teaching at this point. To be sure, the nature of apocalyptic and the degree of its influence on Paul are debated; but Paul gives many explicit indications in both the structure of his argument and in his vocabulary that he is deeply influenced by apocalyptic conceptions in

---

64. Gk. ἐκ νεκρῶν ζῶντας.

65. Gk. ὡσεί; for the point, see Dunn.

66. Gk. ἀνάστασις νεκρῶν.

67. See esp. Meyer; Lietzmann; Schlier. Paul, of course, says nothing here about any stage between the final restoration of Israel and the enjoyment of eschatological life. But nothing in the verse contradicts the conception either (contra, e.g., Davies, 297-98; cf. n. 1 on p. 298). If one is convinced (as I am) on the basis of other texts, such as Rev. 20, that the NT predicts an "interim" stage of eschatological fulfillment between the parousia and the eternal state — a "millennium" — then Paul's outline of events in this chapter need not be a problem. As is often the case in the NT, Paul here telescopes eschatological events, omitting those not immediately relevant to his argument.

68. See, e.g., Cranfield.

Rom. 9–11, and especially in 11:12-32.[69] Yet most Jewish apocalyptic thinking focused on the events leading to, and bringing in, the end of history. A standard apocalyptic pattern featured the restoration of Israel as the event that would bring in the eschatological consummation.[70] Since we are justified in thinking that Paul builds his teaching here on apocalyptic, a reference to resurrection at the end of history seems likely.

Therefore, as Israel's "trespass" (vv. 11, 12) and "rejection" (v. 15) trigger the stage of salvation history in which Paul (and we) are located, a stage in which God is specially blessing Gentiles, so Israel's "fullness" (v. 12) and "acceptance" (v. 15) will trigger the climactic end of salvation history. Paul insists on the vital, continuing significance of Israel in salvation history, against tendencies among Gentile Christians to discard Israel from any further role in the plan of God. However, Paul is silent about the timing of these events. Indeed, many commentators think that Paul's own role in this process (vv. 13-14) suggests that he was sure that the culmination of this process would take place within his lifetime.[71] But, as we have seen, Paul's view of his role in the process was much more modest. Like the rest of the NT, Paul leaves the timing of these events in the hands of God.

2. The Interrelationship of Jews and Gentiles: A Warning to Gentile Believers (11:16-24)

16Now if the first fruits are holy, then so is the lump. And if the root is holy, then so are the branches.

17Now if some of the branches have been cut off, and you, a wild olive branch, have been grafted in among them and become partakers of the rich root[1] of the olive tree, 18do not boast over the branches.

69. Käsemann's commentary gives classic expression to this conviction. See also Johnson, *Function*, esp. pp. 124-31. On Paul's apocalyptic worldview and the doctrine of resurrection, see Beker, 152-63.

70. See D. C. Allison, Jr., "The Background of Romans 11:11-15 in Apocalyptic and Rabbinic Literature," *Studia Biblica et Theologica* 10 (1980), 229-34; idem, "Romans 11:11-15: A Suggestion," *Perspectives in Religious Studies* 12 (1985), pp. 23-30. He refers to *T. Dan* 6:4; *T. Sim.* 6:2-7; *T. Jud.* 23:5; *T. Moses* 1:18; *2 Apoc. Bar.* 78:6-7; 4 Ezra 4:38-43; *b. Sanh.* 97b, 98a; *b. Shabb.* 118b; *Sifre Deut.* 41. Acts 3:19-20 may presuppose this tradition (cf. Johnson, *Function*, pp. 125-26).

71. See, on v. 15, Dunn, 2.658.

1. The text found in UBS[4] and NA[27], and on which this translation is based, is τῆς ῥίζης τῆς πιότητος, "the root of the fatness." It is attested in the two primary Alexandrian uncials, א (original hand) and B, in the secondary Alexandrian uncial C, in the uncial Ψ, and in a few minuscules. Three variants that avoid this rather awkward combination of words, and which are therefore probably scribal corrections, are extant. (1) τῆς ῥίζης καὶ τῆς πιότητος, "the root and the fatness" (the second [Byzantine] corrector

But if you are to boast, remember that it is not you who supports the root, but the root that supports you. 19You will say then, "Branches have been broken off in order that I might be grafted in." 20True. They were broken off because of lack of faith, and you stand because of faith. Do not think highly of yourselves, but fear. 21For if God did not spare the natural branches, neither2 will he spare you. 22See therefore the goodness and the severity of God. For those who have fallen, there is severity, but for you, the goodness of God — if indeed you remain in that goodness; otherwise you, too, will be cut off. 23And those also, if they do not persist in their lack of faith, will be grafted in again. For God is able to graft them in again. 24For if you, who have been cut from the wild olive tree you belonged to by nature, have been, against nature, grafted into the cultivated olive tree, how much more will these who are natural branches be grafted into their own olive tree.

The argument of v. 16, that the "part" of something can convey holiness to the "whole," is transitional.3 On the one hand, it reinforces the hope for a

---

of ℵ, the secondary Alexandrian MSS A, 33, 81, and 1739, and the second corrector of one western uncial, D, as well as in the majority text; it is also attested in most of the ancient translations). It is the textual basis for the KJV "the root and fatness." (2) τῆς πιότητος, "the fatness" (read in P46, the original hand of D, two other western uncials [F and G], and in some minuscules and ancient translations). (3) τῆς ρίζης, "the root" (the reading assumed, apparently, by Ambrosiaster). The second reading is supported by Godet (p. 406), but most scholars support the reading we have adopted (cf., e.g., S-H, 328; Michel, 349-50 n.; Metzger, 526).

2. UBS4 and NA27 include, although in brackets, the words μή πως before οὐδέ, "neither." The effect of this addition would be to add a nuance of uncertainty to the construction: "neither, perhaps" (cf. BAGD, 519). The addition has widespread textual support, including P46, the secondary Alexandrian MS 33, Ψ, the western uncials D, F, and G, and the majority text. Metzger (pp. 526-27) defends the decision of the UBS committee to include the words in the text on the grounds that (1) μή πως is typically Pauline; (2) scribes may have omitted it because they thought it was unnecessary or a problem with the future verb (cf. also Meyer [2.198] and Godet [407]). However, the omission of the words has very strong support in the Alexandrian textual family (the primary uncials ℵ and B, the secondary MSS C, 81, and 1739), and this may be a case in which the rule "the shorter reading should be preferred" should be followed (see, e.g., S-H, 329; Murray, 2.88; Cranfield, 2.569 n. 6).

3. See Cranfield, 2.563; Dunn, 2.652. Some translations (NIV, NRSV) put a paragraph division between vv. 16 and 17 (as do the NA27 and UBS4 Greek texts). But TEV and NJB, as well as almost all the commentaries (e.g., Godet, 398; S-H, 318; Michel, 344; Käsemann, 304; Wilckens, 2.241; Murray, 2.84), place the division between vv. 15 and 16. If a choice has to be made, the latter is the better option because v. 16 is more closely related to vv. 17ff. than it is to vv. 11-15.

spiritual renewal of Israel that vv. 11-15 have implied: the holiness of "part" of Israel is good reason to anticipate a "fullness" and "acceptance" for the whole of Israel. On the other hand, v. 16 paves the way to vv. 17-24 by introducing the metaphor of the root and the branches that dominates these verses. As Paul develops this metaphor, he compares the root of the tree to the patriarchs and the promise of God to them, the "natural branches" to Jews, and "wild olive tree shoots" to the Gentiles. As these identifications suggest, the tree itself represents the people of God in the broadest sense of that concept — a people spanning both ages of salvation history and both major ethnic/religious groups, Jews and Gentiles. Paul makes two points with this olive tree image.

The first, and most obvious, is hortatory. Throughout this text he continues (cf. v. 13) to address the Gentile Christians in Rome directly, using the second person singular to make his address all the more pointed.[4] The olive tree image makes clear that the Gentiles' very spiritual existence depends on their partaking of the tree whose indispensable nourishing roots are planted in the soil of Jewish patriarchs and promises and to which, therefore, Jews naturally belong. This being the case, any boasting on the part of the Gentile Christians is clearly out of place: whether it be boasting over Jews (v. 18) or boasting about their own spiritual accomplishments (vv. 19-22).[5]

Paul's second purpose is didactic. By emphasizing the ease with which natural branches can be grafted back into "their own" olive tree (vv. 23-24), Paul provides further support for his key theme in 11:11-32: hope for a spiritual future for Israel.

16 The imagery of root and branches forges an obvious connection between this verse and what follows. The connection with vv. 11-15 is not as obvious but can be readily supplied.[6] For Paul's sketch of the future of salvation history includes one critical stage that is introduced without explanation or substantiation: the spiritual restoration of Israel ("their fullness" [v. 12]; "their acceptance" [v. 15]). This Paul now provides by arguing that the holiness that characterized the beginnings of Israel is an indelible mark on that people, fraught with significance for her present and her future.

Paul uses two parallel metaphors, each arguing from the part to the whole, to make this point. The first is drawn from Num. 15:17-21. In this

---

4. Some scholars (e.g., Aletti, *Comment Dieu est-il juste?* pp. 191-92) continue to think that this address is a purely rhetorical device, stemming from the diatribe, and that no actual audience is intended.

5. Scholars debate the exact reasons for Gentile-Christian arrogance toward Jews. Some suggest that ancient anti-Semitism might have played a role (e.g., Davies, "Paul and the Gentiles," pp. 135-37). But the problem in Rome and in the early church generally was based more on religious differences than on ethnic ones.

6. The δέ indicates here, then, a loose transition: hence the "now" in our translation.

passage, the Lord commands the people of Israel, after they enter the promised land, to offer to the Lord a donation from the "first fruits"[7] of the "lump of dough"[8] that they use to bake their bread. Paul's point is that the holiness of this first part of the dough extends to the whole lump of dough.[9] To what set of circumstances does Paul intend this metaphor to apply? Since Paul gives no hint, it seems reasonable to look for our answer to the second metaphor in the verse, which appears to be parallel to the first. Here we are given help in interpreting the elements in the metaphor by the context and by other Jewish texts. The "branches," as vv. 17-18 reveal, are the Jews.[10] Paul does not so clearly identify the "root," and this has given scope to various suggestions, including Christ,[11] Jewish Christians (the remnant),[12] and the patriarchs. But the last of these receives decisive support from the imagery of vv. 17-18, the somewhat parallel concept in v. 28 — God loves Israel "because of the fathers" (cf. also 9:5) — and from Jewish texts in which Abraham and the patriarchs are called a root.[13]

---

7. Heb. רֵאשִׁית, "first," "chief part," "choice part"; LXX ἀπαρχή, "first fruits," usually denoting an initial stage of something that gives promise of more to come. The word is common in both secular Greek and in the OT to denote the initial or representative portion of a commodity that was to be offered in sacrifice to God (cf., e.g., Lev. 2:12 [grain]; 23:10 [the harvest]; Deut. 18:4 [grain, wine, the fleece of sheep]). This "first fruits" was often reserved for the priests (e.g., Num. 18:8). See A. Sand, *EDNT* I, 116.

8. Heb. עֲרִסָה, whose meaning is uncertain (cf. BDB 791); LXX φύραμα, "lump," "dough" (cf. Rom. 9:21; 1 Cor. 5:6, 7; Gal. 5:9).

9. The text in Numbers does not indicate that this "first fruits" of the dough had any affect on the lump of dough as a whole; nor do other OT or Jewish texts clearly assert such a relationship generally between "first fruits" and the remainder (contra, e.g., Cranfield, who refers to Lev. 19:23-25, and Käsemann, who refers to Philo, *Special Laws* 1.131-44). Paul may therefore apply to this circumstance a principle derived from elsewhere; Dunn, e.g., notes that Jews thought the temple conveyed holiness to all of Jerusalem (he cites Neh. 11:1, 18; Isa. 11:9; 48:2; 66:20; Jer. 31:23, 40; Ezek. 20:40) and that the Pharisees apparently sought to extend the temple's holiness throughout the land by their scrupulous observances (2.658-59). Perhaps Paul is also influenced by the principle "a little leaven leavens the whole lump" (1 Cor. 5:6; the word here is also φύραμα).

10. It might be argued that the branches are Jewish Christians only since, according to vv. 17-24, they only now remain in the tree. But Paul is not yet here developing the contrast between branches that remain and those that are "cut off" (see M. M. Bourke, *A Study of the Metaphor of the Olive Tree in Romans XI* [Washington, D.C.: Catholic University of America, 1947], pp. 72-73).

11. Ellison, *Mystery of Israel,* pp. 86-87.

12. Barrett (who allows for possible reference to Christ also); P. von der Osten-Sacken, *Christian-Jewish Dialogue: Theological Foundations* (Philadelphia: Fortress, 1986), pp. 106-7; Johnson, *Function,* p. 98.

13. E.g., *1 Enoch* 93:5, 8; Philo, *Heir* 279 (Abraham); *Jub.* 21:24 (Isaac). Most commentators take this position; cf., e.g., Chrysostom; Godet; Cranfield; Fitzmyer.

But is this also what Paul is teaching in his first metaphor? Can we conclude from the apparent parallelism that "first fruits" represents the patriarchs and "lump of dough" the Jewish people? Almost all scholars agree on the second point: "lump of dough" stands for the Jews.[14] Opinion on the identification of the "first fruits" is more divided. Most scholars are led by the parallelism to identify the "first fruits" with the patriarchs.[15] But some think that the "first fruits" is Adam[16] or Christ (cf. 1 Cor. 15:20, 23),[17] while a significant (and growing) number think it is Jewish Christians, the remnant.[18] Advocates of this last view note that Paul elsewhere uses the word "first fruits" to refer to "first converts" (Rom. 16:5; 1 Cor. 16:15; 2 Thess. 2:13), and that the OT and Jewish thinkers view the remnant as a down payment on a greater blessing of the Jewish people. If we make this identification, then v. 16 would have even more transitional force than we have recognized, with v. 16a picking up the argument of vv. 1-10 and v. 16b leading into vv. 17ff. While the choice is a difficult one, I think that the traditional identification of the "first fruits" with the patriarchs is more likely. The parallelism, while not decisive, is certainly important; but more important is the lack of solid support in the OT or in Jewish theology for the idea that the remnant would have a "sanctifying" effect on the people of Israel as a whole.

Both of the metaphors in v. 16, then, assert that the "holiness" of the patriarchs conveys to all of Israel a similar holiness. In according such significance to the patriarchs, Paul of course does not mean that Abraham, Isaac, and Jacob possessed any qualities that earned spiritual benefits for themselves and their descendants. As both the OT and Paul make clear (see esp. Rom. 4 and Gal. 3), the patriarchs convey spiritual benefits on their descendants only as recipients and transmitters of the promises of God. Their "holiness" consists in their having

14. Lenski and Dunn, however, think that Paul may refer to all the spiritual descendants of the patriarchs, whether Jewish or Gentile (cf. Rom. 4:16-19).

15. Cf., e.g., Chrysostom; Godet; S-H; Murray; Michel; Käsemann; Wilckens; Schlier; Bourke, *Olive Tree,* pp. 75-76.

16. An opinion based on a fairly widespread Jewish tradition that connected Adam with "first fruits" (see K. H. Rengstorf, "Das Ölbaum-Gleichnis in Röm 11, 16ff.: Versuch einer weiterführenden Deutung," in *Donum Gentilicium: New Testament Studies in Honour of David Daube* [ed. E. Bammel, C. K. Barrett, and W. D. Davies; Oxford: Clarendon, 1978], pp. 128-35).

17. Some church fathers took this position (Schelkle); cf. also Barrett (in combination with Jewish Christians).

18. This view was adopted by some in the early church (Schelkle); cf. also Gaugler; Leenhardt; Barrett; Bruce; Cranfield; Fitzmyer; Hafemann, "Salvation of Israel," p. 51; Osten-Sacken, *Christian-Jewish Dialogue,* pp. 106-7; Johnson, *Function,* pp. 98-99; Bell, *Provoked to Jealousy,* pp. 118-20. Dunn includes Gentile as well as Jewish believers of Paul's day.

been set apart by God for this salvation-historical role.[19] Moreover, the word "holy" *(hagios)* is taken from OT sacrificial language. The word will not, then, have the technical sense of "set apart by God for salvation" that it usually has in Paul but will connote a being "set apart" by God for special attention in a more general way.[20] Paul is not here asserting the salvation of every Israelite but the continuing "special" identity of the people of Israel in the eyes of the Lord.

17 This continuing special relationship between God and Israel is, however, reason to hope that Israel might one day be spiritually renewed, hope that Paul enunciates in vv. 23-24. First, however, he exploits the metaphor of root and branches to chastise and warn Gentile Christians (vv. 17-22).

Verse 17 is the protasis (the "if" clause) of a conditional sentence, whose apodosis (the "then" clause) comes in v. 18a: "do not boast over the branches." The condition in this case is one that Paul obviously views as fulfilled (note that TEV turns the condition into an assertion).[21] There are two parts of this condition. First, "some[22] of the branches have been cut off." Here in a new image Paul restates the essential tragedy that sparks Rom. 9–11: Jews, the recipients of God's blessings through their ancestry, have been severed from those blessings — through both God's hardening (cf. vv. 7b-10)[23] and their own unbelief (cf. v. 20). Second, however, we find "grafted in"[24] among the branches that remain[25] other branches — branches that come from "a wild olive tree."[26] With this image, as

19. See J. L. Burns, "The Future of Ethnic Israel in Romans 11," in *Dispensationalism, Israel and the Church: The Search for Definition* (ed. C. A. Blaising and D. L. Bock; Grand Rapids: Zondervan, 1992), pp. 203-7.

20. Bourke, *Olive Tree*, pp. 67-72, 77. Paul uses words from the ἁγιαζ- root in a similar way in 1 Cor. 7:14; cf. G. D. Fee, *The First Epistle to the Corinthians* (NICNT; Grand Rapids: Eerdmans, 1987), pp. 300-301.

21. The combination of εἰ with an indicative verb does not itself, however, denote a "factual" condition; this can be determined only by context (see, e.g., Zerwick, 303-6).

22. Paul uses τινες not because he knows that the number of branches that have been cut off is small but because he wants to stress to the Gentiles that not all the branches have been cut off. See also 3:3; 11:14.

23. The verb ἐξεκλάσθησαν, "have been cut off," is a "divine passive," suggesting that God is the one who has done the cutting off. See Wilckens.

24. Gk. ἐνεκεντρίσθης, from ἐγκεντρίζω. The verb occurs only in the passage in the NT and is a technical arboricultural term (BAGD).

25. Arguing that the antecedent of αὐτοῖς must be the cut-off branches mentioned earlier in the verse, some commentators insist that ἐν must mean "in place of" (e.g., Stuart; Ziesler; Wilckens). But it seems preferable, especially if we give συγκοινωνός the meaning I have suggested, to think that ἐν means "among" and that the antecedent of αὐτοῖς in Paul's mind is the branches that still remain on the tree (e.g., S-H; Michel; Murray; Käsemann; Cranfield; Dunn; Fitzmyer; Donaldson, " 'Riches for the Gentiles,' " p. 84 n. 14).

26. Gk. ἀγριέλαιος. The word is an adjective and may be used as one here: individual Gentiles (σύ) partake of the quality of the wild olive (BAGD [?]; Meyer; Godet). But it is probably used substantivally, with Paul's language being somewhat imprecise.

Paul's direct address makes clear (see v. 13), he refers to Gentile Christians. As Gentiles, they have no "natural" relationship to the patriarchs and the promises given to them. Only by God's grace (v. 22) and their faith (v. 20) have they been able to become "fellow participants" (with Jewish Christians)[27] of the "rich root of the olive tree."[28]

Two aspects of Paul's metaphor in v. 17 require further comment. First is the significance of Paul's choice of the olive tree to fill out the imagery of root and branches. This probably reflects both its use as a symbol of Israel in the OT and Judaism[29] and the fact that the olive tree was "the most widely cultivated fruit tree in the Mediterranean area."[30] The "wild olive tree," by contrast, was notoriously unfruitful, and Paul's comparison of Gentiles to it may be intended to prick the Gentiles' pride and sense of superiority.[31] The second point calling for attention is Paul's reference to the practice of grafting branches from a wild, or uncultivated, tree into a cultivated one — the reverse of the usual process. Some scholars find here

27. The word συγκοινωνός, "participant," "partner," takes a genitive after it to indicate that in which one shares: here τῆς ῥίζης, "the root." Paul could simply mean, then, that Gentile Christians participate in the root. However, while Paul's other uses of the word are not conclusive (1 Cor. 9:23; Phil. 1:7), it is likely that he would in this context want to stress the participation of the Gentile Christians *with* Jewish Christians in the root. See, e.g., Cranfield.

28. Paul's series of three genitives — τῆς ῥίζης τῆς πιότητος τῆς ἐλαίας — requires unpacking (and note the textual variant that would break the series). The first is required by the preceding word συγκοινωνός, while the third denotes either possession or source. The second, τῆς πιότητος (a NT hapax, πιότης means "fatness," "richness" [of plants]), may be epexegetic — "the root, that is the richness that comes from the olive tree" (e.g., Michel; Cranfield) — but is probably qualitative — "the rich root that belongs to the olive tree" (so most English translations; cf. Murray).

29. See esp. Jer. 11:16: "'A green olive tree, beautiful with valuable fruit,' the LORD called your name, but with the voice of a great storm he will set fire to it, and its branches will be broken [as BDB translate רָעֻעֹ]" (see J. M. Scott, "Paul's Use of Deuteronomic Tradition," *JBL* 112 [1994], 662-63). Note also Hos. 14:5-6: "I will be like the dew to Israel; he shall blossom like the lily, he shall strike root like the forests of Lebanon. His shoots shall spread out; his beauty shall be like the olive tree, and his fragrance like that of Lebanon." References to Israel as "God's planting" are more frequent (see *1 Enoch* 10:16; 93:2, 5, 8, 10; *Jub.* 16:26; 21:4; *Pss. Sol.* 14:3-4; 1QS 8:5; 11:8; 1QH 6:15-16; 8:5-7, 9-10). See, e.g., Str-B, 3.290; Rengstorf, "Das Ölbaum-Zeichnis," pp. 128-35. Schoeps (242 n. 5) thinks Philo's remark about proselytes in *Rewards and Punishments* 152 might be the basis for Paul's image. Philo writes that God, in accepting proselytes, "takes no account of the roots [τὰς ῥίζας] but accepts the full-grown stem, because it has been changed from a weed into fruitfulness."

30. Dunn. Davies, noting the paucity of OT references to Israel as an olive tree, argues that a Roman synagogue called "the synagogue of the olive" may have played a role in Paul's choice ("Paul and the Gentiles," pp. 137-44).

31. Davies, "Paul and the Gentiles," pp. 137-44; Dunn.

evidence of Paul's urban roots — he simply did not know arboriculture.[32] Others have rushed to Paul's defense, citing evidence in ancient sources showing that farmers did occasionally graft a wild olive shoot into a cultivated tree.[33] Still others argue that Paul has knowingly cited a practice that is "contrary to nature" as a way of illustrating the grace of God at work in the incorporation of Gentiles into the people of God (see "against nature" in v. 24).[34] None of these conclusions is warranted. Writers and speakers frequently transgress the natural boundaries of a metaphor in their application of it. We should therefore be content to recognize that Paul has allowed the theological process he is illustrating to affect the terms of his metaphor. We cannot be sure, then, whether he knows he is citing an actual arboricultural practice or not; and we certainly cannot draw any theological conclusions from the fact.[35]

18 The prohibition "do not boast over the branches" completes the conditional sentence begun in v. 17. The verb "boast over" combines the ideas of sinful pride and arrogant superiority: "boast in triumphant comparison with others."[36] The "others" over whom the Gentile Christians are not to exult are "the branches." But does Paul have in mind the branches that have been broken off the tree (unbelieving Jews),[37] the branches that remain in the tree (Jewish Christians), or both?[38] Probably both. Paul's comparison between the Gentile Christians who stand in God's grace by their faith with Jews who have been cut off because of their unbelief (vv. 20-22) shows that he must have unbelieving Jews in mind. Yet 14:1–15:13 manifests a concern to reconcile Jews and Gentiles within the church; and Paul almost certainly has this situation in mind even here.

Gentile-Christian boasting over Jews is probably not the result of

---

32. "Paul had the limitations of a town-bred man" (Dodd; cf. also Lietzmann).

33. See esp. W. M. Ramsay, "The Olive-Tree and the Wild Olive," in *Paul and Other Studies in Early Christian History* (London: Hodder and Stoughton, 1908), pp. 219-50; and A. G. Baxter and J. A. Ziesler, "Paul and Arboriculture: Romans 11.17-24," *JSNT* 24 (1985), 25-32. Cf. also Dunn. The ancient texts cited are Columella, *De re rustica* 5.9.16 and Palladius, *De insitione* 53-54. Since the purpose of this practice was to rejuvenate a decaying olive tree, Paul's theological point might then be that the incorporation of Gentiles would serve to bring new life to the people of God (Baxter and Ziesler, ibid.; Ziesler; Volf, *Paul and Perseverance,* p. 175).

34. Rengstorf, "Das Ölbaum-Zeichnis," pp. 145-46; S-H; Viard.

35. Godet; Murray; Käsemann; Barrett; Cranfield; Schmeller, *Paulus und die "Diatribe,"* pp. 313-14.

36. R. Bultmann, *TDNT* III, 653. The word (κατακαυχάομαι) occurs only rarely outside the Bible; it occurs elsewhere in the NT with a similar sense in Jas. 2:13 and 3:14.

37. R. Bultmann, *TDNT* III, 654; Michel; Barrett; Murray.

38. Godet; S-H; Cranfield; Dunn.

anti-Semitism generally,[39] but of a mistaken reading of the course of salvation history. These Gentile Christians appear to have concluded that the unprecedented degree in which the doors of salvation were open to Gentiles after the coming of Christ meant the closing of those same doors to Jews. At the same time, these Gentile believers were apparently convinced that they belonged to a new people of God that had simply replaced Israel. Those Jews who believed, they apparently assumed, could become part of *their* community and on *their* terms (see 14:1–15:13). It is to this kind of attitude that Paul responds in vv. 18b-22, where he expands on the basic imagery of v. 17 to back up his prohibition of Gentile-Christian boasting.

He begins with another conditional sentence, in which, for the sake of argument, he assumes that, despite his prohibition, the Gentile Christians will insist on continuing to boast over Jews. In that case, Paul warns: "remember[40] that it is not you who supports the root, but the root that supports you." Gentile Christians who boast over Jews are demonstrating an attitude of disdain for the Jewish heritage. Yet it is that very heritage upon which the Gentile Christians themselves depend for their own spiritual standing. For "the root" that gives spiritual nourishment to Jewish and Gentile believers alike is the patriarchs as recipients and transmitters of the promises of God. And that root is not only of historical interest. As the present tense Paul uses here indicates, the root of the patriarchs continues to be the source of spiritual nourishment that believers require.[41] There is only one root and only one tree; branches, whether Jewish or Gentile, that do not remain attached to that tree are doomed to wither and die. Here again we see the careful balance of Paul's argument in Romans. Physical descent from the patriarchs does not, in itself, bring salvation (2:25-29; 9:6b-29); Jews are in the same position as Gentiles, held under sin's power (2:1–3:20) and needing to respond to God in faith to be saved (3:21–4:25). Yet salvation comes only to those who are of "Abraham's seed": the people of God are one, and that people has both a Jewish root and a continuing Jewish element.

19-20 In good diatribe style, Paul now puts a further argument on the lips of a hypothetical Gentile Christian who seeks to justify his feeling of

---

39. Contra, e.g., Davies, who thinks that ancient anti-Semitism played a role in the Roman situation ("Paul and the Gentiles"). Nor is it clear that Paul here directs his remarks against "pneumatics," Christians who prided themselves on their spiritual attainments as partakers of the new age (contra Michel, e.g., 350-51).

40. Some language such as this must be supplied in the apodosis of the sentence: we have here an instance of brachylogy, an omission of words that are not required by the grammar but must be supplied to understand the thought (see BDF 483).

41. Contra, e.g., Mussner (*Tractate,* p. 24), the root that supports Gentile Christians is not Israel (see, for criticisms of this view, Walter, "Römer 9–11," pp. 181-82; Hofius, "Das Evangelium und Israel," p. 309 n. 43).

superiority over the Jews: "Branches have been broken off in order that I[42] might be grafted in." Paul responds in v. 20 with a qualified agreement.[43] He does not straightforwardly deny the point that the Gentile Christian has made; for, indeed, as Paul himself has argued, the hardening of Jews has led to the extension of salvation to Gentiles (vv. 11-15). But Paul also argues that this salvation is, in turn, designed to stimulate Jews to jealousy as the means of their spiritual restoration. God's purposes in "cutting off" natural branches extend far beyond the inclusion of Gentiles. It is the egotism of Gentile Christians who present God's manifold plan as having the salvation of themselves as its focus that Paul wishes to expose and criticize.

Another facet of the egotism of the Gentile Christians is their sense of pride in having attained a place in the people of God. This attitude Paul seeks to deflate by reminding them that it is faith that makes the difference. It is because of their lack of faith[44] that so many Jews have been "cut off"; and it is through faith[45] that the Gentile Christian has attained a standing[46] within the people of God. What Paul says here to the Gentile Christian echoes what he said earlier to the Jews.[47] In response to the Jews' tendency to boast in their status and accomplishments, Paul emphasized that the gracious nature of God's dealings with human beings excluded all boasting. It is faith, and faith alone — characterized by humility and receptivity — that is the only way to establish or to maintain a relationship with God (3:27–4:5). Recognizing that every spiritual benefit comes as a sheer gift from our gracious God, the Gentile Christian must stop thinking so highly of his or her accomplishments[48] and take up an attitude of fear. This basic biblical concept combines reverential respect for the God of majesty and glory with a healthy concern to continue

---

42. The pronoun ἐγώ in the Greek probably carries some emphasis, manifesting the self-centered concern of the Gentile Christian objector.

43. Gk. καλῶς. Some think that this reply is simply ironical (e.g., Michel), but most agree that it combines real agreement with a degree of qualification (e.g., Cranfield; Dunn; Wilckens; Käsemann).

44. τῇ ἀπιστίᾳ is a causal dative; see BDF 196(1); Käsemann.

45. τῇ πίστει might also be causal, but since it relates to the Gentile Christian's continuing relationship to God, it is probably instrumental (R. Bultmann, *TDNT* VI, 218; Dunn).

46. Gk. ἕστηκας. Paul elsewhere uses this verb to express one's spiritual status; see esp. Rom. 5:2; 1 Cor. 7:37; 10:12; 15:1; 2 Cor. 1:24. The perfect form may suggest that one's status is the result of a prior act (e.g., Dunn), but it may simply accentuate the present state one is in.

47. See esp. Dunn.

48. Gk. ὑψηλὰ φρόνει, lit. "think high thoughts." The expression can have a positive meaning — dwell on lofty concepts — but is used by Paul in Rom. 12:16 with a negative nuance — think too highly of oneself (cf. also ὑψηλοφρονεῖν in 1 Tim. 6:17).

to live out of the grace of God in our lives (see esp. Phil 2:12; also 2 Cor. 5:1; 7:1, 11, 15; Col. 3:22).

21 Paul now explains[49] why the Gentile Christian should fear: "if God did not spare the natural branches, neither will he spare you." A failure to continue in faith — thus a failure to display an appropriate "fear" of God — has led to judgment[50] for many Jews. And if God so judged Jews, who had a natural connection to the tree and its sustaining root, he will surely judge those who have been grafted in as alien branches.

22 In this verse, Paul states in more theological language an implication[51] that picks up a number of points he has made in vv. 17-21. His emphasis on God's "goodness"[52] makes clear that the representative Gentile Christian Paul addresses has been "grafted into" God's people (vv. 17 and 19) and thus "stands" (v. 20) in faith through God's gracious initiative. The reference to God's "severity," on the other hand, reinforces the note of condemnation found in the "not spared" of v. 21.[53] By denoting those upon whom God's severity is visited as "those who have fallen," Paul draws our attention back to an even earlier verse (v. 11).[54] But Paul's main purpose in this verse appears at its end: to repeat his warning to the Gentile believer who may (like the Jew; cf. 2:4-5) presume on God's goodness. For the goodness of God is not simply a past act or automatic benefit on which the believer can rest secure; it is also a continuing relationship in which the believer must remain. "Otherwise"[55] — that is, if[56] the believer does not continue in the goodness of God — the believer will, like the Jew, be "cut off" — severed

49. Cf. the γάρ, "for."

50. "Not sparing" seems to have this meaning here, as the parallel warning to the Gentiles suggests; cf. also the same construction (οὐ with φείδομαι) in 2 Pet. 2:4, 5. Hays (p. 61) suggests that Paul may "echo" his earlier reference to God "not sparing" his own Son (8:32): Israel, like Christ, undergoes punishment vicariously for the world (see the argument of vv. 11-15). But the allusion seems forced.

51. Note the οὖν, "therefore."

52. Gk. χρηστότης. See the notes on 2:4.

53. The word ἀποτομία occurs only here in biblical Greek, but Paul uses its cognate ἀποτόμως ("severely") to qualify the chastisement meted out by Christian ministers in 2 Cor. 13:10 and Tit. 1:13. The most important influence on Paul's use of the word here may be *Wisdom of Solomon,* in which both ἀποτόμως and another cognate, ἀπότομος ("severe"), are used to describe the nature of God's judgment (5:20, 22; 6:5; 11:10; 12:9; 18:15).

54. Paul may use "fall" (πίπτω) here because it forms a natural contrast with "stand" (ἵστημι); see 14:4 and 1 Cor. 10:12.

55. Gk. ἐπεί; for this meaning, see Turner, 318.

56. When speaking of events in the past tense (vv. 17, 21, and 24), Paul appropriately uses the "simple" conditional construction (εἰ with indicative); both here and in v. 23, referring to a future contingency, he uses ἐάν with the subjunctive. (Note, however, the simple condition in v. 18b.)

forever from the people of God and eternally condemned. In issuing this warning, Paul echoes a consistent NT theme: ultimate salvation is dependent on continuing faith; therefore, the person who ceases to believe forfeits any hope of salvation (cf. also Rom. 8:13; Col. 1:23; Heb. 3:6, 14).[57]

23 Paul has stressed God's equal treatment of both Jew and Gentile in judgment: just as Jews who do not believe are "cut off," so Gentiles who do not continue in God's goodness will be "cut off." In vv. 23-24, he uses this same principle of equal treatment positively to offer hope for the eventual spiritual renewal of Jews. "Those also"[58] can be grafted back into the olive tree "if they do not persist in their lack of faith." In speaking of such a regrafting, Paul again reveals how little he is concerned to stick to the details of actual olive cultivation in his metaphor. It is not the logic of nature that explains this regrafting, but the *theo*logic of the God who "gives life to the dead and calls things that do not exist as if they did" (4:17; cf. also *dynatos* in v. 21); the "power of God" that is work in the gospel (1:16).[59] Paul's stress on God's ability here may seem redundant; but he is probably thinking of the attitude of certain Gentile Christians who might question the appropriateness of God extending his grace to those who had already been cast off.[60]

24 Even though Paul has stretched the limits of his metaphor to the breaking point, he continues to exploit it to give further reason[61] for God's ability to restore Jews who turn from unbelief to belief. Paul utilizes the familiar "how much more" argument. He reminds Gentile Christians that

---

57. Does this then mean that a genuine Christian can lose his faith and thus be eternally condemned? Certainly it is possible to infer this from Paul's warning. But it is no necessary inference. For there is clearly an element of phenomenology in the metaphor that Paul uses throughout these verses. While the olive tree represents the true, spiritual people of God, those who are said to belong to this tree are not only those who, through their faith, are actually part of the tree but also those who only appear to belong to that tree. This is evident from the fact that Paul speaks of unbelieving Jews as having been "cut off" from the tree (v. 17). In reality, these Jews had never been part of the tree at all; yet to preserve the metaphor he is using, Paul presents them as if they had been. In the same way, then, those Gentiles within the church at Rome — and elsewhere — who appear to be part of God's people, yet do not continue in faith, may never have been part of that tree at all. See, for this general approach, Calvin. Other commentators deny any implications for the doctrine of the perseverance of the saints by arguing that Paul's warning is directed to the Gentiles as a people rather than to individuals (cf. Hodge; Godet). Volf, on the other hand, claims that the threat of being "cut off" need not be God's final word on the individual — just as Jews who are cut off may be grafted in again (cf. v. 17 and vv. 23-24), so Gentiles who are cut off may be grafted in again (*Paul and Perseverance*, pp. 198-99).

58. Gk. κἀκεῖνοι δέ — marking an emphatic subject change.

59. See Fitzmyer.

60. Murray.

61. Cf. the γάρ, "for."

they, who belong to a wild olive tree[62] by nature,[63] have been cut off from that tree and grafted into the cultivated olive tree (cf. v. 17).[64] Now if God can so graft branches into the cultivated olive tree that do not naturally belong to it,[65] he is certainly able to graft back into this tree those branches who do belong to that tree by nature — the Jews. For it is, after all, "their own"[66] tree.

We must allow for Paul's hortatory purpose in evaluating this "how much more" argument. For just as Paul dwelt on Jewish sin in chap. 2 to counter Jewish boasting over Gentiles, so he now accentuates Jewish advantages to counter Gentile boasting over Jews. Paul does not mean that it is easier to save a Jew than a Gentile or that the Jew, by reason of being a Jew, can make any claim on God; for this would be to give the Jew an "advantage" in salvation that Paul has plainly denied (see chap. 2). Every person, Jew or Gentile, stands under sin's power (3:9) and can be saved only by a special act of God's grace. Just like Gentiles, Jews can be saved only if they are grafted by God into the tree. But even when cut off from the parent tree because of unbelief, they retain the stamp of their origin. They belong to that people which God has chosen, through which he has manifested himself to the world, and to which he remains committed (11:1-2). Their quality as "natural branches" does not itself qualify them for grafting onto the tree. But, as branches that trace their origin to a "holy" root (v. 16), their regrafting is easier to understand than the grafting in of those alien, wild olive branches.

Paul skillfully mixes theology and exhortation in this paragraph. His olive tree metaphor makes an important contribution to our understanding of the people of God. It is notoriously easy to squeeze more theology out of such a metaphor

---

62. ἀγριέλαιος. In v. 17, this word may be used as an adjective; here it is clearly a substantive (BAGD).

63. Gk. ἐκ τῆς κατὰ φύσιν ἐξεκόπης ἀγριελαίου. The sequence of words is confusing. ἐξεκόπης, a masculine singular aorist passive participle, is exepegetic of σύ, "you." ἐκ τῆς ἀγριελαίου (a feminine noun) describe that from which the branch (the word is assumed) has been cut. Differences arise, however, over the way κατὰ φύσιν fits into this sequence. Many translations (e.g., NRSV: "what is by nature a wild olive tree"; cf. also NIV; NASB) and commentators (e.g., Käsemann; Barrett) take it to modify ἀγριελαίου. But Cranfield's objection that it is tautologous to call a wild olive tree wild "by nature" is justified; it is better to take as modifying the way in which the "cut-off branch" belongs to the tree (cf. also Dunn).

64. καλλιέλαιον. This cultivated olive tree is contrasted with the wild olive tree as early as Aristotle, *Plant.* 1.6, p. 820b, 40 (BAGD).

65. Gk. παρὰ φύσιν. Paul's contrast is therefore straightforward: Gentiles are like branches that belonged "by nature" to a wild olive tree but that have now been grafted, "against nature," into a cultivated olive tree.

66. Gk. ἴδιος.

than it is intended to convey. But basic to the whole metaphor is the unity of God's people, a unity that crosses both historical and ethnic boundaries. The basic point of the metaphor is that there is only one olive tree, whose roots are firmly planted in OT soil, and whose branches include both Jews and Gentiles. This olive tree represents the true people of God.[67] The turn of the ages at the coming of Christ brought an important development in the people of God: the object of one's faith became clearer and more specific and the ethnic makeup of that people changed radically, as God extended his grace in vastly increased measure to Gentiles.[68] But Paul's metaphor warns us not to view this transition as a transition from one people of God to another. Gentiles who come to Christ become part of that community of salvation founded on God's promises to the patriarchs. And "messianic Jews," following in the footsteps of their believing ancestors, belong to this same community.

The picture Paul sketches reveals the danger of the simple and popular notion that the church has "replaced" Israel. For this formula misses the stress Paul places on historical continuity in the people of God. Paul suggests that the church, defined as the entire body of believers in Jesus Christ, is simply the name for the people of God in this era of salvation history — as "Israel" was the name of that people in the previous age. To be sure, the dual nature of OT Israel — both spiritual and national — complicates the matter, but in neither sense does the church simply "replace" Israel. As a spiritual entity, Israel is organically connected to the church; and as a national entity, as Paul has made clear (11:1-2), Israel continues to exist as the object of God's care and attention. Perhaps a better word to describe the movement from OT Israel to NT church is the same word that the NT so often uses to denote such relationships: "fulfillment."[69] We thereby capture the necessary note of continuity — the church is the continuation of Israel into the new age — and discontinuity — the church, not Israel, is now the locus of God's work in the world.

---

67. See, e.g., Bourke, *The Metaphor of the Olive Tree,* p. 79 (who also gives history of interpretation, pp. 84-103); Hofius, " 'All Israel Will Be Saved,' " p. 32; Fitzmyer; W. D. Davies, "Paul and the People of Israel," *NTS* 24 (1977-78), 31.

68. Davies puts it well: "The advent of the Messiah, therefore, raised acutely the question of the constitution of the people of God: is it made up of those who have faith in the Messiah or those who observe the tradition? Paul redefined the Law and Israel in terms of Jesus the Messiah. The Messiahship of Jesus is the point of departure for Paulinism, and the inevitable accompaniment, the criticism of the Law, its method. But its concern, outcome and end became — it might well be argued, from the beginning — the redefinition of the true nature of the people of God" ("Paul and the People of Israel," p. 5).

69. See the similar proposals of Hagner — the church is the "true Israel, if not the new Israel" ("Paul and Judaism," p. 123) — and B. Witherington III (*Jesus, Paul and the End of the World: A Comparative Study in New Testament Eschatology* [Downers Grove: InterVarsity, 1992], pp. 117-28).

What is particularly pernicious in the "replacement" model is the assumption so easily made that "church" = Gentiles. This assumption was apparently beginning to be made by Paul's contemporaries. And it has certainly been embraced by many Christians throughout history, contributing (albeit often inadvertently) to the anti-Semitism that has too often stained the name of Christ.[70] To be sure, the gospel, with its exclusive claim about salvation, is unavoidably a "stumbling block" to Jews. The NT can justly be said, therefore, to be "anti-Judaic," in the sense that its claims leave no room for the claims of "Judaism" to mediate salvation through torah. But the NT is *not* "anti-Semitic," that is, hostile to Jews as such.[71] We must remember that, for Paul, the church was both rooted in the Jews and heavily populated by Jews. The coming of Christ did not for him involve ethnic subtraction, as if Jews were now eliminated, but addition, with Gentiles now being added to believing Jews. Paul's boundary for the people of God is a religious one — faith in Jesus Christ — not an ethnic one. We must not become so focused on the theology of Paul's teaching here that we miss its purpose: to criticize those of us who are Gentiles for arrogance toward believing and unbelieving Jews and to remind us that our own spiritual heritage is a Jewish one.

3. The Salvation of "All Israel" (11:25-32)

25*For I do not want you to be ignorant, brothers and sisters, about this mystery, in order that you might not be wise in your own estima-*

---

70. The significance of Paul's teaching for this matter is correctly emphasized by van Buren: "Whether the church understood Paul is therefore a question central to the church's reconsideration of its relationship to the Jewish people" (*A Theology of the Jewish-Christian Reality,* 1.277).

71. See particularly D. A. Hagner, "Paul's Quarrel with Judaism," in *Anti-Semitism and Early Christianity: Issues of Polemic and Faith* (ed. C. A. Evans and D. A. Hagner; Minneapolis: Fortress, 1993), pp. 128-50. This distinction is a vital one. For R. R. Ruether (*Faith and Fratricide: The Theological Roots of Anti-Semitism* [New York: Seabury, 1974]) and others have argued that the exclusive christological claims advanced by the NT make Christianity unavoidably "anti-Semitic"; only by jettisoning traditional Christianity can we therefore avoid anti-Semitism. As Hagner and others point out, such a line of argument confuses anti-Semitism (race hatred) with anti-"Judaism" (denial of Judaism's claims to mediate salvation). In fact, it is anachronistic to speak of Paul's "anti-Judaism," for the very nature and definition of Judaism were still being debated in Paul's day (see J. D. G. Dunn, *The Parting of the Ways between Christianity and Judaism and Their Significance for the Character of Christianity* [London: SCM, 1991], pp. 143-61). One must speak in a more limited way of Paul's anti-"one variety of Judaism" (see also Hagner, "Paul's Quarrel," pp. 128-29). For general discussions of the history of Jewish-Christian interaction, see H.-J. Schoeps, *The Jewish-Christian Argument: A History of Theologies in Conflict* (3d ed.; New York: Holt, Rinehart and Winston, 1963); Jocz, *Jewish People.*

tion[1]: *that a hardening has come partially on Israel until the fullness of the Gentiles comes in. 26And in this way all Israel will be saved, just as it is written:*

The deliverer will come from Zion
    to turn away ungodliness from Jacob;
27and this is my covenant with them,
    when I remove their sins.[a]

28*According to the gospel the Jews are enemies on your behalf, but according to election they are beloved because of the fathers. 29For the gifts and the call of God are irrevocable. 30For just as you at one time disobeyed God and now have received mercy because of their disobedience, 31so also they have disobeyed for the sake of mercy for you in order that they also might now[2] receive mercy. 32For God has shut up all[3] to disobedience in order that he might have mercy on all.*

a. Isa. 59:20-21; 27:9

1. NA[27] and UBS[4] tentatively adopt the reading παρ' ἑαυτοῖς, "before themselves," "in the judgment of themselves," which has some Alexandrian support (ℵ, C, 33, and 81), some western support (D), and the support of the majority text. Two other readings are found in the MS tradition: ἐν ἑαυτοῖς (some Alexandrian support [B and A]; cf. also several minuscules); and simply ἑαυτοῖς (the early papyrus P[46], the Alexandrian 1739, Ψ, and the later western uncials F and G). Several commentators support the reading ἐν ἑαυτοῖς, arguing that παρά was introduced by assimilation to 12:16 (Meyer, 2.198; S-H, 334; Godet, 410; Wilckens, 2.252), while others prefer the simple ἑαυτοῖς (Michel, 354 n. 5; Cranfield, 2.574 n. 2). We are inclined to accept this last alternative, the "shorter reading," although the meaning is very little affected by our decision.

2. NA[27] and UBS[4] tentatively include νῦν, "now," following the potent combination of the primary Alexandrian uncials ℵ and B and a part of the western tradition (the original hand and third corrector of D). In this they are followed by most of the commentators (Käsemann, 316; Cranfield, 2.585; Michel, 358; S-H, 338; Fitzmyer, 628; Schlier, 343; Morris, 425; Barrett, 226). Other commentators (e.g., Godet, 415; Meyer, 1.198; Wilckens, 2.261-62) prefer to omit the word, a variant with equally strong support: the early papyrus P[46], the Alexandrian MSS A, 81, and 1739, the first corrector of D, the secondary western uncials F and G, Ψ, and the majority text. (Receiving little modern support is the reading ὕστερον, found only in a number of minuscules.) The former reading has strong early attestation, fits neatly into Paul's balanced sentence, and is — at least superficially — the "most difficult." On the other hand, the balanced structure achieved when the word appears may have been precisely the reason why a scribe added it. On the whole, however, the arguments in favor of inclusion slightly outweigh those for omitting it.

3. A few MSS (the early papyrus P[46vid], the original hand of the western uncial D, and the later western uncials F and G) read the neuter τὰ πάντα (F and G omit the article) in place of the masculine τοὺς πάντας. But this alternative lacks solid MS support and is suspect as an assimilation to the wording of Gal. 3:22.

In these verses Paul brings the argument of vv. 11ff. to its climax. This argument comes in response to the notion that Israel had "stumbled" so as to "fall" irretrievably (v. 11). Not so, Paul has contended. For Israel's "stumble" has been but the first act in an unfolding salvation-historical drama. In this drama Israel and the Gentiles take turns on center stage. Israel, the focus of salvation history throughout the OT, has now, as a result of the gospel, given place to the Gentiles: because of Israel's "trespass," salvation has come to the Gentiles (vv. 11), and God's riches and the blessing of reconciliation have come to the world (vv. 12, 15). But the Gentiles will, in turn, be replaced in the limelight by Israel, as her "defeat" gives way to her "fullness" (v. 12), her rejection to acceptance (v. 15). The Jews, like branches that retain the qualities of the tree from which they were cut, can be grafted back in again (vv. 16-24).

In vv. 25-32 Paul rehearses this salvation-historical drama for a final time.[4] But he draws our special attention to this restatement by introducing it as a "mystery." And, in contrast to his earlier sketches of the drama of God's work with the Gentiles and Israel, he now focuses especially on the last act of the drama, the heart of the mystery: the restoration of Israel. "And in this way all Israel will be saved" (v. 26a) is the center of this paragraph. Verse 25 stresses the temporal limits on the present situation to explain *how* "all Israel will be saved": in a final act *after* the hardening of Israel is removed and the destined number of Gentiles enter the kingdom. Verses 26b-32 back up Paul's climactic prediction about Israel's salvation by showing that (1) it is confirmed by Scripture (vv. 26b-27); (2) it is rooted in God's unswerving faithfulness to his promise and his election (vv. 28-29); and (3) it manifests God's impartiality to all people, as the capstone of the drama of salvation history (vv. 30-32).

But 11:25-32 is not only the climax of 11:11-32; it is also the climax to all of Rom. 9–11.[5] This is revealed particularly in the themes that Paul develops in vv. 28-32. Here we find juxtaposed the two apparently conflicting factors that give rise to the argument of these chapters: Israel's current hostile relationship with God (v. 28a; cf. 9:1-3) and God's expressed and irrevocable

---

4. The similarity between the sequence Paul has sketched in vv. 11-24 and what he describes in vv. 25-27 should, along with the lack of any textual evidence whatsoever, more than suffice to show how misguided is the attempt of C. Plag to find in these verses a later addition to the letter (*Israels Weg zum Heil. Eine Untersuchung zu Römer 9 bis 11* [Arbeiten zur Theologie 1.40; Stuttgart: Calwer, 1969], pp. 41-66; contra Plag, see P. Stuhlmacher, "Zur Interpretation von Römer 11.25-32," in *Probleme biblischer Theologie: Gerhard von Rad zum 70. Geburtstag* [ed. H. W. Wolff; Munich: Kaiser, 1971], p. 562; Wilckens 2.252). Nor is there sufficient evidence to show that Paul is quoting an earlier "oracle" (contra, e.g., Schmithals, 402-3).

5. See, e.g., Aletti, *Comment Dieu est-il juste?* p. 183.

promises to Israel (v. 28b; cf. 9:4-5; 11:1-2).[6] Paul suggests that the resolution of this tension is to be found in a divinely given insight ("mystery") into the way in which God's purposes are working themselves out in salvation history. Israel's present hostility toward God, manifested in her general refusal of the gospel (cf. 9:30–10:21), is itself part of God's plan, for it is the result of God's act of hardening ("hardening has come" in v. 25b; cf. 11:7b-10; 9:17-18). But this hardening is both limited ("partially" in v. 25b; cf. 11:3-7) and temporary ("until" in v. 25b), designed both to allow Gentiles to "come in" (vv. 25b, 30; cf. 11:11-15) and to stimulate Israel herself to repentance (v. 31; cf. 11:11). It is by means of this salvation-historical process that God's faithfulness to his promises to Israel is manifested. That faithfulness presently takes the form of a preservation of a remnant (11:3-6). But in the future God's unwavering commitment to Israel will be spectacularly revealed in the salvation of the nation as a whole (v. 26a). At the same time, Paul suggests, this salvation of Israel in the last days will vindicate God's impartiality (v. 32). For Israel's present hardening could suggest an imbalance in God's treatment of ethnic groups, as if he preferred Gentiles to Jews. The last day, however, will reveal that God has treated all equally: "imprisoning" all in disobedience — Gentiles before Christ; Jews since Christ's coming — so that he could have mercy on all — Gentiles in the present age; Jews (making up for their small numbers now), in great numbers at the end of the age.[7]

This profound theological mystery has a specific practical purpose. Paul continues to address the Gentile Christians in Rome in these verses (he uses the second person plural throughout [vv. 25, 28, 30-31]; cf. v. 13). And he leaves no doubt about what he wants his readers to learn from this mystery: to stop thinking so highly of themselves in comparison with Jews (v. 25a). We who are Gentiles should likewise take these verses as a reminder that we are only part of the great salvation-historical plan of God and that that plan has its climax in the salvation of Israel.

25 The "for"[8] at the beginning of this verse ties vv. 25-32 to v. 24: hope that natural branches will be grafted in again is well founded, *for* Paul

---

6. 11:28 thus duplicates the tension Paul has hinted at in 9:1-5. These texts form an inclusio, framing the argument of chaps. 9–11.

7. Beker therefore emphasizes the way in which 11:25-32 bring to a climax the argument of the letter as a whole: ". . . the total sweep of the argument of Romans is held together by the theme of the peculiar interaction between Israel's particularity and the universality of the gospel for the Gentiles" (cf. the "for all who believe" and "for the Jew first" in 1:16) ("The Faithfulness of God and the Priority of Israel in Paul's Letter to the Romans," *HTR* 79 [1986], 14; cf. also idem, "Romans 9–11 in the Context of the Early Church," *The Princeton Seminary Bulletin,* Supplemental Issue 1 [1990], 44-45; Dunn, 2.677).

8. Gk. γάρ.

has been given the knowledge of the mystery that. . . .[9] But since the hope expressed in v. 24 is a theme that pervades vv. 11-24, this "for" ultimately connects vv. 25-32 with the whole preceding argument.[10] Paul draws attention to the importance of the mystery he is about to reveal with the formula "I do not want you to be ignorant, brothers and sisters."[11] Paul uses the word "mystery" with a technical theological meaning derived from Jewish apocalyptic. In these writings "mystery" usually refers to an event of the end times that has already been determined by God — and so, in that sense, exists already in heaven — but which is first revealed to the apocalyptic seer for the comfort and encouragement of the people of Israel.[12] Paul also speaks of a mystery as something that had been "hidden" from God's people in the past but had now been revealed in the gospel.[13] Usually the mystery involves an event or insight associated with Christ's coming and the preaching of the gospel, but here and in 1 Cor. 15:51 it refers to an event at the end of history.

Considering Paul's other uses of the term "mystery," we are justified in thinking that Paul here assumes the notion of revelation: "I do not want you to be ignorant, brothers and sisters, about this mystery *that has been revealed to me*. . . ." How was this mystery revealed to Paul? Some scholars,

9. Stuart; Meyer.

10. See, e.g., Cranfield; Dunn.

11. See the note on 1:13.

12. This definition is a loose paraphrase of Wilckens's excellent summary (2.253). This use of the word "mystery" is found first in Daniel (2:17-18, 27-30, 47; the Aramaic word is רָז), with reference to the content of the dreams of King Nebuchadnezzar. It is expressly said in this context that "the God of Heaven" is the revealer of these mysteries (v. 28). A typical example of the word in Jewish apocalyptic comes in *T. Levi* 2:10: "And when you [Levi, being addressed by an angel] have mounted up there [to "another heaven"], you shall stand near the Lord. You shall be his priest and you shall tell forth his mysteries to men. You shall announce the one who is about to redeem Israel." See also, e.g., 4 Ezra 10:38; 12:36-38; 14:5; *1 Enoch* 9:6; 41:1; 46:2; 103:2; 104:10, 12; 106:19; *2 Apoc. Bar.* 48:3; 81:4; *T. Jud.* 16:4; 1QS 3:23; 4:18; 9:18; 11:3, 5, 19; 1QH 1:21; 2:13; 4:27-28; 7:27; 11:10; 12:13; 1QpHab 7:5, 8, 14; and the survey in G. Bornkamm, *TDNT* IV, 813-17). The term μυστήριον was a very significant one in Hellenistic religion (cf. the "mystery" religions), but Paul's use of the term is rooted in the OT and Judaism (see esp. R. E. Brown, *The Semitic Background of the Term "Mystery" in the New Testament* [FBBS 12; Philadelphia: Fortress, 1968]; J. Coppens, " 'Mystery' in the Theology of Saint Paul and Its Parallels at Qumran," in *Paul and the Dead Sea Scrolls* [ed. J. Murphy-O'Connor; New York: Crossroad, 1990], pp. 132-58). Demurring, however, from the parallel between 11:25 and Jewish apocalyptic is Sänger, "Rettung der Heiden und Erwählung Israels," pp. 107-15.

13. Rom. 16:25 [v.l.]; 1 Cor. 2:1, 7; 4:1; 15:51; Eph. 1:9; 3:3, 4, 9; 6:19; Col. 1:26, 27; 2:2; 4:3; 1 Tim. 3:9, 16. Paul also uses the word in 1 Cor. 13:2; 14:2; Eph. 5:32; and 2 Thess. 2:7, but without the clear technical sense of these other occurrences. See also Matt. 13:11 = Mark 4:11 = Luke 8:10; Rev. 1:20; 10:7; 17:5, 7.

particularly those who find a tension between the teaching about Israel in 11:25-32 and the earlier parts of Rom. 9–11, suggest that Paul received a prophetic insight into this matter as he wrote these chapters.[14] But this view assumes more tension in Paul's argument in these chapters than is warranted. Better is the suggestion that Paul came to understand this mystery through study of the OT in light of the gospel.[15] But, while meditation on the OT was probably an important source for Paul's understanding, as the OT quotation in vv. 26b-27 suggests, the apocalyptic flavor of the word "mystery" points to the involvement of a special divine revelation as well.[16]

Paul interrupts his discussion of this mystery with a reminder to his readers that his purpose is ultimately a very practical one. He divulges this mystery, he says, "in order that you might not be wise in your own estimation."[17] As vv. 17-21 show, Paul's concern is with Gentile Christians who are boasting over Jews and Jewish Christians because of their assumption that they — the Gentiles — had ousted the Jews as the focus of God's purposes in history. "Wise in your own estimation," then, will refer not to a sense of superiority engendered by spiritual giftedness or accomplishments,[18] but to an attitude of ethnic pride and exclusiveness.[19]

Paul now returns to the "mystery," using a *hoti* ("that") clause to specify its contents. This clause runs through the end of v. 25, but it is not

---

14. Noack, "Current and Backwater," pp. 165-66; for the idea of prophetic insight, see also D. Zeller, "Christus, Skandal und Hoffnung. Die Juden in den Briefen des Paulus," in *Gottesverächter und Menschenfeinde?* (ed. H. Goldstein Horst; Düsseldorf: Patmos, 1979), pp. 272-73; U. B. Müller, *Prophetie und Predigt im Neuen Testament: Form-geschichtliche Untersuchungen zur urchristlichen Prophetie* (SzNT 10; Gütersloh: Gerd Mohn, 1975), pp. 225-32.

15. E.g., Hübner, *Gottes Ich und Israel,* pp. 113, 121 (he cites Isa. 45:25); O. Betz, "Die heilsgeschichtliche Rolle Israels bei Paulus," *TBei* 9 (1978), 20 (he cites Isa. 6:1-13); Hofius, " 'All Israel Will Be Saved,' " p. 38; Cranfield; Stuhlmacher.

16. Hübner, *Gottes Ich und Israel,* pp. 120-21; Dunn; Wilckens. Paul is similar to apocalyptic Jewish traditions on another point as well: he, like them, is granted a revelation into God's plan for the people of Israel in response to a struggle to understand the meaning of Israel's present weakness and suffering (see Johnson, *Function,* pp. 124-25; Müller, *Prophetie,* pp. 225-32; Dunn, 2.678-79).

17. If, as I have suggested (see the note on the translation), we read here simply the dative ἑαυτοῖς, it will have the sense "before yourselves," "in your own estimation" (the third person plural reflexive pronoun being used, as usually in the NT, for the second person; cf. Z-G, 485). If ἐν or παρά is added, however, the meaning will be the same (see BAGD on παρά). Paul may be alluding to Prov. 3:7: "Do not be wise in your own eyes [μὴ ἴσθι φρόνιμος παρὰ σεαυτῷ]; fear the Lord, and turn away from evil" (cf., e.g., Bruce; Käsemann; Dunn; Schlier).

18. Contra, e.g., Michel and Käsemann, who find allusion here again to "pneumatics."

19. Cf. Wilckens.

clear whether it includes the first part of v. 26 or not.[20] This question is somewhat moot, however, since "in this way" at the beginning of v. 26 shows that v. 26a is closely related to v. 25b. Paul, then, describes the mystery in three separate clauses:

1. "a hardening has come partly on Israel"
2. "until the fullness of the Gentiles comes in"
3. "[A]nd in this way all Israel will be saved"

What is not clear is the relative weight to be assigned to these clauses. Or, in other words, what is the real "core" of the mystery? The fact of Israel's hardening?[21] The fact that Israel's hardening is only partial and temporary?[22] The fact that "all Israel will be saved"?[23] Or some combination of these?[24] An important clue in answering this question is the sense of something new in Paul's argument that his use of the word "mystery" suggests. This consideration would seem to rule out the fact of Israel's hardening since Paul had plainly taught it earlier (11:7b-10). It also suggests that the focal point of the mystery is not the salvation of all Israel since this was an expectation widely held among Jews in Paul's day. What stands out in vv. 25b-26a, what Paul has not yet explicitly taught, and what entails a reversal in current Jewish belief, is the sequence by which "all Israel" will be saved: Israel hardened *until* the Gentiles come in and *in this way* all Israel being saved.[25] Some OT and Jewish texts predict that Gentiles will join the worship of the Lord in the last day; and some of them suggest that it is the Lord's glory revealed in a rejuvenated and regathered Israel that will stimulate the Gentiles' interest.[26] But wholly novel was the idea that the inauguration of the eschatological age would involve setting aside the majority of Jews while

---

20. Several commentators insist on both grammatical and contextual grounds that v. 26 begins a new sentence (S-H; Meyer; Denney; Kuss; cf. also KJV; NRSV; NIV; TEV), but most commentators (cf. most clearly Cranfield and NA[27]; UBS[4]; RSV; NASB; REB) connect it with v. 25b. See the survey of possibilities in Refoulé, *Tout Israël*, pp. 31-32.

21. E.g., Hahn, "Römer 11.26a," p. 224.

22. Kuss; Murray; Schlier.

23. Michel; Cranfield.

24. Some (e.g., Godet; Fitzmyer; Hofius, "Das Evangelium und Israel," p. 311; Wilckens) simply note these three parts without distinguishing among them. C. Cooper, on the other hand, thinks the mystery is that Israel can be saved in the same way that Gentiles are ("Romans 11:25, 26," *RestQ* 21 [1978], 84-94).

25. See, for this general approach, Wilckens; Beker, 333-35; Lübking, *Paulus und Israel*, p. 123; Refoulé, *Tout Israël*, pp. 71-73.

26. For this so-called "eschatological pilgrimage motif," see the note at the introductory material to 11:11-32.

Gentiles streamed in to enjoy the blessings of salvation and that only when that stream had been exhausted would Israel as a whole experience these blessings.

Turning to the individual stages of the mystery, we find Paul reaffirming his interpretation of Israel's present obduracy in terms of divine hardening.[27] But he also reminds us of God's continued faithfulness in preserving a remnant by indicating that the hardening has come only "partially"[28] on Israel. And not only is Israel's hardening partial — it is also temporary. For, Paul reveals, Israel's hardening will last only "until the fullness of the Gentiles comes in." Indeed, some scholars have questioned whether Paul implies any change in Israel's condition of hardening, it being suggested that Paul is teaching only that Israel's hardening will continue "right up to" the last day. No removal of that hardening is then envisaged.[29] The Greek construction Paul uses could mean this, but it more naturally suggests a reversal of the present situation: Israel's partial hardening will last only *until* the fullness of the Gentiles comes in — and then it will be removed.[30] But decisive for this interpretation is the context, for Paul has

---

27. Gk. πώρωσις; cf. the cognate verb πωρόω in v. 7 and the note there.

28. The Greek phrase is ἀπὸ μέρους, "in part" (BAGD). There has been considerable debate over whether this phrase is adjectival, modifying Ἰσραήλ — "hardening has come on part of Israel" (Barrett; Käsemann), or adverbial, modifying either the verbal concept present in πώρωσις — "a partial hardening has come on Israel" (Dunn) — or γέγονεν — "a hardening has come partially on Israel" (Godet; Michel; Schlier). The last of the alternatives is most likely syntactically (ἀπὸ μέρους is adverbial in its four other Pauline occurrences [Rom. 15:15, 24; 2 Cor. 1:14; 2:5]), but the difference in meaning is not great. However we take the syntax, it is clear that Paul is placing a numerical limitation on Israel's hardening (cf. Wilckens; Hofius, "Das Evangelium und Israel," p. 312).

29. E.g., Calvin; Lenski; M. H. Woudstra, "Israel and the Church: A Case for Continuity," in *Continuity and Discontinuity,* p. 236; H. Ponsot, "Et ainsi tout Israel sera sauvé: Rom., XI,26a," *RB* 89 (1982), 412-13. Cf. also Wright, who argues that hardening in apocalyptic literature always has judgment as its object; therefore, we should expect Paul's "until" to mean that Israel will remain hardened in part until she passes into the judgment (*Climax of the Covenant,* p. 249).

30. The preposition ἄχρι occurs 48 times in the NT (the relative pronoun ᾧ following it is short for τοῦ χρόνου ᾧ). Eleven do not fall to consideration here because they involve a spatial rather than a temporal concept. Of the 37 remaining occurrences, 25 rather clearly denote a period of time that will come to an end and be followed by a change of those circumstances denoted (Luke 1:20; 4:13; Acts 1:12; 3:21; 7:18; 13:11; 20:6, 11; 22:22; 27:33; Rom. 1:13; 1 Cor. 11:26; 15:25; Gal. 3:19; 4:2; Phil. 1:6; Heb. 3:13; 6:11; Rev. 2:25, 26; 7:3; 15:8; 17:17; 20:3, 5). Significantly, 14 of these are followed by an aorist verb (as in Rom. 11:25), while only two of ten occurrences of ἄχρι where it means "right up to" use the aorist (Matt. 24:38 = Luke 17:27; cf. also Acts 2:29; 23:1; 26:22; Rom. 5:13; 8:23; 1 Cor. 4:11; 2 Cor. 3:14; Phil. 1:5).

throughout vv. 11-24 implied that Israel would one day experience a spiritual rejuvenation that would extend far beyond the present bounds of the remnant ("their fullness" contrasted with "their defeat" in v. 12; "their acceptance" contrasted with "their rejection" in v. 15; the "holiness" of even the broken-off branches in v. 16; the hope that these branches might be grafted in again in v. 24).[31]

The temporal limit of Israel's hardening is the "coming in" of the "fullness of the Gentiles." "Coming in" probably refers to entrance into the kingdom of God, the present messianic salvation.[32] "Fullness of the Gentiles" is harder to decipher. As we noted in discussing the term "fullness"[33] in v. 12, the word consistently has a qualitative meaning in the Bible — "fulfillment," "completion," "fullness." Some scholars therefore think that "fullness of the Gentiles" means simply the "full blessing" that God intends to bestow on the Gentiles,[34] or perhaps the "completion" of the Gentile mission.[35] But the imagery of "coming in" does not fit this concept very well. Furthermore, Paul is probably borrowing here another concept from

31. So most commentators. See, e.g., Godet; Murray; Cranfield.

32. Paul's use of εἰσέρχομαι here appears to be modeled on the frequent use of this verb in the Gospels to denote entrance into the kingdom or into eternal life; see especially the absolute uses of the verb in Matt. 7:13; Luke 13:24; 23:13 (e.g., S-H; Murray; Dunn). Some scholars argue that the verb reflects the "eschatological pilgrimage motif," according to which Gentiles would in the last days "enter into" Jerusalem (cf. Stuhlmann, *Eschatologische Maß*, pp. 166-67; R. D. Aus, "Paul's Travel Plans to Spain and the 'Full Number of the Gentiles' of Rom. XI 25," *NovT* 21 [1979], 251-52; Dunn; Wilckens). A few scholars suggest, in analogy to the language used at Qumran, that Paul might be referring to the idea of "entering into" the covenant community of Israel (following the imagery of vv. 17-24; cf. Hofius, "Das Evangelium und Israel," p. 313; Refoulé, *Tout Israël*, pp. 82-83).

33. Gk. πλήρωμα.

34. See esp. Murray; note his interpretation of v. 12.

35. Advocates of this interpretation point especially to 15:16-19, where the verb cognate to πλήρωμα, πληρόω, is used with reference to Paul's "fulfillment" of preaching in the eastern Mediterranean (cf. also Col. 1:27). These interpreters think that Paul views his own preaching as the event that will bring to a completion the Gentile mission. Those so converted through this mission are themselves the "offering" (Rom. 15:16) that Paul is bringing to Jerusalem (cf. 15:30-33) in order to fulfill the expectation of an eschatological entry of Gentiles into Jerusalem. Paul, then, sees himself as a central figure in salvation history, whose mission to the Gentiles will usher in the end times. See also Mark 13:10: "And the gospel must first [before 'the end'] be preached to all the nations." (See esp. Munck, 47-51; Aus, "Paul's Travel Plans," pp. 235-37, 260-61; Hübner, *Gottes Ich und Israel*, pp. 112-13.) However, this interpretation goes far beyond the evidence of 15:16-19 and, indeed, misrepresents Paul's teaching there rather seriously (see the notes on those verses). And, as we have seen (see the note on 11:14), Paul himself is much less optimistic about the results of his own ministry than this view would suggest.

Jewish apocalyptic: the idea of a fixed number of people whom God has destined for salvation.[36] These considerations suggest that the Gentiles' "fullness" involves a numerical completion: God has determined to save a certain number of Gentiles, and only when that number has been reached will Israel's hardening be removed.[37] The "fullness of Israel" (v. 12) is therefore matched by a "fullness of the Gentiles." Interpreted along these lines, Paul's brief sketch of salvation history in v. 25b resembles very closely Jesus' prediction of the sequence of events that would follow his death and resurrection:

> For there shall be great distress on the earth and wrath on this people, and they shall fall by the edge of the sword and they shall be taken captive into all nations, and Jerusalem will be trodden down by the Gentiles, until [*achri*] the times of the Gentiles be fulfilled [*plēroō*]. (Luke 21:23b-24)

26a   The first clause of v. 26 is the storm center in the interpretation of Rom. 9–11 and of NT teaching about the Jews and their future. Three issues must be settled: the meaning and reference of *houtōs* ("in this way"); the reference of *pas Israēl* ("all Israel"); and the time and manner of all Israel's salvation *(sōthēsetai)*.

We have four basic options in the interpretation of the word *houtōs*. First, it might have a temporal meaning: "And then [after the events depicted in v. 25b] all Israel will be saved."[38] But Fitzmyer seems to be right: "a

36. See, e.g., 4 Ezra 4:35-37:

> Did not the souls of the righteous in their chambers ask about these matters, saying, "How long are we to remain here? And when will come the harvest of our reward?" And Jeremiel the archangel answered them and said, "When the number of those like yourselves is completed; for he has weighed the age in the balance, and measured the times by measure, and numbered the times by number; and he will not move or arouse them until that measure is fulfilled."

See also Rev. 6:11; 7:4; 14:1; *2 Apoc. Bar.* 23:4; 30:2; 75:6; *Apoc. Abr.* 29:17; cf. J. van Oorschot, *Hoffnung für Israel: Eine Studie zu Römer 11,25-32* (Theologie und Dienst 55; Giessen: Brunnen, 1988), p. 22.

37. The translation "full number" (NRSV; NIV) or "complete number" (TEV), therefore, captures the essence of the idea. For this interpretation see, e.g., Theophylact, who paraphrases "all those foreknown"; cf. also Michel; Kuss; Schlier; Dunn; Refoulé, *Tout Israël*, pp. 83-85. Others give the phrase a numerical meaning but do not think that election comes into the picture: the "full number" are simply a representative number of Gentiles (cf. Godet; Meyer; Leenhardt).

38. Stuart; Barrett; Käsemann; Corley, "The Jews, the Future and God," p. 51. Many other scholars (e.g., Michel; Dunn; Schmitt, *Gottesgerechtigkeit*, p. 111; A. Feuillet, "L'espérance de la 'conversion' d'Israël en Rm 11,25-32: l'interprétation des versets 26 et 31," in *De la Tôrah au Messie* [ed. M. Carrez et al.; Paris: Desclée, 1981], pp. 486-87) find some temporal nuance in the word.

temporal meaning of *houtōs* is not otherwise found in Greek."[39] Second, *houtōs* could introduce a consequence or conclusion: "And in consequence of this process [v. 25b] all Israel will be saved."[40] This use of *houtōs* is attested in Greek and in Paul, but it is rare, and there seems no good reason to abandon the usual meaning of the word, which is to denote the manner in which an action takes place.[41] A third option understands *houtōs* to have this meaning and connects it with the "just as it is written" formula that follows: "It is in this way that Israel will be saved: namely, just as it is written. . . ."[42] But Paul never elsewhere pairs *houtōs* and "just as it is written." Therefore the fourth option — taking *houtōs* to indicate manner and linking it with what comes before — is to be preferred: "And in this manner all Israel will be saved."[43] The "manner" of Israel's salvation is the process that Paul has outlined in vv. 11-24 and summarized in v. 25b: God imposes a hardening on most of Israel while Gentiles come into the messianic salvation, with the Gentiles' salvation leading in turn to Israel's jealousy and her own salvation. But this means that *houtōs*, while not having a temporal *meaning*, has a temporal *reference*: for the manner in which all Israel is saved involves a process that unfolds in definite stages.[44]

But what is the "all Israel" so destined to be saved? We can best answer that question by examining the interpretive possibilities, beginning with the word "Israel" and then moving on to the word "all."

Pauline usage makes it possible to define "Israel" as (1) the community of the elect, including both Jews and Gentiles; (2) the nation of Israel; or (3) the elect within Israel. The first of these options received some support in the very early church and became especially widespread in the post-Reformation period[45] but has received less support in the modern pe-

---

39. Neither LSJ nor BAGD indicate a temporal meaning for the word; and the two NT examples of a temporal meaning often cited (Acts 17:33; 20:11) are better explained in other ways.

40. Dodd; Michel; Fitzmyer; Hofius, " 'All Israel Will Be Saved,' " p. 35; Volf, *Paul and Perseverance,* pp. 179-80; Kim, *Origin,* pp. 83-84.

41. Only four of the 74 occurrences of οὕτως in Paul seem to have this "logical" or "consecutive" meaning (Rom. 1:15; 6:11; 1 Cor. 14:25; 1 Thess. 4:17). The others all indicate manner.

42. BAGD; Stuhlmacher, "Interpretation," pp. 559-60; Gaston, "Israel's Misstep," p. 143; van Oorschot, *Hoffnung,* p. 24.

43. So, e.g., S-H; Godet; Wilckens; Dunn; J. Jeremias, "Eine vorwiegend sprachliche Beobachtungen zu Röm 11,25-36," in Lorenzi, *Israelfrage,* p. 198.

44. See, e.g., Hofius, "Das Evangelium und Israel," p. 315; Bell, *Provoked to Jealousy,* pp. 134-36.

45. Some Fathers used this verse to support the universality of salvation, interpreting "all Israel" as the entire spiritual Israel (Fitzmyer cites Irenaeus, Clement of Alexandria, Theodore of Mopsuestia, and Theodoret; cf. also Schelkle). Among the Re-

riod.[46] Moreover, this lack of support seems to be justified.[47] Paul has used the term "Israel" ten times so far in Rom. 9–11, and each refers to ethnic Israel.[48] This clearly is the meaning of the term in v. 25b, and a shift from this ethnic denotation to a purely religious one in v. 26a — despite the "all" — is unlikely. But another factor is even more damaging to the idea that Paul uses Israel in v. 26a to refer to the church generally: the hortatory purpose of Rom. 11:11-32. Paul's view of the continuity of salvation history certainly allows him to transfer the OT title of the people of God to the NT people of God, as Gal. 6:16 probably indicates (cf. also Phil. 3:3).[49] And this same theology surfaces in Romans itself, as Paul argues that Abraham's "seed" consists of faithful Jews *and Gentiles* (4:13-18). But the difference in purpose between Rom. 11 and these other texts makes it unlikely that Paul would make the semantic move of using Israel to denote the church here. In both Galatians and Rom. 4 Paul is arguing that Gentiles, as Gentiles, can become recipients of the blessings promised to Abraham and full members of the people of God. Paul's application to Gentiles of OT people-of-God language is perfectly appropriate in such contexts.[50] But Paul's purpose in Rom. 11 is almost the opposite. Here, he counters a tendency for Gentiles to appropriate for themselves exclusively the rights and titles of "God's people." For Paul in this context to call the church "Israel" would be to fuel the fire of the Gentiles' arrogance by giving them grounds to brag that "*we* are the true Israel."[51]

The choice between the other two options is more difficult to make. Paul uses "Israel" in Rom. 9–11 of both the nation generally and of the elect from within Israel, as 9:6b succinctly reveals: "not all who are from Israel [the nation] are Israel [the elect]." If Paul uses "Israel" here in the latter sense,

---

formers, Calvin took this view, but it became especially widespread among Protestant Continental theologians in the late sixteenth and seventeenth centuries.

46. Although see Barth, *CD,* Part 34, p. 300; Jeremias, "Sprachliche Beobachtungen," pp. 199-200; P. E. Hughes, "The Olive Tree of Romans XI," *EvQ* 20 (1948), 44-45; Whiteley, *Theology,* p. 97; Ponsot, "Tout Israel," pp. 413-15; Judant, *Les deux Israël,* pp. 194-201; Chilton, "Romans 9–11," pp. 27, 31, 34; Martin, *Reconciliation,* p. 134; Wright, *Climax of the Covenant,* pp. 249-50.

47. Although they interpret the phrase differently in different places, both Origen (in his commentary on Matthew [*PG* 13.1485]) and Augustine (cf. *PL* 35.1347 and *City of God* 20.29) apply the phrase to ethnic Israel (Fitzmyer); cf. also Chrysostom. This was the standard view among English Puritans (Murray, *The Puritan Hope,* e.g., p. 43).

48. 9:6b (twice), 27 (twice), 31; 10:19, 21; 11:2, 7, 25.

49. See the note on 9:6.

50. Hence, in the same context in Galatians, Paul also transfers the word "law" from Moses to Christ (6:2).

51. My point is not that Paul would deny that this is the case; Gal. 6:16 and Phil. 3:3 show conclusively that he would be quite happy to use this language — but only in a certain rhetorical situation. That rhetorical situation is entirely different in Rom. 11.

he would be affirming that all elect Jews would be saved.[52] Some have dismissed this interpretation because it would turn Paul's prediction into a purposeless truism: after all, by definition those who are elect will be saved. But this objection is not decisive. As we have seen, Paul's focus is not so much on the *fact* that all Israel will be saved as on the *manner* in which it will be saved. A more serious objection to this interpretation is that it requires a shift in the meaning of "Israel" from v. 25b to v. 26a since the Israel that has been partially hardened is clearly national Israel. For this reason, and also because of the usual meaning of the phrase "all Israel" (see below), I incline slightly to the view that Israel in v. 26a refers to the nation generally.

What, then, is the significance of Paul's emphasis that it is *all* the nation of Israel that will be saved? A few scholars have insisted that this must indicate the salvation of every single Jew.[53] But Paul writes "all Israel,"[54] not "every Israelite" — and the difference is an important one. "All Israel," as the OT and Jewish sources demonstrate, has a corporate significance, referring to the nation as a whole and not to every single individual who is a part of that nation.[55] The phrase is similar, then, to those

52. See, e.g., Lenski; Ridderbos; Hendriksen; C. M. Horne, "The Meaning of the Phrase 'And Thus All Israel Will Be Saved' (Romans 11:26)," *JETS* 21 (1978), 331-34; and esp. Refoulé, *Tout Israël,* pp. 135-42, 179-81.

53. E.g., Meyer, who thinks that the salvation is a future event, insists that Paul predicts that all Israelites who are uncoverted at that time will be saved. Cf. also, apparently, Bell, *Provoked to Jealousy,* pp. 136-45.

54. According to classical Greek standards, the anarthrous πᾶς 'Ισραήλ would mean "each Israel" (a distributive sense). But these standards are by no means always upheld, and it is obvious that the phrase is used here in a collective sense (see on this Conybeare and Stock, *Grammar,* 63; BDF 275 [1]; Turner, 199-200).

55. The phrase πᾶς 'Ισραήλ occurs 136 times in the LXX; πᾶς ὁ 'Ισραήλ five times; ὁ πᾶς 'Ισραήλ once (the usual Hebrew is כָּל־יִשְׂרָאֵל); and there are similar expressions, such as πᾶς οἶκος 'Ισραήλ. Few of these refer to every Israelite (although cf. 3 Kgdms. [1 Kings] 22:17; 1 Chron. 21:5; 29:21; Mal. 3:24; 1 Esdr. 7:8; 8:7; 8:92). Sometimes, to be sure, the scope of the phrase is limited clearly by the context (e.g., Num. 16:34: "And all Israel that was around them fled from their voice, for they were saying, 'Lest the earth devour us' "). But there are many examples of the corporate and even representative nature of the phrase; see, e.g., Josh. 7:25: "And Joshua said to Achan, 'Why did you bring trouble on us? The Lord is bringing trouble on you today.' And all Israel stoned him with stones"; 2 Kgdms. (2 Sam.) 16:22: "And they pitched a tent for Absalom on the roof, and Absalom went in to the concubines of his father before the eyes of all Israel"; cf. also 1 Kgdms. (1 Sam.) 7:5; 25:1; 3 Kgdms. 12:1; 2 Chron. 12:1; Dan. 9:11. The frequently cited Jewish text, although of course post-Pauline, is *m. Sanh.* 10:1: "All Israelites have a share in the world to come. . . . And these are they that have no share in the world to come. . . ." However, the relevance of this text to Rom. 11:26 is doubtful because the Mishnah text, unlike Rom. 11:26, explicitly qualifies the meaning of "all" in the context. On the general and corporate meaning of the phrase generally, see Stuhlmann, *Eschatologische Maß,* pp. 168-78.

that we sometimes use to denote a large and representative number from a group; that is, "the whole school turned out to see the football game"; "the whole nation was outraged at the incident." A more difficult issue is whether "all Israel" refers to the nation as a whole as it has existed throughout history (a "diachronic" sense)[56] or to the nation as a whole as it exists at one moment in history (a "synchronic" sense).[57] In favor of the former is the "all," which, it could be argued, is hardly justified if Paul has in mind only the nation at one moment of time, excluding the many millions of Jews who have lived at other periods. But usage of the expression "all Israel" and the perspective from which Paul writes favor the synchronic sense. No occurrence of the phrase "all Israel" has a clearly diachronic meaning. And Paul, we must remember, is not consciously thinking in terms of the passing of many centuries before these events are completed, but of a potentially very short time.[58]

We conclude that Paul is probably using the phrase "all Israel" to denote the corporate entity of the nation of Israel as it exists at a particular point in time. We must note, however, that the interpretation that takes the phrase to refer to the elect among Israel throughout time deserves consideration as a serious alternative.

We turn, finally, to the question of the time and manner of "all Israel's" salvation. Many points that I have already made in the course of my interpretation of vv. 11-24 and of vv. 25-26a in particular make clear that Paul places this event at the time of the end.

(1) The prediction of v. 26a seems to match the third step in the salvation-historical process that Paul describes throughout these verses ("their fullness" [v. 12]; "their acceptance" [v. 15]; the grafting in again of natural branches [v. 24]; cf. also vv. 30-31). Since Paul makes clear that this reinte-

---

56. See, e.g., Hofius, " 'All Israel Will Be Saved,' " p. 35; Mussner, " 'Ganz Israel wird gerettet werden,' " pp. 241-45; Rese, "Römer 11," p. 429; Bell, *Provoked to Jealousy,* pp. 140-43; Fitzmyer (?).

57. E.g., Luther, *Scholium* on 11:25; Godet; S-H; Michel; Murray; Cranfield; Dunn; Volf, *Paul and Perseverance,* pp. 184-85. In a break with their Reformed tradition, the English Puritans held strongly to the belief in a future conversion of Jews, a belief that fueled their missionary zeal (see Murray, *Puritan Hope,* pp. 175-77).

58. We do not mean by this that Paul was certain, or that what he writes in Rom. 11 requires, that the coming of Christ and wrapping up of human history would take place within his own generation or within a very short period of time (as many scholars think). But we must take seriously the fact that Paul, like other NT authors and, indeed, Jesus himself (cf. Mark 13:32//Matt. 24:36) did not know when the consummation of the kingdom would take place. Paul seems to have hoped that the consummation would be soon. At least we must recognize that our own perspective, twenty centuries after the prediction, is quite different from Paul's.

gration of Israel is in contrast to the situation as it exists in his own time — when Israel is "rejected" — it must be a future event.

(2) The specific point in the future when this will occur is indicated by Paul's probable connection between Israel's "acceptance" and the eschatological resurrection of the dead (v. 15).

(3) The implication of v. 25b is that the current partial hardening of Israel will be reversed when all the elect Gentiles have been saved; and it is unlikely that Paul would think that salvation would be closed to Gentiles before the end.

We may add to these points two others drawn from v. 26 itself. First, the OT quotation that Paul cites in v. 26b-27 to confirm the truth that "all Israel will be saved" probably refers to the second coming of Christ (see below). Second, the hope of a spiritual rejuvenation of the nation of Israel is endemic in the OT prophets and in Jewish apocalyptic. This rejuvenation is often pictured as a regathering of Jews that reverses the judgment of Israel's exile and that ushers in the eschatological age. Paul — and the rest of the NT — teaches that the coming of Christ has brought the fulfillment of many of these prophecies about Israel's renewal. But Paul's language in Rom. 11 seems deliberately calculated to restate this traditional hope for Israel's renewal. His point seems to be that the present situation in salvation history, in which so few Jews are being saved, cannot finally do full justice to the scriptural expectations about Israel's future. Something "more" is to be expected; and this "more," Paul implies, is a large-scale conversion of Jewish people at the end of this age.[59] The corporate significance of "all Israel" makes it impossible to reckon the actual percentage of Jews living at that time who will be saved. But the contrast between the remnant and "all Israel" would suggest a significantly larger percentage than was the case in Paul's day. Nor is it possible to be precise about the exact timing of the conversion of Israel in comparison

59. It should be noted that, even if we adopt the viable alternative intepretation of "all Israel will be saved" as a reference to the ultimate salvation of all the elect from the people of Israel throughout history, a great end-time conversion of Jews is not excluded. Verse 26a would then simply summarize the process by which Jews are saved that Paul has described throughout this chapter. And this process, Paul has plainly hinted, will involve a reversal of the current "partial hardness" of Israel, a new mercy extended to Jews that we are not in this age seeing (see vv. 30-31). Thus, on this alternative interpretation, v. 26a does not directly state the salvation of a last generation of Jews, but it still presupposes it.

The OT/Jewish tradition that Paul uses usually makes prominent reference to a restoration to the land as integral to the eschatological rejuvenation of Israel. Some think that Rom. 11 includes this physical dimension of Israel's restoration (e.g., W. C. Kaiser, Jr., "Kingdom Promises as Spiritual and National," in *Continuity and Discontinuity*, pp. 302-3). But we find no evidence of this; accepting such a hope as part of NT eschatology will require evidence in texts other than Rom. 11.

with other events of the end times,[60] although the fact that it will take place only after the salvation of all elect Gentiles suggests that it will be closely associated with the return of Christ in glory.

How will this eschatological salvation of "all Israel" happen? Several scholars have argued recently that the absence of any specific christological language in Rom. 11 is very significant for this question. They think that this absence is deliberate and that Paul is implying that Israel will be saved in a "special way," a different way than the faith in Christ required of Gentiles for salvation.[61] The most extreme form of this view finds in Rom. 11 the exegetical basis for a "bi-covenantal" theology, according to which Gentiles are saved in *their* ("new") covenant by faith in Christ while Jews are saved in *their* (Mosaic) covenant by their adherence to torah. Such a view, allowing as it does for both the Jew and the Christian to affirm the integrity of each other's religion, has proved quite attractive to our "post-holocaust" and pluralistic age. But Paul knows nothing of it. He teaches that salvation can be found in one place only: within the one community made up of those who believe in Jesus Christ. There is only one tree, and one becomes attached to this tree by faith: Jews can be grafted back in only if they do not persist in

---

60. Some scholars think that the Jews will be converted through a mission to Jews after the conclusion of the mission to the Gentiles (e.g., Becker, *Paul,* pp. 469-72). Murray (*Puritan Hope,* pp. 39-55) notes that the Puritans, who almost unanimously held to a future conversion of Israel, were quite divided over its timing, arguing about whether it would take place only after the Gentile mission and about its relationship to the millennium.

61. The Germ. *Sonderweg,* "special way," has therefore been used to describe this approach. Prominent advocates of this general approach are K. Stendahl, "Paul among Jews and Gentiles," "The Apostle Paul and the Introspective Conscience of the West" (both reprinted in *Paul among Jews and Gentiles*), and "Christ's Lordship and Religious Pluralism," in *Meanings: The Bible as Document and as Guide* (Philadelphia: Fortress, 1984), pp. 233-44; Mussner, 'Ganz Israel wird gerettet werden,' " pp. 245-53; idem, "Heil für alle," pp. 207-14; Gager, *Origins of Anti-Semitism,* pp. 261-62; Gaston, "Israel's Misstep," pp. 147-49; van Buren, *Theology,* 1.240. Cf. also Barth, *People of God,* pp. 52, 71; Hall, *Christian Anti-Semitism,* pp. 57-93, 113-27 (he insists that Jews must embrace the gospel, but he defines the gospel not in terms of Christ but in terms of its inclusive message); K. Haacker, "Das Evangelium Gottes und die Erwählung Israels. Zum Beitrag des Römerbriefs zur Erneuerung des Verhältnisses zwischen Christen und Juden," *TBei* 13 (1982), 70-71; P. Lapide (and P. Stuhlmacher), *Paul, Rabbi and Apostle* (Minneapolis: Augsburg, 1984), pp. 47-54; Theobald, "Kirche und Israel," pp. 13-14; Rese, "Rettung der Juden," pp. 422-31; Klappert, "Traktat," pp. 80-86. The specifics of the manner of salvation differ, some arguing that Israel will be saved apart from response to the preaching of Christ but nevertheless through Christ in some indefinite way. (This was also the view of most "classic" dispensationalists.) Hofius, e.g., suggests that Israel will be saved as Paul was: through the revelation of Christ from heaven ("Das Evangelium und Israel," pp. 319-20).

unbelief (v. 23).[62] Nor can the absence of the name of Christ in Rom. 11 justify the conclusion that this faith need not be faith in Christ. Paul has defined the faith he is talking about here quite adequately in the first ten chapters of the letter: it is faith in Jesus Christ (see esp. 3:22, 26; 10:4-13). As Paul has made clear in the immediately preceding chapter, faith is inextricably tied to Jesus and his resurrection victory (10:9), and it is this faith that brings salvation to Gentile and Jew alike (10:10-13).[63] Jews, like Gentiles, can be saved only by responding to the gospel and being grafted into the one people of God. Paul has certainly not forgotten his great summary of the theme of his letter as he writes chap. 11: "For I am not ashamed of the gospel, for it is the power of God for salvation for all who believe, *for the Jew first,* and then for the Gentile" (1:16).[64] The end-time conversion of a large number of Jews will therefore come about only through their faith in the gospel of Jesus the Messiah.[65]

62. Lübking (*Paulus und Israel,* 116) rightly emphasizes the importance of this verse for resolving the dialectic of Rom. 9–11: while God promises salvation to Israel (11:26), this salvation comes only as individual Jews believe.

63. See, e.g., Beker: "Scholars who — for the sake of an irenic Jewish-Christian dialogue — concentrate exclusively on 11:25-36 and neglect its basic connection with 9:1–11:24 transgress the hermeneutical rule of the relation of the parts to the whole" ("Romans 9–11," p. 48).

64. Criticisms of the "Sonderweg" interpretation of Rom. 11:26 are numerous. The best, perhaps, is R. Hvalvik, "A 'Sonderweg' for Israel: A Critical Examination of a Current Interpretation of Romans 11.25-27," *JSNT* 38 (1990), 87-107. See also Beker, "Romans 9–11," pp. 48-52; Becker, *Paul,* pp. 469-72; Hübner, *Gottes Ich und Israel,* pp. 116-20; E. P. Sanders, "Paul's Attitude toward the Jewish People," *USQR* 33 (1978), 180-83; Stuhlmacher, "Interpretation," pp. 562-64; W. S. Campbell, "Salvation for Jews and Gentiles: Krister Stendahl and Paul's letter to the Romans," in *Studia Biblica 1978 III,* pp. 65-72; Segal, *Paul the Convert,* pp. 130-33, 148-49, 279-81; Richardson, "Paul, God, and Israel," pp. 189-92; Hahn, "Römer 11:26a," pp. 221-30; Lübking, *Paulus und Israel,* pp. 125-28; E. Grässer, "Zwei Heilswege?" in *Der Alte Bunde im Neuen. Exegetische Studien zur Israelfrage im Neuen Testament* (WUNT 2.35; Tübingen: Mohr, 1985), pp. 212-30; Zeller, "Christus, Skandal und Hoffnung," pp. 270-78. Wright is correct when he points out that "bi-covenantal theology" is an ultimately unstable "halfway house" on the road to full-blown religious pluralism (*Climax of the Covenant,* p. 254).

65. The logical implication of this theology is that — paradoxically — it is the refusal to preach the gospel to Jews that is anti-Semitic (cf. Bell, *Provoked to Jealousy,* pp. 354-55). For one would then refuse to the Jews alone the sole means of salvation. At the same time, the certainty with which Paul can predict this mass conversion assumes that God is ultimately the one who "calls" these Jews to salvation (see 9:6b-29!). Only on such an assumption can a future mass conversion of Jews be known to be certain (see Dinkler, "Historical and Eschatological Israel," p. 122). Paul's prediction here therefore illustrates from another angle the harmony in his thinking between a full-fledged doctrine of sovereign divine election and the indispensability of human response in faith for salvation.

26b-27 As Paul has done in the conclusions of each of the other main parts of his argument in Rom. 9–11 (cf. 9:25-29; 10:21-21; 11:8-10), he reinforces his teaching with a composite quotation from the OT. He quotes Isa. 59:20-21a in vv. 26b-27a and a clause from Isa. 27:9 in v. 27b. Both parts of the quotation follow the LXX closely, with one notable exception: where the LXX of Isa. 59:20 says that "the redeemer will come *for the sake of* [*heneken*] Zion," Paul says "the redeemer will come *out of* [*ek*] Zion."[66] And not only does Paul's reading differ from the LXX, it differs also from the Hebrew text and from every known pre-Pauline text and version.[67] How are we to account for this variation? Paul may have inadvertently assimilated this text to others in the OT that speak of Israel's deliverance as coming "from Zion" (cf. Ps. 13:7; 53:7; 110:2).[68] He may have deliberately changed the wording to make a point: to show that Christ, "the redeemer," originates from the Jewish people (cf. 9:5);[69] to show that the final "missionary" to the Gentiles, Christ, comes, like the present missionaries to the Gentiles, from Jerusalem (cf. 15:19);[70] or to show that Christ will save Israel by coming from the "heavenly" Zion at his parousia.[71] Or Paul may, in fact, be faithfully quoting from a form of the LXX text that we no longer have.[72]

---

66. The LXX of Isa. 59:20-21a reads καὶ ἥξει ἕνεκεν Σιων ὁ ῥυόμενος καὶ ἀποστρέψει ἀσεβείας ἀπὸ Ιακωβ. καὶ αὕτη αὐτοῖς ἡ παρ' ἐμοῦ διαθήκη, εἶπεν κύριος. This rendering differs from the MT at two points. First, it translates the Hebrew participial construction לְשָׁבֵי, "to those who turn," with a finite future verb, ἀποστρέψει, "he will turn." The LXX formulation accords well with Paul's emphasis on divine condescension in Israel's salvation. The second difference is more difficult to explain. Where the MT has the preposition לְ, the LXX has ἕνεκεν. The לְ is probably local — "to Zion" (BDB, 511) — in which case the LXX rendering could have arisen as a scribal misreading of an original εἰς (B. Schaller, "ΗΞΕΙ ΕΚ ΣΙΩΝ Ο ΡΥΟΜΕΝΟΣ. Zur Textgestalt von Jes. 59:20f. in Röm 11:26f.," in *De Septuaginta. Studies in Honour of John William Wevers on His Sixty-Fifth Birthday* [ed. A. Pietersma and C. Cox; Toronto: Benben, 1984], pp. 201-6). Less likely is the possibility that לְ has the more general sense "with respect to" and that the LXX is an interpretive paraphrase (Alexander, *Commentary,* p. 377). Paul's dependence on the LXX in his quotation of Isa. 27:9 is more obvious, for the LXX ὅταν ἀφέλωμαι αὐτοῦ τὴν ἁμαρτίαν differs significantly from the MT. Paul's change is necessary to match the plural αὐτοῖς in his quotation of Isa. 59:21a in v. 27a.

67. The few MSS of the LXX that have ἐκ are clearly influenced by the form of Rom. 11:26 itself.

68. Meyer; Leenhardt; Bruce; Cranfield.

69. E.g., Murray; Fitzmyer; Johnson, *Function,* pp. 162-63.

70. Wilckens.

71. S-H; Käsemann; Dunn (with other factors).

72. See esp. Schaller, "ΗΞΕΙ ΕΚ ΣΙΩΝ Ο ΡΥΟΜΕΝΟΣ," pp. 201-6; Koch, 175-78. C. D. Stanley (" 'The Redeemer will come ἐκ Σιων'; Romans 11:26-27 Revisited," in *Paul and the Scriptures of Israel* [ed. C. A. Evans and J. A. Sanders; JSNTSup 83; Sheffield: Sheffield Academic Press, 1993], pp. 133-36), on the other hand, thinks that Paul's rendering reflects Diaspora Jewish traditions.

The last alternative must certainly be taken seriously, but it is perhaps on the whole best to think that Paul is assuming the tradition that surfaces in Heb. 12:22, according to which "Zion" is associated with the heavenly Jerusalem, the site of Christ's high-priestly ministry.[73] If so, he probably changes the text in order to make clear that the final deliverance of Israel is accomplished by Christ at his parousia.[74]

While, therefore, the "redeemer" in Isa. 59:20 is Yahweh himself, Paul probably intends to identify Christ as the redeemer.[75] It is when Christ comes "out of" heaven that he will "turn away ungodliness from Jacob" and thus fulfill the covenant with Israel.[76] In light of Paul's reference to the patriarchs in the next verse and his extensive use of the OT traditions about God's covenant with Abraham, we are justified in assuming that he would identify this covenant with the promise-covenant that God entered into with Abraham and his descendants. Paul, of course, insists that this covenant has been fulfilled in the first coming of Christ and his provision for both Jews and Gentiles to enter, by faith, into the people of God (Gal. 3; Rom. 4). But, in a pattern typical of the NT, Paul suggests that this covenant with Abraham still

73. Note Gal. 4:26, where Paul refers to the "Jerusalem above" to which Christians belong. Paul does not use "Zion" with any theological significance. He only uses the term once elsewhere, in a quotation of Isa. 28:16 in Rom. 9:33. It would make sense to interpret "out of Zion" in 11:26 in light of this earlier text (cf., e.g., B. W. Longenecker, "Different Answers to Different Issues: Israel, the Gentiles and Salvation History in Romans 9–11," *JSNT* 36 [1989], 117 n. 21), but it is difficult to see how it helps explain Paul's reference here. "Zion" occurs in the NT only elsewhere in quotations of Zech. 9:9 in Matt. 21:5; John 12:15; in another quotation of Isa. 28:16 in 1 Pet. 2:6 and in Rev. 14:1: "And I looked, and behold the Lamb, standing on Mount Zion, and with him the 144,000 who had his name and the name of his Father written on their foreheads."

74. Cf. Stuhlmacher, "Interpretation," p. 561.

75. See the similar language in 1 Thess. 1:10: ". . . Jesus, the one who delivers us [ὁ ῥυόμενος] from the wrath to come." Cf., e.g., S-H; Kuss; Wilckens; Cranfield; Hofius, "Das Evangelium und Israel," p. 318. Isa. 59:20-21 is interpreted as a reference to the Messiah in the targum (Str-B, 3.293), but the late date of the tradition renders its applicability to Paul's understanding questionable (Dunn). Other scholars think that Paul might be referring to Christ's first coming (Lenski; Wright, *Climax of the Covenant,* pp. 250-51; D. Zeller, "Israel unter dem Ruf Gottes (Röm 9–11)," *Internationale Katholische Zeit-schrift* 2 [1973], 296; Räisänen, "Römer 9–11," pp. 2919-20; Luz, 294-95) or to a deliverance by Yahweh himself (Gaston, "Israel's Misstep," p. 143; Stanley, " 'The Redeemer will come ἐκ Σιων,' " pp. 137-38).

76. Some commentators think that Paul may also allude to the "new covenant" prophecy of Jer. 31:31-34 (e.g., Murray; Morris; Fitzmyer). But the verbal similarity to Isa. 27:9 is much closer. Refoulé (*Tout Israël,* pp. 94-107) argues, on the basis of the OT and Jewish traditions, that we must translate this clause "remove the ungodly from the midst of Jacob [e.g., the remnant]." Paul would therefore not be referring here to a forgiveness of sins among Israel in general but to a final purifying of the people before the end.

awaits its final consummation — a consummation that will affect Israel in particular.

Paul uses a clause from Isa. 27:9 to interpret this covenant in terms of the forgiveness of sins. Some similarity in wording between this verse and Isa. 59:20-21 probably helped draw Paul's attention to this verse; but more important is the context from which it is taken. For Isaiah 29, like Isa. 59:20–60:7, predicts that Yahweh will deliver "Jacob" from her exile/sins, bringing the scattered people back to their own city.[77] Isaiah 29 notes that the judgment God has brought on Israel (in the Exile) is different from the judgment God brings on other nations: for Israel's judgment, it is implied, will be both temporary and sanitive (vv. 7-8). The prophet therefore foresees "days to come" when "Jacob shall take root, Israel shall blossom and put forth shoots, and fill the whole world with fruit" (v. 6); when God will regather his people and the exiles will return to "worship the LORD on the holy mountain at Jerusalem" (vv. 12-13). The parallel between this scenario and Paul's teaching in 11:11-32 that the hardening of Israel is temporary and intended to lead to her ultimate deliverance cannot be missed. Moreover, by focusing on "the forgiveness of sins" as integral to the fulfillment of God's covenant with Israel, Paul ties this final deliverance to the cross, where the price for these sins has been paid (cf. 3:21-26). With this quotation, then, Paul not only suggests *when* Israel's deliverance will take place; he also makes clear *how* it will take place: by Israel's acceptance of the gospel message about the forgiveness of sins in Jesus Christ.

28 The lack of any connecting word between vv. 27 and 28 (asyndeton) suggests that a break in Paul's argument occurs here. With the obvious shift in thought between vv. 32 and 33, then, verses 28-32 becomes a discrete paragraph. The immediate purpose of this paragraph is to ground and elaborate Paul's prediction of Israel's final salvation. Paul does this by highlighting God's purpose of showing mercy to Israel, the central theme of vv. 28-32 (it is the climactic point in each of the arguments: cf. vv. 28b, 31b, and 32b). It is because God has chosen Israel to be his "beloved" that he will bring salvation to the people in the last day. But the paragraph also rounds off Paul's discussion in chap. 11. His assertion of Israel's election (v. 28b) brings his argument back to where it began (vv. 1-2), while vv. 30-31 summarize the process of interaction between Gentiles and Israel that Paul has throughout vv. 11-27 highlighted as the vehicle by which God manifests this election. Finally, however, these verses serve to recapitulate and wrap up the argument of chaps. 9–11 as a whole. Paul's assertion of Israel's dual status in v. 28

---

77. See Stuhlmacher, "Interpretation," pp. 560-61; Hübner, *Gottes Ich und Israel,* pp. 119-20. Stanley (*Paul and the Language of Scripture,* pp. 169-70) thinks that the combination of Isa. 59:20-21 and 27:9 may have been traditional.

succinctly summarizes the dilemma that drives the whole argument of these chapters: the Israel now at enmity with God because of the gospel is nevertheless the Israel to whom God has made irrevocable promises of blessing. In broad terms, as 9:30–10:21 has elaborated the former, negative side of this dilemma, so 9:6b-29 and 11:1-27 have explained the second, positive, side.[78]

Though v. 28 is not formally connected with the previous context, an implicit connection is forged by the need to supply the subject of v. 28 from v. 27: "them," the (unbelieving) Israelites. The two clauses of v. 28 are parallel in structure:

> "According to the gospel"   "enemies"   "because of you"
> "According to election"   "beloved"   "because of the fathers"

"Enemies according to the gospel" succinctly summarizes the point that Paul has made in 9:30–10:21: through their failure to respond to the revelation of God's righteousness in Christ, the heart of the gospel, Israel as a whole has failed to attain the eschatological salvation manifested in the gospel. "According to" will then express the standard by which Israelites can be judged to be "enemies."[79] The word "enemies" can have an active sense — "those who hate God"[80] — or a passive meaning — "those hated by God."[81] Most commentators favor the latter because of the parallel word "beloved," which obviously has a passive meaning. However, we must be careful not to insist on a parallel in meaning where Paul may intend only a parallel in form;[82] and the word "enemies"[83] often has an active sense in Paul. Perhaps, then, as in the somewhat parallel 5:10, it is best to give the word both an active and passive sense, captured adequately in the English word "enemies."[84] This

---

78. Cf. Schmitt, *Gottesgerechtigkeit,* p. 111. In addition to the point of contact mentioned above, note also the verbal parallels: ἐκλογή (v. 28; cf. 9:11; 11:5, 7); πατέρας (v. 28; cf. 9:5); κλῆσις (v. 29; cf. καλέω in 9:7, 12, 24, 25, 26); ἀπειθέω (vv. 30-31; cf. 10:21); ἐλεέω (vv. 30-32; cf. 9:15, 18).

79. As BAGD define this use of κατά with accusative: "the norm according to which a judgment is rendered, or rewards or punishments are given" (II.5.β.; although they classify the word here differently). See also Michel.

80. So Schlier; Dunn (?); Munck, *Christ and Israel,* p. 138; Hofius, "Das Evangelium und Israel," p. 321. F. Mussner argues that we should not assume that God is either the object or the subject of the word ("Sind die Juden 'Feinde Gottes'? Bemerkungen zu Röm 11,28," in *Dynamik im Wort* [Stuttgart: Katholisches, 1983], pp. 235-40). But the parallel ἀγαπητοί — "beloved by God" — makes clear that the hostility of the Jews in v. 28a is with God.

81. E.g., Godet; Michel; Murray; Kuss; Cranfield; Refoulé, *Tout Israël,* pp. 199-200.

82. This point is emphasized especially by Dunn.

83. Gk. ἐχθροί.

84. Wilckens; Käsemann. See, further, the note on 5:10.

meaning effectively captures the dual note Paul has sounded throughout Rom. 9–11 when speaking of Israel's failure: "hated," hardened," and "rejected" by God (cf. 9:13, 17-23; 11:7b-10, 15, 25); for their part, disobedient, unbelieving, and stubborn (9:31-32; 10:3, 14-21; 11:11, 12, 20, 23, 30-31).

The importance of not insisting that the formally parallel elements have the same meaning is especially clear in comparing the two "because of" phrases. For the latter one clearly has a causal sense — Israel is "beloved" *because of* the fathers (the patriarchs; cf. 9:5) — while the former must have a final sense — Israelites are "enemies" *for the sake of* you [Gentile Christians]; for instance, as Paul has argued previously, God has "hardened" Israel so that salvation could be extended to the Gentiles (cf. vv. 11, 12, 15, 17).[85] In saying that God's love for Israel is "based on" the patriarchs, Paul is not of course suggesting that the patriarchs have done anything to merit God's love for themselves or their descendants. As Gal. 3 and Rom. 4 make clear, the significance of Abraham and the other patriarchs in the plan of salvation rests not on their own actions but on the gracious promises that God has made to them. So it is not because of the patriarchs in and of themselves that the Jews are still beloved; it is because of the promises God made to them. As it is by the standard of the gospel that the Jews are now judged to be enemies of God, so it is by the standard of "election" that they are loved by God.

Some think, because of the way that Paul describes election in 9:6b-13 — an act by which God brings people into relationship with himself — that Paul must be referring here to the remnant.[86] But a switch in subject in mid-verse, from the Jews who are God's enemies in light of the gospel, to Jews who are beloved by God as elect members of the remnant, seems unwarranted.[87] It is better, then, to understand the election Paul speaks of here to be the same corporate election of the people of Israel as a whole that he referred to in vv. 1-2.[88] This election, as I argued at that point, is that choosing of Israel as a nation which the OT frequently emphasizes, a choice that does not mean salvation for every single member of the nation, but blessings for

---

85. See, e.g., Michel; Käsemann; Wilckens; Dunn. On the "final" meaning of διά, see BDF 222; and, for a similar variation in the meaning of two formally parallel occurrences of διά, see 4:25.

86. Meyer; Lenski; Refoulé, *Tout Israël,* pp. 214-15; Dreyfuss, "Le passé et le présent d'Israel," p. 143; Hafemann, "Salvation of Israel," p. 53.

87. Equally unwarranted would be a shift in the temporal reference of the assumed verb, as if Paul were saying that the Jews were *now* enemies with respect to the gospel, but would *in the future* be beloved because of election (as seems to be suggested by Stuhlmacher, "Interpretation," pp. 564-65 and Longenecker, "Different Answers").

88. See, e.g., Calvin; Murray; Cranfield; Fitzmyer (?). Godet, on the other hand, defines election here as God's gracious but resistible call to all Jews to respond to the gospel and so be saved.

the nation as a whole. All Jews, therefore, are "beloved of God"; but, as Paul has made clear, this status will eventuate in salvation only for those whom God individually chooses for salvation in this age (the remnant) and in the last days ("all Israel").

29 Paul now grounds the last part of v. 28: the Jews, despite their rejection of the gospel, remain God's beloved "because[89] the gifts and the call of God are irrevocable." The "call" of God clearly refers to the election according to which the Jews are beloved.[90] The "gifts" may then be combined with "call" as one idea — "the benefits of God's call"[91] — or be taken as a distinct category — "the gifts and the call of God."[92] The relationship between this paragraph and 9:1-5 suggests that Paul would intend "gifts" to summarize those privileges of Israel that he enumerated in 9:4-5. God's "call," then, is probably to be seen as one of the most important of those gifts: "the gifts and especially, among those gifts, the call of God."[93] The rare word "irrevocable"[94] emphasizes the point that Paul made at the beginning of his argument: "The word of God has not failed" (9:6a). However, while this initial statement of God's faithfulness to his promises was defensive — just because Israel has not believed, *"it is not as though"* God is not faithful — this second assertion is positive — Israel still has a place in God's plan *because* God is faithful. In this way Paul marks the movement of his argument. He began with a defense of God's word and constancy against a Jewish assumption of assured access to God's grace (9:6b-29); he ends with a defense of Israel's continuing privileges on the basis of God's word against a Gentile assumption of superiority.

30 Verses 30-31 explain how God's continuing elective love of the Jews will be manifest.[95] The argument recapitulates the process that Paul has described several times already, according to which God works out his purposes of salvation in history through an oscillation between Jews and Gentiles (cf. vv. 11-12, 15, 17-24, 25). Paul uses the familiar "just as" — "so also" logic to argue that the sequence of "disobedience" — "mercy" experienced already by the Gentiles (v. 30) will also be experienced by the Jews (v. 31). Paul again uses formal parallelism to enhance this similarity in treatment, with

---

89. Gk. γάρ.

90. The Gk. for "call" is κλῆσις, cognate to the word for "election" (ἐκλογή).

91. Calvin; Käsemann.

92. E.g., Cranfield.

93. E.g., Michel.

94. Gk. ἀμεταμέλητος, lit. "without regret"; cf. the only other occurrence in biblical Greek, in 2 Cor. 7:10: "godly pain brings a repentance that leads to salvation and *brings no regret.*"

95. Käsemann; Schlier.

a chiasm linking the end of v. 30 and the beginning of v. 31 (see the discussion below):

v. 30	v. 31
"Just as"	"so also"
"you"	"they"
"at one time"	"now"
"disobeyed God"	"have disobeyed"
	"for (dative) the sake of mercy for you"
"and now"	"in order that [now]"
"you have received mercy"	"they might also receive mercy"
"because of (dative) their disobedience"	

As the second person plural verbs and pronouns show, Paul continues to address the Gentile Christians in Rome. He reminds them in v. 30 of their own experience. They were at one time "disobedient" to God, as Paul has shown at length in 1:18-32 (and cf. 2:8, where "disobedience" is one reason why God's wrath falls on both Jew and Gentile alike). Paul undoubtedly characterizes the Gentiles' sin in terms of disobedience because this renunciation of God is equally applicable to both Jews and Gentiles (see the reference to Israel's "disobedience" in 10:21). "But now you have received mercy." "But now" signals, as so often in Romans and in Paul, the salvation-historical movement from the old era to the new. It is not so much, then, the conversion of each of the Gentile Christians that Paul alludes to as the shift from the era when Gentiles were "alienated from the commonwealth of Israel, and strangers to the covenants of promise, having no hope and without God in the world" (Eph. 2:12b) to the present era in which God's righteousness has been manifested "for all who believe," whether Jew or Gentile (1:16; 3:22; 10:11-13). Yet Paul's particular emphasis in this verse is on the last phrase, in which he reminds the Gentiles that the mercy they have experienced came as a result of the disobedience of "them," the Jews.[96] As Paul has already made clear, it was Israel's "trespass," her "rejection," that made it possible for the gospel to be preached to and received by the Gentiles (vv. 12, 15, 17).

31   To form the hinge of his argument, Paul now looks at the situation he has described at the end of v. 30 from the perspective of the Jews. Note the chiastic arrangement:

---

96. Gk. τῇ τούτων ἀπειθείᾳ. The dative is probably a causal dative (BDF 196; Z-G, 486; Wilckens; Fitzmyer), although Turner (243) and Moule (*Idiom Book,* p. 44[?]) suggest that it might be temporal: "at the time of their disbelief."

733

"you received mercy   because of their disobedience"
"they have disobeyed   for the sake of mercy for you"

This diagram assumes that the phrase I have translated "for the sake of mercy for you"[97] modifies the first verb in the verse, "disobeyed."[98] But this point is highly disputed. Many, perhaps most, commentators argue that it should go with the verb "receive mercy"[99] at the end of the verse, yielding a translation such as that found in the NIV: "so they too have now become disobedient in order that they too may now receive mercy *as a result of God's mercy to you.*"[100] Supporters of this arrangement cite three main arguments: (1) it makes for better parallelism between the two verses, for each would have a dative modifier of the verb "receive mercy" in the second clause; (2) it would enhance the parallelism in a second way, allowing the two phrases, "[through] their disobedience" (v. 30b) and "[through] mercy to you," to have the same (instrumental) meaning; (3) it fits better the scenario that Paul has sketched earlier in the chapter, where the mercy ultimately received by the Jews comes as a result of their jealousy of the Gentiles' salvation.

None of these arguments is at all decisive. The first is perhaps the strongest; but, as our diagram above suggests, Paul may well be utilizing the well-known device of chiasm in his arrangement of the last clause of v. 30 and the first of v. 31. The second presumes that two units that are structurally parallel must also be parallel in meaning. But we have already seen that this need not be the case (see v. 28). Taking "mercy to you" as an instrumental modifier of "receive mercy" certainly fits with the scenario Paul has outlined earlier (the third argument); but it fits equally well to take it as a dative of advantage with the verb "disobeyed." "They have disobeyed for the sake of mercy for you" would then match "their trespass means riches for the world," "their defeat means riches for the Gentiles" (v. 12), and "their rejection means reconciliation for the world" (v. 15). Since, then, the arguments in favor of taking "mercy to you" with "they will receive mercy" are not compelling,

---

97. Gk. τῷ ὑμετέρῳ ἐλέει.

98. The initially strange pairing of νῦν with an aorist verb (ἠπείθησαν) is readily explained, the aorist being used, as it regularly is, to picture as a whole a state that began in the past and continues into the present (see BAGD, 545; Moule, *Idiom Book,* p. 13). See also Porter, who uses such occurrences of the aorist to question the temporal denotation of the aorist (*Verbal Aspect,* p. 227).

99. Gk. ἐλεηθῶσιν.

100. Italics mine; cf. also KJV; RSV; NRSV; NASB; NJB. Cranfield provides the best defense of this view; but cf. also Godet; S-H; Michel; Murray; Fitzmyer; Feuillet, "L'espérance de la 'conversion' d'Israël en Rm 11,25-32," pp. 487-91. Most who take this view think the dative is instrumental, but a few (e.g., Fitzmyer) think it is causal; cf. the NIV quoted above.

we should follow the most natural reading of the syntax[101] and take the phrase with the verb "disobeyed": "they disobeyed for the sake of mercy for you."[102]

As Paul has shown in his earlier sketches of the process of salvation history, however, the Jews' disobedience is not God's final word about them. "They have not stumbled so as to have fallen" (v. 11). The Jews' disobedience, precisely because it leads to the inclusion of the Gentiles, has the purpose[103] that they, too, might receive mercy. What is surprising about this purpose statement is the adverb "now."[104] For it seems clear from other places in the chapter that Paul does not think that Israel is "now" experiencing the mercy that he hopes (and predicts) they one day will (cf. vv. 12, 15, 24, 25-26). Some commentators, indeed, think that this "now" here is one clue among many others that Paul is not thinking in this chapter of a great future conversion of Jews.[105] But I am convinced that the verses I have cited are conclusive for the futuristic interpretation. That being so, it seems best to treat Paul's "now" as an expression of imminence, expressing his conviction that this final manifestation of God's mercy to Israel could take place "now, at any time." It need not mean that the event will infallibly take place within a few years,[106] but it reveals that typical NT perspective which views the new era of fulfillment as already having dawned and all the events belonging to that era as therefore near in time. The salvation experienced by the Gentiles means that Israel is "now" in the position to experience again God's mercy.[107]

32 Paul now makes a final comment on this process by which God has used the disobedience of the Gentiles and the Jews to bring about mercy to both Jews and Gentiles.[108] The image of God "enclosing"[109] in disobe-

---

101. We would normally expect τῷ ὑμετέρῳ ἐλέει to modify the verb in the clause where it is placed rather than a verb from which it is separated by a ἵνα. But, as advocates of the alternative view rightly point out, words to be construed with a verb dependent on ἵνα do sometimes precede the ἵνα (Cranfield cites, in the NT, Acts 19:4; 2 Cor. 2:4; Gal. 2:10; Col. 4:16; and cf. LSJ).

102. See, e.g., Barrett; Kuss; Käsemann; Wilckens; Schlier; Dunn; Refoulé, *Tout Israël,* pp. 217-19; Müller, *Gottes Gerechtigkeit,* p. 47. Some who understand the syntax this way, however, take the dative as causal (BDF 196).

103. Gk. ἵνα.

104. We are assuming here that the νῦν is the correct reading. See the note on the translation above.

105. See esp. Judant, *Les deux Israël,* pp. 111-25.

106. Contra those who see in this verse another indication that Paul was certain the parousia would occur within his own lifetime (e.g., Käsemann; Michel).

107. Schlier. See the references to "the present time" in Rom. 3:26; 8:18; 11:5.

108. Some scholars think that v. 32 brings to a climax Paul's argument in the epistle thus far (e.g., Achtemeier; Dunn; Beker, "Faithfulness of God," p. 14). But this too greatly simplifies chaps. 1–8 and applies the verse too broadly.

109. The Gk. verb is συγκλείω, meaning, according to its roots, "close up to-

dience reminds us of Paul's language about God "handing over" Gentiles to the consequences of their sins in chap. 1 (cf. vv. 24, 26, and 28).[110] And as there, this "enclosing" probably involves God's decision to "confine" people in the state that they have chosen for themselves. But God's punishment, while still a punishment, has an ultimately redeeming purpose: to bestow mercy.

Interpretations of this verse go astray when it is wrenched from its context. One glaring and serious example of such a misinterpretation is the view that Paul is here teaching a salvific universalism: as God has confined every single person in sin, so he will have mercy — save — every single person.[111] But such a conclusion is obviously contradictory to Paul's teaching elsewhere to the effect that there are people who will not in the end be saved. Paul may, then, mean simply that God's mercy is potentially available to all.[112] But a reference to an offer of mercy here does not square well with Paul's emphasis throughout Rom. 9–11 on the God who is sovereignly working in salvation history to accomplish his purposes — and not least in the showing of mercy (cf. 9:15-16). When we put this verse in its context we get a very different result. Paul is commenting on the process that he has outlined in vv. 30-31 (and several other times in this chapter). That being the case, "all" might refer to the unbelieving Jews about whom he has been speaking in v. 31.[113] But we can hardly eliminate from Paul's reference the Gentiles in the church at Rome whom Paul has been addressing throughout this section.[114] Considering the corporate perspective that is basic to chap. 11, then, it seems best to think that "all" refers to "all the groups" about which Paul has been speaking; for example, Jews and Gentiles.[115] Paul is not saying that all human beings will be saved. Rather, he is saying that God has imprisoned in disobedience first Gentiles and now Jews so

---

gether" (cf. Luke 5:6, with reference to fish in a net). The verb is then frequently used in Hellenistic Greek to mean "imprison" (cf. BAGD, M-M), and from this the metaphorical usage here and in Gal. 3:22, 23 ("shutting up in sin") develops. Paul may be dependent on the LXX, where the verb is used (followed by εἰς) of God's act of "enclosing," or "giving over," people to their enemies (Ps. 31:8) or to the plague (Ps. 78:50) or to death (Ps. 78:62); cf. Dunn.

110. Cf. Godet.

111. Origen was an early advocate of such a view, holding that there would in the end be an ἀποκατάστασις ("restoration") of all things. He was opposed, however, among others, by Augustine (see *City of God* 21.24). Modern advocates of the universalistic interpretation of this verse include Dodd. Cranfield and Dunn argue that universalism cannot be ruled out.

112. Alford; Meyer.

113. Cf. Zahn; Refoulé, *Tout Israël,* pp. 233-35.

114. So, correctly, Cranfield.

115. Calvin; S-H; Denney; Murray; Schmidt; Wilckens; Müller, *Gottes Gerechtigkeit,* p. 48. The Greek is τοὺς πάντας, the article perhaps emphasizing the collective, or corporate, aspect.

that he might bestow mercy on each of these groups of humanity. How many from each of these groups will ultimately be saved Paul does not say.

In our comments on v. 28, we noted how vv. 28-32 wrap up the argument of chaps. 9–11 as a whole. But these verses also bring to a climax a line of thinking that appears to create tension with what Paul teaches earlier in these chapters and, indeed, in his writings elsewhere. For in chap. 9 Paul seems to teach that God elects individuals on the basis of his pure grace, without any consideration of ethnic origin — a perspective consonant with Paul's vision of the church of Jew and Gentile as the fulfillment of God's promises to Abraham (Rom. 4; Gal. 3). Yet in chap. 11 Paul seems to smuggle back into salvation history the principle of ethnic privilege that he excludes in chap. 9 and elsewhere: Jews, just because they are Jews, can look forward to a time when a great number of them are saved.

Many scholars despair of reconciling these two viewpoints and conclude that Paul expresses contradictory viewpoints on this matter.[116] They believe that Paul's thinking on this issue may have developed over time (even from the time he wrote chap. 9 to the time he wrote chap. 11!)[117] or that his teaching in chap. 11, as elsewhere, is directed to specific practical purposes with little concern about consistency.[118] But this conclusion — one that calls into question Paul's right to inform on this or on any issue — is unnecessary. For this negative opinion about Paul's consistency in his teaching about Israel's election fails to give due attention to larger theological presuppositions and frameworks of reference that enable us to solve the apparent contradiction at the conceptual level.

A critical frame of reference in Paul's treatment of Israel's salvation is a distinction between corporate and individual election.[119] Those traditional

---

116. See most bluntly Räisänen, "Paul, God, and Israel," pp. 192-96. See also van Buren, "Church and Israel," p. 5: ". . . that strange text, Romans 9–11, with its . . . flat contradictions." See also Dodd; Schmithals, 408; Ziesler, 237; Hübner, *Gottes Ich und Israel,* pp. 122-24; Watson, 168-70; Beker, "Romans 9–11," pp. 45-48.

117. See the note on 11:26, which refers to those who think that Paul received the "mystery" of 11:26 in a special revelation as he composed Rom. 11. See also Moffatt (*Grace,* p. 269), who thinks the ethnic concern for Israel in chap. 11 involves a modification of Paul's teaching about grace. It is common to posit development in Paul's thought over time, from the supposedly "harsh" attitude toward Israel in 1 Thess. 2:13-16 to the supposedly positive attitude expressed in Rom. 11 (see, e.g., R. Penna, "L'évolution de l'attitude de Paul envers les Juifs," in *L'Apôtre Paul,* p. 419). Especially radical are those who find the allegedly different attitudes toward Israel in chaps. 9 and 11 to be evidence that different authors were at work (cf. M. Widmann, "Der Israelit Paulus und seine antijüdischer Redaktor: Eine literarkritische Studie zu Röm. 9–11," in *"Wie gut sind deine zelte, Jaakow . . .": Festschrift zum 60. Geburtstag von Reinhold Meyer* [ed. E. L. Erlich and B. Klappert; Gerlingen: Bleicher, 1986], pp. 150-58).

118. See esp. Watson, 170-73.

119. See the commentary on 11:2.

explanations that treat Rom. 9–11 as an exposition on predestination have overemphasized the individual perspective. But some contemporary approaches err in the opposite direction. The situation Paul confronted required him to integrate the two perspectives, or, better, to interpret one in the light of the other. Paul inherited from the Scriptures and his Jewish heritage the teaching of a corporate election of all Israel. But his experience of and understanding of the gospel required a revision, or addition, to this perspective. That not all Jews were responding to the gospel did not itself overturn the traditional understanding of Israel's election; for that tradition never insisted that Israel's election required the salvation of every single Israelite. On the other hand, the relatively small number of Jews responding to the gospel must at least have pushed the boundaries of that tradition. But it was the great influx of Gentiles — as individuals, not as a "people" — that broke those boundaries altogether. Thus Paul, like some other Jewish thinkers before him (e.g., the Qumran covenanters[120]), had to develop a concept of individual election within, or alongside of, the corporate election of Israel.

Once we recognize that Paul must deal with both individual and corporate election in Rom. 9–11, it is no "harmonizing expedient" to ask which perspective Paul might have in mind in a given text. Paul has framed his discussion in Rom. 9–11 with reassertions of the continuing validity of Israel's "corporate" election (9:4-5; 11:28b-29; cf. also 11:1-2). But Paul's key task is to explain how individual election qualifies the nature and significance of this corporate election.[121] This he does in 9:6-29. This text does not revoke Israel's election,[122] but shows that it does not have a necessary salvific significance. Within the corporate election of Israel, there is operating, Paul shows, an election of individuals. This individual election in Paul's day is being extended to Gentiles and restricted to a remnant among Israel. But his focus is on his own time in salvation history.[123] "Only the remnant will be saved" is not Paul's final word on the salvation of Israel.

Nor does Paul's teaching about the freedom of God to elect whomever he chooses mean that God cannot take into consideration ethnic identity; only

120. Cf. Seifrid, *Justification*, pp. 85-89.

121. Cf. Hofius: "Paul fully acknowledges that God's election and rejection within Israel is *set in the broader framework* of God's election of *all* Israel . . ." (" 'All Israel Will Be Saved,' " p. 32; cf. also Osten-Sacken, *Christian-Jewish Dialogue*, pp. 70-72).

122. Contra, e.g., Watson, 164, 228 n. 10.

123. Indeed, B. Longenecker argues that it is the contrast between the present and the future in salvation history that explains the difference: in the present time, God does not take into account ethnic distinction, but in the future he will (see *Eschatology and the Covenant*, pp. 256-65; and "Different Answers"). But Paul seems to suggest that God is even in this age taking into account ethnic distinctions: hardening "most" of Israel and bringing in the "full number" of Gentiles.

that ethnic identity is never the *basis* for God's choice.[124] There is, therefore, nothing contradictory to chap. 9 if Paul in chap. 11 affirms that God, in faithfulness to his own pledged word, will choose to save a great number of Jews in the last days. Paul's reassertion of this traditional hope contradicts his teaching in Rom. 9 only if that chapter claims that the election of Israel is exhaustively fulfilled in the remnant of Paul's day or if it teaches that God cannot take ethnic identity in account in his decision about whom to save. But Paul affirms neither of these there.

It is true that Paul's teaching about a final ingathering of Jewish people has no parallel elsewhere in his writings. But this may be explained by the contingent character of all Paul wrote. In most of the situations where Paul taught about Israel or the Jews he was concerned to establish the right of Gentiles to enter fully into the people of God — usually against a Jewish-oriented attempt to exclude them or to impose inappropriate restrictions on them (e.g., Rom. 3–4; Galatians; Phil. 3). Only in Rom. 11, apparently, did Paul face a situation in which he needed to remind Gentile Christians of the continuing significance of Israel's election.[125]

F. CONCLUSION: PRAISE TO GOD IN LIGHT OF HIS AWESOME PLAN (11:33-36)

> 33*O the depth of the riches and of the wisdom and of the knowledge of God!*
> *How unsearchable are his judgments*
> *And inscrutable his ways!*
> 34*For who has known the mind of the Lord?*
> *And who has been his counselor?*[a]
> 35*Or who has given to him in advance, so as to give back to him?*[b]
> 36*For from him and through him and for him are all things.*
> *To him be the glory forever. Amen.*

a. Isa. 40:13
b. Job 41:3

---

124. Räisänen badly misunderstands Paul and the traditional view of God's sovereign election when he asserts that "sovereignty entails that God's action is incalculable" ("Paul, God, and Israel," p. 193). God's sovereignty in election means that nothing outside himself can force his hand to save; not that he cannot act in election to fulfill his previous decisions.

125. Ultimately, of course, one would want to seek to integrate Paul's perspective in Rom 11:25-32 with his teaching elsewhere. This is no easy task (and 1 Thess 2:13-16 is particularly difficult — for which see the recent discussion in Hagner, "Paul's Quarrel," pp. 130-36). But a recognition of the contingency of those writings goes far to mitigate the differences.

Paul appropriately concludes one of his most profound and difficult theological discussions with a hymn in praise of God for his purposes and plans. Many readers of this response to the theological argument of Rom. 9–11[1] think that Paul is communicating a sense of frustration: confronted with the mysteries of election and the future of Israel, Paul confesses that the truth of these matters can be known finally only by God himself. Certainly in these chapters Paul touches on matters, such as the interplay of divine sovereignty and human responsibility, that are ultimately beyond our ability as humans to understand fully; and Calvin's warning about our limitations at this point are well taken. But we must not push this line of interpretation too far. For Paul, after all, claims to have received revelation into a "mystery" concerning the future of Israel that gives us access to the mind of God. Throughout Rom. 9–11, while certain points remain hard to understand, Paul is claiming to be transmitting truth to which his readers are to respond. And Paul certainly teaches elsewhere that in Christ, and through the Spirit, we have access to "the secret and hidden wisdom of God" (1 Cor. 2:6-16).[2] We should, then, perhaps understand Paul's praise to be motivated not so much by the hiddenness of God's ways but by the (admittedly partial) revelation of those mind-transcending ways to us.

This expression of praise falls into three strophes: v. 33, containing three exclamations about God's wise plan; vv. 34-35, featuring three rhetorical questions that emphasize human inability to understand God's ways; and v. 36, containing a declaration about the ultimacy of God that calls forth a final doxology. This arrangement of the material, the short, roughly parallel lines, and some unusual vocabulary suggest that we should treat the passage as a hymn.[3] Paul probably composed it himself, borrowing extensively from OT wisdom traditions, apocalyptic, and Hellenistic Jewish teachings.[4]

---

1. The focus on God the Father in the doxology matches very well the emphases of Rom. 9–11, and this suggests that Paul intends the doxology to conclude these chapters only (Murray, 2.104-5; Käsemann, 318; Cranfield, 2.589; Schlier, 348; contra, e.g., Bruce [211] and Fitzmyer [632], who take it as the conclusion of chaps. 1–11).

2. See U. Wilckens, *TDNT* VII, 518. As Schnabel (*Law and Wisdom,* pp. 250-51) puts it: "God's inscrutable riches, wisdom and knowledge are closely linked with Jesus Christ who not only knew and knows God's works and plan in contrast to man, but embodied, i.e., revealed and effectively realized, God's wisdom in bringing salvation to man."

3. See especially the analyses of E. Norden, *Agnostos Theos: Untersuchungen zur Formgeschichtlichte religiöser Rede* (Leipzig/Berlin: Teubner, 1913), pp. 240-46; G. Bornkamm, "The Praise of God: Romans 11:33-36," in *Early Christian Experience,* pp. 105-11. Note also the triads: in addition to the three strophes, we find three words dependent on "depths" (v. 33), three questions (vv. 34-35), and three prepositional phrases in v. 36a (Dunn, 2.698).

4. Wisdom concepts are especially clear in vv. 34-35; apocalyptic parallels in v. 33, and a Hellenistic Jewish tradition in v. 36. Some think that Paul may have taken over a

33 The particle "O" shows that the first line in Paul's hymn is an exclamation, an emotional assertion of awe.[5] Paul's awe is stimulated by his contemplation of the "depth," or the inexhaustible magnitude,[6] of three divine qualities.[7] These qualities are not intrinsic "attributes" of God, but are what some theologians have called "communicable" attributes of God: aspects of God's character that have partial parallels among human beings and that involve God's interaction with the world he has created. "Riches" might refer generally to the infinite resources of God, but, in light of 11:12, probably connotes especially God's kindness as it is expressed in the blessing he brings on undeserving sinners — both Jew and Gentile alike.[8] God's wisdom is an extremely rich biblical theme. But Paul is undoubtedly thinking of God's wisdom as it has been revealed and expressed in his plan for the salvation of human beings.[9] "Knowledge of God" clearly means God's knowledge of us and not our knowledge of God.[10] The occurrence of the cognate verb "foreknow" in 11:2 (cf. also 8:29) suggests that God's knowledge here is that special relational "knowing" which comes to expression

---

hymn from the synagogue (e.g., Johnson, *Function,* pp. 164-73), but it is more likely that he assembled elements from various traditions to compose it himself (Bornkamm, "Praise of God," p. 105; M. Barth, "Theologie — ein Gebet (Röm 11,33-36)," *TZ* 41 [1985], 331-32).

5. BDF 146(2); BAGD.

6. Gk. βάθος. The word is always used metaphorically in Paul. In Rom. 8:39, used absolutely, it probably refers to hell (see our comments there); in Eph. 3:18 Paul speaks of the "depth" of love; while in 1 Cor. 2:10, the verse most relevant to Paul's use here, he says that "the Spirit searches all things, even the depths of God."

7. Some think that the second two genitive words in the verse, σοφίας and γνώσεως, are dependent on πλούτου, yielding the translation "O the depth of the riches both of the wisdom and knowledge of God" (KJV; cf. also NASB; NIV; cf. Calvin; Godet; Fitzmyer). But, recognizing that πλοῦτος is used absolutely already in Rom. 11 (v. 11), it makes better sense to view πλούτου, σοφίας, and γνώσεως as coordinate, each dependent on the word βάθος: "O the depth of the riches and wisdom and knowledge of God!" (NRSV; cf. also TEV; REB; S-H; Käsemann; Kuss; Wilckens; Cranfield; Dunn).

8. And see Rom. 10:12b: "The same Lord is Lord of all, *richly blessing* [πλουτῶν] all who call on him." Paul usually adds to πλοῦτος a genitive of content: riches "of glory" (Rom. 9:23; Eph. 1:18; 3:16; Phil. 4:19; Col. 1:27); "of liberality" (2 Cor. 8:2; 1 Tim. 6:17); "of grace" (Eph. 1:7); "of goodness" (Rom. 2:4); "of Christ" (Eph. 3:8); and "of assurance" (Col. 2:2). Only in Rom. 11:12 (twice) and here does he use the word absolutely.

9. See especially Paul's discussion of the true Christian "wisdom" in 1 Cor. 1:17–2:16, a wisdom whose focus is the fulfillment of God's plan in the crucified Christ. Note also the collocation of "mystery" with Christ and "wisdom" and "knowledge" in Col. 2:2-3.

10. That is, the genitive θεοῦ is subjective.

in his election of individuals to salvation (and perhaps also of Israel to her corporate blessing).[11]

The second and third lines of Paul's hymn are both introduced with another exclamatory particle, "How!"[12] Paul's stylistic care is evident here again. The two lines are syntactically parallel — predicate adjective-article-subject-possessive pronoun (the copulative verbs are assumed) — and both predicate adjectives begin with the same letters (anex-).[13] The first of these adjectives, anexeraunēta, is rare but seems to mean "unfathomable," "unsearchable."[14] Paul applies this description to God's "judgments," which will not refer here, as the word usually does in Paul, to God's judicial decisions, but to his "executive" decisions about the direction of salvation history.[15] The word "ways" in the last line has essentially the same meaning; they, too, Paul exclaims, are "inscrutable."[16] In synonymous parallelism, then, the second and third lines of Paul's hymn extol God's providential control of salvation history as something beyond human understanding.[17]

34-35 The second strophe in Paul's hymn comprises three questions, the first two of which come from Isa. 40:13[18] and the third (in v. 35) from (perhaps) Job 41:3.[19] It is possible that each question relates, in reverse order,

11. Cf., e.g., Bornkamm, "Praise of God," p. 107; Cranfield; Wilckens; Dunn; Fitzmyer.

12. Gk. ὡς. See BAGD (IV.6) for this use of the word.

13. The Greek is:

ὡς ἀνεξεραύνητα τὰ κρίματα αὐτοῦ
καὶ ἀνεξιχνίαστοι αἱ ὁδοὶ αὐτοῦ.

14. The word is not found in the NT or LXX, but is used in Symmachus's translation of the OT (Prov. 25:3 and perhaps Jer. 17:9). It may be a Hellenistic Greek variation of the classical word ἀνεξερεύνητος, "not to be searched out" (LSJ).

15. The Greek is κρίμα. Only here and in 1 Cor. 6:7 does Paul use this word in the plural. For a parallel use of the word in this way, see Ps. 19:10; 36:7; 119:75 (Schlier); cf. also Sir. 17:12.

16. Gk. ἀνεξιχνίαστος; cf. also Eph. 3:8; Job 5:9; 9:10; 34:24; Pr. Man. 6.

17. A frequently cited parallel text to v. 33 is 2 Apoc. Bar. 14:8-9: "O Lord, my Lord, who can understand your judgment? Or who can explore the depth of your way? Or who can discern the majesty of your path? Or who can discern the beginning and the end of your wisdom?" This text comes in a passage that wrestles with much the same issue that occupies Paul in Rom. 9–11: the destiny of the people of God in light of apparent calamity. On the apocalyptic background of vv. 33-35, see Johnson, Function, pp. 168-71.

18. Paul's rendering is close to the LXX, which paraphrases the MT slightly.

19. Paul's wording differs significantly from the LXX, leading to the suppositions that Paul (1) translates from the Hebrew (Meyer; Dunn); (2) translates from a version attested in the targum (Wilckens); or (3) uses a non-LXX Greek version (Michel, who notes that Paul's only other quotation from Job also differs from the LXX [see 1 Cor. 3:19]). Some MSS of the LXX (Sinaiticus and Vaticanus) add this wording after Isa. 40:14; but this is an obvious case of a LXX translator or scribe borrowing from Paul.

to one of the exclamations in v. 33. "Who knows the mind of the Lord?" would then expand the inscrutable ways of God, "Who has been his counselor?" would draw out the implications of his unsearchable judgments, and "Who has given to him in advance, so as to give back to him?" would suggest an implication of God's riches (= his kindness and mercy).[20]

The questions in these verses are obviously rhetorical, expecting the answer "no one." The first two stress that no human being can understand what God is doing in the world. But, as the wisdom tradition from which these questions are drawn teaches, what no human being can understand, "wisdom" can.[21] And since Paul sees Christ as the embodiment of wisdom, we are probably justified in adding to our expected answer "no one" a qualification: "no one, except Jesus Christ, who has revealed to us in his own person the plan of God for salvation history" (see the reference to the mystery in 11:26). The third question moves from the issue of our knowledge of God's plan to the way in which we experience it. No one, Paul claims, is ahead of God in giving,[22] as if[23] to earn a recompense[24] from him. Paul thus reminds us that it is only by God's grace that we can experience the "depth of riches" that his plan is designed to communicate.[25]

36 Paul's affirmation of the centrality of God in all of creation may relate specifically to v. 35 — no one is in a position to demand anything from God, for[26] he is . . .[27] — but probably reflects on all of vv. 33-35. The concept of God as the source *(ek)*, sustainer *(dia)*, and goal *(eis)* of all things is particularly strong among the Greek Stoic philosophers. Hellenistic Jews picked up this language and applied it to Yahweh; and it is probably, therefore, from the synagogue that Paul borrows this formula.[28] An ancient and widespread interpretation finds a reference to the Trinity in the three prepositional phrases. But this view is now, correctly, almost universally rejected. Paul is clearly speaking of God the Father; and his purpose is to underline the uniqueness and sovereignty of God that has been the focus of these verses.

20. See, e.g., Käsemann; Wilckens; Fitzmyer.
21. See, for this approach, Liebers, *Das Gesetz als Evangelium,* pp. 139-40.
22. Gk. προδίδωμι, used only here in the NT.
23. The καί has a consecutive nuance: "so that" (Wilckens).
24. Gk. ἀνταποδίδωμι. Cf. also Luke 14:14; Rom. 12:19; 1 Thess. 3:9; 2 Thess. 1:6.
25. See esp. Calvin.
26. Gk. ὅτι.
27. E.g., Meyer.
28. See Norden, *Agnostos Theou,* pp. 240-50. Dunn lists the most important parallel texts. An example of the Stoic tradition comes from the second-century Roman emperor Marcus Aurelius: ἐκ σοῦ πάντα, ἐν σοὶ πάντα, εἰς σὲ πάντα ("from you are all things, in you are all things, for you are all things") (*Meditations* 4.23); cf. also Philo, *Special Laws* 1.208. Paul offers a similar formula about God in 1 Cor. 8:6; and cf. the application of this language to Christ in Col. 1:16-17.

What should be our response to our contemplation of God's supremacy in all the universe? Like Paul's, doxology.[29]

V. THE TRANSFORMING POWER OF THE GOSPEL: CHRISTIAN CONDUCT (12:1–15:13)

In this final main section of the body of the letter, Paul shifts his focus from instruction to exhortation; from "indicative" to "imperative." Commands are rare in chaps. 1–11 (see 6:11-13, 19; 11:18, 20). Of course Paul would have been the first to emphasize that all that he teaches in Romans has an eminently "practical" significance. For if we take to heart the truth of the gospel that he has presented, we will have a transformed worldview that cannot but affect our lives in uncounted ways. Paul has made this clear already in chap. 6, where he shows how our union with Christ in his death and resurrection leads to our "walking in newness of life" (v. 4) and demands that we "present ourselves to God as those who are alive from out of the dead" (v. 13). But Paul knows that it is vital to flesh out these general principles about the transforming power of the gospel. This he does in 12:1–15:13, as he urges Christians to manifest the power of the gospel in specific areas of day-to-day life.[1]

Romans 12:1–15:13 is therefore integral to the letter and to its purposes. It is not an appendix, a last-minute "add-on" relatively unrelated to the real — theological — heart of the letter.[2] For, as we have seen, Romans, while thoroughly theological and carefully argued, is not a doctrinal treatise. It is Paul's grandest exposition of the gospel. The gospel unleashes God's power so that people, by embracing it, can be rescued from the disastrous effects of sin, being pronounced "righteous" in God's sight and having a secure hope for salvation from wrath in the last day. But, as Paul has made clear in Rom. 6, deliverance from the power of sin is inseparable from deliverance from its penalty. Union with Christ in his death and resurrection provides both. For Jesus Christ is the Lord; and thus to believe in him means at the same time a commitment to obey him (cf. "the obedience of faith" in

---

29. Paul interjects other similar doxologies in his letters; cf. Rom. 16:27; Gal. 1:5; Eph. 3:21; Phil. 4:20; 1 Tim. 1:17; 2 Tim. 4:18.

1. The exhortations of 12:1–15:13 are built on the entire argument of the letter, but most scholars recognize a particularly close relationship with chap. 6 (see, e.g., Murray, 2.109; Cranfield, 2.593-94; Wilckens, 3.2; and the notes on 12:1-2).

2. Schmithals also separates these chapters from 1-11, but for literary reasons: he argues that "Romans B," the hypothesized second of the two different letters he finds in our present Romans, begins here (pp. 417-24).

1:5 and 16:26; note also "obedience of the Gentiles" in 15:18). The "imperative" of a transformed life is therefore not an optional "second step" after we embrace the gospel: it is rooted in our initial response to the gospel itself. To eliminate this part of Romans would be therefore to omit an indispensable dimension of the gospel. The transition from Rom. 11 to Rom. 12 — which mirrors similar transitions in Ephesians (4:1) and 1 Thessalonians (4:1) — is not, therefore, a transition from "theology" to "practice," but from a focus more on the "indicative" side of the gospel to a focus more on the "imperative" side of the gospel.[3] "What God has given to us" (Rom. 1–11) gives way to "what we are to give to God." But even as we put it this way, we must quickly add the qualification that what we are to give to God cannot be produced independently of God's continuing gracious provision. God's "giving" to us is not simply a past basis for Christian obedience; it is its continuous source. "Indicative" and imperative" do not succeed each other as two distinct stages in Christian experience, but are two sides of the same coin.

One of the most striking features of Rom. 12:1–15:13 is the way in which its various themes resemble teaching that Paul gives elsewhere. The following chart outlines some of the main parallels:

The need for transformation by the renewing of the mind (12:1-2)	Eph. 4:17-24
The unity of the body of Christ despite its diversity of gifts (12:3-8)	1 Cor. 12; cf. Eph. 4:11-17
The central demand of love (12:9-21)	1 Thess. 4:9-12; 1 Cor. 13
— as the fulfillment of the law (13:8-10)	Gal. 5:13-15
The need for spiritual wakefulness in light of the Day of the Lord (13:11-14)	1 Thess. 5:1-11
Reconciliation between "weak" and "strong" Christians over issues of food (14:1–15:13)	1 Cor. 8–10

Significantly, the only section of 12:1–15:13 not included in the list above, Paul's demand for submission to government (13:1-7), has significant parallels with the teaching of Jesus (cf. Mark 12:13-17 and pars.) and with early Christian instruction (cf. 1 Pet. 2:13-14). Other parallels with

---

3. See Käsemann: "Our salvation is grounded in the creator's claim on us and this is apparent in exhortation as the reverse side of our salvation" (p. 323). For similar conclusions about the relationship of "indicative" and "imperative" in relation to Rom. 12:1–15:13, see Furnish, *Theology and Ethics,* esp. p. 106; Ortkemper, 149-56; M. Parsons, "Being Precedes Act: Indicative and Imperative in Paul's Writing," *EvQ* 88 (1988), 99-127; W. Schrage, *Ethik des Neuen Testaments* (NTD 4; Göttingen: Vandenhoeck & Ruprecht, 1982), pp. 156-61.

Jesus' teaching and the teaching of the early church are found throughout these chapters.[4] Many scholars conclude from these parallels that Paul in Rom. 12:1–15:13 is simply rehearsing typical early Christian ethical emphases with little concern for the specific situation of the Roman Christians.[5] Moreover, this emphasis on the gospel's provision for obedience in daily life fits with Paul's overall purpose in Romans, the explanation and defense of "his" gospel. Against those who might object that the abandonment of the law as a code of conduct (cf. 6:14, 15; 7:1-6) leads to license, Paul argues that the gospel itself provides sufficient ethical guidance for Christians. Through the renewal of the mind that the gospel makes possible, Christians can know and do the will of God (12:2); and by following the dictates of love, they can accomplish all that the law itself demands of them (13:8-10).[6]

There is some truth in this picture, as the lack of reference to specific issues and the abbreviated, almost proverbial nature of some of the sections (e.g., 12:9-21) indicate. But there is also evidence that Paul is writing with at least one eye on the situation of the church in Rome.[7] Romans 14:1–15:13 is almost certainly addressed to a specific problem in the Roman Christian community;[8] and the lack of a clear parallel in Paul's other letters to his exhortation to obey government authorities (13:1-7) suggests that this passage, too, may have particular relevance to the Roman Christians. As is the case,

---

4. Some parallels with Jewish and Greek moral instruction are also present. For example, W. T. Wilson finds many parallels, in both structure and content, between Rom. 12 and various Jewish wisdom texts (*Love without Pretense: Romans 12:9-21 and Hellenistic-Jewish Wisdom Literature* [WUNT 2.46; Tübingen: Mohr, 1991], pp. 91-126).

5. M. Dibelius's influential understanding of "parenesis," a genre in which traditional moral teaching was passed on with little regard for theological integration or the circumstances of the addressees, plays an important role here (cf. *From Tradition to Gospel* [New York: Scribner's, n.d.], p. 238). Furnish has shown that Paul's ethics are more closely integrated with his theology than Dibelius thought (see *Theology and Ethics*), but many scholars still regard the exhortations of 12:1–15:13 as basically unrelated to the specific needs of the Christians in Rome. See esp. C. H. Dodd, "The 'Primitive Catechism' and the Sayings of Jesus," in *More New Testament Studies* (Grand Rapids: Eerdmans, 1968), pp. 11-13; R. J. Karris, "Romans 14:1–15:13 and the Occasion of Romans," in Donfried, 81-84. See also Ridderbos, *Paul,* pp. 275-77, who, while admitting that we find no "systematic ethic" in Paul, notes that texts like Rom. 12:3-21 point to a "a certain line of thought" that might represent his typical emphases.

6. See C. J. Roetzel, "Sacrifice in Romans 12–15," *WW* 6 (1986), 412-18; Wilson, *Love without Pretense,* pp. 206-7. Dunn, similarly, stresses the way in which Paul in these chapters sketches the kind of life expected of the "redefined" people of God (2.705); cf. also Leenhardt, 300.

7. See, e.g., Wedderburn, *Reasons,* pp. 75-87.

8. See the introduction to 14:1–15:13 for substantiation.

then, with Romans as a whole, Paul in these chapters adapts his general description of the gospel and its implications for the situation he addresses in Rome.[9]

Paul's exhortation falls into two parts: injunctions relating to Christian conduct generally in chaps. 12–13 and guidelines for a specific problem affecting the Roman community in 14:1–15:13.[10] Paul's general exhortations in chaps. 12–13 are framed by texts that bring out the eschatological context in which Christians are to display their redeemed character.[11] Paul here presupposes the "realm transfer" imagery that he has used especially in Rom. 5–8 to describe the Christian's situation: transferred from the old realm of sin into the new realm of salvation, we are people who belong now to "the day," but who must still struggle against the forces of darkness since we still await the culmination of our salvation (13:11-14). Our task, then, is to conduct ourselves as those who belong to the day and to resist the pressure to conform to the old realm from which we have been saved (12:2). The exhortations that fall between these two texts take up various issues of importance for the early Christian community, including, no doubt, the Roman community. The exhortations display various specific points of contact with one another but do not fall into any neat arrangement.[12] Paul begins by encouraging Christians to assess their place within the community and their ministry to it accurately and soberly (12:3-8). There follow a series of short, proverbial, injunctions that loosely develop the theme of Christian love (12:9-21). Paul then enjoins obedience to governmental authorities (13:1-7) before turning back again to love, which he elevates as the virtue that provides for the true and complete fulfillment of all the commands of the law (13:8-10).

9. See Ortkemper, 11-18. J. Moiser argues that Paul's concern to unite the Roman community in order to provide support for his mission work in Spain drives everything that Paul says in these chapters ("Rethinking Romans 12–15," *NTS* 36 [1990], 571-82). Minear (pp. 82-90) also finds specific relevance for the Roman church, but against the evidence of the text (see esp. 12:3) he thinks that Paul is addressing only the "strong" in chaps. 12–13.

10. Most commentators suggest such a division; see, e.g., Godet, 421; Käsemann, 323; Michel, 365; Schlier, 349.

11. Cf., e.g., Furnish, *Theology and Ethics,* pp. 215-16; Ortkemper, 5; O. Merk, *Handeln aus Glauben: Die Motivierungen der paulinischen Ethik* (Marburger Theologische Studien 5; Marburg: N. G. Elwert, 1968), pp. 166-67.

12. Contra, e.g., Godet (p. 423), who thinks the exhortations are "systematically arranged," and Dunn (2.706), who posits a chiastic arrangement of 12:1–15:16. However, Leenhardt (p. 300) and S-H (p. 351) go too far in the other direction, emphasizing the loose and spontaneous organization.

A. THE HEART OF THE MATTER: TOTAL TRANSFORMATION (12:1-2)

1Therefore I exhort you, brothers and sisters, through the mercies of God, to present your bodies as a sacrifice — living, holy, and well pleasing to God, your true worship. 2And do not conform to this age, but be transformed through the renewing of your mind, so that you can approve what is the will of God, that is, what is good, well pleasing, and perfect.

Romans 12:1-2 is one of the best-known passages in the NT. Its fame is justified: here Paul succinctly and with vivid imagery summarizes what the Christian response to God's grace in Christ should be. The verses have a pivotal role in Romans. On the one hand, they look back at the argument of chaps. 1–11. While Paul ultimately has in view all of these chapters, verbal and thematic links point to two texts as particularly significant. The first is Rom. 1, whose downward spiral of false and foolish worship (cf. v. 25) and corrupted minds (cf. v. 28) now finds its reversal in the Christians' "reasonable" worship and renewed mind.[13] The second is Romans 6, whose brief mention of the need for Christians to "present" themselves (vv. 13 and 19) as those "alive from the dead" (v. 13) is here reiterated and expanded.[14] At the same time, 12:1-2 stand as the heading for all that follows in 12:3–15:13.

1 "Therefore"[15] must be given its full weight:[16] Paul wants to show that the exhortations of 12:1–15:13 are built firmly on the theology of chaps. 1–11.[17] The English verb "exhort" captures well the nuance of the Greek *parakaleō* in contexts such as this.[18] Its semantic range lies somewhere between "request" and

---

13. See esp. C. Evans, "Romans 12.1-2: The True Worship," in Lorenzi, *Dimensions,* pp. 30-31.

14. See, for these relationships generally, M. Thompson, *Clothed with Christ: The Example and Teaching of Jesus in Romans 12.1–15.13* (JSNTSup 59; Sheffield: Sheffield Academic Press, 1991), pp. 79-85; D. Peterson, "Worship and Ethics in Romans 12," *TynBul* 44 (1993), 276-79.

15. Gk. οὖν.

16. E.g., Cranfield; Wilckens; contra those who view οὖν as a simple transitional particle (e.g., Käsemann; C. J. Bjerkelund, *Parakalô: Form, Funktion und Sinn der parakalô-Sätze in den paulinischen Briefen* [Bibliotheca Theologica Norvegica 1; Oslo: Universitetsforlaget, 1967], pp. 161-68; Evans, "Romans 12.1-2," pp. 11-12).

17. Most commentators think that Paul refers back to the argument of the entire epistle (e.g., Godet; S-H; Murray; Cranfield), but some think the reference is immmediately to 11:35-36 (Meyer), to chaps. 5–8 (Schlier; Zeller [chaps. 6–8]), or to chaps. 5–11 (Dunn).

18. Paul's 54 uses of παρακαλέω fall into three categories: (1) "comfort" (14 occurrences; cf., e.g., 2 Cor. 1:4); (2) "beseech" (a personal request; nine occurrences; cf., e.g., 2 Cor. 12:8); and (3) "exhort."

"command": an exhortation comes with authority, but the authority of a preacher who is the mediator of God's truth rather than the authority of a superior issuing a command.[19] "Through the mercies[20] of God" underscores the connection between what Paul now asks his readers to do and what he has told them earlier in the letter that God has done for them. All that Paul has written in the letter thus far may be summed up under the heading of the mercy of God in action. Paul has just summarized that universal mercy of God (11:30-32) and expressed praise to God for it (11:33-36). Now he calls Christians to respond. The preposition "through" is better translated here "because of" (TEV) or "in view of" (NIV): it indicates not the means by which Paul exhorts but the basis, or even the source, of the exhortation.[21] Ultimately Paul is simply the instrument through whom "the mercy of God" is itself exhorting us. As Paul puts it in 2 Cor. 5:20, he is an "ambassador for Christ," one through whom God himself exhorts his people.[22] What Paul calls for in v. 1 — and, by extension, in all of 12:2–15:13 — is no more (and no less!) than the appropriate and expected response to God's mercy as we have experienced it. Yet this response is no simple "tit for tat" bargain, as if we grudgingly "pay God back" for what he has done for us. For God's mercy is not a matter of past benefits only, but it continues to exercise its power in and through us. That God's mercy does not automatically produce the obedience God expects

19. "The exhortation is distinguished from a mere verbal appeal by this reference back to the work of salvation as its presupposition and basis" [he is referring to "through the mercy of God"] (O. Schmitz, *TDNT* V, 795). See also H. Schlier, "Vom Wesen der apostolischen Ermahnung nach Römerbrief 12,1-2," in *Die Zeit der Kirche* (2d ed.; Freiburg: Herder, 1958), pp. 75-78, and his commentary, 351-53; Cranfield 2.597. Bjerkelund has compared Paul's use of παρακαλέω to its use in Hellenistic literature (*Parakalô*), suggesting that Paul often uses it to introduce key points in his argument. See also the survey of A. Grabner-Haider, *Paraklese und Eschatologie bei Paulus: Mensch und Welt im Anspruch der Zukunft Gottes* (NTAbh n.s. 4; Münster: Aschendorff, 1968).

20. I reflect in my (literal) translation the fact that the Greek word Paul uses here, οἰκτιρμῶν, is plural (cf. also KJV; NASB; RSV; NRSV). But Paul picks up the plural form from the LXX, which uses it to translate a Hebrew word (רַחֲמִים) that has a singular meaning. With, then, NIV; TEV; REB, and most commentators (e.g., Käsemann; Cranfield), it is probably best translated in English with a singular.

21. See the other occurrences of διά following παρακαλέω in Paul: Rom. 15:30 ("I exhort you *through* our Lord Jesus Christ and *through* the love of the Spirit"); 1 Cor. 1:10 ("I exhort you, brothers, *through* the name of our Lord Jesus Christ"); and 2 Cor. 10:1 ("I myself, Paul, exhort you *through* the meekness and gentleness of Christ"; the use of διά in 2 Cor. 5:20 is different). In each case, the object of διά is that which is ultimately making the appeal that is expressed. See, e.g., Schlier, "Ermähnung," pp. 78-80; Bjerkelund, *Parakalô*, pp. 162-67; Grabner-Haider, *Paraklese und Eschatologie*, pp. 48-49, 117; Käsemann; Wilckens. Some think that Paul's construction might reflect the Lat. *per* (e.g., BDF 223[4]; Turner, 267; Zahn; Michel; Cranfield), but this is not clear (Schlier).

22. See Furnish, *Theology and Ethics*, pp. 99-102.

is clear from the imperatives in this passage. But God's mercy manifested in his Spirit's work of inward renewal (see v. 2) does impel us toward the obedience that the gospel demands.[23]

We experience God's mercy as a power that exerts a total and all-encompassing claim upon us: grace now "reigns" over us (5:21). It is therefore entirely fitting that our response is to be one that is equally total and all-encompassing: the presentation of our entire persons as a sacrifice to God.[24] Some scholars think that Paul's use of the aorist tense to state this demand indicates that he thinks of this presentation as a "once-for-all" act.[25] But the aorist tense itself does not indicate this; and there is no reason in the context to think that Paul would view this presentation as an offering that we make only once. Paul simply commands us to make this offering, saying nothing about how often it needs to be done.

Paul's use of sacrificial imagery here fits a pattern found throughout the NT. Christians no longer offer literal sacrifices; for Christ has fulfilled and thus brought to an end the OT sacrificial system. But the centrality of sacrifice in ancient religion made it a natural and inevitable vehicle for the early Christians to express their own religious convictions. At the same time, the NT use of cultic language has an important salvation-historical and polemical function, claiming for Christianity the fulfillment of those institutions so central to the OT and to Judaism.[26] Christians offer no bloody sacrifice on an altar; but they offer "spiritual sacrifices" (1 Pet. 2:5), such as the "sacrifice of praise to God, which is the fruit of lips that acknowledge his name" (Heb. 13:15). In Rom. 15:16, Paul describes his own missionary work in cultic terms (see also Phil. 2:17; and note Phil. 3:3 and 4:18). In Rom. 12:1, however, the sacrifice we offer is not some specific form of praise or service, but our "bodies" themselves. It is not only what we can give that God demands; he demands the giver.[27] "Body" can, of course, refer to the physical body as such,[28] and the metaphorical associations

---

23. See, e.g., G. Dehn, *Vom christlichen Leben. Auslegung des 12. und 13. Kapitels des Briefes an die Römer* (Neukirchen/Vluyn, Neukirchener, 1954), pp. 12-14.

24. The shift from the plural σώματα ("bodies") to the singular θυσίαν ("sacrifice") could indicate that Paul thinks of this presentation as having a corporate dimension, involving the service of the entire Christian community together (e.g., G. Smiga, "Romans 12:1-2 and 15:30-32 and the Occasion of the Letter to the Romans," *CBQ* 53 [1991], 268-70). But θυσίαν is probably a distributive singular.

25. E.g., Godet, who contrasts the "once-for-all" requirement of v. 1 with the "continuous incessant" acts demanded in v. 2 (where present tenses are used).

26. The OT and other Jewish authors also used sacrificial language metaphorically (cf., e.g., Ps. 50:14, 23; 51:16-17; 141:2; Sir. 35:1; Tob. 4:10-11; 12:12; 2 Macc. 12:43-44; Jud. 16:16; 4 Macc. 6:29; 1QS 9:3-5; cf. J. Behm, *TDNT* III, 186-87), but, as Dunn points out, these texts do not, as do the NT texts, assume the abolition of the literal cult.

27. Wilckens.

28. It is given a prominently physical sense by, e.g., Godet; S-H; Murray; Gundry, 34-36.

with sacrifice make it an appropriate choice here. But Paul probably intends to refer to the entire person, with special emphasis on that person's interaction with the world.[29] Paul is making a special point to emphasize that the sacrifice we are called on to make requires a dedication to the service of God in the harsh and often ambiguous life of this world. The sacrificial context makes it likely that the verb "present," unlike its somewhat parallel occurrences in 6:13 and 19, means "offer as a sacrifice."[30]

Paul qualifies the sacrifice that we offer with our bodies with three adjectives.[31] Each of the three continues the sacrificial metaphor. Many commentators, noting the many points of comparison with Rom. 6, give "living" a theological sense, "as those who have been brought to new spiritual life" (cf. 6:11, 13).[32] This would make good sense if the adjective modified "our bodies." But it does not; it modifies "sacrifice." This being the case, it is more likely to refer to the nature of the sacrifice itself: one that does not die as it is offered but goes on living and therefore continues in its efficacy until the person who is offered dies.[33] "Holy" is a regular description of sacrifices; it implies here that the offering of ourselves to God involves a being "set apart" from the profane and a dedication to the service of the Lord.[34] Such a sacrifice is "well pleasing to God."[35]

At the end of v. 1, Paul adds an appositional phrase that qualifies the whole exhortation that Paul has just given: offering ourselves as a sacrifice is our "*logikēn* worship."[36] The meaning of the word *logikēn* is notoriously

29. On this "theological" meaning of σῶμα, particularly in Paul, see the notes on 6:6. See here Calvin; Barrett; Käsemann; Cranfield; Dunn; Fitzmyer; Ortkemper, 23-24.

30. The verb παρίστημι does not have this sense in biblical Greek but does in extrabiblical Greek (BAGD).

31. All three follow the noun they modify, θυσία, as I have brought out, somewhat awkwardly, in my translation. But by putting the first adjective, ζῶσαν ("living"), before the noun, many English translations (e.g., KJV; NIV; NASB; NRSV) give it a prominence that Paul does not.

32. Calvin; S-H; Cranfield; Murray; Schlier; Wilckens; Thüsing, *Per Christum in Deum,* pp. 94-95.

33. Parallel uses of the adjective "living" are John 6:51: "I am the *living* bread that has come down from heaven . . ."; and 1 Pet. 1:3, "*living* hope." See Hodge; Dunn.

34. The metaphorical context makes clear that "holy" has primarily cultic associations (Käsemann; Dunn); but for Paul the ultimate significance of this being "set apart" has, of course, moral implications (see Cranfield).

35. εὐάρεστον τῷ θεῷ; Paul uses the same phrase to refer to a metaphorical sacrifice in Phil. 4:18.

36. A few commentators think that τὴν λογικὴν λατρείαν ὑμῶν ("your *logikēn* worship") is in apposition to θυσίαν ("sacrifice") only (e.g., Hodge; Barrett). But it makes better sense to see the phrase in apposition to the entire exhortation, beginning with παραστῆσαι (cf., e.g., S-H; Denney; Ortkemper, 26).

difficult to pin down. The word *logikos* (the lexical form of the adjective *logikēn*) does not occur in the LXX and only once elsewhere in the NT, where its meaning is also debated: 1 Pet. 2:2, where Peter exhorts his readers to "long for the pure *logikon* milk." The word does, however, have a rich background in Greek and Hellenistic Jewish philosophy and religion. Arguing that God and human beings had *logos* (reason) in common, some of the Greek philosophers of the Stoic school emphasized that only *logikos* worship could be truly appropriate worship. They contrasted this "rational" worship with what they considered to be the superstitions that were so typical of Greek religion.[37] Hellenistic Jews took over this use of the term, applying it sometimes to the mental and spiritual attitude that was necessary for a sacrifice to have any merit before God.[38] Still later, the word was applied directly to sacrifice in the gnostic Hermetic writings.[39]

Considering this background and the context, we arrive at four main possibilities for the connotation of *logikos* here: (1) "spiritual," in the sense of "inner": a worship that involves the mind and the heart as opposed to a worship that simply "goes through the motions"[40]; (2) "spiritual" or "rational," in the sense of "appropriate for human beings as rational and spiritual creatures of God": a worship that honors God by giving him what he truly wants as opposed to the depraved worship offered by human beings under the power of sin (see Rom. 1:23-25);[41] (3) "rational," in the sense of

---

37. See the evidence listed in G. Kittel, *TDNT* IV, 142 and Ortkemper, 28-33. The sense of λογικός as it is used in these texts is especially clear in this statement of Epictetus: "If I were a nightingale, I should be singing as a nightingale; if a swan, as a swan. But as it is, I am a rational being [λογικός], therefore I must be singing hymns of praise to God" (1.16.20-21).

38. The clearest example is Philo, *Special Laws* 1.277: ". . . that which is precious in the sight of God is not the number of victims immolated but the true purity of a rational spirit [πνεῦμα λογικόν] in him who makes the sacrifice"; cf. 1.272: "And indeed though the worshippers bring nothing else, in bringing themselves they offer the best of sacrifices, the full and truly perfect oblation of noble living, as they honour with hymns and thanksgivings their Benefactor and Saviour, God. . . ." See also *T. Levi* 3:6, which refers to angels who "present to the Lord a pleasing odor, a rational [λογικός] and bloodless oblation."

39. Several passages speak of a λογικὴ θυσία; for the texts, see Cranfield.

40. Note the contrast in Rom. 2:28-29 between the Jew "in appearance only" and the Jew "in the hiddenness [of the heart]." See, for this general approach, Zahn; Barrett; Black; Bruce; Ziesler; Ortkemper, 27; J. M. Nielen, "Die paulinische Auffassung der λογικὴ λατρεία (rationabile obsequium; Röm. 12,1) in ihrer Beziehung zum kultischen Gottesdienst," *TGl* 18 (1926), pp. 696-97.

41. Although they differ in detail, see Lietzmann; Dunn; Evans, "Romans 12.1-2," pp. 17-21; H. D. Betz, "The Foundations of Christian Ethics According to Romans 12:1-2," in *Witness and Existence: Essays in Honor of Schubert M. Ogden* (ed. P. E. Devenish and G. L. Goodwin; Chicago: University of Chicago, 1989), pp. 63, 69; idem, "Christianity

"acceptable to human reason": a worship that "makes sense," as opposed to the "irrational" worship of God through the offering of animals;[42] (4) "reasonable," or "logical," in the sense of "fitting the circumstances": a worship that is appropriate to those who have truly understood the truth revealed in Christ.[43]

This last connotation, while probably implied, does not go far enough, ignoring too much of the rich background of the term that we have sketched. The third is also a questionable explanation, assuming as it does that the OT sacrificial system, for instance, was, or would have been, viewed by Paul as an irrational form of worship.[44] Choosing between the first two alternatives is difficult and perhaps not necessary. Certainly Paul does not suggest, as the reference to "bodies" makes clear, that true Christian worship is a matter only of inner attitude.[45] But the inner attitude is basic to acceptable worship, as Paul makes clear in v. 2 by stressing the "renewing of your mind." And it is just this involvement of the mind, renewed so that it can again understand God aright, that makes this worship the only finally appropriate and true worship. In light of this, and recognizing that each of the usual translations "spiritual" (NIV; NASB; NRSV) and "reasonable" (KJV) misses an important part of the meaning, it would be best to follow TEV and translate "true worship."[46]

The word "worship" *(latreia)* continues the cultic imagery of the verse.[47] Paul probably chooses the term deliberately to create a contrast between the Jewish and Christian form of worship. For Christians, there is

---

as Religion: Paul's Attempt at Definition in Romans," *JR* 91 (1991), pp. 337-39; P. Seiden-sticker, *Lebendiges Opfer (Röm 12,1): Ein Beitrag zur Theologie des Apostels Paulus* (NTAbh 20; Münster: Aschendorff, 1954), pp. 260-63.

42. Chrysostom; S-H; Lagrange; Haldane; Gifford; Fitzmyer.

43. Godet; Cranfield; Peterson, "Worship and Ethics," pp. 273-75; Newton, *Concept of Purity,* p. 71.

44. See the appropriate objection of Roetzel along these lines ("Sacrifice," pp. 414-15).

45. Cranfield.

46. See Wilckens. Paul's use of the term may have a polemical edge: in contrast to the superstitious practices of the pagans, the mystical integration with the *logos* in Hermetic worship, and the continuation of the "shadow" of the cult in Judaism, Christians in offering themselves to the God who redeemed them offer the only "true" worship (see Schlier, who stresses the contrast with the Hermetic conception).

47. Its one other occurrence in Paul is a reference to the Jewish cult (9:4), the only other NT occurrences (John 16:2; Heb. 9:1, 6) have a cultic connotation, and it has this reference in all but one of its nine LXX occurrences (Exod. 12:25, 26; 13:5; Josh. 22:27; 1 Chron. 28:13; 1 Macc. 1:43; 2:19, 22. 3 Macc. 4:14 is the exception). The cognate verb λατρεύω is also a religious term, referring to "serving" (1:9; 2 Tim. 1:3) or "worshiping" (Rom. 1:25; Phil. 3:3) God.

no more "cult" or "sacrifice" in any literal sense.[48] While the Jew looked to the Jerusalem temple and its cult as the center of worship, the Christian looks back to the once-for-all sacrifice of Christ. Christians are all priests (1 Pet. 2:5; Rev. 1:6; 5:10; 20:6), forming together the temple where God now reveals himself in a special way.[49] But Paul does not "spiritualize" the cult; rather, he extends the sphere of the cultic into every dimension of life.[50] Thus the Christian is called to a worship that is not confined to one place or to one time, but which involves all places and all times: "Christian worship does not consist of what is practiced at sacred sites, at sacred times, and with sacred acts. . . . It is the offering of bodily existence in the otherwise profane sphere."[51] Chrysostom comments: "And how is the body, it may be said, to become a sacrifice? Let the eye look on no evil thing, and it hath become a sacrifice; let thy tongue speak nothing filthy, and it hath become an offering; let thine hand do no lawless deed, and it hath become a whole burnt offering." Regular meetings together of Christians for praise and mutual edification are appropriate and, indeed, commanded in Scripture. And what happens at these meetings is certainly "worship." But such special times of corporate worship are only one aspect of the continual worship that each of us is to offer the Lord in the sacrifice of our bodies day by day.[52]

2 By using the vague conjunction *kai* (usually translated "and"; cf. KJV and NASB), Paul leaves open the exact relationship between vv. 1 and 2. The two verses could be coordinate, issuing two parallel but separate exhortations.[53] But v. 2 is probably subordinate to v. 1, giving the means by which we can carry out the sweeping exhortation of v. 1.[54] We can present our bodies to the Lord as genuinely holy and acceptable sacrifices only if we "do not conform to this world" but "are transformed by the renewing of the

---

48. Hence Dunn is right to label the later tendency to describe the Lord's Supper as a sacrifice as a departure from the Pauline (and NT) perspective.

49. 1 Cor. 3:9, 16-17; 6:19; 2 Cor. 6:16; Eph. 2:19-22; 1 Pet. 2:5.

50. Cf. Roetzel, "Sacrifice," pp. 415-16. He intriguingly compares Paul's concept to that of the Pharisees, who, it has been alleged by several prominent scholars, had as their program the extension of the purity of the cult into everyday Jewish life.

51. Käsemann.

52. We may again quote Käsemann: "[Woship services and the sacraments] are no longer, as in cultic thinking, fundamentally separated from everyday Christian life in such a way as to mean something other than the promise for this and the summons to it. . . . Either the whole of Christian life is worship and the gatherings and sacramental acts of the community provide equipment and instruction for this, or these gatherings and acts lead in fact to absurdity" (p. 327). See also Peterson, "Worship and Ethics."

53. Zahn, e.g., thinks that v. 1 is directed mainly to Jewish Christians and v. 2 to Gentile Christians. Fitzmyer is representative of others who argue that v. 1 focuses on external ("bodily") service and v. 2 on internal ("noetic") commitment.

54. Evans, "Romans 12.1-2," p. 25.

mind."[55] The salvation-historical framework that is so basic to the development and expression of Paul's understanding of the Christian life (see particularly Rom. 5–8) comes to the surface very plainly here.[56] "This world," literally "this age,"[57] is the sin-dominated, death-producing realm in which all people, included in Adam's fall, naturally belong. But it is "to deliver us from the present evil age" that Christ gave himself (Gal. 1:4); and those who belong to Christ have been transferred from the old realm of sin and death into the new realm of righteousness and life.[58] But this transfer, while decisive and final, does not isolate us from the influence of the old realm. For while belonging to the new realm, we continue to live, as people still in the "body,"[59] in the old realm. Paul's command that we "not conform to this world," then, builds on the theology of Rom. 5–8 (and of Rom. 6 especially) and calls on us to resist the pressure to "be squeezed into the mold" of this world and the "pattern" of behavior that typifies it (see 1 Cor. 7:31).

Because the verb "conform" is in the present tense, many scholars think that Paul wants his readers to "*stop* conforming" to this world.[60] But Paul's generally positive attitude toward the Romans' spirituality (cf. 15:14) makes this doubtful.[61] Also uncertain is the voice of the verb and its significance. It could be passive — "do not be conformed" (KJV; NASB; NRSV)[62] — or middle, with a reflexive idea — "do not conform yourselves" (TEV) — but, perhaps most likely, whether middle or passive in form, it has a simple ("intransitive") active significance — "do not conform" (NIV; REB; NJB).[63]

The second, positive, imperative in the verse, however, has a clearly passive meaning: "be transformed." The neat verbal paronomasia found in most English translations (con*formed*/trans*formed*) is not present in Greek,

---

55. The shift from παρακαλέω plus infinitive (v. 1) to imperatives (v. 2) is found elsewhere in Paul; see Rom. 16:17.

56. See esp. Nygren for this emphasis.

57. Gk. αἰών. The word can refer to the "world" in a spatial sense (cf. BAGD), but typically in Paul it has a temporal nuance, referring to "this age" as the period of time in world history characterized by the domination of sin and Satan (1 Cor. 1:20; 2:6, 8; 3:18; 2 Cor. 4:4; Gal. 1:4; Eph. 1:21; 2:2; 1 Tim. 6:17; 2 Tim. 4:10; Tit. 2:12).

58. Rom. 5:17, 21; 6:2-6, 14, 17-18, 22; 7:2-6; 8:2, 9.

59. Cf. the reference to σῶμα in v. 1.

60. E.g., Wilckens; Cranfield. The supposition that the present imperative when negated denotes the need to stop an action one is engaging in (durative *Aktionsart*) is widespread even in the grammars; cf., e.g., Turner, 74-75.

61. Porter thinks that Paul uses the present tense rather to draw attention to the importance of the prohibition (*Verbal Aspect,* pp. 351-60); but this is also unlikely. See, for further remarks on tense in Greek commands, the notes on 6:12 and 13.

62. Dunn.

63. See Turner, 57, who notes that Hellenistic Greek manifested a tendency to use the middle and the passive voice with an active meaning.

where verbs from two separate roots are used. Most older commentators and many recent ones are sure that this change in root signifies a change in meaning also. They argue that the verb translated "conform"[64] connotes a superficial resemblance, whereas the verb translated "be transformed"[65] refers to an inward and genuine resemblance. As Morris puts it, then, "Paul is looking for a transformation at the deepest level that is infinitely more significant than the conformity to the world's pattern that is distinctive of so many lives."[66] However, as Barrett notes, "conformity to this age is no superficial matter." More important, the lexical basis for the distinction is not solid.[67] Therefore the shift in root probably reflects no difference in meaning; and, somewhat ironically, the use of the same root to translate both verbs in English reflects closely enough the meaning of the Greek terms. The tense of the verb is again present; and in this case the fact that the renewing of the mind is a continuing process justifies us in thinking that Paul uses this tense to stress the need for us to work constantly at our transformation.

"The renewing of your mind" is the means by which this transformation takes place. "Mind" translates a word that Paul uses especially to connote a person's "practical reason," or "moral consciousness."[68] Christians are to adjust their way of thinking about everything in accordance with the "newness" of their life in the Spirit (cf. 7:6).[69] This "re-programming" of the mind

---

64. Gk. συσχηματίζομαι, which uses the σχημ- root.

65. Gk. μεταμορφόω, which uses the μορφ- root.

66. Others (e.g., Chrysostom; Leenhardt) think that συσχηματίζομαι implies the transitory nature of this world. Among those who find a distinction of some kind are Godet; S-H; Michel; Murray; Dunn; R. A. Culpepper, "God's Righteousness in the Life of His People. Romans 12–15," *RevExp* 73 (1976), 452. J. B. Lightfoot, in an extended note in his Philippians commentary, presented the classic case for a consistent NT distinction between words built on the σχημ- root and those built on the μορφ- root (*Philippians,* pp. 127-33).

67. Paul can certainly use verbs from the σχημ- root to indicate a superficial and outward transformation; cf. his references in 2 Cor. 11:13 and 15 to false apostles, who "masquerade" as apostles of Christ and servants of righteousness, and in 2 Cor. 11:14 to Satan, who "disguises" himself as an "angel of light." But a similar superficial or outward conformity is difficult to suppose in Phil. 3:21, where Paul says that God will "transform" (μετασχηματίζομαι) our "body of humility" into a "body of his glory"; and note that Paul uses a word from the μορφ- root in the same verse to refer to the same concept. Similarly, a difference between μορφή and σχῆμα is difficult to sustain in Phil. 2:6-7. Among those who do not think the two verbs are different in meaning in Rom. 12:2 are Barrett; Wilckens; Cranfield; Evans, "Romans 12.1-2," pp. 25-26.

68. Denney. The Greek is νοῦς. See the note on 1:28.

69. The Greek word in Rom. 12:2 is ἀνακαινώσει (a dative of instrument; cf. Turner, 240); Paul uses the word in a similar way in Tit. 3:5 and the cognate verb in 2 Cor. 4:16 (our inner person being renewed day by day) and Col. 3:10 (the new [person] being

does not take place overnight but is a lifelong process by which our way of thinking is to resemble more and more the way God wants us to think. In Rom. 1:28 Paul has pointed out that people's rejection of God has resulted in God's giving them over to a "worthless" mind: one that is "unqualified" (*adokimos*) in assessing the truth about God and the world he has made. Now, Paul asserts, the purpose[70] of our being transformed by the renewing of the mind is that this state might be reversed; that we might be able to "approve" (*dokimazō*) the will of God. "Approving" the will of God means to understand and agree with what God wants of us with a view to putting it into practice.[71] That Paul means here by "the will of God" his moral direction is clear from the way Paul describes it: this will is that which is "good," "acceptable [to God]," and "perfect."[72]

Paul's teaching about the Christian's source for finding the moral will of God in this verse deserves attention. Paul has made clear earlier in the letter that the Christian no longer is to look to the OT law as a complete and authoritative guide for conduct (see Rom. 5:20; 6:14, 15; 7:4). What, Paul's first readers and we ourselves today might ask, is to be put in its place? Paul answers: the renewed mind of the believer. Paul's confidence in the mind of the Christian is the result of his understanding of the work of the Spirit, who is actively working to effect the renewal in thinking that Paul here assumes (cf. Rom. 8:4-9).[73] And it is important to note that Paul's confidence in our ability to determine right and wrong is not unbounded. He knows that the renewal of the mind is a process and that as long as we are in these

---

renewed in knowledge according to the image of the one who created it). Particularly significant for the argument of the letter is the way this phrase picks up καινότητι πνεύματος ("newness of Spirit") from 7:6 and καινότητι ζωῆς ("newness of life") from 6:4. See also Eph. 4:23: "be renewed [ἀνανεοῦσθαι] in [or by] the spirit of your mind [νοός]" (the use of the verb ἀνανέομαι in this verse demonstrates that a hard-and-fast distinction between the roots νε- and καιν- is as difficult to sustain as one between μορφ- and σχημ-).

70. The Greek construction εἰς τό with the infinitive probably denotes purpose here (Michel) rather than result (as Lenski thinks).

71. Ziesler paraphrases "discover in order to carry out." On the Greek verb δοκιμάζω, see the note on 1:28.

72. The three adjectives are probably in apposition to τὸ θέλημα τοῦ θεοῦ, as the translation above and most English translations suggest (Murray; Käsemann; Cranfield; Schlier), rather than direct descriptions of it, as KJV translates: ". . . what is that good, and acceptable, and perfect will of God" (this view is defended by, e.g., Godet).

73. See Westerholm, 243; and on this general subject, D. J. Moo, "Putting the Renewed Mind to Work," in *Renewing Your Mind in a Secular World* (ed. J. D. Woodbridge; Chicago: Moody, 1985), pp. 145-60; Fee, *God's Empowering Presence,* pp. 596-97.

bodies we need some revealed, objective standards against which to measure our behavior.[74] Hence Paul makes clear that Christians are not without "law," but are under "the law of Christ" (Gal. 6:2; 1 Cor. 9:19). This "law" has its heart in Jesus' own teaching about the will of God, expanded and explicated by his appointed representatives, the apostles. But Paul's vision, to which he calls us, is of Christians whose minds are so thoroughly renewed that we know from within, almost instinctively, what we are to do to please God in any given situation. We need "law"; but it would be to betray Paul's call to us in these verses to substitute external commands for the continuing work of mind-renewal that is at the heart of God's New Covenant work.[75]

B. HUMILITY AND MUTUAL SERVICE (12:3-8)

3*For I say through the grace that was given to me to every person among you, that you not think beyond what is necessary to think but that you think with sober thinking, as God has measured to each a measure of faith.* 4*For even as we have many members in one body, and all the members do not have the same function,* 5*so also we, who are many, are one body in Christ, and individually members of one another.* 6*And since we have gifts that differ according to the grace that was given to us, let us use them accordingly: if prophecy, according to the analogy of faith;* 7*if service, in service; if one is a teacher, in teaching;* 8*if one is an exhorter, in exhorting; one who shares with others, in simplicity; one who presides, with diligence; one who shows mercy, in gladness.*

The main point of this paragraph is the command in v. 3: Christians are "to regard themselves with sober judgment." The discussion of the diversity of gifts and their uses within the one body of Christ in vv. 4-8 provides the basis for this command. Understanding that Christians belong to one another in one body and have in common the same grace of God (v. 5) and faith (vv. 3, 6) will help to stifle exaggerated ideas about one's own status or ministry. And recognition of the significant contribution made by each member of the body

---

74. Schnabel, therefore, suggests that Paul combines in his ethics the perspectives of the legal and wisdom traditions: "The Christian ethic according to Paul is neither legalistic nor antinomistic — it is a heteronomous sapiential ethos realizing the correlation of law and wisdom in the horizon of God's salvational action in and through Christ" (*Law and Wisdom,* pp. 310-42 [342]).

75. Cf. Longenecker, 195-96: the Christian requires for ethical guidance both the subjective "mind of Christ" and the objective "law of Christ."

of Christ will prevent one from thinking too highly (or too lowly) of him- or herself.[1]

What place does this teaching have within Rom. 12? And what prompts Paul to include it here? No specific relationship with vv. 1-2 is evident,[2] but this call to Christian humility and unity is certainly one important manifestation of the transformation in thinking that should characterize the believer. Perhaps Paul is especially concerned that believers not take too individualistic an approach to transformation. Thus he wants us to recognize that the transformation of character is seen especially in our relationships with one another.[3] Paul may, then, have included this teaching here simply because it was an important part of his understanding of Christian behavior, as the parallels with 1 Cor. 12 and, to a lesser extent, Eph. 4:1-16, suggest.[4]

But the parallel with 1 Cor. 12 could also suggest that Paul is directing his comments to the same kind of people as those with whom he had to deal in Corinth: "pneumatics," Christians who overvalued certain more evident or spectacular manifestations of the Spirit.[5] This supposition gains force when we remember that Paul is writing from Corinth. Nevertheless, Romans itself gives little evidence that this issue was important to Paul at this point; at the most, perhaps, the Corinthian experience led Paul to recognize the potential for spiritual pride and consequent disunity in the Spirit's gifts to the church. We must also reckon with the possibility that Paul emphasizes the importance of each Christian judging himself accurately in order to prepare the way for his rebuke of the weak and strong parties in Rome (14:1–15:13).[6] However, vv. 3-8 do not speak to the issue of judging one another that is the key issue in Rom. 14:1–15:13. Therefore, a concern for Roman bickering does not seem to have been the main motivation for these verses. Probably, then, Paul writes what he does here mainly because it was integral to his understanding of the way in which the gospel was to transform the lives of Christians. Here, he suggests, is

---

1. On the way in which the concept of unity and diversity gives to the paragraph its cohesion, see J. S. Bosch, "Le corps du christ et les charismes dans l'épître aux Romains," in Lorenzi, *Dimensions,* pp. 51-52.

2. Although, as Fee points out (*God's Empowering Presence,* p. 604), the "thinking" language of vv. 3-8 (φρονέω and its cognates) may be conceptually related to λογικήν and νοός in 12:1-2.

3. See Schlatter, 335.

4. See, e.g., Leenhardt, 308; Dunn, 2.726; Ortkemper, 43-44; U. Brockhaus, *Charisma und Amt: Die paulinische Charismalehre auf dem Hintergrund der frühchristlichen Gemeindefunktionen* (Wüppertal: Theologischer, 1972), pp. 195-97.

5. See esp. Käsemann, 333; cf. also Michel, 366, 373; Schmithals, 438; Althaus, 125-26.

6. See Wedderburn, *Reasons,* pp. 78-81.

one specific example of the will of God for the Christian who has been transferred into the new age.

3 By connecting this new paragraph to vv. 1-2 with a "for," Paul suggests that the exhortations he now gives are concrete instances of the transformed way of life to which the believer is called. In light of Paul's reference to his apostolic status in the phrase "through the grace given to me,"[7] "I say" must refer to an authoritative request, parallel to "I exhort" in v. 1.[8] Paul addresses this admonition not to any specific group or kind of person in the Roman community, but to "every person" among them. (Contrast 11:13-32, where Paul scolds the Gentile Christians for arrogance.) Paul's admonition is built on a wordplay that is difficult to bring out in English, although I have tried in the translation above, quite awkwardly, to do so. The key term, which Paul uses in both its simple ("think") and in two compound forms ("think beyond"; "sober thinking"), is *phroneō*.[9] This verb, which is a favorite of Paul's and which we have met before in Romans,[10] connotes not so much the act of thinking in itself (the intellectual process) but the direction of one's thinking, the way in which a person views something.[11] In this verse, it is clear that Paul is using the verb to denote the way in which a person views him- or herself. In contrast to the overestimation of ourselves to which we are so prone, Paul insists that we are to view ourselves in a "sober" manner[12] — in accordance with a true and objective estimate, the product of the "renewed mind" (12:2).

But a true and objective estimate of ourselves requires that we have an accurate and objective standard against which to measure ourselves. And this, Paul says, we have, for God has "measured to each one[13] a measure of

7. The personal pronoun μοι and the parallels in Rom. 1:5 and 15:15 suggest strongly that "the grace given to me" refers to Paul's apostolic calling (as also in 1 Cor. 3:10; Gal. 2:9; Eph. 3:7, 8) rather than to the grace Paul has received in common with others (though Leenhardt, Hodge, and Morris argue for the latter).

8. Käsemann; Cranfield; Wilckens. Cf. also Rom. 2:22; 1 Cor. 7:8; Gal. 1:9; 5:2.

9. ὑπερφρονεῖν . . . φρονεῖν . . . φρονεῖν . . . σωφρονεῖν. The paronomasia is found elsewhere in Hellenistic literature.

10. Rom. 8:5; 11:20; cf. the cognate noun in 8:6, 7, and 27 and the adjective in 11:25.

11. See the notes on 8:5.

12. The infinitive construction εἰς τὸ σωφρονεῖν does not indicate purpose (contra Turner, 143), but modifies φρονεῖν, stating the way in which one is to "think." See the note on 1:20. Paul uses σωφρονέω (cf. also 2 Cor. 5:13) and its cognates σωφρονίζω (Tit. 2:4), σωφρονισμός (2 Tim. 1:7), σωφρονῶς (Tit. 2:12), σωφροσύνη (1 Tim. 2:9, 15), and σώφρων (1 Tim. 3:2; Tit. 1:8; 2:2, 5) to denote a quality of steady, clearheaded understanding of the believer and his or her world that recognizes the truth of the gospel. The word group denoted a cardinal virtue among the Greeks, from whom it found its way into Hellenistic Jewish literature (see U. Luck, *TDNT* VII, 1097-1102).

13. The Gk. ἑκάστῳ is an abbreviation of ἕκαστος ὡς αὐτῷ: "each, as [God has given] him" (Michel).

faith." The meaning of the phrase is uncertain, with two possibilities deserving consideration.

(1) In light of the discussion of the spiritual gifts that follows, the phrase might refer to the differing "measures" of faith God has assigned to each believer.[14] This interpretation matches the closest parallel expression in Paul (2 Cor. 10:13), and fits the context (see esp. "proportion of faith" in v. 6b). But its interpretation of "faith" is strained. This faith might refer, as it has throughout Romans thus far, to the basic Christian response to the gospel.[15] But it is difficult to think that Paul would consider this faith as given by God in different measures to Christians.[16] Recognizing this, many supporters of this interpretation think that the faith Paul refers to is, or relates especially to, the differing capacities God gives to people for their service of the community.[17] But this interpretation of the word "faith" is questionable; and, in any case, Paul has not prepared us for the use of this word in Romans.

(2) If faith is, then, basic Christian faith as given equally by God to all, then the "measure of faith" could refer to this shared faith as the standard by which Christians are to regard themselves. Our faith *is* the measure.[18] On this view God has not given a different measure to each Christian but has given to each Christian the same measure. Dunn and others criticize this interpretation because it does not recognize the distributive implications of the verb *merizō*, "measure" or "apportion." But this second interpretation faces fewer difficulties than the first and should be accepted. "Measure of faith," then, should be compared in this paragraph not to the many different "gifts" that God distributes to believers, but to the one common grace from which they stem (v. 6). It is that faith which believers have in common as fellow members of the body of Christ that Paul here highlights as the standard against which each of us is to estimate himself.

14. On this view, μέτρον refers to a "measured quantity" (as in Eph. 4:7, 13, 16; 2 Cor. 10:13; John 3:34 [?]; cf. BAGD; K. Deissner, *TDNT* IV, 632-33) and the genitive πίστεως is partitive.

15. Käsemann; Michel; Schlier; Dunn; Ortkemper, 45-46; R. Jewett, *Christian Tolerance: Paul's Message to the Modern Church* (Philadelphia: Westminster, 1982), pp. 59-63.

16. Dunn adduces Rom. 4:19-20 and 14:1 in support of the notion that faith in Paul is "variable." But while Paul recognizes that faith can be weak or strong, he does not imply — indeed, his exhortations contradict the notion — that it is God who gives believers that "degree" of faith. See also Godet and Murray, who suggest rather strained interpretations to deal with this problem.

17. Barrett; Zahn; Bruce; Huby. "Measure of faith" becomes then almost equivalent to one's χάρισμα, "gift."

18. μέτρον will then mean "means of measurement," "standard" (as in Matt. 7:2; 23:32; Mark 4:24; Luke 6:38; Rev. 21:15, 17) and πίστεως will be a genitive of apposition. For this view see esp. Cranfield (and cf. his article "μέτρον πίστεως in Romans 12:3," *NTS* 8 [1961-62], 345-51); Wilckens; Fitzmyer; Bosch, "Le corps du Christ," pp. 53-54.

4-5   In these verses Paul uses the imagery of the human body to bring out both the diversity and the unity of the Christian community. Paul's comparison of the church to a body is familiar from his other letters. He first uses the comparison in 1 Cor. 12, and it is found in its most developed form in Ephesians and Colossians. Scholars have labored long and hard to pin down the exact source of Paul's "body of Christ" metaphor.[19] But so natural is the imagery and so widespread was it in the ancient world that Paul may well have picked up the comparison from his general environment, molding it into its final form, of course, under the influence of his theology.[20] Paul's use of the metaphor in this text has most in common with 1 Cor. 12:12-31. In both these passages Paul compares individual Christians to "members" of the human body. And it is not only the basic metaphor that 1 Cor. 12 and this text have in common; Paul also applies the metaphor to the same basic issue. As in 1 Cor. 12, where Paul uses the body metaphor to (among other things) rebuke the arrogance of some members of the body who prided themselves on possessing more important gifts (vv. 22-26), so here in Rom. 12 Paul uses the metaphor to back up his exhortation that believers not think more highly of themselves than they should.[21]

Paul sketches the basis for his comparison in v. 4 ("just as"): "we have[22] many parts in one body, and all the parts do not have the same function."[23] Verse 5 then draws the conclusion ("so also"): "we, who are many,[24] are one body in Christ, and individually members of one another."[25]

19. Others in Paul's day compared the political community to the human body; cf. the well-known parable of Menenius Agrippa found in the Roman historian Livy (2.32; cf. Epictetus 2.10.4-5). Many other influences are alleged to have contributed to Paul's conception, including gnostic "primal man" myths, Jewish speculation about Adam, eucharistic reflection, and redemptive-historical conceptions of Christ as "inclusive" person. See the survey of options in Käsemann, 336-38 and Dunn, 2.722-24 especially; and in much more detail, Ridderbos, *Paul,* pp. 362-87; Best, *One Body;* L. Cerfaux, *The Church in the Theology of Paul* (New York: Herder, 1959); E. Schweizer, *The Church as the Body of Christ* (Richmond: Knox, 1964); E. Percy, *Der Leib Christi* (LUÅ 38.1; Lund: Gleerup, 1942).

20. Cf. Beker, 307-9, who emphasizes that the "body" image is one of many that Paul uses to convey the nature of Christian relationships.

21. V. 3; note the γάρ ("for") at the beginning of v. 4.

22. Paul presumably uses the first plural verb to state what he and his readers together know generally to be the case.

23. Gk. πρᾶξιν. Paul uses the word elsewhere to mean "act" (Rom. 8:13; Col. 3:9); here it means "function" (BAGD).

24. οἱ πολλοί ("the many") is in apposition to the understood subject of the verb ἐσμεν. Paul uses the word "many" because his focus is on plurality rather than on universality (e.g., "all").

25. The phrase at the end of v. 5, καθ' εἷς, is an idiomatic expression in later Greek, meaning "each one" (BDF 305); εἷς is indeclinable (Z-G, 487).

Paul, working from the assumption of the unity of the body,[26] argues for the need to recognize a healthy diversity within that one body. The overall thrust of the letter and the specific exhortation in 14:1–15:13 might suggest that Paul has especially in view the conflict between Jew and Gentile. But he gives little evidence of this in the context. It seems rather that, as in 1 Cor. 12, it is the diversity of gifts and the temptation to comparison and false pride that comes with that diversity that is his chief concern.

One matter that is not clear in this passage is whether Paul is thinking of the local church or of the church universal. The omission of "apostles" from the list of gifts that follows (contrast 1 Cor. 12:28 and Eph. 4:11) might suggest that he has the local church only in view (where there would, at that point in time, be no apostles in the technical sense of that word). But we must qualify "local church" to mean the Christian community in Rome, for chap. 16 makes clear that the Christians in Rome, all of whom Paul addresses in the letter (cf. 1:7), met in several "house churches." Our oneness in Christ, Paul reminds us, extends beyond those with whom we meet weekly for worship, embracing all who call on the name of the Lord.

6   Paul continues to echo his teaching in 1 Cor. 12, as he turns next to discuss the way in which gifts exemplify diversity in unity. But if the general logical progression is clear enough, the syntactical progression is not. The problem is twofold: (1) what is the relationship between v. 6 and v. 5? and (2) what verbs, if any, are we to supply in vv. 6b-8? The participle that opens v. 6[27] could indicate that the verse is subordinate to v. 5: "We, who are many, are one body in Christ, . . . having gifts that differ according to the grace given to us."[28] But in most English translations and commentaries v. 6 begins a new sentence. But, to turn to the second question, how are we to understand this new sentence? We can allow the participle to stand as the ruling verb throughout vv. 6-8. In this case, after mentioning the diversity of gifts in v. 6a, Paul in vv. 6b-8 cites illustrations of them: as NRSV translates, "We have gifts that differ according to the grace given to us: prophecy, in proportion to faith; ministry, in ministering; the teacher, in teaching; the exhorter, in exhortation; the giver, in generosity; the leader, in diligence; the compassionate, in cheerfulness." With this understanding of the syntax, vv. 6-8 have a purely "indicative" function: Paul is describing the way in which God, in his grace, has distributed different gifts to his people as a means of building the unity of the body.[29]

The difficulty with this view is that it does not sufficiently account for the phrases that Paul appends to each gift ("in proportion to faith," "in

---

26. Cf. Ridderbos, *Paul,* p. 376.
27. Gk. ἔχοντες, lit. "having."
28. Cf. Moulton, 183-84; Denney; Dunn.
29. See esp. Dunn.

service," etc.). These seem out of place in an enumeration of gifts. These qualifications of each gift appear to reflect an underlying hortatory sense: for example, "if a person has the gift of prophecy, *let him or her use it* in proportion to faith."[30] In agreement, then, with most commentators, we should assume an ellipsis in vv. 6b-8 that must be filled with an imperative verb (as in NASB and RSV; see my translation above) or series of imperative verbs (KJV; NIV; TEV; REB; NJB).[31] Paul is then not just listing gifts; he is exhorting each member of the community to use his or her own gift diligently and faithfully to strengthen the body's unity and help it to flourish.

But before turning to exhortation, Paul reminds us of the wonderful blessing of the varied gifts that he has given the church. "We have different gifts," Paul asserts, and his assumption that these gifts are operative in the Roman church, which Paul has neither founded nor visited, shows that the operation of gifts was widespread, if not universal, in the early church. Believers possess different *charismata* ("gifts"); but each one is the product of God's *charis* ("grace"), which all believers have in common. Again Paul stresses the combination of diversity within unity that makes the church so rich and strong.[32] But if the gifts are to bring these positive benefits, they must be used rightly — not for self-aggrandizement (cf. v. 3) but in accordance with their true nature. It is this that Paul focuses attention on in the series of exhortations in vv. 6b-8.

Two of the gifts Paul mentions in these verses — prophecy and teaching — are also found in other lists of gifts in Paul.[33] The gifts in v. 8, however, have no linguistic equivalent in the other lists, although the ministries they denote could well correspond to, or overlap with, some of the gifts listed elsewhere. These texts suggest that Paul, and presumably the early church generally, recognized a small number of well-defined and widely occurring gifts along with an indefinite number of other less-defined gifts, some of which may not have been manifest everywhere and some of which may have overlapped with others.

---

30. See Meyer.

31. The ellipsis of verbs is not uncommon in Greek. Perhaps we could put the ellipsis here in the category of "formulae and proverbs that tend to be expressed in laconic form" (BDF 480[5]). See also Godet; S-H; Michel; Murray; Barrett; Schlier; Wilckens; Cranfield. NASB keeps ἔχοντες subordinate to this understood imperative, interpreting it as a causal participle: "since we have . . ." But it is better to treat it as a circumstantial participle and give the statement of the diversity of gifts full weight on its own (see NIV; Schlatter; Schlier; Cranfield).

32. On the Pauline teaching about χαρίσματα, see H. Schürmann, "Die geistlichen Gnadengaben in den paulinischen Gemeiden," in *Ursprung und Gestalt: Erörterungen und Besinningen zum Neuen Testament* (Düsseldorf: Patmos, 1970), pp. 236-73.

33. Prophecy in 1 Cor. 12:7-10, 28 and Eph. 4:11; teaching in 1 Cor. 12:28 and Eph. 4:11.

Paul places the six gifts he mentions into two groups of three each.[34] It may be significant that the first example is that of the gift of prophecy, since it occurs in second position in 1 Cor. 12:28 and Eph. 4:11 (where "apostles," not found here, come first). As 1 Cor. 14 especially reveals, Paul prized this gift very highly. NT prophecy could include predictions of the future (cf. Acts 11:28; 21:10-12), but this was not its essence. More broadly, rather, NT prophecy involved proclaiming to the community information that God had revealed to the prophet for the church's edification (see esp. 1 Cor. 14:3, 24-25, 30). The truth revealed by the prophet did not come with the authority of the truth taught by the apostles, for prophetic speech was to be scrutinized by other prophets (1 Cor. 14:29-32).[35]

But Paul suggests in this verse the need for each prophet to use the gift rightly: each is to prophesy "in accordance with the *analogia* of faith." *Analogia* is a term drawn from the world of mathematics and logic, where it denotes the correct proportion or right relationship.[36] Prophesying, Paul is saying, is to be in "right proportion" to faith. As in the similar phrase in v. 3b, the question here is what "faith" means. Perhaps the most obvious possibility is that Paul refers to the special "charismatic" faith God gives to each prophet. Paul would then be urging that prophets be sure to prophesy in accordance with the degree of faith that they have received: they are to transmit to the church all that God has given them to say, but no more than what God has given them to say.[37] As we argued in v. 3, however, this interpretation of faith does not have a solid basis in Paul. The majority of interpreters think that faith here is not our act of believing but that which we believe:[38] Christian teaching.[39] It would certainly make good sense for Paul to insist that prophets assess what they are saying against the standard of Christian truth. And "faith" can have this objective sense in Paul.[40] But the

---

34. The first three (vv. 6b-8a) are each introduced with εἴτε ("if," "whether"); the last three have no introductory particle.

35. For this view of the nature of NT prophecy see W. Grudem, *The Gift of Prophecy in 1 Corinthians* (Washington: University Press of America, 1982; cf., in revised form, *The Gift of Prophecy in the New Testament and the World Today* [Westchester: Crossway, 1988]); cf. also D. E. Aune, *Prophecy in Early Christianity and the Ancient Mediterranean World* (Grand Rapids: Eerdmans, 1983).

36. See LSJ. The word does not appear in the NT or LXX. Josephus, however, says that the porticos on the temple in Jerusalem were in "right proportion" to the temple as a whole (*Ant.* 15.396); cf. also Philo, *Virtues* 95.

37. S-H; Michel; Murray; Dunn; Fee, *God's Empowering Presence,* pp. 608-9.

38. Lat. *fides quae creditur,* "the faith that one believes."

39. E.g., Calvin; Käsemann; Wilckens; Schlier; Fitzmyer; Ortkemper, 73-74. Exegetes and theologians in the Middle Ages and Reformation built on this phrase the concept of "the analogy of faith," the hermeneutical principle that Scripture must be interpreted on the basis of other Scripture. See, e.g., Melanchthon's treatment of the phrase in his commentary on Romans.

40. It is debated whether the word has this meaning in the earlier letters of Paul

meaning is relatively rare and is not found elsewhere in Romans. On the whole, then, we are inclined to side with Cranfield, who argues that faith refers, as usual, to basic Christian faith and that "the *analogia* of faith" is essentially the same as the "measure of faith" in v. 3: the standard implied in one's own belief in Christ. Prophets, Paul is saying, are to make sure that their utterances are in right proportion to their faith in Christ.

7 The second gift is that of "serving" or "ministering." Words from the root *diak-* were originally used to denote "waiting at table," a connotation that was preserved into the NT period (see Luke 17:8). The words refer to service to others of a personal nature and often carried, in both the Greek and Jewish worlds, nuances of subservience and lack of status.[41] But Jesus described his own intention in terms of service and urged his followers to emulate him (Mark 10:45 and pars.). "Service" then became a standard way describing the work that Christians do on behalf of others and to the glory of God; the translation "minister" brings out this religious connotation. Paul uses "service" words to denote Christian "ministry" in general,[42] the ministry of Christ,[43] his own specific ministry and that of others,[44] the specific ministry of collecting money for the saints in Jerusalem,[45] and a special office or function within the church (the *diakonos,* "deacon").[46] Paul never elsewhere mentions "service" as a distinct gift, and some commentators think therefore that he uses it very generally here, of any kind of ministry that a Christian might have.[47] But the other gifts in these verses involve specific functions. Probably, then, Paul thinks of a specific gift of service that qualifies a person to fill the office of "deacon," a ministry that apparently involved especially organizing and providing for the material needs of the church.[48] In urging Christians who have this gift of "service" to use it "in

---

(although cf. Gal. 1:23), but it clearly does in the Pastoral Epistles (see, e.g., 1 Tim. 1:4, 19a; 3:9; 4:1, 6; 6:21). See, e.g., R. Bultmann, *TDNT* VI, 213-14 (whose list of references is, however, very generous).

41. See H. W. Beyer, *TDNT* II, 81-83.

42. Rom. 15:25; 1 Cor. 3:5; 12:5; 16:15; 2 Cor. 3:3, 6, 7, 8, 9 (twice); 4:1; 6:4; 11:15, 15, 23; Eph. 3:7; 4:12; 6:21; Col. 1:7, 23, 25; 4:7; 1 Tim. 1:12; 4:6; 2 Tim. 1:18; 4:11; Phlm. 13.

43. Rom. 15:8; Gal. 2:17.

44. Rom. 11:13; 2 Cor. 5:18; 6:3; Col. 4:17; 2 Tim. 4:5.

45. Rom. 15:31; 2 Cor. 8:4, 19, 20; 9:1, 12, 13.

46. Rom. 16:1 (see the notes there); Phil. 1:1; 1 Tim. 3:8, 10, 12, 13. Only in Rom. 13:4 does Paul use words from the διακ- root to describe a "service" that is not carried out by a Christian.

47. Huby; Viard; Schlier; Ortkemper, 74-76.

48. E.g., Godet; S-H; Murray; Käsemann; Wilckens; Cranfield. Dunn thinks the meaning lies somewhere between "service" generally and serving as a deacon specifically. Wilckens suggests that διακονίαν might be the "heading" for the last three gifts, with προφητείαν the heading for "teaching" and "exhorting"; see the summary of ministries

service,"[49] Paul is emphasizing the importance of recognizing the gift and using it in accordance with its true nature. The gift of "service" should not become an occasion of pride (v. 3) but should be the foundation for heartfelt and sacrificial "serving" of others. Perhaps Paul is also concerned that those who have a certain gift might seek to minister in areas outside their sphere of giftedness and so neglect the gift that they have been given.

Paul mentions the gift of "teaching" in two of his other lists of gifts (1 Cor. 12:28, 29; Eph. 4:11), and in both places it is listed immediately after "prophecy." Here Paul refers to "the teacher" rather than to the gift of teaching. Why he changes from abstract nouns in describing the first two gifts — "prophecy," "service" — to personal designations for the last four is not clear.[50] While both prophecy and teaching are speaking gifts that are intended to exhort the church, they are distinguishable. "Prophecy," as we have seen, has a revelatory basis: the prophet speaks the words that God "puts into his mouth." Teaching, on the other hand, involves the passing on of the truth of the gospel as it has been preserved in the church.[51] Again, Paul is concerned that those who have the gift of teaching faithfully use that gift.

8 The word translated "exhorter"[52] could also be translated "comforter," or "encourager" (NIV; TEV). But coming immediately after "teacher," the word probably denotes the activity of urging Christians to live out the truth of the gospel.[53]

Paul changes his syntax yet again in his enumeration of the last three gifts[54]; and again it is hard to find any reason for the change. "The one who

---

in 1 Pet. 4:11 under the heading of "speaking" (λαλέω) and "serving" (διακονέω). The former is possible; but "prophecy" in Paul is a specific gift and cannot be used as a heading for the others. Bosch thinks that διακονία must refer to the "ministry of the Word" because of its location between "prophecy" and "teaching" ("Le corps du Christ," pp. 64-65). But there is no evidence that Paul has constructed his list with such care.

49. The ἐν indicates manner (Z-G, 487).

50. Dunn suggests that Paul viewed teaching as an activity regularly done by specific individuals; but the same is apparently true of prophecy.

51. The sense of the special ministry of teaching becomes especially evident in the Pastoral Epistles; see esp. 2 Tim. 2:2; also 1 Tim. 1:10; 6:3; 2 Tim. 3:10; Tit. 1:9; 2:1, 7, 10. 1 Tim. 3:2 and 5:17 suggest that elders/overseers are especially active in teaching. On teaching in the NT see esp. K. Rengstorf, *TDNT* II, 138-65 and H. Greeven, "Propheten, Lehrer, Vorsteher bei Paulus: Zur Frage der 'Ämter' im Urchristentum," *ZNW* 44 (1952-53), 1-43.

52. Gk. παρακαλῶν. On the meaning of this verb, see the note on 12:1.

53. See esp. Schlatter; on this sense of παρακαλέω, see v. 1. On the noun παράκλησις, see the note on 15:4.

54. He drops the introductory particle εἴτε (whose sense, however, continues in force) and changes the way he qualifies the use of the gifts, from ἐν with a noun cognate to the word denoting the gift to ἐν with a distinctive noun.

shares"[55] could denote one who distributes the resources of the church as a whole[56] or one who shares his or her own resources with those less fortunate.[57] A decision between the two is difficult, but perhaps the qualification "in simplicity" fits better the situation of one who is sharing one's own goods. "Simplicity" translates *haplotēs,* a word that means "singleness" (of purpose; hence "simplicity"; cf. 2 Cor. 11:3; Eph. 6:5; Col. 3:22).[58] However, when used of giving, the meaning of the word shades over into "generosity," that is, a giving that displays a singleness of heart and intent (2 Cor. 8:2; 9:11, 13).[59] Either meaning fits the present context very well. But it might be better to stick with the basic and well-attested meaning "simplicity."[60] Paul is encouraging the one who gives to others to do so straightforwardly and without ulterior motives.

The fifth kind of gifted person Paul exhorts is *ho proïstamenos.* The word may denote a person who presides over something or a person who comes to the aid of others.[61] Noting that Paul sandwiches this gift between two others that refer to giving, some commentators argue for the latter meaning.[62] But the meaning "give aid" is not well attested for this verb, and Paul does not appear to use the verb with this meaning elsewhere. Probably, then, we should translate "one who presides." But presides over what? Paul does not say, and this leads a few scholars to think that Paul may intend to denote any person who is in a position of leadership, whether that be in the home or the church.[63] Others try to do justice to the context by arguing that Paul is referring to those persons who presided over the charitable work of the church.[64] But Paul twice elsewhere uses this verb (once absolutely) to denote

55. Gk. μεταδιδούς.

56. Calvin; Käsemann; Schlier.

57. Godet; S-H; Murray; Cranfield; Dunn; Ortkemper, 80-81. W. C. van Unnik argues that what one "shares" here is not material possessions but the Word of God ("The Interpretation of Romans 12:8: ὁ μεταδιδοὺς ἐν ἁπλότητι," in *On Language, Culture, and Religion: In Honor of Eugene A. Nida* [ed. M. Black and W. Smalley; The Hague: Mouton, 1974], pp. 169-83). But the meaning "share material goods" for μεταδίδωμι is well attested (see Luke 3:11; Eph. 4:28) and makes better sense in the context.

58. See also esp. *T. Issachar,* which holds up ἁπλότης, in the sense of "singleness" or "integrity," as a key moral virtue.

59. Silva ("New Lexical Semitisms," pp. 253-54) suggests that this shade of meaning may be partly due to Semitic influence.

60. See KJV; cf. Godet; Murray; Käsemann; Cranfield; Dunn; Black (who cites the use of the word in *T. Issachar*). Contra NIV; NRSV; TEV; cf. BAGD (though with a note).

61. See BAGD.

62. Michel argues that the word is used in the technical sense "act as a patron" (cf. the related word προστάτις in 16:2); cf. also BAGD; Dunn.

63. S-H; Alford. Paul uses the word to refer to "managing" one's home in 1 Tim. 3:4, 5, 12.

64. See Cranfield especially; also Lagrange; Leenhardt; Godet; Wilckens.

768

the "leaders" of the local church (1 Thess. 5:12; 1 Tim. 5:17). It is probably this ministry, usually associated with the elders/overseers (see 1 Tim. 5:17) that Paul has in mind here.[65] Paul exhorts the leaders in the community to pursue their calling with "eagerness" or "diligence."[66]

Paul turns finally to the one with the gift of "showing mercy."[67] Pinning down the exact nature of this ministry is not easy; as Dunn points out, this is the only place that Paul uses the verb "show mercy" of human beings. Noting that the word "mercy" is used in the NT to describe the very important Jewish pious activity of almsgiving — providing materially for the poor (cf. Matt. 6:3) — Dunn suggests that Paul might be thinking specifically of this ministry here.[68] But the connection of the word "mercy" with Jewish almsgiving is not widespread enough to justify this restriction of the reference. Probably, then, we are to understand the ministry very generally and include within it any act of mercy toward others, such as visiting the sick, caring for the elderly or disabled, and providing for the poor.[69] Those who are active in such ministries of mercy should be especially careful, Paul advises, to avoid a grudging or downcast attitude, but they should strive to minister with "cheerfulness."[70]

C. LOVE AND ITS MANIFESTATIONS (12:9-21)

> 9*Let love be sincere.*
> *Abhor what is evil;*
> *cling to what is good.*
> 10*In brotherly love, be heartfelt in your love to one another;*
> *in honor, go ahead of one another;*
> 11*in zeal, do not be lazy.*
> *Be set on fire by the Spirit;*
> *serve the Lord.*[1]

65. Calvin; Murray; Käsemann; Fitzmyer.
66. Gk. σπουδή; cf. also Rom. 12:11; 2 Cor. 7:11, 12; 8:7, 8, 16.
67. Gk. ὁ ἐλεῶν.
68. Dunn.
69. Calvin; Godet; Murray; Käsemann; Cranfield; Wilckens. This interpretation has the additional advantage of distinguishing this last gift from the fourth, "sharing with others."
70. Gk. ἱλαρότητι; cf. 2 Cor. 9:7.
1. A group of MSS from the "western" textual family (the original hand and third corrector of D, F, and G) read, in place of "serving the Lord" (κυρίῳ), "serving the time" (καιρῷ). Many scholars favor this western reading, arguing that it is far more likely that scribes would have changed the unusual "serving the time" to the obvious "serving the Lord" than that the reverse took place (see Godet, 435; Michel, 384-85; Käsemann, 346). If this word is read, then Paul would be urging Christians to "use advantageously the [present] time" (cf. Paul's exhortation to "redeem the time" in Eph. 5:16 and Col. 4:5). But the phrase "serving the

12*Rejoice in hope;*
bear up under tribulation;
be devoted to prayer.
13*Participate in meeting the needs of the saints;*
pursue hospitality.

14*Bless those who persecute you;*[2]
bless and do not curse.

15*Rejoice with those who rejoice;*
weep with those who weep.

16*Think the same thing toward one another;*
do not think highly of yourself, but associate with the lowly;
do not become proud in your own estimation.

17*Do not repay evil for evil.*
Take thought for what is good in the sight of all people.
18*If possible, to the extent that it depends on you, be at*
peace with all people.
19*Do not avenge yourselves, beloved ones, but give*
place to wrath; for it is written, "I will avenge,
I will pay back,"[a] *says the Lord.*
20*But "if your enemy is hungry, feed him; if he thirsts, give*
him something to drink; for by doing this you will be
heaping coals of fire on his head."[b]
21*Do not be overcome by evil, but overcome evil with the good.*[3]

---

time" in ancient Greek had the negative connotation of opportunism, and it is almost impossible that Paul could have written this. Probably, then, "serving the Lord" (found in P[46], all the Alexandrian witnesses [‫א‬, A, B, 33, 81, 1739], Ψ, and the majority text) is original and was changed in some MSS through error (cf. esp. Cranfield, 2.634-36; also S-H, 362; Wilckens, 2.21; Schlier, 376-77; Dunn, 2.737; Ortkemper, 93-94).

2. ὑμᾶς ("you") is missing in two very important MSS (P[46] and the primary Alexandrian uncial B; cf. also the secondary Alexandrian minuscule 1739) and a few others. This shorter text could very well be original, the word having been added by assimilation to Matt. 5:44 (Cranfield, 2.640; Wilckens, 3.22). But it makes little difference to the meaning since some such object must in any case be assumed.

3. We have formatted this text to reveal its structure, in which we follow closely the proposal of D. A. Black, "The Pauline Love Command: Structure, Style, and Ethics in Romans 12.9-21," *Filologia Neotestamentaria* 1 (1989), 3-21. The structural relations are clearer in the Greek:

9 Ἡ ἀγάπη ἀνυπόκριτος.
    ἀποστυγοῦντες τὸ πονηρόν,
    κολλώμενοι τῷ ἀγαθῷ,
10   τῇ φιλαδελφίᾳ εἰς ἀλλήλους φιλόστοργοι,

770

a. Deut. 32:35
b. Prov. 25:21-22a

Four features of this passage are particularly noteworthy. (1) Its style. Paul fires off a volley of short, sharp injunctions with little elaboration. The omission of finite verbs in most of these injunctions in the Greek text makes the abruptness of these injunctions even more pronounced.[4] Related to the rapid-fire style of this section is (2) its loose structure. There are few conjunctions or particles to indicate the flow of thought, and it is often not clear on what principle (if any) Paul has organized his various admonitions. And the connections among several of the sayings appear to be verbal rather than logical.[5] The apparently haphazard arrangement makes it especially difficult to pinpoint (3) the theme of the passage. Many commentators content themselves, therefore, with a very general heading: for example, "Maxims to Guide the Christian Life" (S-H). Finally, (4) the text reflects several diverse texts and tradi-

---

        τῇ τιμῇ ἀλλήλους προηγούμενοι,
11   τῇ σπουδῇ μὴ ὀκνηροί,
        τῷ πνεύματι ζέοντες,
        τῷ κυρίῳ δουλεύοντες,
12   τῇ ἐλπίδι χαίροντες,
        τῇ θλίψει ὑπομένοντες,
        τῇ προσευχῇ προσκαρτεροῦντες,
13   ταῖς χρείαις τῶν ἁγίων κοινωνοῦντες,
        τὴν φιλοξενίαν διώκοντες.
14   εὐλογεῖτε τοὺς διώκοντας [ὑμᾶς],
        εὐλογεῖτε καὶ μὴ καταρᾶσθε.
15   χαίρειν μετὰ χαιρόντων
        κλαίειν μετὰ κλαιόντων
16   τὸ αὐτὸ εἰς ἀλλήλους φρονοῦντες,
        μὴ τὰ ὑψηλὰ φρονοῦντες ἀλλὰ τοῖς ταπεινοῖς συναπαγόμενοι.
        μὴ γίνεσθε φρόνιμοι παρ᾽ ἑαυτοῖς.
17   μηδενὶ κακὸν ἀντὶ κακοῦ ἀποδιδόντες,
        προνοούμενοι καλὰ ἐνώπιον πάντων ἀνθρώπων:
18   εἰ δυνατὸν τὸ ἐξ ὑμῶν, μετὰ πάντων ἀνθρώπων εἰρηνεύοντες:
19   μὴ ἑαυτοὺς ἐκδικοῦντες, ἀγαπητοί, ἀλλὰ δότε τόπον τῇ ὀργῇ,
        γέγραπται γάρ: ἐμοὶ ἐκδίκησις, ἐγὼ ἀνταποδώσω, λέγει κύριος.
20   ἀλλὰ ἐὰν πεινᾷ ὁ ἐχθρός σου, ψώμιζε αὐτόν: ἐὰν διψᾷ, πότιζε αὐτόν:
        τοῦτο γὰρ ποιῶν ἄνθρακας πυρὸς σωρεύσεις ἐπὶ τὴν κεφαλὴν αὐτοῦ.
21   μὴ νικῶ ὑπὸ τοῦ κακοῦ ἀλλὰ νίκα ἐν τῷ ἀγαθῷ τὸ κακόν.

4. Of the 31 imperative verbs in the NRSV (which sticks closely to the structure of the Greek), only nine translate imperatives in the Greek (vv. 14a, b, c; 16d; 19b; 20a and b [quoting the OT]; 21a, b). The others translate verbless clauses (vv. 9a; 10a; 11a), infinitives (vv. 15a and b), and participles (vv. 9b, c; 10b; 11b, c; 12a, b, c; 13a, b; 16a, b, c; 17a, b; 18; 19a).

5. See, e.g., the way διώκω ("pursue," "persecute") joins the otherwise disparate vv. 13 and 14.

tions: the OT (vv. 16c, 19c, 20), the teaching of Jesus (vv. 14, 17, 18, and 21, especially),[6] early Christian instructions to new converts, and various Jewish and even Greek ethical and wisdom sayings.[7]

Some scholars offer a simple explanation for these features: Paul is using a style known as "parenesis."[8] Found in both Greek and Jewish writings, parenesis "strings together admonitions of a general ethical content." Parenesis is characterized by eclecticism (borrowing from many sources) and by a lack of concern for sequence of thought and development of a single theme.[9] That this passage resembles and may even deserve categorization as parenesis is clear. But parenesis is so broad a category that, even if we make this identification, several key issues remain unresolved.

One such issue is the relationship between these admonitions and the Roman congregation. Parenesis is usually thought to have a very general audience; and this could also fit 12:9-21 very well since many commentators think that Paul in chaps. 12–13 is providing a general summary of his ethical teaching. However, several scholars have recently argued that the admonitions in this section have the situation of the church in Rome very much in view.[10] Such a focus would explain why Paul excludes certain important ethical topics (e.g., holiness in sexual relations) while focusing on issues that affect personal relationships: love and care for fellow Christians (vv. 10a, 13), humility and a common mind-set (vv. 10b, 15-16), and love toward our enemies (vv. 14, 17-21). I think the evidence suggests that we steer a middle course between these positions. Paul's selection of material suggests that he may have at least one eye on the situation of the Roman church. But there are no direct allusions; nor does he use the vocabulary characteristic of his discussion of the weak and the strong in 14:1–15:13. Moreover, the parallels between the sequence

---

6. The case for conscious reference to the teaching of Jesus has been made especially well by J. D. G. Dunn, "Paul's Knowledge of the Jesus Tradition: The Evidence of Romans," in *Christus Bezeugen: Für Wolfgang Trilling* (ed. K. Kertelge, T. Holtz, and C.-P. März; Freiburg/Basel/Vienna: Herder, 1990), pp. 193-207; Stuhlmacher, "Jesustradition im Römerbrief?" 240-50; and, in greatest detail, Thompson, *Clothed with Christ.* Others, while noting similarities between Paul's teaching and Jesus', argue that Paul is simply citing common Christian tradition, without consciously alluding to Jesus (e.g., N. Walter, "Paulus und die urchristliche Jesustradition," *NTS* 31 [1985], 498-522, esp. 501-2).

7. Wilson (*Love without Pretense,* e.g., p. 143) has drawn attention to the parallels with various Jewish wisdom passages.

8. See, most clearly, Michel, 381-82.

9. See, e.g., M. Dibelius, *A Fresh Approach to the New Testament and Early Christian Literature* (New York: Scribner's, 1936); cf. also his *James* (Hermeneia; rev. H. Greeven; Philadelphia: Fortress, 1976), pp. 3-11 (the words quoted above are on p. 3).

10. See esp. Wedderburn, *Reasons,* pp. 81-82; Jewett, *Christian Tolerance,* pp. 93-94; Black, "Pauline Love Command," pp. 13-14.

of exhortations here and in other Pauline texts also suggest that Paul may be rehearsing familiar early Christian teaching. Note especially how Paul, as in 1 Cor. 12–13, follows a discussion of gifts with a reminder of the importance of love.[11] And, as we have seen, many of Paul's specific exhortations find parallels in other early Christian material. These parallels do not suggest that Paul has taken over one or more "blocks" of traditional material but that he is weaving together from many different sources central emphases in the early church's catechetical instruction.[12]

A second issue that requires further examination is the matter of structure. Many scholars are convinced that the text is not as loosely organized as has been previously thought, particularly when style and not just content is considered. The most persuasive proposal has been set forth by D. Black,[13] and I reproduce his scheme as best I can in my translation of the text above. According to Black, "let love be genuine" (v. 9a) is the heading for the entire section. There follows in vv. 9b-13 a chiastically arranged series of exhortations, in a 2-3-2-3-2 pattern.[14] Verses 14, 15, and 16 each display internal stylistic and verbal unity but are relatively unrelated to each other. The text concludes with another chiasm devoted to the issue of the Christian treatment of enemies. At the extremes of the chiasm are vv. 17a and 21, which share the key word "evil." Moving in one step, we find in vv. 17b-18 and v. 20 exhortations about the way Christians are to treat non-Christians. And at the middle of the chiasm is v. 19, which contains the key prohibition of vengeance. Black's rhetorical analysis follows many more traditional analyses in dividing the text into two major sections, vv. 9-13 and 14-21.[15] But some uncertainty

---

11. Note also that v. 9a stresses the importance that love be "genuine," suggesting that Paul is concerned that Christians exercise proper discrimination in their understanding and application of love. This is similar, then, to the stress on a similar point in 1 Cor. 14. See also 1 Thess. 5:19-22, which moves from exhortation to the use of spiritual gifts (vv. 19-20; cf. Rom. 12:6-8), to the need for discrimination (v. 21a; cf. Rom. 12:9, "sincere"), to a call to hold onto the "good" and avoid "evil" (vv. 21b-22; cf. Rom. 12:9b). For these parallels, see esp. Dunn, 2.740.

12. See, e.g., Wilckens, 3.18-19; Dunn, 2.737. Contra, e.g., C. H. Talbert, who thinks that vv. 9b-13 may have been a Semitically flavored tradition that Paul has taken over ("Tradition and Redaction in Romans XII.9-21," *NTS* 16 [1969-70], 84-91). Talbert cites Paul's use of participles for imperatives as evidence of his use of a Semitic source. But even if Semitic influence is granted (which is not clear; see the note on v. 9), the participles do not point to a single source (see Wilson, *Love without Pretense,* pp. 157-60).

13. See "Pauline Love Command." Of course, many other proposals for the structure of the section as a whole, or parts of it, have been advanced. See, e.g., Dunn, 2.738; Michel, 383; Schmithals, 449; Wilson, *Love without Pretense,* pp. 175-76.

14. All these begin with the definite article in Greek.

15. See, e.g., Chrysostom, Homily 22 (p. 506); Käsemann, 345; Cranfield, 2.629; Wilckens, 3.18; Dunn, 2.738.

about this division was always present because the content of these sections did not seem to match this division. Particularly troublesome is the way in which Paul seems to move from inner-Christian relationships (vv. 9b-13) to relationships with non-Christians (v. 14), back to inner-Christian relationships (vv. 15-16), and back again to relationships with non-Christians (vv. 17-21).[16] Black's analysis provides something of an answer to this problem by recognizing that the middle of the passage, vv. 14-16, consists of three relatively independent exhortations.[17]

Two final and related unresolved matters are the issues of theme and relationship to context. Black's structural proposal highlights the opening call for genuine love in v. 9a as the overall topic of the section. And most scholars would agree that love, which Paul spotlights again in 13:8-10 as the fulfillment of the law, is basic to the section.[18] But it is basic not in the sense that every exhortation is a direct exposition of what love is, but basic in the sense that it is the underlying motif of the section. Paul is not always talking specifically about love, but he keeps coming back to love as the single most important criterion for approved Christian behavior.

What relationship does this section have to what has come before it? A few scholars think that vv. 9-21 continue the discussion of community relationships in vv. 3-8,[19] perhaps with special reference to the community's exercise of gifts.[20] But v. 9, which is not tied syntactically to vv. 3-8, creates a break, both in style and in content. We are, then, to view vv. 9-21 as a further elaboration of that "good" which the person who is being transformed by the renewing of the mind approves of (v. 2).

9 The opening words are not explicitly linked to anything in the previous context, and there is no verb in the Greek. Paul says, literally, "sincere love."[21] These words are the heading for what follows, as Paul proceeds in a series of participial clauses to explain just what sincere love

16. See, e.g., Ortkemper, 8-9. This problem leads some scholars to propose that the key division in the text comes between vv. 16 and 17 (Lagrange, 301; Huby, 422; Viard, 265; Morris, 454; Schmithals [444] is similar, though he sees v. 16 as transitional).

17. Black himself thinks that vv. 14-16 all relate to inner-Christian relationships ("Pauline Love Command," pp. 18-19). But this is unlikely for v. 14.

18. See, e.g., S-H, 360; Michel, 382; Dunn, 2.739; Schlier, 373; Fitzmyer, 652; V. P. Furnish, *The Love Command in the New Testament* (Nashville: Abingdon, 1972), p. 103; Wilson, *Love without Pretense,* pp. 143-44; even Käsemann, who denies on p. 343 that the expression of love in v. 9a is the heading of the section, admits on p. 349 that ἀγάπη determines the beginning and the end of vv. 9-21 and repeatedly comes into view throughout the text.

19. See esp. Achtemeier, 196, 200.

20. See esp. Käsemann, 343-44.

21. Gk. ἡ ἀγάπη ἀνυπόκριτος.

really is. Yet the addition of an imperative verb in all major English translations — for example, NRSV: "let love be genuine" — is not off the mark. As in the similar phrases in vv. 6b-8, Paul's purpose is to exhort, not simply to describe. Love for others, singled out by our Lord himself as the essence of the OT law (Mark 12:28-34 and pars.) and the central demand of the New Covenant (John 13:31-35), quickly became enshrined as the foundational and characteristic ethical norm of Christianity.[22] The love of Christians for others was grounded in, and enabled by, the love of God expressed in the gift of his Son (see esp. John 13:34 and 1 John 4:9-11).[23] Paul has already in Romans reminded us of this love (see 5:5-8). The early Christians chose a relatively rare term to express the distinctive nature of the love that was to be the foundation of all their relationships: *agapē*.[24] This is the term Paul uses here, the definite article (in the Greek) signifying that he is speaking about a well-known virtue.[25] In fact, so basic does Paul consider love that he does not even exhort us here to love but to make sure that the love he presumes we already have is "genuine." In urging that our love be genuine, Paul is warning about making our love a mere pretense, an outward display or emotion that does not conform to the nature of the God who is love and who has loved us.[26]

In the second part of v. 9, we find two more exhortations, each put in the form of a participial clause. Why Paul chooses to express these admoni-

22. See also, e.g., 1 Thess. 4:9; Gal. 5:13-14; 1 Cor. 13; Jas. 2:8-9; 1 Pet. 1:22; 1 John 2:7-11; 3:10-18; 4:7-12, 18-21; and see particularly, in Romans, 13:8-10.

23. Thus, as Furnish points out, love is a necessity — it is an indispensable mark of the "new creation" in Christ (*Love Command,* pp. 93-95).

24. The noun ἀγάπη is rare in nonbiblical Greek before the 2d-3d centuries A.D. It occurs 20 times in the LXX, 11 times with reference to love between humans (2 Kgdms. 1:26) and especially for love between men and women (2 Kgdms. 13:15; Eccl. 9:1, 6 [?]; 11 times in Canticles [the Song of Songs]; Jer. 2:2 [though with application to Israel's love for God]), but also with reference to God's love (Wis. 3:9) and our love for wisdom (cf. Wis. 6:18; the reference in Sir. 48:11 is not clear). The verb ἀγαπάω, on the other hand, was much more common in NT times (over 250 occurrences in the LXX), denoting all kinds of relationships. Claims, therefore, that the word ἀγάπη is distinctively Christian, or that it denotes a distinctive Christian virtue, are not accurate; it is better to say that the early Christians chose the word (perhaps because of unwanted nuances in other words for "love" in Greek) to convey their particular understanding of the nature of love.

25. BDF 258(1); Turner, 177.

26. The Greek word ἀνυπόκριτος literally means "without hypocrisy," e.g., not playing the part of an actor on the stage. Paul's indebtedness to general early Christian teaching is evident here again since the same adjective is applied to love in 2 Cor. 6:6, 1 Tim. 1:5, and 1 Pet. 1:22 (it also occurs in 2 Tim. 1:5, describing faith, and in Jas. 3:17, describing "wisdom from above").

tions with participles continues to be debated,[27] but it may be that he does so in order to indicate the close relationship of the exhortations with the original demand for "genuine love."[28] "Genuine love," Paul is saying, will "abhor what is evil" and "cling to what is good."[29] Both verbs are very strong: "abhor" could also be translated "hate exceedingly,"[30] and "cling" can be used to refer to the intimate union that is to characterize the marriage relationship.[31] "Genuine" Christian love, Paul is suggesting, is not a directionless emotion or something that can be only felt and not expressed. Love is not genuine when it leads a person to do something evil or to avoid doing what is right — as defined by God in his Word. Genuine love, "the real thing," will lead the Christian to that "good" which is the result of the transformed heart and mind (v. 2).

10 The two exhortations in this verse share a focus on the relations of Christians to "one another." They also share a similar structure: each begins

27. Three explanations for the use of participles with an apparently imperatival thrust have been offered. (1) The participles are not used independently but depend on another verb in the context (e.g., G. B. Winer, *A Treatise on the Grammar of NT Greek Regarded as a Sure Basis for NT Exegesis* [3d ed.; Edinburgh: T & T Clark, 1882], p. 442). (2) NT imperatival participles reflect the use of participles in tannaitic Hebrew to express admonitions (see esp. D. Daube, "Appended Note: Participle and Imperative in I Peter," in *The First Epistle of Saint Peter,* by E. G. Selwyn [2d ed.; Grand Rapids: Baker, 1981 {= 1947}], pp. 467-88; idem, *The New Testament and Rabbinic Judaism* [London: Athlone, 1956], pp. 90-97; Black, "Pauline Love Command," p. 17; C. K. Barrett, "The Imperative Participle," *ExpTim* 59 [1948], 165-66; P. Kanjuparambil, "Imperatival Participles in Rom 12:9-21," *JBL* 102 [1983], 285-88; Moule, *Idiom Book,* pp. 179-80). (3) NT imperatival participles are a natural development from within the Greek language itself (Moulton, 180-83; H. G. Meecham, "The Use of the Participle for the Imperative in the New Testament," *ExpTim* 58 [1947], 207-8; Porter, *Verbal Aspect,* pp. 370-77 [who has a fine survey of the state of the question]). The strain necessary to attach these participles to another verb renders (1) unlikely, while the late date of the clearest evidence for the use of the participle to express admonitions in Hebrew makes (2) questionable. The third alternative should, then, probably be accepted.

28. Other scholars suggest that Paul may use the participle because it is less forceful, more "diplomatic" than an imperative (N. F. Miller, "The Imperativals of Romans 12," in *Linguistics and New Testament Interpretation: Essays on Discourse Analysis* [ed. D. A. Black; Nashville: Broadman, 1992], esp. pp. 173-74; Wilson, *Love without Pretense,* pp. 161-63; Thompson, *Clothed with Christ,* p. 90).

29. For the connection of the participles with the original demand for "sincere love," see, e.g., Godet; Michel; Jewett, *Christian Tolerance,* p. 94; contra Cranfield, who thinks they are independent.

30. As commentators since Chrysostom have recognized, the ἀπο- in ἀπο-στυγοῦντες makes the verb emphatic (cf. also S-H; Cranfield). The word occurs only here in biblical Greek.

31. The verb κολλάομαι occurs elsewhere in Paul only with reference to sexual relations (1 Cor. 6:16, 17; cf. also Matt. 19:5). See Jewett, *Christian Tolerance,* pp. 101-4.

with a reference to the virtue about which Paul gives instructions — "with reference to brotherly love," "with reference to honor"[32] — moves on to the reciprocal emphasis ("one another") and concludes with the imperatival element.[33]

After introducing all the exhortations in vv. 9-21 with a call for sincere love, Paul now narrows his focus, admonishing Christians to be "devoted" (philostorgoi) to one another in "brotherly love" (philadelphia). Both key terms in this exhortation, which share the philo- stem, convey the sense of family relationships.[34] Paul here reflects the early Christian understanding of the church as an extended family, whose members, bound together in intimate fellowship, should exhibit toward one another a heartfelt and consistent concern.

The general meaning of the second exhortation in this verse is clear enough: Christians are to be anxious to recognize and give credit to other believers. But its exact meaning is debated. The verb Paul uses here means "go before," often with the additional nuance that one goes before to show the way to someone else.[35] Taking the verb in this basic sense, many early translations and commentators as well as more recent ones think Paul means something like "surpassing one another in showing honor."[36] Others, however, suggest that the verb might here have an unusual sense, "consider better,"[37] and so translate "in honor preferring one another."[38] Each interpretation has its weaknesses; I, however, prefer the former since the second assumes an otherwise unattested meaning for the verb. Paul is then calling on

32. The datives τῇ φιλαδελφίᾳ and τῇ τιμῇ are datives of respect (Moule, Idiom Book, p. 46; Z-G, 487).

33. The first has no explicit verb at all, requiring us to supply something like "show yourselves" before the adjective φιλόστοργοι (Z-G, 487). The second returns to the imperatival participle (see the note on v. 9).

34. This nuance is basic to the term φιλαδελφία, which is used only sporadically in the NT (cf. 1 Thess. 4:9; Heb. 13:1; 1 Pet. 1:22; 2 Pet. 1:7). φιλόστοργος occurs only here in the NT and only once in the LXX (4 Macc. 15:13; the noun φιλοστοργία is found in 2 Macc. 6:20 and 4 Macc. 15:6, 9, and the adverb φιλοστόργως in 2 Macc. 9:21). This word group was applied to several different spheres of relationship in the Hellenistic period (Michel) but retained the familial flavor of loving and solicitous concern (see C. Spicq, "ΦΙΛΟΣΤΟΡΓΟΣ (A propos de Rom., XII,10)," RB 62 [1955], 497-510).

35. The verb is προηγούμαι, which occurs only here in biblical Greek; on the definition, see BAGD.

36. Cf. RSV; NRSV; Chrysostom; BDF 150; Dunn; Fitzmyer; Jewett, Christian Tolerance, p. 108.

37. These take the simplex ἡγούομαι to mean "consider," and the προ- to denote superiority.

38. KJV; NASB; NIV; S-H; Käsemann; Michel; Cranfield; Wilckens. Reference is often made to Phil. 2:3, "in humility consider [ἡγούμενοι] others as better than yourselves" (which, however, does not use the same verb as we have in Rom. 12:10).

Christians to outdo each other in bestowing honor on one another; for example, to recognize and praise one another's accomplishments and to defer to one another.

11 As the verse division suggests, the first exhortation in this verse, "in zeal, do not be lazy," could well be taken with the exhortation that follows, "be set on fire by the Spirit."[39] But, as we have seen (see the introduction to this section), the style of this exhortation has more in common with the exhortations in v. 10. Probably, then, we should relate Paul's warning about laziness in zeal to his call for us to love and esteem one another in v. 10.[40] Paul does not specify the object of the unflagging zeal that he calls for, but we should perhaps think of the "rational worship" to which we are called.[41] The temptation to "lose steam" in our lifelong responsibility to reverence God in every aspect of our lives, to become lazy and complacent[42] in our pursuit of what is "good, well pleasing to God, and perfect," is a natural one — but it must be strenuously resisted.

The idea of "zeal" is continued in the image of "being set on fire"[43] in the second exhortation. Paul might here be urging Christians to maintain a strong and emotional commitment to the Lord in their own spirits.[44] But the spirit to which Paul refers is more likely, in light of the parallel reference to the Lord in v. 11c, the Holy Spirit.[45] On this view, Paul is exhorting us to allow the Holy Spirit to "set us on fire":[46] to open ourselves to the Spirit as he seeks to excite us about the "rational worship" to which the Lord has called us.

The exhortation to "serve the Lord" might at first sight seem like an anticlimax, too obvious and too broad to have any real application. But a closer look at the context suggests otherwise. The encouragement to be "set on fire by the Spirit" is, as church history and current experience amply attest, open to abuse. Christians have often been so carried away by enthusiasm for spiritual things that they have left behind those objective standards of Christian

---

39. See, e.g., Murray.

40. See Black, "Pauline Love Command," pp. 7-8; Furnish, *Love Command,* p. 104 (who notes that σπουδή ["zeal"] qualifies love in 2 Cor. 8:8; cf. also 8:16).

41. Cranfield.

42. The Greek word ὀκνηρός can refer to the causing of idleness (e.g., Phil. 3:1) or to the possession of idleness (as here and in Matt. 25:26). See BAGD.

43. The verb ζέω means "boil, seethe," and was used figuratively with reference to emotions and desires (BAGD). Cf. Acts 18:25, where Apollos is said to be "fervent in spirit" (ζέων τῷ πνεύματι).

44. Godet; S-H; Murray. The dative τῷ πνεύματι will then be local: "in the spirit [of each one of you]." Fee (*God's Empowering Presence,* pp. 611-12) thinks that the basic reference is to the human spirit, but with allusion also to the Holy Spirit.

45. Calvin; Barrett; Käsemann; Cranfield; Schlier; Dunn.

46. This interpretation takes the dative τῷ πνεύματι as instrumental: "by the Spirit."

living that the Scriptures set forth. This, it seems is Paul's concern; and he seeks to cut off any such abuse by reminding us that being set on fire by the Spirit must lead to, and be directed by, our service of the Lord. It is not the "enthusiasm" of self-centered display (such as characterized the Corinthians) but the enthusiasm of humble service of the Master who bought us that the Spirit creates within us.[47]

12 The three admonitions in this verse are closely related in both style and content. For hope, endurance, and prayer are natural partners. Even as we "rejoice in hope,"[48] gaining confidence from God's promise that we will share the glory of God, we recognize the "down side": the path to the culmination of hope is strewn with tribulations. Paul, ever the realist, knows this; and so here, as he does elsewhere, he quickly moves from hope to the need for endurance.[49] At the same time, we realize that our ability to continue to rejoice and to "bear up under" our tribulations is dependent on the degree to which we heed Paul's challenge to "persist[50] in prayer." (Note that Paul moves from hope to endurance to prayer also in Rom. 8:24-27.)

13 Paul concludes his first series of exhortations with a call for Christians to put into practice the love and concern for one another that he has mentioned earlier (v. 10).[51] In the first exhortation Paul uses the verbal form of the very familiar NT *koinōnia,* "fellowship." Paul, however, is not urging us to have fellowship with the saints, but to have fellowship with, to participate in, the "needs" of the saints. These "needs" are material ones: food, clothing, and shelter.[52] Therefore, the fellowship we are called to here

---

47. See esp. Cranfield. Some English versions make this connection clear by subordinating the call to "be set on fire by the Spirit" to this last exhortation; cf., e.g., REB: "With unflagging zeal, aglow with the Spirit, serve the Lord" (cf. also TEV).

48. The dative τῇ ἐλπίδι might be causal (BDF 196; Z-G, 487; Cranfield; Wilckens; Fitzmyer) or instrumental (Michel; Murray), in which case hope would be the basis or reason for our joy: "rejoice because of the hope you have" (cf. REB: "let hope keep you joyful"; cf. also TEV). But it is better, in light of Rom. 5:2b and 8:24, to take the dative as local (Käsemann; Schlier): hope is the object in which we rejoice.

49. See also Rom. 5:2b-3; 8:24-25; 1 Cor. 13:7; 1 Thess. 1:3.

50. The verb προσκαρτερέω, "occupy oneself diligently with something" (W. Grundmann, *TDNT* III, 618), is also used with reference to prayer in Acts 1:14; 2:42; 6:4; and Col. 4:2.

51. Thus, although v. 13 is related to v. 9b stylistically (see the analysis in the introduction to the section), it is related to v. 10 in terms of content (note also that φιλοξενία ["hospitality"] picks up the φιλο- root from v. 10).

52. The only other occurrences of this word in the plural in the NT have this material focus (Acts 6:3; 20:34; 28:10; Tit. 3:14; cf. also Acts 2:45; 4:35; Eph. 4:28; Phil. 2:25; 4:16; 1 John 3:17; Rev. 3:17). The parallel between Paul's exhortation and the practice of the early church, which displayed its κοινωνία (2:42) by pooling its resources and thus providing for everyone who had need (χρεία; 2:44-45) is striking.

is the sharing of our material goods with Christians who are less well-off.[53] Some scholars think that Paul might be thinking specifically of the Jewish Christians in Jerusalem (cf. 15:25, 26) to whom Paul was bringing money collected from the Gentile churches (cf. 15:30-33).[54] But, while we should not of course exclude these Christians from Paul's reference, there is nothing to suggest that he has them particularly in mind here.[55]

Another dimension of Christian love is the practice of hospitality. The need to give shelter and food to visitors was great in the NT world, there being few hotels or motels. And the need among Christians was exacerbated by the many traveling missionaries and other Christian workers. Hence the NT frequently urges Christians to offer hospitality to others (see 1 Tim. 3:2; Tit. 1:8; Heb. 13:2; 1 Pet. 4:9). But Paul does more than that here; he urges us to "pursue" it — to go out of our way to welcome and provide for travelers.

14 A break in the passage occurs here, marked by a change in both style — from the imperatival participles of vv. 9-13 to the imperatives of v. 14[56] — and topic — from relations among Christians in vv. 10-13 to relations of Christians with non-Christians in v. 14. There is a verbal connection with v. 13: "pursue [hospitality]" and "persecutors" translate the same Greek verb.[57] More important, however, is the thematic connection with v. 9: blessing persecutors is one manifestation of that "sincere love" which shuns evil and clings to the good. And it is certainly one of the most striking exhibitions of that transformed way of thinking which is to characterize believers (v. 2). In the Scriptures, "blessing" is typically associated with God; he "possesses and dispenses all blessings."[58] To "bless" one's persecutors, therefore, is to call on God to bestow his favor upon them. Its opposite is, of course, cursing — asking God to bring disaster and/or spiritual ruin on a person. By prohibiting cursing as well as enjoining blessing, Paul stresses the sincerity and single-mindedness of the loving attitude we are to have toward our persecutors.

While persecution in various forms — from social ostracism to legal action — was almost unavoidable in the early church, we have no evidence that the Roman Christians were at this time going through any special time of persecution. Paul is probably, then, issuing a general command, reflecting

---

53. See the use of this verb in 15:17; Gal. 6:6; Phil. 4:15; and 1 Tim. 5:22. See Fitzmyer.

54. Black; Ziesler; Dunn.

55. Barrett; Schlier. Far less is it clear that Paul has in mind those Jewish Christians who had been expelled by Claudius and were now returning to the city (contra Jewett, *Christian Tolerance*, p. 110).

56. This change in style may be due to the tradition that Paul depends on in v. 14 (see below); but it may also reflect a new urgency (see Godet).

57. διώκω. Such verbal links are typical of parenesis.

58. H. W. Beyer, *TDNT* II, 756.

once again a staple item in the list of early Christian exhortation (see 1 Cor. 4:12; 1 Pet. 3:9). It was Jesus himself who first enunciated this demand of the kingdom, and there is good reason to think that Paul deliberately alludes here to Jesus' own saying. Note the similarities:

> Matt. 5:44: "Love your enemies and pray for *those who persecute you.*"
>
> Luke 6:27-28: "Love your enemies, do good to those who hate you, *bless* those who curse you, pray for those who abuse you."

Paul seems to combine these two forms of Jesus' saying from the "Sermon on the Mount/Plain," suggesting perhaps that he quotes here a pre-Synoptic form of one of Jesus' best-known and most startling kingdom demands.[59] For Jesus' command that his followers respond to persecution and hatred with love and blessing was unprecedented in both the Greek and Jewish worlds.[60] Paul's dependence on Jesus' teaching at this point is bolstered by the fact that he appears to allude in this same paragraph to other portions of Jesus' teaching on love of the enemy from this same "sermon" (cf. vv. 17a and 21).[61] Paul does not, of course, identify the teaching as coming from Jesus. But this may indicate not that he did not know its source, but that the source was so well known as to require no explicit mention.

15 Paul changes both style and topic yet again, suggesting (as we noted in the introduction to the section) that this part of Paul's parenesis

---

59. See esp. D. Wenham, "Paul's Use of the Jesus Tradition: Three Samples," in *The Jesus Tradition Outside the Gospels* (ed. D. Wenham; Gospel Perspectives 5; Sheffield: JSOT, 1985), pp. 15-17. See also D. C. Allison, "The Pauline Epistles and the Synoptic Gospels: The Pattern of the Parallels," *NTS* 28 (1982), 11-12; Dunn, "Paul's Knowledge," pp. 200-202; Stuhlmacher, "Jesustradition," pp. 247-48; Thompson, *Clothed with Christ*, pp. 96-105; Davies, 138. A few scholars have suggested that the dependence runs the other direction; i.e., that the synoptic saying is borrowed from Paul (e.g., J. Sauer, "Traditionsgeschichtliche Erwägungen zu den synoptischen und paulinischen Aussagen über Feindesliebe und Wiedervergeltungsverzicht," *ZNW* 76 [1985], 17-21). But such a view not only presumes the inauthenticity of Luke 6:27-36 and pars.; it does not explain the traditions-history satisfactorily (see Thompson, *Clothed with Christ*, pp. 103-5).

60. Thompson (*Clothed with Christ*, pp. 97-98) notes that nowhere in pre-Christian Greek literature do we find "blessing" (εὐλογέω) as a response to "cursing" or "reviling."

61. While recognizing the allusions to Jesus' teaching throughout the paragraph, Thompson (*Clothed with Christ*, pp. 109-10) questions whether Paul intended his readers to recognize the allusions. But it is likely that the Roman Christians were already familiar with Jesus' teaching on these points, so that Paul's "paraphrase" of it would have been immediately understood as such.

combines several relatively independent sayings. In style, the imperative verbs of v. 14 give way to imperatival infinitives in v. 15.[62] And Paul shifts from exhortation about the relation of Christians to those outside the community (v. 14) back to their relation to fellow Christians (vv. 15-16). Indeed, identifying with others in both their joys and their sorrows is an appropriate way for Christians to demonstrate the sincerity of their love to non-Christians as well as Christians.[63] But Paul's exhortation here seems to pick up his assertion about the mutual and intimate relations of the members of the body of Christ in 1 Cor. 12:26: "And if one member suffers, all the members suffer together; and if one member is honored, all the members rejoice together."[64] Love that is genuine will not respond to a fellow believer's joy with envy or bitterness, but will enter wholeheartedly into that same joy. Similarly, love that is genuine will bring us to identify so intimately with our brothers and sisters in Christ that their sorrows will become ours.

16 The transition from v. 15 to v. 16 is a natural one: the mutual sympathy that Paul calls for in v. 15 is possible only if Christians share a common mind-set.[65] The "one another" language of v. 15 picks up the same theme from v. 10, while the use of the root *phron-* ("think") in all three admonitions in this verse reminds us of Paul's demand for the right kind of "thinking" among Christians in v. 3. These parallels make it clear that v. 16 is about the relations of Christians with one another.[66] Paul's first exhortation uses language that he uses elsewhere to denote unity of thinking among Christians.[67] However, his wording here suggests not so much a plea for Christians to "the think the same thing *among* one another," but to "think the same thing *toward* one another."[68] Paul's point might then be that

---

62. The use of an independent infinitive with imperatival force is found as early as Homer and is very common in the papyri, though rare in the NT (cf. also Phil. 3:16; BDF 389; Turner, 78; Moule, *Idiom Book,* pp. 126-27).

63. Thus, some commentators think that Paul may be continuing in v. 15 to speak about the relation of Christians to non-Christians (Chrysostom; Cranfield; Dunn; cf. also Furnish, *Love Command,* p. 106).

64. Wilckens; cf. also Murray; Michel; Schlier. Such mutuality is frequently enjoined in Jewish wisdom texts. See, e.g., Sir. 7:34: "Do not fail those who weep, but mourn with those who mourn"; cf. also Job 30:35 (LXX); *T. Issachar* 7:5; *T. Zebulun* 7:4; *T. Joseph* 17:7 (Dunn; Wilson [*Love without Pretense,* pp. 173-75] claims that the combination of themes in vv. 15-21 duplicates several wisdom texts). It is interesting to note, however, that almost all these sayings speak of identification with others in their sorrow or tribulation and not in joy.

65. The two verses are therefore to be connected (Gifford) rather than treated as separate (Michel).

66. Calvin; Godet; Wilckens; Dunn; contra Leenhardt; Cranfield.

67. Gk. τὸ αὐτὸ φρονεῖν; cf. 15:5; 2 Cor. 13:11; Phil. 2:2; 4:2.

68. The preposition Paul uses here is εἰς. Contrast, e.g., 15:5, where he uses ἐν

Christians should display the same attitude toward all other people, whatever their social, ethnic, or economic status.[69] However, while Paul might emphasize here the outward display of our "thinking," it does not force us to adopt a meaning for the basic phrase that is different from its sense in its other occurrences in Paul. He is calling us to a common mind-set. Such a common mind-set does not mean that we must all think in just the same way or that we must think exactly the same thing about every issue, but that we should adopt an attitude toward everything that touches our lives that springs from the renewed mind of the new realm to which we belong by God's grace (see v. 2).

As Paul recognizes elsewhere (see esp. Phil. 2:2-4), the biggest barrier to unity is pride. Therefore, Paul next warns us about "thinking exalted things," that is, "thinking too highly of ourselves."[70] Our overly exalted opinion of ourselves, leading us to think that we are always right and others wrong and that our opinions matter more than others, often prevents the church from exhibiting the unity to which God calls her. The positive antidote to such pride, Paul says, is association with "the lowly." It is not certain what Paul means by this positive exhortation. The adjective "lowly" could be neuter, in which case Paul might be urging Christians, in contrast to being haughty, to devote themselves to humble tasks.[71] But "lowly" could also refer to persons, in which case Paul would be exhorting believers to associate with "lowly people," that is, the outcasts, the poor, and the needy.[72] A decision between these two options is impossible to make; both fit the context well and both are paralleled in the NT.

ἀλλήλοις after τὸ αὐτὸ φρονεῖν; in none of Paul's other uses of the phrase does it have a prepositional addition.

69. See TEV: "Have the same concern for everyone"; cf. also NEB; Chrysostom; Huby; Zahn; Murray.

70. The Greek neuter plural ὑψηλά could refer to "high positions," in which case Paul would be prohibiting the desire to associate with people in exalted positions (Godet). But the verb φρονέω hardly allows this meaning; the phrase τὰ ὑψηλὰ φρονοῦντες, rather, means the same as the similar phrase ὑψηλὰ φρόνει in 11:20 (see Cranfield; Dunn; Fitzmyer).

71. In favor of this rendering is the neuter τὰ ὑψηλά, which is placed in contrasting parallelism with τοῖς ταπεινοῖς; cf. TEV: "accept humble duties"; S-H; Murray; Michel; Schlier. Some (e.g., Michel) think that Paul might be directing this exhortation especially to "enthusiasts," who were interested only in the more spectacular and glamorous aspects of Christian experience and service.

72. Godet; Cranfield; Käsemann; R. Leivestad, "ΤΑΠΕΙΝΟΣ — ΤΑΠΕΙΝΟ-ΦΡΩΝ," *NovT* 8 (1966), 45-46. As Käsemann emphasizes, ταπεινός does not refer to an inner attitude of "humility" but to external status of circumstances. The OT has much to say about God's special concern for such people (see, e.g., Judg. 6:15; Ps. 10:18; 34:18; Isa. 14:32; 49:13; Zeph. 2:13; cf. Jas. 4:6), a concern that we, children of the Father, are to exhibit.

But in either case Paul emphasizes the degree of our involvement with "the lowly" by using a verb that could be translated "be carried away with."[73]

The word *phronimos* in the final exhortation in the verse continues the rhetorically striking use of the root *phron-*. The person who is *phronimos* is characterized by "thinking" and is therefore "wise." The quality denoted by the word is therefore a positive one.[74] It becomes negative only when the standard by which we judge our wisdom is our own. It is this subjectivity and arrogance that Paul warns us about here: "do not be wise in your own eyes."[75]

17 After two verses that exhort Christians about their relations to one another, Paul concludes his delineation of the manifestations of "genuine love" (v. 9a) with admonitions about the attitude Christians are to adopt toward non-Christians (vv. 17-21).[76] As in v. 14, where Paul first touched on this topic, his focus is on the way Christians are to respond to non-Christians who persecute and in other ways "do evil"[77] to us. Thus the prohibition of retaliation in v. 17a expands on Paul's warning that we are not to curse our persecutors in v. 14b. Here again, Paul's dependence on Jesus' teaching is clear. For not only did Jesus exhort us to love and pray for our enemies; in the same context he also warns us not to exact "eye for eye, and tooth for tooth" (Matt. 5:38).[78]

---

73. The Greek verb used here, συναπάγω, is rare, occurring only once in the LXX (Exod. 14:6) and twice elsewhere in the NT (Gal. 2:13; 2 Pet. 3:17). In its two other NT occurrences, it is followed by a dative of instrument, but the dative here in Rom. 12:16 cannot be instrumental. Presumably, then, it is dative because of the συν- prefix of the verb, in which case the verb here will have an "associative" flavor. See LSJ; BAGD; MM; W. Grundmann, *TDNT* VIII, 19-20.

74. Cf. Matt. 7:24; 10:16; 24:45; 25:2, 4, 8-9; Luke 12:42; 16:8; 1 Cor. 4:10; 10:15; 2 Cor. 11:19.

75. Cf. Rom. 11:25 and Prov. 3:7. Gk. παρ' ἑαυτοῖς, where παρά means "in the sight of" (Moule, *Idiom Book,* p. 52).

76. See the analysis in the introduction to this section for the integrity and movement of thought of vv. 17-21 (for which see Black, "Pauline Love Command," pp. 11-12). See also Ortkemper, 106.

77. The word for "evil" here is κακός, in contrast to πονηρός in v. 9b. While the two can sometimes be distinguished, it is doubtful whether there is any difference in meaning here.

78. Wenham, "Paul's Use," pp. 17-18. Wenham notes that vv. 17-20 have a number of parallels (more conceptual than verbal) with Matt. 5:38-43. This kind of "paraphrasing" of the teaching of Jesus seems to have been standard in the early church; see, e.g., another variation of these themes in 1 Thess. 5:15 and 1 Pet. 3:9. Allison thinks that Paul may have in mind the form of Jesus' teaching on these points that we now find in Luke 6:27-36 ("The Pauline Epistles," pp. 11-12). See also Dunn, "Jesus' Knowledge," pp. 200-202; Davies, 138. Thompson (*Clothed with Christ,* p. 107) is more skeptical about an allusion to Jesus' teaching, noting that the prohibition of retaliation is found widely in Judaism (see *Jos. and As.* 23:9; 28:4, 14; 29:3). But probability of dependence on Jesus' teaching comes from the pattern of allusions in these verses.

In a pattern similar to that in vv. 14 and 16, the negative prohibition "Do not repay evil for evil" is paired with a positive injunction: "Take thought for what is good in the sight of all people." The verb "take thought" is probably emphatic: "Doing good to all is something to be planned and not just willed."[79] The translation "in the sight of all people" is disputed; many commentators, doubting that Paul would allow non-Christians to set the standard for what Christians do, prefer to translate "Take thought to do good things *to* all persons."[80] But there is no clear parallel for this interpretation of the Greek word involved. Cranfield suggests a different alternative: that Paul is urging us to display "in the sight of all people" the good things that we do. Non-Christians do not set the standard for "the good"; they are the audience. But this, also, is an unusual way to translate the Greek.[81] We should, then, take Paul's words at face value: he wants us to commend ourselves before non-Christians by seeking to do those "good things" that non-Christians approve and recognize. There is, of course, an unstated limitation to this command, one that resides in the word "good" itself. For Paul would certainly not want us to have forgotten that the "good" that he speaks of throughout these verses is defined in terms of the will of God (v. 2).

18   The close relation between this exhortation — "If possible, to the extent that it depends on you, be at peace with all people" — and the last one in v. 17 is obvious: both urge Christians to pursue behavior that will have a positive impact on "all people." Jesus himself commended "peacemakers" (Matt. 5:9) and urged his followers to "be at peace with one another" (Mark 9:50, where "one another" probably refers to people generally rather than to the disciples only). Although much less clear than the allusions in vv. 14, 17, and 21, this may, then, be another allusion to the teaching of Jesus.[82] We do not know whether there was any special need to exhort the Roman Christians to live at peace with their fellow-citizens. Paul's reasons for including this admonition here, along with the similar one at the end of v. 17, may be more related to the logic of what he has been saying. For his encouragement to Christians to bless persecutors (v. 14) and not repay evil for evil (v. 17a) assumes that Christians are in conflict with the world around them. To a

79. Käsemann; cf. 2 Cor. 8:21; 1 Tim. 5:8.

80. These commentators think that the Gk. ἐνώπιον can have the significance of a dative (Michel; Käsemann; Schlier; Wilckens; Ortkemper, 107-8).

81. See especially the close parallel to the wording here in 2 Cor. 8:21: προνοοῦμεν γὰρ καλὰ οὐ μόνον ἐνώπιον κυρίου ἀλλὰ καὶ ἐνώπιον ἀνθρώπων; "For take thought for what is good not only before the Lord but also before people." Here ἐνώπιον κυρίου shows that ἐνώπιον must mean "before" in the sense of approval (Dunn; also Fitzmyer).

82. Dunn, "Paul's Knowledge," pp. 200-202. Wenham suggests that Paul may be alluding generally to Jesus' teaching about nonretaliation (Matt. 5:39b-42; cf. "Paul's Use," pp. 17-18).

considerable extent, Paul recognizes, such conflict is inevitable: as the world hated Jesus, so it hates his followers (John 16:33). Paul acknowledges that much such conflict is unavoidable by adding to his exhortation to "be at peace" the double qualification "if possible, to the extent that it depends on you."[83] But Paul does not want Christians to use the inevitability of tension with the world as an excuse for behavior that needlessly exacerbates that conflict or for a resignation that leads us not even to bother to seek to maintain a positive witness.

19 After this excursus in which Paul exhorts Christians to relate positively to the world (vv. 17b-18), Paul returns to admonish us about the way we are to react to the pressure that the world brings upon us. "Do not avenge yourselves" moves one step beyond "do not repay evil for evil" (v. 17a). Confronted with someone who is wronging us, we might be tempted to harm our adversary by doing a similar wrong to him. But the temptation becomes more subtle when we seek to "baptize" such a response by viewing it as a means by which to execute a just and deserved judgment on our oppressor. Perhaps because he understands the strength of this temptation, Paul reminds us that we are "beloved": people who have quite undeservedly experienced the love of God.[84] Rather than taking justice into our hands, we are to "give place to wrath." Paul does not explicitly say whose wrath this is, and it is possible to think that he refers to the wrath of the adversary, or our own wrath,[85] or the wrath executed by governmental authorities (see 13:4).[86] But Paul certainly intends to refer to the wrath of God, as the definite "the wrath" and the OT quotation that follows show.[87] It is not our job to execute justice on evil people; that is God's prerogative, and he will visit his wrath on such people when he deems it right to do

---

83. The former may refer to the conduct of others and the latter to the constraints imposed on us by our own situation (Godet; Murray; Schlier). But the second may simply elaborate the first. In the phrase τὸ ἐξ ὑμῶν, τό is probably an accusative of respect (Moule, *Idiom Book,* pp. 33-34): "if possible, with respect to that which depends on you."

84. Wilckens.

85. Stuart; Haldane; E. R. Smothers, "Give Place to the Wrath (Rom. 12:19): An Essay in Verbal Exegesis," *CBQ* 6 (1944), 205-15 (although he thinks that Paul means that we are to calm our own wrath so as to give way to God's).

86. Leenhardt (although he thinks that it is the wrath of God that the authorities execute).

87. δότε τόπον, "give a place," may be a Semitism (see Sir. 4:5; 13:22; 19:17; 38:12; cf. Michel; Dunn). It is used literally in Luke 14:9 and metaphorically in Eph. 4:27, where Paul urges us not to "give place" to the devil. The idea in this latter text is "give opportunity to" (cf. RSV), and this meaning fits Rom. 12:19 very well: "give opportunity to the wrath of God." Almost all modern commentators adopt this interpretation.

so.[88] The prohibition of vengeance is found in both the OT[89] and Judaism,[90] but it tends to be confined to relations with co-religionists.[91] Paul's prohibition of vengeance even upon enemies is an extension of the idea that reflects Jesus' revolutionary ethic.[92]

Paul buttresses his exhortation to defer to God in matters of retributive justice with an OT quotation highlighting God's determination to exact vengeance. The words are from Deut. 32:35,[93] but the theme is quite widespread, and it might be that Paul has in view some of the other texts enunciating this theme as well.[94] This may explain the cumbersome addition at the end of the quotation, "says the Lord," since these words appear in some of the prophetic announcements of God's vengeance.[95]

20 Paul continues quoting the OT: the exhortation in v. 20 is a straightforward rendering of Prov. 25:21-22a.[96] Paul was probably drawn to this text for several reasons. First, the reference to the "enemy" may have attracted his attention since the teaching of Jesus on which he depends throughout these verses exhorts us to "love our enemies" (Matt. 5:43 = Luke 6:27). Second, feeding and giving water to our enemy is similar to the action Jesus recommends as the expression of this love: turning the other cheek;

---

88. Since Paul normally places the visitation of God's wrath at the last judgment, many commentators think that it is this eschatological revelation of wrath to which he refers here. But Rom. 1:18 makes clear that God's wrath, though decisively revealed in the last day, is even now operative. This makes it possible that Paul is leaving unspecified here the exact time or nature of God's wrath.

89. Lev. 19:18a; 2 Chron. 28:8-15; Prov. 20:22; 24:29.

90. *T. Gad* 6:7; 1QS 10:17-18.

91. See, e.g., CD 9:2.

92. See Wilckens; Schlier; Dunn.

93. Paul's wording differs, however, from both the LXX — ἐν ἡμέρᾳ ἐκδικήσεως ἀνταποδώσω ("in the day of vengeance, I will recompense") — and the MT — לִי נָקָם וְשִׁלֵּם ("vengeance is mine, and recompense"). Koch (pp. 77-78) thinks that Paul may be quoting from memory an early Christian form of the text. But Paul's wording is close to the targumic tradition, especially to *Targum Neofiti* and the *Fragmentary Targum* (cf. Str-B, 3.300; Wilckens). Paul may, then, be quoting a variant Greek text to which the later targums give indirect testimony (see Michel; Stanley, *Paul and the Language of Scripture,* pp. 171-73).

94. See, e.g., Jer. 5:9; 23:2; Hos. 4:9; Joel 3:21; Nah. 1:2.

95. See, e.g., Jer. 5:9: "Shall I not punish them for these things? says the LORD." On this view, λέγει κύριος is virtually part of the quotation. See Dunn. For another interpretation of this phrase, see Ellis, who thinks that it is a remnant of the original prophetic origin of the saying (*Paul's Use of the Old Testament,* pp. 107-12).

96. Paul's wording agrees exactly with that of LXX MS B, but B differs from the two other most important MSS, A and S, at one point, translating ψώμιζε in place of the roughly synonymous τρέφε. The reading of B has probably been assimilated to Paul's wording. The LXX and the Hebrew of the MT are similar.

giving our shirts to those who ask for our coats; giving to those who beg from us (cf. Luke 6:29-30). And, third, such a response to our enemies is a practical way of putting into action our "blessing" of those who persecute us (v. 14) and a specific form of "doing good in the sight of all people" (v. 17b).

The text indicates that acting in this way toward the enemy will mean "heaping coals of fire on his head." What is intended by this imagery is not clear, either in Proverbs or in Paul. The Greek for the phrase "coals of fire" occurs only two other times in the LXX, neither of which is metaphorical (Isa. 47:14; Prov. 6:28). However, when used metaphorically in the OT, the words "coals" and "fire" usually refer to God's awesome presence, and especially to his judgment.[97] Paul may then view our giving of food and water to the enemy to be means by which — if such actions do not lead to repentance — the enemy's guilt before the Lord will be increased, leading in turn to an increase in the severity of his or her judgment. Paul, of course, would not mean, on this view, that we are to act kindly toward our enemy with the *purpose* of making his or her judgment more severe. Paul would simply be noting that our good actions can have this result.[98]

Understood in this way, this view of the text cannot be cavalierly dismissed as "sub-Christian," for there is biblical precedent for the idea.[99] The major difficulty with the view is that it does not fit well in the context. In vv. 17-21, Paul has been urging that Christians avoid a spirit of retaliation; yet, however qualified, this first interpretation comes close to encouraging just such an attitude. Moreover, the teaching of Jesus from which Paul draws so much of what he says in these verses contains no such idea. Most modern commentators have therefore concluded that Paul views "coals of fire" as a

97. ἄνθρακας, "coals" (from ἄνθραξ, "charcoal"), is a true metaphor only in 2 Sam. 14:7 (referring to a child). But in several other texts it is part of an imagery that refers to God's awesome power (2 Sam. 22:9, 13; Ps. 18:8, 12) and to his judgment (Ps. 140:10; Isa. 5:24; cf. also Job 41:11, 12; Ps. 120:4).

98. This view was widespread in the early church (cf., e.g., Chrysostom), but has not been popular recently. See, however (with variations), Haldane; Zeller; S. Légasse, "Vengeance humaine et vengeance divine en Romains 12,14-21," in *La Vie de la Parole: De l'Ancien au Nouveau Testament: Etudes d'exégèse et d'herméneutique bibliques offertes à Pierre Grelot* (ed. Departement des Etudes Bibliques de l'Institut Catholique de Paris; Paris: Desclée, 1987), pp. 281-90; S. Segert, " 'Live Coals Heaped on the Head'," in *Love and Death in the Ancient Near East: Essays in Honor of Marvin H. Pope* (ed. J. H. Marks and R. H. Good; Guilford, CN: Four Quarters, 1987), pp. 159-64; K. Stendahl, "Hate, Non-Retaliation, and Love: I QS x,17-20 and Rom. 12:19-21," *HTR* 55 (1962), 343-55; and esp. J. Piper, *Love Your Enemies: Jesus' Love Command in the Synoptic Gospels and in the Early Christian Paraenesis* (SNTSMS 38; Cambridge: Cambridge University, 1979), pp. 115-18.

99. See esp. Piper, *Love Your Enemies*, pp. 117-18.

metaphor for "the burning pangs of shame."[100] Acting kindly toward our enemies is a means of leading them to be ashamed of their conduct toward us and, perhaps, to repent and turn to the Lord whose love we embody.[101] While the linguistic basis for this view is not all that one would wish, it is probably the best alternative. Paul is giving us a positive motivation for acts of kindness toward our enemies. He does not want the prohibition of vengeance (v. 19) to produce in us a "do-nothing" attitude toward our persecutors.[102] However, Paul is not claiming that acts of kindness toward enemies will infallibly bring repentance; whatever degree of shame our acts might produce, they may be quickly pushed aside and produce even greater hostility toward both us and the Lord.

21 Paul rounds off his series of admonitions about the Christian's response to hostility with a final, general summons: "Do not be overcome with evil, but overcome evil with the good." The double use of the word "evil"[103] links this verse with v. 17a in a chiastic arrangement. Evil can overcome us when we allow the pressure put on us by a hostile world to force us into attitudes and actions that are out of keeping with the transformed character of the new realm. Paul urges us to resist such temptation. But, more than that, sounding a note typical both of this paragraph and of the teaching of Jesus that it reflects, he urges us to take a positive step as well: to work constantly[104] at triumphing over the evil others do to us[105] by doing good. By

---

100. Some scholars have traced the metaphor to an Egyptian practice of carrying a tray of burning coals on one's head as a sign of contrition; see esp. S. Morenz, "Feurige Kohlen auf dem Haupt," in *Religion und Geschichte der alten Agypten. Gesammelte Aufsätze* (Weimar: Hermann Böhlaus, 1975), pp. 433-44. For other suggestions for the origin of the metaphor as a reference to shame, see J. E. Yonge, "Heaping Coals of Fire on the Head," *The Expositor,* series 3, vol. 2 (1885), 158-59; A. T. Fryer, "Coals of Fire," *ExpTim* 36 (1924-25), 478; J. Steele, "Heaping Coals of Fire on the Head (Pr. xxv.22; Ro. xii.20)," *ExpTim* 44 (1932), 141.

101. This view was also popular in the early church, being held by, e.g., Origen and Augustine. Almost all modern commentators hold some form of this view; see also Furnish, *Love Command,* pp. 107-8, and W. Klassen, "Coals of Fire: Sign of Repentance or Revenge?" *NTS* 9 (1962-63), 337-50. Calvin, however, claims that the image connotes shame, with the result of that shame — greater degree of guilt or repentance — not being specified. Cranfield holds a somewhat similar view. Some commentators have cited the targum in favor of a positive interpretation, since it adds to the verse in Proverbs the words "and will make him your friend" (e.g., Dunn).

102. Hence the ἀλλά ("but") at the beginning of the verse; see Dunn.

103. Gk. κακός.

104. The present tense of the imperative νίκα probably indicates that the action is to be continual (see Dunn).

105. The κακός in this verse is almost certainly the evil others do to us rather than the evil of our own vindictiveness (see Murray).

responding to evil with "the good" rather than with evil, we gain a victory over that evil. Not only have we not allowed it to corrupt our own moral integrity, but we have displayed the character of Christ before a watching and skeptical world.[106] Here, Paul suggests at the end of this important series of exhortations, is a critical example of that "good" *(agathos)* which Paul exhorts us to display in this section of the letter (see 12:2).

D. THE CHRISTIAN AND SECULAR RULERS (13:1-7)

1Every soul is to be submissive to the governing authorities.[1] For there is no authority except by God, and the existing authorities have been appointed by God. 2So that the one who resists the authority is resisting the ordinance of God. And those who resist will bring judgment on themselves. 3For the rulers are not a cause of fear to the good work but to the bad. Now do you want to avoid fear of the authority? Do good, and you will receive praise from him. 4For he is God's servant for you, for the good. But if you do what is bad, fear. For he does not bear the sword in vain. For he is God's servant, an avenger who brings wrath on the one who practices what is bad.

5Therefore it is necessary to be submissive, not only because of wrath but also because of conscience. 6For also, because of this, you are paying taxes. For they are servants of God, devoted to this very thing. 7Pay back to everyone what you owe: taxes, to whom you owe taxes; custom duties to whom you owe custom duties; respect to whom you owe respect; honor to whom you owe honor.

In contrast to the loosely connected series of exhortations in 12:9-21, we find in 13:1-7 a coherent and well-organized argument about a single topic: the need for submission to governing authorities. This argument comes on the scene quite abruptly, with no explicit syntactical connection with what has come before it[2] — and not much evidence of any connection in subject matter

---

106. See, in this respect, the similar exhortations in 1 Peter (2:11-12, 15; 3:16-17; 4:12-19).

1. The valuable early papyrus P[46], along with a significant part of the western MS tradition (the original hand of D, F, and G), read πάσαις ἐξουσίαις ὑπερεχούσαις ὑποτάσσεσθε, "be submissive to all the governing authorities." The variant does not have sufficient external support to be considered seriously (UBS[4] gives the usual text an "A" rating, indicating the editors thought it was "certain" [UBS[3], however, gave it only a "C" rating]); in any case, the meaning is not affected.

2. E.g., there are no particles or conjunctions in 13:1 to link this and the following verses to the end of chap. 12. Such a situation (asyndeton) is relatively unusual in Greek.

objections

either. In fact, vv. 8-10, highlighting the centrality of love for the Christian ethic, seem to relate to vv. 9-21, which also focus on love and its outworkings. When we add to these points the allegedly un-Pauline vocabulary of the passage, we can understand why some scholars think that a redactor has added 13:1-7 to Paul's original letter to the Romans.[3] Other scholars do not go so far. They think that Paul himself included this section here but that he was quoting an already developed Christian tradition. On either view, however, Rom. 13:1-7 is viewed as an "alien body" within 12:1–13:14.[4] Not only does it interrupt Paul's elaboration of the nature and centrality of love, but it seems to give unqualified endorsement to an institution that belongs to an age that is "passing away" (13:11-14) and to which we are not to be conformed (12:2).

But Paul's teaching about the transitory nature of this world might be precisely why he includes 13:1-7. His purpose may be to stifle the kind of extremism that would pervert his emphasis on the coming of a new era and on the "new creation" into a rejection of every human and societal convention — including the government. Paul had had to respond to such extremism before. In fact, Paul writes to the Romans from the city in which this extremism appears to have had its boldest manifestation: Corinth (cf. 1 Corinthians). One can well imagine Christians arguing: "The old age has passed away; we are 'a new creation in Christ' and belong to the transcendent, spiritual realm. Surely we, who are even now reigning with Christ in his kingdom, need pay no attention to the secular authorities of this defunct age." If Rom. 13:1-7 is directed to just such an attitude, Paul may have inserted it here as a guard against those who might draw the wrong conclusions from his concern that Christians avoid conformity to "this age." For all that is present in the world around us is not part of "this age," or at least not part of it in the same way. To the degree that this age is dominated by Satan and sin, Christians must resolutely refuse to adopt its values. But the world in which Christians continue to live out their bodily existence (see 12:1) has not been wholly abandoned by God. As a manifestation of his common grace, God has established in this world certain institutions, such as marriage and government, that have a positive role to play even after the inauguration of the new age.[5]

---

3. Schmithals, 458-62; O'Neill, 207-9; J. Kallas, "Romans XIII.1-7: An Interpolation," *NTS* 11 (1964-65), 365-74; W. Munro, *Authority in Paul and Peter: The Identification of a Pastoral Stratum in the Pauline Corpus and 1 Peter* (SNTSMS 45; Cambridge: Cambridge University, 1983), pp. 56-67; idem, "Romans 13:1-7: Apartheid's Last Biblical Refuge," *BTB* 20 (1990), 161-68.

4. The phrase is Käsemann's (352). See also Michel, 393-94.

5. This explanation for Rom. 13:1-7 was common in the early church (see, e.g., Chrysostom, Homily 23 [p. 511]; Pelagius, 136) and is also held, in a variety of forms, by a number of modern scholars; see esp. Ridderbos, *Paul,* pp. 320-23; U. Wilckens, "Römer 13,1-7," in *Rechtfertigung als Freiheit,* pp. 226-30; Käsemann, 350-51 (the text counters "enthusiasts"); Nygren, 426-27; Fitzmyer, 663; R. Walker, *Studie zu Römer 13,1-7* (The-

Recognizing how Paul's teaching about the need for Christians to respect governing authorities in 13:1-7 fits into his overall theology of the Christian's life in this world helps explain its presence at this point in Paul's exhortations. Submission to government is another aspect of that "good" which the Christian, seeking to "approve" the will of God, will exemplify (cf. 12:2).[6] The specific contextual trigger for Paul's teaching about government and its role in this world may have been 12:19. Forbidding the Christian from taking vengeance and allowing God to exercise this right in the last judgment might lead one to think that God was letting evildoers have their way in this world. Not so, says Paul in 13:1-7: for God, through governing authorities, is even now inflicting wrath on evildoers (vv. 3-4).[7]

I think these considerations are sufficient to explain why Paul includes 13:1-7 in his letter to the Romans. But many scholars are not convinced of this. They think that there must have been a situation in the church at Rome, of which Paul was aware, that led him to include this exhortation. Scholars have proposed several scenarios,[8] but the most likely is that the Roman

---

ologische Existenz Heute 132; Munich: Kaiser, 1966), pp. 57-58; H. Schlier, "The State according to the New Testament," in *The Relevance of the New Testament* (New York: Herder and Herder, 1968), pp. 229-30; W. Schrage, *Die Christen und der Staat nach dem Neuen Testament* (Gütersloh: Gütersloher, 1971), pp. 51-52; H. von Campenhausen, "Zur Auslegung von Röm. 13: Die dämonistische Deutung des ἐξουσία-Begriffs," in *Aus der Frühzeit des Christentums: Studien zur Kirchengeschichte des ersten und zweiten Jahrhunderts* (Tübingen: Mohr, 1963), pp. 81-101.

6. R. Heiligenthal, "Strategien konformer Ethik im Neuen Testament am Beispiel von Röm 13.1-7," *NTS* 29 (1983), 57; Wilckens, "Römer 13,1-7," pp. 209-10; V. P. Furnish, *The Moral Teaching of Paul: Selected Issues* (Nashville: Abingdon, 1979), p. 126; Murray, 2.146; G. Delling, *Römer 13,1-7 innerhalb der Briefe des Neuen Testaments* (Berlin: Evangelische, 1962), pp. 67-68.

7. Wilckens, "Römer 13:1-7," pp. 209-10; C. K. Barrett, "The New Testament Doctrine of Church and State," in *New Testament Essays* (London: SPCK, 1972), pp. 14-15; Black, 180; S-H, 366. T. C. De Kruijf ("The Literary Unity of Rom 12,16–13,8a: A Network of Inclusions," *Bijdragen, tijdschrift voor filosofie en theologie* 48 [1987], 319-26) argues that Paul marks off 12:17–13:7 as an integral unit about relationships with outsiders; cf. also Viard, 273.

8. Many scholars cite the violent anti-Roman Jewish Zealot movement as a possible influence on the Christians in Rome — a tendency that the Christians must resist if they are not to be identified, and condemned, with the Jewish community (cf. E. Bammel, "Romans 13," in *Jesus and the Politics of his Day* [ed. E. Bammel and C. F. D. Moule; Cambridge: Cambridge University, 1984], pp. 366-75; M. Borg, "A New Context for Romans XIII," *NTS* 19 [1972-73], 205-18; R. A. Culpepper, "God's Righteousness in the Life of his People. Romans 12–15," *RevExp* 73 [1976], 456-57; Calvin, 477; Harrison, 136). However, as Käsemann notes (p. 350), there is little evidence for Zealot or Zealot-like agitation in Rome at this date. J. Moiser suggests that Claudius's expulsion of Jews (and Jewish Christians) in A.D. 49 might have led to resentment against the state and the temptation to rebel against it ("Rethinking Romans 12–15," *NTS* 36 [1990], 571-82).

Christians had been infected by their fellow citizens with a resistance to paying taxes to an increasingly rapacious Roman government.[9] It would be because of this background that Paul concludes his teaching about submission to government with a plea to pay taxes (vv. 6-7). However, evidence for a tax rebellion in Rome as early as 56-57 (the date of Romans) is sparse; and if Paul was concerned about the Roman Christians not paying taxes, it is peculiar that he would commend them for doing just that in v. 6b.[10] Nor do we need to posit a situation in Rome to explain Paul's exhortation to pay taxes. The paying of taxes was then, as now, the most pervasive and universal expression of subservience to the state. More important, Paul is probably in this paragraph continuing his allusions to the teaching of Jesus. And it was, of course, the paying of taxes that formed the basis for Jesus' famous pronouncement about "rendering to Caesar what is Caesar's and to God what is God's" (Mark 12:13-17 and pars.).

Paul's teaching also has a number of striking similarities to 1 Pet. 2:13-17.[11] This suggests that Jesus' teaching about the relationship of the disciple to the state was the basis for a widespread early Christian tradition, which Paul here takes up and adapts.[12] Paul certainly casts this tradition in

9. The Roman historian Tacitus refers to resistance against the payment of "indirect" taxes in the middle 50s, culminating in a tax revolt in A.D. 58 (*Ann.* 13.50ff.). If Paul knew of these tendencies, his purpose in 13:1-7 would be to counsel the Roman Christians to demonstrate their loyalty to the Roman government by paying both the "indirect" and the "direct" tax (cf. v. 7). For this scenario, see esp. J. Friedrich, W. Pöhlmann, and P. Stuhlmacher, "Zur historischen Situation und Intention von Röm 13,1-7," *ZTK* 73 (1976), 153-59; also F. Laub, "Der Christ und die staatliche Gewalt: Zum Verständnis der 'politischen' Paränese Röm 13,1-7 in der gegenwärtigen Diskussion," *MTZ* 30 (1979), 257-65; Dunn, 2.759; idem, "Romans 13:1-7 — A Charter for Political Quietism?" *Ex Auditu* 2 (1986), 66; Furnish, *Moral Teaching,* pp. 131-35.

10. See Wilckens, 3.34; K. Weiss, *TDNT* IX, 82-83.

11. The 1 Peter text has a number of key words and concepts in common with Rom. 13:1-7: ὑποτάσσω ("order under, submit") as the basic command; ὑπερέχω ("supreme"), used to denote governing powers; the purpose of government as being ἐκδίκησιν κακοποιῶν ("taking vengeance on evildoers") and ἔπαινον ἀγαθοποιῶν ("giving praise to doers of good"); the exhortation to give "honor" (τιμάω) and "fear" (φοβέομαι). See also 1 Tim. 2:1-2, which commands believers to pray for kings and "all those placed over [ὑπεροχῇ] us, in order that we might lead a quiet and peaceful life in all piety and godliness"; and Tit. 3:1, which exhorts us to "submit" (ὑποτάσσεσθαι) to "rulers, authorities" (ἀρχαῖς, ἐξουσίαις). A parallel with 1 Thess. 5:15, which demands obedience to church leaders in a context that bears many similarities to Rom. 13, is less likely (contra Campenhausen, "Zur Auslegung von Röm. 13," pp. 96-100).

12. A. F. C. Webster, "St. Paul's Political Advice to the Haughty Gentile Christians in Rome: An Exegesis of Romans 13:1-7," *St. Vladimir's Theological Quarterly* 25 (1981), 262-73; Wilckens, 2.39-40 and "Römer 13:1-7," pp. 211-14; Friedrich, Pöhlmann, and Stulhmacher, "Zur historischen Situation," pp. 134-35; Michel, 396-97.

language drawn from Greco-Roman government;[13] and submission to government was certainly encouraged in many Greco-Roman circles. But, as is usually the case, the concepts Paul teaches here have their roots in the OT and Judaism.[14]

The line of thought in the paragraph is as follows[15]:

General command: "submit to the authorities" (v. 1a)
> First reason ("for") for submission: they are appointed by God (v. 1b)
> Consequences ("so that") of resisting the authorities: God's judgment (v. 2)
> Second reason ("for") for submission: rulers are God's servants to reward good and punish evil (vv. 3-4)
Reiteration ("therefore") of general command, with abbreviated reference to reasons for submission (v. 5):
> "because of [fear of] wrath" and
> "because of conscience"
Appeal to practice: the Roman Christians are paying taxes (v. 6)
Specific command ("because of this"): pay your taxes and respect the authorities! (v. 7)

1 Paul gets right to the point: "Every soul is to be submissive to the governing authorities." In typical OT and Jewish fashion, Paul uses "soul" (*psychē*) to denote not one "part" of a human being (soul in distinction from body or spirit) but the whole person. The translation "every person" (NRSV; NASB; REB) or "everyone" (NIV; TEV; NJB) is therefore entirely justified.[16] The basis of Paul's own authority — an apostle of the gospel — as well as the audience of the letter indicates that his immediate reference must be to Christians. But we should probably not limit the reference to Christians only. Submission to governing authorities is especially incumbent on Christians

---

13. See esp. A. Strobel, "Zum Verständnis von Rm 13," *ZNW* 47 (1956), 58-62, 80-90; cf. also Käsemann, 353; Schlier, 393; Merk, *Handeln aus Glauben,* pp. 162-64.

14. Wilckens, "Römer 13,1-7," pp. 223-26; cf. also Friedrich, Pöhlmann, and Stuhlmacher, "Zur historischen Situation," pp. 135-46, who stress Paul's indebtedness to both Greco-Roman and Jewish traditions. It must be noted, on the other hand, that Rom. 13:1-7 lacks many of the typical features of Jewish treatments of the state (e.g., emphasis on martyrdom; cf. F. Neugebauer, "Zur Auslegung von Röm. 13,1-7," *KD* 8 [1962], 152-59). This does not invalidate Paul's dependence on the OT and Jewish teaching, but it shows that he has selected only the most basic of their teachings.

15. This differs in only a couple of points from the analysis of R. H. Stein, "The Argument of Romans 13:1-7," *NovT* 31 (1989), 325-43.

16. See also Rom. 2:9; Acts 2:43; 3:23; Rev. 16:3.

who recognize that the God they serve stands behind those authorities, but it is required even for those who do not know this.[17]

"Governing authorities" (cf. also NRSV; NIV; NASB; NJB) translates a phrase that is central to the interpretation of the paragraph. Like our "authority," *exousia* refers broadly in secular and biblical Greek to the possession and exercise of (usually legitimate) power. As an abstract noun, the word usually denotes the concept of authority. Jesus' well-known words in Matt. 28:18 use the word in a typical way: "All *authority* in heaven and on earth has been given to me." But the word can also have a concrete application, in which case *exousia* denotes a sphere over which authority is exercised (e.g., a "dominion"; cf. Luke 23:7) or the being who exercises authority.[18] The latter is clearly how the word is used in Rom. 13:1. The NT refers to two different kinds of "beings" who exercise authority: a person in government (a "ruler")[19] and spiritual "powers."[20] A few scholars have argued that Paul may be referring at least partially to spiritual beings in Rom. 13:1.[21] But this

17. Wilckens; Fitzmyer; Stein, "Argument," p. 326; Walker, *Römer 13,1-7*, pp. 8, 11-12; contra, e.g., Schlier; Cranfield.

18. ἐξουσία occurs approximately 72 times in the LXX and 93 in the NT. The large majority of occurrences are abstract (as in Matt. 28:18) and, as might be expected, in the singular. In the LXX, only Dan. 3:2 and 7:27 use ἐξουσία in the plural with a concrete application. The meaning of the word in the former verse is uncertain, while in 7:27 it refers to spheres of authority, e.g., "dominions." Cf. also Luke 23:7: Jesus was from "the authority [ἐκ τῆς ἐξουσίας] of Herod."

19. See Luke 12:11 — "And when they bring you before the synagogues (τὰς συναγωγάς) and the rulers (τὰς ἀρχάς) and the authorities (τὰς ἐξουσίας), do not be anxious about how or what you will answer and what you will say" — and Tit. 3:1: "Remind them to be submissive to ruling authorities (ἀρχαῖς ἐξουσίαις) [or "rulers and authorities"; note the textual variant]. . . ." This same meaning of the plural ἐξουσίαις is found in secular Greek (see the references in G. Foerster, *TDNT* II, 563 nn. 16 and 17) and in Josephus (*J.W.* 2.350).

20. See Eph. 3:10; 6:12; Col. 1:16; 2:15; 1 Pet. 3:22; and, in the singular, Eph. 1:21 and Col. 2:10. In all but the 1 Peter text, ἐξουσία(ι) is paralleled with ἀρχή/αί. This use of ἐξουσία does not seem to have any precedent and may reflect the influence of Hebrew (see G. Foerster, *TDNT* II, 565, 571).

21. This identification was first, apparently, proposed by M. Dibelius (*Die Geisterwelt im Glauben des Paulus* [Göttingen: Vandenhoeck & Ruprecht, 1909]), though he later retracted it (cf. "Rom und die Christen im ersten Jahrhundert," in *Botschaft und Geschichte: Gesammelte Aufsätze II* [Tübingen: Mohr, 1956], 177-228). It was accepted and developed by several other scholars (e.g., K. L. Schmidt, "Das Gegenüber von Kirche und Staat in der Gemeinde des Neuen Testaments," *TBl* 16 [1937], cols. 1-16; G. Dehn, "Engel und Obrigkeit," in *Theologische Aufsätze Karl Barth zum 50. Geburtstag* [ed. E. Wolf; Munich: Kaiser, 1936], 90-109; idem, *Vom christlichen Leben*, p. 72; C. E. B. Cranfield, "Some Observations on Romans 13:1-7," *NTS* 6 [1959-60], 241-49 [retracted in his commentary]), but attained considerable attention through its advocacy by K. Barth (cf. *Church and State* [London: SCM, 1939], 23-36) and O. Cullmann (*The State in the*

is unlikely.[22] As parallel terms in this context suggest (cf. "rulers" [*archontes*] in v. 3), the "authorities" occupy positions in secular government. Paul qualifies them as "governing" in order to indicate that they are in positions of superiority over the believers he is addressing.[23]

New Testament [New York: Harper & Row, 1956], 55-70). See also C. Morrison, *The Powers That Be: Earthly Rulers and Demonic Powers in Romans 13:1-7* (SBT; London: SCM, 1960), who emphasizes the degree to which the material and the spiritual were intertwined in the first century; and W. Wink, who, while recognizing the difficulty of lexical identification, nevertheless thinks that spiritual powers would have been part of Paul's conception of the secular rulers he discusses in Rom. 13 (*Naming the Powers: The Language of Power in the New Testament,* vol. 1: *The Powers* [Philadelphia: Fortress, 1984], pp. 45-47). The importance of the lexical point is that it provides for these scholars both a christological basis for Paul's exhortation and an implicit justification for disobedience of the state. They argue as follows: as was typical in the ancient world, Paul assumed that behind the secular governing authorities stood angelic beings. This conceptual context, coupled with the lexical evidence that Paul uses ἐξουσία in the plural to refer to spiritual beings (the exception is Tit. 3:1, which most of these scholars would not in any case consider Pauline), justifies us in thinking that Paul intends a double reference with ἐξουσίαι in Rom. 13:1: both the human rulers and the spiritual beings that stand behind them. Ultimately, then, the Christian's submission to "the authorities" must be seen in light of Christ's subduing of these authorities. We are justified in obeying them as long as they recognize and manifest the fact of their subjection; but when they rebel against this subjection, we Christians are justified in ignoring them.

22. Four points, in particular, are fatal to the Barth-Cullmann approach. (1) When ἐξουσίαι refers to spiritual beings in Paul, it always occurs with ἀρχαί. The omission of the latter in Rom. 13:1 calls into question the value of the lexical parallels. (2) Other terms in Rom. 13:1-7 that are parallel to ἐξουσίαι cannot have such a double meaning (see ἄρχοντες in v. 3; διάκονος in v. 4). Paul throughout the passage uses terms drawn from Greco-Roman government and administration, and we would expect ἐξουσίαι to have a similar background (see, e.g., Strobel, "Verständnis," pp. 67-79). (3) The attempt to introduce a christological basis for Paul's exhortation is to seek to introduce what simply is not there. Paul explicitly grounds his commands in *theo*logy, pointing to God's appointment of the authorities as the foundation for Christian submission. (4) It is almost impossible that Paul would have commanded Christians to submit to (often evil) spiritual beings. For these points, and others, see W. Carr, *Angels and Principalities: The Background, Meaning and Development of the the Pauline Phrase kai archai kai hai exousiai* (SNTSMS 42; Cambridge: Cambridge University, 1981), pp. 115-21; V. Zsifkovits, *Der Staatsgedanke nach Paulus in Röm 13,1-7, mit besonderer Berücksichtigung der Umwelt und der patristischen Auslegung* (Wiener Beiträge zur Theologie 8; Vienna: Herder, 1964), pp. 57-64; Delling, *Römer 13,1-7,* pp. 20-34; Campenhausen, "Zur Auslegung von Röm. 13," pp. 81-96. Some theologians and scholars have thought that governing authorities in the church might be included among the ἐξουσίαι (see, e.g., Pelagius; Luther; and, among modern authors, cf. A. B. Ogle, "What Is Left for Caesar? A Look at Mark 12:13-17 and Romans 13:1-7," *TToday* 35 [1978], 254-64); but the vocabulary of the passage points decisively toward a reference exclusively to secular rulers.

23. See 1 Tim. 2:2, οἱ ἐν ὑπεροχῇ, "those who have power" (cf. also Wis. 6:5). This explanation, which takes ὑπερεχούσαις to have comparative force (the authorities

Paul calls on believers to "submit"[24] to governing authorities rather than to "obey" them; and Paul's choice of words may be important to our interpretation and application of Paul's exhortation. To submit is to recognize one's subordinate place in a hierarchy, to acknowledge as a general rule that certain people or institutions have "authority" over us. In addition to governing authorities (cf. also Tit. 3:1), Paul urges Christians to submit to their spiritual leaders (1 Cor. 16:16) and to "one another" (Eph. 5:21); and he calls on Christian slaves to submit to their masters (Tit. 2:9), Christian prophets to submit to other prophets (1 Cor. 14:32), and Christian wives to submit to their husbands (1 Cor. 14:34 [?]; Eph. 5:24; Col. 3:18; Tit. 2:5).[25] It is this general posture toward government that Paul demands here of Christians. And such a posture will usually demand that we obey what the governing authorities tell us to do. But perhaps our submission to government is compatible with disobedience to government in certain exceptional circumstances. For heading the hierarchy of relations in which Christians find themselves is God; and all subordinate "submissions" must always be measured in relationship to our all-embracing submission to him.[26]

"surpass" or "excel" [ὑπερέχω] the believer), is preferable to taking the word as a superlative (which would suggest that Paul refers to the superior "authorities," e.g., the highest Roman authorities; see, perhaps, 1 Pet. 2:13; for this perspective, see Godet; Cranfield; contra Barrett; Black [cf. NEB]). See also E. A. Judge, who suggests that ἐξουσίαι might denote those in government who were particularly in contact with the Christians ("Origin," 9-10). The view of S. E. Porter ("Romans 13:1-7 as Pauline Political Rhetoric," *Filologia Neotestamentaria* 3 [1990], 122-24) that ὑπερεχούσαις means "superior" in a qualitative sense, and thus limits Paul's demand for submission to "just" officials, must be rejected because it builds on uncertain lexical evidence.

24. The Greek verb is ὑποτάσσω. The specific form here, ὑποτασσέσθω, could be middle (cf. G. Delling, *TDNT* VIII, 42; Murray), but it is probably passive since the aorist form of the verb is always passive (cf. BAGD; Cranfield).

25. Paul also uses ὑποτάσσω of the relationship of people to the law (Rom. 8:7), of creation to "vanity" (Rom. 8:20), of Jews (negatively) to the righteousness of God (Rom. 10:3), and (with allusion to Ps. 8:6), of "all things" to Christ (1 Cor. 15:27-28; Eph. 1:22; Phil. 3:21). The verb also occurs in Luke 2:51; 10:17, 20; Heb. 2:5, 8; 12:9; Jas. 4:7; 1 Pet. 2:13, 18; 3:1, 5, 22; 5:5.

26. See Fitzmyer: ". . . submission in earthly matters as an expression of the Christian's relation to God and his order of things. . . . Such submission is clearly measured by the form of human government in which one resides; it would carry nuances dependent on the form of monarchic, democratic, or republican state." On this interpretation of ὑποτάσσω, see also Cranfield; Morris; Barrett, "New Testament Doctrine," p. 16; S. Hutchinson, "The Political Implications of Romans 13:1-7," *Biblical Theology* 21 (1971), 53-55; E. Jüngel, " 'Jedermann sei untertan der Obrigkeit . . .' Eine Bibelarbeit über Römer 13,1-7," in *Evangelische Christen . . . in unserer Demokratie: Beiträge aus der Synode der Evangelischen Kirche in Deutschland* (ed. E. Jüngel, R. Herzog, and H. Simon; Gütersloh: Mohn, 1986), pp. 25-30; Furnish, *Moral Teaching,* p. 127; Porter, "Romans 13:1-7," pp. 120-22. See also my comments at the end of this section.

Verse 1b gives the reason[27] why we are to submit to governing authorities: "there is no authority except by God, and the existing authorities have been appointed[28] by God."[29] In light of *exousiai* in v. 1a, "authority" will refer to the individual human ruler.[30] Paul's insistence that no ruler wields power except through God's appointment reflects standard OT and Jewish teaching. Daniel tells the proud pagan king Nebuchadnezzar that God was teaching him that "the Most High is sovereign over the kingdom of mortals; he gives it to whom he will and sets over it the lowliest of human beings" (4:17).[31] Paul's dependence on this tradition and his all-inclusive language ("there is no authority except") make clear that he is asserting a universally applicable truth about the ultimate origin of rulers. From a human perspective, rulers come to power through force or heredity or popular choice. But the "transformed mind" recognizes behind every such process the hand of God. Paul brings home this general principle in the last clause of the verse.[32] The believers in Rome are to recognize that the specific governmental officials with whom they have dealings[33] — "the ones that now exist,"[34] as Paul puts it — are "appointed," or "ordained," by God.

27. Cf. Gk. γάρ.

28. Gk. τάσσω, "appoint, order, put someone over"; cf. Matt. 28:16; Luke 7:8; Acts 13:18; 15:2; 22:10; 28:23; 1 Cor. 16:15.

29. The presence of the preposition ὑπό in both clauses suggests that we should read back into the first clause a form of the verb τάσσω, which Paul uses in the second clause. The connection between the command of v. 1a and its basis in v. 1b through the use of words built on the ταγ- stem — ὑποτασσέσθω-τεταγμέναι (perfect passive from τάσσω) — should be noted (cf. also ἀντιτασσόμενος and διαταγῇ in v. 2).

30. Contra Chrysostom, who thinks that ἐξουσία denotes the principle of rulership and that Paul is therefore not affirming the divine origin of every human ruler.

31. Cf. the similar refrain in 4:25, 32; 5:21; also 1 Sam. 12:8; Jer. 2:7, 10; 27:5-6; Dan. 2:21, 37-38; Prov. 8:15-16; Isa. 41:2-4; 45:1-7. Post-OT Jewish sources are just as explicit. See Wis. 6:1-3:

> Listen, therefore, O kings, and understand; learn, O judges of the ends of the earth. Give ear, you that rule over multitudes, and boast of many nations. For your dominion was given you from the Lord, and your sovereignty from the Most High, who will search out your works and inquire into your plans.

See also Josephus, *J.W.* 2.140: "no ruler attains his office save by the will of God"; Sir. 4:27; 10:4; 17:7; *1 Enoch* 46:5; *Ep. Arist.* 224; *2 Apoc. Bar.* 82:9; and cf. Str-B, 3.303-4.

32. The δέ introducing it is probably ascensive: "and even" (see Godet).

33. E. A. Judge ("Cultural Conformity and Innovation in Paul: Some Clues from Contemporary Documents," *TynBul* 35 [1984], 9-10) suggests that the ἐξουσίαι are the officials who administer authority (an authority derived from the ἀρχαί). Zsifkovits (*Staatsgedanke,* pp. 64-65) notes that ἐξουσίαι translates Lat. *potestates,* a term that broadly covered a range of Roman government officials.

34. Gk. αἱ οὖσαι, "the ones being."

2   In v. 1a Paul has stated a positive consequence of God's appointment of human rulers: we are to submit to them. Now he asserts two related negative consequences[35] of the same theological truth. Since God has appointed human rulers, the person who opposes them is opposing, is "in a state of rebellion against,"[36] the "ordinance" of God.[37] And such opposition will ultimately lead to eternal condemnation. As submission denotes a recognition of government's position over the Christian by God's appointment, so resistance is the refusal to acknowledge the authority of government.[38] It denotes the attitude of one who will not admit that government has a legitimate right to exercise authority over him or her. Those who take up this attitude[39] "will bring judgment on themselves."[40] "Bringing judgment"[41] could refer to the action of the secular ruler, with the implication (spelled out in v. 4b) that God's own judgment is present in the punishment meted out by the ruler.[42] But Paul's argument has not advanced this far. It is better to understand the judgment here to be the eschatological judgment of God: those who persistently oppose secular rulers, and hence the will of God, will suffer condemnation for that opposition.[43]

35. See the Gk. ὥστε, "so that," "as a consequence."

36. The verb is the perfect ἀνθέστηκεν, connoting a state of resistance (see Porter, *Verbal Aspect,* p. 396).

37. "Ordained" and "ordinance" capture the wordplay in Greek between τεταγ-μέναι in v. 1b and διαταγή in v. 2. The word διαταγή occurs once in the LXX (Ezra 4:11) and once elsewhere in the NT (Acts 7:53; cf. διατάσσω, "ordain," in Gal. 3:19 and Heb. 2:2). The word refers to the act of God's appointment, not to an eternal "ordinance" of God (see Walker, *Römer 13,1-7,* p. 23). Schlier suggests that Paul may intend a certain irony here since he claims that the word was used of the "orders" that rulers issue; Paul would therefore be saying, in effect, that the rulers themselves are "under orders." But Wilckens questions whether the word is used this way.

38. Paul uses two different verbs for this concept in the clause: ἀντιτάσσω, "oppose," "resist" (only here and in Acts 18:6, Jas. 4:6, and 1 Pet. 5:5 [the latter quoting Prov. 3:34] in the NT); and ἀνθίστημι, which cannot be distinguished in meaning here from the former.

39. The perfect participle ἀνθεστηκότες connotes a persistent refusal to recognize government's role in the divine hierarchy (and not just an occasional failure), as is clear not so much from the tense but the context (see Dunn). Note Eph. 6:13 for a similar use of the verb.

40. "Against themselves" reflects the decision to take ἑαυτοῖς as a dative of disadvantage (BDF 188[2]).

41. The Greek phrase κρίμα λήμψονται, "receive judgment," is a Semitism (Black; cf. also Mark 12:40; Luke 20:47; Jas. 3:1).

42. S-H; Godet; Calvin; Murray; Cranfield; Zsifkovits, *Staatsgedanke,* pp. 72-73; H. Merklein, "Sinn und Zweck von Röm 13,1-7: Zur semantischen und pragmatischen Struktur eines umstrittenen Testes," in *Neues Testament und Ethik: Für Rudolf Schnackenburg* (ed. H. Merklein; Freiburg: Herder, 1989), p. 245.

43. Wilckens; Dunn; Michel; Stein, "Argument," pp. 331-32; Delling, *Römer 13,1-7,* pp. 64-65. Four of the five other occurrences of κρίμα in Romans refer to eschatological judgment (2:2, 3; 3:8; 5:16; the exception is 11:33, where the reference is to God's acts in history).

3-4 If "bring judgment" in v. 2b refers to a historical judgment that is mediated by the secular rulers, than vv. 3-4 could further explain this situation.[44] But if the judgment of v. 2b is God's final judgment, then we must view vv. 3-4 as a second reason why Christians are to submit to governing authorities.[45] Not only has God appointed them (v. 1b), but he has also entrusted to them an important role in maintaining order in society. By punishing those who do wrong and rewarding those who do good, secular rulers are carrying out God's purposes in the world. Christians, therefore, are to submit to the secular rulers. For "rulers,"[46] Paul explains, are not a "cause of fear"[47] to those who are persistent in doing good[48] but only to those who do evil. Christians need only do the good that they are called to do under the gospel (cf. 12:2, 9, 17, and 21) if they want to avoid fear of the authorities.[49] In fact, Paul concludes, doing good will not only bring freedom from fear; it will even result in praise from the rulers.[50]

44. Verses 3-4 might then explain the judgment of v. 2b (Meyer) or the prerogative of rulers to exercise that judgment (Haldane; Murray); or it might elaborate further the concept of a divinely ordained society (Dunn).

45. Calvin; Schlier; Cranfield; Stein, "Argument," pp. 332-33.

46. Gk. ἄρχοντες. Paul uses the word only three other times, once in the singular (Eph. 2:2: "the ruler of the authority of the air" [= Satan]) and twice in the plural (1 Cor. 2:6 and 8: "the rulers of this age"). Many scholars have taken the Corinthian occurrences as references to spiritual beings, but a reference to human rulers and leaders is probable (see Carr, *Angels and Principalities,* pp. 118-20; Fee, *1 Corinthians,* pp. 103-4). This is certainly the usual meaning of ἄρχων in the NT.

47. φόβος usually refers to the actual feeling of fear in the NT, but here it must denote the "source of fear" (cf. BAGD; *GEL* [25.254] translate "cause those who do good to fear").

48. The Greek is τῷ ἀγαθῷ ἔργῳ, "the good work." As in 2:7, the phrase probably has a collective sense (S-H), and the context suggests that it is a personification (Murray). The same observations will apply also to τῷ κακῷ.

49. The clause θέλεις δὲ μὴ φοβεῖσθαι τὴν ἐξουσίαν could be conditional — "if you wish not to fear the authority . . ." (cf. NJB; BDF 471[3]; Turner, 319; Barrett) — or a question — "do you wish not to fear the authority? . . . (most English translations; S-H; Murray; Dunn). Syntax does not decide the matter, and either fits perfectly well in the context.

50. A few interpreters have thought that the "praise" (ἔπαινος) is from God (e.g., Origen, Augustine, Pelagius; cf. Zsifkovits, *Staatsgedanke,* pp. 78-80; Walker, *Römer 13,1-7,* pp. 36-37), but the antithetical parallel to "fear" (which is clearly fear of the secular ruler) requires that it be the ruler that bestows the praise. Paul may be thinking specifically of the practice of Roman authorities of publishing on inscriptions the names of "benefactors" of society (cf. e.g., Käsemann; Wilckens; Schlier; W. C. van Unnik, "Lob und Strafe durch die Obrigkeit: Hellenistisches zu Röm 13,3-4," in *Jesus und Paulus,* pp. 334-43; Heiligenthal, *Werke as Zeugen,* pp. 107-8). This being the case, Paul might intend the "doing good" in this verse to refer specifically to the activities of Christians as "good citizens" in the societies where they live (cf. Strobel, "Zum Verständnis von Rm 13," p. 79; B. W. Winter, "The Public Honouring of Christian Benefactors: Romans 13.3-4 and

Verse 4 is framed by two assertions in which Paul characterizes the ruler as a "servant of God." The first elaborates the positive function of the ruler — praising those who do good — which Paul has described in v. 3b. The second explains the negative function of the ruler — punishing evil — which Paul touched on in v. 3 and explains in more detail in v. 4b. In both these functions, the secular ruler is carrying out God's purposes, as his *diakonos*. Paul usually uses this word to refer to a Christian in his capacity as a willing "servant," or "minister," of the Lord and of other Christians. But people can also "serve" God, his purposes, and his people unconsciously. So it is with secular rulers, who, appointed by God (v. 1b), "administer" justice in keeping with divine standards of right and wrong.[51] On the positive side, rulers, by bestowing praise (v. 3b), encourage Christians to do what is good (v. 4a).[52]

Paul now turns again to the negative role of the ruler, showing why he is a "cause of fear" to those who do evil (cf. v. 3a). It is because the ruler "does not bear the sword in vain." Scholars have argued about the exact background and significance of the phrase "bear the sword," but none of the specific connotations suggested seems to be well established.[53] Probably, then,

---

1 Peter 2.14-15," *JSNT* 34 [1988], 87-103). While public benefaction should not be eliminated from the reference, the broader context of Rom. 12–13 suggests that it cannot be limited to this either.

51. διάκονος was used in secular Greek to denote a civic official (MM); cf. its application to court officials in Esth. 1:10; 2:2; 6:3 and to King Nebuchadrezzar in Jer. 25:9. See also Wis. 6:4. The outstanding OT example is, of course, the pagan king Cyrus (Isa. 45:1). The idea that secular rulers administer divine justice is not confined to Jewish or Christian circles; see, e.g., Plutarch, "Rulers are ministers of God for the care and safety of mankind, that they may distribute or hold in safe keeping the blessings and benefits which God gives to man" (*Princip. Inerud.* 5.13.22–14.2, quoted in Black). In light of this evidence, the argument about whether διάκονος here has a purely secular meaning (e.g., Käsemann) or a quasi-religious meaning (e.g., Barrett) is moot. The word *means* "servant," "minister," and no more; it is the qualifying genitive θεοῦ that indicates the ultimately "religious" significance of this service.

52. This interpretation of σοὶ εἰς τὸ ἀγαθόν assumes that σοί is a dative of advantage dependent on θεοῦ διάκονος — "he is God's servant *for your benefit*" — and that εἰς τὸ ἀγαθόν is equivalent to a purpose clause, with "you" as the understood subject (see Michel; Wilckens; Morris; Delling, *Römer 13,1-7*, pp. 58-59). This reading is preferable to the usual interpretation (reflected in most English translations) that the "good" is something bestowed on the believer by the government — either general peace and order (Althaus; Dunn; Fitzmyer) or ultimate spiritual good (cf. Rom. 8:28; see Cranfield) — because ἀγαθός in the context always describes Christian behavior, as does its opposite, κακός.

53. Several scholars point to the Roman *ius gladii,* the "authority (possessed by all higher magistrates) of inflicting sentence of death (cf. Tacitus, *Histories,* iii.68)" (Barrett; cf. also Michel; Lagrange; Leenhardt). But this practice seems to have been confined to the power of Roman provincial governors to condemn to death Roman citizens serving

Paul uses the phrase to refer generally to the right of the government to punish those who violate its laws.[54] For the purpose of his argument at this point, Paul is assuming that the laws of the state embody those general moral principles that are taught in the word of God.[55] The "evil" that the civil authorities punish, therefore, is evil in the absolute sense: those acts that God himself condemns as evil.[56] Only if this is so can we explain how Paul can see the government's use of the sword as a manifestation of its role as "God's servant." At the same time, this suggests that the "wrath" that the governing authority inflicts on wrongdoers is God's wrath.[57] When the civil authority punishes wrongdoers, the authority, acting as God's servant, is "an instrument of vengeance"[58] through whom God is executing his wrath on human sin. For, as Rom. 1:18 shows, the final eschatological outpouring of God's wrath on sin is even now, in the course of human history, finding expression. The "vengeance" that is prohibited to individual Christians (12:19) is executed by God's chosen servants, the secular authorities.

5 Paul sums up his argument in vv. 1-4: "Therefore[59] it is necessary to be submissive [to governmental authorities], not only[60] because of wrath but also

in the military (cf. A. N. Sherwin-White, *Roman Society and Roman Law in the New Testament* [Oxford: Clarendon, 1963], pp. 8-11); it would hardly be relevant to the Roman Christians (cf., e.g., Dunn). Others cite Philo's use of μαχαιροφόροι, "sword-bearers," to refer to Egyptian police officials (*Special Laws* 2.92-95; 3.159-63) (Wilckens); still others, the military power wielded by Rome (Cranfield; Harrison; Borg, "New Context," pp. 216-17 [in keeping with his view of the text as a whole, he sees a reference specifically to military suppression of Jewish rebellion]).

54. Friedrich, Pöhlmann, and Stuhlmacher, "Zur historischen Situation," pp. 140-44; Murray; Schlier; Fitzmyer. The phrase does not, then, directly refer to the infliction of the death penalty; but in the context of first-century Rome, and against the OT background (Gen. 9:4-6), Paul would clearly include the death penalty in the state's panoply of punishments for wrongdoing (see, e.g., Murray; Dunn).

55. Why this is so, and why Paul fails to deal with those times when secular rulers do *not* enforce biblical morals but rather reward what is evil and punish what is good, will be discussed at the end of this paragraph.

56. Cf. Wilckens; Cranfield; contra, e.g., Michel and Käsemann, who think that the reference is only to political/social offenses.

57. See, e.g., Calvin; S-H; Michel; Murray; Käsemann; Schlier; Dunn; contra, e.g., Delling, *Römer 13,1-7,* p. 59, who thinks that the wrath is the magistrate's. Part of the background for Paul's concept is the widespread OT teaching about God's use of pagan nations and rulers for executing wrath (often on Israel); cf. Isa. 5:26-29; 7:18-20; 8:7-8; 10:5-6; etc.

58. Gk. ἔκδικος. BAGD translate here "avenger" (cf. also 1 Thess. 4:6; Wis. 12:12; Sir. 30:6; Josephus, *J.W.* 5.377); cf. MM and Käsemann, who note the Hellenistic background for the word, where it can denote a "representative agent for wrath."

59. Gk. διό.

60. Gk. οὐ μόνον, οὐ (instead of the expected μή after the infinitive ὑποτάσσεσθαι) being used because of the stereotypical phrase (Burton, 481).

because of conscience."[61] The two "because of" phrases summarize the reasons for submission that Paul has developed in vv. 1b-4. "Because of wrath" encapsulates Paul's reminder in vv. 3-4 about the punitive function of secular rulers. It is the Christian's recognition of this function, and the consequent fear of suffering wrath at the hands of the secular official, that should motivate submission (cf. NIV: "because of possible punishment"). But this is only the minor reason for Christian submission, as Paul's "not only . . . but also" sequence indicates. A more basic reason for Christian submission is "because of conscience." "Conscience" refers here to the believer's knowledge of God's will and purposes.[62] Christians know what Paul has just taught: that secular rulers are appointed by God (v. 1b) and that they function therefore as his servants (v. 4).[63] The "necessity" for Christians to submit to government is therefore no mere practical expedient, a means of avoiding punishment; it arises ultimately from insight into God's providential ordering of human history.[64] Such submission is part of that "good, well-pleasing, and perfect" will of God discovered by the renewed mind (cf. also 1 Pet. 2:13, where the believer is to submit to "every human institution" "because of the Lord"). "Not being conformed to this world" does not require Christians to renounce every institution now in place in society. For some of them — such as government and marriage — reflect God's providential ordering of the world for our good and his glory.

6 "Because of this" could be parallel to the "therefore" at the beginning of v. 5 and refer to vv. 1b-4: because God has appointed secular rulers and they are his servants, "you are paying taxes."[65] However, while it amounts

---

61. Bultmann thinks this verse must be a post-Pauline addition to the text ("Glossen," p. 200). But his basis for this judgment, the allegedly un-Pauline use of συνείδησις ("conscience"), is groundless.

62. On Paul's use of συνείδησις, see the note on 2:15. Based on the claim that "conscience" always has a retrospective function in Paul, Pierce (*Conscience*, pp. 65-71) argues that "because of conscience" here means because one wants to avoid the painful knowledge that one has violated the will of God (cf. also Jewett, *Paul's Anthropological Terms*, pp. 439-41). But it is not clear that Paul always uses the term this strictly; and it is probably better to think that conscience functions prospectively, as a guide to Christian conduct (cf. Thrall, "ΣΥΝΕΙΔΗΣΙΣ," p. 624; Eckstein, *Syneidesis*, pp. 291-300; Cranfield; Michel; Wilckens; Barrett; furthermore, as Dunn points out, a prospective significance of the phrase is clear however we translate).

63. Stein ("Argument," pp. 338-39) and Merklein ("Sinn und Zweck von Röm 13,1-7," p. 250) suggest that "because of conscience" refers especially to vv. 1b-2. But the phrase must certainly include reference as well to the important immediately preceding emphasis on the ruler as "God's servant" (v. 4).

64. "Necessity" (Gk. ἀνάγκη) frequently refers to a requirement that arises from God's governance of the universe (cf. W. Grundmann, *TDNT* I, 345-47; Zsifkovits, *Staatsgedanke*, pp. 93-94).

65. Lietzmann; Stein, "Argument," pp. 340-41. Godet takes it with all of vv. 1-5.

to the same thing (since "conscience" summarizes these points from vv. 1b-4), it is better to see "because of this" picking up the immediately preceding phrase: "because of conscience" "you are paying taxes."[66] A few commentators think that *teleite* might be an imperative: "you must pay taxes."[67] But Paul's addition of "for"[68] to "because of this" shows rather conclusively that the verb must be an indicative, because Paul almost always uses this word to introduce the ground or explanation of a previous statement.[69] Here Paul is suggesting that the Roman Christians should acknowledge in their own habit of paying taxes to the government an implicit recognition of the authority that the government possesses over them.

In the second part of the verse Paul reiterates the fact that this authority stems ultimately from God and that paying taxes is therefore a matter of "conscience." Paul again calls secular rulers "servants of God" (see v. 4), but now he uses a different term, *leitourgos*. This word was used frequently in the LXX to refer to people who served in the temple,[70] and in the NT it always refers to those who are "ministering" for the sake of the Lord.[71] Paul may therefore choose to use this word to indicate that secular rulers, even if unknowingly, are performing a religious function.[72] This may, however, build too much on the use of the word *leitourgos* since it was used widely in Greek at the time to denote public officials of various kinds (cf. our "public servant").[73] In any case, as in the case of *diakonos* in v. 4, the addition "of God" makes clear the ultimately sacred nature of the "secular" ruler's "service."[74] Therefore the payment of taxes becomes a responsibility that the Christian

66. S-H; Murray; Cranfield; Walker, *Römer 13,1-7*, p. 49. Merklein ("Sinn und Zweck von Röm 13,1-7," p. 251) thinks it refers to all of v. 5.

67. Zahn; Tholuck; Schmithals; cf. NJB.

68. Gk. γάρ.

69. See, e.g., Schlier; Cranfield; Dunn. We have no syntactical basis for comparison since only here in the NT do we find the sequence διὰ τοῦτο γάρ.

70. Num. 4:37, 41; 1 Sam. 2:11, 18; 3:1; Ezra 7:24; Neh. 10:40; Isa. 61:6. However, the word refers more broadly to those who "serve" the Lord or his people in various ways (Ps. 102:21; 103:4; 2 Kings 4:43; 6:15) as well as to court officials (2 Sam. 13:18; 1 Kings 10:5; 2 Chron. 9:4).

71. λειτουργός refers specifically to cultic "ministry" in Heb. 8:2; 10:11 and (probably) Rom. 15:16; and to "ministry" more generally in Phil. 2:25 and Heb. 1:7. The cognate λειτουργία (from which we get the word "liturgy") denotes cultic service in Luke 1:23; Heb. 8:6; 9:21; and "ministry" generally in 2 Cor. 9:12; Phil. 2:17 (with sacrificial allusions); Phil. 2:30. The verb λειτουργέω refers to ministry in general: Acts 13:2; Rom. 15:27; cf. also the adjective λειτουργικός in Heb. 1:14.

72. Godet; Meyer; Black.

73. See some of the LXX references noted above; and cf. Strobel, "Zum Verständnis," pp. 86-87; Michel; Käsemann; Wilckens; Cranfield; Schlier.

74. Barrett.

owes to God himself. This is underscored in Paul's additional description of the rulers as those who "devote themselves[75] to this very thing."[76] Paul may think of the "thing" to which the rulers devote themselves as their promoting of good and restraining of evil (vv. 3-4),[77] their collecting of taxes (v. 6a),[78] or, perhaps most likely, their service itself ("servants of God").[79]

7 Verse 7 has no explicit link to the context, but its call for the discharge of one's obligations is probably intended to bring the general call for submission to rulers in vv. 1-6 to a practical conclusion. This makes it likely that the "everyone" to whom we are to "pay back" our obligations is limited by the context to secular officials and rulers.[80] By using the language of the discharge of a debt,[81] Paul suggests that the "service" that government renders to us places us under obligation to the various authorities. Paul spells out four kinds of "obligations" that we may owe to the authorities: "direct" taxes,[82] "indirect" taxes,[83] "respect," and "honor." Paul's call to "give back"

75. Gk. προσκαρτεροῦντες (the verb is also found in Mark 3:9; Acts 1:14; 2:42, 46; 6:4; 8:13; 10:7; Rom. 12:12; Col. 4:2). The participle could be periphrastic, dependent on εἰσιν ("for the servants of God are appointed for this very thing"; cf. Porter, *Verbal Aspect,* p. 479), but the importance of the designation of the rulers as "servants" makes it more likely that εἰσιν is independent.

76. This translation, similar to most English translations, takes εἰς αὐτὸ τοῦτο with προσκαρτεροῦντες. It is rare (if not unprecedented) for this verb to be followed by εἰς (it usually takes the dative), but the alternative — to take εἰς αὐτὸ τοῦτο with λειτουργοί, with προσκαρτεροῦντες independent ("servants for this very purpose, devoting themselves"; argued for by, e.g., Godet; S-H) — seems less likely (so most commentators).

77. Barrett.

78. E.g., Murray; Cranfield; Wilckens; Dunn; Fitzmyer; Porter, "Romans 13:1-7," p. 135.

79. W. Grundmann, *TDNT* III, 618; Stein, "Argument," p. 342. More unlikely than any of these suggestions is V. Riekkinen's view that the clause introduces v. 7: "remembering all this, give everybody what is due . . ." (*Römer 13: Aufzeichnung und Weiterführung der exegetischen Diskussion* [Helsinki: Suomalainen Tiedeakatemia, 1980], p. 215).

80. Godet; Michel; Käsemann; Murray; contra, e.g., Denney; Tholuck; Merklein, "Sinn und Zweck von Röm 13,1-7," p. 252.

81. The Gk. ὀφειλή, "debt," occurs often in the papyri with reference to financial debts; cf. Matt. 18:32. Paul uses the word once else to denote the sexual "obligation" owed by spouses to one another (1 Cor. 7:3). It is indistinguishable from ὀφείλημα in the NT (see Matt. 6:12 and Rom. 4:4). See F. Hauck, *TDNT* V, 564. The verb Paul uses — ἀποδίδωμι, "give back," "repay" — fits well with this imagery of obligation.

82. Gk. φόρος (= Lat. *tributa*). Cf. the previous verse and Luke 20:22; 23:2.

83. Gk. τέλος (= Lat. *portoria*), which also has this meaning in Matt. 17:25. "Indirect" taxes would include customs duties, fees for various services, and so on. The two words for taxation that Paul uses here are found together in other texts (cf. BAGD).

taxes to the secular rulers is reminiscent of Jesus's demand that his disciples "give back to Caesar what is Caesar's" (Mark 12:17).[84] Since Jesus pairs this obligation to Caesar with our obligation to God — "give to God what is God's" — some interpreters think that Paul may do the same. They suggest that the "fear" we are to render might not be, as in vv. 3-4, terror of the punishment that the ruler might inflict, but reverence toward God himself.[85] However, the parallel traditions do not provide enough basis to find here an application of the word different from that in v. 3-4.[86] But dependence on the gospel tradition, along with the perennial significance of taxation as *the* concrete sign of the authority of a state, probably does explain why Paul brings up the subject of taxes at the end of this paragraph.

It is only a slight exaggeration to say that the history of the interpretation of Rom. 13:1-7 is the history of attempts to avoid what seems to be its plain meaning.[87] At first glance, and taken on its own, this passage seems to require that Christians always, in whatever situation, obey whatever their governmental leaders tell them to do. Almost all Christians recoil from this conclusion. Our own sad experience of situations like the Holocaust during World War II suggests that genuine Christian devotion to God must sometimes require *disobedience* of the government. Moreover, this sense finds support within the NT itself. The classic text is Acts 5:29, in which Peter and John respond to the Jewish leaders' order to stop teaching in Jesus' name: "We must obey God rather than men" (see also Acts 4:18-20). Equally important is the book of Revelation, in which keeping the commandments of God in the face of governmental pressure to the contrary is the central demand placed on loyal believers.

84. See also the parallel texts in Matthew (22:21) and Luke (20:25); the verb in both cases is ἀπόδοτε (as also in the parallel texts in Matthew [22:21] and Luke [20:25]; Luke also uses the word φόρος [20:22]). Dependence on Jesus' teaching here is denied by some scholars (e.g., Käsemann; Fitzmyer), but it seems to be solidly established (see, e.g., F. F. Bruce, "Paul and 'The Powers That Be'," *BJRL* 66 [1984], 92-93; Allison, "Pauline Epistles," pp. 16-17; Thompson, *Clothed with Christ,* pp. 111-20; Stuhlmacher, "Jesustradition," p. 248; Dunn, "Paul's Knowledge," p. 202; Davies, 138).

85. This interpretation was defended in the early church by Origen and Tertullian (cf. Zsifkovits, *Staatsgedanke,* p. 103) and is thought to be possible by Viard; Harrison; Cranfield; Wilckens; Ziesler. Note also the distinction in 1 Pet. 2:17 (which comes in a passage that has many similarities to Rom. 13:1-7) between "fearing" (φοβέομαι) God and "honoring" (τιμάω) the emperor.

86. Murray; Käsemann; Dunn; Merklein, "Sinn und Zweck von Röm 13,1-7," pp. 253-54.

87. For a history of interpretation, see Riekkinen, *Römer 13,* pp. 2-202; Wilckens, 3.43-66. L. Pohle provides a survey and exegetical analysis of the major comtemporary interpretations: *Die Christen und der Staat nach Römer 13: Eine typologische Untersuchung der neueren deutschsprächigen Schriftauslegung* (Mainz: Mattias-Grünewald, 1984).

Clearly, a willingness to resist the demands of secular rulers, when those conflict with the demand of the God we serve, is part of that "transformation" of life which Paul speaks about in these chapters. But how, then, can Paul apparently speak so absolutely about our need to "be submissive to the authorities"? Theologians and exegetes who have wrestled with this question have come up with several answers, which we will now survey briefly (moving from the least to the most likely).[88]

(1) Paul does not demand such submission at all. The text is a late addition to Romans, put in when the original radical demands of the gospel had been lost sight of and Christians were seeking accommodation with the world.[89] This desperate expedient has no textual basis.

(2) Paul is naive about the evil that governments might do or demand that we do. The apostle's experience with governmental authorities, as Acts makes clear, had been rather positive: on several occasions, secular rulers acknowledged Paul's right to preach the gospel. Moreover, Paul was writing Romans during the early years of Nero's reign, a period of Roman stability and good government (quite in contrast to Nero's later bizarre and anti-Christian behavior). But Paul knew the history of the often harsh treatment meted out to Israel by pagan nations, recorded both in the OT and in inter-testamental Jewish literature. And he certainly knew that it was governmental leaders who put to death Jesus the Messiah, his Lord. Moreover, many of the Christians to whom he writes in Rome had recently been forced by the Roman emperor to leave their homes and businesses and live in exile. Surely Paul was not so naive as to ignore these blunt reminders of government's capacity to do evil.[90]

(3) Paul was demanding submission to the government only for the short interval before the kingdom would be established in power.[91] This view assumes the "consistent," or *konsequente,* view of early Christian eschatology

---

88. For other interpretations, see the historical surveys in, e.g., Riekkinen, *Römer 13;* W. Bauer, " 'Jedermann sie untertan der Obrigkeit,' " in *Aufsätze und kleine Schriften* (ed. G. Strecker; Tübingen: Mohr, 1967), pp. 262-84; Pohle, *Dei Christen und der Staat;* W. Affeldt, *Die weltliche Gewalt in der Paulus-Exegese. Röm. 13,1-7 in den Römerbrief-kommentaren der lateinischen Kirche bis zum Ende des 13. Jahrhunderts* (Forschungen zur Kirchen- und Dogmengeschichte 22; Göttingen: Vandenhoeck & Ruprecht, 1969); B. C. Lategan, "Reception: Theory and Practice in Reading Romans 13," in *Text and Interpretation: New Approaches in the Criticism of the New Testament* (ed. P. J. Hartin and J. H. Petzer; NTTS 15; Leiden: Brill, 1991), 145-69. A. Molnar has illustrated a variety of attempts by late medieval commentators to avoid a universal application of the demand for submission ("Romains 13 dans l'interprétation de la première Réforme," *ETR* 46 [1971], 231-40).

89. See the introduction to the section for bibliography.

90. Rightly emphasized by Schrage, *Die Christen und der Staat,* pp. 52-53.

91. See, e.g., Dibelius, "Rom und die Christen," p. 184.

and ethics made famous by A. Schweitzer. Such an interpretation does not do justice to the NT and must read into Rom. 13:1-7 an eschatological focus that is simply not there.[92]

(4) Paul demands submission to "authorities," interpreted as both secular rulers and the spiritual powers that stand behind them, only as long as those authorities manifest their own submission to Christ. We have already argued that this interpretation is linguistically impossible (see the notes on v. 1).

(5) Paul is demanding submission to secular rulers only of the Roman Christians and only in the immediate situation they are facing. Finding in the passage a universally applicable norm for the Christian's attitude toward government is simply an overinterpretation that fails to take into account the specific local nature of the text.[93] There is, of course, some truth in this point; and vv. 6-7 are thought by many to suggest that Paul is especially concerned to address an immediate problem in the Roman community (see the introduction to this section). But even if this is the case (and it is not clear either way), vv. 1-2 are hard to get around. Paul here goes out of his way to emphasize the universal scope of his demand: "every soul" is to submit; there is "no authority" except by appointment of God. The text does not clearly teach the divine ordination of government in general; for Paul speaks throughout concretely of governmental authorities and not about the concept or the institution of government. But, in keeping with the OT and Jewish tradition (see the notes on v. 1), he does make clear that God stands behind every governmental authority whom the Christian encounters. Application to situations beyond those in Rome in Paul's day is entirely valid.[94]

(6) Paul demands submission to government only as long as the government functions as Paul says it should function in vv. 3-4. The government that rewards good and punishes evil deserves Christian obedience; but the government that begins doing the reverse forfeits its divine prerogative, and

---

92. See particularly Neugebauer, "Zur Auslegung," pp. 160-66.

93. E.g., with various twists and emphases, Michel, 395-97; Wilckens, 3.40-42; Leenhardt, 328; Käsemann, 354, 359; idem, "Principles of the Interpretation of Romans 13," in *New Testament Questions,* pp. 196-216; Bammel, "Romans 13," 366-75; R. Heiligenthal, "Strategien konformer Ethik," pp. 55-61; A. J. Hultgren, "Reflections on Romans 13:1-7," *Dialog* 15 (1976), 269.

94. On the divine ordination of government, see, e.g., Calvin, *Institutes* 4.20.2. On the universal applicability of the text, see, e.g., H. Schlier, "Die Beurteilung des Staates im Neuen Testament," in *Die Zeit der Kirche* (2d ed.; Freiburg: Herder, 1958), pp. 6-9. Note also J. Kosnetter, "Röm 13,1-7: Zeitbedingte Vorsichtsmassregel oder grundsätzliche Einstellung?" *SPCIC* 1.347-55; Ridderbos, *Paul,* pp. 321-24; and, more cautiously, K. Aland, "Das Verhältnis von Kirche und Staat nach dem Neuen Testament und den Aussagen des 2. Jahrhunderts," in *Neutestamentliche Entwürfe* (TBü 63; Munich: Kaiser, 1979), pp. 26-123.

Christians are free to disobey it.[95] To be sure, Paul does not explicitly make our submission conditional on the way a government acts: vv. 3-4 are simply descriptive. But we must ask why Paul can describe government in such an unrelieved positive light when he knew very well that many governments do not, in fact, behave in this manner. And the answer may be that Paul is describing government as it *should* be. Perhaps, then, we are justified in thinking that Paul would require Christians to submit to government when it behaves in the way God intended it to behave. Thus, when a government arrogates to itself divine powers (as in the Revelation), Christians are no longer bound to it.[96]

(7) Paul demands a "submission" to government: not strict and universal obedience. "Submission," as we pointed out in the exegesis of v. 1, denotes a recognition of the place that God has given government in the ordering of the world. The Christian submits to government by acknowledging this divinely ordained status of government and its consequent right to demand the believer's allegiance. In most cases, then, Christian submission to government will involve obeying what government tells the Christian to do. But government does not have absolute rights over the believer, for government, like every human institution, is subordinate to God himself. The ultimate claim of God, who stands at the peak of the hierarchy of relationships in which the Christian is placed, is always assumed. This means, then, that Christians may continue to "submit" to a particular government (acknowledging their subordination to it generally) even as they, in obedience to a "higher" authority, refuse to do, in a given instance, what that government requires. In a similar way, the Christian wife, called on to "submit" to her husband, may well have to disobey a particular request of her husband if it conflicts with her allegiance to God.[97]

Balance is needed. On the one hand, we must not obscure the teaching of Rom. 13:1-7 in a flood of qualifications. Paul makes clear that government is ordained by God — indeed, that every particular governmental authority is ordained by God — and that the Christian must recognize and respond to this fact with an attitude of "submission." Government is more than a nuisance to be put up with; it is an institution established by God to accomplish some of his purposes on earth (cf. vv. 3-4). On the other hand, we must not read

95. The view is very common; cf., e.g., J. Hering, " 'Serviteurs de Dieu': Contribution a L'exégèse pratique de Romains 13:3-4," *RHPR* 30 (1950), 31-40; Stuart, 401; Achtemeier, 205; Leenhardt, 323-25.

96. Whether a government can become so demonic that the Christian has the right not only to refuse to obey it but also actively to seek its overthrow (e.g., revolution) is a matter we cannot go into here.

97. Judge makes similar comments about the "ranks" that Gal. 3:28 speaks about, noting how the NT encourages Christians to recognize the continuing validity of the socio-political order ("Cultural Conformity," p. 9).

Rom. 13:1-7 out of its broad NT context and put government in a position relative to the Christian that only God can hold. Christians should give thanks for government as an institution of God; we should pray regularly for our leaders (cf. 1 Tim. 2:1-2); and we should be prepared to follow the orders of our government. But we should also refuse to give to government any absolute rights and should evaluate all its demands in the light of the gospel.

E. LOVE AND THE LAW (13:8-10)

8*Owe nothing to anyone, except to love one another. For the one who loves the other person has fulfilled the law.* 9*For the series of commandments, "you shall not commit adultery," "you shall not murder," "you shall not steal,"*a *"you shall not covet"*b1 — *and if there is any other commandment — is summed up in this commandment: "you shall love your neighbor as yourself."*c 10*Love does no wrong to the neighbor; therefore love is the fulfillment of the law.*

  a. Deut. 5:17-19; cf. Exod. 20:13-15
  b. Deut. 5:21; Exod. 20:17
  c. Lev. 19:18

Paul cleverly uses the idea of "obligation" to make the transition from his advice about governing authorities (vv. 1-7) to his exhortation to love for the neighbor (vv. 8-10). In v. 7 Paul urges, "pay back what you owe to everyone." Paul then repeats this exhortation in v. 8a, but adds to it a significant exception: the obligation of love for one another. In this demand for love, Paul suggests, we find an obligation that can never be discharged, a "never-ending debt" (Bengel). We will never be in a position to claim that we have "loved enough." Yet, while joined to vv. 1-7 by means of the notion of obligation, vv. 8-10 are connected by their content to 12:9-21, where Paul expounded the meaning and outworking of "sincere love."2 These verses therefore return to the "main

1. The unusual order and selection of commandments in v. 9 has created some confusion in the text. Several Fathers (Marcion, Clement, Origen) omit the commandment "you shall not covet"; an important early uncial of the Alexandrian family (‭א‬), a later Alexandrian witness (81), as well as other MSS, lectionaries, and early versions, insert the commandment "you shall not testify falsely" (οὐ ψευδομαρτυρήσεις) between "you shall not steal" and "you shall not covet"; one lectionary and several Fathers substitute "you shall not testify falsely" for "you shall not covet"; and Chrysostom omits "you shall not covet" altogether. All these variants (none of them strongly attested) are due to assimilation to the OT text.

2. Attempts to find a connection between vv. 1-7 and 8-10 in content (e.g., that vv. 8-10 highlight love as an important motivation for our obedience to governing authorities [Calvin, 484] or that vv. 8-10 bring another perspective on justice [Godet, 446]) are strained.

line" of Paul's exhortation after the somewhat parenthetical advice about government in 13:1-7. But these verses look forward as well as backward. In their insistence that love for others fulfills the law, Paul lays groundwork for his rebuke of the strong and the weak (14:1–15:13), who are allowing debates about the law to disturb the love and unity that they should be exhibiting.[3]

The obligation of love for another (v. 8b) is the key point in the paragraph. Paul highlights the importance of love in vv. 8c-10 by presenting it as the "fulfillment" of the law.[4] This point also serves the larger purpose of the letter — the explanation and defense of the gospel — by guarding Paul's gospel at a potential point of vulnerability. For the claim that Christians are "not under the law" (6:14, 15) could open the way to the assumption that Paul's gospel leads to a "do whatever you want" libertinism. Paul rejects any such conclusion by asserting that obedience of the central demand of the gospel, love for the neighbor, provides for the law's complete fulfillment.[5]

In a manner typical of the exhortations throughout Rom. 12–13, Paul fashions these verses from traditional material. The emphasis on love for the neighbor as a central obligation of the law may have its roots in the Hellenistic synagogue.[6] But far more important for Paul is the fact that Jesus himself singled out the love command (Lev. 19:18) as one of the two commandments on which "all the law and the prophets hang" (Matt. 22:34-40//Mark 12:28-34//Luke 10:25-28; cf. also John 13:34-35). Paul, then, undoubtedly depends on Jesus' teaching in these verses.[7] The traditional character of the connection between love and the law is seen also in the parallel to this text in Gal. 5:13-15. Following a pattern typical of Rom. 12–13, then, Paul here reiterates in his general exhortation of the Roman Christians a point he has made before.

---

3. See esp. 14:15 — "If your brother is grieved because of a dispute about food, you are no longer walking according to love" — and the reference to the "neighbor" in 15:2. See Räisänen, 64; Fitzmyer, 677.

4. The connection between "love" and "law" is characteristic of the paragraph, as Paul relates them together in a roughly chiastic pattern: love (v. 8b) — love (v. 8c) — law (v. 8d) — law ("commandments"; v. 9a) — love (v. 9b) — love (v. 10a) — law (v. 10b); cf. A. L. Bencze, "An Analysis of 'Romans XIII.8-10'," NTS 20 (1974), 90-92; Schmithals.

5. Stuhlmacher, 210-11, especially emphasizes the polemical application of vv. 8-10.

6. See especially the detailed treatment of this background in K. Berger, Die Gesetzauslegung Jesu I (WMANT 40; Neukirchen/Vluyn: Neukirchener, 1972), cf. esp. pp. 50-51, 99-136; cf. also Käsemann, 361; Schmithals, 472-73.

7. See, e.g., Dunn, "Paul's Knowledge," p. 202; Thompson, Clothed with Christ, pp. 121-40. Allison, "Paul's Knowledge," pp. 16-17, noting that Jesus' teaching about Caesar (e.g., Mark 12:13-17) and about the love command (e.g., Mark 12:28-34) come close together in the Synoptic tradition, suggests that Paul might be using a tradition in which these topics were joined.

8 The need for Christians to discharge their obligations forms the transition between vv. 1-7 and vv. 8-10. In v. 7a, Paul urged Christians to "pay back" their "debts" *(opheilas)* to everyone, especially (in that context) to the governing authorities. In v. 8a, Paul repeats this demand: "Owe [*opheilete*] nothing to anyone."[8] This command does not forbid a Christian from ever incurring a debt (e.g., to buy a house or a car); it rather demands that Christians repay any debts they do incur promptly and in accordance with the terms of the contract. Prompt payment of debts, however, is simply a transitional point in these verses. Paul's real interest emerges in the next clause: that Christians "love one another."[9] What is the relationship between this demand for love and the preceding demand that Christians "owe nothing to anyone"? The words that connect these two commands[10] could be adversative; we would then translate v. 8a, "Owe nothing to anyone; *but* you ought to love one another."[11] However, the words can also denote an exception; and, from early times, commentators have generally preferred this explanation, translating as in the NRSV, "Owe no one anything, except to love one another." I also prefer this interpretation, since it gives the debated words the meaning they usually have in Paul and creates a transition between the two commands that is both natural and striking.[12] As Origen put it, "Let your only debt that

---

8. The verb ὀφείλω that Paul uses here often refers to financial obligations but was at an early time extended to include moral and religious obligations as well (F. Hauck, *TDNT* V, 559-61). It can therefore mean both "owe" (in which case it is usually followed by an accusative denoting what is owed) and "be obliged to" (in which case it is usually followed by an infinitive stating the obligation). Paul generally uses the word in the latter sense (Rom. 15:1, 27; 1 Cor. 4:8; 5:10; 7:36; 9:10; 11:7, 10; 2 Cor. 11:1; 12:11; 12:14; Gal. 5:12; Eph. 5:28; 2 Thess. 1:3; 2:13 — in each of these verses [with the exception of 1 Cor. 4:8, 2 Cor. 11:1, and Gal. 5:12, which use a fixed form of the verb] ὀφείλω is followed by an infinitive). Only here and in Phlm. 18 does he use it in the sense "owe," with that which is owed stated in the accusative.

9. The article (τό) before the clause ἀλλήλους ἀγαπᾶν may be anaphoric, Paul "referring back" to the well-known command of Jesus (Godet; BDF 399[1]). On the other hand, the article could be used simply to make the following phrase into a substantive (as τό at the beginning of v. 9 does); cf. Robertson, 243; BDF 267 indicate that the article is often used in Greek to introduce quotations.

10. Gk. εἰ μή.

11. On this interpretation, as the translation above indicates, the meaning of the verb ὀφείλω shifts from "owe" in v. 8a to "ought," "be obliged" in v. 8b (where, although it does not occur, it must be supplied from the previous clause). This shift in meaning could, as our preceding note indicates, find some basis in the syntax, since we have an infinitive (ἀγαπᾶν) in v. 8b. See, e.g., F. Hauck, *TDNT* V, 564; Michel; Murray; Barrett; Schlatter; Ortkemper, 126-27. Black notes that the double meaning of ὀφείλω matches its Aramaic equivalent and that the radicals of that verb are the same as the verb "to love."

12. The combination εἰ μή occurs 26 times in Paul, and 23 mean "except" (Rom. 7:7 (twice); 9:29; 11:15; 13:1; 1 Cor. 1:14; 2:2, 11 (twice); 7:17; 8:4; 10:13; 12:3; 14:5;

is unpaid be that of love — a debt which you should always be attempting to discharge in full, but will never succeed in discharging."[13]

Pauline use of "one another"[14] in similar contexts shows that the command to love here is restricted to love for fellow Christians.[15] Nevertheless, the universalistic language that both precedes — "no one" — and follows — "the other" — this command demands that the love Paul is exhorting Christians to display is ultimately not to be restricted to fellow Christians.[16] We are called to love "the other"; and, as Jesus' parable of the Good Samaritan so vividly illustrates, this "other" may be someone quite unknown to us or even hostile toward us (Luke 10:25-37). As Paul has already made clear, "sincere love" (12:9) means that we are to "bless our persecutors" (12:14) and seek to do good to *all* people (12:17).

In the second part of the verse, Paul explains[17] why love for one another is the Christian's one outstanding debt: "the one who loves the other person has fulfilled the law."[18] By using the phrase "the other" to specify the object of our love,[19] Paul emphasizes that we are called to love specific individuals with whom we come into contact. At the same time, he hints that these

---

15:2; 2 Cor. 2:2; 12:5, 13; Gal. 1:19; 6:14; Eph. 4:9; Phil. 4:15; 1 Tim. 5:19); only in Rom. 14:14, 1 Cor. 7:17, and Gal. 1:7 does the combination probably mean "but." Furthermore, as Cranfield notes, the alternative interpretation demands not only that ὀφείλω have a different meaning in v. 8b than it does in v. 8a, but that it also have a different mood (imperative in v. 8a; indicative in v. 8b). See also S-H; Dunn; S. Lyonnet, "La charité plénitude de la loi (Rm 13,8-10)," in Lorenzi, *Dimensions,* pp. 152-53.

13. Cf. S-H.

14. Gk. ἀλλήλους.

15. As the reciprocal nature of the word suggests, ἀλλήλους (and ἀλλήλοις), when preceded by a command, always in Paul denotes fellow Christians. See esp. 1 Thess. 3:12 and 5:15, which explicitly command actions toward both "one another" (fellow Christians) and "all" (non-Christians). See, e.g., Lietzmann; Dunn; contra, e.g., Cranfield; Wilckens.

16. For a similar view, see Murray; Dunn.

17. Cf. the γάρ, "for."

18. Cranfield suggests that this clause may explain why the debt of love must always remain outstanding: because to be done with love would mean the fulfillment of the law, a task impossible for human beings. But this explanation is both oversubtle and overlooks the fact that Paul does, in fact, claim that Christians fulfill the law (cf. 8:4).

19. An alternative translation, which takes τὸν ἕτερον as a modifier of νόμον, is "the one who loves has fulfilled the other law," the "other law" being the Mosaic law (as opposed to the Roman law or to the commandment of love) or the other love command (of God) (see Zahn; W. Gutbrod, *TDNT* IV, 1071; Leenhardt; W. Marxsen, "Der ἕτερος νόμος Röm. 13,8," *TZ* 11 [1955], 230-37; Merk, *Handeln aus Glauben,* p. 165). However, while ἕτερος can occur in attributive position (between the article and its substantive; cf. Robertson, 748), it usually does not. More seriously, this rendering would leave the verb ἀγαπάω without an object — an unprecedented situation in Paul.

individuals may be people who are different from us.[20] As the repetition of the point in v. 10 makes clear, Paul's claim that the one who loves the other "has fulfilled" the (Mosaic[21]) law introduces a central point in this paragraph.[22] What does Paul means by this claim?

(1) He may simply be highlighting the centrality of love *within* the law. On this view, Paul is teaching that loving other people is necessary if we are to claim truly to have "done" what the law demands. Paul's purpose is not to minimize the importance and continuing relevance of the other commandments but to insist that love must ever be the guiding principle in our obedience to these other commandments.[23] But I question whether this view does justice to the word "has fulfilled." Paul reserves the word "fulfill" for Christian experience; only Christians, as a result of the work of Christ and through the Spirit, can "fulfill" the law.[24]

(2) The word "fulfill," then, suggests that Paul is thinking about a complete and final "doing" of the law that is possible only in the new age of eschatological accomplishment.[25] Christians who love others have satisfied the demands of the law *en toto;*[26] and they need therefore not worry about

20. The article specifies — we are to love that particular "other" person with whom we come into contact (see Michel; Cranfield; Dunn) — while ἕτερος suggests distinction or difference (Barrett; for parallels to this use of ἕτερος, see 2:1, 21; 1 Cor. 4:6; 6:1; 10:24, 29; 14:17; Phil. 2:4).

21. That Paul is speaking here again about the Mosaic law, the torah, is clear both from the larger context of Romans (where the Mosaic law is constantly at issue) and the immediate context (the list of commandments in v. 9); contra those (e.g., Lenski) who overemphasize the lack of an article and think Paul is discussing "law" in general.

22. The assertion in v. 9 that the love command "sums up" the law makes a different, though related point, as we will see.

23. See, particularly clearly, Murray, representing at this point the mainstream "Reformed" tradition. See also Ortkemper, 128-29; Dunn; Ridderbos, *Paul,* pp. 280-81.

24. See the notes on 8:4. F. W. Danker thinks that word has a commercial flavor here ("Under Contract: A Form-Critical Study of Linguistic Adaptation in Romans," in *Festschrift to Honor F. Wilbur Gingrich* [ed. E. H. Barth and R. E. Cocroft; Leiden: Brill, 1972], pp. 96, 111). The context could support such a nuance (cf. vv. 6-8a), but Paul's theological application of the term elsewhere does not betray such an idea.

25. The perfect tense of the verb πεπλήρωκεν may also suggest this point. Some scholars think this is a "gnomic" perfect — e.g., "the one who loves the other is fulfilling the law" (Robertson, 897; Michel; Käsemann) — while others think it preserves its allegedly natural significance of a process resulting from an action — e.g., "the one who loves has just then entered into the state of having fulfilled the law" (S-H). But the perfect tense probably simply denotes a state: "the one who loves is in the state of fulfilling the law."

26. Obviously, loving others does not fulfill those parts of the law that state our obligations to God. But Paul is thinking, in this context, only of the law as it dictates our conduct toward other human beings.

any other commandment.[27] We must emphasize, however, that such complete and consistent loving of others remains an impossibility, even for the Spirit-filled believer: we will never, short of glory, truly love "the other" as we should. This means that it would be premature to claim that love "replaces" the law for the Christian, as if the only commandment we ever needed to worry about was the command of love. For as long as our love remains incomplete, we may very well require other commandments both to chastise and to guide us.[28] What the source of those commandments may be is, of course, another question; and this Paul touches on in the next verse.

9 Paul now supports his contention that loving others fulfills the law by arguing that the commandments of the law are "summed up" in the "word"[29] found in Lev. 19:18: "love your neighbor as yourself."[30] Paul cites as illustrations of the commandments he has in mind abbreviated references to the seventh, sixth, eighth, and tenth commandments from the Decalogue.[31] His addition "and if there is any other[32] commandment" makes clear, however, that he includes other commandments: probably, as the context would suggest, all those commandments of the law that relate to our relations with other human beings.[33] Various Jewish authors refer to the commandment to love the neighbor in Lev. 19:18, but it was given no special prominence in Judaism generally. Probably, therefore, the central position that Paul gives the commandment echoes Jesus, who paired Lev. 19:18 with Deut. 6:5 as the com-

27. See Nygren; Fitzmyer; Schmithals.

28. "The law protects love from the subjectivism and self-deception to which the Christian is constantly exposed, not because he is 'unjust,' but because he is human" (Deidun, 224).

29. The use of the word λόγος for a commandment has precedents in Judaism, especially in relation to the "Ten Commandments," often called the "Ten Words" (cf. Exod. 24:28; Deut. 10:4; Philo, *Heir* 168; *Decalogue* 32; Josephus, *Ant.* 3.138). It is doubtful, therefore, whether there is any special significance in the term here (contra Schmithals).

30. Paul's quotation follows the majority LXX text exactly, which in turn adequately renders the Hebrew.

31. This order is the same as that found in MS B of the LXX in Deut. 5:17-18; in the Nash Papyrus (a first- or second-century-B.C. scrap of text with the Ten Commandments); it is reflected in several other Jewish and early Christian sources (Luke 18:30; Jas. 2:11; Philo, *Decalogue* 24; 36; 51; 121-37; 167-71; *Special Laws* 3.28; Clement of Alexandria, *Stromateis* 6.16). It may be an order popular in Diaspora Judaism (Dunn); Koch (p. 34) thinks that B may be the original LXX text here.

32. This is probably one of the many places in which ἕτερος has lost its original "dual" emphasis (Turner, 197).

33. Stuhlmacher argues that early Jewish sources (e.g., Philo, *Decalogue* 18-19; Josephus, *Ant.* 3.89, 93; *m. Tamid* 5:1) demonstrate the centrality of the Decalogue in the NT period; only with the Christian "appropriation" of the Decalogue did later Jews downplay its significance.

mandments on which "all the law and the prophets hang" (Matt. 22:34-40).[34] Paul undoubtedly also follows Jesus (see the parable of the Good Samaritan, Luke 10:25-37) in interpreting the "neighbor" in the commandment to refer to other persons generally and not (as the original text of Lev. 19:18 might indicate) to the fellow Jew.[35] The "as yourself" in the commandment does not command or give an excuse for egotism or selfishness. It simply recognizes that people do, as a matter of fact, love themselves. It is this deep concern for ourselves that should characterize our attitude toward others.

Paul denotes the relationship of the love command of Lev. 19:18 to the rest of the commandments with the verb "sum up."[36] The imprecision of this term is reflected in the contradictory theological conclusions that are drawn from Paul's assertion. Thus, H. Räisänen claims that Paul teaches here the "radical reduction" of the law to the love command,[37] while T. Schreiner concludes that the verse shows that some OT commandments are still applicable to believers.[38] At issue, then, is whether, in "summing up" the OT commandments about our relations to others, the love command *replaces* these commandments or whether it simply *focuses* them by setting forth a demand that is integral to each one of them. When we remember that Paul has earlier in Romans proclaimed the Christian's freedom from the "binding authority" of the Mosaic law (6:14, 15; 7:4; 8:4), the former alternative seems to be closer to the truth. The Christian, who belongs to the New Covenant people of God, is no longer "under the [Mosaic] law," the law for the Old Covenant people of God; he is under a "new law," "the law of Christ" (see Gal. 6:2

---

34. Dunn.

35. Some Jews understood רֵעַ in the "narrower" sense, "fellow Israelite" (cf. the Targum and *Sifra* on Lev. 19:18), while others applied it more broadly (cf. Lev. 19:34; *T. Zeb.* 5:1; *T. Asher* 5:7; *T. Naph.* 5:2). See Berger, *Gesetzauslegung*, pp. 99-136; A. Nissen, *Gott und der Nächste im antiken Judentum: Untersuchungen zum Doppelgebot der Liebe* (WUNT 15; Tübingen: Mohr, 1974), pp. 304-8. The interchange between a "lawyer" and Jesus in Luke 10:25-29 implies that many teachers of the law in Jesus' day held to a "narrow" meaning of the term.

36. The Greek verb is ἀνακεφαλαιόω. The term occurs in the NT only elsewhere in Eph. 1:10, where Paul describes the plan of God for the fullness of times as consisting in the "summing up" in Christ of all things; it does not occur in the LXX. The word was frequent in literary Greek, where it often refers to the summation or conclusion of a book or speech (H. Schlier, *TDNT*, III, 681-82).

37. Räisänen, 27; similar, though not so extreme in all details, are A. Lindemann, "Die biblischen Toragebote und die paulinische Ethik," in *Studien zum Text und zur Ethik des Neuen Testaments. Festschrift zum 80. Geburtstag von Heinrich Greeven* (ed. W. Schrage; Berlin: de Gruyter, 1986), pp. 262-63; Westerholm, 201-2; Deidun, 153.

38. Schreiner, *The Law and Its Fulfillment*, pp. 149-50; cf. also Thielmann, *From Plight to Solution*, pp. 89-90; Martin, *Christ and the Law*, p. 151; W. Schrage, *Die konkreten Einzelgebote in der paulinischen Paränese* (Gütersloh: Mohn, 1961), pp. 255-56.

and 1 Cor. 9:19-21).[39] And central to this new law is a command that Christ himself took from the Mosaic law and made central to his new demand: the command to love our neighbors as ourselves (cf. Gal. 6:2 with 5:13-14).

10   While not explicitly connected with v. 9, the first statement in v. 10 clearly explains what Paul has asserted in that verse. The reason why the love command can "sum up" the law is that "love does no wrong to the neighbor." For not doing wrong to others or, positively, doing good to others, is exactly what the OT commandments about our relationship with other human beings aims at. "Therefore,"[40] Paul concludes, "love is the fulfillment of the law." Opinions on the meaning of this assertion depend considerably on the decisions one reaches about the similar statements in vv. 8 and 9. Murray, for instance, argues that Paul is here presenting love as the virtue that brings our obedience of the law to its "full measure" *(plērōma).*[41] But the proximity of the cognate verb *plēroō* ("fulfill") in v. 8b — which matches v. 10b in a chiastic arrangement — suggests that *plērōma* here has the active meaning "fulfilling."[42] It is also likely that v. 10b repeats the idea of v. 8b: that the Christian who loves, and who therefore does what the law requires (vv. 9-10a), has brought the law to its culmination, its eschatological fulfillment.[43]

F. LIVING IN LIGHT OF THE DAY (13:11-14)

11*And do this, knowing the time: that it is already the hour for you*[1]

39. It is important to stress that here, as throughout Romans, Paul is speaking of a very definite law: the law of Moses, the torah. He is not therefore claiming that love renders irrelevant all other commandments; only that love for others has, for the New Covenant people of God, taken center stage away from the Mosaic law. As Gal. 6:2, 1 Cor. 9:19-21, and the many commands in Paul's letters themselves indicate, Paul by no means thinks that the love command is the only commandment of relevance to Christian believers.

40. Gk. οὖν.

41. Cf. also Lenski.

42. See, e.g., S-H; Käsemann; Wilckens; Cranfield; G. Delling, *TDNT* VI, 305. See the notes on 11:12 for the meaning and usage of πλήρωμα.

43. Lagrange; Ziesler; Feuillet, "Loi de Dieu," p. 55; Deidun, 153.

1. Several early and important witnesses (P[46] [probably], the secondary Alexandrian MSS 33 and 1739, the western uncial D, Ψ, and the majority text) read ἡμᾶς ("us") in place of ὑμᾶς ("you"); the latter is found in the two most important Alexandrian uncials (ℵ [original hand] and B), three other Alexandrian MSS (A, C, and 81), P, and many minuscules and Fathers — two early versions and Origen have no corresponding word at all. The variation, involving only one letter in the Greek text and often hardly affecting the sense, is very common in the NT manuscript tradition. The ἡμῶν ("our") later in the verse might suggest that Paul would have used the first person plural here also; but perhaps it is more likely that a scribe would have changed an original ὑμᾶς to ἡμᾶς to achieve uniformity (Metzger, 529; Godet, 449; Cranfield, 2.680).

to rise up from sleep. For our salvation is now nearer than when we believed. 12*The night is far along; the day is drawing near. Therefore put off*[2] *the works of darkness; put on the weapons of light.* 13*Walk decently, as in the day, not in carousings and drinking bouts, not in sexual excesses and licentiousness; not in strife and jealousy.* 14*But put on the Lord Jesus Christ and make no provision for the flesh, to carry out its desires.*

Paul brings to a close his general exhortations to the Roman Christians by focusing on the same point with which he began: a call for a totally new way of living in light of the eschatological situation. In 12:1-2, Paul urges Christians to give themselves as living sacrifices, adopting a lifestyle in keeping with the new era to which they belong. In 13:11-14, he exhorts Christians to clothe themselves with Christ himself (v. 14) and with that behavior (v. 12b) fitting for those who live already in the light of the great "day" of final salvation that is soon to dawn (vv. 11-12a).[3] The earlier text encourages Christians to look at the present in light of the past: by virtue of Christ's death and resurrection, the "old age" has been transcended by a new one. The Christian is to live out the values of that new age, appropriating the power available in the gospel to renew the mind and transform conduct. The text now before us shifts the perspective, encouraging Christians to look at the present in light of the future. For, while transferred by God's grace into the new realm of righteousness and life, Christians still await full and final salvation (cf. 5:9-10), "the redemption of the body" (cf. 8:23). The transformation that the gospel both demands and empowers flows from the work of Christ already accomplished. But it also looks ahead to the completion of the process on that day when we will be fully "conformed to the image of [God's] Son" (8:29).[4] Christians are not only to "become what we are"; we are also to "become what we one day will be."

---

2. In place of ἀποθώμεθα, "let us put off" — read in the major Alexandrian uncials (ℵ, B), other Alexandrian MSS (A, C, 33, 81, and 1739), Ψ, the western uncial D (second corrector), and the majority text — P[46], along with the "western" tradition (original hand and third corrrector of D, F, and G), reads ἀποβαλώμεθα, "let us throw off." Zuntz (p. 94), Cranfield (2.685), and Wilckens (3.76) defend this alternative, impressed with the combination of the western tradition and P[46], and arguing that an early scribe substituted for it the more familiar ἀποθώμεθα. But it is not at all uncommon for P[46] to line up with the western tradition, and Paul never uses this verb anywhere else (cf. Metzger, 529-30).

3. The way in which the eschatological focus of 12:1-2 and 13:11-14 functions as a kind of inclusio for chaps. 12–13 is widely recognized; see the notes on 12:1-2; and especially here, Michel, 412; Leenhardt, 338; Wilckens, 3.78; Thompson, *Clothed with Christ,* p. 151.

4. See Ridderbos, *Paul,* pp. 267-68.

Verses 11-14 fall naturally into two parts: the "indicative" section, in which Paul reminds us of the nature of the "time" (vv. 11-12a); and the "imperative" section, in which he summons us to action in light of the "time" (vv. 12b-14). The imperatives occur in three pairs of contrasts:

"put off . . . / put on . . ." (v. 12b);
"walk decently . . . / not in . . ." (v. 13);
"put on the Lord Jesus Christ / make no provision for the flesh" (v. 14).

Appealing to the imminence of Christ's return as a basis for exhortation is a common NT pattern, rooted in Jesus' own teaching.[5] And the specific parallels in wording between this paragraph and other Pauline texts (esp. 1 Thess. 5:1-10) confirm the traditional nature of what Paul is here telling the Roman Christians.[6]

11-12a   The phrase that introduces this next paragraph, "and this,"[7] might be an idiom used to create a transition — "besides this" (NRSV)[8] — but it is probably elliptical, with an imperative such as "do"[9] to be supplied — cf. NIV: "And do this, understanding. . . ."[10] Many commentators add an ascensive nuance to the phrase — "and do this *especially* as you recognize . . ."[11] — but there seems no good grammatical basis for it. The "this"

---

5. See esp. 1 Pet. 4:7; Jas. 5:8-9. On the influence of Jesus' eschatological discourse (Mark 13 and pars.) on Paul's teaching, see esp. D. Wenham, "Paul and the Synoptic Apocalypse," in *Gospel Perspectives I* (ed. R. T. France and D. Wenham; Sheffield: JSOT, 1981), pp. 345-75. Contact (perhaps indirect) between this paragraph and Jesus' teaching is also posited by Thompson, *Clothed with Christ,* pp. 141-49. He notes that calls to stay "awake" and avoid sleep in eschatological contexts are not found in Judaism; but they are in the teaching of Jesus (cf., e.g., Mark 13:33-37).

6. Both Rom. 13:11-14 and 1 Thess. 5:1-10 use the day/night and light/darkness metaphors together with both eschatological and moral reference; and both speak of salvation as future and call for the "putting on" (of virtues and Christ in Romans; of spiritual "armor" in Thessalonians). The need to "wake from sleep" (ἐξ ὕπνου ἐγερθῆναι — v. 11) also resembles the puzzling "saying" of Eph. 5:14: "awake [ἔγειρε], O sleeper, and rise from the dead, and Christ will shine on you." Many think this saying could stem from early Christian baptismal liturgy and suggest accordingly that Rom. 13:11-14 also reproduces, at least in part, this liturgy (e.g., Wilckens, 3.75; Schlatter, 395-96; Schmithals, 479-82; Stuhlmacher, 212).

7. Gk. καὶ τοῦτο.

8. See also KJV; NJB; S-H; Murray; Cranfield; Dunn. Appeal is made to 1 Cor. 6:6, 8; Eph. 2:8; Phil. 1:28, but none of these is parallel to Rom. 13:11.

9. Gk. ποιεῖτε.

10. See also NASB; TEV; Moulton, 182; Michel; Wilckens. Godet adds an indicative verb: "and this you fulfill, recognizing. . . ."

11. The view is as early as Theodoret, who paraphrased with μάλιστα, "especially"; cf. also A. Vögtle, "Paraklese und Eschatologie nach Röm 13:11-14," in Lorenzi, *Dimensions,* pp. 179-80; Michel; Wilckens; Schlatter.

could refer back immediately to the love command in vv. 8-10,[12] but it probably alludes to all the exhortations in 12:1–13:10.[13] All that Paul has set forth as the will of God for our sacrificial service in the new age of redemption is to be done because we understand[14] the "time," or "opportune moment,"[15] in which we live.

Paul then adds three statements in which he explains[16] just what he means by the "time." His first and third assertions share the metaphor of night giving way to day: "it is already[17] the hour for you to rise up from sleep"[18] (v. 11b) and "the night is far along[19]; the day is drawing near" (v. 12a). In a society governed by the sun rather than by the convenience of artificial lighting, people rose at dawn. Only slackards would keep to their beds after the first glow of daylight. Early rising was especially necessary in the Near East, where the bulk of work needed to be done before the heat of midday. Paul wants no slackards among his readers. Christians are to be alert and eager to "present their bodies as a living sacrifice." But Paul does not use the darkness/light, night/day imagery simply as an illustration drawn from daily life. For in using these contrasts, Paul is drawing on a broad tradition in which these contrasts were used as metaphors for moral and eschatological conditions. Basic to Paul's application is the OT/Jewish "the day of the Lord," adapted by the early Christians to denote the time of Christ's return in glory

12. Murray; Fitzmyer.

13. Godet; Barrett; Cranfield; Baumgarten, *Paulus und die Apokalyptik,* p. 209.

14. εἰδότες is a causal participle (cf. Stuart).

15. καιρός. While καιρός cannot always be neatly distinguished from χρόνος, the former does often connote "opportunity" and is generally used in eschatological contexts (see J. Barr, *Biblical Words for Time* [SBT; London: SCM, 1969], p. 127).

16. Cf. the Gk. ὅτι.

17. It makes better sense to take ἤδη, "already," with ὥρα (Cranfield) than with ἐγερθῆναι (as does, e.g., S-H).

18. This is the only verse in the NT that uses ὕπνος in a metaphorical sense; the verb καθεύδω, on the other hand, is used to denote "spiritual laziness and indifference" (1 Thess. 5:6; Eph. 5:14; cf. Mark 13:35-36; Matt. 24:43; Luke 12:39). No noun form of this verb occurs in the NT, however; so Paul undoubtedly uses ὕπνος as a noun-form equivalent to καθεύδω in this metaphorical sense. Sleep as a metaphor for spiritual insensitivity is widespread in the ancient world (cf., e.g., Philo, *Migration of Abraham* 222; *Dreams* 1.117; 2.106, 133, 160, etc.), but was particularly popular with the gnostics. But while the gnostics applied the concept within a cosmological and anthropological dualism (people needed to become illuminated and awake from the spiritual ignorance of this world), Paul is oriented historically and eschatologically (see esp. E. Lövestam, *Spiritual Wakefulness in the New Testament* [LUÅ 55.3; Lund: Gleerup, 1963], pp. 25-27).

19. The verb προκόπτω usually means "progress" in the NT (in Paul: Gal. 1:14; 2 Tim. 2:16; 3:9, 16); here it has a temporal nuance: "be advanced," "be far along" (BAGD; cf. Josephus, *J.W.* 4.298, "as the night advanced"). Paul probably uses the aorist because he wants simply to state the "advancement" of the time of the night.

and the believer's final redemption.[20] "The day" of v. 12a is certainly a reference to this "day of the Lord/Jesus Christ."[21] The "night," then, probably also hints at, by contrast, "the present evil age" (cf. Gal. 1:4).[22] While not as certain, it is also possible that "the hour" in v. 11b has eschatological connotations.[23] To "rise from sleep," then, means to reject "absorption in the present night-age," to avoid conformity with the present evil age (cf. 12:2).[24]

The central explanatory statement of "the time" is a straightforward assertion of what these metaphors hint at: "our[25] salvation is now nearer than

20. Paul uses several variations of this common early Christian reference: "the day of the Lord Jesus Christ" (1 Cor. 1:8); "the day of our Lord Jesus" (2 Cor. 1:14); "the day of Jesus Christ" (Phil. 1:6); "the day of Christ" (Phil. 1:10; 2:16); "the day of the Lord" (1 Cor. 5:5; 1 Thess. 5:2; 2 Thess. 2:2); "the day of redemption" (Eph. 4:30); "the day of wrath" (Rom. 2:5); "the day when God judges" (Rom. 2:16); "the evil day" (Eph. 6:13); "that day" (2 Thess. 1:10; 2 Tim. 1:12, 18; 4:8); "the day" (Rom. 13:12, 13; 1 Thess. 5:4). These phrases all go back to the OT "day of the Lord," the time of eschatological judgment and salvation (cf., e.g., Isa. 27; Jer. 30:8-9; Joel 2:32; 3:18; Obad. 15-17).

21. Although some patristic commentators thought that the "day" referred to Christ (cf. K. H. Schelkle, "Biblische und Patristische Eschatologie nach Röm., XIII, 11-13," in *Sacra Pagina: Miscellanea Biblica Congressus Internationalis Catholici de re Biblica* [2 vols.; ed. J. Coppens, A. Descamps, and E. Massoux; BETL 12-13; Paris: Gabalda, 1959], 1.364-65).

22. Lövestam has shown how widespread in early Judaism was the use of the contrasts night/day and darkness/light to describe the contrast between "this age" and "the age to come" (*Spiritual Wakefulness,* pp. 10-24). See, e.g., *1 Enoch* 58:

> The righteous ones shall be in the light of the sun and the elect ones in the light of eternal life which has no end (v. 2). . . . The sun has shined upon the earth and the darkness is over. There shall be a light that has no end. . . . For already darkness has been destroyed, light shall be permanent before the Lord of the Spirits, and the light of uprightness shall stand firm forever and ever before the Lord of the Spirits (v. 6).

The Qumran covenanters constantly use the contrast "children of light"/"children of darkness" (see esp. 1QM).

23. ὥρα often occurs in phrases simply denoting a short period of time; this is the case in all the other occurrences of the word in Paul (1 Cor. 4:11; 15:30; 2 Cor. 7:8; Gal. 2:5; 1 Thess. 2:17; Phlm. 15), and it gives good reason to think that Paul may use the word here in this simple, prosaic sense (cf. Cranfield). But ὥρα does have eschatological nuances in the NT (John 4:23; 5:25; 12:34; 1 John 2:18; Rev. 3:3, 10) and in the OT (Dan. 8:17, 19; 11:35, 40), and the context may favor such a nuance here (cf. Schlier; Dunn).

24. See Lövestam, *Spiritual Wakefulness,* pp. 34-35.

25. ἡμῶν could go with ἐγγύτερον — "salvation is now nearer *to us* than when we believed" (NRSV; REB; NASB; Wilckens; Cranfield) — but it probably goes with ἡ σωτηρία — "*our* salvation is now nearer than when we believed" (KJV; NIV; TEV; Michel; Dunn); for when ἔγγυς occurs in eschatological statements in the NT, it is never followed by a genitive object.

when we believed."[26] Some Christians might find it puzzling that Paul places "salvation" in the future for believers. But, in fact, Paul regularly uses "salvation" and its cognates to denote the believer's final deliverance from sin and death. Some commentators argue that salvation here refers to each individual believer's entrance into heaven at death or at the time of the parousia.[27] But Paul's imagery in this passage is not individual but salvation-historical. The "salvation" must be the completion of God's work on behalf of the church at the time of Christ's return.[28]

Many scholars think that Paul's statement here, along with many similar ones in the NT, shows that the early Christians were certain that Christ was going to return within a very short period of time. And, since Paul's imperatives are, to some extent, based on this premise, the failure of Christ to return as soon as Paul expected requires that we critically evaluate the continuing validity of those imperatives.[29] Paul certainly betrays a strong sense of expectation about the return of Christ (e.g., Phil. 4:5) and can even speak at times as if he will be alive at that time (e.g., 1 Thess. 4:15). But nowhere does he predict a near return; and, more importantly, he does not ground his exhortations on the conviction that the parousia would take place very soon but on the conviction that the parousia was always imminent — its coming certain, its timing incalculable. "On the *certainty of the event,* our faith is grounded: by the *uncertainty of the time,* our hope is stimulated, and our watchfulness aroused."[30] Christ's return is the next event in God's plan; Paul knew it could take place at any time and sought to prepare Christians — both in his generation and in ours — for that "blessed hope."[31]

---

26. ἐπιστεύσαμεν is probably an ingressive aorist, noting the entrance into belief; cf. NRSV, "when we became believers"; REB, "when first we believed." See Cranfield.

27. Many of the patristic commentators took this view (cf. Schelkle, "Biblische und Patristische Eschatologie," pp. 365-66); cf. also Stuart; Haldane; Hodge; Lenski.

28. See the notes on 5:9.

29. See, e.g., Käsemann; G. Dautzenberg, "Was bleibt von der Naherwartung? Zu Röm 13,11-14," in *Biblische Rand Bemerkungen: Schülerfestschrift für Rudolf Schnackenburg zum 60. Geburtstag* (ed. H. Merklein and J. Lange; Augsburg: Echter, 1974), pp. 361-74. Dunn, who thinks that Paul does speak out of a certainty of a near parousia, nevertheless (somewhat unconvincingly) denies that this invalidates the exhortations based on it.

30. Alford.

31. For this general perspective see esp. A. L. Moore, *The Parousia in the New Testament* (NovTSup 13; Leiden: Brill, 1966); Ridderbos, *Paul,* pp. 487-97; and, on this passage, Godet, 449-50; Murray, 2.167-69; Cranfield, 2.683-84. On the related issue of apocalyptic and imminence, see I. H. Marshall, "Is Apocalyptic the Mother of Christian Theology?" in *Tradition and Interpretation in the New Testament,* pp. 32-42; Beker, 176-81; J. A. Baird, "Pauline Eschatology in Hermeneutical Perspective," *NTS* 17 (1970-71), 314-27.

12b   The first pair of imperatives that Paul builds on the imminence of Christ's return uses the imagery of changing clothes: "putting off" one set in order to "put on" another. This language was widely used with metaphorical associations in the ancient world, and the NT writers adopt it as a vivid way of picturing the change of values that accompanies, and is required by, conversion to Christ.[32] Many scholars think that the eschatological imagery of night giving way to day that Paul has just used (vv. 11b, 12a) influences Paul's choice of this metaphor here: Christians are to put off their "night" clothes and put on their "day" clothes.[33] The connection is possible, although the metaphor is so widespread that there is no need to posit such a point of contact.[34] Equally common as an image of morality is the contrast between darkness and light that Paul uses to characterize what Christians are to "put off" and "put on." Particularly significant here is that in the OT, Judaism, and the NT, the contrast is extended into eschatology, with darkness characterizing the present evil age and light the new age of salvation.[35] The darkness of night, as the time when those bent on evil and mischief are particularly active, becomes an image for the evil realm, that "old age" which continues to exert its influence and to which Christians are not to be conformed (12:2). The light/darkness contrast is, of course, a natural extension of the day/night imagery of vv. 11-12a; cf. also 1 Thess. 5:4-5: "But you, brothers, are not in *darkness,* that *the day* [the "day of the Lord"; cf. v. 2] should overtake you as a thief. For you are all sons of *light* and sons of *the day.* We are not of *the night,* neither of *the darkness.*" The "works of darkness" that Paul urges us to renounce are therefore those activities that are typical of that evil realm.[36] In their

32. The contrast with both verbs occurs also in Eph. 4:22, 25; Col. 3:8, 12. ἀποτίθημι in this sense is found also in Jas. 1:21; 1 Pet. 2:1; ἐνδύω in Eph. 6:11, 14; 1 Thess. 5:8. Significantly, these latter three all have as their object "armor" or a specific piece of armor. Some scholars (e.g., Black; Michel) think the imagery may reflect the ritual change of clothes associated with the early Christian baptismal liturgy. But there is no evidence for the ceremony being this early (Dunn).

33. E.g., Althaus; Schlatter; Dunn. Lenski betrays an all-too-typical misinterpretation of the aorist tense by insisting that Paul here demands a "once-for-all" putting off and putting on. Only contextual factors could indicate any such nuance; lacking them here, we must view the aorist hortatory subjunctives as simply demanding that these actions be taken — perhaps as often as necessary. (Fanning, *Verbal Aspect,* pp. 362-63, notes the prevalence of the aorist with verbs of "clothing" and suggests that in this verse, and in v. 14, Paul is capturing a process in a single image.)

34. Michel points out that it was not apparently the custom for people to put on one set of clothes in place of another for the day (cf. also Cranfield).

35. See esp. Amos 5:18, 20; Isa. 60:19-20; *1 Enoch* 10:5; 92:4-5; 108:11; *2 Apoc. Bar.* 18:2; 48:50; and, esp. Qumran, where "the sons of the light" were sharply distinguished from "the sons of darkness" in an eschatological context (e.g., 1QS 1:9; 2:16; 3:13; 1QM 1:1, passim). In the NT, see, e.g., Matt. 4:16; 1 Pet. 2:9; Rev. 22:5.

36. The genitive τοῦ σκότους is probably qualitative; cf. Cranfield.

place, we are to put on "the weapons[37] of light," weapons appropriate for those who have been "delivered from the dominion of darkness" and been "qualified to share in the inheritance of the saints in light" (Col. 1:13, 12). We need such weapons both to defend and to extend the light.[38] Paul switches from the term "works" to "weapons" because, as Calvin notes, "we are to carry on a warfare for the Lord."[39]

13 Paul now derives a second pair of contrasted commands from his teaching about the nearness of the Lord's return. This contrast employs the very popular imagery of "walking" as a way of speaking about one's daily conduct.[40] Our manner of life, Paul urges, is to be "decent," a word that suggests a decorous and "becoming" deportment, a lifestyle "appropriate" to those who live in the full light of the day.[41] Paul's addition of the phrase "as in the day" may simply accentuate this metaphor,[42] but the use of the same term in v. 12 with reference to the "day of Christ" strongly suggests that Paul intends more than a metaphor. But it is not clear whether Paul is also carrying over from v. 12 the futurity of the day — in which case he would be urging us to "walk decently *as if* we were in the day"[43] — or whether he has shifted to the present element of that "day" — in which case, he is exhorting us to "walk decently as those who are in the day."[44] The latter alternative is, however, more in keeping with Paul's typical combination of the "already" and the "not yet" in his eschatological perspective. Christians eagerly wait for the coming of the day (in its final phase) even as they experience, by faith, the power and blessings of that day in its present phase.

In contrast to the "decent" conduct that we are to exhibit, Paul lists three pairs of vices that we are to avoid. It seems evident that Paul has chosen

---

37. ὅπλα could mean "instruments" (cf. Godet, who thinks the reference is to "the garments of the laborious workman"), but the parallel text in 1 Thess. 5:8 strongly argues for the meaning "weapons" (and see the notes on 6:13).

38. The genitive φωτός is again probably descriptive; cf. Cranfield.

39. Calvin.

40. On the NT use of περιπατέω and its background in Judaism, see the note on 6:4. Paul does not explicitly contrast two imperative verbs in this verse; but the hortatory subjunctive περιπατήσωμεν governs both εὐσχημόνως (the positive command) and the series of datives beginning with [μὴ] κώμοις.

41. Paul uses the adverb εὐσχημόνως also in 1 Thess. 4:2 with the verb περιπατέω and in 1 Cor. 14:40. The corresponding adjective, εὐσχήμων, occurs in 1 Cor. 7:35 and 12:24; the noun εὐσχημοσύνη in 1 Cor. 12:23. (The concentration of these terms in 1 Cor. is probably no accident; and it suggests, by way of contrast with the Corinthians' errors, the flavor of the terms.)

42. E.g., Black.

43. E.g., Barrett. Godet combines this with the metaphorical allusion.

44. Cf. Cranfield; Wilckens; Ridderbos, *Paul,* p. 493. Käsemann: "you do in fact stand under the sign of the new day."

the first two pairs especially to match the metaphor of darkness/night that he has been using; for excessive drinking[45] and sexual misbehavior[46] are especially "sins of the night." "Strife"[47] and "jealousy"[48] do not so naturally fit here; and Paul may have chosen them with a view ahead to his rebuke of the Roman Christians for their divisiveness and mutual criticism (cf. 14:1–15:13).

14 Paul's final pair of contrasted imperatives are not so obviously related as those in vv. 12b and 13. The positive command picks up the verb "put on" from v. 12b. Now, however, what we are to put on is not a suit of armor but Christ himself. The exact meaning of what Paul intends is not easy to pinpoint. But perhaps we should view the imperative in light of his understanding of Christ as a corporate figure. As a result of our baptism/conversion, we have been incorporated into Christ, sharing his death, burial, and (proleptically) his resurrection (Rom. 6:3-6). Our "old man," our corporate identity with Adam, has been severed (Rom. 6:6); and in its place, we have become attached to the "new man" (Col. 3:10-11; Eph. 2:16), Jesus Christ himself (cf. Eph. 4:13), whom we have "put on" (Gal. 3:27). But our relationship to Christ, the new man, while established at conversion, needs constantly to be reappropriated and lived out, as Eph. 4:25, with its call to "put on the new man" makes clear. Against this background, Paul's exhortation to "put on the Lord Jesus Christ"[49] means that we are consciously to embrace Christ in such

45. κῶμος originally referred to a festal banquet, but took on a negative meaning, "excessive feasting," "carousing" (cf. also Wis. 14:23; 2 Macc. 6:4; Gal. 5:21; 1 Pet. 4:3; cf. Dunn). μέθη (13 LXX occurrences; Luke 21:34; Gal. 5:21) means "drunkenness" (cf. also its cognates: μέθυσος, "drunkard" [1 Cor. 5:11; 6:10]; and μεθύω, "be drunk" [Matt. 24:49; John 2:10; Acts 2:15; 1 Cor. 11:21; 1 Thess. 5:7; Rev. 17:2, 6]). The close association (hendiadys) here between κῶμος and μέθη may suggest that the former refers here specifically to a "drinking bout" (BAGD).

46. Paul links κοίτη ("sexual intercourse" [cf. the notes on Rom. 9:10]; here sexual excesses) with ἀσελγείαις, "acts of licentiousness" (a general term for "unseemly" behavior of all kinds, though often with reference to sexual immorality [H. Bauernfeind, *TDNT* I, 490; cf. Wis. 14:26; 3 Macc. 2:26; Mark 7:22; 2 Cor. 12:21; Gal. 5:21; Eph. 4:9; 1 Pet. 4:3; 2 Pet. 2:2, 7, 18; Jude 4]).

47. Gk. ἔρις; cf. also Rom. 1:29; 1 Cor. 1:11; 3:3; 2 Cor. 12:20; Gal. 5:20; Phil. 1:15; 1 Tim. 6:4.

48. ζῆλος can have a neutral or even positive meaning, "zeal" (cf. John 2:17; Rom. 10:2; 2 Cor. 7:7, 11; 9:2; 11:2; Phil. 3:6; Heb. 10:27), but it also refers, as here, to "jealousy" or "envy" (1 Cor. 3:3; Gal. 5:20; Jas. 3:14, 16). Note that ζῆλος and ἔρις occur together also in 1 Cor. 3:3 and in the list of vices in Gal. 5:19-21. What we have in this verse, then, is a mini "vice list," such is often used by NT authors to characterize sinful and unchristian conduct (cf. Rom. 1:29-31).

49. Paul's use of the full expression τὸν κύριον Ἰησοῦν Χριστόν, and especially his inclusion of κύριος ("Lord"), stresses the totality of the act and its implications for all of life (cf. Murray).

a way that his character is manifested in all that we do and say.[50] This exhortation appears to match the exhortation at the beginning of this section, "be transformed by the renewing of the mind," suggesting that it is into the image of Christ that we are being transformed (cf. 8:29).[51]

As the negative counterpart to "put on the Lord Jesus Christ," Paul warns us, "make no provision[52] for the flesh, to carry out its desires."[53] "Flesh"[54] might have a neutral meaning here, Paul's point being that we should not pay special attention to the demands of our human nature so as to let them dominate us.[55] But the term more likely lies more toward the negative end of its spectrum of meaning: "flesh" as that principle and power of life in this world which tends to pull us away from the spiritual realm.[56] As he does in Galatians (cf. 5:13-26), Paul implies concern that his proclamation of freedom from the law (vv. 8-10) might lead to a licentious lifestyle. Thus he urges his readers, in place of the law, to embrace Christ — who, through the Spirit, provides completely for victory over the flesh.

G. A PLEA FOR UNITY (14:1–15:13)

Paul wraps up his exhortations with a lengthy plea for mutual acceptance. The command to "receive" fellow believers begins the section (14:1) and is repeated again at its climax (15:7). Paul accentuates the theme of mutuality

---

50. See esp. Ridderbos, *Paul,* pp. 223-24; cf. also Dunn. Dunn also refers to Dionysius of Halicarnassus, who, referring to an actor, says that he "put on Tarquin" (τὸν Ταρκύνιον ἐνδύεσθαι), e.g., "played the part of Tarquin." The text may help explain the origin of the metaphor, but the meaning that Paul gives it is rooted in his particular view of salvation history. The aorist tense of the imperative again (cf. v. 12b) does not indicate a "once-for-all" act but simply states the necessity of acting (note that Paul's command here seems to match his command in 12:2 to "be transformed by the renewing of your mind"; a command that is in the present tense; see the note on v. 12).

51. See Thompson, *Clothed with Christ,* pp. 151-52. Both Thompson and Dunn ("Paul's Knowledge," p. 198) suggest that Paul would also be thinking of Christians modeling their behavior according to the pattern of Christ's life.

52. Paul uses the middle, ποιεῖσθε, because it was customary with the object πρόνοιαν, "provision" (BAGD; Zerwick, 227). πρόνοια, which was used outside the NT of God's "foresight," occurs in the NT only with reference to human foresight, concern, or provision (cf. Acts 24:2; BAGD).

53. εἰς ἐπιθυμίας could conceivably be the object of ποιεῖσθε πρόνοιαν, but this construction is usually followed by the genitive (cf. σαρκός). εἰς ἐπιθυμίας is therefore a separate clause, probably with a consecutive meaning (see Godet).

54. Gk. σάρξ.

55. E.g., Godet.

56. E.g., Murray; Michel; Käsemann; Cranfield. Dunn holds a more nuanced view (see the notes on 1:3), which has much to be said for it (see also Denney).

sounded in this last verse — "receive one another" — with three other "one another" references: "do not judge *one another*" (14:13); "let us pursue those matters that lead to peace and to edification for *one another*" (14:19); "May the God of endurance and of comfort give to you the power to think the same thing among *one another* according to Christ Jesus" (15:5). These exhortations to mutual acceptance and concern are directed specifically to two groups of Christians: those who are "weak in faith" (14:1; cf. 15:1) and those who are "strong in faith" (15:1). Two, and probably three, issues divide these two groups: (1) the "strong" eat all kinds of food while the "weak" eat only vegetables (14:2); (2) the "strong" make no distinction among days while the "weak" value some days more than others (14:5); and (3) the "strong" drink wine while the "weak" abstain (14:21; cf. 14:17).[1]

Two general issues must be cleared up before the details of Paul's exhortation can be understood: (1) the reason why Paul includes this exhortation in his letter to the Roman Christians; (2) the underlying basis for the differences in practice between the two groups.

With respect to the first issue, the most natural explanation for this extended plea for mutual acceptance is that Paul knew of a division between "strong" and "weak" in the Roman church and writes what he does to heal that division. But many scholars reject this explanation. They argue three points. (1) Rom. 12:1–15:13 is general parenesis, an outline of the gospel ethic that is engendered by the gospel itself and not by the needs of a particular community. (2) The impressive number of verbal and conceptual parallels with 1 Cor. 8–10 confirms that 14:1–15:13 is, like the rest of this section, general parenesis. Paul is here giving a generalized version of his advice to the Corinthians about their disputes over idol meat. (3) The difficulty in pinning down the precise religious motivations for the practices of the "weak" suggests that Paul is not describing an actual state of affairs but an idealized situation.[2]

However, these arguments are not sufficient to overturn the natural presumption that Paul is addressing a real problem in the Roman community. (1) Romans 12:1–15:13 is not simply general parenesis; Paul chooses themes and adds nuances with at least one eye on the situation in Rome (see the introduction to Rom. 12:1–15:13). (2) The parallels with 1 Cor. 8–10 are clear

---

1. To be sure, Paul mentions "drinking wine" only as as example and does not clearly identify it as an issue dividing the Roman Christians. But Paul probably brings it up precisely because it was another point of tension.

2. For these points, see esp. Karris, "Romans 14:1–15:13," pp. 65-84; W. A. Meeks, "Judgment and the Brother: Romans 14:1–15:13," in *Tradition and Interpretation in the New Testament,* pp. 290-300; F. Vouga, "L'Épître aux Romains comme document ecclésiologique (Rm 12–15)," *ETR* 61 (1986), 489-91; Furnish, *Love Command,* p. 115; S-H, 399-403; Leenhardt, 344-46.

and extensive.[3] But the degree of similarity causes the equally obvious differences to stand out all the more.[4] Karris and others argue that the differences reveal that Rom. 14:1–15:13 generalizes from the specific situation Paul addressed in Corinth.[5] But Paul's focus on abstention from all meat — which was not a major issue in the early church — suggests rather that the differences are occasioned by the different situations that Paul is addressing.[6] (3) Identifying the religious reasons for the practices of the "weak" that Paul notes is admittedly not easy. But I think it is possible to suggest a scenario that would explain the data (see the next paragraphs). Romans 14:1–15:13, therefore, while naturally picking up themes from throughout the letter, is occasioned specifically by Paul's need to address a current problem in the Roman community.[7]

Explanations of the root issue in Rom. 14:1–15:13 fall into six major categories.

(1) The "weak" were mainly Gentile Christians who abstained from meat (and perhaps wine), particularly on certain "fast" days, under the influence of certain pagan religions.[8]

(2) The "weak" were Christians, perhaps both Jewish and Gentile, who practiced an ascetic lifestyle for reasons that we cannot determine.[9]

(3) The "weak" were mainly Jewish Christians who observed certain

3. Convenient summaries of the parallels are found in Karris, "Romans 14:1–15:13," pp. 73-75; Wilckens, 3.115; Cranfield, 2.692-93; cf. also J. Dupont, "Appel aux faibles et aux forts dans la communauté Romaine (Rom 14,1–15,13)," SPCIC 1.357-66.

4. As, e.g., the issue of idolatry, which is basic to the problem in 1 Corinthians (cf. 8 and 10:1-22), but which is not even mentioned in Romans.

5. Karris, "Romans 14:1–15:13," pp. 73-77; Meeks, "Judgment and the Brother," pp. 292-93. For instance, Karris thinks that the presence of seven imperatives in the first person plural or third person singular (as opposed to six in the second person plural) reveals the general nature of the polemic. But, as Wilckens (3.110) notes, the shift in person is stylistic; its says nothing about the nature of the problem.

6. See, e.g., Wedderburn, Reasons, pp. 30-35.

7. This is not to say, however, that the dispute between the "strong" and the "weak" is the reason for the letter.

8. See esp. M. Rauer, Die 'Schwachen' in Korinth und Rom nach den Paulusbriefen (Biblische Studien 21; Freiburg: Herder, 1923), pp. 76-184. Somewhat similar are Lagrange, 335-40 and Käsemann, 367-68. Specific influences on the Roman Christians may have been Orphism (cf. Lagrange) or the (neo-)Pythagoreans (who avoided eating anything with a "soul"; cf. Diogenes Laertius 8.38; Philostratus, Vita Apollonii 1:8; cf. J. Behm, TDNT II, 690). An incipient form of gnosticism may also have been involved. Some later gnostics abstained from eating flesh (cf. Irenaeus, AH 1.24.2; Eusebius, H.E. 4.29); and many scholars detect a developing gnostic influence on the false teachers at Colossae and Ephesus (see 1 Timothy). Other scholars think that the days that the weak were concerned about were lucky and unlucky days determined by astrology.

9. Lenski, 812-13; Murray, 2.172-74; Achtemeier, 215.

practices derived from the Mosaic law out of a concern to establish righteousness before God.[10]

(4) The "weak" were mainly Jewish Christians who followed a sectarian ascetic program as a means of expressing their piety. This program may have been the product of syncretistic tendencies.[11]

(5) The "weak" were mainly Jewish Christians who, like some of the Corinthians, believed that it was wrong to eat meat that was sold in marketplace and was probably tainted by idolatry.[12]

(6) The "weak" were mainly Jewish Christians who refrained from certain kinds of food and observed certain days out of continuing loyalty to the Mosaic law.[13]

Four considerations make the sixth alternative the most likely.

First, there is abundant evidence that the dispute between the "weak" and the "strong" was rooted in differences between Jews and Gentiles. The relationship between these two groups has been a leitmotif of Romans since chap. 1; and the conclusion of this section, in which Paul emphasizes the inclusion of both Jews and Gentiles in the one new people of God (15:8-13), brings this motif into Paul's plea for reconciliation between the "strong" and the "weak."[14] Confirmation of a basically Jewish origin for the position of the weak comes from Paul's use of the term *koinos,* "common," "unclean," to describe (implicitly) the "weak" Christians' attitude toward food (14:14). For this term had become a semitechnical way of describing food prohibited

---

10. Cf. Barrett, 256-57.

11. See, e.g., Meyer, 2.296-98; Hodge, 417; Althaus, 138; Black, 190-91. Strongest evidence for this identification comes from a comparison with the program of the apparently syncretistic (perhaps a mixture of Judaism and incipient gnosticism) false teachers that Paul combats at Colossae and Ephesus. The former advocated abstinence from food, drink, and the observance of certain days (2:16, 21), while those at Ephesus demanded the avoidance of "foods" (1 Tim. 4:3) and may have influenced Timothy to stop drinking wine (cf. 1 Tim. 5:23). Jewish sectarian asceticism is attested in many other places. The "therapeutae," a sect of Jews in Egypt, were vegetarians and drank only "spring water" (see Philo, *The Contemplative Life* 37); and some early Jewish Christians were said to have abstained from eating flesh: James the brother of the Lord (cf. Eusebius, *H.E.* 2.23.5) and the Ebionites (Epiphanius, *Haer.* 30.15).

12. Nygren, 442; Ziesler, 323-26.

13. While always defended, this view has become the most popular in recent years. See, e.g., Calvin, 491-92; Wilckens, 3.79, 111-13; Cranfield, 2.694-97; Dunn, 2.799-802; Segal, *Paul the Convert,* 231-33; Tomson, *Paul and the Jewish Law,* pp. 236-58; Watson, 94-95; idem, "The Two Roman Congregations: Romans 14:1–15:13," in Donfried, 203-15; Wedderburn, *Reasons,* pp. 31-35; H.-W. Bartsch, "Die antisemitischen Gegner des Paulus im Römerbrief," in *Antijudaismus im Neuen Testament?* (ed. P. W. Eckert, N. P. Levinson, and M. Stöhr; Abhandlungen zum christlich-jüdischen Dialog; Munich: Kaiser, 1967), pp. 33-34.

14. Karris's attempt to dismiss the significance of this text for the issue ("Romans 14:1–15:13," pp. 80-81) is not successful.

under the Mosaic law (see Mark 7:2, 5; Acts 10:14). Moreover, the NT provides abundant evidence that the OT food laws constituted a prime issue in the early Christian communities.[15] This consideration rules out alternatives 1 and 2. It also create difficulties for alternative 4 since those sectarian Jews who abstained from meat and wine usually did so not primarily because of concern about violating the Mosaic law but under the influence of ascetic religious principles derived from non-Jewish sources (and often, indeed, antithetical to the OT/Jewish worldview).[16]

Second, Paul's plea for understanding and acceptance of the "weak" within the community makes clear that they were not propagating a view antithetical to the gospel. This makes it impossible to view them as Jews who believed that observance of the law was necessary for salvation. It also makes it unlikely that the "weak" were sectarian Jews who adopted an ascetic regime under the influence of other philosophical and/or religious tendencies.[17] This consideration rules out alternative 3 and creates difficulties for alternative 4.

Third, Paul's failure to mention "food sacrificed to idols" (*eidōlothyta;* cf. 1 Cor. 8:1) and his reference to the observance of special days and abstention from wine make it unlikely that the dispute in Romans can be confined to the issue of food offered to idols.

Fourth, positively, the practices Paul attributed to the "weak" can be explained as a result of concerns to observe certain requirements of the Mosaic law. Abstention from meat and wine is, of course, not required by the Mosaic law.[18] But scrupulous Jews would sometimes avoid all meat in environments

15. See Mark 7:19b (Mark's editorial comment); Acts 10, 15; Gal. 2:11-15. Segal claims that "the conflict between those who practiced some form of Jewish custom and those who did not was the most significant issue within Christianity's first two generations" (*Paul the Convert,* p. 150). Cf. also Dunn (2.800-801), who correctly emphasizes the centrality of food laws and Sabbath observance in maintaining the unique and separate status of the Jewish people.

16. Note, e.g., Philo's description of the "therapeutae" (see n. 10 above): "For as nature has set hunger and thirst as mistresses over mortal kind they propitiate them without using anything to curry favour but only such things as are actually needed and without which life cannot be maintained. Therefore they eat enough to keep from hunger and drink enough to keep from thirst but abhor surfeiting as a malignant enemy both to soul and body" (*The Contemplative Life* 37).

17. If a pre-gnostic or other pagan tradition lay behind the habits of the "weak," we would have expected Paul to be more harsh with them — as he is toward such people in Colossians and 1 Timothy (see Tholuck, 416; Murray, 2.173). It is just possible, however, that the degree of influence from these other sources was slight enough that Paul is able to encourage toleration of their practices.

18. The law prohibited Israelites from eating certain kinds of meat (cf. Lev. 11; 20:25; Deut. 14:3-21) and any meat "with the blood in it" (cf. Lev. 17:10-16; 19:26; Deut. 12:15-25), while only Nazirites were required to abstain from wine (cf. Num. 6:2-4; Judg. 13:4-5; 16:7; Amos 2:11-12).

where they could not be sure that the meat had been prepared in a "kosher" manner.[19] And Jewish Christians in Rome, who were perhaps ostracized from the Jewish community because of their faith in Christ and had been forced to settle in strange parts of the city after their exile (by the decree of Claudius), may have been in precisely this kind of environment.[20] Similarly, Jews would sometimes abstain from wine out of concern that it had been tainted by the pagan practice of offering the wine as a libation to the gods.[21] Finally, of course, the Mosaic law stipulates the observance of many special religious days: the weekly Sabbath and the major religious festivals. And many first-century Jews also observed weekly fasting and prayer days.

These considerations suggest that the "weak" were Jewish Christians (and probably also some Gentile "god-fearers"[22]) who believed that they were still bound by certain "ritual" requirements of the Mosaic law. Paul's exhortation in 14:1 to the Roman community to "receive" these who are "weak in faith" makes clear that this group was in the minority. And, typical of such scrupulous minorities, these "weak" Christians were "condemning" those other Christians who did not follow their rules (14:3). This other group, who perhaps called themselves "the strong," was probably composed mainly of Gentile Christians, along with some more "liberated" Jewish Christians, such as Paul himself (cf. 15:1). They believed that the coming of Christ had brought an end to the ritual requirements of the Mosaic law; and, like many such "enlightened" majorities, they tended to "despise" and look down on the "weak" (14:3). It is possible that the "strong" and the "weak" occupied rival congregations and that Paul's purpose in this section is to unify the two groups into one congregation.[23] But the degree of mutual recrimination and the real power of the "strong" to harm the "weak" suggest rather that Paul writes to bring unity to an existing congregation, or, more likely, to a number of "house" congregations.[24]

19. See especially the example of Daniel, who "resolved that he would not defile himself with the royal rations of food and wine" (Dan. 1:8; cf. also Dan. 10:3); cf. also Tob. 1:10-12; Jud. 12:2, 19; Add. Esth. 14:17; *Jos. and As.* 7:1; 8:5; Josephus, *Life* 14; *m. 'Abot* 3:3.

20. See Watson, 94-95.

21. See Dan. 1:3-16; 10:3; Add. Esth. 14:17; *T. Reuben* 1:10; *T. Jud.* 15:4; *Jos. and As.* 8:5; *m. 'Abod. Zar.* 2:3; 5. Cf. Wilckens, 3.95-96; Dunn, 2.827.

22. Roman writers note the popularity of both the Sabbath and Jewish food laws even among Gentiles (cf. Juvenal, *Satirae* 14.9b-10b; Horace, *Satirae* 1.9.67-72; Ovid, *Remedia Amoris* 219-20; *Ars Amatoria* 1.76, 415-16; cf. Leon, *Jews of Ancient Rome,* pp. 12-13; P. Lampe, *Die stadtrömischen Christen in den ersten beiden Jahrhunderten: Untersuchungen zur Socialgeschichte* [2d ed.; WUNT 2.18; Tübingen: Mohr, 1989], pp. 54-60).

23. See esp. Watson, 97; idem, "The Two Roman Congregations," p. 206.

24. See esp. Karris, "Romans 14:1–15:13," p. 79: Paul "is not trying to create a community out of the disarray of 'the weak' and 'the strong' communities, but is concerned to show how an established congregation can maintain its unity despite differences of opinion."

Paul agrees in principle with the "strong": "I know and am persuaded in the Lord Jesus that nothing is unclean in itself" (14:14a; cf. also 14:20; 15:1). But he spends no time developing this point. His concern is not so much with the "rights" and "wrongs" of this particular issue but with the "peace" and "mutual edification" of the body of Christ (cf. 14:19). And he makes clear that those who pride themselves on being the "strong" have a special responsibility toward this end. It is they, those who truly sense their liberty on these matters, who are to put their exercise of that liberty in perspective and to subordinate it to the far more important "good" of their fellow believers' edification and salvation (14:15-21). In this they are to imitate their Lord, who subordinated his own interests for the sake of those — both circumcised and uncircumcised — that he came to redeem (15:3, 8-12).

Those who think that Paul writes Rom. 14:1–15:13 without specific knowledge of such a problem in Rome are right to note that the general situation we have sketched in the last three paragraphs is one that would have been found in many of the early Christian communities. It is also true that this section is internally consistent with the theme and development of the letter. For the division between the "strong" and the "weak" is a practical example of the problem of the relationship between Jew and Gentile, law and gospel, OT and NT, that is basic to Romans. We find worked out in detail in these chapters the exhortation of Rom. 11:17, that Gentile Christians should not "boast over the natural branches." And some of the exhortations of chaps. 12–13 have at least a general relationship to what Paul teaches in 14:1–15:13. The diversity within unity of the body of Christ (12:3-8) undergirds Paul's call for tolerance between "weak" and "strong"; the importance of love for the "neighbor" (13:8-10; cf. also 12:9-21) informs Paul's call to the "strong" to restrict the exercise of their liberty for the sake of their "neighbor," the "weak" Christian (15:2; cf. 14:13-23).[25] We do not think these connections are numerous or specific enough to justify the thesis that Rom. 1–13 (or even 12–13) has as its main purpose preparing the ground for Rom. 14:1–15:13. But they do show that Rom. 14:1–15:13, without diminishing its specific application to a problem in Rome, also fits naturally into Paul's exposition and defense of the gospel. We find even in this hortatory section, therefore, further confirmation of our thesis that Romans is a general exposition of the gospel occasioned by specific needs in the Roman community (see the introduction to the commentary).

Paul's call for mutual acceptance in the Roman community falls into four larger sections. Each combines exhortation with theological rationale.

---

25. Several commentators think that "love" is the key connection between 12:1–13:14 and 14:1–15:13; cf., e.g., Wilckens, 3.79; Stuhlmacher, 223; Zeller, 222.

14:1-12 — Both "strong" and "weak" Christians need to stop condemning each other because it is the Lord, and he alone, who has the right to assess the believer's status and conduct.

14:13-23 — The "strong" Christians must be careful not to cause the "weak" Christians to suffer spiritual harm by their insistence on exercising their liberty on disputed matters. For such insistence violates the essence of the kingdom, which is to manifest love and concern for one another.

15:1-6 — The "strong" Christians should willingly tolerate the tender consciences of the "weak" Christians, seeking thereby to foster unified praise of God in the community. Christians should exhibit such concern for others because of the example set for them by their Lord.

15:7-13 — Both "strong" and "weak" Christians should receive each other as full and respected members of the Christian community, for God himself has shown, in fulfillment of Scripture, that he accepts both Jews and Gentiles as his people.

1. Do Not Condemn One Another! (14:1-12)

1Receive the one who is weak with respect to faith, and not for the purpose of quarrels over disputed matters. 2One person believes he can eat all things, while another eats vegetables. 3Let the one who eats not despise the one who does not eat; and let the one who does not eat not judge the one who eats, for God has received him.

4Who are you who is judging the household servant of another? It is to his lord that he stands or falls. But he will stand, for the Lord[26] is able to cause him to stand. 5For[27] one person judges one day to be more important than another day, while another judges each day to be the same. Let each one be thoroughly convinced in his own mind. 6The one who observes the day, observes it to the Lord. And the one who eats, eats to the Lord, for he gives thanks to God. And the one

---

26. In light of its weak attestation (the western uncials D, F, and G, the secondary Alexandrian minuscules 33, 81, and 1739, and the majority text), the variant θεός is probably an assimilation to the same word in v. 3.

27. External testimony alone suggests that we should omit the γάρ; for the combination of P[46], the bulk of the Alexandrian tradition (B, 33, 81, and 1739), Ψ, and the western tradition (D, F, and G; cf. also the majority text) is very strong (e.g., Cranfield, 2.704; Dunn, 2.796). But internal evidence favors its inclusion, the supposition being that an early scribe dropped the γάρ because he recognized that its normal causal meaning did not make sense (cf. Metzger, 530-31; Lietzmann, 110; Michel, 425). We lean very slightly to the inclusion of γάρ, following the original hand of ℵ, the secondary Alexandrian uncial A, P, and a few other MSS.

*who does not eat, does not eat to the Lord, and he gives thanks to God. 7For no one of us lives to himself, and no one dies to himself. 8For if we live, we live to the Lord, and if we die, we die to the Lord. Therefore whether we live or whether we die, we are the Lord's. 9For it is for this reason that Christ died and came to life,*28 *in order that he might be Lord over both the dead and the living.*

*10Now why are you judging your brother? Or you also: why are you despising your brother? For we all must appear before the judgment seat of God.*29 *11For it is written,*

As I live, says the Lord, to me every knee will bow
*and every tongue will praise God.*a

*12Therefore each of us will give account of himself to God.*30

a. Isa. 45:23

This paragraph divides into three sections: vv. 1-3, 4-9, and 10-12. The divisions between the sections are marked with similar rhetorical questions, each using the second person singular: "Who are you31 who is judging the servant of another?" (v. 4a); "Why are you judging your brother?" (v. 10a). It is evident, then, that Paul has arranged the three sections in a classic "ring

28. The MS tradition contains a number of alternatives and additions to the words ἀπέθανεν καὶ ἔζησεν: (1) ἀπέθανεν καὶ ἀνέστη — "died and arose" (found in the sister western uncials F and G); (2) καὶ ἀπέθανεν καὶ ἀνέστη καὶ ἔζησεν — "and died and arose and lives" (the first corrector of the western D, the secondary Alexandrian MSS 33 and 81, Ψ, and the majority text [including the second corrector of ℵ]); (3) ἔζησεν καὶ ἀπέθανεν καὶ ἀνέστη — "came to life and died and arose" (the original hand and second corrector of D). But the text is well supported (it is found in the two great Alexandrian uncials, ℵ [original hand] and B, as well as in the secondary Alexandrian C and 1739, and a few other MSS). The other readings are corruptions under the influence of the formula πιστεύομεν ὅτι Ἰησοῦς ἀπέθανεν καὶ ἀνέστη (1 Thess. 4:14); cf., e.g., Metzger, 531; Bengel, 3.176.

29. Although widely attested, the variant Χριστοῦ ("Christ") is not strongly supported (the later Alexandrian MSS C, 33, and 81, Ψ, the second [Byzantine] corrector of ℵ, two other uncials, and the majority text). It is therefore probably an assimilation to the familiar text of 2 Cor. 5:10: τοὺς γὰρ πάντας ἡμᾶς φανερωθῆναι δεῖ ἔμπροσθεν τοῦ βήματος τοῦ Χριστοῦ, "for we must all appear before the judgment seat of Christ."

30. The last words of the verse, τῷ θεῷ ("to God"), are omitted in the important primary Alexandrian uncial B, in the secondary Alexandrian minuscule 1739, and in the sister western bilinguals F and G. The omission could be original, later scribes feeling it necessary to complete the text (cf. Käsemann, 373). But the omission of the words renders the text perhaps too difficult; we should probably follow the primary Alexandrian ℵ, the secondary Alexandrian MSS A, C, 33, and 81, Ψ, the western uncial D, and the majority text and include it (cf. Cranfield, 2.711; Dunn, 2.796).

31. Gk. σύ.

composition."[32] The first (vv. 1-3) and the third (vv. 10-12) state in almost identical language the main point of the paragraph: the "strong" are not to "despise" the "weak"; the "weak" are not to "judge" the "strong" (cf. vv. 3a and 10a). In the central section, vv. 4-9, Paul provides the theological foundation for these commands: every Christian is a servant of the Lord; and it is to that "master," and not to any other fellow servant, that the believer must answer.[33]

1 Paul concludes his exhortation to the "strong" and the "weak" with a plea for mutual acceptance (15:7). But he begins by urging that the community "receive the one who is weak with respect to faith." By making the "weak" in faith the object of this command, which appears to be directed to the community as a whole, Paul implies that the "strong" were the dominant element in the Roman church.[34] This fits with our identification of the "strong" as mainly Gentile Christians, since Paul treats the church in Rome as predominantly Gentile (see the introduction). To "receive" the "weak" is not simply to accord them official recognition as church members. The verb means "receive or accept into one's society, home, circle of acquaintance" (BAGD), and implies that the Roman Christians were not only to "tolerate" the "weak" but that they were to treat them as brothers and sisters in the intimate fellowship typical of the people of God.[35]

Paul's description of those who are to be received, "the weak with respect to faith,"[36] obviously carries a pejorative connotation: it is certainly better to be "strong" than to be "weak"![37] It was probably the "strong" in

---

32. See, e.g., Schmithals, 495.

33. These verses are marked by a heavy use of the dative case to state the one "with reference to whom" or "for whom" the believer acts: τῷ ἰδίῳ κυρίῳ (v. 4); κυρίῳ, κυρίῳ, τῷ θεῷ, κυρίῳ, τῷ θεῷ (v. 6); ἑαυτῷ, ἑαυτῷ (v. 7); τῷ κυρίῳ, τῷ κυρίῳ (v. 8).

34. For convenience' sake, we are using the term "strong" to describe those Christians in Rome who held the view opposite to the "weak," even though Paul does not himself use this terminology until 15:1.

35. See, e.g., Schlier; Cranfield; Michel; Dunn. The verb is προσλαμβάνω (lit., "take alongside oneself"). It occurs eight other times in the NT, but the closest parallels to Rom. 14:1 are in Acts 18:26; 28:2; and Phlm. 17 (the only Pauline occurrence outside of these chapters; cf. also Matt. 16:22; Mark 8:32; Acts 17:5; 27:33, 36). The present tense of the imperative might suggest a continuing attitude of acceptance.

36. The singular τὸν ἀσθενοῦντα ("the one who is weak") is clearly generic, Paul citing one person as representative of the group; cf. e.g., Turner, 22. The dative is the first of many in Rom. 14 that is not easy to classify; but it is probably best to treat it (as our overliteral translation suggests) as a dative of respect (cf. Z-G, 490; Lenski). Moule, *Idiom Book,* p. 44, on the other hand, suggests that it might be a "metaphorical local" use of the case.

37. See, e.g., Chrysostom.

Rome who described those with whom they disagreed in this way.[38] Yet the phrase is not as negative as it may seem at first sight. Crucial here is the meaning of the word "faith" in this description. Paul uses the language of faith to describe the dispute between the two groups at both the beginning (vv. 1, 2) and end (vv. 22, 23) of chap. 14.[39] The words certainly have some reference to that basic response to God in Christ demanded by the gospel which "faith" and "believe" have denoted throughout Romans.[40] Yet this distinctively Christian notion of faith has (at least implicitly) the person of Jesus Christ as its object: to "believe" is to entrust oneself to a person. Explicitly in v. 2, however, "believe" has the notion "believe that something is legitimate." Paul is not therefore simply criticizing these people for having a "weak" or inadequate trust in Christ as their Savior and Lord.[41] Rather, he is criticizing them for lack of insight into some of the implications of their faith in Christ. These are Christians who are not able[42] to accept for themselves the truth that their faith in Christ implies liberation from certain OT/Jewish ritual requirements. The "faith" with respect to which these people are "weak," therefore, is related to their basic faith in Christ but one step removed from it. It involves their individual outworking of Christian faith, their convictions about what that faith allows and prohibits.[43] Paul's decision to use the pejorative phrase "weak in faith" makes clear where his sympathies lie. We cannot avoid the impression (though his pastoral concerns lead him to keep it implicit) that Paul would hope that a growth in Christ would help those who were "weak" become "strong."

In the meantime, however, Paul is concerned with the unity of the church. This is why he not only urges the "strong" to "receive" the "weak" but to receive them with the right motivation and in the right spirit. Don't, Paul says, welcome the "weak" simply "for the purpose[44] of quarrels over

38. See G. Stählin, *TDNT* I, 492; Wilckens.

39. The noun πίστις in vv. 1, 22, and 23; the verb πιστεύω in v. 2.

40. See esp. Dunn. The suggestions of Tomson (*Paul and the Jewish Law,* p. 243), that "weak" is best translated (noting the similarity to rabbinic discussions) as "delicate," and of Jewett (*Christian Tolerance,* pp. 29-30), that it be translated "conservative," move too far away from the connection with basic Christian faith.

41. Contra, e.g., Denney.

42. Note the contrast δυνατός/ἀδύνατος in 15:1.

43. See R. Bultmann, *TDNT* VI, 218-19; cf. also esp. Cranfield, 2.697-98, 700; Fitzmyer, 688-89. Paul's use of the participle ἀσθενοῦντα, in place of the adjective ἀσθενής, may add to this nuance, suggesting a faltering of faith "at a given moment and in a special case" (Godet). And, while we must be careful not simply to read 1 Cor. 8–10 into Rom. 14–15, the undeniable parallels between the sections give some weight to the fact that the word that stands in 1 Cor. 8–10 in place of "faith" is "conscience" (cf. 8:7, 10, 12; 10:25, 27, 28, 29).

44. Gk. εἰς probably denotes purpose.

disputed matters."[45] The "disputed matters" are those differences of opinion respecting the eating of meat, the observance of days, and the drinking of wine that Paul mentions later in the chapter (vv. 2, 5, 21). Paul wants the "strong" to receive the "weak" into full and intimate fellowship, something that could not happen if the "strong," the majority group, persist in advancing their views on these issues, sparking quarrels and mutual recrimination.[46]

2 Paul now cites one of the "disputed matters": "One person believes he can eat all things, while another eats vegetables."[47] In light of v. 21 ("it is good not to eat meat") "eats vegetables" must mean "eats *only* vegetables," that is, is a "vegetarian," a person who eats no meat. As we have suggested in the introduction to 14:1–15:13, the "weak in faith" probably decided to avoid meat altogether out of a concern to maintain OT laws of purity in a pagan context where "kosher" meat was not easily obtained. Other believers, however, did not share this concern to maintain purity, no doubt because they were convinced that, as New Covenant Christians, they were no longer obligated to the OT laws involved. When Paul therefore says that these Christians "believe to eat all things" (a literal translation), he is using "believe" in an unusual way. It may mean simply "have confidence,"[48] but the probable connection with the word "faith" in v. 1 (cf. also vv. 22-23) suggests that we

---

45. The two words in this phrase, διαχρίσεις and διαλογισμῶν, can each be translated in a couple of ways, opening up a wide range of possibilities for the interpretation of the phrase. But there are two main options. (1) Take διαχρίσεις to mean "passing judgment" and διαλογισμνῶν to mean "doubts" or "scruples," the genitive being objective: "passing judgment over [the weak Christian's] doubts" (cf. LSJ ["judicial decisions"]; NIV; NASB; S-H; Murray; Cranfield; Wilckens; Dunn). (2) Take διαχρίσεις to mean "quarrels" and διαλογισμῶν to mean "opinions," the genitive again being objective: "quarrels over opinions" (cf. NRSV; TEV; REB; BAGD; *GEL* 33.444; Godet; Barrett; Michel; Schlier; Fitzmyer). διάχρισις occurs only once in the LXX (Job 37:16) and twice elsewhere in the NT, where it means "distinguishing, discerning" (1 Cor. 12:10; Heb. 5:14). But the act of discernment passes easily into that of "stand in judgment over"; and the cognate verb διαχρίνομαι means "pass judgment" in Acts 10:20; 11:2; Jude 9. But the practice of "discerning" can also involve quarrels (a meaning διάχρισις has in the reading of uncial D in Acts 4:32). διαλογισμός occurs more frequently in the NT, referring (a) to the process of reasoning, or its result, "thought," "opinion" (Matt. 15:19; Mark 7:21; Luke 2:35; 5:22; 9:47; Rom. 1:21; 1 Cor. 3:20; Jas. 2:4) or (b) to "doubts," "disputes" (Luke 9:46; 24:38; Phil. 2:14; 1 Tim. 2:8 [(cf. BAGD)]. NT usage slightly favors the first alternative; but the plural form of διαχρίσεις finally tips the scales slightly in favor of the second.

46. Since it is the weak in faith who is to be received, it is almost certainly the "opinions" or "scruples" of the weak that Paul refers to (contra Käsemann).

47. "One person" translates the Greek relative pronoun ὅς, which occasionally occurs in Hellenistic Greek in such a clause in place of the article (e.g., ὁ μέν . . . ὁ δέ); cf. Turner, 36.

48. BDF 397(2); Michel; Fitzmyer.

should not eliminate all connotations of specifically Christian believing. The word probably, then, combines the connotations of "believe" and "believe that": this Christian, Paul is saying, has the kind of ("strong") Christian faith as to lead him or her to think that it is legitimate to eat anything. REB captures the sense well: "one person may have faith 'strong' enough to eat all kinds of food" (cf. also NIV; TEV).[49]

3 Paul has begun by urging the "strong" to accept the "weak" (v. 1). But he is well aware that both groups are at fault. He therefore rebukes each side in the dispute, continuing to use the generic singular as a way of particularizing his concern. "The one who eats" (that is, "the one who eats all things" [v. 2] = the "strong") is not to "despise" the one who does not (the "weak"). And the "one who does not eat" (the "weak") is not to "judge" the one who does (the "strong"). Paul's choice of verbs to describe the attitudes of each group is no doubt deliberate. "Despise" connotes a disdainful, condescending judgment,[50] an attitude that we can well imagine the "strong" majority, who prided themselves on their enlightened, "liberal," perspective, taking toward those whom they considered to be foolishly "hung up" on the trivia of a bygone era. The "weak," Paul suggests, responded in kind, considering themselves to be the "righteous remnant" who alone upheld true standards of piety and righteousness and who were "standing in judgment"[51] over those who fell beneath these standards. Paul calls on each side to stop criticizing the other.

At the end of the verse Paul states the ultimate reason why such mutual criticism is out of place: "God has received him." Here we find Paul's theological "bottom line" in this whole issue, one that he elaborates in vv. 4-9 and states again at the climax of his argument (15:7). Christians have no right to reject from their fellowship those whom God himself has accepted.

---

49. See BAGD; Schlier. πιστεύω is followed by an absolute infinitive in the NT only one other time, Acts 15:11b: πιστεύομεν σωθῆναι καθ' ὅν τρόπον κἀκεῖνοι: "we believe [that] we will saved in the same manner as they."

50. The verb is ἐξουθενέω; see Luke 18:9; 23:11; Acts 4:11; Rom. 14:10; 1 Cor. 6:4; 16:11; 2 Cor. 10:10; Gal. 4:14; 1 Thess. 5:20. It sometimes carries with it the nuance of "reject with contempt" (Acts 4:11, with reference to the Jews' treatment of Jesus; 1 Thess. 5:20, with reference to prophecies [BAGD]; note also some LXX occurrences, where God is said not to "despise" the repentant sinner [e.g., Ps. 51:17]), and this nuance may be present here also.

51. Gk. κρίνω, one of a series of words from the κρίνω stem that play a central role in chap. 14: διάκρισις (v. 1); κρίνω (v. 3b, 4a, 5a [twice], 10a, 13a, 13b, 22b); διακρίνω (v. 23a); κατακρίνω (v. 23b). The verb κρίνω, from its usual Greek meaning "decide," "make a judgment about" (see F. Büchsel, *TDNT* III, 922), takes on several specific connotations in the NT (BAGD). In Rom. 14, Paul uses it with at least three distinct meanings: "stand in judgment, condemn" (vv. 3b, 4a, 10a, 13a, 22b); "prefer, give precedence to" (v. 5a); "determine" (v. 13b).

They must "receive" those whom God has "received."[52] In 15:7, Paul uses this principle to urge both the "weak" and the "strong" to "receive one another." Here, however, he uses the principle specifically to undergird his command that the "weak" stop standing in judgment over the "strong."[53]

4 Paul elaborates this critical theological foundation of his exhortation to the "strong" and the "weak" in vv. 4-9. "God has received him"; it is God to whom each believer must answer, and God whom each believer must strive to please. This point is obviously applicable to both the "strong" and the "weak"; the "you" whom Paul directly addresses in diatribe style in v. 4a may, then, represent both "weak" and "strong" believers.[54] But the description of this person as "the one who judges" picks up the language Paul used to rebuke the "weak" believer in v. 3. Moreover, the beginning of v. 4 sounds a great deal like Paul's rebuke of the self-satisfied Jew in 2:1 — "Therefore you are without excuse, O human being, whoever you are, who is judging" (cf. also v. 3).[55] This makes it likely that Paul in v. 4a is addressing the Jewish-oriented "weak" believer, whose attitude toward Christians who do not follow the law's ritual guidelines is similar to that of many Jews toward "law-less" Gentiles.[56]

The very wording of the opening of the rhetorical question reveals the heart of Paul's concern: "Who are *you* who is judging . . . ?"; that is, "Who do you think you are, you who are putting yourself in the position of judge over another believer?" No one has the right to judge a fellow believer because each believer is a "household slave,"[57] one who belongs to "another."[58] It

---

52. In the interests of guarding against an illegitimately broad application of this principle, it is vital to stress that Paul commands us here to receive *those whom God has received.* In other words, Paul limits his plea for tolerance to those who can rightly claim a saving relationship with God through Jesus Christ, involving all those doctrinal and practical requirements that Paul and the NT elsewhere insist must be present for such a genuine saving relationship to exist.

53. The close connection (see the γάρ, "for") between the last clause of v. 3 and the command that the weak stop judging the strong requires that the αὐτόν in this last clause refer to the "strong": the weak is to stop judging the strong because God has received *him* (the strong). So most commentators, although Käsemann and Fitzmyer (see also Jewett, *Christian Tolerance,* pp. 31, 153) think that Paul might be referring to both weak and strong.

54. E.g., Käsemann.

55. The similarity is clearer in the Greek, since Paul uses the same participial form — ὁ κρίνων — as in 14:4. See esp. Meeks, "Judgment and the Brother," pp. 294-97; Dunn.

56. See, e.g., S-H; Murray; Barrett; Cranfield; Dunn.

57. Gk. οἰκέτης, used only here in Paul (cf. also Luke 16:13; Acts 10:7; 1 Pet. 2:18).

58. Gk. ἀλλότριον, a perhaps more emphatic way of expressing the point than if Paul had used ἕτερος (cf. Käsemann). It is used with οἰκέτης in Josephus, *Ant.* 18:47; Dio Chrysostom 14 (31), 34, and is a natural antonym to ἴδιος in the next clause (BAGD). A

is "with reference to"[59] that "other," "his own master [*kyrios*]," that he must "stand or fall." The slavery imagery makes clear that *kyrios* has its normal secular meaning of "master."[60] But Paul undoubtedly expects his Christian readers to see also an allusion to their ultimate Lord (see Rom. 10:9). This title, indeed, is central to the theological argument of vv. 4-9.[61] The use of "stand" and "fall" metaphorically elsewhere and the application of the terms

---

few commentators (e.g., Black) think that ἀλλότριον might mean "foreign," "alien," the reference being to the Gentile servant. But the context shows that the implied contrast is between two masters, not between two kinds of servants.

59. The dative τῷ ἰδίῳ κυρίῳ is usually classified (with many of the datives in vv. 6-8) as a dative "of advantage," yielding the sense "it is his own master whose interest is involved, who is concerned, in his standing or falling" (Cranfield; cf. also BDF 188[2]; Turner, 238; Wilckens; Schlier). But Dunn is right: the issue here is not the "benefit" derived by the Lord from the Christian's service but the integrity of the relationship between "lord" and servant. The dative is better seen, then, as a dative of reference (cf. also S-H). Less likely is a dative of instrument: "*by* his own master he stands or falls."

60. See KJV; NIV; NASB; NJB. NRSV uses "lord," but keeps it lower case to distinguish it from "Lord" later in the verse. REB and TEV, on the other hand, use "Master," implying a more direct reference to *the* Lord.

61. The referent of "lord" (κύριος) throughout this passage is not easy to determine. Paul uses the title nine times (and the verb "lord it over" [κυριεύω] once), significantly interchanging it with God (θεός) and Christ (Χριστός):

v. 3c — "*God* has received him"
v. 4 — "to his own *lord* he stands or falls"; "the *Lord* will cause him to stand"
v. 6 — "observes the day to the *Lord*"; "eats to the *Lord*"; "gives thanks to *God*"; "does not eat to the *Lord*"; "gives thanks to *God*"
v. 8 — "we live to the *Lord*"; "we die to the *Lord*"; "we belong to the *Lord*"
v. 9 — "*Christ* died and came to life, in order that he might also be *lord* over both the dead and the living"
v. 10 — "we must all appear before the judgment seat of *God*"
v. 11 — "As I live, says the *Lord*"; "every tongue will praise *God*"
v. 12 — "give account to *God*"

This interchange could suggest that "the Lord" refers to God the Father throughout. But this is difficult because the verb "lord it over" in v. 9 must have Christ as its subject; and this, in turn, suggests that "Lord" in the closely related v. 8 must also refer to Christ. The references in vv. 4c and 6 are more difficult to be certain about, but both probably also refer to Christ. "The Lord" in v. 11, on the other hand, coming in an OT quotation, probably refers to Yahweh (see the notes on these verses for further discussion). (For this general interpretation, see esp. Thüsing, *Per Christum in Deum*, pp. 34-36.) On the other hand, the ease with which Paul interchanges the titles suggests (1) that he may not have been been intending to distinguish clearly in each case his referent, and (2) the degree to which he thought of Christ, Lord, and God on equal terms (contra, e.g., Dunn, who unsuccessfully argues that Christ is in a subordinate relationship to God in the passage).

here to the relationship of slave to master suggest that they refer to approval/disapproval; we may compare the English "stand in favor with"/"fall out of favor with."[62] It is the Lord, not the fellow Christian, whom the believer must please and who will ultimately determine the acceptability of the believer and his or her conduct.

In the last clause of v. 4, the "secular" meaning of *kyrios* gives way to its theological use: the believer whose behavior is being judged "will stand,[63] for *the* Lord is able to cause him to stand." "The Lord" may here refer to Christ,[64] although this is not certain. Paul here expresses confidence that the "strong" believer will persist in the Lord's favor. Perhaps Paul's intention is to suggest to the "weak" believer that the Lord's approval is attained not by following rules pertaining to food but by the Lord's own sustaining power: "is able"[65] "points both to the possibility and the power of grace."[66]

5 Paul interrupts[67] his theological argument to cite another point on which the "weak" and the "strong" disagree: the evaluation of "days." Paul does not explicitly relate this dispute over days to the "strong" and "weak." But we may be relatively certain that the "weak" believer was the one who

---

62. See especially Paul's use of these terms in 1 Cor. 10:12 — "let anyone who thinks he stands be careful lest he fall." Note also Rom. 11, where Paul denies that Israel has "fallen" (v. 11), reminds the Gentile believers that they "stand by faith" (v. 20), and contrasts that state with "those who fall" (v. 22). In each of these contexts, "stand" (ἵστημι) means to keep one's spiritual status, while "fall" (πίπτω) means to fall away from that status (see also the use of ἵστημι in 2 Cor. 1:24; Eph. 6:11, 13, 14; Col. 4:12). Paul is not, then, referring here to moral success or failure (contra BAGD); nor is he referring directly to the verdict of the last judgment (see esp. Murray). But allusion to the judgment cannot be excluded entirely, for the believer's current "standing in God's favor" or "falling from that favor" clearly have significance for that ultimate verdict (see Calvin; Barrett; Thüsing, *Per Christum in Deum,* pp. 34-35).

63. Many commentators insist that σταθήσεται (a future passive) be given a passive meaning: "he shall be made to stand [e.g., by the Lord]" (see KJV; NRSV; NJB; Michel; Käsemann; Schlier; Cambier, "Liberté," p. 61). But ἵστημι shares with other verbs in Hellenistic Greek a tendency to use the passive with an intransitive meaning. Since a passive rendering of the verb would tend to duplicate what Paul says in the next clause, it is preferable to give the verb here such an intransitive meaning: "shall stand" (cf. NIV; NASB; TEV; REB; Zerwick, 231; Turner, 57; Leenhardt; Cranfield; Wilckens; Dunn). Nor is there any reason to think that Paul is predicting that the Christian will be made to stand after a fall (contra, e.g., Käsemann; Schlier).

64. See, e.g., Thüsing, *Per Christum in Deum,* p. 34; Murray; Dunn; W. Foerster, *TDNT* III, 1090-91; Merk, *Handeln aus Glauben,* p. 168.

65. Gk. δυνατεῖ.

66. Käsemann.

67. If, as we have suggested, the textually uncertain γάρ is kept, it will have a general continuative force (see Lietzmann; Z-G, 473; Schlier).

was "judging"[68] "one day to be more important than[69] another day," while the "strong" believer was "judging each day to be the same."[70] Pinning down the exact nature of this disagreement over "days" is difficult since Paul does not elaborate. Some expositors trace the problem to the influence of the pagan environment, which might have led some Roman Christians to distinguish "lucky" and "unlucky" days,[71] or to practice days of abstinence in accordance with certain Greco-Roman religious cults.[72] But we have seen good reason to trace the root issue between the "strong" and the "weak" to Jewish concerns about the law. And the observance of days was, of course, important in the OT and in Judaism. Whether the specific point at issue was the observance of the great Jewish festivals, regular days of fasting,[73] or the Sabbath is difficult to say. But we would expect that the Sabbath, at least, would be involved, since Sabbath observance was, along with food laws (cf. vv. 2-3), a key Jewish distinctive in the first century, and surfaced as a point of tension elsewhere in the early church (see Gal. 4:10 [?]; Col. 2:16).[74] It is typical of Paul's approach to the dispute in Rome that he does not commend, or command, one practice or the other, but exhorts each believer to be "thoroughly convinced in his own mind."[75]

6 Paul now uses this dispute about days to launch back into the theological rationale for his rebuke of judgmental attitudes. Verse 4, where

---

68. The Greek verb is κρίνω, continuing Paul's focus on this word and its cognates in chap. 14 (see n. 50). Paul has used it to refer to the weak believer's condemnatory evaluation of the strong believer (vv. 3-4); here, with the word ἡμέραν ("day") as its object, it will mean "prefer," an extension of its basic sense of "separate," "distinguish" (BAGD).

69. The Greek is ἡμέραν παρ' ἡμέραν, with παρά meaning "more than" (cf. BDF 236[3]): the weak believer "prefers [one] day more than [another] day."

70. The Gk. κρίνει πᾶσαν ἡμέραν is elliptical: "judges every day" (lit.) must mean "judges every day to be the same." Almost all commentators assume that it was the "strong" who were treating every day the same. However, De Lacey ("Sabbath/Sunday Question," p. 182) thinks that it was the "weak" who were treating every day the same, refusing to join the "strong" in their observance of festive occasions.

71. E.g., Käsemann.

72. Leenhardt. S-H and Jewett (*Christian Tolerance,* pp. 31-32) think the reference is intentionally vague, allowing application to any scrupulousness about "holy days."

73. E.g., R. Dederen, "On Esteeming One Day Better than Another," *AUSS* 9 (1971), 16-35.

74. See esp. Dunn; also Barrett; Michel; contra, e.g., Murray; Denney; Dederen, "On Esteeming," pp. 16-35. As Stuhlmacher correctly notes, inclusion of Sabbath observance among the matters of dispute in Rome demonstrates that it was not considered by Paul to be an obligation binding on Christians; this suggests, further, that the early church did not take over the Decalogue as a whole. Reference to early Christian observance of "the Lord's Day," on the other hand, is almost certainly not present (contra, e.g., Haldane).

75. Gk. πληροφορείσθω; see the note on Rom. 4:21.

Paul began this rationale, came in a context where Paul was criticizing the "weak" believers. Now, however, by citing examples of the behavior of both the "weak" and the "strong," Paul makes clear that his argument applies equally to both. The first example Paul cites could refer to both the "strong" and the "weak," if we were to give the verb *phroneō* a general or neutral meaning: "The person who *holds an opinion about* the day, *holds that opinion* to the Lord."[76] But the word probably here means "to be concerned about," "observe," in which case the reference will be to the "weak" believer.[77] Paul then returns to the issue with which he began, referring first to the "strong" believer — "the one who eats" — and then to the "weak" again — "the one who does not eat." In each of these instances, Paul notes, the believer — whether "strong" or "weak" — does what he or she does "to the Lord," that is, "in the interest of," "for the benefit of," the Lord.[78] The believer who sets aside certain days for fasting, or who observes the Sabbath, does so because he or she sincerely believes this honors the Lord. Similarly, both the believer who eats anything without discrimination and the believer who refuses to eat certain things "give thanks" to God at their mealtimes[79] and are motivated in their respective practices by a desire to glorify the Lord.

7 In v. 4 Paul compared the Christian to the slave who is dedicated "to his or her own master (or lord)." He applies this comparison to specific activities of "strong" and "weak" Christians in v. 6 — observing days "to the Lord"; eating and abstaining "to the Lord." Now, in vv. 7-9, Paul gives

76. Dunn (as possible).

77. See, e.g., Michel; Murray; Schlier; Cranfield. Godet likewise thinks the reference is to the weak Christian, but supports a weakly attested variant (only the uncial Ψ and the majority text) that adds a contrasting reference to the strong Christian.

78. The datives are almost universally — and correctly — taken as datives of "advantage" (see, e.g., Turner, 238). The interchange with θεός in this verse could suggest that κύριος refers to God the Father. But the obvious similarity between the thought expressed with the dative κυρίῳ in this verse and in v. 8 (where, because of v. 9, κύριος almost certainly refers to Christ) makes a reference to Christ more likely (cf., e.g., Meyer; Murray). Nor is the lack of article with κύριος in this verse (contrast vv. 4 and 8) a big problem for identifying the Lord as Christ. To be sure, when κύριος denotes Christ in Paul, it more often has the article (approximately 130 times). But Paul uses anarthrous κύριος to denote Christ at least 80 times; it refers to God the Father only 12 times, and all of those in OT quotations (as in v. 11). One can usually find a reason in the context for Paul to omit the article with κύριος when it refers to Christ: 21 times it comes with other anarthrous titles; 47 times it is the object of a preposition. Does the placement of the title before the verb in each case in this verse explain the lack of an article?

79. This is one of the earliest references to the Christian practice of giving thanks at mealtime (see also Acts 27:35; 1 Cor. 11:24; 1 Tim. 4:3[?]; *Did.* 10:1-6); it is, of course, an extension of the Jewish practice (see esp. Deut. 8:10; and, in the NT, Mark 8:6 and par.; 14:23; John 6:11, 23).

a general theological explanation for this comparison.[80] Christ's death and resurrection have established him as Lord over all believers; and believers must therefore recognize that all their activities are done "for the benefit of" that Lord — and not for the benefit of any other Christian who may presume to judge us or any of our actions. These verses are therefore the heart of Paul's rebuke of the Roman Christians for their judgmental attitudes (vv. 1-12).[81]

Paul begins with a negative point: "For no one of us lives to himself and no one dies to himself." Paul probably uses both "live" and "die" to make the point as comprehensive as possible: nothing at all that a Christian does is done "with reference to himself alone" or "for his own benefit." The implicit comparison is not with other human beings — as if Paul were think-ing, in the words of John Donne, "No man is an island, entire of itself; every man is a piece of the continent, a part of the main. . . ." Rather, as the context makes clear, the comparison is with the Lord. Paul develops this point in v. 8, the positive counterpart to v. 7.

8 That no Christian lives or dies "to himself" is clear[82] from the truth, which Christians confess, that "if we live, we live to the Lord, and if we die, we die to the Lord." We can easily understand how Christians "live to the Lord": all parts of believers' lives — their thoughts, actions, ambitions, decisions — are to be carried out with a view to what pleases and glorifies the Lord. But what does it mean to "die to the Lord"? A few interpreters think that Paul might be using "die" in a spiritual sense, as in Rom. 6:3-6.[83] But nothing in the context would suggest such a nuance. Paul must be referring to physical death. In this regard, he probably has in mind the fact that the circumstances of the believer's death, as of his life, are determined not by his will or in consideration of his own interests, but are wholly in the hands of the Lord, who sets the time for death in accordance with his own interests and purposes.[84] The last sentence of the verse summarizes: "Therefore whether we live or whether we die, we are the Lord's." The change in grammatical construction (from "to the Lord" to "of the Lord"[85]) broadens the idea: not only does the believer live and die "in the Lord's interests"; in

---

80. The γάρ at the beginning of v. 7 therefore introduces the entire argument in vv. 7-9 as the basis for Paul's assertions in v. 6 that both "strong" and "weak" do what they do "to the Lord."

81. See, e.g., Michel; Käsemann. The parallels between these verses and other NT texts, as well as the formulaic wording of, e.g., v. 9a, suggest that Paul is here paraphrasing a widespread early Christian tradition (see, e.g., Schmithals; Schlier; Käsemann).

82. Verse 8 explains why (note the γάρ) the believer does not live or die "to himself" (v. 7).

83. Viard; cf. also Chrysostom, although he is not clear on the matter.

84. See Murray.

85. A shift in Greek from the dative (τῷ κυρίῳ) to the genitive (τοῦ κυρίου).

both life and death he or she also belongs to the Lord. The union with the Lord Christ,[86] with all its benefits, that the believer enjoys in this life will continue after death with, indeed, an even fuller measure of blessing (cf. 8:18, 31-39).

9 Paul's theological reasoning continues: whether we live or die, we "belong to the Lord," because it was this for very reason[87] that Christ died and "came to life,"[88] namely, to "become lord"[89] of both the dead and the living. Paul is reminding the Roman Christians of a well-known truth; see 2 Cor. 5:15: "And he died on behalf of all, in order that those who live might live no longer to themselves[90] but to the one who died[91] on their behalf and was raised." Here also Christ's death and resurrection stimulate Christians to live "for the Lord" rather than "for themselves." But Paul tailors the tradition for its particular function at this point in Romans. For one thing, he departs from the more customary "Christ died and was raised" (cf. 1 Thess. 4:14; 1 Cor. 15:3-4; Rom. 8:34[92]) to use a formula unique in the NT: "Christ died and came to life." Presumably Paul does this in order to forge the closest possible link between Christ's redemptive acts — his death and "coming to life" — and the two most basic parts of Christian experience — life and death.[93] The same purpose explains the unusual word order "the dead and the living" at the end of the verse: Paul simply maintains the order that he used in depicting Christ's work on behalf of Christians (v. 9a).[94] This is not to say, however, that Paul intends Christ's death to have particular relationship to his

86. κύριος in this verse almost certainly refers to Christ, considering the close relationship between this verse and v. 9, where Christ's death and resurrection are explicitly mentioned (cf., e.g., S-H; Murray; Cranfield; Dunn).

87. The antecedent of τοῦτο in the phrase εἰς τοῦτο is the ἵνα clause that follows. The inclusion of this phrase lends emphasis to this idea (see the paraphrase above; cf. Dunn).

88. The aorist ἔζησεν is ingressive; see similar uses of this same form in Luke 15:31; Rev. 20:4, 5.

89. κυριεύω means simply "be lord" (BAGD; cf. Luke 22:25; Rom. 6:9, 14; 7:1; 2 Cor. 1:24; 1 Tim. 6:15), but the aorist κυριεύσῃ is almost certainly ingressive (e.g., Cranfield).

90. Gk. ἑαυτοῖς.

91. Gk. τῷ . . . ἀποθανόντι.

92. The first uses a form of ἀνίστημι; the second two a form of ἐγείρω. The presence of Χριστός in Rom. 8:34 may help explain why Paul uses that title here (in departure from κύριος, used throughout the passage); cf. Dunn.

93. Gifford; Murray; Dunn.

94. The phrase "the living and the dead" occurs three times in the NT: Acts 10:42; 2 Tim. 4:1; 1 Pet. 4:5 (cf. also Matt. 22:32//Mark 12:27//Luke 20:38); the phrase "the dead and the living" only here. A few think that this order may suggest that "dead" has a spiritual meaning — Christ as Lord of both those who have died [to sin] and now live (cf. Rom. 6:2-12) (cf. Leenhardt) — or that Paul intends a chiasm with v. 8 (Lagrange). But an imitation of the word order at the beginning of v. 9, with perhaps an intended emphasis on "dead" — Christ is Lord even of the dead, as well as the living (cf. Dunn) — is more likely (cf., e.g., S-H; Morris).

lordship over the dead and his "coming to life" over the living.[95] It is Christ's death and resurrection *together* that establish his lordship over all people, including especially here Christians, whether they are living or dead.[96] In teaching that Christ's redemptive work *established* his lordship, Paul is not of course denying that Christ has eternally exercised lordship. But, as usual, Paul's focus is on that unique exercise of "kingdom" power and rule that were established only through Christ's death and resurrection and the appropriation of the benefits of those acts by individual persons in faith.[97]

10 With the emphatic return to the second person singular diatribe style — *"you"*[98] — Paul signals his return to exhortation after the theological rationale of vv. 7-9. He first rebukes the representative "weak" Christian in the same terms he used in v. 4a (and cf. also v. 3b): "Who are you who is judging[99] your brother?"[100] He then adds, for the first time, a direct rebuke of the "strong" Christian, again duplicating the language he used to describe the "strong" Christian's attitude in v. 3: "Or you also, why are you despising[101] your brother?" Paul's direct and lively style creates the picture of the apostle shifting his gaze from the "weak" to the "strong" as he publicly chastises these representative Christians from the Roman community.[102] Each, Paul suggests by using the term "brother" (which becomes central to the argument of vv. 13-23), is guilty of casting doubt on the status of a fellow member of the spiritual family. No believer has such a right. For, in an extension of the central theological argument of vv. 7-9, Paul reminds the Roman Christians that "we all must appear[103] before the judgment seat[104] of God." Paul may be warning the believers that they stand in danger of suffering

95. Contra Bengel; Bruce; Moule, *Idiom Book,* p. 195 (tentatively). Cf. Kramer, *Christ, Lord, Son of God,* p. 193.

96. See, e.g., Althaus; Barrett; Cranfield.

97. Murray calls this the "lordship of redemptive relationship" and refers to Acts 2:36; Rom. 8:34; and Phil. 2:9-11.

98. Gk. σύ.

99. Gk. κρίνεις.

100. It is possible, though not certain, that Paul alludes here to Jesus' rebuke: "Judge not, and you will not be judged" (Luke 6:37); cf. Allison, "The Pauline Epistles," pp. 11-12; Davies, 138.

101. Gk. ἐξουθενεῖς.

102. So most commentators (cf., e.g., Bengel; Godet; S-H; and see R. L. Omanson, "The 'Weak' and the 'Strong' and Paul's Letter to the Roman Christians," *BT* 33 [1982], 113).

103. The Greek verb is παρίστημι, which can denote standing in court before a judge (cf. MM; BAGD; Acts 27:24).

104. Gk. βῆμα; it denotes a secular scene of judgment in Matt. 27:19; John 19:13; Acts 7:5; 12:21; 18:12, 16, 17; 25:6, 10, 17. Paul is the only NT author to appropriate the term for theological purposes; cf. also 2 Cor. 5:10.

God's judgment for their sinful criticism of one another. But, in light of vv. 7-9, we think it more likely that he is reminding them that it is God, and not other Christians, to whom each believer is answerable. In "judging" and "despising" others, therefore, they are arrogating to themselves a prerogative that is God's only. He will pronounce his judgment over every believer's status and actions on that day when "each will receive good or evil according to the things that he or she has done in the body" (2 Cor. 5:10).[105]

11 In confirmation that God, and God alone, will judge all people and their actions on the last day, Paul cites Isa. 45:23: "As I live, says the Lord, to me every knee will bow and every tongue will praise[106] God." The appropriateness of the application of this text to the matter discussed in 14:1-12 is enhanced when we note that it is surrounded by statements of the Lord's unique sovereignty: "I am God, and there is no other" (v. 22b); "Only in the Lord, it shall be said of me, are righteousness and strength" (v. 24a). Paul introduces the quotation with his usual formula, "it is written," and reproduces the LXX fairly closely.[107] However, there is an exception: the opening words of Paul's quotation, "As I live, says the Lord," do not occur in Isa. 45:23. These words are, however, found in a number of OT texts, including Isa. 49:18.[108] Why does Paul add them here? Some interpreters think that this is Paul's way of identifying the "Lord" *(kyrios)* in the OT quotation with Christ.[109] Paul uses *kyrios* with reference to Christ throughout vv. 4-9, and, in his other allusion to Isa. 45:23 (in Phil. 2:11), he relates the confession of

---

105. Some MSS assimilate this verse to 2 Cor. 5:10 — which speaks of the "judgment seat of Christ" — by reading Χριστοῦ in place of θεοῦ. The shift of terminology does not imply that Paul conceives of two separate "judgment seats" but that he views God and Christ as so closely related that he can shift almost unconsciously from one to the other — a noted feature of these verses (cf Thüsing, *Per Christum in Deum,* pp. 35-36).

106. The Greek word here is ἐξομολογέω, which usually means "confess," a meaning some commentators want to give the word here (e.g., Fitzmyer; and cf. Phil. 2:11, where it seems to have this meaning also). But the word is used in the LXX, with a dative following, to mean "praise" (cf. 2 Sam. 22:50; 1 Chron. 29:13; Ps. 85:12; 117:28, etc.; cf. S-H; Käsemann; Dunn).

107. The text printed in Rahlfs (based on MSS A, Q, and the corrector of S [א]) differs from Paul's wording only in transposing πᾶσα γλῶσσα and ἐξομολογήσεται. But very good MSS (B and the original hand of S) read in place of ἐξομολογήσεται, ὀμεῖται, "swear," a reading closer to the literal meaning of the Hebrew (תִּשָּׁבַע, "swear [an oath of allegiance]"; cf. BDB). M. Black surmises that the reading of A, Q, and the corrector of S is a later variant that might have arisen from reading שׁבע as שׁבח, "praise" ("The Christological Use of the Old Testament in the New Testament," *NTS* 18 [1971-72], 8).

108. Most scholars think that Paul alludes directly to Isa. 49:18; but the phrase occurs 22 times in the LXX, and Paul may not have any particular text in mind (Stanley, *Paul and the Language of Scripture,* pp. 176-77).

109. E.g., Hodge; Black (cf. also his "Christological Use," 8).

"every tongue" to the fact that "Jesus Christ is Lord."[110] And there is precedent within Romans itself for the identification of *kyrios* in the OT with Christ (see 10:13). Yet Paul does not usually identify the *kyrios* of his OT quotations with Christ; and his focus within this paragraph seems to have shifted from Christ to God the Father.[111] Probably, then, we should not read an implicit christological identification into the reference to *kyrios* in the quotation. Paul may introduce these words inadvertently because of a slip in memory;[112] or he may have deliberately added them to accentuate the words that follow.[113]

12 Paul summarizes vv. 10c-11: "Therefore each of us will give account[114] of himself to God." "*Each* of us" carries on the universalistic emphasis of the previous verses: "we must *all* appear before the judgment seat of God" (v. 10c); "*every* knee will bow"; "*every* tongue will confess" (v. 11). But, as the first person plural ("we") of v. 10c and the "us" here indicate, Paul is especially concerned to remind Christians that they will be among those who must "give an account" of their behavior before the sovereign and all-knowing judge of history. This reminder, with which Paul concludes this part of his exhortation, is two-pronged. On the one hand, as Paul has emphasized earlier (vv. 4, 10), it shows why it is wrong for a Christian to stand in judgment over another: "Do not judge your brother, for God will judge him." But the fact of judgment to come also reminds believers that they will have to answer before the Lord for their own behavior: "Do not judge your brother (and so sin), for God will judge *you*."[115]

2. Do Not Cause Your Brother to Stumble! (14:13-23)

> 13*Therefore, let us no longer be judging one another. But judge this rather: not to place a stumbling block or hindrance before your brother.* 14*I know and am persuaded in the Lord Jesus that nothing is unclean in itself. But to the one who reckons it to be unclean, to that person it is unclean.* 15*For if through food your brother is caused pain, you are no longer walking in love. Do not because of food destroy one for whom Christ died.* 16*Therefore let not your good be blasphemed.*

110. See, e.g., Wilckens; Stuhlmacher.

111. Note the references at the end of vv. 10 (τοῦ θεοῦ), 11 (τῷ θεῷ), and 12 (τῷ θεῷ [?]). See esp. Dunn; and also, e.g., Cranfield.

112. Cranfield; Gifford.

113. Stuhlmacher.

114. Gk. λόγον, which takes on here the commercial sense of "account," "settlement" (BAGD; cf. also Matt. 12:36; Luke 16:2; Acts 19:40; Phil. 4:17 [probably]; Heb. 13:17; 1 Pet. 3:15; 4:5).

115. See Godet.

17*For the kingdom of God is not eating and drinking but righteousness and peace and joy in the Holy Spirit.* 18*For the one who serves
Christ in this is pleasing to God and esteemed by people.*

19*Therefore, let us pursue*[1] *those things that make for peace and the
edification of one another.* 20*Do not, on account of food, tear down the
work of God. All things are indeed clean, but it is wrong for a person
to eat while causing another to stumble.* 21*It is good not to eat meat
or to drink wine or to do anything else in which your brother might
be caused to stumble.*[2] 22*The faith that*[3] *you have, keep to yourself
before God. Blessed is the one who does not judge himself in what he
approves.* 23*But the one who doubts when he eats is condemned, for it
is not out of faith. And everything that is not out of faith is sin.*[4]

Although Paul begins vv. 1-12 with a plea to the "strong" and quickly moves
on to address both the "strong" and the "weak" (v. 3; cf. also v. 10), his
focus is on the "weak" (vv. 3b-4; and the argument of vv. 7-9, while relevant
to both groups, is especially applicable to the "weak"). Paul balances this
focus by concentrating in vv. 13-23 almost exclusively on the "strong." On

1. Deciding between the indicative διώκομεν and the subjunctive διώκωμεν is
difficult. The former has the stronger external support (the two best uncials of Paul's letters,
the primary Alexandrian witnesses ℵ and B, in addition to the secondary Alexandrian uncial
A, the western uncials F and G, and several other MSS) and is arguably the more difficult
reading (see, e.g., S-H, 392; Michel, 436; Käsemann, 378; Dunn, 2.816; Stuhlmacher, 226).
But the subjunctive, read by the secondary Alexandrian MSS C, 33, 81, and 1739, Ψ, the
western D, and the majority text, is by far the better reading in the context and should
probably be preferred (with most modern English translations and most commentators
[e.g., Godet, 462; Meyer, 2.296; Schlier, 416; Cranfield, 2.720-21; Wilckens, 3.94; cf. also
Metzger, 532]).
2. To the single word προσκόπτει (found in the first [Byzantine] corrector of ℵ,
the secondary Alexandrians A, C, 81, and 1739, and a few other MSS), a significant number
of MSS add ἢ σκανδαλίζεται καὶ ἀσθενεῖ (the Alexandrian MSS B 33[vid], P[46vid], the
western uncials D, F, and G, Ψ, and the majority text [including the second corrector of
ℵ]; one MS, the original hand of ℵ, reads λυπεῖται alone). A few commentators support
the longer reading (e.g., Meyer, 2.296; Godet, 463), but it is almost certainly a secondary
expansion (cf. Cranfield, 2.725).
3. Several manuscripts, including the western uncials D, (F), and G, the secondary
Alexandrian MSS 81 and 1739, Ψ, and the majority text, omit the relative pronoun here;
and several commentators think this was the original text (Meyer, 2.296; Godet, 463). This
might be the more difficult reading, but the strong external support for the inclusion of ἥν
renders this latter reading the more likely (cf. S-H, 393; Michel, 438; Käsemann, 378;
Cranfield, 2.726; Metzger, 533).
4. Some MSS add here the doxology, 16:25-27, which is placed at different points
in the MS tradition of chaps. 15–16. For this variant and other related ones, see the
introduction.

the negative side, Paul exhorts the "strong" not to use their liberty in such a way that they would cause their weaker brothers to suffer spiritual harm (e.g., "stumble"; cf. vv. 13b, 20b-21; cf. also vv. 15a, 15c, and 20a). Positively, Paul urges the "strong" to recognize that their freedom on these matters ("their good" in v. 16) must be governed by love for their fellow believers (v. 15) and concern for the "building up" of the body of Christ (v. 19). Structurally, Paul's exhortation to the "strong" takes a form that resembles the one he has used in vv. 1-12. Again his basic exhortation is found at the beginning and at the end of the text — "don't cause a weaker Christian to stumble" (vv. 13b-16 and vv. 19-23) — while a central section sets forth the basic theological rationale for his exhortation — the nature of the kingdom of God (vv. 17-18).[5] Further, the basic points Paul makes in the two exhortation sections are in chiastic order:

A Warning about stumbling blocks (*proskomma*) — v. 13b
B Nothing is "unclean" (*koinos*) in itself — v. 14a
C Do not "destroy" one for whom Christ died — v. 15b

C' Do not tear down "the work of God" — v. 20a
B' All things are "clean" (*katharos*) — v. 20b
A' Don't do anything to cause the fellow believer to stumble — v. 21[6]

13 "Let us no longer be judging one another" is transitional.[7] The exhortation sums up vv. 1-12 while preparing for the new focus in vv. 13-23. Both the "strong" Christian and the "weak" Christian, Paul has made clear, are to stop standing in judgment over one another; for God has accepted each one, and it is to their master, the Lord who has redeemed them, and not to any fellow servant, that they are answerable. In the second half of the verse,

---

5. An alternative arrangement, advocated by many commentators (e.g., Wilckens, 3.90; Stuhlmacher, 226), is to divide the paragraph into two basic sections, vv. 13-18 and 19-23. Suggesting this arrangement is the similarity between v. 13a and v. 19 — both using a hortatory subjunctive (κρίνωμεν; διώκωμεν) and ἀλλήλους — the strong resumptive ἄρα οὖν in v. 19, and the similarity in content between the sections. My suggestion is similar to, but not identical with, Dunn's (2.816), who also sees a threefold structure, vv. 13-15, 16-18, and 19-21, with vv. 22-23 a sort of appendix.

6. Similar ideas about chiastic structure are suggested by Dunn, 2.816; Schmithals, 495; Thompson, *Clothed with Christ,* pp. 200-207.

7. Cf., e.g., Käsemann. Thompson (*Clothed with Christ,* pp. 163-73) thinks that Paul may allude to Jesus' prohibition of judging (Matt. 7:1//Luke 6:37a) since absolute prohibitions of judging are not found in Greek literature nor (at least clearly) in Jewish literature. See also Davies, 138.

however, Paul turns to the "strong" in faith, using a play on the word *krinō* to forge his transition. In the first part of the verse, this verb means "condemn"; in the second half, however, it means "determine," "decide."[8] Rather than "judging" (condemning) others, the "strong" in faith are to "judge" (decide)[9] "not to place a stumbling block or cause of offense before their fellow believer." "Stumbling block" translates a word that refers to that which causes a person to trip or stumble. The word took on a metaphorical sense and is always used in the NT with reference to spiritual downfall.[10] Similar is the origin and use of *skandalon,* "cause of offense." It, too, originally denoted a literal "trap," but it came quickly to have a metaphorical meaning, "occasion of misfortune," "cause of ruin."[11] The words are essentially synonymous here.[12] Paul neither here nor anywhere in this paragraph delineates the exact manner in which the "strong" believer might cause "spiritual downfall" to the "weak" believer. But Paul's concern to remind the "strong"

8. See BAGD.

9. The shift from first person plural to second person plural and from the present tense to the aorist tense (κρίνωμεν/κρίνατε) lends urgency to this second verb; cf. NRSV: "resolve instead never to put a stumbling block or hindrance in the way of another" (cf., e.g., Barrett; Lenski, on the other hand, again overinterprets the aorist, claiming that "one act, final and permanent," is indicated).

10. The original literal sense of the verb προσκόπτω (from which πρόσκομμα is derived), "fall, fall over something," can be seen in Matt. 7:27: "the rain came down and the floods came and the winds blew and that house *fell.*" The -μα ending on πρόσκομμα would normally indicate that it denotes the result of the action of falling or tripping. But, like many such nouns in Hellenistic Greek, it can also refer to the activity of falling or stumbling or even, as here, the cause of that stumbling (cf. G. Stählin, *TDNT* VI, 745-47; BAGD). The word occurs 11 times in the LXX, usually with metaphorical significance. Three of the five occurrences of the word in the NT come in the context of the words λίθον προσκόμματος καὶ πέτραν σκανδάλου from Isa. 8:14 (cf. Rom. 9:32, 33; 1 Pet. 2:8); the other comes in a passage (1 Cor. 8:9) that offers many conceptual parallels to Rom. 14–15.

11. The Greek word is σκάνδαλον (from the verb σκανδαλίζω). Its metaphorical significance is especially due to its use in the LXX (21 occurrences) to translate מוֹקֵשׁ and מִכְשׁוֹל (G. Stählin, *TDNT* VII, 340-41). Str-B (3.110-12) suggest that Lev. 19:14 was a seminal verse for the metaphorical significance of the word. It refers to the cause of spiritual downfall in all its NT occurrences: Matt. 13:41; 16:23; 18:7 (three times); Luke 17:1; Rom. 9:33; 11:9; 16:17; 1 Cor. 1:23; Gal. 5:11; 1 Pet. 2:8; 1 John 2:10; Rev. 2:14. Jesus' warnings about giving "causes of offense" (σκάνδαλα) to others (Matt. 18:7; Luke 17:1-2; cf. σκανδαλίζω in Mark 9:42) may have influenced Paul's warning here (cf. Allison, "The Pauline Epistles," pp. 14-15; Dunn, "Paul's Knowledge," p. 203; S-H; Dodd; Cranfield). Thompson (*Clothed with Christ,* pp. 174-84), however, is more cautious, noting that Paul's phrasing could well derive from the OT and Jewish tradition.

12. The two words overlap considerably in the LXX (see G. Stählin, *TDNT* VII, 341); note also the parallelism between the two suggested by their use together in Isa. 8:14. See especially the careful linguistic analysis in Müller, *Anstoss und Gericht,* pp. 32-35; also, e.g., Murray; Michel; Schlier; Wilckens; contra, e.g., Godet; Lenski.

believers that food, while in theory "clean," might be "unclean" to the "weak" believer (v. 14), coupled with his concluding assertion that a person who acts against "what he believes" commits sin, suggests that he is thinking of the possibility that the "strong" believers' exercise of liberty might create pressure on the "weak" believers to do what their consciences were telling them not to do and so fall into sin and potential spiritual ruin.[13]

14 In this verse Paul lays the groundwork for the suggestion, implicit in his exhortation of v. 13b, that the behavior of the "strong" could bring spiritual harm to the "weak." Paul begins by stating a fundamental principle — one to which the "strong" would no doubt give an enthusiastic "Amen!": "I know and am persuaded in the Lord Jesus that nothing is unclean in itself." "Unclean" translates a word that means "common." But Jews began using the word to denote those things that, by virtue of what they considered inappropriate contact with the ordinary, secular, world, were ritually defiled or unclean.[14] Paul clearly uses the word here in this sense, as the antonym "clean" *(katharos)* in the parallel v. 20 makes clear. This connotation of the word "common" or "unclean" also makes clear that Paul is not here claiming that there is nothing at all that is absolutely evil or sinful. His statement must be confined to the point at issue: ritual defilement as defined by OT/Jewish law.[15]

It is not clear what role "the Lord Jesus" has in this emphatic declaration of Paul's. Three possibilities deserve consideration: (1) "I know *through my fellowship with the Lord Jesus* that nothing is unclean"[16]; (2) "I know *through my understanding of the truth revealed in the Lord Jesus* that nothing is unclean"[17]; (3) "I know *through the teaching of the Lord Jesus on earth* that nothing is unclean."[18] Good evidence can be marshaled for this

---

13. See esp. J. Murray, "The Weak and the Strong," *WTJ* 12 (1949-50), 144-49. Some commentators (e.g., Godet) think that the early Christian "love feast," the sharing together in a meal at the time of the Lord's Supper, might be the occasion on which such difficulties would arise.

14. Note especially the parallelism between κοινός and ἀκάθαρτος in Mark 7:2, 5 and Acts 10:14; see also Acts 10:15, 28; 11:8, 9; Heb. 10:29 (the adjective is used in a different, nontechnical sense in Acts 2:44; 4:32; Tit. 1:4; Jude 3; Rev. 21:27). The cognate verb κοινόω has this meaning in all its NT occurrences: Matt. 15:11, 18, 20; Mark 7:15, 18, 20, 23; Acts 10:15; 11:9; 21:28; Heb. 9:13. κοινός is not used in this way in the earlier parts of the LXX; but see, e.g., 1 Macc. 1:47, 62; and Josephus, *Ant.* 12.112; 13.4.

15. See, e.g., Cranfield; Dunn.

16. See the NIV: "As one who is in the Lord Jesus, I am fully convinced that no food is unclean in itself." Note also S-H; Dodd; Murray; Morris; Fitzmyer.

17. Note the REB: "All that I know of the Lord Jesus convinces me that nothing is impure in itself." See, generally, Godet (Christ's redemptive work as the basis for liberty). Wilckens and Käsemann refer to the authority of Jesus as passed on in the early community.

18. Dunn, "Paul's Knowledge," p. 203; Thompson, *Clothed with Christ,* pp. 185-99; Michel; Cranfield (?).

last interpretation. Jesus' teaching about true defilement was so important that Mark (writing in Rome at about this time?) added his own editorial comment to make the point clear to his readers: "And so he declared all foods clean" (Mark 7:19b). Paul's "in the Lord Jesus" rather than his usual "in Christ [Jesus]" might also point to the historical Jesus. And a reference to this teaching of Christ's would fit with Paul's propensity to allude to the teaching of Jesus in this part of Romans. In the last analysis, however, this interpretation reads quite a bit into the phrase "in the Lord Jesus." Perhaps, then, view 1 or 2, or a combination of them, is preferable.

The "strong" in faith would certainly agree with this declaration of liberty; indeed, their position may well be the result of their acquaintance, directly or indirectly, with Paul's own bold stance on these matters.[19] But, as he does in the very similar Corinthian situation (see 1 Cor. 8:4-7), Paul quickly adds a complementary and qualifying truth: "But[20] to the one who reckons something to be unclean, to that person it is unclean." What Paul wants the "strong" to realize is that people differ in their ability to internalize truth. The fact that Christ's coming brought an end to the absolute validity of the Mosaic law (cf. 6:14, 15; 7:4), and thus explicitly to the ritual provisions of that law, was standard early Christian teaching. And, at the intellectual level, the "weak" Christians may themselves have understood this truth. But Paul wants the "strong" in faith to recognize that people cannot always "existentially" grasp such truth — particularly when it runs so counter to a long and strongly held tradition basic to their own identity as God's people.

15 Verse 14, supplying the theoretical basis for Paul's use of the language of spiritual downfall in v. 13, is somewhat parenthetical. Verse 15, accordingly, probably relates especially to v. 13:[21] Don't put a stumbling block in the way of a brother (v. 13b), . . . "for"[22] this is just what you are doing — by insisting on exercising your freedom to eat food, you bring pain to your

---

19. Paul's greeting of Prisca and Aquila in Rom. 16:3 shows that there were at least some "Pauline" Christians in the Roman community. Remember also that Paul worked with this couple in Corinth, where there is reason to think that the Christians had taken to an extreme some of Paul's slogans about Christian freedom (see particularly in this regard 1 Cor. 6:12; 8:1-3; 10:22).

20. The Gk. εἰ μή probably means "but" (e.g., BDF 448[8]; Zerwick, 470; Michel; Käsemann; Cranfield; Dunn) rather than "except" (Gifford; Wilckens; O. E. Evans, "Paul's Certainties. III. What God Requires of Man — Romans xiv.14," *ExpTim* 69 [1957-58], 201-2).

21. Michel; Käsemann; Schlier; Cranfield. Murray, on other hand, connects it with vv. 13-14, while S-H connect it with a suppressed thought: "You must have respect therefore for his scruples, although you may not share them, for. . . ."

22. The γάρ does not give the basis for v. 13, but explains it.

fellow believer and thereby violate the cardinal Christian virtue of love. The "pain" that the "strong" believer causes the "weak" believer is more than the annoyance or irritation that the "weak" believer might feel toward those who act in ways they do not approve.[23] Its relationship to the warnings about spiritual downfall in vv. 13b and 15b show that it must denote the pain caused the "weak" believer by the violation of his or her conscience.[24] The eating of the "strong," coupled with their attitude of superiority and scorn toward those who think differently, can pressure the "weak" into eating even when they do not yet have the faith to believe that it is right for them to do so. And by doing what does not come "out of faith," the "weak" sin (v. 23) and suffer the pain of that knowledge. In behaving as they are, then, the "strong" are ignoring what Paul has set forth in 12:9-21; 13:8-10 as basic to Christian conduct: love for "the neighbor."

Paul sharpens his point by issuing a direct command: "Do not because of food[25] destroy[26] one for whom Christ died." This command raises the stakes in two ways. First, instead of speaking generally about the "spiritual harm" (v. 13b) and "pain" (v. 15a) that the "strong" might cause the "weak," Paul stresses that their actions can "destroy" them. "Destroy" might refer to the spiritual grief and self-condemnation that the "weak" incur by following the practices of the "strong" against their consciences.[27] But Pauline usage suggests rather that Paul is warning the "strong" that their behavior has the potential to bring the "weak" to ultimate spiritual ruin — failure to attain final salvation.[28] If Paul is not simply exaggerating for effect, perhaps he thinks

23. Contra, e.g., BAGD; Godet.

24. Cf. Murray, "The Strong and the Weak," pp. 147-48; S-H; Cranfield; Dunn. Barrett thinks that both the sin of violating the conscience and annoyance are involved. Somewhat similar to the use here are those occurrences of the same verb in 2 Corinthians to denote the "pain" caused the Corinthians by his letter to them (cf. 2:2, 4, 5; 6:10; 7:8, 9, 11); Paul also uses the verb in Eph. 4:30; 1 Thess. 4:13.

25. The dative $\tau\tilde{\omega}$ βρώματι might be causal (cf. διὰ βρῶμα earlier in the verse; Turner, 242) or instrumental (Moule, *Idiom Book,* p. 44).

26. Paul may use the present tense ἀπόλλυε because he envisages the destruction as already underway (and the strong are to stop doing it) or, perhaps more likely, because he conceives of the spiritual destruction as a process.

27. See esp. Volf, *Paul and Perseverance,* pp. 85-97.

28. Every time Paul uses the verb ἀπόλλυμι with a personal object, it refers to spiritual ruin (with three possible exceptions): Rom. 2:12; 1 Cor. 1:18; 8:11; 15:18; 2 Cor. 2:15; 4:3; 2 Thess. 2:10; the possible exceptions are 1 Cor. 10:9, 10; 2 Cor. 4:9. See also the use of the cognate noun (e.g., Phil. 1:28: 3:19). He uses the verb with an impersonal object only in 1 Cor. 1:19. See, e.g., Michel; Cranfield; Dunn. Two theological nonimplications of taking ἀπόλλυμι to refer to ultimate spiritual destruction should be noted. First, the word is applied to the spiritual realm as a metaphor: it does not suggest the annihilation of the person. Second, Rom. 14:15 does not refute the doctrine of the perseverance of the saints because (1) Paul does not make clear that the person who might be destroyed is

that the "weak" in faith might be led by the scorn of the "strong" to turn away entirely from their faith.

Second, Paul accentuates the matter by reminding the "strong" in faith about the tremendous sacrifice that Christ had already made to provide for the salvation of that "weak" believer. If, Paul implies, Christ has already paid the supreme price for that "weak" Christian, how can the "strong" refuse to pay the quite insignificant price of a minor and occasional restriction in their diet?

16 This verse, returning to the second person plural address of v. 13b (after the second person singular in v. 15), rounds off the opening paragraph in this section.[29] The prohibition in the verse is a conclusion[30] that Paul draws from what he has just said in vv. 14-15. Freedom from the dietary laws is a "good" thing, a legitimate implication of the coming of Jesus the Messiah and the New Covenant. But if the Christian were to use that freedom in such a way that a fellow believer was put in spiritual danger, that "good" would quickly become something that would be "blasphemed" — that is, it would become the cause of other people reviling and defaming that which is a divine gift.[31] I am therefore assuming that "the good thing" refers to the freedom enjoyed by the "strong"[32] rather than, more generally, to Christian teaching, or the kingdom of God, or faith.[33] I think the possessive pronoun, "your," points in this direction since it most naturally refers to the "strong" (cf. v. 15). On this view, it is more likely that those who are "blaspheming" the good are the "weak"[34] rather than non-

---

genuinely regenerate (although this conclusion must be drawn by those who adhere to limited atonement since the person is one "on whose behalf Christ died") since the NT can use ἀδελφός of one who appears to be a believer; and (2) Paul does not say that the destruction will actually take place — he warns that this would be the ultimate consequence if the sin goes unchecked (cf. Murray, 2.191-92; Dunn, 2.820). As Hodge (424) puts it: "Believers (the elect) are constantly spoken of as in danger of perdition. They are saved only, if they continue steadfast unto the end. If they apostasize, they perish. . . . Saints are preserved, not in despite of apostasy, but from apostasy."

29. Contra, e.g., Dunn, who thinks the verse opens a new paragraph.

30. Cf. Gk. οὖν, "therefore."

31. The Greek verb βλασφημέω refers basically to the reviling or despising of the "gods" (cf. Acts 19:37); hence it is regularly used in the NT with respect to God, his name, the Spirit, and Christ (Matt. 9:3; 26:65; 27:39; Mark 2:7; 3:28, 29; 15:29; Luke 12:10; 22:65; 23:39; John 10:36; Acts 26:11; Rom. 2:24; 1 Tim. 1:20; 6:1; Jas. 2:7; 1 Pet. 4:4; Rev. 13:6; 16:9, 11, 21). By derivation, it can then also refer to "things which constitute the significant possession of Christians" (BAGD); cf. Tit. 2:5; 2 Pet. 2:2. Perhaps the most significant parallel, however, is 1 Cor. 10:30, where Paul argues that "strong" believers should not be "blasphemed" if they exercise their freedom properly.

32. With, e.g., Calvin; Godet; S-H; Michel; Murray; Käsemann; Wilckens; Fitzmyer.

33. See, e.g., Cranfield; Schlier; Dunn.

34. Cf. S-H; Michel; Wilckens.

Christians.[35] Paul is warning the "strong" Christians that their insistence on exercising their freedom in ceremonial matters in the name of Christ can lead those who are spiritually harmed by their behavior to revile the legitimate freedom that Christ has won for them.

17 In verses 17-18, Paul provides the theological underpinnings for his imperatives in vv. 13-16 and 20-23.[36] The "strong" need perspective; and this is just what Paul tries to give them here. For the "strong" are placing too high a value on Christian freedom from ceremonial observances. By insisting that they exercise their liberty in these matters, they are causing spiritual harm to fellow believers and are thereby failing to maintain a proper focus on what is truly important in the kingdom of God. Theirs, paradoxically, is the same fault as that of the Pharisees, only in reverse: where the Pharisees insisted on strict adherence to the ritual law at the expense of "justice, mercy, and faith" (Matt. 23:23), the "strong" are insisting on exercising their freedom from the ritual law at the expense of "righteousness and peace and joy in the Holy Spirit." For these are the qualities, Paul reminds the "strong," that are what the kingdom of God is all about — not "eating[37] and drinking." At the same time, of course, while not explicitly directed to them, this theology would be important for the "weak" also to hear — and act upon.

This is the first time in the passage that Paul has said anything about "drinking." He may add the word here simply because it is a natural complement to "eating."[38] But it is also possible, in light of the reference in v. 21, that drinking wine was another issue that separated the "strong" and the "weak." We would therefore assume that it was the "weak" who abstained from drinking wine, while the "strong" insisted on using their liberty to do so. But it is important to note that, supposing this to be the case, the "weak" would have abstained not because they were afraid of the intoxicating or enslaving potential of alcohol, but because they were afraid that the wine had been contaminated by association with pagan religious practices.[39]

35. Cranfield, Dunn, and Stuhlmacher all think Paul might refer to non-Christians.

36. See, e.g., Cambier, "La liberté chrétienne," p. 68.

37. Paul's shift from βρῶμα (v. 15) to βρῶσις here may not be significant, but this may be a place where the old distinction between these two endings is observed, with the latter indicating the action of eating (cf. Bengel; Dunn).

38. "Eating and drinking" are, of course, a natural combination; cf., e.g., Matt. 6:25; 11:18, 19; and, in Paul, 1 Cor. 9:4; 10:7; 10:31; 11:22. The mention of "drinking" in 1 Cor. 10:31, toward the end of Paul's discussion of food sacrificed to idols and without any indication that this was a problem in Corinth, may especially suggest that in Rom. 14–15 also, Paul introduces "drinking" simply as a hypothetical matter.

39. See esp. Murray, 2.260-61 on this.

Paul does not often refer to the kingdom of God;[40] and his use of the concept here, in a context with so many allusions to the teaching of Jesus, may reflect his dependence on Christ's own emphasis on the true nature of the kingdom.[41] Paul's way of describing the kingdom, however, reflects his own theological emphases. "Righteousness"[42] is, of course, a central theme of Romans, where it usually refers to the "justifying" action of God in Christ and the resultant status enjoyed by believers. And since Paul is not contrasting two types of human behavior — eating and drinking on the one hand versus "right" action on the other — many scholars think he is using the term in this sense.[43] But the context focuses on relations among believers. Probably, then, the main reference here is to "ethical" righteousness — right behavior within the community of believers.[44] "Peace," as v. 19 strongly suggests, will have a similar horizontal meaning: harmony and mutual support of the believers with one another.[45] It is when these blessings are experienced that the community will also be characterized by "joy." All three blessings come as a result of the believer's experience of the Holy Spirit.[46]

18 Paul now underscores the point that he has just made[47]: "righ-

---

40. Elsewhere only in 1 Cor. 6:9, 10; 15:50, 54; Gal. 5:21; Eph. 5:5; Col. 4:11; 1 Thess. 2:12; 2 Thess. 1:5 (all these [with the possible exception of 1 Thess. 2:12] refer to the future state of the kingdom established by Christ at his return); 1 Cor. 4:20 (the only other clear reference in Paul to the present kingdom of God [cf., however, Col. 1:13: "the kingdom of his beloved Son"]). On the kingdom in Paul, see further K. P. Donfried, "The Kingdom of God in Paul," in *The Kingdom of God in Twentieth Century Interpretation* (ed. W. Willis; Peabody, MA: Hendrickson, 1987), pp. 175-90.

41. See, e.g., Thompson, *Clothed with Christ*, pp. 200-207; Dunn, "Paul's Knowledge," pp. 203-4.

42. Gk. δικαιοσύνη.

43. Cf., e.g., Calvin; Michel; Cranfield; Wilckens; Dunn. Differences of emphasis relate to differences in interpreting Paul's overall concept of "righteousness" and "the righteousness of God."

44. E.g., Godet; S-H; Barrett; Murray; Stuhlmacher.

45. See also 12:18. Scholars line up on this issue as they did on the definition of "righeousness" (see the previous note).

46. I think it more likely that ἐν πνεύματι ἁγίῳ modifies all three qualities and not just χαρά (cf. Godet; Käsemann; Wilckens; Schlier; Fitzmyer; contra, e.g., Michel [who refers to 1 Thess. 1:6]; Cranfield). As Schmithals rightly emphasizes, all three qualities are eschatological gifts of the Spirit. That Paul depends on his exposition of the gospel in Romans for this summary is suggested especially by its similarity to Paul's transitional encapsulation of the argument of chaps. 1–4 in Rom. 5:1-2: "Having, therefore, been *justified* [Gk. δικαιόω] by faith, we have *peace* with God through our Lord Jesus Christ, through whom we also have access to this grace in which we stand; and we *rejoice* [Gk. καυχάομαι] in the hope of the glory of God."

47. Cf. Käsemann, in contrast, e.g., to Michel, who thinks that Paul here draws a parenetic conclusion from v. 17.

teousness, peace, and joy" are central to life in the kingdom, "for[48] the one who serves Christ in this" both pleases[49] God and is "esteemed[50] by people." The question here is the antecedent of the pronoun "this." Many commentators think that it refers to the virtues of "righteousness, peace, and joy,"[51] but the singular form of the word is against this. Others suggest a reference to the Holy Spirit,[52] but the Spirit is a subordinate idea in v. 17. Still others think the antecedent is a principle or concept that emerges from v. 17: the promotion of peace,[53] or the "matter" that Paul has been speaking about.[54] I prefer to interpret "this" as the proper kingdom focus that Paul has delineated in v. 17, with the phrase as a whole denoting the manner of service: "the one who serves Christ by focusing on those matters that are truly central to the kingdom."[55] Paul's description of the believer as one who is "serving Christ" reminds us of his characterization of the believer as a servant who is required to satisfy the demands of his or her master (vv. 4, 7-8). And by making the believer's service of *Christ* the means of honoring *God,* Paul places Christ and God in a relationship that is typical of this whole section. It is only as the "strong" submit to Christ and the demands of his kingdom in this matter of ceremonial observances that they will meet with God's approval. At the same time, by following Christ in love and putting "righteousness, peace, and joy" ahead of "eating and drinking," the "strong," rather than being "blasphemed" by the "weak," will be esteemed by them.[56]

19 After his "indicative" interlude, Paul turns back to "imperative," exhorting the Roman Christians to put into practice in their relationships with

---

48. Gk. γάρ.

49. Gk. εὐάρεστος; cf. 12:2, where Paul speaks of the "pleasing"/"acceptable" (Gk. εὐάρεστον) will of God.

50. Gk. δόκιμος, which usually means "approved (by a test)," hence "genuine" (cf. Rom. 16:10; 1 Cor. 11:19; 2 Cor. 10:18; 13:7; 2 Tim. 2:15; Jas. 1:12), but which may have here the sense "esteemed," "respected" (BAGD; cf. Philo, *Creation* 128; *Joseph* 201; Josephus, *Ag. Ap.* 1.18; cf. Käsemann).

51. So also the majority of commentators; cf., e.g., S-H; Käsemann; Cranfield; Fitzmyer. A weakly attested variant (though accepted by Godet) here is the plural τούτοις, changed no doubt to reflect this interpretation.

52. Wilckens.

53. Michel.

54. Dunn.

55. Paul uses ἐν τούτῳ six other times; in all, the antecedent of τούτῳ is a "matter" or "circumstance" denoted in the previous context (cf. 1 Cor. 4:4; 7:24; 11:22; 2 Cor. 5:2; 8:10; Phil. 1:18). The occurrence in 1 Cor. 4:4 comes close to the "manner" idea that I am suggesting for Rom. 14:18.

56. The dative τοῖς ἀνθρώποις indicates that the agent of the verbal idea in δόκιμος. "Approval" or "respect" from other people is the opposite of βλασφημείσθω in v. 16; and those who approve the "strong" will therefore be the "weak."

each other the principles of the kingdom that he has just set forth (vv. 17-18).[57] This verse, then, introduces the concluding section of commands in this paragraph (vv. 19-23), a section that matches, in both structure and, to a lesser extent, content, the opening series of exhortations (vv. 13-16). Having made "peace" a basic feature of the kingdom of God (v. 17), Paul now exhorts the Roman Christians to "pursue"[58] "those things that make for peace."[59] This "peace," more clearly here than in v. 17, is horizontal: peace with other Christians. As v. 20 makes clear, Paul is still addressing the "strong": he calls on them to maintain the kind of attitude and behavior with respect to the matters of dispute in the Roman church that will foster harmony between the two factions. Paul exhorts them also to pursue "those things that make for edification of one another."[60] Paul probably is thinking more of the edification, or "building up," of the church as a whole than of the edification of individual believers.[61] "Those things" that edify the church are probably, then, a more specific way of describing "those things" that lead to peace. The strong believers will foster peace in the community by making the interests of the church as a whole their priority.

20 Paul now uses a more direct and forceful style (the second person singular imperative) to urge a representative "strong" believer not to "tear down the work of God." This prohibition is the flip side of the positive exhortation to "pursue . . . those things that make for edification" (v. 19b); for "tear down" is a natural antonym of "build up."[62] "The work of God,"

---

57. Note the strong consecutive phrase ἄρα οὖν.

58. Paul uses the hortatory subjunctive διώκωμεν (assuming this to be the correct reading; see the note on the translation above).

59. The genitive τῆς εἰρήνης is loosely objective; see BDF 266(3): "what makes for peace" (the parallel genitive τῆς οἰκοδομῆς has the same function). "Pursue peace" is a common Semitism (cf., in the NT, Rom. 12:18; Heb. 12:14; cf. also 1 Pet. 3:11 [= Ps. 35:14]).

60. εἰς ἀλλήλους, "toward one another," could go with both τὰ τῆς εἰρήνης and τὰ τῆς οἰκοδομῆς, but it probably modifies only the latter.

61. See, e.g., Käsemann; Wilckens; Dunn; contra, e.g., Godet; Cranfield sees reference to both the edification of the individual and the community. The Greek word is οἰκοδομή. Its literal meaning is "act of building," "building" (see Matt. 24:1; Mark 13:1, 2). Paul uses the word metaphorically, either with reference to a "building" (1 Cor. 3:9; 2 Cor. 5:1; Eph. 2:21) or, more often, of the act of spiritual building: edification, strengthening, and growth of faith (Rom. 15:2; 1 Cor. 14:3, 5, 12, 26; 2 Cor. 10:8; 12:19; 13:10; Eph. 4:12, 16, 29; see, e.g., O. Michel, *TDNT* V, 144-47). While the "building up" of individual believers is, of course, important, Paul seems to think especially of the collective strengthening of the church as a whole (cf., e.g., 1 Cor. 3:9; 14:5, 12; Eph. 4:12, 16).

62. The Greek verb καταλύω refers, literally, to the tearing down of a building (Matt. 24:2; 26:61; 27:40; Mark 13:2; 14:58; 15:29; Luke 21:6; Acts 6:14), but is used most often in the NT of a figurative "tearing down" or "abolishing" (Matt. 5:17; Luke 9:12; 19:7; 23:2; Acts 5:38, 39; Gal. 2:18; 2 Cor. 5:1). Paul uses καταλύω and οἰκοδομέω as opposites in Gal. 2:18.

accordingly, probably refers to the Christian community rather than to the individual "weak" believer.[63] Paul is warning "strong" believers that they can seriously damage the church — destroy its unity and sap its strength — through their attitudes and actions toward the "weak." And they cause this damage "for the sake of food" — because they persist in behaving in a certain way in a matter that is peripheral, at best, to the kingdom of God. To be sure, Paul admits, the strong believers are right to think that they possess the freedom as the New Covenant people of God to eat and drink without any restriction from the Old Covenant law — "all things are clean."[64] But, as he did earlier when making the same point (v. 14), Paul immediately qualifies this assertion of liberty. In the former verse, Paul's qualification had to do with the perception and attitude of the "weak" believer: "to the one who reckons something to be unclean, to that person it is unclean." And this may be what Paul means here also, if we translate, with the NJB, "but all the same, any kind [of food] can be evil for someone to whom it is an offense to eat it."[65] In favor of this reading is the close parallelism thereby attained between vv. 14 and 20 (and we have noted that Paul seems to intend a certain parallelism between vv. 13b-16 and 19-23).[66] But context and grammar make it more likely that the "person who eats" here is the "strong believer." Paul is therefore warning the "strong" believer that it is wrong for him or her to eat "while causing offense" or "if it causes [another] to stumble"; cf. NRSV: "it is wrong for you to make others fall by what you eat."[67]

21 Paul again uses antonyms to elaborate: as it is "wrong"[68] for the strong believer to eat while causing offense to the weaker brother, so it is

---

63. S-H; Barrett; Käsemann; Schlier; Dunn; contra, e.g., Godet; Murray; Cranfield; Fitzmyer. Michel suggests that the reference may be to the work of Christ on the cross (cf. v. 15b). E. Peterson seeks to draw a closer relationship to the idea of "building up" in v. 19 by arguing that ἔργον here means "building" ("'Έργον in der Bedeutung 'Bau' bei Paulus," *Bib* 22 [1941], 439-41).

64. Gk. καθαρός, used in the LXX with reference to ritually "clean" food (cf., e.g., Gen. 7:2-3, 8; 8:20; Lev. 4:12; 6:11; 7:19; Ezra 6:20; Mal. 1:11). In the NT, see Luke 11:41 and the extended uses in John 13:10, 11; Acts 18:6; 20:26.

65. The Greek sentence is incomplete; we are probably to supply the form τὸ ἐσθιεῖν (derived from τῷ ἀνθρώπῳ τῷ . . . ἐσθίοντι) as the subject of the clause (cf., e.g., Cranfield; Wilckens). It is clear that the διά introduces an "attendant circumstance" (BDF 223[3]; Turner, 267; Zerwick, 114; cf. διὰ γράμματος καὶ περιτομῆς in 2:27). Thus: "For the person who eats through, or with offense, eating is wrong."

66. See, e.g., Godet; Murray; Michel; Wilckens; Ridderbos, *Paul,* p. 291.

67. So almost all other modern English translations; cf. S-H; Käsemann; Cranfield. A reference to both the strong and the weak believer (e.g., Barrett; Dunn) is unnecessarily complicated.

68. Gk. κακός, v. 20b.

"good"[69] "not to eat meat or to drink wine[70] or to do anything"[71] that might cause that brother to stumble. As v. 17 sums up the central theological point, so this assertion states the basic practical point that Paul makes in vv. 13-23.[72] The "stumbling" will again (cf. vv. 13b, 20b) consist in the "weak" in faith, under pressure from the arguments and example of the "strong," doing what they still think is wrong. The issue of "eating" has been central to the argument from the beginning, but this verse clarifies what is meant in v. 2 — "eats vegetables," that is, "is a vegetarian, abstaining from meat" — and elaborates the brief references to "food" and "eating" throughout this paragraph (vv. 15, 17, 20). As I argued in the introduction to 14:1–15:13, the "weak" probably abstained from meat because they feared that it would not meet the ritual requirements of the OT law. Paul's reference here to "drinking wine" probably implies that the same believers avoided wine out of similar concerns: for wine was widely used in pagan religious libations (see also v. 17). But Paul clearly intends to make the principle he states here as widely applicable as possible by adding "or anything else." The believer who seeks the peace and edification of the church should gladly refrain from activities that[73] might cause a fellow believer to suffer spiritual harm.

22 Paul continues to address the representative "strong" Christian. "You" is emphatic: "as for you,[74] the faith that you have, keep to yourself[75] before God!" This is the first time since the beginning of the chapter that Paul has used the language of faith to characterize the parties in the dispute. As in v. 1, "faith" does not refer to general Christian faith but to convictions about the issues in dispute in Rome that arise out of one's faith in Christ. Paul is not, then, telling the "strong" Christian to be quiet about his or her faith in Christ — a plea that would be quite out of place in the NT! Nor is he neces-

---

69. Gk. καλόν.

70. Many scholars think that the aorist form of the infinitives φαγεῖν and πιεῖν implies that Paul is urging the strong to abstain only on particular occasions (e.g., BDF 338[1]; Barrett; Ziesler; Morris; Cranfield is hesitant). It is likely that, as in 1 Cor. 10:23–11:1, Paul commands abstention only in situations in which definite offense to the "weak" might occur; but the aorist tense of the infinitives is not a good basis for the argument.

71. The sentence is elliptical at this point, with the second μηδέ used absolutely. But it was common to use the word in this way by itself, with the word "other" assumed (BDF 480[1]).

72. Michel. As Cranfield notes, the lack of explicit connection with v. 20 (asyndeton) accentuates the principial and authoritative character of the statement.

73. ἐν in the phrase ἐν ᾧ probably has a causal sense (Turner, 253), with the antecedent of the relative pronoun not being expressed: "It is good . . . not to do anything because of which your fellow believer might stumble."

74. Gk. σύ. The translation here assumes that we are to read the relative pronoun ἥν (see the note on the translation above).

75. For this translation of ἔχε κατὰ σεαυτόν, see BAGD, 406.

sarily requiring "strong" believers never to mention their views on these matters or to speak of their sense of freedom before others. As the context suggests, the silence that Paul requires is related to the need to avoid putting a stumbling block in the way of the "weak." This will mean that the "strong" are not to brag about their convictions before the "weak" and, especially, that they are not to propagandize the "weak."

The blessing that Paul adds at the end of the verse can be taken in two different ways. (1) Paul might be commending believers who have no reservations about their own beliefs on these disputed matters and therefore have no cause to "reproach" themselves for their conduct. See TEV: "Happy is the person who does not feel guilty when he does something he judges is right" (cf. also REB). In this case, Paul may have in mind both "strong" and "weak" believers,[76] or, more likely, "strong" believers only.[77] (2) Paul might be encouraging "strong" believers to "walk in love" toward their "weak" fellow believers and so give themselves — or God — no reason to "condemn" themselves.[78] The first alternative is preferable. The latter interpretation would make good sense if Paul intended this blessing as a basis for his plea for silence in v. 22a, but he does not indicate any such relationship.[79] But he does suggest a relationship between vv. 22b and 23;[80] and this connection suggests that, as he warns "weak" believers about acting against what they believe in v. 23, so in v. 22b he commends "strong" believers for acting on the basis of faith. Moreover, Paul's use of the word "approve"[81] also favors a reference to the "strong." Paul's point, then, is that the "strong" should be content with the blessing God has given them in enabling them to understand the liberty that their faith provides them, without feeling it necessary to flaunt that liberty before their "weaker" fellow believers.

23 In contrast to the Christian who acts from conviction is the "weak" Christian "who has doubts" or "who wavers."[82] The doubts of such

---

76. Käsemann; Fitzmyer.

77. Godet; S-H; Murray; Cranfield; Dunn (although he allows for the second view also).

78. Haldane; Michel; Schlier; Wilckens.

79. No particle or conjunction (e.g., a γάρ ["for"]) connects vv. 22a and 22b.

80. Cf. the particle δέ in v. 23.

81. As BAGD define δοχιμάζει here; it is obviouly not a natural way to depict the views of the "weak" who decisively *disapprove* of the practices at issue. As in v. 21, the phrase ἐν ῷ is dependent on an assumed antecedent of ῷ ("that in which"); ἐν is perhaps instrumental.

82. Gk. διαχρινόμενος, from διαχρίνω (Paul carries on the sequence of χριν-words). The verb can mean "decide, determine" (so usually in Paul; cf. 1 Cor. 4:7; 6:5; 11:29, 31; 14:29) or "doubt, waver," often as the opposite of faith (see Rom. 4:20; Mark 11:23//Matt. 21:21; Jas. 1:6; Jude 22). Here it is clearly the latter.

Christians arise from the fact that they do not have a strong enough faith to believe that they can ignore the ritual elements of the OT law. Doubters such as this, Paul says, are "condemned"[83] when they eat. This is not simply a subjective self-condemnation; as the reference to sin later in the verse makes clear, Paul refers to God's disapproval of such an act.[84] Condemnation comes not because of the eating itself; as Paul has already explained (vv. 14, 20), eating anything one wants is quite all right for the believer. Rather, what brings God's condemnation is eating when one does not have the faith to believe that it is right to do it. This, Paul claims, is "sin."[85] Why? Because,[86] Paul goes on to explain, "everything that is not out of faith is sin." Paul here asserts a general theological principle. But it is necessary to describe accurately just what that principle is. Most important is to realize that "faith" here almost certainly has the same meaning that it has elsewhere in this chapter (vv. 1, 22): "conviction" stemming from one's faith in Christ.[87] Paul is not, then, claiming that any act that does not arise out of a basic trust and dependency on Christ is sinful, true as that may be.[88] What he here labels "sin," rather, is any act that does not match our sincerely held convictions about what our Christian faith allows us to do and prohibits us from doing. "For a Christian not a single decision and action can be good which he does not think he can justify on the ground of his Christian conviction and his liberty before God in Christ."[89] Violation of the dictates of the conscience,[90] even when the

---

83. The perfect κατακέκριται, which is clearly "timeless" here, may emphasize the state of condemnation (Porter, *Verbal Aspect,* p. 269).

84. The Greek word is κατακέκριται. Paul's four other uses of the verb κατακρίνω all refer to divine condemnation (Rom. 2:1; 8:3, 34; 1 Cor. 11:32); it will not, then, refer here simply to human self-condemnation (contra, e.g., Volf, *Paul and Perseverance,* p. 91; cf., correctly, Stuhlmacher: "takes upon him- or herself the condemnation of God's judgment"). The perfect form probably indicates the state that would result from the fulfillment of the condition (ἐὰν φάγῃ); it could, of course, then, denote future action (see BDF 344; Zerwick, 257).

85. Paul surely uses ἁμαρτία here in a general way, "act of sin," "transgression" (Wilckens) and implies nothing about the state of sin that reigns over all people (cf. Cranfield).

86. Gk. γάρ.

87. Chrysostom; S-H; Murray; Cranfield; Fitzmyer; contra, e.g., Godet; Dunn.

88. Augustine, e.g., used this verse to argue that any act of a non-Christian must be sinful (*Contra Julianum* 4.32). His use of the verse is probably invalid because of the special nuance of "faith," but it should not be rejected on theological grounds as quickly as many modern scholars do. For it is surely true, in one sense, that all acts done by believers and nonbelievers alike that are not motivated by, and arise from, trust and dependence on Christ are sinful. See Dunn.

89. Ridderbos, *Paul,* p. 291.

90. While Paul does not use the word "conscience" here, we are justified by the parallel in 1 Cor. 10:25-30 to bring it into the present discussion.

conscience does not conform perfectly with God's will, is sinful. And we must remember that Paul cites this theological point to buttress his exhortation of the "strong." The "strong," he is suggesting, should not force the "weak" to eat meat, or drink wine, or ignore the Sabbath, when the "weak" are not yet convinced that their faith in Christ allows them to do so. For to do so would be to force them into sin, to put a "stumbling" block in their way (cf. vv. 13, 20-21). First, their faith must be strengthened, their consciences enlightened; and then they can follow the "strong" in exercising Christian liberty together.

3. Put Other People First! (15:1-6)

> 1*But we who are strong ought to bear the weaknesses of those who are without strength*[1] *and not please ourselves.* 2*Let each of us please his neighbor for good, for edification.* 3*For even Christ did not please himself but, just as it is written, "The reproaches of those who reproached you have fallen on me."*[a] 4*For whatever was written beforehand was written for our instruction, in order that through endurance and through the comfort of the Scriptures we might have hope.* 5*Now may the God of endurance and comfort give to you to think the same thing among one another, according to Christ Jesus,* 6*in order that you might with one accord, with one mouth, glorify the God and Father of our Lord Jesus Christ.*

> a. Ps. 69:9b

The opening verses of chap. 15 continue Paul's exhortation to the "weak" and the "strong" in chap. 14, but the relationship between the two is disputed. Some commentators posit a tight connection and would eliminate the usual paragraph break placed between the chapters. They see the first person plural exhortation in v. 1, with its grounding in vv. 2-3, as the conclusion to the argument of 14:20-23.[2] At the other extreme are those who think that 15:1 marks a significant transition from a narrow focus on the dispute between the "weak" and the "strong" in Rome to a broader exploration of the principles Christians should follow in any such disputes.[3] We prefer to steer a middle course. Paul gives no indication that he intends to shift his focus from the specific problem of disunity

---

1. Cf. NASB.
2. E.g., Schmithals, 509; cf. also Wilckens, 3.100, who thinks that 15:1-3 concludes both 14:20-23 and the entire chapter.
3. E.g., Godet, 467; Michel, 441; Käsemann, 381; Schlier, 419. Cranfield (2.731) sees this to be a possibility; Dodd (221) thinks that vv. 1-2 round off the discussion about the "strong" and the "weak," with v. 3 beginning the transition into a more general issue.

in the Roman church. But the introduction of new vocabulary[4] and new arguments suggests that 15:1 marks a new stage in the discussion.

This paragraph runs through v. 6. Paul begins by exhorting his fellow
"powerful" believers in Rome to "bear" the weaknesses of their less powerful
fellow believers and not to "please themselves," that is, to use their sense of
Christian liberty selfishly (v. 1). On the contrary, the "powerful" or "strong"
are to "please" others (v. 2), following the example of their Lord and master,
Jesus Christ, who put others before himself when he bore the reproaches of
human beings directed against God (v. 3). Having used a line from Ps. 69 to
describe Christ's bearing of reproach (v. 3b), Paul adds a general assertion about
the applicability of the OT to Christian experience, focusing on its purpose of
strengthening believers' hope (v. 4). A concluding "wish-prayer" returns to the
root issue, as Paul prays that God might give to the Roman Christians a common
mind-set (v. 5), which would enable them to praise God with a strong and united
voice (v. 6). Thus the paragraph is basically a call to the "strong" in Rome to
follow Christ's example of loving service of others as a means of bringing unity
to the church. We find the same pattern of teaching in Phil. 2:1-11, where Paul
pleads for believers to follow Christ's example in preferring other's interests to
their own in order to bring unity to the community.

1 We have at the opening of this paragraph a shift in style. Dominant
in the exhortations of chap. 14 is Paul's use of the second person singular to
address a representative "weak" or "strong" believer. First person plural
exhortations occur only as brief interruptions to this style (vv. 13a, 19). In vv.
1-4, however, Paul uses the first person plural form of address as his mainstay.
But this change in style does not signal a change in address: Paul continues
to address the "strong" believers, as he has in 14:13b-23. Now, for the first
time, he names them, implicitly including himself among them: "we who are
strong."[5] The context requires that we delimit the significance of this description to the specific issue that Paul has been discussing: these Christians are
"strong" or "capable" *(dynatos)* with respect to the faith to believe that certain
practices are legitimate for believers. Conversely, then, those whom Paul here
designates as the *adynatōn* are believers who are "incapable" of realizing that
their faith in Christ has freed them from certain ritual observances.[6]

---

4. Most significant is the shift from the word "weak" (ἀσθενῆς) to describe the
"rigorists" in Rome to the word "powerless," "unable" (ἀδύνατος).

5. The identification comes as no surprise since Paul has already aligned himself
with the views of the "strong" (14:14, 20).

6. See esp. *GEL* 74.22. Paul's shift from ἀσθενέω/ἀσθενῆς (14:1-2) to ἀδύνατος
to describe these believers is probably simply stylistic, his use of δύνατος for the "strong"
making it natural for him to use its morphological antonym (contra, e.g., Godet, who takes
the change as a sign that Paul is now broaching a new, broader, topic). And δύνατος is a
natural semantic antonym of ἀσθενῆς; cf., e.g., 2 Cor. 12:10; 13:9.

Those who pride themselves on their "strength" are obliged,[7] Paul says, to use that strength to "bear the weaknesses"[8] of those who are "without strength" in this matter. Paul is not urging the "strong" simply to "bear with," to tolerate or "put up with," the "weak" and their scruples.[9] For Paul uses this same verb in Gal. 6:2 (and cf. v. 5) in a similar way, urging believers to "bear one another's burdens and so fulfill the law of Christ [i.e., love for one another; cf. 5:14]."[10] In this light, what Paul is exhorting the "strong" to do is willingly and lovingly to assume for themselves the burden that these weak believers are carrying. See REB: "Those of us who are strong must accept as our own burden the tender scruples of the weak." This does not necessarily mean that the "strong" are to adopt the scruples of the "weak." But what it does mean is that they are sympathetically to "enter into" their attitudes, refrain from criticizing and judging them, and do what love would require toward them. Love demands that the "strong" go beyond the distance implied in mere toleration; they are to treat the "weak" as brothers and sisters.[11] Negatively, it means that the "strong" are not to "please[12] themselves." Lying just below the surface here is what becomes explicit in v. 3: that this "carry-ing" of the weaknesses of other believers is to be done in imitation of the Lord Christ, who himself "carried" our infirmities (Matt. 8:17, quoting Isa. 53:4[13]) and did not come to be served but to serve (Mark 10:45 and pars.).

2 Rather than "pleasing ourselves," "each of us," Paul goes on to say, should "please the neighbor." By using the phrase "each of us," Paul may expand his address to include all the believers in Rome, whether "weak"

---

7. Gk. ὀφείλω. Paul uses this verb elsewhere, followed with an infinitive, to denote an obligation incumbent on Christians by virtue of their faith in Christ (cf. Rom. 15:27; 1 Cor. 11:7, 10; 2 Cor. 12:14; Eph. 5:28; 2 Thess. 1:3; 2:13). See also the note on 13:8.

8. Gk. ἀσθενήματα; the word occurs only here in the NT.

9. Contra, e.g., Barrett, who translates "endure" (cf. Rev. 2:2-3).

10. The Greek verb is βαστάζω, "bear, carry." It is used in the NT both literally (e.g., Luke 22:10, where Jesus tells the disciples to look for a man "carrying [βαστάζων] a water jar") and metaphorically (e.g., Acts 15:10, where Peter describes the law as "a yoke . . . which neither our fathers nor we have been able to bear [βαστάσαι]"). All of Paul's uses of the verb are metaphorical: Rom. 1:18; Gal. 5:10; 6:2, 5, 17.

11. See esp. Murray; Wilckens.

12. Gk. ἀρέσκω, used by Paul also in Rom. 8:8; 1 Cor. 7:32, 33, 34; 10:33; Gal. 1:10; 1 Thess. 2:4, 15; 2 Thess. 4:1; 2 Tim. 2:4. The most important parallel comes in the similar discussion about the "strong" and the "weak" in 1 Cor. 8–10: "Just as I try to please [ἀρέσκω] all people, not seeking my own advantage, but that of the many, in order that they might be saved" (10:33).

13. The verb here is the same — βαστάζω — and note that the previous line uses the word ἀσθενεία ("weakness"): αὐτὸς τὰς ἀσθενείας ἡμῶν ἔλαβεν ("he carried our weaknesses"). See, on this parallel, esp. Michel; Black; and, at greatest length, Thompson, *Clothed with Christ*, pp. 208-12. (Käsemann doubts the allusion but without good reason.)

or "strong."[14] Evidence for this inclusiveness can be found at the end of the paragraph, where Paul clearly includes the entire Roman community (cf. vv. 5-6). But the relationship between vv. 1 and 2 — not pleasing ourselves/pleasing the neighbor — and the similarity between v. 2 and Paul's exhortations to the "strong" in 14:13-23 (cf. the "good" with v. 16 and "edification" with v. 19) suggest rather that Paul continues in v. 2 to address the "strong" only.[15] The "neighbor" will, then, be the "weak" fellow believer.[16] By using the term "neighbor," Paul makes clear that he bases his plea to the "strong" on the love command.[17] The "strong" believer "walks in love" when he or she "pleases" rather than "pains" the "weak" believer (cf. 14:15). Paul thus applies to this particular issue his earlier general teaching about the centrality of love for the Christian life (13:8-10).

Picking up another key motif in his earlier exhortation, Paul asserts that the purpose of pleasing others is "the good."[18] This "good" is the good of the individual "weak" believer: his or her spiritual profit,[19] in contrast to the spiritual harm that the insensitive and selfish behavior of the "strong" might cause (14:15, 20). But Paul defines this "good" more specifically in a second clause: "edification," or "building up."[20] As in 14:19, this word takes us out of the narrowly individualistic realm. For the spiritual profit of the "weak" believer is at the same time to the advantage of the Christian community as a whole, as its unity in praise and service is enhanced.[21] These two statements of purpose also define what Paul means by "pleasing" others. What is involved is not the "pleasing people" *rather than God* that Paul elsewhere condemns (Gal. 1:10; Col. 3:22; 1 Thess. 2:4; Eph. 6:6), but a "pleasing" fellow believers *rather than ourselves.*

14. E.g., Godet; Huby; Morris; Schmithals.

15. Murray; Michel; Käsemann; Cranfield; Wilckens; Schlier; Stuhlmacher.

16. Lenski. The love command, as Jesus made quite clear (Matt. 5:43), demands that Christians love all people; but, contra, e.g., Morris, this universal scope does not seem to be present here.

17. "Neighbor" (Gk. πλησίον) occurs in the NT 16 times; and all but three are found in quotations of, or allusions to, the love command of Lev. 19:18 (Matt. 5:43; 19:19; 22:39; Mark 12:31, 33; Luke 10:27, 29, 36; Rom. 13:9, 10; Gal. 5:14; Jas. 2:8; 4:12; the exceptions are John 4:5; Acts 7:27, and Eph. 4:25).

18. See Rom. 12:2, 9, 21; 13:3, 4; cf. also 8:28.

19. Morris. Eschatological salvation is included (Cranfield), but the concept is broader than that (Dunn).

20. Gk. οἰκοδομή. This second clause, πρὸς οἰκοδομήν, elaborates the first, εἰς τὸ ἀγαθόν (cf., e.g., S-H; Barrett; Käsemann). The prepositions are used interchangeably to denote purpose (Murray); contra, e.g., Godet, Stuart, who think that εἰς introduces a limitation ("in respect to that which is good"), and Bengal, 3.181, who thinks that εἰς denotes the "internal end" and πρός the "external."

21. Fitzmyer.

3 In 1 Cor. 10:33–11:1, when dealing with a debate among believers in Corinth similar to that in Rome, Paul cites his own practice of "pleasing all others . . . so that they might be saved" and then quickly adds that he is himself acting in imitation of Christ. Paul here moves directly from an exhortation to "please the neighbor" to the example of Christ (although he implicitly refers to his own practice with the form of address). The "strong" should not think that their "giving into" others is incompatible with their "strength"; for even[22] the Messiah[23] "did not please[24] himself." We might have expected at this point an explicit reference to Christ's giving of his life for the sake of sinful human beings — the "weak" (cf. 5:6). Instead, after a typical introductory formula, Paul puts words from Ps. 69:9b on the lips of Jesus: "The reproaches of those who reproached you have fallen on me."[25] "Me" in the quotation is Christ; "you" is God[26] — Paul has Jesus saying that the reproaches, or insults, of people that were directed at God fell on himself instead. Why Paul uses this particular quotation is not clear since we have no reason to think that the "strong" were enduring "reproaches." Probably Paul viewed it as a convenient way to (1) make clear that the sufferings of Christ were ordained by God and in his service;[27] and (2) allude to Jesus' supreme example of service on the cross. For the reference to Christ's "not pleasing himself" is almost certainly to the crucifixion.[28] NT writers often apply language from Ps. 69 to the passion of Jesus,[29] and Paul probably thinks of the "reproaches" born by Christ as those tauntings Jesus

---

22. Probably the best translation of καί here (cf. KJV; NIV; NASB; Morris).

23. The article with Χριστός may emphasize its titular significance (cf. Käsemann; Michel; Dunn; Cranfield [?]).

24. Gk. ἤρεσεν, a "constantive" aorist (BDF 332[13], though we doubt their particular application of the word).

25. The text Paul uses is identical with the majority LXX tradition (68:10b in the LXX).

26. Contra those who try to fit the quotation better to its application by identifying σε with a human being (e.g., S-H; Lietzmann).

27. Schlatter.

28. Merk, *Handeln aus Glauben,* p. 171; Michel; Käsemann; Wilckens; contra those who think the reference is to Jesus' entire earthly life (BDF 332[13]; Barrett; cf. also Dunn, who refers both to Jesus' earthly life and the passion) or to the entire "Christ event," including especially the incarnation (cf. Phil. 2:6; Cranfield; Schmithals).

29. It is quoted or alluded to in Matt. 27:34, 48//Mark 15:35-36//Luke 23:36//John 19:28-29; John 2:17; 15:25; Acts 1:20; Rom. 11:9. Note especially Jesus' quotation of the first half of this same verse to defend his "cleansing" of the temple: "Zeal for your house has consumed me" (John 2:17); see, on this, Dodd, *According to the Scriptures,* pp. 57-58; Ellis, *Paul's Use of the Old Testament,* p. 139; and, on the use of this psalm in the NT, Moo, *Old Testament,* pp. 233-34, 243-44, 249-52, 275-80, 285-300; Lindars, *New Testament Apologetic,* pp. 99-108.

endured at the time of his crucifixion (see 27:27-31, 39-41 and pars.).[30] Paul therefore implicitly appeals to Jesus' giving of himself in service to others as a model to imitate. As Chrysostom says: "He had power not to have been reproached, power not to have suffered what He did suffer, had He been minded to look to His own things." At the same time, perhaps, Paul may be trying to get the "strong" to put their own "suffering" in perspective: occasionally abstaining from meat or wine or observing a special religious day should not seem like much of a burden in comparison with what Christ had to suffer for the sake of others.

4 In a brief detour from his main argument,[31] Paul reminds his readers that the use he has just made of the OT is entirely appropriate: "for whatever was written beforehand was written for our instruction."[32] Paul here crisply enunciates a conviction basic to his ministry and to the early church generally. The OT, though no longer a source of direct moral imperative (6:14, 15; 7:4), continues to play a central role in helping Christians to understand the climax of salvation history and their responsibilities as the New Covenant people of God.[33]

The instruction Christians gain from the Scriptures has many purposes. One of these, Paul asserts in the second part of the verse, is that "we might have hope."[34] The introduction of hope at this point might also seem to be a detour in Paul's argument. But two connections with the context may be noted. First, hope is especially needed by Christians when facing suffering (cf. 5:2-5; 8:20, 24-25). And Paul has broached the general problem of Christian suffering by citing the reproaches born by Christ as a model for the "strong" believers to imitate.[35] The subordinate phrases Paul adds to his main purpose statement

---

30. The Greek verb ὀνειδίζω used here is also used of the "mocking" of Jesus by those crucified with him (Matt. 27:44//Mark 15:32). It may also be significant that the word is used to depict the suffering that disciples of the Lord must be expected to endure (Matt. 5:11//Luke 6:22; 1 Pet. 4:14), as is the cognate noun ὀνειδισμός (Heb. 10:33; cf. 11:26). Note esp. Heb. 13:13, where Christians are exhorted to "bear the reproach that he endured."

31. The shift in focus leads Schmithals (pp. 511-13) to suggest a rearrangement of the paragraph, in the order vv. 1-4a, 7, 4b, 5-6.

32. The Greek word is διδασκαλία, which becomes a keynote of the Pastoral Epistles (1 Tim. 1:10; 4:1, 6, 13, 16; 5:17; 6:1, 3; 2 Tim. 3:10, 16; 4:3; Tit. 1:9; 2:1, 7, 10; other Pauline occurrences are in Rom. 12:7; Eph. 4:14; Col. 2:22).

33. See also, in Paul, Rom. 4:24; 1 Cor. 9:10; 10:11; 2 Tim. 3:16.

34. Gk. ἐλπίδα ἔχωμεν; this combination is regularly used to denote Christian growth in hope (see also Acts 24:15; 2 Cor. 10:15; Eph. 2:12; 1 Thess. 4:13; 1 John 3:3). The present tense ἔχωμεν probably indicates the maintenance and strengthening of hope: "go on hoping" (cf. Cranfield; Dunn; cf., however Porter, *Verbal Aspect*, p. 329, for a different explanation based on his "aspect" theory).

35. See Denney.

bear out this emphasis: "through [i.e., with] endurance"[36] and "through the comfort[37] of the Scriptures."[38] Reading the OT and seeing its fulfillment in Christ and the church fosters the believer's hope, a hope that is accompanied by the ability to "bear up" under the pressure of spiritually hostile and irritating circumstances. But to return to the initial point: Paul signals his intention to talk about Christian suffering by using here two key terms, "endurance" and "comfort," that he regularly uses when discussing the trials of believers.[39]

A second reason for Paul to bring "hope" into the discussion here emerges when we remember that many, perhaps most, of the "strong" were Gentiles. As such, apart from Christ, they were "without hope" (Eph. 2:12). Now, however, they have been "brought near," wild branches grafted into the promises and people of God (cf. Rom. 11:17-24). By strengthening their "hope," therefore, the Scriptures help these "strong" believers become more secure about their place in the people of God. At the same time, they are given the very practical reminder that this hope focuses on *one* people of God, made up of both Jews and Gentiles and of "strong" and "weak" (a point that Paul develops in vv. 8-13).[40] If the "strong" believers, therefore, wish to maintain

36. Gk. διὰ τῆς ὑπομονῆς. See the note on 5:3. The preposition διά here denotes an "attendant circumstance" to the main idea, "that we might have hope" (so most modern commentators; Barrett, however, suggests that it might be causal — "because we practice endurance"). REB translates "in order that . . . we might maintain our hope with perseverance."

37. Gk. διὰ τῆς παρακλήσεως. Similar to its cognate verb παρακαλέω (see the note on 12:1), the noun παράκλησις can mean either "exhortation" or "comfort." Some scholars prefer the former meaning here (e.g., Barrett; Stuart). But the majority of commentators prefer, rightly, "comfort" (e.g., Käsemann; Murray; Cranfield; Schlier; Wilckens; cf. also BAGD). As Calvin says, "consolation is more suitable to patience, for this arises from it; because then only we are prepared to bear adversities in patience, when God blends them with consolation."

The preposition διά in this phrase, in contrast to the first phrase, has its usual instrumental meaning, denoting the "comfort" or "encouragement" that comes from the Scriptures as the means by which Christians' hope is strengthened (a causal meaning [suggested by Käsemann, Schlier, and Dunn] is similar).

38. τῶν γραφῶν is a genitive of source (e.g., Alford). It is difficult to decide whether to attach this phrase to παρακλήσεως only — "through endurance and the comfort that comes from the Scriptures" (e.g., Michel; Käsemann; Cranfield; Wilckens) — or to both ὑπομονῆς and παρακλήσεως — "through the endurance and comfort that come from the Scriptures" (e.g., Godet; Murray). The repetition of the preposition and the definite article favors the former alternative; and especially is this so if, as I have argued, we give διά different meanings in the two phrases. Note also 1 Macc. 12:9: "since we have as encouragement [παράκλησιν] the holy books in our hands."

39. On ὑπομονή, see the note on 5:3. Paul uses παράκλησις in a context of suffering in 2 Cor. 1:4, 5, 6, 7; 7:4, 13; 2 Thess. 2:16.

40. For this general point, see Käsemann and, especially, Dunn.

their hope, they must work to put into effect the unity of the people of God, within which they experience their own salvation.

5 Verses 5-6 contain a "prayer-wish," a prayer of intercession that Paul offers to God and records for the benefit of the Roman Christians. By sharing the contents of his prayer with the Romans, Paul uses it as an indirect means of exhortation.[41] With this prayer, then, Paul returns to his central concern throughout 14:1–15:13: restoring the unity of the Roman church.[42] Paul links this "prayer-wish" to v. 4 by addressing God as "the God of endurance and comfort," or, we may legitimately paraphrase, "the God who is the source of endurance and comfort."[43] "God alone is doubtless the author of patience and of consolation; for he conveys both to our hearts by his Spirit: yet he employs his word as the instrument."[44] Paul signals his intent to begin bringing his exhortation to the "strong" and the "weak" to a conclusion by using a second person plural verb to address the entire community[45] and by introducing the "one another" theme that occurs at crucial junctures in the exhortation (cf. 14:13a; 15:7).

Paul prays specifically that God might give[46] to the Roman Christians the ability "to think the same thing."[47] In light of Paul's insistence that both the "strong" and the "weak" respect one another's views on the debated issues, we must not think that Paul prays that the two groups may come to the same opinion on these issues. He is, rather, asking God to give them, despite their differences of opinion, a common perspective and purpose.[48] Paul's concern is not, at least primarily, that the believers in Rome all hold the same opinion of these "matters indifferent"; but that they remain united in their devotion to the Lord Jesus and to his service in the world. The unity, therefore, as Paul prays, should be "according to Christ Jesus." This might mean that the unity should be in accordance with the will, or spirit, of Christ,[49]

---

41. Murray.

42. Wiles suggests that Paul's description of God as "the God of comfort" (παράκλησις) may allude to the opening of the hortatory section (12:1, παρακαλέω), and even to the opening of the letter (cf. 1:12) (*Paul's Intercessory Prayers*, p. 81).

43. The genitives τῆς ὑπομονῆς and τῆς παρακλήσεως probably denote those virtues that God gives believers. Paul often so qualifies God when he addresses him in prayer; cf. Rom. 15:13, "the God of hope"; and Rom. 15:33; 16:20; 2 Cor. 13:11; Phil. 4:9; 1 Thess. 5:23, "the God of peace."

44. Calvin.

45. Gk. ὑμῖν. Paul has not used the second person plural to address the community since 14:1.

46. Gk. δώη, an aorist optative (the optative is often used in wishes; cf. Zerwick, 355).

47. Gk. τὸ αὐτὸ φρονεῖν. See also Rom. 12:16; 2 Cor. 13:11; Phil. 2:2; 4:2.

48. See, e.g., Cranfield.

49. Käsemann; Cranfield.

or that it should be in accordance with the example of Christ (cf. v. 3).[50] But this may be a case where it is better to avoid such fine distinctions; Paul may well want to include both these specific ideas as part of a general inducement to think "according to Christ Jesus."[51]

6 Unity among the Roman Christians is important, and Paul uses many words seeking to encourage it. But this unity has a more important ultimate object: the glory of "the God and Father of our Lord Jesus Christ."[52] Only when the Roman community is united, only when the Christians in Rome can act "with one accord"[53] and speak "with one voice,"[54] will they be able to glorify God in the way that he deserves to be glorified. Divisions in the church over nonessentials diverts precious time and energy from its basic mission: the proclamation of the gospel and the glorifying of God.

4. Receive One Another! (15:7-13)

> 7*Therefore receive one another, just as Christ has received you,*[1] *to the glory of God.* 8*For I say that Christ has become a servant of the circumcision for the sake of the truth of God, to confirm the promises*

---

50. Haldane.

51. Wiles, *Paul's Intercessory Prayers,* pp. 81-82; Michel; Murray; Dunn. On the significance of the order of the titles — Χριστὸν Ἰησοῦν — see the note on 1:1.

52. The Gk. τὸν θεὸν καὶ πατέρα τοῦ κυρίου ἡμῶν Ἰησοῦ Χριστοῦ could be construed, as in the KJV, "God, even the Father of our Lord Jesus Christ" (θεόν being absolute; cf. many older commentators [e.g., Gifford; Stuart; Meyer]) or "the God and Father of our Lord Jesus Christ" (θεόν governing τοῦ κυρίου; so most modern versions and commentators). The latter rendering is preferable: it fits the syntax (articular θεόν and anarthrous πατέρα); it has precedent in Pauline usage (Eph. 1:17: ὁ θεὸς τοῦ κυρίου ἡμῶν Ἰησοῦ Χριστοῦ, "The God of our Lord Jesus Christ"); and it is theologically unobjectionable (see, e.g., Matt. 27:46 and pars.).

53. Gk. ὁμοθυμαδόν, originally a political term (H. W. Heidland, *TDNT* V, 185), is used especially often by Luke in descriptions of the early church (Acts 1:14; 2:46; 4:24; 5:12; 15:25; cf. also 7:57; 8:6; 12:20; 18:12; 19:29). Paul therefore prays that the Roman church might exhibit the unity that characterized the first Spirit-filled church.

54. Gk. ἐν ἑνὶ στόματι; the ἐν is instrumental (Turner, 252).

1. In place of ὑμᾶς, "you," several manuscripts, including the primary Alexandrian uncial B, read here ἡμᾶς, "us" (see also the western uncial D [original hand]). A few scholars think this reading might be original, a scribe having replaced an original ἡμᾶς with ὑμᾶς under influence from the second person plural pronouns in vv. 5-6 (e.g., Godet, 470; Michel, 447). But ὑμᾶς is better attested (it is read in the primary Alexandrian uncial ℵ, the secondary Alexandrian MSS A, C, 33, 81, and 1739, Ψ, the western uncials D [corrector], F, and G, and the majority text), and a scribe might have been equally likely to change to the first person plural for liturgical reasons (see, e.g., S-H, 397; Käsemann, 385; Murray, 2.203; Cranfield, 2.739; Wilckens, 3.105; Dunn, 2.844).

made to the fathers, 9*and so that the Gentiles might glorify God for the sake of his mercy, even as it written,*

> *Because of this I will praise you among the Gentiles*
> *and in your name I will sing praises.*ᵃ

10*And again it says,*

> *Rejoice, Gentiles, with his people.*ᵇ

11*And, again:*

> *Praise, all you Gentiles, the Lord,*
> *and let all the peoples praise him.*ᶜ

12*And again Isaiah says,*

> *The root of Jesse shall come, even the one who arises*
> *to rule the Gentiles. On him the Gentiles will hope.*ᵈ

13*Now may the God of hope fill you with all joy and peace as you believe, in order that you might abound in hope by the power of the Holy Spirit.*

> a. Ps. 18:49 (= 2 Sam. 22:50)
> b. Deut. 32:43
> c. Ps. 117:1
> d. Isa. 11:10

The opening words express the main point of this paragraph: "receive one another." Paul thereby returns to the theme with which he opened his exhortation to the "weak" and the "strong" (cf. 14:1). But there is an important difference: in 14:1, he urged the Roman community to "receive the person who is weak in faith." Here, however, he exhorts every believer to receive every other believer. Most of the rest of the paragraph supports this key command: the Roman Christians are to "receive one another" because (1) Christ has "received" them (v. 7b); and (2) Christ has acted to bring God's blessing to both Jews (v. 8) and Gentiles (v. 9a), in fulfillment of Scripture (vv. 9b-12). Paul concludes with a "wish-prayer." The whole paragraph, with its opening basic command, reference to Christ and Scripture in support of the command, and concluding prayer, closely resembles 15:1-6.[2]

---

2. This resemblance led a number of literary critics in the nineteenth century to suggest that vv. 7-13, or 8-13, were out of place and belonged somewhere else, perhaps at the conclusion of chap. 11 (see Wilckens, 3.104 for a survey). Schmithals (pp. 511-13, 519-21) holds a similar theory, arguing that 15:8-13 is the conclusion to "Romans A," while 15:1-4a, 7, 4b-6, is the conclusion to "Romans B."

The similarity of 15:7a to 14:1 suggests that Paul intends 15:7-13 to be the conclusion to his exhortation to the "weak" and the "strong."[3] But many disagree, arguing that the breadth of themes in 15:7-13 suggests that it is the conclusion to the hortatory section, beginning at 12:1,[4] or to the entire letter.[5] And it is true that this paragraph alludes to many of the themes that have dominated Romans: God's faithfulness to his promises to Israel (v. 8; cf., e.g., 1:2; 3:1-8; 9:4-5; 11:1-2, 28); the inclusion of Gentiles in the people of God (v. 9a; cf., e.g., 3:21-31; 4:12-17; 9:24-25, 30; 10:9-13; 11:28-30); and the broader themes of hope, joy, peace, faith, and the Holy Spirit (v. 13; cf. passim).[6] But many of the letter's key themes are also omitted (e.g., justification, victory over sin, the law, and death). I think it is preferable, then, to see Paul's allusion to some of the larger themes of the letter as a means of buttressing his final appeal to the "strong" and the "weak." He sets the local conflict in Rome against the panorama of salvation history in order to stimulate them to obedience.[7] As I argue in the introduction, this exhortation to the two groups in the Roman church is not the main driving force of the letter; but it is one of the key converging motivations that led Paul to write about the gospel the way that he has in Romans.

Paul's emphasis on the inclusion within the people of God of both Jews and Gentiles is not, then, simply an exemplary parallel to the problem of the "weak" and the "strong";[8] it gets to the heart of that problem. For, while some of the "strong" were Jews (e.g., Paul himself) and some of the "weak" may have been Gentiles, the dividing line between these two groups was basically the issue of the continuing applicability of the Jewish law. And this made it inevitable that the two parties would split along basically ethnic lines. Paul's "broadening" of perspective, as he reminds his readers of the New Covenant inclusion of Jews and Gentiles, provides the basic theological undergirding for his plea that the "strong" and the "weak" at Rome "receive one another."

7 "Therefore"[9] gathers up the threads of Paul's entire exhortation to the "strong" and the "weak." Similarly, his command that believers in both groups "receive one another" brings the section to its climax. As in 14:1, "receive" means more than "tolerate" or "give official recognition to"; Paul wants the Roman Christians to accept one another as fellow members of a family, with all the love and concern that should typify brothers and sisters.

---

3. See, e.g., Cranfield, 2.739; Wilckens, 3.104.

4. See, e.g., Cambier, "Liberté," p. 81; Ziesler, 336-37.

5. Dodd, 222; Dunn, 2.844-45; Hays, 70.

6. See Käsemann, 384-85; and esp. Dunn, 2.844-45.

7. Wilckens, 3.107.

8. Contra, e.g., Althaus, 145; Karris, "Romans 14:1–15:13," pp. 80-81. Cf. also S-H, 397, Lenski, 866, and Ziesler, 338, who think that Paul moves here into a new and broader topic. For the view I have adopted, see esp. Michel, 442; Murray, 2.203.

9. Gk. διό.

In 14:3, Paul prohibited "weak" Christians from judging their "strong" fellow believers on the grounds that *God* had "received" them. Now, however, he grounds a similar command on the truth that "*Christ*[10] has received you." Here we have yet another instance of Paul's close association of God and Christ in this part of Romans. The conjunction that Paul uses to introduce this theological reminder, *kathōs,* usually indicates a comparison; and, were we to adopt this meaning here, Paul would be teaching that believers should accept one another *in the same manner* as Christ has accepted us.[11] But *kathōs* here probably has its more rare causal sense.[12] Paul would then be insisting that Christians treat one another as the fellow members of the family of God that they all truly are. "Mutual love ought to reign supremely in a church wholly composed of the Lord's well-beloved."[13]

The final phrase, "to the glory of God," is a statement of purpose: "in order that God might be glorified."[14] The difficulty is to decide whether this is the purpose of believers' receiving each other[15] or of Christ's receiving us.[16] Perhaps, since the former is the leading idea, and since Paul has already drawn a connection between unity and the glorifying of God (v. 6), we should attach the phrase to the initial imperative, "receive one another."

8-9a The sense-redundant opening verb, "I say," has a rhetorical purpose, signifying that what follows is an especially "solemn doctrinal declaration."[17] This declaration, found in vv. 8-9a and supported with scriptural citations in vv. 9b-12, summarizes one of the central motifs of the letter: that God has fulfilled the promise of the Abrahamic covenant by bringing Gentiles into the people of God through the gospel. Paul reminds the Roman Christians of this truth in order to encourage them to "receive one another."[18] For the barrier between "strong" and "weak" is at root the

---

10. The article may again (as in v. 3) suggest that Paul wants to accentuate the titular significance of Χριστός, "the Messiah" (e.g., Käsemann).

11. See, e.g., Dunn.

12. E.g., Käsemann; Cranfield; Schlier.

13. Godet.

14. See NIV: "in order to bring praise to God." A few commentators (e.g., Tholuck) have suggested that εἰς has a local sense and that δόξαν τοῦ θεοῦ denotes the state of glory to which God is leading the believer (θεοῦ, then, being perhaps a possessive genitive); hence, "as Christ received you into God's glory." But, with all modern English translations and almost all commentators, I believe that εἰς indicates purpose, that δόξαν refers to the glory believers ascribe to God, and that θεοῦ is an objective genitive.

15. Godet; Cranfield; Wilckens; Stuhlmacher.

16. Thüsing, *Per Christum in Deum,* p. 42; S-H; Murray; Käsemann; Schlier. Several attach the phrase to both clauses: Calvin; Barrett; Dunn.

17. Cranfield.

18. So, e.g., Murray; Cranfield. Others (e.g., Godet; Wilckens) construe this theological assertion as an explanation of "Christ has received you."

barrier between Jew and Gentile, a barrier that Christ's ministry dismantled. Paul makes this clear by showing that Christ provided both for the fulfillment of God's promises to the Jews (v. 8) and for the inclusion of Gentiles in glorifying God (v. 9a). But the precise syntactical relationship between these two assertions is not clear. There are two basic options:

(1) Paul might intend most of v. 8 and v. 9a as two parallel assertions dependent on "I say":

I say:
a. that Christ has become a servant of the circumcision for the sake of the truth of God, in order to confirm the promises to the fathers;
b. and that the Gentiles are glorifying God for the sake of his mercy.[19]

(2) Paul might intend v. 8b and v. 9a as two parallel purpose expressions dependent on v. 8a:

I say that Christ has become a servant of the circumcision for the sake of the truth of God,
a. in order to confirm the promises made to the fathers;
b. and in order that the Gentiles might glorify God for the sake of his mercy.[20]

Despite Cranfield's claim that it is a "syntactical horror,"[21] the second alternative is preferable. As Käsemann notes, the awkward ("horror" is an exaggeration) syntax arises from Paul's desire to maintain a critical theological balance basic to Paul's argument in Romans: the equality of Jew and Gentile and the salvation-historical priority of the Jew (e.g., 1:16b: the gospel is "for all who believe," but "for the Jew first").[22] Paul accomplishes this here by using parallel statements to describe the benefit that both Jews and Gentiles derive from Christ's mission — promises made to the Jewish patri-

19. On this view, the infinitive δοξάσαι ("glorify") in v. 9a is parallel to γεγενῆσθαι ("became") in v. 8, both being used in noun clauses dependent on λέγω. See esp. Cranfield, who provides his usual full list of options, and also Godet. Wilckens adopts this syntax but takes the verb δοξάσαι as an implied imperative: the Gentiles "are to glorify" God for his mercy.

20. This reading takes the infinitive δοξάσαι ("glorify") in v. 9a to be dependent, along with βεβαιῶσαι ("confirm"), on εἰς τό. See NRSV; REB; TEV; and most commentators (e.g., S-H; Barrett; Murray; Käsemann; Schlier).

21. He is referring specifically to the change of subject from the first purpose clause — "in order that [Christ] might confirm . . ." — to the second — "in order that the Gentiles might glorify. . . ."

22. See also D. W. B. Robinson, "The Priesthood of Paul in the Gospel of Hope," in Reconciliation and Hope, p. 232; Theobald, "Gottesbild," pp. 151-52; Beker, 331-32, 343.

archs are confirmed and Gentiles are enabled to glorify God for his mercy to them — while at the same time subordinating the blessing of the Gentiles to Christ's mission to the Jews in confirmation of God's faithfulness. Thus Paul implicitly reminds the "weak," mainly Jewish Christians, that the "strong," mainly Gentile Christians, are full members of the people of God: they, "wild olive shoots," have been "grafted in" (11:17). At the same time, however, he reminds the "strong" that the status they enjoy rests on a Jewish foundation: "the root supports you" (11:18).

Having sorted out the syntax, I turn now to the details. Paul's assertion that Christ has become a servant to[23] "the circumcision," the Jews,[24] reflects Jesus' own sense of calling "to the lost sheep of the house of Israel" (Matt. 15:24), a calling that Paul alludes to by asserting that Christ was "born under the law that he might redeem those under the law" (Gal. 4:4b-5a). But by using a perfect tense — "has become"[25] — Paul implies that Christ's ministry to Jews is not confined to his earthly life or sacrificial death,[26] but continues even now, as the benefits of his death are appropriated by Jews.[27] This ministry, Paul goes on to say, was "for the sake of the truth of God," or, as we might paraphrase, "in order to show[28] that God is faithful."[29] Paul elaborates this idea in a purpose clause: "to confirm[30] the promises to the fathers." The use of the same words, "confirm the promises," in Rom. 4:16 might suggest that the promises are those made to Abraham and intended to embrace all his "seed," Gentile and Jewish believers alike.[31] But in

23. Gifford and Gaston, "Inclusion," p. 133, construe περιτομῆς as a genitive of origin: Christ is a servant who has come from the circumcision — in other words, he is Jewish. But this is not Paul's point here.

24. A few scholars take the word περιτομή as a reference to the rite of circumcision itself (e.g., S-H), but this seems clearly to be one of those many places where Paul refers to the distinctive Jewish rite as a way of denoting the Jews themselves (see the note on Rom. 3:30; cf. BAGD; Käsemann; Cranfield; Wilckens; Dunn).

25. Gk. γεγενῆσθαι (a poorly attested variant substitutes the aorist, γένεσθαι).

26. The use of διάκονος here to describe Christ may allude to Mark 10:45: "The Son of man came not to be served [διακονηθῆναι] but to serve [διακονῆσαι] and to give his life as a ransom for the many" (see, e.g., Thompson, *Clothed with Christ,* pp. 233-34; Dunn).

27. See Barrett; Morris.

28. See BAGD for this meaning of ὑπέρ here.

29. For the use of ἀλήθεια and cognates to refer to God's "faithfulness," see the note on 3:7.

30. Gk. βεβαιόω. In this context, it connotes "proving promises reliable by fulfilling them" (Cranfield; cf. BAGD; Michel; Wilckens). See the similar use in 4:16.

31. See Thüsing, *Per Christum in Deum,* pp. 43-44. If this were the case, the purpose clause in v. 9a would be subordinate to v. 8 as a whole:

> I say that Christ has become a servant of the circumcision for the sake of the truth of God,
>> in order to confirm the promises made to the fathers,
>> and so that the Gentiles might glorify God for the sake of his mercy.

9:5 and 11:28, Paul applies the language of "promise" and "fathers" (i.e., the patriarchs) to the Jewish people specifically. Probably this is Paul's intention here also. Matching God's purpose in confirming his promises made to the Jews is God's purpose in causing the Gentiles to glorify God "for the sake of his mercy," that is, because of the mercy that he has shown to them (see 11:29-30 especially).[32]

9b Paul uses his customary "as it is written" to introduce a series of four OT quotations. Common to all the quotations is the link-word "Gentiles," and the first three also feature the praise of God.[33] These elements suggest that Paul may intend the quotations to provide OT support for his assertion in v. 9a about the Gentiles glorifying God.[34] But the second quotation, from Deut. 32:43 LXX (v. 10), links Gentiles and Jews together in the praise of God, while the fourth, from Isa. 11:10, bases the Gentiles' hope in God on the Jewish Messiah. Probably, then, the quotations support vv. 8-9a as a whole.[35] Paul cites every part of the OT — the "writings" (vv. 9b and 11), the "law" (v. 10), and the "prophets" (v. 12) — to show that the inclusion of Gentiles with Jews in the praise of God has always been part of God's purposes.

The first quotation is from Ps. 18:49, or possibly 2 Sam. 22:50.[36] Paul may cite this text simply because it speaks of God being "praised"[37] among the Gentiles. But the speaker is David, and it is possible that Paul read the psalm typologically (as in his use of Ps. 69 in v. 3).[38] Thus Paul may cite the

---

32. Paul's pairing of ἔλεος and ἀλήθεια in parallel prepositional phrases may evoke the familiar OT combination of God's "truth [or faithfulness] and mercy" (חֶסֶד וֶאֱמֶת); cf. Michel; J. Dupont, "Rm 15,1-13: Imiter la charité du Christ," *Assembles du Seigneur* 4 (1961), 21. Some scholars suggest a contrasting use of the two words, "faithfulness" applying to God's commitment to Israel, "mercy" to the purely gracious extension of God's promise to the Gentiles (e.g., Schlatter). But the syntax suggests that "faithfulness" applies equally to Jews and Gentiles; and it is questionable whether such a distinction is theologically accurate.

33. Several scholars (e.g., Michel; Morris) find a gradation in the series of quotations, but this is not evident. Other scholars (e.g., Wilckens) think, without sufficient evidence, that Paul may be citing a pre-formed tradition. The "chain" of quotations here is similar to the rabbinic *haraz* form (e.g., Ellis, *Paul's Use of the Old Testament,* p. 97).

34. See, e.g., Murray.

35. See, e.g., Cranfield; Morris.

36. The LXX text of these two verses is identical, except for the placement of the vocative κύριε, which Paul omits (2 Sam. 22 reproduces the text of Ps. 18). With this exception, Paul's text reproduces the LXX exactly; and the LXX, in turn, is a faithful rendering of the Hebrew. Since Paul cites the Psalms so often, Ps. 18 is more likely his source (Koch, 34-35; contra, e.g., Schlatter).

37. For the meaning "praise" for the Greek verb ἐξομολογέω, see the note on 14:11.

38. It may be for this reason that Paul omits κύριε from his quotation; for it might

verse as a claim of the risen Christ. And this possibility gains credence when we note the context of the verse that Paul quotes. For David's praise of God "among the Gentiles" is stimulated by the fact that God has given him victory over Gentile nations. God has made him "the head of the nations," so that a "people whom I had not known served me" (v. 43). It would fit Paul's purposes perfectly if he were attributing to Christ this praise of God for the subduing of the Gentiles under his messianic rule. Through his death and resurrection, Gentiles who had not known the righteous rule of the Lord can now be brought into submission to him, glorifying him for his mercy to them. This opening quotation would then match the last in the series, both focusing on the way in which the Jewish king/Messiah has brought Gentiles into submission.

10 Paul introduces his next quotation with a brief linking phrase, "and again it[39] says." This second quotation is from Deut. 32:43 in the Septuagint version or from a text similar to it.[40] Like Ps. 18:50, this text speaks about the praise of God for his acts in subduing other nations/enemies. But an advance from the first quotation is evident, for the Gentiles are now themselves praising God — and doing it "with his people," namely, Israel. So what the OT text calls on the Gentiles to do, they now, through God's mercy to them in the gospel, are able to do — join Israel in praise of God.

11 "And again" picks up the formula used in v. 10. Paul quotes another OT verse — Ps. 117:1 — that calls on Gentiles to praise "the Lord."[41] It is surely no accident that the second (and only other) verse of this psalm cites God's "mercy" *(eleos)* and "truth" *(alētheia)* as reasons for this praise (cf. vv. 8-9a).

12 Paul varies his introductory formula by citing the author of the next quotation (Isa. 11:10). Paul's wording is again very close to the LXX,[42]

---

have suggested that the speaker was addressing Christ. See, e.g., Wilckens; Cranfield. We do not, however, need to view the text as a "prophetic utterance by Christ" (as Hanson *Studies,* p. 155, thinks).

39. The implied subject of λέγει is almost certainly "Scripture" rather than David.

40. The LXX differs considerably from the MT at this point; Paul's wording reproduces exactly the third line of the LXX text of the verse. But the LXX rendering may rest on a Hebrew Vorlage, attested in a Qumran scroll (4QDeut[a]; cf. Fitzmyer; note that the NRSV uses the LXX in preference to the MT at several points in translating this verse). A few scholars (e.g., Calvin) have thought that Paul might be paraphrasing Ps. 47:5.

41. Paul again follows the LXX (a straightforward rendering of the MT), varying from it only in reversing the order of πάντα τὰ ἔθνη and τὸν κύριον and in adding καί. In the second line, "all the peoples" (πάντες οἱ λαοί), who are urged to praise the Lord, are probably also the Gentiles (contra, e.g., Wilckens, who thinks the reference is to both Gentiles and Jews).

42. Paul differs only in omitting the words ἐν τῇ ἡμέρᾳ ἐκείνῃ ("in that day"), which come immediately after ἔσται in the LXX.

although in this case the LXX differs from the MT. For the Hebrew speaks of the root of Jesse standing "as a signal to the peoples" and of the Gentiles "inquiring" of him.[43] With its reference to the shoot of Jesse "arising" — a possible allusion to Jesus' resurrection[44] — to "rule" the Gentiles and to the Gentiles' "hoping" — a key word in this section (cf. vv. 4, 12) — the LXX rendering obviously suits Paul's purposes better than the MT. Nevertheless, the basic meaning of the text is the same in both versions; either would allow Paul to make the point he wants to make: that the Gentiles' participation in the praise of God (vv. 9b-11) comes as a result of the work of "the root of Jesse," a messianic designation.[45] Increasing the appropriateness of the quotation for Paul is the immediately following reference in Isa. 11 to God's gathering of the "remnant" of Israel from among the nations.[46]

13 Paul rounds off his exhortation in this paragraph, and his entire exhortation to the "strong" and the "weak," with a final "prayer-wish." In this prayer, Paul brings together many key elements from his exhortation and from the letter as whole.[47] As he did in vv. 5-6, Paul characterizes God in the address of his prayer-wish with a concept drawn from the immediate context. As the Gentiles have now come to "set their hope" on the root of Jesse, so Paul prays to the "God who gives hope."[48] In praying that this God might "fill[49] you with all joy and peace as[50] you believe," Paul is undoubtedly thinking specifically of the "weak" and the "strong" in the Roman community. He does not want the differing conclusions that they draw from their "believing" in Christ (cf. 14:1-2, 22) to take away that

---

43. The Hebrew of the MT is: וְהָיָה בַּיּוֹם הַהוּא שֹׁרֶשׁ יִשַׁי אֲשֶׁר עֹמֵד לְנֵס עַמִּים אֵלָיו גּוֹיִם יִדְרֹשׁוּ, which the NRSV renders "On that day the root of Jesse shall stand as a signal to the peoples; the nations shall inquire of him." On the basis of the LXX changes to the MT, B. Frid suggests an alternative, though unlikely, translation of Rom. 15:11 ("Jesaja und Paulus in Röm 15,12," *BZ* 27 [1983], 237-41).

44. Paul uses the same Greek verb that occurs here, ἀνίστημι, to refer to Christ's resurrection in 1 Thess. 4:14 and to the resurrection of believers in 1 Thess. 4:16 (and perhaps Eph. 5:14); cf. Käsemann; Schlier; Dunn.

45. "Root" is used as a messianic designation in Jer. 23:5; 33:15; Sir. 47:22; 4QFlor 1:11; 4QPat 3-4; Rev. 5:5; 22:16, usually in conjunction with the name David. In these texts, while we usually translate "root," the Greek word ῥίζα refers to a "shoot, springing from the root" (BAGD).

46. See Hays, 73.

47. Wiles, *Paul's Intercessory Prayers,* pp. 84-89.

48. The phrase ὁ θεὸς τῆς ἐλπίδος probably has this general sense (cf. REB; TEV; and, e.g., Cranfield) rather than, e.g., "the God in whom we hope" (Calvin), or "the God who both gives hope and in whom we hope" (Murray; Dunn).

49. Gk. πληρώσαι, an optative used to express a wish (see the note on v. 5).

50. Turner, 145 (cf. also Z-G, 493) think that the ἐν here might be causal — "because you believe" — but the usual temporal sense of the preposition (when followed by an infinitive) makes better sense in this context.

"peace"[51] and "joy" which they should be experiencing as joint participants in the kingdom of God (cf. 14:17). It is only as the "God of hope" fills them with these qualities that they will be able to "abound in hope," to realize in their community the hope of a new people of God in which Jews and Gentiles praise God with a united voice (cf. 15:6, 7-12). All this can happen, however, only "by[52] the power of the Holy Spirit" (see, again, 14:17).

Paul's remarks in 14:1–15:13 are directed to a set of very specific issues in the Roman (and first-century) church. All three specific issues are still debated by Christians: whether it is necessary to abstain from meat and from wine, and to observe the Sabbath and other "holy" days. But only on the issue of Sabbath observance is there a real parallel. For it was out of continuing reverence for the Mosaic law that some of the Roman Christians adopted these practices. But modern Christians who, for example, abstain from all alcoholic beverages do so not because they fear ritual contamination. Some abstain because they are leery of a product that has had such a sad history of "enslaving" those who partake (see the principle of 1 Cor. 6:12b). Many others do not drink because they do not want to set a bad example for others who might not be able to handle alcohol. Abstinence on these grounds may be a laudable course of action; but it has little basis in Paul's argument in these chapters. For the "weak" here are not those who cannot control their drinking. They are people who are not convinced that their faith in Christ allows them to do a particular thing. They are not "weak" in respect to handling alcohol; they are "weak" in respect to their faith (14:1). And Paul urges the "strong" to abstain, not because their example might lead the "weak" to drink to excess but because their example might lead the "weak" to drink and so to violate their conscience (14:22-23). Only, therefore, where the contemporary Christian is convinced that his drinking (or eating meat) might lead another to drink (or eat meat) in violation of his conscience is Paul's advice truly applicable to the matter of alcohol.[53]

But the value of this section is not limited to Paul's advice on these specific issues.[54] For Paul here sets forth principles that are applicable to a range of issues that we may loosely classify as *adiaphora:* matters neither required of Christians nor prohibited to them. Carefully defining these *adiaphora* is vital. On the one hand, not all issues can be put in this category. Paul

51. In the context, the reference is probably to peace among the members of the community (Käsemann; Dunn) rather than to "peace of mind" (Murray; Cranfield).
52. The Greek preposition ἐν has an instrumental force (Käsemann; Schlier), although it might shade also into a locative nuance — "in and through" (Dunn).
53. See also, e.g., Murray.
54. Ridderbos, *Paul,* p. 276.

considered certain matters pertaining to the gospel to be basic and nonnegotiable, and he fought like a tiger for them (cf. Galatians). To apply Paul's plea for tolerance in this chapter to these issues would be to surrender the heart of Christianity.[55] On the other hand, there are issues that are in this category of "things indifferent," and on these Christians are willingly and lovingly to "agree to disagree." Inflexible commitment to the basics; complete flexibility on the *adiaphora:* this was the posture of Paul that he would like every one of us to emulate.

Paul makes three specific points, each one built solidly on general theological truth.

(1) Paul was a realist: he knew that we have to deal with people "where they are." In his day Jewish Christians who had lived all their lives believing the law of Moses to be God's last and absolute word could not always align their consciences with the truth about the end of the law's authority. For such believers, while eating meat that might not be kosher was not "sin" in the absolute sense, it continued to be "sin" *for them* (cf. 14:14, 20). In much the same manner, believers in our day cannot always "internalize" the liberty of the gospel on all matters. On one or more practices on which the gospel gives freedom, these believers continue to have scruples. To them, Paul says: "Don't violate your conscience." And his theological justification? — "anything not done on the basis of faith is sin" (14:23). Paul would undoubtedly hope that such believers would "grow out of" their prejudice. But until they do, Paul does not want them to do anything that their consciences are telling them not to.

(2) For whatever reason (greater spiritual maturity; background; personality), other believers will not share the scruples of these believers. They do not find any bar at all in their conscience to the practice that some of their fellow believers abhor. To them, Paul says: "Don't use your freedom in a way that brings spiritual harm to a fellow believer" (14:13b, 20-21). And his theological justification cuts to the heart of what the gospel is all about. For the Christian, like the Christ he or she follows, should not be seeking to please him- or herself, but others (15:2-3). That same Christ is their Lord, who demands that those who belong to his kingdom "walk in love" (14:15), pursue peace with others (14:17, 19), and do everything they can to "build up" their fellow disciples (14:17, 19). Rather than "building up" fellow believers, Paul makes clear that the "strong" can run the risk of "tearing down" and causing spiritual harm to the "weak." Such harm will be caused these believers when

---

55. I think that Jewett's monograph *Christian Tolerance* may open the door to this danger. He suggests, e.g., that the only limit on tolerance is that one must stay consistent with one's own faith in responsibility to God (pp. 132-33) without making clear that our "faith" on these matters must be rooted in the absolute truth of the gospel.

those who have no scruples insist on exercising their liberty in front of the "weak" in such a way as to pressure them into doing what their consciences are forbidding them.

To be sure, Paul does not want the "strong" to walk around in constant fear lest something they do might "injure" a "weak" believer; little would be left of Christian liberty were this to be the case. We are probably justified in introducing here some of those limitations that Paul brings up in the parallel 1 Cor. 8–10 passage, where he urges the "strong" to go ahead with their legitimate behavior as long as no "weak" Christian is being harmed (1 Cor. 10:25-29). I may know, for instance, that some believers do not think a certain practice "right" for Christians. I should not refrain for that reason, but only if I think that my practice might bring spiritual harm to other believers. Finally, we must emphasize: Paul is not advocating that any Christian give up his or her liberty (which no human being can take from the believer); he is advocating only that we be willing, for the sake of others, to give up our *exercise* of Christian liberty. In Luther's famous formulation, "A Christian man is a most free lord of all, subject to none. A Christian man is a most dutiful servant of all, subject to all."[56]

(3) Paul's "bottom line" is the unity of the church. As we have indicated, this unity is not to be pursued at any price; but Paul is adamant about not allowing differences among believers about the *adiaphora* to injure the oneness of the body of Christ. Therefore, negatively, Paul tells those with scruples not to condemn believers who think differently (14:3, 10, 13a). Paul suggests that "weak" as well as "strong" believers should be able to recognize the difference between those matters required by the gospel and those that are not. And the "weak," while not enjoying the sense of liberty that the "strong" have, are not to condemn the "strong" for exercising that liberty. At the same time, he warns the "strong" about looking down on the "weak" (14:3, 10; cf. v. 13a). Those who consider themselves "enlightened" are always tempted to treat with condescension and even scorn those who are less "enlightened." Paul warns the "strong" not to succumb to this tendency. Paul's theological justification for this warning to both "weak" and "strong" is the central Christian affirmation "Christ is Lord" (14:4-9). Christians are slaves who owe absolute allegiance to their master — and only to their master; not to fellow slaves. No fellow believer, apart from Christ's own revelation and teaching in the gospel, has the right to call us to account.

Paul expresses this same point positively in the climax of the section: "Receive one another, just as Christ has received you" (15:7). Each of us must recognize that we have been "received" by Christ, as a matter of pure grace; and that same grace has reached out and brought into the kingdom

---

56. From *On the Freedom of a Christian Man*.

people from all kinds of races, nations, and backgrounds, and with all kinds of prejudices (see 15:8-12). Such differences should never be allowed to disturb the unity of the church.

VI. THE LETTER CLOSING (15:14–16:27)

Paul's sustained argument about the nature and implications of the gospel is at an end. So he returns to where he began, speaking of the Roman Christians and of his own ministry and plans (cf. 1:1-15). He thereby completes the "epistolary frame" around his portrait of the gospel.

The elements that Paul includes in this final section of the letter are typical of his letter conclusions:

Paul's Travel Plans	15:14-29	1 Cor. 16:1-9
Request for Prayer	15:30-32	cf. Eph. 6:18-20; Col. 4:3-4; 1 Thess. 5:25; 2 Thess. 3:1-2; Phlm. 22
Prayer-Wish for Peace	15:33	2 Cor. 13:11c; Gal. 6:16; Eph. 6:23; Phil. 4:9; 1 Thess. 5:23; 2 Thess. 3:16
Paul's Associates	16:1-2	1 Cor. 16:10-12, 15-18; Eph. 6:21-22; Col. 4:7-9; 2 Tim. 4:20
Exhortation to Greet One Another	16:3-15	1 Cor. 16:20b; 2 Cor. 13:12; Phil. 4:21a; (Col. 4:15); 1 Thess. 5:26; 2 Tim. 4:19; Tit. 3:15b
The "Holy Kiss"	16:16a	1 Cor. 16:20; 2 Cor. 13:12a; 1 Thess. 5:26
Warning/Exhortation	16:17-19	1 Cor. 16:13-14, 22; 2 Cor. 13:11b; Gal. 6:12-15 (?); Eph. 6:10-17 (?); Col. 4:17
Eschatological Wish/Promise	16:20a	1 Cor. 16:22b; 1 Thess. 5:24
Concluding "Grace"	16:20b	1 Cor. 16:23; 2 Cor. 13:14; Gal. 6:18; Eph. 6:24; Phil. 4:23; Col. 4:18c; 1 Thess. 5:28; 2 Thess. 3:18; 1 Tim. 6:21b; 2 Tim. 4:22b; Tit. 3:15b; Phlm. 25
Greetings from Paul's Associates	16:16b, 21-23	1 Cor. 16:19-20a; 2 Cor. 13:13; Phil. 4:21b-22; Col. 4:10-14; 2 Tim. 4:21b; Tit. 3:15a; Phlm. 23-24
Doxology	16:25-27	Phil. 4:20

Two things are evident from this chart.[1] First, while Paul tends to include certain elements in his letter closings, there is considerable variation both in the items that he includes and the order in which he places them. We should not, then, be surprised if Paul includes some elements in his conclusion to Romans that are not found elsewhere (e.g., the warning about false teachers; the doxology?) or excludes some that he often includes (e.g., an affirmation about the authenticity of the letter; cf. 1 Cor. 16:21a; Gal. 6:11; Col. 4:18; 2 Thess. 3:17a). These variations may well point to specific circumstances surrounding the composition of Romans. Second, the conclusion to Romans is by far the longest of Paul's letter closings — matching in that respect its counterpart, the letter opening.

A. PAUL'S MINISTRY AND TRAVEL PLANS (15:14-33)

Paul's travels are the leitmotif of this section and identify it as a discrete literary unit.[2] It falls into three basic parts, marked by the address "brothers" in vv. 14 and 30 and the transitional "therefore" in v. 22.[3] In vv. 14-21, Paul alludes to his past travels — "from Jerusalem around to Illyricum" (v. 19b) — to explain why he has written to the Roman Christians. His focus shifts to his future travel plans in vv. 22-29. Here Paul tells how he intends to "pass through" Rome on his way to Spain after delivering the collection to Jerusalem. Verses 30-33 are closely tied to this last matter, as Paul asks the Roman Christians to pray for that visit to Jerusalem. This section therefore reveals the degree to which Paul's past ministry and especially his anticipated itinerary shape the content and emphases of the letter.[4] A certain degree of reflection on the stage of ministry Paul has completed; concern about his reception by Jews and Jewish Christians in Jerusalem; preparation for his visit to Rome — all these contribute to the way in which Paul explains and applies his gospel in this letter.

The way in which the letter opening and closing "frame" the body of

---

1. For a similar chart, see Dunn, 2.854.

2. Käsemann, 389. Note also R. Funk's form-critical identification of this section as "apostolic parousia" ("The Apostolic *Parousia:* Form and Significance," in *Christian History and Interpretation,* pp. 249-68 [cf. p. 251]).

3. Most scholars so divide the section (see, e.g., Jervis [*Purpose of Romans,* p. 120], who identifies vv. 14-21 as the "writing" unit and vv. 22-32 as the "visit" unit). But a few place a break between vv. 24 and 25 (e.g., Morris, 508, 516; Fitzmyer, 710; Moiser, "Rethinking Romans 12–15," p. 581).

4. See on this esp. Jervis, *Purpose of Romans,* pp. 158-63; P. Müller, "Grundlinien paulinischer Theologie (Röm 15,14-33)," *KD* 35 (1989), 214-34.

Romans is seen all the more clearly when we note the way in which the contents of 15:14-33 match those of 1:1-15, and especially 1:8-15[5]:

Commendation of the Romans	15:14	1:8
"Apostle to the Gentiles"	15:15b-21	1:3, 13
Hindrance in visiting Rome	15:22	1:13a
"Indebtedness"	15:27	1:14
Desire to minister for mutual blessing	15:29	1:11-12
Prayer	15:30-32	1:9-10

1. Looking Back: Paul's Ministry in the East (15:14-21)

14*But I myself am confident, my brothers and sisters, concerning you, that you yourselves are full of goodness, being filled with all knowledge, able also to admonish one another.* 15*Now I have written to you on some points rather boldly,[6] reminding you because of the grace that was given to me by God* 16*with the purpose that I might be a minister of Christ Jesus to the Gentiles, serving the gospel of God as a priest, in order that the offering of the Gentiles might be acceptable, sanctified by the Holy Spirit.* 17*Therefore I have this[7] boasting in Christ Jesus with respect to the things of God.* 18*For I will not dare to speak of anything that Christ has not accomplished through me for the obedience of the Gentiles, in word and deed,* 19*in the power of signs and wonders, in the power of the Spirit.[8] As a result, from Jerusalem*

---

5. These parallels have long been noticed; cf., e.g., Chrysostom, Homily 29 (pp. 542-45).

6. The MSS tradition is divided between the forms τολμηρότερον (P[46], the Alexandrian MSS ℵ and C, Ψ, the western D, F, and G, and the majority text) and τολμηροτέρως (the Alexandrian A and B, and a few minuscules). Many commentators prefer the latter (e.g., S-H, 405; Käsemann, 391; Michel, 456; Schlier, 428; Cranfield, 2.753), while a few follow UBS[4] (although the editors do not mention the variant) in reading the former (Wilckens, 3.111; Dunn, 2.855). The meaning remains the same.

7. "This" translates the definite article τήν, which is read in the primary Alexandrian uncial B, in the secondary Alexandrian MSS C and 81, in the western uncials D, F, and G, and in some minuscules. Its omission in other manuscripts (e.g., the primary Alexandrian ℵ, the secondary Alexandrian A, Ψ, and the majority text) is probably secondary (cf. Käsemann, 393; Cranfield, 2.757; Dunn, 2.856; contra, e.g., Godet, 479; S-H, 406).

8. Most manuscripts include after πνεύματος ("Spirit") either θεοῦ ("of God") (e.g., P[46], the primary Alexandrian ℵ, Ψ, the western D [first corrector], and the majority text) or ἁγίου ("holy") (e.g., the secondary Alexandrian MSS A, 33, 81, and 1739, the western D [original hand], F, and G, and several important minuscules). The strength of the external support tends to favor the reading θεοῦ (cf. Metzger, 537; Fitzmyer, 713), but

and around to Illyricum I have fulfilled the gospel of Christ, 20*in this
way making it my intention to preach the gospel where Christ has not
been named, in order that I might not build on another's foundation,*
21*but, even as it is written,*

> *Those to whom it has not been announced concerning him
> will see, and those who have not heard will understand.*a

a. Isa. 52:15

As he did in the letter opening (cf. 1:11-12), Paul again displays sensitivity
about presuming to write to a church that he had neither founded nor pastored.
Hence the commendation and almost apologetic tone of vv. 14-15a. But, as
he also did in the opening (cf. 1:5, 14), Paul quickly tempers this hesitancy
with an assertion of his right to address the Roman church: as a mainly Gentile
congregation, it lies within the sphere of apostolic responsibility that God has
allotted him (vv. 15b-21).[9]

14 Paul's address, "brothers and sisters,"[10] signals the transition to a
new topic. After exhorting the Roman Christians at length (12:1–15:13), Paul now
commends them for their spiritual maturity. Undoubtedly Paul walks on eggshells
in his desire not to offend the Christians in Rome by assuming an authority over
them that they would not recognize.[11] But there is no reason to think that Paul is
insincere in what he says of them here.[12] Through trusted co-workers (e.g., Prisca
and Aquila; cf. 16:3), Paul had access to good information about the Roman
Christian community — information about both its problems and its strengths.
Thus he can say, emphatically, "I *myself*[13] am convinced"[14] that "you *your-*

---

internal evidence strongly favors the simple πνεύματος, though read in only one — albeit
important — uncial, B (cf. Lietzmann, 115; S-H, 407; Cranfield, 2.758).

9. While he overplays his hand, Stuhlmacher is probably right to discern here again
a polemical background: Paul must dispel doubts and diffuse resistance to him among the
Roman Christians (pp. 236-37; cf. also Käsemann, 390).

10. Gk. ἀδελφοί. Paul uses this address only sparingly in Romans (cf. 1:13; 7:1,
4; 8:12; 10:1; 11:25; 12:1; 15:30; 16:17).

11. As Käsemann puts it with some exaggeration, he is "undisguisedly wooing
the readers." S. N. Olson shows how other ancient writers would use an expression of
confidence in their readers to gain adherence to their ideas ("Pauline Expressions of
Confidence in his Addressees," *CBQ* 47 [1985], 282-95 [cf. 292-93]).

12. See esp. Cranfield, who objects to those who suggest that Paul uses the literary
category of the *captatio benevolentiae* simply as a diplomatic insincerity.

13. Gk. αὐτὸς ἐγώ. Paul uses the emphatic nominative pronoun to underscore the
sincerity of his conviction (cf. Cranfield; Dunn), probably because he is afraid that the rest
of the letter might have given the opposite impression (Godet).

14. "Am convinced" translates the perfect passive πέπεισμαι. On the meaning of
this form, see BAGD.

selves[15] are full of goodness, being filled with[16] all[17] knowledge." "Goodness" translates a rather rare word that can denote general "uprightness" in conduct or, more specifically, "kindness" and "generosity" toward others.[18] In so general a commendation, it should probably here be given the broadest possible meaning.[19] The Roman Christians' "goodness" flows from their comprehensive understanding of the Christian faith ("all knowledge").[20] Indeed, so complete is their understanding that they are "able to admonish one another."

15 But[21] if their knowledge of the faith is so extensive, why has Paul bothered to write them so long a letter? Paul admits that he wrote[22] "rather boldly"[23] in certain parts[24] of the letter, but he did so by way of reminder.[25] We may again spot a bit of diplomatic exaggeration in this assertion. But certainly the Romans would not be fooled by Paul into thinking that they

---

15. Paul may use the emphatic pronoun (Gk. αὐτοί) to suggest that the Roman Christians have experienced their spiritual birth and growth apart from Paul's (or anyone else's?) apostolic labors (cf. Käsemann; Schlier).

16. Gk. πεπληρωμένοι, the perfect connoting that the Roman Christians are in the condition of being filled (Burton, 154).

17. Whether or not we read the article before γνώσεως, πάσης will connote the idea of "the whole range of" (cf. Dunn).

18. The word is ἀγαθωσύνη. It occurs only in biblical Greek (16 times in the LXX) and in related literature (cf. LSJ) and only in Paul in the NT. It means "uprightness," "goodness" in Eph. 5:9 and 2 Thess. 1:11 and (perhaps) "generosity" in Gal. 5:22.

19. See, e.g., S-H; Wilckens; Dunn; Michel; contra, e.g., Käsemann and Cranfield, who think it denotes "honesty in dealings with others" and, e.g., Denney, who translates "charity."

20. Cf. S-H; Murray; Wilckens; Cranfield. As several commentators point out, the virtues Paul mentions here would be particularly necessary for the Roman Christians to overcome tensions between "strong" and "weak" (S-H; Murray; Schmithals). But it is not clear that Paul is thinking of that issue specifically.

21. The δέ is probably slightly adversative.

22. The aorist ἔγραψα is not "epistolary" because it refers here to the "past" act of writing the earlier part of the letter to which Paul refers (cf. BDF 334; Turner, 73).

23. τολμηρότερον is a comparative adverb from τολμηρός, "bold." Turner, 30, sees this as an instance of the comparative being used for the positive; but, in any case, there is general agreement on the translation "rather boldly" (BAGD).

24. The phrase ἀπὸ μέρους (found also in 11:25; 15:24; 2 Cor. 1:14; 2:5) could modify τολμηρότερον — "boldly in some measure" (Hodge; Murray) — or ἐπαναμιμνήσκων — "remind of things they know to a certain degree" (Godet), but it probably modifies the main verb, ἔγραψα. It must then refer to "parts" of the letter in which Paul has written "rather boldly." But any more specific identification of these parts — e.g., 12:1–15:13 (Cranfield) or 14:1–15:13 (Wilckens; Schmithals) — is impossible.

25. The ὡς before ἐπαναμιμνήσκων indicates manner, with the verb "write" assumed (cf. BAGD, I.2.a). NRSV "by way of reminder" is therefore better than NIV "as if to remind you." The verb ἐπαναμιμνήσκω occurs only here in the NT, but its simple form is common.

already knew everything contained in this letter — unless, indeed, they were a collection of the most insightful theologians who ever lived! Paul must intend his language seriously; and what he is saying is that the things he has taught them and exhorted them to do all derive from the faith that they hold in common with Paul. In his letter Paul has done nothing but to explicate, for them in their circumstances, the implications of the gospel.[26]

But however much Paul might want to tiptoe carefully around the Romans' sensibilities, he will not surrender his right to address them, and to address them with authority. For, as he indicates in the last part of this verse, his "bringing to their remembrance" gospel truths is based on "the grace that was given to [him] by God."[27] By this, of course, Paul does not mean that general divine grace that underlies and empowers all of Christian existence. As in 1 Cor. 3:10; Gal. 2:9; Eph. 3:2, 7, 8, Paul refers to that special gift of God's grace which established him as an apostle; cf. 1:5, "the grace of being an apostle."

16 Of special relevance for the matter of Paul's authority over the Roman Christians is the purpose[28] for which God called Paul to be an apostle: that he might be "a minister of Christ Jesus to the Gentiles." As God indicated in his initial call of him (Acts 9:15; cf. Rom. 1:5; Gal. 1:16), Paul was given a special responsibility for the Gentiles: a call that the Jerusalem apostles duly recognized (Gal. 2:1-10). The Roman church, a mainly Gentile church (cf. 1:6-7, 14-15), therefore lies within the scope of Paul's apostolic authority. However, it is interesting that Paul does not in v. 16 name himself an "apostle" but a "*leitourgos* of Christ Jesus." With this word, Paul may simply be describing himself as a "servant" or "minister" of Christ.[29] But the sacrificial language in the last part of the verse makes it more likely that he intends the term to connote *priestly* ministry specifically.[30] Thus Paul goes on to describe

---

26. See esp. Wilckens.

27. We follow, e.g., Käsemann and Cranfield, in connecting διὰ τὴν χάριν τὴν δοθεῖσάν μοι with ἐπαναμιμνήσκων ("reminding") rather than directly with ἔγραψα ("I have written"). But since ἐπαναμιμνήσκων is subordinate to ἔγραψα, the difference in meaning is virtually nonexistent.

28. We take εἰς τὸ εἶναι to indicate purpose (cf., e.g., Cranfield; Schlier).

29. Cf. Schlatter.

30. See the notes on 13:6 for the meaning of λειτουργός and related words. The term refers to a priest, or priests, in 2 Esdr. 20:36 (= Neh. 10:39); Isa. 61:6; cf. also Sir. 7:30; *Ep. Arist.* 95; *T. Levi* 2:10; 4:2; 8:3-10; 9:3; Philo, *Life of Moses* 2.94, 149; *Special Laws* 1.249; 4:191; *Allegorical Interpretation* 3.175; *Posterity* 184. Cranfield, following Barth *(Shorter),* thinks that Paul here presents himself as a Levite, in subordinate service to Christ the High Priest. But while λειτουργός often refers to the Levites in the LXX, the context here makes a reference to priestly service clear (so almost all commentators). See, further, H. Schlier, "Die 'Liturgie' der apostolischen Evangeliums (Römer 15,14-21)," in *Das Ende der Zeit: Exegetische Aufsätze und Vorträge* (Freiburg/Basel/Vienna: Herder, 1971), pp. 171-76.

his "ministry" here as consisting in "serving the gospel of God[31] as a priest."[32] The purpose of this ministry, further, is that "the offering[33] of the Gentiles might be acceptable." The "offering" might be the praise, or obedience (cf. v. 18), of the Gentiles,[34] but it is more likely to be the Gentiles themselves (cf. NIV, "that the Gentiles might become an acceptable sacrifice").[35] Paul therefore pictures himself as a priest, using the gospel as the means[36] by which he offers his Gentile converts as a sacrifice acceptable to God.[37] The language of "priest" and "sacrifice" here is, of course, metaphorical; Paul makes no claim to be a "priest" or to be offering sacrifice in any literal sense. This is made altogether clear by his reference to the Gentiles themselves as the sacrifice.[38] In keeping with the rest of the NT, Paul assumes

31. θεοῦ is a source genitive (Turner, 211): "the gospel that comes from God."

32. The construction is difficult, but τὸ εὐαγγέλιον is probably an accusative of respect; cf. the similar construction in 4 Macc. 7:8 (v.l.): τοὺς ἱερουργοῦντας τὸν νόμον, "those who serve the law as priests." See, e.g., Dunn. The verb ἱερουργέω does not occur in the LXX or elsewhere in the NT, but it is used frequently in Philo and Josephus, always with the meaning "offer sacrifice" (G. Schrenk, *TDNT* III, 252). This renders Cranfield's looser translation, "serve with a holy service," very unlikely.

33. Gk. προσφορά, which can mean the *act* of offering (cf. Acts 24:17; Heb. 10:10, 14, 18) or, as here, what is offered (cf. also Acts 21:26; Eph. 5:2; Heb. 10:5, 8; cf. BAGD). The word is common in Sirach in the LXX (nine out of 13 LXX occurrences).

34. In this case, the genitive τῶν ἐθνῶν is subjective. See, e.g., A.-M. Denis, "La fonction apostolique et la liturgie nouvelle en esprit," *RSPT* 42 (1958), 405-6; R. Dabelstein, *Die Beurteilung der 'Heiden' bei Paulus* (BBET 14; Frankfurt: Peter Lang, 1981), pp. 112-14; Robinson, "Priesthood of Paul," p. 231; Elliott, *Language and Style,* pp. 91-92; Dunn (as possible).

35. Cf. also NRSV; NASB; REB; TEV; as well as the great majority of commentators (e.g., Michel; Käsemann; Cranfield). On this view, the genitive τῶν ἐθνῶν is epexegetic. Not only does this interpretation fit the context well, but it also accords with the probable background for Paul's conception: Isa. 66:19-20, where God proclaims that in the last days he would send survivors from the nations to declare his glory among the nations and bring all their kindred "from all the nations as an offering [LXX ἐκ πάντων τῶν ἐθνῶν δῶρον] for the Lord" (cf. Murray; Aus, "Paul's Travel Plans," pp. 236-37; Hultgren, *Paul's Gospel,* pp. 133-34; J. Ponthot, "L'expression cultuelle du ministère paulinien selon R 15,16," in *L'Apôtre Paul,* pp. 254-62).

36. Calvin says that the gospel is "like a sword by which the minister sacrifices men as victims to God."

37. Though not explicit, the sacrificial imagery makes it clear that the one before whom the sacrifices are εὐπρόσδεκτος, "well pleasing," is God (cf. 1 Pet. 2:5; the word does not occur in the LXX and only in 15:31; 2 Cor. 6:2; 8:12 elsewhere in the NT).

38. See Hodge: "Paul . . . no more calls himself a priest in the strict sense of the term, than he calls the Gentiles a sacrifice in the literal meaning of that word." On the word ἱερουργέω in this sense, see C. Wiéner, "Ἱερουργεῖν (Rm 15,16)," *SPCIC* 2.399-404.

an eschatological transformation of the OT cultic ministry, in which animal sacrifices are replaced by obedient Christians (cf. 12:1) and the praise they offer God (Heb. 13:15), the temple by the community of believers (e.g., John 2:21; 1 Cor. 6:19; 1 Pet. 2:5), and the priest by Christians (1 Pet. 2:5, 9) or Christian ministers.[39] But one thing has not changed: to be "pleasing to God," sacrifices must still be "sanctified." And so, Paul acknowledges, it is ultimately God himself, by his Holy Spirit, who "sanctifies"[40] Gentiles, turning them from unclean and sinful creatures to "holy" offerings fit for the service and praise of a holy God.[41]

17 This verse is closely related to vv. 15b-16: this boasting I do — in claiming so central a role in God's purposes for the Gentiles[42] — is perfectly legitimate, for it is a boasting "in Christ Jesus" and "with respect to the things of God."[43] Paul condemns boasting in one's own achievements (cf. 3:27; 4:2-3); but Paul's priestly ministry to the Gentiles is not of his own doing — it is the work of God's grace in his life.

18 Paul now further justifies his "boasting," explaining specifically how it is a boasting that is "in Christ Jesus."[44] With perhaps an intentional glance at his earlier use of the cognate adverb in v. 15 ("rather boldly"), Paul claims that he would not "be so bold"[45] as to speak "of anything other than

---

39. On this theme, see esp. Newton, *Concept of Purity.* Paul did not, then — as some Hellenistic Jews did — "spiritualize" the sacrifices; he "eschatologized" them. See, e.g., P. T. O'Brien, *Consumed by Passion: Paul and the Logic of the Gospel* (Homebush West, Australia: Lancer, 1993), pp. 31-32; Käsemann; Dunn; Schlier; Michel.

40. Paul here uses the passive form, ἡγιασμένη, as he often does (see 1 Cor. 1:2; 6:11; 7:14 [twice]; 1 Tim. 4:5; 2 Tim. 2:21). In the OT, see esp. Ezek. 36:22-28, which predicts the day when God would "sanctify his name" among the Gentiles.

41. See O'Brien, *Consumed with Passion,* pp. 31, 50-51.

42. The connection with the preceding verse is especially clear if, as I have argued above (see the note on the translation), we read the definite article τήν before καύχησιν. For the article acts almost like a demonstrative pronoun, pointing back to vv. 15b-16 (e.g., Käsemann; Cranfield; Dunn).

43. τά makes a substantive out of the following prepositional phrase. The accusative, as in the identical phrase in Heb. 2:17, is an accusative of reference, or an adverbial accusative (BDF 160; Turner, 221). The "things" to which Paul refers will look backward to vv. 15b-16 rather than forward to vv. 18-19 (contra Jervis, *Purpose of Romans,* p. 123).

44. See Cranfield. Verse 17 is a hinge verse in the paragraph, drawing a conclusion from vv. 15b-16 and setting up Paul's further discussion in vv. 18ff. (see S. N. Olson, "Epistolary Uses of Expressions of Self-Confidence," *JBL* 103 [1984], 591). Some interpreters think that Paul's reticence to "boast" may reflect his desire not to be classed as an "enthusiast," a Christian worker who took undue pride in his spiritual gifts and accomplishments (e.g., Michel, 458-59). But Paul does not give evidence of any such concern (cf. Käsemann, 393; Dunn, 2.862).

45. Gk. τολμήσω; cf. τολμηρότερον in v. 15.

what Christ accomplished"[46] through him.[47] What Paul earlier alluded to — "grace given to me by God," "sanctified by the Holy Spirit" — he now makes clear: the success of his ministry is due entirely to divine enablement. Christ is the active "worker" in the things of which Paul is speaking; Paul is simply the instrument.[48]

At the end of the verse, Paul specifies the goal of what Christ has accomplished through him — "obedience of the Gentiles" — and its means — "by word and by deed." In making the Gentiles' obedience the object of his ministry, Paul sounds again a key note in this paragraph and in Paul's initial introduction of himself to the Romans; cf. 1:5: "through [Christ Jesus our Lord] we have received grace and apostleship for the obedience of faith of the Gentiles." And "obedience" will therefore have the same meaning here as in this earlier verse, denoting comprehensively the believers' response to the Lord Jesus Christ, including, but not limited to, faith. "Word and deed" is a natural combination, occurring frequently in extrabiblical Greek and in the NT.[49] It subsumes all Paul's apostolic activity under the heading of speaking and doing.

19 The first part of this verse continues Paul's description of the means by which Christ has "accomplished" things through him. "By word and by deed" (v. 18b) is the general summary of these means; the two "by"[50] phrases at the beginning of v. 19 go into more detail. It is tempting to connect the first of these phrases with "by deed" and the second with "by word" in a chiastic arrangement. Paul would then be identifying the "deed" part of his ministry with "signs and wonders" and the "word" part of his ministry as accomplished by "the power of the Spirit."[51] However, Paul would obviously attribute all that he accomplishes in ministry — whether "by word" or "by

---

46. Paul uses the verb κατεργάζομαι. In many contexts, it is indistinguishable in meaning from the more common ποιέω (see the note on 7:15); here, however, it carries a certain emphasis: "produce," "work out" (cf. Dunn).

47. The syntax of the verse is complicated, the singular object after λαλεῖν, τι ("something") being filled out with a clause introduced with a genitive plural relative pronoun (ὧν . . .). But once we recognize that the relative pronoun is plural "according to the sense" — referring to the many different "things" alluded to by τι — the meaning resolves itself into something like "anything other than what Christ accomplished" (cf. Z-G, 494; Cranfield; and most English versions). Barrett suggests that Paul intends a contrast not only between things accomplished by himself and by Christ but also between things accomplished by himself and by others. But there is no indication of such a second contrast here (cf. Ziesler).

48. We see here again, then, an implicit trinitarianism (cf. Murray).

49. See BAGD; in the NT elsewhere: Luke 24:19; Acts 7:22; Col. 3:17; 2 Thess. 2:17.

50. Gk. ἐν, which is instrumental in both phrases.

51. See, e.g., Bengel; Leenhardt; Michel.

deed" — to the power of the Spirit. This makes it more likely that "by the power of the Spirit"[52] refers to all the means of ministry that Paul identifies in vv. 18b-19a.[53] And, while "the power of signs and wonders"[54] probably relates to the "deeds" part of Paul's ministry, it is unlikely that Paul intends the phrase as a complete description of his "work." For there is no good reason to confine the term "deed" or "work"[55] to miraculous works only;[56] and Paul's apostolic "work" included many other kinds of activities.

"Signs and wonders" is standard biblical phraseology for miracles, the former term connoting the purpose of the miracle and the latter its marvelous and unusual character. The phrase occurs especially often in descriptions of the miracles at the time of the Exodus and in the history of the early church.[57] Paul may then choose to illustrate his apostolic work with this phrase in order to suggest the salvation-historical significance of his own ministry.[58] For Paul is not just another apostle; he is *the* apostle to the Gentiles, the one chosen to have a unique role in opening up the Gentile world to the gospel. Many scholars think that Paul's conception of his role goes even further: that he thinks of his offering up the Gentiles and/or their gifts (e.g., the collection; cf. vv. 25-28) as fulfilling the prophetic predictions about the pilgrimage of the nations to Jerusalem at the climax of salvation history.[59] However, we have seen reason to doubt whether Paul views his role as so narrowly eschatological (see, e.g., our comments on 11:14).[60] That Paul saw himself as a significant figure in salvation history, with a central role in the Gentile mission,

52. The genitive πνεύματος may be epexegetic — "the power that is the Spirit" (e.g., Käsemann; Schlier) — but is more likely subjective — "the power exercised [through me] by the Spirit"; cf. Godet.

53. Meyer; Murray; Cranfield.

54. "Power" (δύναμις) does not refer to a miracle (as it does often in the Gospels and occasionally in Paul [cf. 1 Cor. 2:4; 12:10, 28, 29; 2 Cor. 12:12 {with σημεῖα, "signs," and τέρατα, "wonders"}]), but, generally, to the divine power "breaking forth in signs and wonders" (Godet; cf. Murray).

55. Gk. ἔργον.

56. Cf. Calvin; Murray; Dunn. On ἔργον in Paul, see the note on 2:6.

57. σημεῖα ("signs") and τέρατα ("wonders") occur together in the LXX 29 times; and 15 refer to the Exodus events (Exod. 7:3, 9; 11:9-10; Deut. 4:34; 6:22; 7:19; 11:3; 26:8; 29:3; 34:11; Neh. 9:10; Ps. 78:43; 105:27; 135:9). In Acts, the phrase refers to the miracles of Jesus (2:22) and then to the miracles accomplished in Christ's name by the apostles (2:43; 4:30; 5:12), including Paul (14:3; 15:12). The phrase also occurs in Mark 13:22; 2 Cor. 12:12; 2 Thess. 2:9; Heb. 2:4.

58. See Dunn; O'Brien, *Consumed with Passion,* p. 142.

59. See esp. Munck, 49-55; also, e.g., Aus, "Paul's Travel Plans," pp. 232-62; Käsemann; Barrett; Schlier; Wilckens; Dunn.

60. See also on this passage, J. Knox, "Romans 15:14-33 and Paul's Conception of His Apostolic Mission," *JBL* 83 (1964), 3-8.

is clear; but that he thought his own efforts would bring that mission to its conclusion is not clear at all.

Paul has identified the initiator and agent of his apostolic work — Christ; its purpose — "the obedience of the Gentiles"; and its means — "in word and deed, in the power of signs and wonders, in the power of the Spirit." Now he identifies its results: "so that from Jerusalem and around to Illyricum I have fulfilled the gospel of Christ." This result statement contains three matters that require comment.

(1) Why does Paul choose Jerusalem and Illyricum as the geographical limits of his previous ministry? We would have expected Paul to identify Antioch as the jumping off point of his distinctive outreach to the Gentiles (Acts 13:1-2). Many scholars think that Paul is thinking more theologically than geographically and that he uses Jerusalem to denote the starting point of the Christian movement.[61] But this suggestion does not square well with the obvious personal and geographical focus of the verse, a focus confirmed by the reference to Illyricum. Probably, then, Paul alludes to his own ministry in Jerusalem.[62] The Book of Acts gives plenty of evidence of such ministry (9:26-30; cf. 26:20), although Paul's own comments (e.g., Gal. 1:18-19, 22) suggest that it was quite brief. But, however brief, Paul can legitimately claim Jerusalem as the geographical beginning point of his ministry. And Illyricum is appropriately chosen as the other limit. The Illyrians inhabited a region north and west of Macedonia; and the Romans carved out a province in the area, occupied today by northern Albania, much of Yugoslavia, and Bosnia-Herzegovina.[63] Paul is probably referring to this province.[64]

61. Cf., e.g., Michel; Cranfield; Wilckens; Müller, "Grundlinien," pp. 216-17; O'Brien, *Consumed with Passion,* pp. 37-38. A. S. Geyser ("Un Essai d'explication de Rom. XV.19," *NTS* [1959-60], 156-59) thinks that Paul uses Jerusalem to symbolize the approval of the 11 apostles of his ministry.

62. See, e.g., Zeller, *Juden,* p. 227; Meyer; Fitzmyer; Dunn (?). ἀπό might suggest that Paul began his preaching not in, but just outside Jerusalem. But the preposition is often equivalent to ἐκ (cf. BAGD, 87). We may also discern a muted allusion to Paul's emphasis in the letter on "the Jew first."

63. See D. B. Madvig, *ISBE* II, 802-3.

64. Noting that neither Paul nor Acts mentions missionary activity of Paul in Illyricum, many scholars think that Paul may be claiming only to have preached "as far as," or "up to the boundaries of" Illyricum. μέχρι, when used spatially, indicates the limits of movement; but when a large geographical region is that limit, it is not clear whether the limit includes or excludes that region. This is the only verse in the NT in which μέχρι has a spatial significance (although see the v.l. in Acts 20:4). Hahn (*Mission,* p. 96) thinks that Illyricum may represent the ancient boundary between the eastern and western empires; but there is no evidence that this was the case. But it is quite possible that Paul ventured into Illyricum during his apparently circuitous trip from Ephesus to Corinth on his third journey (Acts 20:1-2). The ancient geographer Strabo (7.7.4) mentions that the Egnatian

(2) Why does Paul add the word *kuklō* to his description of his travels from Jerusalem to Illyricum? The word means "circle" or "ring."[65] It may, then, indicate the "ring" around Jerusalem, for instance, the environs of the city where Paul first began to preach.[66] But the word is always used in the NT as an adverb.[67] Some scholars think that Paul retains the allusion to a circle, viewing his movement from Jerusalem to Illyricum as an "arc"[68] or as one part of a larger "circle" of apostolic preaching.[69] But literal reference to a "circle" is absent from the word's NT occurrences; it usually means simply "around," "about."[70] The closest parallel is Mark 6:6b, where Jesus is said to have "traveled round about the villages, teaching." Probably, then, Paul intends simply to indicate that the journey he describes was not a direct one, but that he moved "around," "in a circuitous route" as he made his way from Jerusalem to Illyricum (cf. KJV and NASB, "round about").[71]

(3) How can Paul claim that he had "fulfilled" the preaching of "the gospel[72] of Christ"[73] in these regions? Does not this language suggest a finality to preaching in the eastern Mediterranean that hardly accords with the relatively small number of churches that had been planted? There are four possible explanations. First, Paul may be claiming to have "filled" *(plēroō)* the regions indicated with the gospel.[74] But this view assumes without warrant that the object of the verb is not "gospel" but "regions" or something of the sort. Second, then, Paul might be speaking of the manner of his preaching: "I have fully and effectively preached the gospel."[75] But this does not do justice to the strength of the verb "fulfill." A third explanation seeks to do just that. Its

---

Way passes through Illyricum on its way from the Adriatic Coast to Macedonia. Knowing Paul's preference to stick to well-traveled Roman roads, then, Paul may easily have preached in the southern regions of Illyricum during the movements mentioned by Luke in Acts 20:1-2. See, e.g., Madvig, *ISBE* II, 802; Godet; Meyer; Haldane; Dodd; Bruce; Barrett.

65. LSJ.

66. So many older commentators: e.g., Godet; Alford; Gifford.

67. See, e.g., Robertson, 295, 296; BAGD. And, as S-H point out, we would have expected the article if this had been the meaning of the word.

68. BAGD; Käsemann; Dunn.

69. See esp. Knox, "Romans 15:14-33," pp. 10-11. Knox thinks that Paul conceives of the Mediterranean world as a great circle, with him having responsibility for preaching in the northern half of that circle. See also Beker, 71.

70. See Mark 3:34; 6:6; Rev. 4:6; 5:11; 7:11.

71. Chrysostom; S-H; Viard; Cranfield.

72. εὐαγγέλιον clearly has here a dynamic sense.

73. The genitive Χριστοῦ is objective: the preaching of the good news *about* Christ (e.g., Michel; Cranfield).

74. Calvin; Haldane.

75. See, e.g., S-H.

advocates note, rightly (see the note on 13:9), that Paul often uses this verb in an eschatological sense. They therefore think that Paul is hinting again at his special role as an eschatological preacher, destined to bring Gentiles into the kingdom and hence usher in the end.[76] But I have already indicated the problems with this view in my comments on the phrase "signs and wonders" earlier in the verse. The fourth explanation, then, seems to be the only reasonable one: Paul claims that he has brought to completion in the regions designated his own special apostolic task of planting strategic churches.[77] As Knox puts it,

> He could say that he had completed the preaching of the gospel from Jerusalem to Illyricum only because this statement would have meant for him that the message had been proclaimed and the church planted in each of the nations north and west across Asia Minor and the Greek peninsula — "proclaimed" widely enough and "planted" firmly enough to assure that the name of Christ would soon be heard throughout its borders.[78]

20 Further support for this last interpretation of "fulfill the gospel of Christ" is found in the connection of v. 19 with v. 20. "In this manner" at the beginning of the verse looks both backward and forward, linking Paul's fulfilling of the gospel in v. 19b with the procedure that he describes in v. 20b-c: "But[79] in this way I am fulfilling the gospel (v. 19b): by striving[80] to preach the gospel where Christ has not been named, lest I build on another person's foundation."[81] By "where Christ has not been named," Paul means places where there is no worship of Christ at all.[82] Paul here indicates that he believed that God had given him the ministry of establishing strategic churches in virgin gospel territory; like the early American pioneers who pulled up stakes anytime they could see the smoke from another person's cabin, Paul felt "crowded" by too many Christians. His purpose was therefore "not to

76. Käsemann; Dunn; Aus, "Paul's Travel Plans," pp. 257-60; Hultgren, *Paul's Gospel,* p. 135; Munck, 51-55.

77. O'Brien, *Consumed with Passion,* pp. 39-43; Godet; Murray; Cranfield.

78. Knox, "Romans 15:14-33," p. 3.

79. Gk. δέ.

80. The participle φιλοτιμούμενον, which modifies πεπληρωκέναι, is modal. The verb φιλοτίμουμαι has the root meaning "love [φίλος] of honor [τιμή]" and therefore might here mean "strive after honor" or "have as one's ambition" (Käsemann; Godet; Meyer). But the papyri indicate a weakening in meaning, especially when followed by an infinitive, to no more than "strive eagerly," "am zealous" (MM); this seems to be the meaning here and its other NT occurrences (2 Cor. 5:9; 1 Thess. 4:11) (cf. Cranfield; Dunn).

81. See especially clearly Dunn; and, in substance, Cranfield; Wilckens.

82. "Name" (ὀνομάζω) means here clearly "name in worship" (cf., e.g., Fitzmyer; contra, e.g., BAGD).

build on another's foundations" (see also 2 Cor. 10:13-18). As he does in 1 Cor. 3:9b-15, Paul uses the metaphor of a building to describe the work of ministry. And, as that passage makes clear, Paul does not intend to say anything disparaging in general about the work of "building on the foundation," for example, further evangelism and pastoral care. It was simply that he knew that his commission from the risen Christ did not include these activities. To adopt Paul's other metaphor from the same passage, he had been given the task of "planting"; others, like Apollos, were there to "water" the fragile new growth (1 Cor. 3:5b-8).

How does Paul's expressed reluctance to build on another's foundations fit with his assumption of some degree of authority over the Roman Christians through this letter and with his anticipated visit to them? That the Roman church lacked "foundations" because it had not yet received the *imprimatur* of an apostle is unlikely — although it is quite likely that the church had not been founded by, nor visited by, any apostle at this point. We should rather recognize that the desire Paul's expresses here is just that, and not an absolute rule. For in pursuing his pioneer church-planting ministry, Paul would often have to engage in other ministry activities or to work with churches that he did not himself found (e.g., Antioch). And, as Paul will explain in the next paragraph, his letter and planned visit to the Roman church are means by which he hopes to advance his pioneering mission work into a new field — Spain.[83]

21 As he so often does, Paul clinches his point with an OT quotation. The quotation is from Isa. 52:15b.[84] Paul has probably chosen to quote this text for at least three reasons. First, it justifies Paul's decision not "to build on another's foundations" (v. 20); for the text speaks of bringing a message to those who have not yet heard.[85] Second, it accords with Paul's sense of calling to Gentiles, since the ones who have not had it announced to them

---

83. See, e.g., P. von der Osten-Sacken, "Erwägungen zur Abfassungsgeschichte und zum literarisch-theologischen Charakter des Römerbriefes," in *Evangelium und Tora: Aufsätze zu Paulus* (Munich: Kaiser, 1987), pp. 120-23.

84. Its wording exactly matches the LXX; at least, it does if we follow the reading adopted in UBS[4] and found in the majority of MSS, and place ὄψονται at the end of the first line. Vaticanus (B), however, places the verb at the beginning of the line, and some commentators (e.g., Cranfield and Dunn) prefer this reading, suspecting the majority reading as an assimilation to the LXX. The LXX translation differs a bit from the MT, which, literally translated, is "For what had not been told to them, they will see; and what they did not hear they will contemplate." The LXX rendering, by adding "concerning him," makes the application to the servant clearer, but it does not materially change the meaning.

85. See S. Pedersen, "Theologische Überlegungen zur Isagogik des Römerbriefes," *ZNW* 76 (1985), 62.

and have not yet heard are "kings" and "nations" (cf. v. 15a). Third, it alludes to the content of Paul's gospel. For Isa. 52:15 is part of the famous fourth "servant" passage, and the "him" concerning whom these Gentiles have not been told is the Servant of the Lord. Paul's pioneering church-planting ministry among the Gentiles is fulfilling the OT prediction about Gentiles coming to see and understand the message about the Servant of the Lord.[86]

2. Looking Ahead: Jerusalem, Rome, and Spain (15:22-29)

22Therefore I also have been hindered these many times from coming to you. 23But now, no more having a place in these regions, and having the desire for many years to come to you, 24as I go to Spain — [1]for I hope to visit you as I pass through and to be helped on my way there by you, if I might first for a while enjoy your company. 25But now I am going to Jerusalem to minister to the saints. 26For Macedonia and Achaia were well pleased to make some contribution for the poor of the saints who are in Jerusalem. 27Indeed, they were well pleased, and they are debtors to them. For if the Gentiles have participated with them in spiritual things, they are obliged also to minister to them in material things. 28Therefore, when I have finished and put a seal on this fruit for them, I will go away through you to Spain. 29And I know that when I come to you, I will come in the fullness of the blessing of Christ.[2]

This paragraph begins (vv. 22-24) and ends (vv. 28-29) and thus has as its main theme Paul's intention to visit Rome. As he did at the beginning of the letter (1:13), Paul semi-apologizes for not having come sooner. Even now, he cannot come immediately, for he must first travel to Jerusalem on an important ministry errand (vv. 25-27). And, while sincere in his desire to visit Rome, Paul makes it clear that Rome is not much more than a stop on his way to his ultimate destination: Spain (vv. 24, 28). Paul here hints at one of his main

---

86. Since Paul implies that it is his mission to announce matters "concerning him," e.g., the Servant, it seems unlikely that he is suggesting here that he sees himself in the role of the Servant (Käsemann; Cranfield; Schlier; Fitzmyer; contra O'Brien, *Consumed with Passion,* pp. 143-44; Michel; Dunn — though I agree with Dunn that Paul elsewhere suggests such an identification).

1. Recognizing the incompleteness of Paul's sentence, the secondary Alexandrian minuscule 33, the second (Byzantine) corrector of $\aleph$, and the majority text add ἐλεύσομαι πρὸς ὑμᾶς, "I will come to you"; cf. KJV. The addition is secondary.

2. The Alexandrian 33, the uncial Ψ, and the majority text (including the second corrector of $\aleph$) add τοῦ εὐαγγελίου ("the gospel") to Χριστοῦ ("of Christ"); cf. KJV. The addition is secondary.

purposes in writing Romans: the need to get help from the Romans for his projected Spanish mission (cf. *propempō* in v. 24).

22 "Therefore" might link this verse with the missionary principle that Paul has just enunciated (v. 20) — I have been hindered in coming to you because I did not want to build on another's foundations[3] — but more likely connects it with his description of his missionary work in the eastern Mediterranean (vv. 17-19, esp. 19b) — I have been hindered in coming to you because I was concentrating on "fulfilling the gospel from Jerusalem to Illyricum."[4] It was the needs of ministry in these regions that "hindered"[5] Paul "many times"[6] from coming[7] to Rome.

23-24a "But now" contrasts the situation in the past, when Paul was prevented by gospel ministry in the east from coming to Rome, with the present situation, in which, having "completed" that ministry (cf. v. 19b), he is free to move on. We would therefore expect Paul to announce in the sentence that begins here his plan to come to Rome. And this seems to have been Paul's original intention, which he hints at in v. 24 — "I hope to visit you as I pass through" — and spells out in v. 28 — "I will go away through you." But, as he sometimes does, he allows subordinate ideas to crop up to such an extent that he never gets around to finishing his sentence. We have here, then, an unfinished sentence.[8] It begins with two parallel participial clauses: "having no longer an opportunity[9] in these regions[10]" and "having

3. Käsemann.

4. E.g., Godet; Cranfield; Wilckens; Schlier.

5. Gk. ἐνεκοπτόμην is an imperfect form, probably with iterative significance; and it is best translated (as many Greek verbs that refer to the indefinite past) with an English perfect tense (Burton, 28). It comes from the verb ἐγκόπτω, used also in the NT in Acts 24:4; Gal. 5:7; 1 Thess. 2:18; 1 Pet. 3:7. It means the same thing here as the verb κωλύω, which Paul uses in a similar way in 1:13.

6. τὰ πολλά is probably temporal — "these many times" (e.g., Godet; S-H; Käsemann; Cranfield); contra, e.g., Zerwick, 74, "to a great extent," Michel, "in all these cases."

7. The genitive article (τοῦ) with the infinitive conveys an ablatival sense (Burton, 401; Zerwick, 386).

8. See, e.g., S-H; Michel; Cranfield; Dunn. Godet avoids this conclusion by adopting a very weak variant, omitting the γάρ in v. 24b and thus making the subordinate clauses in vv. 23-24a depend on ἐλπίζω. English versions handle the problem in different ways. Only the NASB retains the syntax of the original, indicating the breaking off of Paul's sentence in v. 24a with a dash (see our literal rendering above). KJV (on the basis of a textual variant; see the note on the translation above), NIV, and TEV add the missing main clause. NRSV and REB turn the second ἔχων ("having") in v. 23 into a finite verb.

9. Gk. τόπον, literally "place." But the word often takes on the metaphorical sense of "possibility," "opportunity," "chance" (BAGD).

10. Gk. κλίμασι; the reference is probably to the "districts" or Roman provinces located "round about" the line from Jerusalem to Illyricum (cf. v. 19b; Paul also uses the

the desire[11] for many years[12] to come to you." Both are probably causal,[13] the former explaining why Paul can now come to Rome and the latter why he plans to. The previous hindrance of ministry in the east has been removed; and Paul's long-held wish to visit Christians at the very seat of the Roman Empire can now be fulfilled. The third subordinate clause (v. 24a) is temporal: "when[14] I go to Spain." This clause could be dependent on the second participial clause in v. 23b — having the desire for many years to come to you when I go to Spain[15] — but it is probably dependent on the assumed main clause — [I will come to you] when I go to Spain.[16]

Parts of Spain (which in the ancient world included all the Iberian peninsula) had been occupied by Rome since about 200 B.C.; but it was only in Paul's lifetime that the Romans had fully organized the entire area. Until recently, scholars seemed confident that there was a significant Jewish presence in Spain by this time;[17] but this is now questioned.[18] Why Paul had chosen Spain as his next mission territory cannot be determined;[19] the most

---

word in 2 Cor. 11:10 and Gal. 1:21). We must, of course, interpret this "lack of opportunity" in terms of Paul's special pioneer church planting ministry. He is not suggesting that there is no more preaching to be done in these regions or that all the nations in the east have been reached (contra Barrett); as Cranfield notes, Paul undoubtedly knew of many "eastern" regions that still required evangelistic ministry (cf. also Dunn).

11. Gk. ἐπιποθίαν, a NT *hapax* (it is a variant reading in 2 Cor. 7:11).

12. The preposition ἀπό in this clause has the same force as an accusative of extent (Zerwick, 70).

13. Cranfield.

14. ὡς has a temporal meaning here; and the addition of ἄν and the use of the subjunctive πορεύωμαι suggest indefiniteness (= ὅταν) (BDF 455[2]; Moule, *Idiom Book*, p. 133; although Turner, 112, takes it as definite).

15. Cranfield; cf. NRSV; NASB; REB.

16. See NIV; TEV. The indefiniteness of the construction is not, then, due to uncertainty about Paul's plans for the visit but to uncertainty about whether his Jerusalem visit will allow him to carry it out.

17. See, e.g., the "old" Schürer (*The Jewish People in the Time of Jesus Christ* [2d ed.; 3 vols.; Edinburgh: T & T Clark, 1890], 3.38); and, e.g., Michel; Käsemann.

18. See esp. W. P. Bowers, "Jewish Communities in Spain in the Time of Paul the Apostle," *JTS* 26 (1975), 395-402; cf. also R. Jewett, "Paul, Phoebe, and the Spanish Mission," in *The Social World of Formative Judaism and Christianity: Essays in Tribute to Howard Clark Kee* (ed. J. Neusner et al.; Philadelphia: Fortress, 1988), pp. 144-47; O. F. A. Meinardus, "Paul's Missionary Journey to Spain: Tradition and Folklore," *BA* 41 (1978), 61-63; Fitzmyer.

19. Aus suggests that Spain would have represented for Paul the OT "Tarshish," the "end of the earth" (cf. Isa. 66) to which Paul must travel to complete his task of bringing Gentiles as an offering to Jerusalem and thus usher in the parousia ("Paul's Travel Plans," pp. 242-46; cf. also Müller, "Grundlinien," p. 218; Black; Stuhlmacher). Dunn suggests that it was the natural extension of Paul's "arc" from Jerusalem to Illyricum.

we can say is that Paul was evidently confident that the Spirit was leading him there.[20]

24b Paul elaborates[21] on what he has hinted at in vv. 23-24a: that he hopes to fulfill his desire to visit[22] the Roman Christians on his projected journey to Spain. Paul also mentioned his intention to visit the Roman church at the beginning of the letter, but he claimed there that his purpose was to "preach the gospel" in Rome (1:15). Now, however, Paul speaks generally of "enjoying their company,"[23] hints at a fairly short stay ("for a while"[24]), and treats Rome as little more than a layover on his trip to Spain ("while passing through"). The best explanation for the difference in emphasis (there is no contradiction[25]) between these two statements is Paul's sensitivity about financial matters. For Paul makes clear in this verse that he hopes his "layover" in Rome will result in his gaining material support from the Roman Christian community for his Spanish mission: the verb *propempō* is a regular technical term for missionary support.[26] Probably, then, Paul is reluctant even to hint at this request for help at the beginning of the letter; only after he has

20. Whether Paul ever arrived in Spain is a point that we can never be certain about. The NT never reports such a visit; and the evidence of the Pastoral Epistles suggests that Paul turned back to the east after his trip to Rome (see also Phil. 1:25-26; 2:23-24, if written [as is likely] from Rome). But an early Christian document, *1 Clement* (cf. 5:7), can be interpreted to suggest that he did reach Spain. See, on the whole matter, Bruce, *Paul,* pp. 447-48.

21. The γάρ ("for") is explanatory.

22. Paul uses the verb θεάομαι, which can mean simply "see," but which can also take on the connotation of "see a person as the basis of friendship and with helpful intent — 'to visit, to go to see' " (*GEL* 34.50). See also 2 Chron. 22:6; Josephus, *Ant.* 16.6; Matt. 22:11 (?) (cf. Cranfield).

23. Gk. ἐμπλησθῶ, from ἐμπίπλημι. The verb means, generally, "to fill" (cf. Luke 1:53; Acts 14:17) or "to satisfy" (John 6:12; Acts 14:17 [?]; 2 Cor. 6:25), and hence here, "to be satisfied with you [ὑμῶν]," e.g., "to enjoy your company" (BAGD).

24. ἀπὸ μέρους has a temporal significance (BAGD).

25. A layover for a relatively short time in Rome on his way to Spain would still afford plenty of opportunity to preach the gospel there. Thus there is no need to suggest that Paul is thinking of different visits in these two texts (as, e.g., Elliott, *Language and Style,* p. 87, suggests).

26. See Acts 15:3; 20:38; 21:5; 1 Cor. 6:6, 11; 2 Cor. 1:16; Tit. 3:13; 3 John 6; cf. F. Vouga, "L'Épître aux Romains comme Document Ecclésiologique (Rm 12–15)," *ETR* 61 (1986), 487; Michel; BAGD; *GEL* 15.72 (Bartsch, "Gegner," p. 29, however, is not convinced that this meaning is established). What kind of support Paul hoped for is not specified. In keeping with the basic meaning of the verb — "accompany," "escort" — he might be hoping for coworkers to join him in the work. Help with the customs and languages of the new territory may also be included; and almost certainly financial and logistical support.

"built a relationship" with the community through his letter does he think it appropriate to bring up the matter.[27]

25 Only one last obligation in the east prevents Paul from fulfilling his desire to visit Rome and then to move on to evangelize in Spain: "But now I am going[28] to Jerusalem to minister[29] to the saints."[30] As Paul makes clear in the following verses, the ministry he intends to have in Jerusalem is a very specific one: sharing with the Jewish Christian community there the money that Paul had gathered from his own mainly Gentile mission churches. This "collection for the saints" was a major focus of Paul on his so-called "third missionary journey"; each letter he wrote on the journey mentions it (cf. also 1 Cor. 16:1-2; 2 Cor. 8–9).[31] By speaking of the collection as a "ministry," Paul points to the fact that it was a means by which Gentile Christians could express in a very practical way their love and concern for their less well-off brothers and sisters.[32] It is the need to bring this collection to Jerusalem that hinders Paul from coming straight to Rome. Paul apparently plans to travel to Rome almost immediately; and this suggests that he is writing from Greece after he had finished gathering the money from the Gentile churches (cf. Acts 20:2-3).

26 Having mentioned his purpose of "ministering" in Jerusalem,

27. See his letter to the Philippians, in which he gets around to thanking the community for its financial help only at the end (4:10-20).

28. The present tense of πορεύομαι probably implies that Paul is even as he writes preparing to leave for Jerusalem (cf. Cranfield; Dunn).

29. The participle διακονῶν could be modal, indicating that Paul goes "in service" of the saints (cf., e.g., Godet; Michel), but it probably expresses purpose (cf. Chrysostom; Cranfield; Wilckens; Schlier; Fitzmyer). J. J. O'Rourke ("The Participle in Rom 15,25," *CBQ* 29 [1967], 116-18) shows that the present tense of the participle is no problem for this interpretation.

30. Many scholars think that Paul uses ἅγιοι ("saints") here as a virtual technical term for the Jerusalem Christians (cf. also 15:26, 31; 1 Cor. 16:1; 2 Cor. 8:4; 9:1, 12), revealing the earliest Christian community's early takeover of this honorary title of the people of God (cf., e.g., K. F. Nickle, *The Collection: A Study in Paul's Strategy* [SBT 48; London: SCM, 1966], p. 138; Barrett; Michel; Schlier; Schmithals; Dunn; L. Cerfaux thinks that the term refers to the leaders of the Jerusalem church [" 'Les Saints' de Jérusalem," in *Recueil Lucien Cerfaux* {2 vols.; BETL 6-7; Gembloux: Duculot, 1954}, 1.392-97]). But this is not clear since every time he uses the term of the Jerusalem Christians its limitation to this particular group of believers is either explicit or clear from the context (cf. Cranfield; Wilckens).

31. For general studies of the "collection," see esp. D. Georgi, *Die Geschichte der Kollekte des Paulus für Jerusalem* (TF 38; Hamburg: Evangelische, 1965); Nickle, *Collection;* K. Berger, "Almosen für Israel: Zum historischen Kontext der paulinischen Kollekte," *NTS* 23 (1976-77), 180-204.

32. Paul uses διακονέω with respect to the collection also in 2 Cor. 8:19, 20, and calls it a διακονία, a "ministry," in 2 Cor. 8:4; 9:1, 12, 13.

Paul now explains[33] what he means by it in vv. 26-28a, before returning to his starting point, his projected trip to Rome and to Spain, in vv. 28b-29. His references to the Roman provinces of Macedonia (= modern northern Greece, Macedonia, and southern Albania/Macedonia) and Achaia (= the bulk of modern Greece) are of course intended to denote the churches that were to be found there (e.g., at Philippi, Thessalonica, Berea, and Corinth).[34] As his letters to the Corinthians suggest, Paul has not been shy about exhorting these churches to participate in the collection. But their participation is, nevertheless, of their own free will: they were "pleased"; they "freely decided" to make a contribution.[35] Paul suggests something of the significance of this contribution by calling it a *koinōnia*, literally, a "fellowship." Here the word clearly means "that which is readily shared,"[36] "contribution," but there is certainly an allusion to the word's common use in Paul to denote the loving intimacy of the Christian community. As Paul makes explicit in 2 Cor. 8:4 and 9:13, the Gentile Christians' contribution to the Jewish Christians in Jerusalem is an expression of this unity and intimacy.[37]

Paul's identification of the recipients of this expression of fellowship, "the poor of the saints in Jerusalem," can be interpreted in three different ways: (1) "the poor saints in Jerusalem" (KJV); (2) "the poor among the saints in Jerusalem" (NIV; NASB; REB; NRSV; cf. TEV);[38] (3) "the poor, that is, the saints in Jerusalem."[39] Both the first two options assume that "poor" is an economic designation. The first, however, suggests that all the

---

33. The γάρ is again explanatory.

34. Cranfield notes that Paul here simply extends into ecclesiology the common practice of denoting the people of nations by the name of the nation. Why Paul mentions only churches from these regions is not clear. Some think that he intentially conceals the scope of the enterprise (e.g., Käsemann) or that he reflects the fact that the Galatian churches, despite his letter to them, had recently rebuffed his efforts to claim them back to his "law-free" gospel (e.g., Luedemann, *Paul, Apostle of the Gentiles*, p. 86; Beker, 72-73). But it may simply be that these were the areas that came to mind because they were closest both to Paul and to the Romans (Dunn).

35. See TEV, "That decision was their own." Cf. G. Schrenk, *TDNT* II, 741; Godet; Cranfield; Wilckens. The verb is εὐδόκησαν, a variant aorist form of εὐδοκέω (e.g., with a lengthening of the ε to form the augment; cf. BAGD), which can mean "be pleased, take delight," "resolve," "determine" (similar Pauline occurrences, with the verb followed by an infinitive, are: 1 Cor. 1:21; 2 Cor. 5:8; Gal. 1:15; Col. 1:19; 1 Thess. 2:8; 3:1).

36. *GEL* 57.101. The construction with the middle form of ποιέω is standard in such expressions (see Z-G, 495).

37. F. Hauck, *TDNT* III, 807.

38. So most grammars (e.g., Turner, 209; Moule, *Idiom Book*, p. 43) and commentators (e.g., Käsemann; Cranfield; Wilckens; Fitzmyer); and cf. Georgi, *Kollekte*, pp. 81-82; Luedemann, *Paul, Apostle of the Gentiles*, p. 79.

39. E. Bammel, *TDNT* VI, 909; Michel (possible); Schlier; Schmithals.

Christians in Jerusalem were poor and that the collection was meant accordingly for them all, while the second suggests that only some of the "saints" were poor and that the collection was directed specifically to them. The third rendering, however, taking "the poor" and "saints" as having the same scope, assumes that "poor" is a theological description, drawn from the OT and Jewish tradition that used the term to denote the "righteous" and taken over by the early Jerusalem church as a self-description.[40] The NT contains passages in which "poor" has this theological nuance.[41] But Paul gives no hint of such a nuance here; and surely an economic meaning is more likely in a context where he talking about a financial contribution.[42] Of the first two alternatives, the second is to be preferred since it explains better why Paul uses both "poor" and "saints."

27 Using the same verb that he used at the beginning of v. 26, Paul reiterates the free choice of "Macedonia and Achaia" to participate in the collection; but he immediately adds, "indeed,[43] they are indebted[44] to them [the saints in Jerusalem[45]]." We can remove the apparent conflict between these assertions if we view the "obligation" Paul speaks of as moral rather than legal.[46] No one was compelling (or had the power to compel) the Gentile Christians to give money to the impoverished Jewish Christians in Jerusalem; they gave "cheerfully" (cf. 2 Cor. 9:7) and without compulsion

---

40. K. Holl ("Der Kirchenbegriff des Paulus in seinem Verhältnis zu dem der Urgemeinde," in *Gesammelte Aufsätze zur Kirchengeschichte,* vol. 2: *Der Osten* [Tübingen: Mohr, 1928], pp. 44-67) was instrumental in inaugurating this interpretation. He refers especially to Gal. 2:10, where he thinks the Jerusalem apostles' request to Paul to "remember the poor" refers specifically to the need for the Gentile churches to express solidarity with the Jerusalem "mother" community in a kind of "tax."

41. E.g., Luke 6:20; Jas. 2:5.

42. For the case against identifying "poor" as a technical name for the early Jerusalem Christians, see esp. L. E. Keck, "The Poor among the Saints in the New Testament," *ZNW* 56 (1965), 100-129; idem, "The Poor among the Saints in Jewish Christianity and Qumran," *ZNW* 57 (1966), 54-78.

43. Gk. καί; cf., e.g., Käsemann.

44. Gk. ὀφειλέται; another verbal parallel to the letter opening; cf. 1:14: "I am under obligation [ὀφειλέτης] to both Greeks and barbarians, to both the wise and the foolish."

45. The antecedent of αὐτῶν is probably τῶν ἁγίων ("the saints") rather than τοὺς πτωχούς (Dunn; contra Cranfield). The noun ὀφειλέτης can be followed by either a genitive or dative word to express the person(s) to whom the debt is owed (BAGD).

46. The lack of compulsion about the collection that Paul emphasizes both here and in 2 Cor. 8–9 suggests that it cannot be viewed as a "tax" on the Gentiles, equivalent to the requirement that Diaspora Jews pay a "temple tax" (cf. E. Bammel, *TDNT* VI, 909; Käsemann; Nickle, *Collection,* pp. 87-93). Berger, however, thinks that the Jerusalem apostles may have viewed the collection differently, as an essential expression of the Gentiles' commitment to Israel ("Almosen").

(2 Cor. 9:5). But Paul did want the Gentile Christians to recognize that they had received much from the Jewish Christians in Jerusalem and that this had placed them under a moral obligation to reciprocate.[47] Specifically, the Gentiles (i.e., Gentile Christians) have "received a share[48] in the spiritual things"[49] of the Jewish Christians — that is, in the gospel and all its associated blessings. Paul alludes here to a central theological theme of the letter: that the salvation enjoyed by the Gentiles comes only by way of the Jewish Messiah and the fulfillment of promises made to Israel (1:16; 4:13-16; 11:17-24; 15:7-8).[50] There is a sense in which the spiritual blessings of the new age belong especially to the Jewish Christians; and Gentile Christians should acknowledge and give thanks for their "sharing" of these blessings with them. And it is by "serving"[51] the Jewish Christians with "material things" that the Gentiles can express their sense of indebtedness and thanksgiving.[52]

These verses reveal that the collection was more than a charitable enterprise; it was a strategic theological/practical enterprise as well.[53] For Paul understands that the Gentiles' status as members of the people of God is inextricably tied to a salvation history that has an indelible OT/Jewish cast. Gentile Christians, many with no previous ties to Judaism and living far from Jerusalem, need to understand this also; and their giving of money to the "saints in Jerusalem" will go a long way toward solidifying this sense of "indebtedness."[54] For their part, Jewish Christians need to understand that salvation

---

47. Some interpreters (e.g., Bengel, 3.189; Calvin, 535-36; Schmithals, 537; Fitzmyer, 723; Nickle, *Collection,* pp. 69-70) think that Paul is subtly inviting the Romans to participate in the collection. But the immediacy of Paul's plans to leave for Jerusalem makes this unlikely.

48. The verb κοινωνέω followed by the dative can mean "give a share of something" (as in 12:13) or, as here, "receive a share of something" (BAGD; S-H).

49. Gk. πνευματικοῖς.

50. See, e.g., Beker, 72; Müller, "Grundlinien," pp. 231-32.

51. Gk. λειτουργῆσαι. The choice of this verb (cf. also Acts 13:2; Heb. 10:11) may suggest that Paul views the collection as an act of worship, since it is often used in the LXX with reference to the cult. But the verb is also used in secular Greek of the work of civil servants (cf. *New Docs.* 1.45). It is possible, though not clear, that the priestly associations of the cognate word λειτουργός from 15:16 are still present here.

52. The "spirit/flesh" contrast here (πνευματικοῖς/σαρκικοῖς) is not, as usually in Paul, a moral one (cf. the notes on 7:5). It is a contrast between the spiritual realm and the material realm; cf. 1 Cor. 9:11: "If we have sown for you spiritual things [πνευματικά], then should we not reap your material things [σαρκικά]?"

53. See, e.g., J. Eckert, "Die Kollekte des Paulus für Jerusalem," in *Kontinuität und Einheit: Für Franz Mußner* (ed. P.-G. Müller and W. Stenger; Freiburg: Herder, 1981), pp. 65-80.

54. Many scholars think that Paul viewed the collection as the fulfillment of the OT predictions about an influx of Gentile gifts into Jerusalem in the last days (see esp.

history has moved on from the days in which God's people were mainly restricted to Israel. Moreover, their willingness to receive a financial contribution from Gentiles will signify their acceptance of this new situation. It is precisely Paul's concern about the Jewish Christians' response to the collection that surfaces in his request for the Roman Christians' prayer (vv. 30-33).

28 Paul now makes the transition back to his "main" point in this paragraph: his projected visit to Spain via Rome. However, as we have seen, Paul gets tangled up in his syntax in vv. 23-24a and so ends up there only implying his plan to make this trip. Now he makes it explicit in the main clause of the sentence: "I will go away through you[55] to Spain." But the timing of this trip depends on the "ministry" to the saints in Jerusalem, as Paul indicates in a compound subordinate clause: "when[56] I have completed[57] this [service[58]] and placed a seal on this fruit for them." The main point Paul makes is clear enough: he cannot leave for Spain until he has delivered the collection. But what he means by "put[ting] a seal on this fruit" is not clear. "Fruit" refers to the collection itself.[59] But what does it mean to "seal" it? Many translations (e.g., NRSV; NIV; TEV; REB) and commentators suggest that Paul simply refers to the safe delivery of the money.[60] But affixing a seal to something is often an official affirmation of authenticity;[61] perhaps, then,

---

Isa. 66:19-20); cf., e.g., Aus, "Paul's Travel Plans," pp. 240-41, 260-61; Georgi, *Kollekte,* pp. 84-86; Richardson, *Israel,* pp. 145-46. But, as in the related interpretation about the "offering of the Gentiles" (v. 16), this is unlikely.

55. Gk. δι' ὑμῶν; Moule, *Idiom Book,* p. 55, translates "via you"; cf. διαπορευό-μενος, "pass through," in v. 24.

56. The "when" has no explicit counterpart in the Greek text; but it is legitimate to add it because the participles are probably temporal.

57. Gk. ἐπιτελέσας. The verb means here simply "complete, finish," with no further connotations (Denney; Cranfield); Paul uses it also in 2 Cor. 8:6, 11, with reference to the collection.

58. τοῦτο, "this," is neuter and refers in a general way to the concept of the collection as Paul has developed it in vv. 26-27.

59. So virtually all commentators; contra, e.g., H.-W. Bartsch, who thinks it refers to the Gentile believers of the Diaspora (". . . wenn ich ihnen diese Frucht versiegelt habe. Röm 15.28," *ZNW* 63 [1972], 95-97) and Nickle (*Collection,* pp. 128-29), who thinks it denotes Paul's ministry. Murray thinks Paul uses the word to suggest that what the Gentiles give to the Jerusalem Christians is the "product" of the spiritual benefits they have received from them.

60. E.g., BAGD; Schlier; cf. Dunn.

61. See, e.g., Esth. 8:8, 10; John 3:33. All three other Pauline uses of σφραγίζω refer to believers being "sealed" with the Holy Spirit, and in each text the idea of "authenticating" believers, "marking" them as truly redeemed, seems to be intended (2 Cor. 1:22; Eph. 1:13; 4:30). In the NT the verb is also used with reference to the "sealing" of the tomb of Christ (Matt. 27:66), the "sealing up" (in order to keep secret) of apocalyptic teachings (Rev. 10:4; 22:10), the "sealing" shut of the abyss (Rev. 20:3), and "marking" so as to identify people (John 6:27; Rev. 7:3, 4 [twice], 5, 8).

Paul, as the "apostle to the Gentiles," intends to accompany those delivering the collection to Jerusalem in order to affirm its integrity and insure that it is understood rightly.[62]

29 As Käsemann puts it, Paul here breathes "a sigh of relief" as he contemplates his eventual visit to the Romans. For by then the collection will, he trusts, be safely delivered, the poor Christians in Jerusalem somewhat relieved of their crushing burden, and a stronger fellowship between Jewish and Gentile believers secured. When he comes to the Romans, then, he will come "in[63] the fullness of Christ's blessing." "Fullness" emphasizes the completeness of the blessing that Paul anticipates in Rome. If we translate literally, this blessing would seem to be one that Paul imparts to the Roman Christians through his ministry.[64] But it might be legitimate to assume that Paul thinks not only of his coming but of the results of his coming; and he may then be alluding to a mutuality of "blessing": Paul ministering to the Roman Christians, and the Christians there encouraging and helping Paul (cf. the mutuality in 1:12).[65]

3. A Request for Prayer (15:30-33)

> 30*Now I urge you, brothers and sisters,[1] through our Lord Jesus Christ and through the love of the Spirit, to strive with me in prayers on my behalf to God,* 31*in order that I might be delivered from those who are disobedient in Judea and that my ministry[2] for Jerusalem might be acceptable to the saints,* 32*in order that, coming to you in joy*

---

62. A. Deissmann notes papyrus texts that speak of "sealing [sacks] of grain" in order to guarantee the correctness of their contents (*Bible Studies* [Edinburgh: T & T Clark, 1901], pp. 238-39; cf. also MM). These texts are close to the idea here of "sealing fruit." For a view similar to the interpretation I have adopted, see Calvin; Murray; Cranfield. Reference to an affirmation on the part of the Jerusalem Christians of Paul's apostleship (cf. L. Radermacher, "σφραγίζεσθαι. Rm 15.28," *ZNW* 32 [1933], 87-89; Viard; Fitzmyer) is unlikely since it is the collection, not Paul, that is sealed.

63. Gk. ἐν, here used to indicate accompaniment (Zerwick, 117).

64. So, e.g., Michel; Murray.

65. Cf. S-H; Barrett; Dunn.

1. Gk. ἀδελφοί. The word is omitted in two very early and important manuscripts, P[46] and the primary Alexandrian witness B, and Zuntz (pp. 197-98) thinks that the omission is original. But all other manuscripts include it, and it fits Paul's usual style (cf. Cranfield, 2.775-76).

2. The primary Alexandrian uncial B and the "western" text (D, F, G) read δωροφορία ἐν, "bringing of a gift in," in place of διακονία εἰς, "ministry unto, or for," which is found in all other manuscripts. The former is an obvious attempt to smooth out the Greek (cf. Metzger, 537-38; contra Nickle, *Collection,* p. 134).

907

through the will of God, I might find rest with you.[3] 33*May the God of peace be with you all. Amen.*[4]

Paul often includes requests for prayer toward the end of his letters (see the introduction to 15:14–16:27). Often, however, those requests are very general. His request here, however, grows directly out of his reference to the collection for the poor among the saints in Jerusalem in vv. 25-28a. Paul asks the Romans to join him in praying for two things: (1) personal safety (v. 31a); and (2) the Jerusalem Christians' willingness to accept the collection (v. 31b). But Paul has not forgotten his visit to Rome; he makes clear that it is through a positive answer to these requests that he will be able to come to Rome with joy and to find rest for his soul there (v. 32). The paragraph concludes with another typical Pauline letter-closing feature: a prayer-wish that God might be with his readers (v. 33).

Paul's deep concern about his upcoming trip to Jerusalem and the success of his great collection enterprise shows through clearly here. It is certainly an exaggeration to think that concern about this enterprise was the motivating factor for his letter to the Romans.[5] But, involving as it did the relations between Jew and Gentile in the early church, it was one of those

---

3. As Metzger (p. 538) puts it, "This verse involves a nest of variant readings." The text after the opening ἵνα is found in five different forms:

1. ἐν χαρᾷ ἐλθὼν πρὸς ὑμᾶς διὰ θελήματος θεοῦ συναναπαύσωμαι ὑμῖν (read by the secondary Alexandrian MSS A, C, 33, 81, and 1739, and by several other MSS);

2. ἐλθὼν ἐν χαρᾷ πρὸς ὑμᾶς διὰ θελήματος Ἰησοῦ Χριστοῦ συναναπαύσωμαι ὑμῖν (read by the original hand of the primary Alexandrian uncial ℵ);

3. ἐν χαρᾷ ἔλθω πρὸς ὑμᾶς διὰ θελήματος θεοῦ (found in P46 and the primary Alexandrian B [which has κυρίου Ἰησοῦ in place of θεοῦ]);

4. ἐν χαρᾷ ἔλθω πρὸς ὑμᾶς διὰ θελήματος θεοῦ καὶ συναναπαύσωμαι ὑμῖν (read in the secondary Alexandrian C, in Ψ, in the second [Byzantine] correction of ℵ, and in the majority text [some of which, however, have the indicative συναναπαύσομαι in place of the subjunctive]);

5. ἐν χαρᾷ ἔλθω πρὸς ὑμᾶς διὰ θελήματος Χριστοῦ Ἰησοῦ καὶ ἀναψύξω μεθ' ὑμῶν (read in the western uncials D, F, and G [the latter two have ἀναψύχω]).

All modern English translations and most commentators favor the first reading, for the following reasons: (1) Paul always speaks of "the will of God"; never of "the will of Jesus Christ" (variant 2); or "the will of Christ Jesus" (variant 5); (2) the subjunctive ἔλθω (variants 3 and 4) is, after ἵνα, a superficially "easier" reading. P46 and B may drop συναναπαύσωμαι, and D, etc., replace it because the verb is used here in an unusual sense.

4. A few manuscripts (the secondary Alexandrian MSS A and 1739, the western uncials F and G, and a few minuscules) omit ἀμήν; and the papyrus P46 replaces it with the doxology read by most MSS in 16:25-27. These variations reflect the complex and debated matter of the ending of the book of Romans (for which, see the Introduction).

5. As Jervell ("The Letter to Jerusalem") argues; see the Introduction for discussion.

converging factors that led Paul to focus so strongly in the letter on the implications of salvation history for Jew and Gentile in the people of God. And, although he does not come right out and say so, what Paul says about the collection may suggest that he is also concerned about the attitude of the Roman Christians themselves to the collection.[6]

30 The fulfillment of Paul's hope to come to the Romans "with the fullness of the blessing of Christ" (v. 29) depends on what will happen when Paul goes to Jerusalem with the collection. And so he "now"[7] "urges" the Roman Christians to pray for him. The word is a strong one,[8] and Paul accentuates it by his twofold qualification: "through our Lord Jesus Christ and through the love of the Spirit." The first "through" might be paraphrased "in the name of": it introduces the authority by which Paul makes his request.[9] The second, on the other hand, identifies the ground of the request.[10] "Love of the Spirit" might mean "the love of the Spirit for us;"[11] but, in a context where relations among Christians have been so central, it probably indicates "the love that the Spirit inspires" (REB; cf. TEV);[12] for example, the love that believers have for one another, a love "that has been poured into our hearts through the Holy Spirit."[13]

Paul's request is that the Roman Christians "strive together"[14] with

---

6. Wedderburn (*Reasons,* pp. 70-75) suggests that Jewish Christians might have distrusted the collection because it lent legitimacy to the law-free gospel while Gentile Christians might have entertained like suspicions because the collection tied them too closely to Jerusalem.

7. Gk. δέ; cf. Godet.

8. παρακαλέω; see the note on 12:1. It should not be weakened to "ask" or "request" (contra Cranfield; cf. Michel; Käsemann; Dunn).

9. See the note on the similar use of διά after παρακαλέω in 12:1; and see, here, BDF 223(4); Wiles, *Paul's Intercessory Prayers,* p. 266; Thüsing, *Per Christum in Deum,* pp. 170-71; Michel; Schlier.

10. Cf., e.g., Cranfield.

11. E.g., the genitive τοῦ πνεύματος may be subjective; cf. Murray; Fitzmyer.

12. A source genitive; so most commentators (e.g., S-H; Barrett; Michel; Cranfield; Dunn; cf. also Z-G, 495).

13. Wiles notes, with some justification, that Paul's prayer here alludes to a number of the letter's key themes (*Paul's Intercessory Prayers,* pp. 264-67).

14. The verb Paul uses here, συναγωνίζομαι, occurs only here in biblical Greek; but its simple form, ἀγωνίζομαι, occurs eight times in the NT. This word means "to engage in conflict," and can be used both literally (e.g., of military battle [cf. John 18:36] or athletic contests [cf. 1 Cor. 9:25]). Particularly important for Paul's use is the application of this word to the spiritual struggle of the righteous person in this life (cf., e.g., Philo, *Husbandry* 112, 119; and cf. 4 Maccabees, where the word refers to the struggles of the martyrs). See E. Stauffer, *TDNT* I, 135-36; V. C. Pfitzner, *Paul and the Agon Motif: Traditional Athletic Imagery in the Pauline Literature* (NovTSup 16; Leiden: Brill, 1967), pp. 16-75. Thus, Paul uses it to describe labor in ministry (Col. 1:19; 1 Tim. 4:10), spiritual "striving" (1 Tim. 6:12; 2 Tim. 4:7), and prayer (Col. 4:12).

him in prayers. Paul's use of the metaphor of fighting or wrestling may imply something about the nature of the prayer that he is requesting: that it involves a "wrestling" with God;[15] or that it must be especially diligent.[16] But Paul's use of the language of "striving" to describe his own ministry might suggest rather that he is inviting the Roman Christians, through their prayers, to participate with him in his "struggle" to complete his ordained missionary work.[17] Though so many are unknown personally to him, Paul can nevertheless ask the Roman Christians to identify with him in his own struggle so that they might sincerely pray on his behalf.[18] As Calvin remarks, Paul "shows how the godly ought to pray for their brethren, that they are to assume their person, as though they were placed in the same difficulties."[19]

31 The first thing that Paul wants the Roman Christians to pray for is his personal safety: "that I might be delivered from those who are disobedient in Judea." "The disobedient" refer to unbelievers;[20] and that Paul had good ground for this request is clear from what happened when he did reach Jerusalem with the collection: the Romans had to take him into custody in order to keep the Jews from killing him (Acts 21:27-36).

But Paul is also concerned about his reception by believers in Jerusalem. Therefore, his second request is that the Roman Christians pray that "my ministry for Jerusalem might be acceptable to the saints." As the parallel language in v. 25 shows, "ministry" (or "service") refers to the collection. And it is possible that this second request might be closely related to the first. For Paul might think that it would be pressure put on the Jewish Christians by their unbelieving fellow Jews that would lead them to reject the collection.[21] But Paul does not draw this connection; and the distrust about Paul and his law-free gospel among Jewish Christians themselves was great enough to give him ample reason for the concern he expresses here.[22] For, while Paul's

---

15. The image may originate in Jacob's wrestling with God (Gen. 32); cf. Black.

16. Murray; Cranfield; Wilckens. Note the use of ἀγωνίζομαι to describe prayer in Col. 4:12.

17. See esp. Pfitzner, *Paul and the Agon Motif,* pp. 120-25. There may be specific allusion to a struggle with spiritual powers (S-H), or, more likely, with the opposition facing him in Jerusalem (cf. Godet; Käsemann; Dunn).

18. ὑπὲρ ἐμοῦ is more naturally taken with προσευχαῖς than with συναγωνίσασθαι (contra Godet).

19. Calvin.

20. See especially the use of this verb (ἀπειθέω) in 10:16, 21; 11:30, 31. Contra Segal (*Paul the Convert,* p. 258), this makes it unlikely that Paul would include Christians in this designation.

21. Schmithals; Dunn.

22. See, e.g., Michel; Wilckens; Dunn. Contra Cranfield, more than normal human sensibilities about receiving charity are at stake.

relationships with the Jerusalem apostles were apparently cordial enough at this point,[23] his own letters reveal that various conservative Jewish-Christian groups continued to be hostile toward him.[24]

32 The purpose clause in this verse could be a third prayer request, parallel to the two in v. 31,[25] but it probably expresses the ultimate goal of those requests:[26] that Paul might "come[27] in joy[28]" to the Roman Christians and find refreshment[29] there with them. "Through the will of God" probably modifies "come" rather than "find rest";[30] but, in either case, Paul thereby reminds his readers that all his plans and hopes are subordinate to the will of God. We find a somewhat ironic confirmation of this in the way in which God "answered" Paul's prayer here. He *was* delivered from the unbelievers in Judea, but only by being locked up by the Romans for two years. The collection *was,* apparently, accepted by the Jewish Christians (or at least most of them [cf. Acts 21:17]), but Paul's subsequent arrest in the temple precincts must have raised Jewish Christians' suspicions about him again. And Paul *did* get to Rome and experience some measure of joy and refreshment (cf. Phil. 1:12-19; 2:25-30), but he arrived there in Roman chains.

33 In the prayer-wish that climaxes the first part (15:14-32) of his letter closing, Paul addresses God as "the God of peace," that is, "the God who gives peace." Paul refers in Romans both to the peace of a new, harmonious relationship with God (cf. 2:10; 5:1; 8:6) and to the peace that should characterize the relations of believers with one another (cf. 14:19). It is difficult, and probably unwise, to restrict the meaning of the word here to one or the other: "peace," like the Hebrew *shalōm,* embraces the panoply of blessings God makes available to his people in the age of fulfillment (cf. also 1:7).[31]

---

23. See, e.g., Acts 21:18-25; Gal. 2:1-10.

24. See especially the evidence from 2 Cor. 10–13, written shortly before Romans.

25. Cf. Wiles, *Paul's Intercessory Prayers,* p. 269.

26. So most commentators, e.g., Michel; Käsemann; Cranfield; Dunn.

27. All modern English translations follow our rendering, putting "come" as a finite verb in parallel with "find rest" as dependent on ἵνα. Some may, of course, be adopting the textual variant that reads ἔλθω in place of ἐλθών (see the note on the translation above). But this translation of the participle is also justified since the participle in Greek, while syntactically subordinate, often expresses a thought that is logically parallel to the verb it modifies. This is the situation here.

28. Gk. ἐν χαρᾷ, in which ἐν is adverbial.

29. The verb, συναναπαύομαι, occurs only here in the NT; and in its only LXX occurrence, in Isa. 11:6, it means "lie down together," "sleep with." Here, as in Eusebius, *H.E.* 4.22.2, it must mean "find rest with," "be refreshed together with" (BAGD; Cranfield).

30. See, e.g., Leenhardt.

31. Cf. Murray; Cranfield.

B. GREETINGS (16:1-23)

Paul does six things in this section: (1) he commends to the Roman Christians
a sister in the Lord, Phoebe (vv. 1-2); (2) he urges the Roman Christians to
greet various of their number (vv. 3-15) and one another (v. 16a); (3) he sends
greetings to the Roman Christians from others (vv. 16b, 21-23); (4) he warns
the believers in Rome about false teachers (vv. 17-19); (5) he assures the
believers of final spiritual victory (v. 20a); and (6) he prays that "the grace
of our Lord Jesus" might be with them (v. 20b). Every one of these topics is
also found in one or more of the concluding sections of Paul's other letters
(see the chart at the introduction of 15:14–16:27). But Paul treats two of these
matters quite differently here than he does anywhere else. In no other letter
does Paul even come close to the number of personal greetings he asks to be
conveyed in vv. 3-15; and in no other letter does he launch so suddenly in the
midst of concluding greetings into a substantial warning about false teachers
(vv. 17-19). But not only are these topics unusual in comparison with Paul's
other letters; scholars also allege that neither fits well into Paul's letter to the
Romans. So large a number of personal greetings seems strange in a letter
written to a church that Paul had never visited. And Paul has said nothing in
the letter previously to prepare us for so urgent a warning about false teachers.

These alleged inconsistencies, along with several important textual
variations, have led a number of scholars to think that Rom. 16 does not
belong to Paul's letter to the Roman Christians. We treated this issue in the
Introduction; here we need only reiterate our conclusion: Rom. 16 is an integral
part of Paul's letter to the Romans. Each of the alleged inconsistencies can
be explained once we (1) recognize the considerable variety found in Paul's
epistolary conclusions; and (2) take into sufficient account certain factors
peculiar to the occasion of Romans (see the introductions to the specific
sections below for details).

1. Commendation of Phoebe (16:1-2)

> 1*Now I commend to you Phoebe, our sister, who is also*[1] *deacon of
> the church at Cenchreae,* 2*in order that you might receive her in the
> Lord in a manner worthy of the saints, and assist her in the matter in
> which she has need of you. For she has herself also been a benefactor
> of many, and of me myself.*

---

1. "Also" translates καί, which is read in P[46] and in much of the Alexandrian
tradition (B, C [original hand], and 81). It should probably be read (cf. Michel, 473;
Cranfield, 2.781).

Paul often brings to the attention of his readers at the end of his letters fellow Christians who may come into contact with his readers (cf. 1 Cor. 16:10-12, 15-18; Eph. 6:21-22; Col. 4:7-9; 2 Tim. 4:20). Only here, however, does Paul request the assistance of a church in the private matter of a fellow believer. Phoebe is mentioned nowhere else in the NT, but it is clear from what Paul says about her here that she was a prominent member of the church at Cenchreae, that she was actively involved in ministry, and that she was planning a trip to Rome. Probably she was the person who carried Paul's letter to the Roman Christians.

1 Letters of commendation were common in the ancient world.[2] People who were traveling in an age with few public facilities often depended on the assistance of people they had never met; and this assistance was easier to be had if the traveler could produce a letter of introduction from someone known to the potential host/assistant. So Paul writes to "commend"[3] Phoebe to the Roman Christians. She is a fellow believer,[4] probably a Gentile,[5] and comes from Cenchreae. Paul would have had plenty of opportunity to get to know her, for Cenchreae[6] is only eight miles from Corinth, where Paul spent 18 months at one point (cf. Acts 18:1-18; cf. v. 11) and is now staying as he writes to the Romans.

But Phoebe is more than an ordinary believer; she is a "servant," or "deacon." The word Paul uses here, *diakonos,* is one that is applicable to any Christian, for every Christian is a "servant" or "minister" of the risen Christ and of other Christians.[7] Paul may, then, simply be highlighting the fact that

2. See C.-H. Kim, *Form and Structure of the Familiar Greek Letter of Recommendation* (SBLDS 4; Missoula, MT: Scholars Press, 1972).

3. Gk. συνίστημι. The word is not common in Greek letters of introduction, but it does occur (cf. 2 Macc. 9:25; MM; BAGD). Paul uses the word in this sense also in 2 Cor. 3:1; 5:12; 6:4; 10:12, 18.

4. Gk. ἀδελφή, "sister," used only rarely in the NT in this sense (cf. also 1 Cor. 7:15; 9:5; Phlm. 2; Jas. 2:15).

5. Her Gentile background is suggested by her name, Φοίβη, which is taken from Greek mythology.

6. Corinth itself lies inland several miles from the sea (the Gulf of Corinth to the northwest and the Saronic Gulf to the northeast). Cenchreae was a seaport on the Saronic Gulf and was connected to Corinth by a series of forts (D. H. Madvig, *ISBE* I, 772). Paul, like other travelers taking ship for the east, left from Cenchreae after his first stay in Corinth (cf. Acts 18:18). Note that 2 Corinthians is addressed to "all the saints who are in the whole of Achaia."

7. See especially the cognate verb διακονέω in 1 Pet. 4:10. Paul uses the word διάκονος 20 other times. Twice he uses it to refer to secular rulers (Rom. 13:4) and twice to describe Christ (Rom. 15:8; Gal. 2:17). Paul uses it especially often to refer to himself and his coworkers (1 Cor. 3:5; 2 Cor. 3:6; 6:4; Eph. 3:7; 6:21; Col. 1:7, 23, 25; 4:7; 1 Tim. 4:6) or to those who sought a position similar to his (2 Cor. 11:15 [twice], 23). Only in Phil. 1:1 and 1 Tim. 3:8, 12 does the word denote an "office."

Phoebe has effectively "served" the church to which she belongs.[8] Others, noting that Paul often applies the term to himself and his coworkers, think that the title here marks Phoebe as the leader and preacher of the church.[9] But the qualification of *diakonos* by "of the church"[10] suggests, rather, that Phoebe held at Cenchreae the "office" of "deacon" as Paul describes it in 1 Tim. 3:8-12 (cf. Phil. 1:1).[11] We put "office" in quotation marks because it is very likely that regular offices in local Christian churches were still in the process of being established, as people who regularly ministered in a certain way were gradually recognized officially by the congregation and given a regular title. Moreover, the NT furnishes little basis on which to pinpoint the ministries carried out by deacons. But based partially on hints within the NT and partially on the later institution of the diaconate, it is likely that deacons were charged with visitation of the sick, poor relief, and perhaps financial oversight.

8. See, e.g., TEV, "who serves the church"; KJV, NIV, and NASB translate "servant"; cf. K. Romaniuk, "Was Phoebe in Romans 16, 1 a Deaconess?" *ZNW* 81 (1990), 132-34; Murray. One of the problems with this view is that Paul seldom — if ever — uses διάκονος of the "service" or "ministry" of Christians generally.

9. E. S. Fiorenza, "Missionaries, Apostles, Coworkers: Romans 16 and the Reconstruction of Women's Early Christian History," *WW* 6 (1986), 425-26; Jewett, "Paul, Phoebe, and the Spanish Mission," pp. 148-49. On this meaning of διάκονος, see E. E. Ellis, "Paul and His Co-Workers," *NTS* 17 (1970-71), 441-43. The first two authors and, to some extent, Ellis, confuse meaning and reference. The meaning of διάκονος in Paul is demonstrably quite general: "servant," especially servant of Christ. Depending on the context, this term can then refer to Christian workers of many different kinds. But there is no warrant to import the reference that the term has when used, e.g., of Paul himself, to Phoebe here.

10. This is the first occurrence of ἐκκλησία in Romans. Paul uses it only in this chapter (cf. also vv. 4, 5, 16, 23), and probably always (v. 23 is debated) of the local church, "Christians in one place gathered to share their common life of worship and discipleship" (Dunn, 2.887).

11. See NRSV; REB ("minister"); and so most commentators (e.g., Chrysostom, Homily 31 [pp. 549-50, 557]; Godet; Michel; Käsemann; Cranfield; Wilckens; Dunn); cf. also D. C. Arichea, Jr., "Who was Phoebe? Translating *diakonos* in Romans 16:1," *BT* 39 (1988), 401-9; P. Richardson, "From Apostles to Virgins: Romans 16 and the Roles of Women in the Early Church," *Toronto Journal of Theology* 2 (1986), 238-39; W.-H. Ollrog, *Paulus und seine Mitarbeiter: Untersuchungen zu Theorie und Praxis der paulinischen Mission* (WMANT 50; Neukirchen/Vluyn: Neukirchener, 1979), 31. We use the term "semi-official" because evidence for a fixed "office," with a definite "job description," is lacking for this early period. We must recognize something of a transitional phase, in which people who regularly involved themselves in certain ministries were beginning to be recognized by the church as more-or-less permanent "servants" (cf. Barrett; Dunn). A few commentators use the term "deaconess" (see RSV); and, at a later date, when the office was officially recognized, the feminine term διακόνισσα was used of "female deacons" (cf. *Apost. Const.* 8.19, 20, 28). But διάκονος is used of female officeholders in the early church (cf. the texts cited in *New Docs.* 2.193-94; 4:239-41); in this period, it was clearly used of both men and women.

2   Paul's purpose[12] in commending Phoebe is twofold. First, he wants the Roman Christians to "receive her in the Lord in a manner worthy of the saints." "Receiving" includes, of course, welcoming Phoebe into fellowship. But it would also mean assisting her to find lodging, food, and the like.[13] The qualification "in the Lord"/"in Christ" is typical of the personal greetings and references in this chapter.[14] We should avoid seeking some exact nuance for the phrase; by it Paul simply means that the Roman Christians are to give Phoebe a "Christian" welcome. The additional qualification, "in a manner worthy of the saints," expands on this same point.[15] Paul's second purpose in commending Phoebe is that the Roman Christians would "assist[16] her in the matter in which[17] she has need of you." The "matter" on which Phoebe requires assistance cannot be determined, although it is possible that a legal dispute is involved.[18]

Paul adds another reason for the Roman Christians to receive and help Phoebe when she comes to them: "she has herself also been a benefactor of many, and of me myself." Considerable debate surrounds the word I here translate "benefactor." The Greek word *prostatis* is found only here in biblical Greek. It comes from a verb that means (1) "care for, give aid to," or (2) "direct, preside over." If Paul is applying to the noun this first meaning of the verb, he would simply be characterizing Phoebe as a "helper" of many Christians (cf. NASB; RSV; NIV).[19] But if we use the meaning of the cognate verb to define *prostatis,* Pauline usage would favor a different rendering. For

12. The verse begins with ἵνα. Moule (*Idiom Book,* p. 145) suggests that this might be an "imperatival" ἵνα.

13. The verb is προσδέχομαι, different from the verb Paul uses in 14:1 and 15:7 (προσλαμβάνω). For the meaning of προσδέχομαι here, see also Luke 15:2; Phil. 2:29 (BAGD; Käsemann).

14. "In the Lord" occurs seven times (cf. also vv. 8, 11, 12 [twice], 13, 22); "in Christ" four times (vv. 3, 7, 9, 10). There is no difference in meaning between them here.

15. The debate about whether this phrase highlights the one to be received or the ones doing the receiving (e.g., Murray) is probably misguided: the phrase modifies the verb and includes both those who receive and those who are received.

16. The Greek verb is παρίστημι. It has a variety of meanings in the NT; cf. 2 Tim. 4:17 for the closest parallel (BAGD).

17. The Greek is awkward, with the antecedent of the relative pronoun ᾧ coming after the pronoun (πράγματι; cf. Turner, 265).

18. The Greek word is πρᾶγμα, a very general term meaning "act, deed, matter." But in 1 Cor. 6:1 it is used to describe a legal dispute; and this meaning would fit this context well (cf. Gifford; Michel; Dunn; Fitzmyer). On the other hand, the indefinite construction Paul uses — ἄν with the subjunctive χρῄζη ("have need of") — might point to the general meaning (cf., e.g., Käsemann; Schlier; Cranfield). The indefinite construction also tells against the suggestion of Jewett ("Paul, Phoebe, and the Spanish Mission," pp. 150-51), that the "matter" was Phoebe's sponsorship of Paul's mission to Spain.

19. See, e.g., Lietzmann; Michel; Käsemann; Schlier.

Paul seems to use the verb only to mean "direct," "preside over." Noting this, some recent scholars have argued that Paul intends to characterize Phoebe as a "leader" of the church.[20] But it is difficult to conceive how Phoebe would have had the opportunity to be a "leader" of Paul. Moreover, the fact that Paul designates her as the leader "of many" rather than as the leader of "the church" (contrast v. 1) suggests that the term here does not denote an official, or even semi-official, position in the local church. The best alternative, then, is to give to *prostatis* the meaning that it often has in secular Greek: "patron," "benefactor."[21] A "patron" was one who came to the aid of others, especially foreigners, by providing housing and financial aid and by representing their interests before local authorities. Cenchreae's status as a busy seaport would make it imperative that a Christian in its church take up this ministry on behalf of visiting Christians. Phoebe, then, was probably a woman of high social standing and some wealth, who put her status, resources, and time at the services of traveling Christians, like Paul, who needed help and support. Paul now urges the Romans to reciprocate.

2. Greetings to Roman Christians (16:3-16)

> 3*Greet Prisca and Aquila, my fellow workers in Christ Jesus,* 4*who risked their neck on behalf of my soul, whom not only I alone but also all the churches of the Gentiles thank.* 5*[Greet] also the church of their house.*
>
> *Greet Epaenetus, my beloved, who is the first fruits of Asia for Christ.*
>
> 6*Greet Mary, who worked hard for you.*
>
> 7*Greet Andronicus and Junia,*[1] *my kindred and fellow prisoners,*

---

20. See, e.g., R. R. Schulz, "A Case for 'President' Phoebe in Romans 16:2," *Lutheran Theological Journal* 24 (1990), 124-26; D. M. Scholer, "Paul's Women Co-workers in the Ministry of the Church," *Daughters of Sarah* 6/4 (1980), 3-6.

21. προστάτις is the feminine form of προστάτης, which is often used in this sense, and sometimes with reference also to one who is the "guardian" of a particular god or religious shrine (BAGD; cf. also Lat. *patronus*). The feminine form of the word has recently been discovered with this general meaning in a second-century papyrus (*New Docs* 4.241-44). The "patron" sometimes had an official legal status; but this is not clear with respect to Phoebe. For this general approach, see Judge, "Cultural Conformity," pp. 20-21; Meeks, *First Urban Christians,* p. 60; Richardson, "From Apostle to Virgin," p. 239; Fiorenza, "Missionaries, Apostles, Co-workers," p. 426; Jewett, "Paul, Phoebe, and the Spanish Mission," pp. 149-50; S-H; Cranfield; Dunn; Fitzmyer.

1. Considerable debate surrounds the name that should be read here; see the notes on the verse. Since the issue hinges on the accent, and most MSS are without accents, the issue is not basically a textual one. However, two MSS (P[46] and minuscule 6) read here Ἰουλίαν, "Julia." But this reading is too weakly supported to be considered seriously.

who are esteemed among the apostles, and who were in Christ before me.

8Greet Ampliatus, my beloved in the Lord.

9Greet Urbanus, our fellow worker in Christ, and Stachys, my beloved.

10Greet Apelles, who is approved in Christ.

Greet those of the house of Aristobulus.

11Greet Herodion, my compatriot.

Greet those of the house of Narcissus who are in the Lord.

12Greet Tryphaena and Tryphosa, workers in the Lord.

Greet Persis, the beloved one, who worked hard in the Lord.

13Greet Rufus, the elect in the Lord, and his mother and mine.

14Greet Asyncritus, Phlegon, Hermes, Patrobas, Hermas, and the brothers and sisters with them.

15Greet Philologus and Julia,2 Nereus and his sister, and Olympas and all the saints with them.

16Greet one another with a holy kiss.

All the churches of Christ greet you.

At the end of his letters, Paul habitually asks the Christians to whom he writes to "greet one another" (Phil. 4:21a; Tit. 3:15b), often by means of a "holy kiss" (cf. 1 Cor. 16:20b; 2 Cor. 13:12; 1 Thess. 5:26). He does so here in Romans also (v. 16a). But what is remarkable about this section is that Paul precedes this customary general exhortation with commands that the church in Rome greet on his behalf 26 individuals, two "families," and three "house churches."3 This procedure is not, however, completely without parallel; see Col. 4:15, where Paul requests that the Colossians convey his greetings to "the fellow believers at Laodicea, and to Nympha and the church in her house," and 2 Tim. 4:19, where Paul asks Timothy to greet "Prisca and Aquila and the household of Onesiphorus." And it may be significant that Colossians, like Romans, is directed to a church that Paul did not personally know. As many have conjectured, then, Paul's extensive request for greetings in Rom. 16 may reflect his desire to mention all the Christians in Rome he knows — a procedure plainly impossible in those letters directed to churches where he has ministered. But the large number of greetings may also have a role in Paul's strategy in Romans. For it is clear that one of the motives in Paul's writing is to secure a welcome for

---

2. A few MSS (the original hand of the secondary Alexandrian uncial C, and the western uncials F and G) read here Ἰουνιαν (see v. 7); P46 has Βηρέα καὶ Ἀουλίαν in place of Ἰουλίαν, Νηρέα.

3. It is not clear whether "those of Aristobulus" and "those of Narcissus" represent house churches or not.

himself when he comes to visit the church and seek support for his Spanish mission. A public recognition — the request for greetings were probably read aloud to the assembled church — of those Christians in Rome whom Paul already knows would encourage them to think favorably of him and remind the church as a whole of the number of "supporters" he already has.[4]

Looking at the structure of the section, and beginning at the end, it is clear that v. 16a and v. 16b stand out — the former because it includes, in summary fashion, all the believers in Rome; the latter because Paul shifts to the indicative mood to pass on the greetings of other churches. Verses 3-15 is really a connected whole; but perhaps a minor transition can be discerned at v. 8, where Paul moves from greetings to people that he knows well (vv. 3-7) to greetings of people that he may know only casually or perhaps even only by reputation (vv. 8-15).[5]

The list of names in this section does not make very interesting reading for most students of Romans. But for those few who are especially interested in the socioeconomic composition of the early church, it is a gold mine. For there was a tendency in the ancient world to give certain names to certain kinds of people; for example, wealthy people high on the social ladder would give their children certain names; slaves or former slaves would use (or be made to use) others. Several such studies of the names in this list have been done; and I will refer to them occasionally in my exegesis. But I might note here two conclusions from the most recent and most thorough such study:[6] (1) a majority of the names are Gentile (confirming the mainly Gentile makeup of the church at Rome);[7] and (2) the majority of the names are those of slaves and "freedmen" (slaves who had been given their freedom), or the descendants of slaves/freedmen.[8] Another point that the list

---

4. See P. Lampe, "The Roman Christians of Romans 16," in Donfried, p. 218; Jervis, *Purpose of Romans,* pp. 151-52; Jewett, "Paul, Phoebe, and the Spanish Mission," p. 153; J. A. D. Weima, *Neglected Endings: The Significance of the Pauline Letter Closings* (JSNTSup 101; Sheffield: JSOT, 1994), pp. 226-28; Käsemann, 412; Wilckens, 3.138; Dunn, 2.908; Fitzmyer, 734.

5. Stuhlmacher, 247.

6. Lampe, *Die stadtrömischen Christen,* pp. 135-53; cf. also idem, "Roman Christians," pp. 216-30. The most important earlier studies are found in Lightfoot's appendix on "Caesar's Household" in his *Commentary on Saint Paul's Epistle to the Philippians,* pp. 174-77; and S-H.

7. Lampe assumes, however, that Paul specifically identifies all the Jewish Christians that he can (cf. also Lietzmann, 119). But this is not true, since Paul does nothing to identify Prisca and Aquila; and the latter, at least, was certainly Jewish.

8. Lampe concludes that four names are definitely not those of slaves or freemen; ten definitely are; and 12 cannot be determined. He further acknowledges that we cannot know whether this pattern obtained for the church as a whole. However, if it did, the composition of the church would mirror rather closely the society as a whole (cf. *Die stadtrömischen Christen,* pp. 141-53; cf. also the brief summary in "Roman Christians," pp. 227-29).

makes clear is the pattern of church organization in Rome, for Paul identifies at least three, and perhaps five, separate house churches (vv. 5, 14, 15; cf. also vv. 10, 11). Early Christians did not have large public facilities for meeting, so they used their own houses. And since even the largest house of the wealthiest Christian would hold no more than seventy or eighty for worship, growth beyond that point required that the Christians split up into house churches.

3-5a   Paul begins sixteen sentences in a row with the second person plural imperative, "greet."[9] And, with the exception of the last of these imperatives, with its reciprocal ("one another") construction, it is clear that Paul is asking the Roman Christians to convey his own greetings to the respective individuals and groups; cf. the REB and TEV, "Greetings to. . . ."[10] The first sentence, in which Paul conveys greetings to Prisca and Aquila, is the longest in the list (vv. 3-5a). This is probably because the couple was in the best position to mediate Paul's ministry to the church in Rome. For Paul had been especially close to this missionary wife-and-husband team. Paul first met them at Corinth, on his second missionary journey. Luke tells us that Prisca (or Priscilla[11]) and Aquila, who was originally from Pontus, had "come from Italy . . . because Claudius had issued a decree that all Jews must leave Rome" (Acts 18:2). In addition to their commitment to Christ, they had in common with Paul a secular trade: tent-making (Acts 18:3). After ministering with Paul for some time in Corinth, Paul dropped them off at Ephesus to begin the work there (Acts 18:18). They were instrumental in bringing Apollos to a better understanding of Christ (Acts 18:26); and Paul joined them in Ephesus for a lengthy ministry (cf. 1 Cor. 16:19). We do not know when they returned to Rome. But it is only natural that they would want to return to their home after Claudius's decree of banishment lapsed at his death (A.D. 54). Whether they returned specifically to resurrect a business,[12] or to help prepare the way for Paul's coming,[13] is impossible to say.

9. The Greek verb is ἀσπάζομαι, which, MM claim, was the *"term. tech.* for conveying the greetings at the end of a letter."

10. Cf. Gamble, 93. As Lampe notes, asking the Romans themselves to convey his greetings may have been a tactic to improve relations in the church ("Roman Christians," p. 218). But Paul does the same thing at the end of Philippians, so we should probably not make too much of the point.

11. Luke prefers "Priscilla," the diminutive form of "Prisca." We do not know why Priscilla/Prisca comes first in four of the six NT mentions of the couple. Scholars have suggested that she may have been the more dominant of the two, the more gifted, the one who brought most money into the marriage, or the one who was most significant for their "home-based" ministry.

12. Dunn, 2.892.

13. Michel, 474; Watson, 105; Lampe, "Roman Christians," p. 220.

What Paul emphasizes as the basis for his greeting is not, of course, any of these prosaic details, but their commitment to both ministry and to Paul. They are "fellow workers,"[14] called to labor in the cause of the gospel along with Paul. In the course of that co-laboring, they "risked their neck"[15] on behalf of Paul's soul; that is, they saved his life.[16] When this happened we have no way of knowing, although one naturally thinks of the riot in Ephesus (Acts 19:23-41).[17] Paul himself therefore has good reason to "give thanks" for them; but so do "all the churches of the Gentiles." We do not know whether these thanks from the Gentile churches are due specifically to Prisca and Aquila's rescue of Paul, the "apostle to the Gentiles,"[18] or, more generally, to their significant ministry in these churches over many years.[19]

And this ministry continues, as Paul hints at the beginning of v. 5. Here Paul adds, after his threefold description of Prisca and Aquila, a second object to the main verb, "greet": "the church of their house." This means "the church that meets in their house."[20] Prisca and Aquila are apparently (as their travels also suggest) a fairly wealthy couple; thus they are able to provide a decent-sized meeting room for a group of Christians in Rome.

5b Epaenetus is mentioned nowhere else in the NT. By calling him "my beloved one," Paul suggests that he knows him personally. But we should not overinterpret "beloved" since Paul clearly tries to say something complimentary about every person he greets. The characterization, while undoubtedly sincere, is also semiformalized.[21] In calling him the "first fruits of Asia," Paul indicates that he was the first convert in the Roman province

---

14. Gk. συνεργοί (cf. also vv. 9, 21; 2 Cor. 8:23; Phil. 2:25; 4:3; Col. 4:11; Phlm. 1, 24). On the meaning of the term, see Ollrog, *Paulus,* pp. 63-72. The term always denotes work in ministry, but the kind of ministry undertaken is not specified; contra, e.g., Fiorenza, "Missionaries, Apostles, Co-workers," p. 430, who argues that the term denotes leaders in the community. See, in general, Ellis, "Paul and His Co-Workers," p. 440.

15. This need not indicate a literal "baring of the neck" to the executioner; the imagery is very similar to our "risking one's neck" (cf. Deissmann, *Light,* pp. 117-18).

16. The Greek word ψυχή refers here, in Hebrew fashion, to the "life" as a whole.

17. E.g., Michel; Cranfield.

18. Cranfield; Murray (?).

19. Dunn.

20. It is just possible that the Greek, τὴν κατ' οἶκον αὐτῶν ἐκκλησίαν, could mean "the church made up of members of their household." But this is less likely. The κατά is not distributive, as if Paul is identifying that part of the Roman church which met in their house (Godet), but it simply means "in" (BAGD II.1.c; M. Gielen, "Zur Interpretation der Formel ἡ κατ' οἶκον ἐκκλησία," *ZNW* 77 [1986], 111-12), the "church" being, as throughout Rom. 16, the "house church."

21. The term is virtually equivalent here, and in vv. 8, 9, and 12, to ἀδελφός, "fellow believer." See esp. Dunn, 2.893.

of Asia, whose cultural center was Ephesus.[22] Paul may, then, mention him here because he was brought to faith through the ministry of Prisca and Aquila, and has now come with them to Rome (as a business associate? or ministry worker?).[23]

6 "Mary" is a very common name, especially among Jews. For this reason, most commentators think that she is Jewish.[24] But the name is also used of Gentiles,[25] so we cannot be certain about her ethnic status. Mary, Paul says, is one who has "worked hard[26] for you."[27] Attempts have been made to identify a semitechnical sense for the verb "work" in Paul, as a reference to early Christian missionary ministry.[28] But a preponderance of references to missionary work in the letters of Paul is to be expected, granted their subject matter. The frequency of reference does not establish a technical meaning for the word.

7 Paul now sends greetings to two fellow Jews,[29] who, as Paul's description indicates, had considerable stature in the early church. Andronicus is a common Greek name, so he must have been a "Hellenistic" Jew. The identity of Andronicus's "partner" is a matter of considerable debate. The problem arises from the fact that the Greek form used here, *Iounian,* depending on how it is accented, could refer either (1) to a man with the name Junianus,

---

22. On this application of the imagery of the "first fruits" (ἀπαρχή), see 1 Cor. 16:15; and see the note on 11:16.

23. See, e.g., Michel; Lampe, "Roman Christians," p. 221; Fitzmyer. Wilckens thinks that he simply belonged to their house church.

24. E.g., Michel; Käsemann. S-H demur, noting that Paul does not identify her as Jewish, as he does a number of others in these greetings (cf. also Lampe, "Roman Christians," p. 225). But Paul is not consistent on this matter, so this argument holds no water.

25. See, for some recent evidence, *New Docs* 4.229-30.

26. Gk. πολλά, "many things." The word here intensifies the verb (Z-G, 496).

27. Gk. εἰς ὑμᾶς, which functions like a dative of advantage (Z-G, 496). Paul's use of the second person form here might suggest that Paul had heard of Mary only indirectly (through Prisca and Aquila?; cf. Lampe, "Roman Christians," p. 220).

28. See esp. A. von Harnack, "κόπος (κοπιᾶν, οἱ κοπιῶντες) im frühchristlichen Sprachgebrauch," *ZNW* 27 (1928), 1-10; note also Scholer, "Paul's Women Co-workers," pp. 3-4; Lampe, "Roman Christians," p. 223. Paul uses the verb in 16:12; 1 Cor. 4:12; 15:10; 16:16; Gal. 4:11; Eph. 4:28; Phil. 2:16; Col. 1:29; 1 Thess. 5:12; 1 Tim. 4:10; 5:17; 2 Tim. 2:6.

29. The Greek term is συγγενεῖς. It has occasionally been argued that the word refers, literally, to Paul's "blood relatives" (Meyer; Liddon; Haldane; Murray) or to his close "companions" (V. Fabrega, "War Junia(s), der hervorragende Apostel (Röm. 16, 7), eine Frau?" *JAC* 27-28 [1984-85], pp. 49-50) or to fellow citizens of Tarsus (W. R. Ramsay, *The Cities of St. Paul* [New York: A. C. Armstrong and Son, 1908], pp. 175-78), but a reference to fellow Jews fits both Paul's usage (see Rom. 9:3 and the note there) and the context.

found here in its contracted form, "Junias" (cf. NIV; RSV; NASB; TEV; NJB); or (2) to a woman with the name of Junia (KJV; NRSV; REB).[30] Interpreters from the thirteenth to the middle of the twentieth century generally favored the masculine identification.[31] But it appears that commentators before the thirteenth century were unanimous in favor of the feminine identification;[32] and scholars have recently again inclined decisively to this same view.[33] And probably with good reason. For while a contracted form of Junianus would fit quite well in this list of greetings (for Paul uses several other such contractions), we have no evidence elsewhere for this contracted form of the name. On the other hand, the Latin "Junia" was a very common name.[34]

30. The UBS[4] and NA[27] Greek New Testaments both accent Ἰουνιᾶν, which would be the contracted form of Junianus. They cite Ἰουνίαν, from "Junia," as a variant. It must be remembered that few of the oldest MSS had any accents at all. The later minuscules, many of which did have accents, reflect the interpretation of the name as masculine that became current from the thirteenth century onward (an exception, however, is the important minuscule 33, which has the feminine form; cf. Lampe, "Roman Christians," p. 223).

31. The first explicitly to identify "Junia(s)" as a man was apparently Epiphanius (A.D. 315-403) in his *Index of Disciples* 125.19-20 (cf. J. Piper and W. Grudem, "An Overview of Central Concerns: Questions and Answers," in *Recovering Biblical Manhood and Womanhood: A Response to Evangelical Feminism* [ed. J. Piper and W. Grudem; Westchester, IL: Crossway, 1991], p. 79). But the reliability of his information is called into question by his identification, in the same passage, of Prisca as a man. The next known person to identify Junia(s) as a man was Aegidius of Rome (A.D. 1245-1316); cf. the history of interpretation in B. Brooten, " 'Junia . . . outstanding among the Apostles,' " in *Women Priests: A Catholic Commentary on the Vatican Declaration* (ed. L. and A. Swidler; New York: Paulist, 1977), pp. 141-44. See also, e.g., Godet; S-H; Meyer; Lietzmann; Gaugler; Althaus; Barrett; Murray; Hendriksen.

32. See the list in Fitzmyer. The only possible exception is Origen, who, according to Rufinus's translation of his commentary in Migne, *PG* 14, 1281B and 1289A, reads a masculine name. But Migne's text (notoriously corrupt) is probably in error; Origen apparently read a feminine name here (cf. Brooten, "Junia," p. 141; Lampe, "Roman Christians," p. 223).

33. See, e.g., Brooten, "Junia," pp. 141-44; Fiorenza, "Missionaries, Apostles, Coworkers," p. 430; Fabrega, "Junia(s)," pp. 48-49; R. R. Schulz, "Romans 16:7: Junia or Junias?" *ExpTim* 98 (1986-87), 109-10; Richardson, "From Apostles to Virgins," pp. 238-39; Lampe, "Roman Christians," pp. 223-24 (though he is more cautious in "Iunia/Iunias: Sklavenherkunft im Kreise der vorpaulinischen Apostel [Röm 16,7]," *ZNW* 76 [1985], 132-34); R. S. Cervin, "A Note Regarding the Name 'Junia(s)' in Romans 16.7," *NTS* 40 (1994), 464-70; Lagrange; Bruce; Cranfield; Wilckens; Dunn; Fitzmyer; Schlier.

34. See, e.g., Lampe, "Roman Christians," p. 223. It should be noted, however, that the Greek form Ἰουνία was *not* a popular name; a search of the *TLG* database came up with only three occurrences outside of Rom. 16:7 (see J. Piper and W. Grudem, "An Overview of Central Concerns," pp. 79-80).

Probably, then, "Junia" was the wife of Andronicus (note the other husband and wife pairs in this list, Prisca and Aquila [v. 3] and [probably], Philologus and Julia [v. 15]).[35]

In addition to their natural relationship ("kindred"), Paul shared with Andronicus and Junia also a spiritual relationship, in both ministry and suffering. For they were Paul's "fellow prisoners." Implied is that their imprisonment, like those of Paul's that we know about, were for the sake of the gospel.[36] But whether they were in prison with Paul at the same time[37] or simply shared with him this kind of experience in the service of the Lord is impossible to say. In two relative clauses Paul draws the attention of the Roman Christians to the stature of this husband and wife ministry team. The first description might mean that Andronicus and Junia were "esteemed by the apostles."[38] But it is more natural to translate "esteemed among the apostles."[39] And it is because Paul thus calls Junia(s) an "apostle" that earlier interpreters tended to argue that Paul must be referring to a man; for they had difficulty imagining that a woman could hold such authority in the early church. Yet it is just for this reason that many contemporary scholars are eager to identify Junia(s) as a woman, for Pauline recognition of a female apostle would support the notion that the NT places no restrictions on the ministry of women.[40]

But many scholars on both sides of this issue are guilty of accepting too readily a key supposition in this line of reasoning: that "apostle" here refers to an authoritative leadership position such as that held by the "Twelve" and by Paul. In fact, Paul often uses the title "apostle" in a "looser" sense:

35. So most of the commentators who identify Junia(s) as a woman.

36. A few scholars have suggested that Paul might use the term συναιχμαλώτος, "fellow prisoner," in a metaphorical sense, "captured for the gospel ministry" (G. Kittel, *TDNT* I, 196-97; Fabrega, "Junia(s)," pp. 50-51), but there is no evidence for this usage.

37. Luke records only one imprisonment of Paul before the writing of Romans: an (interrupted) overnight incarceration in Philippi (Acts 16:24-34); but Paul himself, writing just before Romans, acknowledges many imprisonments (2 Cor. 11:23); and many scholars think that Paul was imprisoned for a time during his Ephesian ministry (Acts 19).

38. The Greek phrase is ἐπίσημοι ἐν τοῖς ἀποστόλοις; on this view, ἐν will have an instrumental force, or be equivalent to the Hebrew "in the eyes of." See, e.g., Meyer; Zahn; Gifford; Hodge; Lenski; Murray.

39. With a plural object, ἐν often means "among"; and if Paul had wanted to say that Andronicus and Junia were esteemed "by" the apostles, we would have expected him to use a simple dative or ὑπό with the genitive. The word ἐπίσημοι ("splendid," "prominent," "outstanding"; only here in the NT in this sense [cf. also Matt. 27:16]) also favors this rendering (cf. esp. S-H).

40. See, e.g., Brooten, "Junia," p. 143; Fiorenza, "Missionaries, Apostles, Coworkers," pp. 430-31; Richardson, "From Apostles to Virgins," pp. 238-39.

sometimes simply to denote a "messenger" or "emissary"[41] and sometimes to denote a " commissioned missionary."[42] When Paul uses the word in the former sense, he makes clear the source and purpose of the "emissary's" commission. So "apostle" here probably means "traveling missionary."[43] Since Paul, in the second relative clause, acknowledges that they were "in Christ" before him, we might infer that Andronicus and Junia were among those early "Hellenistic" Jews in Jerusalem[44] and that, like Peter and his wife (cf. 1 Cor. 9:5), they moved about in the eastern Mediterranean (where they encountered and perhaps were imprisoned with Paul), seeking to bring men and women to faith in Christ.

8 "Ampliatus" was probably a slave or freedman[45] and may be the Ampliatus referred to in a catacomb inscription.[46] On "my beloved one," see v. 5b; on "in the Lord," see v. 2.

9 "Urbanus" is also probably a slave or freedman[47] but, unlike Epaenetus and Ampliatus (*"my* beloved one," vv. 5, 8) and Prisca and Aquila (*"my* fellow workers," v. 3), Paul may have known him only by reputation (*"our* fellow worker").[48] We know nothing about "Stachys."

10 "Apelles" is a relatively rare name, and we know nothing else about him. Paul honors him by saying that he is "approved" in Christ. By this Paul might mean that he had proved himself in a difficult test of faith or, simply, that he was a respected believer.[49]

---

41. See 2 Cor. 8:3; Phil. 2:25.

42. The phrase is E. E. Ellis's ("Paul and His Co-Workers," in *Dictionary of Paul and His Letters* [ed. G. F. Hawthorne and R. P. Martin; Downers Grove: InterVarsity, 1993], p. 186). See especially the probable distinction in 1 Cor. 15 between "the twelve" (v. 5) and "all the apostles" (v. 7); also 1 Cor. 9:5-6; Gal. 2:9; Acts 14:4, 14. Even Paul's reference to the teachers bothering the Corinthians as false "apostles" (11:5; 12:11) implies a broader use of the term. And note the evidence from the early church: *Did.* 11:4; *Herm. Vis.* 3.5.1; *Sim.* 9.15.4; 16.5; 25.2. On the whole matter, see esp. J. B. Lightfoot, *The Epistle of St. Paul to the Galatians* (rpt.; Grand Rapids: Zondervan, n.d.), pp. 95-99; R. Schnackenburg, "Apostles Before and During Paul's Time," in *Apostolic History and the Gospel,* pp. 287-303.

43. See, e.g., Lightfoot, *Galatians,* pp. 97-98; B. Bacon, "Andronicus," *ExpTim* 42 (1930-31), 300-304; Meeks, *First Urban Christians,* pp. 131-33; Calvin; Godet; Michel; Käsemann; Cranfield; Wilckens; Dunn; Fitzmyer; Schlier.

44. Wilckens.

45. Lampe, "Roman Christians," p. 228; cf. Lightfoot, *Philippians,* p. 174.

46. See esp. S-H.

47. Lightfoot (*Philippians,* p. 174), indeed, conjectures that he may have been part of "Caesar's household" (cf. Phil. 4:22), that is, the imperial staff.

48. See, e.g., Michel; Murray; Cranfield; Schlier.

49. The Greek term δόκιμιον often denotes the proven character that results from a test (see the note on 5:4 [δοκιμή]); and several commentators think Paul uses it in this sense here (Godet; Murray; Dunn [?]). But in Rom. 14:18 it seems to mean simply "approved," "esteemed."

"Those who are of Aristobulus" are probably members, especially slaves, of the household of a man named Aristobulus. By not greeting Aristobulus directly, Paul implies that he was not a believer. Indeed, he may be dead since there is some reason to identify this Aristobulus with the brother of King Herod Agrippa I; and this Aristobulus died in A.D. 48 or 49.[50]

11 The identification of Aristobulus with the Herodian family gains some strength from the fact that Paul next greets a man who was apparently a freedman (and a Jew) in the service of one of the Herods. This, at least, is the only likely explanation of the name "Herodion," which is otherwise unattested in Rome.[51]

Paul may continue to think of Roman Christians who were socially prominent or who had connections with those who were. For Narcissus is the name of a well-known freedman who served the Emperor Claudius and who committed suicide just before Paul wrote Romans.[52] As in v. 10, the people Paul greets will have been members of Narcissus's household.

12 Tryphaena and Tryphosa were probably slaves or freedwomen[53] and may have been sisters.[54] Their names come from a word that means "delicate" or "dainty"; but it is unclear whether Paul deliberately intended the irony involved in calling them "those who worked in the Lord."[55]

"Persis," probably also a slave or freedwoman,[56] is also "beloved" (see v. 5) and "worked hard in the Lord" (see v. 6).

13 "Rufus" may be the son of Simon of Cyrene, who carried the cross of Christ part of the way to Golgotha.[57] In calling Rufus "the elect one," Paul may intend to single him out as a specially "outstanding" or "choice"

---

50. Agrippa went to Rome, accompanied by his brother, as a hostage. Aristobulus never held public office (cf. Josephus, *Ant.* 18.273-76; *J.W.* 2.221). On the identification, see Lightfoot, *Philippians,* p. 174-75; it is supported by most commentators since Aristobulus is a rare name in Rome (cf. Lampe, "Roman Christians," p. 222). Käsemann is not convinced, but he shows unnecessary scepticism about identifying those greeted here with people known from other sources.

51. Lampe, "Roman Christians," p. 226.

52. Tacitus, *Ann.* 31.1; Cassius Dio, *Rom. Hist.* 60.34; cf. also Lightfoot, *Philippians,* p. 175; Calvin.

53. Lampe, "Roman Christians," p. 228. Both names, as Lightfoot (*Philippians,* p. 176) notes, are found at about Paul's time for servants in the imperial household.

54. It was common to give children names from the same Greek root.

55. On κοπιάω, see v. 6; on "in the Lord" see v. 2.

56. The name comes from "Persia" and perhaps denotes a slave captured in that region.

57. Mark identifies Simon as "the father of Alexander and Rufus" (Mark 15:21), perhaps to connect him with two well-known Christians in Rome, from where Mark is probably written. Rufus was, however, a fairly common name (Lampe, "Roman Christians," p. 226). Favoring the identification are Lightfoot, *Philippians,* p. 176; Godet; Cranfield; Dunn; doubting it are Käsemann; Schlier.

believer.[58] But probably Paul simply means that he was a Christian, "chosen" as all Christians are.[59] Paul also conveys greetings to Rufus's mother, who had on some occasion also apparently provided hospitality and care to Paul.

14 We know nothing specifically about "Asyncritus, Phlegon, Hermes, Patrobas," and "Hermas" except that Hermes was probably a slave or freedman.[60] The additional phrase "and those with them" refers to other Christians who met in the same house church as they did.

15 The pairing of the masculine "Philologus" with the feminine "Julia" suggests to most commentators that they were husband and wife.[61] "Nereus" (a masculine name) and "his sister" may then have been their children. They, too, have apparently made their house available for Christians to meet in. Paul knows only one other member of their house church by name, "Olympas," mentioning the others only generally: "all the saints with them"[62] (as in v. 14).

16 ˙ Having conveyed greetings to perhaps every individual believer and house church that Paul knew about in Rome, he now adds a final catchall: "Greet one another with a holy kiss." Such requests are standard at the end of Paul's letters (cf. 1 Cor. 16:20; 2 Cor. 13:12; 1 Thess. 5:26; cf. 1 Pet. 5:14). The kiss was a common form of greeting in the ancient world generally and in Judaism especially.[63] Evidence from the second century indicates that the "kiss of peace" had by that time entered into the typical Christian liturgy as a standard feature.[64] Whether this was true as early as Paul's day is hard to say; but many commentators think that Paul may here be envisaging a worship gathering in which his letter is being read aloud and which is concluded with such a kiss.[65]

Paul also often passes on greetings from other churches. Only here, however, are the greetings sent, generally, from "all the churches of Christ."[66]

---

58. Godet; S-H; Murray; Barrett. Dunn thinks that the word suggests that Rufus had been chosen for some special task and theorizes that it might have something to do with his father's carrying of Christ's cross.

59. See esp. Cranfield, who notes that Paul uses other terms, such as "beloved" (see my notes on v. 5), in this list without any special emphasis.

60. Hermes "is among the commonest of slave-names" (Lightfoot, *Philippians,* p. 176).

61. See, e.g., Cranfield; Fitzmyer. Both names occur frequently to denote members of the imperial court (Lightfoot, *Philippians,* p. 177).

62. The placement of πάντας in this phrase, τοὺς σὺν αὐτοῖς πάντας ἁγίους, is unusual; but it must be equivalent to πάντας τοὺς ἁγίους σὺν αὐτοῖς (Moule, *Idiom Book,* p. 93).

63. See G. Stählin, *TDNT* IX, 121-22; 125-27; S. Benko, *Pagan Rome and the Early Christians* (Bloomington, IN: Indiana University, 1984), pp. 79-102.

64. Justin, *Apol.* 1.65.

65. See, e.g., Michel, 478; Cranfield, 2.796; Wilckens, 3.137; Schlier, 446.

66. The genitive τοῦ Χριστοῦ here is a classic example of a genitive that defies narrow classification; Turner (p. 212), with others, calls it a "mystical" genitive, but

The designation is probably not universal, however; Paul refers to those churches that he has been instrumental in planting in his ministry "from Jerusalem to Illyricum."[67] By conveying greetings from so many of the churches, Paul again hints at his strategy to bring the Roman church into the sphere of churches that know and support him.[68]

As interesting as these greetings might have been for the first-century Christians (for who does not like to hear his or her name read aloud and honored?), modern readers are to be forgiven for thinking that this section of Romans is not the most edifying in the letter. We don't learn much about Christian theology or the Christian life from a list of names! But there are two indirect lessons to be learned from it. First, Paul's reference to coworkers (vv. 3, 9; cf. v. 7) reminds us that Paul was not a "lone ranger" kind of missionary. At every point in his ministry, Paul depended on a significant number of others who were working along with him. And if Paul needed such help, how much more do we. There is no room in modern ministry for the lone ranger approach either.

Second, Paul's mention of nine women in this list reminds us (if we needed the reminder) that women played an important role in the early church. Moreover, five of these women — Prisca (v. 3), Junia (v. 7), Tryphaena and Tryphosa (v. 12), and Persis (v. 12) — are commended for their labor "in the Lord." Ministry in the early church was never confined to men; these greetings and other similar passages show that women engaged in ministries that were just as important as those of men. We have created many problems for ourselves by confining "ministry" to what certain full-time Christian workers do. But it is important that we not overinterpret this evidence either. For nothing Paul says in this passage (even in v. 7) conflicts with limitations on some kinds of women's ministry with respect to men such as I think are suggested by 1 Tim. 2:8-15 and other texts.[69]

3. A Warning, a Promise, and a Prayer for Grace (16:17-20)

> 17Now I am urging you, brothers and sisters, to watch out for those who cause dissensions and stumbling blocks against the teaching that you learned; turn away from them. 18For people such as these are not

---

perhaps "general" would be a better description. It suggests that the churches are "related to" Christ but in no single, particular manner.

67. Fitzmyer.

68. See esp. Wilckens, 3.137-38.

69. See especially D. Moo, "What Does It Mean Not to Teach or Have Authority over Men?" in Recovering Biblical Manhood and Womanhood, pp. 179-93.

serving our Lord Christ but their own belly; and through smooth talk and fine words they are deceiving the hearts of the unwary. 19*For the report of your obedience has reached everyone. Therefore I am rejoicing in you; but I want you to be wise with respect to the good but innocent with respect to what is evil.*

20*And the God of peace will soon crush Satan under your feet. May the grace of our Lord Jesus[1] be with you.[2]*

We group these verses together for convenience' sake; for they really fall into three separate parts: a warning about false teachers (vv. 17-19); a promise of deliverance (v. 20a); and a grace wish (v. 20b). The last of these has parallels in Paul's other letters: he includes such a grace wish at the end of all of his letters. And the second element, the promise of deliverance, has at least partial parallels in 1 Cor. 16:22b — "Our Lord come!" *(marana tha)* — and 1 Thess. 5:24 — "Faithful is he who called you, and he will do it." The first section, however, is not typical of Paul's letter endings; only here does he launch into an attack on false teachers, an attack, moreover, that interrupts Paul's greetings (vv. 3-16, 21-23). Added to this form-critical problem is another from within Romans itself: Paul has not said anything in the letter to this point that would suggest that there was any problem with false teachers. For these reasons, a few scholars argue that these verses do not belong in Paul's letter to the Romans at all.[3]

But there is no textual basis for omitting the verses; and the problems are not nearly as great as some have made them. While Paul does not elsewhere warn about false teachers at such length in his letter endings, he does include exhortations and warnings (cf. 1 Cor. 16:13-14; 2 Cor. 13:11b; Col. 4:17; cf. also Gal. 6:12-15; Eph. 6:10-17).[4] And 3:8 at least alludes to opponents of Paul.[5] He may delay specific mention of false teachers to this point because they had not yet come to Rome and/or because Paul had just heard about the threat.[6]

---

1. Several MSS (the secondary Alexandrian witnesses A, C, 33, 81, and 1739, Ψ, and the majority text) add Χριστοῦ, "Christ." The shorter reading, which has strong and early support (P[46] and the two primary Alexandrian witnesses, ℵ, and B) should be followed.

2. Several, mainly western, MSS (D, F, G) omit the grace prayer-wish entirely, putting in its place a similar grace wish that other MSS put after v. 23.

3. K. Erbes, "Zeit und Zeil der Grüße Röm 16,3-15 und der Mitteilungen 2 Tim 4,9-21," *ZNW* 10 (1909), 146; Jewett, *Christian Tolerance,* pp. 17-22; O'Neill, 252-53; Schmithals, 550-51; Ollrog, "Abfassungsverhältnisse," pp. 221-44.

4. See, e.g., Gamble, 52; Wiles, *Paul's Intercessory Prayers,* pp. 95-97; Jervis, *Purpose,* pp. 152-53; Seifrid, *Justification by Faith,* p. 198; Michel, 479; Wilckens, 3.139.

5. Stuhlmacher (252-53) argues plausibly that Paul has the same group in mind in both texts.

6. For the latter, see Wilckens, 3.143.

Identifying these false teachers is almost impossible.[7] This is because Paul is concerned to characterize them rather than to identify them.[8] He therefore presses into service certain stock imagery that communicates to the Romans the decisive points: they are divisive, self-centered, persuasive, teach what is contrary to the gospel, and must therefore be avoided at all costs. In an attempt to integrate the section with the rest of the letter, a few scholars have thought that the warning might relate to the dispute between the "strong" and the "weak" (14:1–15:13).[9] But Paul's strong denunciation in this text is completely different from anything we find in the earlier passage. The two identifications that have had the most support are (1) (gnostic) libertines;[10] and (2) Judaizers.[11] Perhaps, since we know that Jewish-oriented teachers plagued Paul throughout his ministry (cf. Galatians; 2 Cor. 10–13; Phil. 3), the latter suggestion has the most to commend it. But Paul simply does not give enough information to enable us to be at all certain. In any case, it seems likely that the false teachers had not yet come to Rome; his purpose is not to get the Roman Christians to exercise "church discipline" against heretical church members but to put them on their guard against such teachers who might make their way to Rome.[12]

17 Paul signals a shift to a different subject with his address, "brothers and sisters."[13] While this warning about false teachers appears to be an abrupt interruption in his closing greetings, it is not unrelated to its context. In conveying greetings from his mission churches to the church at Rome (v. 16b), Paul is probably reminded of the doctrinal threats that those churches have had to confront.[14] He is worried that the same threat might be impending in Rome. "I urge" translates *parakaleō,* a verb that Paul has used with varied shades of meaning in Rom. 12–16.[15] The translation "look out

---

7. Many scholars think that Paul may issue a generic warning that would cover any kind of false teaching that might crop up in Rome (e.g., Seifrid, *Justification by Faith,* p. 199; Cranfield, 2.800-801; Schlier, 446; Dunn, 2.904).

8. See esp. Wilckens, 3.144. Cf. also Michel, 472, 479. Verses 17-19 have many parallels with two similar Pauline warnings: Phil. 3:17-21 and Gal. 6:11-16.

9. Donfried, "Short Note," pp. 51-52; Black, 212-13; Barrett, 285 (?).

10. See, e.g., Dodd, 242-43, and esp. Schmithals, 560, and at greater length in his "Die Irrlehrer von Rm 16:17-20," *ST* 13 (1959), 51-69.

11. Godet, 496; S-H, 429; Stuhlmacher, 252-53; and esp. Wilckens, 3.141, 144-45.

12. See Seifrid, *Justification by Faith,* pp. 199-200; M. H. Franzmann, "Exegesis on Romans 16:17ff.," *Concordia Journal* 7 (1981), 14; Godet, 496; S-H, 429; Murray, 2.234-35; contra, e.g., Watson, 210-12, who finds here evidence of a Roman Jewish-Christian congregation antagonistic to the "Gentile-oriented" congregation focused on Prisca and Aquila.

13. Gk. ἀδελφοί. See the note on 15:30.

14. Godet, 496; Cranfield, 2.797-98.

15. See the note on 12:1; cf. also 12:8; 15:30.

for" brings out the warning nuance that the verb *skopeō* has here (cf. also NRSV and REB: "keep an eye on").[16] Those whom the Roman Christians are to "look out for" are "those who cause[17] dissensions and stumbling blocks against the teaching that you learned." The definite article — "those" — suggests that Paul has in mind a definite group of people and one that the Romans will recognize when (and if) they come there; but it need not mean that they were known to the Romans.[18]

As we noticed in the introduction to this section, Paul's description of these false teachers is very general. As false teachers usually do, they create disunity in the Christian community.[19] But more serious is their heretical doctrine. They create, Paul says, "stumbling blocks," which translates a word that Paul uses in Romans to refer to a spiritual problem that has the potential of leading to damnation.[20] By further describing these stumbling blocks as being "against the teaching that you learned,"[21] Paul makes clear that he is thinking mainly of false doctrine. The seriousness of the threat they pose demands a correspondingly serious response from the Roman Christians: they must "turn away from them"; "shun" them.[22] Again, Paul is not necessarily implying that the false teachers are already present.[23] His point is that the Roman Christians must be on their guard against them and be determined to avoid them should they appear.

18 Paul explains[24] further why it is so necessary to "turn away from" these teachers. He gives two reasons. First, "people such as these[25] are not serving our Lord Christ but their own belly." What Paul means by "serving their belly" is not clear. Paul uses similar language to describe false teachers in Phil. 3:19 — "their god is their belly" — but the identity of the false teachers in that text is as uncertain as in this one. Some scholars think the reference should be taken in its most straightforward sense and that Paul refers

---

16. The verb means "observe," "pay attention to," and Paul elsewhere uses it with a positive nuance (2 Cor. 4:18; Gal. 6:1; Phil. 2:4; 3:17).

17. Gk. ποιοῦντας, a substantival participle coming at the end of the clause.

18. I therefore steer a middle course in the interpretation of the article between Wilckens, who insists that it indicates that the false teachers were known to the Romans, and Dunn, who thinks that it is simply stylistic (cf. also Godet).

19. "Dissensions" translates διχοστασίας, a word that occurs only twice else in biblical Greek (1 Macc. 3:29; Gal. 3:20; it is v.l. in 1 Cor. 3:3).

20. See 9:33; 11:9; 14:13; cf. esp. Müller, *Anstoß,* pp. 46-67.

21. The phrase is parallel to the τύπον διδαχῆς of 6:17.

22. Gk. ἐκκλίνω, which is common in the LXX but rare in the NT (cf. also Rom. 3:12; 1 Pet. 3:11). The present tense probably suggests that the Roman Christians must be constant in their vigilance.

23. Contra, e.g., Franzmann, "Exegesis," pp. 15-16. See Cranfield; Wilckens.

24. See the γάρ, "for."

25. Gk. τοιοῦτοι, which has a qualitative force (cf. BAGD).

to gluttony and, by metonymy, to a greedy and dissipated lifestyle.[26] Others, however, think that Paul refers to the Jewish tendency to put too much stock in food laws.[27] Most think, however, that "belly" has virtually the same meaning here as the word "flesh" often does in Paul; "serving their belly" would then refer to egocentrism.[28] Perhaps a combination of the first and third views makes best sense: these false teachers are interested in their own pleasure.[29] In any case, the decisive point is really the negative one: they are *not* serving "our Lord Christ."

A second reason why it is important for the Roman Christians to shun these people is that they "deceive the hearts of the unwary." To be "innocent" and "guileless"[30] can be a good thing; but it can also leave people open to the subtle machinations of those who would take advantage of them. It is this that Paul is concerned about. For Paul well knows that these false teachers are clever at dressing up their heresies in "smooth talk and fine words."[31] Those who are not on the watch for these people and who do not listen closely enough to what they are teaching might be led astray and into ultimate spiritual ruin.

19   Paul suggests that v. 19 explains or gives the basis for something in v. 18.[32] How it does so is not, however, immediately clear. But perhaps the clue lies in what seems to be an intentional play on the idea of "innocence."[33]

---

26. E.g., Godet; W. Schmithals, *Paul and the Gnostics* (Nashville: Abingdon, 1972), pp. 231-32.

27. Barrett; Fitzmyer (?).

28. See, e.g., Cranfield; Michel; Käsemann; Wilckens; Schlier.

29. See Dunn; and note the translation "appetites" in almost all modern English versions. Perhaps this meaning finds some confirmation in 1 Cor. 6:13, a "slogan" of the Corinthians: "foods for the belly, and the belly for foods." Paul's only other use of the word is in Gal. 1:15, where he refers to the "belly," i.e., "womb," of his mother.

30. The Greek word Paul uses here, ἄκακος, can have a very positive nuance, as when Christ is called "innocent" in Heb. 7:26 (the only other NT use of the word; cf. BAGD). But it clearly has something of a pejorative meaning here (cf. Cranfield): note KJV, "simple"; NRSV, "simple-minded"; NIV, "naive."

31. Gk. διὰ τῆς χρηστολογίας καὶ εὐλογίας. As most recognize, the construction is a hendiadys, in which the two nouns are mutually interpreting. χρηστολογία occurs only here in the Greek Bible, and means "smooth, plausible speech" (BAGD; Black's suggestion of a complicated allusion to "Christ" is too subtle by half). εὐλογία, on the other hand, occurs frequently, and everywhere else in the NT with the positive sense, "blessing." But the word can mean "fine speaking" (BAGD), and Paul apparently uses it here with deliberate irony: they conceal the content of what they say in attractive rhetorical flourishes. (The suggestion that Paul is alluding here to a sectarian christological "eulogy" [cf. R. Trevijano, "Εὐλογία in Paul and the Text of Rom. 16,18," *SE* 6 {1973}, 537-40] cannot be accepted.)

32. Cf. the γάρ, "for."

33. See Calvin. It is a play on the same concept rather than on the same word because Paul uses different words for "innocent" in v. 18b (ἀκάκος) and in v. 19b (ἀκεραίος); and this might be an objection to my interpretation. But perhaps Paul changes

Paul warns that the false teachers are adept at deceiving the "innocent" (v. 18b). And he issues this warning just *because* the Roman Christians have such a universal[34] reputation for being "obedient," that is, innocent. Paul rejoices in this, for it is, of course, a good quality. But[35] at the same time, he wants them to combine this innocence with "wisdom" about what is good[36] and to confine their "innocence" to what is evil. In other words, Paul is recognizing and encouraging the Roman Christians' "innocence" in one sense — their freedom from sin as a result of their obedience to the gospel message — while he subtly warns them about another kind of "innocence" — the kind that lacks wisdom and discernment about truth and error. As Bruce puts it, they should not be "so 'simple-minded' as to swallow whatever is offered." Understood in this way, Paul probably alludes to Jesus' saying about being "wise as serpents and innocent as doves" (Matt. 10:16), for the meaning is much the same.[37]

20 The promise of deliverance in the first part of this verse may be a general promise, completely independent of Paul's warning about false teachers in vv. 17-19.[38] On the other hand, it could be part and parcel of that warning, Paul concluding with a promise that God would give the Roman Christians victory over those Satan-inspired heretics.[39] But perhaps a mediating position is best, in which we view the promise as a general one, similar to others that occur in Paul's letter endings, but with obvious relevance to the false teachers that Paul has just warned the church about. The language of the promise may allude to the "proto-evangelium" of Gen. 3:15d: "you [Adam, or his seed] will strike his [the serpent's] heel."[40] If our interpretation is

---

words to hint at the difference in meaning that I suggest (or because v. 19b picks up the same word that Jesus used in a similar saying). Other interpreters think that γάρ in v. 19 is parallel to the one in v. 18, both supporting the command "shun" them in v. 17b (e.g., Z-G, 496); or that it connects v. 19 to v. 18 in a different way: e.g., that Paul thinks the false teachers will aim at Rome precisely because of their reputation (Godet); or that Paul reminds them of the reputation that they must uphold (Cranfield).

34. πάντας must, of course, be restricted by its context to "all the other Christians who have heard about you."

35. The δέ at the beginning of this clause is therefore adversative.

36. εἰς (τὸ ἀγαθόν) means "with respect to" (Meyer); cf. also εἰς (τὸ κακόν) at the end of the verse.

37. See, e.g., Stuhlmacher. Matthew has the same word for "innocent" that Paul uses — ἀκέραιος — but a different one for "wise" — φρόνιμος, in contrast to σοφός. ἀκέραιος occurs only in these two verses and in Phil. 2:15 in the NT.

38. Cranfield; Dunn.

39. Cf., e.g., Wilckens; Fitzmyer.

40. Godet; Michel. It must be said, however, that the language of Paul's promise is not that close to that of Gen. 3:15. Nor are the alleged (e.g., Schlier, 449-50) Jewish parallels to Gen. 3:15: *Jub.* 23:29; *T. Mos.* 10:1; *T. Levi* 18:37; *T. Sim.* 6:6; cf. also the twelfth benediction in the *Shemoneh Esreh.*

correct, the promise of victory over Satan, while including victory over the false teachers of vv. 17-19, is much broader, extending to the final eschatological victory of God's people when Satan is thrown into the "lake of fire."[41]

Paul's prayer-wish that "the grace of our Lord Jesus be with you" finds a parallel in every other letter he wrote; and it also takes us back to the beginning of the letter (cf. 1:7).

4. Greetings from Paul's Companions (16:21-23)

21*Timothy, my fellow worker, greets you; as do Lucius and Jason and Sosipater, my kindred.* 22*I, Tertius, who has written this letter, greet you in the Lord.* 23*Gaius, the host of me and all the church, greets you. Erastus, the city treasurer, greets you; as does Quartus, the brother.*[1]

Paul usually passes on greetings from fellow workers or local Christians at the end of his letters. But he usually joins them with the greetings he himself extends to his addressees. (The only exception is 2 Timothy, where he interrupts the greetings with some remarks about his fellow workers [4:19-21].) Because these greetings from associates are so typical in his letters, it is unlikely that they were added as an afterthought.[2] Rather, as we have seen, the greetings Paul conveys from "all the churches" (v. 16b) sparked his concern about the potential of the false teachers who plagued those churches to disrupt the Roman community also. Thus he departs from his normal epistolary practice to interject a warning about these false teachers before returning to his usual end-of-the-letter format.[3]

---

41. See, e.g., Michel; Cranfield; Dunn; contra those who think Paul is looking for an immediate victory over Satan's forces in history (e.g., Schmithals, *Paul and the Gnostics,* p. 235; Wiles, *Paul's Intercessory Prayers,* p. 95; Calvin; Harrison; Morris). Paul's prediction that the victory over Satan will come "quickly" (ἐν τάχει) is no problem for the eschatological view once we appreciate rightly the NT concept of imminence (see the notes on 13:11-14).

1. A number of MSS, including the "western" uncials D, F, and G, Ψ, and the majority text, add after v. 23 a grace wish: ἡ χάρις τοῦ κυρίου ἡμῶν Ἰησοῦ Χριστοῦ μετὰ πάντων ὑμῶν. Ἀμήν (there are minor variations among these witnesses, particularly in the names of Christ); and the KJV therefore has, as v. 24: "The grace of our Lord Jesus Christ be with you all. Amen." But the verse is omitted in the earliest and most important MSS (P[46], ℵ, B, the secondary Alexandrian uncial C, P[61], 0150, and a few minuscules) and is clearly a later addition to the text.

2. Contra Wilckens, 3.140.

3. The break in the sequence of greetings has sparked theories about dislocations or interpolations in the text (cf. the introduction to vv. 17-20 and, on vv. 21-23, Schmithals, 563-64). But no textual evidence for such interpolations exists; and the theories assume a rigidity in Paul's letter-ending format that his letters simply do not bear out.

21 Timothy, whom Paul simply introduces here as "my fellow worker" (cf. also vv. 3 and 9), was Paul's closest ministry associate. A native of Lystra, in South Galatia, Timothy joined Paul's missionary team at the beginning of the second missionary journey (Acts 16:2-3). Timothy worked with Paul throughout the rest of that journey (cf. Acts 17:14-15; 18:5). He was perhaps left behind in Greece or Macedonia when Paul returned to Palestine, and met up with Paul again when he returned to these regions on the third missionary journey.[4] He was later with Paul during his Roman imprisonment[5] and worked with the apostle after his release in the eastern Mediterranean again (cf. 1 and 2 Timothy). As this verse makes clear, then, Timothy was with Paul during his stay in Greece at the end of the third missionary journey (cf. Acts 20:3-4). Timothy's importance can be gauged from the fact that Paul introduces him as "co-author" of six of his letters (2 Corinthians; 1 Thessalonians; 2 Thessalonians; Philippians; Colossians; Philemon). Paul probably does not do so in Romans because Timothy is unknown to most of the Roman Christians and because at stake in the letter is Paul's unique apostolic mission to the Gentiles.[6]

"Lucius" has been identified with "Lucius of Cyrene," a prophet/teacher in the church at Syrian Antioch (Acts 13:1)[7] or with Luke the evangelist ("Luke" can be a variant of "Lucius").[8] But neither identification is very likely.[9] "Jason," on the other hand, is very likely the Jason who gave hospitality to Paul during his brief and tumultuous stay in Thessalonica (Acts 17:5-9).[10] And "Sosipater" is almost certainly the "Sopater" of Beroea whom Luke tells us accompanied Paul when he left Greece toward the end of the third missionary journey (Acts 20:4).[11] Paul tells us that all three of these men were fellow Jews;[12] and they probably were also delegates from the Pauline churches selected to escort Paul with the collection for the poor among the saints in Jerusalem.[13]

---

4. Paul does not mention Timothy in 1 Corinthians, written from Ephesus, but he is included as coauthor of 2 Corinthians, written from Macedonia.

5. See Col. 1:1; Phlm. 1; and Phil. 1:1, 19-23 (assuming that Philippians was written from Rome).

6. See Godet.

7. Godet.

8. Cf. BDF 125(2); Stuart; Schmithals; Dunn (?); Stuhlmacher (?).

9. See Bruce; Käsemann; Schlier; Fitzmyer.

10. Godet; Michel; Cranfield; Wilckens; contra, e.g., Käsemann; Schlier.

11. Sosipater (Σωσίπατρος) is a variant of Sopater (Σώπατρος).

12. Gk. συγγενεῖς, on which see v. 7. It is not completely clear whether this designation applies to all three or only to the last two (cf. Cranfield).

13. See, e.g., Michel; Wilckens; Dunn; Fitzmyer. Käsemann objects, arguing that Jewish Christians would not have represented Paul's "Gentile" churches. But perhaps this is just why some Jewish Christians were selected: to demonstrate to the Jerusalem saints that the Pauline churches were not exclusively Gentile.

22 Tertius is otherwise unknown to us. He identifies himself in this verse as Paul's "amanuensis" for Romans: the one who "wrote down" what Paul dictated.[14] After his hard work, Paul gives him the opportunity to extend Christian[15] greetings to the Roman Christians in his own name.

23 "Gaius" was a common name; and at least three different men in the NT bore it: Gaius "of Derbe" (Acts 20:4; cf. 19:29); a Gaius from Corinth (1 Cor. 1:14); and a Gaius who was a church leader in Asia Minor (3 John 1). The Gaius whom Paul greets here was almost certainly Gaius of Corinth, since Paul was writing Romans from Corinth. He may very well be identified also with Titius Justus, who gave Paul lodging on his first stay in Corinth (Acts 18:7).[16] The role that Gaius played in Corinth is not completely clear, for Paul's description of Gaius could mean either that he was the "host"[17] of the entire church in Corinth[18] or that he was the "host" to any Christian from "the whole church" who might pass through Corinth.[19] Certainty is impossible, but the second option might be preferable since it is unlikely that the entire church at Corinth would have met in one house.

"Erastus" may be the same Erastus whom Paul sends from Ephesus to Macedonia during the third missionary journey (Acts 19:21-22; cf. also 2 Tim. 4:20).[20] But the identification is complicated by the existence of an inscription in Corinth that names an Erastus as "aedile" of the city. The term that Paul uses here to describe Erastus, *oikonomos,* identifies him as a financial officer in the city government (BAGD: "treasurer"); and it is not clear whether this title would be equivalent to "aedile."[21] If not, it is still possible that

14. On this meaning of γράφω, see BAGD. It was customary for ancient authors to use a scribe to write out their letters; and authors gave to their scribes varying degrees of freedom in the actual wording of the contents. (See, e.g., R. N. Longenecker, "Ancient Amanuenses and the Pauline Epistles," in *New Dimensions in New Testament Study,* pp. 281-97; R. E. Richards, *The Secretary in the Letters of Paul* [WUNT 2.42; Tübingen: Mohr, 1991], esp. pp. 170-72.) Most scholars agree that the directness of the style of Romans, as well as its similarity to the style of Galatians and 1 Corinthians, suggests strongly that the wording of Romans is Paul's own. Tertius probably simply copied out Paul's dictation.

15. ἐν τῷ κυρίῳ ("in the Lord"), which probably modifies ἀσπάζομαι ("greet") rather than γράψας ("write"); cf. Cranfield.

16. His full name would then have been Gaius Titius Justus, Gaius being his praenomen (cf. Bruce).

17. Gk. ξένος. The word usually means "stranger," "alien," but it can also mean "host" (BAGD).

18. BAGD; Althaus; Dunn; Gielen, "Zur Interpretation"; Fitzmyer.

19. See, e.g., Käsemann; Wilckens.

20. Cf., e.g., Fitzmyer.

21. The aedile was appointed for one year and was responsible for the city streets and buildings and for certain finances. The identification of Lat. *aedile* and Gk. οἰκονόμος

Erastus, having served as "treasurer," was promoted to aedile at a later date.[22] On the whole, the identification of Paul's Erastus with the Erastus named in this inscription is probable.[23]

"Quartus" is not found elsewhere in the NT; Paul simply identifies him as a fellow believer.[24]

C. CONCLUDING DOXOLOGY (16:25-27)

> 25Now to the one who is able to strengthen you according to my gospel and the preaching of Jesus Christ, according to the revelation of the mystery that has been kept secret for long ages, 26but now has been manifested and made known through the prophetical writings according to the command of the eternal God for the obedience of faith for all the nations, 27to the only wise God be the glory, through Jesus Christ, for ever.[1] Amen.[2]

is questioned by many (e.g., H. J. Cadbury, "Erastus of Corinth," *JBL* 50 [1931], 42-58; G. Theissen, *The Social Setting of Pauline Christianity* [Edinburgh: T & T Clark, 1982], pp. 77-78). But D. W. J. Gill shows that the identification is possible ("Erastus the Aedile," *TynBul* 40 [1989], 293-301).

22. See Theissen, *Social Setting,* pp. 77-78; Meeks, *First Urban Christians,* pp. 58-59; Bruce.

23. See also A. D. Clarke, "Another Corinthian Erastus Inscription," *TynBul* 42 (1991), 146-51.

24. Gk. ἀδελφός, "brother." A few think that the word could here be used of a physical relationship to Erastus or Tertius (e.g., Bruce), but this is unlikely.

1. The addition of τῶν αἰώνων to αἰῶνας (e.g., "forever and ever") in some MSS (the primary Alexandrian uncial ℵ, the secondary Alexandrian uncial MSS A and 81, the western D, and a few other MSS) is a secondary expansion (contra, e.g., Käsemann).

2. This concluding doxology has a checkered textual history. It is missing entirely in the sister western bilinguals F and G, it is placed after 14:23 in Ψ, 0209, and some minuscules, it is placed after 15:33 in others (P46 and minuscule 1506), and in still others it is placed both here and after 14:23 (the secondary Alexandrian A, the Byzantine P, uncial 0150, and a few minuscules). This uncertainty about its placement has raised doubts in the minds of critics about its authenticity. But far more serious are the doubts raised by its contents. The language of these verses is said to be un-Pauline, with wording such as χρόνοις αἰώνιος σεσιγημένοι ("silent for eternal ages"), γραφῶν προφητικῶν ("prophetical writings"), and τοῦ αἰωνίου θεοῦ ("the eternal God") that is foreign to him and that is typical of a later period. Many find this supposition confirmed by the resemblance between the language of the doxology (esp. "mystery") and the allegedly later and post-Pauline letters to the Ephesians and to the Colossians. Finally, Paul never elsewhere concludes a letter with a doxology. For these reasons, and others, a large majority of recent scholars think that the doxology is a post-Pauline addition to Romans, perhaps originating at the time when Marcion allegedly butchered the text of the letter. See, e.g., Barrett, 286; Dodd, 245-46; Käsemann, 422, 427-28; Gaugler, 2.416-17; Cranfield, 2.808; Wilckens,

Paul ends his majestic letter to the Romans with a doxology in praise of the God who has in the gospel of Jesus Christ revealed the climax of salvation history. Paul deliberately echoes in these verses the language and themes of the letter, and particularly its opening section:

"Who is able" (power)	cf. 1:4, 16
"Strengthen you"	1:11
"[my] gospel"	1:1, 9, 16; cf. 2:16
"revelation"/"manifested"	1:17; 3:21
"prophetical writings"	1:2; 3:21
"obedience of faith"	1:5
"all the nations (Gentiles)"	1:5; passim

3.147; Bruce, 267-68; Black, 215; Schlier, 451; Dunn, 2.912-13; Fitzmyer, 753; B. W. Bacon, "The Doxology at the End of Romans," *JBL* 18 (1899), 167-76; Zuntz, 227-29; Manson, "To the Romans," p. 8; K. Aland, "Die Schluss und die ursprüngliche Gestalt des Römerbriefes," in *Neutestamentliche Entwürfe*, pp. 284-301; Donfried, "Short Note," p. 50; J. K. Elliott, "The Language and Style of the Concluding Doxology to the Epistle to the Romans," *ZNW* 72 (1981), 124-30; Ollrog, "Abfassungsverhältnisse," p. 227.

The arguments for the exclusion of this doxology are therefore formidable; but there are arguments on the other side as well. First, the MS support for including the doxology at this point is strong: the primary Alexandrian witnesses ℵ and B, the secondary Alexandrian MSS C, 81, and 1739, the western D, P[61], and many minuscules. Second, the language of the doxology demonstrates remarkable parallels to the language of Romans, and especially to its opening. These parallels are usually attributed to the later redactor, who sought to fit the doxology to the style of the letter. But they could also point to Paul's own authorship. Third, the differences from Paul's own style are largely eliminated if we maintain the Pauline authorship of Ephesians and Colossians. Fourth, it does not seem credible that Paul would end his letter with "Quartus, the fellow Christian." Thus the many older scholars who maintained the authenticity of the doxology (e.g., Hort, in *Biblical Essays,* pp. 322-29; Alford, 2.471; Godet, 506-9; S-H, 423; Meyer, 2.363-67; Liddon, 232) are joined by a number of modern supporters as well (Murray, 2.262-68; Lenski, 926-27; Huby, 516-20; Nygren, 457; Schmidt, 265-66; Hendrikson, 2.521-22; Harrison, 171; Stuhlmacher, 244-46, 256; L. Gaugusch, "Untersuchungen zum Römerbrief. Der Epilog [15,14–16,27]," *BZ* 24 [1938-39], 263-65; T. Fahy, "Epistle to the Romans 16:25-27," *ITQ* 28 [1961], 238-41; Weima, *Neglected Endings,* pp. 218-19; and cf. L. Hurtado, "The Doxology at the End of Romans," in *New Testament Textual Criticism: Its Significance for Exegesis. Essays in Honor of Bruce M. Metzger* [ed. E. J. Epp and G. Fee; Oxford: Clarendon, 1981], pp. 185-99).

A decision is very difficult; but we are slightly inclined to include the doxology as part of Paul's original letter. The differing placements of the doxology, and its omission in some MSS, can be accounted for by the textual disruptions of the last chapters of the letter. The language and style are not un-Pauline. The biggest obstacle in the way of accepting the doxology is Paul's general practice of adding doxologies in the midst of his letters. But the ending of Romans shows enough differences from the other letters that this is not that large a problem.

| "only God" | 3:29-30 |
| "wise God" | 11:33-36 |

Prominent here again is the theme of the revelation of the gospel as the pinnacle of salvation history and as a message of universal applicability. Paul ends as he began.[3] Paul clearly intends to stimulate the Roman Christians' praise of God by reminding them of what he has told them of God's wonderful plan for their salvation in Jesus Christ.

Paul uses a repeated threefold structure to enhance the liturgical tone of the doxology: note "gospel," "preaching," and "revelation" in v. 25b, the three participial modifiers of revelation — "kept secret," "manifested," and "made known." Perhaps it is the very complexity of this arrangement that lands Paul in syntactical difficulties; for vv. 25-27 are one long incomplete sentence.[4]

25 Addressing God in a dative construction ("to") is typical of doxologies.[5] Paul begins, however, not by naming God, but by characterizing him as the one who "is able to strengthen you." What Paul hopes to do when he comes to Rome (1:11), he acknowledges to be possible only through divine aid. "According to my gospel"[6] might modify "able": God is able to strengthen you, as my gospel says he is.[7] But it should probably be taken with "strengthen," in which case it might denote the means of the strengthening ("through")[8] or the norm in accordance with which the strengthening takes place ("in accordance with," "in").[9] But perhaps we need not decide between these options: Paul's point is that the gospel is the source of the strengthening.[10]

"Preaching of Jesus Christ," which we can paraphrase "preaching[11] about Jesus Christ,"[12] is a further definition of "my gospel."[13] And "according to the revelation" could be a third, roughly parallel, description of the

---

3. See, e.g., Bengel, 3.197; Michel, 486; Stuhlmacher, 256.

4. E.g., an "anacolouthon." See Denney, 725. Attempts to avoid this conclusion by supplying a verb (e.g., Godet, 506) are neither necessary nor persuasive. See further the notes on v. 27.

5. See, e.g., Eph. 3:20; Jude 24-25.

6. On "my gospel," see 2:16.

7. Cf. Godet.

8. S-H (?).

9. Käsemann; Murray.

10. Cf. Dunn.

11. Gk. κήρυγμα; the word occurs only here in Romans, but cf. κηρύσσω in 10:8, 14, 15 (used in connection with gospel).

12. Ἰησοῦ Χριστοῦ is clearly objective, a subjective genitive — "preaching done by Jesus Christ" (suggested by Schlatter; G. Friedrich, *TDNT* II, 731) — being out of place.

13. The καί is explicative (Wilckens).

same message.[14] But it is better to subordinate this phrase to "preaching,"[15]or "gospel and preaching,"[16] or, perhaps best, "gospel"[17]: the gospel is "in accordance with," "based on," the revelation of the mystery. Paul speaks of the gospel as consisting in the "revelation of the righteousness of God" in his statement of the theme of the letter (1:17). Here he echoes this revelatory concept. Paul has used "mystery" in 11:25,[18] but its application here to the basic content of Paul's gospel and preaching is closer to Paul's use of the term in passages such as 1 Cor. 2:7, Eph. 3:3-9, and Col. 1:26-27.

The rest of v. 25 and all of v. 26 are taken up with a threefold description of this "mystery." First, Paul says, it was "kept secret[19] for long ages."[20] Here Paul reflects a motif typical in apocalyptic: the hiddenness of God's plan and purposes. This hiddenness, as Paul will make clear in v. 26, does not mean that one could have no knowledge of the content of the mystery. What it means, rather, is that one could not fully understand it nor — and this is the special emphasis — experience it.

26 Following a typical NT salvation-historical scheme,[21] Paul indicates that the mystery that has been "kept secret" has "now been manifested."[22] The "and" that follows this clause suggests that the four prepositional modifiers in the verse all go with the third participle Paul uses to describe the mystery, "made known" at the end of the verse.[23] These last two participles are obviously very close in meaning;[24] perhaps Paul uses both for stylistic reasons (to keep his threefold scheme) or to accentuate the idea. The first of the prepositional phrases describes the means though which the mystery was made known: "through the prophetical writings."

14. Cf. Meyer.

15. S-H; Cranfield.

16. Godet; Murray.

17. E.g., Bengel.

18. See the note there on the meaning and background of μυστήριον in Paul.

19. Gk. σεσιγημένου, from the verb σιγάω, "be silent"; the form is perfect, hence stressing the state of "secrecy" of the mystery in the past. Paul uses this verb elsewhere only in 1 Cor. 14:28, 30, 34; on its meaning here, see BAGD.

20. Gk. χρόνοις αἰωνίοις. The dative is temporal (Wilckens), and the plural χρόνοις here means "a rather long period of time composed of several shorter ones" (BAGD). There may be allusion to the "eternity" of God's plan (cf. Murray).

21. See esp. 1 Cor. 2:7-9; Eph. 3:5, 9-10; Col. 1:26-27; 2 Tim. 1:9-10; Tit. 1:2-3; 1 Pet. 1:10.

22. The Greek verb is φανερόω, used in a similar way in Rom. 3:21. In that verse, Paul accentuates the state of manifestation (perfect tense); here, simply, its occurrence (aorist tense).

23. See, e.g., Godet; Cranfield; Dunn.

24. Paul's use of τε (instead of καί or δέ) to connect them hints at the close connection of the two.

Since we would expect the gospel, or the NT, to be the source of this revelation, some scholars think that Paul may allude here to the apostles' writings or to the Scriptures as a whole.[25] But Paul has made sufficiently clear that the mystery of God's work in Christ, while not experienced or understood in its fullness in the OT period, was nevertheless "testified to" by the OT (cf. esp. 1:2; 3:21). "Prophetical writings" will therefore refer to the OT.[26] "According to[27] the command of the eternal God"[28] stresses that it was God's own determination to make known the mystery at the time that he did. The "command" is not any specific historical divine command,[29] but refers to the expression of God's will.[30] The last two prepositional phrases indicate the purpose of the mystery being "made known" — that people might come to believe and obey the gospel[31] — and the object of its being made known — "all the nations." Paul returns for the last time to a theme with which the letter opened (1:5) and to which he has continually returned: the universal applicability of the gospel of Jesus Christ.

27 Paul finally returns to the construction[32] with which he opened his doxology, identifying now the "one who is able" as "the only wise God."[33] God's "wisdom," as in 11:33, has to do with his "wise" plan for salvation history, now understood, lived out, and given thanks for by the saints. This plan, of course, culminated in a person and his work: God's Son, Jesus Christ

25. Godet thinks that Paul refers to the apostles' teaching. But this view is especially popular with those who think that the doxology was added by a later redactor. Included in the phrase could then be the letters of Paul themselves (cf. Käsemann; Wilckens). Appeal is made to the similar phrase in 2 Pet. 1:20, προφητεία γραφῆς, "prophecy of Scripture," which is also thought by these scholars to reflect conditions at the end of the first century.

26. See Dunn; Stuhlmacher.

27. κατά here merges the ideas of "according to" and "because of"; cf. BAGD, 407.

28. αἰώνιος θεός occurs only here in the NT, but it is common in the OT (cf. Gen. 21:33; Isa. 26:4; 40:28) and in Judaism (e.g., Bar. 4 passim). See Dunn.

29. Contra Godet, who thinks it refers to the "Great Commission," and Fitzmyer, who sees in it an allusion to Paul's call.

30. See Cranfield. Paul uses the word "command" (ἐπιταγή) similarly in 1 Tim. 1:1; Tit. 1:3; 2:15; cf. also 1 Cor. 7:6, 25; 2 Cor. 8:8.

31. On the meaning of the phrase ὑπακοὴν πίστεως, see 1:5.

32. The dative μόνῳ σοφῷ θεῷ ("to the only wise God") is in apposition to τῷ δυναμένῳ ("to the one who is able") in v. 25.

33. This interpretation of the words μόνῳ σοφῷ, assumed in all modern English translations and supported by most of the commentators (e.g., Murray; Schlier; Cranfield), is preferable to translating "the only and wise God." This description of God is very common in Philo and picks up the biblical wisdom tradition (cf. esp. J. Dupont, "ΜΟΝΩΙ ΣΟΦΩΙ ΘΕΩΙ [Rom., XVI,27]," *ETL* 22 [1946], 362-75).

(cf. 1:3-4). It is therefore appropriate that the saints give glory to God[34] "through Jesus Christ."[35]

34. The syntax of the last part of this verse is made difficult by the presence of the relative pronoun ᾧ. Some MSS accordingly eliminate it, an obvious secondary attempt to remove the problem (contra BDF 467; S-H). Some scholars think that it is simplest to begin a new sentence with the relative pronoun and that its antecedent is "Jesus Christ" (Barrett). But this would leave the entire doxology hanging in mid-air; the antecedent must be "only wise God," and Paul simply adds the relative pronoun because he has lost track of the progress of the sentence.

35. It is better to take διὰ Ἰησοῦ Χριστοῦ with what follows (cf. Schlier) than with what precedes (Meyer).

INDEX OF SUBJECTS

INDEX OF AUTHORS

945

951

Wiles, G. P., 558, 871, 872, 880, 909,
911, 928, 933
Wiles, M. F., 207
Willer, A., 97
Williams, C. S. C., 8
Williams, S. K., 21, 70, 182, 190, 220,
222, 224, 225, 235, 236, 239, 273,
633, 637
Wilson, J. P., 528
Wilson, R. R., 597
Wilson, W. E., 239
Wilson, W. T., 746, 772, 773, 774, 776,
782
Windisch, H., 62
Winer, G. B., 776
Winger, M., 146, 173, 249, 276, 464, 474
Wink, W., 796
Winslow, O., 540
Winter, B. W., 800
Wintle, B. C., 128
Wisse, S.-H. F., 308
Witherington, B., III, 709
Wollebius, J., 325
Wolter, M., 291, 293, 297, 298, 301,
308, 310
Wonneberger, R., 221, 227
Woudstra, M. H., 717
Wrede, W., 23, 89
Wright, N. T., 12, 24, 26, 41, 46, 85,
101, 213, 215, 248, 293, 294, 348,
420, 426, 438, 456, 460, 463, 480,
484, 485, 552, 567, 573, 577, 628,
646, 653, 683, 694, 717, 721, 726, 728
Wuellner, W., 15, 39
Würthwein, E., 464

Yonge, J. E., 789
Young, N. H., 221, 235
Ysebart, J., 365

Zahn, T., 10, 42, 43, 44, 52, 53, 58, 68,
76, 97, 109, 129, 137, 149, 150, 170,
182, 200, 205, 283, 322, 345, 361,
370, 371, 408, 411, 421, 425, 441,
455, 473, 507, 514, 515, 524, 529,
536, 567, 571, 573, 613, 624, 625,
637, 643, 652, 694, 736, 749, 752,
754, 761, 783, 804, 813, 923
Zeller, D., 17, 18, 71, 68, 220, 231, 234,
567, 604, 605, 617, 637, 662, 672,
677, 687, 694, 715, 726, 728, 748,
788, 832
Zerwick, M., 139, 283, 304, 317, 341,
385, 466, 512, 701, 826, 841, 853,
860, 863, 871, 899, 900, 907
Zerwick, M., and Grosvenor, M., 51,
54, 59, 109, 339, 558, 579, 593, 645,
692, 715, 733, 762, 767, 777, 779,
835, 841, 880, 892, 903, 909, 921,
932
Ziegler, J., 614
Ziesler, J. A., 72, 88, 80, 87, 222, 262,
345, 386, 405, 435, 482, 565, 569,
616, 625, 659, 694, 701, 703, 737,
752, 757, 780, 806, 817, 829, 861,
874, 892
Zimmerli, W., 228
Zsifkovits, V., 796, 798, 799, 800, 803,
806
Zuntz, G., 7, 818, 907, 937
Zwingli, U., 416

INDEX OF SCRIPTURE REFERENCES

INDEX OF SCRIPTURE REFERENCES

2:7	134	11	880	43:10	41
3:7	715, 784	11:1	46	45:1-7	798
3:34	799	11:6	911	45:1-12	847
6:28	788	11:9	699	45:8	650
8:15-16	798	11:10	46, 878	45:9	602, 650
8:21	650	12:2	66	45:9-10	602
10–13	81	14:13	654	45:22	847
10:20	680	14:24	581	45:23	847
11:5	102	14:32	783	45:24	847
17:15	264	16:14	108	45:25	87
19:21	581	24:4	514	46	85
20:13	120	24:20	687	46:3	66, 73, 81, 82,
20:22	787	25:1	581		223
24:12	136	25:9	66	46:13	653
24:29	787	26:4	940	47:11	465
25:3	742	26:14	318	47:14	788
25:14	302	27	821	48:2	699
25:21-22	787	27:9	727, 728, 729	48:13	281
30:4	654	28:16	304, 620, 628,	49:6	66, 162
31:6	557		630, 645, 659,	49:13	783
			660, 682, 728	49:18	847
ECCLESIASTES		28:22	614	50	85
1:14	136	29	729	50:5-8	73
4:6	690	29:6	729	50:7-8	659
7:20	203	29:7-8	729	50:7-9	542
9:1	775	29:10	681, 682	50:8	80, 82, 87
9:6	775	29:12-13	729	51:1	621
		29:16	601, 602	51:1-2	256
ISAIAH		29:17	169	51:1-7	621
1:7-9	616	31:8	688	51:5	81, 223, 653
1:9	569, 616, 674	32:15	169	51:6	81, 223
2:2-3	684	32:42	529	51:8	81, 223
5:7	80	35:2	226	51:11	519, 557
5:16	83	35:10	519, 557	52:5	166
5:23	80, 264	37:33	318	52:7	66, 299, 529,
5:24	788	38:19	81, 82		663, 664, 665
5:26-29	802	40:5	108	52:10	66
6:1-13	715	40:8	581	52:15	897, 898
6:9	668	40:9	43	53	336, 540, 664
6:9-10	682	40:13	742	53:1	664, 665
6:10	682	40:14	742	53:4	866
7:3-9	615	40:18-19	369	53:5	288
7:9	615	40:28	940	53:11	288, 345
7:18-20	802	41:2-4	798	53:12	288
8:7-8	802	41:4	281	54:5-8	82
8:14	620, 628, 630,	41:8	584	54:10	299
	851	42:6-7	162	55:3-5	274
9:33	682	42:7	43	55:6	660
10:5-6	802	42:25	715	55:10-11	650
10:22	83, 614, 676	43:6	499	56:6-7	684
10:22-23	614, 616	43:7	139	59	204
10:23	609, 614	43:9	·87	59:7	204

969

INDEX OF EARLY EXTRABIBLICAL LITERATURE

7:8	890	44:19	256	15:7	602, 603
15:6	777	44:19-21	256	16:24	514
15:9	777	44:21	274	17:11	152
17:16	564	45:5	625	18:4	162
17:20-22	558	45:23-24	632	18:15	706
17:21-22	235	47:22	677, 880	18:22	563
17:22	235	48:11	775	19:6	514
18:3	505				
18:10	223	**Tob.**			
		1:10-12	831	**PSEUDEPIGRAPHA**	
Pr. Man.		3:1	519		
6	742	3:10	557	*Apoc. Abr.*	
8	256	4:10-11	750	29:17	719
		12:12	750	29:19	21, 171
Sir.		13:11-13	684		
4:5	786	14:6-7	684	*2 Apoc. Bar.*	
4:27	798			13:9	499
7:30	889	**Wis.**		14:8-9	557, 742
7:34	782	2:6	114	14:13	274
10:4	798	2:11	625	15:8	512
10:20	693	2:23	137	21:4	281
11:7	600	2:24	324	21:20	134
11:10	621	3:8	171	23:4	324, 719
12:6	587	3:13	579	28:2	823
13:22	786	3:16	579	29	514
16:6	116	3:17	169	30:2	719
17:7	798	5:5	499	32:6	514
17:11	439, 625	5:17	514	35:3	557
17:12	742	5:20	706	44:12	514
19:17	786	5:22	706	48:3	714
23:2	238	6:1-3	798	48:8	281
25:24	324	6:4	801	48:20-24	160
26:8	116	6:5	706, 796	48:42	324
26:29	377	6:18	775	48:50	823
27:8	621	9:6	169	51:3	274
27:24	587	11:10	706	54:5	633
30:3	688	11:14	133	54:15	324
30:6	802	11:15	133	54:19	324
30:13	116	11:15-16	111	57:2	150, 208, 256,
33:13	602	11:23	133		514
34:7	572	12:9	706	59:6	133
35:1	750	12:12	602, 802	75:6	719
35:12	143	12:15	128	78:6-7	696
36:12	499	13:1	125	81:4	714
38:12	786	13:8	125	82:9	798
39:8	625	13:13	110	85:9	131
39:25	529	13:14	109, 125		
39:27	529	14:9-10	587	*Apoc. Mos.*	
41:7	600	14:12	113	21:6	226
42:18	152	14:23	825		
44:12	563	14:26	115, 825	*As. Mos.*	
44:18	563	15:1-2	133	5:3	4, 112

Plutarch
Princip. Inerud.
5.13.22-14.2   801

Pseudo-Xenophon
Re Publica Athen.
1.11   427
2.11   427

Strabo
7.7.4   894

Suetonius
Life of Claudius
25.2   4

Tacitus
Ann.
13.50   793
31.1   925
Histories
3.68   801

Thucydides
2.18.5   117
2.40.4   263

Xenophon
Cyr.
7.5.45   300
Eq. Mag.
7.10   238